MOTOR CONTROL AND LEARNING

A Behavioral Emphasis

FIFTH EDITION

Richard A. Schmidt, PhD, Professor Emeritus

Psychology Department
University of California, Los Angeles
and
Human Performance Research
Marina del Rey, California

Timothy D. Lee, PhD

Department of Kinesiology
McMaster University, Ontario, Canada

HUMAN KINETICS

Library of Congress Cataloging-in-Publication Data

Schmidt, Richard A., 1941-
  Motor control and learning : a behavioral emphasis / Richard A. Schmidt and Timothy D. Lee. -- 5th ed.
    p. ; cm.
  Includes bibliographical references and indexes.
  ISBN-13: 978-0-7360-7961-7 (hard cover)
  ISBN-10: 0-7360-7961-0 (hard cover)
  1. Movement, Psychology of. 2. Motor learning. I. Lee, Timothy Donald, 1955- II. Title.
  [DNLM: 1. Motor Activity. 2. Motor Skills. 3. Learning. WE 103]
  BF295.S248 2011
  152.3--dc22

                          2010044051

ISBN-10: 0-7360-7961-0 (print)
ISBN-13: 978-0-7360-7961-7 (print)

The Web addresses cited in this text were current as of August 2010, unless otherwise noted.

Acquisitions Editor: Myles Schrag; **Managing Editor:** Melissa J. Zavala; **Assistant Editors:** Antoinette Pomata and Steve Calderwood; **Copyeditor:** Joyce Sexton; **Indexer:** Andrea J. Hepner; **Permission Manager:** Dalene Reeder; **Graphic Designer:** Bob Reuther; **Graphic Artist:** Denise Lowry; **Cover Designer:** Keith Blomberg; **Photographer (cover):** © Yuri Kadobnov/AFP/Getty Images; **Photographer (interior):** © Human Kinetics, unless otherwise noted; **Photo Production Manager:** Jason Allen; **Art Manager:** Kelly Hendren; **Associate Art Manager:** Alan L. Wilborn; **Art Style Development:** Joanne Brummett; **Illustrations:** © Human Kinetics; **Printer:** Sheridan Books

Printed in the United States of America   10   9   8   7   6   5   4   3   2   1

The paper in this book is certified under a sustainable forestry program.

Human Kinetics
Web site: www.HumanKinetics.com

United States: Human Kinetics, P.O. Box 5076, Champaign, IL 61825-5076
800-747-4457
e-mail: humank@hkusa.com

Canada: Human Kinetics, 475 Devonshire Road Unit 100, Windsor, ON N8Y 2L5
800-465-7301 (in Canada only)
e-mail: info@hkcanada.com

Europe: Human Kinetics, 107 Bradford Road, Stanningley, Leeds LS28 6AT, United Kingdom
+44 (0) 113 255 5665
e-mail: hk@hkeurope.com

Australia: Human Kinetics, 57A Price Avenue, Lower Mitcham, South Australia 5062
08 8372 0999
e-mail: info@hkaustralia.com

New Zealand: Human Kinetics, P.O. Box 80, Torrens Park, South Australia 5062
0800 222 062
e-mail: info@hknewzealand.com

E4689

CONTENTS

PART II Motor Control

133

PART III Motor Learning

325

PREFACE

Most of us have marveled at one time or another about how the most highly skilled performers in industry, sport, music, or dance seem to make their actions appear so simple and easy—performed with incredible efficiency, smoothness, style, and grace. Like the first four editions of this text (Schmidt, 1982, 1988; Schmidt & Lee, 1999, 2005), the fifth edition of *Motor Control and Learning: A Behavioral Emphasis* was written for those who would like to understand how it is that these performers can achieve such artistry while we, as beginners in a similar task, are clumsy, inept, and unskilled. This book was written particularly as a textbook for university or college undergraduate and graduate students taking courses in human performance or motor learning, primarily in fields such as kinesiology or psychology. However, students in other fields, such as the neurosciences, physical therapy, occupational therapy, speech therapy, biomedical or industrial engineering, human factors or ergonomics, and sport, will also find many of the concepts contained here to be of interest, as movement behavior is a part of all of them. And for those who are, or who are becoming, practitioners in these fields, the principles of motor behavior outlined here should provide a solid basis for tasks such as designing human–machine systems, developing training programs in sport or industry, or teaching progressions in dance or music.

The emphasis of the text is behavioral. That is, the primary focus is on movement behavior that can be observed directly, as well as on the many factors that affect the quality of these performances and the ease with which they can be learned. In this sense, the book has strong ties to the methods and traditions of experimental psychology. Yet, at the same time, we focus on the neurological and biomechanical processes out of which these complex movement behaviors are crafted. Brain mechanisms that allow the detection of errors, spinal cord processes that are capable of generating patterns of skilled activities in locomotion, and various biomechanical factors that act to determine the nature of our movement behaviors are all important if we are to understand highly skilled performance. This blending of behavioral, neurophysiological, and biomechanical analyses reflects the fact that the fields of motor behavior and motor learning, movement neurophysiology (or motor control), and biomechanics are rapidly moving together toward the shared understanding of complex movement behaviors.

This edition of the text retains the same goal of presenting an up-to-date review of the state of knowledge in movement control and learning, and it does so with a format similar to that of the previous editions. We have directed considerable effort toward including the most recent knowledge from a number of rapidly developing subfields, and each chapter has been revised extensively in light of these newer concepts. In addition to including more than 280 new references to work published since the last edition (in 2005), we have also endeavored to pay homage to some of the important early research developments in the various areas. One of the features introduced in the previous two editions was sidebars highlighting specific research issues throughout the book. We have created more of these sidebars in this fifth edition with the idea that certain material requires a more detailed treatment to ensure understanding than is typical of passages in the text. Some of these sidebars highlight quotations from selected historical papers; other sidebars highlight careers of key researchers in motor control and learning; and still others deal with various applications of specific concepts in motor control and learning.

eBook available at HumanKinetics.com

Some chapters from the previous edition have been reduced in order to lessen complexities in the text without sacrificing the in-depth coverage or richness of the concepts. And we have expanded other chapters and sections to present new, exciting areas of research that have emerged since the previous edition. Many new figures have also been included to help illustrate and emphasize concepts and data that are difficult to communicate effectively in words. Practical examples from areas such as human factors, sport, therapy, and music are provided to illustrate motor control and learning concepts and provide suggestions for application. As before, the fifth edition reflects a logical progression so that later chapters build upon concepts presented in earlier chapters, with the final result being a consistent, defensible framework of ideas about motor skills. Having such a framework, or point of view, is important for those who wish to use the information presented here, both so that contributions to new applications may be made and so that the design of new skills research is facilitated.

The book is divided into three parts. Part I provides an introduction to research and fundamental concepts that are important to understanding motor behavior. The first chapter, a brief history of the field, is followed by a presentation of methods in movement research in chapter 2, focusing on various paradigms and statistical techniques used in the study of movement behavior. In chapter 3 the human is regarded as a processor of information, and we focus on the many ways that information is dealt with in motor behavior. The concept of attention is the focus of chapter 4, with particular emphasis on the role of attention in motor behavior.

Part II deals with motor control. Chapter 5 views motor control from a closed-loop perspective, in which the sensory contributions to movement control are examined, with particular emphasis on new research regarding the role of vision. In chapter 6, the focus shifts to contributions of the central nervous system to movement control, with emphasis on preorganized actions that involve motor programs and generalized motor programs. Some principles related to speed and accuracy are presented in chapter 7, together with a discussion of theoretical concepts that integrate the central and sensory contributions to movement control. Chapter 8 presents a discussion of the factors involved in movement control that make coordination both easy and difficult to achieve. The final chapter in this part contains a discussion of factors that determine skill differences between people and among groups of people, with emphasis on important themes about abilities and the prediction of skills.

Part III deals with the acquisition of skill, or motor learning. Chapter 10 concentrates on some special methodological problems for studying learning. The effects of practice, the structure of the practice session, and the many variables under the control of a teacher, coach, or therapist are discussed in chapter 11, while feedback contributions to learning are included in chapter 12. In both of these chapters, much new information is covered that demands important changes in our understanding of the processes involved in practice and the ways in which these influence learning. Chapter 13 presents various theoretical treatments of motor learning. And finally, chapter 14 deals with the factors associated with the retention and transfer of skills.

ACKNOWLEDGMENTS

Throughout the long process of this revision, a number of people provided very highly valued input. Judy Wright of Human Kinetics provided encouragement and many valuable suggestions for not only this revision, but on previous editions of the book as well. Her recent retirement closes an important chapter not only for the publisher, but also for the expression of ideas presented in this book. Judy, we wish you an energetic and successful next dance.

Thanks also go to our editors, Melissa Zavala and Antoinette Pomata, for their excellent work on the project. We called upon a number of colleagues to read specific sections of the book. The many suggestions made by Ramesh Balasubramaniam, Ian Franks, Waclaw Petrynski, Gwen Gordon, and Laurie Wishart were invaluable in making these revisions. The final manuscript is much better as a result, and we are grateful for their time and effort.

PART I

INTRODUCTION TO MOTOR BEHAVIOR

This first part introduces the field of motor control and learning. In chapter 1 the area is described, and the important distinctions separating motor control and learning from other, related fields of study are made. Then, a brief history of the field is given, showing how knowledge about movements from psychology and kinesiology, as well as from the neurosciences, has been combined. The second chapter deals with the various scientific methods used for studying motor skills. Here, we explain the tools of motor behavior research, focusing on the various ways in which motor behavior and skill can be measured. Chapter 3 presents the information-processing approach, which is fundamental to understanding how humans think and act. The last chapter in this section describes attention and its role in motor behavior.

CHAPTER 1

EVOLUTION OF A FIELD OF *STUDY*

Movement is a critical aspect of life. Without movement, we could not feed ourselves, we could not reproduce, and we would not survive. Our capacity to move is more than just a convenience that enables us to walk, play, or manipulate objects; it is a critical aspect of our evolutionary development, no less important than the evolution of our intellectual and emotional capacities. Some assert that our highly developed cognitive capacities evolved so that we could make the movements essential to survival—those involved in the construction of shelter, the making of tools, and communication. Surely the study of movement needs no further justification than its significance in terms of the evolution of humankind.

Movement takes many forms. Some forms can be regarded as genetically defined, such as the way in which people control their limbs or the ability of centipedes to coordinate their legs. Other examples include the "scratch reflex" of dogs or the rapid blink of the eye in response to an unexpected puff of air. Here, the patterns of action appear to be determined by genetic makeup, through growth and development, or in both ways; and these actions appear to be quite stereotypical for members of the same species. A second class of movements can be thought of as "learned"—for example, those involved in controlling an automobile, operat-

ing a typewriter, or performing a triple twisting somersault from the diving board. These learned movements are often termed *skills*. They are not inherited, and mastering them requires long periods of practice and experience. Guthrie (1952) perhaps provided the best definition of skills: "Skill consists in the ability to bring about some end result with maximum certainty and minimum outlay of energy, or of time and energy" (p. 136). Skills are especially critical to the study of human behavior, as they are involved in operating machines in industry, controlling vehicles, preparing meals, playing games, and so on. Skills and genetically defined movements can range from very simple (e.g., snapping fingers or blinking eyes) to very complex (e.g., pole-vaulting).

This book is about all these kinds of movements, whether primarily genetically defined or learned through practice. In particular, we will be concerned with how these various movements are *controlled*—how the central nervous system is organized so that the many individual muscles and joints become coordinated. We will also be concerned with how sensory information from the environment, the body, or both is used in the control of movement. The scientific field of study that addresses these issues is known as *motor control*—the study of the control of movements in humans and animals.

In this book, we add one important aspect to motor control that is sometimes not included—the study of how movements are *learned*, that is, how movements are produced differently as a result of practice or experience. Indeed, much evidence suggests that many of the movements already mentioned consist of a complex combination of genetic determinants coupled with modifications made through practice or experience. Understanding how movements are learned is the major concern of a field of study called *motor learning*. We see no good justification, however, for separating the study of motor learning from the study of movement or of motor control in general, as this artificial separation inhibits the understanding of both issues. For these reasons, as the title reveals, the subject matter of the book is motor control *and* learning.

Understanding Movement

How can knowledge and information about movement be acquired? A logical way to proceed would be to study some relevant aspect of the movement-control process using scientific methods. But which processes should be examined? One possibility would be to focus on the nature of biochemical interactions that occur within cells as individuals move. Or we could focus on the cell itself, asking how cells interact with each other in the control of movement. In a similar way, we could consider groups of cells, such as a whole muscle, the spinal cord, or the nerves, and ask how these relatively more complex structures are involved in movement control. Another possibility would be to focus on the movements of the freely moving animal or human, concentrating on the factors that determine movement accuracy, the choice of movement, or the patterns of action. Along the same lines, we could study movement in an even more global context, asking questions about the role of movement in society, the choice of certain skilled occupations or sports, movement in groups or teams, and so on.

Clearly, there are various ways to consider the same phenomenon. They involve the study of a phenomenon on different *levels of analysis*, and analogous levels are present in any area of scientific concern. Illnesses, for example, can be considered at levels that range from the biochemical and neurological determinants of disease through the historical and sociological effects of illnesses on entire societies. Because these various ways of considering a single problem are so diverse, a given scientist usually focuses on one, or at most two, of these levels of analysis.

A Behavioral Level of Analysis

The focus of this text is primarily at the *behavioral* level of analysis, centering on *cognitive*, information-processing concepts. The major goals will be to understand the variables that determine motor performance proficiency and to understand the variables that are most important for the learning of movement behaviors. We also want to understand how such information can be used in the solution of certain practical problems such as those involved in the design of equipment that humans must operate, in the selection of individuals for occupations, in the teaching of skills in sport and industry, and in the rehabilitation of skills after injury or stroke.

This behavioral level of analysis, however, is more interesting and complete when combined with two other fields of study, each representing a deeper level of analysis. The field of *biomechanics* concerns the mechanical and physical bases of biological systems. Certainly in order to understand movement we must understand something of the body itself, with all its joints, levers, and associated mechanical characteristics. The field of *neurophysiology* concerns the functioning of the brain and central nervous system and the ways in which they control the contractions of muscles that move the limbs. The study of movement will be addressed at various levels of analysis—but as the subtitle of the book suggests, the emphasis is at the behavioral level.

Emphasizing Movements

In considering movements, especially skills, it is often difficult to isolate a movement from its environment. In driving a car, for example, there are the coordinated actions involved in changing gears (clutch, accelerator, shift lever, etc.) as well as the movements involved in steering. These parts of the skill are the means through which the driver *affects* his environment. But skills are also *affected by* the environment. For example, whether or not there are turns in the road or whether snow is present influences the driver's interactions with the vehicle controls. Such reciprocal relations between the environment and the individual make it very difficult to pinpoint the various determinants of motor behavior, because the interaction of the many motor control and environmental factors is extremely complex and difficult to study with experimental procedures.

The approach taken in this text is to focus on the mutual interactions between the environment and the motor system. A large portion of this approach deals with the behavior and capabilities of the motor system to produce movements, studied more or less independently of the role of sensory or environmental information. But at the same time, the role of environmental information such as vision, and the ways in which it is processed and used to guide movements, is important. In any case, we are deliberately not concerned with skills in which the quality of the *movement* components per se is almost irrelevant to the outcome (as in playing chess).

In deciding which skills to include in our field of study, it is helpful to consider the probable limiting factors in the performance. In the chess example, intellectual decision making seems to be the important factor and should not be included in this treatment. In a marathon, or in weightlifting, the factors seem to be more closely related to cardiovascular fitness and strength, respectively—also not within the confines of the present field of study. We will emphasize skills in which the focus is on the capabilities to use environmental information in the complex control of the limbs.

Potential Applications

Given an understanding of some of the processes underlying the control of movements, where can these principles be applied? High-level sports, games, and athletic events come to mind as areas for application, as these activities often involve the same kinds of processes that are studied in the area of motor control and learning. But potential generalizations should not be limited to these kinds of activities. Many apparently genetically defined actions such as walking and maintaining posture are under consideration here. How these movement capabilities, when disrupted by injuries or disease, can be improved by treatments emphasizing the learning of *new* movement patterns—the subject matter of *physical therapy*—is also an application area. Many industrial skills,

such as using a lathe, typing, woodcarving, and handwriting, are of critical importance to this field of study. Artistic performances, such as the playing of musical instruments, the creation of a painting, or the production of a dance, are certainly under the heading of motor behavior as treated here. The use of voice, whether by the vocalist in an opera or by the student learning a new language,[1] is also a motor task, as the sounds are controlled by muscular activity of the vocal apparatus in ways analogous to the control of the hands and fingers of the skilled typist. The potential applications for the principles discovered in the field of motor control are present in nearly every aspect of our lives.

Origins of the Field

In an examination of the early research on movement and learning, it will be evident that the field, as we know it today, emerged from two isolated bodies of knowledge. These two areas are (a) the branch of neurophysiology primarily concerned with the neural processes that are associated with (or are causes of) movements, with only slight reference to the movements themselves; and (b) the branch of psychology and related fields primarily concerned with high-level skills with very little reference to the neurological mechanisms involved. For nearly a century, these two fields developed knowledge at different levels of analysis but with little mutual influence. Only toward the end of the 1970s did the two fields begin to come together. For the reader interested in more detail on these historical developments, see Irion (1966), Adams (1987), and Summers (1992, 2004).

Early Research

A fascinating account of some of the early insights regarding actions and movement appears in a review by Meijer (2001). In this historical paper, Meijer traces the origins of a number of ideas within current thinking to philosophers such as Plato, Aristotle, and Galen. Some of the earliest empirical investigations of motor skills were performed around 1820 by the astronomer Bessel (cited by Welford, 1968), who tried to understand the differences among his colleagues in recording the transit times of the movements of stars. This skill involved estimating the time required for the image of a star to move through the crosshairs of a telescope. Bessel was interested in the processes underlying this complex skill, as well as in the reasons some of his colleagues estimated accurately and others could not. Considerably later, studies addressed the visual contributions to hand movements in localizing targets (Bowditch & Southard, 1882). Leuba and Chamberlain (1909) studied the accuracy of limb-positioning movements; Fullerton and Cattell (1892) examined force reproducibility; Stevens (1886) studied timing; and Judd (1908) studied transfer of learning with dart-throwing tasks. Some researchers used experimental methods to study expertise in sport performance (Scripture, 1894; see also Fuchs, 1998). An important trend was established by Bryan and Harter's (1897, 1899) work on receiving and sending Morse code; periods of no improvement (plateaus) between segments of improvement were identified, and considerable debate about the existence and interpretation of these plateaus continued for some decades (e.g., Book, 1908/1925; Keller, 1958). Galton (see Boring, 1950) studied the relationships among strength, steadiness, and body configuration in over 9,000 British males and females; Book (1908/1925) examined typing skills for very large samples of subjects ranging widely in ability and age. Retention of skills over long intervals of no practice was an important theme, and typing was a convenient way to study it (e.g., Bean, 1912; Swift & Schuyler, 1907). A remarkable series of studies on the retention of typing skill, initiated by Hill, Rejall, and Thorndike (1913), showed "savings," in terms of practice time or the amount of practice, involved in the relearning of typing skill after two consecutive 25-year periods of no practice (Hill, 1934, 1957).

One of the earliest systematic approaches to the understanding of motor skills was used by Woodworth (1899), who sought to identify some of the fundamental principles of rapid arm and hand movements. This work, together with that of Hollingworth (1909), uncovered principles about visual-motor performance that remain a topic of current debate (e.g., Elliott, Helsen, & Chua, 2001; Newell & Vaillancourt, 2001b). Some other research, published in German and French, went unnoticed in the English literature for many years. Work on such topics as memory for movements, speed–accuracy trade-offs, and phase transitions in bimanual movements appeared in German and French publications during the middle and late 1800s. Some of this research is summarized by Worringham (1992).

A major influence of the time was Thorndike (1914), who was concerned with processes underlying the learning of skills and other behaviors. His Law of Effect, which continues to have its influences in psychology, states that responses that are rewarded tend to be repeated. Responses that are not followed by a reward tend not to be repeated. This idea formed the cornerstone for much of the theorizing about learning that was to follow in the 20th century (Adams, 1978). Thorndike was also a pioneer in the area of individual differences, in which the focus is on the differences among individuals surrounding practice (see chapter 9).

Most of the work mentioned here originated from the field of psychology, and much of the field of motor behavior today is the legacy of this early thinking and research. But the early research, which is similar in method to at least some of today's work, marked a severe break in tradition from the pre-1900 views of behavior. The pre-1900 research often involved *introspection*, including subjective self-reports of feelings that were unobservable. Skills were studied only because they were thought to provide "access to the mind." As the 19th century ended, there was a shift to more systematic and objective approaches to the study of skills. And, of equal importance, skills were beginning to be studied because investigators wanted to know about the skills themselves.

Toward the end of this period, the number of studies involving skills increased slightly. Some of these concerned handwriting proficiency, ways in which practice sessions could be structured to maximize motor learning, and whether or not skills should be "broken down" into their components for practice. Skills research placed greater emphasis on industrial applications (Gilbreth, 1909; Stimpel, 1933). So-called time-and-motion studies analyzed production-line assembly movements; such research became the target of criticism by workers because of the strict standards of performance it imposed on them. There was rising interest in the most efficient ways to perform tasks such as carrying mortar and shoveling coal and in methods of improving the conduct of work in extremely hot environments; these studies became the early contributions to the emerging fields of human factors and ergonomics. Some early theories of learning were published (e.g., Snoddy, 1935), and work by physical educators interested in sports and athletic performances emerged (e.g., McCloy, 1934, 1937). An interest in factors associated with growth, maturation, and motor performance began to surface; and studies by Bayley (1935), Espenschade (1940), McGraw (1935, 1939), and Shirley (1931) led the way to the formation of the subarea that we now call *motor development* (see Thomas, 1997, for a historical review).

The evolution of the study of the physiological or neural bases of movement paralleled work in the motor behavior area during this period, but without much formal contact between the fields. The characteristics and contraction properties of muscle tissue were a topic of early study by Blix (1892-1895) and Weber (1846; see Partridge, 1983), who identified "spring-like" properties of muscle that were later "rediscovered." Jackson conducted early investigations of the neural control of movement in the 1870s, well before the advent of electrophysiological techniques that were to revolutionize the field. But what led to the development of various electrophysiological methods was the discovery by Fritsch and Hitzig (1870) that the brain is electrically excitable. These methods gave rise to studies by Ferrier (1888) on the responses in the brain's cortex to movements, as well as to the work by Beevor and Horsely (1887, 1890) on sensory and motor areas of the brain.

One of the more important influences in the neural control area was the work on reflexes at about the end of the 19th century by Sherrington and his coworkers. Sherrington studied and classified the major responses to stimuli presented to the extremities, and he believed that most of our voluntary movements resulted from these fundamental reflexes. Sherrington is credited with the creation of a number of classical concepts of motor control, most of which influence thinking today. For example, he first talked of *reciprocal innervation,* the idea that when the flexors of a joint are activated, the extensors tend to be automatically deactivated, and vice versa. Also, Sherrington coined the term *final common path,* which referred to the notion that influences from reflexes and sensory sources, as well as from "command" sources in the brain, eventually converge at spinal levels to produce the final set

of commands delivered to the muscles. Indeed, Sherrington's early writings (e.g., Sherrington, 1906) remain relevant today (see tributes to his work in Gallistel, 1980; Stuart, Pierce, Callister, Brichta, & McDonagh, 2001).

Sherrington was one of those involved in research on the perception of movement. Various sensory receptors were identified, such as the Golgi tendon organ, thought to signal changes in muscle *tension,* and the muscle spindle, thought to be involved in the perception of muscle *length* and hence joint position. Sherrington coined the now-common term *proprioception,* which refers to the sense of body position and orientation thought to be signaled by the various muscle and joint receptors together with receptors located in the inner ear.

Somewhat later, scientists conducted research on various brain structures. Herrick (1924) proposed numerous hypotheses about the functions of the cerebellum, many of which seem at least reasonable today. Also, patients with accidental cerebellar damage were studied (e.g., by Holmes [1939]) in an attempt to pinpoint some of the movement-control deficits associated with this structure. Other brain structures, studied in patients with various kinds of brain damage, became subjects of interest (Adrian & Buytendijk, 1931).

Early neural control research mainly involved very simple movements. Indeed, experimenters sometimes isolated nerve–muscle preparations or used animals with various degrees of experimentally induced spinal cord damage; here the concern about movement was usually secondary to interest in the neurological processes. When movements were studied, the movement was often not considered in much detail; and measures of the speed, accuracy, or patterns of movement were usually missing from these reports. The motor behavior work, on the other hand, typically involved very complex actions (e.g., typing, telegraphy) but with very little emphasis on the underlying neural or biomechanical mechanisms that controlled these actions.

We can see an exception to this general separation of the neural control and motor behavior areas in the research of two important physiologists in the 1930s and 1940s. During this period, Nikolai Bernstein and Erich von Holst published a number of seminal papers that have had a significant impact on motor control theorizing today (for more on Bernstein see "Nikolai Bernstein"). Unfortunately, many scientists involved in the study of movement, from both behavioral and neural control areas, were unaware of the contributions made by Bernstein and von Holst until translations of their work appeared in English—Bernstein's work had been published in Russian, von Holst's in German. Their early papers reappeared in English in the late 1960s and early 1970s (see Bernstein, 1967, 1996; Whiting, 1984;

Nikolai Bernstein

At the same time that Ivan Pavlov dominated the field of Russian physiology during the 1920s and 1930s, Nikolai Bernstein, in relative obscurity, was publishing his remarkable discoveries on movement coordination. The differences between Pavlov and Bernstein could not have been more dramatic. For Pavlov, the movements of an animal were seen as a passive bundle of conditioned reflexes; for Bernstein, movements were active and goal directed. Pavlov was proudly supported by the Russian government; Bernstein lost his job because of his criticisms of Pavlov's research.

There has been a remarkable rise in interest in Bernstein's ideas since the English translation of some of his papers in 1967. One of his ideas that has received considerable attention has been called the *degrees of freedom problem.* The issue concerns the fact that the motor system has many different independent parts that move—too many for an individual to control separately at a conscious level. One problem for the motor control scientist is to explain how so many degrees of freedom are coordinated in such an elegant manner if only a few of them are regulated at a conscious level. Parts of chapters later in this book are devoted to this problem.

FIGURE 1.1 Nikolai A. Bernstein (1897-1966).

Reprinted, by permission, from Fizkultura Sports Publishers.

Another important contribution, to be discussed in detail later, concerns the problem of learning a new movement pattern. Again, Bernstein used the degrees of freedom concept to great advantage. His idea was that, in the early stages of skill acquisition, learners tend to "freeze" the nonessential body parts by reducing the number of degrees of freedom so that they can concentrate on the essence of the action. The elegance of movement is seen when skill develops, and coincides with the "release" and "exploitation" of the degrees of freedom.

Perhaps the most telling evidence of Bernstein's influence on current motor control theorizing is the fact that the journal *Motor Control* has published over a dozen English translations of Bernstein's papers since 1998 and that a biennial conference celebrating his legacy continues to this day.

Selected Bibliography

Bernstein, N.A. (1967). *The co-ordination and regulation of movements.* Oxford: Pergamon Press.

Bernstein, N.A. (1996). On dexterity and its development. In M.L. Latash & M.T. Turvey (Eds.), *Dexterity and its development.* Mahwah, NJ: Erlbaum.

Whiting, H.T.A. (Ed.). (1984). *Human motor actions: Bernstein reassessed.* Amsterdam: Elsevier.

Further Reading

Bongaardt, R. (2001). How Bernstein conquered movement. In M.L. Latash & V.M. Zatsiorsky (Eds.), *Classics in movement science* (pp. 59-84). Champaign, IL: Human Kinetics.

Bongaardt, R., & Meijer, O. (2000). Bernstein's theory of movement behavior: Historical development and contemporary relevance. *Journal of Motor Behavior, 32,* 57-71.

Feigenberg, I.M., & Latash, L.P. (1996). N.A. Bernstein: The reformer of neuroscience. In M.L. Latash & M.T. Turvey (Eds.), *Dexterity and its development* (pp. 247-275). Champaign, IL: Human Kinetics.

von Holst, 1937/1973; Gallistel, 1980). Thus, while the two areas were being blended in Russia and Germany, these trends were not seen in the United States or England, where most of the work on movement was being conducted. Ironically, it was the translation of this work many years later, and the attention that it received (e.g., Turvey, 1977), that served as a significant catalyst to the merging of the neural control and motor behavior areas.

Postwar Research

World War II had profound effects on the world, and it is not surprising that it also had major effects on movement research. One of the earliest and most direct effects can be traced to the need to select the most suitable people for pilot training, which resulted in the creation of the U.S. Army Air Force's Psycho-Motor Testing Program, initiated by Arthur Melton in the early stages of the war (see Melton, 1947, for a description of some of this work). Important studies were conducted on underlying motor, perceptual, and intellectual abilities as they related to the selection of pilots and other military personnel (see chapter 9). Similar studies were conducted in England. In addition, scientists studied gunnery, physical training in the heat and cold, vehicle control, and many other issues related to combat performance.

When the war ended in 1945, the prevailing attitude in the United States was that the efforts related to selection and training of military personnel should not be abandoned. Consequently, this research continued for many years (e.g., Druckman & Bjork, 1991, 1994). The military research effort was sustained when Arthur Melton created (in 1949) the U.S. Air Force Human Resources Research Center, which carried on many of the wartime programs but also expanded to include studies of more general interest. A major contribution of this program was Fleishman's work on individual differences and abilities (e.g., Fleishman, 1965, 2004). The wartime programs, devoted to personnel selection and motor abilities, had not resulted in the success in pilot selection that had been anticipated. Researchers began to realize that training—not selection—was perhaps more important to the development of proficient pilots. Hence, much attention was directed toward procedures for teaching motor skills, the transfer of motor skills from one activity to another, and the retention of skills (chapter 14).

In addition to the formal laboratories that were supported by defense funds, research relevant to the military was given increased federal funding. This funding, in the form of contracts, grants, and training programs, was responsible for a shift of attention among psychologists toward motor behavior research. The directions imposed by federal funding agencies had, and continue to have, a profound influence on the behaviors studied and the research questions asked. The area of motor behavior was important at the time, and a great deal of funding was directed toward it, convincing a large number of psychologists to become interested in research in this area.

A second major influence in the creation of the boom in motor behavior research in the postwar period was the emergence of various theories of learning, most notably that of Hull (1943). In scientific inquiry, theories generally provide an organization of the conceptual issues and findings as well as strong suggestions for future research. Theories stimulate and provide focus for the research of others, and Hull's theory was no exception. His was a general learning theory, applying to animals and humans and to verbal and motor behavior, and it was often tested with motor tasks. A major emphasis of the theory was the fatigue-like process associated with long practice periods. The theory attempted to explain how fatigue and recovery processes combined to determine the learning of motor skills, and many scientists worked with motor tasks to test Hull's predictions. Most of this work has relevance to the distribution of practice (see chapter 11) or to the effects of fatigue on performance and learning. Hull's theory later proved to be an inadequate account of the processes and variables that determine motor learning and performance. However, theories like Hull's provide strong directions for research and contribute experimental data for use by future generations, even though the original theory may be shown to be inadequate.

As the complexity of machines increased in this period and industrial methods became more complicated, it became obvious that the capabilities of humans to operate machinery effectively were being exceeded. For example, a number of serious airplane accidents that were initially attributed to "pilot error" were eventually traced to the way in which the instruments and controls in the cockpit were arranged (Chapanis, 1965; Fitts & Jones, 1947; Schlager, 1994). Thus, shortly after the war, a study of man–machine interactions, variously termed *human factors, ergonomics,* or *engineering psychology* (a subarea of industrial psychology), emerged. The guiding concepts were that humans were an important component in most of the machinery involved in industry, and that such machinery must be designed with humans in mind. Although this thinking began in the military, it is now seen in automobile design (Lee, 2008), the organization of assembly lines and work spaces, the design of home appliances and computer workstations, and many other areas (Chapanis, 1999; Jagacinski & Flach, 2003; Karwowski, 2001; Wickens & Hollands, 2000). Professional societies and journals were founded in the mid-20th century and continue to flourish today (Cooke, 2008; Waterson & Sell, 2006).

This period also saw a great deal of experimental effort in England. One of the most important contributions was by Craik (1948), who proposed that we consider the brain as a kind of computer in which information is received, processed, and then output to the environment in the form of overt actions of the limbs. An important part of this general idea is the notion of *central intermittency,* by which the human movement is seen as a series of discrete bursts rather than as continuous (as it might appear). Craik's idea paved the way for other English psychologists such as Welford, who in 1952 proposed the still-relevant *single-channel hypothesis* of attention (see chapter 4). Also, a great deal of work was done in ergonomics, on training and conditions of practice, and on hand movement control, particularly with respect to anticipation and timing (Poulton, 1950).

The ideas about central intermittency and the analogies of the brain to the computer were accompanied by similar new directions in psychology and related fields. One of the new ideas was represented by Wiener's (1948) book *Cybernetics,* which outlined an information-processing basis for human behavior. Also, Shannon and Weaver's (1949) *The Mathematical Theory of Communication* established important principles of information processing that later led to systematic attempts to study the motor system in terms of its capabilities and limitations in processing information (see Hick's law in chapter 3). In keeping with the information-processing basis for behavior suggested by Craik and others, Fitts (1954) established some now-famous fundamental relations among characteristics of aiming movements—their movement time, their movement extent, and their accuracy (see chapter 7 and "Paul Fitts"). The discovery of these two laws of behavior was an important advance in research, tied together by information theory (Seow, 2005).

In the middle of this postwar period, a great deal of motor behavior research was being conducted—enough that Robert and Carol Ammons, themselves researchers in this area, created a journal in 1949 titled *Perceptual and Motor Skills Research Exchange.*[2] The journal now publishes both motor and nonmotor research, but during its early years it served as a major outlet for motor behavior work. In addition, *Research Quarterly,*[3] a physical education research journal, and the *Journal of Experimental Psychology*[4] published a great deal of motor behavior research during this period.

Toward the end of the postwar period, the number of psychologists interested in motor behavior research gradually declined, while the number of physical educators interested in the study of motor skills greatly increased. The psychologists' lack of interest may be attributed to decreased federal support for motor behavior research, disillusionment with Hull's theory, and increasing interest in other types of human behavior such as verbal learning and memory. This trend away from motor behavior research reached its peak in the mid-1960s when an "academic funeral" sponsored by Ina and Edward Bilodeau was held at Tulane University. Renowned motor behavior psychologists gathered to hear the "last rites" and to bid each other farewell as each moved on to different research topics in psychology. The eulogies were recorded in a volume titled *Acquisition of Skill* (Bilodeau, 1966), which well describes the attitude of the times.

Motor behavior research was dead, or so the psychologists thought; but they did not consider a man named Franklin Henry, trained in psychology and working in the Physical Education Department at Berkeley, who had a continuing interest in motor behavior research (see "Franklin Henry" on p. 12). Together with A.T. Slater-Hammel and other leaders in physical education, these new motor behavior scientists organized the North American Society for the Psychology of Sport and Physical Activity (NASPSPA) and the Canadian Society for Psychomotor Learning and Sport Psychology. These groups flourished in the 1970s. During this period, two books devoted strictly to motor behavior and motor learning

Paul Fitts

FIGURE 1.2 Paul M. Fitts (1912-1965).

Probably no empirical discovery in the area of motor control is better known than Fitts' law, which states that the time observed to complete an aimed movement depends on a simple mathematical relationship between the distance to move and the size of the intended target (see chapter 7). Called "Fitts' law" out of respect for its originator, this formulation was an early attempt to apply mathematical and information-processing principles to the understanding of human movements, and it suggested that more complex limb control could be understood by future application of such methods and thinking. The mathematical equation described in Fitts' law characterizes the trade-off between speed and error during simple aiming movements in a way that has remarkable generalizability.

But Fitts' law was just one of many legacies of a psychologist whose research had many implications for activities of daily living, especially for equipment design. Fitts' early research on the effects of the spatial compatibility between work-space displays and the controls used in responding to these displays had a profound influence on the then-emerging field of ergonomics and human factors (see chapter 3). In later years, Fitts also wrote about perceptual–motor learning, suggesting that learning involves a progression through various stages, each with distinctive characteristics regarding the capabilities of the human to process information (see chapter 13). Paul Fitts was widely regarded as a leader in his area of research when he died unexpectedly in the mid-1960s at the age of 53, well before his full potential could be realized.

Selected Bibliography

Fitts, P.M. (1954). The information capacity of the human motor system in controlling the amplitude of movement. *Journal of Experimental Psychology, 47,* 381-391.

Fitts, P.M. (1964). Perceptual-motor skills learning. In A.W. Melton (Ed.), *Categories of human learning* (pp. 243-285). New York: Academic Press.

Fitts, P.M., & Seeger, C.M. (1953). S-R compatibility: Spatial characteristics of stimulus and response codes. *Journal of Experimental Psychology, 46,* 199-210.

Further Reading

Pew, R.W. (1994). Paul Morris Fitts, 1912-1965. In H.L. Taylor (Ed.), *Division 21 members who made distinguished contributions to engineering psychology* (pp. 23-44). Washington, DC: APA.

were published, one in England (Knapp, 1963) and one in the United States (Cratty, 1964). Many more followed (including the first edition of this book in 1982).

Not all psychologists of the period were bored with motor behavior research. Fitts and Peterson (1964) presented influential experiments on limb movement accuracy; Bilodeau and Bilodeau (1961), Adams (1964), and Noble (1968) wrote needed reviews of motor behavior research; Adams (1968) wrote a theoretical treatment of the role of sensory feedback in movement learn-

ing; and Keele (1968) wrote an often quoted review of motor control (see "Steve Keele" on p. 13). But these were the exceptions. As the 1970s approached, the cluster of scientists in physical education and (to a limited extent) psychology began to evolve in new directions. Posner and Konick (1966) and Adams and Dijkstra (1966) presented seminal articles dealing with short-term memory for movements; Henry and his students (e.g., Henry & Rogers, 1960) were interested in motor programs; Posner (1969) studied attention and movement control; Pew (1966) examined

Franklin Henry

Fittingly acknowledged as the father of motor behavior research in physical education, Franklin Henry advocated an approach using psychological techniques, laboratory tasks, and careful measurement. Unlike most psychologists, he used whole-body activities (as well as the psychologists' traditional fine-motor tasks) in his research, and many of these tasks included very rapid motor actions representative of activities in sports and games. One of Henry's most important contributions to motor control research was the "memory drum theory," and his experiments in 1960 provided rather convincing evidence that measures of reaction time (RT) were sensitive to the "complexity" of the action that was to be produced (see chapter 3). Among Henry's many other contributions was the controversial idea that individuals possess many independent abilities. He argued that the so-called all-around athlete is not someone who has a very "strong" general motor ability, but rather someone who has inherited many specific, highly effective capabilities. His innovative research methods showed that

FIGURE 1.3   Franklin M. Henry (1904-1993).

there was very little correlation between an individual's performances on two or more tasks, even if these tasks seem to be very similar in an assumed underlying ability (e.g., dynamic vs. static balance; see chapter 9). Henry educated many doctoral students who subscribed to his general method and point of view as they assumed positions in physical education departments during the college growth boom of the 1960s. Many of these scholars created PhD programs and trained more students in this basic tradition, with the result that Henry's influence became pervasive by the 1970s and continues today.

Selected Bibliography

Henry, F.M. (1968). Specificity vs. generality in learning motor skill. In R.C. Brown & G.S. Kenyon (Eds.), *Classical studies on physical activity* (pp. 341-340). Englewood Cliffs, NJ: Prentice Hall. (Original work published in 1958)

Henry, F.M., & Harrison, J.S. (1961). Refractoriness of a fast movement. *Perceptual and Motor Skills, 13,* 351-354.

Henry, F.M., & Rogers, D.E. (1960). Increased response latency for complicated movements and a "memory drum" theory of neuromotor reaction. *Research Quarterly, 31,* 448-458.

Further Reading

Snyder, C., & Abernethy, B. (Eds.) (1992). The creative side of experimentation: Personal perspectives from leading researchers in motor control, motor development, and sport psychology. Champaign, IL: Human Kinetics.

practice and automaticity; and Adams (1971) initiated a return to theorizing about motor learning. These emphases provided strong leadership for the motor behavior area in the 1970s.

As in the early period, the neural control and motor behavior scientists were nearly oblivious to each other; but important contributions

were being made in neural control that would later be influential in joining the two areas. One of the more important contributions was the work on muscle spindle mechanisms by Merton (1953; Marsden, Merton, & Morton, 1972), to be discussed in chapter 5. While the specific mechanisms proposed by Merton now appear

Steve Keele

FIGURE 1.4 Steve Keele (1940-2005).

Courtesy of Betty Jean Keele.

The 1960s marked a critical time in the history of motor behavior research, as many psychologists shifted their focus to issues of cognition, such as memory and attention. Psychology appeared to have abandoned the study of motor behavior, with a few notable exceptions. The appearance of Keele's motor control literature review in 1968 created renewed interest in important issues such as the motor program and the role of vision in movement regulation. His paper (with Michael Posner) on the period during a movement that is required to process and act on visual information remains one of our favorites for its simple, elegant methods of answering a difficult question. Keele's book, *Attention and Human Performance,* published several years later, situated movement prominently within a late-filter theory of attention, reminding psychologists that movement is not just a simple "output" in the human-computer metaphor (Rosenbaum, 2005). Updated and expanded reviews of motor control in later years were considered mandatory reading for students in this area. Keele's later research interests included important contributions to our understanding of individual differences, timing, and sequence learning.

Selected Bibliography

Keele, S.W. (1968). Movement control in skilled motor performance. *Psychological Bulletin, 70,* 387-403.

Keele, S.W. (1973). *Attention and human performance.* Pacific Palisades, CA: Goodyear.

Keele, S.W. (1986). Motor control. In K.R. Boff, L. Kaufman, & J.P. Thomas (Eds.), *Handbook of perception and performance* (pp. 30.1-30.60). New York: Wiley.

Keele, S.W., Jennings, P., Jones, S., Caulton, D., & Cohen, A. (1995). On the modularity of sequence representation. *Journal of Motor Behavior, 27,* 17-30.

Keele, S.W., & Posner, M.I. (1968). Processing of visual feedback in rapid movements. *Journal of Experimental Psychology, 77,* 155-158.

Further Reading

Ivry, R.B., Mayr, U., Corcos, D.M., & Posner, M.I. (2006). Psychological processes and neural mechanisms for action: The legacy of Steven W. Keele. *Journal of Motor Behavior, 38,* 3-6.

Keele, S.W. (1983). This week's citation classic. *Current Contents, 37* (Sept. 12), 20.

---

to be incorrect (Houk, 1979; Smith, 1977), Merton's original ideas about automatic regulation of movement are reasonable in very general terms. Merton was one of the first to measure movements *and* neurophysiological processes in the same investigation, creating a beginning for a blend of behavior and neurological emphases that was to follow. At about the same time, a great deal of research was devoted to the sensory receptors associated with movement perception and kinesthesis. Skoglund (1956) published a classic paper showing that the various receptors in a joint capsule appear to be activated at certain specific joint angles, suggesting that these receptors have a large role in the perception of joint position.

Numerous studies on the nature of muscle and its contractile and mechanical (e.g., spring-like) properties were also completed during these postwar years, and these studies attracted the attention of contemporary researchers in motor behavior and motor control (Rack & Westbury, 1969). These mechanical characteristics of muscle and of the motor apparatus were utilized by scientists in the Moscow laboratories who were following the earlier tradition of Bernstein. The extensive work on movement control by this group, originally published in Russian and thus generally unknown to American and British researchers, attracted a great deal of attention through various translations (e.g., Gelfand, Gurfinkel, Tomin, & Tsetlin, 1971; Kots, 1977). This research has special relevance for the control of locomotion and provides important links between the neural control mechanisms and behavioral principles. But despite these efforts, by 1970 almost no association existed between the behavioral scientists interested in more global and complex skills and the neurophysiological scientists interested in simple movements and neural control.

The End of the Century

The 1970s brought massive changes in the field of movement control and learning. The strict stimulus–response (S-R) orientation that had had such a strong foothold during most of the century was overshadowed by the cognitive, information-processing approach. The publication of two books during the 1960s—Miller, Galanter, and Pribram's (1960) *Plans and the Structure of Behavior* and Neisser's (1967) *Cognitive Psychology*—had a large impact on the field of experimental psychology in general and, later, on motor behavior too. The move toward cognitive psychology was a reaction to S-R theories of behavior. Ideas about mental and motor processes, together with many methods and paradigms for understanding them, took the place of S-R theories. Perhaps more than anything else, the books by Miller and colleagues and Neisser popularized the study of mental processes such as response selection and movement programming, whose existence must be *inferred* from the behaving individual rather than directly observed (see also Baars, 1986; Miller, 2003).

Influenced by cognitive psychology, the motor behavior field seemed to undergo a transition from a *task orientation*, which focuses primarily on the effects of variables on the performance or learning of certain motor tasks (or both), to a *process orientation*, which focuses on the underlying mental or neural events that support or produce movements (Pew, 1970, 1974b; Schmidt, 1975b, 1989a). Humans were considered processors of information, and this approach was an attempt to understand how movement information is coded and stored, how actions are represented in memory, and how information about errors is processed so that learning can occur.

Led by such researchers as Adams and Dijkstra (1966) and Posner and Konick (1966), the process orientation helped to create the area of *short-term motor memory*—the study of the processes underlying memory loss in simple movements over short periods of time. Many studies were conducted in this area during the late 1960s and early 1970s (see chapter 14). Studies were also completed on information-processing activities during the learning of simple motor tasks (see chapter 12).

More importantly, theorizing returned to motor behavior and learning, a style of inquiry that had been relatively dormant since the failure of Hull's (1943) theory. Adams sparked the interest in theory when he presented a feedback-based theory of verbal learning (Adams & Bray, 1970), followed the next year by a similar theory devoted to motor learning (Adams, 1971) (see "Jack Adams"). Pew (1974a) returned to the old idea of a movement *schema* (Bartlett, 1932)—the abstract hypothetical structures responsible for movement control and evaluation, to be discussed in chapter 13. And, one year later, the schema theory for the learning of simple motor skills was presented (Schmidt, 1975b). Together, these theoretical ideas generated a great deal of interest in motor skills, as this text makes evident later.

The motor behavior field not only changed its direction, but also grew rapidly. Formal courses of study in universities flourished, and new journals appeared. In 1969, Schmidt founded the *Journal of Motor Behavior*, which was closely followed in 1975 by the *Journal of Human Movement Studies*, created by the English motor behavior scientist John Whiting (see "H.T.A. (John) Whiting" on p. 16). A review journal titled *Exercise and Sport Sciences Reviews* was created in this period, and it devoted a major portion of its space to motor behavior research. Two more journals devoted to the study of motor control also appeared before the turn of the century; *Human Movement Science* appeared in 1982 and *Motor Control* in 1997. And throughout this time, the psychological journals (e.g., *Journal of Experimental Psychology: Human Perception and Performance, Psychological Research, Psychological Bulletin, British Journal of Psychology, Psychological Review, Human Factors,* and *Ergonomics*) continued to publish motor behavior research. As the field grew, motor behavior textbooks proliferated. More than 30 textbooks written subsequent to Knapp's (1963) and Cratty's (1964)

Jack Adams

FIGURE 1.5 Jack A. Adams (1922-2010).

Courtesy of Jack Adams.

One of the landmark advances in the developing field of motor learning was the publication of "A Closed-Loop Theory of Motor Learning" in the *Journal of Motor Behavior* in 1971. This paper described one of the very first theories directed specifically at *motor* learning and presented numerous testable hypotheses that became the focus of a considerable number of research studies in the 1970s. Although many of the tenets of closed-loop theory were later found to need revision (see chapter 13), which is the case for most theories that are scrutinized carefully, Adams' theory was clearly a catalyst that moved the research "bar" in motor learning much higher. But the 1971 theory was only one of many contributions to motor learning research that Adams made in a long and fruitful career. His early work on psychological warm-up effects as a source of memory decrement in practice (e.g., Adams, 1961) led to one of the very first of many investigations on short-term memory for movement information (Adams & Dijkstra, 1966). Throughout his research career, Adams maintained an interest in the application of motor learning research in the area of human factors and ergonomics, beginning with his work at Lackland Air Force Base in Texas. Later he turned his attention to the effects of modeling and observational learning (e.g., Adams, 1986), again spearheading a rise in research activity in that area. Perhaps his most lasting legacy, however, will be as a research historian—Jack Adams' ability to accurately and concisely synthesize volumes of research history into manageable chunks of understandable knowledge will serve students of motor control and learning for many years to come. His 1964 paper in the *Annual Review of Psychology* and the 1987 paper in the *Psychological Bulletin* remain as landmark reference works in motor behavior.

Selected Bibliography

Adams, J.A. (1961). The second facet of forgetting: A review of warm-up decrement. *Psychological Bulletin, 58*, 257-273.

Adams, J.A. (1964). Motor skills. *Annual Review of Psychology, 15*, 181-202.

Adams, J.A. (1971). A closed-loop theory of motor learning. *Journal of Motor Behavior, 3*, 111-150.

Adams, J.A. (1987). Historical review and appraisal of research on the learning, retention, and transfer of human motor skills. *Psychological Bulletin, 101*, 41-74.

Further Reading

Schmidt, R.A. (1990). Distinguished scholar award to Jack Ashton Adams. *NASPSPA Newsletter, 15*, 4-5.

Schmidt, R.A. (2011). Jack Adams, a giant of motor behavior, has died. *Journal of Motor Behavior, 43*, 83-84.

work were published, as were a large number of edited volumes on more specific topics.

The 1970s were the beginning of a long-needed merger between the neural control and the motor behavior scientists. Many people were trained formally in both motor behavior and neural control, and these people completed the bridge between the two levels of analysis. More and more behavior-oriented scientists began to ask questions

about movement control and made increased use of various electrophysiological and biomechanical techniques to understand the functions of the central nervous system in movement. The neural control scientists were shifting from studies that examined only the neural mechanisms to studies investigating these mechanisms during complex movements. Much of this latter work was done with animals, principally monkeys

H.T.A. (John) Whiting

Another pioneer who had tremendous influence on motor behavior research was H.T.A. (John) Whiting. Like Franklin Henry in the United States, discussed earlier in the chapter, Whiting introduced traditional psychological techniques to the study of human motor control in the performance of sport tasks. His research on catching performance was the first to demonstrate that continuous vision of a ball in flight is not necessary in order to support accurate performance (see chapter 5). Whiting's book, *Acquiring Ball Skill* (1969), was one of the first psychologically oriented texts to be devoted to the study of motor skills. Later Whiting turned his attention to the study of learning in the Bernstein tradition (see chapter 13). During this time Whiting also founded and served as the editor of the *Journal of Human Movement Studies* and, later, *Human Movement Science.* Another important legacy was the many graduate students Whiting supervised at Leeds during the 1960s and 1970s, and then at the Free University of Amsterdam in the Netherlands during the 1980s and 1990s. Many of these scientists continue to carry on Whiting's legacy today.

FIGURE 1.6 H.T.A. (John) Whiting (1929-2001).

Courtesy of Vrije Universiteit.

Selected Bibliography

Vereijken, B., Whiting, H.T.A., & Beek, W.J. (1992). A dynamical systems approach to skill acquisition. *Quarterly Journal of Experimental Psychology, 45A,* 323-344.

Whiting, H.T.A. (1969). *Acquiring ball skill: A psychological interpretation.* London: Bell.

Whiting, H.T.A., Gill, E.B., & Stephenson, J.M. (1970). Critical time intervals for taking in flight information in a ball-catching task. *Ergonomics, 13,* 265-272.

Further Reading

Savelsburgh, G., & Davids, K. (2002). "Keeping the eye on the ball": The legacy of John Whiting (1929-2001) in sport science. *Journal of Sport Sciences, 20,* 79-82.

Snyder, C., & Abernethy, B. (1992). *The creative side of experimentation: Personal perspectives from leading researchers in motor control, motor development, and sport psychology.* Champaign, IL: Human Kinetics.

and cats. Records from electrodes implanted in the brain, spinal cord, or muscle were taken while the animal was engaged in motor activity. Representing this approach are Grillner and his colleagues (1972, 1975) and Smith and her colleagues (1986), who studied locomotion in cats; Evarts (1972, 1973), who studied a number of separate brain structures in monkeys; and Houk (1979) and Granit (1970), who studied the gamma motor system in monkeys and humans.

The essential feature of all this work is the strong attempt to find an association between movement behaviors and neurological processes in order to provide a more complete understanding of how movements are controlled. This emphasis marked a refreshing change from the earlier research in which the movements per se were hardly considered. The association between motor behavior and motor control resulted in several reviews written toward the end of the 1970s, such as those by Brooks (1975, 1979, 1986), Grillner (1975), Wetzel and Stuart (1976), and Gallistel (1980). Behaviorists and neurophysiologists participated in a number of scientific meetings, and the results appeared in edited volumes (e.g., Gandevia, Proske, & Stuart, 2002; Stelmach & Requin, 1980, 1992; Swinnen, Heuer, Massion, & Casaer, 1994).

An additional change occurred toward the end of the century—one far more subtle than those just mentioned. Rather than remaining a mere blending of two different fields, the field of motor control acquired an independent identity. It became a field of study in its own right, complete with its own journals and methods for asking research questions and collecting data. Such methods involve the use of sophisticated techniques for recording and analyzing movements (such as electrophysiological recordings), cinematographic and three-dimensional analyses, measurement of the kinematics of movement, and advanced methods for examining the involvement of brain structures, integrated with the more traditional techniques for studying learning (e.g., Corcos, Jaric, & Gottlieb, 1996; see also chapter 2).

The influence of Bernstein (and others) resurfaced in the writings of a number of scientists who conducted motor control research (e.g., Greene, 1972; Kelso, 1995; Kugler & Turvey, 1987; Reed, 1988; Turvey, 1977). According to Turvey (1990), Bernstein's legacy resulted in two rounds of theorizing and experimentation. The first round dealt with the degrees of freedom problem—research addressing how a system with many independent parts could be controlled without the need for an executive "decision maker." The second round extended Bernstein's thinking on coordination and the degrees of freedom problem to a search for laws and principles of self-organization. Much of this work uses physical biology as its basis. The dynamical-systems perspective (e.g., Kelso, 1995) suggests that coordinated movement evolves over time as a function of the interaction among the body parts, and between the body parts and the physical world. Also associated with this view are the ideas that perception and action are functionally inseparable—that understanding the motor system depends on understanding the physical principles of our actions and how they interact with biological functions. Advocates of these traditions showed a reluctance to use cognitive–psychological styles of inquiry with hypothetically defined brain mechanisms such as memory, motor programs, schemas, and the like. This approach contributed a different emphasis to the attempt to understand motor behavior (e.g., Anson, Elliott, & Davids, 2005).

The late 1970s and early 1980s were also characterized by a general decline in interest in *motor learning,* with a corresponding increase in issues of movement control or human performance. This was unfortunate, because the issues involved in learning have perhaps the most practical application to training, rehabilitation, and teaching in general. But there was a renewed interest in learning toward the end of the century, sparked in part by counterintuitive findings regarding how practice scheduling (Shea & Morgan, 1979; Lee & Magill, 1983b; Magill & Hall, 1990) and augmented feedback (Salmoni, Schmidt, & Walter, 1984; Schmidt, 1991a) could be organized to optimize the learning environment. Much of this work is described in chapters 11 and 12.

Motor Control and Learning Research Today

The integration of motor control research that developed toward the end of the 20th century continues today. For example, behavioral studies of motor control and learning now appear in journals that in the past were strictly oriented toward neuroscience (e.g., *Experimental Brain Research, Neuroscience Letters, Journal of Neuroscience*), and neuroscience-oriented studies appear in journals that were formerly primarily behavioral (e.g., *Journal of Motor Behavior, Human Movement Science*). Studies of the specific brain mechanisms involved in the performance of movement tasks have appeared in specialist journals (e.g., *NeuroImage*) and represent a rapidly growing approach to the study of motor control. Studies of motor control and learning also continue to be published in journals devoted to specific professional topics (e.g., *Physical Therapy, Human Factors*), and this list continues to expand to include journals that did not previously publish motor behavior articles (e.g., *American Journal of Surgery*). New societies (e.g., International Society of Motor Control) and journals (e.g., *Motor Control, Frontiers in Movement Science and Sport Psychology*) have emerged. In short, more research in the area of motor control and learning is being published now than ever before. And that research is being conducted by researchers who have a greater diversity and breadth of knowledge than ever before.

The computer, employed in relatively few laboratories for research investigations prior to the 1980s, is now used almost universally for conducting research and organizing data. Analyses that used to take many hours can now be performed in a matter of minutes. In short, the *capacity* to conduct research of very high quality has grown at a dizzying rate.

This is an exciting time for research in motor control and learning, an area of literature now so broad in scope that it would seem to be more and more difficult for the student to remain aware of the most recent publications. Ironically, however, it has never been easier to retrieve research information in this area. The Internet, which did not even exist at the time the second edition of this book was published, has revolutionized the way in which motor behavior research is made public. E-mail alerting services deliver the tables of contents of new journal issues as soon as they are published and previews of soon to be published papers. Almost all journals are now available in electronic formats, and the articles are available to consumers at the click of a mouse. Moreover, many journals are not only publishing current issues in electronic formats but also archiving all of their pre-electronic issues. General search engines (such as Google) and specialized search engines (such as Google Scholar, PubMed, Web of Science) make the literature retrieval for a particular topic, author, or paper very fast and effective. The Internet has also made databases easy to access. Carlton and colleagues (1999) described a Web-based laboratory, for example, where a student can retrieve and analyze a set of data that addresses a particular research topic.

However, the student of motor behavior must also be aware, now more than ever, that what is available online can be of variable quality. Respected journals maintain the peer review process, whereby a paper submitted for publication undergoes careful scrutiny by a small committee of established peers ("referees") before it can appear in press under the journal's title. This scrutiny is maintained regardless of whether the published work appears in paper or electronic format. However, not all articles that one can retrieve on the Internet have undergone this peer review process. As in the previous centuries, the best and most influential research articles are almost always those that have undergone careful and rigorous scientific scrutiny.

It is impossible to know what changes will emerge in the next decade. Perhaps these words will no longer be available in paper format. Regardless of the changes that occur, however, the lessons of history tell us that the scientific disciplines combining to define *motor control and learning* will continue to undergo refinement with further accumulation of knowledge and application.

Summary

This text is fundamentally concerned with movements of human beings. Some of these movements are probably genetically defined while others are *skills*, requiring practice or experience. Even though most of the field of human behavior deals in one way or another with movement, in this text we focus primarily (but not exclusively) on those movements in which cognitive involvement is relatively slight, and for which the nature of the movement itself—rather than the choice of the movement from already learned alternatives—is the primary determinant of success. We focus on movements that do not have a heavy concentration on cardiovascular endurance or strength, as these activities seem to be more closely aligned with other fields of study. Finally, the focus is on many different movements that fall within the categories mentioned, such as those in musical performance, work, industry, and sport and other activities of daily living.

The field of movement control and learning, viewed from a historical perspective, emerged from the separate but parallel fields of motor behavior and neurophysiology. Both fields showed steady growth through the beginning of World War II, then increased in growth and sophistication after the war and through the 1960s and 1970s. The two fields, however, were largely separated until the early 1970s, when they began to share common problems and methods. Motor learning research, largely forgotten during the '70s, reemerged as a strong research area toward the end of the century. Today the computer (and the Internet) has revolutionized the way in which research is conducted and disseminated.

Student Assignments

1. Answer the following questions and bring the information to class for discussion:
   a. How does a behavioral level of analysis of motor control and learning differ

from biomechanical and neurophysiological levels of analysis?

b. If you could interview one of the people featured in the highlight boxes (Bernstein, Fitts, Henry, Keele, Adams, Whiting), what would you ask him about motor control and learning?

c. What has the proliferation in publication outlets contributed to our current understanding of research in motor control and learning?

2. Find a research article authored by any of the six people listed in question 1b. Are the findings of that research article still relevant today?

Web Resources

These are some of the professional organizations that promote research in motor control and learning through newsletters and annual conferences:

www.naspspa.org

www.scapps.org

www.i-s-m-c.org

These journals specialize in publishing research in motor control and learning:

www.tandf.co.uk/journals/titles/00222895.asp

www.humankinetics.com/MC/journalAbout.cfm

www.elsevier.com/wps/find/journaldescription.cws_home/505584/description#description

Notes

[1] Learning the rules (grammar) of a language would probably not be of much relevance for the area of motor control, but learning to make the guttural sounds involved in German or the nasal sounds inherent in French could logically be included in the area of motor control (MacNeilage, 1970).

[2] Now called *Perceptual and Motor Skills*.

[3] Now called *Research Quarterly for Exercise and Sport*.

[4] Now subdivided into five different journals (one of which is entitled *Journal of Experimental Psychology: Human Perception and Performance*).

CHAPTER 2

METHODOLOGY FOR STUDYING MOTOR PERFORMANCE

A major goal of this book is to present not only relevant principles and theories about the nature of motor performance, motor control, and motor learning but also the research evidence that supports (or, in some cases, refutes) these principles and theories. In evaluating this evidence, it is necessary to understand some of the methods involved in the research and the ways in which the motor behaviors are measured, so that we can more effectively establish the relevance of the evidence to the particular principle or theory in question. Later in the book (chapter 10), we focus on the methods and paradigms used specifically in the study of motor *learning*.

Classification of Motor Skills

In any field of study, the objects under investigation are usually classified according to some scheme or framework in order to simplify discussion. The field of motor behavior is no exception. Classification of movements and motor tasks is important for two fundamental reasons. First, in the research literature on motor behavior and control, various terms are used to describe the tasks and movements. These terms must be understood if we are to communicate about the field. The second reason is that the laws of motor behavior seem to depend on the kinds of performances

(i.e., the class of task) under consideration. That is, the relation between certain independent and dependent variables is often different for one class of task or behavior when compared to another. Without classification, the laws of motor control would be far more difficult to understand.

Movement behaviors have been classified in various ways. Two important classification schemes are the discrete/continuous/serial dimension, which is based on the particular *movements* made, and the open/closed dimension, which is determined by the *perceptual* attributes of the task.

Discrete, Continuous, and Serial Skills

Discrete movements are those with a recognizable beginning and end. Kicking a ball, throwing, striking a match, and shifting gears in a car are examples (figure 2.1). The end of the movement is defined by the skill in question, not arbitrarily by the time at which an observer ceased examining it, as would be the case for swimming or jogging, for example. Discrete skills can be very rapid, requiring only a fraction of a second to complete (e.g., kicking, blinking an eye); but they can also require much more time for completion, as in writing your signature. Discrete skills can also be quite cognitive. For example, one laboratory task is to press one of four buttons when one of four lights comes on; the problem for the subject is to decide which button to press in response to which light. Thus, the decision about which button to push is paramount, and the "how" of pushing the button is clearly secondary in importance. While many discrete skills have large verbal–cognitive components, there are certainly examples of discrete skills that are highly "motor" as well.

Continuous movements—defined as those that have no recognizable beginning and end, with behavior continuing until the movement is arbitrarily stopped—are at the opposite end of the continuum (in figure 2.1). Swimming, running, and steering a car are examples of tasks that have arbitrary ends. Continuous tasks tend to have longer movement times than do discrete tasks (they might even continue all day). This, however, should not be taken as basic to their definition.

A common class of continuous skills, both in everyday experience and in the laboratory, involves tracking tasks. The tracking task is characterized by a pathway (track) that the individual intends to follow and a device that the person attempts to keep on the track via certain limb movements. In steering a car, for example, the track is the road, and the device is the car, steering wheel, and so on. A very common laboratory example involves two cursors on a computer monitor. One of the cursors is moved by the experimenter (or by the computer), and it can move in either a predictable or an uncertain way on the screen. The second cursor is moved by the subject via a hand control, and the subject's task is to minimize the distance (or error) between the two cursors.

Two kinds of tracking tasks are used commonly in motor behavior research: *pursuit* tracking and *compensatory* tracking. In pursuit tracking, experimenter-produced actions of the target and the subject's own movements are both displayed. The previously mentioned task of steering a car is a good example of pursuit tracking. In compensatory tracking, the experimenter-produced variations in the track are combined with the subject's movements to produce a single displayed value, and the subject's goal is to maintain this value at some constant location. Practical examples of compensatory tracking are often seen in aircraft instruments, such as the glide slope indicator. Here only the difference between the proper altitude and the actual altitude is displayed; and when the pointer is in the middle of the screen, the pilot's altitude is correct. Compensatory tracking tasks are almost always more "difficult" than pursuit tracking tasks, particularly if the behavior of the track is irregular and unpredictable.

Tracking tasks also vary in terms of the aspect of the display that the subject controls. The most simple is the zero-order, or positional, display. If the subject moves the handle from one position to another and then stops, the indicator on the display moves a proportional amount and also

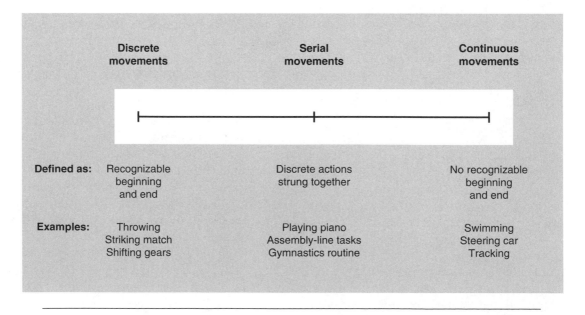

Discrete movements	Serial movements	Continuous movements
Defined as: Recognizable beginning and end	Discrete actions strung together	No recognizable beginning and end
Examples: Throwing Striking match Shifting gears	Playing piano Assembly-line tasks Gymnastics routine	Swimming Steering car Tracking

FIGURE 2.1   The discrete/serial/continuous classification for motor behavior.

stops; that is, the handle movements control the *position* of the pointer. In *first-order,* or velocity control, movement of the handle causes changes in the *velocity* of the pointer. Moving the handle further in one direction causes the velocity of the pointer to increase in the same direction, and stopping the handle movement off center results in a constant velocity of pointer movement. In a second-order task, the movements of the control produce changes in the pointer's *acceleration.* Keeping the handle centered produces zero acceleration, but moving the handle to a new position off center accelerates the pointer in the same direction. Each of these kinds of tracking tasks is used in research, and there are real-world examples of each in various control systems (see Poulton, 1974, for more details).

One final type of tracking task is step tracking. In this task, the track "jumps" from one fixed location to another, often unpredictably, and the subject's task is to move the control as quickly as possible to correct this sudden change in the track's location. Step tracking tasks can be either pursuit or compensatory.

Serial movements are neither discrete nor continuous, but usually are comprised of a series of individual movements tied together in time to make some "whole." These types of movements appear in the center of the continuum in figure 2.1 because they can be rather long in duration but are not stopped arbitrarily. Examples are starting a car, preparing and lighting a wood fireplace, and many tasks involved in production lines in industry. Serial tasks can be thought of as a number of discrete tasks strung together, and the order (and sometimes timing) of the actions is important.

Open Versus Closed Skills

Environmental predictability during the performance provides another basis for classifying movement skills (Poulton, 1957; Gentile, 2000). *Open skills* are those for which the environment is constantly (perhaps unpredictably) changing, so that the performer cannot effectively plan the entire movement in advance (figure 2.2). A good example is the penalty shot in ice hockey. While skating toward the goalie, the player may make a general decision about whether to go left or right, but the final decision may depend on what the goalie does. Another example is driving on a busy freeway. Although you may make a general plan about what you want to do, such as pass another car, your precise plans must be left flexible enough to deal with unexpected actions of other drivers. Success in open skills is largely determined by the extent to which the individual is successful in adapting the planned motor behavior to the changing environment. Often this adaptation must be extremely rapid, and the effective responder must have many different actions ready to implement.

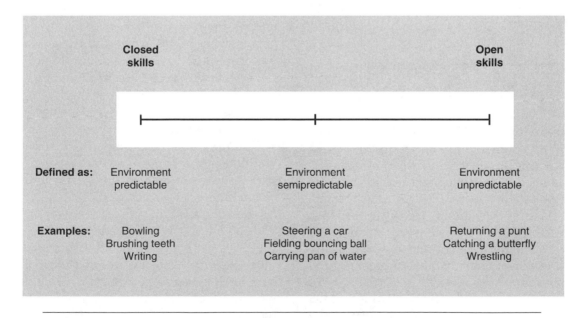

FIGURE 2.2   The open/closed continuum for motor behavior.

Closed skills, for which the environment is predictable, are at the other end of the continuum shown in figure 2.2. An environment may be predictable because it is almost perfectly stable—for example, the environment in which one performs skills like archery, bowling, or signing one's name to a check. An unstable yet predictable situation can also arise when the environment is variable but the changes are very predictable, or have been learned as a result of practice, or both; examples are juggling and industrial production-line tasks. Here, the essential feature is that the environment for the next few seconds or so is essentially predictable, so that the movement can be planned in advance. Of course, some skills have environments that are semi-predictable, and these can be classified somewhere between the ends of the open/closed continuum in figure 2.2. Farrell (1975) has provided additional distinctions that help us to classify movements on this dimension. The observation that open skills seem to require rapid adaptations to a changing environment, whereas closed skills require very consistent and stable performances in a predictable environment, raises interesting questions about how the two classes of skills might best be learned and taught. Should the methods for teaching open and closed skills be different? Do different individuals perform better in one of these skill classes or the other? Are the laws of performance different for the two kinds of skills? Evidence suggests that some of the answers to these questions are yes, and we will discuss these issues in more detail in later chapters.

Basic Considerations in Measurement

A fundamental issue in any science concerns how the behaviors of the objects of study are measured, and motor behavior is no exception. We often need to operationalize *skills* so that we can assign numerical values to certain performances based on the quality of the movements. Scientists must be able to measure the degree of skill exhibited by a performer in scientifically acceptable ways. Some of the criteria for good measurement systems are (a) the objectivity of the system, (b) the reliability (or stability) of the measuring system, and (c) the validity of the system.

Objectivity

The term *objectivity* is important in measurement because of the scientific demand that observations be subject to public verification. A measurement system is objective to the extent that two observers evaluating the same performance arrive at the same (or very similar) measurements. For example, using a tape measure to determine the distance a javelin was thrown yields very similar results regardless of who reads the tape. By comparison, evaluation of performances such as diving, gymnastics, and figure skating is more subjective—although elaborate scoring rules, complete with certification tests for judges, help make it more objective. From the point of view of research in motor behavior, it is important to use performances in the laboratory for which the scoring can be as objective as possible; and this necessarily limits the usefulness of some tasks for providing an understanding of motor behavior in general.

A second aspect of objectivity relates to the *sensitivity* of the measuring device to changes in the skill of the performer. How high did the girl jump when she set the school record in the high jump? The record books report that she jumped 5 ft 6 1/2 in. (168 cm). But it is more accurate to say that she jumped *at least* 5 ft 6 1/2 in. The measurement system for the high jump (and for the pole vault) indicates only whether or not the bar was knocked off during the jump, and it is possible that the successful jumper cleared the bar by 6 in. In such situations, the scoring system is somewhat *insensitive* to the variations in the performer's actual level of skill.

In this example, the scale of measurement itself was acceptable in terms of sensitivity; in fact, we often see high jump officials measuring the height of the bar very carefully, perhaps to the nearest 1/4 in. Yet this method is not totally objective, as we have just argued. However, sometimes the scale of measurement itself is lacking in precision. Often, continuous measures are artificially categorized, as in hit/miss scoring for basketball and golf putting. For these examples the details of the movement, together with information about the performer's skill level, can be lost in the oversimplified measurement method. Such methods make it more difficult to determine whether an individual has improved on the task with practice, or to identify which of two individuals is the more skilled performer—both of which may be critical questions in the study of movement.

Reliability

A second aspect of the measurement system that is important to motor behavior is *reliability*—the extent to which the measurement is repeatable under similar conditions. A lack of reliability can result from random technological error, such as the stretch in measuring tapes, errors in clocks, and human errors in reading instruments. These errors, while they might seem to be important sources of unreliability, probably contribute very little to unreliability as long as a researcher uses quality recording apparatus and careful procedures. The most important source of unreliability manifests itself when the performer does not perform the same action twice in exactly the same way. Some of these *intrasubject* variations are caused by momentary changes in the internal state of the subject (degree of attention, fatigue, or boredom, for example), while others are caused by systematic changes, such as alterations in strategy, the amount of practice, and the like. Both of these factors tend to obscure the constructs that scientists are attempting to measure.

Experimenters seek to minimize these sources of variability through experimental control in the testing situation. Researchers typically use written or prerecorded instructions in order to eliminate variability in what and how information is presented; they use testing rooms that are either silenced or sound deadened; subjects are tested one at a time to eliminate variability due to another person's presence in the room; and the entire experimental session is often quite formal and impersonal. This is the primary reason some researchers tend not to measure skills in everyday settings—at a ball game or on an industrial production line, for example. In these situations, the environment is not well controlled; there are many sources of variation from other players or workers, from changes in the score of the game, from the level of proficiency of opponents, from day-to-day changes in the weather, and so on. Primarily for reasons of experimental control, motor behavior tends to be most profitably studied in the laboratory, away from these sources of variability. To be sure, there is a trade-off in this approach: Laboratory studies tend to make the situation less natural and more artificial, and the measures taken are not quite as directly related to practical situations, but the alternative of studying skills during a game adds sources of variation that reduce the reliability of the measures.

The procedures mentioned can reduce variability in experimental settings. But even when the task is well learned and simple, when the experimental situation is well controlled, and when the subject is trying to do well, there remains a great deal of variability because biological systems are inherently somewhat unstable. Experimentally, the best method for countering this type of variability is to record many observations of the "same" behavior on the same subject, taking the average of a large number of measurements under essentially identical conditions. With this procedure the variations in the subject's performance tend to "average out," raising the reliability of the measurement system, so that the mean of a large number of observations more closely represents the construct being measured.

Validity

Another aspect of the measurement process is *validity*, the extent to which the test measures what the researcher intends it to measure. An important aspect of validity (called *construct validity*) is the extent to which the measures taken actually reflect the underlying construct of interest. We would be reasonably comfortable with a 10 min typing test to operationalize typing skill, but we would perhaps be less comfortable with a measure of finger tapping speed to assess typing skill. There are, on the other hand, situations in which validity does not seem to present much of a problem. One of these involves what are often called *face valid* tests, which are so obviously measures of the concept of interest that they usually are not questioned. For example, if we wish to determine which member of a group of individuals has most skill in javelin throwing (a construct), we might have them all throw the javelin as a standardized test.

Another class of measurement situations in which the importance of validity is minimal is in experiments on motor learning (Schmidt, 1989a). In these situations, an arbitrary task is created that represents a motor performance novel to the subject, and the experimenter studies how the subject attempts to learn it or what variables influence that learning. The particular constructs being measured (e.g., balance, timing, movement speed) frequently are not very important to the experimenter, because the primary focus is on the variables that affect performance and learning generally.

Measuring Motor Behavior

In the field of motor behavior and control, measurement can be approached in essentially three different ways. At the most general level, we can describe how well a movement achieved some environmental goal that was inherent in the task (e.g., whether or not a target was struck). Here the emphasis is on the *outcome* of movement. At a more specific level, we may be concerned with quantifying the actual movements the person made. In this case, the focus of analysis is describing the movement itself. The third level of analysis entails the study of the brain and central nervous system prior to and during the production of movement. At this level, researchers are interested in the neural activities involved in planning and executing movements.

Describing the Outcome of Movements

The first aspect of measurement in motor behavior is quantification of the extent to which a given movement achieved the goal that was intended or instructed. For example, did the movement result in striking the target, or was the movement made at the right time? Such measures generally concern the movement in relation to some object or to another performer in the environment, although some movements (e.g., modern dance, diving) may not be so closely associated with other environmental elements. The achievement of such environmental goals can be assessed in essentially four fundamental ways—through measures of (a) error, (b) time and speed, (c) movement magnitude, and (d) performance on secondary tasks.

Measures of Error for a Single Subject

Many performances require the subject to perform some action with maximum accuracy. Thus, the performance measures represent the degree to which the target was not achieved—a measure of error. The accuracy goal can be imposed in many ways; for example, subjects can be asked to move with a certain amount of force, hit a certain spatial target, move at a certain speed, or perform some

act at a particular time (e.g., hitting a baseball). A particular force, distance, speed, or time can be defined as the subject's target; then, deviations of the subject's performances with respect to this target are measured. The level of analysis that is least sensitive comprises dichotic outcomes, such as when the performances are scored as hit/miss or right/wrong, as in shooting a basketball or judging which of two lifted weights is heavier. We can refine the accuracy score by dividing the possible outcomes into hit/almost hit/miss or by dividing a bull's-eye into 10 or more zones, for example. But motor performance is complex, and more sophistication in the measurement of accuracy is usually required.

In the discussion that follows, assume that a single performer is striving for accuracy in arriving at some target (e.g., a force, a speed, a location in space) and that the movement outcomes can be placed along some measurable dimension (e.g., kilograms, centimeters per second, centimeters) as in figure 2.3. Let the correct value along this dimension—the target—have the value T. The values that the performer actually achieves are abbreviated by x_i, where i is a subscript notating a particular trial (i.e., the ith trial). For example, x_{23} is the score on the 23rd trial. In the simple formulas that describe these fundamental statistical accuracy scores, the symbol Σ means "the sum of." For example, Σx_i means to add up all of the values x_i, where i ranges progressively from 1 through n, with $n = 5$ in the following example:

$$\Sigma x_i = x_1 + x_2 + x_3 + x_4 + x_5 \qquad (2.1)$$

In the following explanation, assume that the target (T) is 100 units and that the individual does not always achieve this target score. In figure 2.3 there are five scores: 93, 103, 99, 105, and 96 units for trials 1 through 5, respectively.

It is obvious that no single trial will be very effective in describing the subject's behavior, as the scores possess a great deal of variability. One solution is to combine these scores to achieve a more representative measure of the subject's capability. In the study of motor behavior, researchers have typically focused on five methods for combining scores into measures of "error," and each one has a slightly different meaning in terms of the performer's capability. These methods are described in the next sections as (a) constant error, (b) variable error, (c) total variability, (d) absolute error, and (e) absolute constant error.

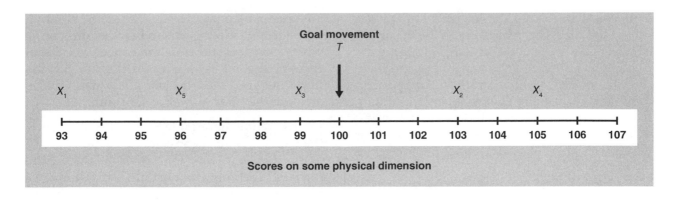

FIGURE 2.3 An arbitrary measurement scale, showing locations of a target *(T)* and of five hypothetical movement attempts ($x_1, \ldots, x_5$).

Constant Error (CE)—Computation The first statistic to be considered as a measure of the subject's accuracy is the *constant error (CE)*, which measures the average error in responding. Its formula is

$$\text{Constant error} = CE = \Sigma\, (x_i - T)\, /\, n \qquad (2.2)$$

where x_i is the score on trial i, T is the target, and n is the number of trials the subject performed. It is very easy to compute this measure from table 2.1, which can serve as a work table for computing all of the statistics presented in this section on error measures. The trial numbers are listed in column A; the scores obtained (x_i) are given in column B. All other values in the table are computed from these initial values (remember that $T = 100$ in this example).

To compute the CE, the numerator calls for finding the difference between each of the scores on the test (x_i) and the target $(T = 100)$; these dif-ference scores are shown in column C, headed $(x_i - T)$. It is important to notice in this column that for CE, the *sign* (+ or −) of the difference is retained. Next, the summation sign calls for adding the values (using the *signed* values) for each of the trials (in this case for each of the five trials), and this sum is presented at the bottom of column C (−4.0). Then the formula calls for dividing by n, the number of trials, in order to get the average CE over trials. The final CE score is −4.0/5, or −0.80.

Interpretation of Constant Error The CE score of −0.80 indicates that, on average, the subject fell slightly short of the target (by 0.80 units). Notice that the CE is given in units that represent the amount *and* direction of deviation relative to the target, sometimes called *bias*. One could also ask for the subject's scores on the average by consulting the mean for column B. Thus, the average

TABLE 2.1. Work Table for Computing Various Components of Movement Error

A Trial	B x_i	C $(x_i - T)$	D $(x_i - M)$	E $(x_i - M)^2$	F $(x_i - T)^2$	G $\lvert x_i - T \rvert$
1	93	−7	−6.2	38.44	49	7
2	103	+3	+3.8	14.44	9	3
3	99	−1	−0.2	0.04	1	1
4	105	+5	+5.8	33.64	25	5
5	96	−4	−3.2	10.24	16	4
Sum	496	−4.0	—	96.80	100	20
Mean	99.2	−0.80	—	19.36	20	4
Square root	—	—	—	4.40	4.47	—

score was 496 / 5 = 99.2 units, meaning that the subject fell short of the target by 99.2 – 100 units, which is also –0.80 units. The CE represents the average magnitude of the movement and measures the direction of the errors on the average.

While a measure of average error bias might, at first, seem satisfying to students as a measure of accuracy, notice that the value computed for the subject (–0.80) was far smaller than the error for any of the single movements that contributed to the average. The movements were scattered a great deal, with the center of movements being roughly the target that was the goal. What the CE does not consider is this amount of scatter, variability, or inconsistency in performance of the movements. Consider a second hypothetical subject with scores of 99, 99, 99, 99, and 100. These scores represent a very small scatter but would result in precisely the same CE score as for the subject we have just been considering (–0.80). For this reason, another measure of error, the variable error, is used to describe the subject's inconsistency.

Variable Error (VE)—Computation   The variable error (VE) measures the *inconsistency* in movement outcome. It is the variability of the subject's performances about the mean value and is calculated by the formula

$$\text{Variable error} = \text{VE} = \sqrt{\Sigma \, (x_i - M)^2 \, / \, n} \qquad (2.3)$$

where x_i and n are defined as in the previous example. The M is the subject's average movement, measured in the same units as the scores for the task, so that for this example the M has the value of 99.2 units. To compute the VE for this subject, use table 2.1 once again. Notice that the formula indicates first to compute the difference between the performance score and the subject's own mean (M), so the first step is to compute the subject's M. As noted in the previous section, the computed M for these trials was 99.2 units. Now, the values in column D of table 2.1 represent the differences between each of the scores on the trials and 99.2 (that is, the difference between each individual score and the mean of all *that person's* scores). For example, 93.0 – 99.2 equals –6.2, the first entry in column D. Since the deviations from the mean for each of the individual trials must cancel each other out, by definition the sum of the values in column D must equal zero. So, the next instruction from the formula is to square each of the values in column D, and these squared values

are given in column E. Next, obey the summation sign and add the squared values, the sum of which (96.80) is shown at the bottom of column E. Then divide this sum by the number of cases ($n = 5$) to get 19.36 and take the square root to arrive at the final answer of 4.40 units.

Interpretation of Variable Error   The VE reflects the variability, or inconsistency, in movements, as can be seen from the "ingredients" in the formula. The important feature is the difference between the subject's score on each trial and his own average score. Thus, if one subject always moves very consistently, the VE will tend to be small. If the subject always receives the same score, even though it is not the correct one (such as a score of 99 on all five trials), then the VE will be zero. This is so because the subject's average score will be 99, and the difference between each of the scores and the average will always be zero as well.

Thus, VE does not depend on whether or not the subject was close to the target, since it is the measure of spread about the subject's *own* average. To illustrate, the VE for the set of scores 43, 53, 49, 55, and 46 achieved during aiming at a target of 100 units will be precisely the same (4.40) as that calculated in the previous example. (We obtained these five new values by subtracting 50 from each of the raw scores in table 2.1.)

Using Constant Error and Variable Error   An additional aspect of error scores is important from the point of view not only of research but also of practical application. Compare two rifle marksmen: Marksman A has a large VE and small CE, whereas marksman B has a small VE and large CE. This situation was described years ago by Chapanis (1951) and is illustrated in figure 2.4 (see "The Relative Importance of Constant and Variable Errors"). Which marksman, A or B, appears to be the more skilled?[1]

The study of motor learning will show that the measure of error that is most sensitive to the effects of practice is consistency (VE); bias (CE) often changes quickly in the first several trials and remains near zero thereafter, even after years of practice. There are some situations, however, in which CE is preferred to VE; but these are specialized applications. Thus, these two measures of error, CE and VE, seem to represent two distinct aspects of performance—bias and variability, respectively. But sometimes it is more desirable

THE RELATIVE IMPORTANCE
OF CONSTANT AND VARIABLE ERRORS

They said it . . .

Alphonse Chapanis was one of the pioneers in the emergence of human factors research. His analysis of errors in movement is as important today as it was over a half century ago.

"Having defined constant and variable errors, we might ask: Which is the more important? Let us return for a moment to the target patterns shot by the two riflemen [figure 2.4]. At first glance, you might say that B is a very inaccurate shooter. And yet any rifleman will tell you that this is not the case at all. B is a much better shooter than A. The reason is this: The large constant error in the trial shots fired by B can be compensated for very easily by simple adjustments in his sights. With suitable corrections in elevation and windage, rifleman B will turn in a perfect score. In rifle shooting, then, constant errors are not the important ones, because they can be very easily adjusted for by changing the position of the sights on the gun. The really important errors are the variable errors. No correction of the sights on A's gun will make all of his shots fall in the center. He is inherently much too variable" (Chapanis, 1951, p. 1187).

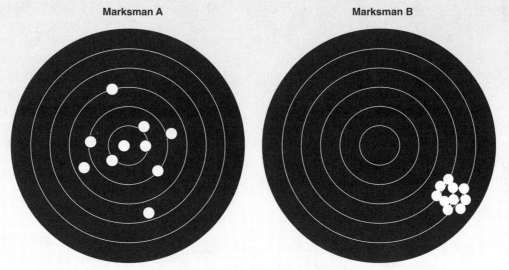

Marksman A   **Marksman B**

FIGURE 2.4   Distribution of rifle shots. Marksman A has a small constant error (CE) and large variable error (VE). Marksman B has a large CE bias, but a small VE.

Reprinted, by permission, from A. Chapanis, 1951, "Theory and methods for analyzing errors in man-machine systems," *Annals of the New York Academy of Sciences* 51: 1181.

to have a single measure of "overall error" that combines both of these performance indicators rather than using separate measures of accuracy and variability.

Total Variability (E)—Computation   The total variability around a target (or error) for a set of movements (labeled E by Henry [1975] and sometimes called *root mean square error*) can be thought of as the measure of "overall error" (see also Chapanis, 1951). E can be defined as the square root of the sum of VE^2 and CE^2, or in the following formula when expressed as E^2:

$$E^2 = VE^2 + CE^2 \tag{2.4}$$

E can also be computed directly from the formula:

$$\text{Total variability} = E = \sqrt{\Sigma\,(x_i - T)^2\,/\,n} \tag{2.5}$$

where x_i, T, and n are defined as before. To apply the formula, we can use table 2.1 again. Notice that the major "ingredient" is the difference between the score and the target $(x_i - T)$, and this difference (with the sign included) is given in table 2.1, column C—the same values used to compute CE. Next, square each of these values;

these squared values are given in column F. The summation sign then says to add the squared values, and the sum (equal to 100) is given at the bottom of column F. Next, divide by n (5), which results in a value of 20; then find the square root. The final value for E is $\sqrt{20}$, or 4.47.

Interpretation of Total Variability The total variability, E, is the total amount of "spread" of the movements about the target, so it represents an overall measure of how successful the subject was in achieving the target. The key to understanding this formula is the expression in the numerator $(x_i - T)^2$. E is based on the sum of a group of squared differences, where each difference is the amount by which the subject missed the target. This contrasts with VE, where the numerator $(x_i - M)^2$ represented the deviations from the *subject's own average*, which is not necessarily equal to the target. In cases when CE is close to zero (i.e., the mean of the trials approximates the aimed-for target [M and T are nearly equal]), then E and VE come to represent very similar aspects of the subject's performance. But, in cases when the CE is very different than the target, then E will represent the combination of this error in bias plus the variability about the CE (i.e., E is a combination of CE and VE).

Absolute Error (AE)—Computation A statistic closely related to the total variability (E) is absolute error (AE), which can also be thought of as a measure of overall accuracy in performance. It is the average *absolute deviation* (without regard to direction, or sign) between the subject's movements and the target, and its formula is as follows:

$$\text{Absolute error} = AE = \Sigma \, |x_i - T| \, / \, n \qquad (2.6)$$

where x_i, T, and n are defined as before. The important difference here is the presence of the vertical bars ($|\ \ |$), which are the symbol for "absolute value of" and mean that we should take away the sign of the difference before summing.

To compute AE, refer again to table 2.1. The first step is to compute the values for the numerator terms, and this is done in column G, headed $|x_i - T|$. Notice that the value in this column is the same as the corresponding value in column C, except for the sign. The summation sign Σ is an instruction to add up the values from each of the n trials (recall that $n = 5$ in this example), and the sum is given at the bottom of column G as 20. The next step is to divide by the number of trials included ($n = 5$), and so the final answer is 4.0.

Interpretation of Absolute Error In providing an interpretation of the AE, it will be helpful to consider the ways in which it is similar to E. First, notice that the numerator is essentially the same for the two statistics, each numerator having a difference between the obtained score (x_i) and the target (T) as the major "ingredient." Second, the x_i values for E and AE (4.47 and 4.0, respectively) are very similar; the two values will be equal only in special circumstances but will be very close in most situations. Third, both of the formulas involve methods for eliminating the sign of the difference between the score and the target; for the AE, the method is to take the absolute value, while for E, the method is to square the values in the numerator.

Absolute Error Versus Total Variability The AE is a very "logical" measure to use to describe the subject's overall accuracy in a task because it is sensitive to the extent to which the subject was "off target." It was used far more commonly than E in the early research and for many different applications. A controversy, however, has arisen about the use of AE (Schutz & Roy, 1973). The mathematical properties of AE have been shown to be a complex combination of CE (accuracy or bias) and VE (variability), and it is difficult to be certain of the relative contribution of each. Because of the precise relation among E, CE, and VE (namely, $E^2 = VE^2 + CE^2$), E is always an exact combination of the variability and bias, and thus is preferred to AE (Henry, 1975). The tendency today, when a researcher wishes to present a combined measure of accuracy and variability, is to prefer E, for two reasons: First, E measures essentially the same component of movement as AE, and second, E is more easily interpreted since it represents a simple combination of CE and VE. However, we will use AE a great deal in this text, because much of the earlier research reported only this measure.

Absolute Constant Error ($|CE|$) One final measure of accuracy is merely a transformation of constant error, CE:

$$\text{Absolute constant error} = |CE| \qquad (2.7)$$

Thus, for a single subject, the absolute constant error ($|CE|$) is just the absolute value of the CE, which is simply 0.80 in the present example. Be careful to note, however, that $|CE|$ is not calculated in the same way as AE. For AE we take the sign away immediately after calculating the difference between a single score and the target, *prior* to summation. For |CE| the sign is not taken away until *after* the average over a series of trials has been calculated.

Interpretation of Absolute Constant Error The situation sometimes arises (e.g., Newell, 1976a) in which approximately half the *subjects in a group* have positive CE scores while the other half have negative CE scores. If one characterizes the average bias for this *group* of subjects by calculating a group mean score (the average score of all the subjects), the positive and negative signs will tend to "cancel" each other out. This could give rise to the misleading conclusion that the average bias for the *group* was nearly zero when in fact every subject in the group might have shown a bias of considerable size. In this case, it is useful to also compute |CE|, which tells the researcher the mean amount of bias for the group of subjects without regard to its direction, and which will not fall prey to this "canceling" effect of the positive and negative CEs. In cases in which group data have been the focus of a researcher's experiment, there has been a trend to report |CE| (as the measure of accuracy) along with VE (as the variability score) (see Schutz, 1977, for more statistical details).

Relationships Among the Error Scores One way to evaluate the relative contributions of the various measures of error is to consider the following cases. At one extreme, when CE is very large (an extreme is the situation in which all the person's movements lie on one side of the target), then the absolute error (AE), the total variability (E), and the constant error (CE) all tend to measure the same component of performance—the bias or directional deviations of the errors. In the following case, the target is again 100, but subject 1 produces five movements, 80, 90, 85, 82, and 87—each smaller than the target. Table 2.2 gives the measures of error for this subject. Notice that the statistics E, CE, AE, and |CE| are all around 15, but that the VE is very much lower at 3.54. This suggests that when the CE is large in either direction, the measures of overall error (E and AE) tend to represent the magnitude of the bias, and VE alone represents the variability.

Now consider subject 2 in table 2.2. This subject has the same spread of outcomes as subject 1, but with much less bias. We obtained these scores by adding 15 to each of subject 1's scores to get subject 2's scores: 95, 105, 100, 97, 102. Table 2.2 gives the error measures of this set of scores. Now notice that the measures of overall error tend to be very close to the VE, all around 3. The CE (and |CE|), however, is now nearly zero. Here the measures of overall error (E and AE) represent the variability of the movements (VE), exactly the opposite of the situation with subject 1.

Therefore, when CE is large in either direction, the measures of overall error (E and AE) tend to represent the amount of bias in the scores. When CE is small, E and AE tend to represent the amount of variability (VE) in the scores. When CE is intermediate in value (with some bias, but with scores falling on both sides of the target), the measures of overall error represent an unknown combination of bias and variability. This should make clear why simply examining overall error statistics does not provide a very complete picture of performance.

Other Measures of Accuracy There are many tasks in the motor behavior literature that could not be scored so simply. A task for which accuracy is important is the *tracking task;* in this case, performance is ongoing, thus preventing the computation of a discrete performance error. A commonly-used tracking task is the *pursuit rotor,* shown in figure 2.5a. There are many varieties of pursuit tracking tasks, and figure 2.5a illustrates just one type. Here, a target (e.g., a small circle) is embedded in the surface of a turntable-like structure that rotates at various speeds. The subject holds a stylus in the preferred hand and attempts to keep its tip in contact with the target as the turntable rotates. A trial might last from 10 s to 1 min, and performance is scored in terms of the amount of time in the trial that the subject

TABLE 2.2. Error Measures for Two Hypothetical Subjects on an Accuracy Task

	E	CE	VE	AE	|CE|
Subject 1	15.61	−15.2	3.54	15.2	15.2
Subject 2	3.55	−0.2	3.54	3.0	0.2

maintained contact with the target. The performance measure is usually called *time on target (TOT)* and can range from zero (if the subject never touched the target) up to a value equal to the duration of a trial (if the subject was always in contact with the target). But notice that time on target can represent a complex combination of bias (if the subject is consistently behind the target, for example) and variability (if the subject is alternately ahead of and behind the target).

Other common variations of tracking tasks are shown in figure 2.5. The *Mashburn task* is shown in figure 2.5*b*. It was designed to simulate certain features of airplane controls. The control panel contains three double rows of lights. One row of each pair is controlled by the movements of the subject (left–right and forward–backward movements of the stick, and right–left movements of the pedals), while the other row of each pair is controlled by the experimenter. The subject attempts to match the experimenter-determined lights with appropriate movements of the controls. The task is

scored in terms of the number of correct matches that can be achieved in a trial of fixed duration.

The *stabilometer* is shown in figure 2.5*c*. The standing subject attempts to keep an unstable platform level; the scores denote either time in balance or the number of times the platform edge touches the floor (indicating extreme loss of balance) during a trial of perhaps 30 s. The number of times a stylus touches the sides of a maze is another example of this kind of measure. Figure 2.5*d* shows the *two-hand coordination task*, in which the subject attempts to follow a target by moving a pointer with two crank handles. One handle controls the right–left movement, and the other controls the forward–backward movement (as in the "Etch-a-Sketch" toy). The score is again TOT, or the amount of time in a trial that the subject was over the target. All these measures, including TOT, are measures of overall error, and they tend to confound the bias with variability in performance.

In each of the foregoing examples, the experimenter does not need to keep a record of the sub-

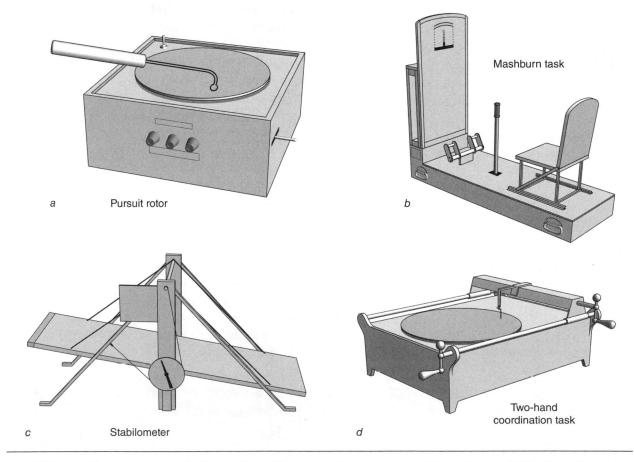

a   Pursuit rotor

Mashburn task

b

c   Stabilometer

d   Two-hand coordination task

FIGURE 2.5   Four movement tasks frequently used in motor behavior research: *(a)* pursuit rotor, *(b)* Mashburn task, *(c)* stabilometer, and *(d)* two-hand coordination task.

ject's actual behavior. However, there are other tracking tasks for which a continuous record of the movements of the subject and the target is kept. From these data a measure of overall accuracy, the root mean square (RMS) error, can be computed. (Notice that RMS error is analogous to E, described earlier. Both are root mean square deviations of the behavior from some target, computed on successive "trials.") Essentially, the RMS error is based on taking small "slices" of time and measuring the deviation of the subject's line from the target at each of these times, as shown in figure 2.6. Depending on the capacity of the recording system, these slices can be taken every few milliseconds or so over the entire course of a 20 s trial, providing many measures of error. To compute the RMS error, square each of these deviations from the track, add up the squared deviations, divide by the number of measures, and then take the square root, giving a measure of the amount of deviation over the course of the trial. Root mean square error in each of these cases represents essentially (but not exactly) the area between the subject's movements and the target, as shown by the shaded portions of figure 2.6. As with TOT, the RMS error is a measure of overall error and is sensitive to both the bias and the variability in performing.

Measures of Time and Speed

The second fundamental way of assessing skills is by measures of time and speed. Basic to this idea is the assumption that the performer who can accomplish more in a given amount of time, or who can produce a given amount of behavior in less time, is the more skillful. These two kinds of measures are essentially the same, since a time measure (time/unit) can easily be converted to a speed measure by taking the reciprocal; that is, 1 / (time / unit) = units / time, which is a measure of speed. Both speed and time measures have been used a great deal in motor behavior research. Reaction time and movement time are common examples, described next.

Reaction Time   Reaction time (commonly abbreviated as RT) is a measure of the time from the arrival of a suddenly presented and unanticipated signal to the *beginning* of the response to it. In the RT paradigm shown in figure 2.7, the subject is given a warning signal, and after a randomly determined *foreperiod* (perhaps ranging from 1 to 5 s), the stimulus is presented. Using the variable foreperiod represents an attempt to prevent the subject from anticipating when the stimulus will arrive (temporal anticipation). Sometimes "catch trials" are used, in which the stimulus is not presented at all; this allows the experimenter to "catch" a subject who is anticipating, and thus its use tends to prevent anticipation. The introduction of catch trials, given randomly perhaps on 15% of the total number of trials in an experiment, improves the experimental control. Also, subjects can be prevented from anticipating which movement to make (i.e., spatial or event anticipation) through the use of two or more choices, so that the

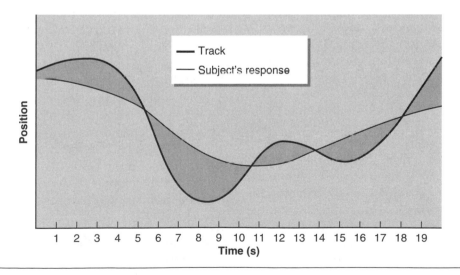

FIGURE 2.6   Hypothetical record from a tracking task, showing the basis for computation of root mean square (RMS) error.

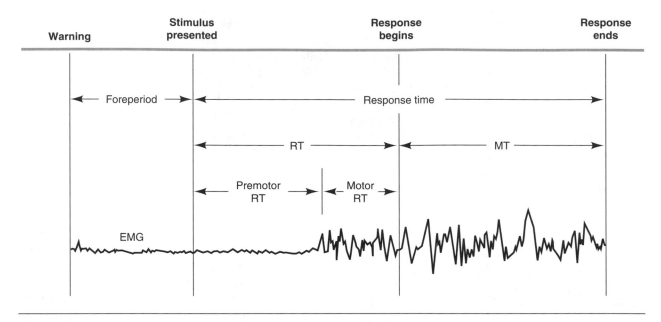

FIGURE 2.7   Critical events involved in the reaction-time (RT) paradigm.

proper response is signaled by the stimulus itself (e.g., red light means move left, blue light means move right); this is termed the *choice-RT* method (when only one option or "choice" is available, this is termed a *simple-RT* method).

Reaction-time measures are common in many sport settings; an example is the interval between the starter's gun and the first movement in a swimming race. This is an example of a simple-RT task in which there is only one response to make. The starter varies the time between the "ready" command and the auditory signal to start in order to reduce temporal anticipation. The decision of a soccer goalie to dive to the left or to the right in a penalty kick is an example of a choice-RT task in sport. Reaction-time measures are also used extensively in the laboratory as measures of information-processing speed (see chapter 3).

One variation of the RT method is to partition the latency of the response initiation into "central" and "peripheral" components (Weiss, 1965). The bottom of figure 2.7 shows a hypothetical electromyographic (EMG) trace taken from a muscle involved in the movement to be made (EMG indicates the electrical activity in a muscle). The EMG is mostly silent during a substantial part of the RT, indicating that the command to move the finger, which is initiated in the brain, has not yet reached the finger musculature. The muscle is activated late in the RT, but no movement occurs for 40 to 80 ms. The interval from

the signal to the first change in EMG is termed "premotor RT" and is thought to represent central processes involved in making the response (e.g., perception, decisions). The interval from the first change in EMG to finger movement is termed "motor RT" and represents processes associated with the musculature itself. Such methods are useful in gaining further information about the effect of an independent variable on RT (e.g., Fischman, 1984).

Reaction-time measures are very common in research on skills, for two basic reasons. First, RT measures are components of real-life tasks (e.g., sprint starts), so they often have high face validity. A more important reason (which we will amplify in chapters 3 and 4) is that RT presumably measures the time taken for mental events, such as stimulus processing, decision making, and movement programming. These two motivations for using RT measures differ considerably. In the first case, RT is a measure studied for its own sake; in the second case, RT allows the researcher to understand the kinds of mental processes that lead to movement (e.g., Posner, 1978). Regardless of the motivation, the measurement of RT is the same.

Movement Time   Movement time (commonly abbreviated as MT) is usually defined as the interval from the initiation of the response (which defines the end of the RT) to the completion of the movement (figure 2.7). Clearly, MT can be just about any value, ranging from a few milliseconds for a very quick movement to several weeks if the movement being studied is jogging from Los Angeles to Chicago. Some sport skills have minimal MT as a goal (e.g., time to run 100 m, or time for a quarterback to "set up" for a pass), and MT is used a great deal in skills research as a result of its overall external validity in these practical settings. Sometimes researchers use RT and MT tasks together in the same performance, as in requiring the subject to lift a finger from a key and move to a button as quickly as possible after a stimulus.

The sum of RT and MT is termed *response time* (figure 2.7). Research has consistently shown that very different processes or abilities are required in reacting quickly as opposed to moving quickly once the reaction is over, and this has justified separating response time into RT and MT. What is frequently called "brake reaction time" in the field of automobile accident analysis is really response time, because it consists of the time used to initiate the foot movement from the accelerator pedal plus the time required to move the foot to the brake pedal and press it.

Often the degree of accuracy in the task must be taken into account when measures of speed are used. A well-known phenomenon in motor behavior is the *speed–accuracy trade-off*, meaning simply that when performers attempt to do something more quickly, they typically do it less accurately. In most measures of speed, therefore, accuracy requirements are kept to a minimum so that speeding up the movement (which is the major goal for the subject) does not seriously affect accuracy. In some situations, though, measures of speed are confounded with measures of accuracy, and the speed with which the subject performs is dependent on the amount of error she is willing to make or the amount of error the experimenter will tolerate. Such trade-offs are particularly troublesome for experimenters, because it is not always clear to subjects how much error will be tolerated, and experimenters are unsure about how to interpret an independent variable that produces increases in speed but decreases in accuracy. One solution to this problem is to hold accuracy constant by various experimental techniques so that a single dependent variable of speed can be assessed (e.g., Fitts, 1954). Another solution is to hold speed constant,

via instructions, so that accuracy can be assessed (e.g., Quinn, Schmidt, Zelaznik, Hawkins, & McFarquhar, 1980; Schmidt, Zelaznik, Hawkins, Frank, & Quinn, 1979).

Measures of Movement Magnitude

A third way of measuring skills is by the magnitude of behavior that the performer produces, such as the distance that a discus was thrown or the amount of weight that was lifted. These measures have particularly important applications to sport settings, as many sports use such measures as the primary determinants of success in the activity. One example of these measures in research is the Bachman (1961) ladder climb task (figure 2.8), which uses a specially constructed ladder. At the beginning of, say, a 30 s trial, the subject begins to climb the (unsupported) ladder without skipping rungs until balance is lost and the subject topples over. The subject quickly returns to the starting position and begins climbing again, and so on until the trial has been completed. The score is the number of rungs accumulated in a given trial. A variant of the task is to climb as high as possible in a single attempt.

The ski simulator (figure 2.9) is a task in which large rubber bands keep a platform centered. The subject's task is to displace the platform as far as possible from side to side using whole-body movements.

FIGURE 2.8 The Bachman ladder climb task.

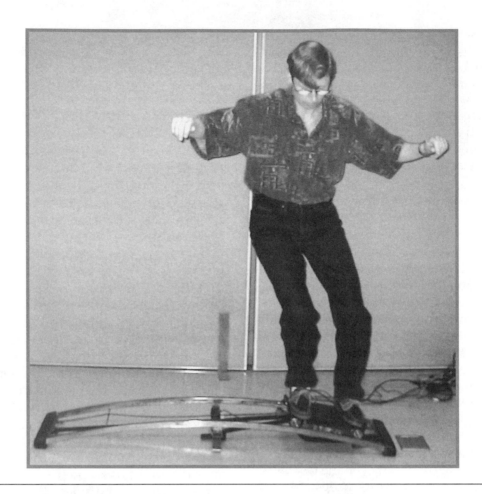

FIGURE 2.9   Ski simulator being used by Gaby Wulf.

Reprinted, by permission, from G. Wulf, 2007, *Attention and motor skill learning* (Champaign, IL: Human Kinetics), 9.

While it might seem that tasks with goals of maximum movement magnitude are considerably different from those requiring speed or accuracy, their fundamental determinants may not be all that different. At first glance, producing maximum movement magnitude would seem simply to be a matter of generating more force. But these skills certainly require precise timing of the forceful contractions and accurate coordination among the various participating limbs. Therefore these precise muscular activities might be essentially the same as those required in tasks that seem to necessitate only accuracy. Of course, inconsistency (in terms of VE) in these processes will degrade performance, and such inconsistency is probably related to the VEs that are seen in the outcomes of simpler tasks.

Measures of Secondary Tasks

There are instances in both practical and research settings in which none of these basic methods of measurement will be sensitive to differences in skill among individuals or to differences in skill caused by some independent variable. Generally these situations involve tasks for which differences in performance are not evident because the tasks are well learned (driving a car down an open road), or involve tasks that do not "tax" the motor system very much because they are so simple (drinking a glass of water without spilling). How are skills assessed in such situations?

One method is to use some measure of critical incidents. In the driving example, accident rates from statistical databases for a particular kind of car, or for certain types of people (e.g., drunk drivers), might be used as measures of skill; with pilots, "near misses" (midair near-collisions) might be used. But these techniques are difficult to utilize in the laboratory because (fortunately) such critical events occur so infrequently. Thus, they are far more useful for groups of people taken over relatively long stretches of time.

Another useful technique is to employ performance on some sort of secondary task, performed simultaneously with the primary task, as a measure of the skill in the *primary* task. For example, Brown (1962) used a verbal task in which the individual was presented with eight-digit numbers at 4 s intervals. Each number contained seven of the same digits as the previous one, and the subject's task was to detect the digit that was different and to provide a response. Errors were counted as omitted responses, incorrect responses, and late responses. In this experiment, Brown obtained measures of performance when subjects performed only this verbal–numerical task, and also when subjects performed this task while driving under various conditions. The mean percentage of correct responses when the verbal task was performed alone was 90.6%. When the task was performed during driving in quiet residential areas, the mean percentage dropped to 83.8%. And when the task was performed in heavy traffic conditions, the percentage again dropped, to 79.5%. Yet it was very difficult to see any differences in vehicle control in light and heavy traffic, largely because driving is so well learned by most people. This secondary task provided evidence about the difficulty of the driving conditions when the driving task itself would not have provided such a measure.

Some experimenters have used RT tasks (so-called *probe tasks*—e.g., Kerr, 1975) inserted during a performance of the primary task. Others have used measures of finger tapping regularity (e.g., Michon, 1966) as the secondary task. In these latter cases, the implication is that these tasks require some of the subject's *limited capacity* to process information; presenting the secondary task simultaneously with the primary task necessitates the use of some of this capacity, and lowers the performance on the secondary task in relation to the amount of capacity demanded by the primary task. (See chapter 4 for more on this assumption and general method.)

Rather than a task, secondary *physiological* measures of effort can be used during the performance of a main task. One technique is to measure pupil diameter by one of various recording methods. Pupil dilation is associated with circumstances in which effort, arousal, or information processing is demanded (e.g., Beatty & Wagoner, 1978; Kahneman, 1973). Similarly, measures of heart rate, heart rate variability, oxygen consumption (as a measure of overall effort), or even EMG from the muscles of the forehead (to indicate the level of concentration) can be used, depending on the particular situation. Neurophysiological techniques, such as the recording of *event-related potentials* from the scalp, are also used. One such potential has been called *P300*, as it occurs as a positive voltage about 300 ms after the presentation of a stimulus (Duncan-Johnson & Donchin, 1982). The latency of the P300 and the magnitude of its amplitude appear to be highly correlated with RT, thus providing an unobtrusive way to measure processing activities (e.g., Radlo, Janelle, Barba, & Frehlich, 2001). In all these cases, the secondary measures become the focus of the investigator, especially when the main task does not provide sensitive measures of the subject's performance.

A variation of this technique is to use a secondary task as a distracter in order to increase the overall "load" on the performer. Normally, fatigue may not have any obvious effect on the well-learned task of driving. However, if the driver is required to perform a simultaneous mental arithmetic task at a predetermined level, then large differences between fatigued and rested driving may be seen. In this situation, unlike the others, the major interest is in the performance of the main task, and the secondary task has increased the sensitivity of the measurement system for the main task. However, care must be taken with these techniques, as Brown (1962) has shown. When truck drivers were fatigued, their performance on the secondary digit detection task actually improved, suggesting that they were devoting less capacity to the driving task and overcompensating by devoting more capacity to the secondary task. While these techniques can be somewhat tricky to use, they have served well in a number of situations.

Describing Characteristics of Movements

Countless methods could be employed to describe movements, depending on the characteristics of the movement that are of interest to the observer. At the most fundamental level, one can use verbal descriptors to characterize movement. For example, movements have been described in dance notation created by Laban (1956) and in terms of units of work behavior called "Therbligs" in early industrial time-and-motion studies (Gilbreth, 1909; note that "Therblig" is the author's name spelled backward, almost). Another way is to illustrate movement with photographs, as was done over a century ago by Muybridge (1887, 1979) using series of still photos (see "The Movement Photographs of Eadweard Muybridge," figure 2.10), or with videotape or digital images. Such methods are of some use in describing or illustrating the basic forms of movement, but

The Movement Photographs of Eadweard Muybridge

In 1887 Eadweard Muybridge published what probably was the first photographic analysis of human and animal locomotion. In some series, Muybridge used 36 separate shutters, arranged so that three different angles could be photographed simultaneously, positioned at the side, front, and rear of the subject. At each angle a series of 12 shutters was electrically arranged to open in a timed sequence after a signal had been sent to the first shutter. Muybridge determined the length of the time intervals on the basis of the speed at which the subject performed the activity (e.g., picking up an object vs. running at full speed). These methods resulted in a sequence of still photographs that produced simulated motion, which one could study further by examining the changes in the action as it evolved over time. In all, Muybridge published 781 plates, each plate a series of photographs of the subject. The subjects were both humans and animals. Humans of all ages, males and females, and of many different body types, performed actions such as walking, running, jumping, skipping, lifting objects, and hammering. Many of the humans were photographed in the nude, which provided rather explicit details of body actions. Animals from a wide range of species were photographed in various natural and contrived settings. It is rumored that Muybridge settled a bet concerning whether or not all of a galloping horse's feet are ever off the ground at the same time. According to his photos, they are. Muybridge's series of still-sequence photographs remains as a magnificent legacy in the history of human and animal motion analysis.

FIGURE 2.10 A famous series of Muybridge photos, clearly revealing a period of time when the horse has no contact with the ground.

have limited value in detailed assessments of performance. Improvements in photographic techniques occurred early in the 20th century; some were pioneered by Bernstein (Bernstein & Popova, 1930/2003). In this section we focus on *kinematics*, a branch of mechanics in physics that involves the description of "pure" motion without regard for the forces and masses that produced the motion. The devices that can be used to collect this information also vary widely, and we will describe some of the more common ones.

Movement Kinematics

As applied to movement behavior, kinematic measures describe the movement of the limbs or the entire body. The locations of various parts of the body during the movement, the angles of the various joints, and the time relations between the movement in one joint and the movement in another are examples of the many ways movement kinematics can be recorded.

Location   Perhaps the most common of the kinematic methods entails recording the locations of the limbs during a movement. An early example of research using movement kinematics is that of Lindahl (1945; see "Lindahl's Study Using Movement Kinematics"). Early in the history of motor behavior and biomechanics, researchers used high-speed cinematography to record

Lindahl's Study Using Movement Kinematics

One of the early investigations using movement kinematics as a research tool was published by Lawrence Lindahl in 1945. His study concerned a very practical problem: an industrial task in which a factory worker operated a machine that cut very thin slices off tungsten rods. The key aspect of the job involved using a foot pedal action that moved an unseen cutting wheel through the tungsten rod. Success at the task required carefully coordinated displacement–time foot actions. Failure to coordinate these actions resulted in wasted material (improperly cut discs) and damage to the equipment (broken wheels). Skilled machine operators made very stereotypical actions of the foot, which Lindahl captured nicely using a writing apparatus that recorded the foot displacements over time (see figure 2.11). These recordings were then used for comparison with the recordings that beginning and less skilled workers produced in their disc-cutting performances. This type of recording, using kinematics as a means to provide objective feedback and goal-related movement information (so-called kinematic feedback), predated modern investigations by about 40 years (see discussion in chapter 12).

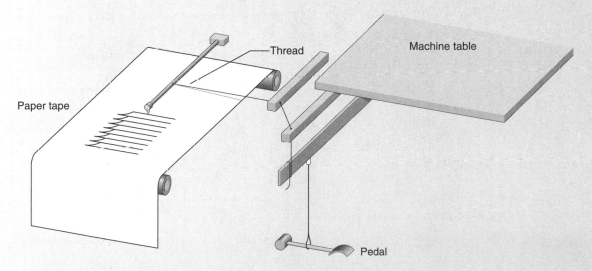

FIGURE 2.11   Experimental setup used by Lindahl (1945) to record kinematics of the disc-cutting task.

movements. Often the subject being filmed wore tape markers over certain landmarks (e.g., the wrist or ankle) so that the locations of these body parts could be studied frame by frame. These positions on successive frames were separated by nearly fixed periods of time, so a graph of the position of the landmark against time could be generated from the data.

Figure 2.12 shows an example of this type of graph, taken from Wadman, Denier van der Gon, Geuze, and Mol (1979). For now, consider only trace a, which represents position; it is derived from the output of a device called a potentiometer that signals angular position. This trace, read from left to right, represents an arm movement of about 17 cm. The movement began at the time when the trace left the horizontal axis. The largest amplitude (about 20 cm) was achieved about 125 ms after the movement started, and then the limb stabilized its position at the final location.

But examining the location of a limb in space may mask some of the more subtle factors that determine its control. For this reason motor behavior researchers often examine variables that

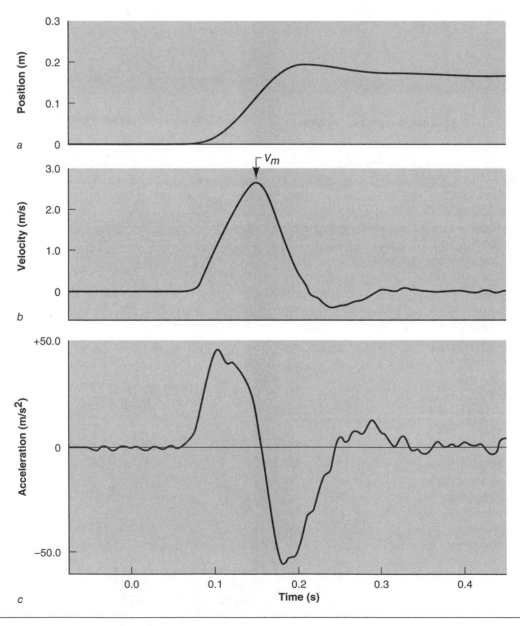

FIGURE 2.12   Position, velocity, and acceleration traces representing a rapid 17 cm elbow extension movement.

Reprinted from W.J. Wadman et al., 1979, "Control of fast goal-directed arm movements," *Journal of Human Movement Studies* 5: 5. By permission of W.J. Wadman.

can be derived from location information—velocity and acceleration.

Velocity   Trace b in figure 2.12 is a record of velocity of the movement at each moment in time, placed on the same time scale as the positional trace for easy comparison. The velocity trace was determined by computer, which read in the position information from the potentiometer and then calculated the slope or inclination of the line at each moment. The slopes (called derivatives) of the positions at each moment in time represent the velocities at corresponding moments, indicating *the rate of change in position*. Then this information is output onto the same record as the position information. Such a trace is useful here in showing that the maximum velocity (V_m) was about 2.7 m/s and that the achievement of maximum velocity occurred at about 75 ms through the movement. Also shown are a gradual increase in velocity until the peak velocity (the midpoint of the movement) is reached and then a decline toward the end. Such a trace gives a more complete description of the movement than does positional information alone.

Acceleration   Trace c in figure 2.12 is a record of the acceleration at each moment of time. This record was also obtained by the computer, which calculated the slope or inclination of the velocity curve at each moment. The slopes of the velocity curve at each moment yield the accelerations and represent *the rate of change in velocity*. This output is plotted along with the other two traces on the same time scale. Initial acceleration lasts about 100 ms until the acceleration trace returns to zero. Then there is a deceleration (a negative acceleration trace) that lasts for about the same length of time. Also, the peak velocity of the movement is achieved at the point at which the acceleration changes to deceleration (where the acceleration curve crosses the zero baseline).

These kinematic variables, with simultaneous recording of position, velocity, and acceleration as a function of time, provide a reasonably complete picture of these movements. Scientists often search for changes in these kinematic variables when certain independent variables are changed—for instance, instructions to the subject or the size of a target to which the person is moving. Examples of this kind of research are provided later in the text.

Coordination Kinematics   In chapter 8 we will focus on movement coordination—how the actions of one body part are controlled together with the movements of another body part. Many types of coordination exist, such as the coordination of two or more joints in one limb (as when one is reaching for a cup) or of different limbs simultaneously (as of the arms and legs during walking), or even more subtle coordinations (such as the movements of the eye and head while one is reaching for a glass in the cupboard). For movements that are oscillatory, one measure of coordination is to describe the temporal *phasing* between the two body parts.

Consider the simple action of tapping two fingers on a table. Suppose we plotted the displacement records of the up-and-down tapping cycles of the right finger along the abscissa and the cycles of the left finger along the ordinate. Plotted separately, each would be represented as a back-and-forth, overlapping straight line along its respective axis. However, to assess how these two fingers are coordinated, the time records of one finger can be plotted relative to the time records of the other finger. At any point in time, the position of the left hand and the position of the right hand are represented as a single data point on the graph. When the points are combined over time they produce one continuous trace, as illustrated in the two examples in figure 2.13 (see also Winstein & Garfinkel, 1989). In figure 2.13a, the two fingers tap the table at approximately the same time, are at maximum height above the table (in the "up" position on the graph) at about the same time, and seem to be moving within their respective cycles at about the same time—the coordinated motions are *simultaneous*. The example in figure 2.13b illustrates *alternate tapping*—one finger taps the table at about the same time that the other finger reaches maximum height, then vice versa. This figure illustrates just two of the types of temporal coordination patterns that exist between oscillating effectors (see chapter 8).

One can also obtain a quantitative measure of temporal coordination by considering the displacements of each cycle over time. This is represented in figure 2.14 in two ways. In figure 2.14a, displacement of one finger is plotted over time—position A represents the finger at the time of a tap, position B is about halfway up, position C represents the "up" point, and position D is halfway back down again. Figure 2.14b represents the same data by plotting these one-finger

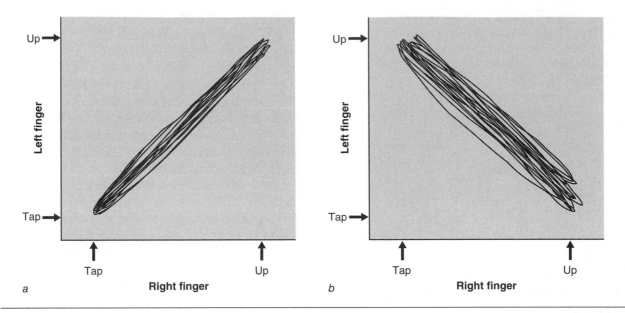

FIGURE 2.13 Sample displacement plots of two fingers moving simultaneously. *(a)* In-phase coordination; *(b)* anti-phase coordination.

displacements against their own velocities (called a phase-plane representation). Now positions A and C represent zero velocity, and positions B and D are the maximum upward and downward velocities, respectively. The value of phase-plane representations is that the position of each finger at any point within its cycle can be described as a

phase angle (Φ) indicating the progress through a cycle, or a circle, containing 360°.

Since the phase planes of each finger can be determined independently, the measure of coordination is simply the difference between the phase angle for the left finger (Φ_L) and the phase angle for right finger (Φ_R). This measure is called

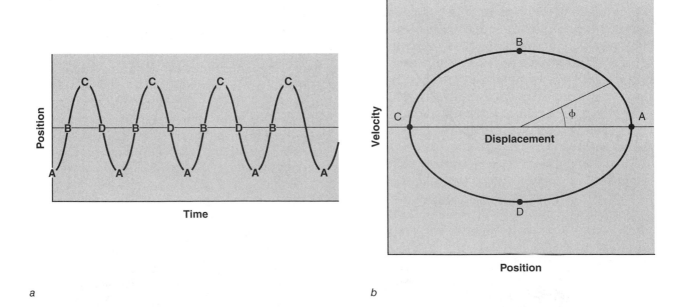

FIGURE 2.14 Repetitive movement of a finger: displacement *(a)* relative to time and *(b)* relative to its velocity.

Figure 2.14a Adapted from Kelso et al. 1985.

Figure 2.14b Adapted from Burgess-Limerick, Abernethy, and Neal 1991.

relative phase, because the measure represents the position of one finger within its cycle relative to the position of the other finger within its cycle.

From figures 2.13*a* and 2.14, it is clear that at any one time, the two phase angles are about the same. That is, when both fingers are "down," each phase angle is 0°; when both fingers are "up," each phase angle is 180°, and so on. Thus, the relative phase ($\Phi_L - \Phi_R$) will always be close to 0° whenever a sample is measured. This simultaneous pattern of coordination is often referred to as moving *in-phase.* However, for figure 2.13*b,* notice that the temporal phasing of one finger is always nearly exactly opposite that of the other finger. That is, when one phase angle is at 0°, the other is at 180°; then when the first is at 180°, the other has reached 360° (or 0°). The relative phase for this series of estimates produces an average relative phase of about 180°, which is sometimes referred to as moving in an *anti-phase* pattern of coordination.

But notice also that there is some variability in the plots presented in figure 2.13. Thus, researchers often calculate the standard deviation of these relative-phase samples in order to supplement the description of a pattern's average relative phase with an estimate of its *stability.* The measure of relative-phase variability is determined in a way similar to that for the measures of VE, discussed earlier in the chapter. Both the mean and standard deviation measures of relative phase will be used to describe important features of coordination in chapter 8.

Movement Measurement Devices

Measurement recording systems, used to collect data about human movement, have undergone many changes over the years. Just as "moving picture" technology evolved from the efforts of Muybridge and others to capture on film the moment-to-moment changes in body positions, new developments in measurement technology have often been created to satisfy the needs of researchers to make recordings with increased precision and economy (in terms of time and effort).

One of the simplest methods to collect body position information is to acquire the information directly through various means. For example, a *goniometer* is a hinged device that, when strapped to the side of a body joint, physically changes in angle along with changes in the joint angle.

Goniometers can be wired with potentiometers that send voltage information (proportional to the joint angle); this can be accumulated and analyzed by a computer. Potentiometers are also used in many other direct measurement devices, such as a computer *mouse,* that signal changes in position when physically moved by the subject. A *graphics tablet* is another device that records the changes in contact positions with the surface.

Muybridge (see "The Movement Photographs of Eadweard Muybridge" on p. 38) is often credited with initiating the analysis of human movement through imaging techniques. High-speed cinematography introduced a way to capture images of moving limbs many times each second. However, frame-by-frame analysis methods were tedious ways of examining changes in locations over time (Bernstein & Popova, 1930/2003). Fortunately, technology has introduced more automated ways of performing these analyses. Such instruments have relieved the scientist of the time-consuming job of reading locations from each frame of film, a method that also made the cost of such analysis systems prohibitive for many years. Computer systems that analyze such data are now more powerful and much cheaper, and the use of these measurement techniques is now the norm.

The most common imaging devices use *video* and *optoelectric* methods. Video methods were straightforward, as movements could be captured on relatively inexpensive videotape using VHS and 8 mm formats. Typically, the subject was recorded on videotape wearing pieces of tape or fluorescent "markers." The locations of these markers were later digitized for analysis. For optoelectric methods, tiny light bulbs (called light-emitting diodes or LEDs) are attached to the subject on various body parts. Light-sensing devices then detect and record automatically the locations of the LEDs during the movement. As illustrated in figure 2.15, an advantage of these newer systems is the capability to record information in three dimensions, providing greater information about movements and greater flexibility in the types of actions that can be studied in experiments.

The most recent advances in movement recording technology have combined the use of robotics and virtual reality environments (see figure 2.16). These systems not only record movement with fine precision, but also have great flexibility to provide diverse perceptual inputs. For example,

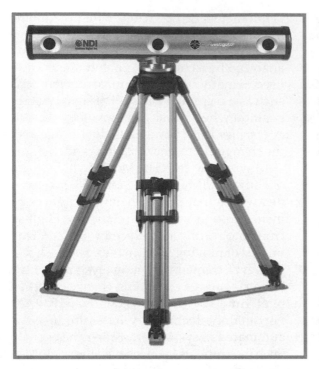

FIGURE 2.15 Three-dimensional optoelectric system.

Photo courtesy of Northern Digital Inc.

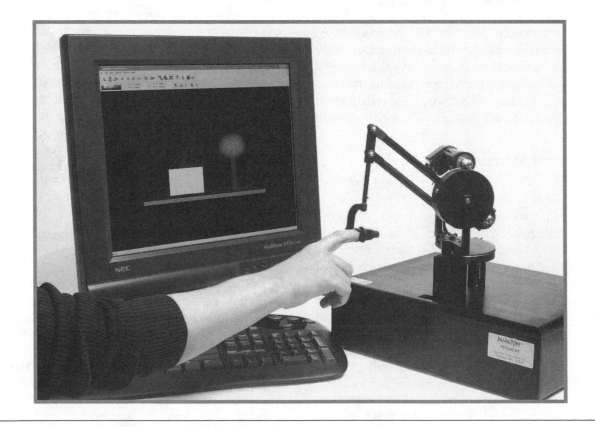

FIGURE 2.16 Robotic system in a virtual environment.

© *SensAble Technologies, Inc.* www.sensable.com/documents/images/premium_3.0_6dof_large.jpg

the robotic system can induce different types and magnitudes of haptic feedback (information about touch) during movement. When combined with virtual reality feedback information, these robotic systems can simulate the look and feel of complex skills (e.g., surgical techniques) without the dangers that might otherwise be present if practice were undertaken in the "real world" (e.g., on a patient).

Electromyography

Another method for describing movement characteristics is to measure the involvement of a muscle in a movement by recording the electrical activity associated with its contraction. The simplest method is to attach (with adhesive collars) recording electrodes to the skin surface over the involved muscle; then, this weak signal from the muscle is amplified and recorded on a polygraph recorder or computer for later analysis. Occasionally subcutaneous electrodes are used; the electrode is placed just under the skin but above the muscle belly. Or a small wire electrode can be embedded *within* the muscle so that electrical activity in small portions of the muscle can be recorded.

A recording using surface electrodes, taken from a study by Carter and Shapiro (1984), is shown in figure 2.17. Subjects were asked to

perform a four-phase movement involving rotation of the right wrist. The record at the top of the figure shows the clockwise (supination) and counterclockwise (pronation) movements. The EMGs are from the pronator teres muscle, which acts as the pronator (counterclockwise), and the biceps muscle, which acts as the supinator (clockwise). Once the movement begins, one can see marked activity in the various muscles; the activity is dependent on the particular action being performed. The pronator teres is the first muscle to act, throwing the wrist into pronation; then the pronator is turned off and the biceps acts to brake the action and reverse it; then the pronator brakes and reverses that action, and so on. These records describe the *temporal patterning* of the movement segments. Information about the intensity of contraction is also provided by the amplitudes in these records, with larger EMG amplitudes being generally indicative of larger forces. However, while the relation between EMG amplitude and force under static, controlled conditions within a given muscle is good, many situations arise that can degrade this relation, so that the amount of force produced is usually not accurately reflected by the amount of EMG being produced.

A record of transformed EMG activity, taken during a rapid elbow extension (from Wadman

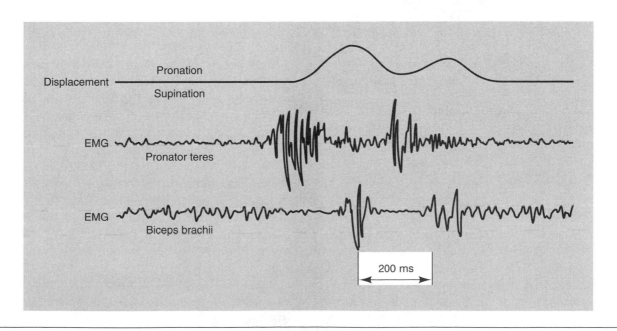

FIGURE 2.17　A typical electromyogram tracing taken during a movement.

et al., 1979), is depicted in figure 2.18. A number of changes were made in the raw EMG signals before they were plotted. First, the EMGs were *rectified*; that is, the negative voltage values were given positive signs so that the resulting record would be completely positive. (Notice that figure 2.18 has two such records, with the biceps record inverted so that the two patterns can be compared more easily.) When the EMG is rectified, the pattern of electrical activity can be seen more readily than with the raw signals shown in figure 2.17. Second, these records were *averaged* for a number of similar movements, mainly so that the important patterns of contractions could be seen over and above the trial-to-trial variations. These patterns are more reliable than are those for a single trial.

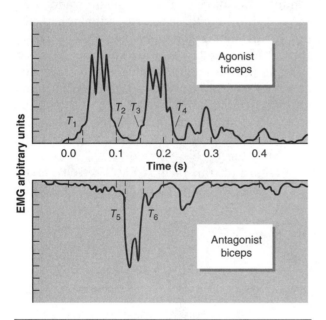

FIGURE 2.18　Rectified and averaged electromyogram signals from the triceps and biceps muscles during a rapid elbow extension.

Reprinted from W.J. Wadman et al., 1979, "Control of fast goal-directed arm movements," *Journal of Human Movement Studies* 5: 10. By permission of W.J. Wadman.

Such records are useful in that they provide one kind of description of what the central nervous system "tells" the muscles to do. In the example shown, it appears that the triceps muscle contracted for about 100 ms; then it turned off and the biceps muscle contracted for about 50 ms; and then the triceps muscle came on again for another burst of about 100 ms. These records are even more helpful if they are superimposed on

other records of kinematic information, so that the changes in the muscle actions can be associated with the resulting actions of the limbs.

Measures of Eye Movements

Motor skills involving the use of the upper limbs constitute a large proportion of our daily activities. How we use our hands and fingers to press the buttons to make a phone call, pick up a cup from the table, or move a mouse-controlled pointer across a computer monitor depends considerably on our visual system. We use vision to determine where we want the hand to go and then to update the relative success of that movement as it approaches the target. Researchers have used eye movement recording systems in their investigations to determine where someone is looking (that is, where the eyes are directed), for example during an aiming movement of the hand or in making a left turn in an automobile. These recording systems can provide accurate measures of what the subject sees, through two video imaging techniques. One camera mounted on the head or helmet of the subject provides an image of the subject's line of vision. This visual gaze is then coordinated with an eye-tracking device that measures the movements of the eyes by means of corneal reflection. The calibration of the two recording devices provides an accurate measure of where the eye is directed during the performance of a motor task, sometimes referred to as point-of-gaze information. One caveat here is that what the person "sees" (i.e., perceives visually) is not perfectly related to where the eye is pointed. In some situations, even though the eye is directed at an object, the object is for various reasons not actually "seen." The mere fact that a person is looking at an object does not guarantee that he actually perceives it.

Figure 2.19 provides a good example of how the information from eye-tracking devices can be coordinated with other information to provide a more informative description of the motor behavior of a subject in a particular task. In the example in figure 2.19, the subject is moving a hand forward to point at a target that is 40 cm away from the initial "home" location. The top half of the figure provides data from the eye-tracking measurement system, showing that the eye performs a rapid relocation from the home position to a point about 4 cm short of the 40 cm target (indicated by the arrow denoting point of

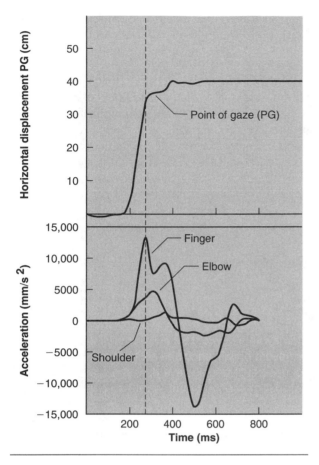

FIGURE 2.19 Acceleration traces of the finger, elbow, and shoulder, relative to the changes in horizontal displacement in point of gaze, during a rapidly aimed movement.

Adapted from Helsen et al. 2000 and 1998.

gaze). The bottom half of the figure illustrates kinematic information regarding the acceleration profiles of the finger, elbow, and shoulder as the upper arm moves toward the target. These kinematics were provided by an optoelectric measurement system that, while separate from the eye-tracking system, was calibrated in real time in order that these measurements could be coordinated later to provide the kinds of data illustrated in figure 2.19. The dotted line in the figure illustrates that the end of the initial rapid-eye movement toward the target (called a "saccade") corresponded very well with the point of peak acceleration of the finger. A second saccade of the eye, initiated about 100 ms later, again corresponded with an increase in the acceleration profile of the finger. Methods such as these have provided a rich source of information about motor behavior, as researchers can associate the movements of body parts with the perceptual information that may be received during action. Such techniques may be informative when one is determining, for example, how visual information is used during action (chapter 5), or how athletes of varying levels of skill use visual information in performance (chapter 9). Figure 2.20 illustrates the use of eye tracking to measure point-of-gaze information during the performance of a golf putt.

Measures of Brain Activity

The most dramatic advances in measurement in recent years have been the various methods of measuring brain activity. Their use in describing the brain activity that underlies motor performance is still in development; and the promise of faster, more flexible, and more accurate advances in technique remains a technological challenge. Each of these techniques has advantages and disadvantages, although changes in methodology are occurring at a rapid pace and many of the current disadvantages may yet be overcome.

Electroencephalography (EEG), which has been around the longest, involves the recording of electrical changes that occur in the brain as recorded from the scalp, more or less as EMG measures electrical activity of a muscle via the skin adjacent to the muscle. Another type of encephalography is known as magnetoencephalography (MEG). As the name suggests, this technique measures changes in the magnetic fields involving brain activities. Both techniques have the advantage of working very quickly, providing precise measures of the timing of mental events. However, their capacity to allow inferences about localized anatomical structures is significantly less than that of other, albeit slower, methods (Haynes & Rees, 2006).

In contrast, methods such as (a) positron emission tomography (PET), (b) single-photon emission computed tomography (SPECT), and (c) functional magnetic resonance imaging (fMRI) are all neural imaging techniques that provide much more detailed information about the localization of brain structure and activity. The latter technique (fMRI) is based on the fact that when a specific part of the brain is active in the processing of information, neural activity increases and consequently oxygenated blood to that region of the brain increases. The fMRI records the "BOLD"

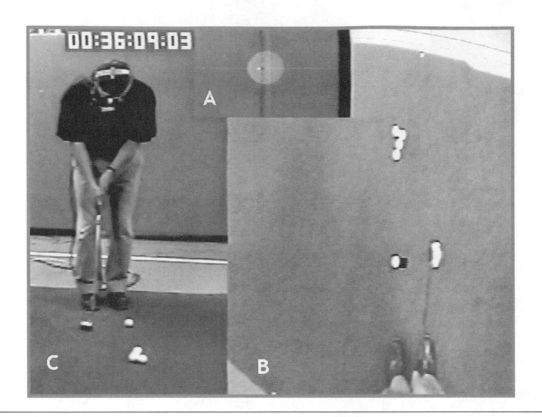

FIGURE 2.20 Eye-tracking setup.

Reprinted, by permission, from J. Vickers, 2007, *Perception, cognition, and decision training: The quiet eye in action* (Champaign, IL: Human Kinetics), 59.

(blood oxygen level dependent) signal as vectors of three-dimensional pixels (called "voxels"), allowing researchers to map the location and volume of brain regions that are actively processing information during task performance. The use of new brain recording techniques in motor control and learning experiments has increased dramatically in the past decade, although some challenges remain, such as temporal resolution and the nature of tasks that can be used with these devices.

Although not a brain activity "measurement" device, an approach to studying brain function that is frequently used today is called transcranial magnetic stimulation (TMS). The TMS method sends a brief pulse through a magnetic coil that has a temporary effect on the region of the brain above which the coil has been positioned. Depending on where the magnetic coil is positioned, the brief pulse can either excite or inhibit the activity of that brain area. In contrast to what happens in nonstimulated trials, the TMS-stimulated locations of the brain are assumed to be active if a change in task performance is observed (see Hallett, 2007, for an excellent primer on TMS). Recent investigations have combined TMS with fMRI so that the effects of stimulation on both behavioral and brain responses can be observed (Sack & Linden, 2003).

These neural imaging and simulation techniques are useful in localizing the parts of the brain that are active during the performance of many activities. Indeed, many motor behavior researchers are including these techniques as routine components of their investigations to provide neural–anatomical evidence that augments the motor behavior data obtained in their experiments.

Measuring and Evaluating Relationships

An important process for evaluating the outcomes of various experimental procedures begins after the main performance measures are generated from the experiment. This process involves determining the relationship between some independent variable and a dependent variable on the basis of the empirical data. One important kind of relationship is linear. In a graph, the dependent variable plots essentially as a straight line with the independent variable.

Linear Relationships

In figure 2.21 we have plotted data from an experiment by Schmidt and colleagues (1979), for which the error (measured as VE and called effective target width, W_e) in hitting a target with a handheld stylus is plotted as a function of the average velocity of the movement. A quick examination of the plot in figure 2.21 indicates that the relationship between these two variables is essentially linear. A line has been placed through the points that seems to represent their general direction, and this line is called the *line of best fit*. The actual placement can be done accurately by various statistical techniques (e.g., regression) or can be done "by eye" for a rough approximation.

The goal in this section is to express this line of best fit in terms of what is known as an *empirical equation*, a kind of shorthand that enables us, with but two numbers, to convey information about a linear relationship for an empirically determined set of data points. These two numbers also will have special meaning in terms of various theories; that is, these numbers will be measures of certain hypothetical constructs. We begin with the general equation for a line:

$$Y = a + bX \qquad (2.8)$$

In this equation, Y represents the values on the y-axis (error), X represents the values on the x-axis (average velocity), and a and b are constants (figure 2.21). The constant a is termed the y-intercept, and it refers to the value of Y when the line crosses the y-axis; here the value is about 2 mm. The constant b is called the *slope* and refers to the amount of inclination of the line. The slope can be *positive* (upward and to the right, as in this example) or *negative* (downward to the right), associated with either positive or negative values of b, respectively. Once these values are specified from a given set of data, the empirical equation that describes the linear relation between values of X and Y can be written.

Computation of Constants

Computation of the constants needed for the empirical equation is simple. After the line of best fit has been applied to the data points, extend it leftward until it crosses the y-axis and read off the y-intercept, or a. In the data shown in figure 2.21, a equals 2.08 mm.

Next, draw two lines, one perpendicular to the y-axis and one perpendicular to the x-axis, forming the shaded triangle as shown. The length of the line forming the base of the triangle will be called ΔX, and the length of the line forming the side of the triangle will be called ΔY. The symbol Δ means "change in"; measures of the changes in Y (6.7 mm) and the corresponding changes in

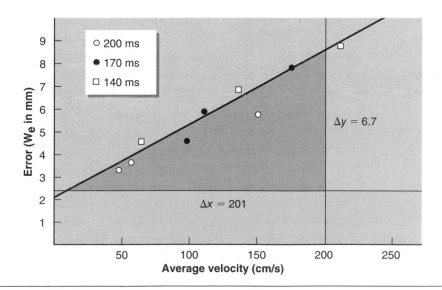

FIGURE 2.21 Graphical method for determining constants for linear empirical equations.

Reprinted, by permission, from R.A. Schmidt et al., 1979, "Motor-output variability: A theory for the accuracy of rapid motor acts," *Psychological Review* 86: 427.

X (201 cm/s) can be seen. Then, the slope of the line is defined as

$$b = \Delta Y / \Delta X \qquad (2.9)$$

That is, the slope is defined as the change in Y divided by the corresponding change in X. Here, the slope (b) is computed as 6.7 / 201 = +0.033. The interpretation of this slope is that each time the value of X increases by 1 cm/s, there is a 0.033 mm increase in the Y value (error).

Uses of Empirical Equations

The slope and intercept are the only two values needed to determine the linear relationship. Putting the slope and the intercept together into the general equation for a straight line results in the empirical equation for these data:

$$Y = 2.08 + 0.033X$$

Having been provided the calculated values of a and b found by a person in California, someone in Munich can reconstruct the line of best fit by using the linear equation. This is done by picking any two arbitrary values of X (say, 50 and 250 cm/s) and calculating the values of Y for these values of X:

$$Y = 2.08 + 0.033 (50) = 3.73 \text{ mm}$$

$$Y = 2.08 + 0.033 (250) = 10.33 \text{ mm}$$

Then, on a new graph, these data points ($X = 50$, $Y = 3.73$; and $X = 250$, $Y = 10.33$) can be plotted, and the line in figure 2.21 drawn between them. Thus, saying that the intercept was 2.08 and the slope was 0.033 can convey a great deal of information about the experimental results to someone who does not have access to the nine actual data points.

In addition, this relation can be used to predict *new* values of error before they are found. If we wanted to choose a velocity value so that the error was only 5.00 mm, we could take the empirical equation and substitute the value of the error as follows, then solve for the value of the velocity:

$$5.00 = 2.08 + 0.033X$$

$$X = (2.08 - 5.00) / (-0.033)$$

$$X = 88.48 \text{ cm/s}$$

Thus, if we wanted the error to be about 5 mm, we would use a velocity of about 88 cm/s. Having an empirical equation makes it possible to predict this result without actually going into the laboratory to measure it directly.

Interpreting Empirical Equations

In addition to the benefits provided by empirical equations in terms of description of experimental results and prediction of new findings, the values of the constants a and b often have special theoretical meaning, depending on the nature of the data collected and the kind of independent variable studied. In the present example, the meaning of the constant a (the intercept) is related to the amount of error for the slowest movement possible, and thus the intercept seems to represent a kind of "background" or "baseline" error. On the other hand, the value of the slope (b) refers to the amount of *increase* in error as the velocity increases, and it represents a measure of the "difficulty" of the task. In this and other similar situations to be discussed later, the slope and intercept describe two distinct features of the task or the subject's behavior.

Correlation and Regression

A statistical tool that is used often in motor behavior research, and that has mathematical properties similar to those of the simple linear regression method, is the *correlation*. The correlation and regression methods are used to establish the degree of *association* between two measures, as seen in the study of individual differences, for example (in chapter 9). For a relatively large group of subjects (e.g., 50), we begin with two different tests administered to each person. The degree to which the performances by individuals on one test are related to the performances of the same individuals on the other test is reflected in the size of the correlation coefficient. The correlation coefficient expresses the amount of shared association that exists between the two data sets, with no implications about whether or not one variable caused the other to change.

Scattergrams

One of the ways in which data from two tests can be described is by a special kind of graph called a *scattergram*. Consider the data shown in table 2.3, which have been plotted on the scattergram in figure 2.22. The two axes in figure 2.22 are the scales of the two tests, respectively; and each of the subjects is represented as a dot, located according to his scores on the two tests. The data are hypothetical scores that might be obtained on a common playground and consist of age (in years) and the time for a 100 m dash (in seconds). In figure 2.22, the scores for these 10 people are

TABLE 2.3. Hypothetical Data for Age and 100 m Dash Performance

| Subjects | 100 M DASH | | |
	Age (years)	Time (s)	Average speed (km/h)
1	13.1	13.5	26.6
2	11.6	12.8	28.1
3	12.2	12.0	30.0
4	16.1	10.5	34.3
5	9.2	16.1	22.4
6	8.5	15.2	23.7
7	8.1	16.0	22.5
8	11.3	14.1	25.5
9	12.2	13.0	27.7
10	7.3	18.0	20.0

Note: Speed data were computed from the time data.

plotted, so that each of the 10 dots on the graph represents each person's joint scores on the two variables (age and running time).

A relationship apparently exists between the score on the age variable and the score on the running test, indicating that as the age score becomes larger, the number of seconds on the running test tends to become smaller, with some exceptions. In general, the 10 subjects showed a relationship

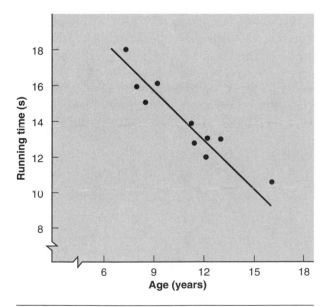

FIGURE 2.22 A scattergram showing the relationship between age and running time. (Data are from table 2.3, and each dot represents one of the 10 subjects.)

between these two variables, and a line could be drawn through the points to represent the "direction" in which the "cloud" of points is oriented. This "line of best fit" can be determined in exactly the same way as discussed earlier for empirical equations, and often involves computing regression equations.

Direction of the Relationship In this example, as the value of the age variable increases, the value of the running time variable tends to decrease. This kind of relationship is called an inverse, or *negative*, relationship, and the equation representing this relationship has a negative slope constant (*b*). In other situations, we might find that as one of the variables increases, the value of the other variable tends to increase as well; this is a direct, or *positive*, relationship. In such cases, the slope constant of the regression equation has a positive value, with the line of best fit sloping upward to the right.

The direction of the relationship shown in such data is often dependent on the scoring system used. Consider the data in table 2.3. In the fourth column we have expressed each subject's 100 m dash scores as average running *speed* (km/h) rather than as the *time* required to travel 100 m. This change in scoring system "inverts" the group of scores, so that the person who had the largest time score has the smallest speed score, and so on. When the age data are plotted against the average running speed scores in figure 2.23, the relationship becomes positive, and the empirical

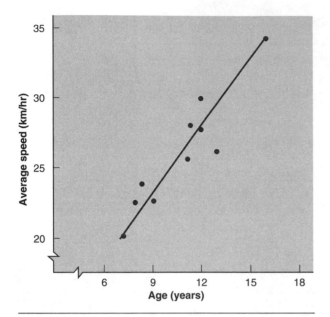

FIGURE 2.23 A scattergram showing the relationship between age and running speed. (Data are from table 2.3, where speed is computed from running time; each dot represents one of the 10 subjects.)

equation would now have a positive slope constant (*b*) rather than a negative one. Thus, a positive relationship is not any "better" than a negative one; the sign simply indicates the direction in which the line of best fit is sloped.

Strength of the Relationship   A second characteristic of the relationship between two variables is its *strength.* By strength, we mean the extent to which the relationship is perfectly linear, or the extent to which all of the subjects' points fall exactly on the line of best fit. Figure 2.24 shows two scattergrams that represent relationships of different strengths. In figure 2.24*a,* the relationship can be considered quite strong because nearly all the points fall close to the line of best fit. In figure 2.24*b,* however, the relationship is not very strong, because the points tend to fall away from the line of best fit. These two aspects, direction and strength, are the primary descriptors used to characterize relationships. They are *independent,* in that a relationship can be either positive or negative *and* either strong or weak.

Predicting From a Relationship   One of the most important reasons scientists want to know the nature of the relationship between two variables is for the purpose of *prediction.* For example, if we know that the relationship between age and running time has been found to be as described in figure 2.22, then on a new group of children we can estimate (or predict) the 100 m time given the age of a person not in the original data set without actually measuring running speed, just as with the linear equations discussed earlier. Such procedures are used extensively in everyday situations, as in predicting the probability of having an automobile accident from one's age,

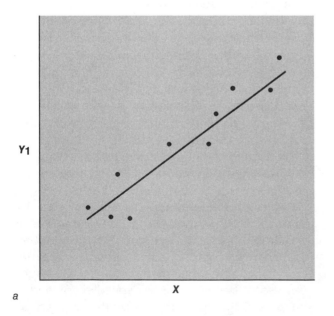

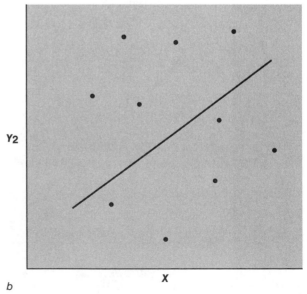

FIGURE 2.24   Hypothetical scattergrams for *(a)* a strong and *(b)* a weak relationship.

or predicting success in graduate school from achievement test scores.

As the strength of the relationship increases, the predictability of one variable from the other increases as well. When the relationship is perfect and all the individual data points fall exactly on the line of best fit, perfect predictions with no error can be made. When the data are related less perfectly, as in the example shown in figure 2.24b, then more error is introduced into the predictions. Thus, the strength of the relationship—but not the direction—is the primary determinant of the extent to which a relationship can be used to predict.

Correlation Coefficient

These concepts of strength and direction of relationships can be quantified using a statistic called the *correlation coefficient*. The correlation, abbreviated *r*, ranges from +1.0 through zero to −1.0. The two important aspects of the correlation are the sign and its absolute size. The sign of the correlation indicates the direction of the relation-

ship, exactly as described in the previous sections. The absolute size of the correlation indicates the strength of the relationship and hence is critical for evaluating the extent to which one can use the relationship to predict. Figure 2.25 shows five hypothetical examples of correlations and the associated scatterplots. Both a +0.90 and a −0.90 correlation are strong relationships, as all the data points fall almost exactly on the lines, although the lines are sloped in opposite directions. Correlations of +0.50 and −0.50 are moderate in strength, and the points fall considerably away from the lines of best fit. A correlation of zero is weakest, indicating that no predictive capability is possible between these two variables. Formulas for the calculation of correlations can be found in most statistics textbooks (e.g., chapter 8 in Thomas, Nelson, & Silverman, 2005; chapter 7 in Vincent, 2005).

A convenient method for comparing the strength of relationships between tests is to square the correlation coefficient and multiply by 100 to

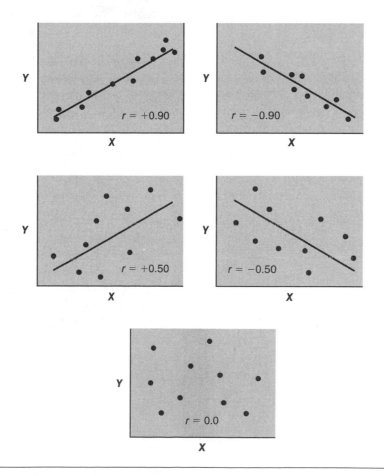

FIGURE 2.25 Scattergrams for hypothetical data showing high, moderate, and low relationships.

convert it into a percentage score. Generally, the square of the correlation coefficient indicates the extent to which two tests can be considered to measure the same thing, and represents the percentage of *shared* variance (or, the percentage "in common") between the two variables. This fits nicely with the earlier discussion of the strength and direction of relationships. The shared variance for two tests that correlate positively (+0.90) or two others that correlate negatively (−0.90) is the same (e.g., $+0.90^2 \times 100 = -0.90^2 \times 100 = 81\%$), indicating that the direction of the relationship (positive or negative) has no effect on the amount of shared variance.

The r^2 value is useful for interpreting the strength of two relationships. For example, suppose two variables correlate with a value of $r = 0.50$ and two other variables correlate with a value of $r = 0.25$. In this case, the r^2 value of the first relationship ($0.50^2 = 0.25$) indicates approximately four times more shared variance than for the second relationship ($0.25^2 = 0.063$), or that the first two tests had approximately four times more in common than did the second pair.

Summary

Motor behavior can be classified according to several dimensions, such as (a) *continuous/serial/discrete*, referring to the extent to which the movement has a definite beginning and end, and (b) *open/closed*, referring to the extent to which the environment is predictable. Most of the tasks used in motor control work fall into one or the other of these basic categories. In measuring movement, experimenters devote attention to a measure's *objectivity* (the extent to which two independent observers achieve the same score), its *sensitivity* to changes in skill, its *reliability* (the extent to which the score is repeatable), and its *validity* (the extent to which the test measures what the experimenter intends it to measure).

The outcome of movements in terms of the environmental goal can be measured in essentially four ways: in terms of errors, speed or time (or both), or magnitude, or with various secondary tasks. There are many ways to measure errors in movement; chief among these are *constant error* (CE, a measure of average error or bias), *variable error* (VE, a measure of inconsistency), *total variability* (E, a measure of overall error), and *absolute error* (AE, also a measure of overall error). Each error measure has a different meaning and is used in different aspects of the measurement process. Measures of speed are used when accuracy is less important (or is controlled) and when rapid actions are critical. Measures of magnitude are used when the *amount* of behavior is critical. A fourth but related measure is based on the analysis of simultaneous secondary tasks, providing a measure of the spare capacity of the performer after she has devoted attention to a primary task.

Movements can be measured in many ways, but common methods involve the calculation of kinematic variables (position, velocity, acceleration) and the recording of the electrical activity from muscles (EMG). Methods used to assess kinematics have changed dramatically with digital technology, and precise measures of sensory–motor control are now the norm. Studies of brain activity are also becoming increasingly popular, and their use in motor behavior research continues to grow. *Linear empirical equations* provide a description of a linear relationship between two variables. The parameters of the equation can be easily estimated, and they provide a means by which the relationship can be used to predict facts that are yet unknown. The parameters can also be useful in describing the direction and strength of the relationship between two variables as indicated by the correlation coefficient.

Student Assignments

1. Answer the following questions and bring the information to class for discussion:

   a. Compile a new list of examples from activities of everyday life that fit each of the following task categories: discrete/open, discrete/closed, serial/open, serial/closed, continuous/open, continuous/closed.

   b. Close your eyes and draw 10 lines as close as possible to 10 cm in length. Do not open your eyes until you are finished. Calculate the following error measures: CE, |CE|, VE, E, and AE.

   c. Discuss the relative importance of reaction time in the following Olympic events: 100 m run, 10,000 m run, 100 m butterfly swim, 400 m relay.

2. Find a research article published in the past five years that uses functional magnetic resonance imaging (fMRI) or transcranial magnetic stimulation (TMS) to better explain basic motor control processes.

Web Resources

This resource is related to reaction-time methodology and the history of RT research:

www.chss.montclair.edu/psychology/museum/mrt.html

This site provides some examples of Muybridge's photographs:

www.masters-of-photography.com/M/muybridge/muybridge.html

Notes

[1] A quantitative analysis of error scores in two dimensions is provided by Hancock, Butler, and Fischman (1995), but is beyond the scope of the present discussion.

CHAPTER 3

HUMAN INFORMATION PROCESSING

Human functioning in the environment can be conceptualized and studied in many ways; one of the most popular is based on the fundamental notion that humans are processors of information. It is assumed that information is available in the environment; that the individual accepts this information into various "storage systems" called memory; and that the information is then "processed" for the purposes of perception, decision making, and action. Human information processing is based on a computer metaphor. According to this metaphor, we "take in" information from outside sources, just as a computer takes in information via input devices. That information undergoes transformations, uses other information stored in memory, and is subject to certain limitations based on the amount processed and the speed of processing that is available; again, this is similar to how a computer processes information. And lastly, the process by which information is "output" has many analogies to the computer—the pro-

cessed information can result in various kinds of movement, just as a computer displays the results of its processing on a monitor or sends it elsewhere as an output. The goal of this chapter is to discuss information processing as it relates to human motor behavior (see also Marteniuk, 1976)—specifically how information is processed for the specific purpose of producing skilled movement.

The Information-Processing Model

The model begins with the input of information from the environment through one or more of the sense organs, and then considers what happens to this information once it is inside the system. A typical "black box" model of the process is shown in figure 3.1. The individual is considered to be the box, and information enters the box from the environment. This information

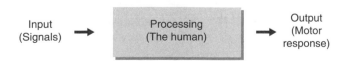

FIGURE 3.1   The simplified information-processing model.

is then processed in various ways, eventually resulting in output as observable motor activity. This *black box model* prevailed in the stimulus–response (S-R) tradition (see chapter 1), in which researchers were primarily concerned with the relationship between what went into the box (the information, or stimuli) and the output from the box (the response). With the emergence of *cognitive psychology*, however, interest began to focus on the processes that occur *within* the box. Obviously, this is an abstract way to study human behavior because it concerns processes and events that are not directly observable. Knowledge about these processes is inferred from the overt behavior of the human under various experimental conditions. Events occurring inside the box can be studied in a variety of ways through use of the cognitive–psychological perspective.

The most common approach to the study of information processing is to consider the durations of these various processes. This *chronometric approach* (see Posner, 1978) makes considerable use of the reaction-time (RT) method, whereby the chief measure of the subject's behavior is the interval between the presentation of a stimulus and the beginning of the response. Many different information-processing activities occur during RT; but if the experiment is designed properly, so that the durations of most other processes are held constant, one can usually infer that an increase in RT resulting from some experimental variable was caused by the lengthening of the duration of a *particular* process. This chapter presents many examples of this type of research and thinking, and the chronometric approach to studying information processing constitutes a large portion of it. Later in the chapter we consider other aspects of information processing that are not necessarily studied using the chronometric approach but are particularly important in the performance of motor skills.

Three Stages of Information Processing

Although the notion of separate stages or processes between a stimulus and a response has been popularized by the cognitive–psychological

viewpoint, the general concept of stages of processing is quite old, dating back to the research of Donders (1868/1969; see "Donders' Subtractive Method"). This thinking, coupled with efforts from cognitive psychology (e.g., Kellogg, 2003; Sanders, 1980; Schweickert, 1993; Sternberg, 1969), has led to the view that various processing stages can be defined and that these stages can be either *serial* (sequential) or *parallel* (simultaneous) in nature.

Donders argued that with use of these methods, the durations of the stages of processing involved in stimulus discrimination and response selection, which are not directly observable, could be estimated in the laboratory. It is remarkable that these insights were developed in 1868, long predating the cognitive revolution in experimental psychology that made use of these and similar concepts.

Donders' general methods and assumptions would later be revived in a classic paper by Saul Sternberg (1969) that generated considerable interest and further research, some of which was involved in understanding motor behavior (e.g., Sanders, 1980). Later thinking and research identified a number of flaws in Donders' subtractive method (see Massaro, 1989, for an analysis of Donders' and Sternberg's logic and methods). But even so, Donders' basic idea that we could examine the duration of stages by subtracting the RTs in various conditions was remarkable, given the time of his work, and served as the foundation for more modern analyses of human information processing.[1]

The Nature of Serial and Parallel Processing

Imagine an automotive plant as a model of information processing, as in figure 3.2. Some stages occur at the same time in different places, such as the fabrication of the electronics, the assembly of the engine, and the assembly of the chassis. But at various times during the overall process, these components are combined to complete the final assembly stage. After final assembly, imagine a test-drive stage, in which the drivers search for problems before the car is sent to the dealers, as yet another stage. This simple analogy contains an example of both parallel processing (simultaneous assembly of the electronics, engine, and body stages), and serial processing (successive

Donders' Subtractive Method

Over a century ago, the Dutch physician F.C. Donders (1868/1969) made the first attempts to measure the time required to complete certain thought processes. Donders' *subtractive method* assumed the existence of a series of separate, nonoverlapping information-processing stages between a stimulus and a response. The notion was that the processing that occurs in stage 1 is separate and distinct from the processing that occurs in stage 2, and that stage 2 processing cannot begin until stage 1 processing is completed. Donders studied this idea using three RT methods that differed in systematic ways.

In the simplest method, termed the *a*-reaction task, the subject was presented with a single, unanticipated stimulus that required a single response (e.g., pressing a key using the right hand in response to the illumination of a red light). This reaction task is now commonly referred to as a *simple*-RT task. In a more complicated task, termed the *c*-reaction task, a subject was presented with two different light stimuli and asked to respond by pressing a key with the right hand if a specific stimulus was illuminated. For example, if the two stimuli were red and blue, then the task might be to respond if the red stimulus was illuminated but to *not* respond to the blue stimulus. This reaction task is today called a *go/no-go* task because the subject is to respond if the specific stimulus is illuminated ("go") but not if the nonspecified stimulus is illuminated ("no-go"). In the third task, called the *b*-reaction task, the subject was again presented with more than one stimulus and asked to make a response that depended on which particular stimulus was presented. For example, a red light might require a key press with a finger on the right hand whereas a blue light would require a left-hand response. This reaction task is known today as a *choice*-RT task.

The logic of Donders' subtractive method was that the three tasks differed in the number of stages involved. All three tasks require stimulus detection (e.g., noting that a stimulus light has appeared). In addition, however, the *b*-reaction involves the processes of discriminating the stimulus that was detected from the possible alternatives that could have appeared, as well as the selection of a specific response. The *c*-reaction, however, requires only discrimination of the stimulus, and no response selection (because the specific response is always the same in the *c*-reaction). Thus, the difference in RT between a *c*-reaction and a *b*-reaction reflects the time to perform response selection. In a similar way, the *c*-reaction involves stimulus discrimination whereas the *a*-reaction does not; only one stimulus is presented in the *a*-reaction, and both of these tasks involve only one response (i.e., no response selection is needed for either). Therefore, the difference in RT between the *a*-reaction and the *c*-reaction should reflect the time for stimulus discrimination. This can perhaps be seen more clearly in table 3.1, which presents an example using these ideas.

TABLE 3.1. Work Table for Computing Various Stages of Processing

Donders' description	Common term	Number of stimulus choices	Number of response choices	Stages of processing	Hypothetical reaction time (RT)
a	Simple RT	1	1	Stimulus detection, response execution	200 ms
b	Choice RT	2	2	Stimulus detection, stimulus identification, response selection, response execution	285 ms
c	Go/no-go RT	2	1	Stimulus detection, stimulus identification, response execution	230 ms
Processing stage	**Subtraction**	**Example**			
Stimulus identification	*c* − *a*	230 − 200 = 30 ms			
Response selection	*b* − *c*	285 − 230 = 55 ms			

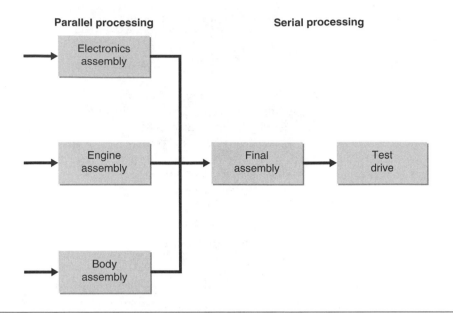

FIGURE 3.2   Examples of serial and parallel processing in an automobile assembly plant.

stages of final assembly and test drive). Thus, this system has both serial and parallel processing, but at different times in the total sequence. In human behavior, many have thought that the total RT has various stages, some of which can be performed in parallel and some of which are performed serially.

At least three stages can be proposed that intervene between the presentation of a stimulus and the production of a response (see figure 3.3). First, the individual must sense that a stimulus has occurred and identify it. This stage is frequently called the *stimulus-identification stage*. Second, after a stimulus has been properly identified, the individual must decide *what* response to make. The decision can be to do one of a number of possible actions, or the stimulus can be ignored in favor of no action at all. This stage is usually called the *response-selection stage*. Finally, after the response has been selected, the system must be prepared for the appropriate action and then initiate that action. This stage is frequently called the *response-initiation stage*, but we will use the term *response-programming stage* to represent the preparations of the motor apparatus and the initiation of the action. More detailed discussion of these stages is presented in the remainder of the chapter.

"Information Processing and Traffic Intersections" (p. 62) presents an example of the potential information-processing activities involved

in the decisions needed to respond to a yellow (caution) light at an intersection. Although many of the experimental methods and research issues discussed in this chapter may seem quite removed from this example, it is probable that the processing of information in lab tasks and many examples of everyday life involves similar activities.

Stimulus-Identification Stage

Think of the stimulus-identification stage as beginning with the presentation (or onset) of an environmental stimulus that must be detected; this stimulus information must then be recognized as a part of an identifiable pattern. These two substages are considered in the following sections.

Stimulus Detection

The occurrence of an environmental stimulus (e.g., light entering the retina of the eye or sound entering the ear) results in neurological impulses that are sent toward the brain. The stimulus is presumably processed further at different levels of analysis until it *contacts memory*, meaning that some memorized aspect of the stimulus is aroused, such as its name or an attribute with which it has been associated in the past (e.g., its red color, as with a stop sign). Considerable processing must occur in order for the stimulus to arouse the proper association in memory

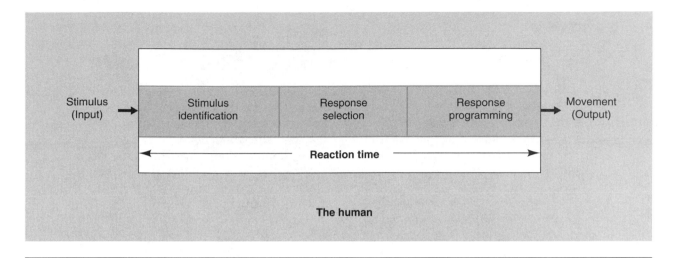

FIGURE 3.3   An expanded information-processing model.

(rather than an improper associate or all possible associates). Scientists working in this area have assumed that the *variables* affecting the stimulus-identification stage relate specifically to the nature of the stimulus. For example, an experimental variable called *stimulus clarity*, which refers to the extent to which the visual stimulus is well defined and "sharp" (vs. out of focus) has been used. With increased clarity, the overall RT is shorter, and this change is attributed to the increased processing speed in the stimulus-identification stage. A variable called *stimulus intensity* (e.g., the brightness of a light stimulus or the loudness of a sound stimulus) is also assumed to affect information-processing time in this stage. Early research that has been replicated many times also revealed that RT is greatly affected by the *modality* of the stimulus—the latency in responding to a visual stimulus is somewhat slower than the time to respond to an auditory or a tactile stimulus. Further, stimuli presented simultaneously in more than one modality (e.g., combined visual + auditory stimuli) will shorten RT relative to either modality presented alone; this is called intersensory facilitation (Nickerson, 1973; Schmidt, Gielen, & van den Heuvel, 1984). Many more effects involving the physical properties of the stimulus have been investigated, much of this research having been conducted many years ago. An excellent summary of the effects of the properties of the stimulus on RT by Woodworth and Schlosberg (1954) remains informative today.

Pattern Recognition

In more realistic tasks, the stimuli that enter the system are seldom as simple as they are in lab RT tasks, and we must usually extract a pattern or feature from the stimuli presented. Often these patterns have to do with such things as the shape of a face—or in sport, with where a baseball is going, how fast it is traveling, and what kind of spin has been put on it. Some of these pattern detections are genetically defined (e.g., related to survival). Others may depend heavily on learning, such as recognizing a developing play in volleyball.

Important studies of chess players demonstrate the influence of learning on pattern detection (deGroot, 1946/1978; Chase & Simon, 1973). In one such study, deGroot asked chess masters and good-to-average chess players to reconstruct the locations of the chess pieces in a half-finished game after viewing the board for 5 s. As one might imagine, the chess masters were far superior to the good-to-average players. It could be argued that the superiority of the chess masters in this task was not necessarily evidence that they had learned to remember chess patterns, but rather that they were just superior, generally, in their inherent perceptual abilities. This last hypothesis is doubtful, however, as a later experiment by Chase and Simon (1973) included an important condition in which the chess pieces were placed on the board in random fashion. With this random arrangement, the chess masters and the average players were about equal in their ability to

Information Processing and Traffic Intersections

An activity that drivers face often while navigating city traffic concerns how to respond when an intersection signal changes color from green to yellow. Experiments in human information processing mirror this example in many ways. The traffic signal represents one of many sources of environmental information to which a driver must attend. A change in the traffic signal from green to yellow is a sensory event that the driver must identify and respond to with a decision. In the simplest case, the response to be selected involves making one of two choices—either to continue on through the intersection or to stop before entering the intersection. In making that decision, the driver quickly must process how fast his car is traveling relative to the distance to be covered (Senders, 1998). In addition to this environmentally available information, the driver must also access information in memory. Recently acquired information might include the proximity of the car behind. More remotely acquired information might include information learned about this particular traffic intersection (such as the width of the intersection and the duration of the yellow phase of the traffic signal) and the quality of the brakes of the car being driven. If the decision is to carry on through the intersection, then a typical driver response is to continue at the same speed or even to accelerate. If the decision is to stop, then the driver must remove the foot from the accelerator and apply it to the brake. In both of these selected responses (accelerate or apply the brake), an action is required that must be generated in the brain and sent to the appropriate musculature for implementation (see Green, 2000, for further discussion).

All of these information-processing activities—identifying that the signal has changed color, selecting which response is appropriate, and programming the response to be made—take *time,* during which the car continues to approach the intersection. It is quite understandable, therefore, why a great deal of research activity has dealt with the temporal components of information processing, an approach some have referred to as the chronometric approach (Posner, 1978).

Two other factors involved in this traffic example are also important components of information-processing activities and are discussed in this chapter. One of these entails *anticipation,* the use of information to prepare a response in advance of the critical stimulus. For example, a driver who saw the traffic light turn green just a short time ago may anticipate that a yellow light will not occur before she enters the intersection, especially when this information is combined with prior information in memory that the green phase of the light is fairly long. The other factor relates to the potential

results if the driver makes an incorrect decision in response to the light (going ahead when a stop was the appropriate response; or stopping when proceeding through the intersection was the correct response). Making the decision to go and making the decision to stop both carry two possible outcomes, one correct and one incorrect. The ability to process information in a way that optimizes the outcome of this decision is the domain of research called *signal-detection* (or *decision*) *theory*. All of these various issues (processing stages, memory, anticipation, and decision theory) represent features that influence indirectly how we control movement.

reposition the pieces (see also Vicente & Wang, 1998). One interpretation is that the processes involved in the stimulus-identification stage were improved in the masters through years of experience in *game* situations and that considerably more information could be accumulated in a single view of the board, but only as long as that information conformed to the normal patterns of chess play.

Analysis of such static situations seems important to many activities; but even more important from the point of view of motor behavior is an ability to extract patterns of movement from the environment. In many situations, how the environment changes from moment to moment will determine which action is most appropriate.

A great deal of environmental movement information is represented as changes in the visual field, and it seems clear that an individual can use this information to provide an unequivocal analysis of movements in an environment or of the environment's movements. Gibson (1966), for example, referred to "optical-flow patterns," which are the patterns made up of the rays of light that strike the eye from every visible part of the environment (see figure 3.4). As the individual or the environment moves, the angles of these rays change predictably to allow the subject to extract a pattern of movement from the changing visual array. For example, you *know* that a ball is coming directly toward your eye if the rates of change of the angles of the rays of light from all edges of the ball are the same. This *looming* can elicit strong avoidance reactions even in children and young animals who have presumably never been hit in the eye, suggesting that at least some kinds of pattern recognitions may be genetically defined. We will discuss these various aspects of visual information processing in more detail in chapter 5.

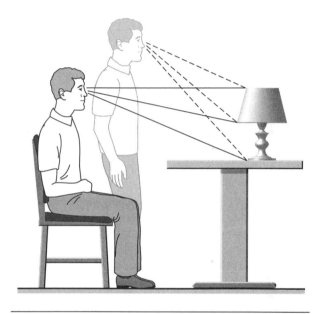

FIGURE 3.4 Optical arrays vary as the location of the observer changes in the environment.

These interpretations are important for many fast-action sports and games. Patterns of opponent position or action arouse meaningful responses that lead to fast action in highly skilled players, while they may go nearly unnoticed by novices. For example, certain patterns of linemen and backfield movement in American football mean the difference between a running and a passing play, and an effective response to this action by the defensive player often depends on recognizing such a pattern quickly and accurately (for reviews see Ericsson, 1996; Starkes & Allard, 1993; Starkes & Ericsson, 2003; Williams, Ward, & Smeeton, 2004).

Response-Selection Stage

As a product of the stimulus-identification stage, the information in the stimulus input has been analyzed, and the individual now has a basis for "knowing" what happened in the environment. In the next stage, response selection, the subject decides what response to make. A baseball outfielder must make rapid decisions about whether to attempt to field a batted ball either before or after it bounces, what direction to move in order to catch it, and what to do with the ball if it is fielded successfully. Such decisions are important and apply to a wide variety of activities in sport, industry, driving, and so on.

Number of Stimulus–Response Alternatives

For over a century (since Donders' contributions), scientists have believed that the processing of information relevant to the selection of a response requires more time when the number of *possible* alternatives is larger. The idea is that if increasing the number of alternatives causes an increase in the choice RT, then the increased RT is associated with changes in the way the information was processed in the response-selection stage.

In the choice-RT paradigm, the subject might be presented, say, with four stimulus lights and instructed that one of the four will be illuminated randomly on a particular trial. Each of the four lights is associated (via instructions from the experimenter) with one of four different responses (e.g., the four stimulus lights are assigned, or "mapped," to buttons located under the four fingers of the right hand). The task is to press the appropriate button as quickly as possible after one of the stimulus lights is illuminated. Usually subjects are not able to predict exactly when the stimulus will occur and are thus prevented from initiating the response in advance. The time from stimulus to response will be sensitive to the speed of information processing responsible for the selecting the appropriate finger.

One of the earliest studies addressing this question was done by Merkel in 1885 (described by Woodworth, 1938). The digits 1 through 5 were mapped to the fingers of the right hand, and the Roman numerals I through V were mapped to the fingers of the left hand. In one set of trials, Merkel used all 10 possible stimulus–response (S-R) pairings, so there were 10 possible stimuli for these trials. On other sets of trials the subject knew which, from the set of 10 stimuli, would be possible (e.g., if there were three possible stimuli, they might be 3, 5, and V), yet only one of these

stimuli was actually presented. (On this set of trials, only 3, 5, and V would be presented, and none of the other stimuli would be involved.) Other sets of trials might involve 1, 3, 5, and VI (four possible stimuli) or 2, 4, VII, VIII, and X (five possible stimuli). Note that, on any given trial, only one of the set of possible stimuli would occur. Merkel studied the relationship between the number of possible S-R pairs (ranging from 1 to 10) and the choice RT.

His basic findings are presented in the left side of figure 3.5, which plots the choice RT against the number of S-R alternatives (or *N*). As the number of alternatives increased, so did the choice RT taken to respond to any one of them. This relationship was *curvilinear*, as is clearly illustrated in the data on the left side of figure 3.5. Note, for example, that as the number of alternatives was increased from 1 to 2, the increase in choice RT was about 129 ms, whereas when the number of alternatives was increased from 9 to 10, the increase in choice RT was only about 3 ms. Even though there was an increase by one in the number of alternatives in both cases (i.e., $1{\rightarrow}2$ vs. $9{\rightarrow}10$ alternatives), the effects on choice RT were very different.

This relationship between number of alternatives and choice RT has been studied a great deal since Merkel made his original observations. The overall conclusion has not changed, although there have been some refinements in technique and much additional theorizing about the causes of the relationship. The most widely known findings and explanations of the effect were apparently produced by two people at about the same time—Hick (1952) and Hyman (1953). The relation they discovered between the number of S-R alternatives and RT has since been termed Hick's law, or sometimes the Hick-Hyman law (Keele, 1986; Proctor & Dutta, 1995).

Hick's Law Hick (1952) and Hyman (1953) studied the relationship between choice RT and the number of S-R alternatives in much the same way Merkel had, using various numbers of lights that were associated with an equal number of keys to be pressed when the appropriate light appeared. As Merkel had found, choice RT increased as the number of possible S-R alternatives increased. The RT values, as well as the overall shape of the function, were consistent with Merkel's findings in figure 3.5. However, what Hick and Hyman discovered was that choice RT appeared to increase

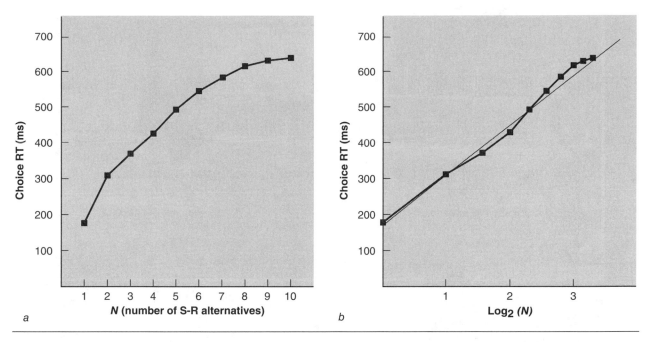

FIGURE 3.5 *(a)* Choice reaction time (RT) as a function of the number of stimulus–response (S-R) alternatives and *(b)* the logarithm of the number of S-R alternatives.

Data from Merkel 1885.

by a nearly constant amount (about 150 ms) every time the number of S-R alternatives was *doubled.* This suggested that the relationship between choice RT and the *logarithm* of the number of S-R alternatives should be linear.

The interpretation here is that the logarithm of the number of S-R alternatives is a measure of the amount of *information* that had to be processed, suggesting that more alternatives required more information processing. In the right side of figure 3.5 we have replotted Merkel's data as a function of the logarithm of the number of alternatives, and we see that these data demonstrate a linear fit too. The formal relation that has come to be known as Hick's law states that choice RT is linearly related to the logarithm to the base 2 (Log₂) of the number of S-R alternatives. In equation form,

$$\text{Choice RT} = a + b[\text{Log}_2\,(N)] \qquad (3.1)$$

where N is the number of (equally likely) S-R alternatives and a and b are the empirical constants. Notice that equation 3.1 is somewhat different from the "typical" linear equation discussed in chapter 2, where $Y = a + bX$; but if X is [$\text{Log}_2\,(N)$], then equation 3.1 means that choice RT is linearly related to $\text{Log}_2\,(N)$.

The data from four subjects in Hyman's (1953) study are presented in figure 3.6; the data of inter-

est at this point in our discussion are the open circles, referring to experiment 1, in which the number of S-R alternatives was varied (plotted as the $\text{Log}_2\,[N]$, or the number of bits of information to process—more on that later). For each subject there was a strong linear trend between the Log_2 (N) and choice RT. The individual linear equation is shown on each subject's graph; for example, for subject G.C., the intercept (a) was 212 ms and the slope (b) was 153 ms. Notice that these empirical "constants" were considerably different for different subjects. Nevertheless, in each case the RT was linearly related to the amount of stimulus information (or $\text{Log}_2\,[N]$).

That the relationship between the choice RT and the logarithm to the base 2 of the number of alternatives should be so clearly linear is of considerable interest in its own right. A linear relationship is the most simple of relationships, and scientists become excited about the possibility that complex behaviors of human beings can be described by such simple expressions. But of even more importance is one interpretation of this relationship: that the time required to make a decision (or to make a choice) about a response is linearly related to the amount of information that must be processed in coming to that decision.

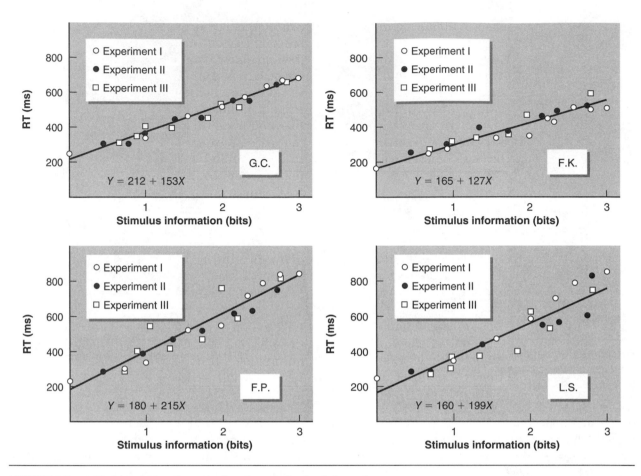

FIGURE 3.6 Choice reaction time as a function of stimulus information.

Reprinted from R. Hyman, 1953, "Stimulus information as a determinant of reaction time," *Journal of Experimental Psychology* 45: 192.

Measuring the Amount of Information For Hick, and other scientists at that time, the notion of *information* was used in a very special way. Information is related to uncertainty and to the amount of uncertainty that is reduced by the presentation of a stimulus. Specifically, the amount of information contained in some signal is measured in *bits* (short for *bi*nary dig*its*). One bit is defined as the amount of information needed to reduce the original uncertainty by half. For example, your friend tells you that she is thinking of one of four numbers (1, 2, 3, and 4), and you are to guess which it is. Then she tells you that the number is even. This last message has reduced the number of choices from four to two (i.e., by half) and has conveyed 1 bit of information. See "Uncertainty and Information Theory" and figure 3.7 for more details and an example about measuring information.

Interpreting Hick's Law Now we will connect the notion of information as the reduction of uncertainty to the logarithm involved in Hick's law. First, the logarithm to the base 2 of some number N is defined as the power to which the base 2 must be raised in order to obtain that number. For example, the Log_2 (8) is 3, since 2 must be raised to the third power to obtain 8 ($2^3 = 2 \times 2 \times 2 = 8$). Other examples are shown in table 3.2 (a more comprehensive table of log values appears in the appendix). Notice that every time N is doubled (say from 4 to 8, or from 8 to 16), table 3.2 shows that the Log_2 of the number increases by 1.

Now, as applied to the RT situation, if N is the number of equally likely S-R alternatives, resolving the uncertainty about N things can be interpreted as requiring Log_2 (N) bits of information. In terms of Hick's law, we can say that choice RT is linearly related to the amount of information needed to resolve the uncertainty about N S-R alternatives. Stated differently, every time the number of S-R alternatives is doubled,

Uncertainty and Information Theory

Scientists who study information processing use the term "information" to refer to the amount of *uncertainty* that has been *reduced* by a signal that was presented. If during a walk in the rain your friend says that it is raining, that "signal" conveys little information because there was little original uncertainty available to be reduced further. But if your friend says that it is raining in the Sahara desert, that signal conveys a great deal of information because (a) the probability that it is raining there is low and (b) you had no previous knowledge that it was raining there. Thus, the amount of information *transmitted* is affected by both (a) the amount of uncertainty prior to the signal's being presented and (b) the amount of reduction of uncertainty. Generally speaking, the amount of information *(H)* is given by a simple equation:

$$H = Log_2(1 / P_i) \qquad (3.2)$$

where P_i is the probability that a given event *(i)* will occur. As the probability of an event *(P_i)* decreases, the amount of information conveyed by a signal describing that event increases; this is why a signal about a rare event (it is raining in the desert) carries more information than a signal about a common event (it is raining in Eugene, Oregon). Figure 3.7 provides a concrete example about how the information in a given situation can be reduced by asking a series of uncertainty-reducing questions (from Attneave, 1959). In the figure is a 4 × 4 matrix of squares, comprising 15 empty squares and 1 square with an "X" inside. If you did not know which of the 16 squares the "X" appeared in but wanted to find out, you could do so by asking four questions (because Log$_2$ 16 = 4 bits, and because 2 × 2 × 2 × 2 = 16), designing each question to reduce the uncertainty by one-half (1 bit). Notice also that it does not matter whether the answer to each of the questions is yes or no—the information gained allows the uncertainty to be reduced by one-half, regardless of the answer.

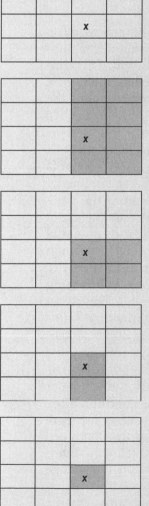

Task: Find the "*x*" in as few questions as possible.

Question #1. Does the *x* appear in the left half of the matrix?
Answer. No.
Information transmitted: The 8 squares on the left side are eliminated and 8 remain (shaded); uncertainty is reduced by half, so 1 bit of information has been transmitted.

Question #2. Does the *x* appear in the bottom half of the remaining squares?
Answer. Yes
Information transmitted: The upper 4 squares are eliminated and the bottom 4 squares remain viable; again, uncertainty reduced by half, and 1 bit is transmitted.

Question #3. Does the *x* appear in one of the two squares in the right side?
Answer. No.
Information transmitted: The right two squares are eliminated and now only two squares remain; again, 1 bit transmitted.

Question #4. Of the two remaining squares, is the *x* in the bottom position?
Answer. No.
Information transmitted: Since we can eliminate the bottom square and no more alternatives remain, we do not need to ask another question – the *x* must be in the only square that has not been eliminated; one more bit transmitted, for a total of 4 bits in the whole task.

FIGURE 3.7 Guess the location of the X in only four questions (from Attneave, 1959).

Adapted from F. Attneave, 1959, *Applications of information theory to psychology: A summary of basic concepts, methods, and results* (New York: Holt, Rinehart & Winston).

TABLE 3.2. Relation Between Number of Alternatives (N) and the Log₂ (N)

Number (N)	Log₂ (N)
1	0
2	1
4	2
8	3
16	4
32	5
64	6
128	7
256	8

the amount of information to be processed is increased by 1 bit, and the time required for choice RT is increased by a *constant* amount. This constant amount is the slope of the Hick equation, *b*.

To this point, we have considered only the circles in figure 3.6 (Hyman, 1953, experiment I); in that experiment, the number of S-R alternatives was varied in order to change the amount of information to be processed. In Hyman's experiment II (the filled circles), the amount of information was varied by changing the *probability* of the stimulus. Remember, as the event becomes less probable, having to process a signal about it conveys more information, as in equation 3.2 (see "Uncertainty and Information Theory"). When information was increased by decreasing the stimulus probabilities, RT again increased linearly. In experiment III, Hyman varied information by changing the sequential dependencies (the probability that a given event [or stimulus] is followed by another event [or stimulus]). The effect was to make a particular stimulus more or less probable just before the presentation of the stimulus for a given trial. The squares in figure 3.6 again show a linear relationship between amount of information and choice RT. If this interpretation is correct, the response-selection stage can be thought of as being involved in reducing uncertainty about alternative responses when a given stimulus is presented.

Interpreting the Intercept and Slope How should we interpret the intercept (*a*) and the slope (*b*) in Hick's law? From the earlier discussion of empirical equations (in chapter 2), recall that the intercept (*a*) was that value of choice RT associated with $\text{Log}_2 (N) = 0$, or the value of choice RT when the line crossed the vertical axis. In the data from various subjects in Hyman's (1953) study (figure 3.6), the average of these intercepts was 179 ms (mean of 212, 165, 180, and 160 ms). Also, recall that when $\text{Log}_2 (N) = 0$, the value of N must be 1 (table 3.2), denoting a situation with only one alternative, in which there is *no* uncertainty about what to do (this is usually called *simple* RT). Consequently, it has been reasonable to interpret the intercept (*a*) of Hick's law as a measure of the overall "speed" of the perceptual and motor system exclusive of any time required for a decision about which response to make. Comparing subject L.S. in figure 3.6 (*a* = 160 ms) with subject G.C. (*a* = 212 ms) might be roughly analogous to comparing a telephone dial-up modem with broadband to surf the Internet (Seow, 2005)—the basic processing speed is different.

Also from Hyman's (1953) data, the slopes of the relation ranged from about 127 ms/bit to 215 ms/bit for the various subjects (figure 3.6). Remember that the slope (*b*) is a measure of the amount of inclination of the line; alternatively *b* represents the amount of increase in choice RT as $\text{Log}_2 (N)$ is increased by one unit (1 bit). So, one additional bit of information resulted in from 127 to 215 ms of additional choice RT for the different subjects. Thus, the slope is the "speed" of decision making by the response-selection stage of processing, measured in units of milliseconds per bit. Seen in this way, the slope and intercept measure two different underlying processes in human performance.

The practical implications of the slope are important and probably obvious. For games in which rapid reaction is important, if the player can double the number of likely alternatives to which the opponent must respond (and the opponent cannot anticipate them), then the player increases by 1 bit the amount of information that must be processed in order for the opponent to respond, and thereby increases by a constant amount the opponent's choice RT in initiating the appropriate response. These kinds of effects are seen in most fast ball games, as well as in reaction situations involved in driving a car, performing various industrial tasks, and so on.

Exceptions to Hick's Law Whereas Hick's law does hold very generally over a wide variety of situations and people, one needs to take a number of other variables into account in order to accurately predict choice RT, and a few situations exist in which the law does not appear to hold at all. The key variable is the subject's *familiarity* with responding to a particular stimulus by means of a specific response. These familiarity effects have been studied in various ways, most notably by examining (a) practice or experience with the task and (b) the nature of the relationship between the stimuli and the associated responses.

In one of the first studies to investigate the role of practice in relation to Hick's law, Mowbray and Rhoades (1959) used a two- and four-choice RT task and found, as had been observed previously by many researchers, that early in practice the four-choice task showed a much slower choice RT than did the two-choice task. However, their study is unique in that they provided their subjects with an incredible 42,000 trials of practice! After this amount of practice, the four-choice RT was reduced to a level essentially equal to that of the two-choice RT. Thus, the slope of the choice-RT function between 1 and 2 bits (i.e., two and four alternatives) was reduced by practice, eventually becoming essentially flat (where $b = 0$). Similar findings were also reported by Seibel (1963). These effects of practice have been the basis for the important notion of automaticity in responding, which we discuss more fully in chapter 4 (see Schneider & Shiffrin, 1977).

Another set of data that can be similarly interpreted was generated by Mowbray (1960). When the task involved digit naming (the number of possible digits was varied, and the RT was measured by a voice microphone), increasing the number of possible digits to be named did not increase the choice RT. The interpretation is that the names of digits are so highly practiced that the association between the digit and the name is nearly direct (i.e., automatic), not requiring further reduction in uncertainty (see also Fitts & Seeger, 1953; Hellyer, 1963).

Similar findings of essentially zero slope for highly overlearned S-R relationships were provided by Leonard (1959). In this study, choice RTs with one, two, four, and eight alternatives were examined, but the situation was quite different from those studied earlier. The subjects placed their fingers on the appropriate number of keys and were instructed to press as quickly as possible on the one key that *vibrated*. The relationship between the stimulus (vibrations) and the response (pressing *that* finger on the key) was very direct. As the number of S-R alternatives increased from two to eight, Leonard found no further increase in choice RT. That is, the relationship was flat (with $b = 0$). When the finger was vibrated, the relation between it and the response was so direct that no additional time was required for decision making about which finger to activate (see also Keele, 1986, for a good review).

Another exception to Hick's law is seen in responses involving rapid movement of the eyes to targets. In experiments by Kveraga, Boucher, and Hughes (2002), subjects responded to stimuli that occurred at from one to eight locations by making either a manual key press, an eye movement (saccade) toward the target, or a saccade away from the target. The authors found that RTs to initiate manual key presses and saccades away from the target corresponded well to Hick's law. However, saccades toward the target were completely unaffected by the number of stimulus alternatives. This finding agrees well with the ideas just discussed, as the saccades toward targets are much more "natural" (and biologically important) than either manual responses or saccades away from a stimulus.

These findings illustrate the importance that the relationship between the stimulus and response can have to response selection. The exceptions to Hick's law suggest that highly overlearned S-R relationships, or relationships that are in some sense biologically "natural," can *facilitate* response selection when multiple alternatives are available. In the next section we examine how this same influence of S-R familiarity can also have *detrimental* effects on response selection.

Stimulus–Response Compatibility

The association between (or the degree of "naturalness" between) a stimulus (or set of stimuli) and the response (or set of responses, called the S-R *ensemble*) has a very important influence on information processing, and was given the term *stimulus–response compatibility* (or simply S-R compatibility) in 1951 by Small (see Small, 1990). For example, when a right-positioned stimulus requires a right-hand response and a left stimulus signals the left, the situation is said to be S-R compatible, as in figure 3.8a. *However,* when a left signal indicates a right-hand response and a right signal a left-hand response (figure 3.8b), this is said to be S-R incompatible, or at least less compatible than the arrangement in figure 3.8a.

The pioneering work on S-R compatibility was conducted by Fitts and his colleagues. An example is illustrated in figure 3.9, a and b (Fitts & Deininger, 1954; Fitts & Seeger, 1953). Figure 3.9a illustrates the basic experimental setup used in these studies. The subject was to move rapidly and accurately from a center home position to one of eight target locations available on the response panel. The specific target was identified by the stimulus pattern on the display visible to the subject. Figure 3.9a illustrates the general layout, where the stimulus information about which response to make is provided via lights, and the subject makes a response with a hand movement on the response panel. Fitts and Seeger used three different stimulus patterns and three response patterns in all nine combinations, illustrated in figure 3.9b.

The organization of the *stimulus* patterns (the left side of figure 3.9b) to indicate which of the eight responses the subject was to make worked as follows. For the top stimulus pattern in figure 3.9b, the light that was illuminated indicated the response—such as "up-left," or "down-right" (see

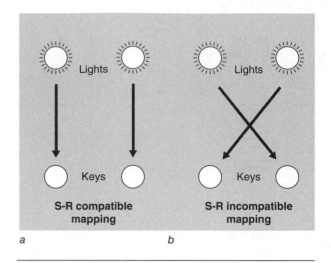

FIGURE 3.8   Stimulus–response (S-R) compatibility is defined by the relationship between the stimuli and the responses to which they are associated.

figure 3.9a). In the second row, the stimulus was presented in a different way. If the upper light was lit, it meant "up," and the right light meant "right." But if the lower *and* right lights came on, this meant "down-right." The third configuration was again different. Here, if the upper light of the vertical pair came on, it meant "up," and the right light of the horizontal pair meant "right."

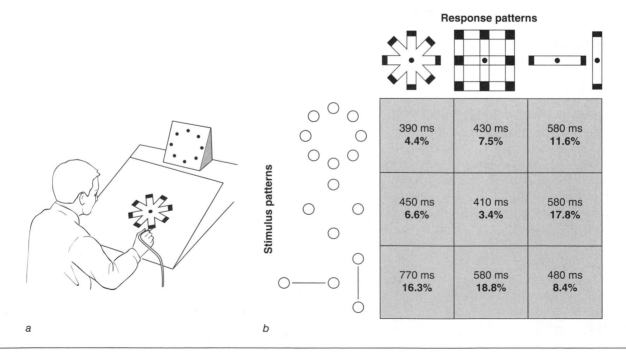

FIGURE 3.9   (a) A subject performing in Fitts and Seeger's (1953) experiment and (b) stimulus–response (S-R) compatibility effects for various stimulus arrays and response panels.

Here, the left light in the horizontal pair *and* the upper light in the vertical pair meant "up-left."

The working of the *response* panels is shown on the top of figure 3.9*b*. In the example at the left, the subject always started in the middle. If the display signaled "up," the response was up; if it signaled "left," the move was left. If "down-right" was signaled, then the movement was along the path downward to the right.

In the second response panel, the subject again started in the middle, but this time could move only along the perpendicular pathways. "Up" meant to move straight up to the center of the upper line, and "left" meant to move to the center of the left line. "Down-right" meant to move to the lower-right corner, either by moving down and then right or by moving right and then down.

Finally, the response panel on the right used two hands, the right hand on the right half and the left hand on the left half. Each hand started at its respective center point. The stimulus pattern "up" meant to make a vertical response up with the right hand (and not move the left hand), and "left" meant to move the left hand to the left (and not move the right hand). Here, though, "down-right" meant to move the right hand down *and* the left hand to the right, and similarly for "up-left."

Now, consider the data shown in the body of the table in figure 3.9*b*—the RTs for the correct responses under that combination of stimulus and response arrangements, and the percentage errors where the subject moved initially in the wrong direction. Consider first the RTs. It is interesting to ask which *stimulus* display pattern is fastest across all the combinations of response arrangements. Examining the RTs, it is clear that the fastest stimulus pattern is different for each of the response arrangements; the shortest RT for the first pattern (390 ms) is for the first response pattern; the shortest RT for the second pattern (410 ms) is for the second response pattern; and the shortest RT for the third pattern (480 ms) is for the third response pattern. The fastest stimulus pattern depended on which response pattern was paired with it.

Next, what is the fastest *response* pattern? The shortest RT for the response pattern on the left (390 ms) is for the top stimulus pattern; the shortest RT for the response pattern in the center (410 ms) is for the center stimulus pattern; and the shortest RT for the right response pattern (480 ms) is for the lower stimulus pattern. Again,

the fastest response pattern depended on which stimulus pattern was paired with it.

This is the essential idea of spatial S-R compatibility. The pattern of the stimulus arrangement seems to be closely linked with the pattern required for the response. The pattern with lights arranged in a circle was fastest when the hand had to make responses radially, but was relatively slow when a two-hand response had to be made. That is, the fastest responses were always on the diagonal in this matrix, where the stimulus requirements seemed aligned with the response requirements.

Next, consider the percentage errors, shown also in figure 3.9*b*, for each of the nine combinations. Again, the stimulus pattern that had the fewest errors depended on the response that was paired with it. Also, the response pattern with the fewest errors depended on which stimulus pattern was paired with it. Note again that the smallest errors were on the diagonal in the matrix where the stimulus and response requirements seemed to be matched. And notice also that some combinations resulted in a *very* high percentage of errors.

Finally, note that these effects cannot be explained by a speed–accuracy trade-off, with some of the combinations having low RTs only because errors happened to be large. To the contrary, with only minor exceptions, the combinations that made the subjects fastest also made them the most accurate—the opposite of a speed–accuracy trade-off. This was truly a remarkable demonstration of the power of having the stimulus and response patterns "go with" each other. This general principle of S-R compatibility has become one of the cornerstones of the field of human factors and ergonomics, and it pervades the design of countless real-world devices for which subjects must make responses based on the patterning of stimuli. In the following sections we describe some of the areas in which S-R compatibility research has been conducted.

Population Stereotypes Many S-R relationships that were originally quite arbitrary "become natural" through practice and experience (e.g., moving a light switch up to turn a light on) and are called *population stereotypes*. Different populations often have their own unique stereotypes, however, resulting in S-R relationships that are quite different from others and sometimes even opposite, such as the movement of the light switch down to turn the lights on in Germany. This relationship seems clumsy to Americans, but it is perfectly natural to Germans who have experienced this relationship throughout their lives.

Spatial and Anatomical Relationships A high degree of S-R compatibility seems to suggest that there is an overlap of the mental representation of the task dimensions associated with the stimuli and the mental representation of the possible responses (Kornblum, Hasbroucq, & Osman, 1990; Weeks & Proctor, 1990). Data of the type shown by Fitts and Seeger (1953) and many others suggest that S-R compatibility occurs because of spatial similarities in the stimulus and response sets. One possible reason for the S-R compatibility effect in figure 3.8 could be that the right limb responds to the right light faster than to the left light because of some anatomical or neural advantage. If this is so, then imagine what would happen if the hands were crossed, so that a subject's right hand was used to press the left button and the left hand used for the right button. This crossed condition is now compatible with respect to the spatial mapping of the stimulus and the *key* to select (as before), but incompatible with respect to the mapping of the stimulus and *hand* to select (i.e., the right stimulus is responded to with the right key, but using the left hand).

Experiments that have addressed this issue (Anzola, Bertolini, Buchtel, & Rizzolatti, 1977; Brebner, Shephard, & Cairney, 1972; Wallace, 1971) reveal that it is the spatial relationship between the location of the stimulus and the location of the response key that is crucial. Regardless of which hand is used (i.e., crossed or uncrossed conditions), performance is faster in the spatially compatible conditions (ensemble *a* in figure 3.8) than in spatially incompatible conditions (ensemble *b* in figure 3.8). This conclusion is supported well by the findings of Brebner and colleagues (1972), shown in figure 3.10. In general, the crossed-hands procedure resulted in slower overall RT than did the uncrossed condition. However, regardless of the position of the hands, when the stimulus light was paired with its spatially compatible response-key position, the RTs were faster than in the incompatible positions (figure 3.10).

Earlier we discussed an exception to Hick's law—making saccades toward visual stimuli (Kveraga et al., 2002). Directing the eyes in response to the presentation of a visual target rep-

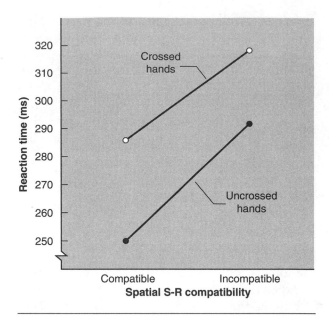

FIGURE 3.10 Effects of stimulus–response (S-R) compatibility and hand location on reaction time (RT).
Data from Brebner et al. 1972.

resents another type of S-R compatibility effect. Reaction times are smaller and errors are fewer when the task is to make the natural response to look *at* the source of a visual stimulus as compared to an *anti-saccade* task, which can be thought of as an incompatible S-R relationship (see Munoz & Everling, 2004, for a review). In the case of the anti-saccade, the natural tendency—that is, to look at the source of the visual stimulus—must be actively suppressed, or inhibited, before the correct response can be made. Presumably, this inhibition requires time.

Stimulus and Response Intensity Another rather straightforward type of S-R compatibility relationship has been found when the force of a response is mapped to the intensity of the stimulus. Subjects in a study by Romaiguère, Hasbroucq, Possamaï, and Seal (1993) were asked to make a weak or strong isometric thumb press in response to a visual stimulus that varied in intensity. The authors found a 50 to 75 ms RT advantage in the compatible condition (in which stimuli low in intensity were paired with weak thumb movements and strong stimuli with strong movements), compared to the incompatible S-R condition (low intensity paired with strong movements). Note, however, that the relation between the stimulus and the response here is more abstract than the more direct physical compatibility relationship that we have considered so far.

A related S-R compatibility effect occurs when different grip actions are made in response to numbers that differ in their magnitude. The left side of figure 3.11 illustrates the two types of responses made by subjects in an experiment by Lindemann, Abolafia, Girardi, and Bekkering (2007)—a precision grip (a pinching action used to pick up small or light objects) or a power grip (a whole-hand grip used to move large or heavy objects). Lindemann and colleagues used a clever design in which these specific grips were used to respond in a choice-RT task regarding the features of a number, presented as the visual stimulus. For example, if the number 2 or 8 was presented (both even numbers), subjects in one condition were to respond with a precision grip; if the number 3 or 9 was presented (odd numbers), then a power grip was required. Quite incidental to making the response was the effect of the *magnitude* of the number and its "compatibility" with the response. As illustrated in the right side of figure 3.11, RT was lower to initiate a precision grip in response to a low number (2 or 3) compared to a high number (8 or 9). Conversely, RT was longer to initiate a power grip to a low number compared to a high number. The compatibility of specific grips to the magnitude of a number may be an example of a more general type of conceptual S-R compatibility effect known as the SNARC effect (the "spatial–numerical association of response codes" effect), which describes a relationship between space and number magnitude

(see Umiltà, Priftis, & Zorzi, 2009, for a review). Some of these types of S-R compatibility effects, which appear to be more "conceptual" than physical (by definition), are considered in the next sections.

Simon Effects   We can also see the influence of S-R compatibility on response selection when the spatial dimension of the stimulus is *irrelevant* to response selection, not unlike the S-R compatibility effects discussed in the previous sections. In an early demonstration of what were later called *Simon effects,* subjects were asked to respond by pressing a right key whenever the verbal stimulus "right" was presented via earphones, and by pressing the left key when the word "left" was presented (Simon & Rudell, 1967). The auditory stimuli were sometimes presented only to the left ear and sometimes only to the right ear. Note that regardless of the ear to which the stimulus was presented, subjects were to respond to the *content* of the message; the spatial location (ear) to which the message was sent was irrelevant to making the correct response. However, the findings revealed that the irrelevant (spatial) feature of the stimulus had a profound effect on response selection and could not be ignored. As figure 3.12 shows, choice RT was faster when the message of the signal and the response were compatible with the spatial origin of the stimulus. These findings, along with others reported since Simon published his initial series of studies, suggest that there is

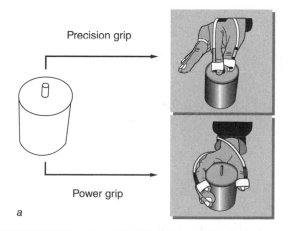

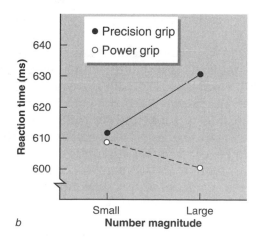

FIGURE 3.11   *(a)* Subjects in the study by Lindemann and colleagues (2007) were cued with a low or high number to pick up an object using either a pinch grip or a power grip; *(b)* RTs were fastest for large numbers using a power grip, but were fastest for small numbers using a pinch grip.

Reprinted, by permission, from O. Lindemann et al., 2007, "Getting a grip on numbers: numerical magnitude priming in object grasping," *Journal of Experimental Psychology: Human Perception and Performance* 33: 1400-1409.

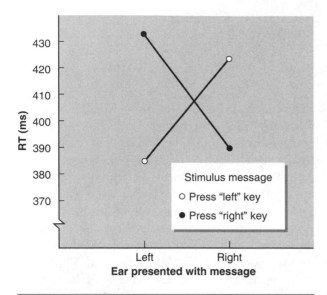

FIGURE 3.12 The Simon effect—the irrelevant stimulus (which ear receives the message) interacts with the information.

Adapted, by permission, from J.R. Simon and A.P. Rudell, 1967, "Auditory S-R compatibility: The effect of an irrelevant cue on information processing," *Journal of Applied Psychology* 51: 302.

interference in selecting a response when the presumably irrelevant stimulus is incompatible with the response. The spatial dimensionality of the stimulus tends to attract the response toward it, which must be inhibited (thus taking extra time) before the correct response can be selected (see also Simon, 1969a, 1969b, 1990).

Although the spatial layout of the S-R ensemble has a critical effect on response selection, this appears to be only a partial explanation of what is happening (Umiltà & Nicoletti, 1990). For example, choice RT to the stimulus word "right" or to a rightward-pointing stimulus arrow is faster when the subject responds with a button press with the right hand or with the word "right" in comparison to arrangements with incompatible relationships (e.g., McCarthy & Donchin, 1981; Weeks & Proctor, 1990). Thus, similar to the effects of number size, verbal stimuli that implicate a spatial relation and responses appear to have dimensions that produce compatibility relationships affecting response selection.

Together, these findings suggest that the response-selection stage is susceptible to compatibility effects when the relationship between the set of stimulus alternatives and the set of response alternatives has a highly learned (or "natural") association (as in the word "right").

Interference is likely to occur when the response is inconsistent with the learned association (for in-depth discussion of theoretical interpretations of various S-R compatibility effects see Cho & Proctor, 2003; Hommel & Prinz, 1997; Kornblum et al., 1990; Proctor & Reeve, 1990; Proctor & Van Zandt, 1994).

Compatibility and Complex Actions When people respond to stimuli that require *complex* actions, the issue of S-R compatibility and response selection seems to be related to the *intentions* of the action. For example, Rosenbaum and colleagues (1990) describe the everyday task of a waiter who wants to turn over an upside-down glass with one hand so that he can pour water from a pitcher into it with the other hand. What will be the initial grasp of the hand—thumb up or inverted with the thumb down? Experiments show that the waiter's initial hand position is usually inverted so that when the glass is turned upright the hand is in the correct holding position, ready to receive poured liquid. The response initially selected by the waiter "trades off" an awkward early posture in order to achieve a posture that is more suited to filling the glass with water. In this case, compatibility between the stimulus (the glass) and the waiter's response (initial hand posture) is defined not in terms of the initial interaction, but rather in terms of the efficiency of the intended *final* position (what Rosenbaum and colleagues have termed the "end-comfort effect"). Also, selection of the method that maximizes the efficiency at movement completion is initiated faster than of one that is more efficient at the action's start (Rosenbaum, 2009; Rosenbaum, Vaughan, Barnes, & Jorgensen, 1992; Rosenbaum, van Heugten, & Caldwell, 1996), especially if the final location has a stringent precision requirement (Short & Cauraugh, 1999). Thus, for more complex actions, S-R compatibility effects may influence the response-selection stage in terms of *how* an action is to be performed, rather than simply about where to move.

Response-Programming Stage

The performer can organize and initiate an action only after having identified the stimulus and selected a response. After response selection, the performer must translate this abstract idea into a set of muscular actions that will achieve the desired action. These processes are thought to occur during the *response-programming stage.* Like the processes in the earlier stages, the events occurring in response programming are probably very complex—requiring that some program of action be *retrieved* from memory, that the program be prepared for activation, that the relevant portions of the motor system be readied for the program (called *feedforward,* or *tuning*), and that the movement be initiated. It is helpful to view the response-programming stage as the final set of processes that allows the individual to communicate with the environment—just as the stimulus-identification stage is viewed as the first stage that allows the environment to communicate with an individual.

Information about the response-programming stage has developed more recently than research regarding the other two stages. It was not until 1960, when Henry and Rogers performed an experiment on the nature of the movement to be produced in RT situations, that conceptualization about the response-programming stage began. The underlying motivation for their experiment was based on Henry's idea that motor programs are stored in memory. When a well-learned action is retrieved from memory, it is "read out" like a series of triggers on a conveyer belt (as in a player piano), with more triggers required for more complex movements (Klapp, 1996). Although the language and analogies have changed over the years, it is interesting and useful to read the theoretical arguments that Henry and Rogers (1960) presented in their paper and to understand why RT was considered a valuable measure of motor program retrieval and preparation (see "Henry and Rogers' 'Memory Drum' Theory of Neuromotor Reaction").

The Henry-Rogers Experiment

Henry and Rogers (1960) studied the nature of the movement to be made using a simple-RT paradigm, in which the subjects knew, on any given trial, exactly which response was required. Over many blocks of trials, Henry and Rogers had the subjects make different movements while keeping the stimulus for the movement, as well as the number of response alternatives, constant (i.e., there were *no* stimulus–response alternatives, or $N = 0$). The apparatus used for the Henry and Rogers experiment is illustrated in figure 3.13. The first task version (movement A) involved merely lifting the finger from a key a few millimeters

---

They said it . . .

HENRY AND ROGERS' "MEMORY DRUM" THEORY OF NEUROMOTOR REACTION

In the following quote from Henry and Rogers (1960), the recall of information for movement is analogous to retrieval of information from a computer's memory buffer. The significance of these statements was probably not fully recognized at the time, even though they were published in the very same year as Miller, Galanter, and Pribram's (1960) book *Plans and the Structure of Behavior.* This book, regarded as one of the major factors leading to the fall of behaviorism, popularized the terms "plans" and "programs" as structures that must precede actions.

"A rich store of unconscious motor memory is available for the performance of acts of neuromotor skill. Added to this are innate neuromotor coordinations that are important in motor acts. The tapping of the store may be thought of broadly as a memory storage drum phenomenon, to use the analogy of the electronic computer. The neural pattern for a specific and well-coordinated motor act is controlled by a stored program that is used to direct the neuromotor details of its performance . . . there should be a longer reaction latency for a complicated movement than for a simpler movement. This is because a more comprehensive program, i.e., a larger amount of stored information, will be needed, and thus the neural impulses will require more time for coordination and direction into the eventual motor neurons and muscles" (pp. 449 and 450).

It was not until years later that Henry and Rogers' ideas became widely cited (Cardinal & Thomas, 2005; Ulrich & Reeve, 2005). These ideas about motor programs are quite prevalent and useful today, as will be evident in later chapters here.

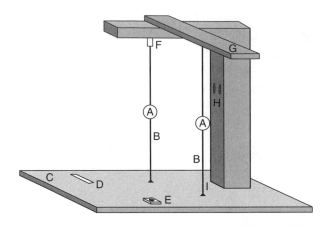

FIGURE 3.13 This apparatus, from Howell (1953), was almost identical to the apparatus used by Henry and Rogers (1960). Explicit details about the apparatus and the three movement tasks are reported in Fischman, Christina, and Anson (2008). (A = tennis balls, B = nylon strings, C = base, D = reaction time, E = button, F = friction contacts, G = sidearm, H = stimulus lights.)

and had essentially no accuracy requirement. For the second version (movement B), the subject lifted the finger from the key and moved approximately 33 cm forward and upward to grasp a tennis ball suspended on a string, which stopped a timer that measured movement time (MT). The third task version (movement C) involved a second suspended ball mounted 30 cm to the left of the first ball. The subject lifted the finger from the key, moved upward to the right to strike the first ball with the back of the hand, moved forward and downward to push a button, and then moved upward to the left to grasp the second suspended ball.[2] Remember, for all three task versions, there were no stimulus and response alternatives for a block of trials. Thus, the processing speed in the stimulus-identification and response-selection mechanisms should always be the same; the only variation among the three task

versions was in the nature of the *movement* to be made. The primary measure, as before, was the (simple) RT, or the interval from stimulus onset until the movement began.

Henry and Rogers' data from the adult subjects are presented in table 3.3. Movement B (single-ball grasp) resulted in a 36 ms longer RT than did movement A. The most complex movement (C) (ball strike, button press, ball grasp) resulted in an additional 13 ms increase in RT compared to movement B. Because the stimuli were not changed for the different movements, nor was the number of choices, these data suggest that the increased RT as the movements increased in complexity was due to an increased amount of time required to *program* the movement in some response-programming stage. Henry and Rogers' original idea was that a more complex set of motor commands, such as would be necessary to control the limb through several movement reversals and to produce striking and grasping actions, would require more neuromotor activities to be coordinated, in turn requiring more time for all of this neurological complexity to be organized during RT. In slightly modified form, this idea still has a great deal of support (see Christina, 1992; Henry, 1980; Klapp, 1977a, 1996).

What is going on in the Henry and Rogers experiment? The obvious conclusion is that RT increased as the *complexity* of the *movement* to be made increased. But what was actually involved in making the movement more "complex"? The careful reader will notice a number of factors that came into play in this regard. Table 3.3 also summarizes a number of potentially relevant factors that differed according to the three experimental conditions in the study. The differences between movements A, B, and C included additional movement parts, increased accuracy demands, and longer movement durations (and perhaps other factors as well). Research conducted since this pioneering experiment suggests that all of these

TABLE 3.3. Experimental Conditions and Results From Henry and Rogers (1960)

Movement task	Number of movement parts	Movement accuracy requirement	Duration of movement	Latency to begin movement (RT)
A	1	No	Very brief	159 ms
B	2	Yes	95 ms	195 ms
C	4	Yes	465 ms	208 ms

factors may have played a role in producing the results seen in the Henry and Rogers experiment.

Number of Movement Parts and Reaction Time
Results similar to the Henry and Rogers (1960) data have been obtained in a number of replications of their study, implicating the addition of movement parts as the primary reason for the increase in RT (e.g., Christina, 1992; Fischman, 1984). Corroborating evidence was obtained from experiments using different tasks. For example, Sternberg, Monsell, Knoll, and Wright (1978) observed that the latency in speaking the first word of a sequence increased by about 10 ms for each word that was added to the sequence (i.e., strings of one, two, three, four, or five words), and by 5 to 15 ms for additional letters to be typed (see also Canic & Franks, 1989). It would appear, however, that the additional movement must be performed as part of a whole ballistic response in order to have an effect on RT. A study by Franks, Nagelkerke, Ketelaars, and van Donkelaar (1998) compared the effect on initiation latency of a single-movement task (elbow extension) and a two-movement task (elbow extension and flexion) in which there was either no pause, a short pause (75 ms), or a long pause (260 ms) between extension and flexion. Elevated RTs were found when the flexion movement followed without delay or with a very brief delay, but not when there was a long delay between the two movements. These results suggested that when there was sufficient time to program the second movement *following* completion of the first movement (and thus not during the original RT), the subject needed only to plan the first movement prior to movement onset, regardless of whether or not it was followed by a flexion. However, with no pause or a brief pause between the two parts, the entire response needed to be programmed in advance, resulting in the observed effect on RT of the additional movement part (see Klapp, 1996, for further discussion).

Movement Accuracy Effects on Reaction Time
At about the same time as Henry and Rogers' work (but quite separate from it), Paul Fitts was investigating movement complexity effects as well, using aiming tasks that varied in target distance and accuracy demands. Although Fitts' primary concern related to the ongoing movement (as revealed by movement time; see chapter 7), he also found that RT increased as the precision requirements of the task increased (Fitts & Peterson, 1964). Findings that RT increases as the target size decreases (thereby increasing the accuracy demands) have since been reported in a number of experiments by Sidaway and his colleagues (e.g., Sidaway, Sekiya, & Fairweather, 1995).

Movement Duration Effects on Reaction Time
In addition to complexity and accuracy demands, the three movements studied by Henry and Rogers (1960) varied in at least one other important respect—their *duration.* From Henry and Rogers' data (table 3.3), notice that the most complex movement required much more time to produce (465 ms) than the simpler one (95 ms). This observation has led various scientists to suspect that the duration of the movement to be produced might be a major variable in the response-programming stage. Klapp and Erwin (1976) asked subjects to make 10 cm movements of a slide along a track, with goal MTs of 150, 300, 600, or 1,200 ms. The number of actions and the accuracy demands of the movement were held constant, but the duration of the movement was varied. As the movement duration increased, the RT to initiate the response increased as well, especially when the movement durations were below 600 ms. Similar effects were reported by Rosenbaum and Patashnik (1980), who varied movement duration of the time a button had to be depressed, and by Quinn, Schmidt, Zelaznik, Hawkins, and McFarquhar (1980), who varied the movement time for aiming responses of a stylus to a target (see Klapp, 1996, for a review).

Response Complexity and Motor Programming

The effect of movement complexity on RT occurs both when the person knows in advance what movement will be made (in simple RT) and when the choice of movement is not known until it is indicated by the stimulus (in choice RT) (see Klapp, 1995, 1996). Regardless of the variations in method and movements, the effect of movement complexity on RT has been interpreted as relating to the time necessary to prepare and initiate the movement during the response-programming stage of RT. Despite over 50 years of research on this topic, the ideas of Henry and Rogers about the process of movement organization during the motor-programming stage remain remarkably valid today.

Anticipation

So far in this chapter, we have discussed information-processing activities in which the performer's task is to respond to generally unanticipated stimulus information. The processing speed, as measured by RT, tends to be relatively slow, giving the impression that humans have severe limitations in information processing. One problem with this line of thinking, though, is that RT is usually studied in highly unrealistic situations, and especially in situations in which the subject is seldom allowed to *anticipate* environmental information. In fact, experimenters go to elaborate lengths to prevent the subjects from anticipating. They often use "catch trials," in which the stimulus is sometimes withheld to "catch" a subject who is anticipating; often use choice-RT tasks, preventing the subject from knowing *what* stimulus is going to occur; or randomize foreperiods (the interval from the preparatory signal to the stimulus presentation) so that the subject cannot predict *when* the stimulus will appear. By employing these methods, researchers try to ensure that subjects are responding to an "unanticipated" signal. Clearly, under these conditions, humans find information processing very difficult indeed.

But in many "real" skills, suddenly presented and unexpected stimuli are the exception rather than the rule. Of course, unexpected events do sometimes occur—and sometimes we even try to make them occur (e.g., faking in sports); but many of the stimuli to which we respond in our daily activities are very predictable. During walking or driving, the stimuli emerge from a generally stable environment that allows us to preview upcoming events with plenty of time to do something about them. And when a signal does arrive, it is often not a discrete event, but rather a *pattern* of sensory information that unfolds before us. Gibson (1966) has emphasized that visual information is really an *optical flow* of stimuli, from which the performer detects important future environmental events (see chapter 5 for a discussion of this idea).

Poulton (1957) has described three different kinds of anticipation. One obvious type is *receptor anticipation*, in which the performer detects the upcoming events with various sensory receptors (e.g., the batter *sees* the ball coming). However, the performer must also estimate how long his

own movement will take, and often he must allow for this interval in initiating the actions; the batter must time the bat swing's initiation so that the bat and ball meet at the proper location over the plate. This is called *effector anticipation*, because the duration of the effector's movement (the body, mainly the arms and bat) must be predicted. Finally, Poulton described what he called *perceptual anticipation*; here the environmental events are not perceived directly, but they are still predictable because the performer has had a great deal of practice with them, such as the regular timing of beats in music or in military drill. In the next sections, we consider important principles related to a performer's capability to anticipate.

Spatial (or Event) Anticipation

One way in which performers can anticipate future activities is by knowing what kinds of stimuli could be presented and what kinds of responses will be required for each of the anticipated stimuli. This class of anticipation has been called *spatial*, or *event*, anticipation. In an experimental study of these processes, Leonard (1953, 1954) and Jeeves (1961) used an apparatus that had trackways arranged as spokes of a wheel. Subjects were asked to move repeatedly from the center position toward lights at the ends of the spokes and back again as quickly as possible. The light indicated the spoke along which the subject was to move. If the next spoke was indicated only after the subject had arrived back at the center position from the previous spoke, subjects could not anticipate which movement to make next, and performance was slow, jerky, and labored. But if subjects were informed about the next spoke when they were at the peripheral end of the previous spoke, they could plan the next movement while they were moving back to the center. Overall, performance was smoother, less jerky, and more rapid. Analogous effects were found by Leonard (1953), whose subjects used advance information to reduce a six-choice RT task to a three-choice task, with associated gains in speed as would be expected from reducing the number of S-R alternatives from six to three (conforming to Hick's law). Many other experiments led to a similar conclusion (see Schmidt, 1968, for a review).

Some experimenters have sought to determine what kinds of information about the upcoming *movement* can be used in advance and how much time can be "saved" by using it. Using the *precuing technique*, Rosenbaum (1980, 1983), Goodman and Kelso (1980), Zelaznik and Hahn (1985), and others have examined tasks in which various aspects of the response could be specified in advance, leaving other aspects unspecified until the stimulus actually arrived; the stimulus then provided the remainder of the information needed to produce the action, as well as the "go" signal. For example, Rosenbaum (1980) used a task in which the response involved up to three types of movement choices: (a) with the right or left arm, (b) toward or away from the body, and (c) to a target that was near to or far from the starting position—an eight-choice RT task (2 × 2 × 2 = 8 alternatives). Rosenbaum found that providing advance information about any one of the three movement features (arm, direction, or extent) reduced the RT by about 100 to 150 ms. Apparently, when the subjects had this advance information they could engage in some response processing before the stimulus arrived, thus "saving" processing time during RT. There seemed to be a greater advantage in receiving information about which arm was to be used (150 ms reduction in RT relative to the no-precue condition) as compared to information about the extent of the movement (100 ms reduction), suggesting that the situation is somewhat more complex than simply reducing the number of alternatives from eight to four. Klapp's (1977b)

work, using a different paradigm, makes a similar point.

One way to think of these effects is illustrated in figure 3.14. If the subject receives advance information about a certain feature of the movement, some of the processing operations normally done during RT can be done in advance, and can be "bypassed" when the reaction stimulus finally arrives. If sufficient information is given so that all the aspects can be selected in advance (e.g., knowing arm, direction, *and* extent in Rosenbaum's situation), then one can think of "bypassing" processing in response selection completely, resulting in what is essentially simple RT. The work of Rosenbaum and others suggests that portions of response programming can be done in advance as well.

It is also interesting to note in Leonard's (1953, 1954) and Jeeves' (1961) studies that advance information allowing partial or complete selection of upcoming actions was presented while the subject was already moving back to the center position. The result should not be particularly surprising, but it does show that one movement can be planned while another is being executed. This is a very important feature of motor control, as it provides a mechanism by which a series of rapid movements can be executed with considerable speed and accuracy.

Anticipating the spatial location of a directed penalty kick in soccer is one example of a situation in which advanced information processing is

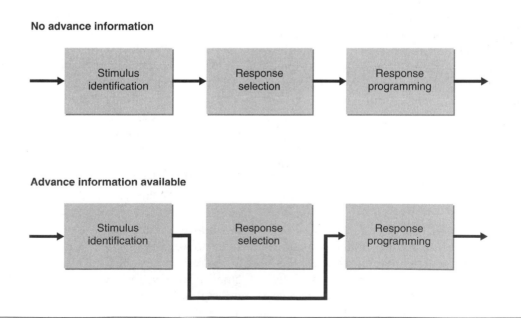

FIGURE 3.14   Bypassing the response-selection stage by processing information in advance.

necessary if a goalkeeper is to have any chance to be successful (Franks & Harvey, 1997). Analyses of the soccer penalty kick have shown that, if a goalkeeper waits until the ball is contacted before deciding which direction to dive, it is virtually impossible to intercept the ball, since the travel time for the ball to reach the goal line (about 600 ms) is roughly equal to the goalkeeper's own movement time (500-700 ms) *after* the decision to move has been made (Franks & Harvey, 1997). Therefore, if she is to be successful, the goalkeeper must pick up advance cues from the kicker regarding the direction in which the ball will travel and must use that information to decide on a response *prior* to the actual delivery of the stimulus (contacting the ball). Analyses of this task have revealed that expert goalkeepers focus on the position of the stance foot (the non-kicking leg) and the relation of both feet to the ball as advance cues, whereas novice goalkeepers use visual search strategies that are much less reliable and useful (Franks & Harvey, 1997; Savelsbergh, van der Kamp, Williams, & Ward, 2005; Williams, 2000).

Temporal Anticipation

The evidence just reviewed on spatial anticipation suggests that the performer can, by knowing some specific information about the response to be produced, bypass or at least shorten some of the stages of information processing. This shortening of RT is rather modest, though, and the responder still has difficulty processing environmental stimuli quickly. The evidence presented in the next sections suggests that if the person can anticipate *when* the stimulus is going to arrive, rather large reductions in RT can occur. Under the proper circumstances, the performer can *eliminate* RT altogether!

Constant-Duration Foreperiods

Imagine a subject in a simple-RT situation (one stimulus and one response) in which a warning signal is followed by a foreperiod, at the end of which is the stimulus onset. Foreperiods may be of a constant duration (e.g., always 3 s), or they may be variable and unpredictable (e.g., 2, 3, or 4 s in random order). It seems obvious that a constant-duration foreperiod will result in the shortest RTs. If these constant foreperiods are relatively short (e.g., less than a few seconds), evidence shows that the subject can respond essentially *simultaneously* with the stimulus after some practice

(provided that the subject knows which response to produce). Quesada and Schmidt (1970) showed that the average RT with a constant 2 s foreperiod was only 22 ms! It seems likely that the person anticipated the temporal onset of the stimulus and began the process of programming and initiating the response before the stimulus came on so that the overt movement occurred at about the same time as the stimulus. Thus, if the foreperiods are both regular *and* short, and all aspects of the response to be made are known in advance, then the subject can (with very little practice) perform the needed processes in advance and emit the overt response essentially simultaneously with the stimulus. This has been termed *early responding* in the literature because the response is triggered early—before the stimulus actually arrives.

On the other hand, when the foreperiod is regular but very long (a few seconds or more), and various features of the response are known in advance, subjects apparently cannot shorten RTs to zero even with extensive practice. Under these conditions, Mowrer (1940) found RTs of about 230 ms. The RTs in these situations with long but regular foreperiods seem to be similar to those in which the foreperiod is short but irregular (thus preventing early responding). When the foreperiods are long (e.g., 12 s), early responding is prevented because the subject cannot anticipate the *exact* stimulus onset when it is so far in the future. The reason is that the internal "timing" for short durations is much less variable than that for long durations.[3] Attempts to anticipate the stimulus onset following a long foreperiod result in too many (very) early responses (by a second or so), which is usually not allowed by the instructions or by the experimenter. All the subject can do is engage in *preparation* and respond very quickly when the stimulus does arrive. Therefore, in situations involving anticipation, a common question is whether it is preparation *or* early responding that is taking place.

Variable-Duration Foreperiods

In simple-RT situations, there is a great deal of evidence that irregular (variable duration) foreperiods averaging about 1 s produce shorter RTs than do longer ones of 2, 3, or 4 s (e.g., Klemmer, 1956; Welford, 1968). This effect seems to be quite small, however, and it is overshadowed by a larger effect that is apparently related to when the subject expects the signal. In these latter situations, the fastest RT is not associated with the shortest foreperiod as would be expected from Klemmer's results, but rather either with the *most probable* foreperiod, or, if the foreperiods are all equally probable, with the center of the range of foreperiods (Aiken, 1964; Mowrer, 1940; Poulton, 1974). Subjects in Mowrer's (1940) study responded to tones presented every 12 s, but occasionally Mowrer presented tones at greater or less than 12 s intervals. The data in figure 3.15 show that the shortest RTs were at the interval that was most expected (12 s), and that longer and especially shorter intervals resulted in slower RTs. It appears that as the end of the expected foreperiods draws near, the subject begins to prepare for the stimulus and response. Because maintaining a prepared state is effortful (and perhaps not possible during these longer intervals), this readiness begins to increase only when the first of the group of stimuli is expected, reaches a maximum at about the center (the most frequently occurring foreperiod), and declines toward the end. Presumably, the subject is most expectant for the signal when it is presented with an average foreperiod, and the RT is somewhat faster as a result. Clearly, this expectancy speeds RT.

Aging Foreperiods

We can see a notable exception to the findings on foreperiod duration in experiments that include *no catch trials* (again, in catch trials, the stimulus—though expected—never arrives; e.g., Drazin, 1961; Rothstein, 1973; Salmoni, Sullivan, & Starkes, 1976). Drazin's data are shown in figure 3.16, which plots the RT against the average foreperiod duration. Here there were variable foreperiods and no catch trials, and the RT decreased as the stimulus was presented later and later in the group of foreperiods. At first, this result seems contradictory to the earlier conclusion that a stimulus presented at the center of the foreperiods elicits the most rapid RT (Aiken, 1964; Mowrer, 1940).

The critical difference is that the studies by Drazin (1961), Rothstein (1973), and Salmoni and colleagues (1976) did not employ catch trials. Without catch trials, the subject can become increasingly expectant for the stimulus as the foreperiod "ages" toward the last possible time of stimulus presentation. Consider an example with four possible (and equally probable) foreperiods (1, 2, 3, and 4 s) and no catch trials. Note that when only 0.5 s of the foreperiod has elapsed, the probability that the signal will appear at the 1 s point is one in four (0.25). After the 1 s interval has passed without presentation of the signal, the probability that the signal will arrive at 2 s is one in three (0.33), and so on, until beyond the passage of 3 s the probability of the signal's arriving at 4 s is

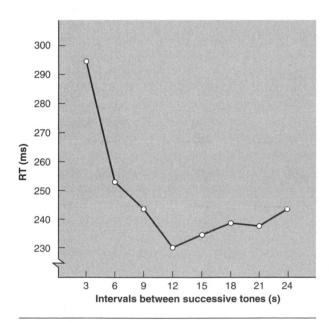

FIGURE 3.15 Minimum reaction time occurs at the most probable interstimulus interval.

Reprinted from O.H. Mowrer, 1940, "Preparatory set (Expectancy): Some methods of measurement," *Psychological Monographs* 52 (233): 12.

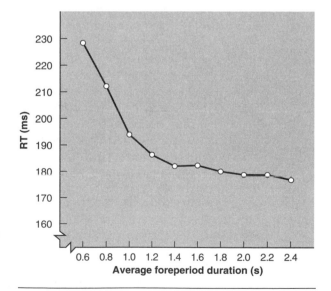

FIGURE 3.16 The aging-foreperiod effect.

Reprinted from D.H. Drazin, 1961, "Effects of foreperiod, foreperiod variability, and probability of stimulus occurrence on simple reaction time," *Journal of Experimental Psychology* 62: 45.

1.0. Thus, the subject has a basis for becoming increasingly expectant as the foreperiod "ages."

Temporal and Spatial Anticipation: Implications

Essentially, anticipation is a *strategy* to reduce the time, or even the stages, of processing that would normally be involved in responding to an unanticipated stimulus. For this reason, in some situations people make attempts to either prevent or enhance such anticipation. For example, the starter in a sprint race attempts to prevent early responding by using a variable-duration foreperiod together with some "catch trials," which requires that the athletes wait for the signal before initiating their response (see "Foreperiods and False Starts in Sprinting"). On the other hand, the dance instructor or the drill leader in the military uses predictable foreperiods so that all the performers can respond simultaneously with the count and with one another. Dance instructors present a 1-2-3-4 count that the pupils know not to respond to, then a second 1-2-3-4; the "1" of the second count is the stimulus to begin. Drill leaders issue a command

Foreperiods and False Starts in Sprinting

A rare event occurred in the 1996 Summer Olympic Games—a sprinter false-started *twice* and was disqualified from the 100 m final. In the second of his false starts, British sprinter Linford Christie appeared to explode out of the blocks with an excellent and legal start. Moments later the start was ruled invalid because Christie had apparently "jumped the gun." His RT, as indicated by the time from the starter's signal until the sudden rise in force of his foot against the blocks, was shorter than the 100 ms minimum value allowed by Olympic standards. Some raised arguments at the time that such standards place too fine a constraint on what might otherwise be an exceptional performance. Was this a fair judgment?

The starter's goal in the sprint is to have all the athletes *reacting* to the sound of the gun, and not responding before it. For this reason the starter attempts to *prevent* anticipations by using variable foreperiods and by sometimes aborting a start when the foreperiod ages too much (a type of catch trial). What the starter observes in the sprint start is forward movement of the athlete in relation to the sound. When that movement occurs before the sound or coincides with it, it is easy to infer that the athlete has anticipated, and the sprinter is rightfully penalized with a false start. The more difficult decision, however, concerns penalizing the sprinter who has initiated the start after the sound of the gun, but not in *reaction* to it. In other words, how fast is too fast?

Numerous experimenters have studied how to optimize RT under various experimental constraints. Simple RTs typically range from about 130 ms to 200 ms or so, depending on the intensity of the stimulus, the effector used in the response, and so on. In the case of the sprint start, however, the time measured is from the presentation of the stimulus until the first change in *force* against the starting block, and additional time is required to actually start the body in motion so that it is visible to the starting official. Also, consider that the laboratory RT values have been achieved under very controlled experimental conditions with responses involving very simple movements (such as finger lifts). The sprint start entails a much more complex coordination of effectors and much larger forces. Consequently, an even longer RT than is typical—not a shorter one—might be expected in the sprint situation.

Still, one could argue that the RTs of world-class sprinters might be expected to be faster than those of the average subjects in an RT experiment. However, though sprint training does improve many speed-related factors, there is only so much that can be shaved off the stages of processing involved in simple RT. The minimum of 100 ms from stimulus to force change as an RT for a sprint start is a conservative criterion that still leaves plenty of time for some anticipation (perhaps up to 100 ms). Anything faster is most likely due to anticipating and "early responding," as discussed in this chapter. When all of the factors affecting sprint RT are combined, we must conclude that Christie was almost certainly guilty of a false start.

(e.g., "Left . . .") to provide the soldiers with event predictability and then later, at a very predictable time, give another command—"Face!"—which is the stimulus to perform the action (a 90° left turn); a good unit will respond as a single person, right on command. Anticipation is also very important in defensive driving skills. Young and Stanton (2007) provide a good review of various individual, vehicle, and situational factors influencing brake response times in driving.

These concepts are also evident in American football, in which the quarterback provides a set of signals for his teammates just before the ball is snapped. The basic idea is for the quarterback to enable his team to anticipate and begin moving before the opposition can do so. According to the principles discussed in the previous sections, the signal count should be predictable, allowing temporal anticipation. For example, the quarterback could bark out distinctive, sharp sounds (such as "two, two, two, two, . . .") such that the timing between the sounds is regular and predictable. Earlier (in the huddle), the team will have been informed that the second "two" is the signal to start the play. This allows all of the offensive team to have nearly perfect temporal and spatial (event) anticipation because they know what is to be done and when to do it. The opposition does not have this capability, which forces them to be delayed by at least one RT before responding. The signal caller should be careful to avoid the aging-foreperiod effect, as an alert defense could predict the temporal onset of the "two" signal with increasing certainty as the count "ages," since the rules do not allow for "catch trials."

Benefits Versus "Costs" of Anticipating

The previous sections have described benefits to performers when they correctly anticipate temporally, spatially, or both. However, the adage that "you don't get something for nothing" holds just as well in motor control laboratories as in anything else, and there are necessarily "costs" of various kinds that result from anticipating.

What happens if we anticipate incorrectly, as occurs when the batter anticipates a fastball but receives a curve ball instead, or the boxer expects a blow from his opponent's left hand but receives one from the right hand? LaBerge (1973) and Posner, Nissen, and Ogden (1978) used a method of estimating the advantages and disadvantages of anticipating called a *cost–benefit analysis.*

In the study by Posner and associates (1978), the subject fixated on the center of a screen and received one of three precues. One second after the precue, a signal would come on at one of two locations on the screen (which could be seen without an eye movement), and the subject's task was to lift a finger from a key as rapidly as possible after stimulus onset. Only one response was ever required (lifting a single finger from a key) regardless of the stimulus location. One of the precues was a plus sign, presented on one-third of the trials, indicating an equal probability that either of the two signal locations could be used (these were called "neutral-precue trials"). On the remaining two-thirds of the trials, however, the precue was an arrow pointing to the left or to the right, meaning that the signal would be presented on the side of the screen to which the arrow pointed; however, this precue was correct on only 80% of the trials. On the remaining 20% of the trials, the subject was "tricked"; the signal would arrive on the side of the screen opposite the one indicated by the arrow. The trials in which the signal arrived on the side indicated by the arrow were called *valid-precue* trials; those in which the arrow pointed away from the eventual signal location were called *invalid-precue* trials.

Posner and colleagues (1978) found that the average RT on the neutral-precue trials was 265 ms. On the valid-precue trials, the average RT was 235 ms, revealing a 30 ms *benefit* to performance for a correct anticipation, relative to the neutral-precue condition. However, when the signal was presented in the location opposite that indicated by the arrow (an invalid-precue trial), the average RT was 304 ms, revealing a 39 ms *cost* of anticipating the direction incorrectly, relative to the neutral-precue condition.

Notice that the cost in this study involved only the detection of the signal, because the response was always the same. But what happens when the task also includes different response alternatives? What are the costs involved in actually *moving* incorrectly? Schmidt and Gordon (1977) used a two-choice RT task in which the subject had to produce a correct amount of force on a lever in a direction indicated by a signal light. In one series of trials, the right and left signals were presented in random order, and subjects could not successfully anticipate the direction of the upcoming response. But in another series of trials, the signals were presented in an alternating order (right, left, right, left, . . .), and the subjects would develop strong spatial anticipation about the next response. In this alternating series, however, a few signals were embedded that were opposite to the direction expected; for example, a series might involve the following responses: left, right, left, right, left, right, *right*—an alternating series in which the subject was expecting the last signal to be a left, not a right.

On those trials in which the subject was anticipating one direction but was presented with the unexpected signal, there were errors on about 64% of the trials. The nature of this effect is illustrated in figure 3.17. These erroneous responses were initiated with a rapid RT (144 ms, on the average); the subject started moving in the incorrect direction (i.e., left) for 144 ms, and only then reversed direction to *begin* to move in the correct direction. Falsely anticipating appears to be a major cause of this kind of error.

Next, if the subject was anticipating left but the right signal came on, and the subject did avoid making an error, then the RT was somewhat longer (276 ms) than it would have been if the person had not been anticipating at all (235 ms). Thus, inhibiting an already planned (incorrect) movement does require time (276 − 235 = 41 ms). This can be thought of as the *cost* of anticipating incorrectly and is very similar to the 40 ms cost found by Posner and colleagues (1978). Interestingly, though, in the Schmidt and Gordon study (1977), there was an 83 ms *benefit* (i.e., 235 − 152) of anticipating correctly, which is somewhat larger than benefits found by Posner and colleagues.

However, more important is the finding that people actually *moved* in the incorrect direction on a majority of the trials (64%) in which they were falsely anticipating. Eventually, they did start moving in the correct direction, but not until 288 ms (144 + 144 ms; see figure 3.17) had elapsed. This was *compounded* by the fact that the person now had farther to go to reach the correct target,

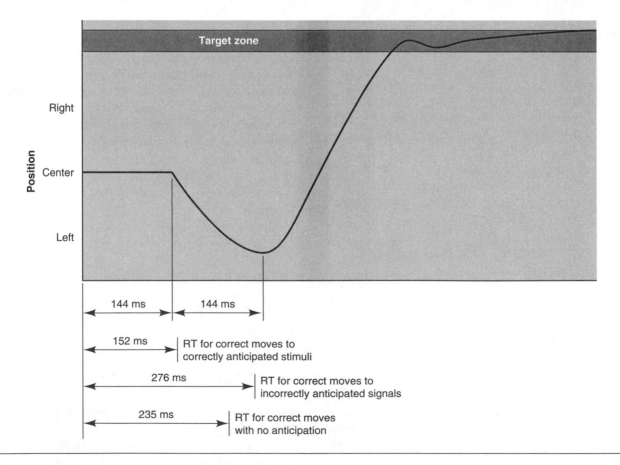

FIGURE 3.17 Movement error caused by false anticipation.

Adapted from R.A. Schmidt and G.B. Gordon, 1977, "Errors in motor responding, "rapid" corrections, and false anticipations," *Journal of Motor Behavior* 9: 107, adapted by permission of the publisher (Taylor & Francis, www.informaworld.com).

so that arriving at the target was delayed even longer. And, in having to move farther to the target, the errant performer was less accurate in hitting the target, because the error in hitting a target is roughly proportional to the movement distance (chapter 7). When we put together all these negative aspects of making an error, it is clear that the cost due to an incorrect anticipation can be quite high.

Many theoretical questions arise from these data on error production, but a major importance of these findings is in their application to various common activities. The pitch count in baseball is used by both batters (Gray, 2002, 2009a) and umpires (MacMahon & Starkes, 2008) to make predictions about the nature of the next pitch. A tennis player anticipating that a shot will be hit to her left moves to the left, only to experience that sinking feeling when the ball is hit to her right. The defensive lineman in American football expects to be blocked to his left so leans or moves to his right, only to find that he is now being blocked to his right, making the task a very easy one for his opponent who was going to block him in that direction anyway. Effective coaching techniques employ the notion that anticipating has certain benefits and costs—and that one can determine whether or not to anticipate in a certain situation by weighing the probable gains against potential losses. In many situations, the benefit of correctly anticipating might be very small compared to the cost of a false anticipation (e.g., when a driver anticipates what another driver may do). In other cases, the reverse is true. Obviously, these factors will depend on the particular activity, as well as on the particular situation (e.g., the score of the game, position on the field, etc.).

Signal-Detection Theory

One of the most important components of motor performance occurs prior to any action at all. Taking in sensory information and making yes/no decisions on the basis of that information is often critical. Deciding whether or not to perform some action (e.g., "Should I turn left at an intersection or wait?"), and whether or not something occurred in the environment (e.g., "Did I see a warning signal or not?"), are examples of this kind of decision making. We discuss these issues further to illustrate a style of decision-making analysis that has been frequently referred to as *signal-detection theory* (Green & Swets, 1966; Swets, 1964).

Signal-detection theory assumes that we make decisions on the basis of what we perceived, and that such perceptual processes are subject to variability and error. As such, decisions are not based on what is actually happening, but on what we *perceive* to be happening, which could be different. Consider the example in which a production-line employee's job is to inspect glassware, searching for flaws or defects in color or shape. The employee examines each piece and, based on what she sees, accepts the good glasses and rejects the flawed ones, which are then destroyed. Table 3.4 presents the four possible outcomes of making a decision about the glass. Here, the two possible decisions to be made by the employee are combined with two "truths" regarding whether or not the glass was actually flawed. In two situations the employee makes a correct decision: when she judges a flawed glass to be flawed (called a *hit*), and when she judges an acceptable glass as acceptable (termed a *correct rejection*).[4] However, in two other cases, the employee makes an error. In one case, she judges an actually acceptable glass as flawed (called a *false alarm*); in the other, she fails to detect the flaw in the glass and judges it as acceptable (called a *miss*).

Signal-detection theory assumes that the "strength" of the perceptual information about which a decision is to be made varies along a continuum, and has a *normal distribution* (i.e., has a dispersion of scores with known statistical properties) as seen in figure 3.18; by convention, the area under these normal curves is taken to be 1.0. There are two curves here, one representing

TABLE 3.4. Four Possible Outcomes of a Decision to See a Flaw in a Glass

		EMPLOYEE'S DECISION	
		No (no flaw)	Yes (flaw in glass)
ACTUAL ("TRUTH")	Glass is not flawed	Correct rejection	False alarm
	Glass is flawed	Miss	Hit

the situation with a (truly) flawed glass (curve on the right in figure 3.18) and one indicating an acceptable glass (curve on the left in figure 3.18); of course, for a given glass, only one of these curves can exist, depending on whether or not it is actually flawed, so only one of these two curves can actually exist at the same time. The x-axis represents a hypothetical measure of the "strength" of the sensory information pointing to the conclusion that a particular glass is flawed, with increased strength (moving to the right along the axis) indicating more (or "stronger") information that a flaw exists. A particular glass has a particular strength for an observer, with some dispersion about the mean because the perceptual processes are variable or "noisy." The y-axis refers to the probability that a certain strength will be perceived on some occasion when the mean strength is at the center of the curve. The y-axis refers to the probability that a particular perceptual strength will occur. In our example, for a given glass, sometimes the glass appears to be more flawed than it is and sometimes it appears to be less flawed. And, for an acceptable glass (left curve), sometimes the unflawed glass even *appears* to be more flawed than an actually flawed one, leading to errors in judgment by our employee.

Setting the Criterion

According to signal-detection theory, the actual process by which humans make decisions occurs when a *criterion* (a kind of cutoff point) is set along the x-axis, as illustrated in figure 3.18. The location of the criterion is usually described by a measure called β (beta; see Green & Swets, 1966, for a formal definition). Here we have the curves for the two glasses, but have added the criterion at 33 "strength units." This criterion is set by the employee as a result of the task instructions, her experience, and various biases she might have about the task. The criterion is a decision rule: Whenever the employee perceives the strength of the signal to be greater than 33 strength units, she makes the decision that the glass is flawed; if the signal is less than or equal to 33 strength units, she decides that the glass is acceptable. This provides a "rule" that the employee uses to make decisions as she examines the various glasses.

The setting of the criterion allows the employee to adjust the sizes of the various kinds of errors she is willing to make (in table 3.4). Suppose that the employee is biased by a perfectionist employer so she feels that a flawed glass should never go undetected. In this case the employee would set the criterion very far to the left (say, around 20—far to the left of the flawed-glass curve in figure 3.18), so that essentially *all* of the actually flawed glasses would be detected and destroyed. The problem with this is that many actually acceptable glasses would be destroyed as well (i.e., those glasses to the right of "20" on the acceptable-glass curve in figure 3.18). On the

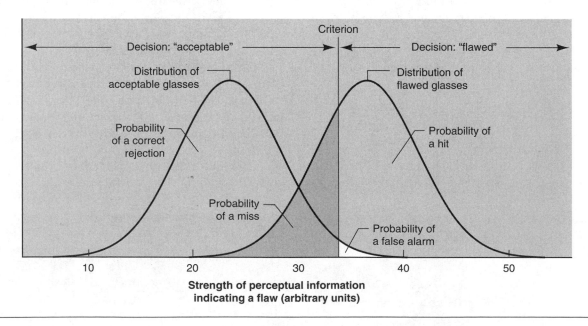

FIGURE 3.18 Basic components of signal-detection theory.

other hand, if maximizing production volume is the employer's goal and some flaws are tolerated, then the employee would set the criterion farther to the right (say, around 40), so that an acceptable glass is almost never judged to be flawed. In doing so, however, she will accept some flawed glasses. Thus, this procedure allows the employee to "trade off" the quality of the glassware for the quantity of glassware produced—a classic issue in manufacturing. Another classic example in signal-detection analysis is the job of the radiologist, which is to detect the presence or absence of a tumor in an X-ray (Swets, Dawes, & Monahan, 2000). There are many other practical examples, especially in situations in which the individual must make a decision based on sensory information.

Misses and False Alarms

Now, with the addition of the criterion, we can relate the curves in figure 3.18 to the types of decisions represented in table 3.4. Consider the rightmost curve, indicating that the glass being judged by the employee is actually flawed. Given the employee's criterion at 33, the probability of detecting that this glass is flawed is represented by the area to the right of the criterion (light gray shaded area), which is about 60% of the area falling beneath the flawed-glasses curve. Note that this is the probability of a *hit*—correctly detecting that the flawed glass is flawed [i.e., p*(hit)* = 0.60]. On the other hand, the probability of judging this glass acceptable is the remaining 40% of the area under the flawed-glasses curve that lies to the left of the criterion (dark gray shading). This is the probability of a *miss*—judging that a flawed glass is acceptable [i.e., p*(miss)* = 0.40].

Next, consider the case in which the employee is examining an actually acceptable glass, represented by the curve on the left in figure 3.18. Here, the probability of judging this glass as flawed is represented by the area under the left curve lying to the right of the criterion (white section), which represents about 15% of the area under the acceptable-glasses curve. This decision is a *false alarm*, because the acceptable glass was judged to be flawed [i.e., p*(false alarm)* = 0.15]. Finally, the probability of judging the good glass to be acceptable is given as the area under the left curve to the left of the criterion (light gray shaded area), which represents the remaining 85% of the area under the acceptable-glasses curve. This was

termed correct rejection, because the acceptable glass was correctly rejected as one being flawed [i.e., p*(correct rejection)* = 0.85].

Reducing Errors

In this kind of analysis, the two types of errors in table 3.4 occur because of *overlap* in the distributions seen in figure 3.18. This overlap can be reduced in essentially two ways, as shown in figure 3.19. We can see one way by comparing the top example in figure 3.19 with the middle example, in which the classes of objects being evaluated are more physically different. Imagine a situation in which the manufacturing process produces glasses that either are essentially perfect or have a massive flaw (e.g., a severe discoloration). Now, the means of the "acceptable" and "flawed" distributions are far apart, resulting in very little or no overlap and essentially no misses or false alarms (middle example). Secondly, overlap can be smaller if the variability of the two distributions is reduced, as seen in the bottom example in figure 3.19, while the means are kept the same distance apart as in the top example. Ways to accomplish this might be to enhance training for the employees, to select people who are very talented perceptually, or to provide more effective lighting or background conditions to facilitate visual detection. There are nearly countless real-world examples. One of these concerns the effect of viewing conditions on signal-detection errors when soccer officials make offside calls; the visual angle at which the play was viewed contributes greatly to the specific types of errors made (Oudejans et al., 2000; see also Baldo, Ranvaud, & Morya, 2002).

The Nature of Decision-Making Errors

One of the advantages of signal-detection methods has to do with evaluation of the nature of the errors that subjects make, as well as evaluation of the effects of various experimental variables (e.g., lighting conditions) on detection. Benefits in accuracy can come in essentially two different ways.

First, consider our example with glassware-flaw detection under different lighting conditions. From figure 3.20 (p. 89), assume that the employee chooses to enhance the lighting in her workplace, and that this enhanced lighting produces a shift in the employee's criterion (i.e., a shift in β), say to the right from 25 to 35 units. This shift in β results in a reduction in false alarms, but at the same time produces an *increase* in misses. These kinds

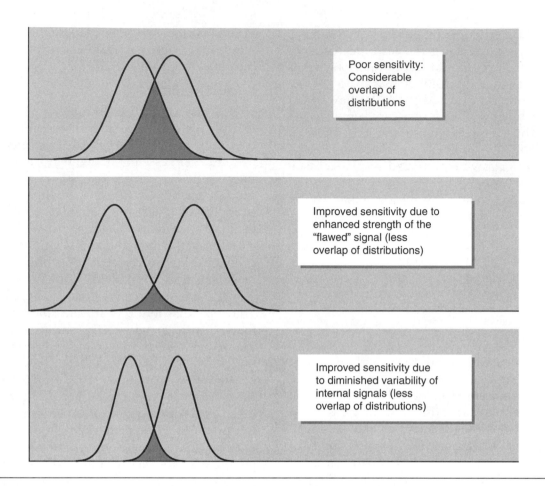

Poor sensitivity: Considerable overlap of distributions

Improved sensitivity due to enhanced strength of the "flawed" signal (less overlap of distributions)

Improved sensitivity due to diminished variability of internal signals (less overlap of distributions)

FIGURE 3.19 Effects of reducing variability in signal-detection judgments.

of changes, and the shift in the types of errors that result, reflect the subject's voluntary choice of criterion (β), perhaps due to lighting choices, or perhaps because of a new directive from the company hierarchy, new ownership, or the like.

Second, the effects of the lighting change might reduce the variability in her detections, as in figure 3.19 (bottom example). This kind of shift reflects a fundamental change in detection *sensitivity* and is independent of a shift in criterion (β). This kind of shift in sensitivity is reflected in a measure called d' ("d-prime"), which represents the amount of separation between the means of the two distributions.[5] Note that when this happens, the number of both misses and false alarms can be reduced because the subject has become a more sensitive "detector" of the flaws.

Finally, experimenters examining decision making usually report both β and d' in their experimental write-ups. In our example, we might have said that the lighting conditions produced a shift in β, but also an increase in d'.

The reader would then know that the improved lighting conditions increased the fundamental detection sensitivity (d'), but also had an effect on the subject's choice of criterion (β).

Memory

So far, our focus has been on what happens to information as it enters the system and is processed, eventually leading to a response. Information must be retained (some would use the word "stored") for future use, perhaps in a way analogous to how information is stored in a computer or library. The persistence of this information that is stored for future processing is called *memory*.

Memory is one of the most controversial and highly debated topics of information processing. Researchers tend to conceptualize ideas and experimental methods according to particular theoretical *frameworks,* and these vary greatly among psychologists. We briefly present one of

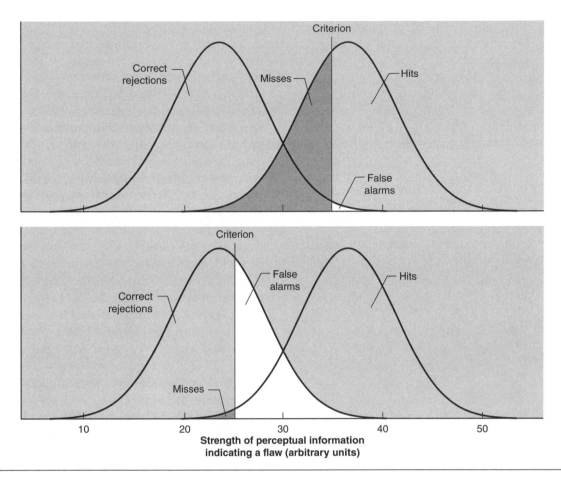

FIGURE 3.20 Effects of shifting the criterion on signal-detection errors.

these frameworks. However, the interested reader should consult the many books on this topic for more complete discussions (e.g., Roediger, 2008a).

In this viewpoint, memory is considered to be a consequence of information processing. When previously processed information influences current information processing, we assume that memory is the reason. Indeed, when viewed this way, it is obvious that everything we do is influenced by memory. The current state of our skills and knowledge reflects previous information processing. Thus, there seems to be no doubt that memories exist. Rather, the debate among psychologists concerns (1) how memory affects the performance of our daily activities and (2) what form these memories might take.

Direct Versus Indirect Influences of Memory

Memory seems to influence our daily activities in two rather distinct and separate ways.

Memory has a direct influence when one makes a deliberate attempt to recollect past experiences for the purpose of facilitating current information processing (e.g., Richardson-Klavehn & Bjork, 1988). For example, one of life's awkward moments occurs when you meet an acquaintance on the street and cannot recall the person's name. In this case, there is a failure to recall a specific memory as a purposeful and explicit means to solve a problem (addressing the person by name). Scientists use terms such as memory *search* and *retrieval* to describe deliberate attempts to use memory in a direct way.

Memory can also have an indirect effect on information processing. For example, in the act of typing, the production of the letters on the computer screen is determined by coordinated actions of the two hands. In this case, the memory for past experience (i.e., learning) in typing is having an indirect impact on the ability to carry out this activity. You do not need to recollect specifically when you last typed, or even when you learned to type, in order for the memory of the skill to influence your performance. One does not have to be conscious that memory is being used in order for it to influence performance. Motor skill can be described mainly in terms of an indirect memory influence. Since this book is about the learning and control of motor skills, our interest in memory is in how it affects current information processing indirectly. However, much of what is known about memory comes from experiments in which subjects are asked to recall or recognize information in a direct manner (i.e., consciously).

In the remainder of this chapter, we describe a rather traditional distinction that psychologists have made among various memory systems, customarily labeled *short-term sensory store (STSS)*, *short-term memory (STM)*, and *long-term memory (LTM)*. In the last chapter of the book (chapter 14, "Retention and Transfer"), we focus on the indirect influences that memory for motor skill has on our daily activities.

Psychologists sometimes refer to these ideas as "box theories" of memory, because the storage systems are often discussed as if they were *places* in which information is stored, which is a common metaphor for memory (e.g., like a computer hard drive or a university library). However, one should note that this is just one way to conceptualize memory—other views discuss memory simply as the persistence of the products of information processing, without taking a stand about memory's location. This reflects one of the many controversies that make the study of memory so interesting (see Roediger, 2008b, for a compelling historical review of the memory literature).

Short-Term Sensory Store

The most peripheral memory is thought to hold massive amounts of information, but only for brief periods of time. When information is presented to the system, STSS accepts it without much recoding and then loses it rather quickly as new information is added. Just as the redness of a burner on an electric stove fades when the burner is turned off, the information in the STSS is thought to fade or *decay* with the passage of time. Such a system can be proposed for each of the stimulus modalities—vision, touch, audition, kinesthesis, and so on.

Some of the earliest and strongest evidence about STSS came from the work of Sperling

(1960). Sperling presented a matrix of three rows of four letters each on a tachistoscope, a device for presenting visual information very briefly and under controlled conditions. The matrix was presented for 50 ms so that the subjective impression was a bright flash of the letters. One of three tones was also presented, indicating which row of four letters the subject was to recall. The tone could be presented 100 ms before the letter matrix was flashed on, simultaneously with the letter matrix, or 150, 300, or 1,000 ms after the matrix appeared.

The number of letters recalled in Sperling's experiment is plotted as a function of the temporal location of the tone in figure 3.21. When the tone was presented before the letters, the recall was about 3.3 letters (out of 4). When the tone was presented 150 ms after the letters, recall was only about 2.3 letters. When the tone was presented after a full second, recall was only about 1.5 letters.

The concept revealed in Sperling's experiment is that all of the letters are delivered by the flash to STSS, where they are stored briefly. However, the subject does not know which of the rows to attend to until the tone is presented. If the tone is presented immediately, the letters are still available and the subject can recall them. But if the

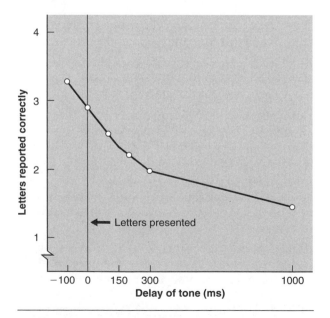

FIGURE 3.21 Number of items correctly recalled as a function of the delay of the tone indicating which row should be recalled.

Reprinted from G. Sperling, 1960, "The information available in brief visual presentations," *Psychological Monographs* 74: 498.

tone is delayed, the letters have begun to decay from STSS and the subject cannot report as many of them. This evidence suggests that (a) STSS is capable of holding all the information presented to it (because the subject could report any of the letters in the row if the tone was presented immediately) and (b) STSS loses information very rapidly with time.

On the basis of later experiments, the information in STSS is thought to have a maximum duration of about 1 s, with a more practical limit of about 250 ms. Also, it involves rather *literal* storage of information, in that the stimulus is recorded in the same way it came into the system in terms of both spatial location and form; this is analogous perhaps to how film records images that enter the lens of the camera (see table 3.5). Contents of STSS are then available for further processing.

Short-Term Memory

Short-term memory is thought to be a storage system for information delivered either from STSS or from LTM. It has a limited capacity and a relatively short duration. Originally, STM was thought of as a kind of "work space" for processing, and one where *control processes* such as decision making, rehearsal, coding, and so on are performed (Atkinson & Shiffrin, 1971). Peterson and Peterson (1959) and Brown (1958) provided evidence for this kind of system that was to have a strong influence on research in memory for the next two decades. In the paradigm developed by Peterson and Peterson, subjects were provided with a single *trigram* (three unrelated letters, e.g., XBF) for a period of study time; then the letters were removed, and the subjects had to count backward by threes from a three-digit number until recall of the trigram was requested, from 0 to 18 s later. The backward counting was intended to prevent the subject from rehearsing the trigram

during the retention interval. Thus, all the subject had to do was remember the trigram after counting backward for up to 18 s.

Peterson and Peterson's results are shown in figure 3.22, where the probability of successfully recalling the trigram is graphed as a function of the length of the retention interval. When the recall was nearly immediate, the probability of recall was about 0.90; but when the retention interval was increased only by a few seconds, there was a marked decrease in the recall. This persisted until, at 18 s, almost no trigrams could be recalled. The evidence suggests the existence of a memory system that loses information rapidly (in about 30 to 60 s) unless the information is *rehearsed* in some way.

Short-Term Memory Versus Short-Term Sensory Store

A major difference between STSS and STM (table 3.5) relates to capacity. Previously we mentioned that the capacity of STSS is very large—practically limitless. However, on the basis of experiments in which subjects have been asked to remember as many members of a list of items as they can, evidence suggests that STM has a capacity (often called the *span* of memory) of only about seven (plus or minus two) items (Miller, 1956). This conclusion, however, depends on the definition of an "item." Sometimes subjects organize separate items into larger groups, so that each group may contain five "items" of its own; this process has been termed *chunking* (Miller, 1956). The idea is that if there are 55 letters to remember (e.g., the number of letters in the first sentence in this paragraph), it would be difficult to remember them as completely separate items without chunking. By chunking the letters into larger, more meaningful groups (words or sentences), one can recall the items more easily. In this sense, the capacity of STM is thought to be seven chunks. Ericsson, Chase, and Faloon (1980) showed that after 175

	MEMORY SYSTEM		
Attribute	**STSS**	**STM**	**LTM**
Storage duration	Less than 1 s	1 s to 60 s	Seemingly limitless
Type of coding	Very literal	More abstract	Very abstract
Capacity	Seemingly limitless	7 ± 2 items	Seemingly limitless

TABLE 3.5. Characteristics of the Three Memory Systems

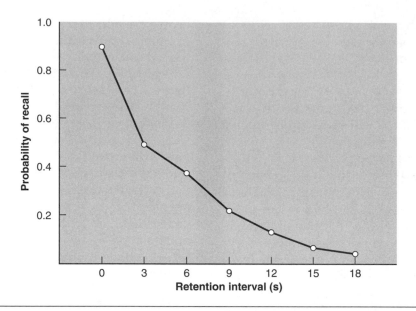

FIGURE 3.22 Probability of correct recall of a single trigram as a function of the retention interval.

Reprinted from L.R. Peterson and M.J. Peterson, 1959, "Short-term retention of individual verbal items," *Journal of Experimental Psychology* 58: 198.

days of practice with a technique for chunking effectively, a subject was able to increase the capacity of STM from 7 to 79 items by creating larger and larger chunks. Therefore, there were probably only about seven chunks or groups of items held in storage at any one time.

Another distinction between STM and STSS (table 3.5) is in the nature of the coding processes. In STM, coding is considered to be abstract. For example, stimuli are given names, and the separate stimuli are often combined in various ways to produce chunks that can reduce the number of separate items in STM. Although many theories of STM do not directly say so, the implication is that STM is related to consciousness; those things in STM are essentially things of which we are consciously aware.

Working Memory

Atkinson and Shiffrin's (1971) earlier notion was that STM comprised a kind of limited capacity "work space" where various operations were performed. More recently, this view of STM has been expanded and incorporated into the notion of *working memory* (e.g., Baddeley, 2003). Although there are differing viewpoints, the essential idea is that working memory is a part of STM where (a) information from STSS can be stored for processing, (b) information from LTM can be retrieved for processing and integrated with information from STSS, and (c) effortful and

limited-capacity conscious processing (*controlled processing*, discussed further in chapter 4) can be performed. Working memory is thought to contain items in a high level of activation for rapid access, but these are lost relatively quickly unless they are attended to, rehearsed, or allocated some of the limited capacity (Anderson, 1990).

For motor behavior, the most important idea is that information processing entailing the choice of actions is involved in working memory, which suggests that working memory is closely related to the response-selection stage mentioned earlier in this chapter. Also, during the response-programming stage, information in the form of stored motor programs—described more fully in chapter 6—or other well-learned information about a task can be retrieved from LTM. In working memory, presumably, environmental information from STSS (such as the locations of seen objects, speed of a flying ball) can be integrated with information from LTM, creating what some term an "action plan" that takes into account one's stored capabilities and the specific environmental demands. The prepared movements are then triggered from working memory to generate muscle contractions and actions.

Motor Short-Term Memory

In a motor analog of verbal STM, Adams and Dijkstra (1966; Posner & Konick, 1966) asked blindfolded subjects to move a slide along a trackway until it struck a fixed stop that defined a criterion target position. Then the subject moved back to the starting position to wait for the remainder of the retention interval (from 10 to 120 s), after which the subject attempted to move the slide to the criterion position with the stop removed. The absolute error in recalling the position increased sharply as the retention interval increased from 10 to 60 s and changed very little thereafter (figure 3.23). These findings closely paralleled the early findings of Brown (1958) and Peterson and Peterson (1959) with verbal materials, in that nearly all the forgetting of the position occurred within the first 60 s, which is interpreted as the approximate upper limit for retention in short-term verbal memory. Chapter 14 presents more about short-term motor memory studies. Long ago, James (1890) proposed the distinction between "primary memory" (what is today called STM) and "secondary memory" (today's LTM), described next.

Long-Term Memory

When items are practiced (or rehearsed), which of course requires information-processing activities, they are in some way transferred from short-term storage to long-term storage, where they can be held more permanently and protected from loss.

An example is learning a new phone number. The first time you hear it, you are likely to forget it quickly if you do not rehearse it. Practice results in the transfer of the number to more permanent storage. In some cases, this storage is indeed permanent. Can you remember what your home phone number was when you were a child? We can.

Long-term memory, of course, provides the capability for making movements that have been practiced before. Some of the variables that appear to determine retention of well-learned acts are discussed in chapter 14. For now we can say that practice leads to the development of "better" or "stronger" (or both) LTM for movement and that these memories are often present after many years, even without intervening use of that stored information. Riding a bicycle is the most often cited example, as people appear to be able to ride acceptably well after 40 years or more with *no* intervening practice.

Another major distinction between LTM and STM relates to the amount of information that can be held (table 3.5). Most argue that STM has a functional capacity of about seven chunks, whereas LTM must have a very large capacity indeed. In the motor realm, the analog of well-learned facts and principles is well-learned motor skills. Thus, the functional capacity of motor LTM must also be very large if it is capable of retaining all of the movements that humans can typically perform on demand.

Summary

We can understand a great deal about the way people move by considering the human as an information-processing system that takes in information from the environment, processes it, and then outputs information to the environment in the form of movements. Using the concepts of subtractive logic first advanced by Donders (1868/1969), *stages of processing* can be defined and studied through the use of RT methods. The first stage, called *stimulus identification*, concerns the reception of a stimulus, preliminary (preconscious) analyses of features, and extraction of patterns from the stimulus array. Variables like stimulus clarity and stimulus intensity affect the duration of processing in this stage. A second stage, called *response selection*, concerns the translation

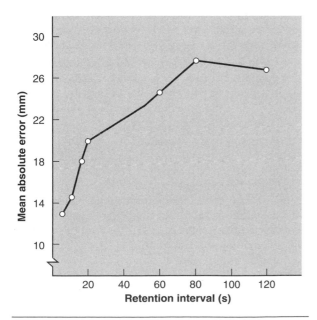

FIGURE 3.23 Absolute error in positioning recall as a function of the retention interval length.

Reprinted, by permission, from J.A. Adams and S. Dijkstra, 1966, "Short-term memory for motor responses," *Journal of Experimental Psychology* 71: 317.

or decision mechanisms that lead to the choice of response. The duration of this stage is sensitive to variables such as the number of S-R alternatives and S-R compatibility (the extent to which the stimulus and response are "naturally" linked). The final stage, called *response programming,* is associated with changing the abstract idea of a response into muscular action. The duration of this stage is related to variables affecting the response, such as response complexity and response duration. Some of the processing in some of these stages can apparently be bypassed by anticipation. Providing both spatial and temporal predictability allows so-called early responding, whereas providing other information leads to increased readiness and faster response.

Another aspect of information processing that considers factors related to making decisions has been termed signal-detection theory and involves two separate types of information-processing activities: setting the criterion for making a decision, and the sensitivity of the system that is used to make the decision. Factors such as the relative importance of the type of error that would result from a wrong decision are major influences on setting the criterion, whereas the skill level of the participant and the nature of the environmental information are major factors in the sensitivity of the information upon which the decision is based.

Parallel to the ideas about stages of processing are concepts about information storage systems, or memory. Motor skills use memory in an indirect way, although much of what we know about memory involves directed remembering. In a common framework, memory can be thought of as consisting of three compartments: a *short-term sensory store (STSS),* capable of storing a large amount of literally coded information for perhaps a second; a *short-term memory (STM,* sometimes discussed as *working memory),* capable of storing only about seven (plus or minus two) abstractly coded items for perhaps 30 s, as well as providing a kind of "work space" for conscious information processing; and a *long-term memory (LTM)* capable of storing very large amounts of abstractly coded information for long periods of time.

Student Assignments

1. Answer the following questions and bring the information to class for discussion:

a. Discuss an everyday-life example of uncertainty that illustrates the concept of information theory.

b. Choose any sport to illustrate the contributions of each of the three stages of information processing.

c. Using the same sport as for question 1b, describe examples of the various kinds of anticipation.

2. Find a research article that uses signal-detection theory to describe processes involved in decision making.

Web Resources

A fun choice-RT game with variable foreperiod delays:

> www.bbc.co.uk/science/humanbody/sleep/sheep/

A number of experiments related to concepts in chapter 3 can be run from this Web site:

> www.artsci.wustl.edu/~rabrams/psychlab/index.htm

Notes

[1] It is fitting that today, F.C. Dondersstraat (which would be translated as "F.C. Donders Street" in English) runs adjacent to Donders' original lab in Utrecht, Holland.

[2] Note that our description of Henry and Rogers' (1960) most complicated task (C) is slightly different than in earlier versions of this book, due to recent revelations about a small error in the describing the apparatus in the original article (Fischman et al., 2008).

[3] This finding is closely related to research on voluntary motor timing, which is discussed in considerable detail in chapter 7. Essentially, the research concludes that producing a string of regular time intervals (e.g., as in drumming) is more variable as the duration of the intervals lengthens (e.g., the variability in producing 1 s intervals is greater than the variability in producing 500 ms intervals). The foreperiod duration effect is similar—anticipating the *end* of a regular foreperiod is more variable as the foreperiod duration lengthens.

[4] Perhaps the use of the labels "hit" and "correct rejection" in this example is confusing. Consider that the employee is searching for a flawed glass and, when she finds one, this is a hit. Accepting a "good" glass is then a correct rejection (i.e., a "good" glass is rejected as being a flawed glass).

[5] Students often find this confusing because the separation (in centimeters) between the means in the top and bottom panels in figure 3.19 is the same. But these are actually measured in standard deviation (Z) units based on the standard deviation of the distributions, and these units are smaller in the lower panel than in the upper panel because the variation of the distributions is smaller. The second panel has a larger d' than the top panel because the separation is greater with similar standard deviations; it is larger in the lower panel than the top panel because of the reduction of standard deviation with a constant mean difference.

CHAPTER 4

ATTENTION AND PERFORMANCE

Attention has always been a topic of major interest to psychologists and motor behavior researchers. Early research and theorizing began in the 19th century (Cattell, 1886; Welch, 1898), and interest in the topic remains high today. Much of the early work involved introspection; for example, William James (1890), one of the most renowned experimental psychologists, wrote:

> Everyone knows what attention is. It is the taking possession by the mind, in clear and vivid form, of one out of what seem several simultaneously possible objects or trains of thought. Focalization, concentration, of consciousness are of its essence. It implies withdrawal from some things in order to deal effectively with others. (pp. 403-404)

But does everyone *agree* on what attention is? Many theorists, such as Norman (1976) and Moray (1970), suggested that different definitions of attention exist, and people use the term in a variety of ways. Consider the task of driving a car. Drivers must be aware of a preplanned route, as well as where they currently are in relation to the route, in order to make appropriate turns at the right times. The driver must also be aware of other traffic (e.g., cars, pedestrians, and bicyclists) and be capable of responding to sudden changes. The control of movement requires another type of attention, although we spend less time and energy thinking about how

to coordinate our limbs in time and space as skill develops. Still other types of attention are required to offset the mental drowsiness that accompanies long periods of driving without rest, or to talk on a cell phone. So, as we read in the quote from William James' description of attention, a number of features of the phenomenon are considered important and reflect various ways to think about the different *types* of attention that may exist.

Types of Attention

There are many different ways to view the concept of attention. One of these is the notion that attention is *limited:* We can attend to only one thing at a time, or think only one thought at a time. In terms of motor behavior, we seem strongly limited in the number of things we can do at a given time, as if the limits to some maximum "capacity" would be exceeded if too much activity were attempted. Another important feature is that attention is *selective:* We can concentrate on one thing or on something else, and can freely shift attention back and forth among numerous things. Here we discuss a few of the types of attention that are particularly relevant in the control of motor skills. Note, however, that the topic of attention entails a very broad research area—much more than can be covered in this chapter. The interested reader is encouraged to seek out some of the many excellent recent reviews for more in-depth discussion of attention (e.g., Baddeley & Weiskrantz, 1993; Folk & Gibson, 2001; Neumann & Sanders, 1996; Pashler, 1999; Shapiro, 2001; Wickens & McCarley, 2008).

Attention and Consciousness

Early in the history of research on human performance, as implied by James' (1890) statement, attention was linked to the notion of consciousness, which is defined loosely as "what we are aware of at any given time." The term "conscious," and in particular the concept of *unconscious behavior,* fell out of favor during the growth of behaviorism after the turn of the 20th century. The measurement of consciousness was troublesome because at the time the only way to understand what was "in" subjects' consciousness was to ask them to introspect, or "search their own minds," and this was far too subjective for the behaviorists' approach to accumulating data and theorizing.

Toward the end of the 20th century, however, the concept of consciousness saw a resurgence in popularity among cognitive neuroscientists, and that interest continues to grow (Cohen & Schooler, 1996; Posner & Petersen, 1990). Examining brain function using methods such as fMRI (functional magnetic resonance imaging) and TMS (transcranial magnetic stimulation) (see chapter 2) has allowed scientists to measure patterns of brain activity, revealing much more objective types of information than had previously been available through methods of introspection (Baars, 1997; Chalmers, 1995; Crick & Koch, 2003; Haggard, Clark, & Kalogeras, 2002). Consciousness has also been linked to the concept of *controlled versus automatic* processing (discussed later in this chapter). Performance on various memory tests (Roediger & McDermott, 1993), and the use of process-dissociation measures (Jacoby, Ste-Marie, & Toth, 1993), suggests an independence between conscious and unconscious influences on behavior. For example, automatic (unconscious) processing appears to be preserved well in older adults, whereas controlled (conscious) processing is quite susceptible to decline with aging (Craik & Jacoby, 1996; Hasher & Zacks, 1988). Performance errors such as *action slips* (Norman, 1981) are often

explained as situations in which an unconscious or automatic action has not been successfully inhibited or counteracted by conscious, controlled processing (Hay & Jacoby, 1996; Reason, 1990; Reason & Mycielska, 1982).

Attention as Effort or Arousal

Another way to operationalize the notion of attention is based on the idea that when people perform attention-demanding tasks such as balancing a checkbook or diving in competitive swimming, they are expending mental *effort* that is revealed in various physiological measures. For example, Kahneman (1973) and Beatty (Beatty & Wagoner, 1978) have used pupil diameter, measured by special techniques that do not interfere with eye movement, as an indirect measure of attention. When subjects are asked to perform various memory tasks, pupil diameter increases when they are under pressure to provide an answer; the increase is larger for more "difficult" tasks. Similarly, it is useful to consider attention as reflected by various physiological measures of arousal, a dimension indicating the extent to which the subject is activated or excited. Kahneman (1973) used physiological measures of skin resistance (resistance to a weak current passed between two electrodes on the skin decreases with increased arousal) and heart rate as indirect measures of the attention demand of various tasks.

Attention as a Capacity or Resource

Another view of attention, and one that is an important component of the information-processing concepts discussed in chapter 3, suggests that humans possess a *limitation* in the *capacity* (or resources) available to handle information from the environment. The idea for the concept of a limited capacity of attention is illustrated in the ability to perform two tasks simultaneously. If one activity *(A)* requires attention, then some (or perhaps all) of the "pool" of limited capacity of attention must be allocated to its performance. Because the amount of this capacity is thought to be limited, some other activity *(B)* that also requires a certain amount of this capacity will compete with *A* for these limited attentional resources. When the combined need for resources exceeds the total amount of attentional capacity available, then *B* will *interfere* with the performance of *A*, and vice versa. Interference could be demonstrated in many ways: (a) *B* could suffer in performance speed or quality while *A* was relatively unaffected; (b) *B* could be unaffected while *A* suffered; (c) both *A* and *B* could suffer; or (d) *B* could be prevented from occurring altogether while *A* was in progress. These patterns of "interference," or competition for attentional resources, could presumably tell us something about the nature of the limitations in capacity.

Interference as a Measure of Attention

If two tasks can be performed as well simultaneously as each can be performed individually, then at least one of them does not require attention, or a portion of the limited capacity. We would say that at least one of the tasks is "automatic." On the other hand, if one task is performed less well when it is combined with some secondary task, then both tasks are thought to require some of the limited capacity. In this instance, both tasks are *attention demanding*. Over the past few decades, this *interference criterion* became the critical test of whether or not a certain task "required attention." Although this test for attention achieved popularity during the cognitive revolution, it is not really a new research method (Welch, 1898).

Structural Interference and Capacity Interference

The simultaneous performance of two tasks can result in interference between them for a variety of reasons, only some of which would be interpretable as interference due to limitations in some central capacity (attention). To confront this problem, researchers have defined two kinds of interference: structural and capacity. *Structural interference* results when physical (or neurological) structures are the source of the decrement. For example, the hand can be in only one place at a time, and interference between handwriting and pressing the buttons to make a phone call with the same hand would be due, at least in part, to this kind of limitation and not necessarily to a limitation in some central capacity. Also, the eyes can focus at only one signal source at a time, and thus detecting two simultaneous visual signals presented in widely different locations could suffer in processing speed because of a structural limitation, again not necessarily due to limitations in attentional capacity. On the other hand, when one can reasonably rule out the possibility that structural interference between two tasks is occurring, then a *capacity interference*—or a decrement in performance due to some limitation in central capacity (i.e., attention)—is inferred.

The concerns about "distracted driving" provide a good example of the difference between structural and capacity interference. Many laws dealing with distracted driving ban the use of *handheld* communication devices, the argument being that the perceptual and motor requirements for communicating with the device create structural interference with the hand and eye movements required for driving. The more important problem, however, is that the task of communication is not simply a structural interference issue—*hands-free* communication devices also interfere with the task of driving because of the attention (capacity interference) required to use them.

Selective Attention

Very closely related to the limited-capacity view is the concept that we can direct (or *allocate*) attention to different inputs or tasks. Selective attention can be either *intentional* or *incidental*, depending on how a specific allocation has been achieved (Eimer, Nattkemper, Schröger, & Prinz, 1996). Intentional selection occurs when we purposefully choose to attend to one source of information (e.g., listening to the radio) while avoiding or inhibiting attention to other sources (e.g., the television or someone talking to us). An involuntary capture of attention usually occurs as a response to an external stimulus—for example, when you suddenly pay attention to a loud or pertinent sound (e.g., the sound of two cars colliding). Theorists sometimes refer to intentional selection as "top-down" processing, and involuntary selection as "bottom-up" processing, to indicate that the orienting of attention is conceptually versus perceptually driven.

Selective attention is readily observed in the patterns of interference already mentioned in dual-task situations. Directing attention toward activity *A* may reveal deficits in the performance of task *B*, although no performance deficit is observed for *A*. However, by shifting the attention to activity *B*, you may observe that activity *A* is now the one that suffers and that performance of *B* is very proficient.

Theories of Attention

If attention is defined as, or measured by, the degree of interference between two tasks, then which kinds of tasks do and do not interfere with each other, and under what conditions might these patterns of interference be expected to occur? Most of the everyday tasks we perform can be thought of as collections of processes involving stimulus input and encoding, response selection and choice, and motor programming and movement control. The fact that two complex tasks interfere with each other (or do not) might not be very meaningful by itself, because it would not be clear what the cause of the interference was or where in the information-processing activities the interference occurred (Jonides, Naveh-Benjamin, & Palmer, 1985). Did the two tasks require response-selection activities at the same time, or did they require movement programming at the same time? As a result, simpler laboratory tasks are used often in this research so that the various processing stages can be more specifically identified and studied. The following theories of attention attempt to explain the patterns of interference found in performing these types of tasks, using various hypothetical structures and processes.

Single-Channel, Filter Theories

Some of the first few theories of attention (e.g., Broadbent, 1958; Deutsch & Deutsch, 1963; Keele, 1973; Norman, 1969; Treisman, 1969; Welford, 1952; see also B. Kerr, 1973), while different in detail, had some important features in common. They all assumed that attention was a *fixed* capacity for processing information and that performance would deteriorate if this capacity was approached or exceeded by the task requirements. These were single-channel theories of *undifferentiated capacity*, in that attention was thought of as a single resource that could be directed at any one of a number of processing operations. Theorists often described single-channel theories as *bottleneck* theories of attention, because the "neck" limits the information that can be later processed and its location determines when interference is likely to occur. Here, as shown in figure 4.1, information flow is left to right, and many operations can occur at the same time in the large part of the bottle; but, at some point, a "bottleneck" is encountered, which allows only one operation

at a time. A major question for these attention theorists was where (e.g., early or late) such a bottleneck, or "filter," was located. These filter theories differed in terms of the kinds of information processing that required attention and, therefore, the location of the bottleneck during the stages of information processing.

Early-Filter Theories

Welford's (1952) theory assumed that *all* processes require attention; in other words, the human could be regarded as a single information channel that could be occupied by one and only one stimulus–response operation (or "channel") at a time. As illustrated in figure 4.1, line 1, Welford's theory located the bottleneck at the earliest stage of information processing. Of course, if only one operation can be done at a time, then *any* task attempted at the same time as another task will interfere (or even be blocked altogether). Thus, this single-channel idea viewed a secondary task as a rather severe source of interference. For this reason, processing in the single channel is defined as attention demanding on the basis of the interference criterion described earlier.

Weaker versions of the single-channel theory denied that *all* the stages of processing require attention, especially the earliest stages, and therefore the location of the bottleneck was moved to a later stage in the sequence of processing. Thus, these other theories (Broadbent, 1958; Deutsch & Deutsch, 1963; Keele, 1973; B. Kerr, 1973; Norman, 1969; Treisman, 1969) presumed that early stages of processing occurred without attention but that attention was required at the later stage(s) of processing. Processing without attention implies *parallel processing*, such that a number of separate signals can be processed simultaneously without interfering with one another. For example, processes that translate sound waves into neurological impulses in the ear, and those that change mechanical stimuli into neurological activity in the movement receptors in the limbs, can occur together, presumably without interference. In other words, these theories assumed that peripheral (mainly sensory) information processing occurs simultaneously and without interference, but the theories differed with respect to the exact information-processing stages at which the interference occurs.

Broadbent (1958) and Deutsch and Deutsch (1963) theorized that a kind of *filter* is located

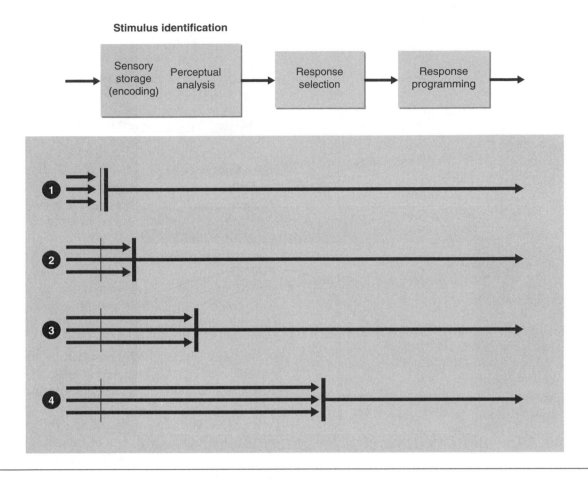

Stimulus identification

FIGURE 4.1   Utilization of attention in various stages of processing, according to various theories. (Line 1 represents the original single-channel theory [Welford, 1952]; line 2 represents Broadbent's [1958] filter theory; line 3 represents the Deutsch and Deutsch [1963] and Norman [1969] theories; and line 4 represents Keele's [1973] theory.)

somewhere along the series of stages of information processing (see figure 4.1, lines 2 and 3). According to these theories, many stimuli can be processed in parallel and do not require attention prior to reaching the filter. When the filter is reached, however, only one stimulus at a time is processed through it (the others being "filtered out"), so that the information processing from then on is sequential, requiring attention in the single channel. The decision regarding which stimuli are filtered out and which one is processed further into the single channel presumably depends on which signal arrives first to the filter, the nature of the activity in which stimuli are expected, and which stimuli are relevant to the task in question.

Lines 2 and 3 in figure 4.1 show the locations of the proposed filter for these two theories. The sensory storage stage is considered the most "peripheral," involving the translation of the physical stimuli into neurological signals. The perceptual analysis stage involves the process that abstracts some preliminary, simple meaning from the stimuli (e.g., perception of right angles, or verticality). (Notice that the stages labeled *sensory storage* and *perceptual analysis* in the language of these theorists can be readily combined to yield the stimulus-identification stage discussed in chapter 3.) Broadbent viewed perceptual analysis and later stages as requiring attention, while Deutsch and Deutsch, Treisman, and Norman saw perceptual analysis as automatic (i.e., not requiring attention), with later stages requiring attention. Thus, these theories are similar, but they differ with respect to where the proposed filter is located in the chain of processes.

Keele's Late-Filter Theory

Keele's (1973) theory of attention places the bottleneck even later in the sequence of stages than the Deutsch and Deutsch theory. According to Keele's concept, information is processed in parallel and thus is attention free through the stimulus-identification and response-selection stages. At this point, *memory contact* is made, in which certain associates of the stimuli are activated, such as items in related categories, items closely associated with the stimulus, or even certain aspects of early preparation for a movement that is to be triggered by the stimulus. In this view, because all such stimuli "contact memory" at about the same time, selective attention must determine which of these memory contacts are to receive further processing. These subsequent operations, such as memory searches, rehearsal, recoding, or readying a movement for production, are the ones that are attention demanding, according to Keele. If two such processes are required at the same time, decrements in performance will occur. Thus, Keele's view is represented as line 4 in figure 4.1, indicating that processing can be in parallel and without interference even through response selection, with subsequent operations requiring attention.

Flexible Allocation of Capacity

In contrast to filter theories, an argument presented by Kahneman (1973) was that the *capacity* of attention could change as the task requirements change. For example, as the "difficulty" of two simultaneous tasks increases, more capacity is used in processing the information. Eventually, when task requirements for processing two streams of information begin to exceed maximum capacity, decrements occur in one or more of the simultaneously presented tasks; that is, interference occurs. Kahneman's theory also differed from the earlier views by suggesting that parallel processing could occur in all of the processing stages, but with some demand on attention at the same time. Kahneman's view that the amount of allocated attention is not fixed creates a number of difficulties for certain secondary-task techniques for measuring spare capacity (see chapter 2), which assume that capacity is fixed.

Other theories of attention have focused on issues of flexibility in information processing. For example, rather than assuming that processes requiring attention can deal with only one stimulus at a time, other theories suggest that these resources can be shared by parallel processing. How they are shared is presumably a function of the relative importance of the tasks, their relative difficulty, and other factors. Trade-offs between proficiency in two simultaneous tasks have been discussed by Norman and Bobrow (1975), Posner and Snyder (1975), and Navon and Gopher (1979).

Multiple-Resource Theories

Some researchers have argued that attention should not be conceptualized as a *single* resource but rather as *multiple pools* of resources, each with its own capacity and each designed to handle certain kinds of information processing. In this view, for example, separate resources would be responsible for selecting the finger to make a movement and for selecting the movement of the jaw to say a word. Hence, these two operations could coincide without interference (e.g., McLeod, 1977; Navon & Gopher, 1979; Wickens, 1976, 1980; Wickens & Hollands, 2000).

Similarly, Shaffer (1971) and Allport, Antonis, and Reynolds (1972) argued that attention can be devoted to separate stages of processing at the same time. Such a position is inconsistent with fixed-capacity theories, in which the processing was thought to be confined to a single stage although it might be possible to perform one or more separate operations in parallel. These views help to explain skill in complex tasks such as typing, simultaneous translations, and sight-reading of music, for which attention is thought to be devoted to input (sight-reading) and output (muscular activation and control) stages at the same time.

Action-Selection Views of Attention

In all of the viewpoints about attention that have been described, the basic assumption is that information-processing activities require some kind of capacity (or "fuel") in order for behavior (skill) to occur. Decrements in performance result when various activities compete for this capacity. Some researchers however, question the validity of this fundamental assumption. Scientists such as Neumann (1987, 1996; see also Allport, 1987, 1993) have criticized the various resource theories and presented a view that is considerably different. Neumann argued that when an animal or human has a certain momentary intention to obtain some goal (e.g., to run, to drink), many stimuli received at this time are processed in parallel in the early stages—the final product of this processing being the selection of a certain action. Then, *as a result* of this selection, certain other processes are *prevented* from occurring, or can occur only with great difficulty. Thus in Neumann's view, interference between two simultaneous tasks occurs not because attention (as a resource) is needed in order to perform various processes; rather, it occurs *because* an action has already been selected, and these other processes are completely or partially blocked. Thus, *selection* is the most basic and fundamental process of attention, not resources or capacity (see earlier discussion of Keele's late-filter theory).

This theory has an interesting ecological aspect, in that if a particular action is important (e.g., escape from a predator) and is selected, then it would seem critical that other possible actions be prevented, at least for a while, until the original action has run its course. The selected action requires certain processes or structures for its completion, and preventing some other action from using them (and thus interfering with them) would ensure that the selected action would, in fact, have a good chance of being completed and of having its goal fulfilled. As we will see in the next sections, this theory is consistent with the general finding that very little interference occurs in processes related to stimulus processing, with most of the interference between tasks occurring in stages related to the planning or production of movements.

Competition for Attention

It is beyond the scope of this text to do a thorough analysis of the extensive literature documenting the patterns of interference among tasks. For our purposes, however, some generalizations about the nature of these patterns, as well as about the situations in which the most and least interference seems to be produced, will enable us to have a reasonable insight into the nature of attention, at least as it relates to the selection and control of movement.

Processing Unexpected Information

In this section, we examine the *competition* that exists for capturing attention—sometimes we are able to block or bypass things to which we do not want to attend, only to find that certain information is processed regardless of our intentions. Three specific research areas have arisen in the literature to demonstrate quite clearly that selective attention can be both *intentional* and *incidental*. The research areas discussed in the next sections include the Stroop effect, the "cocktail party phenomenon," and inattention blindness.

The Stroop Effect

A very interesting and powerful effect that helps us understand intentional and incidental information processing is the so-called *Stroop effect*, named after the psychologist who first identified the phenomenon (Stroop, 1935).[1] Many hundreds of research articles on the effect have been published since this classic article appeared, and the Stroop effect is now commonplace in numerous applications (MacLeod, 1991). The typical experiment involves at least two important conditions. In both, the subject is asked to watch a display and perform a simple task: to name the *ink color* in which a word is printed. In one condition, subjects are presented with a neutral word and asked to name the color in which it is printed (e.g., for the word "house" printed in blue ink, the subject's response would be "blue"). In the second condition, the word name is itself a color (e.g., for the word "blue" printed in blue ink, the subject's response would be "blue"). Typically, the time to respond by naming the color is very fast when the word and target color are the same, or *congruent*. However, when the word name and the color in which it is printed are not the same, or *incongruent*, the subject's response is typically delayed in time and quite prone to error (e.g., for the word "green" printed in blue ink, the subject's response should be "blue," but it is often incorrectly given as "green" or is delayed in time so that the error can be suppressed). This finding—namely that the color meaning of the word interferes with the naming of the ink color in which the word appears (if the two are incongruent)—represents the basic Stroop effect (many variations exist; see MacLeod, 1991, and MacLeod & MacDonald, 2000, for examples).

Why should an irrelevant dimension of the display (the name of the word) interfere with the intentional act of naming the color of the ink? Why cannot the subject simply focus on the color of the ink and ignore the word that the letters spell? One possibility is that since the processing speed for identifying the name of a color is slower than for naming a word (e.g., Fraise, 1969), the name of the word is more quickly readied as a response than is the name of the color. However, a clever experiment by Dunbar and MacLeod (1984) produced evidence that argued against this interpretation. In their studies, Dunbar and MacLeod presented the word names as you might see them in a mirror (reversed). Under these types of conditions, identifying the name of the word was much slower than naming the color. Nevertheless, the Stroop effect was still present when these mirror-oriented word names were presented in incongruent colors. Thus, the simple "speed of processing" explanation is insufficient to explain the Stroop effect. The resistance of the Stroop effect to conform to these and other theoretical predictions likely explains why psychologists have maintained a fascination with the nature of this attentional interference. A popular view is that the subject's inability to ignore the irrelevant message is evidence that the irrelevant signal (color name) and relevant signal (ink color) are processed in parallel, perhaps without any interference in the early stages of processing.

The "Cocktail Party Problem"

Another important illustration of the intentional and incidental effects of sensory-information processing is provided by the *dichotic-listening paradigm*. In a typical dichotic-listening experiment, the individual is presented (via headphones) with a different message in each ear. The subject's task is to ignore one of the messages and to concentrate on (and later report about) the other. Normally, subjects are very skilled at concentrating on the intended message (termed "shadowing" the message) and ignoring the message being presented to the other ear. However, when a message cannot be ignored, the implication is that it is being processed through the stimulus-identification stage whether the individual tries to ignore it or not, perhaps without attention being required for that processing.

The dichotic-listening paradigm is a formal way to study the "cocktail party problem" described by Cherry (1953). At large, noisy parties, attending to one conversation while ignoring the many other conversations is often quite difficult. But, with effort, the various potentially "interfering" conversations can be tuned out, just as they can in dichotic-listening experiments. Situations occur, however, in which the ongoing

discussion in one of these unattended conversations cannot be ignored, such as when your name is spoken. In this case, some feature of the ignored message "gets through" to conscious processing—it captures our attention.

The findings from the dichotic-listening paradigm led to the suggestion that all of the auditory stimuli are processed through stimulus identification in parallel and without attention, and that some mechanism operates to prevent attention from being drawn to unwanted sources of sound. When the sound is particularly relevant or pertinent to us (e.g., our name or a danger alert, such as the sound of a car's horn), the stimulus is allowed to "pass through" for additional processing and attention. Perhaps stimuli from the environment had entered the system simultaneously and had been processed to some superficial level of analysis, with only those relevant (or pertinent) to the individual being processed further. Of course, this further processing will usually require attention, implying that two such activities cannot be done together without interference. Like the evidence from the Stroop effect, the evidence from these observations argues against the early-selection models of attention presented in figure 4.1.

Inattention Blindness and Change Blindness

The "cocktail party phenomenon" is a nice illustration of how intentional and incidental human information processing coexist in daily activities. We can selectively filter out unwanted information yet be receptive to pertinent information when it arises. Another example of the competition for sensory-information processing illustrates a potentially dangerous consequence of selective attention—when intentional processing inhibits or prevents the processing of a critical sensory event. This failure to process incidental information is a frequent complaint in vehicle–bicyclist traffic accidents: The driver is looking for an available parking space or a specific street sign and fails to see the cyclist who is directly in front of the car. These are called "looked-but-failed-to-see" accidents (Hills, 1980) because the drivers often claim that they had been looking in the general direction of the accident victim but did not see the bicyclist at all (Herslund & Jørgensen, 2003; Koustanaï, Boloix, Van Elslande, & Bastien, 2008).

One of the common reasons given for looked-but-failed-to-see accidents relates to the findings from studies using *selective-looking* paradigms. Essentially, these methods use the visual analog of the dichotic-listening paradigm (Neisser & Becklen, 1975) to investigate the cause of *inattention blindness*—the failure to see certain visual stimuli when focusing on other stimuli. Typically, subjects in a selective-looking paradigm are asked to focus on (and report on) the activities occurring in a visual display, but later are asked to report on other (normally obvious) visual events that occurred at the same time. For example, subjects in a study by Simons and Chabris (1999) watched a video showing a basketball being passed among three players dressed in white shirts and another ball being passed among three players dressed in black shirts. The subject's task was to count the passes made by the team dressed in white and ignore the activities of the other team. What made this experiment particularly interesting was that an unusual event occurred about halfway through the video—a person dressed in a gorilla costume walked through the middle of the two teams, stopped and faced the camera, then continued walking off screen. The "gorilla" was in perfect focus and was superimposed on the images of the ball game players—as if two separate movies were being projected onto a screen at the same time. After the trial, subjects were asked how many passes were made, then questioned as to whether anything unusual had happened during the trial. Astonishingly, about half of the subjects tested were completely unaware of the "gorilla." An important additional finding was that if subjects were not engaged in a primary task (e.g., counting the passes), then nearly all of them reported the unusual event. The intentional task of processing specific information selectively in the visual-search task (the ball game information) made the subjects unaware of other events that were occurring in the same visual field, even if the event was unusual (for other examples see Chabris & Simons, 2010; Driver, Davis, Russell, Turatto, & Freeman, 2001; Hyman, Boss, Wise, McKenzie, & Caggiano, 2010; Memmert & Furley, 2007; Simons, 2000).

A variant of this paradigm, illustrating what is called *change blindness*, reveals a similar effect. Subjects in a change-blindness study are typically shown a series of still photos (or a video) of a scene in which a portion of the visual display disappears or changes significantly over time.

Subjects in the experiment often miss or fail to see the change (see Rensink, 2002; Simons & Rensink, 2005, for reviews). In one dramatic live demonstration of change blindness, an actor stops a person on the campus of a university to ask directions (see figure 4.2). While the subject (the person who is providing directions) explains the route to the actor, two people holding a large door walk between them. The actor is then *replaced* by one of the door carriers, who assumes the role of the lost actor after the door passes. Although the two actors look somewhat alike, they are clearly two different people. Yet nearly half of the subjects in the study failed to recognize the change. The change-blindness phenomenon reflects a strong role of memory, and expectation, as to what we attend to and what we become aware of (consciously). Similar to what occurs with the inattention-blindness effect, top-down processes play a very important role in attention and awareness.

Together, the results of experiments on the Stroop effect, the "cocktail party phenomenon," and inattention or change blindness illustrate that humans are capable of searching selectively and attending to specific information in the environment. Sometimes this intentional processing facilitates performance by filtering out unwanted information. At other times the process can have adverse consequences if the filtered information becomes important for task performance. Awareness appears to be a kind of confluence of top-down and bottom-up processes (Most, Scholl, Clifford, & Simons, 2005).

Automatic and Controlled Processing

Whereas a number of "early" processes (stimulus encoding, feature detection, and so on) can apparently be conducted in parallel and without attention, it is clear that other processes prior to choosing an action cannot. For example, if you are asked to detect whether the name of your home town has a *t* in it, various mental operations are required in order for you to come to the answer, and common experience tells you that performing them would be detrimental to a number of other tasks that might be called for at the same time (e.g., remembering your friend's phone number). This kind of processing is what Schneider and Shiffrin (1977) have

FIGURE 4.2   Failure to detect changes to people in a real-world interaction.

Reprinted from D.J. Simons and D.T. Levin, 1998, "Failure to detect changes to people in a real-world interaction," *Psychonomic Bulletin & Review* 5: 644-649. By permission of D.J. Simons and D.T. Levin.

called *controlled processing*. This type of processing is (a) slow; (b) attention demanding, in that other similar tasks interfere with it; (c) serial in nature; and (d) strongly "volitional," in that it can be easily stopped or avoided altogether. But Schneider and his colleagues (Schneider, Dumais, & Shiffrin, 1984; Schneider & Fisk, 1983; Schneider & Shiffrin, 1977) have also argued for another class of information processing: *automatic processing*. This form of information processing is qualitatively different from controlled processing: Automatic processing (a) is fast; (b) is not attention demanding, in that other operations do not interfere with it; (c) is parallel in nature, with various operations occurring together; and (d) is not "volitional," in that it is often unavoidable (Underwood & Everatt, 1996).

Schneider and his colleagues studied these processes using a variety of visual-search tasks. In one example, Schneider and Shiffrin (1977, experiment 2) gave subjects two types of comparison stimuli. First, subjects were presented with a memory set that consisted of one, two, or four target letters (e.g., *J D* represents a memory

set size of two). After the presentation of the memory set, they received a "frame" of letters that could also be composed of one, two, or four letters (e.g., *B K M J* represents a frame size of four). If either of the two letters in the memory set was presented in the frame (as *J* is in this example), the subject was to respond by pressing a "yes" button as quickly as possible; if none of the letters from the memory set was in the frame, a "no" button was to be pressed. Subjects practiced under one of two conditions. In *varied-mapping* conditions, on successive blocks of trials the memory set would be changed. This meant that a given letter in the frame sometimes would be a target, and on other blocks of trials it would not be a target. Thus, seeing a *J* in the frame, for example, would in one block of trials lead to a "yes" response and in another block lead to a "no." On the other hand, with *consistent-mapping* conditions, a given letter in the frame was either always a target or never a target, leading to a consistent response when it was detected (i.e., either "yes" or "no," but never mixed responses in different blocks of trials).

Figure 4.3 illustrates the results for the "yes" responses from these conditions after considerable practice for a memory set size of four. The varied-mapping condition (open circles) shows a strong effect of the frame size, with reaction time (RT) increasing approximately 77 ms per item in the frame. On the other hand, there was virtually no effect of frame size on RT in the consistent-mapping condition. Both early in practice and later in practice, for the *varied*-mapping conditions, search of the frame for a target letter seemed to be slow, serial, and strongly influenced by the number of items to be searched; these features typify controlled processing. But after much practice with *consistent*-mapping conditions, the processing was much faster, appeared to be done in parallel, and was not affected by the number of items to be searched; this is typical of automatic processing. In other experiments using very similar tasks, Schneider and Fisk (1983) reported that after considerable practice with consistent-mapping conditions, subjects could do these detections simultaneously with other secondary tasks without interference. However, sometimes these detections became unavoidable, as if they were triggered off without much control. One subject told of interference with her usual schoolwork (reading about history) after being in the experiment; an *E* (a target letter in the experiment) would unavoidably "jump out" of the page and distract her.

For various reasons, however, the concept of automaticity is not perfectly clear. One problem is that if a process is to be truly automatic, then performance of *any* other simultaneous task should be possible without interference. Neumann (1987), in a review of this topic, argues that no information-processing activity has ever been shown to be interference free across all secondary tasks. Whether or not interference is seen—as well as the amount of interference—seems to depend on the nature of, or the relationship between, the two tasks (McLeod, 1977; Schmidt, 1987). Second, the findings of Schneider and colleagues showing no "resource cost" demands (i.e., no effects of frame size in figure 4.3), in fact, sometimes do show a very small, positive slope for the consistent-mapping conditions, suggesting that these tasks are not completely interference free. Recent thinking suggests that the controlled/automatic dimension may better be thought of as a *continuum* (MacLeod & Dunbar, 1988; Moors & De Houwer, 2006; Underwood & Everatt, 1996).

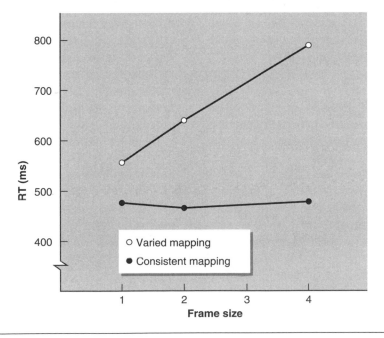

FIGURE 4.3   Reaction time (RT) to detect target letters in a letter matrix of one, two, or four letters (frame size) for varied- and consistent-mapping conditions; more letters to be searched led to no increase in RT for the consistent-mapping condition, suggesting automatic processing.

Certain information-processing activities are attention free with respect to *certain kinds* of secondary tasks, and the problem is then to define which kinds of tasks will and will not interfere with what other kinds of tasks (Neumann, 1987). Various theoretical models have been developed that expand this view of automatic processing as a continuum, from memory-retrieval (Logan, 1988) and parallel-distributed processing perspectives (Cohen, Dunbar, & McClelland, 1990), for example.

The study of automatic processing, and of the ways in which it is developed with practice, has strong implications for understanding control in skills. Many processes in skills, whether they be the detection of individual letters or words as you read this sentence, or the recognition of patterns of automobiles in traffic, can, with extensive practice, become faster and more efficient. Such gains in skilled situations are of course extremely important, in that information-processing loads are reduced so that the performer can concentrate on other aspects of the situation (e.g., the meaning of a poem, navigation in driving), processing is much faster, and many processes can be done in parallel. On the other hand, such automatic processing can occur only with some "cost," which is often seen when attention is drawn to the wrong place (distraction) or when an inappropriate movement is triggered (e.g., you respond to your opponent's "fake" in tennis).

Interference and Movement Production

Whereas the general findings are that many "early" stages of information processing can be done in parallel and without much interference from other tasks, the situation appears to be distinctly different with respect to the organization and initiation of movements. Research studies from various sources point independently to the view that *only one* movement can be initiated at a time. We turn next to the various lines of evidence for single-channel processing during these "late" stages of information processing.

Psychological Refractory Period

Probably the most important evidence for single-channel processing emerges from the *double-stimulation paradigm,* in which the subject must respond to two closely spaced stimuli that require different responses. An example of this paradigm is shown in figure 4.4. The subject is presented with a sound (stimulus 1, or S_1) that requires a response by the right hand (response 1, or R_1). After a very brief interval, a light is presented (S_2) that requires a response by the left hand (R_2). The two stimuli are presented in different modalities and require responses by different hands (to minimize structural interference). The stimuli are usually separated by at least 50 ms, and they may be separated by as much as 500 ms or even more; that is, the second stimulus could, in some situations, come well after the response to the first stimulus is completed. The separation between the onsets of the two stimuli is called the *stimulus onset asynchrony* (SOA). Further, the arrival of the signal onsets is usually randomly ordered, so that the subject cannot predict the occurrence or timing of a given stimulus (either S_1 or S_2) on a given trial. Thus, both stimuli must enter the information-processing system and be processed separately.

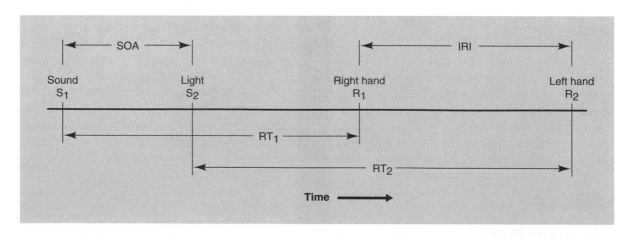

FIGURE 4.4 The double-stimulation paradigm (SOA = stimulus onset asynchrony, IRI = interresponse interval).

Experimenters have been interested especially in the RT to the *second* of the two stimuli (RT$_2$) because it provides an indication about how the processing of the second stimulus has been affected by the ongoing processing of the first. The critical comparison is between RT$_2$ when preceded by a response to S$_1$ versus RT$_2$ when S$_1$ is not presented at all; that is, the "control RT$_2$" is a measure of RT$_2$ when the subject does not have S$_1$ presented at all.

Using this method, experimenters have shown repeatedly that the processing of S$_1$ (through to R$_1$) is generally *un*influenced by the presence of S$_2$. However, the response to the second of the two closely spaced stimuli (i.e., S$_2$) is influenced by the presence of S$_1$. Here, the general finding is that RT$_2$ with S$_1$ present is considerably longer than RT$_2$ in the control condition (where S$_1$ is not present). Apparently the processing of S$_1$ and R$_1$ causes a great deal of interference with the processing of S$_2$ and R$_2$. This important phenomenon was discovered by Telford (1931), who named it the *psychological refractory period (PRP)*.[2] The findings from Davis (1959), presented in figure 4.5, are typical of the PRP effect. In this example, S$_2$ followed S$_1$ by an SOA of 50 ms. The control RT$_2$ (RT for S$_2$ in separate trials in which S$_1$ was not presented) was 124 ms. However, when S$_2$ followed S$_1$, the RT$_2$ was 258 ms—about twice as long as the control RT$_2$. Thus, the presence

of S$_1$ and R$_1$ caused a marked increase in RT$_2$. In other studies, the amount of increase in S$_2$ caused by S$_1$ and its processing can be 300 ms or more (Creamer, 1963; Karlin & Kestenbaum, 1968), making the RT for the second stimulus very slow—around 500 ms!

Another important result in studies of refractoriness is the effect of the length of the SOA on R$_2$. Figure 4.6, also containing data from the Davis (1959) study, plots the values of RT$_2$ for various values of the SOA, which ranged from 50 ms to 500 ms. Notice that, because the RT$_1$ was about 160 ms in this data set, all the SOAs greater than or equal to 200 ms occurred when the second stimulus was presented after the subject had responded to the first (see also figure 4.5). In figure 4.6, we see that as the SOA was increased from 50 ms to 300 ms, RT$_2$ was shortened systematically, until there was no delay at all (relative to the control RT$_2$ shown in the figure) with the longer SOAs. The most important points from figure 4.6 are that (a) the delay in RT$_2$ decreased as the SOA increased and (b) there was considerable delay even though R$_1$ had already been produced (i.e., at SOAs of 200 ms or more).

One major exception to this generalization about the effect of the SOA should be mentioned. If the second signal follows the first one very quickly, with an SOA as short as, say, 10 ms,

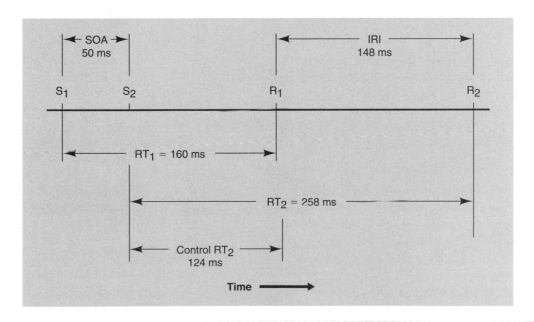

FIGURE 4.5   A demonstration of psychological refractoriness.

Adapted from Davis 1988.

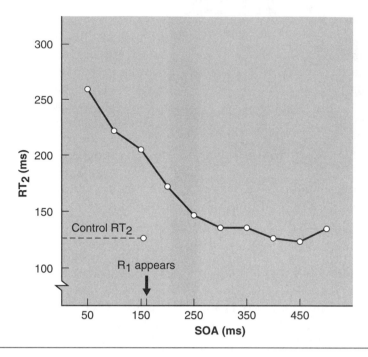

FIGURE 4.6 Refractoriness decreases as the stimulus onset asynchrony (SOA) increases.
Adapted from Davis 1988.

then the two signals are apparently dealt with as a single, more complex stimulus (called a *grouping* effect). The two signals elicit the two responses at about the same time but with a slightly greater RT for both than if only one of the responses had to be made to a single stimulus (see Welford, 1968). To explain this phenomenon, some writers (see Welford, 1968) have suggested the idea of a "gate" that "slams closed" about 50 ms after the presentation of S_1, presumably to prevent a second signal from entering the information-processing mechanisms and interfering with the response to the first signal. If a second signal comes before this point, the first and second signals are processed together as a unit, and the two responses are grouped.

The Single-Channel Hypothesis

A major contribution to the understanding of human information processing in motor tasks was made in 1952 when Welford proposed the *single-channel hypothesis* to account for the well-known findings about psychological refractoriness (see line 1 in figure 4.1). In his version of the theory, Welford hypothesized that if S_1 entered the single channel and was being processed, then processing of S_2 had to be delayed until the single channel was cleared—that is, until the response to S_1 had been started. This was a strict serial-

processing model, because S_1 and S_2 could not be processed together without interference.

How does this theory explain psychological refractoriness such as that seen in figures 4.5 and 4.6? Referring back to figure 4.5, S_2 was presented 50 ms after S_1, and RT_1 was 160 ms. Thus, $160 - 50 = 110$ ms remained before the completion of RT_1 when S_2 was presented. According to the single-channel hypothesis, processing of S_2 must be delayed until the channel is cleared. Thus the predicted RT_2 will be the control RT_2 plus the 110 ms delay, according to the single-channel view. Note from the data that the control RT_2 was 124 ms, which makes the estimate of RT_2 in the double-stimulation situation $124 + 110 = 234$ ms. If you look up the actual value of RT_2 (258 ms) given in figure 4.6, you will see that the predicted RT_2 (234 ms) is fairly close. Thus, the duration of RT_2 was thought to be the control RT_2 plus the amount that RT_2 overlapped with RT_1 or

$$RT_2 = \text{Control } RT_2 + (RT_1 - \text{SOA}) \qquad (4.1)$$

We can see in figure 4.5 and equation 4.1 that, as the size of the SOA increases, there is less overlap between the two RTs, and the predicted value of RT_2 decreases. This accounts for the finding that the RT_2 decreases as the SOA increases, as shown in figure 4.6 and in other research (Welford, 1968).

Evidence Against the Single-Channel Hypothesis

While the original single-channel hypothesis accounts for some of the data, a considerable amount of evidence has suggested that the theory is not correct in its details. According to the single-channel hypothesis, RT_2 lengthens as a direct function of the amount of overlap between RT_1 and RT_2, as can be seen in equation 4.1. The first concern was that even when there was *no* overlap between RT_1 and RT_2 (that is, when S_2 occurred after the subject had already produced a response to S_1), there was still some delay in RT_2. Look at figure 4.6. When the SOA was 200 ms, so that S_2 occurred 40 ms after R_1, there was still some delay in RT_2 (about 50 ms) that did not disappear completely until the SOA had been lengthened to 300 ms. How can there be refractoriness, according to the single-channel view, when the RT_1 and RT_2 do not overlap at all?

Welford (1968) suggested that after R_1 is produced, the subject directs attention to the movement, perhaps to feedback from R_1 to confirm that the movement was in fact produced correctly before processing S_2. Thus, according to Welford's view, attention was directed to feedback from R_1 after the response, which delayed RT_2, just as the attention produced during the time from S_1 to R_1 did.

But this explanation could not solve other problems. In the double-stimulation paradigm, as the SOA decreases, say, from 150 to 50 ms (in figure 4.5), the overlap between the two stimuli increases by exactly 100 ms; the single-channel model assumes that the delay in RT_2 is a direct function of this overlap, so the model predicts that RT_2 should be increased by exactly 100 ms in this example. Generally, the increase in RT_2 in these situations has been much smaller than expected on the basis of the model (Davis, 1959; Kahneman, 1973; see Keele, 1986, for a review). These effects are probably attributable to the fact that some processing of S_2 was being completed while S_1 and its response were being processed, which, strictly speaking, is contrary to the single-channel hypothesis.

Moderating Variables in Psychological Refractoriness

Various factors act to change, or modify, the effects just seen in double-stimulation situations. Some of these variables are practice, stimulus or response complexity, and stimulus–response (S-R) compatibility (see also Pashler, 1993, 1994).

Effects of Practice Practice has marked effects on the exact nature of the delay in RT_2 in this paradigm. Gottsdanker and Stelmach (1971) used 87 sessions of practice, 25 min each, in the double-stimulation paradigm for a single subject. They found that the amount of delay in RT_2 steadily diminished from about 75 ms to 25 ms over this period. But the delay was never quite eliminated, suggesting that refractoriness might have a permanent, structural basis in the information-processing system.

Complexity of Stimulus 1 Karlin and Kestenbaum (1968) found that the delay in RT_2 was strongly affected by the number of choices involved in RT_1. When S_1 was a simple RT (one stimulus, one response), with an SOA (until S_2) of 90 ms, the amount of delay in RT_2 was approximately 100 ms. However, when the first response was a two-choice RT, the delay was approximately doubled, so that RT_2 was over 500 ms. A five-choice S_1 produced an even larger delay, increasing RT_2 to about 630 ms (Keele, 1986). Because increasing the complexity of S_1 affects its processing time according to Hick's law (chapter 3), the magnitude of the delay in RT_2 apparently depends on the duration of processing for S_1.

Stimulus–Response Compatibility An important moderating variable is S-R compatibility, or the relationship between the stimuli and responses to be made (see chapter 3). Greenwald and Schulman (1973) varied the compatibility of the first response (S_1-R_1). In a compatible condition, S_1 was an arrow pointing to the left or right, and R_1 was a hand movement in the indicated direction. In a less compatible (or less "direct") condition, S_1 was the visually presented word "left" or "right," and R_1 was again the manual response in the indicated direction. Thus, reading the word "left" or "right" required transformations from the stimulus to the response that were more complicated and less "natural" than seeing the arrows (see chapter 3). In both conditions, S_2-R_2 was unchanged; S_2 was the number 1 or 2 presented auditorily, and R_2 was the vocal response "one" or "two." Figure 4.7 gives the results; C on the horizontal axis refers to the control RT_2 with no S_1 or R_1 required. When S_1-R_1 was not compatible (open circles), RT_2 was lengthened considerably and refractoriness was increased as the SOA decreased, as we have seen before (e.g., in

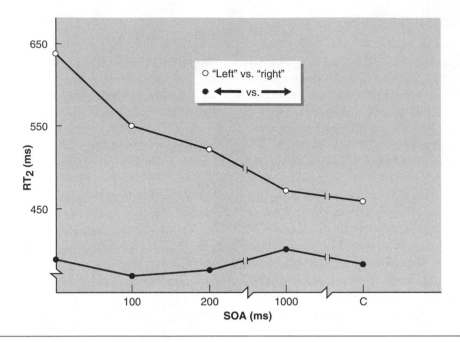

FIGURE 4.7 Reaction time (RT) to the second of two closely spaced stimuli at various stimulus onset asynchronies (SOAs) as a function of the stimulus–response (S-R) compatibility of the first reaction; the compatible arrow stimuli produced no refractoriness for the second reaction.

Adapted, by permission, from A.G. Greenwald and H.G. Schulman, 1973, "On doing two things at once: Elimination of the psychological refractory period effect," *Journal of Experimental Psychology* 101: 74. Copyright © 1973 by the American Psychological Association.

figure 4.6). But when S_1-R_1 was compatible (filled circles), there was no lengthening of RT_2 at any of the SOAs. If the compatibility among the stimuli and responses is very high, the usually devastating effects of the first signal and its response can be reduced or even completely eliminated.

Implications of Refractoriness for Practical Situations

We have seen that the second of two closely spaced reactions can suffer considerably in processing speed, and this fact can have important practical implications. For example, consider many fast-game situations, which often involve offensive and defensive players. Here, we often see the offensive player "fake" an opponent by displaying the initial parts of one action (e.g., a slight movement to the right) followed quickly by a different action (e.g., a movement to the left) that is actually carried to completion (such as what the hockey player is trying to do to the goalie in figure 4.8). If the defensive player responds to the first move, a full RT (about 150-220 ms) will be required, *plus* the added delay caused by refractoriness, before the defensive player can even *begin* to respond to the second move. Thus, RT to the second move could be as long as 500 ms

(see Creamer, 1963; Karlin & Kestenbaum, 1968), which is a very long time in fast games such as basketball and hockey and daily activities such as driving in high-speed traffic. But this is not the only problem. If the player has "taken the fake," (i.e., responded fully to S_1), then he not only will suffer a delay in the RT to the "real" movement (S_2), but also must overcome the momentum that the first movement has produced—plus make up any distance that he may have been traveled in the wrong direction (see also figure 3.17 on p. 84).

Based on findings from the PRP literature, a basic principle of faking is that the actual move should follow the fake by enough time that the second move is treated separately rather than grouped with the first one. Thus, the SOA should probably be around 50 ms or longer. Also, the second move must not follow the fake by so long that the refractory effects of responding to the fake have dissipated—probably not more than 250 ms (see figure 4.6). It would be interesting to study effective fakes in sport to discover whether the most effective SOAs correspond with estimates from experimentation. Such intervals may represent a part of natural defensive actions in other species. Watch a rabbit being chased by a dog. The rabbit runs with unpredictable directional changes,

FIGURE 4.8 Classic example of a psychological refractory period (PRP): The shooter is trying to draw the goalie out of position by faking the delivery of the shot.

probably using intervals between directional changes that are highly effective in confusing the dog. Refractoriness might be an important survival mechanism in animals other than humans.

Separation Between Responses

Evidence about psychological refractoriness suggests that the perceptual–motor system has difficulty responding to closely spaced stimuli,

and that responses must therefore be separated considerably in time. How closely in time can two responses be produced, provided that they are not grouped and produced simultaneously? Kahneman (1973) examined this separation—called the *interresponse interval (IRI)* in figure 4.4—as it is affected by bringing the stimuli closer to each other in time. In figure 4.9, we have plotted some of the data from Smith's (1969) study, as Kahneman

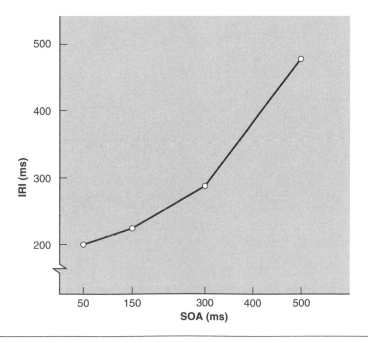

FIGURE 4.9 The relation between the interresponse interval (IRI) and the stimulus onset asynchrony (SOA).

Data from Smith 1969; adapted from Kahneman, 1973.

(1973) did. The SOAs were 50, 150, 300, and 500 ms, and the separations between responses (i.e., the IRIs) that resulted from these intervals are plotted.

As the SOA decreased (moving leftward on the graph), the interval between the two responses decreased, but only to a certain point. It appears that no matter how small the interval between stimuli, provided they are not grouped so that their responses are emitted simultaneously, an approximately 200 ms separation occurs between sequential responses. This is a most important result and suggests that if a signal "gets into" the information-processing stages up to a certain point, a response to it is generated. If another stimulus is presented soon afterward, indicating that the system should do some *other* action, the second action must wait for at least 200 ms before it can be initiated.

Given this general principle, why is it that skilled piano players can produce many movements of the fingers in which the separation between movements is far less than 200 ms? Surely this observation contradicts the notion that a response can be emitted only every 200 ms. We will discuss this in detail in chapter 6, but for now, the issue mainly concerns the definition of a "response." The system can prepare a "response" to a given stimulus that in itself is complex and involves many movements in rapid succession. The "response" that is planned in the response-programming stage is still just one response, but it may have many parts that are not called up separately. This can be thought of as *output chunking*, whereby many subelements are collected into a single unit, controlled by what is called a *motor program* (Keele, 1973; Schmidt, 1976a). Also, according to this general view, these programmed outputs occur in discrete "bursts" separated by at least 200 ms. These discrete elements are difficult to view directly, however, because the muscles and limbs smooth out the transitions between them, giving the impression that we respond continuously. In essence, then, many different *movements* can be separated by less than 200 ms if these movements are all contained in one "response."

It is fortunate that S_2 cannot get into the system to disrupt the preparation of a response to S_1. When preparing a response to a dangerous stimulus, subjects will be successful only if they can process the information and produce the movement without interference from other conflicting signals. Consequently, rather than seeing refractoriness only as a "problem" to be overcome by the motor system in producing rapid-fire actions, we can also view refractoriness as protective. It tends to ensure that responses to important stimuli are appropriate and complete. This is consistent with Neumann's (1987, 1996) view of attention as discussed earlier, according to which interference can be the result of an action having been selected.

Inhibition of Return

Another finding in the literature that reveals an interference "after-effect" following the orienting of attention has been termed *inhibition of return* (Posner & Cohen, 1984). The typical sequence of events is illustrated in figure 4.10. A trial begins with the presentation of an orienting cue—a type of warning cue that requires no overt response but simply alerts the subject that a stimulus will follow shortly, either at the same location or at a different location. An imperative signal occurs after a variable SOA either at the originally oriented cue location (top of figure 4.10) or at an uncued location (bottom of figure 4.10). The subject's goal is simply to make a response as fast as possible to the imperative signal. In comparison to the situation with the double-stimulation paradigm (figure 4.4), no response is required to the orienting cue. But, similar to what we see with the PRP effect, the length of the SOA appears be the critical determinant of how quickly the subject will respond to the imperative signal.

The results from the original Posner and Cohen studies (1984), which have been replicated often, are shown in figure 4.11 (p. 116). Two important effects emerge as a function of the SOA. First, if the imperative stimulus occurs at the same location as the orienting cue *and* with a short SOA (less than 200 ms), then RT is facilitated relative to an imperative stimulus location that is different than the orienting cue (the open symbols have less RT than the filled symbols in figure 4.11). This is the *beneficial effect* of orienting the subject's attention toward the location at which the imperative cue occurred, even though no overt response was required. More important, however, is what happens when the imperative signal occurs 300 ms or more after the orienting cue. In this case, completing the orienting response to the precue *delays* a response to the orienting (cued) location, compared to the RT in response to the cue that

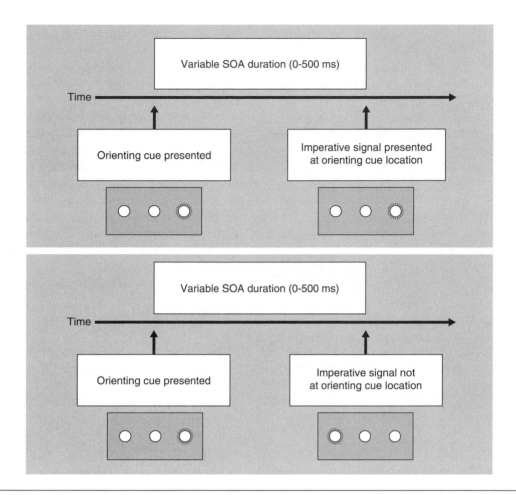

FIGURE 4.10 Events of the typical inhibition-of-return (IOR) paradigm. Top: The imperative signal occurs in the same location as the orienting cue. Bottom: The imperative signal occurs in a location other than the orienting cue location.

Adapted, by permission, from M.I. Posner and Y. Cohen, 1984, Components in visual orienting. In *Attention and performance X: Control of language processes*, edited by H. Bouma and D.G. Bouwhuis (Hillsdale, NJ: Erlbaum), 531-556.

was not at the orienting location (the open symbols now have more RT than the filled symbols in figure 4.11).

The "inhibition of return" seems to be a protective mechanism that prevents returning attention to a previous orienting cue that captured attention but did not require a response. Hypotheses differ regarding the mechanisms involved in producing the inhibition-of-return effect. Some suggest that inhibition of return is caused by an attention shift, whereby the previously attended-to cue loses salience (importance) after being fully processed (e.g., Fecteau & Munoz, 2003). Such a view would explain how one searches a map for a particular location, or searches a page for Waldo in a "Where's Waldo" scene. The start of the map search combines both top-down (directed search) and bottom-up (something that appears to "jump" off the map) features of orienting salience.

Once that location has proven not to be the target of the search, its previous importance is inhibited, thereby allowing other potential locations to rise in salience. Another suggestion is that the inhibition has a motor basis—having made a saccadic eye movement to the precue makes a response to the same cue slower than to a new target location (Fischer, Pratt, & Neggers, 2003). Klein has provided reviews of this extensive literature (Klein, 2000, 2004; Taylor & Klein, 1998).

Revised Single-Channel View

In sum, a single channel does seem to exist, contrary to the conclusion presented earlier in the section about the (original) single-channel hypothesis. But the single channel does not appear to apply to all stages of processing as Welford's (1952) version of the theory stated. Rather, it appears that parallel processing can

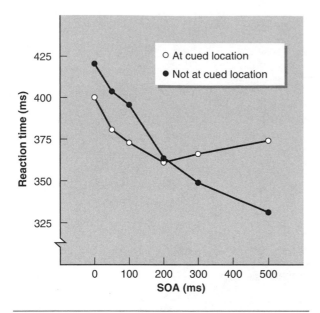

FIGURE 4.11 Effects of the relation between the orienting cue location and stimulus location as a function of stimulus onset asynchrony (SOA): the inhibition-of-return (IOR) effect.

Adapted, by permission, from M.I. Posner and Y. Cohen, 1984, Components in visual orienting. In *Attention and performance X: Control of language processes*, edited by H. Bouma and D.G. Bouwhuis (Hillsdale, NJ: Erlbaum), 531-556.

here) represents the bottleneck where single-channel processing occurs. According to the model in figure 4.12, the processing of S$_2$ in response selection and programming must wait (as indicated by the horizontal line) until S$_1$ has cleared this stage. In other words, only one response at a time can be selected and programmed. Further processing of the second of two closely spaced stimuli is put on hold until the response selection and programming for the first stimulus are complete. This leads us to ask whether the response-selection stage or the response-programming stage (in our terms in chapter 3; different from Pashler's), or both of the stages, might be the precise location of the bottleneck in processing.

Attention During Movement

To this point, we have examined attentional processes present during the RT period, which, of course, takes place prior to movement. But one can conceptualize a "stage" of processing, following response programming, in which the individual carries out the movement and keeps it under control. Strictly speaking, it is not a stage in the sense of the other stages, as it does not occur during RT (see chapter 3). Nevertheless, it is important to consider the attentional characteristics of these processes.

In thinking about our own skilled movements, we are left with the impression that skills require conscious awareness for their performance. We

occur during the early stages of information processing and that a single channel is properly placed during the stages in which decisions are made about the response. Pashler (1993, 1994) has presented persuasive evidence suggesting that the response-selection stage (which, for Pashler, includes response programming as we define it

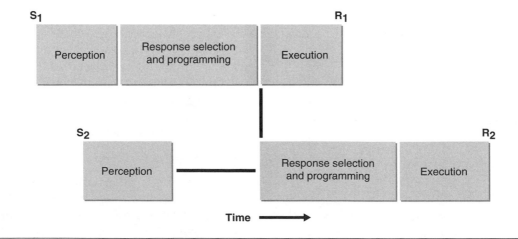

FIGURE 4.12 Pashler's bottleneck theory. Response selection and programming for the second stimulus must wait until the selection and programming of the first response are complete.

Adapted, by permission, from H. Pashler, 1993, "Doing two things at the same time," *American Scientist* 81(1): 52.

must be careful with these analyses, though, because we cannot be sure whether it is the movement itself that requires awareness or the programming and initiation of future movements (e.g., in a dive, when to "open up" to enter the water). We are in a weak position for determining the extent to which movements themselves require consciousness when we use only the methods of introspection.

On the other hand, sometimes it seems that a particular movement is performed without awareness (some consider such movements "automatic"), especially when it is a part of a well-learned sequence (e.g., a part of a dance routine). People who routinely drive a car with a standard transmission sometimes find, when driving an automatic transmission car, that they attempt to depress the "clutch" at a stop sign even though the car has no clutch pedal. Do you typically realize that you have produced this movement only after having done so? Have you ever found, in buttoning your shirt and thinking sleepily about the upcoming day's activities, that you are performing the motions even where a particular button is missing? Have you ever left the house and wondered if you turned off the burner on the stove? These examples, plus many others that come to mind, suggest that not all movements require attention for their performance while some seem to require considerable attention. Some of these "mindless" aspects of performance are described by Langer (1989).

When a movement requires a great deal of attention, what exactly is involved? As we mentioned earlier, attention could be devoted to the response-programming stage for future elements in a long sequence. Attention also could be devoted to other aspects of the environment. In driving, for example, the movements themselves might be carried out with minimal attention; instead, attention is directed to traffic patterns and other relevant features of the environment. Another possibility is that we pay attention to our movements to fine-tune their control—to carry out any necessary corrections, which can be thought of as "responses" as well. We consider some of these questions in the following sections.

The Secondary-Task Technique

An effective tool for evaluating the role of attention in simple movements involved *secondary* tasks, introduced in chapter 2. In the secondary-task technique, the subject performs a *primary* task for which the attention demand is of interest. But the subject is also occasionally presented with another task. These secondary tasks are of two types: *continuous* and *discrete.*

Discrete Secondary Tasks

In the discrete secondary task, a stimulus, called a *probe*, is presented at various times or places in the performance of the primary task, and a quick response to the probe is made with an effector not involved in the main task. The probes are often auditory, and the response may be either manual or vocal. This secondary-task method has been called the "probe technique" and is the subject of a large literature within the study of movement control (Abernethy, 1988, 2001). We discuss some details of this method later in the chapter.

Continuous Secondary Tasks

Continuous secondary tasks are those that are performed together with and throughout the duration of the primary task. Experiments reported by Welch (1898), for example, assessed maximum handgrip strength during the simultaneous performance of various tasks, such as reading, writing, arithmetic calculations, and various visual and auditory perception tasks. In all cases the maximum force output during the control trials (with no secondary task) was greater than when the task was performed simultaneously with another task. Importantly, Welch (1898) was the first to show that different dual-task situations created different "amounts" of interference. For instance, grip-strength performance was more proficient when subjects added two numbers, compared with multiplying two numbers, leading to the conclusion that the multiplication task demanded more of the subject's attention than did the addition task.

As an example, one research area that frequently uses continuous secondary tasks has to do with the attention demands of gait and posture. Beginning with the research of Kerr, Condon, and McDonald (1985), numerous researchers have assessed attention demands of standing balance under various conditions (see review by Woollacott & Shumway-Cook, 2002). Balance and gait control represent increasing challenges with advances in age, as falls often result in major health concerns. Although there are many contradictions among the findings of these studies, an important association exists between dual-task performance (and thus attention demand) and incidents of falling among the frail and elderly (Beauchet et al., 2009). Thus, the use of the secondary-task method may have important clinical implications for early detection of at-risk individuals.

In some experiments, the experimenter is interested in discovering how the subject coordinates the execution of two (or more) simultaneous movements. In this case, it is not the attention demands of one or the other that are of interest per se; rather, the primary concern is how the two tasks become regulated in space and time. You are probably well aware of the difficulty in rubbing your stomach with one hand while patting your head with the other. Of course, doing either of these tasks by itself is easy for most of us; but when we attempt them together, the two hands are particularly difficult to control, and a great deal of mental effort seems to be required. In another example (Klapp et al., 1985), it is particularly difficult to tap a regular rhythm with your left (nonpreferred) hand while tapping as quickly as you can with your right (preferred) hand. Such effects are not limited to these clever little demonstrations. In many piano performances, the two hands must perform with different rhythms for a short while, and most pianists claim that this is one of the most difficult tasks in these pieces. *Rubato* involves the gradual speeding or slowing of one hand with respect to the other, also considered a very advanced technique in piano playing (Peters, 1985).

In these examples, the two tasks are internally generated and not "driven" by any obvious environmental signal. It would thus seem that not all of the interference we observe among tasks has to do with the processing of environmental stimuli leading to a response. Rather, an additional source of interference might have to do with the control of the limbs per se. Although it is tempting to attribute an attentional "overload" explanation to these and related effects, the issue is much more complex than this. In fact, later in the book we devote an entire chapter to the problems of simultaneously coordinating the actions of two or more effectors (chapter 8).

The Probe Technique

This secondary-task method assumes a fixed (nonchanging) attentional capacity. The "pie chart," illustrated in figure 4.13, is an effective way to illustrate this fixed-capacity model. The "whole pie" represents the total attentional capacity available. If the capacity required for the primary task is low (about 75% of the fixed capacity, as illustrated in the diagram on the left in figure 4.13), then the capacity remaining for processing the probe stimulus will be relatively large, which should lead to a probe RT that will be fast. However, if the primary task demands a much larger proportion of the fixed capacity (say, about 90%, as illustrated on the right side of figure 4.13), then much less of the spare capacity remains for the probe stimulus, and its processing will be slower. Thus, the early work of this kind assumed that the duration of the

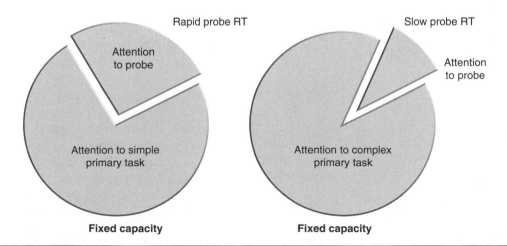

FIGURE 4.13   Assumptions of the probe reaction-time (RT) task: With fixed total capacity, attention to the probe decreases as the complexity of the primary task increases.

Reprinted from M.I. Posner and S.W. Keele, 1969, Attentional demands of movement. In *Proceedings of the 16th Congress of applied physiology* (Amsterdam, Amsterdam: Swets and Zeitlinger). By permission of M.I. Posner.

probe RT could give an indication of the attention requirements of the main task.

In an early study by Posner and Keele (1969), subjects made 700 ms wrist-twist movements of a handle through a range of 150°, attempting to move a pointer to either a large or a small target area. The experimenters presented probe signals at various points during the movement—at the start or at 15°, 45°, 75°, 105°, or 135° of handle movement. The probe RTs are plotted in figure 4.14 as a function of their location within the movement. The horizontal line represents the no-movement, control probe RT (i.e., RT in the absence of a primary task). Several features of this figure are important to note. First, the finding that the probe RTs were always larger than the corresponding values of the control probe RT was taken as evidence that performing the primary task (making the pointing movements) generated interference—that is, they required attention. Next, probe RT for both tasks showed a U-shaped function; there was a marked slowing of the probe RT at the beginning of the movement, with somewhat less slowing at the end. This finding suggests that attention to the movement is strongest at the beginning, that a "relatively" attention-free portion occurs near the middle, and that attention is used near the end again,

perhaps due to positioning the pointer accurately in the target zone. Finally, note that the probe RT increased as the target size decreased, especially near the end of the movement, suggesting that the movement became more attention demanding as end-point precision increased (see also Ells, 1973; Salmoni, Sullivan, & Starkes, 1976). In another of Posner and Keele's (1969) experiments, blindfolded subjects made a movement to a stop, which required essentially no target accuracy; the movement was analogous to pushing a door closed. In this example, there was no increased probe RT beginning at any of the later points during the movement, implying that this movement used no attention once it was initiated.

The probe technique has been used in a number of ways in attempts to assess the attentional demand involved in performing various jobs (Ogden, Levine, & Eisner, 1979); in the control of posture and gait (Abernethy, Hanna, & Plooy, 2002; Ojha, Kern, Lin, & Winstein, 2009; Woollacott & Shumway-Cook, 2002); and in various sport-related activities such as catching a ball (Populin, Rose, & Heath, 1990; Starkes, 1987), shooting a pistol (Rose & Christina, 1990), receiving tennis and volleyball serves (Castiello & Umiltà, 1988), and skating and stick-handling skills in hockey (Leavitt, 1979). A very important and recent

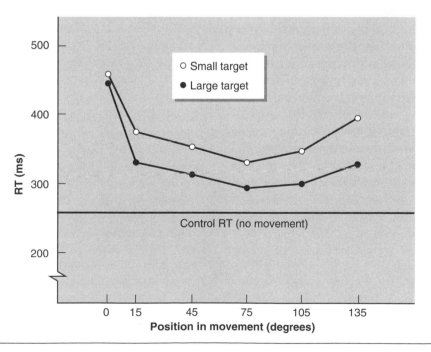

FIGURE 4.14   Probe reaction time (RT) elicited at various points in movements to large and small targets.

Reprinted from M.I. Posner and S.W. Keele, 1969, Attentional demands of movement. In *Proceedings of the 16th Congress of applied physiology* (Amsterdam, Amsterdam: Swets and Zeitlinger). By permission of M.I. Posner.

addition to this literature involves the attention demands of time sharing during driving, which we consider in more detail later in this chapter.

Problems With Secondary Tasks

A number of potential problems with the secondary-task paradigm require that interpretation of these experiments be made with caution. First, the method assumes a fixed, unitary capacity, which is, of course, contrary to Kahneman's (1973) views and contrary to the idea of *pools* of resources discussed earlier. Second, McLeod (1977, 1980) has identified a number of other difficulties. One of these was shown in his finding that a probe RT with a manual response interfered with a simultaneous tracking task, whereas a probe RT with a vocal response hardly interfered at all. If the probe RT actually measures some general, "spare," central capacity (attention), why was more of this capacity available when the only change was in the nature of the movement to be made in response to the probe?

Interpretation of results from continuous dual-task experiments involves a similar issue. A study by Yardley, Gardner, Leadbetter, and Lavie (1999) illustrates this point well. In this experiment, subjects attempted to stand perfectly still on a platform while performing various secondary tasks. Of importance was the difference observed in balance when subjects were asked to count backward by 7s from a three-digit number. When subjects performed the counting task *silently*, the investigators observed no increase in postural sway compared to the single-task control condition. However, when subjects counted backward out loud, postural sway increased dramatically, but no more so than when they simply repeated a three-digit number over and over. Yardley and colleagues concluded that it was not the attention demanded by the secondary task that interfered with performance; rather, increases in postural sway were more likely due to the extraneous postural movements caused by vocalizing aloud, or the attention demanded by the act of speaking, or both.

Whatever the exact nature of the interference might be, clear interference is found when various secondary tasks are paired with a variety of different primary tasks. These experiments seem to tell us that various movement tasks require many of the same processes that auditory–manual probe tasks do, and *not* that some undifferenti-

ated capacity is or is not used. Conversely, findings that the secondary-task performance is not elevated by the primary task do not necessarily mean that the primary task is automatic; rather, they indicate that the particular processes needed in the secondary task are not also involved in *that* primary task. Of course, other secondary tasks could probably be found that *would* interfere with the primary task (Neumann, 1987); if so, this would force us to conclude that the primary task is not automatic after all.

What has usually been meant by the conclusion that a task can be performed "automatically" is that it can be performed without interference from other mental tasks involving (conscious) information-processing activities. This fits with our subjective experiences about "automatic" movements that are performed without consciousness. But, as has been said previously (Neumann, 1987; Schmidt, 1987), it is probably best to think of automaticity *with respect to* some other simultaneous secondary task(s).

Action-Centered Interference

A different way to examine interference effects during movement was introduced by Tipper, Lortie, and Baylis (1992). This experimental approach relates to the everyday problems of interference that one encounters when reaching for an object in a cluttered environment, such as reaching for a paper on a desk that has other papers scattered on it, or reaching for an apple in a basket containing various fruits (Castiello, 1996). The questions of interest relate to how potentially distracting objects in the environment produce interference effects in either the preparation or the execution of movement.

The task for subjects in studies by Tipper and colleagues (1992) was to respond to the illumination of a light by pushing one of the buttons located on a table directly in front of them. As illustrated in figure 4.15, the buttons were arranged in three rows of three buttons each; near each button were two lights—a red light indicated that the button should be pushed, and a yellow light indicated a distracter (nontarget) button that was simply there and was to be ignored. Response times to move from the home button to the target location were very fast in conditions in which none of the distracter lights were illuminated when a target light appeared. However, on some trials, a yellow light was illuminated at the same

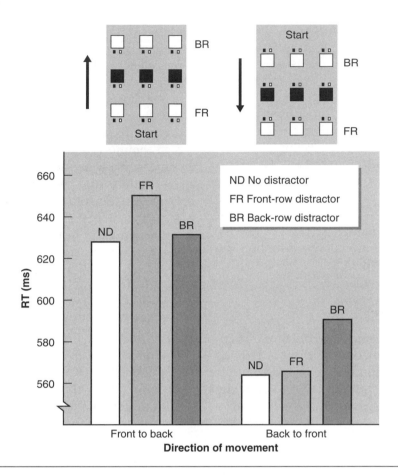

FIGURE 4.15   Action-centered interference in various arrangements of targets and distracters.

Adapted, by permission, from S.P Tipper, C. Lortie, and G.C. Baylis, 1992, "Selective reaching: evidence for action-centered attention," *Journal of Experimental Psychology: Human Perception and Performance* 18: 893, 896. Copyright 1992 by the American Psychological Association.

time that a red target light appeared. The critical issue addressed by Tipper and colleagues was whether the distracters (the yellow lights) would affect response time to reach the target button, and if so, which distracter locations would have the largest effects.

Two sets of results are presented in figure 4.15. On the left are the findings for a layout in which the subject's hand was moving away from the front of the table (which was the "start position") to contact a target in the middle row (i.e., one of the filled boxes). In this condition, only the distracters in the *front row* (FR) interfered with response time compared to a no-distracter (ND), control condition. When distracters appeared in the back row (BR), the response time was almost the same as in the no-distracter, control condition—hence, there was essentially no interference. Tipper and colleagues were able to reverse this pattern of findings by having movements start at the back of the table and move toward the sub-

ject (arrangement at upper right of figure 4.15). In this configuration, compared to no-distracter conditions, targets in the middle row were now unaffected by distracters in the front row, but were severely interfered with by distracters in the back row (back and front as viewed from the subject's perspective). Therefore, in both spatial arrangements, the interference was largest when the distracter was located *between* the start and end points of the movement, but not when it was located "beyond" the target.

The findings of Tipper and colleagues (1992) have been replicated and extended in a number of experiments showing that selective visual interference during movement is highly dependent on the nature of the action (e.g., Howard & Tipper, 1997; Meegan & Tipper, 1998; Pratt & Abrams, 1994). The "amount" of interference produced by a particular distracter appears to depend on its functional significance to the intentions of the main action (Weir et al., 2003; Welsh

& Pratt, 2008). For example, when distracters are located close to a target, they tend to have the largest interference effect on the kinematics of the grasping hand (Jervis, Bennett, Thomas, Lim, & Castiello, 1999; Mon-Williams, Tresilian, Coppard, & Carson, 2001). In contrast, objects located along the path of the movement tend to have larger effects on the kinematics of the reaching action (Mon-Williams et al., 2001). This view suggests a rather radical departure from interference effects during movement as implied by various capacity views of attention. Rather, the findings support Neumann's (1996) view that the nature of the selected action drives attention and determines which potential factors will or will not cause interference.

Distracted Driving

"Several years ago I observed what I believe to be the all-time record for distracted drivers. Driving north on I-95 into Baltimore, I was passed by a male driver who was holding a Styrofoam cup and a cigarette in one hand, and a cellular tele-phone in the other, and who had what appeared to have been a newspaper balanced on the steer-ing wheel—all at approximately 70 miles per hour" (Ambrose, 1997).

With increasing frequency, one hears anecdotal reports of traffic accidents that occurred while a driver appeared to be using some type of hand-held communication or entertainment device. The controversy was fueled by an analysis of acci-dent reports and cell phone call records, which revealed a fourfold increase in accident risk when the driver had been using a cell phone at the time of the incident (Redelmeier & Tibshirani, 1997). The researchers compared the elevated risks of distracted driving to the dangers of driving under the influence of intoxicants (see also Strayer, Drews, & Crouch, 2006).

Lawmakers in many countries around the world have debated how to deal with the issue of distracted driving, and researchers have responded with a wealth of data to inform them. Although this is a current "hot" topic, investiga-tions on cell phone use were initiated by Brown,

---

They said it . . .

I.D. BROWN ON DISTRACTED DRIVING

Research on talking on a phone during driving, though a topic of considerable recent research activity, was investigated many years ago by Brown and colleagues (1969). As evident in the following quotes, their theoretical orientation was clearly concerned with attention. Although single-channel theory (according to which switching between tasks is necessary in order to carry out more than one task) dominated their thinking, their hypotheses and findings remain as relevant today as they were in 1969. It is unfortunate that their plea for additional research on specific outstanding issues was not taken up in earnest for more than two decades.

"Having to use a hand microphone and having to manipulate push buttons to make or take a call will be inconvenient and may impair steering, gear changing, or other control skills. This is a problem which may be solved by engineering advances and is not the concern of the pres-ent paper. A more important and lasting problem arises from the hypothesis that man can be considered to act as a single communication channel of limited capacity. The prediction from this hypothesis is that the driver will often be able to telephone only by switching attention between the informational demands of the two tasks. Telephoning could thus interfere with driving by disrupting visual scanning, since visual and auditory information would have to be transmitted successively. It could also interfere by overloading short-term memory and impairing judgment of relative velocity. . . ." (p. 419).

"The general conclusion must be that some mutual interference between the concurrent tasks is inevitable under conditions of telephoning while driving on the road. The results suggest that, although more automated control skills may be affected minimally by this division of attention, some perception and decision skills may be critically impaired. The extent to which this impairment is a function of the driving task, the informational content of the telephone message, and the individual characteristics of the driver must remain a subject for further research" (pp. 423-424).

Tickner, and Simmons (1969) over 40 years ago. Their subjects made safety margin judgments (whether or not the car could fit through gaps) by either driving through or around markers on the road). On some trials the subjects also performed a reasoning task via a hands-free telephone. Performing the reasoning task while driving elevated the frequency of gap judgment errors by almost 13%. (See the authors' concerns about this increase in "I.D. Brown on Distracted Driving.")

Sending and receiving text messages is an obvious source of structural interference during driving—one cannot fully scan the driving environment while looking at a communication device, and the texting hand is not available for other subtasks. But what are the dangers in simply *talking* on a cell phone during driving? Are handheld cell phones more dangerous than hands-free units, and is the whole issue of interference from cell phones related only to structural interference (i.e., looking at the screen, entering keystrokes)? Is talking on cell phone more dangerous than carrying on a conversation with a passenger in the car? We consider these and other issues in the next sections (see also reviews by Caird, Willness, Steel, & Scialfa, 2008; Collet, Guillot, & Petit, 2010a, 2010b; Haigney, & Westerman, 2001; Horrey & Wickens, 2006; McCartt, Hellinga, & Bratiman; 2006).

Does Cell Phone Use Affect Driving?

The degree to which driving is compromised by cell phone conversation appears to depend on at least three factors: the *driving environment*, the *characteristics of the driver*, and the *nature of the conversation* in which the driver is engaged. The decrement in driving performance during talking on a cell phone has been found to increase with increased traffic demand (Lee, Caven, Haake, & Brown, 2001; Strayer, Drews, & Johnston, 2003) and environmental complexity (Strayer & Johnston, 2001). Also, a greater performance decrement is observed under dual-task driving conditions for older drivers compared to younger drivers (Alm & Nilsson, 1995; Hancock, Lesch, & Simmons, 2003; McKnight & McKnight, 1993), although there is some discrepancy in the literature regarding the role of practice. Some studies suggest that practice lessens driving distraction (Brookhuis, de Vries, & de Waard, 1991; Chisholm, Caird, & Lockhart, 2008; Shinar, Tractinsky, & Compton, 2005), whereas others suggest that the distraction remains about the same (Cooper & Strayer, 2008). However, there is no evidence that the distraction from cell phones is eliminated with practice. Also, conversations that require a larger number of reasoning operations impair performance more than tasks involving fewer operations (Briem & Hedman, 1995).

In sum, the impact of the driving environment, driver experience, and the nature of the conversation is consistent with general attentional capacity limitations in performance discussed earlier in this chapter. However, more complex driving environments usually impose greater visual demands on the driver, and some have argued (e.g., Strayer et al., 2003) that secondary-task performance interferes with visual attention processes, causing an effect like *inattentional blindness* (see our earlier discussion in this chapter; Yantis, 1993). Cell phone conversation reduces the capacity to perceive changes in the visual environment such as traffic patterns (Trbovich & Harbluk, 2003).

Cell Phone Use Versus Other Driver Distractions

Cell phone use is only one of many potential distractions in driving (Cohen, 1997). Conversations with other passengers, listening to and adjusting audio equipment, and reading instrument panels and mirrors are just a few of the ways in which attention might be distracted. The research is not entirely clear, however, on how these other sources of distraction influence driving (Consiglio, Driscoll, Witte, & Berg, 2003; Irwin, Fitzgerald, & Berg, 2000; Strayer & Johnson, 2001). Tasks that require the driver to divert visual attention from the outside to the inside environment (e.g., tuning a radio) appear to be detrimental to performance (McKnight & McKnight, 1993), presumably because hazards to driving come mainly from the outside. The intensity and complexity of the cognitive/visual processes are important contributors to interference, and not simply the manual handling of the device as many have believed.

One of the arguments frequently raised against legislation on cell phone use during driving suggests that the distraction is no greater than talking with a passenger (which is both common and legal). In an epidemiological study, McEvoy, Stevenson, and Woodward (2007) found that the accident-risk odds rose by a factor of 1.6 when one passenger was in the vehicle and by a factor of 2.2 with two or more passengers. However, those increases were much less than the accident risk associated with cell phone use, which rose by a factor of 4.1. These findings are supported by experimental evidence (Drews, Pasupathi, & Strayer, 2008) suggesting that in-vehicle conversations among passengers tend to be considerably less hazardous for drivers than cell phone conversations. Another argument is that the passenger can adjust the conversation (or stop it altogether) in demanding driving situations; obviously, this is not possible for the person on the other end of the cell phone conversations. Also, some argue that the passenger can provide comments that benefit safety ("Look out for the bicyclist!"), even during conversations with the driver.

Handheld Versus Hands-Free Cell Phones

Despite the preponderance of legislation that bans handheld cell phone use during driving but permits the use of hands-free units, almost all experimental studies on the topic have shown that both are about equally detrimental to driving performance (Consiglio, Driscoll, Witte, & Berg, 2003; Lamble, Kauranen, Laakso, & Summala, 1999; Strayer & Johnston, 2001; Törnros & Bolling, 2005). In reviewing the evidence regarding distraction with the use of hands-free and handheld phones, Ishigami and Klein (2009) conclude simply that "the epidemiological and the experimental studies show a similar pattern: *talking* on the phone while driving impairs driving performance for both HH (handheld) and HF (hands-free) phones" (p. 163, emphasis added). Moreover, given the evidence that drivers tend to compensate more for the potential distraction of a handheld unit (e.g., by driving more slowly), Ishigami and Klein argued that driving and talking with a hands-free unit might even be *more* dangerous than with a handheld phone because of the driver's mistaken belief that a conversation with a hands-free device is not attention demanding.

Focus of Attention

In this section we turn the discussion around and ask, What is the effect on movement when we specifically direct our attention to different sources of information, such as the internal sources of the feedback that naturally arise during movement or an object in the environment that represents the outcome goal of an action? In other words, what is the effect when we vary the "focus" or object of our attention?

Internal Versus External Attentional Focus

Views about how one can direct attention optimally during action have been around since at least the late 19th century (see "Cattell and Bernstein on Focus of Attention"), although empirical studies on the topic are relatively recent. However, the more recent research in this area has shown that the suspicions of Cattell and Bernstein were rather accurate—that experts benefit from an "external" focus of attention, whereas less skilled performers benefit from an "internal" focus of attention.

In most investigations, the definition of "internal" involves instructions to the subject to focus on some aspect of the motor skill, such as how a movement is being executed or the sensory consequences of the movement. For an "external" focus of attention, experimenters often ask subjects to focus on an object in the environment or on some expected outcome of the action, such as where a golf ball went after a putt (see Wulf, 2007, for a review). One obvious limitation of this type of research is the lack of any hard evidence that the subject has accurately followed the experimenter's instructions. Therefore, it is very important that instructions be clear, concise, and repeated often to encourage subjects to focus their attention as directed.

In studies by Beilock and her colleagues, golfers in an internal-focus condition made putts while concentrating on the motion of the putter and saying the word "straight" aloud when the ball was contacted (Beilock, Bertenthal, McCoy, & Carr, 2004; Beilock, Carr, MacMahon, & Starkes, 2002). In another condition, the golfers performed their putts while monitoring simultaneously in order to detect when (or if) a tone was presented, which presumably generated an external focus. The results were dramatic. Expert golfers showed more skill in the external than the internal condition, whereas the opposite was the case for novice golfers.

CATTELL AND BERNSTEIN ON FOCUS OF ATTENTION

They said it . . . .

James Cattell's work and writing on attention predated and anticipated many of the research issues that would later become prominent in mainstream experimental psychology (after the demise of the behaviorist tradition). Bernstein's book *(On Dexterity and Its Development)* was written in the 1940s in Russian. Discovered and translated into English many years later, this text is written in a style geared toward a wide audience (Feigenberg & Latash, 1996) and contains many practical examples and illustrations of motor control and learning in sport and daily life. In the following quotes, Cattell and Bernstein address the issue of attentional focus. Note that both advocate what is referred to today as an "external" focus of attention, but only for skills that are well learned. In addition, their theoretical rationale, that focusing "internally" would be disruptive to automatic movements, shares many similarities with current thinking.

"In the practiced automatic movements of daily life attention is directed to the sense impression and not to the movement. So, in piano playing, the beginner may attend to his fingers but the practiced player attends only to the notes or to the melody. In speaking, writing and reading aloud, and in games and manual work, attention is always directed to the goal, never to the movement. In fact, as soon as attention is directed to the movement, this becomes less automatic and less dependable" (Cattell, 1893).

"Consciously watching the movements of a teacher and intent attention toward one's own movements make sense only at the beginning of the process of skill development, when the motor composition of the skill is being defined. After the automations have already been elaborated and switched out of consciousness, it is useless and even detrimental to chase them behind the movement curtain. One needs to trust the level of the muscular–articular links; most of the time, our confidence is justified.

"So, what should be in the focus of our attention during the final phases of skill development? There is a very definite answer. The attention should be focused on a level where consciousness resides and which takes the responsibility for movement success in its major and most important components. Therefore, one should concentrate on the *desire to solve a motor problem as accurately and expediently as possible.* This desire will lead to basic, meaningful corrections for the whole movement. For example, the attention of a person who has learned to ride a bicycle should be fixed not on his legs or arms but on the road in front of the bicycle; the attention of a tennis player should be directed at the ball, the top edge of the net, the movements of the opponent, but certainly not at his own legs or on the racket. Such *concentration on the problem* maximally mobilizes the leading level with all its abilities" (Bernstein, 1996, p. 203).

Perkins-Ceccato, Passmore, and Lee (2003) had subjects perform pitch shots (in golf) under conditions in which they were asked to focus either on the force required to swing the club (internal focus) or on the intended target (external focus). As an additional encouragement to focus as directed, after each shot the golfers were asked to make a performance estimate regarding the amount of the force just produced (internal focus) or the accuracy of the shot relative to the target (external focus). Similar to what Beilock and colleagues (2002, 2004) observed, high- and low-skilled golfers performed differently as a function of the instructed focus of attention. As illustrated in figure 4.16, the low-skilled golfers benefited from internal focusing instructions whereas the high-skilled golfers were more skillful in the external-focus conditions. Similar results have been obtained for soccer dribbling (Ford, Hodges, & Williams, 2005) and baseball batting tasks (Castenada & Gray, 2007; Gray, 2004). However, Flegal and Anderson (2008) reported that an internal focus disrupted golf putting performance only for higher-skilled golfers; the intervention had no effect on the lower-skilled golfers' performance. Overall, in most studies, an external focus tends to enhance high-skilled golfers' performance, and some studies show that an internal focus benefits low-skilled golfers' performance.

For skilled performers, these findings suggest that directing attention *toward* production of the movement itself has a detrimental impact on performance (although it may be equally correct to say that directing attention *away* from producing the movement itself has a beneficial impact on performance—these influences have not been separated). Researchers agree that this effect is primarily related to attentional mechanisms that change as skill develops, although there is disagreement about specific theoretical issues as to how this happens. Beneficial effects of external focus of attention instructions have been demonstrated in a number of *learning* experiments by Wulf and her colleagues, using an assortment of laboratory (e.g., stabilometer; see chapter 2) and sport tasks (reviewed in Wulf, 2007; Wulf, McNiven, & Shea, 2001; Wulf & Prinz, 2001). In many studies the subjects were novices at the beginning of the study and developed skill over several sessions of practice. As discussed in the later chapters of this book, motor learning is frequently thought to involve the cognitive (or verbalizable) attention to movement during the early stages of learning, and these processes diminish or drop out completely as skill develops. Directing attention back to the movement,

therefore, may have an interference effect on the movement control processes that are relevant for advanced performers. In essence, when the expert "breaks into" the preprogrammed action with consciously based information processing, abandoning the elegant programs and routines she has learned over many years, this may produce the jerky, slow, and hesitant actions characteristic of a novice. These findings also add an important component to various considerations about how to conduct practice sessions and to provide augmented feedback, as discussed further in chapters 11 and 12, respectively.

Choking and Attentional Focus

Most of us have personal experiences with performing under *pressure*—situations in which we perceive a special expectation to perform well. The feeling of pressure may occur because of the importance of the performance (e.g., a concert recital) or because of various other factors related to the event (e.g., presence of an audience; performance-outcome incentives, etc.). Sometimes the performer lives up to these expectations; but when performance fails to do so, the unfortunate label of "choking" is often applied. Of interest in the present context is a common tendency for performers to refocus their attention inward when put in these situations, often leading to "choking under pressure."

In one of the first investigations conducted in this area, Baumeister (1984) found a 25% drop in performance when subjects were approached at a video arcade and asked simply to achieve their best score possible in a one-trial performance test. Interestingly, these findings were attributed to the shift toward an "internal performance process" (Baumeister, 1984), anticipating much of the attentional focus literature to follow. "Reinvestment theory" presents a similar view—motor skills that have been learned to an advanced level are disrupted when individuals revert to a form of conscious movement control (Masters, 1992; Masters & Maxwell, 2008). Reinvestment theory has much in common with a view of learning discussed in greater detail in chapter 13 called "progression–regression" processes (Fuchs, 1962), which theorizes that learners *regress* to previous level of control processes after a long retention interval or when faced with pressure situations. Reinvestment may be seen as a reversion to an internal focus (Perkins-Ceccato et al., 2003) or

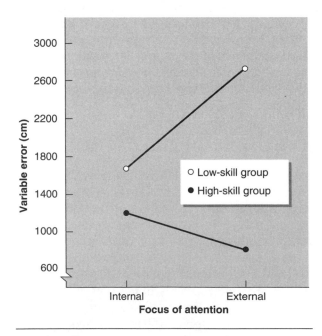

FIGURE 4.16 Effects of focus of attention in low- and high-skilled golfers.

Adapted, by permission, from N.P. Perkins-Ceccato, S.R. Passmore, and T.D. Lee, 2003, "Effects of focus of attention depend on golfers' skill," *Journal of Sports Sciences* 21: 593-600, by permission of the publisher (Taylor & Francis Ltd, http://www.informaworld.com).

controlled-processing style of movement control (Shiffrin & Schneider, 1977). Beilock and Carr (2001) proposed a view that has many similarities to reinvestment theory, although they suggest that choking in the performance of motor skills may be caused by different mechanisms than in the performance of cognitive skills (Beilock, 2008, 2010; Beilock, Kulp, Holt, & Carr, 2004).

Ironic Effects of Attentional Focus

Another counterproductive effect of focused attention is called the *ironic effect.* An anecdotal example of the effect is the golfer who stands at the tee, faced with out-of-bounds looming to the right. If the golfer mentally concentrates on the thought "Don't hit it to the right," the result that seems to occur often is that the performer does what is not desired. Wegner (1994, 2009) has made a more thorough analysis of such situations.

An experiment that illustrates ironic effects was reported by Wegner, Ansfield, and Pilloff (1998) using a handheld pendulum. With the arm extended outward from the body, subjects held a nylon line, at the end of which was a weighted object 2 cm above a glass plate. On the glass plate were grid lines with the *x*- and *y*-axes clearly visible and with a green target in the middle. One (control) group of subjects was instructed to try to hold the pendulum as steadily as possible over the green target for 30 s. The other (experimental) group was given the same instructions, but was also told "You should *not* let it move in the direction paralleling the horizontal line"—that is, in the left-to-right direction. The experimental group produced more movements along the forbidden (horizontal) axis and slightly less movement along the ignored (vertical) axis than the control group (who were not given any "forbidden axis" instructions). These findings lend some empirical support to the anecdotal feeling that trying to *avoid* a particular behavior paradoxically leads to that very behavior. Sport psychologists often spend many hours with their clients to practice positive imagery techniques, perhaps with the goal of avoiding the kinds of ironic behaviors noted by Wegner and his colleagues (Janelle, 1999; Singer, 2000).

Attention and Anxiety

In this final section of the chapter we shift emphasis to some important aspects of human perfor-

mance related to arousal and anxiety and their relationship to ideas about attention. Anxiety is common, as in an important game or match or when we are threatened with harm in some way. How do high-anxiety conditions affect the processing of information necessary for successful performance?

Consider this true story. An airline pilot with over 20,000 h of flying experience returned to San Francisco after an all-night flight from Hong Kong. He drove home to Oakland (20 miles away), slept for a few hours, and then drove to the local airport to check out his private plane for a flight. With his family of three aboard, he left for a destination a few hours away, watched an automobile race there, and late at night began the return flight. At about 2:00 a.m. he radioed that his heater was not working and that he was above a layer of clouds over the Oakland airport. A pilot with his experience would, in this situation, be expected to perform a relatively lengthy (20 to 30 min) instrument approach through the clouds to the airfield, but instead he radioed that he was looking for a "hole" in the clouds, presumably to avoid the instrument approach. The plane crashed a few minutes later, killing all aboard, after a wing broke off.

What happened? We might guess that the pilot was very fatigued from the overseas flight, from the two other flights that day, and from the car race; he was also cold and in a hurry to get home. The fatigue and cold led to a bad decision to find a "hole." Also because of the fatigue, the pilot may have been handling the plane badly, perhaps becoming disoriented and diving too steeply through the "hole," and the wing failed. Similar examples come from underwater diving, as pointed out by Norman (1976) and Bachrach (1970):

> A woman enrolled in a diving course but lacking experience, was reported to have . . . drowned while diving for golf balls in a twelve-foot [pool]. When her body was recovered, she was wearing her weight belt, and, in addition, was still clutching a heavy bag of golf balls. (p. 122)

Again, something went wrong. Perhaps fatigue and cold led to panic. What effects do anxiety and panic have on information processing in these situations, causing people to abandon highly practiced techniques and resort to the skill level of an inexperienced beginner? We consider some possible answers to these questions in the next few sections.

Arousal and *anxiety*, along with related terms such as *motivation* and *stress*, generally refer to states of activation that differ along a number of dimensions. Someone who is "psyched" or "pumped up," or otherwise in a highly energized state of activation, may be referred to as highly aroused or in a state of high anxiety. How does arousal or anxiety, or the combination, influence performance? This relationship has been characterized in a number of ways, each with some supporting evidence. We review each of these characterizations briefly in the next sections (more in-depth analyses are presented in Gould & Krane, 1992; Weinberg & Gould, 2011; Woodman & Hardy, 2001; Zaichkowsky & Baltzell, 2001).

The Inverted-U Principle

One of the oldest and certainly one of the most interesting aspects of arousal and performance was discovered by Yerkes and Dodson (1908) in studying discrimination learning in mice. They found that increased intensity of electric shocks delivered to the mice reduced the number of trials required to acquire the discrimination criterion, but only up to a point. Beyond this point, further increases in the intensity of the shock increased the number of trials to reach criterion. If the shock was arousing, then there appeared to be an optimal level of arousal; that is, the relationship between shock intensity and performance followed an inverted U-shaped function. The principle has been called the Yerkes-Dodson law, after its originators or, more commonly, the *inverted-U principle* (Duffy, 1962). A general visual description of this principle is presented in figure 4.17.

Weinberg and Ragan (1978; see also Klavora, 1977; Martens & Landers, 1970; Sonstroem & Bernardo, 1982) have provided evidence for the inverted-U phenomenon in movement behavior. They asked college males to throw tennis balls at a 5 cm target located 6.1 m away. After 10 trials of initial practice, subjects were asked to fill out a questionnaire, and they then received one of three statements. In the high-stress condition, the subject was told that 90% of the population of college males would have performed better than he did. In the moderate-stress condition, he heard that 60% of the population would have had better performances than his. In the low-stress condition, the subject was told that only 30% of the population was better at throwing. Because the subjects, who were junior high school–aged

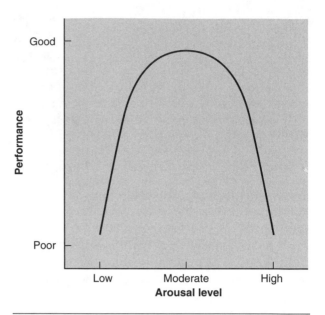

FIGURE 4.17   The inverted-U relation between arousal and performance.

males, were also told that this task was an important indicator of success in most sport tasks involving throwing (which is not actually correct, as we shall see in chapter 9), such (false) statements about their level of performance were expected to be variably arousing. Indeed, arousal data indicated that this was the case.

The throwing scores for the subjects in these three stress conditions are illustrated in figure 4.18. Increased arousal from the low-stress to the moderate-stress condition produced strong gains in performance; but further increases in arousal produced a *decrease* in throwing proficiency relative to that in the moderate-stress condition. Consistent with the inverted-U principle (compare figures 4.17 and 4.18), there was a clear optimal level of arousal for the performance of this motor task.

The inverted-U principle suggests that there is no simple relation between the level of stress and the quality of performance. How often do coaches and sportscasters suggest that an athletic performance was very good because the athlete or team was "up" for the game (see Nideffer, 1976)? The common, everyday belief seems to be that the more "up" we are, the better we perform, which is not usually the case. Although the inverted-U principle has *some* explanatory power, the relation between arousal, anxiety, and performance is much more complex than this.[3]

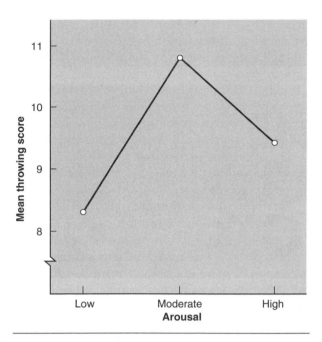

FIGURE 4.18 Throwing proficiency as a function of three stress conditions.

Adapted from Weinberg and Ragan 1978.

Perceptual Narrowing

The idea of perceptual narrowing has been described by Kahneman (1973) and others. With this notion, increased arousal causes narrowing of the attentional focus, with a progressive elimination of input from the more peripheral (or unexpected) aspects of the environment. The term *peripheral* need not refer to events that are actually "in" the periphery (e.g., as in peripheral vision); it refers to events that are relatively improbable. It just so happens that, with vision, events that are expected are usually in our central vision (because we direct our gaze toward them), and events that are improbable occur in peripheral vision.

In addition to the reduced range of cues that can be attended to as arousal increases, there is an increase in the number of shifts in attention to different input sources. Some researchers (e.g., Kahneman, 1973) have referred to this effect as increased *distractibility*. Thus, high levels of arousal are likely to cause the individual to direct attention to many different sources from moment to moment, with some of these sources providing irrelevant information and causing the relevant signals to be missed. Apparently, the individual must discriminate between relevant and irrelevant cues during performance, and one effect of high arousal is deterioration in the quality of such discrimination.

Considerable evidence is available to support the notion of perceptual narrowing in a variety of tasks (see Kahneman, 1973). In an interesting practical setting, Weltman and Egstrom (1966) studied novice scuba divers in air on a pool deck, in a controlled swimming pool, and in the ocean. The divers performed two main tasks (arithmetic and a dial-detection task). Responding to a light stimulus presented in peripheral vision in the diving masks was measured with a secondary task. As the subjects were moved from the air to the pool to the ocean conditions, large (300% to 400%) increases in time to detect these peripheral signals were found; the performance in response to light stimuli presented in central vision was hardly affected. The focus of attention was clearly narrowed with increased stress. Janelle, Singer, and Williams (1999) reported similar findings for a simulated driving task.

Easterbrook's Cue-Utilization Hypothesis

Easterbrook's (1959) hypothesis uses a notion similar to perceptual narrowing to account for the inverted-U relation. This viewpoint assumes that the individual takes in cues, from the environment or from his own movements, that support future performances. There are presumably many relevant and irrelevant cues available in the environment, and the most relevant for performance are located in central vision (where we are looking). With low arousal, the *selectivity* for the cues is poor, as the visual field is wide and many relevant, and irrelevant, cues can be detected to generate action. With an increase in arousal to moderate levels comes a reduction in the number of cues used (because of the narrowing of focus), so that there is a shift to an area where relevant cues are more prevalent and irrelevant cues are less prevalent. As the performer approaches an optimal level of arousal, the most effective combination of attention to relevant cues and minimal inclusion of irrelevant cues occurs. However, with a further increase in the arousal level comes a further restriction in the range of cues used; many relevant cues are now not included, and performance deteriorates. This may have occurred with both the pilot and scuba diver discussed earlier.

Hypervigilance, or Panic

When the stress conditions become more severe, the responses of human performers can be even more severely disrupted. Many of these disrupted responses occur in true emergency situations, such as earthquakes, fires, battlefields, and other life-threatening situations. As such, they are difficult to study directly, and one must usually rely on various kinds of postevent measures to understand them.

Such situations often stem from what Janis, Defares, and Grossman (1983) call *hypervigilance* or what one might loosely term "panic." The contributing conditions seem to be (a) a sudden and intense stimulus, (b) a potentially life-threatening outcome, and (c) a situation in which time to take an appropriate action is quickly running out. All of these seem to be present in most cases of a kind of vehicle accident termed "unintended acceleration" (Schmidt, 1989b, 1993; see chapter 6, p. 203, "Pedal Misapplication Errors"), in which the driver panics when she mistakenly presses the accelerator rather than the brake, and the car accelerates unexpectedly (and with no intention on the driver's part). The individual appears to freeze, perhaps because attention is so narrowed that no alternative actions are considered. It could also be that the driver considers many alternatives but, because of the increased distractibility, none long enough to initiate a solution; she "dithers" until it is too late. Also, the person tends to choose the action that is highest in the response hierarchy—the most common, "natural," or highly practiced action (e.g., pressing the brake when the vehicle spins on ice). Moreover, the individual tends to persevere, producing the same response repeatedly, even though this action has not had the desired effect. These situations are not as rare as they might appear, as evidenced by analyses of numerous vehicle accidents (Perel, 1976). Further, they might also occur in highly stressful sport events, industrial tasks, theater or night club fires, and so forth, with outcomes that are much less dramatic or not so easily analyzed.

Summary

Even though attention has had a long history of thought in psychology, we are still unclear about its nature and the principles of its operation—indeed, even its definition. Many theorists think of attention as a single, undifferentiated, limited capacity to process information; others argue that attention is really a number of pools of capacity, each specialized for separate kinds of processing. The successful performance of various tasks together is presumably limited by these capacities; therefore, attention demand is usually estimated indirectly by the extent to which tasks interfere with each other. Processing of sensory stimuli (or performing other processes early in the sequence) can apparently occur in parallel, with little interference from other tasks. But processes associated with response selection or with response programming or initiation interfere greatly with other activities.

Characteristics of attention play an important role in motor performance. Psychological refractoriness—the delay in responding to the second of two closely spaced stimuli—provides evidence that some single channel, or bottleneck, in processing exists in the response-selection or response-programming stage, before which processing is parallel and after which processing is serial. Other limitations in attention, such as the Stroop effect, inattention blindness, and inhibition of return, reveal that attending selectively to some information may have consequences that are not intentional. Other evidence, based on secondary-task techniques, suggests that attention demands are highest at both the initiation and termination stages of movements, particularly when the end of the action has an important precision component. The use of cell phones and other in-vehicle devices during driving provides an excellent example of attentional limits on daily activities. Some evidence suggests that directing one's attention to movement or environmental cues may differ according to one's skill level.

Performance is influenced by arousal, and several hypotheses have been suggested to explain this relationship. The mechanisms that appear to limit performance under stress are related to the decrease in cue utilization and the failure of decision-making processes, especially under the most stressful conditions called hypervigilance, or panic.

Student Assignments

1. Prepare to answer the following questions in class discussion:
   a. Using examples from a sport, illustrate three different aspects of the concept of attention.

b. Provide examples of inattention blindness in driving.

c. Find two other types of Stroop effects that have been studied in the research literature.

2. Find a research article not covered in the book on the effects of talking on a cellular phone during driving.

Web Resources

Stroop effect demonstration:

http://faculty.washington.edu/chudler/words.html

Original paper by J. Ridley Stroop:

http://psychclassics.yorku.ca/Stroop/

Test your ability to multitask:

www.nytimes.com/interactive/2009/07/19/technology/20090719-driving-game.html

Inattention blindness:

www.dothetest.co.uk/basketball.html

Video showing a danger of texting while walking:

www.tinyurl.com/videodangers2

Notes

[1] Actually, the basic phenomena underlying the "Stroop effect" had been studied for about a half century before Stroop published his work in 1935, beginning with Cattell (1886; see MacLeod, 1991, for a historical review).

[2] In a way, this label is unfortunate. The original idea was that the delay in the subject's response to the second of two closely spaced stimuli is analogous to the delay when a single nerve fiber is stimulated electrically twice in rapid succession in physiological experiments. If the second stimulus is very close to the first (within about 5 ms), no response at all will result from the second stimulus. This effect has been termed the *absolute refractory period,* meaning that the nerve is insensitive to additional stimulation while it is refractory, and it "recovers" from the effects of the first stimulus. These neuronal processes probably have little to do with the psychological refractory period, as the time course is much longer in the behavioral work (e.g., 200 ms).

[3] Note that even the original findings of Yerkes and Dodson (1908) were actually more complex than is traditionally depicted by this inverted-U function. They indeed found an inverted-U relationship between increases in shock intensity and the number of trials required to reach criterion discrimination performance. However, this was true only for moderate and degraded lighting conditions. When full lighting was provided, making the discrimination relatively "easy" (i.e., choosing between a white and black door), there was no inverted-U relationship. Rather, the relationship was linear—the number of trials to reach criterion decreased as shock intensity increased. Thus, even Yerkes and Dodson's data were more complex than this "simple" inverted-U relationship.

PART II

MOTOR CONTROL

The human motor system is a very complex whole with many interacting pieces, processes, and mechanisms. To attempt to understand the entire system as a whole would be extremely difficult. For this reason, scientists generally study various parts of the system in isolation. These are often studied as independent modes of control—fundamentally different ways in which the system's parts can work together. In chapter 5, the focus is on the role of sensory information; we consider the ways in which information from the environment influences, or even determines, movement behavior. In chapter 6, we examine the central control and representation of action in situations in which sensory influences do not have a particularly strong role. Chapter 7 deals with various laws and models regarding the principles of speed and accuracy, especially as they pertain to the control of relatively "simple" movements. This analysis is extended in chapter 8 to more complex tasks involving the coordination of more than one effector. Part II ends with a discussion in chapter 9 of factors that tend to make individuals differ from each other in their skilled behaviors.

CHAPTER 5

SENSORY CONTRIBUTIONS TO MOTOR CONTROL

One of the ways in which motor control is achieved relies heavily on the concept that we use *sensory* (or *afferent*) *information* to regulate our movements. This can be information that tells us about the state of the environment, about the state of our own body, or about the state of our body with respect to the environment. A way to think about how sensory information is used in the control of action is to consider the moving human as a type of *closed-loop* system. A closed-loop system depends heavily on the involvement of particular types of sensory information as it executes its function. Such sensory information, when discussed in the context of closed-loop motor control, is often termed *movement-produced feedback,* or simply *feedback,* implying that the sensory information to be considered has arisen as the *result* of performed actions. Of course there are many other forms of sensory information that are not associated with the performed movements, and these are usually considered under the more general heading of sensation and perception. In this chapter we discuss the various kinds of sensory information that can be used in the control of movement.

Closed-Loop Control Systems

One way of attempting to understand motor control has been to consider sensory contributions in ways analogous to mechanical systems' control. *Closed-loop* systems are important in many situations, especially those that require a system to "control itself" for long periods of time (in contrast, see chapter 6 for a discussion of *open-loop* systems). A diagram that illustrates how a simple closed-loop system works is shown in figure 5.1. First, input about the system's goal is provided to a *reference mechanism.* In a home heating system, the overall goal might be to achieve and maintain a certain temperature in the house. The reference mechanism in this system is the specific temperature setting, say 68° F—the temperature setting can be changed without affecting how the system operates. Next, the reference mechanism samples the environment that it is attempting to control to determine the current temperature. This information from the environment is usually termed *feedback.* The reference mechanism then compares the value of the goal (e.g., 68°) to that of the sample obtained from the environment (current temperature), and an *error* is computed, representing the difference between the actual and desired states. The error is information that is passed to an *executive level,* where decisions are made about how to reduce the error. If the error is large enough, instructions are sent from the executive level to the *effector level,* and a mechanism that has some effect on the environment is activated—in this case, the heater. The heater

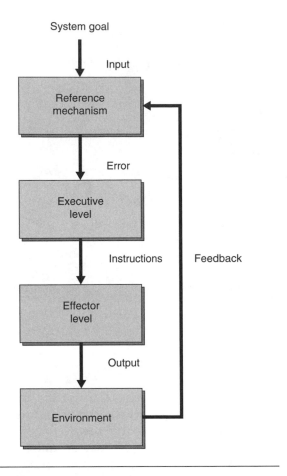

System goal

Input

Reference
mechanism

Error

Executive
level

Instructions   Feedback

Effector
level

Output

Environment

FIGURE 5.1   Elements of the typical closed-loop control system.

raises the temperature of the room, and this raised temperature will be sampled periodically. When the difference between the actual and desired temperatures is zero, the executive level shuts off the heater. In such a way, the heater cycles between being on and off as a function of the actual room temperature and thus maintains the system goal. Such systems are termed *closed loop* because the loop of control from the environment to decisions to action and back to the environment again is completed, or closed.

How does this model of the closed-loop system relate to the human motor control system? For now, think of the reference of correctness and the executive level as being contained in the stages of information processing, so that the system can receive and process feedback information following the stimulus-identification stage, and then program instructions to the musculature to reduce the error in the response-programming stage. Instructions are then given to the effector level,

usually thought of as the muscles or as a program of action that actually controls the muscles. Then, the information obtained from the various muscle, joint, and tendon receptors, as well as from the eyes, ears, and so on, is sent back to the reference mechanisms for analysis, and decisions about future action are again made. Notice that, with this feedback loop (and the stages of processing), the implication is that *all* feedback is processed in this way—requiring attention (and consciousness). As we will learn later in this chapter, some (if not most) feedback for action is processed reflexively, "below" the level of consciousness (see Ghez & Krakauer, 2000; Pearson & Gordon, 2000b).

The various sources (or receptors) of sensory information that are available during movement are traditionally classified into three groups (after Sherrington, 1906). Perhaps the least important for our purposes is the class of receptors called *interoceptors.* They tell us about the states of our internal organs, as with "hunger pains," and have questionable relevance for motor behavior. The remaining two classes of receptors are divided according to whether they provide information about the movement of objects in the environment *(exteroceptors)* or information about our own movements *(proprioceptors).* The roots *extero* and *proprio* refer to events outside one's body and events in one's own body, respectively.

Vision

Certainly the most critical receptor for supplying information about the movement of objects in the outside world is the eye. Therefore, we begin our discussion with the richest and most important feedback information used in the control of movement.

How Vision Provides Information

Subjectively, we all know that darkness critically impairs the performance of many tasks, although we also know that vision is not essential for all motor performances. People who are blind learn to move in the environment with remarkable facility, although they are at a large disadvantage in many situations. In terms of human performance, vision provides information about the movements of objects in the environment, as well as about the movement of one's body in that environment, and much of motor control involves tailoring our motor behavior to meet these visually presented environmental demands.

Dorsal and Ventral Visual Streams

Concerning vision as an exteroceptive system (for detecting events in the outside world), we have long known that central vision (involving visual acuity, contrast, object identification, and consciousness) is a major sensory component of many types of motor behavior. However, evidence and theorizing argue for the existence of two distinct streams of visual processing. The lines of evidence to support these different streams come from a wide range of levels of analysis, using various techniques and subjects in the research. Indeed, even the names for the two visual streams differ markedly, with such proposed dichotomies as cognitive versus motor vision, explicit versus implicit vision, object versus spatial vision, overt versus covert vision (Bridgeman, 1996), and focal versus ambient vision (Trevarthen, 1968). We will refer to the two visual streams in terms of the anatomical distinction proposed by Ungerleider and Mishkin (1982)—the *dorsal* and *ventral* visual stream dichotomy (e.g., see the review and commentaries in Norman, 2002; also Creem & Proffitt, 2001).

In one of these systems (the ventral system), the primary input is limited to central vision. This information requires contrast, focus, and sufficient light. This system is specialized for object identification and (conscious) perception of the environment. Thus, the ventral system is sensitive to what the person is looking at or focusing on (or both). In the other system (the dorsal system), the visual input is full field (nearly 180°), does not require focus, and seems to operate effectively even in very low-light situations. We can think of the retina of the eye as the recipient of rays of light from all parts of the field of vision. For any given position of the eye, a unique combination of these rays allows specification of the eye in space. More importantly, when the eye moves through space (as during walking), the angles of these rays change in predictable ways. These changes in the light rays—termed "optical flow" because the angles of these rays change continuously, or "flow"—specify the nature of the eye's movement (and thus the person's movement) in space. We'll come back to optical flow and movement shortly.

Anatomically, both the dorsal and ventral streams are thought to project visual information from the environment by means of the retina to the primary visual cortex in the brain. From there, however, the dorsal stream sends information to the posterior parietal cortex, whereas the ventral stream projects to the inferotemporal cortex (Ungerleider & Mishkin, 1982). Of particular interest to researchers in motor behavior are the roles afforded by the two streams. Whereas ventral stream processing has been considered responsible for providing cognitive information about objects in the environment (e.g., object identification), processing by the dorsal stream is proposed to provide information specifically for the visual control of movement (Goodale & Milner, 1992; Goodale & Humphrey, 2001; Milner & Goodale, 1993, 1995). Thus, a generalization that has been the topic of hot debate is that ventral stream processing is *vision for perception* (identification) whereas dorsal stream processing is *vision for action* (Jeannerod, 1997; Jeannerod & Jacob, 2005; Milner & Goodale, 2008).

The nature of the information processed appears to be a key component of the distinction. For the ventral stream, information that is central to the identification and recognition of objects is crucial—this includes information picked up from the environment and information stored in memory. In contrast, the dorsal stream is particularly attuned to information about how we control our motor system to interact with an object. As Norman (2002) pointed out, however, it is important to keep in mind that a complementary relationship exists between visual processing in the two streams. For example, when looking for a hammer we use ventral stream information to recognize the hammer and dorsal stream information to pick it up (Norman, 2002). In the next sections, we review some of the evidence that supports the existence of two streams of visual information processing.[1]

Evidence for Two Visual Streams

Classifying things is easy. Before a classification is accepted, however, scientists usually demand strong evidence that it facilitates understanding. One of the strongest kinds of evidence is a *dissociation*, in which the effect of some independent variable on one hypothesized construct (e.g., ventral stream) is different than the effect of the same variable on the other construct (e.g., dorsal stream). Support for the separation of hypothesized constructs is strong when clear dissociations are found. In the study of distinct streams of visual processing, dissociations have been found in two types of research investigations.

Perception–Action Dissociations in Brain-Injured Patients   Strong evidence that favors the dissociation between perception vision and action vision has been found in patients who have specific damage to parts of the brain involved in the processing of visual inputs. For example, patients who had a type of brain injury resulting in what is called *optic ataxia* were able to recognize an object, but were unable to use this same visual information to guide their hand accurately to the object (Perenin & Vighetto, 1988). In contrast, patients with a type of disorder called *visual agnosia* were unable to recognize common objects, yet could use the visual information to grasp the objects accurately (Goodale & Milner, 1992; Goodale, Milner, Jakobson, & Carey, 1991). This dissociation in the ability of patients to use vision for one task but not the other represents a very important finding in support of visual stream separation. Researchers have also relied both on experiments with animals (e.g., Schneider, 1969; Trevarthen, 1968; Ungerleider & Mishkin, 1982) and on behavioral experiments involving healthy individuals to further study these visual streams.

Perception–Action Dissociations in Behavioral Studies   An important early study in the behavioral identification of the two visual streams was conducted by Bridgeman, Kirch, and Sperling (1981). They used an induced-motion paradigm, in which small movements of a surrounding background (a "frame") in a given direction made it appear that a fixed target element within it moved in the opposite direction. Under these conditions, subjects would say (i.e., they perceived, consciously) that the (actually stationary) target moved back and forth through about 2.5° of visual angle. This is a measure of the bias in the ventral processing system. Bridgeman and colleagues then suddenly extinguished the target and background, and the subject's task was to move the hand to point to the last location of the target, providing a measure of the dorsal system's accuracy. These pointing movements (to the *actual* position of the target) were largely unaffected by the movement of the background. In this way, Bridgeman and coworkers found that the movement of the background biased the visual information used for (conscious) perception of

the target's position but did not bias the visual information used for action. Another experiment used the reverse procedures: now, the target actually moved, and the background-frame moved in the opposite direction by such an amount that the subject perceived (consciously, but erroneously) that the target was stationary. When the target and background were extinguished, the pointing tended to be to the actual location of the target, not to the position that the subject perceived consciously.

This effect is actually a *double* dissociation: (1) The moving background (or frame) altered the conscious perception of the fixed target position but not the pointing direction, and (2) the altered actual position of the target (whose location was perceived as fixed because of the moving background) did not bias the pointing direction. Similar double dissociations have also been shown for static images in which an off-centered frame biases the perceptual judgment of a particular stimulus target but does not bias a subject's reach toward the target (Bridgeman, Gemmer, Forsman, & Huemer, 2000).

These important findings, in which a subject-viewed stimulus resulted in a perception vision bias but not an action vision bias, have been the basis for a large number of empirical investigations involving visual *illusions.* Many of these studies used a similar experimental paradigm in which subjects were asked to make perceptual judgments and actions involving various visual illusions as targets. Figure 5.2 illustrates four of these visual illusions.

In investigations of the Ebbinghaus-Titchener illusion[2] (figure 5.2*d*), subjects are asked to point to a circle in the center of surrounding circles (a two-dimensional version of the task), or to grasp a cylindrical disc that is located in the middle of surrounding discs (a three-dimensional version). In this illusion, the Ebbinghaus-Titchener display creates a bias to perceptual vision that makes the center circle surrounded by a ring of small circles appear larger than the center circle surrounded by a ring of large circles, even though the two center circles are identical in size. Most studies, however, have shown a dissociation of the effect of the illusion on perceptual versus action vision—the illusion has no influence on action vision, evaluated either as the movement time to point at the circles or as the size of the grasp used to pick up the center object; sometimes, the bias is much smaller than the effect on perceptual judgments of these circles (Aglioti, DeSouza, & Goodale, 1995; Haffenden & Goodale, 1998; Haffenden, Schiff, & Goodale, 2001). Similar perception vision and action vision dissociations using the other visual illusions have also been found for the Müller-Lyer illusion (figure 5.2a) (Otto-de Haart, Carey, & Milne, 1999), the Ponzo illusion (figure 5.2b) (Bartlett & Darling, 2002; Ellis, Flanagan, & Lederman, 1999; Ganel, Tanzer, & Goodale, 2008), and the horizontal–vertical illusion (figure 5.2c) (Servos, Carnahan, & Fedwick, 2000).

Note, however, that much controversy exists regarding the interpretation of visual illusion dissociations (e.g., Bruno, 2001; Carey, 2001). Some of the behavioral dissociations are found only under restricted and specialized experimental conditions (e.g., Fischer, 2001; Franz, Bülthoff, & Fahle, 2003; van Donkelaar, 1999; Westwood, Dubrowski, Carnahan, & Roy, 2000; Wraga, Creem, & Proffitt, 2000), and sometimes are not found at all (e.g., Meegan et al., 2004). Comprehensive reviews of this research area conclude that visual illusions appear to have a

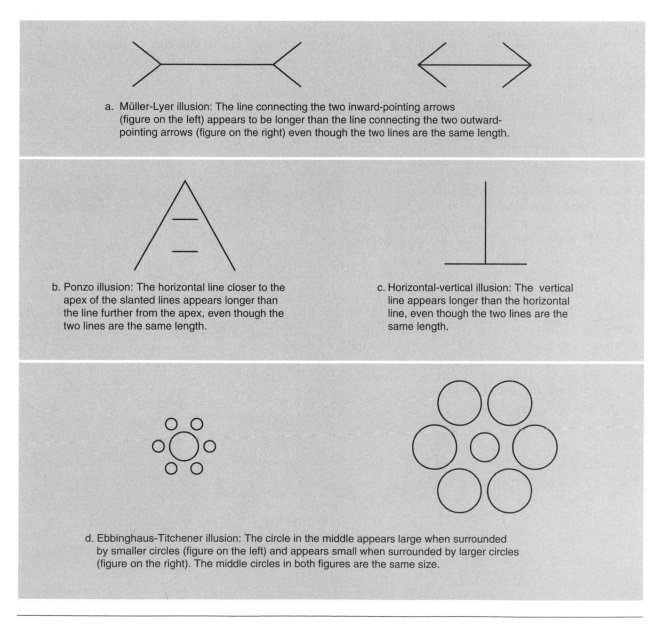

a. Müller-Lyer illusion: The line connecting the two inward-pointing arrows (figure on the left) appears to be longer than the line connecting the two outward-pointing arrows (figure on the right) even though the two lines are the same length.

b. Ponzo illusion: The horizontal line closer to the apex of the slanted lines appears longer than the line further from the apex, even though the two lines are the same length.

c. Horizontal-vertical illusion: The vertical line appears longer than the horizontal line, even though the two lines are the same length.

d. Ebbinghaus-Titchener illusion: The circle in the middle appears large when surrounded by smaller circles (figure on the left) and appears small when surrounded by larger circles (figure on the right). The middle circles in both figures are the same size.

FIGURE 5.2 Various visual illusions used in aiming tasks. (a) Müller-Lyer illusion, (b) Ponzo illusion, (c) horizontal–vertical illusion, (d) Ebbinghaus-Titchener illusion.

larger influence on perception than on action, although both appear to be influenced in similar ways by the visual information (Bruno, Bernardis, & Gentilucci, 2008 ; Bruno & Franz, 2009). Consequently, while some researchers feel that these behavioral data support the distinction between separate streams of visual processing, others are less convinced. For example, Glover (2002, 2004; Glover & Dixon, 2001) presented evidence that a perceptual tilt illusion affected action during the movement planning stage but not during the execution of the movement, leading to the view that differences in the use of action vision are dissociated between the planning and execution stages. In contrast, Smeets and Brenner (2001; Smeets, Brenner, de Grave, & Cuijpers, 2002) argue that object orientation in the environment affects visual processing *strategies,* and does not imply separate streams of vision. It seems that further experimental evidence will be needed before we have a clear understanding of what these behavioral studies suggest regarding ventral and dorsal visual stream processing.

Visual Information About Time to Contact

Another important issue related to the general topic of how visual information is provided has to do with the processing of dynamic information—visual information that changes over time, sometimes at a very rapid rate. For example, in passing another automobile, we are bombarded with various sources of visual inputs that change at different rates: the stationary environmental information that we drive past (such as road signs); the car that we are passing; the car that is coming rapidly toward us in the opposite lane; and the information within our own car, which is traveling at the same speed as ourselves. All these sources of information represent visual cues that we must perceive accurately in order to execute a safe pass.

Considerable research in motor behavior has been directed at a subset of skills involved in the perception of dynamic visual information. Many of these skills are used in ball games and require *interceptive* actions such as catching or striking. The moving object provides various types of information, such as its position in space and the way its position is changing over time (e.g., in the case of a pitched ball in baseball). However, probably the most important and frequently studied skill relates to the use of temporal information about *when* the object will arrive. This is called time-to-contact (T_c) information.

An important view regarding how T_c is perceived was formulated by David Lee (1980, 1990; Lee & Young, 1985; see also Purdy, 1958), and relates quite closely to the concept of *visual proprioception* and to the work of James Gibson (1966, 1979; see "Visual Proprioception" on p. 142). Consider an object, such as a ball, that is moving directly toward your eye, as shown in figure 5.3. If the angles of the light rays from the edges of the ball (i.e., α_1 and α_2) are increasing at the same rate (with respect to straight ahead), this information specifies that the ball is moving directly toward your eye. Such information,

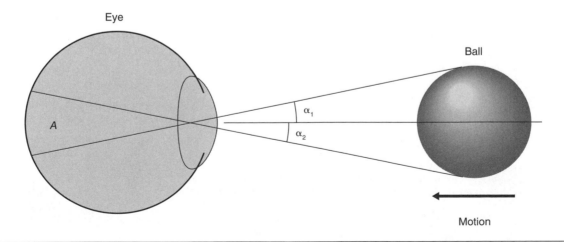

FIGURE 5.3   Diagram of a ball approaching an eye, showing the size of the image *(A)* it projects on the retina; at any moment, the time until contact is proportional to tau, which is directly proportional to the retinal size *A* divided by *Å*, the rate of change of *A* (i.e., tau = *k A / Å*).

called *looming*, usually elicits strong avoidance reactions that appear to be nearly "automatic," or at least difficult to inhibit, especially in infants. But in addition, Lee's work shows that these changes in visual information tell the viewer about the amount of time remaining until contact will be made (Lee, 1976, 1980, 1990, 2009; Lee & Young, 1985). In figure 5.3, the edges of the ball cast a retinal image of size A, which increases in size as the ball comes closer; also, the more rapidly the ball approaches, the faster the image will be expanding. Let's abbreviate this rate of expansion occurring at some moment (or the derivative of A with respect to time) as $\dot{A}$, where the dot above the letter means the "rate of change of." Lee defines "proportionate rate of expansion" as simply the rate of expansion $\dot{A}$ divided by the size of the retinal image A (or $\dot{A}/A$), which is a measure of the rate of change at some moment as a proportion of the size of the retinal image A. Lee (1976) showed mathematically that the reciprocal of this ratio, or $A/\dot{A}$, is directly proportional to T_c. This is true regardless of the size of the object, the velocity at which it travels, or its distance from the eye. That is, time to contact (or T_c) is defined as

$$T_c = \text{tau (or } \tau\text{)} = k\,A\,/\,\dot{A} \qquad (5.1)$$

where k is a proportionality (slope) constant. In other words, T_c is proportional to the reciprocal of the proportionate rate of expansion of the retinal image. This makes common sense. At a given distance, an object has a retinal size of A; the rate of change in the object's retinal image $(\dot{A})$ will be larger the faster it is traveling. This makes the denominator in equation 5.1 larger and hence tau smaller, indicating that there will be less time until the object contacts the eye.

More recently, Lee (1998) formulated a general theory of how tau is used in the control of movement. In this view, all goal-directed actions require the closing of a *gap*. For example, running to catch a ball requires the closing of two gaps: (1) the gap between the ball's initial position and its point of interception and (2) the gap between the catcher's initial position and the point of interception. Lee has suggested that *tau coupling* is one component of a general tau theory—that the closure of the two gaps occurs at the same relative rate (Lee, Georgopolous, Clark, Craig, & Port, 2001). This view follows closely the earlier theoretical formulations and retains the elegant concept that a relatively simple transformation of optical flow allows the specification of important temporal events in the environment. It is a relatively simple theory in the sense that perception does not depend on the "computation" of either distance or velocity cues per se. In a later section we will see how ideas regarding T_c have been used to explain various features of motor control.

Time Required to Process Visual Feedback

Consider the following situation: Someone is working at night in a toolshed, striking the head of a nail with a hammer. Now imagine that the electrical power to the shed is lost and all the lights go out just as the hammer starts its downward swing to contact the nail. How does the sudden loss of vision affect the accuracy? Would accuracy have been affected any more or any less if the hammer had not yet started its downward swing, or if the size of the nail had been larger or smaller, or if the swing had been faster or slower? For over a century, experimenters have studied research questions addressing situations such as these using various theoretical and experimental approaches.

Moving to Stationary Targets

An initial estimate of the time required to process visual feedback was provided more than a century ago by Woodworth (1899). The research was motivated by his view that aiming movements consist of a two-component process. In the *initial-impulse* phase (also termed the *ballistic-* or *programmed-movement phase* by later researchers), Woodworth suggested that movements are initiated by an impulse that drives the limb toward the target. Once the movement is under way, the second phase provides an opportunity to correct any spatial error that may have occurred in the intended path of the limb. Woodworth called this second component the *current-control phase*, during which the subject uses visual feedback to *home in* on the target, making fine corrective adjustments as needed in order to land on the target. According to Woodworth, the successful completion of this second phase of the movement can occur only if there is sufficient time to process the error arising from the analysis of the visual feedback and to issue an efferent signal that will alter the spatial course of the movement. Thus,

Visual Proprioception

Figure 5.4 illustrates one of James Gibson's concepts about how changes in head position contribute to changes in the angles of light rays entering the eye (Gibson, 1966, 1979). The pattern of rays experienced is called the *optical array,* and it provides a unique specification of the location of the eye in space. The changes in the optical array when the eye is moved from one place to another are called the *optical flow,* implying that the visual environment "flows past us" as we move around. An important point is that the particular patterns of flow specify distinct kinds of movements of the eyes with respect to the environment. For example, if the angle between the light rays from two sides of an object is constant over time, this specifies that you are not moving with respect to that object. If the angle between these rays is increasing, then you are moving toward the object; if it is decreasing, you are moving away from it. Also, if the angles from two sides of an object (with respect to straight ahead) are increasing at the same rate, the eye is moving toward the center of the object (e.g., your eye(s) are moving toward the center of a picture on the wall). In conditions in which the angles from both sides of an object are changing in the *same* direction, if the rate of increase in the angle of the rays from the right side of the object is greater than the rate of increase from the left side and continues in this way, you will pass the object so that it is on your right side.

The optical flow generated as you move in the environment also tells you about the *environment itself* in ways that could not be achieved if you were stationary. For example, imagine looking out the window at two telephone poles as illustrated in figure 5.4. Which of them is closer? The question is difficult to answer if you remain still, because the poles appear to be nearly the same thickness and height. But if you move your head sideways you can tell immediately. You will notice that one of the poles seems to "move more quickly" as you change head position. This, of course, is the same as saying that the angles of the rays received from one object changed more quickly (α_1 in the figure) than did those from the other (α_2), implying that pole 1 is closer than pole 2. Thus, the visual system, through movement of the entire head, body, or both, can provide rich information about the nature of the environment. In this view, vision is not merely an exteroceptive sense, passively providing information about the environment. It is also a proprioceptive sense telling us about our own movements. As well, vision is dependent on movement in some situations for informing us about the environment. In this way, vision and movement are very closely and reciprocally linked. Excellent discussions of this basic idea are found in Gibson (1966, 1979) and Lee (1980; Lee & Young, 1985), the latter showing relevance to many situations, including sport-related motions and bird flight.

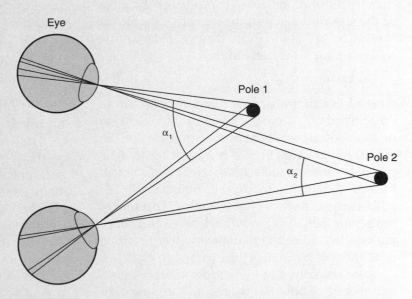

FIGURE 5.4   The detection of distance: The angles of the light rays from the distant pole change less than those from the near pole as the head and eyes are moved.

R.S. WOODWORTH ON MANUAL AIMING

R.S. Woodworth became one of the most noted American experimental psychologists of his time. The topic of his doctoral dissertation was motor control, and in 1899 he published the results of a large number of experiments on the topic of "accuracy of voluntary movement." In this work, Woodworth touches on a wide array of topics related to the control of movement: the use of vision, handedness, biomechanical factors, fatigue, practice, and so on. One of his most lasting contributions has been the two-component model of movement aiming (i.e., initial adjustment vs. current control), and Woodworth's ideas remain at the forefront of theorizing today (Elliott et al., 2010; Elliott, Helsen, & Chua, 2001; Newell & Vaillancourt, 2001b). In the following quote from Woodworth's dissertation (Woodworth, 1899), note how effortlessly he moves between topics that would later become the center of much of our present understanding of these processes.

"If the reader desires a demonstration of the existence of the 'later adjustments' which constitute the most evident part of the 'current control,' let him watch the movements made in bringing the point of his pencil to rest on a certain dot. He will notice that after the bulk of the movement has brought the pencil near its goal, little extra movements are added, serving to bring the point to its mark with any required degree of accuracy. Probably the bulk of the movement is made by the arm as a whole, with little additions by the fingers. If now the reader will decrease the time allowed for the whole movement, he will find it more difficult, and finally impossible, to make the little additions. Rapid movements have to be made as wholes. If similar movements are made with eyes closed, it is soon found that the little additions are of no value. They may bring us further from the goal as likely as nearer" (p. 54).

Woodworth reasoned that aimed movements with vision should be more accurate than those made without vision, but *only if* there is sufficient time to use the visual feedback. Movements that are completed before visual feedback can be processed would be expected to result in target dispersions that are equally inaccurate for blind and sighted aims. The critical question, then, is, What is the minimum amount of time required to process visual feedback? A number of experiments using more or less the same experimental method as Woodworth's have addressed this question. Therefore, we will examine the Woodworth (1899) study in some detail (see also "R.S. Woodworth on Manual Aiming").

Woodworth (1899) To assess the minimal time required to process visual feedback, Woodworth asked his subjects to make back-and-forth movements of a pen. The goal for each action was to produce a movement equal in length to the preceding one. A strip of paper moved beneath the subject's pen at a constant velocity; thus a record of the previous movement could be used as the target for the next and served also as a permanent record that could be used later to calculate mea-

sures of error. Movements were performed with eyes open or closed, paced by a metronome at speeds of 200 to 20 cycles per minute (i.e., movement times [MTs] that ranged from 300 ms to 3 s per cycle, respectively). Aiming was done only in one direction—the return movement was made to a physically restricted stop. Thus, the values of available time to process visual feedback from the stop to the intended target were about half of the total cycle time, or between 150 ms and 1.5 s (Carlton, 1992).

The average errors (similar to absolute error [AE]; see chapter 2) in the eyes-open and eyes-closed conditions are illustrated by the open and filled circles in figure 5.5. As seen on the far left side of this figure (short MTs), the eyes-open and eyes-closed conditions produced equivalent average error. As shown on the right side of the figure (long MTs), the availability of vision in the eyes-open condition resulted in much lower average error, relative to the eyes-closed condition and relative to short MTs with the eyes open. The critical point in the graph occurs when the eyes-closed and eyes-open conditions begin to depart in terms of average error. This departure point represents the time when vision of the target

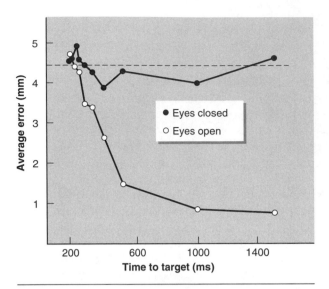

FIGURE 5.5 Aiming errors in moving to targets with the eyes open and closed.

Adapted from Woodworth 1899.

significantly reduces average error compared to the average performance of the eyes-closed condition (represented by the dotted line in figure 5.5). This point of departure occurs between movements of 215 ms duration and movements of 250 ms duration. That is, movements with durations of 250 ms or longer could benefit from the availability of vision (as seen by reduced error), but movements with durations of 215 ms or less did not benefit when vision was available. Notice that, for this task, the estimate of the time to process visual feedback seems to be about the same as in responding to a visual stimulus in a *choice* reaction-time (RT) task.

Keele and Posner (1968) Although Woodworth's empirical and theoretical contributions are considered landmarks in motor control research (Elliott et al., 2001; Newell & Vaillancourt, 2001b), there were some peculiarities. The repetitive, back-and-forth nature of the task meant that subjects had to aim at the target and prepare to reverse the movement (to start it) at about the same time, making the role of vision more complex than in an aimed movement that simply terminates at the target, such as using a computer mouse to move a cursor onto a screen icon. As well, the nature of the task required subjects to try to match the previous movement they had made; the target was more ambiguous than, for example, hitting a nail with a hammer or striking a computer key with a finger (Meyer,

Smith, Kornblum, Abrams, & Wright, 1990, describe other peculiarities).

In another well-known experiment, Keele and Posner (1968) overcame these problems by using a discrete-task version of Woodworth's research strategy. They trained their subjects to move a stylus to a small target about 15 cm away. Knowledge of results about MT was provided, and subjects were trained to move as closely as possible to assigned MT goals (150, 250, 350, and 450 ms). On certain randomly determined test trials, the experimenters turned off the room lights as soon as the stylus left the starting position, so that the entire movement was made in the dark.

Keele and Posner's results are illustrated in figure 5.6, revealing the probability of missing this target as a function of the vision condition and the *actual* average MTs. In the 150 ms MT condition (the actual MT was 190 ms), about as many target misses were recorded when the lights were on (68%) as when the lights were off (69%). As the MTs increased, an advantage emerged when the room lights were on, consistent with the view that vision can be used when sufficient time is available for detecting and correcting errors.

Visual Feedback Uncertainty Despite the changes in the design of their study, Keele and

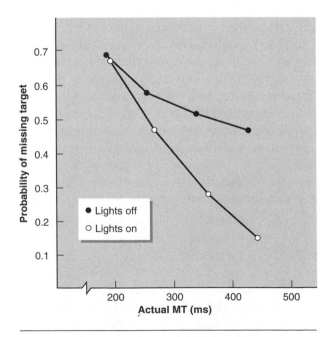

FIGURE 5.6 Percentage of target misses with room lights on and off during movements of various durations.

From Keele and Posner 1968.

Posner's estimate of the time required to process visual feedback information (between 190 and 260 ms) was very similar to the estimate suggested by Woodworth (1899). But *uncertainty* about whether or not visual feedback would be available on a trial seems to have played an important role in the experiment of Keele and Posner (1968). In their methodology, the room lights went off unexpectedly on some trials in a randomly determined order. Perhaps if subjects knew in advance that vision would or would not be available, their attention might have been focused more appropriately, and the estimate of the time to process visual feedback might be considerably less than in situations in which subjects are "surprised" by the presence or absence of vision. If the subject could never fully expect to have vision available, then a strategy designed to employ vision might be avoided in favor of an alternative strategy. The unpredictability of vision in Keele and Posner's study may have prevented subjects from using vision to its fullest when it was available. Thus, visual processing time in the study may have been overestimated.

To address this issue, Zelaznik, Hawkins, and Kisselburgh (1983) and Elliott and Allard (1985) performed experiments similar to Keele and Posner's except that in some conditions the subjects knew in advance when vision would or would not be available. Elliott and Allard (experiment 1) used a series of trials in which the room lights were either left on or were turned off at *random* (as in Keele & Posner), and another series of trials in which room lights were manipulated in a *blocked* order (i.e., entire sets of trials were done either with or without vision). For movements made as fast as possible (225 ms), the availability of vision increased target aiming accuracy only when trials were blocked; no differences were found between vision and no-vision conditions when the trials were randomized (i.e., when visual feedback availability could not be anticipated). These findings raised the possibility that unpredictability and frequent switches between vision and no-vision conditions reduced processing efficiency (Cheng, Luis, & Tremblay, 2008).

Zelaznik and colleagues (1983) also found that visual feedback could be used more quickly in predictable trials than when it was presented randomly. The findings from their third experiment are illustrated in figure 5.7. In this study, all trials were conducted in a blocked (predictable)

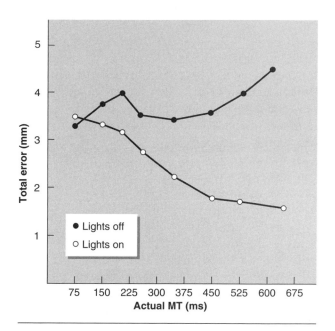

FIGURE 5.7   Target accuracy (total variability, E) in a stylus-aiming task as a function of movement time (MT) and lighting conditions.

Adapted from H.N. Zelaznik, M. Hawkins, and L. Kisselburgh, 1983, "Rapid visual feedback processing in single-aiming movement," *Journal of Motor Behavior* 15: 217-236.

order. No advantage for the availability of visual feedback was found when MTs were about 75 ms; however, clear differences were present for MTs of about 150 ms and longer. These data suggest that vision, when its presence can be expected, can be used in far less time than the minimum suggested by Woodworth (1899) and by Keele and Posner (1968), perhaps with visual processing times as short as 100 ms. In other experiments, Zelaznik and colleagues showed that the advantage for the lights-on condition remained even if the procedures were reversed so that the lights were off initially but would come on suddenly.

Other studies support the contention that the visual processing values obtained by Woodworth (1899) and Keele and Posner (1968) were overestimates of the minimum time to process visual information. Carlton (1981a) prevented visual feedback during the initial 75% of the distance to the target; he found that vision could be used in as little as 135 ms (see also Carlton, 1979, 1981b; Spijkers & Lochner, 1994). Smith and Bowen (1980) showed that distorted or delayed visual information caused disruptions in movement accuracy when the MTs were only 150 ms, also suggesting that visual processing time was far faster than had been previously measured. Similar results were reported by Elliott and Allard (1985, experiments 2 and 3). Suddenly perturbing the *location* of a visible target (immediately after the movement to the "old" target is begun) also resulted in very fast movement corrections, with latencies of about 100 ms (Paulignan, MacKenzie, Marteniuk, & Jeannerod, 1991; Pélisson, Prablanc, Goodale, & Jeannerod, 1986), although perturbing the target *size* necessitates considerably longer processing times (Paulignan, Jeannerod, MacKenzie, & Marteniuk, 1991).

When vision is available and MTs are sufficiently long to use that information, what is typically observed is a *correction* in the trajectory of an aimed movement to improve its end-point accuracy. Technological advances in movement analyses toward the end of the past century permitted researchers to examine the kinematics of these movements (see chapter 2) to make refined estimates of when subjects were using visual information. Reviews of this research by Carlton (1992), Glencross and Barrett (1992), Elliott and colleagues (2001), and Khan and colleagues (2006) include discussions of a number of related methodologies used to investigate the time to process visual feedback. When all this evidence is taken together, it suggests that no single, *absolute* estimate of the time to process visual feedback is likely to be correct. The nature of the task, the type of visual information available, the predictability of this information, and so on all affect the speed and effectiveness with which we use visual information in aiming.

Intercepting Moving Targets

Hitting a nail with a hammer is an example of just one type of action in which vision is used in motor control; the object is stationary, and the goal of the action is to make contact with the object (defined as a "closed" skill in chapter 2). Now consider another class of skills in the situation in which the environment is changing during the action (called "open" skills in chapter 2). Does processing visual information about *moving objects* differ from that for stationary objects (Pélisson et al., 1986)?

An early study by Whiting, Gill, and Stephenson (1970) suggests that the answer might be yes. In this experiment, a ball was dropped from a 3 m height to an angled trampoline-like spring, which bounced the ball another 3 m toward the subject, who attempted to catch it. Trials were conducted in a completely darkened room, and a small bulb inside the ball could be lit for periods of 100, 150, 200, 250, or 300 ms after it hit the trampoline. With a ball flight time (from the point when the ball left the trampoline until the catch was attempted) of 400 ms, these viewing times left the subject without sight of the ball for periods of 300, 250, 200, 150, or 100 ms prior to hand contact, respectively. The proportion of balls caught in each of the vision conditions is presented in figure 5.8. Although performance under the most favorable condition was not as accurate as in a control condition in which all the room lights were on[3] (represented by the dotted line in figure 5.8), Whiting and colleagues found that catching performance improved as the viewing time became longer—even when the 150 and 100 ms conditions were compared! Thus, one conclusion is that visual information of the ball flight could be used in as little as 100 ms to improve catching performance (see Savelsbergh & Davids, 2002; Savelsbergh & Whiting, 1996; and Savelsbergh, Whiting, & Pijpers, 1992, for discussion of related experiments).

One potentially confounding factor in the study by Whiting and colleagues (1970) was that the length of the viewing period covaried with the amount of time without vision; the greater the time with vision, the less time without it, and vice versa. An experimental approach that allows examination of the independent contribution of these factors uses *stroboscopic* conditions. The stroboscopic conditions are simulated with the use of goggles that can be alternately opened and closed during ball flight to provide periodic "snapshots" of visual information. Using this method, Elliott, Zuberec, and Milgram (1994) examined the independent contributions of the length of time that the goggles were open and the length of time that vision was not available (goggles closed). Interestingly, Elliott and colleagues found that the most important contribution to catching performance was *not* the amount of time vision was available, but rather the time *between* the visual snapshots of the ball (i.e., the length of time without vision). Subjects could perform well with as few as 20 ms of available vision of the ball as long as no more than 80 ms intervened between "snapshots" (see also Assaiante, Marchand, & Amblard, 1989). Apparently, longer periods without vision updating can support performance during aiming at stationary targets (Elliott, Chua, & Pollock, 1994). These findings do not constitute rejection of ear-

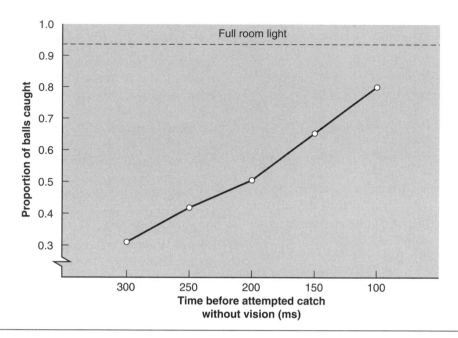

FIGURE 5.8   Number of balls caught in full room light and in conditions in which lights have been extinguished prior to attempted catch.

Adapted from H.T.A. Whiting, E.B. Gill, and J.M. Stephenson, 1970, "Critical time intervals for taking in flight information in a ball-catching task," *Ergonomics* 13: 269.

lier estimates of the minimum time to process visual information. Rather, they serve to reject the idea that a minimum amount of *continuous* visual information is needed. These findings suggest that visual information can be processed *intermittently* (or quasi-continuously), using very short durations of information (these ideas are reviewed in Elliott, Binsted, & Heath, 1999).

One can raise the argument that experimental occlusion of vision is not a natural approach to examining the speed of visual processing. In other words, in our example of the toolshed, the lights do not go out very often. Critics of this approach have used a number of alternative paradigms in which the use of visual feedback information is inferred from the adjustment (homing in) actions that occur during the preparation for object contact. For example, Bootsma and van Wieringen (1990) found that expert table tennis players could use visual information about the moving ball to adjust their forehand drive in the last 105 to 156 ms of ball flight (depending on the individual). Estimates ranging from 50 to 135 ms were reported by Lee, Young, Reddish, Lough, and Clayton (1983) in a task that required subjects to jump to hit a falling ball. Longer estimates for responding to changes in the path of a ball after a perturbed bounce have also been obtained (about

190 ms in McLeod, 1987; 150-190 ms in Carlton, Carlton, & Kim, 1997). The longer delay times in these latter two studies, however, may be attributable to the unexpectedness of the change in flight path and the larger objects that were being manipulated (a cricket bat in McLeod, 1987; a tennis racket in Carlton et al., 1997).

Interpreting the Evidence

It seems that vision, under various conditions, can be processed for motor control in considerably less time than our usual estimates of RT to a visual stimulus would suggest. One interpretation of these differences in visual processing time estimates is that the various experimental conditions appear to introduce *strategic* differences in the ways subjects prepare for specific types of visual information. For example, Glencross and Barrett (1992) suggest that in some situations, subjects may make *deliberate* errors (e.g., undershooting the target) in the initial movement phase, perhaps in order to reduce the uncertainty of the information specified by the visual feedback (see also Barrett & Glencross, 1989; Carlton, 1981a). With use of this strategy, the *amount of information* to be processed in the visual display is reduced because the direction of the corrective action is highly predictable.

Another interpretation is related to the hypothesis of two visual systems proposed by Trevarthen

(1968) and Schneider (1969), discussed earlier in the chapter (see also Aschersleben & Müsseler, 1999). According to the dissociation (Goodale & Milner, 1992), much of the visual information for movement control is handled by the dorsal system, which is thought to be nonconscious and spatially oriented (Bridgeman et al., 1981; Pélisson et al., 1986). However, various experimental manipulations of visual feedback processing time may require use of the ventral visual system. Thus, it may be that the motor control studies using stationary stimuli have forced the subjects to use the (slower) ventral system, which is not the system they would normally use in "real" environmental skill situations. What is clear is that the time to use visual information changes as a function of the characteristics of the target and the goals of the movement (Carlton, 1992). In the next sections we describe other evidence related to the role of vision in motor control.

Vision and Anticipatory Actions

Situations in which the movement goal involves an interaction with a *changing* environment include cases in which the individual, the environment (or an object in the environment), or both are moving. For example, in ball sports, there are times when the performer must stand still and *intercept* a moving object (as in batting a ball) or must move to intercept a ball in flight (as in catching a forward pass in American football). Activities such as running or driving a car involve situations in which the motion of the individual results in a changing visual array. In all cases, information about the changing environment is used to prepare *anticipatory actions* that allow people to complete the task (such as catching a ball or avoiding objects in their path). The issue that we deal with next concerns how these actions become specified by the changing environment.

Interceptive Control

Most of the research on the role of vision during interceptive activities has involved a moving object, as in catching or striking a ball. According to Savelsbergh and colleagues (Savelsbergh & Whiting, 1996; Savelsbergh et al., 1992), the primary use of vision is to specify information about (1) *when* to intercept an object, in particular, temporal information about T_c; and (2) *where* to go to intercept it, information about the spatial characteristics of the ball flight. Research sug-

gests that the visual system specifies these types of information in different ways.

Temporal Information   As mentioned previously in the chapter, there now appears to be considerable evidence that T_c can be specified by tau (Lee et al., 1983; but see also Abernethy & Burgess-Limerick, 1992). An experiment by Savelsbergh, Whiting, and Bootsma (1991) illustrates how tau is used to specify *when* to carry out the hand actions required for grasping a moving ball. Subjects were positioned with their elbow on a table and their wrist locked into a position such that a ball that swung on a pendulum would come directly into contact with the subject's palm. The only task was to time the catch of the ball with a grasping action; there was no spatial uncertainty. The experiment used 5.5 and 7.5 cm balls; a third ball was 5.5 cm but was covered with a balloon that could be inflated to appear to be the size of the 7.5 cm ball. Once the ball was released, the balloon *deflated* from 7.5 to 5.5 cm over the period of the ball flight (which was about 1.7 s).

A plot of the relative size of these objects is shown in figure 5.9*a* for a constant ball size (A) and with the deflating balloon (B). As the balls (A) approached the subject, the retinal image increased in size about 1,200%, but the retinal image of the deflating balloon (B) expanded only about 500%. Thus, the rate of expansion for the balls was considerably faster than for the balloon. The average apertures of the hand changed as subjects prepared to catch the moving objects during the final 200 ms, as illustrated in figure 5.9*b*. Throughout the final 200 ms of ball flight, the hand aperture was larger in anticipation of catching the large ball (L) compared to the small ball (S). But, for the deflating balloon (B), at 200 ms before contact, the hand had an aperture between the sizes of the large and the small ball; and as the balloon decreased to the size of the small ball, so did the hand aperture. Postexperiment interviews indicated that the subjects were not aware of the deflating properties of the balloon; the scaling of hand aperture to the moment-to-moment size of the deflating balloon might have occurred without conscious awareness.

One interpretation is that T_c is used by the subject via the expansion of the optical flow, and that the catching actions were scaled in anticipation of intercepting the object with a temporally precise grasp. However, as cautioned by Abernethy and Burgess-Limerick (1992), the fact that this experiment and others (e.g., Lee, Lishman, &

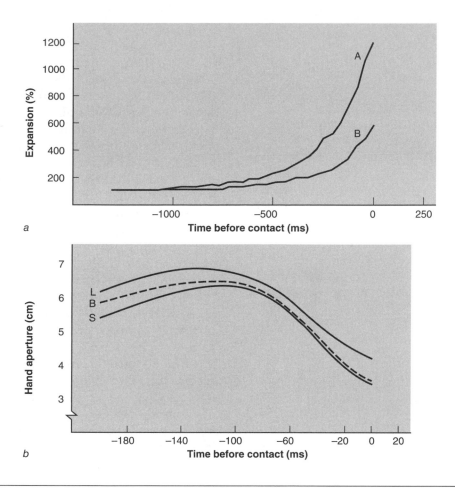

a

b

FIGURE 5.9 Temporal coordination of hand aperture with apparent ball size; zero point on horizontal axis indicates contact with ball. *(a)* Apparent rate of expansion during ball flight (A = constant ball size, B = deflating balloon). *(b)* Hand aperture changes prior to contact (L = large ball, B = deflating balloon, S = small ball).

Adapted, by permission, from G.J. P. Savelsbergh, H.T.A. Whiting, and R.J. Bootsma, 1991, "Grasping tau," *Journal of Experimental Psychology: Human Perception and Performance* 17: 317 and 321. Copyright © 1991 by the American Psychological Association.

Thomson, 1982; Savelsbergh, Whiting, Pijpers, & van Santvoord, 1993) provide evidence *consistent* with the use of tau does not rule out the possibility that T_c can be specified in other ways as well (see also Cavallo & Laurent, 1988; Rock & Harris, 2006; Smeets, Brenner, Trébuchet, & Mestre, 1996; Stewart, Cudworth, & Lishman, 1993; Tresilian, 1995, 1997, 1999; Wann, 1996).

Spatial Information   A difficult task faced by an outfielder in baseball is judging where to go to catch a batted ball, especially when the ball is hit directly at the outfielder. It is not uncommon, even among the most highly skilled players, for an outfielder to run forward to catch a ball, only to stop, reverse and run backward after realizing he has made a mistake. What information is used to make these decisions about *where to go* to catch the ball?

McLeod and Dienes (1993, 1996), following earlier work by Chapman (1968; see also Michaels & Oudejans, 1992; Todd, 1981), suggest that the angle of elevation of gaze (α) between the fielder and the ball is used as the key information for making decisions about where to go to intercept the ball. The sequence of illustrations in figure 5.10 describes McLeod and Dienes' (1996) analysis. Figure 5.10*a* shows how α is computed in relation to a fielder in baseball or cricket. Given the path of the ball in figure 5.10*a*, the fielder determines that movement toward the ball (to decrease *x*) is required before the ball hits the ground (as *y* approaches 0). The fielder's forward movement is depicted in figure 5.10, *b* and *c* (further decreasing *x*), as the ball falls toward the ground (further decreasing *y*). In moving forward, the fielder must keep the angle of gaze

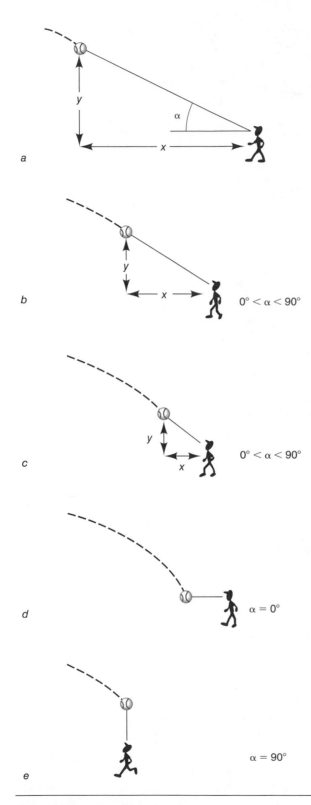

FIGURE 5.10 How a fielder uses the angle of elevation of gaze to decide whether to run forward or backward to catch a ball.

(α) between 0° and 90°. If α ever becomes 0° (i.e., $y = 0$ and $x > 0$), then the ball will land in front of the fielder (figure 5.10d). Likewise, if α ever equals 90° (i.e., $x = 0$ and $y > 0$), then the ball will go over the fielder's head (figure 5.10e). But how does the fielder *use* this information to make the catch?

A considerable amount of research now suggests that the fielder will arrive at the correct place to catch the ball if he adjusts running speed according to visual information (Lenoir, Musch, Thiery, & Savelsbergh, 2002; McLeod & Dienes, 1993, 1996; McLeod, Reed, & Dienes, 2001; Michaels & Oudejans, 1992; Oudejans, Michaels, Bakker, & Davids, 1999). According to McLeod and colleagues, fielders accelerate and decelerate their running speed based on successive samples of vertical gaze (α, position of the height of the ball relative to eye level) and horizontal gaze (δ, position of the ball relative to its origin M, home plate in the case of catching a hit baseball). Specifically, where fielders must run to the left or right (i.e., if the ball is not hit directly at the fielder), they adjust their running speed so that their horizontal gaze (δ) increases at a constant rate and the rate of increase in their vertical gaze (α) decreases steadily, as illustrated in figure 5.11 (McLeod, Reed, & Dienes, 2003, 2006;

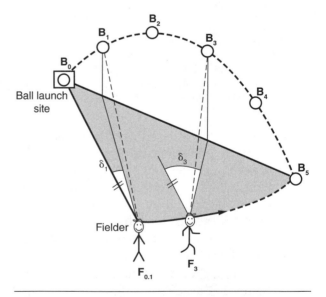

FIGURE 5.11 Running to catch a fly ball. Running speed of the fielder is adjusted in order to maintain a constant rate of increase in the horizontal gaze (δ), the gaze angle relative to the origin of the hit) and to maintain a steadily decreasing rise in the rate of the vertical angle of gaze (α, height of the ball).

Reed, McLeod, & Dienes, 2009). Of course, this strategy does not guarantee that the fielder will successfully make the catch, only that the fielder will be in the right position to try to do so.

Controlling Whole-Body Actions

The work by McLeod and others represents just a small part of a much larger research field dealing with the control of the body as a whole, as in balance and in locomotion. Early thinking about postural control tended to focus on mechanisms that are seemingly obvious contributors to the skills, such as the vestibular apparatus in the inner ear. The receptors are sensitive to deviations from the vertical, to the orientation of the body in space, and to the accelerations applied to the head when the body is moved. All these aspects of balance possibly could be signaled by these receptors.

A second class of processes for the control of balance includes the various receptors associated with the joints and muscles. These processes are discussed in more detail later in this chapter; but for now, consider that in posture, the system is organized to maintain particular angles (which implies muscle lengths) for the joints associated with a particular position of the body in space. When the body begins to lose this posture, the movement of the joints away from the goal position can be sensed by the joint receptors, or perhaps by the stretch of the muscles that control the joint, or by both. Also, there could be tactile sensation from the feet or toes indicating loss of balance. Each of these receptors, alone or in some combination, could conceivably provide the input necessary in order for the person to sense a loss of balance and could provide a basis for initiating a correction. Numerous chapters in the volume by Gandevia, Proske, and Stuart (2002) review this evidence in considerable detail (see also Rossignol, Dubuc, & Gossard, 2006; Shumway-Cook & Woollacott, 2007; Woollacott & Jensen, 1996).

Vision and Balance   A third source of feedback about balance was emphasized by David Lee (see Lee, 1980, for a review). Earlier in this chapter we discussed the concept of visual proprioception, noting that it tells us where our eyes (and therefore our head and body) are in space and how they are moving (if they are) via analysis of the patterns of optical flow received from the surrounding surfaces and elements in the environment (see p. 142, "Visual Proprioception"). Could vision be involved in the control of balance? One

common finding, as pointed out by Lee (1980), is that people who are blind are generally less stable in posture than are sighted people; those without sight sway more when they stand. Also, sighted people sway more when they have their eyes closed versus open. This suggests that vision might have a role in balance (see also Shumway-Cook & Woollcott, 2007, chapter 9).

But more convincing evidence for this assertion comes from some of Lee's experiments (Lee & Aronson, 1974). Lee used a "moving room" apparatus whereby a person stood on a stationary floor in a three-sided "room" with walls (suspended from a ceiling) that could be moved backward and forward as a unit without movement of the floor. The experimenters studied the effect of this wall movement on the posture and sway of the subject (figure 5.12 shows the general

FIGURE 5.12   Experimental apparatus and paradigm for the "moving room." Dr. Lee is second from left.

Reprinted, by permission, from D.N. Lee and E. Aronson, 1974, "Visual proprioceptive control of standing in human infants," *Perception and Psychophysics* 15: 530.

arrangement). With small children as subjects, moving the wall a few centimeters toward the subject caused loss of balance, resulting in a rather ungraceful sitting response and great surprise on the part of the child. Moving the walls away from the child caused a drastic forward lean, which resulted in a stumble or a fall. When adult subjects were studied, the effect was less dramatic; but increases in sway, in-phase with the direction of the wall movement, could be seen.

How can this be explained? Remember, the floor of the room was fixed, so that the movements of the walls could not have exerted *mechanical* influences on the position of the subjects. The mechanisms associated with the joint angles and muscle lengths, as well as the vestibular apparatus, also were not directly affected. The most reasonable explanation is that moving the wall toward the child changed the optical flow and the optical array. If the child was using this information as a source of feedback, she could have interpreted the changed visual array as a loss of balance and consequently produced a compensation in the opposite direction. The walls appearing to move closer to the eye would, if the room were "normal," provide an optic array signaling that the person was falling forward, and a compensation to move backward would be expected. This is just what Lee found: Moving the wall toward the subjects caused them to fall backward. Nashner and Berthoz (1978) showed that responses to the changed optical flow could be generated in about 100 ms (from optical change to change in postural muscles' electromyograms), which shows that these compensations are very fast and automatic and do not involve the stages of processing discussed in chapter 3.

Vision and Locomotion The role of vision during walking and running also seems to be greatly influenced by the optical flow of information; much of the thinking about how we use this information continues to be influenced by Gibson (1958, 1966, 1979; see also Warren, 1998, for a review of Gibson's perspective and Wann & Land, 2000, for a different perspective). We walk down busy streets and through crowded corridors and rarely bump into things or people. We walk on surfaces that have different textures and give them very little attention. But obviously we depend on vision to make our way through the environment. Is vision in this context used in the same way as discussed in the previous sections?

Consider jogging along an irregular path. In this case the placement of the feet with each step is much more critical than, say, on the smooth surface of a running track; to avoid injury, the jogger's goal is to try to step on ground points that indicate good footing and to avoid unstable footings (such as tree roots and loose debris). If the jogger is running at a constant velocity, how is stride length altered in order to step selectively on good ground footings?

Warren, Young, and Lee (1986) had two experienced athletes run at a constant velocity on a treadmill. At various times visual targets appeared on the treadmill, and the runner's task was to try to step on these targets by altering stride lengths as appropriate. The running kinematics revealed that almost all the variations in stride length were attributable to changes in the *vertical impulse* applied at takeoff. An increase in the vertical impulse propels the center of gravity farther upward and thus lengthens the time the lead leg spends in the air; thus, with forward velocity constant, the stride length will also increase. According to Warren and colleagues (1986), the vertical impulse necessary to achieve a specific distance is determined by the difference in the times to contact (T_c) of the takeoff and target points, also called the tau gap ($\Delta \tau$). Since the runner is moving at a constant velocity, the tau gap specifies the duration, and hence the length, of the stride required for the foot to go from the first to the second target (see also Hollands, Marple-Horvat, Henkes, & Rowan, 1995; Patla, 1989; Patla, Robinson, Samways, & Armstrong, 1989; Warren & Yaffe, 1989).

Of course, vision supplies much more than T_c information about how to walk without colliding with objects. Environmental cues provide information about *how* we must accommodate our actions. For example, in walking through *apertures* such as doorways, there is a critical ratio between the aperture and shoulder width: For any aperture less than about 1.3 times the shoulder width, humans will generally rotate their upper body in order to increase the effective passage width (Warren & Whang, 1987). When we step over obstacles, a critical height value also appears to be evident. There is even evidence that the leading leg uses a greater clearance difference if the obstacle is fragile (Patla, Rietdyk, Martin, & Prentice, 1996). Many more examples have been investigated (e.g., Higuchi, Takada, Matsuura, & Imanaka, 2004). However, the main point here is that vision is used in complex ways in order that we may locomote through the environment safely and efficiently (Patla, 1997, 1998).

Audition

Another of the senses traditionally classified as exteroceptive is hearing, or audition. Certainly, audition has a strongly exteroceptive role, informing us about the nature of movements in our environment—the direction of approach of a bicyclist in the dark, the sound of the starter's gun, and so on. But at the same time, like vision, audition can tell us a great deal about our own movements.

As we all know, most of the movements we make in the environment produce sounds, such as the sound of footsteps when we are jogging or the sound of our own speech. The nature of these sounds, then, provides us with a great deal of information about our actions—for example, crunching sounds tell us about the kind of terrain we are jogging on, and beeps from the telephone or automatic teller machine sometimes tell us whether or not we are using the keypad correctly. Sounds serve an important role in sporting events as well. Judges use the sound of a diver as he enters the water as one indication of performance. The "crack of the bat" provides clues to the outfielder regarding how solidly a ball has been struck in baseball. Golfers can often tell what part of the club face has made contact with the ball on the basis of auditory cues. And yet, with all of this sensory feedback available to the performer, the role of audition and how it is used in motor performance remains a largely understudied research area (but see Gray, 2009b; Roberts, Jones, Mansfield, & Rothberg, 2005, for some exceptions).

To some extent, audition and vision are very similar, providing both exteroceptive and proprioceptive information. There are obvious differences, of course. In general, auditory information is processed faster than visual information, but vision seems to provide more useful information than audition. But there are some suggestions that the two types of information as used in similar ways. For example, while flying in a dark cave, bats use acoustic information to orient themselves; sounds from objects (exteroceptive feedback) and from their own movements (exproprioceptive feedback) provide information for orienting them within the cave. Lee (1990, 1998,

2009) suggested that animals (including humans) can determine T_c auditorily by using tau in exactly the same way as described earlier—except that tau is based on the acoustic-flow field rather than the visual-flow field (see also Ashmead, Davis, & Northington, 1995; Jenison, 1997).

Proprioceptors

In the next section we review the set of sensors that provide proprioceptive information (or kinesthesis) about the movement of the body. Although they do not seem to be as salient for movement control as vision is, these sensors are fundamental in their importance for closed-loop control (Abbs & Winstein, 1990; Latash, 2008b). In the first section we outline briefly their anatomy and function, and later we describe their role in motor control.

Vestibular System

Located in the inner ear are sensors that provide information about movements of the head. One aspect of head movement that is critical for motor control is its orientation with respect to gravity; that is, whether the head is upside down, tilted, and so on. Such information is provided by the labyrinthine receptors such as the *otolith* organs— two small structures located in the inner ear (the *saccule* and *utricle*) that signal information about the orientation of the head with respect to gravity. If the head is spinning (e.g., in a somersault), they provide information about the rate and direction of spin. Located near the otolith organs are three fluid-filled half circles, called the *semicircular canals*. Because the canals are oriented in each of the major planes of the body (frontal, sagittal, horizontal), these structures are in a position to sense particular directions of movement, as well as rotation. All these vestibular structures contain thick fluid that moves when the head position changes. The movement of the liquid bends tiny hairs that send information to the central nervous system, informing about movements of the head. As one might imagine, these structures are important in balance, as well as in movements for which the person requires information about forces and accelerations applied to the head (e.g., in flying a plane, doing a somersault; for further discussion see Kelly, 1991; Lackner & DiZio, 2000).

Muscle Receptors

Two main types of receptors provide complementary information about the state of the muscles. The *muscle spindle* is located in the fleshy part of the muscle body and is most active when the muscle is *stretched*. The *Golgi tendon organ* is located in the junction between the muscle and tendon and is most active when the muscle is producing *force* (Gordon & Ghez, 1991; Pearson & Gordon, 2000a).

Muscle Spindles

Lying between the fibers of the main muscles of the body are small spindle-shaped (cigar-shaped) structures that are connected in parallel with the muscles in such a way that they are stretched

when the main muscle is stretched. The spindle consists of three main components: small muscle fibers called *intrafusal (muscle)* fibers (meaning *in the spindle*) that are innervated by *gamma (γ) efferent (motor)* neurons. The spindles can activate *type Ia* and *type II afferent (sensory)* neurons.[4] The fibers in the main muscles are called *extrafusal fibers* (meaning *outside the spindle*). The intrafusal fibers are made up of two types, bag and chain fibers, whose polar ends provide a tension on the central region of the spindle, called the *equatorial region*. The sensory receptors located here are sensitive to the length of the equatorial region, mainly when the spindle is stretched (because the whole muscle is stretched, including the spindle). The major neurological connection to this sensory region is

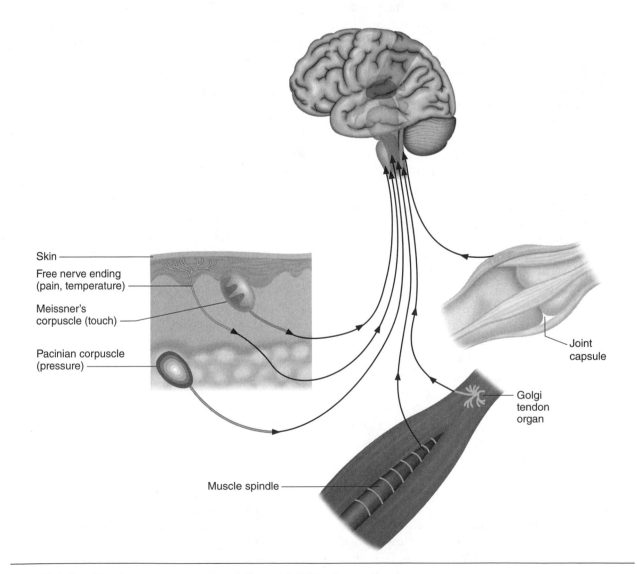

FIGURE 5.13   Muscle receptors: muscle spindle and Golgi tendon organ.

Reprinted, by permission, from J. Wilmore and D. Costill, 2007, *Physiology of sport and exercise*, 4th ed. (Champaign, IL: Human Kinetics), 93.

the *Ia afferent fiber*, whose output is related to the length of the equatorial region (thus signaling joint position information indirectly), as well as to the rate of change in length of this region (velocity information). The spindle connects to the alpha motor neurons for the same muscle, providing excitation to the muscle when it is stretched. This is the basis for the so-called "stretch reflex" discussed later in this chapter. Thus, the spindle appears to have a strong role in movement regulation (Vallbo, 1974; Pearson & Gordon, 2000b).

There has been a great deal of controversy about what the spindle actually signals to the central nervous system (see Gandevia & Burke, 1992, and commentaries). A major conceptual problem in the past was that the output via the Ia afferent that presumably signals stretch or velocity is related to two separate factors. First, Ia afferent output is increased by the elongation of the overall muscle via elongation of the spindle as a whole. But, second, the Ia output is also related to the stretch placed on the equatorial region by the intrafusal fibers via the gamma motor neurons. Therefore, the central nervous system would have difficulty in interpreting changes in the Ia output as due to (a) changes in the overall muscle length with a constant gamma motor neuron activity, (b) changes in gamma motor neuron activity with a constant muscle length, or perhaps (c) changes in both (see "Muscle Spindles and the Gamma Loop" on p. 164).

The system works to disentangle these factors by making use of the gamma motor system and the intrafusal muscle fibers. If the muscle should contract actively (and thus shorten), the stretch of the equatorial region of the spindles would be reduced, and the Ia afferents would decrease their activity. Under such conditions, the spindle would become insensitive to any additional, perhaps unexpected, muscle stretch. However, at the same time the overall muscle is activated (via the alpha motor neurons), the gamma motor system activates the intrafusal fibers, which applies tension to the equatorial region of the spindles. This process has been termed *alpha–gamma coactivation*. This process acts to compensate for the (active) change in the overall muscle, so that the spindle can register changes in muscle length that are not caused by active shortening (e.g., from an unexpected external source).

Another problem was a lack of strong evidence that the Ia afferent fibers actually send information to the sensory cortex of the brain, where other sensory events were thought to be registered. This was suggested by Gelfan and Carter's (1967) research on humans undergoing operations involving wrist tendon repair under local anesthetic only. When the tendons and connected muscles were passively stretched and the subjects were asked what they felt when the tendon was pulled, they usually reported no sensations or sensations that were inconsistent with the direction of tendon pull. Primarily for these reasons, an older view held that the muscle spindles were not important for the conscious perception of movement or position.

Data from Goodwin, McCloskey, and Matthews (1972) and others (Rogers, Bendrups, & Lewis, 1985; Sittig, Denier van der Gon, & Gielen, 1985a) have helped to change this point of view. In these studies, intact subjects had a rapid vibration applied to the biceps tendon at the elbow. The blindfolded subject was asked to "track" the (experimenter-determined) passive movements of the vibrated arm with corresponding active movements of the other arm; thus, the subject had to perceive where the right arm was and match the (consciously felt) position with movements of the left arm. The vibration of the tendon produces a small, rapid, alternating stretch and release of the tendon, which affects the muscle spindle and distorts the output of the Ia afferents from the spindles located in the vibrated muscle. Goodwin and colleagues (1972) found as much as 40° misalignment of the vibrated arm with the nonvibrated arm. The interpretation was that the vibration distorted the Ia afferent information coming from the same muscle, which led to a misperception of that limb's position and hence to improper (conscious) decisions about the positioning of the opposite limb. The argument, then, is that this information from the Ia afferent actually did reach consciousness and thus the Ia afferent was the basis for knowing the limb's position. (To control for the possibility that the vibration merely influenced the structures in the joint capsule of the elbow, the authors placed the vibrator over the triceps tendon; now, the misalignment occurred in the opposite direction, as would be expected if the perception of the Ia afferent output from the triceps muscle were being disrupted.) Such evidence supports the idea that the muscle spindle provides information about limb position and velocity (Sittig, 1986;

Sittig et al., 1985a, 1985b)—quite a different view from that held earlier. There is still some question whether or not the spindle is sufficiently sensitive to detect small positional changes, and thus it may be only one of a number of sources for detecting position (see Kelso & Stelmach, 1976).

Golgi Tendon Organs

The other receptor for muscle information is the Golgi tendon organ; these organs are tiny receptors located in the junction where the muscle "blends into" the tendon (figure 5.13b). They seem to be ideally located to provide information about muscle tension because they lie in series with (i.e., between) the force-producing contractile elements in the muscle and the tendon that attaches the muscle to the bone.

The Golgi tendon organ has been shown to produce an *inhibition* of the muscle in which it is located, so that a stretch to the active muscle would cause the same muscle to decrease its tension somewhat. Also, the early finding that a very large stretch of the muscle (near physiological limits) appeared to be required to induce activity in the Golgi tendon organ led to speculation that the sensor was primarily a protective device that would prevent the muscle from contracting so forcefully that a tendon would rupture.

However, the work of Houk and Henneman (1967) and Stuart (e.g., Stuart, Mosher, Gerlack, & Reinking, 1972) has provided a different picture of the functioning of the Golgi tendon organ. First, anatomical evidence revealed that each organ is attached (in series) to only a small group of from 3 to 25 muscle fibers—not to the entire muscle as had been suspected. Thus, the various receptors were sensing forces produced in different parts of the muscle. Moreover, only a few (up to 15) different motor units[5] were represented in the muscle fibers attached to a single tendon organ, so that the tendon organ now appeared to be in a very good position to sense the tensions produced in a limited number of *individual* motor units—not from the whole muscle. This work has also shown, contrary to earlier beliefs, that the tendon organs can respond to forces of less than 0.1 g (Houk & Henneman, 1967). Such evidence suggests that the Golgi tendon organs are very sensitive detectors for active tension in localized portions of a muscle, in addition to having the well-known protective function noted earlier (see Jami, 1992, for further discussion).

Joint Receptors

Each of the joints of the various limbs is surrounded by a sheath called a joint capsule, which is primarily responsible for holding the lubricating fluid for the joint. Embedded within the joint capsules are different kinds of receptor cells known as the *joint receptors.* They are located primarily on the parts of the joint capsule that are stretched the most when the joint is moved, which originally led investigators to believe that these receptors were involved in the perception of joint position. Studying the cat hindlimb, Skoglund (1956) found individual receptors that were active at very specific locations in the range of limb movement (e.g., from 150° to 180° of joint angle for a particular cell). Another receptor would fire at a different set of joint angles, and so on. Presumably, the central nervous system could "know" the joint angles by detecting which of the joint receptors were active.

These conclusions have been seriously challenged, however (see Kelso & Stelmach, 1976, for a review). A number of investigators (e.g., Burgess & Clark, 1969) have found that only a small proportion of the joint receptors fire at specific angles; rather, most of the joint receptors tend to fire near the extremes of joint movement. Further, other researchers have found that the nature of the firing pattern is dependent on whether the movement is active or passive (Boyd & Roberts, 1953) and on the direction of motion of the joint (see Smith, 1977). The fact that the firing pattern of the joint receptors is dependent on factors other than the simple position of the limb has dimmed enthusiasm for the hypothesis that the joint receptors are the means by which the system senses joint position.

Cutaneous Receptors

Other receptors related to movement perception are located in various places in the skin. Although such receptors can signal many separate states of the body, such as pain, pressure, heat, cold, or chemical stimuli, the important ones for movement control are those receptors that signal information about touch and, to some extent, deep pressure. In addition, pain sensations certainly constitute important information for specific kinds of movement behaviors.

Different kinds of cutaneous receptors exist: some close to the surface and others much deeper, some in glabrous (hairless) skin and others particular to hairy skin. One of these, called the Pacinian corpuscle, is located deep in the skin and is stimulated by deep deformation such as would be produced by a blow or heavy pressure. Other kinds of receptors in the skin include the Meissner corpuscles, Merkel's discs, Ruffini's corpuscles, and "free nerve endings." The last provide especially strong signals when hairs on the body are deformed by light touch, as they are located close to the hair follicles. Near the surface of glabrous skin (such as that of the lips and the palms of the hands) is a particularly strong concentration of Meissner corpuscles and Merkel's discs. The fingertips have one of the highest concentrations of cutaneous receptors on the body, which provide information about the surfaces of objects through touch (Martin & Jessell, 1991).

Input to the Central Nervous System

Input from the various receptors comes together in the periphery into *spinal nerves,* collections of individual neurons (both sensory, or afferent, and motor, or efferent) that carry information toward and away from the spinal cord. These nerves branch into two roots near the cord, called the *dorsal roots* (posterior, or back) and *ventral roots* (anterior, or front), where they contact the spinal cord separately. At this point, there is almost complete division of the neurons into afferent (or sensory) neurons that enter via the dorsal roots and efferent (or motor) neurons that leave the cord via the ventral roots. Once inside the cord, the afferent neurons can either *synapse* (connect) with other neurons whose cell bodies are in the central gray matter, or travel to higher or lower levels in the cord or to the brain in one of the many tracts that form the white matter adjacent to the gray matter.

The major pathways for transmitting signals from the periphery to the brain are the spinal tracts, located alongside the vertebrae that make up the spinal column. There are 8 cervical, 12 thoracic, 5 lumbar, and 5 sacral vertebrae, defining a number of *segments* of the spinal cord. Except for the input from the structures in the head and neck (for our purposes here, mainly from the eyes, ears, and vestibular apparatus, entering through one or more of the 12 cranial nerves), the input to the central nervous system is through the *dorsal roots,* which collect and guide the input to the spinal cord at each segment. Each segment serves a particular region of the body.

Ensemble Characteristics

Proprioception enables us to tell with remarkable accuracy where our limbs are and how they are acting, but how do the various receptors mentioned in the previous sections contribute to our motor control capabilities? An important concept is that any one of the receptors in isolation from the others is generally ineffective in signaling information about the movements of the body. This is so because the various receptors are often sensitive to a variety of aspects of body motion at the same time. For example, the Golgi tendon organs probably cannot signal information about movement, because they cannot differentiate between the forces produced in a static contraction and the same forces produced when the limb is moving. The spindle is sensitive to muscle length, but it is also sensitive to the rate of change in length (velocity) and to the activity in the intrafusal fibers that are active during active contractions; so the spindle confounds information about position of the limb and the level of contraction of the muscles (force). And the joint receptors are sensitive to joint position, but their output can be affected by the tensions applied and by the direction of movement, or by whether the movement is active or passive (Paillard & Bruchon, 1968).

As a solution to this problem, many have suggested that the central nervous system combines and integrates information in some way to resolve the kind of ambiguity in the signals produced by any one of these receptors (e.g., Wetzel & Stuart, 1976). Producing an *ensemble* (meaning a grouping *together*) of information by combining the various separate sources could enable the generation of less ambiguous information about movement (Gandevia & Burke, 1992). How the central nervous system does this, and which sources of information are most strongly represented in which situations, are important questions for the future. It is easy to imagine how all or most of these sensory inputs would be involved in a skill such as that shown in figure 5.14. We turn now to the ways in which these various sources of sensory information contribute to movement control (see the various chapters in the volume by Kandell, Schwartz, & Jessell, 2000, for a good tutorial review).

FIGURE 5.14 An inverted iron cross move on the still rings—where optical flow and other sources of feedback are almost certainly critical.

Proprioception and Motor Control

The closed-loop ideas presented earlier regarding human performance have been considered in various ways (see Krakauer & Ghez, 2000), but one of the more common is to think of the closed-loop system as a system that contains the stages of information processing and conscious decision making discussed in chapter 3. (Of course, it is clear—to be discussed later in this chapter—that there are other embedded closed-loop systems that do not involve consciousness.) It is useful to consider the executive level of this system as consisting of the information-processing stages

discussed in the previous two chapters. This idea is illustrated in figure 5.15. An original command for action, such as an external stimulus or an internal self-generated "go" signal, starts the action by progressing through the stimulus-identification, response-selection, and response-programming stages, eventually leading to evocation of the movement commands to the muscles. This portion of the closed-loop model is similar to that involved in an open-loop system.

The difference becomes apparent, however, when one considers the actions just *subsequent* to this first aspect of the movement. First, a *reference of correctness* is generated that will serve as the standard against which the feedback from the performance is judged. This reference of correctness is also termed *feedforward* information (see "When Can We Tickle Ourselves?" on p. 175). We can think of this reference as a representation of the feedback qualities associated with moving as planned or as intended; it is analogous to the value to which you set your thermostat in your home heating system or to the compass heading for the automatic pilot of a ship. The reference of correctness represents the state of the feedback associated with the correct movements of the limbs during the intended action; it specifies the sensory qualities of *a goal*. According to the model presented in figure 5.15, muscle contractions cause the muscles, limbs, and body to move, producing changes in the environment as a result. Each of these actions generates information. The contracting muscles and the movement of the body produce sensations from the various receptor systems described earlier. Then, via the reference of correctness, the system can compare the feedback it receives with the feedback it expects to receive. If feedback from the two sources is the same, the implication is that the movement is correct and that no adjustments are necessary. But if a difference exists between the feedback received and the reference, then an error is signaled and a correction is required.

Influence of Movement Duration

Closed-loop models such as the one in figure 5.15 are conceptualized in essentially two ways, depending on the nature of the motor skill. For rapid movements, feedback provides a basis for knowing (i.e., consciously) whether a movement

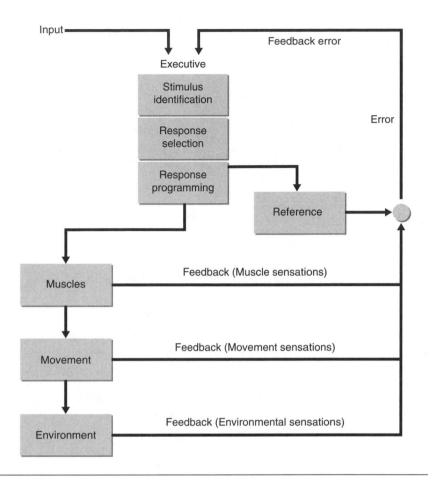

FIGURE 5.15 The expanded closed-loop model for movement control.

produced was correct or not. For example, after a golf ball is hit, the sensations from the swing are available in memory for a brief period of time and can be analyzed. A professional golfer probably can tell a great deal about the direction and distance of the golf shot just from the feel and sound of it. A second way in which the closed-loop ideas in figure 5.15 are used concerns the control of ongoing movements. These kinds of models have obvious relevance to continuous skills, such as steering a car down a highway. Think of the reference as evaluating the set of sensations associated with moving at a particular speed or with maintaining a certain distance behind another car. If one of these goals is not met, the feedback received and the reference do not match, and an error is fed back to the executive level to compute a correction. Thus, these closed-loop models view the control of a car on a highway as a series of corrections that keep the vehicle safely on the road.

Control of Long-Duration Movements

The closed-loop model presented in figure 5.15 has been very useful for describing certain kinds of movements. The model seems to have the most relevance for tasks that require a great deal of time, because the processes involved in the analysis of the error information are relatively slow. Also, the model best relates to movements in which something is *regulated* at some constant value, such as keeping the car at a particular speed by monitoring the speedometer or keeping an airplane on the proper glide path when guiding it onto the runway. These are called *tracking* movements (chapter 2), and they constitute an important class of motor behavior. Tracking tasks have received considerable study, much of this work having been directed to problems in vehicle control, gunnery, and the like. An excellent review of the research on tracking was provided by Poulton (1974); it has been updated by Hammerton (1989), Wickens and Hollands (2000), and Jagacinski and Flach (2003).

There are many different mathematical and physical models of tracking behavior; the major differences relate to how the system uses feedback information and how the system initiates a correction when errors are detected (see Jagacinski & Flach, 2003, for an excellent review). The most important generalization from this research is that if the models are used in computer or mechanical *simulations* of the human (in which the device is controlled in ways analogous to those in figure 5.15), these nonliving devices seem to "come alive" to behave in ways nearly indistinguishable from their human counterparts. For example, when we perform a laboratory tracking task, approximately 200 ms elapses between the appearance of an error and the initiation of a correction back toward the center of the track. Such lags and the character of the correction can be modeled very well, and the statistical agreement between the actual and simulated movements is quite good for this kind of task. This evidence does not prove that humans actually track this way, but the agreement between theoretical predictions and data is very strong, and alternative theories cannot boast of similar success.

Changing the Reference of Correctness

We can extend this idea somewhat (as Adams, 1971, 1976a, 1977, has done) to account for how the individual makes a limb movement such as would be involved in sawing a board or in reaching for a mug of beer. Here, the reference of correctness is not a single state as in the earlier examples, but rather a *set of states* that changes at each moment in time. Because the reference is constantly changing, it can be matched against the feedback from the moving limb, which is also changing as the movement progresses, so that errors in the movement's *trajectory* can be detected and corrected. This kind of mechanism is the basis for Adams' (1971) theory of learning, according to which the subject learns a set of references of correctness that the closed-loop system is to "track" during the movement. We will have more to say about Adams' ideas later in the book when we discuss learning theory (chapter 13).

But these kinds of models have serious limitations. Engineers can design robots and other machines to behave in this way, using what they call *point-to-point computation* methods. The posi-

tion of the limb at each point in space and at each time in the movement is represented by a reference of correctness, and the system can be made to track this set of positions across time to produce an action with a particular form. But the system must process information very rapidly, even for the simplest of movements. All these references of correctness must be stored somewhere, which creates difficulties when we realize that each point will be different if the movement begins from a slightly different place or if it is to take a slightly different pathway through space.

Engineers have generally found these methods very inefficient for machine (robot) control; such findings have led many motor behavior researchers (see Greene, 1972; Kelso, 1995; Turvey, 1977) away from these kinds of control processes to explain human skills. But there is still the possibility that the system might operate in this way at certain times or for certain skills that demand very high precision (e.g., threading a needle or slicing a loaf of bread). Also, such a mechanism might serve as the basis for *recognizing* errors at various places in the movement as it is carried out, without actually being the basis for controlling it. After a tennis stroke the performer could say that the elbow was bent too much on the backswing, and thus have the basis for making a correction in the movement on the next attempt. Finally, there is ample evidence that the system makes use of reflexive mechanisms (i.e., without using the information-processing stages), mechanical mechanisms (Bizzi, Accornero, Chapple, & Hogan, 1982), or both to hold itself on the proper track; these possibilities are discussed later in the chapter.

A compromise view is that only *certain positions* in the movement are represented by references of correctness. One view is that feedback from the movement when it is at its end point is checked against a reference of correctness; then corrections are initiated to move the limb to the proper position if it is not already there. These views of motor control hold that the limb is more or less "thrown" in the direction of the end point by some kind of open-loop control, and that the limb then "homes in on" the target by closed-loop control (a view reminiscent of Woodworth, 1899; see "R.S. Woodworth on Manual Aiming" on p. 143). Here, the actual trajectory of the limb is determined by how the limb is "thrown," in combination with mechanical factors such as gravity, friction, and muscle forces. In this view, the trajectory is not determined by point-to-point computation as would be explained by a purely closed-loop system.

Control of Rapid Movements

One of the most important points to have emerged from the evidence presented in chapters 3 and 4 was that the information-processing mechanisms, which lie at the very heart of the closed-loop system in figure 5.15, require a great deal of *time* in order for stimuli to be processed to yield a response. So far we have assumed that each error signal the system receives must be processed in these stages and that the response (a correction) can follow only after all the stages of processing have been completed. Thus, a correction is seen in the same way as any other response to a stimulus. It requires a great deal of time and attention.

But there is a problem. In the closed-loop models such as that shown in figure 5.15, rapid actions do not provide sufficient time for the system to (a) generate an error, (b) detect the error, (c) determine the correction, (d) initiate the correction, and (e) correct the movement before a rapid movement is completed. The left jab of the great boxer, Muhammad Ali, is a good example. The movement itself was about 40 ms; yet, according to our discussion earlier in this chapter, visually detecting an aiming error and correcting it during the same movement should require about 100 to 150 ms—the time necessary to complete the activities of the stages of information processing. The movement is finished before the correction can begin. For this reason, the closed-loop models of movement behavior do not seem well suited to explaining rapid movements.

Chapter 6 will raise this and other limitations to the closed-loop models again. For now, suffice it to say that the closed-loop mechanisms involving the stages of processing appear to have a very difficult time explaining rapid movements. Because these models have much credibility with respect to very slow movement and posture and have little with respect to rapid movement, it is possible that there are essentially two fundamentally different kinds of movements: fast and slow. We return to this distinction in chapter 6.

Reflexive Closed-Loop Control

In considering closed-loop control of movement, we dealt only with the kind of closed-loop model in which the determination of the correction was produced by conscious information-processing mechanisms, without considering the idea that the central nervous system contains closed-loop mechanisms that do not require any attention. Many examples are possible, such as the control of body temperature and the regulation of breathing during sleep. In this section we discuss evidence that these nonconscious mechanisms are involved in the control of voluntary movements as well.

Latencies of Corrections

An experiment by Dewhurst (1967) is representative of a number of studies on this problem. The subject was asked to hold the elbow at a right angle to support a light weight attached to the hand. The subject could monitor the performance through vision of a display that signaled elbow angle. The experimenter recorded the position of the arm together with the rectified electromyographical (EMG) activity in the biceps muscle as the subject performed. Unexpectedly the weight attached to the hand was then increased, and naturally the hand began to move downward. After a brief period, the subject increased the EMG activity to the biceps muscle, which increased its force output and brought the limb back to the right-angle position. Given that the lowered arm represents an error relative to the goal (of keeping the arm at a right angle), how much time will elapse before a correction is made, as would be seen by an increase in the elbow flexors' EMG? Note that if the subject must process the visual or kinesthetic feedback (or both) from the arm through the information-processing stages, there should be no change in the biceps EMG for approximately 150 to 200 ms.

Figure 5.16 shows the essential results. The weight was added at the point in time indicated by the arrow, and the limb began to move downward immediately. The records show a small burst of EMG about 35 to 40 ms after the weight was added and a larger irregular burst beginning about 50 ms afterward. Just after this second burst of EMG, the limb began to move back to the target position. This change in EMG represents a clear correction for the added weight, yet this correction was initiated far more quickly than can be explained by a closed-loop process that requires information processing as shown in figure 5.15. Rather, the correction is thought to be due to the operation of reflexes in lower, probably spinal, levels in the central nervous system.

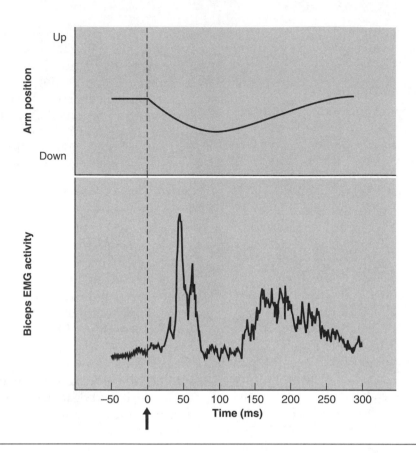

FIGURE 5.16 Movement and rectified electromyogram record showing the latencies of two reflex-based corrections.

Reprinted, by permission, from D.J. Dewhurst, 1967, "Neuromuscular control system," *IEEE Transactions on Biomedical Engineering* 14: 170, © 1967 IEEE.

Consciousness and Reflexive Corrections

Another aspect of reflexive corrections for errors, aside from their apparent rapidity, is that they might not require attention as other corrections seem to. Evidence for this notion was provided in a study by Henry (1953), in which subjects had to regulate the force they applied to a handle. The basic arrangement is shown in figure 5.17. The standing subject (blindfolded in the experiment) is pushing against a handle attached to a mechanical device that could alter the position of the handle continuously. The arrangement was such that if the subject was not pressing against the handle, the handle would move forward and backward unpredictably. But a spring had been placed between the machine and the handle, so that by modulating the force produced at each moment, the subject could maintain the handle in a constant position.

Henry used three conditions. In one condition, the subject's task was to keep the *pressure* against the handle fixed by varying the position of the handle. When the handle pushed against the subject, the correct response was to "ease up," so that the pressure between the handle and the subject's hand was held constant. In the second condition, the subject was to compensate for the changing pressures exerted by the handle so that a constant *position* of the handle was maintained, but with the exertion of constantly changing pressure. A third condition was used to assess the conscious *perception* of change; the subject attempted to hold the arm immobile, reporting through a left-finger movement when a change in the pressure exerted by the apparatus was sensed. The pressure changes were different for different segments in the testing period, and Henry could obtain an estimate of the amount of change that was required for conscious perception of change.

Henry (1953) found that the "threshold" force needed for an appropriate adjustment depended strongly on *what* the subject was asked to control. When the subject was asked to report a conscious change, a force of 0.559 dynes was required for detection. But when the subject was asked to hold

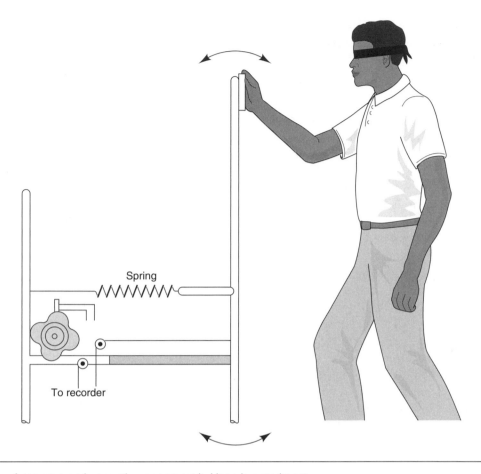

FIGURE 5.17   Apparatus and general arrangement in Henry's experiment.

Reprinted with permission from *Research Quarterly for Exercise and Sport*, vol. 24, pg. 177. Copyright © 1953 by the American Alliance for Health, Physical Education, Recreation and Dance, 1990 Association Drive, Reston, VA 20191.

the *position* constant, a force change of only 0.296 dynes was successfully detected and responded to; apparently, in this constant-position condition, subjects were responding to forces too small to be detected consciously. Even more striking was the finding that position changes associated with a force change of only 0.029 dynes produced successful modifications in movement control. Thus, the motor system, in holding a constant *position* against the apparatus, could respond to a change that was considerably less than the change necessary for conscious awareness (i.e., 0.029 vs. 0.559 dynes). In the constant-pressure condition—and particularly in the constant-position condition—the motor system was responding to stimuli that were too small to be detected consciously. As compared to the change required to adjust to a change in position, the change had to be 19 times larger for conscious detection. These small adjustments were apparently made without the subject's awareness.

Experiments like the ones just described show two important things about movement control. First, studies like Dewhurst's (1967; see also Houk & Rymer, 1981; see Lee, Murphy, & Tatton, 1983, for a review) demonstrate that the corrections for suddenly presented changes in position can be initiated with correction latencies of 30 to 80 ms— far more rapidly than would be expected based on conscious-processing estimates. This kind of result suggests that the information-processing stages, at least as shown in figure 5.15, are not involved in these actions. Second, the data from Henry (1953) and others show that subjects can make adjustments for changes in position—and perhaps for changes in tension—so small that the subject cannot even perceive them consciously. These data also indicate that the stages of information processing are not involved, because at least some of these stages are thought to entail conscious processing and attention in the sense discussed in chapter 4. Both of these lines of evidence suggest that these kinds of corrections are produced via reflexive mechanisms that do not concern the stages of processing.

Muscle Spindles and the Gamma Loop

The mechanisms responsible for the effects just described probably involve the muscle spindle, the small, cigar-shaped structure located between and in parallel to the main fibers of the skeletal muscles (review figure 5.13*a*). The (simplified) neurological connections of the spindle to the spinal cord are illustrated in figure 5.18. Recall from figure 5.13*a* and associated text that the muscle spindles are specialized to detect changes in muscle length. The tension on the equatorial (sensory) region, and thus the output of the Ia afferent neurons, is adjusted via the gamma motor system (and intrafusal muscle fibers) for contractions of the main muscle. Thus, at essentially any point in the action's trajectory, the muscle spindles are set to respond to a muscle length that is different from that anticipated (or intended). Such changes in the muscle length could be caused by unexpected loads applied to (or removed from) the limb's movement, or by the inherent variability of the main muscle's contractions (see the discussion of force variability in chapter 7), or both. Thus, it appears that the muscle spindles and the gamma system provide a means for correcting small changes in the external loads—and that such changes are fast, are not mediated by the stages of processing in figure 5.15), and are automatic in the sense that they do not require attention.

The information from the Ia afferent is sent to several places: From figure 5.18, we see that the Ia afferent signals synapse with the alpha motor neurons in the same muscle to generate greater (or lesser) muscle force to compensate for small changes in load. These signals are also sent upward to various sensory regions in the brain that could mediate more elaborate and complex corrections (e.g., the cortex, cerebellum, or both; Ghez & Thach, 2000). These compensations are effective mainly for small changes in loads; we all know that if we attempt to lift an "empty" box that is actually full of bricks, we stop lifting almost immediately and attempt the action again with a completely new pattern of action.

This process is the basis of what has been called the *monosynaptic stretch reflex*. You experience an example of this reflex when a neurologist lightly strikes your patellar tendon with a small rubber

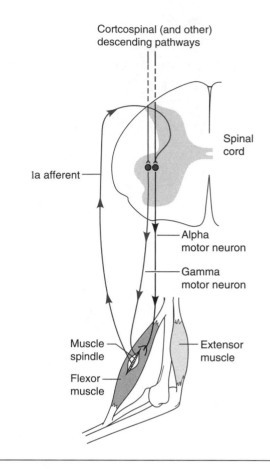

FIGURE 5.18 Simplified diagram of the alpha and gamma motor system connections.

Reprinted from K. Pearson and J. Gordon, 2000, Spinal reflexes. In *Principles of neural science*, 4th ed., edited by E.R. Kandel, J.H. Schwartz, and T.M. Jessell (New York: McGraw-Hill), 722. With permission of The McGraw-Hill Company.

"hammer" just below the kneecap with the knee flexed. The resulting "knee-jerk reflex" is caused by the rapid stretch of the quadriceps muscle, which stretches the spindles in the muscle. This increases the firing of the Ia afferent transmitted to the cord, increasing the alpha motor neuron firing rate, which causes the muscle to contract. This is an *autogenetic reflex*, because it causes an action in the same muscle that was stimulated. The loop time, or the time from the initial stretch until the extrafusal fibers are increased in their activation, is about 30 to 40 ms in humans. Because this 30 to 40 ms value corresponds with the latency for the first burst of EMG shown in the Dewhurst (1967) experiment (see figure 5.16), this monosynaptic mechanism is probably responsible for this first compensation for the added weight. This information may explain how Dewhurst's (1967) subjects responded so quickly to the added weight. It also helps to explain why Henry's (1953, figure 5.17) subjects were able to make corrections for position that they could not even perceive; some of the corrections for changes in position occur in the spinal cord, without the conscious involvement of the information-processing stages.

Notice also that the reflex activity (figure 5.18) is more complicated than simply activating the one muscle that was stretched. When the neurologist's hammer strikes the tendon, that muscle is stretched, leading to increased firing in the Ia afferent fibers from its spindles. These Ia afferents transmit their signal into the dorsal roots, where the Ia synapses with several other neurons. First, it synapses with the alpha motor neurons that activate that muscle via the monosynaptic stretch reflex. Second, the Ia synapses with other alpha motor neurons (not shown) for muscles acting as synergists for this action (muscles oriented to aid in the action). Third, the Ia synapses with Ia inhibitory interneurons (not shown), which in turn synapses with the alpha motor neuron for the antagonist muscle (here, the triceps) and inhibits its action. This reflex-based inhibition of the muscle acting in opposition to the muscle stimulated is called *reciprocal inhibition.* Thus, the stretch from striking the tendon with a rubber hammer has (a) increased activation in the muscle that was stretched (the agonist), (b) increased activation in synergistic muscle(s), and (c) inhibited activity in the muscle acting as an antagonist—all rapidly, automatically, and without consciousness. Also, if this had occurred in the legs, the stretch reflex (say, for right-knee flexion) would have produced increased activities in the *left*-knee extensors, and, via reciprocal inhibition, decreased activity in the left-knee flexors (see Pearson & Gordon, 2000b, for more details), presumably to allow the individual to provide postural support when the right knee was flexed reflexively.

This kind of reflexive adjustment is applicable to situations other than those in which the limbs are being held in a static position. Numerous investigations have shown that these processes seem to keep an ongoing movement on course. For example, Marsden, Merton, and Morton (1972) had subjects move the last joint of the thumb back and forth in time to a metronome. At an unpredictable time, the movement of the thumb was resisted. The result was an additional burst of EMG within 30 ms of the perturbation. It is impressive that this occurred when the

perturbation occurred at *any* location or time in the thumb's cycle. Similar findings have been shown in the breathing cycle by Sears and Newsom-Davis (1968); when the resistance to airflow was suddenly changed at various places in the cycle, the EMG in the intercostal muscles (which control the rib cage volume) increased in activity with a latency of 30 ms, regardless of when in the cycle the resistance to airflow was changed. Nashner and Woollacott (1979) have presented similar findings for the situation in which the ankle joint is unexpectedly perturbed during normal walking. One interpretation of these findings is that there is a reference of correctness that "moves with" the overall movement so that, at any time in the movement, the limb's desired or planned location can be specified (Schmidt, 1976a). Thus, it appears that the muscle spindles—because they work in concert with the alpha and gamma systems as described earlier—are able to provide information about whether the limb is in a position different from that specified, even during the execution of an action, and can induce rapid, automatic, reflex-based corrections if it is not.

More recent research has added considerably to our understanding of these reflexive processes in movement control. There is considerable evidence that the reflexive response is not always autogenetic, in that the effects of a stimulus (such as a sudden stretch) can be seen in many of the participating muscles—not just in the one(s) stimulated (Pearson & Gordon, 2000b). Thus, these reflexive activities can be viewed as rapid, automatic, involuntary, and *coordinated* responses to disruptive stimuli.

We can conceptualize the function of these reflexes as directed at ensuring that the original *goal* of the action is achieved in the event of a perturbation to it during execution. Consider a task in which you are to repeatedly touch the tip of your right thumb to the tip of your right index finger. That is, both digit tips are moving toward the goal of touching each other. Now, imagine the application of a perturbing force that resists (only) the thumb's movement somewhat. We would expect automatic, rapid changes in the thumb musculature—and this is what you see. But, in addition, we will observe changes in the *index finger* musculature that are coordinated with the changes in the thumb musculature; this happens even though the index finger was not perturbed at all. One way to explain such findings is that the motor system has set up the goal of touching the two digit tips; the thumb's progress toward that goal is slowed by the perturbation. So, the index finger's action is also adjusted (sped up), presumably so that the goal of digit touching is achieved (see Pearson & Gordon, 2000b, for a more complete discussion).

Control of Muscle Stiffness   We have seen how the muscle spindles are involved not only in the maintenance of static positions (e.g., posture), but also in maintaining the trajectories of various limbs involved in a goal-directed action. But the spindle seems also to be related to the control of muscle *stiffness*, which is probably very important in the control of posture and other movements. Stiffness, one of the measures used by engineers (and others) to describe the characteristics of elastic materials (e.g., springs), is defined in terms of the amount of tension increase that is required to increase the length of the object by a certain amount (one unit). Engineers define stiffness more precisely as the change in tension divided by the resulting change in length, or the slope of the length–tension relationship. If a spring is very stiff, a great deal of tension is needed to increase its length by a given amount; for a less stiff spring, less tension is required. This is important in our context because the muscle seems to provide a compliant (springy) interface between the performer and the environment.

When we maintain posture, the muscles supporting the skeleton are contracting under the

influence of the gamma loop just described. This is conceptualized in figure 5.19, which shows a bone in equilibrium being supported by two opposing muscles producing force (equal and opposite joint torques). If the system is perturbed, causing the bone to move downward, the muscle on the right side of the diagram is lengthened slightly, causing the stretch reflex described earlier. Perhaps even more important, because the contracting muscle is a "springy" substance, more tension is produced in it by purely *mechanical* means as its length increases. Furthermore, this mechanical change in tension is *instantaneous*, just as the change in tension in a metal spring would be if it were stretched. Such increases in tension have the effect of opposing the perturbation, bringing the system back to the original position. Nichols and Houk (1976) have provided evidence that the muscle spindle is responsible for the maintenance of muscle stiffness when the muscle is stretched, so that the muscle can continue to act as a spring in the control of posture and similar movements (see also Houk, 1979; Houk & Rymer, 1981).

Long-Loop Reflexes   Have another look at figure 5.16. In addition to the monosynaptic reflex activity (the EMG activity that began with a latency of about 30 ms), there is another kind of activity responsible for the more sustained burst that occurred about 50 ms after the weight was added, and yet more starting at about 130 ms. This second burst at about 50 to 70 ms occurs too rapidly to be explained by the stages of informa-

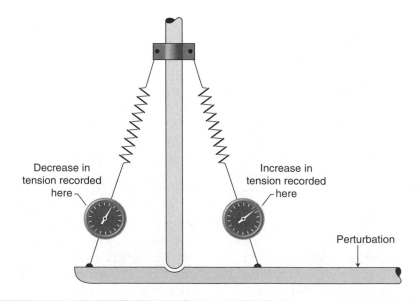

FIGURE 5.19   Muscle–spring model with gauges for measuring tension in the "tendons" as a perturbation is applied.

tion processing, yet it is apparently too slow to be accounted for by the monosynaptic stretch reflex. The early burst at 30 ms was very brief and did not result in much actual increase in force, whereas the burst at 50 to 80 ms was larger, was more sustained, and probably resulted in the force changes necessary to move the limb back toward the horizontal position. The response at 130 ms is probably the RT response, mediated by the stages of processing. The response to muscle stretch with a latency of 50 to 70 ms has been termed the *long-loop reflex* (also called the *functional stretch reflex*).

The long-loop reflex fits neatly into the overall picture of segmental limb control. When the spindle is stretched and the Ia afferent is increased in its activation, the information is fed back to the spinal cord where it activates the alpha motor neuron and the same (and functionally related) muscle (review figure 5.18). This signal is also sent to higher segmental levels in the cord, to the brain, or both. Information from the Ia afferent is integrated with other information in sensory and motor centers in the brain that can initiate a more complete or more complex response to the imposed stretch. Because the information travels to a higher center to be organized, and because more information needs to be considered and more synapses are involved, the reflex requires more time—50 to 70 ms rather than 30 to 40 ms for the monosynaptic reflex.

Something appears to be regained, however, with the loss in time. First, the EMG activity from the long-loop reflex is far stronger (producing more force change) than that involved in the monosynaptic stretch reflex. Second, because the reflex is organized in a higher center, it is more *flexible* than the monosynaptic reflex. For example, Evarts (1973) has shown that, if the subject in a task similar to Dewhurst's (1967) is told to "resist" the stretch, a burst pattern like that in figure 5.16 occurs. If the subject is told to "let go," so that when the weight is added the subject simply lets her arm be moved by it, the second burst (presumably due to the long-loop reflex) nearly disappears but the first burst remains, unaffected. It appears that *prior instructions* can change the reflexive response to a given stimulus (the added weight) so that the reaction is appropriate for the particular situation. The monosynaptic reflex, residing at a very low level in the spinal cord, can probably not be modulated by prior instructions (at least to any great degree). It is fortunate that we are constructed in this fashion, as there are situations in which we must resist very strongly when perturbations occur. Other situations arise in which a very strong resistance would mean a serious accident; in skiing over bumps, for example, failing to "let go" would result in a very stiff leg musculature when a very compliant (springy and supple) one would be more desirable.

Triggered Reactions

So far, we have seen three distinct processes leading to increased EMG in response to perturbations such as an added weight. These are the monosynaptic stretch reflex (30 to 50 ms latency), the long-loop reflex (or functional stretch reflex, 50-70 ms), and of course the voluntary RT response discussed in chapter 4 that begins at about 130 ms in Dewhurst's (figure 5.16) study.[6] Crago, Houk, and Hasan (1976) argue, however, that there is yet a fourth kind of response that falls between the 50 to 70 ms long-loop response and the voluntary RT latency. They call these responses *triggered reactions:* prestructured, coordinated reactions in the same or in closely related musculature that are "triggered" into action by various receptors. Such reactions have latencies from 80 to perhaps 200 ms, and the latencies are far more variable than are those of the faster reflexes. Presumably the triggered reaction is like a "very fast RT," perhaps bypassing some of the stages of information processing because the reaction to the stretch is stereotyped, predictable, and well practiced. The performer does not have to spend much time in processes like response selection and programming, and the reaction is just "triggered off" almost as if it were automatic (see Schmidt, 1987).

What evidence is there for this kind of control? Crago and colleagues (1976) have shown that portions of the response to an unexpected stretch perturbation were faster than RT (as we have seen before), but also that the latencies increased as the number of stimulus–response alternatives increased from one to two; here, the perturbation was (a) always a flexion (i.e., a one-choice task) or (b) either a flexion or an extension (i.e., a two-choice task). We usually think of processes involved in resolving choice as being "located" in a response-selection stage (Hick's law, chapter 3); these results suggest that, unlike the monosynaptic stretch reflexes, the responses might be mediated in some way by the stages of information processing. Perhaps some of the processes

TABLE 5.1. Four Kinds of Responses to Environmental Stimuli During Movement, and Some of Their Differing Characteristics

Response type	Loop time (in ms)	Structures involved	CATEGORY ANALYSIS	
			Modified by instructions	Affected by number of choices
Myotatic reflexes (autogenetic)	30-50	Spindles, gamma loop, same muscles	No	No
Long-loop reflexes (autogenetic)	50-80	Spindles, cortex or cerebellum, same muscles	Yes	No
Triggered reactions (not autogenetic)	80-120	Various receptors, higher centers, and associated musculature	Yes	Yes
Reaction time (not autogenetic)	120-180	Various receptors, higher centers, any musculature	Yes	Yes

are bypassed, leading to latencies shorter than "normal" RT latencies. Table 5.1 summarizes these several processes. More research is clearly needed to clarify these issues.

Tactile Feedback

Recently, we have seen evidence of the initiation of reflex-like control by the cutaneous receptors in the skin. We have long known that the cutaneous receptors can be the trigger for withdrawal responses—as in jerking your hand from a hot surface (Johansson & Westling, 1991; Johansson & Flanagan, 2009).

The Wineglass Effect Suppose you are washing dishes and raise an object to check its cleanliness—for example, holding the stem of an expensive wineglass between your fingertips. If the glass begins to tip or slip (because of the wet surface), a common reaction is to increase the grip of force with your fingers to stop it. Using a laboratory analog of this basic idea, Johansson and Westling (1984, 1988, 1990; Westling & Johansson, 1984; see also Ghez & Krakauer, 2000, and Johansson & Westling, 1991) have studied the motor reactions to stimuli indicating loss of grip. They asked subjects to lift small objects (having various degrees of surface friction) between the thumb and index finger and hoist them with an elbow flexion action. The stimuli indicating that the object is slipping are a set of tiny vibrations in the skin of the fingers, which we detect through the cutaneous receptors. After the onset of a slip (which can be measured by vibration sensors in apparatus), subjects showed an increase in the EMG in muscles responsible for

finger gripping force, and with a latency of only about 80 ms (see also Cole & Abbs, 1988). These reflexes were fast enough to prevent a noticeable movement of the object, and often the subject did not even know that a slip had occurred. Sometimes, several of these slips and catches were seen in a single lift of the object, each with very short latencies. In addition to the increase in gripping forces, there was at the same time a corresponding *decrease* in the EMG in the elbow flexors, as if the system were reducing the slippage by decreasing the hand's upward acceleration. All this resulted in a beautifully coordinated response to the slipping, which was evidenced in a number of joints—not just in the structures directly affected by the stimulus. The reaction was very fast and probably nonconscious, and seemed to have the overall "goal" of reorganizing the system slightly to complete the action successfully (i.e., lifting without dropping). Thus, in this example, as well as in others mentioned here, the stimulus does not (only) *directly* affect the muscles that make the response as in the example from Dewhurst (1967); that is, the response to the stimulation is not (simply) autogenetic, but rather is coordinated across several muscles and joints.

Object Manipulation In addition, it appears that cutaneous receptors can provide sensitive feedback about the fingers' contact with objects being manipulated. One example involves anesthetizing (via needle injections) the tips of the thumb, index, and middle finger. Before the injection, the subject could remove a wooden match from a matchbox and light it by striking it against the side of the matchbox—a very common, unremarkable action requiring about 8 s. However, after the anesthetic was injected, which eliminated cutaneous feedback from the fingertips temporarily, this task became very difficult; the subject dropped matches several times and produced very clumsy and "labored" actions, eventually succeeding in lighting the match in about 29 s. In addition, it appeared that the subject made extensive use of visual feedback after the injections, but this apparently did not make up for the loss of tactile sensation, perhaps because the visual feedback was far slower than the reflex-like feedback from the cutaneous receptors (Johansson & Flanagan, 2009).[7]

Other Reflexes

Many reflexes can be elicited in humans, and some scientists have suggested that these reflexes play important roles in movement control. For example, Fukuda (1961) collected photographs of athletes, dancers, and other performers in specific situations, such as the baseball player illustrated in figure 5.20 who is jumping and stretching his gloved hand high in the air to catch a ball. In this example the positioning of the outstretched hand and extended leg on the one side of the body, together with the flexed arm and leg on the other side of the body, closely resembles the *tonic neck reflex*, which is often seen in infants. When the head is turned to the left, the left arm becomes extended and the right arm curls up alongside the neck. Fukuda's observations, illustrated in examples from baseball among others, perhaps suggest that built-in reflex patterns might represent basic components of various skilled actions in adult motor behavior. In support of Fukuda's argument, if subjects turned their head toward the hand that was active in a force production task, the force was increased as compared to when the head was turned away (Hellebrandt, Houtz, Partridge, & Walters, 1956; Shea, Guadagnoli, & Dean, 1995). The interpretation was that turning the head supposedly activates the tonic neck reflex that provides a reflex-based facilitation of the alpha motor neurons on both sides of the body.

However, in this baseball example (figure 5.20), it is possible that the player is in this position simply because he is looking at and reaching for the ball, not because the reflexes are producing the classic tonic neck pattern. Fukuda presents a suggestive set of findings, but the crucial evidence is lacking to link these reflexes as observed in isolation and in childhood directly with the movement patterns seen in adults. A review of the possible role of reflexes in movement is provided by Easton (1972, 1978).

FIGURE 5.20 A baseball player reaching for a ball, showing a pattern resembling the tonic neck reflex.

Reproduced with permission from T. Fukuda et al., *Acta Oto-Laryngologica*, 1961; 161: 1261-1263. ©1961 Informa Healthcare. "Studies on human dynamic postures from the viewpoint of postural reflexes."

Speech Perturbations

Another example of triggered reactions was provided by Abbs and Gracco (1983; Abbs, Gracco, & Cole, 1984) and by Kelso, Tuller, Vatikiotis-Bateson, and Fowler (1984). In Abbs' work, the subjects were asked to utter nonsense syllables such as /afa/ and /aba/. Try /aba/, for example; the lips must be open to make the initial vowel sound, and then they must come together briefly to make the stop consonant /b/. In their experiments, Abbs and colleagues (1984) would occasionally perturb the lower jaw (during the utterance of /aba/) with a small downward force pulse that prevented the lower lip from rising to make contact with the upper lip in its normal position, and the EMG from the musculature in the *upper* lip and its position were measured. When the perturbation was applied, EMG increased in the *upper* lip musculature, which moved the upper lip downward, all with a latency of about 25 to 70 ms. Notice that, as in the wineglass example, this is not an autogenetic response, because the response to the stimulation does not occur (only) in the stimulated muscle and seems to be organized with the "purpose" of completing the *action* of making the proper sound (which required lip closure for success). Furthermore, the reaction seems to be dependent on practice, as it is difficult to argue that making the particular sound /aba/ is genetically determined; this feature of susceptibility to practice might be yet another distinguishing characteristic of triggered reactions. However, this effect is analogous to the so-called *reflex-reversal phenomenon* in the study of locomotion; in locomotion, it is difficult to argue that learning plays a large role. In this situation, the same stimulus elicits one reflex when the leg is in the swing phase, and a different reflex when the leg is in the stance phase. See chapter 6 for a fuller discussion.

The Role of Reflexes in Skilled Actions

It is interesting to think about the possible role of the various reflexes in the control of movement, and the evidence for such contributions is mounting steadily. At this point, there is considerable evidence for the involvement of reflex-like processes in voluntary motor behavior. We have seen stretch reflexes, reflex reversals, cutaneous feedback effects, triggered reactions, and ambient vision effects. All of these have the property of providing stereotyped (if sometimes somewhat complex) responses to stimuli, and all with latencies far shorter than our usual estimates of reaction time. Thus, it is difficult to argue that the stages of processing (identification, selection, programming; see chapter 3) have any role in these reactions. This evidence, taken together, suggests that these reactions are automatic (nonconscious) responses, which seem to have the property of

ensuring that the original action is carried out faithfully even in the face of small perturbations.

This idea can be summarized from the flowchart in figure 5.21. Here, we attempt to show that many simultaneous feedback loops appear to be involved in one way or another in movement control. One of these—the outermost loop, shown as a heavy line in figure 5.21—involves the stages of processing, reaction time (M_3 response), and attention as we argued in chapter 3. However, in the present chapter we have provided evidence for various reflex-like processes that appear not to involve the stages of processing. The innermost loop is the M_1 response, probably the most rapid of all, traversing from an involved muscle to the spinal cord and back to that muscle. Feedback from cutaneous receptors in the fingertips is involved in nonconscious control, and this feedback can also be conceptualized as operating mainly nonconsciously, as we have discussed (Johansson & Flanagan, 2009). The M_2 response also travels to the spinal cord, but extends as well to somewhat higher levels than the M_1 response. Triggered reactions arising from receptors in various muscles or from the environment can also be thought of as providing input to some level of the spinal cord. Finally, ambient vision can influence (at least) balance nonconsciously, certainly not involving the stages of processing.[8]

Feedforward Influences on Motor Control

In this section we consider evidence that the motor system operates with a feed*forward* control mode. This term—coined to contrast with the concept of feed*back*—is usually defined as the sending of a signal that (a) readies the system for the upcoming motor command or (b) readies the system for the receipt of some particular kind of feedback information (or does both). Such processes appear to occur frequently, and we will consider a few examples. Notice that the reference mechanisms illustrated in figures 5.15 and 5.21 are examples of a feedforward process.

Saccadic Eye Movements

Numerous situations exist in which the idea of feedforward control appears to be involved in the production and evaluation of human behavior.

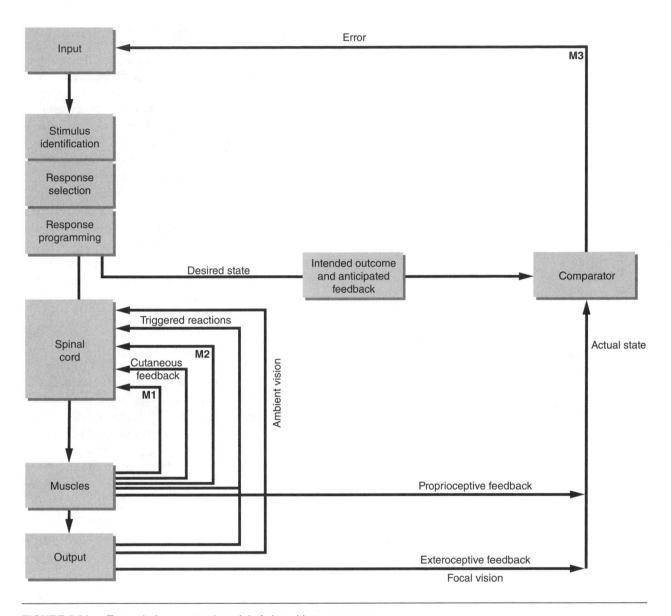

FIGURE 5.21 Expanded conceptual model of closed-loop processes.

One of the earliest notions of feedforward control concerned the mechanisms of visual perception after the eye made a *saccade*—a very rapid, jerky movement of the eyes from one position to a new position. Of course, the light patterns falling on the retina are different before, during, and after the saccade. But how does the person know whether the eye moved in a stable world or whether the world moved, with the eye remaining stationary? The pattern of stimulation (optical flow pattern) on the retina could be exactly the same in both cases.

The answer suggested by von Holst (1954; von Holst & Mittelstaedt, 1950), Sperry (1950), and others (e.g., Gallistel, 1980) was that the visual perceptual system was informed about the upcoming movement of the eye ahead of time, so that the pattern of changed visual input could be evaluated properly. This advance (feedforward) information was termed *corollary discharge,* or *efference copy,* by these authors (see also Evarts, 1973, and Kelso, 1982, for reviews).

The idea is that a "copy" of the motor (efferent) command to the eye muscles is also sent to some other location in the brain, where it is used to evaluate the incoming visual feedback signals and to "correct for" the fact that the image on the retina is about to move. Thus, the individual perceives the environment as stable because she "knows" that the eye has moved via a saccade. How such a system works is the subject of much debate, but many scientists have argued that some such mechanism must exist in order for the individual to interpret incoming visual signals correctly.

Efference Copy in Limb Control

The efference copy mechanism appears to have a parallel in the control or evaluation of limb movements. First, as pointed out by Evarts (1973), there is neurological evidence that information destined for the muscles is also sent to places in the brain that are primarily sensory in nature. Perhaps the purpose of such activities is to "tell" the sensory system what was ordered by the motor system and to ready it for receipt of the feedback. Thus, the idea of efference copy is much like the establishment of the reference of correctness against which the feedback signals will be compared. One component of this feedforward must simply be the knowledge *that* the person moved voluntarily (as opposed to passively), so that the person can distinguish feedback from movement as due to active motion versus passive motion.

Related to this example is the well-known heightened kinesthetic sensitivity when the subject is moving *actively* versus passively (Brodie & Ross, 1985). Do this experiment. Take a few different grades of sandpaper, and rank them in terms of roughness by rubbing them with your index finger (eyes closed). First, move your finger actively over the surfaces. Then have someone hold your finger and move it over the surface in the same way, but without your active muscular involvement. You will likely find that your perception of roughness is much impaired when you are moved passively. Why? One answer is that when the motor system sends the commands to move actively, it also sends an efference copy of the commands to sensory areas in the brain to enable proper evaluation of the feedback. But when the finger is moved passively, no motor commands are issued to the muscles; hence there is no efference copy, and the "same" feedback signals from the finger are not perceived as accurately (for further evidence and discussion, see Lederman & Klatzky, 1997, 2009).

Preparatory Postural Reactions

Consider a situation in which a standing subject awaits a signal to raise the arm (with a weight in the hand) quickly from a relaxed position at the side to a position in front of the body, as if to point straight ahead. According to earlier discussions about such actions, the commands for the shoulder muscles are generated after an RT of about 150 to 200 ms or so following an external "go" signal. But if the subject is in a balanced stance, a sudden movement of the (loaded) arm forward and upward will cause a shift in the person's center of gravity, and he will lose balance unless some compensation is provided prior to or along with the movement itself. When is such compensation produced—before, during, or after the action?

Belen'kii, Gurfinkel, and Pal'tsev (1967; see also Cordo & Nashner, 1982) recorded the EMG activity from the support muscles of the legs as well as the prime-moving shoulder muscles in this rapid arm-raise task (performed as a reaction to a stimulus). After the stimulus came on, the first signs of EMG activity occurred in the large muscles in the back of the leg (biceps femoris) on the opposite side of the body from the intended action—and these changes occurred about 60 ms *before* any EMG was seen in the shoulder muscles. The actions of the EMGs in the legs could not have been caused by an imbalance resulting from the movement of the arm, because these changes occurred before the first EMG changes in the shoulder did and even longer before any movement in the shoulder occurred. It is possible to consider these changes as an example of feedforward control, in which the motor system sends commands to the spinal levels associated with the leg musculature prior to the arm action; the purpose is to "prepare" the legs so that the body does not lose balance when the arm finally moves, or to ready the motor unit pools in the spinal cord for the upcoming signal to contract (called *spinal tuning*), or both.

Another, related view is that the changes in the patterns of EMGs in the legs prior to action could be considered a part of the coordination of the entire action, beginning with change in the legs. W. Lee (1980), using this same task, found that the temporal aspects of the EMGs are quite closely linked, with the various muscles acting in the same order and with a nearly constant pattern of action for various trials (see chapter 8 for more evidence related to the processes involved in coordination). This supports the idea that the feedforward information is an integral part of the overall control system (discussed later in this chapter), or part of the motor program for action as we discuss in the next chapter.

Detection and Correction of Errors

What role does feedforward information play in the detection and correction of errors? It is thought that this feedforward information is, first of all, information *that* a movement was ordered. Also, this feedforward information presumably contains the expected sensory consequences of the movement just ordered. As an example, if you ask a friend to call your home phone while you look on, then in some way you "know" that the phone at home is ringing even though you cannot hear it directly. Knowing that your friend has placed the call is almost as reliable as hearing the telephone ring. In this way, feedforward information can be thought of as a variant of feedback.

If feedforward (or efference copy) could, in this general way, be evaluated as a kind of sensory information, then the idea is that it can be evaluated against a reference of correctness just as feedback can be evaluated. If the subsequent analysis of the efference copy in relation to this

reference indicated that there was *going to be* an error, a correction could be initiated and a new movement command could be sent. This has the advantage of initiating the correction much more quickly than would be the case if feedback from the (errant) movement was evaluated; and the correction could even be given before the errant movement was initiated, or at least before the movement could "do much damage" in the environment.

Various experiments appear to provide evidence for such processes. For example, Angel and Higgins (1969) used a step tracking task in which the target would move suddenly in discrete steps to the left or right; the subject's task was to follow the target movement with appropriate limb movements. When the subject is highly motivated to minimize RT, she will move in the wrong direction occasionally, reverse the move, and then move rapidly to the correct target. Figure 5.22 is a diagram of a typical corrected trial, showing the incorrect initial movement (beginning at point B) and the subsequent correction (beginning at point C). Interestingly, the correction times, measured as the interval from the beginning of the incorrect movement until the beginning of the correction (from B to C in the figure), were as short as 90 ms. The subjects could not have been processing movement feedback from proprioception or

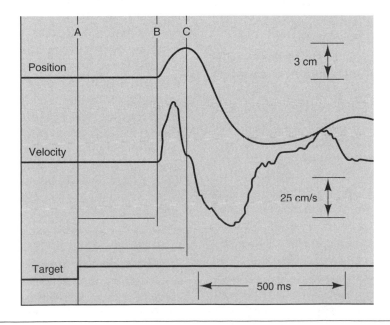

FIGURE 5.22   Position (top) and velocity (center) traces showing an error with "rapid" correction toward the target.

Reprinted, by permission, from R.W. Angell and J.R. Higgins, 1969, "Correction of false moves in pursuit tracking," *Journal of Experimental Psychology* 82: 186. Copyright © 1969 by the American Psychological Association.

vision in the stages of processing, because the correction for the false move was made more rapidly than could be accounted for by the usual feedback-processing mechanisms. Perhaps the subjects were using a central feedback loop based on efference copy as a basis for initiating these corrections.

We discussed these so-called "rapid error corrections" earlier (in chapter 3). But, the hypothesis of efference copy–based "rapid" corrections just mentioned can also be explained in other ways. For example, when the subject moves, he feeds forward the expected sensory consequences of the display. That is, if the subject guesses "left," he will feed forward the expected sensory (visual) consequences of the left signal coming on, and then trigger off the (incorrect) action with a very fast RT (152 ms). However, if the proper response is "right" on that trial, then what the subject expects to see (the left signal being on) is not matched by the signal that actually appeared (the right signal). This mismatch is the "stimulus" indicating that the response will surely be an error, and corrective actions to move left are initiated then, using the stages of processing in the "usual" way. If so, the latency of the onset of the correction is not really very "rapid." In the Schmidt-Gordon data (see figure 3.17 on p. 84), this correction had a latency of 276 ms (from signal onset to reversal in direction, or from A to C in figure 5.22). Thus, in this interpretation, these "rapid" corrections are not rapid at all, and we need not invoke efference copy explanations to explain them.

The notion of efference copy also has the difficulty of explaining how efferent (or motor) information can be compared against sensory information (see Schmidt & Gordon, 1977). The problem is that the "language" of the motor information is in terms of which muscles to contract, when, in what order and timing, and with what force (discussed further in chapter 6). The sensory information arising from the action is in the form of limb movement, joint positions, and muscle forces. So, how can the system compare the information about motor commands with the information about movement feedback if these signals are in different codes? For several authors, this problem requires that the feedforward information be in the same code as the sensory information, which is the basis for the reference of correctness seen in figure 5.15 (see Schmidt, 1975b) and a class of models discussed next.

Forward Models of Motor Control

Consider the simple example of being tickled. Most of us have body parts that are responsive to touch and that result in mild to extreme sensations when brushed lightly. With only a few exceptions (see "When Can We Tickle Ourselves?"), those responses are completely avoided when the same tickling movements are produced by our own actions. Why? A class of theories of motor control known as *forward models* provides a fairly simple explanation of why we are unable to tickle ourselves (for overviews see Desmurget & Grafton, 2000; Shadmehr & Krakauer, 2008; Wolpert, Ghahramani, & Flanagan, 2001; Wolpert, Miall, & Kawato, 1998). The basic idea is that when a limb movement is initiated, a "model" of the *predicted* consequences of the action is also generated. This is called a "forward" model because it is a prediction of the movement's sensory consequences before the actual sensory consequences have been generated. If the actual sensory consequences match the expected consequences (as they would if we try to tickle ourselves), this evokes no tickling response. But, when someone else tickles us, the actual sensory consequences do not match the expected consequences, because the expected consequences of the (other person's movement) do not exist for comparison, and the result is the tickling sensation.

In other kinds of actions, once the movement is begun, the predicted and actual consequences are compared and corrections for discrepancies between them can be initiated with minimal time delays. Thus, forward models of motor control avoid many of the processing delays that are implicit in traditional feedback-based theories of control. And, unlike feedforward-based theories, forward models have the advantage of using actual feedback in error correction processes to avoid the problem of motor and sensory coding states as mentioned in the previous section.

Summary

Closed-loop systems involve the comparison of feedback against a reference of correctness, the determination of an error, and a subsequent correction. The receptors for the feedback supplied to closed-loop systems are the eyes, ears, and vestibular apparatus, as well as the Golgi tendon

When Can We Tickle Ourselves?

Most of us have certain areas of our bodies that are particularly susceptible to tickling. Stimulation of these areas results in a mixture of feelings that often includes both excitement and discomfort. Perhaps somewhat surprisingly, the act of tickling has become a study of interest to motor control scientists. The reason is simple: Although we respond to tickling by someone else, we do not respond when we attempt to tickle ourselves (Claxton, 1975; Weiskrantz, Elliott, & Darlington, 1971), unless this is done under special circumstances. Why is this so?

Some researchers suggest that the inability to tickle ourselves is related to predictive processes involved in motor control. According to Blakemore, Wolpert, and Frith (1998, 2000), the act of producing a movement that would normally stimulate a ticklish part of the body produces an *expectation* of the sensory consequences of the action. This expectation has the effect of *canceling* the sensations that would normally arise if the area is stimulated by the subject, but cannot cancel those sensations that arise when the subject is stimulated by another agent. Support for this comes from studies using functional magnetic resonance imaging (fMRI); brain activity during tickles shows less activation under self-generated than externally generated tickles (Blakemore et al., 2000).

In another study, however, Blakemore, Frith, and Wolpert (1999) employed a robotic device that could be used to generate a tickling sensation externally or could be manipulated by the individual. As expected, higher ratings of "tickliness" were found on external- than on self-generated tickle trials, even when the machine provided the tickles. However, in some trials the robot did not execute the movement until a brief period of time (100, 200 or 300 ms) had elapsed after the subject had commanded the tickle. The 100 ms lag resulted in a greater feeling of tickliness compared to immediately experienced self-tickles. Moreover, lags of 200 and 300 ms produced as much sensation of tickliness as externally produced tickles. One explanation for this finding was that the predictive information fed forward in expectation of certain sensory consequences had a rather short "shelf life," essentially as short-term (visual) sensory store (STSS) does, as discussed in chapter 3. Perhaps this rapid decay in memory quality is characteristic of feedforward information generally. Other explanations are equally plausible, however, and further research is warranted to sort out this interesting phenomenon.

organs, the muscle spindles, the joint receptors, and touch receptors in various places in the skin. All these sources provide input to the central nervous system, and then the information is presumably combined for the purpose of analysis of movement.

Vision provides the richest source of information for closed-loop control. Vision can be used in a variety of ways, providing information about errors in movement as well as predictive information so that potential errors can be anticipated and avoided. Closed-loop control models seem to have their greatest strength in explaining movements that are slow in time or that have very high accuracy requirements (or both). Tracking tasks are most obviously related to closed-loop processes. These closed-loop models have difficulty explaining the kinds of corrections seen in very rapid movements, however, and this fact leads to the suggestion that two fundamentally

different kinds of movements exist: slow and fast. However, strong evidence exists for closed-loop reflexive control in limb movements. Most of this work suggests involvement of the muscle spindle and the gamma loop, but other receptors are involved as well. Such reflexive corrections can be classified as (a) the monosynaptic stretch reflex (latency = 30-50 ms), (b) the long-loop or transcortical (or functional) stretch reflex (latency = 50-80 ms), (c) the triggered reaction (latency = 80-120 ms), and (d) RT (latency = 120-180 ms or longer).

Feedforward control models involve the delivery of information to some other part of the system to "prepare it" for incoming sensory information or for an upcoming motor command (as in spinal tuning). Thus, feedforward information serves an important role in error detection and correction, often occurring in anticipation of the error.

Student Assignments

1. Prepare to answer the following questions during class discussion:

   a. Describe the closed-loop operation of any human-made device of daily living (e.g., a furnace).

   b. Describe the anatomical parts and what each contributes to the stretch reflex.

   c. What are the psychophysiological cues that humans use for depth perception?

2. Find a recent research article (within the past five years) that compares the effect of a visual illusion on perception and motor control.

Web Resources

How the sensory systems function:

   http://pathology.mc.duke.edu/neuropath/nawr/sensory.html

A gallery of visual illusions:

   http://dragon.uml.edu/psych/illusion.html

Basic information about the brain and central nervous system:

   http://faculty.washington.edu/chudler/introb.html

Notes

[1] Anatomical and neurophysiological evidence that supports the two visual stream proposal is reviewed by Norman (2002) and Bear, Connors, and Paradiso (2001, chapter 10).

[2] Some authors refer to this illusion as the Ebbinghaus illusion while others refer to it as the Titchener illusion (see also footnote 1 in Fischer, 2001).

[3] Performance in the various vision conditions may have reached a ceiling level. Thus, direct comparison to performance in the control condition with full room lighting is problematic because of the richer sources of contextual cues provided, which appear to be particularly important for reducing spatial errors (Montagne & Laurent, 1994). Whiting and colleagues (1970) also noted that subjects used a different catching strategy in the full room lighting condition whereby they would move with the ball and delay their attempts to make the catch, thereby gaining themselves an additional 100 ms or so of ball flight information.

[4] The root *fusal* means fusiform or spindle-shaped; so intrafusal fibers are muscle fibers within the spindle, and the extrafusal fibers are those outside the spindle—that is, the fibers of the muscle in which the spindle is embedded. The Greek letter gamma (γ) refers to the spindle system (the intrafusal fibers are thus innervated by the gamma motor neurons; the alpha motor neurons innervate the extrafusal fibers). The term Ia refers to the fact that the sensory (afferent) fiber emerging from the spindle is a large type I afferent; the a refers to the fact that this fiber comes from the spindle (type Ib fibers come from the Golgi tendon organs). Type II afferents are smaller in diameter and conduct impulses more slowly than the type I afferents.

[5] A motor unit is defined as an alpha motor neuron and all of the muscle fibers that it innervates. In humans, the number of fibers supplied by one alpha motor neuron might vary from a few (in muscles requiring fine control—in the hand, larynx, eyes) up to several thousand (in muscles requiring only gross control—in the trunk). There could be from a few to several hundred motor units in any one muscle (see Leob & Ghez, 2000).

[6] This 120 ms value in figure 5.16 is considerably shorter than the typical RT latency discussed in chapters 3 and 4. But in figure 5.16, the latency is measured by the EMG change, whereas in chapters 3 and 4 the RT is measured with respect to the movement, which usually occurs with an additional delay of at least 50 ms.

[7] A video of this demonstration is available at www.hp-research.com/videos.shtml.

[8] This diagram is not meant to be correct anatomically. For example, visual information probably travels to high levels in the central nervous system (visual cortex) and is certainly not "housed" in the spinal cord, per se. Rather, this diagram should be taken as a set of functional pathways—some of which involve the stages of processing and some of which do not.

CHAPTER 6

CENTRAL CONTRIBUTIONS TO MOTOR CONTROL

The focus in the last chapter was primarily on the role of sensory mechanisms. Motor control was considered as a closed-loop system, dependent on feedback either (a) for online corrections mediated by the stages of processing, or (b) for corrections or compensations in the action that are reflex based and not mediated by the stages of processing. In contrast to this closed-loop viewpoint is an open-loop system, in which the instructions for movement are structured in advance and are executed without regard to the effects they may have on the environment. That is, the behavior of the open-loop system is not sensitive to feedback.

A good example of an open-loop system is the traffic signal at a major intersection. The pattern of red and green lights is controlled from a program that handles this sequence without regard to moment-to-moment variations in traffic patterns. Because there is no feedback from the traffic conditions back to the executive, there can be no immediate modification in the pattern if an accident occurs or if traffic is particularly heavy. However, even though the program for the traffic lights is inflexible, we should not get the idea that it must be simple. The program can be structured so that the north–south street has a 20% longer green light duration than the east–west street during rush hours, with this relation being altered in midday when the traffic pattern is often dif-

ferent. But the only way modifications in timing can occur is for the programmer to structure them into the program in advance.

Open-Loop Processes

A diagram of a typical open-loop system is shown in figure 6.1. The executive and effector mechanisms can be thought of in the same way as for the closed-loop system in figure 5.1 on page 136, but the feedback loop and the reference of correctness are missing (the feedback pathway is "cut" or

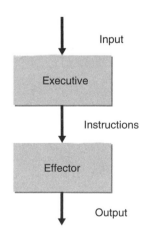

FIGURE 6.1   Elements of the typical open-loop control system.

"open," as when a switch is open—hence the label "open loop"). The executive is "programmed" to send certain instructions at particular times to the effector, and the effector carries them out without the possibility of modification if something goes wrong. In this chapter, we emphasize the open-loop processes and central representations involved in motor control, for which sensory influences play a much less dominant role.

Response-Chaining Hypothesis

One of the earliest explanations of movement control was the *response-chaining hypothesis* (sometimes called the reflex-chaining hypothesis) proposed by the 19th-century psychologist William James (1890). The basic idea is illustrated in figure 6.2. James assumed that a movement began with a muscular contraction caused by an external or internal signal. This first contraction generated sensory information (which he termed *response-produced feedback*), which we discussed in detail in chapter 5. James regarded this feedback as stimulus information (just like that from any other stimulus such as light or sound), which served as the *trigger* for the next contraction in the "chain." The second contraction then produced its own response-produced feedback, which triggered the third contraction, and so on until all the contractions in the sequence were completed. The feedback could come from various sources (e.g., muscle spindles, joint receptors, or even vision or audition), and it could trigger responses in the same or in different limbs. With such a mechanism, James hypothesized how certain actions

appear in the proper order in skills, as the chain ensured that the second contraction did not occur before the first one. Also, James thought that this mechanism could account for the *timing among* the various contractions so important for skilled actions; such timing (or more precisely, *relative timing*) would be determined by the temporal delays in the various sensory processes and could be relatively consistent from response to response to produce stereotyped actions. Although such a model seems appropriate for serial tasks (starting the car, buttoning a shirt), there is no conceptual reason why the model could not explain discrete actions, such as speech and throwing, by assuming that the responses triggered are the contractions of individual motor units. Viewed in this way, the response chain shown in figure 6.2, which consists of four units of behavior, might last only 100 ms, or it might continue for a few seconds.

James (1890) recognized that when *skilled* movements were produced, they did not seem to require much consciousness for their control. Under the response-chaining hypothesis, movements could be viewed as requiring attention only for the initiation of the first action, with the remainder of the actions being run off "automatically." Also, in James's view of *learning* motor skills, the acquisition of the associations between a given feedback event and the next action is the fundamental basis for improvement in skill.

The response-chaining hypothesis is really a variant of an open-loop control mode, in spite of the presence of feedback. Remember that in a

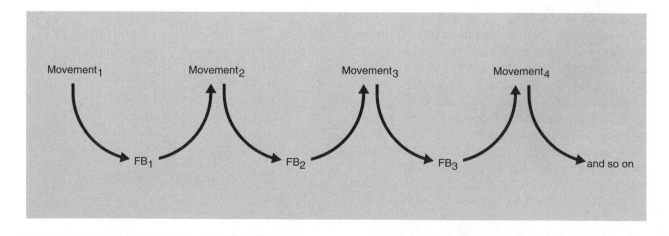

FIGURE 6.2 The response-chaining hypothesis. (The response-produced feedback from earlier portions of the action serves as a trigger for later portions.)

closed-loop system (chapter 5), the executive level is acting on the *error* that is produced, and such errors are computed as the difference between the actual state and the desired state defined by the reference of correctness. In the response-chaining hypothesis, though, there is no reference of correctness against which feedback is compared—the feedback simply serves as the trigger for the next act in the sequence. It is open loop because the original stimulus sets the chain in motion, and the following events are determined by the learned associations between feedback and the next act in the sequence. Also, open-loop movements cannot be modified if something goes wrong or if the environment changes, as is the case for a closed-loop model.

One way to test the response-chaining hypothesis is to examine the role of sensory information in the production of movement. Of course, if the sensory information is eliminated (or delayed or degraded in quality), then the result should be a loss of skill, or even paralysis, because the *trigger* mechanisms have been disrupted. In the next sections, we review some evidence about feedback degradation in relation to this hypothesis.

Deafferentation

There are both temporary methods for interrupting the flow of sensory information into the spinal cord (e.g., the blood pressure cuff technique, the injection of local anesthetics) and permanent procedures, called *deafferentation*. Nearly all of the afferent input to the spinal cord enters through the dorsal roots on the posterior side of the cord. In an operation called a *dorsal rhizotomy*, the back of the animal is entered surgically, and the muscles are carefully moved to expose the dorsal roots. Then, at the particular spinal level of interest, the dorsal roots are cut, essentially preventing any sensory information at that spinal level from reaching the cord in the future. Note that this procedure leaves intact the *efferent* (or motor) part of the system, which exits the cord via the ventral roots, and allows the muscles to be activated as before the operation; but, of course, it eliminates the feedback from the muscles. This procedure can be done at a single spinal level or at multiple levels—with additional deafferentation at each successive level progressively eliminating more and more of the animal's sensations from the periphery. The operation can be done

unilaterally or bilaterally, thereby eliminating the feedback from one or both sides of the body. These procedures have been performed on mice, cats, monkeys, and numerous other species in order to study the movement control that occurs in the deafferented state.

While normally these procedures are limited to animal experiments, a number of examples of deafferented humans have also been reported. Lashley (1917), in a study we will describe in detail later, assessed a patient with a gunshot wound to the lower spine. The lesion had the same effects as surgical deafferentation, and it left the motor innervation of the subject intact. Also, patients with complete or near-complete loss of sensory information due to degenerated afferent pathways (sensory *neuropathy*), but with intact motor systems, have made significant contributions to this area (e.g., Bonnet, Carello, & Turvey, 2009; Gordon, Ghilardi, & Ghez, 1995; Rothwell et al., 1982; Sanes, 1990; Teasdale et al., 1993). Finally, Kelso, Holt, and Flatt (1980) have studied arthritic patients who have had the joints of the fingers replaced with artificial ones. This operation removes the joint and the joint capsule in which the joint receptors are located. Thus, while this is not really a deafferentation procedure in the strictest sense, it does provide a situation in which feedback from the moving limb is disrupted.

Deafferentation Studies

One of the earliest investigations using surgical deafferentation was conducted by Sherrington (1906). He severed the dorsal roots in a monkey so that only the sensations from a single forelimb were lost; the remainder of the body had normal sensory feedback. A major finding was that after recovery from surgery, the monkey never used the limb, keeping it tucked against the chest and using the other limbs to eat and ambulate. For decades, this finding was regarded as support for the response-chaining hypothesis, because eliminating the feedback seemed to eliminate movement altogether, as it should if the hypothesis is correct.

But Sherrington's conclusions were later challenged by a number of separate lines of evidence. On the one hand, considerable research was completed on the control of locomotion in lower organisms such as fish, snakes, frogs, insects, and birds (for reviews of this early work, see Grillner,

1975; Pearson, 1976). Some of this research involved severing the afferent (sensory) pathways for various segments of the animal's system. The conclusions generally were that movements are not seriously disrupted. For example, Wilson (1961) deafferented locusts, stimulating the insect electrically with a pulse near the head region, and wing movement patterns resembling flying resulted. The patterns were decreased in amplitude and frequency as compared to normal flight patterns, but clear rhythmic activity nevertheless continued.

Why were the locust's movements so well accomplished, when Sherrington's monkey did not move the deafferented limb at all? Could it be that monkeys are fundamentally different from the lower species in terms of their motor systems? This is probably not the answer, as studies subsequent to Sherrington's on humans and monkeys have tended to show that some movements are not strongly interrupted by deafferentation. For example, Lashley (1917), in his study of the patient in whom a gunshot wound to the spine had rendered the legs deafferented, asked the patient to perform various positioning movements without vision. While sitting on the edge of an examination table, the patient was asked to extend the knee to 45°, and the error in producing the movement was compared to that of a "normal" control subject. Lashley found that the deafferented subject and the normal subject could do the positioning task about equally well.

How can the apparently contradictory findings of Sherrington and Lashley be reconciled? One possibility is that the deafferented monkey *chose not* to use the affected limb, which is quite different from saying that the monkey *could not* use it. You know how it feels when you sleep on your arm the "wrong way," or when your jaw is anesthetized after a trip to the dentist; the sensation is strange and unpleasant, and we might prefer not use these effectors in these situations unless it was important to do so.

Later Deafferentation Studies

In a series of studies, Taub and his colleagues (see Taub & Berman, 1968, or Taub, 1976, for reviews) and Bizzi (e.g., Polit & Bizzi, 1978) used surgical deafferentation affecting various portions of monkeys' bodies. After Taub and Berman's monkeys had both forelimbs deafferented and had recovered from the operation, they were able to move the limbs *nearly* normally—activities such as climbing, swinging, eating, and grooming were different only in minor ways from those of the normal animals. The deafferented monkeys did, however, show some deficiencies in very fine manipulations, such as those that would be required to pick up a small piece of food. Perhaps this is related to the role of the cutaneous receptors in these movements (see chapter 5; also, Frank, Williams, & Hayes, 1977). The conclusion to be drawn from these studies is that feedback from the moving limb is not *essential* for movement to occur, but that it undoubtedly aids the accuracy of movement in most situations.[1] However, these findings do seem to contradict the expectations of the reflex-chaining hypothesis, which claims the necessary involvement of feedback in the normal conduct of movement.

Deafferentation in Humans

Provins (1958) studied the role of joint receptors from the fingers by injecting anesthetic directly into the joint capsule. Although the subjects could not feel the movements of their fingers, there was nevertheless a strong capability to move; but the accuracy suffered somewhat compared to that in the condition without the anesthetic. Very similar findings were obtained by Kelso (1977; Kelso et al., 1980) in studies involving the joint afferents from the hand. When the feedback from the joint afferents was blocked either by Laszlo's (1967) cuff technique (see below, and Kelso, 1977) or in patients who had artificial finger joints (Kelso et al., 1980), little or no loss in movement positioning accuracy occurred without vision. Of course, these studies involved normal afferent feedback from the muscle spindles located in the finger muscles in the forearm, and it could be that this was the source of feedback that allowed for accurate control. All these studies imply that the joint afferents are not essential for movement, as is often believed (e.g., Adams, 1977).

Using an anesthetic block of the gamma loop and other pathways from the right arm in humans, J. Smith (1969; Smith, Roberts, & Atkins, 1972) found that dart throwing and grip strength tasks were only minimally disrupted by this kind of deafferentation. Although some impairments in performance occurred, the most important point is that the movement could be produced even though feedback was not available from the moving limb.

Many studies have been done using the so-called cuff technique popularized by Laszlo (1967). Here, a blood pressure cuff is inflated around the upper arm, blocking blood flow to the lower arm; after about 20 min, the feedback sensations from the lower arm and hand are temporarily lost; but for a few minutes, the motor capabilities remain largely intact. In a series of studies using tasks such as rapid finger tapping, handwriting, aiming, and limb positioning, impairments were found in performance under the cuff conditions. However, the movements, although impaired, still could be produced, contrary to the expectations from a response-chaining hypothesis (see also Chambers & Schumsky, 1978; Kelso, Stelmach, & Wannamaker, 1976; Laszlo & Bairstow, 1979).

Studies involving patients with sensory neuropathy have yielded similar conclusions, although these individuals often have severe difficulties in performing many activities of daily living. For example, the patient studied by Rothwell and colleagues (1982) reported that he had trouble feeding and dressing himself and could not hold a pen in his hand. Yet figure 6.3a illustrates that he could control his hands to touch the thumb to each fingertip sequentially without visual feedback, at least for a short period of time. The photos shown in figure 6.3b reveal that this activity could not be maintained for very long, however; performance had deteriorated considerably after 30 s, when these photos were taken.

Another example involves a woman known in the literature as GL, who is completely without

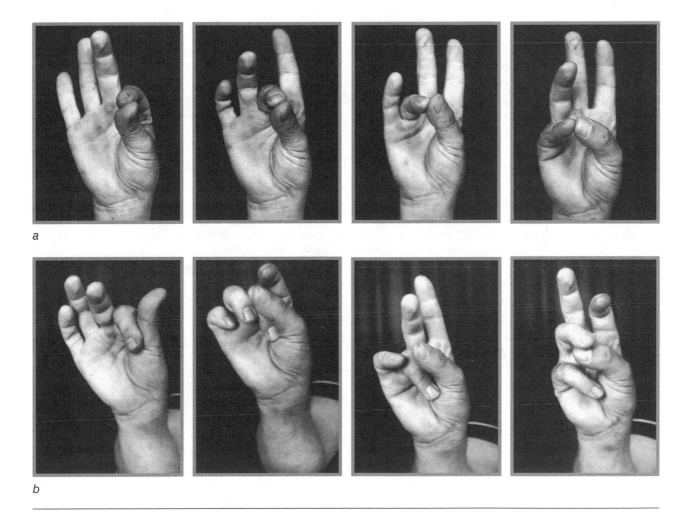

a

b

FIGURE 6.3 *(a)* A patient with sensory neuropathy could touch his thumb and fingers without vision quite well early in the sequence, but *(b)* performance was disrupted markedly after 30 s.

Reprinted, by permission, from J.C. Rothwell et al., 1982, "Manual motor performance in a deafferented man," *Brain* 105: 523.

information about touch, tendon vibration, and proprioception but has normal visual feedback and efferent pathways. GL is able to carry out her activities of daily living quite well using constant visual feedback (Bard et al., 1999; Blouin, Gauthier, Vercher, & Cole, 1996; Hepp-Reymond, Chakarov, Schulte-Mönting, Huethe, & Kristeva, 2009). From the perspective of the response-chaining hypothesis, sensory neuropathy patients demonstrate remarkable capabilities to perform skilled actions (Sanes, Mauritz, Dalakas, & Evarts, 1985).

Implications for the Response-Chaining Hypothesis

Even though work with various kinds of deaf-ferentation has shown that feedback from the responding limbs is not necessary in order for actions to occur, the evidence was sometimes taken incorrectly to mean that feedback in general is *never* used in movement control. The deaf-ferented animals were not completely normal in their movement, especially when the fine control of finger action was required. We saw (in chapter 5) the effects of having the fingertips anesthetized on performance of simple tasks such as striking a match. Also, it is possible, as Adams (1971, 1976b) has said, that other kinds of feedback (e.g., vision) could be substituted for the lost sensations in the deafferented animal. And finally, there are many cases in which feedback is almost certainly used in movement, such as those that we discussed in chapter 5. On strict experimental grounds, the evidence does not really say that the response-chaining hypothesis is incorrect. But the fact that movements can occur in the absence of any movement-produced feedback at all strongly indicates that the response-chaining hypothesis is not a very complete account of movement control. Other mechanisms of motor control have to be used to explain the available evidence.

Central Control Mechanisms

We need motor control mechanisms that explain how movements can occur in the absence of sensory feedback in order to deal with some of the evidence just described. In the next sections, the role of sensory processes is more or less reduced in prominence. Keep in mind, however, that various mechanisms of motor control can be isolated for study in the various paradigms, although none seems to operate independently during most everyday activities. It is important for students to understand these mechanisms, but the real problem in understanding motor behavior is to appreciate how these processes work together toward smooth, elegant, and energy-efficient performance (see also Cruse, Dean, Heuer, & Schmidt, 1990).

Central Pattern Generators

A number of extensive reviews summarize the evidence about the control of locomotion and gait in a variety of animals (Dietz & Duysens, 2000; Grillner, 2007; Grillner & Wallén, 1985, 2002; Goulding, 2009; Marder, Bucher, Schulz, & Taylor, 2005; Pearson & Gordon, 2000a; Zehr & Stein, 1999) and humans (Zehr, 2005). One important topic in this literature concerns so-called *spinal preparations* in cats and other animals. In this procedure, the spinal cord is cut at a level below the brain so that the higher (supraspinal) centers cannot influence lower ones, and often the cord is deafferented below the level of the cut as well (see Pearson & Gordon, 2000b). If the prepared cord is then stimulated only briefly below the cut, the cord displays a definite *periodicity* in terms of the activity in the efferent fibers emerging from its ventral side. Thus, the spinal cord is seemingly capable of producing a rhythm that can be present even without input from the brain or higher centers, and without feedback from the limbs. With reference to gait patterns, a popular view, termed the *half-center* model (Brown, 1911), suggests that interneurons (wholly within the spinal cord) alternately stimulate the flexor and extensor motor neurons in a pattern more or less like the one that would be displayed in locomotion. Apparently, the spinal cord has complex neural circuitry that is capable of producing these oscillations. These circuits have come to be called *central pattern generators*.

A schematic diagram of how such a simple spinal generator might be structured is shown in figure 6.4. Many alternatives exist, and the central pattern generator illustrated in figure 6.4 is only a simple illustration. In this structure there could be a neural network in the cord made up of four interneurons (the cord undoubtedly uses many more). Input from some higher center (a chemical or electrical signal for the spinal animal) initiates a cyclical pattern of excitatory motor neural activ-

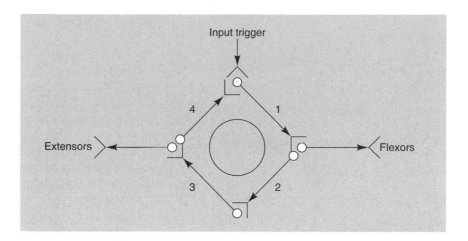

FIGURE 6.4   A simple possibility for the connections of interneurons forming a central pattern generator.

ity. Neuron 1 is activated, which activates neuron 2, and so on, until neuron 4 activates neuron 1 again to start the cycle all over again. This continuous cycling process would go on indefinitely or until some other process turned it off. Further, if neuron 1 synapses with another neuron that drives the flexor muscles, and neuron 3 synapses with another that drives the extensors, every time around the cycle the flexors and extensors will be activated. This basic concept of simple oscillating circuits helps to illustrate how a neural network could be expected to produce rhythmic patterns of activity such as gait or breathing in animals.

Showing that the spinal cord has some slow rhythmic capability is interesting, but to what extent is this activity involved in gait control? A very important surgical preparation in cats has allowed considerable insight into this process. This preparation is called the mesencephalic (midbrain) preparation (Shik, Orlovskii, & Severin, 1968). The cat receives a cut of the spinal cord in the midbrain, which totally severs the lower levels of the cord from the higher, supraspinal centers. The cerebellum, the small structure behind the midbrain, is left intact, connected to the spinal cord side of the cut. In this state, the cat is (presumably) unable to sense any stimulation from the body (because the afferent pathways to the cortex are severed) and is unable to perform voluntary movements of the legs. Shik and colleagues used a mechanism that supported the cat above a treadmill, as shown in figure 6.5.

A number of important observations have come from this preparation. First, when stimulated with a brief electrical current or a chemical at the level of the cut, the animal on a moving treadmill began to produce stepping movements that resembled normal locomotion in cats. This stepping continued for some time after the stimulus was discontinued. As the treadmill sped up, the cat walked faster, even trotting or galloping. It appears that some spinal generator(s) for walking must be activated by a higher source and that, once initiated, the pattern of flexion and extension continues without further involvement from the supraspinal centers. Because the mesencephalic animal cannot sense the activity occurring in its limbs, such stepping activity must be independent of the animal's feedback of the activity.

As it turns out, a stimulus from the higher center in the midbrain is not the only way to initiate the spinal generators for stepping. Using the same apparatus, Shik and Orlovskii (1976) studied the cat's behavior when the treadmill was turned on. At first, the legs would trail off behind the animal; then suddenly the animal would initiate stepping, with the total pattern of activity generated as a unit. As the treadmill increased in speed, the animal would walk faster, with only minor differences in the pattern of activity from that observed in the normal cat, plus some unsteadiness. As the treadmill increased in speed further, the cat would suddenly break into a trot pattern. Occasionally the cat could be made to gallop. (Remember, there is no control from the higher centers and no stimulus from higher levels in the cord to turn on the spinal generators.) These results indicate that the afferent input from the feet and legs, which are at first dragged by the treadmill, is sufficient to initiate stepping. Once

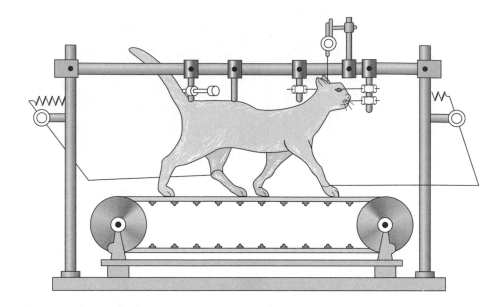

FIGURE 6.5   Mesencephalic (midbrain) cat supported on a treadmill as used in the study of spinal mechanisms in gait.

Reprinted from *Biofizika*, Vol. 11, M.L. Shik, G.N. Orlovskii, and F.V. Severin, "Locomotion of the mesencephalic cat elicited by stimulation of the pyramids," Copyright 1966, with permission from Elsevier Science.

the pattern generators are activated, the speed of the oscillation appears to be controlled by the rate at which the treadmill moves the cat's legs and feet. When the limbs are being moved so rapidly by the treadmill that a walk pattern is no longer effective in keeping up, the afferent information presumably triggers a new pattern—the trot. An analogous set of findings has been produced by Smith and her colleagues (Carter & Smith, 1986; Smith, 1978; Smith et al., 1986).

As a result of this evidence, as well as the evidence reviewed by Grillner (1975), several models of gait have emerged. The general features of these models are shown in figure 6.6. The box in the center of the diagram represents a central pattern generator, and it can be activated or deactivated by supraspinal centers. In some cases, this higher-level input appears to be but a single pulse that will turn on the generator, with no further higher-level activity necessary in order for the oscillator to continue to operate. In other cases, a continuous input (not necessarily a rhythmic one) appears to be necessary, with the action in the generator continuing only as long as the input continues.

The activity in the generator can also be turned on by sensory input. While the generator is operating, the activities in the flexor and extensor muscles are coordinated, and feedback from the responding limbs also can serve to modify the

output; this is shown by the two-way arrows from the various muscles to the spinal generator. And, finally, a number of spinal generators are thought to exist, perhaps one for each of the four limbs in the stepping cycle of the cat, so that the operation of the separate oscillators must be coordinated (coupled) by interneurons. Thus, in the diagram a connection is shown from another oscillator to indicate this kind of control.

A number of important concepts emerge from this work on pattern generators. First, for the control of gait and other stereotyped actions in a variety of species (e.g., swimming in lamprey; tail

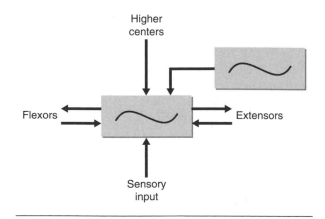

FIGURE 6.6   Spinal generator model for gait, showing input to oscillators from sensory sources, from higher centers, from other oscillators, and from moving limbs.

flipping or escape reactions in lobsters; grooming in mice), strong evidence exists that these patterns are controlled by "prewired" pattern generators that can handle most of the details of the actions. They can be turned on by a variety of sources of stimulation, and they can continue until they "run down" or are stopped by some other source of input. While the basic pattern is quite stereotyped, in "higher" animals (such as cats), extensive modification of the basic pattern is possible, either from higher centers to make the whole pattern more rapid or more forceful, or from lower feedback sources (e.g., from the leg or foot) that serve to alter the particular pattern of force applied to conform to variations in terrain. And, finally, these pattern generators do not require the conscious awareness of the animal in order to operate. Once initiated, they can apparently continue without involvement of the higher centers. However, in the operation of these generators during running, for example, attention seems to be required, perhaps to evaluate the upcoming terrain or to keep the oscillator running (e.g., Duysens & Van de Crommert, 1998; Van de Crommert, Mulder, & Duysens, 1998).

Reflex Involvement in Locomotion

Throughout the history of motor skills research, considerable debate has centered on the role of reflexes, and our discussion about genetically defined activities such as locomotion would be incomplete unless we considered reflex involvement (see also chapter 5). The following sections present some of these diverse viewpoints.

Maintaining the Original Pattern

The focus in the next few sections concerns the ways in which feedback activity of various kinds cooperates with the central programs for action. We are only now beginning to understand the important principles of these sensory–motor interactions.

An older notion of control in locomotion was that the patterns of limb action *consisted* of fundamental reflex activities (e.g., Easton, 1972). This was somewhat different from the reflex-chaining hypothesis in that the component reflexes were thought to be the identifiable, genetically defined patterns that we see so often in infants, whereas the reflex-chaining hypothesis involves any chained activity—even those that are learned. A good example of these genetically defined

reflexes is *reciprocal inhibition*, whereby the flexors of a joint tend to be automatically inhibited when the extensors are activated. With the *crossed-extensor reflex*, the extensors of one knee are activated when the flexors of the opposite knee are called into action. When we step on a tack, the flexors in the affected leg take the weight off the tack, while the extensors in the opposite leg help to prevent falling. Another example is the *tonic neck reflex*, in which turning the head to the right causes facilitation in the arm flexors on the left and in the arm extensors on the right (see chapter 5).

That these reflexes *exist* is not in question. They are especially easy to identify in infants, and they have been used in the diagnosis of various neurological disorders. But to say that gait and other movement behaviors *consist* of the various reflexes implies a model in which the motor system is always *reacting* to peripheral stimulation. A more reasonable viewpoint, based on the evidence on central pattern generators, is that reflexes ensure that the pattern of activity specified by the central pattern generator is carried out effectively in the face of unexpected changes in the environment. The muscle spindle and gamma systems seem to fill this role. One function of the gamma system is to maintain muscle stiffness (i.e., its mechanical, spring-like properties) in the face of various unexpected changes in muscle length because of changes in joint position(s) (Nichols & Houk, 1976). If an animal steps on a patch of ground that is higher than expected, the "springy" muscles allow extensors to yield without collapsing, maintaining a smooth gait without a fall. The view is that reflexes are *prepared* to operate if the system is perturbed but do not have a particularly important role under normal circumstances (Grillner, 1975).

Reflex-Reversal Phenomena

An important variation of the concept of triggered reactions (discussed in chapter 5) is the concept of reflex reversals described in relation to locomotion by Forssberg, Grillner, and Rossignol (1975). In the locomoting cat, when a light touch or a weak electrical shock is applied to the top of the foot during the flexion portion of the swing phase of the gait cycle (i.e., the time at which the animal is lifting the foot in preparation for the swing forward), an abrupt increase in the flexion response occurs (with an extension response in the opposite foot), as if the cat were trying to lift its foot to avoid an obstacle (such as a rock) that would cause it to trip. (This crossed-extensor pattern is not voluntary, as it can be shown to exist in the mesencephalic cats described earlier; thus, the response is spinal in origin.) However, when the *same stimulus* is applied to the foot during the phase of the gait cycle in which the foot is on the ground (the stance phase), essentially no reaction, or perhaps a slight extra extension, takes place in the stimulated foot—a response *opposite* that shown in the swing phase of the step cycle. Because the same stimulus causes two different patterns of action depending on the phase of the stepping cycle, this effect has been termed the *reflex-reversal phenomenon.*

Frequently (but see some exceptions in chapter 5), a reflex is thought of as a *stereotyped response* caused by a particular stimulus (e.g., the blink of an eye when a puff of air is presented). Yet the evidence just cited in locomotion indicates that the response to the stimulus depends on the location of the limb in the stepping cycle and is not simple and stereotyped. Thus, a simple view of reflex control cannot explain these effects. This kind of evidence has been explained (e.g., Grillner, 1975) based on the assumption that the spinal generators for locomotion, in addition to providing efferent commands to the relevant musculature, also provide feedforward signals to other locations in the cord that serve to modify the actions of various reflexes. The sense of this control is that if the pathways to the extensors of the right leg are being activated (during the

stance phase), then the reflex that would serve to lift the leg in response to a tap is inhibited by the central generator. However, this pathway is activated when the flexors are activated (in the flexion phase). In this way, the pattern generators involve the already structured reflex pathways so that they contribute maximally to the animal's overall movement goals (see also Hasan & Enoka, 1985).

The role of reflexes in human posture and locomotion is also starting to emerge. Zehr and Stein's (1999) excellent review on the topic identified a number of situations in which the role of reflexes changes either as a function of the *task* being performed or due to a *specific phase* of the activity within the current task. For example, pain reflex responses are diminished during standing as postural load is increased (a task-related modulation of the cutaneous reflex), whereas the functional importance of cutaneous and muscle reflexes changes between the parts of the step cycles within the task of locomotion. Figure 6.7 illustrates these changes within locomotion as summarized in Zehr and Stein's (1999) review. Cutaneous reflexes involved in corrections for a stumble and foot-placing reactions dominate the swing and swing-to-stance phases of the step cycle. Muscle reflexes involved in weight support, stability, timing, and unloading dominate the stance and stance-to-swing phases (see Zehr & Stein, 1999, for details).

Other studies of the role of reflexes in humans have been conducted in research on the motor

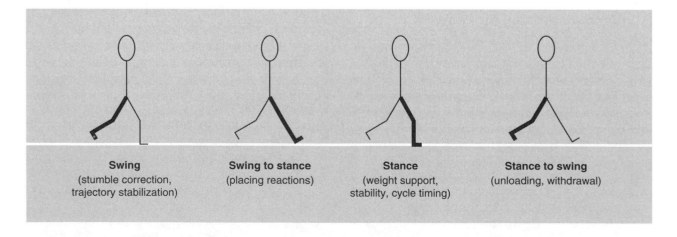

Swing
(stumble correction,
trajectory stabilization)

Swing to stance
(placing reactions)

Stance
(weight support,
stability, cycle timing)

Stance to swing
(unloading, withdrawal)

FIGURE 6.7   The phase-dependent role of reflexes in locomotion. Cutaneous reflexes dominate the swing and swing-to-stance phases, and muscle reflexes dominate in the stance and stance-to-swing phases.

control of speech (Abbs & Gracco, 1983; Abbs, Gracco, & Cole, 1984; Kelso, Tuller, Vatikiotis-Bateson, & Fowler, 1984). These are also discussed in chapter 5. Subjects in the study by Kelso and colleagues said simple sentences, such as "It's a /baez/ again" or "It's a /baeb/ again," and received an unexpected downward perturbation to the jaw during the target syllable /baez/ or /baeb/. When /baez/ was to be spoken, a perturbation to the jaw evoked a rapid compensation in the tongue muscles but not in the lip, whereas the same perturbation during /baeb/ produced the reverse pattern—a compensation in the lip but not the tongue; this compensation occurred on the *very first* trial. As in the work on locomotion, the same stimulus (here the jaw perturbation) produced rapid responses (about 30 ms latency) that were very different depending on the action being produced (i.e., the specific word). But, unlike the changes observed in the locomotion studies, these speech modifications were probably learned along with speech, as it is difficult to imagine how this capability could have been a part of an inherited pattern as was the case for locomotion. These rapid sensory–motor processes seem to serve the general purpose of ensuring that the overall *goal* of the particular movement being attempted at the time is maintained, with the modifications necessarily being different for different movement goals (Schmidt, 1987).

The "Smart" Spinal Cord

Early in the thinking about motor control, the spinal cord tended to be viewed as a "freeway" that simply carried impulses back and forth from the brain to the peripheral receptors and muscles. Gradually, as many spinal activities were isolated and studied (e.g., Sherrington, 1906), the spinal cord came to be regarded as considerably more complex—and has even been considered as an organ. The evidence that the spinal cord contains central pattern generators for gait and other movements continues to point toward the cord as a complex organ where much of motor control is structured. Further, evidence suggests that the spinal cord is responsible for considerable integration of sensory and motor information, as shown by the following example.

Figure 6.8 shows a frog making a wiping response to a noxious stimulus placed on the "elbow." Fukson, Berkinblit, and Feldman (1980; Berkinblit, Feldman, & Fukson, 1986), like others before them, showed that the frog is capable of performing these hindlimb responses when spinalized (i.e., with a transection that separates the cortex from the intact spinal cord). The response always begins with a movement of the hindlimb toe to the region of the shoulder area, followed by a rapid wiping action that is aimed at the elbow. It is interesting that the animal can use sensory information from one part of the body (the elbow)

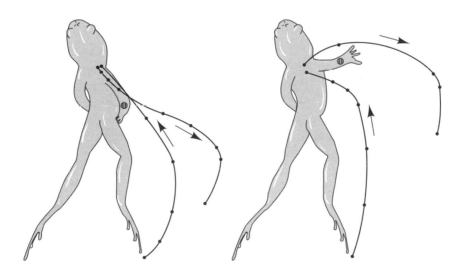

FIGURE 6.8 In the spinal frog, the hindlimb response to wipe an acid stimulus from the "elbow" is aimed to various elbow positions without the involvement of voluntary control from the cortex.

Reprinted with permission from O.I. Fukson, M.B. Berkinblit, A.G. and Feldman, 1980, "The spinal frog takes into account the scheme of its body during the wiping reflex," *Science* 209: 1261. Reprinted with permission of AAAS.

to trigger an action pattern in some other part (the hindlimb), even when spinalized. What is of more interest, however, is that the animal produces different wiping movements depending on the location of the elbow at which the response is aimed. That is, the central pattern generator for this response appears to modify its action depending on the sensory information from the forelimb indicating the position of the stimulus—the cord "knows" where the limbs are. Remember, the frog had no cortical involvement in this response, and thus no awareness of the limbs' actions, so this integration of sensory information was done at very low levels, perhaps completely within the spinal cord. Such observations indicate that the spinal cord is a very "smart" organ indeed.

Another example, from the work of Smith and colleagues (1986) on spinalized cats, is particularly impressive. When a piece of tape was placed on the walking cat's hind paw, a stereotyped paw-shake program was initiated in which the cat lifted the foot and shook it rapidly and violently for about 10 to 13 cycles, apparently for the purpose of shaking the tape loose. Of course, because of the spinal section, this stereotyped program must have been initiated through peripheral stimulation from the foot and controlled by the spinal cord. But even more remarkably, the spinal cat could walk on the treadmill (another program) and shake the paw at the same time, triggering the paw shake when the limb was in the swing phase of locomotion and turning it off when the foot was on the ground in support. Somehow the spinal cord, without the help of a higher center, "knew" how to coordinate these two actions simultaneously to achieve the double goals of removing the tape and walking without falling.

Human Skills

The evidence and ideas presented that support the concept of a central pattern generator were produced in animals. Suggestions that central pattern generators also operate in humans have sparked considerable debate, and to date the evidence is not entirely clear on the issue (MacKay-Lyons, 2002). We might expect that central pattern generators likely would operate in humans to some extent (see Zehr, 2005, for more discussion).

The movements studied in the cat mentioned previously are probably genetically defined and "prewired." To what extent are motor programs for movements like throwing a football structured in the same way? Are there programs in the spinal cord that can handle the production of a football pass if they are activated by a pulse from the midbrain, or do programs that are not genetically defined have some different origin? These questions are difficult to answer, as almost no research with animals has used tasks or skills that we could consider learned, or that are not genetically defined. One hypothesis is that the control of learned and genetically defined actions is fundamentally the same, but no good evidence is available on this question. Instead, we turn next to evidence about the role of central control mechanisms—*motor programs*, specifically—that has been generated in behavioral studies with humans.

Central Control of Rapid Movements

Consider a very rapid limb movement in which the pattern of action is initiated and completed in less than 150 ms. There are many examples of movements like this, such as a key press in typing (<100 ms) and, in sport, the bat swing in baseball (~140 ms) and boxer Muhammad Ali's left jab (40 ms). Because these discrete tasks are so highly represented in our everyday activities, they have been studied in laboratory settings in an attempt to understand how they are controlled.

A laboratory study might involve beginning with the elbow in one position and then rapidly extending it so that the hand comes to rest at or near a target 30 cm away. Although at first this movement appears to be very simple, the kinds of neurological activities associated with it are elegant and complex. Although many examples could be presented, one in a study by Wadman, Denier van der Gon, Geuze, and Mol (1979) makes the point particularly well. Figure 6.9 shows a pattern of electromyographic (EMG) activity in this elbow extension task; this kind of pattern is common in many investigations using fast movements such as this. The EMGs from the triceps (the agonist) and the biceps (the antagonist) are shown. The "raw" EMGs from the muscles have been *rectified*, meaning that the negative swings of the EMG signals have been changed to positive values, and these positive values are plotted as a function of time in the action. The occurrence of peaks in the rectified EMGs represents periods of heightened activity in the muscle in question.

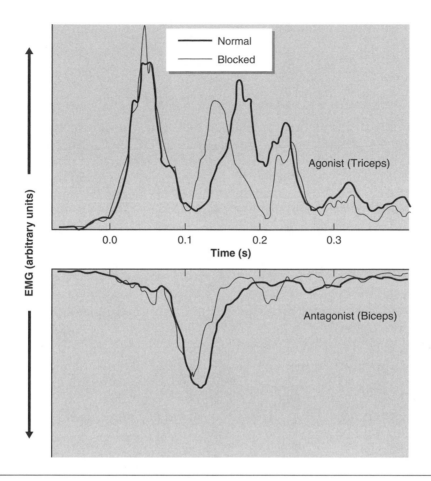

FIGURE 6.9 Agonist (triceps) and antagonist (biceps) electromyographic activity in a rapid elbow extension action.

Reprinted from W.J. Wadman, 1979, "Control of fast goal-directed arm movements," *Journal of Human Movement Studies* 5: 10. By permission of W.J. Wadman.

Also, the record for the biceps (the antagonist) has been turned "upside down" so it can more easily be compared to the triceps record.

The distinctive triple-burst EMG pattern is prominent in figure 6.9, first identified in the 1920s by the German physiologist Wachholder (see Sternad, 2001; Sternad & Corcos, 2001). A burst of the agonist (triceps) muscle occurs first, and then the agonist is turned off and the antagonist (the biceps here) is turned on, presumably to bring the limb to a stop. Then, near the end of the action, the antagonist muscle is turned off and the agonist comes on again, probably to cause the limb to be "clamped" at the target, dampening the oscillations that could be produced. The exact nature of this pattern of EMG activation depends on various task-related parameters (Sternad & Corcos, 2001).

A question of interest for these kinds of actions is how the motor system controls the timing of these events—how does it "know" when to turn off the triceps activity and turn on the biceps activity? This question becomes much more complex when applied to skills for which many muscles turn on and off at particular times, such as in pole-vaulting and swinging a sledgehammer. The closed-loop account of movement behavior involving the stages of information processing could account for these features of the movement by indicating that the system monitors the position of the limb (perhaps by sensing the joint angle) and waits until the limb is at some particular position before turning off the triceps and turning on the biceps. That is, the system could use the feedback from the responding limb to trigger the end of activity in one muscle and initiate activity in the other.[2] However, a number of fundamental difficulties arise with this idea about the control of actions, as discussed next.

The Degrees of Freedom Problem

One difficulty for the closed-loop model, and for any other model holding that the contractions of the various muscles are handled by direct commands from higher centers, was raised by the Russian physiologist Nikolai Bernstein (see "Nikolai Bernstein" on p. 8). Bernstein's idea was that if the information-processing system were involved in the production of all the decisions about each of the muscles participating in a motor act, it would be difficult to imagine how this would explain all of the mental work involved in producing even a simple act like that shown in figure 6.9. The fundamental concern is that the system has too many *independent states* that must be controlled at the same time. These independent states are called *degrees of freedom*.

As an example, consider a simple arm movement. Each joint is capable of moving independently, having at least one degree of freedom that must be controlled in an action. And some joints have two degrees of freedom, such as the shoulder, which can (a) allow the hand to move in a half sphere with the elbow "locked" and (b) rotate the shaft of the arm, independently. The degrees of freedom problem is compounded further because each joint has a number of muscles acting on it, and each of these muscles is made up of hundreds of motor units that also must be controlled. All of the independently moving parts would lead to an impossible situation for the central nervous system if it had to control these degrees of freedom individually by conscious decisions (see also Greene, 1972; Whiting, 1984).

In searching for answers about how we control movement, a good question is "How can the very many degrees of freedom of the body be regulated in the course of activity by a minimally intelligent executive intervening minimally?" (Kugler, Kelso, & Turvey, 1980, p. 4). The idea is that an executive level should not be thought of as having much responsibility for the control of the many degrees of freedom; there are simply too many degrees of freedom for even an intelligent executive to control and yet still have capability left over to do anything else.

On other grounds, for many years scientists have thought that *actions* are controlled, not the individual degrees of freedom such as muscles or motor units. When we perform an action, we seem to be aware of the goal of the movement, its global action pattern, and its effect on the environment; but we are hardly aware at all of the particular muscles used and are never aware of the particular motor units involved. Therefore,

if the executive does not have the responsibility for controlling the degrees of freedom, how *are* the many degrees of freedom controlled, and how can the elegant, skilled organization of the muscles and joints be achieved?

This general question has been of fundamental concern since scientists began to think about movement skills. One solution has been to postulate a structure, subordinate to the executive, which can account for the particular organization required among the separate degrees of freedom. These theoretical structures, called *motor programs* by many (e.g., Brooks, 1979, 1986; Henry & Rogers, 1960; Keele, 1968, 1986; Keele, Cohen, & Ivry, 1990; Lashley, 1917; Schmidt, 1975b, 1988), have the capability to influence the activity of the many independent degrees of freedom so that they act as a single unit. If this temporary organization can be imposed on the system, then the problem for the executive will have been simplified so that only a single degree of freedom will need to be controlled. In other words, the executive level is thought to control the selection of a motor program, ready it for action, and initiate it at the proper time. Once under way, the program controls the activity of the individual degrees of freedom involved in the movement. In this sense, the executive is freed from the task of solving the degrees of freedom problem.

This kind of solution to the degrees of freedom problem sounds very simple—in fact, too simple. Explaining how all the degrees of freedom are controlled by inventing some theoretical structure (here, the motor program) does not really answer the question of control at all. The question of exactly how the various degrees of freedom are coordinated still must be addressed. The debate about the nature of this reduction in controllable degrees of freedom—in terms of what variables are controlled, when, and how—represents a truly fundamental problem for researchers in motor control. We will consider some of these questions later in this chapter and again in chapters 7 and 8.

Agonist–Antagonist Patterning

Another argument against the idea that some executive level *directly* terminates the triceps burst of EMG and initiates the biceps burst (figure 6.9) relates to the time available for generating these events. The information-processing stages require considerable time in order for an individual to produce a response to an environmental stimulus, such as the offset of the triceps EMG and the onset of the biceps EMG. Although this model might be acceptable for very slow movements, if the action is very fast (as in the example in figure 6.9), the movement will be over before one of these stimulus–response processes can be completed. Something else must be involved in the activation of the various muscle groups.

This argument, however, does not rule out the possibility that the patterning has been influenced by reflexive adjustments, handled at lower levels in the motor system. As discussed in chapter 5, such processes are far faster than those involved in the stages of processing, and they might be rapid enough to account for the control entailed in these very fast actions. A number of models based on lower-level reflex control have been proposed (e.g., Adamovich & Feldman, 1984; Feldman, 1986), and considerable debate has centered on this question. Some available data, however, seem to suggest that these models are not correct either.

Wadman and colleagues' (1979) experiment had a very important, additional condition that we have not yet described. When the subject had become accustomed to the apparatus and movement task (a rapid, 150 ms, elbow extension to a target), on particular trials the lever was unexpectedly *locked* mechanically at the starting position so that no movement of it could occur. Figure 6.9 shows the EMG patterns available from these "blocked" trials, superimposed on the patterns from the "normal" trials. For approximately 110 ms after the initial agonist EMG burst, the two EMG patterns were nearly identical, with only minor modifications in the patterning afterward. The most important feature of figure 6.9 is that the onset of the antagonist (biceps) EMG occurred at the expected time on these "blocked" trials—that is, it occurred at approximately the same time in the blocked trials as it did in the "normal" trials. Magill, Schmidt, Young, and Shapiro (1987) and Shapiro and Walter (1982) obtained similar results for fast movements.

Several have argued that unexpectedly blocking the limb from moving would result in reflex-like responses from various proprioceptors, and hence the EMG patterning of the blocked action cannot tell us about the originally planned pattern of action. We agree, to a point. But, what

impresses us is essentially the reverse of this: The antagonist (here, biceps) EMG is turned on even though no movement of the limb occurred. The fascinating question is thus, What *did* turn on the EMG in the antagonist? Feedback (e.g., vision) from the movement could not have been processed by the stages of processing; the stages are too slow and, in any case, there was no movement. Reflex activities associated with joint movement could not do this, as there was no movement and hence no usable output from the various proprioceptors. The dynamics of the moving limb cannot be responsible for activating the antagonist, as the limb did not move and, in addition, had its dynamics severely disrupted. We are left with one theory that can handle these findings: The motor program for action was prepared in advance to govern the timing in the action, and this program continued to "run" even though the limb was blocked. That is, the answer to the question "What turned the antagonist on at the proper time (even though the limb was blocked and prevented from moving)?" is *The motor program did.*

Using considerably slower movements, Angel (1977) found that the antagonist EMG disappeared when the movement was blocked; this suggests that sufficient time was involved for feedback to higher levels, or reflex activities, or both to have an effect on the action. This also provides evidence for the long-held view that "fast" and "slow" movements are controlled in fundamentally differently ways. Simply, fast movements seem to be controlled open loop, whereas slow movements appear not to be. We will return to these ideas several more times later.

Startled Actions

Another line of evidence, using a very different experimental paradigm, supports the conclusions we have just drawn from the study by Wadman and colleagues (1979). Our usual reaction to a loud, unexpected sound signal is a *startle response*, which is characterized by a sudden, fast, automatic, generalized, stereotypical reaction that includes a rapid eye blink and flexion of the neck muscles; this response is clearly one of the reflex-like actions that result from certain stimuli. Valls-Solé, Rothwell, Goulart, Cossu, and Muñoz (1999) asked subjects to perform a large number of trials involving a movement task similar to the task used by Wadman and colleagues (1979). On a few of these trials, the visual stimulus was accompanied by a very loud (130 dB) auditory signal. As expected, the loud stimulus produced the typical startle reflex responses. Unexpectedly, however, the startle response was also accompanied by the action that the subjects were prepared to make—all of the features of the triple-burst pattern seen in "normal" trials, including magnitude and timing of the EMG patterns, were also observed in these "startle" trials. However, the response was initiated about 100 ms *earlier* than in the "normal" trials! The premotor reaction times (RTs) (see chapter 2), which had averaged 171 ms on the normal trials, were reduced to 77 ms on the startle trials. And, even though the subject also produced the typical startle response (eye blink and neck reflexes), all of the movement events, including magnitude and timing of the EMG patterns, were identical to those in the normal trials.

One interpretation of these findings is that the prepared movement was still released "voluntarily," just much earlier because auditory stimuli result in faster RTs than do visual stimuli or because the more intense stimuli produce faster RTs than less intense stimuli (Woodworth & Schlosberg, 1954). Carlsen, Dakin, Chua, and Franks (2007) provided evidence against such an interpretation, however, when they separated startle trials that produced an accompanying EMG activation in the neck (sternocleidomastoid muscle) from those trials that did not (presumably, the former trials were ones in which an actual startle response occurred). Figure 6.10 illustrates their main results. Even though louder auditory stimuli produced faster premotor RTs than softer stimuli (by about 20 ms), the trials that produced a neck response (indicating a startle) resulted in premotor RTs that were 20 to 30 ms shorter than in trials without the startle response indication. Also, responses in these "true" startle trials were independent of the loudness of the stimulus—all stimuli that produced a true startle response had premotor RTs of about 80 ms. This suggests that a startle had a role in these findings.

Another possible explanation for the results of Valls-Solé and colleagues is that, since the visual and auditory stimuli were presented together, there was an intersensory facilitation effect, in which the two stimuli somehow "combined" to produce a facilitation (Gielen, Schmidt, & van den Heuvel 1983; Schmidt et al., 1984). However,

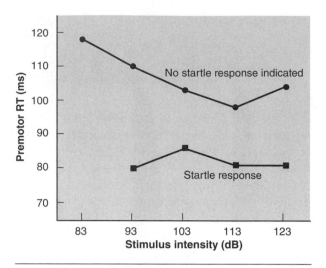

FIGURE 6.10 Increases in stimulus intensity produce faster premotor reaction times (RTs) in the absence of a startle response. In the presence of a startle response indicator (sternocleidomastoid muscle electromyographic activity), premotor RTs were reduced by 20 to 30 ms and immune to stimulus intensity effects.

With kind permission from Springer Science+Business Media: *Experimental Brain Research*, "Startle produces early response latencies that are distinct from stimulus intensity effects," Vol. 176, 2007, pgs. 199-205, A.N. Carlsen, C.J. Dakin, R. Chua, and I.M. Franks, figure 1.

two pieces of evidence argue against such an interpretation. First, the premotor RTs (77 ms) and RTs (104 ms) were much shorter than would be expected for a voluntary response. And, second, in the postexperiment questioning, two-thirds of the subjects claimed that "something other than their own will was making them move" (Valls-Solé et al., 1999, p. 935), even though none of the subjects was aware of the speed-up.

Valls-Solé and colleagues (1999) argued that the motor program is stored in subcortical structures of the brain (see Valls-Solé, Kumru, & Kofler, 2008, for a review of the evidence). The presentation of the startle stimulus results in an involuntary "release" of the motor program, in advance of the voluntary initiation that would have occurred in response to the regular (visual) stimulus. Valls-Solé and colleagues' (1999) procedures and findings have been replicated using similar tasks (e.g., Carlsen, Chua, Inglis, Sanderson, & Franks, 2004; Oude Nijhuis et al., 2007; Siegmund, Inglis, & Sanderson, 2001) and also using saccadic eye movement responses (Castellote, Kumru, Queralt, & Valls-Solé, 2007). These results provide another convincing line of support for the idea that fast movements are organized in advance via motor programs.

Inhibiting Actions

In the next sections we examine some of the evidence about the performer's capabilities to *inhibit* a movement, even before it has been initiated. This information is closely related to the findings presented in chapter 4 (e.g., psychological refractoriness), and the two kinds of findings seem to blend well to provide a picture of what happens during the course of a rapid action.

Anecdotal Evidence

Evidence from personal experience is quite difficult to interpret, for the strong possibility exists that what we think we do is not what actually occurs, leading to a false picture of movement control processes. Even so, some of our common observations guide us to experiments in which the ideas can be studied more carefully.

Long after his work with the wounded patient, Lashley (1951) provided an example of a skilled pianist playing a piano with a broken key that could not be depressed. As the pianist played a string of notes, the attempts to press the broken key did not interrupt the sequence of actions at all. In fact, only after the entire sequence was completed did the individual notice and remark that the key was broken. This suggests that the actions do not appear to be structured with feedback to "verify" that a certain finger movement has been made before the next one is commanded. The feedback appeared to be only minimally involved in the production of the movement sequence (see also Gordon & Soechting, 1995). Another example is buttoning a shirt, an activity

that sometimes continues in its fine detail even if a button is missing. Again, feedback from the fingers is probably not critically involved in the production of this sequence of movements. But, this seems to contradict the finding that striking a match was seriously impaired by anesthetic applied to the cutaneous receptors of the fingertips. More work is needed in this area to resolve these uncertainties.

The British psychologist Bartlett expressed similar views about the lack of role for feedback in certain ball sports. Bartlett (1958) suggested that the "launching" of an action signals a *point* (or *region*) *of no return*—beyond which attempts to modify the action are largely unsuccessful. In the next sections, we describe some experimental approaches to examine these issues.

Inhibiting Rapid Discrete Actions

Henry and Harrison (1961) presented one of the first experimental analyses of these questions. They asked subjects to begin with a finger on a key located at their hip and, at a "go" signal, to move the arm forward and upward to trip a string located in front of their right shoulder. Subjects were instructed to do this as quickly as possible. The simple RT in these control trials was 214 ms on the average, and the movement time (MT) was slightly shorter, at 199 ms. On some trials, a second, "stop" signal would occur, indicating that the subject should *avoid* tripping the string or at least try to begin to slow the limb as quickly as possible. The "stop" signal could come on at one of four times: 110, 190, 270, and 350 ms after the "go" signal. Figure 6.11 shows the timing of

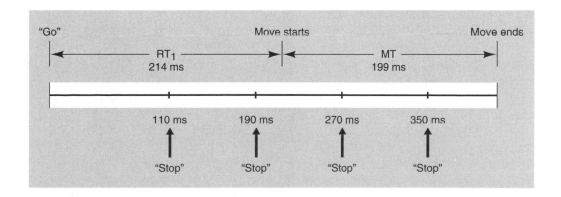

FIGURE 6.11   A time line showing the critical events in the Henry-Harrison experiment. ("Stop" signals were presented at various times after an initial "go" signal.)

the essential details of the experiment, indicating where the "stop" signals could come on relative to the observed RT and MT durations.

The primary result of interest to Henry and Harrison was the time taken to *begin* to decelerate the limb after the "stop" signal was presented. They found that only when the "stop" signal was given at the very earliest of the presentation times (the 110 ms location) was there a tendency for the subjects to even *start* to slow the movement before it had been completed. But the more interesting feature of these data is the subject's response in the 190 ms condition. Notice here that the "stop" signal came on 24 ms *before* the movement even started, and yet the movement was carried out without interruption. That is, a signal presented before the movement was not effective in modifying that particular movement, even when the movement lasted for 199 ms (see also Gao & Zelaznik, 1991).

If the information-processing stages are too slow to be involved in the details of a particular action, and segmental reflexive control is not involved either, then (as we have argued earlier in this chapter) these movements must be *preprogrammed*, structured in advance, and run off as a unit without much modification from events in the environment. An additional interpretation is that, once some internal "go" signal is issued, the action occurs and cannot be stopped, as in pulling the trigger on a gun. The initiation of the internal "go" signal represents the point of no return. When the (external) "stop" signal was presented 104 ms before the overall response was to begin, the response began anyway, and an additional 110 ms or so was required to even begin to modify it.

Logan has performed many of the recent experimental and theoretical analyses using this "stop signal" paradigm (reviewed in Boucher, Palmeri, Logan, & Schall, 2007; Logan, 1994; Verbruggen & Logan, 2008). In one of these studies, skilled typists were asked to type phrases as rapidly as possible, but to stop their typing upon presentation of a "stop" tone (Logan, 1982). In general, the typists produced one to two additional letters after the "stop" tone occurred (about 200 ms of MT), regardless of the specific position within the word at which the tone was presented. However, there were several notable exceptions; one occurred with the word "the." Logan (1982) found that typists would almost always produce the entire "the," and the *space* after it, and that this occurred even when the "stop" signal was provided on the last letter of the previous word. Given that "the" is the most frequently used word in the English language (Kucera & Francis, 1967), typists have probably developed a very highly overlearned motor program for typing it—one whose entire execution is difficult to inhibit after the internal "go" signal has been issued. At what point in the RT to a signal are we committed to action? In other words, when does the point of no return occur? An experiment by Slater-Hammel (1960) helps to answer this question; as well, it supports some of the other points just made about movement programming.

Inhibiting Anticipatory Actions

Slater-Hammel (1960) asked subjects to watch a sweep timer that made one revolution per second and to respond by lifting a finger from a key to stop the clock at the moment when the timer reached "8" on the second revolution (i.e., 1.8 revolutions after the clock hand started). The subject could not, of course, wait until the clock hand had actually arrived at "8" before planning and initiating the movement, because the finger lift would be far too late. So the subject's task on these trials was to anticipate the movement of the clock hand, together with the lags in the information-processing and neuromuscular systems, so that the finger was lifted at precisely the correct time. Slater-Hammel added an interesting condition, however. Occasionally, unpredictably from the viewpoint of the subject, the experimenter would stop the clock hand before it reached "8." The subject was instructed to *not* lift the finger from the key if this happened—that is, to do "nothing." Slater-Hammel set up the experimental conditions such that the primary task (stopping at the "8") was required on about 75% of the trials. On the remaining trials, the clock hand could stop randomly at some point prior to the target point at "8." The critical events of the experiment are illustrated in figure 6.12.

The measure of most interest to Slater-Hammel was the probability of the subject's *inhibiting* the finger lift successfully as a function of the time before "8" when the clock hand was stopped by the experimenter. Figure 6.13 presents the probability of successful inhibition as a function of the time before "8" when the clock hand stopped. If the clock hand stopped 250 ms before "8," the subject would probably have had no trouble

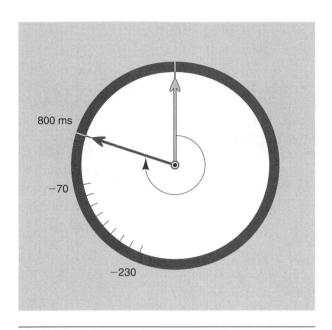

FIGURE 6.12   The task used by Slater-Hammel (1960). The sweep hand of the chronoscope normally made a full revolution in 1 s (1,000 ms). The subject's primary task was to stop the sweep hand of the chronoscope on its second revolution precisely on the 800 ms mark by lifting a finger off a response key. If, however, the sweep hand stopped prior to the 800 ms point, then the subject was to try to inhibit the finger lift.

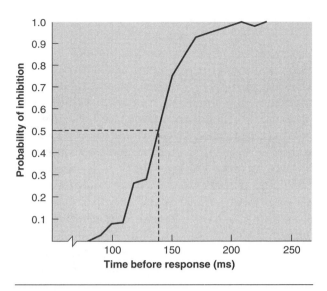

FIGURE 6.13   The probability of successfully inhibiting an anticipated finger lift as a function of the interval before the critical event.

Reprinted with permission from *Research Quarterly for Exercise and Sport*, vol. 31, pg. 226. Copyright 1960 by the American Alliance for Health, Physical Education, Recreation and Dance, 1900 Association Drive, Reston, VA 20191.

inhibiting the movement, as the stages of processing would seem to have ample time to inhibit it. Conversely, if the clock hand stopped only 50 ms before the clock reached "8," the subject should never have been able to inhibit the movement. That is essentially what Slater-Hammel found. But notice that as the time before "8" decreased from about 170 ms, the probability of successfully inhibiting the movement decreased sharply; the probability was about 0.5 when the interval before "8" was 140 ms. Another way to state this finding is to say that if the clock hand stopped 140 ms before "8," the subject could successfully inhibit the response about half the time. In our interpretation, this result says that, at 140 ms before the finger lift (on average), the subject irrevocably triggered the action.

However, this conclusion needs to be adjusted slightly. Although this median (50%) point occurred at 140 ms before "8," Slater-Hammel's subjects responded a little late on average (constant error = +26 ms, responding at the 826 ms point on the clock, rather than at the "8," or 800 ms mark). Because our first estimate of the point of no return (140 ms) presumed that subjects

responded to the primary task with no error (i.e., assuming a CE = 0), we must therefore add (as Slater-Hammel [1960] did) the 26 ms to the 140 ms to obtain 166 ms as the estimate of the time before "8" that the internal "go" signal must have been produced. Thus, these data provide one estimate of a point of no return at 166 ms before the action.

A number of important interpretations may be derived from this thinking. First, the finding that the subject could not inhibit a movement once it was internally planned and initiated supports the observations made about the Henry and Harrison (1961) study and the typing of the word "the" shown by Logan (1982). Apparently, once the subject has *committed* to action, the movement occurs even when some signal is presented in the environment shortly afterward indicating that the action should not be performed. As mentioned in chapter 4, inhibiting preplanned actions requires time and attention, an idea supported by these data.

Students do this experiment in the laboratory sections of our courses; they *see* that the clock hand has stopped, but their hand then responds anyway. The subjective feeling is that they do not have control over the hand, where "they" refers to "their consciousness." The point of no return appears to represent the point at which conscious control of the hand has been transferred, with the hand now subservient to the motor program instead (Osman, Kornblum, & Meyer, 1990; see also De Jong, Coles, Logan, & Gratton, 1990). These ideas of conscious control, and related concepts such as "intention" or "will," which were the source of philosophical debate for centuries, have resurfaced in recent years (e.g., Haggard, 2008; Libet, 1985) thanks to modern techniques used to record what the subject is doing in various "stop signal" tasks. Among such measures are the EMG activity of the effectors (McGarry & Franks, 1997), including activities in the motor neuron pools in the cord (H-reflexes; McGarry, Inglis, & Franks, 2000), and various measures of neurophysiological activity (Band & van Boxtel, 1999). Sometimes actions are either completely inhibited or not (i.e., they are performed as originally intended). In other instances, however, researchers have identified responses that have been interrupted, for example by means of a partial reduction of motor neuron pool activation (e.g., McGarry & Franks, 1997). Findings such as these have resulted in a controversy regarding the location of the point of no return—some arguing that the location is at a high level of the central nervous system such as the cortex (Band & van Boxtel, 1999; van Boxtel & Band, 2000), with others suggesting that it is at a lower level in the central nervous system (McGarry & Franks, 2000).

Regardless of the exact location of the point of no return, a theory of how the process works applies equally well. The theory, developed by Logan (1994; Band, van der Molen, & Logan, 2003; Boucher et al., 2007; Logan & Cowan, 1984), regards the inhibition of action as a kind of *horse race*. One horse, the "start horse," represents a command that is sent to the motor neuron pool to execute the preprogrammed response. The other horse, the "stop horse" represents a command sent to halt the execution. The horse that reaches the "finish line" first (here, the lower centers involved with movement production) "wins"—thereby determining whether or not the movement is executed or inhibited. In this way, it is possible to model situations in which total and partial inhibition and execution occur (Boucher et al., 2007; McGarry, Chua, & Franks, 2003; McGarry & Franks, 1997). Extensions of this research have been used to explain more complex actions, such as "checking" a swing in baseball batting (see "The Checked Swing in Baseball").

Programming Rapid Movements in Advance

In chapter 3, we introduced the idea that in a response-programming stage the person selects, organizes, and initiates a program of action that will produce a series of muscular activities resulting in an action. According to this model, the program must be structured completely (or almost completely) in advance, before the movement can be initiated, and very little modification will occur in the movement for the next few hundred milliseconds or so. We saw evidence for this also in situations in which the limb was blocked from moving, with the pattern of EMGs being unaffected (as compared to unblocked moves) for the next 100 ms or so (Wadman et al., 1979). We also saw evidence that a startling stimulus can "release" a complete, preplanned action far earlier than would be the case if it was released "normally" via the stages of processing (Valls-Solé et al., 1999). Another line of support for this hypothesis is the evidence that certain variables, related to the "complexity" of the movement to be made (i.e., the number of limbs or movement segments, the movement's duration, or both), tend to affect the time between stimulus and the beginning of the movement (i.e., the RT; Henry & Rogers, 1960). More complex, and longer-duration (but still rapid) movements produce longer RTs (Christina, 1992; Klapp, 1996). It has not been possible to explain how these effects could occur except by the hypothesis that the movement is programmed in advance, with these variables affecting the duration of the stage necessary for completing this preprogramming (Henry & Rogers, 1960; Schmidt, 1972b; Schmidt & Russell, 1972). Many of these ideas are far from new; the original notion dates back to thinking by James (1890) and Lashley (1917), and more recently to Henry and Rogers (1960), Keele (1968), Schmidt (1976a), and Brooks (1979). Early thinking on how motor programs might be structured is credited to Karl Lashley (see "K.S. Lashley on 'Motor Programs'" on p. 198; see also Rosenbaum, Cohen, Jax, Weiss, & van der Wel, 2007).

As a result of this thinking, at least two levels can be distinguished in the motor system: (a) an executive level (including the information-processing stages) for selecting, organizing, and preparing and initiating a complex pattern of muscular activities and (b) an effector level

The Checked Swing in Baseball

Batting in baseball is a good example of a case in which inhibitory processes are likely to operate. In baseball it is not uncommon to observe "checked swings"—the batter has started to swing, but at some point after the pitcher has released the ball, the batter decides otherwise and tries to stop the swing instead. If the "inhibit swing" decision occurs soon enough, the bat can be stopped before it crosses the plate (after this point, if the ball is not contacted, the swing is considered an attempted swing and is called a strike). But how is this inhibition process carried out?

Recall that Slater-Hammel measured only two kinds of behavior—release of the key or not. In baseball batting, these two behaviors would be analogous to (a) the full swing and (b) the non-swing, or fully inhibited swing. However, studies of baseball batting have revealed two other types of swing behavior, called (c) *partial response* and (d) *interrupted outcome* (Gray, 2009a; McGarry & Franks, 2003). The partial response occurs when the batter initiates bat movement toward the contact point with the ball (above the plate) but with less velocity than in the full swing (see the lighter dashed line in figure 6.14). With the interrupted outcome, the swing is initiated with the same velocity as the full swing but undergoes a sudden alteration in kinematics prior to its completion (see the darker dashed line in figure 6.14).

Using a batting simulation task in which batters were instructed to swing only at pitches that were predicted to arrive in the strike zone, Gray (2002, 2009a) found that "stop signals" were executed based on pitch predictions and three distinct types of ball information. Gray modeled pitch predictions (pitch speed and location) using variables that baseball players frequently rely upon to make predictions about an upcoming pitch (e.g., the ball–strike count; location and speed of recent pitches). The earliest ball information used to determine if a pitch would arrive out of the strike zone was the *launch angle* of the ball as it left the pitcher's hand; this was used most frequently for pitches that resulted in a fully inhibited swing. The discrepancy between the predicted and actual *speed* of the pitch as it approached the strike zone was used in the majority of cases that resulted in a partial response. And the discrepancy between the actual and predicted *horizontal height* (above the plate) of the pitch was the information picked up latest in the ball flight trajectory, resulting in the most frequent occurrence of interrupted outcomes.[3]

Of most importance for the batter, however, were the results of these attempts to inhibit the swing—95% of the partial responses resulted in a successfully checked swing (i.e., stopped before the bat crossed the plate), whereas only 41% of the interrupted outcome swings were checked successfully. Therefore, different ball flight characteristics (speed and location) were most frequently associated with specific inhibitory processes (partial responses and interrupted outcomes, respectively), which dramatically affected the probability of swinging at a pitch that was out of the strike zone. These analyses provide an understanding of how inhibition processes are regulated in everyday, complex activities based on the interaction of visual information and prior expectations.

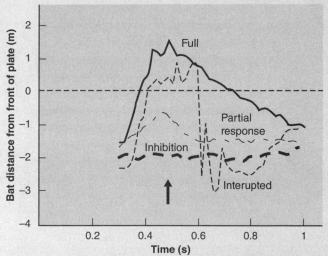

FIGURE 6.14   Sample bat displacement–time profiles for four types of baseball batting swings: *(a)* full, *(b)* interrupted, *(c)* partial, and *(d)* fully inhibited. The arrow represents the point when the ball crossed the plate. FOP = front of plate.

K.S. LASHLEY ON "MOTOR PROGRAMS"

They said it . . .

Karl Lashley's (1951) paper, "The Problem of Serial Order of Behavior," represented a death blow to the behaviorists' influence on views of motor control. In this seminal paper, Lashley described an early and very clear implication for an open-loop central control mechanism. Although he did not specifically refer to the term "motor program," Lashley set the stage for a strict view of the motor program. An early definition was "a set of muscle commands that are structured before a movement begins, and that allows the entire sequence to be carried out uninfluenced by peripheral feedback" (Keele, 1968, p. 387).

Lashley said, "A series of movements is not a chain of sensory-motor reactions . . . I had the opportunity to study a patient who had a complete anesthesia for movements of the knee joint, as a result of a gunshot wound of the cord (Lashley, 1917). In spite of the anesthesia, he was able to control the extent and speed of movements of flexion and extension of the knee quite as accurately as can a normal person. The performance of very quick movements also indicates their independence of current control. "Whip-snapping" movements of the hand can be regulated accurately in extent, yet the entire movement, from initiation to completion, requires less than the reaction time for tactile or kinesthetic stimulation of the arm, which is about one-eighth of a second, even when no discrimination is involved. Such facts force the conclusion that an effector mechanism can be preset or primed to discharge at a given intensity or for a given duration, in independence of any sensory controls" (pp. 122-123).

He also said, "I believe that there exist in the nervous organization, elaborate systems of interrelated neurons capable of imposing certain types of integration upon a large number of widely spaced effector elements. . . . These systems are in constant action. They form a sort of substratum upon which other activity is built" (pp. 127-128).

(motor programs and the muscular system) for actually controlling or producing the patterns as they unfold. We can further distinguish these two levels by examining two distinct types of errors that can occur in performance, which we describe later in the chapter. That said, however, we have already presented evidence that such a view can explain only a limited set of movement situations, as many examples can be cited in which feedback processes seem to interact with open-loop processes in the production of movement. A more complete approach to motor programming would be to ask *how* the sensory processes operate together with (i.e., cooperate with) these open-loop processes to produce skilled actions. We turn to some of these ideas in the next sections.

Sensory Information and Motor Programs

The next sections deal with various functions of feedback in movement control. We can conceptualize these functions as acting before a movement, during a movement, and after a movement.

Prior to the Movement

One of the major roles of sensory information is almost certainly to provide information about the initial state of the motor system prior to the action. Consider this simple example: You must know whether you are standing with your left or right foot forward in order to initiate a walking pattern (Keele, 1973). The spinal frog (figure 6.8) requires sensory information from the forelimb in order to direct the hindlimb to the elbow during the wiping response. Such information is presumably provided by afferent feedback from the various proprioceptors, and it would seem to be critical for the selection and adjustment of the proper action. We argued in chapters 2 and 3 that these processes are very important for open types of skills, for which the nature of the environment is unpredictable or constantly changing.

Polit and Bizzi (1979), using deafferented monkeys, showed that when the initial position of the shoulder changed prior to the elbow action, a systematic error in pointing to the target position occurred. This is understandable from figure

6.15, because changing the shoulder angle as shown necessarily affects the *elbow angle* (from θ_1 to θ_2) required for pointing at a target in a given position in space. If the monkey programmed a given elbow angle, then the *equilibrium-point mechanism* (chapter 7) would achieve that angle, and the arm would not be pointing to the proper target. These monkeys did not learn to point to the target, even after considerable practice. By contrast, normal, intact monkeys learned in a few trials to compensate for the shifts in the shoulder position. The interpretation is that the intact animals had feedback from the shoulder joint and could adjust the angle at the elbow to compensate for the change in the shoulder angle. Thus, these data suggest that feedback about the initial positions of the joints is required when pointing to a position in space if the environment is not perfectly predictable.

Another role of afferent information involves what a number of authors have called *functional tuning* (Fitch, Tuller, & Turvey, 1982; Turvey, 1977). Recall that the spinal apparatus and resulting limb force output could be affected by change in the head position, much as would be expected on the basis of the idea that the tonic neck reflex was involved in the action (Hellebrandt, Houtz, Partridge, & Walters, 1956). In this example, afferent information from the neck influences the spinal mechanisms prior to action, thereby facilitating or inhibiting them. But a more compelling reason for assuming that premovement tuning must occur relates to some simple facts about the nature of

the motor apparatus. In figure 6.16 are two diagrams of a hypothetical rapid movement. In both cases, the movement involves flexion of the elbow a distance of 45°, beginning with the arm straight. In figure 6.16*a*, the upper arm is positioned 45° below the horizontal, so that a flexion of the elbow will result in the forearm's being horizontal at the end. In figure 6.16*b*, the upper arm is 45° above horizontal, so that the forearm will be vertical at the end. The same command signal delivered to the biceps muscle group will not "work" in both situations, for two reasons. First, a force is required to hold the forearm against gravity at the target position in the first situation, but not in the second. Second, more force is required to move the forearm against gravity in the first example relative to the second. A logical conclusion from this simple example is that the motor system must "know" the position the shoulder is in prior to the action so that the command to the elbow flexors can produce the required 45° movement. How this happens is not entirely clear, but *that* it happens seems nearly obvious.

Consider another complicating factor facing the motor system in producing a movement. Figure 6.17 is a schematic diagram of the muscle attachments involved in a simple movement. This time, imagine that the movement is an extension movement in which the elbow is to be moved through 45°. Notice that the triceps muscle, which is the primary elbow extensor, is attached to the humerus in two places (internal and external heads) and to the scapula of the shoulder area (the

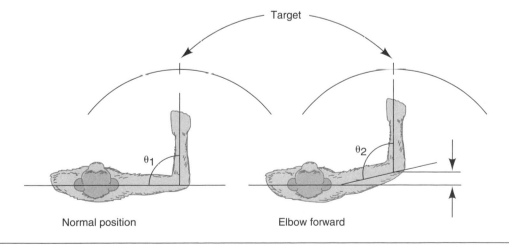

FIGURE 6.15   In pointing to a target, the equilibrium point of the elbow is dependent on the angle at the shoulder.

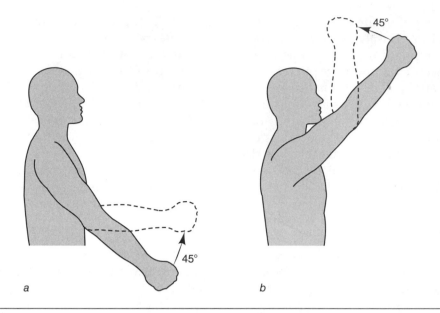

FIGURE 6.16 Two 45° elbow flexion movements that appear to require different commands for the action and different forces at their end points because of the effects of gravity.

long head). Thus, the triceps muscle performs two actions when it contracts: It extends the elbow and it tends to extend the shoulder joint, pulling the humerus back. Therefore, when the triceps is contracting to produce the 45° movement, one of the muscles that flexes the shoulder must contract so that the shoulder joint is stabilized and only the elbow moves. Thus, during this simple extension movement, the motor system must "know" that a two-jointed muscle is involved and produce some compensatory stabilization. The amount of stabilization will be dependent on the shoulder angle because of the length–tension relation (chapter 7).

The picture that emerges from these observations is that a "simple" 45° movement of the elbow joint is not really that simple at all, at least in terms of the motor system. In addition, other complicated aspects of the muscle need to be considered by the motor system, such as

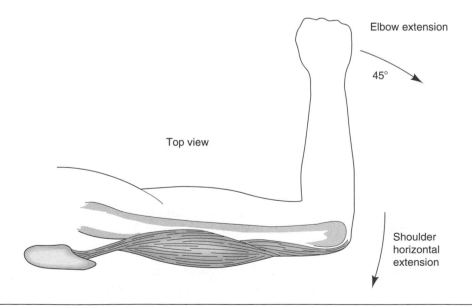

FIGURE 6.17 Complexity in a 45° elbow extension movement caused by the fact that the triceps muscle both extends the elbow and horizontally extends the shoulder.

the nonlinear relationship between the muscle force and limb velocity, together with aspects of the contraction process that make the motor system very difficult to predict and control (Partridge, 1979, 1983). We all know that our nervous system controls our limbs beautifully in these "simple" situations. How it does so is exciting to ponder.

One role that feedback seems to have during movement production is a monitoring function, whereby the feedback from the movement is taken in and processed but not necessarily used in the control of the action unless something goes wrong. It is probable that a long string of actions dealing with finger movements in piano playing is programmed and carried out open loop. Feedback from the fingers is returned to the central nervous system for analysis, as if the central nervous system were "checking" for errors. If no errors appear, then the feedback is ignored. But if the feedback indicates that an error has occurred, attention can be directed to that feedback source, and an appropriate correction may be initiated. Reflexive corrections may also be generated, as discussed in chapter 5.

A second way to view feedback is that it may be intricately involved in the physical control of the limb. We mentioned a number of examples of this in the preceding chapter. The possibility exists that a constantly changing reference of correctness is specified by the gamma motor neurons to the muscle spindles and that their actions result in a continuous set of corrections to keep the movement on the proper course. The feedback could be involved in the determination of the end location of a movement if the reference of correctness were set for this position. And in repetitive movements, the feedback from early segments of the sequence can provide adjustments for the later segments.

Following the Movement

Extensive feedback is also delivered to the central nervous system after a movement. Such information can be evaluated, presumably, by the stages of information processing in order to determine the nature (or "quality") of the movement just made. Information about whether or not the movement achieved the environmental goal and about its smoothness, its level of force or effort, or its form or style is derived from sensory feedback. A major role for such information is in the adjustment of the movement on the *subsequent* trial,

perhaps to reduce the errors made on the present trial. As such, this information has a considerable relevance to the acquisition of skills, as discussed in the final part of this book dealing with motor *learning* (chapters 12 and 13 in particular).

Types of Motor Program Errors

If, as we suspect, the motor system can be conceptualized as consisting of two major parts (an executive level and an effector level), we can ask about the origins of errors in each—including their causes, their detection, and their correction. We conceptualize the motor system as being capable of making essentially two distinct types of errors. Each of these errors involves feedback in distinctly different ways for their detection and correction. We discuss these two kinds of errors in the next sections.

When a person makes a rapid movement, there are really two goals (Schmidt, 1976a). First, there is an environmentally defined goal, such as changing gears in a standard transmission car or doing a somersault from a diving board. A second goal (or subgoal) can be defined in terms of the muscular activities required to produce the desired outcomes in the environment—that is, to produce the first goal. For example, a person must contract the muscles in the arm and torso in one of a limited number of ways in order to change gears smoothly, and only certain patterns of muscular activity will result in a somersault. Essentially, how to generate such a subgoal is the problem facing the performer.

We can view the subgoal as a pattern of action that is structured in both space and time. Such a pattern of action will determine where a particular part of the body will be at a particular time after the movement starts. If this spatial–temporal pattern in the muscles and limbs (the subgoal) is produced accurately, then the environmental goal will be achieved. This process can go astray in essentially two ways.

Errors in Program Selection

Given the assumptions about the spatial–temporal goal, the first kind of error that the person might produce can be defined as an error in *program selection.* This kind of failure to achieve the environmental goal results from the performer's choice of action. This error can happen in a number of ways (Reason & Mycielska, 1982). First, the person can produce the wrong pattern of action: for example, heading versus kicking a ball in soccer, moving right when a left move is appropriate, or moving when it might be important to stand still. The outcomes are the result of apparently intentional decisions about what to do and, in our terms, represent inappropriate *choices* of a program of action. Such errors can arise from a variety of sources, such as a faulty perception of the environment (e.g., the speed of an oncoming car by a pedestrian crossing the street) or an error in the choice of a goal (e.g., to pass to teammate A when a pass to teammate B would have been better).

How does a person make a correction for an error in program selection? According to the evidence presented earlier, the person must issue a *new* motor program, as the "old" one will not achieve the goal in the environment. Hence, the information-processing stages must be initiated again; a new program must be selected in the response-selection stage, and it must be programmed in the response-programming stage. Because all of these stages are relatively slow, the result is that a new pattern of action in a rapid motor skill usually cannot be selected before the movement has been completed and the error has occurred. If the movement has a somewhat longer MT, however, then a correction for an error in selection is possible during the action.

Errors in Program Execution

An error in program execution is fundamentally different from an error in program selection (Schmidt, 1976a). An error in execution can occur if the person produces a program of action appropriate for the environment but some unexpected event occurs that disrupts the movement. This can happen, for example, if the contractions specified by the motor program are not quite achieved by the muscles, perhaps because of inconsistencies in the spinal cord where it is determined which of the many motor units are to be activated. The basketball player attempting a free throw shot selects the proper action (making no selection error), but random noise in the central nervous system often causes the shot to miss its target because of an error in execution. Sometimes the mass or friction of the objects in the environment is not estimated quite accurately before the action, such as when you pick up a nearly empty milk carton that you thought was nearly full; the initial part of the action is much too rapid. Sometimes the resistance offered by the environment increases

unexpectedly, slowing the action and making it miss its mark. Many other examples can be used of course, including one that occurs occasionally in driving (see "Pedal Misapplication Errors").

These influences do not make the *originally* intended movement pattern incorrect, as some compensation that will achieve the originally planned spatial–temporal goal will still result in the achievement of the environmental goal. Thus, the correction for an error in movement execution may not require a new motor program, since the original pattern of action defined by the "old" program will be correct if the motor system can compensate for the unexpected environmental influences. This implies that because the system does not have to select a new motor program, the correction for an error in execution does not require all the stages of information processing and will be far more rapid than correcting for an error in program selection.

What is the evidence for this kind of correction, and is the correction for error in execution fundamentally different than that for an error in selection? Consider the example from Dewhurst (1967; figure 5.16) presented in the preceding chapter; recall that the subject was instructed to hold a weight with the elbow at a right angle. When weight was suddenly added, a correction followed in the biceps EMG within about 30 ms, and a more sustained correction followed in about 50 to 80 ms. The corrections were far faster than can be explained by the production of a new program of action; hence it seems reasonable to believe that the original program of action was modified in some way. More importantly, the person did not have to select a new program of action to compensate for the added weight, as the original spatial–temporal goal was still appropriate; the goal before the weight was added was "Hold the elbow at right angles," and the goal afterward was still the same; the subject seemed only to require additional muscular tension in order to comply with the "old" goal. Thus, it appears that the corrections served the purpose of maintaining the *original* pattern of action and did not result in the generation of a new one. Consequently, the corrections had a far shorter latency than would be expected if it had been necessary to produce a new pattern (see chapter 5 for other examples).

What about the role of consciousness in corrections for errors in selection? As you will recall from chapter 5, Henry (1953; figure 5.17) asked

Pedal Misapplication Errors

The concept of two types of errors (selection and execution) has a wealth of applications to real-world situations, one of which is automobile accidents. Consider the following situation.

A driver enters his car (with automatic transmission) and prepares to drive forward. He reports that he started the car, placed his right foot on the brake, and shifted the transmission to Drive. The car roared away under what seemed to be full throttle, and the brakes were completely ineffective in stopping the car ("The brake pedal went to the floor") until the car struck a wall after about 8 s of travel. The driver claims that the car malfunctioned, but a subsequent inspection of the vehicle (by experts, car makers, three federal government agencies, or independent research firms) reveals nothing wrong with the car. Incidents essentially like this have occurred more than 10,000 times since the mid-1980s and are now referred to as *unintended acceleration* cases, involving *pedal misapplication errors.* What can be going on here?

A leading theory to explain these events is that the driver in some way placed his foot on the accelerator pedal rather than the brake (see Reinhart, 1994; Schmidt, 1989b, 1993). But why would a driver with, in some cases, 50 years of driving experience choose the wrong pedal after never having done so before? The important word in this question is "choose." It is certainly difficult to imagine that the driver made an error in the choice of the accelerator pedal rather than the brake—what we call here a selection error—and, in fact, the driver emphatically claims not to have done so.

Rather, imagine that the driver intends to press the brake as usual, and the executive level programs and initiates an action to do so. The executive passes control to the program, and the program controls the muscles and limbs, while the executive shifts attention to vision or other sources of information relevant for driving. However, (a) because the driver is slightly misaligned after having just entered the car or (b) because of variability in the neuromuscular processes (see chapter 7, impulse variability)—or because of both—the foot on this occasion turns out to be aimed at the accelerator rather than the brake that was the intended goal, and a pedal error occurs. This represents an error in execution, as the correct action was selected and produced but it was executed or aimed (or both) inappropriately. Now, when the shift lever reaches Drive, the car lurches forward, and the startled driver's response is to press harder on the "brake." But, because his foot is actually on the accelerator, the car goes faster, he presses harder, it goes even faster, and so on, until the car hits the wall.

In these situations, the driver "knows" (incorrectly, however) that his foot was on the brake because that is where the executive level ordered the foot to go. Lower-level processes have caused the error, and the executive level has no information about them. The driver's response to the unexpected acceleration is to make a very fast correction at the execution level (to press the "brake" harder), a kind of triggered reaction that actually makes the situation worse. Because of the hypervigilance (or "panic"; see the related discussion in chapter 4) associated with the unexpected acceleration, he does not consider that the foot is on the accelerator, hence does not make any of a number of actions that would stop the car (e.g., switch off the ignition, shift to Neutral, etc.), which would have required initiation of a new action (see also Schmidt, 2010).

Such views are now commonly accepted in examples of unintended acceleration (e.g., Department of Transportation, 2000; Lococo & Tucker, 2011). These analyses of such automobile accidents have involved our current understanding of the separation between errors in selection and errors in execution, the factors that control their corrections, and the separation between levels of hierarchical control. These concepts are critical in a number of analogous real-world situations.

subjects to try to maintain the position of a lever in response to unexpected changes in the pressure it exerted against the hand. He showed that subjects were able to compensate for changes in position that were some 20 times smaller than changes they could consciously detect. The subjects were responding to changes in position that they could not perceive—that is, they were responding *unconsciously.* Also, Johansson and Westling (1984; Westling & Johansson, 1984) showed that if subjects began to lose grip on an object held between the fingers, compensations (in the fingers and in the elbow) could be made in approximately 30 ms, apparently without conscious awareness. In these examples, the person did not have to select a new program of action when the stimulus occurred, because the original pattern of action was still acceptable. Force changes within the context of this pattern of behavior were required, however, to maintain the movement's overall goals. These were accomplished very quickly and without awareness, and can be thought of as corrections for errors in execution.

Program Selection Errors Versus Execution Errors

Table 6.1 summarizes some of the fundamental features of errors in program selection and program execution, listed so that their differences can be seen more easily. These differences are important, because without testable distinctions between these error categories it would make little sense to consider them as separate classes (see also classifications of reflex responses in chapter 5 for a similar analysis, especially table 5.1).

From table 6.1, we can see that the latencies of the two kinds of corrections are quite different; the selection errors require 120 to 200 ms or more in order for a correction to begin, and the execution errors can be corrected far more quickly, in 30 to 50 ms. Also, a new spatial–temporal goal is needed to correct an error in selection, whereas the original pattern of action can continue while an error in execution is being produced. We know that selecting and initiating a new motor program (needed to correct an error in selection) requires attention and consciousness in the sense defined

in chapter 4 and that this process will interfere greatly with certain other (cognitive) processes attempted at the same time; hence only one such correction can be done at a time. Correcting for an error in execution, on the other hand, is automatic with respect to cognitive information-processing activities, and many such corrections could presumably be done at the same time in parallel and without interference—some in the arms, some in the legs, and so on. Hick's law clearly applies when one is correcting for errors in selection (chapter 3), with the latency increasing as the number of possible corrections increases. For errors in execution, on the other hand, the number of possible errors is probably not a factor, and so Hick's law would not be expected to apply.[4] All these differences, taken together, clearly argue that corrections of motor program errors are of at least two fundamental types.

Triggered Reactions

The classification scheme in table 6.1 is now rather old (Schmidt, 1976a, 1983), and newer research suggests it may be somewhat too simple to account for all the evidence. One good example involves triggered reactions, as discussed in chapter 5. We saw that triggered reactions were faster than RT, did not seem to require conscious processing, and did not seem to involve the selection of a new movement program—all of which would at first glance seem to place them into the category of corrections for errors in execution. But the notion of errors in execution implies that the correction serves to bring the limbs back to the original spatial–temporal goal, or *trajectory* originally selected, after a perturbation (Cooke, 1980). Yet the evidence on triggered reactions shows that the response to various perturba-

TABLE 6.1. Characteristics of Corrections for Erors in Selection and Execution

Characteristic	Selection	Execution
Latency of correction?	120-200 ms	30-50 ms
Old spatial–temporal goal OK?	No	Yes
New program selected?	Yes	No[a]
Attention required?	Yes	No
More than one at a time?	No	Yes
Hick's law apply?	Yes	No?

[a]Provided that the deviation from the spatial–temporal goals is not very large.
Adapted from Schmidt 1983, 1987.

tions is a *new* pattern of action, with a trajectory fundamentally different from the one that was occurring before the stimulus. When a given perturbation was applied, we saw altered lip and tongue trajectories in human speech (Abbs et al., 1984; Kelso et al., 1984), new hindlimb trajectories in cat locomotion (Forssberg et al., 1975), and different, coordinated patterns of elbow and finger movements in lifting tasks (Johansson & Westling, 1984; Westling & Johansson, 1984), all with very short latencies.

It is tempting to suggest that triggered reactions ensure that the *original goal* of the action is achieved—not necessarily that the *original trajectory* of the limbs is achieved. This suggestion implies that a particular trajectory of the limbs may not be as important as achieving the environmental goal. Of course, there are many ways in which the motor system can achieve a particular environmental goal; and when perturbed, the system seems to shift from one of these alternatives to another, with a very short latency. This capability to solve a problem with several action patterns is often termed *motor equivalence* (see figure 6.18, p. 209). This combination of features seems to suggest that triggered reactions fall somewhere between correction for errors in execution and correction for errors in selection, sharing features of both categories or perhaps even forming a third category. It may be that when the perturbation is small, a correction for an error in execution can occur to bring the limbs back on the target trajectory; if the perturbation is somewhat larger, a triggered reaction results in another trajectory, but without the need for reprogramming the movement using the stages of information processing; and if the perturbation is even larger, a correction for an error in selection is generated, which of course involves the stages of processing.

Hierarchical Levels of Control

From the previous sections it is clear that there is considerable evidence for a central open-loop mechanism, structured before the movement is initiated, that serves to organize and control limb movements in coordinated actions. Yet substantial evidence also suggests that feedback from the responding limbs can, through a variety of mechanisms, modify the movement in various ways. Some of the lower-level reflex activities serve to keep the movement "on track," and triggered reactions and reflex reversals alter the

trajectory quickly while seeming to maintain the overall movement goal in the environment. Feedback from the touch receptors in the skin can also modify the ways in which the gamma loop functions in movement control (Merton, 1972).

This large body of evidence suggests a centrally organized structure that is capable of handling most of the details of the action but is also very sensitive to movement-produced sensory information from a variety of sources. One way to view this blending of open- and closed-loop functioning is to consider a hierarchical control, in which a higher-order, open-loop control structure has "under" it a set of closed-loop processes that ensure the movement's intended goal in the face of various perturbations. If a signal appears in the environment indicating that the higher-order program is no longer relevant, the highest levels in the system (the stages of processing) become involved in stopping it, or initiating a different program, or perhaps both. But if smaller perturbations occur that do not involve an alteration in the fundamental movement goal, these can be handled by lower levels in the hierarchy, presumably while the original higher-level program continues to operate. This is a classic example of one form of *hybrid control* in which a closed-loop system is embedded within an open-loop system.

These thoughts lead to a modified, less restricted definition of a motor program, one that is in keeping with the literature on feedback process but yet retains the essential feature of the open-loop concept: *The motor program is an abstract representation of action that, when activated, produces movement without regard to sensory information indicating errors in selection.* Once the program has been initiated, the pattern of action is carried out even if the environmental information indicates that an error in selection has been made. Yet during the program's execution, countless corrections for minor errors in execution can be produced that serve to ensure that the original goal is carried out faithfully. Grillner (1975) has said essentially the same thing with respect to the control of gait:

> Perhaps it is useful to regard the relevant reflexes as *prepared* [italics added] to operate but without any effect as long as the movement proceeds according to the set central program. At the same instant when the locomotor movements are disturbed (small hole, a slippery surface, etc.) the reflexes come into operation to compensate. (p. 297)

This idea is similar in many ways to the concept of a *coordinative structure* discussed by Greene (1972), Fitch and colleagues (1982), Turvey (1977), and Berkinblit and Feldman (1988). In both the motor program and coordinative structure concepts, the many degrees of freedom in the musculature are reduced by a structure that organizes the limbs to act as a single unit. Also, both notions involve the tuning of spinal centers, corrections for errors in execution, and freedom of the executive level from the details of what occurs at lower levels in the motor system.

Similar ideas along these lines were expressed many years ago by Bernstein (see "Nikolai Bernstein" on p. 8). In one of his works, Bernstein (1996) described in detail a four-level, hierarchical system that was responsible for providing the capability for dexterity without overwhelming the role of consciousness. Level A in Bernstein's scheme refers to neck and trunk tone, responsible for the automated control of posture. Level B (the level of muscular–articular links) refers to the level at which coordinative structures, or *synergies*, operate (Turvey & Carello, 1996). The higher levels—C (space) and D (actions)—are devoted to the problems of perception and intention, respectively (Turvey & Carello, 1996).

Greene's (1972) point of view was similar to Bernstein's and emphasized the hierarchical nature of motor control. Greene suggested that at the highest levels of the system, the global aspects of the movement are represented in the form of a goal (e.g., shoot a basket). The control of movement is passed down through progressively lower levels until all the particular decisions about which motor units to fire are defined at the muscle level. The higher levels in the system do not have any direct control over muscle contractions; they have control only over adjacent levels of control that eventually result in those contractions. This idea is related to the motor program view, stated earlier here, in which only two levels exist—an executive and a program or effector. Greene's view suggests that there are more than these two levels.

Along these lines, the highest level specifies what Greene called a "ballpark" movement, which would result in any of a number of movements that are generally capable of producing the intended goal; they are "in the ballpark," as Americans would say. As the system passes control to lower levels, the individual details of the actions are defined by the initial conditions of the limbs, the posture of the performer, the relations with respect to gravity, and a host of other factors of which the highest level of the system is not aware. These lower functions then determine the ultimate movement that will result, on the basis of these lower-level interactions with feedback, tuning, and other factors. In short, the "ballpark response" becomes increasingly more specified at each lower level in the motor system.

Problems With the Motor Program Notion

The advantage of the motor program notion as a theory of movement control is that it provides order to a large number of separate findings, such as the inability to use certain kinds of feedback and the kinds of corrections that can and cannot be made. But the ideas about programs that we have stated so far have other logical drawbacks that must be considered. The next section deals with two of the most important: the *storage problem* and the *novelty problem*.

The Storage Problem

Given that an animal can produce a motor program "on command" and initiate it, *how many* such programs must the organism have at its disposal in order to move as it does? Recall that a motor program is thought to result in commands to muscles that define a particular pattern of action. In this view, if the pattern is to be changed (e.g., from an overhand to a sidearm throwing pattern), then a totally new program must be produced. Imagine all the ways to produce a throwing action, each of which must have a separate program.

MacNeilage (1970) identified this problem in the context of speech production. According to programming theories of speech, each sound that a human can produce (called a *phoneme*) is governed by a separate program; in order to speak, we string together these separate programs in a way that follows the "rules" of intelligible speech. This solution seemed to be a good one— since there are only about 44 sounds in English, we should require only 44 programs. The difficulty is that the actions of the mouth, jaw, tongue, and so forth for a particular sound are different depending on the sound that precedes it, as well as the sound that is to follow it. That is, to make the sound of a *t*, the musculature must make one of two different movements depending on whether the word is "eat" or "boat," as you can easily discover for yourself when you say these two words and note the actions of your own tongue. And, depending on the previous sound, the program for the next sound must vary for similar reasons. Thus, the 44 programs for tongue movement for the various sounds must be multiplied by the number of different sounds that could precede and follow each of these sounds. This notion—called *context-conditioned variability*—led MacNeilage to estimate that a very large number of programs must be stored in memory in order for us to speak as we do. Considering all the various accents, inflections, and combinations, as well as any foreign language sounds, he estimated that about 100,000 programs would be required for speech alone.

It is possible that the brain *can* store 100,000 programs for speaking, of course, as long-term memory has a very large capacity. But when we consider the number of ways in which we move other than for speech, and the interaction of previous and subsequent states for each of these movements, there would have to be a nearly countless number of programs in long-term memory. How (and/or where) are all of these programs stored in the central nervous system?

This original motor program notion stated earlier seems unwise for several reasons. First, many mechanical or electronic control systems can have a serious storage problem, and it is crippling to them; examples are libraries that have to cope with tons of paper and computer systems that have to store programs for every kind of computation. They simply run out of room for storage. A second reason relates to the belief that our motor system evolved in such a way that it was simple to operate and efficient in terms of storage. To store a complex program for every movement is not a simple and elegant way for a system to have evolved (e.g., Schmidt, 1975b; Turvey, 1977). There must be a better way to conceptualize the storage of motor programs.

The Novelty Problem

The next concern about this original motor program notion is related to the storage problem, but it takes a slightly different form. The basic issue is not how we retain learned movements, but rather how we make *new* movements. Consider a movement like this: Beginning in a standing position, jump up from both feet, touching your head with the right hand and your leg with your left hand before you land. Certainly, most of us could do this on the first try. If you had never done that particular movement before and if the action required a previously learned program for its execution, then where did the program come from? It is difficult to assume that the program was genetically defined (as walking might be), because such an action does not seem particularly essential to our survival. And you could not have learned it through practice, as this was the first time that you produced this action. A logical dilemma arises about the motor program notion when we consider novel movements.

The same sort of problem exists for more common skills. If you were to study a series of 50 shots in tennis, examining the fine details of the feet, hands, and body, you would probably find that no two movements were *exactly* the same. This is compounded by the fact that the ball never has exactly the same velocity, the same location on the court, or the same height on two occasions. Therefore, it is unlikely that any two tennis strokes could be exactly the same. If no two shots are exactly the same, then the programs must also be different. Thus, according to this analysis at least, every shot is "novel" in the sense that it has never been produced in exactly that way before. When you make a movement, you do not simply repeat a movement that has been learned earlier.

On the other hand, a given golf or tennis stroke is certainly very similar to strokes that you have made in the past. For example, some people have an atypical style of hitting a golf ball that is characteristic of them and no one else, and a popular touring (golf) professional's style is easily recognized (e.g., Jim Furyk or Ryan Moore). Thus, it is not fair to say that every golf stroke is absolutely new, as considerable practice and experience have led to the production of that action, and this experience tends to make the actions similar and characteristic of that individual.

Writing more than 70 years ago, Bartlett (1932) made the following observation about tennis strokes: "When I make the stroke I do not, as a matter of fact, produce something absolutely new, and I never repeat something old" (p. 202). His point summarizes the issues in this section very well. When making a stroke, you do not make a movement that is absolutely new, because that movement will depend on your past learning. But you do not exactly repeat an old movement either, as any particular movement will be slightly different from all the others that you have made in the past. In this sense, the stroke is considered novel, yet at the same time, dependent on previous experience.

One weakness of the earlier idea about the motor program notion is that it does not explain how the individual can produce a novel movement or how a movement such as a particular tennis stroke is somehow slightly different, yet characteristic of all earlier ones. If our theories about movement programs are to have an application to everyday motor behavior, then they must be able to explain these common phenomena.

The Need for Revision

These two rather persistent problems—the storage problem and the novelty problem—pose rather severe limitations for the motor program idea as it has been stated previously. One solution has been to introduce a modification to the fundamental programming notion, one that retains all the attractive aspects of programming that have been discussed so far but also provides a solution to the two problems. This kind of thinking led to Schmidt's idea (1975b, 1976a) that a motor program should be considered as *generalized*.

Generalized Motor Programs

The idea of a *generalized motor program* (abbreviated GMP) is that a motor program for a particular *class* of actions is stored in memory and that a unique pattern of activity will result whenever the program is executed. In order for the program to be executed, certain *parameters* must be supplied to the program that define how it is to be executed for that particular instance. The program is considered generalized because choosing different parameters will alter the output, in terms of movements of the limbs, but these movements will differ in only certain ways. But, before we describe how such a system might operate, it will be helpful to consider an example of a generalized program for a different application.

A Computer Model

Perhaps the best example of a generalized program comes from computer science. Consider a program that calculates means, such as the "function" feature in Microsoft Excel. This type of program is "generalized" in such a way that it will calculate the mean for sets of values that differ in terms of the number (*n*) of them to be considered. Note that the set of operations that is to be done with these values is fundamentally similar regardless of the number of scores we have; that is, add up all of the values and then divide by the number of them you have. To run the function you simply specify the number of data points over which the mean is to be calculated—the number of values is one of the *parameters* that must be applied to the execution of the statistical function. Once these are specified, the program is executed for this particular number of scores.

How does this kind of program solve the storage and novelty problems? First, the storage problem is reduced because, for this class of computing problem, only one program needs to be stored in the system for each function (i.e., calculating the mean), and each program can generate its results for a wide range of possible numbers of data points. So, rather than having separate programs to calculate the mean of 2, 3, 4, 5, . . . , 1,000 numbers, we need only one program that is generalized; providing it with a parameter value (e.g., 8 or 800 data points, or some different number) enables the generalized program to produce the result easily.

With respect to the novelty problem, notice that the program for means and standard deviations can produce results for data that it has never been used for previously. One simply specifies the proper parameters, and the program is executed perfectly. The program can compute the mean for a number of scores that it has never confronted previously. In this sense, the generalized program provides one kind of solution to the novelty problem—it can produce a result it has never produced before.

Invariant Features

A motor program is thought to be responsible for the production of a pattern of action, expressed in both space and time. When we examine patterns of action carefully, we see that various aspects of them are easy to change while other aspects remain almost completely fixed from movement to movement. It is not always obvious which aspects of the movement are fixed and which are easily changed; but examining the movement in certain ways, or with certain theoretical biases, can reveal these features (Schmidt, 1985).

A classic example of ways in which movements demonstrate both fixed and modifiable features is one of our most common movement patterns, *handwriting*. This demonstration was presented many years ago (apparently independently) by Lashley (1942; see Bruce, 1994) and Bernstein (1947; reproduced in Keele, Cohen, & Ivry, 1990 [their figure 3.5]), and more recently by Merton (1972) and Raibert (1977). All these demonstrations suggest basically the same thing. Figure 6.18 is a reproduction of the handwriting samples published by Lashley (1942). Two right-handed, blindfolded subjects wrote the words "motor equivalence"[5] normally (with the right hand), with the nondominant (left) hand, and with either hand attempting to produce a mirror image of the words (these have been reversed in the figure to appear as normal). The subject represented in figure 6.18*a* even wrote the words with the pencil held by the teeth.

These handwriting samples are different in obvious ways—they are of different sizes and show a different amount of "shakiness" in some cases. The MT taken to complete each word was probably not the same either. But in all samples for each individual there are many remarkable similarities. A certain "style" is seen in all of them, such as the little curl at the start of the *m* for the subject illustrated in figure 6.18*a*, and the way the downstroke of the *q* is made by the subject in figure 6.18*b*. Some aspects of these written words appear to be *invariant,* even when the effector used or the size or speed of the writing is changed. In this figure it appears that the spatial pattern was invariant—the shapes of the letters. Lashley noted:

> In spite of the clumsiness, the general features of the writing, individual differences in the forming of letters and the like, are characteristically maintained. The mechanics of writing is a sequence of movements in relation to bodily position, not a set pattern of special groups of muscles. (1942, p. 317)

You can see a similar phenomenon if you do this yourself. First, write your signature in your "normal" way, as if signing a document or a

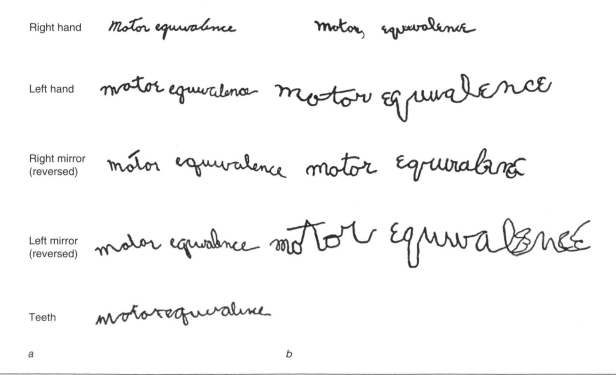

FIGURE 6.18   Examples from two subjects writing the words "motor equivalence" with different effectors.

From K.S. Lashley, 1942, The problem of cerebral organization in vision. In *Biological symposia. Vol. VII. Visual mechanisms*, edited by J. Cattell (Lancaster, PA: Jaques Cattell Press), 301-322.

check. Second, write your signature roughly 10 times larger on a blackboard with chalk. Just by looking at the two signatures, you should be able to see that they are "the same," signed by the same person. (If you want to be more elegant, take a digital photo of both signatures and enlarge or reduce one of them so that they are the same size, and then overlay them.) Now, note that you usually write the small signature with your fingers, with the "heel" of your hand fixed to the writing surface; naturally, with your hand fixed, your elbow and shoulder are fixed also. But, in the blackboard signature, your fingers are mainly fixed, and the writing is done with the elbow and shoulder. The "same" signature was written by completely different joints and muscles.

Although the interpretation of these kinds of demonstrations has been called into question (Latash, 1993, 1999), in-depth analyses support the conclusion that something in the performer's memory is common to all these handwritten samples (Wright, 1990). Some abstract structure has expressed itself, regardless of the variations in handwriting speed or size or in the particular limb or muscles used to write the words. Schmidt (1976a) theorized that those features that are invariant, and that in some ways are *fundamental* to these written words, are structured in the GMP; those aspects of the movement that are relatively superficial (speed, size, the limb used) are thought to be parameters of the program. Remember the computer analogy: The ways in which the means are calculated is invariant and fundamental to the program—the number of scores to be averaged is not fundamental, and this constitutes a parameter of the program. These examples with handwriting seem to be showing something similar and perhaps invariant.

If these observations are correct, how can the structure of the motor program be conceptualized so that the invariant features of handwriting are held constant across a wide variety of other changes? In the next section, we consider one possibility that has abundant evidence to support it—the *impulse-timing view*.

Impulse-Timing View

One straightforward viewpoint about the structure of GMPs is the *impulse-timing view*. The fundamental idea is that the motor program provides pulses of motor neuron activity to the relevant

musculature. These pulses produce patterns of contractions in the muscles that can be seen in EMG records or in records of force produced. The amount of force produced is related in a complex way to the amount of neurological activity, and the duration of the force and its temporal onset are determined by the duration of the neurological activity and the time of its occurrence. The major role of the motor program is to "tell" the muscles when to turn on, how much force to use, and when to turn off. Thus, the motor program ultimately controls force and time.

Impulses

The combination of (or the product of) force and time constitutes what is called an *impulse* in physics. A common physical principle is that the amount of movement produced in an object (such as a limb) is determined by the force(s) acting on it and the duration over which the force acts; the impulse is the product of force and time. Therefore, the impulse-timing view assumes that the GMP controls movement by controlling impulses—bursts of force spread out over time to the appropriate muscles.

In figure 6.19 are three hypothetical, idealized records of the forces produced by a muscle over the time that this muscle is acting on the limb. At each moment of the contraction, the muscle is producing a different force against the bone; the resulting curve in figure 6.19 is called the *force–time curve*—a record of the force produced over time. The impulse is the shaded *area* under the force–time curve. From mathematics, this area is frequently called the *integral*, or the *integral of force over time*.

In the figure, notice that the area under the force–time curve for impulse *a* can be reduced in half by changing the amplitude of the force for a given amount of time (as in impulse *b*), or by changing the duration of the impulse for a given amplitude (as in impulse *c*), or both. From physics, the velocity of the object (or limb, beginning at rest) after the impulse has ended its action will be directly proportional to the size of the impulse. Thus, impulses *b* and *c* in figure 6.19 would theoretically produce the same velocity at the end of their respective actions (because their areas are equal). And the velocity of the limb with impulse *a* would be twice as large as for the other two, because its area is twice as large. According to this view, the motor program controls a feature of

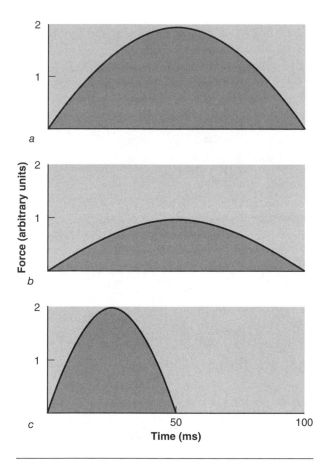

FIGURE 6.19 Hypothetical impulses seen as the area under force–time curves. (Impulses *b* and *c* have half the size that impulse *a* does, but impulse *b* is achieved by halving the force with time constant, and impulse *c* is achieved by halving the time with force constant.)

muscular contraction that is known to be a direct cause of movement—impulses.

If it is correct that the motor program determines impulses, then it is reasonable to assume that the motor program is capable of producing a group of impulses, each one in a different muscle group and each one at a different time, resulting in a pattern of activity that produces a complex, skilled movement. Remember, producing impulses in muscles is really nothing more than defining the time of onset and offset (i.e., the durations) of the relevant contractions, as well as their forces. Once these are defined, the movement is defined, given a fixed environment of course. Even so, defining these impulse sizes and durations should not be seen as simple, because many factors must be considered by the central nervous system, as discussed earlier (see figures 6.16 and 6.17).

Invariant Features and the Impulse-Timing View

Given a model of impulses patterned in time to produce a movement, what features of the action must remain invariant? What aspects of these impulses are the same from one handwriting sample to another, and which of them can vary while maintaining a given pattern of activity? The evidence favors two, and perhaps three, features that remain invariant.

Order of Events One aspect of the patterns shown in figure 6.18 that seems not to vary is the sequence or *order* of events (Lashley, 1951). In each sample, some event occurred before some other event in making a letter or word, and this order was fixed for all of the samples. We assume that the order of muscular contractions for this sequence of events in a given program is fixed. A basic assumption of the impulse-timing view of motor programming is that within the structure of a given program is an invariant order of the various elements. Notice that this is not the same as saying that the order of *muscles* contracting is fixed in the program. The muscles that produced the writing with the teeth are obviously different from those that produced the writing with the hand, and yet the sequence and the pattern were the same. Clearly, the motor program does not contain the order of muscles; rather, it seems to order the *events* (here, upstrokes, downstrokes, etc.) that occur during the movement.

Relative Timing A second aspect of the program that is thought to be invariant is the *temporal structure* of the contractions, usually termed *relative timing*. The temporal structure of a series of events (in this case, a series of actions) can be represented in a number of ways, but one of the most common is to evaluate the structure in terms of what is called *relative time*. In figure 6.20 are hypothetical examples of records taken from two similar actions. This particular record contains EMGs, but the record could have been defined in terms of movements of the limbs, the forces produced, or other characteristics that capture in some way the nature of the movement pattern produced. The hypothetical muscles whose EMGs are shown were chosen because they act at different times in the movement sequence. The sequence begins with a strong burst of EMG from muscle 1; then muscle 1 appears to be turned off and muscles 2 and 3 are activated, with muscle

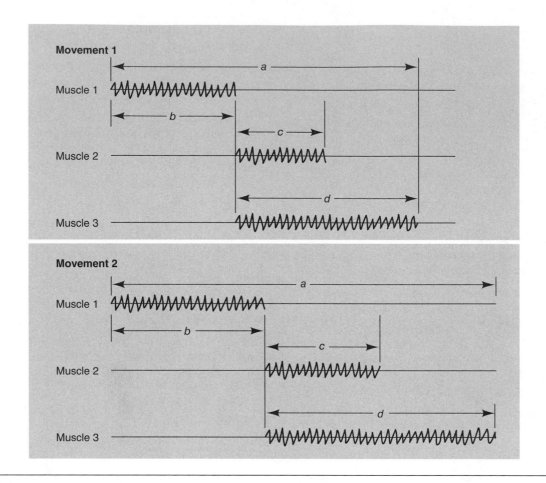

FIGURE 6.20 Hypothetical electromyogram (EMG) records from two similar movements differing only in movement time (MT). (Phasing, or relative timing, is defined by the ratios of the EMG durations among various muscles, e.g., *b/c, c/a,* and so on.)

2 ceasing its activity before muscle 3 does. How can this temporal pattern of events in these three participating muscles be described?

One method is to measure the durations of the various elements within the sequence. Shown in the figure are two similar movements, but one of them (movement 2) has a longer MT than the other. If these two records are evaluated with respect to the durations of the relevant contractions (EMGs), then interval *a* can be defined as the duration of the contraction of the muscles in the entire action, interval *b* is the duration of contraction of muscle 1, interval *c* is the duration of contraction of muscle 2, and interval *d* is the duration of contraction of muscle 3. One way to evaluate the temporal structure of these events is to produce ratios of these various times. The sequence for movement 1 has a ratio of interval *c* to interval *d* of 1:2, or 0.50. That is, interval *d* is twice as long as interval *c*. Also, interval *b* is one

and one-half times as long as interval *c*, making their ratio 1.5:1, or 1.5. Similar ratios can be computed for any two intervals in the sequence.

Another common ratio is that of an element in the sequence relative to the overall length of the sequence. For example, in the movement 1 sequence the ratio of interval *d* to the overall length of the sequence (interval *a*) appears to be about 0.60; thus, muscle 3 is contracting for about 60% of the entire movement. This is the usual use of the term "relative time": the duration of one event divided by the duration of the entire action.

The fundamental idea of these ratios is this: The temporal structure is measured by (or characterized by) the values of these ratios. If all the ratios for analogous pairs of events are the same in two separate movements, then we say that the temporal structures are the same. Thus, any two movements with the same order of contractions (perhaps that shown in figure 6.20) and the same ratios of muscle action to total MT (e.g., 0.45, 0.30, and 0.60 for muscles 1, 2, and 3) have the same temporal structure. Further, these two movements are assumed to be produced by the same GMP, for which relative timing is invariant (or fixed).

Movements 1 and 2 in figure 6.20 have this characteristic. The proportion of total MT for each muscle is the same in the two movements, even though the *amount* of time that each muscle is contracting is different for the two movements. Movements 1 and 2 are thought to be governed by the same motor program because their relative timing is the same. According to this idea, if two movements have different relative timings, then they are governed by different GMPs.

Relative Force   A third important feature of GMPs is *relative force,* which simply means that the amounts of force produced by any two muscles remain in constant proportion from movement to movement. If in movement 1, muscle 1 produced 2 kg of peak force and muscle 2 produced 4 kg, the ratio of these two forces would be 1:2, or 0.50. In another movement using the same program, these proportions should be the same, but perhaps with forces of 2.5 kg for muscle 1 and 5 kg for muscle 2. The ratio remains 1:2, or 0.50.

This feature (relative force) of the movement sequence would seem to remain invariant for the patterns of handwriting in the examples in figure 6.18. We can see this in two ways. First, in this kind of model, the height of a given letter is determined in part by the amount of force applied to the limb during the impulse applied by the motor program. But the heights of the letters remain in almost constant proportion to each other as the various letters in a given sentence are considered. For both subjects in Lashley's example (figure 6.18), the *t* is always about twice the height of the *o* that follows it. The forces that produced these letter heights may have been in constant proportion in the sequence as well.

The Phonograph Record Analogy

It is sometimes helpful in understanding motor control theories to consider a *model* that has many of the same features as the theory. A good model for the GMP is the phonograph record. On the record, structured as invariant features, are three things. First is the order of the events, for example, specifying that a drumbeat comes before a guitar riff, and so on. Next is the relative timing. Think of relative timing as the rhythm, so that the time between any two events on the record divided by the total record time is a constant. For phonograph records, the ratio between the durations of any two events is always fixed. Also, the relative force is fixed. For example, the first drumbeat may be twice as loud as the second one. What is embedded on the record is a code that is translated into sound when the record is played on an audio system. It may be helpful to conceptualize GMPs as records, because in many ways they behave in the same general way, and these similarities allow us to visualize the GMP idea more vividly.[6]

But we know that the record can be played in various ways to produce different sounds. It can be played rapidly or slowly, loudly or softly, with the sound equalizer adjusted in various ways, and so on. Yet a given song can still be recognized because the *pattern* of the sounds produced is invariant, even though some of the superficial features of the pattern may have varied. The actual muscles that produce the action (here, the particular speakers that will be driven) are certainly not "on" the record, because the record can be played on any audio system. In the next section, we discuss some of these more superficial features of movements. These aspects of movement are considered the *parameters* of the GMP.

Parameters of Generalized Motor Programs

Motor program theorists have argued that there are a limited number of parameters that can be applied to a GMP. The evidence is strongest for parameters that are responsible for establishing the overall duration, the overall force, and muscle selection. We discuss these next.

Overall Duration Parameter

The basic idea of an overall duration parameter is that, while the motor program contains relative timing and sequencing information, it can be executed slowly or rapidly depending on the overall duration parameter assigned, just as increasing the speed of the phonograph turntable speeds up the entire sequence of sounds as a unit.

Initial evidence for an overall duration parameter appeared in an unpublished study by Armstrong (1970b). Subjects were asked to learn to move a lever through a particular spatial–temporal pattern. Figure 6.21 shows a tracing of the position of the lever as a function of time in the 4 s movement. Armstrong noticed that when the subject made the movement too rapidly, the entire sequence was made too rapidly, as if the entire movement record was "compressed," with all parts of the movement shortened by the same relative amount, or in the *same proportion*. Although Armstrong did not compute the proportions suggested in figure 6.21, a critical test of the idea is that the time interval between some peak *a* and some other peak *b* divided by the time for the entire movement is about the same in the two movements shown in the figure. Such findings gave initial insight into the possibility of an underlying GMP, with an overall speed parameter that retained the invariant relative timing in the movement pattern, which could be parameterized to allow the total duration of the movement to be made longer or shorter (see Pew, 1974a, for an early discussion of this work).

Following Armstrong's (1970b) and Pew's (1974a) suggestions, Summers (1975) and Shapiro (1977, 1978) examined similar questions in tasks in which the experimenter could instruct the subject to change the overall speed intentionally (remember that movement durations made by subjects in Armstrong's study changed accidentally). Shapiro's paradigm involved practice at

a task that required precise spatial–temporal patterning of pronation/supination of the wrist. Thus, to be successful the subjects had to make a series of actions with criteria defined in both space and time. The temporal structure of the action for Shapiro's (1977) study is shown in figure 6.22, here called the "test" trials. The proportion of the total MT (which was 1,600 ms) occupied by each of the nine wrist-twist segments is plotted as the line marked with open squares. After considerable practice, Shapiro asked her subjects to speed up the movements but to keep the pattern the same; the pattern of proportions for these "compressed" trials is shown as the line with filled circles in figure 6.22. Notice that the proportions of time for the various segments were almost exactly the same for the "test" trials and the "compressed" trials, but that the MT in the latter was decreased to 1,300 ms, on the average. Essentially, Shapiro showed that the subjects could decrease the time of this well-learned movement sequence as a unit, keeping the relative timing in the movement (defined by the proportions) constant. Again, these findings support the view that a movement-duration parameter can be applied to some fundamental program so that the given pattern can be sped up or slowed down as a unit.

Even more remarkable was another finding that both Summers (1975) and Shapiro (1977,

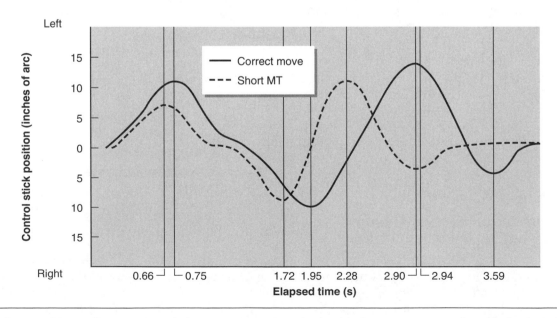

FIGURE 6.21 The position–time record of an arm movement task, showing the correct move and a move in which the overall movement time (MT) was too short.

Reprinted from T.R. Armstrong, 1970, "Training for the production of memorized movement patterns," *Technical Report* 26: 35.

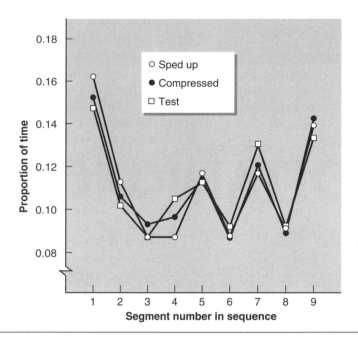

FIGURE 6.22 Proportion of total movement time (MT) required to traverse each segment in a wrist-twist movement. (Normal trials had a goal of 1,600 ms; compressed trials were sped up using the same phasing; speeded-up trials were sped up while subjects attempted to ignore the earlier-learned phasing.)

Adapted from Shapiro 1977.

1978) obtained. They asked their subjects to make the movement as rapidly as possible and to *ignore* the relative timing that they had learned in the earlier practice trials. In figure 6.22, the line with open circles represents these "sped-up" trials; again, the pattern of proportions was almost identical to that for the normal trials. Subjects were able to speed up the movements, but they were apparently unable (or at least unwilling) to do so with a different relative timing (see also Carter & Shapiro, 1984; Verwey & Dronkert, 1996).

There are many other examples of absolute and relative timing in the literature. Terzuolo and Viviani (1979, 1980) studied the typing of various words, examining the relative timing characteristics. Figure 6.23 has a diagram showing various temporal records in typing the word "enclosed," when the word was embedded in various places in standard prose. In figure 6.23a, the time of occurrence of each of the letters is plotted for 42 different trials. Each horizontal row of dots represents the time of occurrence for each letter for one trial. The trials are presented in the same order in which they occurred in the experimental session, and no recognizable pattern of relative timing appears. In figure 6.23b, though, the trials have been reordered so that the trial with the shortest overall MT (843 ms) is at the top, and the trial with

the longest MT (1177 ms) is at the bottom. Notice that the onset times of the various letters "line up" on the sloped lines, as if the longest trials were simply "stretched" versions of the shortest ones. Notice also that the relative time of occurrence of a given letter in the word "enclosed" is almost constant from attempt to attempt.

Similar findings have been produced by Shaffer (1980, 1984) in a study of typing and piano playing, by Roth (1988) using an overarm throwing movement, and by Heuer, Schmidt, and Ghodsian (1995) using a bimanual task in which each arm produces a different pattern, with the two arms being coordinated. All these data support the notion that a given overall sequence can be sped up or slowed down as a unit while the relative timing in the sequence is maintained (i.e., relative timing was invariant). Again, these data are consistent with the view that the same GMP produced the different instances of typing the word "enclosed" in figure 6.23 by applying a slightly different duration parameter each time the word was typed.

One more type of research paradigm has provided evidence that is important to consider. A series of studies by Wulf, Shea, and colleagues used a research strategy in which variables known to affect learning produced different

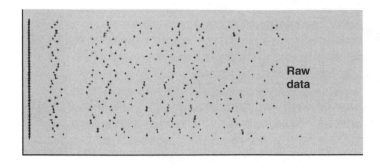

a

b

c

FIGURE 6.23 Temporal structure in typing the word "enclosed." *(a)* Letters are shown in the same order in which they were originally typed; *(b)* the same letters are ordered in terms of their overall movement time (MT); *(c)* the letter durations are expressed as proportions of overall MT.

Reprinted from *Neuroscience*, Vol. 5, C.A. Terzuolo and P. Viviani, "Determinants and characteristics of motor patterns used for typing," pg. 1092, Copyright 1980, with permission of Elsevier.

effects depending on what was learned or measured (much more will be described about learning variables in chapters 11 and 12). This strategy attempts to look for patterns of *dissociations* in learning (see also the same idea in the study of the two visual systems, discussed in chapter 5), such that a particular learning variable has different effects on the learning of relative timing (a measure of GMP performance) as compared to its effects on overall duration (a measure of parameterization) (DeJaeger & Proteau, 2003; Shea & Wulf, 2005). According to some studies,

experimental variations of practice have the effect of *increasing* the accuracy of relative timing (as measured in retention and transfer tests) (Lai & Shea, 1998; Lai, Shea, Wulf, & Wright, 2000; Shea, Lai, Wright, Immink, & Black, 2001; Wright & Shea, 2001; Wulf & Schmidt, 1989; Wulf, Lee, & Schmidt, 1994; Wulf, Schmidt, & Deubel, 1993). At the same time, these studies also showed that those same experimental variables degraded the scaling of absolute-duration performances (see also Wulf & Schmidt, 1996), which is a measure of the accuracy of parameterization. The overall findings appear to show some inconsistencies (cf. Wulf & Lee, 1993; Wulf & Schmidt, 1994b, 1997), however, and more work seems needed to clarify these effects. But overall, there is ample evidence that some factors have different effects on the learning of relative timing versus the parameterization of absolute timing, justifying their theoretical separation (see Shea & Wulf, 2005, for a review).

These results are examples of *double dissociations* as we discussed in chapter 5. Such double dissociations provide very strong evidence that two proposed theoretical structures are actually different empirically. The interpretation is that variables affecting the learning of program variables (such as relative timing, relative force, and sequencing) are not the same variables as those that affect the learning of parameter-assignment processes. Hence, these kinds of results strongly support the theory that program development and parameter assignment are theoretically (and actually) separate processes.

Overall Force Parameter

A second parameter proposed for implementing a GMP is an overall force parameter that modulates the amounts of force produced by the participating muscles. The force parameter is involved with determining how forcefully the relevant muscles will contract when they are recruited by the program. The evidence for the existence for such a parameter is weak, but logically a force parameter is included in the model (see also Schmidt, 2003).

Pew (1974a) described, as an example, a post office in which a conveyer belt carried small packages to be sorted by an employee. The person picked up the package and, with a "set shot" that might be considered good form for a basketball player, tossed the package into one of about 15 equidistant bins for later delivery to different postal zones. This package-sorting "system" required a number of processes on the part of the performer. First, because the bins were equal distances from the person, the final velocity (as the package left the hand) of each package needed to be approximately the same in order for each package to reach its bin, regardless of its weight. But a package with a larger mass will require the application of more force at a *given* duration in order to achieve the desired terminal velocity. Thus, the performer must choose a force parameter that can be applied to the generalized "set shot" program. Presumably, the person would pick up the package, heft it to determine its mass, and then select a force parameter for the generalized program that would achieve the proper goal. The program could be run when the force and duration parameters had been selected.

Another example that supports the concept of an overall force parameter comes from Hollerbach (1978). Figure 6.24 shows the acceleration tracings from a subject writing the word "hell" two times, one word being twice the size of the other. The accelerations are, of course, directly proportional to the forces that the muscles are producing during the action. The tracings have the same temporal pattern, yet the accelerations in the tracing for the larger word are uniformly larger than those for the smaller word. It appears that the forces applied to the pen were simply increased (scaled) while the original temporal pattern was maintained. Of course, increasing the force leads to increased distance that the pen travels; hence, the word is larger with the same spatial–temporal pattern. Similar interpretations can be made from a study of handwriting by Denier van der Gon and Thuring (1965), who showed that when the friction of the pen on the writing surface was increased, a systematic decrease in the writing size resulted but with no change in the pattern of letters produced.

In the examples just cited, the overall force parameter applies to all of the participating muscles proportionally, keeping the relative forces applied to the limb proportional. This concept is very much like the overall-duration parameter, which is applied to the sequence as a whole. A less restrictive view is that the force parameter can be applied to various actions in the sequence without affecting other actions in the body. For example, walking with a heavy backpack would seem to require that more force be applied to the muscles that operate against gravity in walking, but the muscles that cause the foot to move through the air in the swing phase would not need to have extra force applied to them. Perhaps a force parameter is selected that applies only to those aspects of the program that require extra force. However, this idea has the disadvantage of requiring the motor system to do more "computing" in

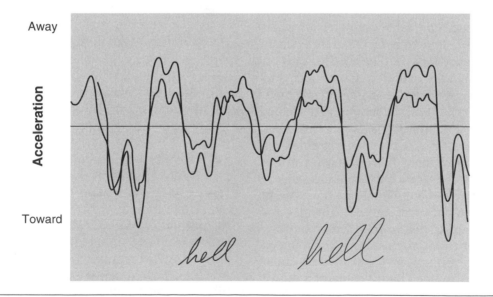

FIGURE 6.24 Vertical accelerations produced in writing the word "hell," with one word having twice the amplitude of the other. (The tracings show a remarkable degree of temporal agreement, with systematic differences in amplitude of acceleration.)

Reprinted, by permission, from J.M. Hollerbach, 1978, *A study of human motor control through analysis and synthesis of handwriting.* Unpublished doctoral dissertation (Cambridge, MA: Massachusetts Institute of Technology).

order to move. Consequently, there appears to be less overall support for the separation of absolute and relative forces than has been seen for the other features of the GMP theory.

Interaction of Duration and Force Parameters

There is a further argument with respect to the necessity for a force parameter, but it is less obvious than the one just given. Consider a movement in which you begin with your elbow straight, flex the elbow to 90°, and then extend it to the straight position again, completing all of the movements in an overall MT of 300 ms. The motor program presumably determines the relative timing of the biceps, the cessation of the biceps and the initiation of triceps (for the reversal), and then the contraction of the biceps again to "clamp" the limb in the final target position. Now consider what would happen if you simply decreased the duration parameter of the program without changing a force parameter. Selecting a shorter duration parameter would cause the program to move through the biceps–triceps–biceps sequence more rapidly while keeping the forces produced by these muscles constant. What would happen to the movement? Because the impulses will be shorter in time, the impulses will be smaller, and the limb will not have moved as far in the time allowed for biceps activity; thus, the movement will reverse itself short of the 90° position. Decreasing a duration parameter while holding a force parameter constant would result in an inappropriate movement in terms of its extent.

One possible remedy is to choose the duration parameter so that the overall MT is correct, and then to choose an overall force parameter that will be sufficient for the limb to move to 90° before reversing itself (Schmidt, Zelaznik, Hawkins, Frank, & Quinn, 1979). If the force parameter is too large, the movement will go too far in the proper amount of time; if the force parameter is too small, the movement will not go far enough. Thus, with this view, movement distance for a given program is determined by a complex combination of duration and force parameters. Clearly, duration and force parameters must complement each other. The selections of the force and duration parameters are not independent, as the particular value of the force parameter will depend heavily on the chosen duration parameter.

Muscle-Selection Parameter

In the analysis of the handwriting examples shown in figure 6.18 (from Lashley, 1942), we argued that the muscles for the particular action could not be stored "in" the GMP, because the same program produced movements in entirely different limbs. Thus, the sequential ordering embedded in the motor program is considered to be *abstract*, with the specific joints and muscles added during the *preparation* (and *parameterization*) of the program. In this case, it is reasonable to think of the specification of muscles (or joints) as another parameter of the motor program.

Additional evidence for this view comes from numerous experiments using a *bilateral-transfer* paradigm. For example, Shapiro (1977) used a wrist-twist task similar to that described earlier, having subjects practice this sequence with the right hand for five days. Then she asked the subjects to make the same movements with the left hand, which had never been used for this pattern before. She found a pattern of activity shown in figure 6.25, in which the well-practiced right-hand pattern is indicated by the open circles and the novel left-hand pattern is indicated by the closed circles. The two patterns are nearly identical, and the case can be made that the program that was generated by practice with the right hand could be produced with the left hand. Further evidence for the preservation of sequence learning during transfer to different effectors has been shown by Keele, Jennings, Jones, Caulton, and Cohen (1995; see also Jordan, 1995; Keele et al., 1990).

In another variant of the bilateral-transfer paradigm, Park and Shea (2002) found that relative force and time transferred from one limb to the other, but absolute force and time did not. Therefore, this could be interpreted to suggest that positive bilateral transfer of the invariant features occurred, not the movement parameters. Stated another way, since bilateral transfer of the properties of the GMP was high this finding supports effector independence of the GMP, but since bilateral transfer of the parameters was low, this finding suggests effector specificity in bilateral transfer of movement parameters (see also Park & Shea, 2003, 2005; Wilde & Shea, 2006). These findings are reminiscent of Lashley's (1942) handwriting examples shown in figure 6.18: The

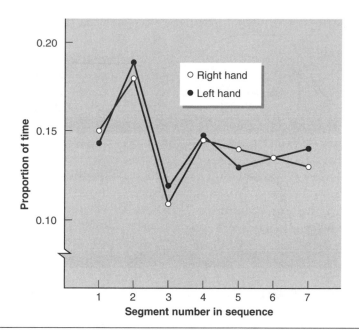

FIGURE 6.25 Proportions of total movement time (MT) required to traverse various movement segments in a wrist-twist task. (The pattern is similar for the practiced right hand and for the unpracticed left hand.)

Adapted from Shapiro 1977.

essential features of the handwriting were maintained when limbs were switched, although the "smoothness" was affected dramatically.

Parameters in the Phonograph Record Analogy

Earlier we presented the analogy between a GMP and a phonograph record, with information about order, relative timing, and relative force structured "in" the motor program ("on" the record) to define a given pattern. To complete the analogy, add the ideas about parameters just discussed. The overall duration parameter is analogous to the speed of the turntable. When the record turns more rapidly, the overall duration of the record's activity decreases, but the relative timing of sounds remains invariant. Next, the overall force parameter can be thought of as the volume control, whereby the same pattern of action can be produced either loudly or softly. This is very much like writing in small or large letters with the pattern of the writing remaining the same. Muscle-selection parameters are analogous to the operation of speakers. If you have an expensive set of speakers in the living room and a cheaper set in the kitchen, choosing one of these will affect the sound quality (and, of course, the location) of the music you are hearing, but will not change the record itself. Here, the speaker is analogous to an effector, in which the same pattern is produced in two different sets of "muscles."

Changing Parameters and Programs

Additional evidence supporting the GMP comes from experiments in which some aspect of the movement has to be changed during the movement. For example, Quinn and Sherwood (1983) had subjects make elbow flexion or extension movements of 400 ms. Occasionally an auditory signal, administered in different blocks of trials, would instruct the subject to either (a) move faster or (b) reverse the movement. The findings, similar to those from earlier studies in this same general paradigm (Gottsdanker, 1973; Vince & Welford, 1967), showed that the latency of the corrections (the interval from the auditory stimulus until the first EMG change) was 100 ms shorter when the movement had to be sped up than when it had to be reversed. Theoretically, with a reversal, the subject has to stop running a given program and select, parameterize, and initiate a different one that will reverse the movement. However, when the movement is sped up, the existing program can be retained, and only a reparameterization is necessary (e.g., with adjusted overall duration and force parameters); the stages involved in program selection and initiation can be bypassed.

Roth (1988) has shown that these principles hold for sport skills studied in the laboratory. For example, the RT to change a tennis ground stroke to a lob (presumably requiring a different program and different parameters) was estimated to be about 600 ms, whereas the RTs to change the direction or length of the ground stroke (presumably requiring only new parameters) were estimated to be about 200 ms less. Analogous results were provided for table tennis and volleyball skills, suggesting that the difference between program *plus* parameter selection versus only parameter selection is general across a variety of movement behaviors (see also Obhi, Matkovich, & Gilbert, 2009; Wright, Black, Park, & Shea, 2001).

Concerns About Generalized Motor Programs

The GMP theory was first proposed more than 35 years ago, and there have been numerous empirical and theoretical examinations of its predictions since then. In general, the theory has held up well. However, as with all theories, some data and analyses do not provide support.

The most contentious issue with regard to GMPs has been the concept of *invariance*, especially as it relates to relative timing. We argued earlier that in order for a timed segment to be considered invariant, its duration, relative to the total duration of the activity, must be constant over a series of separate executions of the program. But have another look at the relative timings for each letter of the word "enclosed" (figure 6.23). Although the relative durations for each letter show rather consistent relative timings, there are still some deviations. The questions that arise are these: Are these deviations meaningful? And how do you decide what is a meaningful deviation?

Statistical Invariance

A qualitative answer to these questions is to draw a straight line through the center of a set of data points (as was done with the absolute timing data in figure 6.23b). If the data were *perfectly* invariant, then all the individual data points would fall exactly on vertical lines—the more data points that are observed off the line, the weaker is the evidence for invariance. In reality, there is very little chance that motor behavior will ever show true, perfect invariance. Therefore, the question becomes, How much deviation from perfection

can be tolerated before we *reject* a conclusion that the data reveal invariance?

One solution to this debate was provided by Gentner (1987). He proposed two statistical methods for assessing relative invariance in a set of data. One method, called the *constant-proportion* test, uses statistical *regression* to assess whether or not the relationship between MT and relative timing has a slope that deviates from zero (see chapter 2 for discussion about regression methods). If relative timing is invariant, then the slope of the regression line will not deviate from zero, either positively or negatively. Gentner's (1987) analysis provided an objective, statistical solution to the problem of assessing invariance. Using these methods, Gentner reanalyzed some previously published data sets and found that, while some studies found support for invariant relative timing, others did not. More recent experiments, using the methods suggested by Gentner, have also produced evidence that is weighted against *perfect* statistical invariance (Burgess-Limerick, Neal, & Abernethy, 1992; Maraj, Elliott, Lee, & Pollock, 1993; Wann & Nimmo-Smith, 1990; but see also Franks & Stanley, 1991).

Are statistical tests appropriate to assess the invariance predictions of relative timing in GMP theory? The answer is unclear. Several questions can be raised from a statistical point of view, such as (a) the appropriateness of accepting the null hypothesis when significant effects are not found (which would be evidence in support of invariance) and (b) the level at which to set the cutoff point for rejection of the null hypothesis. Gentner suggested that a level of $\alpha = 0.05$ is appropriate; however, a case could be made for more or less stringent levels.

Central Versus Peripheral Invariance

Heuer (1988, 1991) has raised another important issue. He suggested that, even in the absence of *measured* invariance, there might still be *central* invariance. Heuer's argument uses the Wing and Kristofferson (1973a, 1973b) distinction between central and peripheral timing as a basis (see chapter 7 for details). The idea is that the timing observed at the output or peripheral level is a combination of a central mechanism that periodically triggers an effector into action and the (somewhat variable) motor delays (such as neural delays and muscle recruitment time) that occur following a central trigger. Heuer (1988) demonstrated that a variable motor delay could result in an absence of invariance in observed performance even though the relative timing of a central timing signal had no variance at all.

Thus, perhaps because of complexities in the muscle properties in fast movements (e.g., Heuer & Schmidt, 1988; Gielen, van den Oosten, & ter Gunne, 1985; Zelaznik, Schmidt, & Gielen, 1986), it is possible that one might not detect invariance at the level of the GMP by searching for invariances in motor output. Perhaps this issue will be resolved only by future research analyzing the brain potentials of action prior to movement output. We will return to the discussion of invariant relative timing when we discuss how the system regulates the coordination of two or more activities at the same time (in chapter 8).

Doubts About Motor Programs

A broader question that has been asked, not just specific to GMP theory, is whether or not the motor program concept remains a relevant or viable theoretical construct at all (Morris, Summers, Matyas, & Iansek, 1994; Summers & Anson, 2009). A number of alternative motor control positions have been described in the past 30+ years, and these have received considerable theoretical and empirical support. Some of these views suggest that the motor program view ascribes too much "intelligence" to a central command center—that much of the evolution of a movement as it unfolds in the course of an action occurs as a natural consequence of the dynamic interactions of the central nervous system, the effectors, the environment, and the task at hand. In other words, the argument is that a complex plan of action that serves to control movement need not be stored in memory and recalled prior to initiating movement.

We share some of these concerns about motor programs, especially as they relate to the ongoing regulation of coordination skills. In chapter 8 we discuss some theoretical alternatives regarding how these skills might be controlled (including a GMP account). However, we also note that many researchers who express doubts about motor programs usually study motor tasks that involve continuous skills, often rhythmical or cyclical (or both) with relatively long durations, for which ongoing regulation, using feedback from the environment and body, would seem critical to successful performance. Of these critics of the motor program concept we ask how, for example,

might a *decentralized* theory of motor control (i.e., a theory that does not involve a central motor program) explain the findings of Wadman and colleagues (1979; discussed earlier here), in which the complex coordination of agonist and antagonist muscle firings was preserved when the limb was blocked in position and prevented from moving at all? If the movement is shaped by the ongoing dynamics, then how could the "normal" pattern of muscle activations occur in the absence of any movement at all? Similarly, how could the findings of Valls-Solé and colleagues (1999), in which an acoustic-startle stimulus "released" a prepared movement almost 100 ms earlier than for a normal RT, be reconciled by a theory in which plans for action do not have a prominent role?

Regarding the divide that separates different theoretical perspectives on how movements are regulated, Steve Keele said: "To a large degree we are simply talking about different kinds of phenomena, and those phenomena have generated very different databases that are not addressed by both classes of theory. It is difficult to pit two 'theories' or perspectives against each other if they do not speak to the same phenomena" (Keele, 1998, p. 404). As we see it, the criticisms of the motor program concept lose strength in argument when a decentralized concept must come to terms with how rapid, ballistic-type tasks are controlled. At the very least, for actions such as these, we feel that the motor program concept provides the most complete and parsimonious account of the research evidence.

Summary

The response-chaining hypothesis proposed by James (1890) was the first open-loop theory for motor control. It held that each action in a sequence is triggered by the movement-produced feedback from the immediately preceding action. Research on the role of feedback in movement performance under various deafferentation conditions has tended to show that sensation from the moving limb is not *essential* for motor performance, although it contributes to the smooth control of many actions. Thus, the response-chaining hypothesis cannot be universally correct.

Motor control scientists have three reasons for believing that movements are controlled by programs: (a) the slowness of the information-processing stages, (b) the evidence for planning movements in advance, and (c) the findings that deafferented animals and humans can produce skilled actions without feedback. This is not to say that feedback is not used in movement. Feedback is used (a) before the movement as information about initial position, or perhaps to tune the spinal apparatus; (b) during the movement, when it is either "monitored" for the presence of error or used directly in the modulation of movements reflexively; and (c) after the movement to determine the success of the response and contribute to motor learning.

An early definition of motor programs as structures that carry out movements in the absence of feedback was found to be inadequate to account for the evidence about feedback utilization during movement. Also, problems were associated with the requirement for storage of many different motor programs (the *storage problem*), as well as with the means by which the motor program could create a novel action (the *novelty problem*). For these reasons, the motor program is thought of as *generalized*—containing an abstract code about the *order of events,* the *relative timing* (or temporal structure) of the events, and the *relative force* with which the events are to be produced.

These generalized motor programs (GMPs) require *parameters* in order to specify how the movement is to be expressed in the environment. Such parameters are the *overall duration* of the movement, the *overall force* of the contractions, and the *muscle* (or limb) that is used to make the movements. With such a model, many different movements can be made with the same program (reducing the storage problem), and novel movements can be produced through selection of parameters that have not been used previously (reducing the novelty problem).

Student Assignments

1. Prepare to answer the following questions during class discussion:
   a. Describe the open-loop operation of any human-made device of daily living (e.g., a microwave oven).
   b. Use an example from sport that illustrates the concept of point of no return.
   c. Provide an example from food preparation activities in the kitchen that illus-

trates the difference between errors of selection and errors of execution.

2. Find a research article that uses relative timing as the main dependent measure. What theoretical issues are investigated with use of this measure in your article?

Web Resources

From the National Transportation Safety Board, featuring unintended acceleration and other examples of movement errors:

www.ntsb.gov/events/boardmeeting.htm

Recent editorial about the role of human error in Toyota automobiles:

www.nytimes.com/2010/03/11/opinion/11schmidt.html

Video of an actual case of unintended acceleration:

www.youtube.com/watch?v=ihDK8ny4ouc

Notes

[1] Four of Taub's monkeys were reexamined 12 years after their surgery, and all revealed considerable functional reorganization of the brain structures responsible for sensory representation (Pons et al., 1991). Thus, it seems that motor and sensory systems may have both short- and long-term methods for adapting to the loss of sensory feedback.

[2] This view could also be related to the reflex-chaining hypothesis. The difference is that the closed-loop model would have the feedback evaluated against a reference of correctness, whereas the reflex-chaining view would have the feedback from the movement trigger the next action directly.

[3] Note that Gray (2002, 2009a) did not manipulate the vertical deviation of the pitch from the strike zone in these batting simulations (i.e., "inside" or "outside" of the strike zone).

[4] The generalizations that errors in execution can be corrected (a) without interference from other similar corrections and (b) with latencies unaffected by the number of possible corrections have not been studied carefully and should be considered with caution.

[5] Lashley had a good reason for choosing these particular words to be written; the term *motor equivalence* refers to the idea that different effectors can be used to achieve the same goal.

[6] Not long ago, a teenaged niece of R.A.S. asked him, "What's a phonograph?" Although the question raises some doubt about the longevity of this analogy, we note that phonograph records have made a resurgence in popularity in recent years.

CHAPTER 7

PRINCIPLES OF SPEED AND ACCURACY

One of the most common errors of movement control occurs when we try to perform a task faster than "normal." Attempts to thread a needle rapidly, to type an e-mail in a hurry, or to pour a glass of milk quickly often result in an increased number of *aiming errors.* These are errors based often on a lack of precision, and they are usually (but not always) studied in tasks involving arm and hand movements.

In this chapter we focus on the fundamental *principles* that pertain to various movement variables and some theoretical ideas that have emerged from them. Such principles are critical to any science, as they describe the relationships among measures of the objects under study. As such, many of the basic *laws* of motor behavior may be seen as analogous to the fundamental principles of physics. The laws relating the mass, velocity, and acceleration of objects when forces are applied to them (the principles of mechanics), for example, have served as the cornerstone of the physical sciences and therefore deserve a special status. In the same way, the field of motor behavior has analogous principles that are somehow fundamental to all the rest: principles that describe, for example, the relationship between the speed at which a limb moves and the resulting accuracy, or the relationship between movement distance and movement time.

Whereas a neat set of simple, elegant principles can be stated for various branches of the physical sciences, we should not expect the same for the behavioral sciences, or for motor control in particular. For a number of reasons, in motor control we find far fewer statements possessing sufficient generality and supporting evidence to have attained the status of a "law." One reason is that the motor control principles have been far more difficult to discover, based as they are on data from biological systems that are more variable ("noisy") and complex than the physical systems. Often the relationships are not obvious and must be "teased apart" from the background noise or variability in order to be observed. The situation is complicated further when different principles are observed for different people (termed individual differences, chapter 9), which seems to suggest that different laws should exist for different individuals or for different classifications of people (children vs. adults, for example). Even so, these motor control principles hold well in many separate sets of data and generalize to a variety of practical situations, and thus represent statements of fundamental knowledge about skilled performance.

One of the most common occurrences in daily activities is known as the *speed–accuracy trade-off.* Common sense tells us that, as we move more rapidly, we become more inaccurate in terms of the goal we are trying to achieve. For example, trying to type too fast or pour a glass of milk too quickly generates annoying mistakes; the adage "haste makes waste" has been a long-standing viewpoint about motor skills. As we will see, however, the speed–accuracy trade-off exists in different forms for different types of movement tasks; the principles of speed–accuracy trade-offs are specific to the goal and nature of the movement tasks.

Three specific types of trade-offs are presented later in this chapter. These relate to situations in which spatial or temporal accuracy, or both, are the primary demands of the movement. Theories of movement control that relate to these trade-offs are presented later in the chapter.

Fitts' Law: The Logarithmic Speed–Accuracy Trade-Off

The first class of speed–accuracy trade-off functions occurs in situations in which the goal is to move a limb (or some other "effector") as quickly as possible to reach or touch a target, doing so with a minimal amount of error. Such is the goal in tasks like typing; moving a mouse-driven cursor to a desktop icon; moving the foot to the brake pedal in driving; and numerous other activities that require rapid movements to push, touch, grasp, intercept, or displace an object.

Early Research

The first major attempt to study scientifically the relationship between the speed of a movement and its resultant accuracy probably came from Woodworth (1899; see chapter 5 and "R.S. Woodworth on Manual Aiming" on p. 143). This work was far ahead of its time in terms of both the ideas examined in experiments and the techniques used. Woodworth proposed that aiming movements are made up of an *initial-adjustment* phase that propels the limb toward the target in an open-loop mode of control (chapter 6) and a *current-control* phase based on visual feedback that causes the limb to "home in" on the target (chapter 5).

At the time Woodworth's experiments were conducted, sophisticated electronic recording techniques were not yet available; so clever methods were devised that provided practical yet precise measurements to answer the research questions. The tasks used by Woodworth involved simple repetitive line-drawing movements to a target. Movement speed was varied by changing the frequency of a pacing metronome. Studies were done with various distances, with the right and left hands, and with the eyes closed and open, in an attempt to uncover some of the fundamental relationships between speed and accuracy. Generally, Woodworth found that accuracy (measured as absolute error) decreased as the movement speed increased, that the left hand was less accurate than the right hand (in right-handed subjects), and that the decrease in accuracy with increased speed was greater when the eyes were open than when they were closed (see "R.S. Woodworth on Manual Aiming," p. 143, and figure 5.5, p. 144). Most of his results have not, in general terms at least, been contradicted in more than a century of research conducted since Woodworth published his results in 1899. Fifty-five years later, the nature of this speed–accuracy relationship was described as a formal mathematical law by Paul Fitts (1954; "Paul Fitts" on p. 11).

Fitts' Research

In 1954, Fitts published a systematic analysis of the relationship between speed and accuracy that has become one of the landmark publications in the history of motor behavior research (Kelso, 1992). In the typical *Fitts paradigm* (or *Fitts task*), a subject is to tap a handheld stylus (a pencil-shaped object) alternately between two target plates as rapidly as possible for a predetermined duration (e.g., 20 s). The two targets are usually rectangular and oriented as shown in figure 7.1. Both the width of the targets (*W*) and the amplitude of the movement between them (*A*) are under the control of the experimenter and therefore can be altered to produce a large number of combinations of *A* and *W*. The task is scored as the number of taps (regardless of whether they are correct) in 20 s, but subjects are cautioned to limit errors (missed targets) to no more than about 5% of their movements. A more general view of the experimental setup is shown in figure 7.2.

Fitts' Law Defined

Fitts found that the relationship between the amplitude (*A*) of the movement, the target width (*W*), and the resulting average movement time (MT) was given by the following equation:

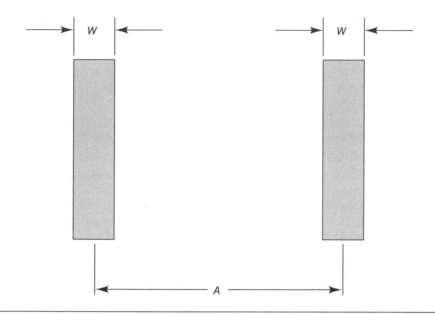

FIGURE 7.1 The Fitts paradigm. (The performer taps a stylus alternately between two targets of width *W* separated by a distance *A*.)

$$MT = a + b[\text{Log}_2 (2A/W)] \qquad (7.1)$$

where MT is the *average* movement time for a series of taps, computed as the trial duration (e.g., 20 s) divided by the number of taps completed in that time. For example, a 20 s trial duration divided by 50 taps in the trial yields 20 / 50 = 0.4 s/tap, or 400 ms/tap as the average MT.

The Fitts equation has the general form of a *linear* equation *(Y = a + bX)*, where *Y* is average MT, *X* is represented by the term $\text{Log}_2 (2A/W)$, and *a* and *b* are the empirical constants of a linear equation. (See also the section on linear empirical equations in chapter 2 and the discussion of Hick's law in chapter 3.) Therefore, a graphical

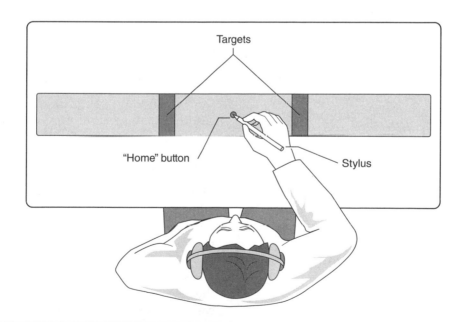

FIGURE 7.2 A subject performing the Fitts tapping task.

plot of average MT against Log_2 ($2A/W$) should be linear (a straight line).

The data from one of Fitts' original experiments are presented in figure 7.3. The values of A and W were varied experimentally by changing the arrangement of the target board (as in figures 7.1 and 7.2) for different blocks of trials, and the resulting MTs were measured after subjects had received some practice at these tasks. Figure 7.3 illustrates the average MTs as a function of Log_2 ($2A/W$), where each of the latter values is computed by taking the values of A and W, dividing them, and looking up the value of the Log_2 ($2A/W$) in the table of logarithms (see appendix). For example, one of the data points in figure 7.3 is associated with a value of 5 on the x-axis. The task values for this particular data point had a target amplitude (A) of 4 in. (10.2 cm) and a target width (W) of 1/4 in. (0.64 cm). Thus, the value $2A/W = 2(4) / 0.25 = 32$. Now, from consulting the table in the appendix, the Log_2 (32) = 5.0. (More simply, the Log_2 of a number is the power to which the base 2 must be raised in order to reach that number; i.e., $2^5 = 32$.)

The data in figure 7.3 indicate that, for the various combinations of A and W used in Fitts' experiment, the average MTs lie almost perfectly on a straight line, except perhaps for the leftmost three data points (representing movements with very short MTs). Notice, for example, that two conditions for which the Log_2 ($2A/W$) = 6.0 had virtually identical MTs (representing two tasks, one with $A = 16$ in., $W = 1/2$ in., and another task with $A = 8$ in., $W = 1/4$ in.). There are similar situations with the other data points plotted for a given value of Log_2 ($2A/W$), such as 3, 4, and 5.

Interpreting Fitts' Equation

What does it mean that the Log_2 ($2A/W$) plots linearly with the average MT in the Fitts task? A closer look at each of the components makes Fitts' equation easier to understand.

The Index of Difficulty   First, notice that the value of Log_2 ($2A/W$) seems to determine how much time was required for each of these movements, so this value seems to be related in some way to how "difficult" the particular combination of A and W was for the subject. For this reason, Fitts called this value the *index of difficulty (ID)*, which is expressed in terms of bits, taken from information theory (see later here, and chapter 3 for a fuller discussion). Thus, in Fitts' terms, the "difficulty" of a movement task was related jointly to the distance that the limb moved and to the narrowness of the target at which it was aimed. In fact, the relationship is even more restrictive than this, as the "difficulty" of the movement is theoretically the same for any combination of A and W that has the same *ratio*. Doubling A and doubling W at the same time result in a value of $2A/W$ that is the same, and hence the same value of Log_2 ($2A/W$) and the same predicted average MT. Another way to say this is that the average MT is linearly related to the ID, where ID = Log_2 ($2A/W$). Thus, Fitts' law could also be written as MT = $a + b$(ID).

The Empirical Constants (*a* and *b*)   Next, the values a and b are the empirical constants—they are required in order for the mathematical equation of the line to fit the observed data from the experimental setting. The constant a is the *y-intercept*, referring to the value of MT where the line of best fit crosses the MT axis. Specifically, the constant a is the value of MT when the ID is zero. But what does it mean to say that a movement has "zero difficulty"? This has been a serious problem for the understanding of the

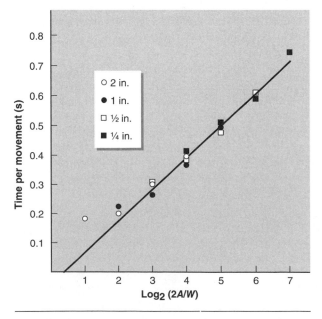

FIGURE 7.3   Average movement time (MT) as a function of the index of difficulty (ID) (Log_2 [$2A/W$]).

Data from Fitts 1954.

ideas surrounding the Fitts task (see Welford, 1968, for a more thorough discussion). For our purposes, a movement with "zero difficulty" is one with a ratio of $2A/W$ of 1.0 (because Log_2 [1] = 0). Therefore, the intercept refers to the situation in which the amplitude is one-half the target width, which results in targets that overlap, so that the subject's task of tapping "alternately" from one target to another actually involves tapping up and down as quickly as possible, with essentially no accuracy requirement.

The constant b is the slope, and it is far more straightforward in its interpretation. Here, the slope refers to the added MT caused by increasing the ID by one unit, which is one *bit* (binary digit; refer to chapter 3). In this sense, the slope refers to the *sensitivity* of the effector to changes in the ID. An example of this comes from Langolf, Chaffin, and Foulke (1976), where the results from a number of different movement situations using the Fitts task were compared. Langolf et al. found that the slope increased progressively as the limb used was changed from the finger to the wrist to the arm. The data from Langolf and colleagues suggest that the larger and more cumbersome limbs (the arms) are more sensitive to the changes in the ID than are the fingers, which can be controlled more precisely.

Differences in the slopes of the Fitts equation have also been shown to be sensitive to many other factors. For example, higher slopes in the Fitts equation are typically found in older adults, suggesting that the impact on average MT of higher IDs is greater for older adults than for younger adults (Goggin & Meeuwsen, 1992; Pohl, Winstein, & Fisher, 1996; Walker, Philbin, & Fisk, 1997; Welford, Norris, & Shock, 1969). The slope of the Fitts equation also can be reduced considerably with practice: B. Kelso (1984) found that the slope was reduced to nearly zero following 40,000 trials conducted over 20 days of practice. Thus, the slope of the Fitts equation represents an interaction of ID with the "controllability" inherent in the system (e.g., the effector characteristics, age of the subject, skill level). However, it is important to keep in mind that even though the slopes and the MT values may be different under various conditions or with different individuals, Fitts' law still holds for any one of these. That is, the average MT for any given limb still plots linearly with the ID, but with different values of a and b.

The Log Term Next, why is a Log term used in the equation, and why is the Log given to the base 2? When the idea was originally published, the theoretical rationale and interpretation was based on a dominant theme of the day—the *information theory* of communication (Shannon & Weaver, 1949; see "Uncertainty and Information Theory" on p. 67). Recall the discussion of Hick's law of choice reaction time (RT) in chapter 3; the equation for that relationship also had a Log_2 term. The $\text{Log}_2 (N)$, in which N was the number of equally likely stimulus–response alternatives, was a measure of the amount of *information* (in bits) required to resolve the uncertainty about N alternatives. The Log_2 term in Fitts' law can be seen in a similar way: $2A/W$ is related to the number of possible *movements,* and the $\text{Log}_2 (2A/W)$ is the information required (in bits) to resolve the uncertainty among them.

The Speed–Accuracy Trade-Off

Fitts' law implies an inverse relationship between the "difficulty" of a movement and the speed (i.e., the time) with which it can be performed. Increasing the ID decreases the speed (i.e., increases the MT). One way to think about this is that the individual in some way "trades off" speed against accuracy, and this trade-off is done so that the rate of information processing is held constant. In addition to this strict view in terms of the constancy of information processing, people presumably have some control over their strategy in moving. They can move very quickly at the "expense" of being less accurate, or they can move very accurately at the "expense" of being slower. In this way, Fitts' law has been fundamental in describing one particular aspect of the speed–accuracy trade-off, or the performer's capability to change the control processes so that speed and accuracy are kept in some balance. In the case of Fitts' law, the subjects were told to "emphasize accuracy rather than speed," and error rates averaged less than 5%. Thus, Fitts' law describes how MT must be traded off, under different values of ID, in order to maintain accuracy. In a later section, we will see how errors are traded off in order to determine the speed of limb movement.

Subsequent Research on Fitts' Law

It may not be obvious why so much attention has been paid to a single principle of motor performance. There appear to be several reasons. First, as we have seen so often, human motor behavior is complex and challenging to understand. Because of this, it is very difficult to provide precise mathematical descriptions of behavior that have general applications. Yet Fitts' law provides just that, and Fitts created it when almost no precise mathematical work was being done in motor behavior. Second, the law appears to relate to many different situations and to a number of variations of the original Fitts task. Thus it appears to represent some fundamental relationship that governs many examples of motor behavior. Third, since the publication of Fitts' law, no investigations have shown it to be fundamentally incorrect, although there now exist alternative ways of dealing with the relation between speed and accuracy. (One way is to change the temporal and spatial accuracy demands of the task, which is described later in this chapter.) In the next few sections we document some diverse research directions and applications that have been inspired by Fitts' law during the past 50+ years.

Modifications to the Fitts Equation

Modifications to the basic Fitts equation have been made in an attempt to achieve a better *fit*—which refers to the amount of variance in the experimental data that can be explained by the equation. Modifications to the definition of the ID by Welford (1968; Welford et al., 1969) and MacKenzie (1989) provided slightly better fit, as too did a consideration of the width of the effector (e.g., a dowel inserted into a target hole) that was being moved into the target area (Hoffmann & Sheikh, 1991). In contrast to the logarithmic relationship between *A* and *W* proposed by Fitts, an exponential relationship described in terms of a *power law* was suggested by Kvålseth (1980), where

$$MT = a(A / W)^b \tag{7.2}$$

Numerous other modifications to the Fitts equation were reviewed by Plamondon and Alimi (1997). And, while many of these have served to improve the overall fit, it should be kept in mind that the Fitts equation often explains well over 90% of the variance in many data sets. Thus, the improvement in accuracy gained by changes to Fitts' equation is relatively small. Fitts' original equation for ID has been very useful in explaining the performance of both one-dimensional tasks (figures 7.1 and 7.2), and two-dimensional tasks (such as the angular moves of a cursor on a computer screen; Murata, 1999). For three-dimensional movements, however, Murata and Iwase (2001) found that Fitts' original definition of ID explained only 56% of the variance in the data. They found a much better fit of the experimental data with an additional term in the definition of ID, compared to Fitts' equation. The inclusion of an additional term that considered the angle of deviation (from vertical) in the z-dimension toward the target [$\sin(\theta)$] improved the amount of explained variance to 73%.

The Discrete Fitts Task

Can the fundamental principle of Fitts' law be applied to other, more "natural" movement situations? Fitts and Peterson (1964) showed that the principle could be applied to a single-aiming task in which a stylus is aimed at a target in a single, discrete move. The subject's task was to make a single move as quickly and accurately as possible to a target of fixed amplitude (*A*) from a starting position and with a given target width (*W*). Consequently, Fitts and Peterson (1964) suggested that people trade off speed for accuracy in discrete tasks in much the same way they do for continuous, cyclical movements. However, recent research suggests that the issue is much more complicated than this (Guiard, 1993, 1997; Schaal, Sternad, Osu, & Kawato, 2004; Smits-Engelsman, Van Galen, & Duysens, 2002). Other research since the time of Fitts' original work has extended his ideas in a number of different ways.

Generality of Fitts' Law

Since the publication of Fitts' law, investigators have studied it in a variety of contexts, revealing that the principle shows remarkable generality and very few exceptions (see "An Exception to Fitts' Law?" on p. 230). For example, in addition to describing the aiming-accuracy principle for young adults, the Fitts relationship holds well for children (Hay, 1981; Schellekens, Kalverboer, & Scholten, 1984) and for older adults (Goggin & Meeuwsen, 1992; Pohl et al., 1996; Walker et al., 1997; Welford et al., 1969). Although Fitts' law was initially based on movements of the upper limbs, the principle has been found to hold when different effectors are compared, such as the foot, arm, hand, and fingers (Drury & Woolley, 1995; Langolf et al., 1976); when movements are conducted underwater (R. Kerr, 1973, 1978) and in space flight (Fowler, Meehan, & Singhal, 2008); and when the movements required are so small that they must be viewed under magnification (Langolf et al., 1976). Fitts' law even applies when tasks are imagined and the movement is not actually produced (Cerritelli, Maruff, Wilson, & Currie, 2000; Decety & Jeannerod, 1996), and when the difficulty of a Fitts task is only perceived (Augustyn & Rosenbaum, 2005; Grosjean, Shiffrar, & Knoblich, 2007).

Fitts' law also applies in the context of everyday activities. In Fitts' (1954) original work, two other experiments were reported in which subjects either placed discs over pegs or inserted pegs into holes, where *A* was the distance between the targets and *W* was the amount of *tolerance* between the size of the hole and the diameter of the peg. With ID defined in this way, the Fitts equation predicted MT very well. Movement-time effects also follow Fitts' law when one compares tasks in which subjects point at, reach for, and grasp objects of different sizes (Bootsma, Marteniuk, MacKenzie, & Zaal, 1994; Marteniuk, MacKenzie, Jeannerod, Athenes, & Dugas, 1987). As well, Fitts' law describes well the positioning movements of various computer-input devices such as keys (Drury & Hoffmann, 1992; Hoffmann, Tsang, & Mu, 1995), joysticks (Card, English, & Burr, 1978), computer "mice" (Card et al., 1978; MacKenzie & Buxton, 1994; Tränkle & Deutschmann, 1991), and head-pointing devices (Andres & Hartung, 1989; Jagacinski & Monk, 1985). Other ergonomics-related situations also appear to have benefited from the study of Fitts' law, such as the length of screwdrivers and crowbars (Baird, Hoffmann, & Drury, 2002) and alterations in the sizes and distances of monitor icons during computer interactions (Balakrishnan, 2004). The review by Plamondon and Alimi (1997) documents many other demonstrations and applications of Fitts' law.

Applications of the Fitts Task

The original Fitts task is a rather strange movement situation, and some have felt that the particular configuration of alternate tapping is not very representative of many real-life tasks (e.g., Schmidt, Zelaznik, & Frank, 1978). Despite its peculiarities, however, the Fitts task (or slight variations of it) have long been found useful as diagnostic measures in therapeutic situations. For example, a common diagnostic tool used by neurologists in clinical examinations is called the "finger–nose test" (Desrosiers, Hébert, Bravo, and Dutil, 1995). In this test the patient is asked to touch his nose, then extend the arm to touch a small target such as the tip of the neurologist's finger, touch the nose, and so on, repeating these alternations as rapidly as possible in a given time frame (e.g., 20 s). The number of successful cycles is counted, and the result is compared to established age-related normative data (Desrosiers et al., 1995). Sometimes this task is used to compare performances of the two upper limbs within an individual who might have neurological damage to one side. This "Fitts-like" task has proven to be a useful, reliable, and valid diagnostic tool (Gagnon, Mathieu, & Desrosiers, 2004; see "Neurological Disorders and Problems in Movement Control" on p. 320).

Importance of Fitts' Law

Lastly, one of the most powerful motivations for scientists working toward an explanation is the existence of a well-established principle or *law*—one that has survived the test of time and has been shown to be applicable to a wide variety of situations or people. Fitts' law certainly meets these criteria. Thus, one natural outgrowth of this work was an attempt to understand the movement control processes that produced the particular relations described by Fitts' law. That is, investigators began theorizing about *why* Fitts' law occurs. We have already mentioned viewpoints based on information theory, whereby the ID was taken by Fitts (1954) to be a measure of the amount of information needed to resolve the uncertainty about the movement. However, dissatisfaction with this theoretical perspective led researchers to propose alternative ways of explaining the kinds of speed–accuracy trade-offs that Fitts and others had observed in their data. These theoretical perspectives are dealt with in later sections of this chapter.

An Exception to Fitts' Law?

In the many hundreds of studies that have examined Fitts' law, only a very few exceptions have been found to the general principle that increases in the ID result in longer MTs. One of those exceptions has been found recently. Adam, Mol, Pratt, and Fischer (2006) had subjects make discrete, aimed movements to one of seven target locations on a computer touch screen. Because the targets always remained the same size, changes in ID were produced by changes in the distance from the home position to the target. For each trial, the specific target to which the subject moved was a green square that appeared on the screen after the subject touched the home position. In one set of conditions, the green target square appeared alone (figure 7.4*a*, line 2). In another condition, the seven possible target locations used were outlined in black and remained on screen at all times. The green target used for any given trial was achieved by coloring one of the target outlines when the subject touched the home position, leaving the other nontargets as unfilled outlines as shown in figure 7.4*a* (line 1).

The results of the study are illustrated in figure 7.4*b*. For trials in which the targets were presented alone (without the seven boxes), a linear increase in MT accompanied increases in ID, as predicted by Fitts' law. This was true also for the condition with the nontarget boxes; but, peculiarly, only for targets 1 through 6. An exception to Fitts' law was found for the most distant (seventh) target, as the MT for this target was *shorter* than that for the previous (sixth) target (which had a *smaller* ID). In a follow-up study, Pratt, Adam, and Fischer (2007) used outlined target contexts of three boxes, rather than seven, but adjusted the target by coloring the leftmost outlined box in one condition, the middle box in another condition, and the rightmost box in a third condition. The results replicated the

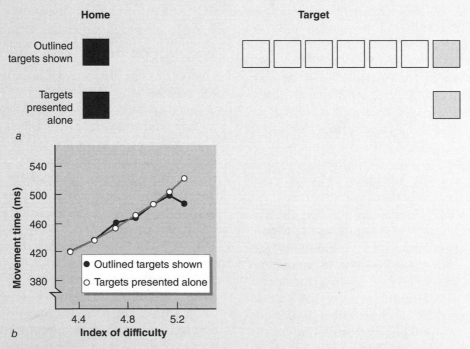

FIGURE 7.4   *(a)* An apparent exception to Fitts' law occurred when subjects moved from the home position to the target located in the farthest right position in the lower panel (line 1, containing the outlined target boxes), compared to movements made when targets were presented alone (line 2). *(b)* The exception is seen as a reduction in movement time to the seventh target position compared to the target with a smaller ID to its left (filled circles in the figure).

Adapted from Adam et al. 2006.

findings from Adam and colleagues (2006)—regardless of the target arrangement and the specific target IDs used, the rightmost of the outlined targets always violated Fitts' law relative to the adjacent target located to the left

So-called exceptions to a well-established principle usually generate much interest, here raising the question about (a) whether Fitts' law needs to be modified, or (b) whether these particular experimental conditions somehow fall outside of the domain of Fitts' law. These findings add an intriguing twist to the nearly ubiquitous finding that MT always follows the ID of the task. Apparently, the visual context in which a target is presented had a modifying effect on the movement, perhaps by defining an end boundary that somehow sped the delivery of the limb to the target. There are other relatively complex findings here, such as the fact that the errors on the seventh target (figure 7.4a) were far larger than on the sixth target, which occurred in both presentation conditions. We are not certain, of course, but this secondary finding might give hints about the underlying explanation here. The effects may also have important consequences for applications of Fitts' law to such tasks as computer monitor designs in which the various nontarget icons are on the display together with a target icon. In any case, these results should provide much fodder for discussion and further research about manual aiming and Fitts' law, as such "exceptions" usually do.

The Linear Speed–Accuracy Trade-Off

As noted in the previous section, the Fitts paradigm involves an unusual movement situation that is not typical of many everyday tasks and that produces one specific type of speed–accuracy trade-off. In an alternate approach, the Fitts paradigm was changed to examine the speed–accuracy effects in tasks that require a single, aimed movement—requiring mainly *preprogrammed* actions.

The Single-Aiming, Constrained Movement-Time Paradigm

The revised paradigm used rapid single-aiming movements of a stylus from a starting position to a target 10 to 60 cm away (Schmidt et al., 1978; Schmidt, Zelaznik, Hawkins, Frank, & Quinn, 1979). But rather than moving as quickly as possible, as in the Fitts and Peterson (1964) experiment, the subjects were asked to complete the movement in a particular *goal movement time (MT)* that was specified by the experimenter. As well, the movements were aimed at a thin target line that did not change in width *(W)*. Thus, both timing accuracy *and* amplitude *(A)* accuracy were required of subjects. Performance of the goal MT was achieved with augmented feedback after each trial about whether the movement was

too fast or slow. Only those movements that conformed to the goal MT (i.e., movements that were within ±10% of the MT goal) were used for analysis.

One experiment used a factorial combination of three movement amplitudes (10, 20, or 30 cm) and three goal MTs (140, 170, and 200 ms), resulting in nine different combinations of A and MT, performed by subjects in separate sessions. Errors were measured as the within-subject standard deviation (SD) of the movement amplitudes, which defined the "spread" or inconsistency of movements aimed at the target (see chapter 2). In keeping with the Fitts tradition, these errors are termed *effective target width* (W_e), which defines the effective size of the "target the subject is using" when moving with a particular MT and A. Notice also that this paradigm is different from the Fitts paradigm in that W_e is the dependent variable, with A and MT being the independent variables; in the Fitts paradigm, MT is the dependent variable, and A and W are the independent variables.

Figure 7.5 shows a plot of W_e for the various combinations of A and MT. There was a clear increase in variability as A increased; the effect was almost linear for the various MTs studied. Also, W_e increased systematically for any given movement distance as the MT decreased. Both increasing A with MT fixed, and decreasing MT with A fixed, imply increases in average velocity

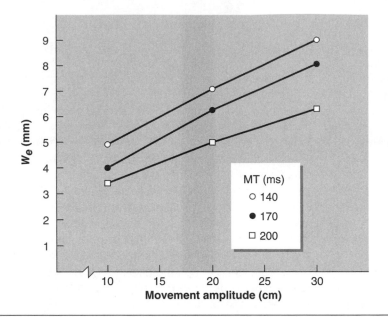

FIGURE 7.5 Effective target width *(W_e)* in a rapid single-aiming task as a function of the movement time (MT) and movement distance.

Reprinted, by permission, from R.A. Schmidt et al., 1979, "Motor-output variability: A theory for the accuracy of rapid motor acts," *Psychological Review* 86: 425. Copyright © 1979 by the American Psychological Association.

(in cm/s). Thus, we can see these data as another example of the principle that increasing movement velocity decreases spatial accuracy (as in Fitts' law), but for very rapid movements in the case of these movements.

This speed–accuracy trade-off can be seen somewhat more easily in figure 7.6, where W_e in figure 7.5 has been plotted as a function of the average velocity, defined as A/MT. Now the relationship between W_e and A/MT is nearly *linear* across a range of movement velocities, and most of the individual data points fall reasonably close to a line of best fit. Thus, the data in figure 7.6 can be expressed in terms of a linear equation in which

$$W_e = a + b \,(A \,/\, MT) \qquad (7.3)$$

For the data in figure 7.6, the value of a (the intercept) was 2.12 mm, and the value of b (the slope) was 0.033 mm for one-unit increases in cm/s. Notice that for very different amplitudes and movement times, but with the ratio of A and MT about the same, the W_e was also about the same.

These effects have been produced in a number of separate experiments using various tasks—even using eye movements (Abrams, Meyer, & Kornblum, 1989; Patla, Frank, Allard, & Thomas, 1985). This linear speed–accuracy trade-off effect

is stable enough for some to name it a law of rapid actions (e.g., Flach, Guisinger, & Robison, 1996; Jagacinski & Flach, 2003; Keele, 1986; Sanders & McCormick, 1993).[1]

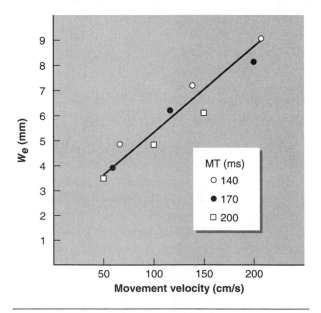

FIGURE 7.6 Effective target width *(W_e)* as a function of the average velocity (*A* / MT).

Reprinted, by permission, from R.A. Schmidt et al., 1979, "Motor-output variability: A theory for the accuracy of rapid motor acts," *Psychological Review* 86: 425. Copyright © 1979 by the American Psychological Association.

Relationship to Fitts' Law

The variables in the single-aiming paradigm are essentially the same as those in the Fitts paradigm (but used slightly differently, as we have seen); and yet the speed–accuracy trade-off is considerably different—*logarithmic* in the Fitts paradigm, and *linear* in the single-aiming paradigm. What are the crucial conditions responsible for producing these two different trade-off functions? Two hypotheses have been suggested, which are related to the key differences between the two paradigms.

Feedback Hypothesis

Remember that the linear speed–accuracy trade-off has been found using single-aiming movement tasks in which the total MT is very brief—probably less than the amount of time required to detect that an error has been made and to issue a correction (e.g., 200 ms or less in the data from Schmidt et al., 1979, in figures 7.5 and 7.6). One obvious hypothesis is that the logarithmic trade-off occurs for movements that are at least partially governed by *feedback-based corrections* (e.g., the Fitts task), whereas the linear trade-off occurs for tasks that are entirely *preprogrammed*. In this view, the two trade-off functions are not in "competition," but rather are functions that describe different emphases on movement control—open-loop versus closed-loop emphases.

This does *not* mean, however, that Fitts' law holds for movements with long MTs and that the linear trade-off holds for movements with short MTs. Whereas MT is certainly a factor in determining whether a movement will or will not be preprogrammed, the hypothesis is that MT provides a *lower limit* for feedback control; that is, movements with very short MTs cannot be under closed-loop control. However, movements with long MTs could be under open-loop control provided that the environment is stable, the task is well learned, errors are not too "costly," and so on. For example, Zelaznik, Shapiro, and McColsky (1981) found that 500 ms movements showed a linear trade-off.

Movement-Time Goal Hypothesis

Another obvious difference between the paradigms that produce the logarithmic and the linear speed–accuracy trade-offs is the intended goal MT. The single-aiming paradigm uses *con-trolled* MTs (i.e., MT goals that are longer than the subjects' minimum MT), whereas in the Fitts paradigm the MT goal is to be as fast as possible while maintaining a high accuracy rate. Some have suggested that requiring the subject to achieve a particular MT goal, per se, causes the shift to a linear speed–accuracy trade-off (Meyer, Smith, & Wright, 1982; Wright & Meyer, 1983). Some evidence favoring this view has been reported by Zelaznik, Mone, McCabe, and Thaman (1988), who found that a relaxation of the *precision* demands in matching the MT goal diminished the strength of the linear speed–accuracy relationship.

What effects might the MT goal have on the motor control processes in these two paradigms? Although the control mechanisms will be the focus of discussion later in this chapter, it is important to note at this point that the single-aiming, MT goal paradigm encourages subjects to adopt a noncorrected, single-impulse control strategy, whereas the ballistic (minimized MT) goal requirements of the Fitts task often result in one or more corrective actions (Jagacinski & Flach, 2003; Meyer, Abrams, Kornblum, Wright, & Smith, 1988; Meyer, Smith, Kornblum, Abrams, & Wright, 1990).

Impressive support for this hypothesis was provided in a clever experiment by Carlton (1994) in which corrective submovements were examined in two movement tasks. Subjects produced a 400 ms goal MT in one task (a timed task), and moved as rapidly as possible in the other task (a ballistic task). For each subject, the dispersion of 95% of the aimed movements in the timed task was used to manufacture the target plate for the ballistic task; that is, a within-subject measure of variability in one task (W_e) was used to determine the size (W) of that subject's target in the other task. With the spatial accuracy demands of each task now closely equated, Carlton found that the ballistic task condition resulted in corrective submovements on 93% of the trials, whereas corrections occurred on less than 20% of trials in the timed task. This difference in the frequency of corrective submovements between the two tasks is even more impressive when one considers that, in the timing task, MT was about 90 ms *longer* than in the ballistic task: If MT were the sole determinant of corrective submovements here, then presumably there should have been more time available for a correction to occur in the timed task.

Thus, it appears that the feedback and the MT goal hypotheses converge on a similar issue regarding the difference between the linear and logarithmic speed–accuracy trade-offs. A linear trade-off appears to occur in movement tasks that encourage a preprogrammed, open-loop control process; a logarithmic trade-off occurs in the performance of tasks that encourage closed-loop, corrective processes. The nature of these control strategies is described in more detail later in this chapter.

The Temporal Speed–Accuracy Trade-Off

Certainly the view is widespread that when we do things faster, we do them less precisely; and, as we have seen in the previous sections, there is considerable evidence to support it. However, the evidence that we have considered so far describes the trade-off that occurs in reference to *spatial* accuracy. What happens when the focus is on *temporal* accuracy? We deal with these situations next.

Discrete Anticipation-Timing Tasks

In tasks requiring anticipation and timing, such as hitting a baseball, the individual must monitor the environmental situation (the flight of the ball) and decide when to swing so that the bat arrives at the plate at nearly the same time as the ball. In chapter 3 we mentioned that these tasks require both *receptor anticipation* (of the ball flight) and *effector anticipation* (of one's internal movement processes). Errors in *timing* result if the bat arrives earlier or later than the ball. What is the effect on errors in timing of increasing the speed (decreasing the MT) of the limb or bat?

Early research on this topic (Schmidt, 1967, 1969b) required subjects to move a slide along a trackway so that an attached pointer would "hit" a target moving rapidly at right angles to the trackway (see figure 7.7), with a follow-through permitted. Accuracy in this task was measured as errors in time—either early or late with respect to the target arrival. Subjects were asked to make a movement that was of "maximal" or "moderate" speed, and four movement distances (15, 30, 45, and 60 cm) were used.

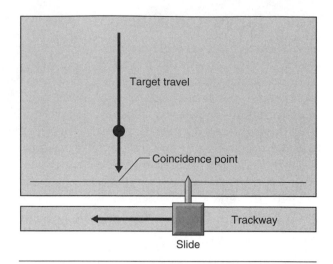

FIGURE 7.7   A coincident-timing task (top view). (A target on a belt moves directly toward the subject, who attempts to move the pointer so that the two "coincide" at the coincidence point.)

Reprinted, by permission, from R.A. Schmidt, 1967, *Motor factors in coincident timing*. Unpublished doctoral dissertation (Urbana, IL: University of Illinois).

In table 7.1, the absolute errors in timing are given as a function of four movement distances (15, 30, 45, and 60 cm) and two movement-speed instructions (to move either at a maximal speed or at a moderate speed). Notice that the absolute error in timing (for any movement distance) was uniformly smaller (20% on the average) for the "maximal" instruction than for the "moderate" instruction. Thus, when the person was performing the task more "violently," with a smaller MT and larger movement velocity, the timing accuracy in these conditions actually *improved*. Such findings seem to contradict the notion of the speed–accuracy trade-off as discussed previously in this chapter.

At least two explanations for these effects are possible. First, when the person moved the handle more rapidly, the movement was initiated when the target was closer to the coincidence point than was the case when the movement was slower. That is, the subject waited longer before initiating the rapid movement. This extra time to view the stimulus may have provided a more accurate receptor anticipation (the estimate of when the target would arrive at the coincidence point), which would permit a more precise estimate of when the person should initiate the movement.

A second explanation is that the rapid movements themselves were more consistent than the

TABLE 7.1. MT, Absolute Error in Timing, and Variable Error in MT as a Function of Movement Distance and Instructions in a Timing Task

| Movement distance | MOVEMENT SPEED INSTRUCTIONS | | | | | |
| | MAXIMAL | | | MODERATE | | |
	MT	AE	MT VE	MT	AE	MT VE
15 cm	76	20	3	139	24	9
30 cm	123	23	7	209	27	13
45 cm	144	25	7	253	30	12
60 cm	206	28	9	274	41	13
Averages	137	24.0	6.5	219	30.5	11.7

Note. AE = absolute error; MT VE = variable error of MT; all measured in milliseconds.
Adapted from Schmidt 1967, 1969c.

slower moves. The variable error (the within-subject SD as discussed in chapter 2) of the MTs (see table 7.1) was about 44% smaller for the rapid movements than for the slower ones. Thus, a second feature of fast movements is more *temporal stability* from trial to trial than for slower movements. This can be seen as an effector anticipation advantage: The person can predict with greater accuracy when the limb will arrive at the target if the movement is rapid because the trial-to-trial variability in the movement's travel time is smaller.

Discrete Movement-Timing Tasks

Newell, Hoshizaki, Carlton, and Halbert (1979) performed a number of experiments on the temporal consistency of movement, and they provided perhaps the best documentation of the effects of MT on discrete timing. They used a ballistic-timing task in which the subject moved a slide along a trackway. The initial movement started a timer, and passing a switch along the trackway stopped the timer. The subject's primary goal was to produce a specific goal MT. Newell and colleagues used a number of MTs (ranging from 100 to 1,000 ms) combined with a number of movement distances (ranging from 0.75 to 15 cm), as can be seen in table 7.2.

The primary dependent measure of interest was the variable error in timing (VE_t), defined as the within-subject SD of the MTs about the subject's own mean, which represents a measure of an individual's inconsistency in timing. As shown in table 7.2, for the 5 cm movements, the inconsistency in movement timing increased markedly as the MT increased from 100 to 1,000 ms (VE_t increased from 10.8 to 125.7 ms). The effect was similar for the 15 cm movements, with VE_t increasing from 9.0 to 91.2 ms. Thus, it appears that this effect is like that seen in anticipation timing (Schmidt, 1967, 1969b); a shorter MT, given the same distance, produces *increased* movement-timing consistency.

TABLE 7.2. Errors in Timing as a Function of Movement Distance and MT

| | MT (ms) | | | | | |
	100		500		1,000	
Distance (cm)	5	15	5	15	5	15
Velocity (cm/s)	50	150	10	30	5	15
Ve_t (ms)	10.8	9.0	74.6	42.8	125.7	91.2
Ve_t/MT%	10.8	9.0	14.9	8.6	12.6	9.1

From Newell et al. 1979.

An even more interesting feature of these findings is that the timing error is *proportional* to the MT. In the fourth line of table 7.2 are the VE_t values divided by the MTs, multiplied by 100 to convert them to percentage values. If the VE_t is proportional to MT, then the $VE_t/MT\%$ values will be similar for any MT from 100 to 1,000 ms. Indeed, this is essentially what happened—the $VE_t/MT\%$ values ranged between 8.6% and 14.9% for all of the combinations of MTs and distances.

This effect of MT can perhaps be thought of as one that follows from the generally held view that short intervals of time are "easier" to estimate or produce than are long intervals of time. To illustrate, do this simple experiment. First, take a stopwatch and, without looking, estimate 1 s (1,000 ms) by pressing the button and releasing it at the appropriate time. Record the actual time for each of 10 trials. Now, do the same task again but use a target interval of 2 s (2,000 ms). You should find that the shorter interval is much "easier" to produce accurately; you should be much closer, on the average, to the target interval with the 1,000 ms task than with the 2,000 ms task. And, if you had calculated VEs for your performances, your VE for the 2,000 ms task should be roughly twice that for the 1,000 ms task. The processes responsible for determining the duration of the intervals are variable, and they seem to be variable in direct proportion to the *amount* of time that is to be produced. Because the movements in the experiments of Newell and colleagues (1979) were, in effect, based on processes that take time, it is reasonable that they should have been variable in time in nearly direct proportion to the amount of time that they occupied.

There is considerable evidence that, generally speaking, the VE_t (or inconsistency) in the production of some interval of time tends to be a nearly constant proportion of the amount of time to be produced, at least within broad limits. For example, Michon (1967) found essentially this effect with rhythmic tapping at different rates; Gottsdanker (1970) found the effect for RT (with subjects who had long RTs having greater within-subject VE_t of their own RTs); and Schmidt and colleagues (1979) found these effects for aiming tasks in which the MTs were controlled. This well-documented finding is an apparent contradiction to the speed–accuracy principles described previously in this chapter. Here, increased speed (by decreasing the MT) produces increases in accuracy in *timing*, whereas earlier we showed that increasing the speed resulted in diminished *spatial* accuracy. The finding that variability in timing is proportional to the duration of the interval to be timed is consistent with a long-held finding in the psychology literature called *Weber's law*.

Temporal Consistency and Movement Velocity

The MT is not the only factor that strongly affects the VE_t—the movement's average velocity (i.e., the movement distance divided by the MT, usually in cm/s) has a strong influence as well. Refer again to table 7.2 (Newell et al., 1979) and consider the VE_t for the various values of movement velocity (second line in the table). Notice that for a given MT (e.g., 100 ms), the movement with the smaller movement distance, and hence the lower movement velocity, has a slightly higher VE_t (10.8 ms for the 5 cm movement, 9.0 ms for the 15 cm movement). This effect is even stronger for the 500 ms and 1,000 ms movements in the same table; the movement with the higher velocity had a smaller timing error, even when the MT was held constant.

To see this effect expressed another way, examine the $VE_t/MT\%$ values presented on the bottom line of table 7.2. Because the division by MT theoretically "cancels out" the effects of MT on the timing error (since these two variables are nearly proportional), any changes in $VE_t/MT\%$ as a function of movement velocity must be due to something *other than* MT. Here, the movements with the longer movement distance (and hence the greater movement velocity) have smaller $VE_t/MT\%$ values. For the three MTs, these values were about 9% for the 15 cm movements and from 10% to 14% for the 5 cm movements. Increasing movement velocity made the movements more consistent in terms of time.

Newell, Carlton, Carlton, and Halbert (1980) studied these velocity effects in experiments that were more thorough than those reported in the earlier paper (see Newell, 1980, for a review). Various movement distances (ranging from 1.5 to 67.5 cm) and MTs (ranging from 100 to 600 ms) were used in combination, producing a set of velocity values that ranged from 5 cm/s to 225 cm/s. The timing inconsistency (VE_t) was studied as a function of these variations in velocity; we have converted these data to the $VE_t/MT\%$ measure here so that they can be compared to the findings in the previous section (see table 7.2). The 1980 data of Newell and colleagues (experiment 3) are shown in figure 7.8, where the $VE_t/MT\%$ is plotted against movement velocity. As the velocity increased, the errors in timing decreased markedly at low velocities, and decreased more gradually with further increases in velocity. Similar effects have been seen in experiments involving wider ranges in velocities and distances (Newell, Carlton, Kim, & Chung, 1993; Jasiewicz & Simmons, 1996). This *velocity effect* is yet another example of the temporal speed–accuracy trade-off.

An interesting application of these findings relates to baseball: As a batter swings "harder" (with a smaller MT, a larger movement distance, or both), the errors in timing should tend to decrease, not increase. Note that this prediction is for errors in *timing* and does not relate to errors in *spatial* accuracy; we consider these issues in more detail later in the chapter.

Repetitive Movement-Timing Tasks

The finding that movement duration becomes more consistent in time as the MT decreases has been shown in tasks in which the subject makes a discrete movement with the intention of achieving a specific goal MT. A similar finding also exists for tasks in which the subjects make a repetitive series of timed movements. For example, Schmidt and colleagues (1978, 1979) studied this problem by having subjects make rhythmic back-and-forth movements of a lever in time to a metronome. The subject exerted timed forces with a strain gauge on the handle. There were four different goal MTs (200, 300, 400, and 500 ms), and the major concern was the variability in the duration of the force bursts (i.e., impulses) produced by muscular action during these movements. The results of this experiment are illustrated in figure 7.9, where the within-subject variability in impulse duration is plotted against the MT imposed by the metronome. The strong, nearly proportional relation found between these two variables is certainly in keeping with the data presented in the previous section about movement durations as a whole.

Synchronization and Continuation Tasks

The back-and-forth, force-burst task used in the studies by Schmidt and colleagues (1978, 1979) represents a variation of repetitive timing tasks that have been studied for over a century (e.g., Bartlett & Bartlett, 1959; Dunlap, 1910; Stevens, 1886; Woodrow, 1932). There are two fundamental versions of this task. The subject's goal in the

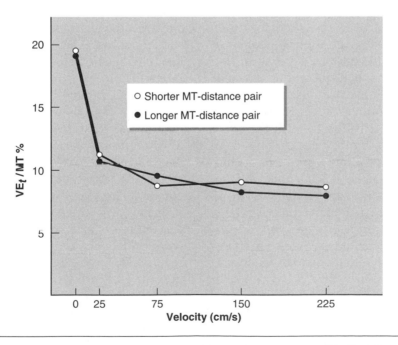

FIGURE 7.8 VE_t (expressed as $VE_t / MT\%$) as a function of the movement velocity. (Dividing VE_t by MT theoretically "cancels out" the effect of MT on errors.)

Adapted from Newell et al. 1980.

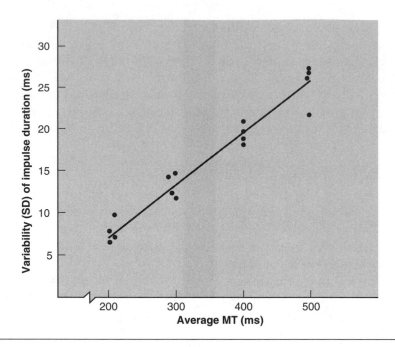

FIGURE 7.9 Variability in impulse duration as a function of the movement time (MT).

Reprinted, by permission, from R.A. Schmidt, H.N. Zelaznik, and J.S. Frank, 1978, Sources of inaccuracy in rapid movement. *Information processing in motor control and learning*, edited by G.E. Stelmach (Champaign, IL: Human Kinetics), 197.

synchronization task is to produce a motor action (such as a finger movement) resulting in a "tap" that coincides with an external perceptible event (such as the auditory beeps of a metronome). In the *continuation task* (Stevens, 1886), a typical trial begins with a series of synchronization taps; then at some point the experimenter turns off the pacing stimulus (e.g., metronome), and the subject's goal is to continue tapping at the same pace. Both the synchronization task and the continuation task have been used in numerous investigations of human motor performance.

One of the curious findings with the synchronization task is a *negative asynchrony*—that is, subjects tend to produce taps prior to the pacing tones. Aschersleben's (2002) review of the evidence shows that the asynchrony is larger in musically untrained than in trained subjects and that the amount of asynchrony can be reduced with practice and augmented feedback (see chapter 12). The suggestion is that negative asynchronies arise due to a closed-loop process in which feedback from the motor output is compared to the auditory stream from the pacing stimulus. If the feedback information is processed more slowly than the pacing-stimulus information, a tap must be produced sooner in order for the central representations of the two auditory

consequences to be perceived as synchronous. Alternative, viable hypotheses exist, however, and the negative-asynchrony effect continues to stimulate a vibrant research area (e.g., Mates & Aschersleben, 2000; Repp, 2001, 2005).

In some respects the continuation task may be considered a simpler version of timing than the synchronization task, in that there is no objective, pacing stimulus to anticipate. For example, Balasubramaniam, Wing, and Daffertshofer (2004) found that movement trajectories were quite "smooth" when subjects produced finger taps in the absence of a pacing signal (see top illustrations in figure 7.10). In contrast, producing finger taps in time with a metronome, either "on the beat" (synchronizing) or "off the beat" (syncopation), resulted in considerable asymmetry in terms of the kinematics. As seen in the middle and bottom illustrations in figure 7.10, the downward deflections of the finger to produce a tap, regardless of whether they were made on or off the beat, were produced much faster than upward movements. These asymmetries were associated with timing accuracy, possibly indicating the use of velocity changes as an error correction strategy (Balasubramaniam, 2006).

However, in other respects the continuation task is more complex than the synchronization

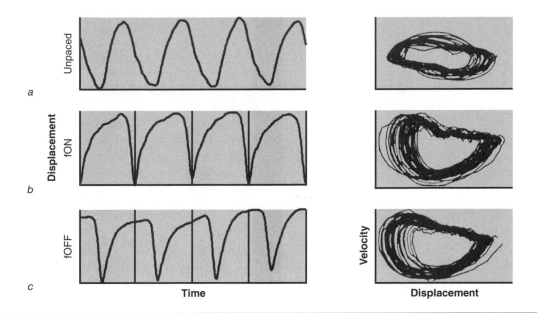

FIGURE 7.10 Finger trajectories in three timing tasks. *(a)* Top figures illustrate a typical position–time graph (left side) and velocity–position graph (right side) for an unpaced tapping condition; *(b)* middle figures illustrate tapping on the beat; and *(c)* bottom figures illustrate tapping off the beat. The top figures illustrate trajectory symmetry, while the middle and bottom figures illustrate much faster velocities in the tap portion of the movement cycle.

With kind permission from Springer Science+Business Media: *Experimental Brain Research*, "Keeping with the beat: Movement trajectories contribute to movement timing," Vol. 159, 2004, pgs. 129-134, R. Balasubramaniam, A.M. Wing, and A. Daffertshofer.

task. In the absence of the pacing stimulus, the subject must establish a central representation of time and adjust performance based on a memory for the pacing rate. Much of the research in the past four decades has been based on an open-loop, hierarchical model of timing performance using the continuation task, which we consider next.

The Wing-Kristofferson Hierarchical Timing Model

Recall that in the continuation task, a subject synchronizes a particular movement (e.g., a tap) with a series of paced tones. After 20 or so tones have been presented, the metronome is stopped and the subject continues to produce 30 or so more taps. Performance of these latter taps is of primary interest. As we have noted several times previously in the chapter, variability in timing is related closely to the MTs of these intertap intervals. As the mean intertap interval decreases, the overall consistency increases. However, something else goes on here as well. In Stevens' (1886) original experiment, a slower intertap interval tended to be followed by one that was faster, and vice versa (e.g., see description in Wing, 1980, and figure 4.2 in Vorberg & Wing, 1996). In other

words, the *adjacent* intertap intervals were found to vary inversely with each other (i.e., they demonstrated a negative covariance or correlation), although intervals that were separated by two or more intervening (i.e., not adjacent) intervals were independent of each other (i.e., they had a covariance of zero).

To account for these and other observations in continuation timing, Wing and Kristofferson (1973b) developed an open-loop, hierarchical model of performance, illustrated in figure 7.11. There are two levels in the hierarchy: a *central timekeeper level* and a *motor implementation level*. The model states that, in the absence of a pacing stimulus, a centrally generated "internal clock" sends pulses via the central nervous system that result in the execution of a movement (e.g., a tap). The internal clock—which can be thought of as similar to the timing generated by the motor program (chapter 6)—is responsible for generating the desired goal durations (C_i); the resulting times between successive taps are the intertap intervals (ITI_i). Any variability in the rate at which the clock times the pulses (or intervals) will result in ITI variance that has a central source. There is a delay, however, from the time a central command is issued until a tap is produced by the motor system.

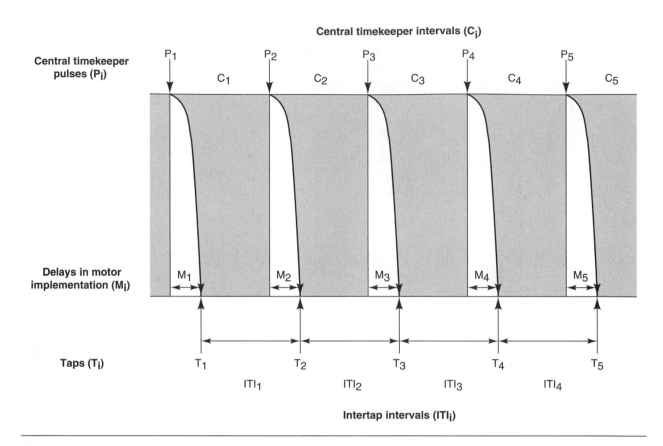

Central timekeeper intervals (C_i)

Central timekeeper pulses (P_i)

Delays in motor implementation (M_i)

Taps (T_i)

Intertap intervals (ITI_i)

FIGURE 7.11   The Wing-Kristofferson hierarchical model of timing. A high-level, central timekeeper produces pulses (e.g., P_i, P_{i+1}, etc.) that generate a time interval (C_i). The duration of each observed intertap interval (ITI_i) is influenced by the C_i and the delays in implementing the motor activity that initiate (M_i) and terminate (M_{i+1}) the ITI. Measures of variability in timing are observed and estimated using statistical techniques.

Adapted from *Tutorials in motor behavior*, A.M. Wing, pgs. 469-486, The long and short of timing in response sequences, edited by G.E. Stelmach and J. Requin, Copyright 1980. By permission of A.M. Wing.

In fact, each ITI is affected by *two* motor implementation delays, because one tap defines the *initiation* of the ITI (M_i) and the next tap defines the *termination* of the ITI (M_{i+1}). Viewed another way, any one motor delay (e.g., M_2) will have an influence on both the preceding interval (ITI_1) and the succeeding interval (ITI_2). Thus, a short M_2 will tend to shorten the preceding ITI and lengthen the next ITI. So, a second source of variation at the motor delay level can add variability to the observed ITIs that is independent of the clock variability. Wing and Kristofferson developed statistical methods for estimating the value of the clock variance and the motor delay variance.

Factors Affecting Clock and Motor Variance

Figure 7.12 presents data from Wing (1980), in which the variance associated with the duration of the ITI has been decomposed into measures of clock variance and motor implementation variance. As the figure illustrates, the variability due to motor implementation processes contributes very little to the total, and the effect is almost entirely due to variability in central (clock) processes.[2]

Wing (2002) has summarized a large number of studies in which processes affecting clock and motor implementation variances were separated. For example, factors such as the age of the subject (Greene & Williams, 1993) and increased cognitive demands due to a secondary task (Sergent, Hellige, & Cherry, 1993) greatly influenced clock variance but had no effect on motor variance. Compared to unimanual tapping performance, adding a second limb so that both limbs are tapping together in continuation has the effect of reducing the ITI variance, almost all of it due to the reduction in clock variance (Drewing & Aschersleben, 2003; Helmuth & Ivry,

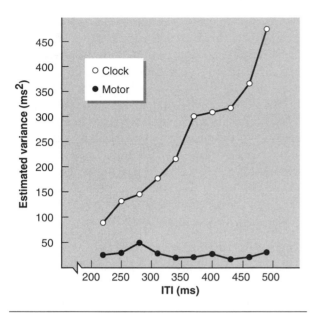

FIGURE 7.12 The effects of the intertap interval (ITI) duration on clock and motor variance.

Adapted from *Tutorials in motor behaviour*, A.M. Wing, pgs. 469-486, The long and short of timing in response sequences, edited by G.E. Stelmach and J. Requin, Copyright 1980. By permission of A.M. Wing.

1996). Interestingly, though, if hand tapping is paired with foot tapping, then clock variance is reduced while motor variance actually increases (Ivry, Richardson, & Helmuth, 2002). Additional practice does reduce motor variance, but not clock variance (Drewing & Aschersleben, 2003). If the length of one of the "effectors" is altered in bimanual timing, then only motor variability is affected (Turvey, Schmidt, & Rosenblum, 1989). The Wing-Kristofferson model has also been useful in contrasting the influence of neural disorders on timing in various patient groups. For example, Ivry, Keele, and Diener (1988) found that patients with one type of lesion in the cerebellum showed increased clock variance whereas another group, with lesions in a different part of the cerebellum, showed elevation only in motor variance.

The Wing-Kristofferson model has proven useful in identifying dissociations in motor timing, which is a very important contribution to understanding processes in motor control. Although various alterations to the model have been proposed over the years (e.g., Collier & Ogden, 2004; Vorberg & Wing, 1996), the original Wing-Kristofferson model remains a powerful and important research tool in studies of motor timing.

Two Types of Timing?

Most of the studies discussed in this section have considered timing tasks involving the tapping of a finger in time to a metronome that either is currently present or was present in the recent past (i.e., Stevens' and Wing-Kristofferson's synchronization and continuation tasks). Timing has been considered to be *explicit* in these tasks in the sense that the nature of the task and the subject's internal timing processes represent compatible goals—the "environment" specifies a time goal that the subject tries to match with specifically timed movements. In studies of individual differences in timing ability, Robertson and colleagues (1999) found that people who are consistent timers for slow tapping rates (e.g., 800 ms per tap) are also consistent timers for fast rates (e.g., 400 ms per tap). That is, the within-trial variabilities in tapping are similar among individuals for the two tasks, resulting in high correlations between people—timing appears to be a type of *general ability* (see also the section "Exceptions to Henry's Specificity Hypothesis" on p. 305). In contrast to this tapping timing task is a circle-drawing timing task (e.g., Robertson et al., 1999), in which subjects produce circles continuously with a defined completion cycle time (e.g., 400 or 800 ms for each revolution). Again, high interindividual correlations exist for the variances in producing timed circles at different cycling rates. However, there is *no correlation* between timed taps and timed circles, suggesting that these two tasks represent different fundamental timing processes. This suggestion is supported by studies involving patients with cerebellar damage, who revealed deficits in performing tapping timing tasks but not circle timing tasks (Spencer, Zelaznik, Diedrichsen, & Ivry, 2003). These and related findings support a dissociation of processes involving these two types of timing tasks (e.g., Studenka & Zelaznik, 2008; Torre & Balasubramaniam, 2009; Zelaznik et al., 2005).

Central Contributions to the Spatial Speed–Accuracy Trade-Off

To this point in the chapter we have presented three relatively different ways in which speed and accuracy are related. Two of these pertain to spatial trade-offs, and one pertains to a temporal trade-off. Some theoretical issues related to timing were presented in the last section, and others will be discussed in more detail in chapter 8. In this section, we concentrate on the spatial trade-off. Two general perspectives have dominated much of the thinking; these perspectives correspond in general to the topics discussed in chapters 5 and 6. With regard to the generation of an impulse to propel a limb toward a target, one perspective has been to consider the importance of *central* contributions. The other perspective has been to examine how *corrective* processes contribute to the speed–accuracy trade-off. In the following sections we discuss the major ideas that have been suggested within these general theoretical approaches.

Keele (1981, 1986) suggested that central processing of rapid aiming movements can be classified under two broad categories. In one category, the thinking is that central commands specify the *distance* that must be traveled to reach a target. Distance programming is assumed by models of impulse variability, whereby the agonist and antagonist muscles produce bursts of force (open loop) that propel a limb a specific goal distance. The other general class of models assumes a programming of commands that specifies a target's *location*. Location programming is assumed by a class of models that specify equilibrium–tension ratios between agonist and antagonist muscle groups.

Impulse-Variability Theory

A number of the principles related to the linear speed–accuracy trade-off form the basis for impulse-variability models of movement control. Two principles are of critical importance: (a) The variability in the *duration* of a group of muscular contractions is directly proportional to the mean duration; and (b) the variability in *force* applied in a group of attempts is an increasing function of the mean force to approximately 65% of maximum, with a leveling off or slight decrease thereafter. The reason these principles have such importance is that they define variability in the two dimensions of the *impulse*—the primary determinant of what the limb will do when muscles attached to it are activated. The notion of the impulse, that is, the forces produced over time, was discussed in chapter 6 (section on the impulse-timing hypothesis). So if, as we have argued earlier, the

impulse is a critical determiner of movement, and variability in impulses is a critical determiner of the variability in movement, then an analysis of the variability of the components of the impulse (variability in force and variability in duration) should allow considerable insight into the sources of spatial errors in movement control—at least in relatively quick actions where feedback processes do not play a major role. Schmidt and colleagues provided the early modeling of these phenomena (Schmidt et al., 1978, 1979), and revisions of the same idea were provided later by Meyer and colleagues (Meyer et al., 1982, 1988).

Force-Variability Principles

In this section we consider factors that produce variability in the amount of force generated by the activation of the motor program. This is an important issue for understanding the processes underlying skillful behavior. All that the muscles can do to bones is to exert force on them, with this application being adjustable in terms of amount of force or in terms of the temporal onset and duration of that force. Complex patterns of force produced *during* a particular contraction are presumably also under the control of the motor system. If the activation sent to the muscles is preprogrammed, then any factors causing the amount of force to deviate from the intended amount of force will cause the movement to deviate from its intended path or fail to meet its goal. Put simply, *muscular forces produce movements, and variability in muscular forces produces variability in movements.*

Schmidt and colleagues (1978, 1979) began a series of studies on the relationship between forces involved in quick, preprogrammed movements and their within-subject variability, and these findings are described next. In relation to slower movements, there has been some interest in these questions for over a century (e.g., Fullerton & Cattell, 1892; see Newell, Carlton, & Hancock, 1984, for a review), although the theoretical orientations of this earlier work were considerably different. The initial issue addressed in the studies by Schmidt and colleagues concerned the relationship between the amount of force produced and the resulting within-subject variability in that force. For example, why did an aiming movement with twice the amplitude (MT constant) produce approximately twice the error in hitting a target (e.g., Schmidt, et al., 1979;

Woodworth, 1899)? According to the generalized motor program (GMP) idea (chapter 6), in order to produce a movement of twice the amplitude, the program would remain the same, but the overall force parameter would be increased so that the limb would travel twice the distance in the same MT. Could it be that when the forces in the limb are increased so that the limb can travel farther, the variability in this force is increased as well, making the output of the movement more variable? This was the hypothesis.

Moderate Force Levels   The subject's task was to produce quick "shots" of force against an immovable handle. Attached to the handle was a strain gauge that measured the amount of force applied; this information was sent to an oscilloscope screen so that the subject could see the force levels. A zero-force level was indicated at the bottom of the screen, and increasing force applied to the handle would move the dot upward. Subjects attempted to produce ballistic "shots" of force that would peak exactly at a target location on the screen, the goal being to produce the same peak force on each trial. The peak force and the within-subject variability (SD) of the peak forces were measured; subjects were asked to produce different amounts of force during separate series of trials.

In figure 7.13, the SD in peak force is plotted as a function of the amount of force the subjects were asked to produce. A clear linear relationship between force and its variability can be seen. In a number of other experiments, force and force variability were found to be linearly related in situations in which the forces were much smaller than indicated in figure 7.13 (40 g elbow flexion measured at the wrist) and also when they were as large as 65% of the subject's maximum (Newell & Carlton, 1985; Schmidt et al., 1978, 1979; Sherwood & Schmidt, 1980).

These results were from static (isometric) contractions, though, and it was not clear that such relationships would occur in actual *movements*, in which the muscle shortens as it is producing force against the bone. Sherwood and Schmidt (1980) examined this issue in an experiment in which forces were recorded during a simple ballistic-timing movement. Again, a linear relationship between force and force variability was found, suggesting that this principle had a strong role in movements. These data certainly supported

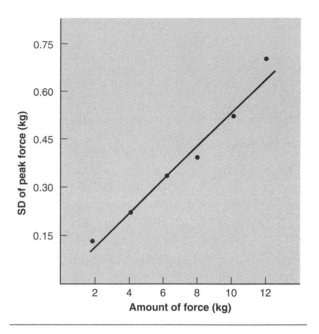

FIGURE 7.13   Variability in peak static force as a function of the amount of force to be produced.

Reprinted, by permission, from R.A. Schmidt, H.N. Zelaznik, and J.S. Frank, 1978, Sources of inaccuracy in rapid movement. *Information processing in motor control and learning*, edited by G.E. Stelmach (Champaign, IL: Human Kinetics), 197.

the speculation that, as the amount of force was increased (in order, for example, to move farther in the same MT), the variability in force would increase in nearly direct proportion, leading to increased variability in the movement's spatial outcome—in this case, in hitting a target accurately.

Near-Maximal Force Levels   Will the linear relationship between force and force variability continue to hold as the forces are increased even further? This is an important question, as many of the skills performed by athletes have very high force requirements, such as those for the forces in the quadriceps muscles generated during a football punt for distance. With such large forces, one might expect that there would be no "room" for variability near the performer's maximum. If the subject actually did produce the theoretical maximum on every trial, there would be no variability (because the SD of a set of constant values is zero). Thus, as the maximum force is approached, one could imagine a point of maximum force variability (perhaps near the middle of the range in force capability) and a gradual decline in force variability (i.e., more consistency) as the forces are increased further. With this reasoning, an inverted-U function should exist between force variability and force across the total range of human force capability.

Figure 7.14 presents the data from another experiment by Sherwood and Schmidt (1980), in which the forces were increased to very near the subject's maximum. The figure shows the variability in peak force as a function of the level of force produced, as before. But in this case a maximum point occurred in force variability, with a strong tendency for decreasing force variability as the forces were increased further. The peak force variability occurred, on the average, at about 65% of maximum force for these subjects; the largest force examined was about 92% of maximum.

Inverted-U or Negatively Accelerating Functions? Some controversy has developed with regard to the inverted-U function shown in figure 7.14. Newell and Carlton (1985, 1988; Carlton & Newell, 1988; Newell et al., 1984) have criticized the procedures used to obtain this inverted-U result on the grounds that the *time* to peak force was not controlled in these experiments. They showed that larger peak forces tend to be associated with a longer time to achieve peak force, and they argued that this should have the effect of producing an artificial inverted U at high force levels. In a subsequent experiment in which the time to peak force was held strictly constant, Sherwood, Schmidt, and Walter (1988) showed that the inverted-U function was no longer as pronounced as indicated in figure 7.14. Thus, perhaps rather than an inverted-U function, the relation between force and force variability follows a curvilinear, *negatively accelerated* function. Beyond about 65% of maximum force, force variability tends to increase at a decreasing rate, leveling off somewhere near the maximum force capabilities (or perhaps decreasing very slightly—Sherwood et al., 1988). Theoretical modeling of force summation characteristics by Ulrich and Wing (1991) suggests that both the inverted-U *and* the negatively accelerated functions may be correct in certain situations.

Modeling the Initial Impulse

It is easy to understand the general idea of impulse-variability principles if one considers only the initial impulse for acceleration in a rapid movement. A good example is the ballistic-timing task, in which the subject moves a slide along a trackway, past a switch at the end, and attempts to achieve a goal MT (initial movement until arrival at the switch). Here the subject is accelerating for the entire (measured) movement, so the movement is governed by the initial impulse for acceleration. When the experimenter changes either the movement amplitude *(A)* or the goal MT, the subject's movement is assumed to be handled by changes in the parameters of the GMP for this rapid action (see chapter 6). Let us examine the effect of variables like movement amplitude and movement time—critical participants in the speed–accuracy trade-off—on the nature of impulse variability in this task.[3]

The Effect of Movement Amplitude Consider what happens to the impulse as the person is asked to move twice as far in the same MT. In this case the movement-duration parameter of the GMP must be fixed, so the duration of the impulse will also be constant. However, the overall force parameter must be doubled so that the force produced will be twice as large as for the shorter movement. From the earlier section on force variability (figure 7.13), we know that as

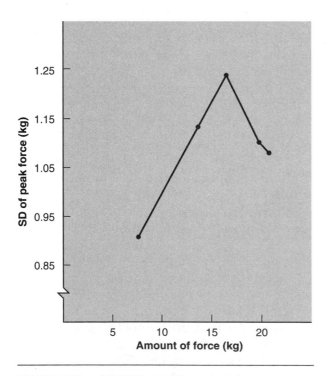

FIGURE 7.14 Variability in peak dynamic force as a function of force produced, including near-maximal force values.

Adapted from D.E. Sherwood and R.A. Schmidt, 1980, "The relationship between force and force variability in minimal and near-maximal static and dynamic contractions," *Journal of Motor Behavior* 12: 75-89, adapted with permission of the publisher (Taylor & Francis Ltd, http://www.informaworld.com).

the amount of force is doubled, the variability is approximately doubled as well. Therefore, with a doubled force but a constant duration, the entire impulse will have twice the variability, with all of the increase in variability occurring because of the changes in the amplitude of the impulse. The overall result is that the impulse variability is linearly related to the movement amplitude:

$$\text{Impulse variability} = k_1 \times (A) \qquad (7.4)$$

where k_1 is an empirical constant, and A is the movement amplitude (the intercept is zero because proportionality is assumed; see the section on empirical equations in chapter 2).

The Effect of Movement Time Next, consider what happens to the impulse as the MT is halved with a constant movement amplitude. From the notions of GMPs, we know that the overall duration parameter will be halved as well, so that all of the impulses in the action will be half their original duration. We know from figure 7.10 that the variability in the duration of an interval is directly proportional to its duration, so halving the duration of the impulse should reduce its variability *in time* by half also. Generally, the temporal variability of an impulse is linearly related to MT:

$$\text{Temporal variability} = k_2 \times (\text{MT}) \qquad (7.5)$$

where k_2 is another proportionality constant (again, the intercept is zero). This is interesting (and somewhat counterintuitive) because the variability of one component (temporal) of the impulse becomes *more* consistent as the MT is shortened, while the variability of another component (force) becomes *less* consistent at the same time.

But along with this shortening of impulse duration as the MT is halved, the impulse must increase in amplitude (force), so that the increased velocity needed for the shorter MT can be achieved. From physics we know that for a movement with twice the velocity (i.e., half the MT), the area of the impulse must be twice as large. But the duration is half as long, so the amplitude must be four times as large (i.e., four times the amplitude together with half the duration yields twice the area). Then, because of force-variability principles (figure 7.14), the force variability is increased by a factor of four as well, so that halving the MT produces a fourfold increase in the *force* component of impulse variability. More generally, the force

component of impulse variability is inversely related to the squared MT, or

$$\text{Force variability} = k_3 \times (1 \, / \, \text{MT}^2) \qquad (7.6)$$

We see that the overall impulse variability is related both (a) directly to the MT in the temporal dimension and (b) directly to $1/\text{MT}^2$ in the force dimension. Combining these two effects of impulse variability (equations 7.5 and 7.6) produces the generalization that

$$\begin{aligned}\text{Impulse variability} &= k_4 \times (\text{MT} \, / \, \text{MT}^2) \\ &= k_4 (1 \, / \, \text{MT}) \qquad (7.7)\end{aligned}$$

That is, total impulse variability is proportional to $1/\text{MT}$.

Amplitude and Movement Time When we combine the effects of A and the effects of MT from equations 7.4 and 7.7, we obtain the relation that

$$\text{Impulse variability} = k \times (A \, / \, \text{MT}) \qquad (7.8)$$

where the total variability in an impulse for accelerating a limb is directly related to the amplitude of the movement *(A)* and inversely related to the duration of the movement (MT). Because the velocity of a movement after an impulse is directly proportional to the size (area) of the impulse, and because the variability in the impulse leads directly to variability in velocity, this relation implies that the variability in the velocity of a movement when an impulse has stopped acting on it will be directly proportional to A/MT as well. This is a key feature in impulse-variability modeling, and many other interesting predictions emerge from it.

Impulse-Variability Principles in Movement Control

The original impulse-variability theory (Schmidt et al., 1978, 1979), which concerned the effects of various movement variables on initial-impulse variability, seems to account relatively well for the behavior of *single* impulses in a number of rapid movement tasks (see Schmidt, Sherwood, Zelaznik, & Leikind, 1985, for a review). As a result, the model accounts fairly well for accuracy in tasks in which only a single impulse is acting, such as the ballistic-timing tasks described at the beginning of this section.

Errors in Ballistic Timing For ballistic-timing tasks, we have already mentioned that the variable error in timing (VE$_t$) has been shown to be nearly proportional to the MT (tables 7.1 and 7.2, figure 7.8). The model also accounts for spatial errors—the error in *position* at the moment that the goal MT has elapsed, or W_e. In this case the model predicts that W_e should be independent of MT, and several experiments show this to be essentially so (e.g., Schmidt, 1994; Schmidt et al., 1979, 1985). Therefore, changing the MT affects mainly timing errors in this timing task, not spatial errors. The principle is just the opposite when *A* is manipulated in this task. Here, increasing *A* causes nearly proportional increases in spatial errors but causes almost no effect in the timing errors.[4] This seemingly curious set of findings is derivable from the model, and is related to the tight connection between space and time in such situations involving tasks in which time is the dependent variable (see, e.g., Newell, 1980; Newell et al., 1984).

Spatial Errors in Very Rapid Movements   Some applications of impulse-variability notions can be seen in a task like hitting a baseball, where the limb seems to be driven by a single impulse, with no deceleration until after the bat passes over the plate and the ball is struck. Here, in addition to being temporally accurate, the batter must be spatially accurate so that the swing will not miss the ball. We can think of such a movement as shown in figure 7.15, where the limb (or limb plus bat) is moving horizontally toward a ball. Assume that the limb is controlled by two muscle groups, A and B, each of

which pulls obliquely on it, their combined action being to move the limb toward the ball. What will be the effect on spatial accuracy of increasing the mass of the bat, with MT constant?

If muscle groups A and B are contracting with less than 65% of maximum force, then increasing the mass of the bat will require increased force output in each of them, and the force variability will increase in both muscle groups at the same time (e.g., figure 7.15). This should result in progressively larger variations in the direction of bat travel and in progressively lower probability that the bat will hit the ball. But what if the forces in the two muscle groups are larger, perhaps greater than 65% of maximum? Here, with increased mass of the bat, there would be (from data in figure 7.14) a decrease (or at least a much smaller increase) in the force variability as the forces are increased, resulting in *increased* consistency of bat travel as the mass is increased.

Schmidt and Sherwood (1982) conducted an experiment that seems to show just that. Subjects made horizontal forward arm swings to attempt to hit a target, with a MT that was to be as close to 200 ms as possible. Figure 7.16 shows the spatial accuracy in hitting the target as a function of the mass added to the handle, measured as VE and total variability (E). As mass was added to the unloaded handle, there was first an increase in spatial errors; but the function soon peaked, so

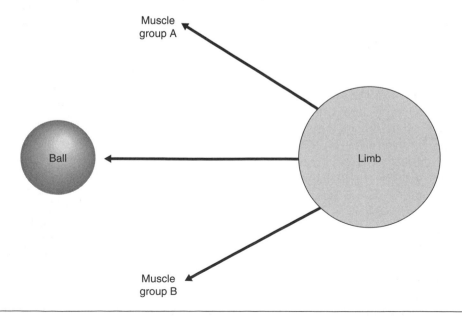

FIGURE 7.15   The limb conceptualized as a mass moved by two forces (muscles) operating in different directions.

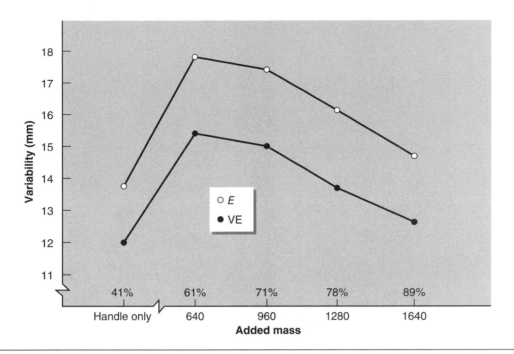

FIGURE 7.16 The effect of added mass on the spatial accuracy of a 200 ms arm swing movement. The values above the x-axis are the percentages of maximum force produced with that added mass.

Reprinted, by permission, from R.A. Schmidt and D.E. Sherwood, 1982, "An inverted-U relation between spatial error and force requirements in rapid limb movements: Further evidence for the impulse-variability model," *Journal of Experimental Psychology: Human Perception and Performance* 8: 165. Copyright © 1982 by the American Psychological Association.

that the errors decreased with further increases in mass. Thus, there was an inverted-U relation between spatial accuracy and mass for this task, with the peak at approximately the mass that resulted in about 60% to 70% of maximum force. This corresponds surprisingly well with the peak in the force/force-variability function found in figure 7.14.

A similar experiment was conducted with variations in MT, this time with the mass held constant. If decreased MT results in increases in force beyond about 65% of maximum, then we should find that making the movement faster results in increased accuracy, not less as would be expected from the speed–accuracy trade-off effect. Figure 7.17 illustrates the results. As the average MT decreased from 158 ms to about 102 ms, there was a progressive increase in the spatial errors, as one would expect. But when the MT was reduced further to 80 ms, requiring approximately 84% of maximum force, there was a decrease in the spatial errors, with the function showing a peak error somewhere near 50% of maximum contraction (102 ms MT). Again, this is compatible with the peak in the force

/force-variability function seen in figure 7.15. It is interesting to note that when the movement was very rapid and required 84% of maximum force, the amount of error was nearly the same as that in a very slow (130 ms) movement.

Both of these results provide exceptions to the speed–accuracy trade-off ideas presented earlier, as increasing speed (or increasing mass) resulted in *increased* accuracy when the movements were very violent. This supports indirectly the impulse-variability model, in which the variability in forces is expected to be a major determiner of the spatial accuracy in these rapid actions. There are also interesting practical implications. Perhaps telling a baseball player to swing slowly to "make contact" would actually result in less spatial accuracy than giving an instruction to swing "hard" (see "Principles of Motor Control Applied to Baseball Batting," where we develop this idea more fully).

Limitations of the Impulse-Variability Theory

One limitation of impulse-variability theory is that it does not account for movement accuracy in aiming tasks (e.g., the linear speed–accuracy

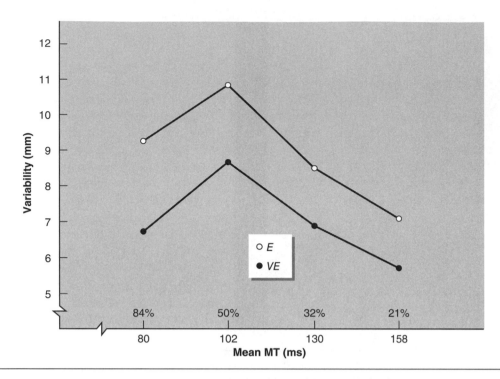

FIGURE 7.17 The effect of movement time (MT) on the spatial accuracy in a horizontal arm swing movement. The values above the x-axis are the percentages of maximum force produced with that movement time.

Reprinted, by permission, from R.A. Schmidt and D.E. Sherwood, 1982, "An inverted-U relation between spatial error and force requirements in rapid limb movements: Further evidence for the impulse-variability model," *Journal of Experimental Psychology: Human Perception and Performance* 8: 165. Copyright © 1982 by the American Psychological Association.

Principles of Motor Control Applied to Baseball Batting

We now attempt to use a number of the principles discussed in this section to understand a complex skill like batting a pitched baseball. Let us review some basic facts about hitting a baseball. In figure 7.18 are data from a number of studies referred to earlier, as well as from Hubbard and Seng (1954). Essentially, it takes about 460 ms for a ball (moving at 89 mph) to travel from the pitcher to the plate. Hubbard and Seng found that the MT of the bat (the time from the first movement of the bat until it reached the plate) was about 160 ms; this is equivalent to about 21 ft (6.4 m) of ball travel.

What would happen if the batter were to reduce the MT of the swing by 20 ms, from 160 ms to 140 ms? Of course, if contact with the ball is made, the ball travels farther and faster, which is usually beneficial in baseball. But, what effect does speeding up the swing have in terms of accuracy?

First, in terms of the decision processes prior to swinging, as the person watches the ball, the most important aspects of the ball's flight are assumedly those closest to the batter. But, by speeding up the swing to 140 ms (see figure 7.18), the batter can view the ball for 20 ms longer. More importantly, those 20 ms occur during the time that the ball is as close as possible to the batter before the ultimate decision has to be made to trigger the action. In this way, the batter should be able to make more accurate predictions about the spatial relation of the ball to the batter when it arrives in the hitting zone, and therefore more effective choices regarding the swing.

What does swinging faster do to the timing of the bat swing initiation? From the discussions about anticipation in chapter 3, in order for the bat to arrive at the plate at the proper time, the batter must anticipate the processes between the final (internal) "go" signal and the end of the movement. This is called *effector anticipation*. Here, this interval begins at the point marked "Decisions end" and ends when the bat reaches the plate. When the MT is 160 ms, this interval is 328 ms, and when the MT is 140 ms it is 308 ms. Because the accuracy in timing an interval is diminished as the interval length increases, more accurate effector anticipation occurs when the swing is 140 ms versus 160 ms, and less variability in the time of swing initiation should result. Schmidt (1969c), using a laboratory task analogous to batting (figure 7.7), found that when MT was decreased, the variability in *when* the bat swing was initiated was decreased as well. A third advantage of swinging more rapidly is that the movement itself is more temporally consistent as the MT is shorter. A number of studies (e.g., Newell et al., 1979, 1980; Schmidt et al., 1979) show decreased MT variability as the MT is decreased. Newell and colleagues (1979, 1980) found a stabilizing effect of movement velocity essentially independent of MT. So, when the batter swings faster, the movements themselves become more temporally consistent.

The combination of increased consistency in the time of swing initiation and in the duration of the swing itself should lead to increased consistency in the time at which the bat arrives at the plate. In the laboratory task mentioned previously (figure 7.7), Schmidt (1969c) found that the temporal accuracy in meeting the "ball" was greater when the MT was shorter (see table 7.1). If the level of muscle contraction in the bat swing is above about 65% of the batter's maximum, then increased swing speed, or increased bat mass with a constant swing speed, should produce *increases* in the spatial accuracy of the swing (see figures 7.16 and 7.17). This is so because with increased levels of contraction there is increased consistency in force production, which results in increased consistency in where the limbs go during the action. These kinds of effects have been shown for laboratory tasks (Schmidt & Sherwood, 1982), as well as in sport-related tasks (Zernicke & Roberts, 1978).

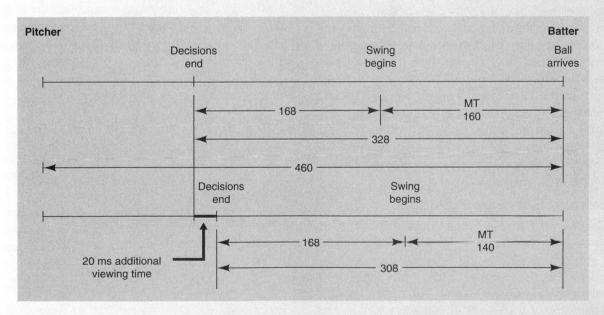

FIGURE 7.18 A time line showing the critical events in hitting a pitched baseball. (The top example has a 160 ms movement time [MT], and the bottom example has a 140 ms MT.)

trade-off) in which a *number* of impulses are presumably combined to produce a complete action (e.g., as in figures 7.5 and 7.6). So, the impulse-variability model falls considerably short of the goal of explaining speed–accuracy phenomena in general. A modification of the theory, using similar assumptions about GMPs, force and time variability, and so on, was provided by Meyer and colleagues (1982). This view does represent an improvement in certain ways, but it suffers from a number of other problems that seem to argue against its adequacy as an account of speed–accuracy effects (see Schmidt et al., 1985; Zelaznik, Schmidt, & Gielen, 1986).

Overall, the impulse-variability theory accounts reasonably well for certain types of ballistic actions that do not require feedback. Thus, the theory provides an important description of some of the centrally generated errors that result in speed–accuracy trade-offs. Later in this chapter we describe a more recent model of Fitts-type tasks by Meyer and colleagues (1988, 1990) that describes how impulse-variability principles are involved in both the initial and corrective portions of aiming movements.

Equilibrium-Point Theories

Alternatives to theories suggesting that movement distances are controlled on the basis of programmed impulses are theories suggesting that the *movement end point* is programmed and that muscle and mechanical properties determine the trajectory. The relation of these theories to speed–accuracy trade-offs per se has not been fully investigated (Latash, 1993; Latash & Gutman, 1993). However, these ideas represent a major theoretical advance regarding the way limb positioning movements are controlled by the central nervous system, so it is important to consider them here.

The Length–Tension Diagram

Muscles, and tendons that connect muscles to bones, have a certain amount of compliance, or *springiness*. In an older view of muscle (e.g., Huxley, 1969), the notion was that the *contractile component* of muscle was responsible for the production of forces and that a *series elastic component* (in the muscular connective tissue and in the tendons) provided elasticity. Although the concept has been known for more than a century (Weber, 1846; see Partridge, 1983), what has been

emphasized more recently is that the contractile portion of muscle has elasticity as well, such that the entire muscle–tendon unit is analogous to a "complicated spring." This concept has influenced thinking about what muscles do when they move bones in skilled actions (see Partridge & Benton, 1981, for a review).

One way to study the properties of muscles is to describe them in terms of a length–tension curve—that is, the relation between a muscle's length and the tension that it is capable of producing at that length under a given level of contraction. In an anesthetized animal, the length of the muscle can be predetermined; the nerve is stimulated artificially so that the level of activation to the muscle can be controlled, and the resulting tension is measured. Such a procedure can produce a family of *length–tension diagrams*, with one curve for each of the levels of contraction that the experimenter uses. Some of these curves from Rack and Westbury (1969) are shown in figure 7.19, in which five levels of activation were used (defined in terms of the number of impulses of electrical stimulus given per second). Notice that at all levels, a generally increasing relationship was found between the length of the muscle and the tension it developed. This relationship is roughly what we would expect if the muscle were a spring attached to a lever (the bone). A fundamental mechanical principle about springs—Hooke's law—is that the tension produced is directly proportional to the amount the spring is stretched (i.e., proportional to the spring's length). Figure 7.20 is a hypothetical length–tension diagram for springs. The four curves represent four different springs, each with a different *stiffness*. Stiffness is the force required to lengthen the spring by one unit (i.e., the change in tension divided by the resulting change in length), represented as the slope of the length–tension curve.

Mass–Spring Mechanisms

The realization by Asatryan and Feldman (1965; Feldman, 1966a, 1966b)[5] that muscles could, in certain gross ways, behave something like complex springs has revealed a possible mechanism for movement control known as *mass–spring* control. Consider a lever, pivoted near one end, with two springs attached on either side. This setup is shown in figure 7.21*a*. Think of the lever as the bone in the forearm; the pivot is the

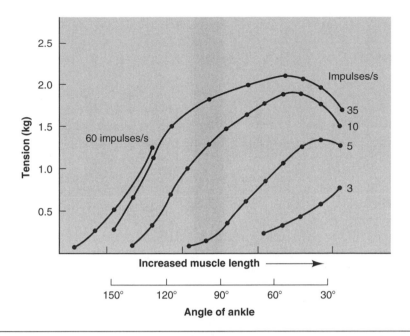

FIGURE 7.19 Tension produced by muscle as a function of the level of activation (impulses per second) and the length of the muscle.

Reprinted, by permission, from P.M.H. Rack and D.R. Westbury, 1969, "The effects of length and stimulus rate on tension in the isometric cat soleus muscle," *Journal of Physiology* 204: 443-460.

elbow joint, and the two springs are the groups of muscles that span the joint—the flexors and the extensors.

In figure 7.21*b* are the hypothetical length–tension curves for these two springs, assuming a constant level of motor activation. Consider what happens when some external force applied

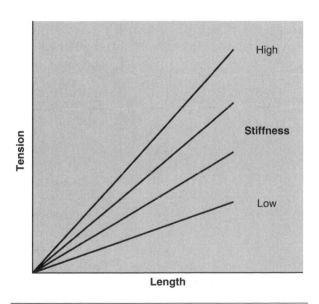

FIGURE 7.20 Idealized length–tension curves as would be produced from four springs, each with a different stiffness.

to the "hand" extends the elbow. First consider the curve labeled "Flexors" in figure 7.21*b*. Here, as the elbow angle is increased from 30° to 180° (i.e., the elbow is extended), a progressively increased tension is produced in the flexors because they are being lengthened (stretched). Also, the curve labeled "Extensors" represents the tension in the extensor muscles. As the elbow extends, the tension in the extensors decreases because the length of the extensors decreases, and the tensions they produce are related to their lengths.

What happens when this force moving the "hand" is suddenly removed? For a given amount of stiffness in the springs, the lever would move to ("spring to") an *equilibrium position* (or *equilibrium point*) in its range, finally stabilizing at a point where it would be held by the opposing actions of the two springs. The equilibrium point is represented by the elbow angle in which the tension (or, more properly, torque at the elbow) from the flexor group is equal and opposite to the tension from the extensor group. In the diagram, the two tensions are equal at only one elbow angle: the elbow angle at which the two length–tension diagrams cross each other, at about 95°. When the system is perturbed, the mass–spring system will tend to move the limb back to the equilibrium

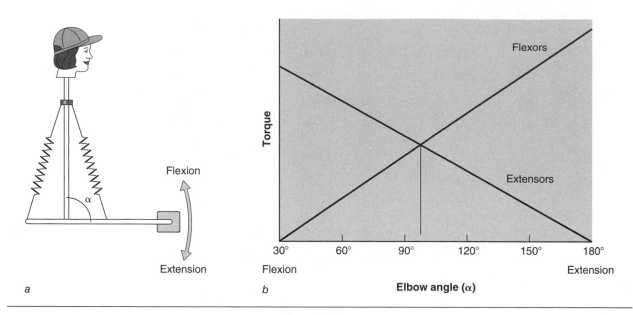

FIGURE 7.21 The mass–spring or equilibrium-point model. *(a)* Muscles seen as springs; *(b)* the length–tension diagrams for the flexors and extensors plotted for different elbow angles, with the intersection being the equilibrium point where the tensions (more properly, torques) in the two muscle groups are equal and opposite.

point, regardless of the amount or direction of the original deflection. This view helps to explain how limbs can be stabilized in one position, as in the maintenance of posture (see also figure 5.19).

Equilibrium-Point Principles (α and λ Models)

The mass–spring view perhaps explains some simple things about how we can hold a limb in one place and how the limb is stabilized after an external perturbation. But how can it explain *movement*? Closely related models have been proposed by Feldman (1966a, 1966b, 1986) and Polit and Bizzi (1978, 1979), which differ in the ways the processes are thought to work. In the λ model (Feldman), illustrated in figure 7.22, assume that the limb is initially at a particular equilibrium position (110°) defined by the two length–tension functions for flexors and extensors (what Feldman called the *invariant characteristic*). When the flexor group is activated, there is a shift from one length–tension function to another (from Flexors$_1$ to Flexors$_2$ in the figure), which occurs because of two distinctly different changes. First, the function is shifted to the left through a change in the *threshold length* (which Feldman labeled λ). This is the muscle length at which the length–tension curve crosses the zero-tension axis (here shifted leftward from λ$_1$ to λ$_2$); it is the muscle length at which the reflex

activities just begin to cause the muscle to contract, with tension increasing progressively as the muscle is lengthened further. Second, the *stiffness* of the muscle is increased as well—seen as the steeper slope of the length–tension function for Flexors$_2$ as compared to Flexors$_1$.

These shifts in the length–tension function result in a change in the equilibrium point from 110° to 80°. But the limb is still at 110°, and not in equilibrium, because the flexors are exerting *a* units of torque, whereas the extensors are exerting *b* units; the difference in torque *(a − b)* begins to move the limb into flexion. This movement continues until the limb is in equilibrium again, this time at the new equilibrium point of 80°, where the two muscle groups are producing torques that are again equal and opposite (*c* units). The analogous process can also occur in the extensor group, or probably in both groups at the same time in most normal movements. So, through appropriate selection of the activation to the muscle groups spanning a joint, and hence a new equilibrium point, the joint can be moved to any position within its anatomical range. The viewpoint has been referred to as an *equilibrium-point model* because the limb moves to the mechanically defined equilibrium point.

At this point, the Polit-Bizzi and Feldman models become slightly different. According to the α model (Polit & Bizzi, 1978, 1979), the

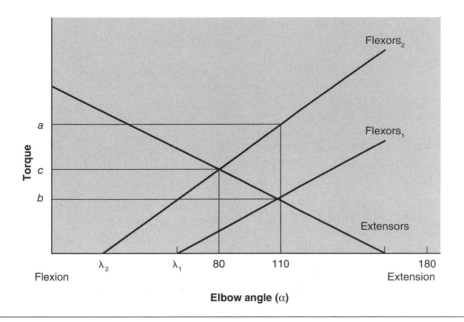

FIGURE 7.22 Length–tension diagrams for the extensors and flexors for various elbow angles at times 1 and 2. (The equilibrium point is shifted from 110° to 80° by increased activation in the flexors to produce a new length–tension relation.)

mechanical characteristics of the muscles enable the limbs to move to the new equilibrium position without any feedback (see the next section for evidence). On the other hand, the λ model (Feldman, 1966a, 1966b, 1986; Feldman & Levin, 1995; Latash, 1993) holds that the feedback from the spindle activities is an essential part of the process, perhaps to ensure that the muscle maintains approximately constant stiffness as Nichols and Houk (1976) suggested. In any case, no feedback to either higher centers or the stages of information processing is needed to move accurately; errors are not detected and corrected as in a closed-loop system. Another difference concerns what the motor system is thought to control. In the α model, the motor system activates only the alpha motor neurons to change the length–tension function; the muscle spindles and the gamma system are uninvolved. In the λ model, the alpha and gamma systems are controlled together, with the muscle spindles being involved in the control of stiffness.

The controversy surrounding the ability of the α and the λ models to explain certain features of limb control has existed for many years and continues to draw diverse opinions. Numerous commentaries have been published, and a number of references represent a good start for the interested reader wishing to gain an appreciation of the differing opinions that exist

on the issue (see Bizzi, Hogan, Mussa-Ivaldi, & Giszter, 1992; Balasubramaniam & Turvey, 2005; Berkinblit, Feldman, & Fukson, 1986; Feldman & Latash, 2005; Feldman & Levin, 1995; Feldman, Ostry, Levin, Gribble, & Mitnitski, 1998; Gottlieb, 1998, 2000; Gottlieb, Corcos, & Agarwal, 1989; Jaric & Latash, 2000; Latash, 1993). For our purposes, however, the equilibrium-point models provide an important contrast to the impulse-timing model of movement control discussed earlier in this chapter. In that model, the critical determiner of the limb's action and trajectory was the amount of force programmed and the *timing* and *duration* of this force. With the equilibrium-point model, the muscle activation is simply changed to a new level, and no preestablished timing of the onsets and offsets of the muscular impulses is involved.

Finally, an important distinction is that, in the equilibrium-point theory, the motor system does not have to "know" where the limb is starting from in order to move it to a new location. As figures 7.21 and 7.22 illustrate, the equilibrium point can be achieved mechanically regardless of the starting position. Thus, the equilibrium-point models are somewhat simpler than the impulse-timing view because only two levels of activation are specified to the muscles. With the impulse-timing view, the system must know where the limb is at the beginning of the movement and then must specify the appropriate durations and intensities of the muscular impulses.

Evidence for Equilibrium-Point Control

Scientists have long known that muscles act like "complicated springs," but the Russian physiologist Feldman (1966a, 1966b; Asatryan & Feldman, 1965) was probably the first to describe relationships between position and torque in human movements, and to propose how mechanical properties might be used in movement control (see footnote 5 at the end of this chapter). Feldman's work was not widely known in the West until it was popularized by Turvey (1977). At about the same time, Polit and Bizzi's (1978, 1979) work in the United States with deafferented monkeys independently supported similar ideas, and some of this evidence is given next.

Experiments With Deafferented Monkeys Polit and Bizzi used monkeys with deafferented forelimbs that were trained to point the hand and an attached lever to a target light. With the hand actions, the monkeys could not, of course, feel the limb move, and they could not see the limb either, as the movements were made in the dark. The major dependent variable was the terminal location of the movement, and Polit and Bizzi studied these moves when the limb was perturbed prior to or during the movement. For example, when the stimulus light was turned on

and the animal looked at it, the experimenters would unexpectedly shift the initial limb position. Sometimes a mass would be applied to the lever unexpectedly, or a brief pulse of force was applied that restrained or aided the movement temporarily.

Typical records of these arm movements are shown in figure 7.23. The top three are from the monkeys prior to deafferentation. An unresisted move is shown in figure 7.23a, and a perturbation is applied (as indicated by the horizontal bar) to aid the movement in figure 7.23b and to resist the movement in figure 7.23c. The same monkeys then performed the movements after recovery from surgical deafferentation. The unresisted move in figure 7.23a appears to be quite like the move before the deafferentation, except that it is slower. When the perturbation was applied to aid the movement (figure 7.23b) or to resist the movement (figure 7.23c), the movement end point was achieved regardless of the direction of the perturbation. Sometimes when the target location was close to the starting position, the perturbation in limb position would take the hand past the target. In these cases the limb moved "backward" toward the target and achieved nearly the same position as when it was unresisted (see also Bizzi, Polit, & Morasso, 1976).

These findings raise some interesting questions. First, the monkeys tended to move directly

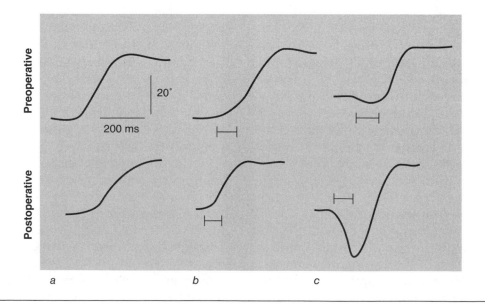

FIGURE 7.23 Elbow movements in normal (top) and deafferented (bottom) monkeys. (The end point is achieved even if a perturbation, indicated by a horizontal bar, is applied during the movement.)

Reprinted with permission from A. Polit and E. Bizzi, 1978, "Processes controlling arm movements in monkeys," *Science* 201: 1236. Reprinted with permission from AAAS.

to the target regardless of the mass that was applied to the limb and regardless of shifts in initial location. All this was accomplished without feedback from limb position to the spinal cord. The hypothesis that the monkey "felt" the change in position, or that reflex processes were involved, cannot explain these findings.

The results also tend to argue against an impulse-timing hypothesis. According to this view, the monkey first determines where the limb is, and the movement is then controlled by the GMP to produce the required impulses. First, if the initial position is shifted, under the impulse-timing view the animal would have to take this into account, because the program (if unaltered) would cause under- or overshooting of the target. Yet, the deafferented animal could not detect this shift, and moved directly to the target. Second, when the monkey's limb was shifted *past* the target position before the movement, the limb moved "backward" toward the target. The impulse-timing hypothesis has the limb moved by a contraction of the agonist first, then of the antagonist, with this order of contraction being specified by the motor program. If so, then the initial movement should have been *away from* the target, not "backward" toward it.

Experiments With Humans The studies just described generated skepticism for a number of reasons. First, it is not certain that these processes found in animals also operate in humans. Second, it is never perfectly clear that deafferentation keeps all sensory movement information from reaching the brain, as bone-conducted vibrations from the movement can be sensed by parts of the body that are not deafferented. Finally, and perhaps most importantly, the monkeys may have adopted an equilibrium-point mode of control simply because Polit and Bizzi deprived them of all their usual movement mechanisms. Do these experiments have relevance for human movement control? Probably, as seen in various experiments with humans.

In experiments with humans, Schmidt (1980; Schmidt & McGown, 1980) had subjects produce rapid elbow flexion movements of a lever to a target. Occasionally, the load on the lever was unpredictably changed before the movement, and the subject moved with the changed load conditions. In the first of these experiments, the lever movement was horizontal, and the lever

mechanism itself would support the weight. The experimenters were interested in the constant errors (CEs) in achieving the target on the "normal trials" (with the expected weight) and on the "switch trials," for which the weight was either added or subtracted unexpectedly.

From table 7.3 (top), when the mass was suddenly increased, the movement end point (the CE, or constant error) was nearly unaffected. The same was true in the mass-subtracted portion of the experiment. However, the MTs shifted considerably, being far longer when the mass was suddenly added and far shorter when the mass was suddenly subtracted. These results are consistent with the equilibrium-point view, as the movements arrived at the target even when the inertial characteristics of the lever were unexpectedly changed, with only the rate of approach to the target position being affected by the load.

A second experiment had the lever movements in the *vertical* plane rather than in the horizontal plane. The equilibrium-point model, in this case, predicts that the movement end point should now be affected by the changed weight since the added weight will bias the equilibrium point downward because of gravity; a weight subtracted unexpectedly will tend to shift the equilibrium point upward. Thus, the prediction is that the limb will undershoot the target when the weight is added and overshoot it when the weight is subtracted, which is different from the prediction of no change in the horizontal-movement experiment where gravity is not involved.

When the weight was added, from table 7.3 we see that the movement in the switch trials was about 5° shorter than in the normal trials. When the weight was subtracted, the limb movement was approximately 8° longer than in the normal trials. Large shifts in MT also occurred, with the added weight slowing the movement and the subtracted weight speeding it. The prediction of an impulse-timing view would be that the limb would come to a stop in the correct time. Interestingly, a reflexive closed-loop model would predict that the movement should achieve its desired end point here, because the limb system would simply move to the position that it "recognizes" to be correct, and added weight should have no effect on the terminal location of the limb—so closed-loop models are contradicted as well.

TABLE 7.3. CE and MT Under "Normal" and "Switch" Conditions for Unidirectional Movements in the Horizontal and Vertical Planes			
Horizontal: mass varied		**Normal trials**	**Switch trials**
Mass added	CE	+6.36°	+6.81°
	MT	187 ms	278 ms
Mass subtracted	CE	+5.78°	+6.28°
	MT	214 ms	180 ms
Vertical: mass varied		**Normal trials**	**Switch trials**
Mass added	CE	+15.82°	+10.40°
	MT	202 ms	243 ms
Mass subtracted	CE	+7.83°	+15.79°
	MT	196 ms	155 ms

From Schmidt and McGown 1980.

Extensions of the Equilibrium-Point Models

Berkinblit and colleagues (1986) proposed a very interesting model for sequential actions on the basis of the wiping reflex in the spinal frog (figure 6.8). They argue that this action is really a *series* of approximately seven discrete positions. The action is achieved by specifying a sequence of equilibrium positions, and each of these positions is achieved exactly as in the equilibrium-point model. This model requires something like a central program to control when each of the

separate equilibrium points is specified, so the model tends to be a compromise between the equilibrium-point models and the motor program models (see Feldman & Levin, 1995; also Rosenbaum, Loukopoulos, Meulenbroek, Vaughan, & Engelbrecht, 1995, for a similar application).

Another application of the equilibrium-point model was described by Hollerbach (1978, 1981), who attempted to simulate handwriting through the use of various mechanical principles. He conceptualized the muscles that move the fingers as

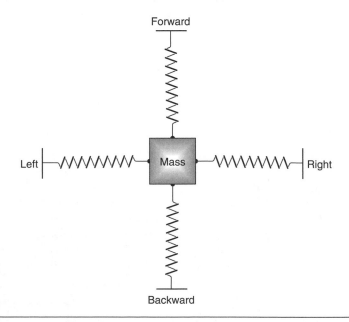

FIGURE 7.24 A mass–spring model for handwriting. (The forward–backward and right–left spring pairs oscillate to produce writing-like patterns of a pencil attached to the mass.)

Reprinted, by permission, from J.M. Hollerbach, 1978, *A study of human motor control through analysis and synthesis of handwriting.* Unpublished doctoral dissertation (Cambridge, MA: Massachusetts Institute of Technology).

springs that move the finger up (toward the top of the page placed horizontally), down, left, and right, as shown in figure 7.24. One important point about the models of Rosenbaum and colleagues and Hollerbach is that treating the muscles as "complicated springs" allows an explanation of how a trajectory is produced with a minimum of complexity in the motor programming.

Limitations of the Equilibrium-Point Models

Most of the support for the equilibrium-point model comes from only one kind of movement—simple, unidirectional positioning tasks (but see Feldman & Levin, 2009, for recent theoretical developments). To what extent is this kind of mechanism involved in movements that use more than one direction of a limb or in movements that involve more than one limb and that must be coordinated?

Schmidt and McGown (cited in Schmidt, 1980) and Schmidt, McGown, Quinn, and Hawkins (1986) investigated this problem with various kinds of movements. One study used the same kind of apparatus and experimental design as just described (table 7.3) for the single-direction moves, but the horizontal movements now involved a reversal in direction. The subject moved in flexion, reversed the move, and extended the elbow past the starting position so that the time from the beginning until the time the starting point was again reached was 300 ms. Mass was unexpectedly added or subtracted from the lever exactly as before. Of interest was where and when the movement reversal occurred under the normal and switch conditions. Was the reversal point determined by equilibrium-point control, so that it would be unbiased in location with added load?

The major results are shown in table 7.4. The reversal point was shorter when the mass was added and longer when the mass was subtracted unexpectedly. Thus, the equilibrium-point model does not seem to account for the results (on rever-

sal position) when the action requires a reversal that must be timed. The impulse-timing model explains these results easily: The motor program "told" the agonist when to turn off, and the movement with added weight could not go as far in this fixed amount of time, so the movement's reversal fell short of its goal.

It is fairly well accepted that the equilibrium-point model is the best account of how a joint achieves its *terminal* position. But there is considerable doubt that this model can account for the events that occur at the very beginning of the movement. Other evidence suggests that the initial trajectories are generated by processes somewhat more complicated than this (Atkeson & Hollerbach, 1985; Hollerbach & Flash, 1982). Also, equilibrium-point models cannot account for the results of Wadman, Denier van der Gon, Geuze, and Mol (1979), in whose experiment the unexpected blocking of the limb resulted in an unaffected agonist–antagonist–agonist EMG pattern (see figure 6.9). It also cannot account for Polit and Bizzi's (1979) experiments in which the monkey pointed at an unseen target by moving the elbow joint: If the *shoulder* joint was moved before the action, the overall pointing direction was grossly incorrect. Overall, neither the equilibrium-point model nor the impulse-timing model is capable of accounting for *all* of the findings.

Correction Models of the Speed–Accuracy Trade-Off

To this point in our discussions about the theoretical basis for rapidly aimed movements, we have ignored the problem of how errors are corrected. However, from previous discussions we know that errors (variability) in centrally generated

TABLE 7.4. CE and MT for "Normal" and "Switch" Trials for the Reversal Movements in the Horizontal Planes			
Horizontal: mass varied		**Normal trials**	**Switch trials**
Mass added	CE	28.3°	25.8°
	MT	139 ms	163 ms
Mass subtracted	CE	24.9°	28.6°
	MT	144 ms	123 ms

Adapted, by permission, from R.A. Schmidt, 1980, "Past and future issues in motor programming," *Research Quarterly for Exercise and Sport* 5: 122-140.

signals are bound to occur. The motor system is inherently "noisy," leading to variability in the generation of impulses or joint positions. Thus, theories describing how these error corrections occur have been important for a more complete understanding of the speed–accuracy trade-off.

The Crossman-Goodeve Model

At the 1963 meeting of the Experimental Psychology Society in England, Crossman and Goodeve presented a feedback-based explanation of Fitts' law. They suggested that Fitts' law could be derived mathematically, on the basis of feedback control in movement (with a number of assumptions), without the need to resort to ideas about information theory as Fitts (1954) had done. This derivation with its associated argument was described in a more accessible form by Keele (1968) and was reprinted in its entirety in 1983.

Crossman and Goodeve (1963/1983) assumed that movement toward a target is made up of two kinds of processes—much as Woodworth (1899) had proposed 50 years earlier—except that the ballistic, distance-covering phase and the feedback-controlled "homing-in" phase were thought to operate in *rapid alternation* during a movement to the target. This mode of control is termed *intermittent* (or *iterative*); hence, their idea has often been termed the iterative-correction model.

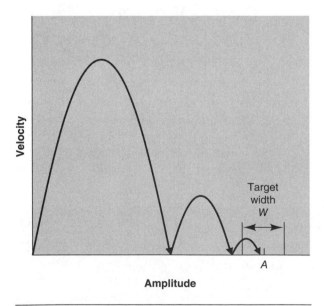

FIGURE 7.25 Crossman and Goodeve's (1963/1983) iterative-correction model of aiming.

The model, illustrated in figure 7.25, is based on the idea that a ballistic, distance-covering phase would operate for a *fixed* period of time, moving the limb a certain amplitude toward the target. This initial phase would have a spatial inaccuracy proportional to the distance that had been moved during that time. Then, feedback processes would evaluate the size and direction of the error and initiate a second ballistic movement that would serve as a correction. This second movement would also have an error proportional to its (much shorter) distance; its error would then be evaluated, another correction would be initiated, and so on until the movement reached the target. Thus, the model is based on rapid alternation between ballistic movement processes and feedback-based corrective processes during the action. The MT, which is the dependent variable in the Fitts equation, was thought to be based on the *number* of these corrective processes that had to be made to achieve the target.

Keele (1968) used Crossman and Goodeve's basic idea and added to it the assumptions that the time between corrections was fixed at 190 ms (Keele & Posner, 1968; see chapter 5) and that the error in each movement was about one-seventh of the total distance moved in each correction. Keele argued that each correction was processed in the stages of information processing, requiring attention, and that aimed movements were made up of a series of such corrections leading to the target. With use of these assumptions, the Crossman-Goodeve model showed a good quantitative fit to some of the experimental data (Keele, 1981).

One major drawback to the Crossman-Goodeve model of rapid aiming movements is related to the speed with which humans can process visual feedback. This was a major theme of chapter 5, and it is one of the most fundamental reasons for believing that very rapid movements must be planned in advance. Another problem relates to the psychological refractory period: Even though it might be possible to make one such correction in 190 ms, it is doubtful that the second and third corrections could also be made this quickly (review discussion of psychological refractory period effects, chapter 4). These and other criticisms of the Crossman-Goodeve theory have been discussed in more detail in several reviews (Schmidt et al., 1978, 1979; Meyer et al., 1982, 1988).

Perhaps the most persuasive argument against the Crossman-Goodeve theory was based on kinematic records of subjects' movement trajectories (Langolf et al., 1976). Transitions between one ballistic segment and the next could be seen as sudden changes in the position or velocity of the limb. Generally, most of the movements studied had one correction (a very few had two), although some had no visible corrections at all, even with MTs of 700 ms. These findings failed to support the hypothesis that a correction occurs every 190 ms.

A side issue here is that Fitts' law, and the speed–accuracy trade-off in general, had usually relied on closed-loop control processes for explanation (e.g., the Crossman-Goodeve view). However, note that one contribution of the impulse-variability theory (Schmidt et al., 1979) is that it provided evidence of speed–accuracy trade-off even when the movements were far too short in time to be explained by feedback-based processes.

Optimized-Submovement Models

The failure of the Crossman-Goodeve theory to handle these and other data was addressed by Meyer and colleagues (1988, 1990) in what they termed the *optimized-submovement* model. Meyer and colleagues began with the idea that the initial segment of an aiming movement was handled by principles of impulse variability as described earlier in this chapter. But then they went on to describe how corrections can be applied to the trajectory after this initial movement to allow the limb to move accurately to a target. In effect, each correction is a new program whose accuracy is governed by impulse-variability principles. This concept is similar to the hypothesis that Woodworth proposed in 1899, but it is made more concrete and experimentally testable by a number of additional assumptions concerning how many such corrections should be expected, and where and under what conditions they should be found in a movement as a function of various movement variables.

Dual-Submovement Model

In most aiming tasks, the processes involved in bringing the limb to the target can be described by two situations that are illustrated in figure 7.26. The first situation (middle curve in figure 7.26) occurs when the initial action (termed the *primary submovement*) requires no correction. The other situation occurs when the initial impulse either undershoots or overshoots the target, requiring a corrective impulse (or *secondary submovement*),

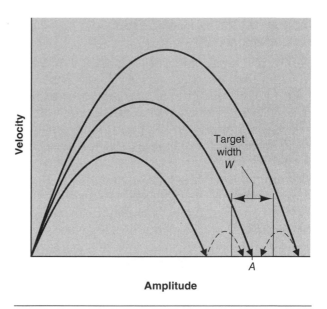

FIGURE 7.26   The optimized-submovement correction model.

Adapted, by permission, from D.E. Meyer et al., 1988, "Optimality in human motor performance: Ideal control of rapid aimed movements," *Psychological Review* 95: 343. Copyright © 1988 by the American Psychological Association.

shown as the dashed lines. Total MT in an aiming task is considered to reflect a strategy whereby a subject attempts to trade off speed for accuracy by *optimizing* the duration of both the initial impulse and, if necessary, the correction. Thus, movement accuracy is achieved in a minimum MT by optimizing the control of the submovement(s)—a nice combination of some of the important open-loop and closed-loop processes discussed in this chapter.

Multiple-Submovement Model

In general, the dual-submovement model fits the experimental data quite well (Meyer et al., 1988). However, Meyer and colleagues also found that corrections occurred more frequently than predicted under some combinations of target amplitude and width. In a revised version of the model, Meyer and colleagues (1990) made additional assumptions to account for the fact that more than one corrective impulse could be made during an aimed movement. This multiple-submovement model was supported by a reanalysis of data from Meyer and colleagues (1988) using a different kinematic analysis protocol (see also Jagacinski & Flach, 2003, chapter 8). This reanalysis confirmed that about 80% of all aimed movements were composed of two or three submovements (i.e., one or two corrections; 43% and 37%, respectively).

How Is a Correction Identified and Measured?

Although Meyer and colleagues' (1988, 1990) models provide a balanced, *hybrid* approach to the issue of open- and closed-loop processes, experimental examination of their predictions places a critical emphasis on the quantitative analysis of corrective submovements. As we have seen before, motor output processes are rather noisy, and often it is not clear how evaluations of kinematic data (e.g., position, velocity, acceleration, or jerk) can discriminate between corrections and motor noise. Various techniques have been used to objectify kinematic data, but it is beyond the scope of the present discussion to describe these analytical techniques (for theoretical discussions underlying these techniques, see Khan et al., 2006, for a recent review and the following references: Carlton, 1979; Chua & Elliott, 1993; Langolf et al., 1976; Meyer et al., 1988; Pratt & Abrams, 1996).

Summary

Three types of speed–accuracy trade-offs were described in this chapter. The earliest formal mathematical statement of this relationship was proposed over 50 years ago by Paul Fitts, called *Fitts' law* in his honor. It says that, in reciprocal movements, the average MT is linearly related to the Log_2 of the ratio of the movement amplitude and the target width. This principle holds for a wide variety of movement situations and types of subjects and is considered one of the cornerstones of motor control.

Force and force variability are strongly related to each other, with the relationship being essentially linear until forces of about 65% of the subject's maximum are achieved. The force variability levels off or even decreases with further increases in force toward the subject's maximum. The laws about MT variability and force variability have been combined into various *impulse-variability* models for movement accuracy: The prediction is that the variability of a movement's initial impulse is linearly related to the ratio of the movement amplitude (*A*) and the MT (*A*/MT), or average velocity.

An analysis of laws of movement timing shows that, as the MT is decreased, an increase occurs in movement-timing consistency. This occurs in addition to the effect of movement velocity,

whereby movement-timing consistency is also increased as velocity is increased. These two effects combined imply that increasing the speed of movements in timing tasks leads to increased temporal consistency, contrary to ideas about the spatial speed–accuracy trade-off. Timing consistency has also been examined in repetitive movement tasks. A model of timing in which variability is due to independent, central, and peripheral sources has been a useful research tool.

Many aiming movements are influenced by central (programmed) mechanisms, closed-loop, corrective actions (both reflexive and intentional), or both. Impulse-variability principles describe how programmed impulses affect the trajectory of a rapid aimed limb movement. A different view is suggested by the *equilibrium-point* model, which holds that the limb moves to a position defined by an equilibrium point between the forces (torques) from the opposing muscles spanning a joint, and that the movement to this position is dependent on the mechanical, spring-like characteristics of the muscles. Such a model is different from an impulse-timing mechanism whereby the amounts of force, as well as the times over which they are applied, are controlled by the motor program.

Early explanations for Fitts' law were based on *intermittent-control* models, in which the commands for action were produced alternately with the analysis of feedback to determine movement corrections. Several lines of evidence, however, suggest that the intermittent-control model is incorrect. More acceptable views indicate that the timing of an open-loop, distance-covering phase and later correction(s) is *optimized* in some way in order to idealize the inconsistency in the distance-covering phase as the forces applied to the limb are increased.

Student Assignments

1. Prepare to answer the following questions during class discussion:
   a. Calculate the Fitts index of difficulty for the following sport tasks: throwing a strike in baseball, scoring a basket from the free-throw line, successfully scoring a field goal from 35 yards in American football, scoring a penalty kick in soccer (assuming no goalkeeper), holing a putt in golf from 30 feet, and

scoring a bull's-eye in darts. (As appropriate, use regulation distances and target sizes to calculate your answers.)

b. Discuss the open-loop and closed-loop processes involved in using a computer mouse to open a desktop icon.

c. Describe the playing of a musical instrument using the concepts of spatial and temporal speed–accuracy trade-offs.

2. Find a research article that investigates or discusses the role of Fitts' law in ergonomics and human factors.

Web Resources

More on Fitts' law:

www.asktog.com/columns/022DesignedTo GiveFitts.html

http://msdn.microsoft.com/en-us/library/ ms993291

More on Weber's law:

www.cis.rit.edu/people/faculty/montag/ vandplite/pages/chap_3/ch3p1.html

Notes

[1] R.A.S. is very appreciative of the label "Schmidt's Law," as some have called it (e.g., Flach, Guisinger, & Robison, 1996; Jagacinski & Flach, 2003; Keele, 1986; Sand-

ers & McCormick, 1993). However, given that most laws are "awarded" posthumously, there is some reluctance in accepting such a tribute at this time.

[2] The observant reader will notice that the measures of variability in figure 7.12 are an order of magnitude higher than those seen in figure 7.9. This occurs because *variance* is the dependent measure in figure 7.12, whereas *standard deviation* is presented in figure 7.9. Since the variance is equal to the squared value of the standard deviation, the results presented in figure 7.12 agree remarkably well with the values in figure 7.9.

[3] The analysis of impulses described here is simplified considerably in order to give an overview of impulse-variability modeling. Space here does not permit a discussion of the numerous assumptions underlying the analyses of impulse variability. For a more complete treatment, see Schmidt and colleagues (1978, 1979, 1985).

[4] These effects are not precisely as predicted by the model, however. For example, changing A does change VE_t slightly, and changing MT does change W_e slightly, in both cases probably because of the effects of velocity discussed earlier (figure 7.8; Newell, Carlton, & Kim, 1994; Newell et al., 1979, 1980).

[5] Feldman (2009) and Latash (2008a) provide historical reflections on the origins of the Asatryan and Feldman (1965) formulation. Related (though generally unacknowledged) views were presented earlier by Wachholder and Altenburger (1927; see Sternad, 2002) and by Crossman and Goodeve (1963/1983). Perhaps these were generally unknown because Wachholder and Altenburger wrote in German and the Crossman-Goodeve model was presented at a conference, and not widely circulated. These ideas were not readily available until many years later.

CHAPTER 8

COORDINATION

In some instances, we seem to be able to produce coordinated actions easily, almost trivially. We engage in countless activities in which our limbs perform different actions at the same time, seemingly without any interference at all (e.g., using a knife and fork; playing piano; walking and chewing gum). In tasks such as throwing and kicking, our upper and lower limbs perform very different functions and movements, all without difficulty.

Yet in other instances, there is substantial interference between the effectors when we try to perform some actions. Well-known cases of interference include the task of patting your head while rubbing your stomach. Both hands seem to "want" to do the same thing, either to rub or to pat, but not to do the different actions as required. Another example comes from Peters (1977), who found that not a single subject, out of 100 who were tested, could recite a nursery rhyme with proper timing while concurrently tapping a different rhythm. Summers, Todd, and Kim (1993) provide further evidence about difficulties in tapping different rhythms with the two hands (producing so-called *polyrhythms,* discussed in more detail later in this chapter). These and many other observations suggest the existence of interlimb coordination processes that facilitate biologically important activities such as locomotion, but that tend to impede more arbitrary skills, which may be culturally important (piano playing, throwing)

or unimportant (rubbing and patting the head and stomach).

We have recognized for several decades now that a major source of interference in interlimb coordination is related to the *temporal* structure(s) of the actions being coordinated (for reviews, see Heuer, 1996; Klapp, 1979, 1981). Actions with the same temporal organization are easily coordinated, with a tight temporal relationship between the limbs, whereas activities with different temporal organizations are not easily produced, if they can be produced at all. There is clearly more to coordination than this, however, as will be seen in the variety of tasks and means by which researchers have attempted to study the fundamental problems of coordination. One important factor in coordination is the duration of the movements being controlled. As we have noted in many of the chapters presented so far, the control processes in discrete skills seem to be very different (in terms of fundamental activities involved) from those underlying continuous skills. This, among other things, has created a vigorous (usually healthy) debate between a group of scientists who think of movement control in terms of self-organizing systems versus a group that thinks in terms of motor program concepts. Indeed, Keele (1998; see "Steve Keele" on p. 13) held the view that this gulf between competing scientific "camps" "is due less to competing conceptualizations of the *same* phenomena than to the *kinds* of phenomena with which different groups of investigators are concerned" (p. 403, emphases added). Keele was referring to the tendency of (a) the self-organizing systems group to study continuous, often rhythmical, skills of (usually) long duration, where processes involving feedback and adjustment for environmental changes can be studied most easily; and (b) the more cognitively based motor program group to study discrete skills of (usually) short duration, where preplanning seems to be critically important and feedback-based adjustments do not.

In chapter 2, we distinguished between discrete and continuous tasks in terms of their beginning and end points. Discrete tasks, such as turning on a light switch or swinging a golf club, have definitive start and end points. In contrast, the start and end of continuous tasks, such as running and driving, are rather arbitrary or context dependent. Discrete tasks are usually (but not always) performed quite rapidly, and considerable theoretical importance is placed on the motor program in preplanning and organizing the body's movements (see chapter 6). In contrast, the role of premovement planning is less important for continuous movements; and other factors such as feedback, error detection, and error correction take on more important roles in the ongoing regulation of control, chiefly because of the additional time allowed for them to occur. Thus, in keeping with the view of motor control—where discrete and continuous skills are performed fundamentally differently—we have organized this chapter by considering the coordination of discrete and continuous tasks in separate sections.

Thus, the understanding of coordination seems to represent different challenges for discrete and continuous tasks. However, keep in mind that the problems encountered in coordinating movements in discrete and continuous tasks share many similarities. The most prominent of these is the *degrees of freedom* problem (Bernstein, 1967): Given that there are more independently moving parts of the body than can be controlled individually, how is the system able to perform actions that coordinate these parts so effectively? The study of coordination in both discrete and continuous tasks points to some fundamental, yet distinct, principles regarding how the degrees of freedom problem is solved.

Discrete Tasks

The focus of discussion in chapter 7 was on the principles by which limb movements, primarily aiming movements, achieved a target with minimum time and maximum accuracy. Although the motor skills that led to the generation of these principles involved relatively "simple" movements (such as repetitive tapping), in reality these movements are far from simple. The following sections also describe relatively "simple" movements, but here the focus instead is on the kinds of organization that must underlie the simultaneous control of the different effectors—that is, the coordination of the various parts of the body.

Eye–Head–Hand Coordination

In chapters 5 and 7 we presented evidence that many tasks involving aiming, including reaching and grasping actions, rely on visual feedback in order to maximize movement end-point accuracy. Visual feedback information is most precise for this kind of task when the eyes can fixate on the target or object for a significant length of time prior to manual contact (e.g., Abrams, Meyer, & Kornblum, 1990). When a target occurs unpredictably, the localization of the target or object to be contacted must be fixated as rapidly as possible in order to provide sufficient time for *processing* the visual information. How is coordination among the eyes, head, and hand achieved in this situation?

Early work with monkeys revealed the existence of a tight relationship between the head and eyes (Bizzi, Kalil, & Tagliasco, 1971). Figure 8.1 illustrates a typical trial in which a monkey turns to look at an unexpected target that has appeared in the periphery of the visual field. From a starting position in which the monkey's eyes and head are pointed straight ahead, the tracings in figure 8.1*a* reveal that, after a brief reaction-time (RT) period, the eyes initially make a rapid *saccade* to fixate the target on the fovea. Movements of the head are initiated at the same time as those of the eyes but are much slower, as can be seen in figure 8.1*b*. As the head moves in the direction of the target, the eyes rotate in a direction *opposite* to the movement of the head. The timing of the opposing motions of the eyes and head is tightly coordinated, so that the fovea remains fixated on the target throughout the head movement. The existence of this coordination between the eyes

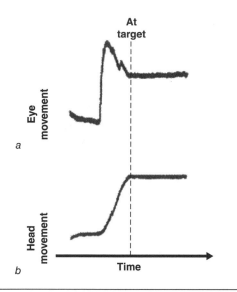

**At
target**

Eye
movement

a

Head
movement

b

Time

FIGURE 8.1 Rotation of the *(a)* eyes and *(b)* head during rapid looking at a target.

Reprinted with permission from E. Bizzi, R.E. Kalil, and V. Tagliasco, 1971, "Eye-head coordination in monkeys: evidence for centrally patterned organization," *Science* 173(3995): 452-454. Reprinted with permission of AAAS. http://www.aaas.org/

and head has been known for a long time and is called the *vestibulo-ocular reflex (VOR)*. In the case of rapid looking, the saccade facilitates a quick identification of the unexpected visual signal. The counterrotation of the eyes maintains the fixation of the target while the head is turning.

A similar relationship among the eyes, head, and hand appears to exist when an intentional manual response is made to a stimulus. Biguer, Jeannerod, and Prablanc (1982) found that the onset of eye movements occurs almost simultaneously with initiation activity of electromyographic (EMG) signals in the arm and neck. This temporal coordination among the *initiation* of eye, head, and limb movements is quite flexible, however, as performance differences arise when instructions do not constrain movement strategies (Abrams et al., 1990; Stahl, 2001) or when instructions emphasize either movement speed or accuracy (Carnahan, 1992; Carnahan & Marteniuk, 1991). In addition to the temporal relationship among eye, head, and limb movements, there is also a *spatial* facilitation when these degrees of freedom interact. Manual aiming is more accurate when the head is free to move than when head position is fixed (Biguer, Prablanc, & Jeannerod, 1984; Vercher, Magenes, Prablanc, & Gauthier, 1994). It remains unclear, however, whether the improved accuracy is due to facilitation from the allowed

movement of the head or a decrement due to the immobilization of the head.

The timing of limb movements is also well coordinated with eye movements during the *termination* of movement toward a target. Using an eye-tracking system (see chapter 2), Helsen, Starkes, and Buekers (1997) found, perhaps not too surprisingly, that an eye saccade always reached and fixated on or near the target before the hand reached the target. Of some surprise, though, was the finding of an invariant relative timing of the saccade and the manual response: Regardless of the amplitude of the movement or the absolute movement time taken to reach the target, the saccade brought the eye onto the target at 50% of the total movement time (see also Starkes, Helsen, & Elliott, 2002). Recall from chapter 6 that evidence of invariant relative timing supported the arguments for a generalized motor program (GMP). A similar argument could explain Helsen and colleagues' findings, such that a GMP coordinates the relative timing of eye and hand movement. In the next section, we show how GMP theory has been developed to explain other types of coordinated discrete actions.

Units of Action

Discrete skills—especially rapid ones—seem to be controlled by a pattern of neuromuscular activity that is largely organized in advance. Of course, this is the essential feature of the theory of motor programs described in chapter 6. While many have debated the relative merits of central versus peripheral contributions to motor control, it seems incontrovertible that at least some fundamental features of the action are specified in advance.

The principles of speed and accuracy discussed in chapter 7 involved actions in which the primary goal was to move an effector from one location to another. Pushing the keys on a telephone and using a keyboard are examples of this type of action. However, there are other, related actions that have a more complex organization, involving serial or parallel (or both serial and parallel) coordination of different muscles and limbs. For example, a computer mouse enables the user to move a cursor to a target, at which time a button click (or double click) initiates the icon's function. Here, one action must be completed *before* another action can be performed. If we consider an action that is somewhat longer in duration and greater in complexity, however, such as serving a tennis ball or shifting gears in a car, it is difficult to claim that such longer sequences are controlled completely by single programs. Nevertheless, it is possible that such actions are composed of a string of programs (each lasting part of a second or more).

Each of these programs might be thought of as a *unit of action*—a "piece" of motor behavior that can be utilized repeatedly in various actions, producing essentially the same movements (but scaled to the environment) each time. For example, we might think of shifting gears in a car from second to third gear as being composed of three units: (1) gas up/clutch down; (2) shift lever up-over-up; and (3) gas down/clutch up. (A racecar driver such as R.A.S. might perform this task as one unit.) And a given unit could be observed in other actions; a clutch-down/gas-up unit could be involved in both a gear change from first to second and a gear change from second to third, while another unit (shift-lever movements) would be different in the two actions. In the next section, we present one possible way to identify such units of behavior, based on GMP concepts.

Identifying Units of Action

The underlying idea for identifying units of action is based on the notion of GMPs, discussed in chapter 6 and in the previous section. To review (see also chapter 6), the GMP is a program with invariant (a) sequencing among muscles, (b) relative timing, and (c) relative forces among the contractions. Superficial features such as overall movement duration and movement size are controlled by parameters that scale (linearly, in this simple view) the surface expression of the GMP's output, yet allow it to retain its invariant structure or pattern.

An invariance in relative timing means that the correlations (within subject, across trials) among the times of various temporal events (or "landmarks") in an action should approach 1.0. Now, to turn the argument around, if an invariance in relative timing happens to be found for a sequence of behavior (i.e., the correlations among landmarks happen to be very close to 1.0), such evidence would be consistent with the hypothesis that a GMP produced that behavior.

Now, consider a longer movement. Suppose that temporal occurrences of the first several landmarks in the movement intercorrelate highly, but that the time of a later landmark does not correlate with any of them. One interpretation would be that the first set of landmarks was governed by a GMP (because relative timing was approximately invariant there) but that the later set of landmarks was not (because the invariance was no longer present). It could be the other way around too, with the group of highly related landmarks being located at the end of the movement, perhaps with all these landmarks being unrelated to a landmark at the start.

This provides the essential idea for the identification of units. A unit is a sequence of behavior with essentially invariant relative timing—that is, it has high correlations among the times of component landmarks. When later landmarks of the action no longer share this invariance (i.e., they do not correlate with landmarks in the earlier portions), this indicates that the first unit has ended, or that there is some sort of boundary between it and the next unit.

Methods in Unit Identification

Schneider and Schmidt (1995; also Young & Schmidt, 1990, 1991) asked subjects to learn a coincident-timing task in which the timed motion of a right-hand–held lever was to coincide with the arrival of a virtual moving object (as in baseball or tennis). After the virtual object began moving, the subject made a small preparatory movement to the right, followed by a backswing to the left, and finished with a striking movement back to the right (a kind of "backhand" action, with a follow-through), with the goal of "hitting" the virtual object with the lever during the second rightward movement.

Kinematic analyses of each trial were used to determine the timing of eight "landmarks" within each trial. These kinematic landmarks (shown as points A, B, C, . . . , H in figure 8.2) were defined as maxima, minima, or zero crossings taken from the position–, velocity–, and acceleration–time records (see chapter 2 on kinematic methods). Within-subject correlations were computed over trials for all of the possible pairs of landmark times. The critical comparisons involved both forward and backward methods of computing the intercorrelations. The forward computation involved the correlation of the first landmark with the second, first with the third, and so on (A-B, A-C, A-D, . . . , A-H). The backward method examined the correlations between the last landmark (H) and all possible earlier landmarks (A-H, B-H, C-H, etc.).

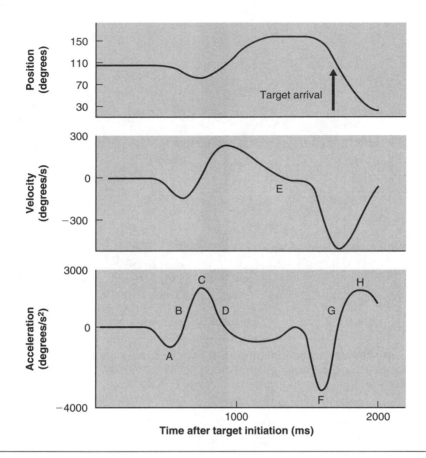

FIGURE 8.2   Kinematic landmarks (A, B, C, . . . , H) taken from the position, velocity, and acceleration profiles of an action are used to search for specific units of action.

Reprinted, by permission, from D.M. Schneider and R.A. Schmidt, 1995, "Units of action in motor control: Role of response complexity and target speed," *Human Performance* 8: 27-39.

If the entire action is governed by a single unit, then all of the correlations (using both the forward and backward methods) should be relatively high, as all intervals would be scaled proportionally in time. The correlations are shown in figure 8.3. On the left, the correlations from the forward method are high among the landmark pairs A-B, A-C, and A-D but are low for the later combinations with A. Using the backward method, the correlations illustrated at the right side of figure 8.3 show that landmark H is highly related to landmarks F and G, but is not related to any of the earlier landmarks. These data suggest that this action has two identifiable units of action, one containing landmarks A-D, and the other containing landmarks F-H, with a boundary between them (between landmarks D and F).

The functioning of these units can perhaps be seen more easily in the acceleration–time

traces in figure 8.4, where these traces for six movements are overlaid. Notice that the traces are all of the same general form (but adjusted with respect to each other in time) for the first portions of the action (A-D, up to about 1,000 ms); the same is true for those in the last part of the action (F-H). However, the traces lose their common form at about 1,000 to 1,400 ms, with the traces crossing over each other. This period of time, according to the analysis, is the transition between units. At this time, the subject has completed the first action (the initial backswing) and is preparing to time the initiation of the forward swing to strike the moving object. Notice also that the first unit (A through D) actually contains two preparatory movements (right, then left; see figure 8.4), indicating that this one unit organizes at least two submovements and involves a change in direction. These general methods have been used in several real-world

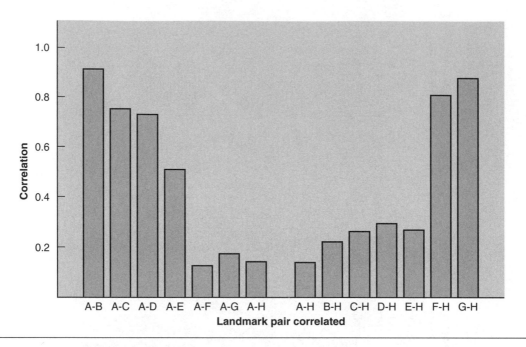

FIGURE 8.3   Correlations of the time of the first landmark (A) with the times of the later landmarks (left side); correlations of the time of the last landmark (H) with the times of the earlier landmarks (right side).

Reprinted, by permission, from D.M. Schneider and R.A. Schmidt, 1995, "Units of action in motor control: Role of response complexity and target speed," *Human Performance* 8: 34.

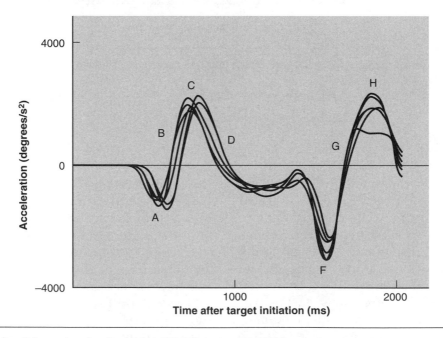

FIGURE 8.4   Visualizing units of action; unit 1 (ABCD) and unit 2 (FGH) are separated by nonsystematic crossovers after point D.

Reprinted, by permission, from D.M. Schneider and R.A. Schmidt, 1995, "Units of action in motor control: Role of response complexity and target speed," *Human Performance* 8: 34.

tasks; for example, researchers in one study analyzed the unit structure involved in lighting a butane cigarette lighter, identifying three sequential elements (Schmidt, Wood, Young, & Kelkar, 1996).

Reaching and Grasping

Another type of unimanual coordination has been studied in situations when limb transport ends in *grasping* an object. The composite photograph

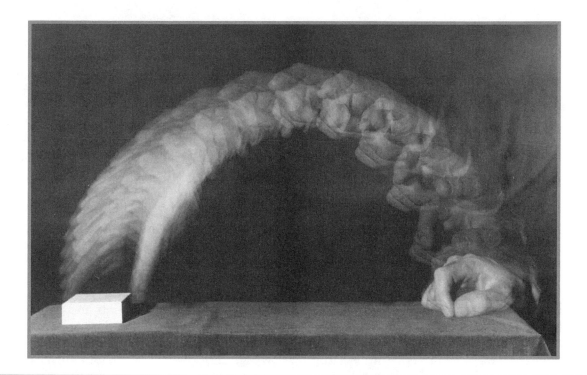

FIGURE 8.5   Composite photograph of the reach/grasp action.

Reprinted from M.A. Goodale and P. Servos, 1996, Visual control of prehension. In *Advances in motor control and learning*, edited by H.N. Zelaznik (Champaign, IL: Human Kinetics), 87. By permission of M.A. Goodale.

in figure 8.5 illustrates how the reach and grasp are coordinated in time and space. The functional *aperture* (separation of the thumb and fingers) of the grasping hand opens during the reach toward the object. Although the hand *could* wait and open once it reached the target, this would likely be an inefficient strategy in terms of economy of effort and time. Typically, the hand reaches its maximum aperture well before object contact, at a peak size that is larger than the width of the target, and then the aperture is fine-tuned to the object's size just prior to contact.

Does this example reflect two separate and independent actions of motor control, as implied by the phrase "reaching and (then) grasping," or is the entire action controlled as one motor program, which seems to be implied by the coordinated relationship between the limb and hand in figure 8.5? This question is at the heart of the research controversy concerning how reaching and grasping are controlled and has motivated two very different theoretical positions about movement planning, one based on temporal relationships and another that concerns spatial relationships involved in acquiring an object.

Temporal Planning in Reaching and Grasping

Jeannerod (1981, 1984) extended the concepts that began with Woodworth (1899) to theorize about the coordination of reaching and grasping. Recall from chapter 5 that Woodworth proposed a two-component model of manual aiming. A ballistic component brought the pencil near the target, and a closed-loop process provided fine adjustments to guide the pencil onto the target. According to Jeannerod, reaching and grasping are organized into the same fundamental components: a *transport* component and a *grip-formation* component. The composite photograph of reaching to grasp an object in figure 8.5 appears to illustrate that the transport component moves the hand into the general vicinity of the target space so that the object may be grasped. The grip-formation component is responsible for preparing the hand to capture the object, and the person's intention regarding what will be done with the object determines how the grip is formed (Jeannerod, 1996; see review by Castiello, 2005).[1]

Jeannerod (1981, 1984) and Arbib (1981; Fagg & Arbib, 1998) developed these ideas further by providing a neurologically plausible rationale for dissociating the transport and grip components. By this view, separate visuomotor channels in the central nervous system (CNS) are responsible for limb transport and grip formation. Jeannerod proposed that each channel independently processes different information in movement planning. From a viewer-centered perspective, an object's *extrinsic* properties (e.g., its distance from the body, its location in space, or both) are used to plan the details of limb transport (e.g., the spatial coordinates of the wrist). Grip formation is determined from the object-centered perspective—the object's *intrinsic* properties (e.g., size, shape, texture) being used to determine the specific details of hand shaping. Coordination of the reach and grasp was hypothesized to follow a *temporal* patterning—where the timing of various kinematic landmarks is scaled proportionally.

By *independent* processing, Jeannerod meant that changes in one type of visual information (i.e., an intrinsic or an extrinsic property) would affect one movement component but not the other. In support of the theory, reaching for objects at various distances from the starting location (extrinsic information) was found to affect the kinematics of the transport component only, but not the grip-formation component (e.g., Jeannerod, 1981; Paulignan, MacKenzie, Marteniuk, & Jeannerod, 1991; but see also Jakobson & Goodale, 1991). Coordination of the two components was

found to be invariant. The occurrence of maximum aperture size was synchronized in time with the peak deceleration of the wrist, regardless of the distance. An idealized trial representing the kinematics as reported by Jeannerod is illustrated in figure 8.6. As shown in the figure, the time to peak grip aperture coincided with the point of peak deceleration of the wrist, at approximately 75% of the overall movement time (MT) (Jeannerod, 1981).

Not all studies have supported the temporal-coordination view of reaching and grasping, however, and the evidence for and against this view is mixed and complex (e.g., Bootsma, Marteniuk, MacKenzie, & Zaal, 1994; Marteniuk, Leavitt, MacKenzie, & Athenes, 1990). As noted by Wing, Turton, and Fraser (1986), research is not necessary to show that arm movements and hand shaping can be performed independently, as each action *can* be done in the absence of the other. When the two are performed together, though, the evidence suggests that reaching and grasping are not independently controlled actions. A common research method that demonstrates this phenomenon involves a perturbation during the action, such as an unexpected change in the location of the object (Gentilucci, Chieffi, Scarpa, & Castiello, 1992; Paulignan, MacKenzie, Marteniuk, & Jeannerod, 1991), in the size of the object (Castiello, Bennett, & Stelmach, 1993; Paulignan, Jeannerod, MacKenzie, & Marteniuk, 1991), in the spatial orienta-

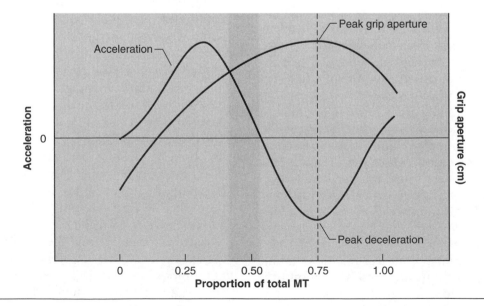

FIGURE 8.6 Illustration of relation between wrist transport kinematics and grip aperture size—idealized trial.
Based on Jeannerod 1981, 1984.

tion of the object (Desmurget et al., 1996), or via a mechanical perturbation of the moving limb itself (Haggard & Wing, 1995). The magnitude of effects observed in these studies was influenced most when a change in the type of grip was required (Paulignan & Jeannerod, 1996). In general, these studies demonstrate that any sudden change in either the perceptual or effector attributes of the action will result in a reorganization of both the reach and grasp components: The coordinated component parts of the action are not reorganized independently (for further discussion see Goodale & Servos, 1996; Jeannerod & Marteniuk, 1992; Paulignan & Jeannerod, 1996). In sum, this evidence does not provide strong support for a temporal view of coordination in the planning of reaching and grasping actions.

Spatial Planning in Reaching and Grasping

An alternative view of movement planning considers reaching and grasping not as separate components of an action, but instead as a coordinated aiming movement. From chapter 7 we know that spatial variability increases if the same movement distance is completed in progressively shorter MTs (Schmidt, Zelaznik, & Frank, 1978; Schmidt, Zelaznik, Hawkins, Frank, & Quinn, 1979). A similar effect appears to apply in reaching for objects. In a study by Wing and colleagues (1986), subjects were asked to grasp an object by reaching for it as rapidly as possible, or reaching for it at a comfortable speed, with or without vision. Under full-vision conditions, the size of the grasp aperture widened as movement duration decreased (735 ms to 376 ms). Further widening of the aperture occurred when the movements were made with the eyes closed. These findings suggested that subjects compensated for anticipated increased spatial variability in limb transport by increasing the size of the grasp, thereby maintaining a constant success rate by adjusting the tolerance for spatial error as needed (see also Wallace & Weeks, 1988; Wallace, Weeks, & Kelso, 1990).

In contrast to a temporal-components view of reaching and grasping, as we discussed previously, Wing (Wing & Fraser, 1983; Wing et al., 1986) suggested that a reach-and-grasp action requires aiming the *thumb* at the object, then shaping the fingers as appropriate to acquire the object. Smeets and Brenner (1999; Smeets,

Brenner, & Biegstraaten, 2002; Smeets, Brenner, & Martin, 2009) extended Wing's idea to suggest that both the thumb and the finger(s) are aimed at specific locations on the object. Importantly, a change in either the position of the object (an extrinsic property in Jeannerod's scheme) or the size of the object (an intrinsic property) is compensated for by simply changing the targeted position for the thumb and finger(s).

A related view by Rosenbaum, Meulenbroek, Vaughan, and Jansen (2001) also considers reaching and grasping as a complex target-aiming task (see also Rosenbaum, Loukopolous, Meulenbroek, Vaughan, & Engelbrecht, 1995; and Rosenbaum, 2009). In their model, a reach-and-grasp action occurs by means of a selection process in which various potential *goal postures* (a forward model of the position adopted by the hand and arm when the object has been grasped, see chapters 5 and 6) are compared with the current posture of the hand and arm. The best candidate posture for the action is then selected, based on a process in which certain movement constraints must be met during the action (e.g., the resulting movement will avoid collisions, and effort is to be economized). Models of the resultant kinematics of this motion-planning view appear to agree quite well with existing data and, together with the Smeets and Brenner theory, provide exciting and potentially significant advances in our understanding of how reaching and grasping are coordinated.

Bimanual Coordination

Using the two hands together is often studied as a different type of coordination than the type we have just examined. Sometimes the hands perform similar actions (e.g., lifting a baby from the crib; steering a car), and sometimes the two actions are different (e.g., holding a bottle with one hand and twisting the cap with the other; using a fork with one hand to stabilize a piece of food while using a knife to cut it with the other hand). How the control of one hand interacts with the control of the other hand while both are moving at the *same time* represents a fundamental problem for scientists who study movement coordination.

The Bimanual Fitts Paradigm

The movement amplitude and size of the target to which a limb is aimed are strong determiners of MT—a relationship identified most commonly with Fitts' law (chapter 7). However, this law was based on experiments in which only one limb was moving. What happens to MT when two limbs are moved? And more importantly, what happens to MT when the task indexes of difficulty (IDs) assigned to the two limbs are different (i.e., incongruent)? These questions were addressed in experiments by Robinson and Kavinsky (1976) and more thoroughly by Kelso, Southard, and Goodman (1979). Subjects in the study by Kelso and colleagues made bimanual aiming movements in which each limb moved to a separate target as rapidly as possible. Two target IDs were used: In an "easy" task, the subject moved a short distance to a large target (ID = 0.8), and in a "difficult" task, the subject moved a long distance to a small target (ID = 3.7).

Kelso and colleagues (1979) found that the answer to the question of having both hands moving depended on which task was examined. The effect of amplitude and target width held true for the limb assigned to the high-ID task. This target was reached in about the same MT (average of 147 ms) regardless of whether the limb moved (a) alone (i.e., "unimanually"); (b) together ("bimanually") with the other limb, which was also moving to a high-ID task; or (c) bimanually but with the other limb moving to a low-ID task. However, amplitude and target width did not always predict MT for the limb moving to a low-ID task. The MT for this limb *changed* depending on the task conditions: (a) The MT was 98 ms when performed unimanually; (b) the MT was slowed slightly (to 105 ms) when the limb was paired with a limb that also moved to a low-ID task; and (c) MT slowed much more (to 130 ms) when the limb was paired with a limb moving to the high-ID task. In summary, incongruent bimanual-task ID conditions influenced the MT for a limb assigned to an "easy" task, but did not influence MT for a limb assigned to a "difficult" task.

These findings were replicated by Fowler, Duck, Mosher, and Mathieson (1991), who used procedures identical to those of Kelso and colleagues (1979, experiment 3) but added another aiming condition in which the task had an even larger ID (of 5.2). However, in both of these studies, it is important to note that the incongruent bimanual MTs for the low-ID task (130 ms in Kelso et al., 1979) remained conspicuously *smaller* than the MTs for the high-ID tasks (147 ms in Kelso et

al., 1979; see also Corcos, 1984; Marteniuk, MacKenzie, & Baba, 1984). Thus, it is probably more appropriate to conclude that the limb that moved to the more "difficult" task exerted a *strong determining influence* on the other limb (Riek, Tresilian, Mon-Williams, Coppard, & Carson, 2003).

This conclusion is supported by the results of a variant of this rapid bimanual-task paradigm. Subjects moved both hands simultaneously the same distance and to the same-sized target, but with a cardboard *hurdle* placed between the home position and the target for one of the limbs only, so that one limb was forced to move with a higher trajectory than the other to get to the target (Goodman, Kobayashi, & Kelso, 1983; Kelso, Putnam, & Goodman, 1983). In the study by Goodman and colleagues, the height of the hurdle for one limb was systematically varied from 0 cm (no hurdle) to 40 cm, while the other limb always moved without a hurdle. The MT findings are presented in figure 8.7. As expected, the MT of the limb going over the hurdle increased markedly with increased height of the hurdle. However, the limb that had *no hurdle* also revealed an increase in its MT as a function of the hurdle height that the *other limb* was assigned to clear, showing the tendency for the two hands to produce a similar pattern. Once again, it is important to note that the increased MTs of the no-hurdle limb were not identical to the increased MTs of the limb that had to clear a hurdle; rather, the MTs of the two limbs were influenced similarly by the hurdle. The size of the difference in MTs of the limbs with and without a hurdle increased with hurdle height, as can be seen by comparing the slopes of the filled and open circle functions in figure 8.7. In the Goodman and Kelso studies (Goodman et al., 1983; Kelso et al., 1983), the effect on the no-hurdle limb was also seen in the kinematic analyses of the movement trajectories. The trajectory required in order for the limb to clear the hurdle was accompanied by a similar *tendency* in the no-hurdle limb (although the effect was not a mirror-image mapping of the two limbs). The bimanual aiming task demands influenced the control of the two limbs in terms of both space and time.

A much stronger temporal interdependence appears to occur with use of a bimanual reaching/grasping task. Subjects in studies by Jackson, Jackson, and Kritikos (1999) reached both hands forward to grasp small wooden dowels. In one experiment, the two dowels were the same size

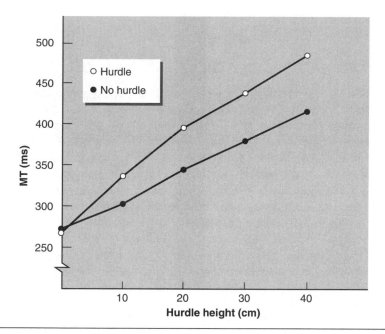

FIGURE 8.7   Movement times (MTs) for two limbs. The two limbs are moving simultaneously toward targets of equal difficulty, but only one limb (open circles) must go over a hurdle that varies in height. But, MT for the other limb, which does not go over a hurdle, also increases (filled circles).

Adapted from Goodman, Kobayashi, and Kelso 1983.

but could be placed either at the same distance from the home position (congruent bimanual task) or at different distances (incongruent task). In another experiment, the dowels were located at the same distance but were either the same size or different sizes. Regardless of the experimental manipulations, the effect on the temporal outcomes was dramatic. When the limbs were required to reach and grasp dowels in the incongruent conditions, all of the temporal measures of the reach-and-grasp actions were nearly identical for both limbs, and were very different compared to the MTs in each task performed unimanually. Although more research needs to be done with this paradigm (see also Jackson, German, & Peacock, 2002), it appears that temporal coupling of the limbs is stronger when a reach-and-grasp action is the goal than in the bimanual Fitts aiming task. Why there is a difference in these effects for reaching/grasping versus the Fitts task is not clear at this point.

Spatial Coordination

Spatial coordination can be observed when two or more body parts are assigned to perform different actions, or arise as the result of a common goal (see "Head–Arm Coordination in Golf Putting"). These effects have been studied in a number of experimental paradigms. Instead of varying target widths (as in the Fitts task), Marteniuk and colleagues (1984) asked their subjects to move as rapidly as possible and as closely as possible to a small target point, and measured the effective target width (W_e in Schmidt et al., 1979; see chapter 7). Marteniuk and colleagues found that one limb tended to overshoot a short target when the other limb moved to a far target. They also observed a small tendency for a limb to undershoot a far target when paired with a limb moving to a short target. Experiments by Sherwood (1991, 1994) suggest that these spatial *assimilation* effects occurred because the *force output* of the limb moving the lesser distance was in some way *biased* by the greater force output required to move the other limb a farther distance.

In all these tasks, the goal was to produce the same action in the two limbs, but with different amounts of distance or slightly different trajectories. The timing of the major force pulses or reversals in direction was nearly identical in the two limbs. In terms of motor programming views, the two limbs could have been controlled by the same GMP, but with different parameters assigned to each of the limbs. These results suggest an interlimb interference, not at the level of the GMP, but rather in terms of the assigned

Head–Arm Coordination in Golf Putting

Coordinating the motions of the arms and head is commonly emphasized in the act of putting in golf, and most experts recommend that the head be kept completely motionless while the arms swing like a pendulum during the putting stroke (e.g., Nicklaus & Bowden, 1974, p. 238; Woods, 2001, p. 37). However, recent research suggests that this recommendation is violated not only by less skilled golfers, but also by expert putters (Lee et al., 2008a, 2008b). Figure 8.8 illustrates the simultaneous velocity profiles of the putter (held by both arms) and the head during the backswing and downstroke of the golf putt (lasting about 1 s in duration). The typical less skilled golfer moved both the head and the putter away from the direction of the putt during the backstroke, and then moved both the head and putter toward the direction of the putt during the downstroke. All the pairs of velocity profiles from the 60 trials in the experiment for one subject are overlaid in figure 8.8a, revealing a head–arm (putter) coordination pattern that was repeated almost identically on each trial. This tight coupling of the head and arms in the *same direction* during the putt resulted in high positive correlations (+0.78; correlations computed within each trial).

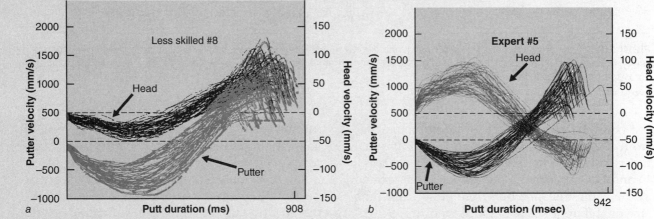

FIGURE 8.8   Velocity profiles of head and putter (arm) movements for *(a)* a typical less skilled golfer and *(b)* an expert golfer. Each figure contains 60 pairs of traces, corresponding to each trial in the experiment.

Reprinted, by permission, from T.D. Lee et al., 2008b, "Do expert golfers really keep their heads still while putting?" *Annual Review of Golf Coaching* 2: 135-143.

A typical set of trials performed by the expert golfers is illustrated in figure 8.8b. Once again, the pairs of velocity profiles are nearly identical on the 60 trials in the experiment for this golfer. However, the major difference, compared to the less skilled golfer, was that the expert golfers moved their head in a direction that was opposite to the motion of the arms during the putt. Experts moved their heads toward the direction of the putt as the backswing moved away from the ball. Then, at the same time the putter reversed its direction, the head reversed its direction too. This tight coupling of the head and arms in the *opposite direction* during the putt resulted in high *negative* (–0.70) correlations of the velocity profiles.

These findings have a number of important implications regarding coordination of degrees of freedom in putting. One implication is that golfers of varying skill level reduce the complexity of the putt by tightly coordinating the motions of the arms and head to act as a GMP. Coordinating the interdependence of the two limbs to act as a single unit of action—both for the less skilled and the expert golfers—is consistent with the evidence that a single GMP governs the coordination of these degrees of freedom (for details see the research of Heuer, Schmidt, & Ghodsian, 1995, discussed later in the chapter). Another implication of these findings is that, during the motor learning process (presumably with practice and augmented feedback), the GMP for the putt undergoes a fundamental change from a same-direction to an opposite-direction coupling of the head and arms. However, it does *not* appear that the skilled golfer keeps the head completely still during the putt, despite how it might appear.

parameters. One question that arises is whether such assimilation would occur when the tasks require different GMPs.

Swinnen, Walter, and colleagues examined interference in tasks that required the upper limbs to perform two completely different patterns at the same time (e.g., Swinnen, Walter, & Shapiro, 1988; Walter & Swinnen, 1990)—that is, in tasks for which a given program controlling the right arm could not have been merely scaled to produce the required action in the left arm. Walter and Swinnen (1990) had subjects produce an 800 ms movement with two reversals in direction with one arm and a unidirectional movement in the other arm. When these actions were done separately, the typical position–time records resembled the traces shown in figure 8.9, *a* and *c*. But when the subjects were asked to produce the two actions simultaneously, evidence of the pattern of the arm performing the complex

movement could be detected in the action of the arm doing the simple movement, although the amount of interference was not sufficient to make the arms produce identical movements (figure 8.9, *b* and *d*). The patterns of forces in the two arms occurred at essentially the same time, as if the pattern of contractions in the complex-movement arm were somehow "overflowing" to the simpler arm action. Furthermore, the interference appeared to be greater when the left arm performed the complex task and the right arm produced the simple task; adding a load to the complex-movement arm tended to increase this bias, and practice reduced the interference (see Walter, Swinnen, & Franz, 1993, for a review).

These authors have discussed their results in terms of what they call structural and metrical *coupling* of the two limbs, with practice serving to uncouple, or *dissociate,* the actions of the arms (e.g., Swinnen, 1992; Walter & Swinnen, 1992). How this

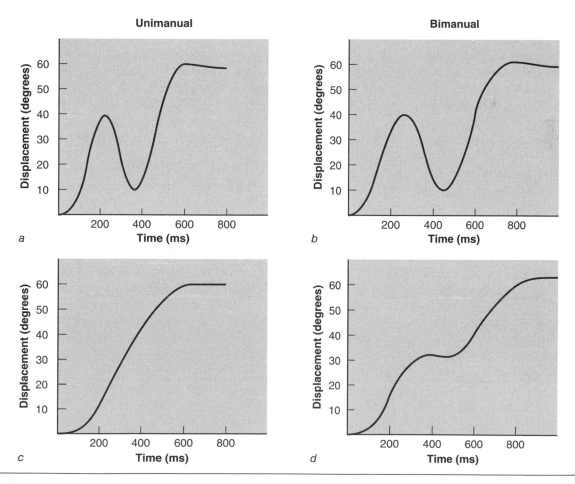

FIGURE 8.9   Bimanual coordination effects for limbs with different displacement–time goals; two-reversal task *(a* and *b),* unidirectional movement *(c* and *d),* unimanual performance *(a* and *c),* bimanual performance *(b* and *d).*

uncoupling occurs, though, is not entirely clear. One possibility is that independent control of each limb is acquired through the development of separate motor programs. This seems unlikely for a number of reasons, most important of which is the evidence presented in chapter 4 that the CNS appears incapable of programming and initiating two different actions at *exactly* the same time. Another possibility is that some different form of *interdependence* emerges that allows the limbs to do slightly different things at the same time.

Heuer, Schmidt, and Ghodsian (1995; also Schmidt, Heuer, Ghodsian, & Young, 1998) studied movement performances in a situation where the two arms produced deliberately different rapid, discrete patterns. The seated subjects moved two horizontal levers with elbow flexion–extension movements to produce specific space–time patterns for each limb. The right arm produced a flexion–extension–flexion pattern through about 70°, while the left arm simultaneously produced a flexion–extension pattern through about 60°, with MTs ranging from 400 to 600 ms. Subjects had considerable difficulty at first, but after several hundred trials they were able to produce the actions very easily.

From the acceleration–time traces, Schmidt and colleagues (1998) defined 12 landmarks, essentially as had been done in the analysis of units described earlier (see figure 8.2). The within-subject (across trials) correlations among all possible pairs of landmarks were then computed (see figure 8.3). The correlations among the landmarks within each arm were generally very high, averaging 0.91 (right) and 0.94 (left), especially when the actions were done as quickly as possible (Schmidt et al., 1998). The relatively high correlations among all of the landmarks suggested that each arm produced a one-unit pattern, as discussed earlier.

The interesting point for coordination, however, concerns the correlations among the landmarks *between* the arms. These correlations were also generally very high, especially when the actions were very rapid, and were nearly the same as those for the individual arms (mean = 0.91). These findings supported the view that the coordination between the two arms was controlled as a single unit (i.e., by a single GMP controlling both hands at the same time, as discussed in an earlier section in this chapter), even though the two limbs produced completely different spatial–temporal patterns. In fact, supporting this single-GMP view, subjects became able to speed up or slow down this entire bimanual pattern on command, changing the left- and right-arm speeds together. But, when instructed to produce the arm movements at different speeds (e.g., speed the right arm and slow the left), subjects found this variant nearly impossible to do (Schmidt et al., 1998). These data imply that the right and left arms were being scaled together in time so that relative timing (both within and between arms) was essentially invariant. In other experiments, where the movements were done even more quickly, the landmarks between the two arms were even more strongly coordinated. Therefore, on the basis of the logic of units of action presented earlier, the separate actions produced by the right and left arms were part of the *same* GMP. This result shows *increased* coupling between the limbs with practice—not decoupling as argued by Swinnen (1992; Walter & Swinnen, 1992), discussed earlier. This finding also provides a basis for the idea that complex, multilimb actions—in which all of the limbs are doing different things, as in pole-vaulting, or the golf-putting example given earlier—can probably be controlled by a single, learned GMP. Apparently, when two limbs do different things at the same time, this does not necessarily mean that they are operating independently.[2]

End-State Coordination

Recall from chapter 3 (see section on "Compatibility and Complex Actions" on p. 74) that, in some situations, we choose rather awkward initial limb postures in order to maximize biomechanical efficiency (or "end-state comfort") at movement completion (Rosenbaum, 2009; Rosenbaum et al., 1990). In these cases, selecting a movement plan to satisfy a specific (end) goal appears to be a natural and spontaneous process. So, how would *two* limbs be coordinated if each had a specific but incompatible end goal? Would the end-state comfort effect be traded off in order to achieve a well-coordinated movement? Surprisingly, individuals do not prefer one coordination pattern to another—they tend to choose the pattern most likely to satisfy a goal that maximizes end comfort for both limbs, as described next.

Kunde and Weigelt (2005) had subjects perform the tasks illustrated in figure 8.10, involving the raising of two blocks from a horizontal to a vertical orientation. These actions could be

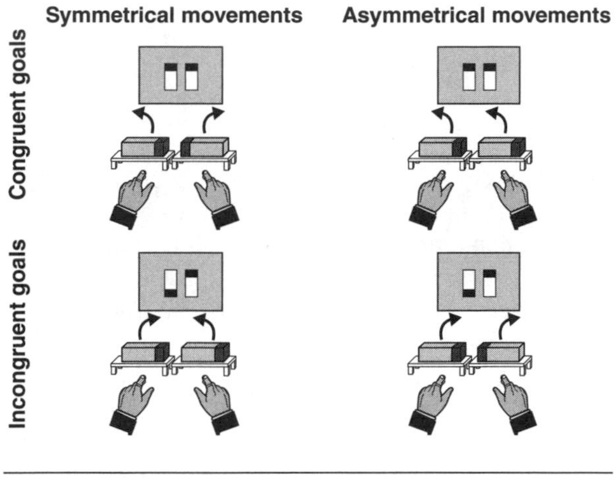

FIGURE 8.10 Subjects performed bimanual movements to raise two blocks, with colored ends, from horizontal to vertical positions. Congruent goals were defined as raising the two colored ends to the same vertical position. Incongruent goals required one colored end to be on top and the other on the bottom of the vertical position. Symmetrical movements involved hand actions in which both raised blocks were turned inward or outward. Asymmetrical movements required both hands to move in the same direction.

Reprinted, by permission, from W. Kunde and M. Weigelt, 2005, "Goal congruency in bimanual object manipulation," *Journal of Experimental Psychology: Human Perception and Performance* 31: 145-156.

performed with either symmetrical or asymmetrical hand movements, resulting in end goals that were either congruent or incongruent with respect to object orientation (see figure 8.10 for details). The main finding was that subjects showed no preference for symmetric over asymmetric hand movements. Rather, the achievement of congruent goals with both hands resulted in responses performed with faster RTs and MTs and fewer errors than incongruent goals, regardless of *how* the actions were performed. Other experiments, in which subjects were allowed to choose the orientation of the hands, revealed that even an uncomfortable coordination pattern was preferred if it maximized end-state comfort (Fischman, Stodden, & Lehman, 2003; Hughes & Franz, 2008; Janssen, Beuting, Meulenbroek, & Steenbergen, 2009; Weigelt, Kunde, & Prinz, 2006). These findings are similar to the results seen in unimanual tasks (Rosenbaum, 2009).

These findings suggest that the nature of the coordination pattern appears to be subservient to the desired end result. In the case of end-state comfort effects, biomechanical efficiency at movement completion appears to take precedence over how the limbs move there.

Continuous Tasks

A recurring issue throughout this book is the difference between discrete and continuous skills in how motor control is achieved. Although some commonalities exist (e.g., timing processes), major differences abound as well (e.g., role of feedback and motor programs). In this section, we will see that many researchers who study coordination in continuous tasks take a fundamentally different view regarding the process of movement control than researchers who study discrete tasks. "Costs and Benefits of Coordinating Two Limbs" (p. 279) presents two little experiments for you to try, which represent examples of some fundamental processes when continuous movements of two or more limbs are performed simultaneously. These phenomena have interested scientists for over a century but have been the topic of intense experimental scrutiny only in recent years.

Early Research

Bimanual coordination of continuous tasks in humans has interested researchers for many years (see "R.S. Woodworth on Coordination"). For example, right-handed subjects in Langfeld's (1915) experiment tapped one finger as rapidly as possible for 30 s—either the index or middle finger of the right or left hand. Between-finger differences on the same hand were small, but between-hand differences were large: Average MTs for the right-hand taps were 181 ms compared with 222 ms for the left hand. This is not too surprising; asymmetries in performance are frequently found when left- and right-hand performances of right-handed people are compared (e.g., Elliott & Roy, 1996; Sainburg, 2005). However, on some trials, subjects were asked to tap one finger on each hand such that the two taps were made *simultaneously* and as fast as possible. When subjects tapped with the same finger on both hands (e.g., the right and left index finger at the same time) the average MT was 208 ms, which represents a 27 ms *decrement* for the right finger (compared to 181 ms in unimanual tapping) but a 14 ms *facilitation* for the left hand (compared to 222 ms). Langfeld (1915) thus showed that, in the process of becoming coordinated, the temporal, "independent behavior" of the two hands changed dramatically. The timing of the two hands became much more interdepen-

R.S. Woodworth on Coordination

They said it . . . .

Much of the current work on coordination has its roots in monographs that were not available in English until quite some time after their original publication. Some of these works were eventually translated and had a very influential effect on English readers when they were published (e.g., Bernstein, 1967; von Holst, 1937/1973). In other cases, contemporary researchers have made us aware of important untranslated works (e.g., Heuer, 1996; Latash & Zatsiorsky, 2001; Worringham, 1992). Another source of 19th-century work on coordination—a brief review published in French by Woodworth (1903)—had not, to our knowledge, been translated into English prior to the third edition of this book. A comparison of the following quoted passage to some of the "modern" work on coordination reveals some remarkable early insights regarding spatial and temporal coordination, which became a dormant issue in research for quite some time.

"It is common knowledge that one can execute with ease simultaneous, corresponding movements with the right and left hand. One must, however, make an effort so that they correspond; if one moves the right hand in mid-air, tracing any shape, one must devote attention to the left hand simply for it to move, for it will trace the symmetrical corresponding shape. The connection is more between the innervation of corresponding muscles on both sides of the body.

"Munsterberg proved that there was another relationship between movements of both sides. When an arm is balanced in front, the other must naturally balance itself, not in front, but behind; there are also other cases in which symmetrical movements on both sides must naturally alternate with one another. It is not less true that it is easy to execute simultaneous movements that correspond on each side.

"Ostermann found that this ease appeared only in bilateral symmetrical movements. If we tried to make simultaneous movement, symmetrical in relation to a horizontal plane, the attempt would result in inexactness and confusion. The attempt had not been "natural" and was executed without confidence, whereas bilateral symmetrical movements were executed with ease and confidence and some achieved exactness.

"Bloch discovered that in order for the symmetrical movements to be executed with ease and precision, both arms have to move at the same time. If one moves an arm toward a certain point, the effort that one will make to place the other arm to the corresponding point will result in inexact movement" (Woodworth, 1903, pp. 97-98).

dent, resulting in a facilitation in performance for the finger on the nondominant hand and a decrement for the finger on the dominant hand.

The struggle between the tendency of one oscillating limb to maintain an independent motor behavior (termed the *maintenance tendency* by von Holst [1937/1973]) and the tendency of its behavior to become coupled with another oscillating limb (which von Holst called the *magnet effect*) captures a critical feature of temporal coordination in continuous skills. As we will see in the next sections, these strong natural tendencies play an important role in the coordination of continuous actions.

Gait Transitions

Watch people as they hurry to catch a bus. They usually choose one of two gaits to get to the bus:

a fast walking gait or a running gait. Each gait has distinct relative timing and biomechanical characteristics. Within a certain range of speeds, either gait will get the job done. What process determines the gait that will be used? As it turns out, this question is not a trivial one; and the answer has provided considerable evidence to support an important view of motor control.

Animal Research

In chapter 6 we discussed the mesencephalic preparation in cats. Walking could be initiated in these spinalized cats on a treadmill; the provided stimulation was not rhythmical and in time with the walking patterns, though. One important finding was that increases in the speed of the treadmill induced changes from a walk to a trot,

Costs and Benefits of Coordinating Two Limbs

Two quick and easy little experiments will demonstrate how moving a second limb along with one that is already moving can have both positive and negative consequences, depending on the task. In the first experiment, using a blackboard and chalk, try to write your name with your nondominant hand, at usual speed but backward (i.e., producing a mirror image of your name). You will probably find that this is very difficult to do and that the pattern is barely legible. Now do the same task again, but this time, do it simultaneously with the dominant hand writing normally, so that the hands are writing in opposite directions. You should find that the pattern of the nondominant hand is much smoother and that the two patterns are roughly similar (but mirror images of each other). More importantly, as you perform the two-handed task, notice how the two limbs seem to be "locked together" (or "coupled"). Even though the nondominant handwriting is somewhat more uncontrolled than the dominant, a characteristic pattern still emerges—the same loops, straight parts, and so on.

Sit in a chair to do the second experiment. Begin by making clockwise circles on the floor with your right foot. Then, while continuing to make circles, draw the number "6" in the air with your right hand. What happened to your foot's movement? In all likelihood, your foot no longer continued to make circles. Now, try this experiment again, combining the right-handed 6s with your left foot making the circles; then again with your left hand making the circles. Now try all three again by making the circles in the counterclockwise direction. Was the circle drawing easier to maintain in any of these six experimental conditions?

In performing these two experiments, notice how the two limbs tend to *want* to be locked together, as if you had lost some control of them and they were being controlled by some other influence. In the handwriting experiment, this tendency has a facilitating effect—the performance of the nondominant limb improves relative to the unimanual (control) condition. In the circle-drawing experiment, this same tendency has a detrimental effect—the performance of the circle declines relative to the control condition. As suggested by the differences in performance in the six circle-drawing conditions, though, the tendencies to couple the limb movements depend largely on the tasks and the effectors that are involved in performing them.

THE FAR SIDE BY GARY LARSON

In the stadiums of ancient Rome, the most feared trial was the rub-your-stomach-and-pat-your-head-at-the-same-time event.

and occasionally to a gallop. Although the animal could not feel its legs while in locomotion, these specific gait patterns, and more importantly, the *qualitative* (or "nonlinear") change from one gait pattern to another, still occurred on occasion.

Gait patterns and the transition between gait patterns in animals with four or more limbs are fascinating to compare across species (e.g., Alexander, 2003, chapter 7). Of particular interest here is the process by which an animal selects a particular speed within each gait, and the process that determines *when* the animal will change gaits. A leading hypothesis is that gait selection and the decision to change gaits are both based on a principle of *minimal energy costs* (Alexander, 2003). Consider the analysis of horse gaits in figure 8.11 (Hoyt & Taylor, 1981). The histograms in the bottom half of figure 8.11 illustrate the frequency of gaits that a horse selected spontaneously when the treadmill speed was changed. These histograms represent a subset of the total range of speeds that the horse *could* select within each gait. Taking this analysis further, Hoyt and Taylor measured the energy cost (defined in terms of oxygen consumption) of horses that were trained to walk, trot, and gallop at a range of speeds on a treadmill (speed now being determined by the experimenter). The data in the top half of figure 8.11 suggest that the energy costs of walking and trotting were rather high at both extremes of the speed ranges within each gait. Moreover,

the maximum energy efficiency, defined at the minimum points on the walk and trot curves, corresponded rather well with the speeds that the horses selected spontaneously when locomoting at different speeds. Hoyt and Taylor (1981) suggested that energy efficiency might represent a basis used by an animal for the selection of specific speeds within a gait, and that energy *inefficiency* serves as the *catalyst* or *trigger* to change gaits.

Human Research

Humans typically use only two gaits, walking and running. The transition between these two gaits occurs between 2.0 and 2.2 m/s (about 4.5 and 4.9 mph), but this can change depending on a number of factors, such as whether the person is accelerating (a walk-to-run transition) or decelerating (run to walk) (Diedrich & Warren, 1995), the rate of acceleration (Van Caekenberghe, Segers, De Smet, Aerts, & De Clercq, 2010), and cognitive load (Daniels & Newell, 2003). On the

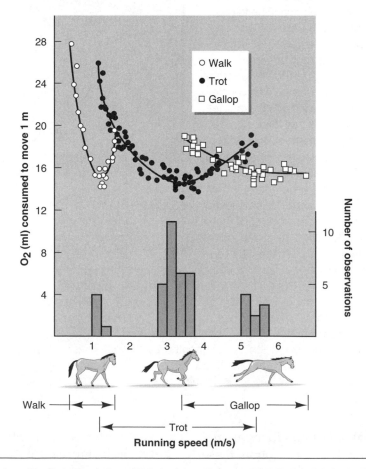

FIGURE 8.11 Oxygen consumption at various speeds in the walk, trot, and gallop gaits of a horse. The histograms just above the *x*-axis represent the preferred speeds that the horse selects in each gait.

Reprinted from *Nature* Vol. 292, D.F. Hoyt and C.R. Taylor, 1981, "Gait and the energetics of locomotion in horses," pgs. 239-240, Copyright 1981. By permission of D.F. Hoyt.

basis of the energy-trigger view from the animal research just presented, one hypothesis would suggest that inefficiency in metabolic costs might be a leading catalyst for this transition. Support for this view would be strong if oxygen consumption levels were drastically different between performances at the pre- and postgait transition speeds. An experiment to test this prediction, however, showed no such drastic change, even when load conditions were added to increase overall energy expenditure (Raynor, Yi, Abernethy, & Jong, 2002).

An alternative view of the trigger process suggests that the gait pattern begins to lose *stability* at speeds beyond the normal transition point (Diedrich & Warren, 1995, 1998a, 1998b). In these experiments, Diedrich and Warren examined the variability in the ankle–hip and ankle–knee segments in terms of within-limb relative phase as subjects walked and ran at speeds that were greater and less than those in the normal transition region. Results from one of these studies are illustrated in figure 8.12. Here the normal transition range appears as the shaded region of the graph, and measures of the SD of relative phase for the ankle–knee segment are plotted for both walking and running at various speeds. (The mea-

sure on the *x*-axis, the so-called Froude number,[3] represents speed normalized for leg length.) The results are clear: For the relative phase in both segments measured, walking became more variable (less stable) at speeds *higher* than the normal transition point, and running became more variable at speeds *lower* than the normal transition point (Diedrich & Warren, 1995; but see also Kao, Ringenbach, & Martin, 2003). Note, however, that these data do not provide clear evidence that pattern instability is necessarily *the trigger* for a gait transition, just that improved stability is concomitant with a gait transition.

Neither the energetic nor the stability hypothesis appears to explain the findings of the role of *vision* on gait transitions, however. In a recent study by Mohler, Thompson, Creem-Regehr, Pick, and Warren (2007), subjects walked on a treadmill that provided an "endless hallway" virtual environment. Walk-to-run and run-to-walk gait transitions were stimulated by increasing or decreasing the treadmill speed periodically over the duration of the trial (which is typical of this research protocol). However, the additional manipulation used by Mohler and associates (2007) was to covary the visual feedback provided by the virtual environment. In a control condition, the virtual visual feedback was matched to the visual array that the subject would have received in a normal environment for that biomechanical speed (a 1:1 correspondence, or 1.0 gain). In two other conditions, the virtual visual feedback was halved (1:2 correspondence, or 0.5 gain) or doubled (2:1 correspondence or 2.0 gain) relative to the actual gait speed. Thus, a slower visual feedback condition resulted in the sensation that gait was slower than was actually the case (and conversely for the faster visual feedback condition). The results of the study are illustrated in figure 8.13. Regardless of the gait transition (walk-run or run-walk), providing the *visual sensation* of a slower gait resulted in a transition that occurred at a faster speed than in the control condition. Conversely, the faster visual feedback condition resulted in gait transitions at speeds less than normal.

Mohler and colleagues' findings provide difficulties for both the energetic and stability gait-transition hypotheses. Since the only manipulation in the study was *virtual* visual feedback (i.e., the treadmill speeds were consistent in all visual conditions), there were no biomechanical or physiological reasons for changes in the

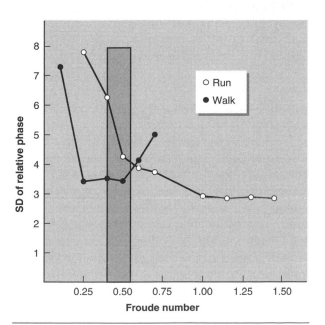

FIGURE 8.12 The variability in ankle–knee relative phasing in walking and running at speeds that were greater and less than the normal transition region (Froude number refers to speed normalized for leg length).

Adapted, by permission, from F.J. Diedrich and W.H. Warren, Jr., 1995, "Why change gaits? Dynamics of the walk-run transition," *Journal of Experimental Psychology: Human Perception and Performance* 21: 183-202. Copyright © 1995 by the American Psychological Association.

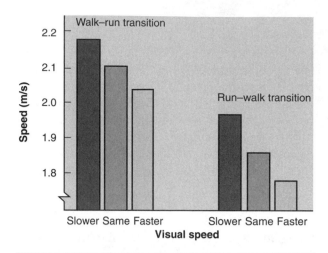

FIGURE 8.13 Effects of actual gait speed and apparent (visual) speed on the point of walk–run and run–walk gait transitions.

With kind permission from Springer Science+Business Media: *Experimental Brain Research*, "Visual flow influences gait transition speed and preferred walking speed," 181, 2007, pgs. 221-228, B.J. Mohler et al.

gait-transition speeds. Therefore, these findings suggest that gait transitions, and perhaps coordination more generally, are based on multisensory information sources.

Temporal Coordination

A considerable research emphasis that has emerged in the past two to three decades is devoted to bimanual coordination of the upper limbs. Some of the initial work was motivated by a desire to understand transitions from one pattern to another more fully; a task involving the continuous cycling of two fingers provided a paradigm to study phase transitions between any two limbs (Kelso, 1995). However, the study of temporal coordination, in general, went far beyond these initial motivations and now represents a complex area of research investigation in itself. In this section we provide an overview of the research issues, paradigms, and theoretical orientations that have emerged in the study of temporal coordination. Much more in-depth treatments of this literature are widely available (Kelso, 1995; Kelso & Engstrøm, 2005; Swinnen, 2002; Turvey & Fonseca, 2009).

Bimanual Timing Patterns

Try this simple experiment (cf. Kelso, 1984). Hold your hands in front of you with the index fingers pointing straight ahead, and make a series of "pinches" by touching the finger to the thumb. Do this with both hands such that you are making one "pinch" about every second with each hand. When we ask students in our classes to do this simple task, with no further instructions, almost everyone does it the same way—the pinches are coordinated such that the fingers and thumbs on both hands are making contact at about the same time. This tendency to produce a recognizable *timing pattern* can be quantified by measuring the relative phase of the between-hand timing (as described in chapter 2). In this case, the "pinch" of the one hand occurs at about the same time within its cycle as does the pinch of the other hand, relative to its cycle. (The difference in phase angles of the two limbs within each of their respective cycles provides a quantitative measure of coordination, called "relative phase"; see chapter 2 and figure 2.14 for more details). Moreover, the maximum opening between the finger and thumb (which occurs about halfway through the cycle) also occurs at about the same time for each hand. The timing of these (and other) kinematic landmarks within each cycle for the two hands result in a mean relative phase of 0°. The standard deviation of individual scores used to calculate the mean provides a measure of the *stability* of the pattern, which is usually very stable for this task (i.e., the SD of these phase angles is typically about 5°-10° around the mean value). The pattern is commonly described as moving *in-phase*, or in *symmetry* (chapter 2). For this task, the in-phase coordination mode is the *preferred*, or most frequently adopted pattern.

Now, holding your hands and moving at about the same speed as before, try performing a different pattern. Make pinching movements with both hands such that the pinches alternate on the two hands. You will probably find that this is also quite easy to do. Since the closing of the pinch for one hand occurs while the other pinch is about halfway through its cycle (i.e., when it is at maximum aperture), the relative phase of this pattern has a mean of 180°. This pattern is commonly known as moving in *anti-phase*, or in *asymmetry*.

Numerous investigators have studied in-phase (0° mean relative phase), anti-phase (180°), and timing patterns with phase relations in between (e.g., 60°, 90°, 150°); the results illustrated in figure 8.14 are typical (Yamanishi, Kawato, & Suzuki, 1980). In this study, subjects tapped their left and right fingers in time with left and

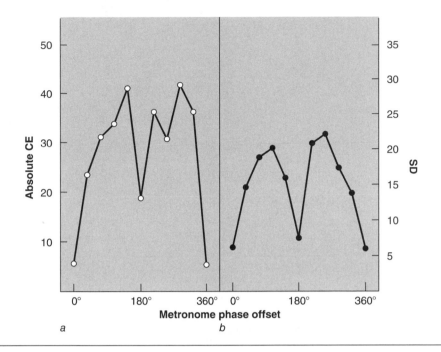

FIGURE 8.14 *(a)* Absolute constant error (|CE|) and *(b)* standard deviation (SD) of relative phase for limbs moving at phase offsets between 0° and 360°.

With kind permission From Springer Science+Business Media: *Biological Cybernetics*, "Two coupled oscillators as a model for the coordinated finger tapping by both hands," 37, 1980, pg. 221, J. Yamanishi, M. Kawato, and R. Suzuki.

right visual metronomes that were set to "beat" at various phase offsets. Measures of relative-phase accuracy and variability are presented in figure 8.14.[4] The in-phase patterns (0° and 360° on the x-axis) and anti-phase pattern (180°) were performed with much greater accuracy (figure 8.14*a*) and with more stability (lower SDs in figure 8.14*b*) than for any of the other phase relations. In addition, there was a slight tendency for the in-phase pattern to be performed with more stability than the anti-phase pattern. The performances of these two timing patterns illustrate natural and stable coordination modes for oscillatory bimanual movements and have been replicated in experiments using finger-oscillation tasks (e.g., Kelso, 1984), finger tapping (e.g., Tuller & Kelso, 1989), wrist rotations (e.g., Cohen, 1971; Lee, Blandin, & Proteau, 1996), swinging pendulums (Schmidt, Shaw, & Turvey, 1993; Turvey, Rosenblum, Schmidt, & Kugler, 1986), and other similar movement coordination tasks. This work has been reviewed by Kelso (1995) and Swinnen (2002; Swinnen & Wenderoth, 2004).

Unintended Phase Transitions Here is another little experiment. Perform the in-phase, pinching pattern as before, starting at a comfortable

timing frequency (e.g., 1 beat/s). Now, gradually speed up the pinching frequency until eventually you are moving as fast as possible. Then repeat the experiment, this time starting with the anti-phase pattern. If your results are similar to those reported by Kelso (1984; Kelso, Scholz, & Schöner, 1986), your data will resemble the results presented in figure 8.15. The open symbols in this figure represent the anti-phase pattern; the filled symbols represent the in-phase pattern. Mean relative phase is presented in figure 8.15*a* and relative-phase variability in figure 8.15*b*. As seen before (Yamanishi et al., 1980; figure 8.14), both timing patterns were performed close to their intended goal and with small variability at low oscillation frequencies.[5] This stable and accurate performance continued for the in-phase pattern as oscillation frequency increased. However, the influence of frequency on the anti-phase pattern was rather startling: At about 2.25 Hz, the timing pattern began to *switch* from anti-phase to an in-phase coordination mode. Notice also that in figure 8.15*b*, the anti-phase pattern actually began to become more variable at about 1.75 Hz, suggesting that the loss in stability somehow precipitated the switch. Subjects in Kelso's experiment had been instructed not to resist these pattern

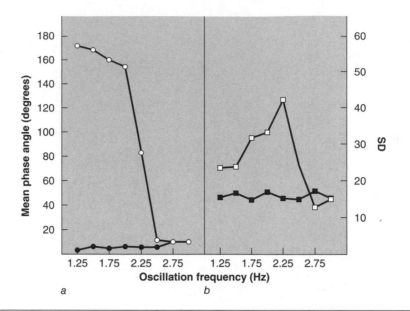

FIGURE 8.15 Bimanual coordination performance for patterns initiated in anti-phase (open symbols) and in-phase (filled symbols) for *(a)* mean relative phase and *(b)* standard deviation (SD).

Reprinted from *Physics Letters A, Vol. 118*, J.A.S. Kelso, J.P. Scholz, and G. Schöner, "Nonequilibrium phase transitions in coordinated biological motion: Critical fluctuations," pg. 281, Copyright 1986, with kind permission of Elsevier.

switches, so once the original anti-phase pattern had become an in-phase pattern at higher speeds, the new mean relative phase remained close to 0° with low variability. This basic set of findings has been replicated many times, using different effector pairs (see Lee et al., 1996, for a review).

Although there are some similarities in the transitions between patterns of bimanual coordination and the gait transitions discussed earlier, there are just about as many differences. For example, a stable in-phase pattern can be performed at all speeds, whereas a stable anti-phase pattern can be performed only at low oscillation frequencies. As well, when changing gaits as the speed increases we do not change from anti-phase to in-phase—that is, we don't start hopping). However, there are many intriguing similarities too. The most important of these is the loss of stability that precedes a phase transition from anti-phase to in-phase. This result is quite similar to the loss in stability that precedes a gait transition at nonpreferred speeds (Diedrich & Warren, 1995). And, in a way similar to what is seen with gait transitions (discussed previously; Mohler et al., 2007; see figure 8.13), the performance of these timing patterns is highly susceptible to visual feedback influences (Mechsner, Kerzel, Knoblich, & Prinz, 2001).

Self-Organization Theory Haken, Kelso, and Bunz (1985) presented an influential model of the results reported in figure 8.15 that has had profound effects on motor control research (for more details see Jeka & Kelso, 1989; Kelso, 1995, 2008; Kelso & Engstrøm, 2005; Wallace, 1996). This model of two coupled oscillators (commonly referred to now as the HKB model) was grounded in the science of dynamics—literally, how physical systems change their states over time. Five important effects depicted in figure 8.15 laid the groundwork for the HKB model. (1) Both the in-phase and anti-phase patterns are performed well at low movement frequencies. The system is said to be *bistable*—there are two stable coordination regimes. (2) At maximal speeds, only the in-phase pattern remains stable; the anti-phase is destabilized and switches to in-phase. Thus, the system underwent a *phase transition* from a bistable to a monostable coordination regime. (3) The process of change for the initially anti-phase pattern is abrupt and qualitative—the change involved a *nonlinear* transition, called a *bifurcation*. (4) The phase transition was instigated by an outside agency (changes in the pacing frequency in this case), called a *control parameter*.[6] (5) The nonlinear phase shift was precipitated by a destabilization of the anti-phase pattern during a *critical period*.

The general purpose of the HKB model was to conceptualize these movement coordination findings (and other, related findings) as a self-organizing system, as in the way the physics of chemical actions might be modeled. By *self-organization,* Haken and colleagues assumed that the degrees of freedom involved in movement were governed by patterns (called "collectives") that were subject to destabilization and transitions. Compared to more cognitively based models or theories of motor control, the key feature of self-organization was a decentralization of the burden of how coordination is achieved. According to this view, the system organizes its degrees of freedom through preferences that undergo transitions as an interaction with the environment within which it performs. The role of cognition is diminished, especially as compared to that in contemporary motor control models. In other words, self-organization is like an orchestra playing without a conductor (Kelso & Engstrøm, 2005).

One critical feature that sets the HKB model (and theoretical approach) apart from many other theories is the role of *variability* in motor control. Recall the discussion of the laws of speed and accuracy in chapter 7: Increases in variability were associated with declines in the efficiency (or effectiveness, or "skillfulness") of the motor control system. In the HKB model, variability is viewed as a characteristic of the current state of the system—that is, instability gives rise to change (Kelso, 1992), and change leads to a more stable state.

The HKB model has had an enormous impact on coordination research, and in the ensuing years hundreds of studies were published in which subjects performed continuous, cyclical tasks. Some of the studies described in the next sections were motivated as direct tests of the HKB model, and other studies were performed as a result of the research that it spawned in the ensuing decades. However, it is important to note that a vast majority of this research has carried on the theoretical tradition to understand coordination as a self-organizing process.

Spatial Orientation and Timing Patterns Swinnen (2002) concluded that interlimb coordination preferences can be summarized into two general categories: an *egocentric* preference, in which synchrony of the timing of two limbs is toward and away from the center of any plane of motion (e.g.,

toward the middle of the chest for upper limb movements in front of the body), and a *directional* preference, in which synchrony of the timing of two limbs is in the same direction along any plane of motion. For bimanual tasks performed in front of the body (e.g., tapping, finger wiggling, and our pinching examples), the egocentric preference (in-phase pattern) dominates over the directional preference (anti-phase). However, a directional preference exists when one is moving an arm and a leg in the up–down direction. But research by Swinnen and his colleagues has demonstrated quite clearly that the relative dominance of these preferences is subject to spatial interactions (Bogaerts & Swinnen, 2001; Serrien, Bogaerts, Suy, & Swinnen, 1999; Swinnen, Jardin, Meulenbroek, Dounskaia, & Hofkens-van den Brandt, 1997; Swinnen et al., 1998).

For example, in one study (Swinnen et al., 1998), subjects moved their right and left limbs in various combinations either along the *x*-axis (left-right, in front of the body) or in the *y*-axis direction (toward and away from the body). In this study, "in-phase" and "anti-phase" were defined in terms of an egocentric referent. Regardless of the spatial trajectory of the limbs, in-phase movements arrived at the egocentrically closest point at the same time and at the point farthest from egocenter at the same time; for anti-phase coordination, one limb arrived at the closest egocentric point at the same time that the other limb arrived at the farthest point from egocenter. As before, when both limbs were moving along the *x*-axis, in a *parallel* (180°) spatial orientation, the egocentric preference (in-phase) dominated performance. However, when one limb moved along the *x*-axis and the other along the *y*-axis, in an *orthogonal* (90°) spatial orientation, the normal stability of these patterns was reversed—anti-phase was more stable than in-phase.

These effects were extended by Lee, Almeida, and Chua (2002) and Welsh, Almeida, and Lee (2005), who used both the parallel and orthogonal spatial orientations as had Swinnen and colleagues (1998); they also included obtuse angles of spatial orientation (such as one limb moving along the *x*-axis and the other at a 120° or 150° spatial orientation to the *x*-axis). When performance was assessed in a high-oscillation frequency condition, the stability of the patterns showed a clear trend, as illustrated in figure 8.16. The shift in

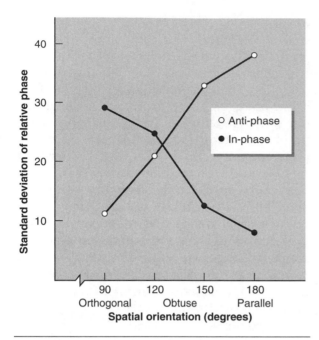

FIGURE 8.16 Effects of spatial orientation on relative-phase variability in upper limb coordination.

With kind permission of Springer Science+Business Media: *Experimental Brain Research*, Spatial constraints in bimanual coordination: Influences of effector orientation," 146, 2002, pgs. 205-212, T.D. Lee, Q.J. Almeida, and R. Chua.

dominance between the egocentric (in-phase) and directional (anti-phase) preferences was mediated by the spatial orientation of the limbs. Findings such as these (see also Amazeen, Amazeen, & Turvey, 1998; Carson, Riek, Smethurst, Párraga, & Byblow, 2000; Salesse, Oullier, & Temprado, 2005)—in which the motor system finds new stable solutions when changed environmental conditions have caused instabilities in the current pattern—have prompted some to suggest modifications to the HKB model (Fuchs & Jirsa, 2000; Newell, Liu, & Mayer-Kress, 2008; Peper, Ridderikhoff, Daffertshofer, & Beek, 2004).

Intention and Attention In the Kelso studies described previously (see figure 8.15), the metronome pacing frequency served as a control parameter to "perturb" the system (by forcing it to move faster or slower); these changes resulted in different effects depending on whether the pattern was stable (in-phase) or unstable (anti-phase). As we mentioned before, the role of cognition in self-organization theory is minimized. But, according to the theory, *intentions* do have a specific role—to stabilize or destabilize a movement pattern in much the same way oscillation frequency and spatial orientation did as described in the previous sections.

To illustrate the role of intentions, let's go back to our bimanual pinching experiment one more time. Start by coordinating your pinching movements in the anti-phase pattern at a relatively slow pace (say, 1 beat/s). At some point, try to switch to an in-phase pattern as quickly as possible. You probably had little difficulty in doing so. Now, trying doing the opposite—try to switch as rapidly as possible from the in-phase pattern to the anti-phase pattern. Experiments of this kind typically show that it takes longer to switch completely from the in-phase mode to the anti-phase mode than vice versa (e.g., Byblow, Lewis, Stinear, Austin, & Lynch, 2000; Carson, Byblow, Abernethy, & Summers, 1996; Kelso, Scholz, & Schöner, 1988; Scholz & Kelso, 1990; Serrien & Swinnen, 1999). Similar differences between the two bimanual coordination modes are seen when a mechanical device is introduced that *perturbs* coordination: The in-phase pattern restabilizes more quickly following a perturbation than the anti-phase pattern (Scholz, Kelso, & Schöner, 1987).

These findings have been interpreted within self-organization theory as being consistent with the unintended phase transitions discussed earlier. The *intention* to switch coordination patterns creates a destabilization of the current pattern, and that destabilization now facilitates the transition to a new pattern. Since the in-phase pattern is a stronger, more stable mode of coordination, intentionally destabilizing this pattern is more "difficult" and takes more time than destabilizing the anti-phase pattern.

The role of intention also highlights a peculiarity associated with some of the research on self-organized coordination. In the early studies by Kelso (1984; Kelso et al., 1986), in which patterns of motion were performed at specified oscillation frequencies, subjects were instructed to let the hands "do what came naturally," and to not intervene intentionally if a pattern destabilized. From one perspective, this instruction is perfect for the study of self-organization—letting the system relax into a pattern that is best suited or "natural" for the given frequency. From another perspective, however, one could argue that the nonlinear phase transition from anti-phase to in-phase occurred because the subjects' *task* had changed—that is, they were no longer intending to perform the original pattern. If the goal of the task was to perform the anti-phase pattern *as well as possible*, then it is peculiar to use an instructional procedure that allows the task goal to change midway through a trial. Indeed, results of studies in which subjects were instructed to try to *maintain* the goal pattern at all times were quite different: There was an overall linear increase in pattern variability, but not a permanent switch to a stable new pattern (Lee, 2004; Lee et al., 1996; Smethurst & Carson, 2003).

The role of intention in bimanual coordination has also been examined in the more traditional sense of attention, as in experiments on mental workload (which was discussed at length in chapter 4). One group of investigators has conducted studies in which in-phase and anti-phase patterns were performed together with a secondary, probe RT task (chapter 4) (for reviews see Monno, Temprado, Zanone, & Laurent, 2002; Temprado, 2004). As might be expected given the foregoing discussion, the performance of an in-phase bimanual pattern was relatively immune to the effects of a secondary task. In contrast, an anti-phase pattern was rather markedly destabilized if priority in the "division" of attention was given to the secondary task. However, performance of an anti-phase task became *more* stable if increased cognitive effort was induced through moderate levels of anxiety (Court, Bennett, Williams, & Davids, 2005). Thus, the effects of attention (in terms of divided attention) converge well with the role of intentions discussed earlier—attention can serve to perturb a stable system, and to maintain either a stable or a destabilized coordination pattern. Inattention has no effect on a highly stable pattern, but gives rise to destabilization and pattern switching for less stable states (see Lee, 2004; Pellecchia, Shockley, & Turvey, 2005; and Shockley & Turvey, 2006 for further discussion on the roles of attention and intention in bimanual coordination).

Perception and Bimanual Timing   One of the important advances in self-organization theory has to do with the critical role played by *information,* which is analogous to its role in other theoretical accounts of motor control. Specifically, information is considered to have a strong influence in coordination stability, arising from intrinsic-feedback sources as well as perception of the environment. In this section we review evidence suggesting that perceptual information is used to stabilize coordination as well as perturb it.

As we have discussed often in the previous sections, simple bimanual coordination patterns differ in stability—in-phase patterns are more stable than anti-phase patterns, which in turn are more stable than all other phase relations (e.g., Yamanishi et al., 1980). Perhaps not surprisingly, researchers have found that a similar relation exists if one merely *perceives* the phase relation of two objects in motion. For example, subjects in a study by Zaal, Bingham, and Schmidt (2000) watched two spheres oscillate on a computer screen, like two illuminated "balls" at the bottom of pendulums oscillating in a darkened room. On each trial the balls could oscillate with a mean relative phasing between 0° and 180°, with a variability ranging from 0° (perfectly stable) to 20° (highly unstable). So, for example, a 180° relative-phase pattern with 0° of variability would resemble the windshield wipers of many cars—moving in a perfectly locked asymmetric coordination mode. In contrast, a pattern with 20° of variability would show considerable random fluctuations in which the pattern deviated from perfect asymmetry, but overall would have a *mean* relative phase of 180°. Following an extensive training period with these stimuli, the subject was simply to judge the pattern's mean relative phase (using a 0-10 Likert scale, with 0 denoting symmetry and 10 asymmetry) or the pattern's phase variability (0 = no variability and 10 = highest variability).

Judgments of mean relative phase were accurate for all subjects—they could identify patterns accurately in symmetrical and asymmetrical motion as well as the relative phase of objects with relative phases between 0° and 180°. However, as illustrated in figure 8.17, perceptual judgments of variability were relatively inaccurate, with some exceptions. For objects moving in-phase (corresponding to 0° on the *x*-axis in the figure), subjects could accurately judge when the pattern was performed with maximal stability (filled square symbols)—as evidenced by the near-zero score, indicating a judgment of no variability. And, subjects perceived added instability quite accurately, too, with correspondingly increased levels of judged variability. In contrast, the anti-phase pattern (corresponding to 180° on the *x*-axis in the figure) was judged to have a moderate level of variability (values around two or three units), regardless of how much actual variability was present. Even so, the anti-phase pattern was perceived to be more stable than all of the other phase relations examined in the experiment; in general, the anti-phase

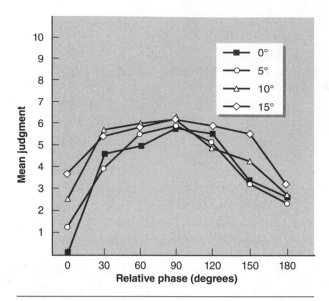

FIGURE 8.17 Judgments of perceived variability for two objects in motion with different mean relative phases (denoted on the *x*-axis) and levels of variability (corresponding to the symbols in the key). Mean judgment was scored on a Likert scale, where 0 represented no variability and 10 represented maximal variability.

Reprinted, by permission, from F.T.J.M. Zaal, G.P. Bingham, and R.C. Schmidt, 2000, "Visual perception of mean relative phase and phase variability," *Journal of Experimental Psychology: Human Perception & Performance* 26: 1209-1220.

pattern received lower judgments of perceived variability (see Wilson & Bingham, 2008, for a review of this research).

One implication of the findings of Zaal and colleagues is that the ability to *perceive* relative phase accurately may contribute significantly to one's ability to *perform* coordinated movements accurately. This implication is supported by results from a study using a related research strategy in which subjects attempted to coordinate movements of one limb with an external object, using perceptual judgments as the basis for stabilizing coordination. Subjects in an experiment by Wimmers, Beek, and van Wieringen (1992) coordinated left and right movements of a lever with a visual metronome that oscillated horizontally across a monitor. The findings revealed many of the same self-organizing properties that had been observed in studies of bimanual coordination discussed earlier (e.g., Kelso, 1984; Kelso et al., 1986).

Very similar effects have been observed when a subject coordinated his or her movements with another person rather than with an inanimate object. For instance, Schmidt, Carello, and Turvey (1990) asked subjects to swing one leg in temporal coordination with another person, who was also swinging one leg (see figure 8.18). The mutual goal between the two subjects resembled the (within subject) bimanual finger-wiggling task used by Kelso (1984). The findings were similar; the antiphase pattern was more variable and difficult to maintain at high movement frequencies than the

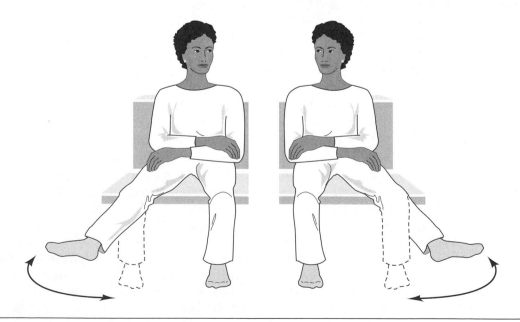

FIGURE 8.18 The between-person coordination task.

Reprinted, by permission, from R.C. Schmidt, C. Carello, and M.T. Turvey, 1990, "Phase transitions and critical fluctuations in the visual coordination of rhythmic movements between people," *Journal of Experimental Psychology: Human Perception and Performance* 16: 229. Copyright © 1990 by the American Psychological Association.

in-phase pattern (Amazeen, Schmidt, & Turvey, 1995; Schmidt, Carello, & Turvey, 1990; Temprado & Laurent, 2004). The importance of these findings is that a similar set of effects emerged when these movements were coordinated, even though each *individual* movement was controlled by a separate nervous system. (We will have more to say about such *social coordination* later in this chapter.)

The importance of perception in coordination was probably revealed most spectacularly in experiments by Mechsner and colleagues (Mechsner, 2004; Mechsner et al., 2001; Mechsner & Knoblich, 2004). These researchers conducted bimanual timing experiments in which the subjects' visual feedback of their upper limbs was manipulated. For example, figure 8.19 illustrates one experiment in which subjects moved two hand-wheels either in-phase or in anti-phase. Instead of viewing these movements directly, the subjects viewed "flags" moving in patterns that were either compatible with the direction of their movements or in opposition to the actual movement patterns. That is, sometimes how they *saw their limbs apparently move* was the mirror image of how the limbs were actually moving. Mechsner and colleagues (2001) obtained a startling result: The actually-produced anti-phase pattern that

FIGURE 8.19 Experimental setup used by Mechsner and colleagues (2001). Subjects moved hands in patterns of in-phase and anti-phase but could only see flags attached to the handles. Typical coordination effects were found when the flags were directionally compatible with the hand movements. However, when one flag moved in the mirror-image direction to the movement of the hand, the typical coordination effects were reversed.

was *perceived* to be in-phase was always the more stable pattern. Mechsner's findings, together with the information presented earlier about the role of perception (see also Franz, Zelaznik, Swinnen, & Walter, 2001; Semjen & Ivry, 2001; Wilson, Bingham, & Craig, 2003), highlight the key role of visual information in stabilizing and destabilizing coordination patterns.

Upper and Lower Limb Coordination

Common activities such as driving, sewing, and playing musical instruments (e.g., the piano and drums) require that we coordinate the timing of our hands and arms with foot and leg movements. In many of these coordinated actions, the dominant pattern of movement is a *directional preference* (both limbs move in the same direction), not the egocentric preference (limbs move toward and away from the center of a plane of motion) that has been observed for many bimanual coordination patterns (Swinnen, 2002). Many of these findings were shown in early experiments by Baldissera and colleagues (1982, 1991; Baldissera, Cavallari, & Tesio, 1994; also Carson, Goodman, Kelso, & Elliott, 1995). For example, subjects in Baldissera and colleagues' (1982) study were asked to coordinate ankle movements in the upward direction (dorsal flexion) or downward direction (plantar flexion) with specific combinations of wrist movements. When the forearm was fixed in the *supine* position (palm of the hand facing up), movements that were coordinated in the *same direction* (i.e., plantar flexion with wrist extension and dorsal flexion with wrist flexion) were more stable than actions coordinated in the opposite direction. However, with the forearm immobilized in the *prone* position (palm facing down), the stronger coordination mode was observed with the opposite pairing of muscle groups: Plantar flexion was now more strongly related to wrist flexion, and dorsal flexion to wrist extension. The common finding among these limb pairings was that the stronger coordination modes occurred for movements in the *same direction*, and regardless of the pairings of flexion-flexion or flexion-extension. The evidence for the differential strength of these particular preferred coordination modes was similar to that for the bimanual modes discussed previously; the weaker coordination pattern showed higher relative-phase variability and frequent unintended transitions to the stronger (same direction) pattern.

For the bimanual patterns discussed previously, one could argue that the in-phase bimanual pattern was more stable because it involved the timing of similar muscular groups (simultaneous flexion and extension), since movements in the same direction (i.e., anti-phase) were *less* strongly coordinated than were movements in the opposite direction. Such an argument fails to explain the findings of Baldissera and colleagues, however, because the coordination strength of the ankle movements with wrist flexion-extension could be *reversed* by simply changing the forearm orientation (i.e., prone or supine). A similar effect of spatial orientation can be seen in the coordination of the wrist and elbow movements within a single arm (Buchanan & Kelso, 1993; Kelso, Buchanan, & Wallace, 1991). This evidence suggests that the pattern of findings for the stability of the different coordination modes is not dependent on the specific muscle groups used, but rather on the *spatial* orientation of the actions.

The effect of spatial orientation in coordinating two limbs is illustrated quite well in studies by Kelso and Jeka (1992) and Serrien and Swinnen (1997a, 1997b). Consider various pairs of limb movements that could be produced in the sagittal plane, as illustrated in figure 8.20. Three different types of interlimb pairings can be produced: those involving *homologous* (same) limb pairs (left and right arms; left and right legs), *ipsilateral* (same side) limb pairs (left leg and arm; right leg and arm), or *contralateral* (diagonal) limb pairs (left leg and right arm; left arm and right leg). These three types of coordination patterns were examined by Kelso and Jeka (1992) under conditions in which the limbs moved either in the same direction or in the opposite direction. The results are illustrated in figure 8.21. In general, the limbs moving in the same direction demonstrated more stable patterns than the limbs moving in opposite directions. But this was true only for upper and lower limb combinations, which were more stable for contralateral pairs than for ipsilateral pairs, especially so when the limbs moved in opposite directions (see also Swinnen, Dounskaia, Verschueren, Serrien, & Daelman, 1995).

Again, notice that for this coordination task (sagittal plane), movement of the two limbs in the same direction was as stable as when they moved in the opposite direction. This effect is quite different from that found for bimanual movements in the frontal plane, as we discussed

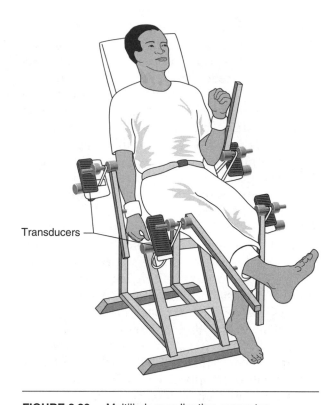

Transducers

FIGURE 8.20 Multilimb coordination apparatus.

Reprinted from *Human Movement Science*, Vol. 12, J.J. Jeka, J.A.S. Kelso, and T. Kiemel, "Spontaneous transitions and symmetry: Pattern dynamics in human four-limb coordination," pg. 635, Copyright 1993, with kind permission of Elsevier.

earlier. Thus, these data strongly imply that the *rules* of movement coordination depend on a number of factors, including the effectors involved, their orientation and planes of motion, interactions with the physical environment, and intended goals.

Complex Timing Patterns

Try the following easy task. Tap the index fingers of both your hands simultaneously on a flat surface. Now, make two taps of the right hand for every single tap of the left hand (i.e., taps of the left hand coincide with every second tap of the right hand—termed a 2:1 rhythm). Then do 3:1 and 4:1 rhythms; all of these should be easy to do when the two hands are performing the same rhythm, that is, when the rhythms are *harmonic*, or integer related (multiples of each other; e.g., Farnsworth & Poynter, 1931; Lashley, 1951).

Temporal coordination becomes much more difficult when the rhythms are not harmonic. For instance, it is very "difficult" to maintain a rhythm with one hand while doing something else as rapidly as possible, such as tapping with the other hand (Klapp, 1979) or speaking a syl-

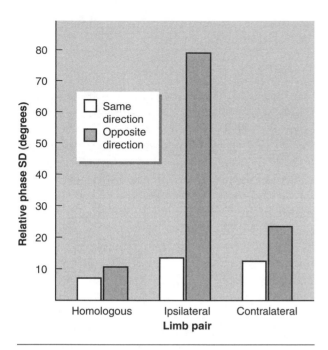

FIGURE 8.21 Standard deviation (SD) of relative phase for various interlimb pairings.

Data from Kelso and Jeka 1992.

lable (Klapp, 1981). Even more "difficult" is the situation in which two concurrent activities have their own rhythms; for example, reciting a nursery rhyme while tapping a rhythm with a different cadence (Peters, 1977).

Recent studies have focused on nonharmonic rhythms, or *polyrhythms,* to identify what makes certain timing patterns so "difficult" to produce. Consider a situation in which one hand produces three beats during a given interval and the other hand produces two beats during the same time interval (a 3:2 polyrhythm). For example, if the time interval is 1,200 ms, the faster hand produces a beat every 400 ms and the slower hand produces a beat every 600 ms. The two beats occur simultaneously only once every 1,200 ms. Although this 3:2 polyrhythm is much harder to perform than any of the harmonic combinations, it is easier to perform than 5:2, 4:3, 5:3, and 5:4 polyrhythms, which are progressively more difficult (Deutsch, 1983; Summers, Rosenbaum, Burns, & Ford, 1993). What is the basis for these control problems?[7]

Figure 8.22 presents data from an experiment by Summers and colleagues (1993), who compared the coefficients of variation (SD divided by the mean, expressed as a percentage) for various polyrhythms as a function of hand speed and musical training. What is evident from this figure is that nonmusicians were most variable in timing the beats of the hand that was moving *more slowly* in these polyrhythms. Summers and colleagues (1993; Summers & Pressing, 1994) explained these findings by considering the faster hand's rhythm

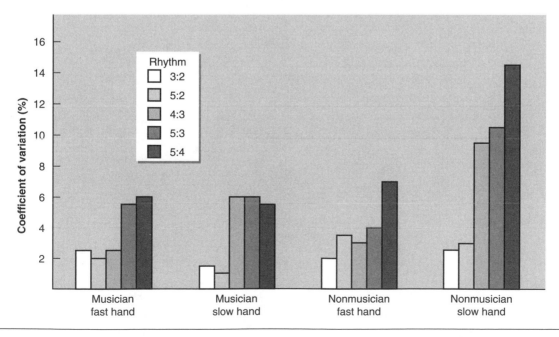

FIGURE 8.22 Variability in temporal coordination for polyrhythms of increasing difficulty in musicians and nonmusicians.

Data from Summers et al. 1993.

as the baseline rhythm. The task of coordinating the polyrhythm involved interspersing the slower beats at specific intervals in between the beats of the faster hand. The bars to the right side of figure 8.22 support the conclusion that the variability in performing a polyrhythm is positively associated with the *number of beats* that the slower hand needs to intersperse between beats of the faster hand (e.g., 5:2 vs. 5:3 vs. 5:4; Deutsch, 1983). Moreover, such a strategy is performed much less effectively by nonmusicians because they tend to intersperse the slow beats at approximately 50% of the interval duration between beats of the faster hand (Summers et al., 1993). This unskilled strategy is rudimentary, although it makes sense because it copes effectively with this situation by drawing upon an *anti-phase* coordination pattern—which, as we have seen, is a relatively natural pattern to adopt. Other strategies can be used, although they require considerable practice in order to

be effective (Bogacz, 2005; Kovacs, Buchanan, & Shea, 2010; Summers, 2002).

Spatial Coordination

Spatial biasing can be observed quite readily in the "pat the head while rubbing the stomach" example ("Costs and Benefits of Coordinating Two Limbs" on p. 279). Someone trying to do this task tends to bias the spatial trajectories of both limbs: The limbs are drawn toward performing one or the other task, or sometimes a novel combination of the two tasks. An experimental version of this coordination task by Franz, Zelaznik, and McCabe (1991) suggests that a novel combination may be the more natural coordination pattern. Here the subjects' task was to draw circles and lines. In some conditions, a single hand drew only one pattern; in other conditions, both hands drew the same pattern; and in another set of conditions, one hand drew a line while the other hand drew a circle. The results from these conditions are illus-

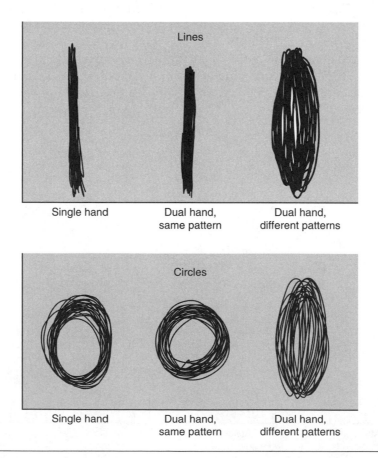

FIGURE 8.23 Drawing lines (upper) and circles (lower) under unimanual and bimanual conditions.

Reprinted from *Acta Psychologica*, Vol. 77, E.A. Franz, H.N. Zelaznik, and G. McCabe, "Spatial topological constraints in a bimanual task," pgs. 142 and 143, Copyright 1991, with kind permission of Elsevier.

trated in sample trials represented in figure 8.23. Both lines and circles were drawn accurately and consistently in the single-hand and dual-hand "same" conditions. However, when the hands drew different patterns, the variability increased dramatically; the circles became more linear, and the lines became somewhat circular.

One recent study suggests that part of the problem encountered during performance of different spatial tasks with the two hands lies in conceptualizing the nature of the two tasks. Franz and colleagues (2001) asked subjects to draw semicircles, one above the other, so that one finger drew a semicircle on top and another finger drew one on the bottom. As expected, the bimanual task was easy to perform when both hands drew "⌒" -shaped semicircles and when both hands drew "⌣"-shaped semicircles. However, the authors found a dissociation in performance when different semicircle orientations were drawn. The task was easy to do when one hand was required to draw a "⌒" on top and a "⌣" below it; however, the task was nearly impossible to do in the reverse configuration. One possibility is that in the former case the spatial representation drawn with the two hands is a full circle, but in the latter it is a nonidentifiable symbol. The dissociation in performance in these two cases occurred despite the fact that the spatial coordinates to produce the two tasks are similar. Perhaps the contribution of a conceptual model provided a strategy that was sufficient to reduce the interference inherent in the task. Or perhaps this effect is related to the strong influences of perception on performance that we discussed earlier. Much more study of spatial coordination effects is needed in order to establish firm principles (see Chan & Chan, 1995; Franz, 1997; Franz, Eliassen, Ivry, & Gazzaniga, 1996; Spijkers & Heuer, 1995; Swinnen, Jardin, & Meulenbroek, 1996).

Social Coordination

Although *interlimb* coordination is organized by the pathways within the CNS (Swinnen, 2002; Swinnen, Heuer, Massion, & Casaer, 1994), this cannot be the case when coordinated actions occur between two (or more) people. Coordinated activities between people often have a well-defined, *explicit mutual goal* (Schmidt, Christianson, Carello, & Baron, 1994), as in music, in sport (e.g., synchronized swimming), and in the

workplace (e.g., when several people join forces to move a heavy object). By "explicit" we mean that the actions of two or more people are choreographed with a specific objective of creating something together that could not be achieved individually, such as the effect on the audience of a ballet duet or the impression made on a judge by a synchronized dive. Predetermined "scripts" that describe the unfolding of a play in football or a duet in ballet often require considerable practice before an acceptable level of coordination is achieved among individuals such as athletes, actors, dancers, and musicians. In many respects, social coordination in these situations mirrors the concept of a GMP, as plans for action that describe the order and timing of events remain invariant, with the parameters (e.g., the specific participant) substituted as needed. How this kind of social coordination is achieved in teams represents an important research area in sport psychology (see Eccles & Tenenbaum, 2004).

Motor control researchers have tended to focus on situations in which coordinated actions arise from mutual goals that are *implicit*—situations in which coordination emerges spontaneously when each person is assigned an individual goal. This is more analogous to a self-organizing system, as we have discussed previously, because coordination arises despite the fact that no intention or goal related to coordination was specified. The nature of the coordination also differs from what we have discussed in previous sections; instead of two (or more) limbs becoming locked in a particular coordination mode (called *absolute coordination* by von Holst, 1937/1973), unintentional coordination between people is characterized as a type of *relative coordination*—the tendency to perform with a relative phase *near* a preferred coordination mode(s), but without being phase locked for extended periods of time (von Holst, 1937/1973).

For example, two people sitting in rocking chairs, with no explicit goal to coordinate their rocking, tended to do so near an in-phase pattern about 30% to 70% of the time (depending on the physical similarities of the two chairs), but only if the subjects were looking directly at each other (Richardson, Marsh, Isenhower, Goodman, & Schmidt, 2007; see also Schmidt & O'Brien, 1997). A greatly reduced tendency toward an in-phase pattern was found when only peripheral vision was available, and relative coordination was eliminated altogether when vision was occluded. Thus, in this task, relative coordination was dependent on the availability of direct visual information (for a review see Schmidt & Richardson, 2008).

But visual information is not the only medium that facilitates social coordination: A conversation between two individuals results in mutual, socially coordinated interactions involving the speaking patterns of the two individuals (see Fowler, Richardson, Marsh, & Shockley, 2008, for a review). Interestingly, shared postural coordination between two individuals was highest when they were engaged in conversation and was influenced by how they spoke to each other (Shockley, Baker, Richardson, & Fowler, 2007), but was not dependent on whether or not the individuals could see each other (Shockley, Santana, & Fowler, 2003).

Coordination can also be studied as a mutual collaboration between more than just a pair of individuals, although such a study is usually designed to investigate explicit cooperation among members of a team, as occurs in sport or the workplace (Eccles & Tenenbaum, 2004). For example, the spontaneous applause that occurs among members of an audience following a concert reveals periods of synchronicity (Néda, Ravasz, Brechet, Vicsek, & Barabási, 2000). We anticipate that more complex forms of unintentional coordination will be studied in years to come.

Summary

Even quite simple movements require the organization of various (potentially independent) moving parts of the motor system. Aiming movements, though simple at one level, involve the coordination of the eyes, head, and hand when perception and action are guided visually. One method of analyzing the organization of discrete tasks is to search for separate *units* of action— parts of action sequences that are independent temporally from other parts of the action. In contrast, reaching/grasping represents a type of discrete movement in which the limb-transport component is quite obviously distinct from that of object manipulation. Evidence suggests that, although these components seem to be separable, their actions are highly interdependent. Two theoretical views of reaching and grasping have been suggested; these differ in terms of the focus on temporal versus spatial factors during movement planning.

Discrete *bimanual* actions have also been an important focus of study. Studies using a two-hand version of the Fitts task reveal considerable influences of one limb's movement on the spatial and temporal actions of the other limb. These influences are even more pervasive if the actions of one limb have increased kinematic complexities. Recent evidence suggests that the development of a new GMP that controls the two limbs simultaneously may be a way in which the motor system solves these coordination difficulties.

The coordination of continuous, cyclical actions represents a contrast to that of discrete actions; in the latter, the GMP seems to play an important role. Some continuous interlimb coordination patterns are more stable than others, and these stable states are subject to change. Important insights regarding pattern organization are revealed by *phase transitions,* in which the destabilization of a pattern leads to a change in the basic form of the pattern. These transitions have been shown in animals and in humans, leading some to suggest that these patterns have a strong *self-organizing* basis, as conceptualized in the HKB model (Haken, Kelso, & Bunz, 1985). Evidence from a number of bimanual and interlimb coordination paradigms has provided support for this view. Other patterns of coordination, such as polyrhythm timing, spatial coordination, and patterns of social coordination, have been the focus of recent investigations and pose exciting challenges for future research.

Student Assignments

1. Prepare to answer the following questions during class discussion:
   a. Describe the coordination components of reaching for and opening a jar of peanut butter.
   b. Describe two different methods by which an artificial limb is used to reach for and grasp objects.
   c. Describe any daily activities that characterize in-phase and anti-phase movements. Describe an activity that either combines in-phase and anti-phase

movements or that characteristically has an alternative phasing.

2. Find a research article that uses the Haken-Kelso-Bunz model as a theoretical basis. Be prepared to explain these concepts using examples from daily activities.

Web Resources

Motor control in zero gravity:

http://mvl.mit.edu/ASTRODYN/html/astrodyn.html

More on the Haken-Kelso-Bunz model:

www.scholarpedia.org/article/Haken-Kelso-Bunz_model

Notes

[1] Different taxonomies have been proposed that extend Napier's (1956) original classification scheme of precision grips versus power grips. However, the choice of which grip to use is determined not by the object but rather by the intentions of the individual regarding how the object will be used (Jeannerod, 1996; Marteniuk, MacKenzie, Jeannerod, Athenes, & Dugas, 1987). For instance, one normally uses a precision grip to write with a pen. However, if one were intending to use the pen to puncture a cardboard box, use of a power grip would be more likely.

[2] This work extends the pioneering research of Wing and Kristofferson (1973a, 1973b), which was discussed in chapter 7. Analyses of the bimanual coordination data here were done with nonoverlapping intervals among the landmarks, which eliminates the bias in the correlations because of overlapping of some of the landmarks. Heuer and colleagues (1995; Schmidt et al., 1998) have developed a theory of bimanual coordination based on GMPs that uses a statistic termed a *covariance ratio*, which is sensitive to the extent to which the hands are coordinated together in time. The covariance-ratio data are consistent with the view that the two hands are controlled by a single GMP, but details of this analysis are beyond the scope of this presentation.

[3] The *Froude number* was discovered in the 19th century by a mathematician and naval architect (William Froude) as a way to characterize the efficiency of boats of different hull lengths. An excellent historical review of the application of the Froude number to gait biomechanics of animals, and other uses, is provided by Vaughn and O'Malley (2005).

[4] The measure of accuracy presented here is different from that presented by Yamanishi and colleagues (1980). They reported constant error, averaged over subjects. However, as noted in chapter 2, the average constant errors for subjects who are biased differently can underestimate the average inaccuracy for a *group*—and these individual differences, in opposite directions of bias, were evident in the data from Yamanishi and colleagues. We have replotted their data in terms of absolute constant error (chapter 2). The results show much the same pattern as the variability data.

[5] Note that mean relative phase is plotted in figure 8.15a, rather than absolute CE as in figure 8.14a. A rough equalization would require a subtraction of 180° from each anti-phase value in figure 8.15a, then a conversion to a positive value.

[6] Use of this term can be confusing here, as we have defined the word "control," as in motor *control,* much differently than as it is used in the term "control parameter." As well, earlier we discussed *parameters* of a GMP (e.g., handwriting in large or small script). A control *parameter* is defined as a nonspecific variable that, when changed, results in a nonlinear change in the behavior of the system as a whole.

[7] Interestingly, the task used by Heuer and colleagues (1995), as described earlier, was a rapid, 3:2 "polyrhythm," which was performed rather easily (after practice). That discrete and continuous versions of a similar task might have remarkably different effects on coordination performance is deserving of more research.

CHAPTER 9

INDIVIDUAL DIFFERENCES AND CAPABILITIES

Why is one person a better gymnast than another, even after the same amount of practice? What are the abilities or aptitudes that contribute to success as a skilled woodworker? How many basic, inherited motor capabilities do humans possess, what are they, and how can they be measured? These are just some of the questions considered by researchers who investigate individual differences—the study of factors that make individuals different from one another. The approach to motor behavior represented by this chapter is a marked departure from the approaches in the previous chapters. With the earlier approach, the concern was for the effect of certain independent variables on certain other dependent variables, using the mean (usually) of a group of people as the measure of primary interest. With individual differences, however, the concern is for how the individuals within a group differ from each other. Because these two scientific traditions are so different in method and goal, they are usually treated as separate points of view. We examine more closely some of the differences between these two approaches in the next sections.

Experimental Versus Differential Approaches

There are a number of fundamental differences between the ways in which motor behavior is studied and understood in the experimental and differential approaches. In the following discussion, we focus on just two of the major differences—the scientific goals and the scientific methods used by the two approaches.

Different Scientific Goals

The most obvious difference between the experimental and differential approaches lies in the goals of these two traditions. The experimental approach is concerned primarily with understanding the effects of certain independent variables (e.g., the target size of an aimed movement) on some dependent variable (e.g., the accuracy of the movement). In this example, the interest is in how aimed movements are regulated in humans generally. A fundamental belief is that humans are not really very different from one another (especially when human-to-human differences are contrasted with human-to-giraffe differences, for example); so when the subjects in a group are treated alike, one can estimate the behavior of a "typical" human by considering the effect of the target size on average accuracy. Through experiments the researcher can hope to arrive at statements such as "decreasing the size of the target will require humans to slow their movement in order to maintain accuracy," as Fitts (1954) did, to cite just one example.

In these kinds of experiments, there is little concern regarding any one individual in the group. Almost no interest is shown in the possibility that one person might use a different strategy than another or have more skill than another. These factors are usually averaged out and are rarely seen in the group data. In fact, if some individual differs "too much" from the mean behavior level of the group (as determined by a statistical procedure), common experimental practice is to remove this *outlier* from consideration. Thus, variations among people are considered "noise," or a nuisance, and many methods are available to eliminate or control such between-subject variations in experiments.

With the differential, or individual-differences, approach, on the other hand, the primary focus is on the differences between or among individuals. Thus, many of the things that the experimentalist considers "noise" in experiments are the very things that the differentialist considers interesting and worthy of study! Generally, the differential approach deals with two basic issues.

First, concern is directed toward the nature of the underlying *abilities* (or *capabilities*), the ways in which these abilities differ in "strength" in different people because of genetic variations or experience, and the ways in which different tasks are interrelated. For example, are tasks involving strength related to other tasks involving accuracy in motion? Does high strength performance on a strength task imply that the person will have low accuracy performance on some other task requiring accuracy? A second problem, closely related to the first, entails *prediction,* or the estimation of performance in one situation based on measurements taken in some other situation. For example, how do intelligence test scores relate to success in graduate school? Or, how does height relate to success in gymnastics?

The differential approach deviates from the experimental approach in that it concerns attempts to explain and predict (a) differences among people rather than (b) general phenomena that are seen in the "average" person. As might be expected, such differences in goals naturally create differences between the points of view of the differentialists and the experimentalists. Indeed, such differences have become so great that the two groups of psychologists are almost totally separated, with separate methods of doing research, statistical designs, goals, textbooks, and scientific journals. These differences were described, and decried, by Cronbach (1957) in his article titled "The Two Disciplines of Scientific Psychology" (see also Underwood, 1975).

Different Scientific Methodologies

The experimentalists and the differentialists answer their respective questions quite differently. While we have already devoted considerable space to the experimental approach, a brief review of its characteristics will help to make clear how it contrasts with the differential approach.

Experimental Methods

Essentially, the "true" experimental method involves the manipulation (or artificial variation) of some independent variable while as many other variables as possible are held constant. This can be done by administering one level of the independent variable to one group of people and another level to another group, and noting the differences in some dependent variable (called a between-subjects or between-groups design). Sometimes only one group of people is used (called a within-subjects design). One level of the independent variable is administered to the group at one time and the other is administered at another time, with differences between the two times (in terms of the dependent variable) being the chief comparison of interest. We have discussed many examples of both of these designs in previous chapters.

In such experiments, the critical comparison is usually between the means of groups of people (or of a single group tested under two different conditions). Typically, no regard is given to the variations among people within the group, except for the usual reporting of statistics that describe the extent to which people differed. Such dispersion statistics are rarely the primary concern in experiments; rather, they are included to ensure that the variations among people were not so large as to obscure or change the conclusions

Origins of Expertise

We often wonder at how some elite performer in some activity or occupation got to be that way. We are tempted to say that such an individual was fortunate to have been born with the "right" abilities (i.e., those needed for performance in his specialty), coupled, of course, with sufficient practice and training. Of these two factors—abilities versus practice—it is our impression that most people seem to place far more credence in genetically determined abilities as the major determinants of elite-level performance.

Such a view is severely challenged in a study by Canadian psychologist Roger Barnsley (Barnsley, Thompson, & Legault, 1992) and others (Dudink, 1994, in Dutch soccer; Helsen, Starkes, & van Winckel, 2000, in Belgian soccer; see Musch & Grondin, 2001, for a review). Here, it is argued that genius (or elite-level performance, or expertise) is not so heavily dependent on inherited abilities, but rather is the product of various important factors that are effective almost by chance alone. (This is all nicely summarized, with more examples, in Gladwell's [2008] book *Outliers,* which we recommend strongly; see also Gladwell's *The Tipping Point* for more.) This view is that the elite performer—rather than being gifted with an extraordinary collection of the "right" abilities—simply happened to be lucky or fortunate enough to exist in an environment where encouragement, coaching, or teaching (or more than one of these), the opportunity for practice and experience, and other factors all converged to make this person great.

There are many examples. In one of these (Barnsley et al., 1992), Canadian Major Junior A league ice hockey players (who are about high school age) and professional ice hockey players were studied. (It almost goes without saying that Canadian ice hockey is played at an extremely high level, and that the Canadians have a highly structured youth hockey system designed to identify and promote promising young players.) Barnsley and colleagues examined the rosters of several Canadian Major Junior A teams, as well as those of several professional hockey teams. These rosters include many statistics such as each player's home town, his right- or left-handedness, his year and month of birth, his height and weight, and so on. Barnsley and colleagues noticed that almost every player at the Major Junior A level and at the professional level was born in the early months of the calendar year (January, February, March, April), and that almost no players were born in the later months (September, October, November, December). This was a very large, and clear, effect. Other than by resorting to some bizarre astrological explanation, how could one explain why the *month* of birth should have any effect at all on hockey performance in these situations?

One interpretation of this finding was as follows. When these elite players were kids, the majority played age-group hockey. In order to be on the 8-year-old team, for example, the player needed to have his eighth birthday during the calendar year (January to December) in question. This meant that a player having his birthday in January could be almost one full year older than a player born in December of that year. This has been termed the "relative age effect," in that those on the team born in January are "relatively older" than those born in December. Of course, especially at the younger ages, older kids are bigger, faster, better skaters, and so on than younger kids; and one year out of eight years can result in a huge difference in skill levels. Therefore, as the hypothesis goes, the older players on the age-group teams (who are bigger, faster, etc.) attracted the attention of the coaches; the coaches then gave the early-month players more coaching, encouragement, practice and playing time, and so on as compared to the relatively younger kids. This bias was then repeated in each subsequent year. So, according to this argument, after several years of preferential treatment, the relatively older kids tended to be playing at the highest levels, while the relatively younger kids were not. This is a kind of "rich get richer" effect.

According to this view, elite performers are not so "special" in terms of their abilities; rather, they just happened to be "lucky" enough to have been born in the "right" month. Of course, this does not say that the birth month is the only factor operating to produce elite performers, as other abilities discussed in this chapter are probably also important. This evidence and interpretation simply reminds us that inherited abilities are not as critically important as we might have once thought.

drawn about the differences between means. Finally, the conclusions that come from these experiments are usually stated in cause-and-effect terms—the variations in the independent variable caused the changes in the dependent variable. As such, experimental methods provide relatively powerful ways of coming to an understanding of one's scientific area.

Differential Methods

The differential methods contrast starkly with those just described, relying substantially on correlational (or associational) techniques whereby the *relationships* between or among variables are studied. In its simplest form, the differential approach uses one group of people and at least two tests measured on each individual. (Remember that the simplest "true" experiment often uses at least two groups of people and one test, or dependent variable.) The primary concern is the extent to which one test (e.g., height) relates to another test (e.g., accuracy) in the same people, with the nature of the relationship being determined by the size and sign of a statistic called the *correlation coefficient* (a discussion of correlation statistics appears in chapter 2). With these correlational methods, the chief concern is the relationship between the two tests, or among several tests if more than two are used. Sometimes the relationship is computed between a group of tests (called a test "battery") and some other single measure. An example is the relationship between a fitness battery (consisting of five subtests) and some other measure, such as probability of becoming a successful firefighter.

A second major method of individual-differences research uses essentially the same logic, but the appearance of the procedures may make it seem that the methods are experimental. Consider a study to determine the relationship between age and throwing accuracy. Typically the researcher chooses one group of people at one age and another group at another age and compares the group means on some "dependent" variable, such as throwing accuracy. This appears to be an experiment, because there are two groups and one dependent variable and the focus is on the group means. But it is not really experimental, because the level of the independent variable (age) is not *manipulated* by the experimenter; that is, the ages of the people in the group were already established when the subjects were chosen. Such

a procedure is a study of the *relationship* between age and throwing accuracy. Such variables (age, in this example) are usually called *individual-difference variables*. Thus, studying which individual-difference variables are related to certain kinds of performances is a primary concern of the differential approach. Indeed, textbooks have been written solely about individual-difference variables, such as life span motor development (e.g., Haywood & Getchell, 2009; Piek, 2006), aging (e.g., Spirduso, Francis, & MacRae, 2005), individuals with various movement disorders (e.g., Weeks, Chua, & Elliott, 2000), and expert–novice differences in sport skill (Farrow, Baker, & MacMahon, 2008; Starkes & Ericsson, 2003). Some of these individual-difference variables will be discussed in more detail toward the end of this chapter (see also "Origins of Expertise").

With the differential approach, conclusions about the results tend to be phrased in language quite unlike that with the experimental approach. In experiments, one might conclude that the independent variable *caused* changes in the dependent variable (because other variables were held constant or "controlled"). In differential studies, however, causation can seldom be inferred logically. The major reason is that many other things may differ, or intervene in the causal nature of the relationship. For example, consider the relationship between children's height and their throwing accuracy. Since weight is usually associated with height, one cannot be certain that a relationship between height and accuracy is really not due to the relation between weight and accuracy. Also, taller people are usually older (if one is considering children), and one could easily confuse the height–accuracy dependency with an age–accuracy dependency. The primary limitation in these studies is that the level of the variable of concern is not *manipulated* (artificially determined by the experimenter). Rather, the variable is allowed to vary naturally, and the scientist measures its value and attempts to understand how it relates to some other variable that is also varying naturally. Such procedures are often called *natural experiments*.

People can differ from each other in at least two fundamental ways. First, two people might be fundamentally and consistently different from each other in some stable characteristic, such as height. Such differences will be enduring and constant across both time and testing conditions.

But the two individuals might also be different in other ways. For example, if on just a single trial, one person makes a successful pool shot and another does not, we might not be willing to say with certainty that the two people are different in pool-shooting capability, as on the next shot the performance success may be opposite. Finding differences between two individuals on some measure of performance does not necessarily indicate that these differences are *reliable*. The stable, enduring differences among people are the subject of this chapter on individual differences. In fact, the definition of individual differences is *the stable, enduring, and underlying differences among people* (Henry, 1959; Schmidt, 1975a). It is critical that measures used in the study of individual differences be reliable, and various methods to assess reliability have been devised (see "Reliability and Individual Differences").

Abilities

Probably the most important topic in the area of individual differences is *abilities*. In this section, we begin by providing a definition of the concept of ability, and then we turn to some of the research indicating the structure of abilities.

Abilities Defined

The term *ability*, which is often used interchangeably with the terms *capability* and *aptitude*, usually

Reliability and Individual Differences

The reliability coefficient provides a way to evaluate the extent to which observed differences among people on some tests are due to individual differences (i.e., stable, enduring differences) or to chance or transitory effects. Reliability is really another use of the correlation, but in this instance the concern is with the correlation of a test "with itself." For example, assume that five subjects each perform six trials on a reaction-time (RT) task. These six scores for each person are divided to form two scores ("halves") for each person according to one of a number of different methods. One common method is called the "odd–even" method; the sum of the odd-numbered trials is computed as one of the scores for each person, and the sum of the even-numbered trials is taken as a second, separate score for each person. The extent to which the odd and even sums for each individual tend to deviate from each other is one measure of the random variations in the individual trial data. Indeed, if there were no random variation at all, the sum of the odds and evens would be exactly the same for a given subject. Next, the across-subjects correlation is computed between the odd and even scores; this correlation is typically called the *reliability coefficient*. Reliability can, theoretically, take on any value between +1.0 and –1.0 (review chapter 2); but, in practical situations, reliability is seldom negative and usually ranges from 0 to +1.0.

One way to interpret reliability is to multiply it by 100 to express it a percentage. The observed variation among people is made up of (a) differences among people in their stable, enduring traits (termed *individual differences*) and (b) random (or other) fluctuations that tend to make people only *appear* to be different. If so, reliability is the percentage of the observed variability due to individual differences. With low reliability of, say, 0.20, only 20% of the observed variation is due to individual differences, with about 80% being due to random (and other) variations.

A primary concern of individual-differences research is the correlation between pairs of tests. Statistically, the size of the correlation between two tests is limited by the reliability of either (or both) of the tests being correlated,[1] so one must be certain that the reliability of each of the tests being correlated is reasonably high. Reliability also represents a measure of the "stability" of the test under different applications. Certainly as the number of trials administered to each subject increases, the performances become more stable, and reliability increases. Not surprisingly, the number of trials that make up a test is a strong determinant of reliability; indeed, if the number of trials is increased enough, the reliability can actually be brought to 1.0 (e.g., Gullicksen, 1950). As easy as this is to do (usually), there is seldom a good excuse for a test with low reliability.

refers to a hypothetical construct that underlies (or supports) performance in a number of tasks or activities. An ability is usually thought to be a relatively stable characteristic or trait. These traits are typically regarded as having been either genetically determined or developed during growth and maturation, and they are not easily modifiable by practice or experience. Abilities represent the "equipment" that a person has at her disposal, determining whether or not a given motor task can be performed either poorly or well.

Abilities are usually inferred from patterns of performance on groups of tasks, largely using correlations as the primary method of measurement. For example, suppose we find that, for a group of individuals, those people who perform well on task A also perform well on task B, and that those who perform poorly on task A also perform poorly on task B. This pattern is what one would expect if tasks A and B were related, or correlated statistically. If two tasks are related, then they might be related because some underlying property or process is included in both. The differential scientist is interested in the possibility that the underlying properties common to these two tasks are abilities—or enduring, stable traits that contribute to the performance of the two tasks.

Abilities Versus Skill

Another way to understand the concept of abilities is to distinguish it from the notion of skill. An ability is a relatively stable, underlying trait that is largely unmodifiable by practice. Skills, of course, can be modified by practice or experience (the last part of this book covers these changes with practice—called motor learning). Thus, abilities underlie or support certain skills. The capability to react quickly may underlie a number of specific skills such as sprint starts in swimming or a quick reaction in driving a car. Also, think of a given skill as composed of a number of different abilities. Thus, the skill of driving a car may be made up of various abilities, such as those involved in vision, an ability to switch attention from one event to another, and an ability to anticipate.

Abilities as Limiting Factors

Abilities can also be conceptualized as representing limitations on performance, or as defining a person's potential for success. Neither of your authors will ever become a professional basketball player regardless of the amount of time and effort we devote to the game, because we do not possess the requisite abilities. Two individuals could have the same skill level at a given time, but one of them could have far greater potential because he has greater abilities for the skill in question. The other person is likely to be frustrated by attempts to improve beyond the limitations defined by his underlying capabilities.

Varieties of Abilities

Abilities can take many forms. One form common to many sports is body configuration. For example, the ability (or trait, if you prefer) of height is important to basketball; similarly, small people rarely succeed in American football, and large people rarely succeed in gymnastics. Such characteristics are surely genetically defined and are almost impossible to modify by training or practice. Another variety of ability is related to certain emotional or personality characteristics. For example, certain personalities are more amenable to team sports than to individual sports, and some people are more excitable or anxious than others. Finally, the abilities that will most concern us here could be called "motor abilities." They are the underlying characteristics that tend to contribute to success in moving the limbs in particular ways such as reaction time, movement speed, and manual dexterity, among many others. These abilities are often not as easy to measure or isolate for study as are abilities relating to body configuration, but they are no less important for understanding why certain people become more skilled than others.

The Structure of Motor Abilities

How many motor abilities are there? What are they, and how can they be measured? These questions have been asked for many years, and the answers have changed systematically as more effective techniques for studying abilities have been developed. First, consider some of the earlier thinking about motor (and cognitive) abilities that has led to present-day beliefs.

General Motor Ability

An early notion about motor abilities—one that is still widespread among people not familiar with the research—was the idea that all motor performances are based on a single, all-encompassing ability (Adams, 1987). This idea goes by different names, such as "athletic ability," "coordination," "motor ability," or a more formal label of "*general motor ability.*" All these terms imply essentially the same thing: that we are structured with a single capability to move, with this capability having relevance to any motor task in which we choose to engage.

These ideas, which were explored largely in the 1930s, were no doubt supported by the common observations (on playgrounds, in athletics, and so on) that certain individuals seemed able to do anything they tried (so-called all-around athletes). A well-known example at the time was Mildred "Babe" Didrikson Zaharias, who won Olympic medals in 1932 in the javelin, high jump, and hurdles. She also excelled in baseball, basketball, and tennis; and later she went on to win 55 amateur and professional events in golf. In contrast, it seemed that other individuals could not do well at any motor task they tried. Given these casual observations, it made sense to postulate an underlying factor relating all the various tasks in sports to one another: a general athletic (or motor) ability.

This idea of general motor ability was probably led by the analogous research on cognitive abilities, which was prevalent in the 1930s. It is beyond the scope of this chapter to present much detail, but one important concept that emerged from this work was that of *intelligence*. It was during the early 20th century that measures of IQ (intelligence quotient) were developed, and educators and parents became strong believers in the predictive power of IQ tests as measures of a child's capacity for "success" in society—a hypothesized general mental ability.

In the 1950s and 1960s, however, the concepts of general intellectual ability and general motor ability both came under serious attack. With respect to motor skills, the threat came from essentially two major sources: (a) the work on individual differences conducted by Henry (see "Franklin Henry" on p. 12) and his students at Berkeley and (b) the research program related to individual differences in pilotry and similar tasks that was conducted by Fleishman and his associates through the U.S. Air Force (see "Edwin A. Fleishman" on p. 309).

Predictions From the General Motor Ability Notion

The general motor ability hypothesis has one important prediction that has been examined frequently, concerning the sizes of the correlations among tests of various skills. Take a group of individuals and test them on task A; after considerable practice the people tend to order themselves on this task from "best" to "worst." According to the general motor ability hypothesis, the "best" performers are most proficient because of a strong general motor ability; conversely, the "worst" performers have a weak general motor ability. Thus, the performance on this task can be taken as a measure of the "strengths" of these subjects' general motor ability. Now, suppose these same people are tested on some other task B. The argument is that, because the individuals who are "best" on task A have a strong general motor ability, then these same individuals should be "best" at task B. Similarly, the individuals "worst" at task A should be "worst" at task B as well.

This kind of prediction can be seen by the hypothetical data in the scatterplot shown in figure 9.1, where each individual is represented by a dot whose position on the scatterplot is determined by scores on each of the two tasks A and B. This pattern suggests a strong relationship between the two tasks, and a high correlation (near +1.0 in this case) between tasks A and B. This is a major prediction of the general motor ability hypothesis. If the correlation turned out to be low (i.e., near zero), this would not support the

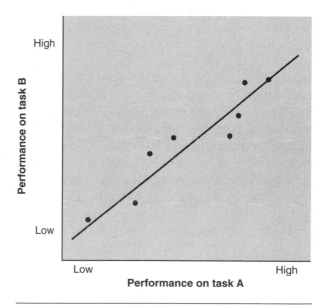

FIGURE 9.1 Hypothetical data presented in a scatterplot showing a relationship between tasks A and B; each subject is represented as a dot, positioned according to the scores on task A and task B.

general motor ability concept. Next let's examine correlations among tasks that have been found in the literature.

Correlations Among Skills

A large number of separate investigations in the published literature deal with the correlations among well-practiced skills, but we discuss only three of these studies in order to give the general idea (for a review see Marteniuk, 1974). One example from Henry's laboratory is a study by Bachman (1961). A group of 320 people practiced two motor tasks that supposedly involved the ability to balance. One of these, the Bachman ladder task (see figure 2.8), required subjects to climb a free-standing ladder. Bachman's second task was the stabilometer (see figure 2.5c). This apparatus was an unstable balancing board on which the subject stood; it pivoted so that the right foot moved down as the left foot moved up. The subject's task was to keep the unstable board still, with feet level. Bachman (1961) found that for various subgroups of subjects (defined by age and gender), the correlations between success on the ladder and success on the stabilometer ranged from +0.25 to −0.15, with most correlations being very close to zero. These results ran contrary to a general motor ability hypothesis, or even to the concept of a general *balance* ability.

Lotter (1960) had subjects perform striking actions of the hand and kicking movements with the foot, and measured reaction and movement times for each. The hand action involved a forward–downward movement to hit a suspended tennis ball as quickly as possible (for the left and right hands separately); the leg movement involved kicking a small plate with a movement similar to a place kick in American football (again, for the right and left legs). The arm–arm correlation was 0.58, and the leg–leg correlation was 0.64. These correlations were considerably higher than those found by Bachman (1961), but note that they involve the same task performed with limbs on opposite sides of the body. The correlations between arm and leg, on the same side of the body (e.g., right arm vs. right leg) or on opposite sides (e.g., left arm vs. right leg), were considerably lower: 0.24, 0.36, 0.23, and 0.18. These findings do not support the general motor ability hypothesis either.

Finally, Parker and Fleishman (1960) had 203 subjects perform a battery of 50 tests in conjunction with an armed services testing program. This produced a 50 × 50 correlation *matrix*, whereby every test is correlated with every other test and the resulting correlations are placed in a large table. The majority of tests correlated about 0.40 or lower with each other; only rarely was there a correlation of 0.50 or higher, which again fails to support the idea of general motor ability.

Many more studies like these have been done. Generally, low correlations are found among different skills. This pattern does not support the notion of a general motor ability or even of general motor subabilities such as balance (Bachman, 1961) or quickness (Lotter, 1960). Marteniuk (1974) published a critical review of the research conducted during the 1950s and 1960s that remains important and relevant today.

Henry's Specificity Hypothesis

In the late 1950s, Henry (1958/1968, 1961) proposed the idea, in direct contradiction to the general motor ability hypothesis, that motor abilities are *specific* to a particular task. Essentially there were three aspects to this hypothesis. First, Henry thought that the number of motor abilities was very large—perhaps in the thousands. Second, he believed that these abilities are independent, so that the strength of any one particular ability is unrelated to the strength of any other ability. Third, each task or skill that we perform depends upon a large number of these abilities. When the task is changed, the particular collection of abilities that supports the performance must change to meet the new task demands.

Probably the most important prediction of the specificity hypothesis is that two tasks, even if they appear to be quite similar (such as throwing a baseball and throwing a javelin), will tend to correlate nearly zero with each other. The groups of abilities that underlie these two tasks are, according to this view, two distinct collections with few or perhaps no abilities in common. Because these abilities are assumed to be independent, the correlation among skills should be zero, or at least very low. As we discussed in the previous section, the evidence supports such a viewpoint.

In addition, the Henry hypothesis predicts that *transfer* among skills should be quite low (Schmidt & Young, 1987). Transfer is defined as the attainment (or loss) of proficiency in one task as a result of practice or experience at some other task (we discuss the concept of transfer in greater detail in chapter 14). If the two tasks have no abilities in common, then no element practiced in one of them will contribute (or transfer) to the other. Generally, the transfer literature supports Henry's hypothesis, showing essentially that motor transfer is generally low and positive.

Exceptions to Henry's Specificity Hypothesis

Although Henry's hypothesis about specificity of individual differences has been widely accepted for many years, recent work by Keele, Ivry, and others indicates that *timing* may represent an exception to Henry's view. This new work suggests that a general "timekeeping" ability underlies performance of a number of tasks. The research focuses on how the temporal aspects of movements are organized in the central nervous system (CNS), and examines correlations among various tasks requiring central control of timing. In one study (Keele & Hawkins, 1982), correlations between maximum rates of tapping by various body parts (finger, thumb, wrist, arm, and foot) ranged from 0.60 to 0.80, considerably higher than the correlations seen in the earlier studies. In another study, Keele, Ivry, and Pokorny (1987) asked subjects to maintain a regular beat by tapping with the finger or arm at 400 ms intervals; the measure of performance was the regularity of tapping, measured by the SD of the produced time intervals. The correlation between the SDs produced with finger and arm tapping was 0.90, suggesting a high degree of commonality between the two tasks. Interestingly, Keele and colleagues also included a task in which subjects were required to produce certain forces with the finger and arm. The correlation between performance in the force production task and in the timing task was about 0.20. The dissociation of performance abilities within the same subjects—showing specificity for the force and timing tasks, but generality across different timing tasks—is evidence against a strict view of Henry's hypothesis.

Support for a common timing ability has been found in a number of studies. For example, Keele, Pokorny, Corcos, and Ivry (1985) found that the correlations between perception of timing and the production of timing were relatively high (with *r*s of about 0.60), suggesting a link between perception and production of action. Williams, Woollacott, and Ivry (1992) found that children

classified as motorically "clumsy" were more variable in both motor and perceptual timing than age-matched controls. Research involving groups of individuals who have neurological damage suggests that the cerebellum may play a specific role in timekeeping ability (Ivry & Corcos, 1993; Ivry & Keele, 1989; Ivry, Keele, & Diener, 1988). These findings have led Keele and Ivry (1987) to suggest a *modular view* of individual differences (see also Jones, 1993). In this view, the brain is organized to perform certain functions rather than certain tasks. *Modules* represent neural systems that support a particular function. A timing module represents a type of timekeeper that functions to support the performance of both perceptual and motor tasks under a wide range of sensory and effector mechanisms.

We note some controversy in this literature, however, as not all studies of motor timing have supported a general timekeeping ability. Only moderate correlations (0.36 to 0.48) were found when the timing of limb and jaw movements were compared (Franz, Zelaznik, & Smith, 1992). Studies in which timed movements were made by tapping, line drawing, and circle drawing showed mostly small correlations; and correlations were significant only when the same tasks were performed at similar timing rates (Robertson et al., 1999; Zelaznik, Spencer, Doffin, 2000).

Factor-Analytic Studies

A second major research thrust uses the factor-analytic method, so called because of a statistical tool termed *factor analysis*. Various investigators have used this general method, but certainly the most active was Fleishman (1964, 1965, 1967; see Fleishman & Bartlett, 1969, for reviews). After a brief discussion of the factor-analytic method, this section presents some of the major findings from this body of research.

Factor Analysis   For factor analysis, typically, a large number of people (e.g., 100 to 200) perform each of a number of tests (e.g., 50). Factor analysis groups the tests into *clusters*, or *factors*, so that the number of factors is considerably less than the number of original tests (e.g., 10 or so, depending on a number of other considerations). The tests that make up a particular cluster or factor have the property of showing relatively high correlations with each other, whereas tests that are members of different factors tend to show low correlations with each other.

This perhaps will be clearer if we consider the diagram in figure 9.2. Say there were 20 tests, and the factor analysis grouped them into five clusters, or factors, each represented by a square. The circled numbers within the squares refer to the test numbers (which are, of course, purely arbitrary), and the numbers on the arrows joining two tests represent the correlation between the two indicated tests. For simplicity, only some of the 20 tests and five factors are shown.

Notice that for Factor I, the tests (1, 8, and 9) show relatively high correlations with each other (0.52, 0.49, and 0.65), indicating that these tests tend to be measures of some common underlying ability. For Factor II, the tests (6, 13, and 18) tend to correlate with each other as well (0.60, 0.48, and 0.50) and therefore tend to measure some common ability. However, a test in Factor I (e.g., test 9) does not correlate well ($r = 0.06$) with any test in Factor II (e.g., test 13). Also, test 6 (in Factor II) and test 2 (in Factor III) do not correlate well with each other ($r = 0.10$). The interpretation is that the tests within a factor tend to measure one or more basic abilities. Each of the factors tends to represent a different set of abilities. In this general way, factor analysis divides a large group of tests into a smaller group of factors, each of which is thought to represent one or more separate abilities.

Identifying the Abilities The next step is to determine what abilities the factors represent. We can illustrate this process with one of Fleishman's (1957) studies, in which 200 people were each given 18 tests. The result of a factor analysis is a *factor matrix,* shown in table 9.1. Across the top are the nine factors that emerged in the analysis, analogous to the clusters or groupings of tests in figure 9.2. On the left side are the tests that were administered, ordered arbitrarily. The numbers in the body of the table are called the *factor loadings,* which indicate the extent to which the test in question is a "measure of" the ability or factor in that column; the factor loading is often thought of as the correlation between the test and the ability that it represents.

For example, consider test 2 (Reaction Time). This test has a high loading (0.60) on Factor I but a relatively small loading on Factor II (−0.15). On the other hand, test 4 (Pattern Comprehension) has a high loading on Factor II (0.66) but a very small loading on Factor I (0.12). Here, we can say that Reaction Time is a measure of Factor I (but not of Factor II), whereas Pattern Comprehension is a measure of Factor II (but not of Factor I). Had we displayed these factors as clusters as in figure 9.2, Reaction Time and Pattern Comprehension would have been represented as members of different clusters.

The values of the factor loadings help the scientist to understand the structure of the abilities that underlie the various tests. Consider Factor IV. Scan the factor loadings for Factor IV, noting which ones are high. All the loadings are less than 0.30 except for two—0.52 for the Mechanical Principles test and 0.65 for General Mechanics. The scientist would be tempted to believe that Factor IV has something to do with mechanical knowledge and to name this factor accordingly. Fleishman named Factor IV "Mechanical Experience." Now look at Factor II. The tests with high loadings are Pattern Comprehension (0.66), Mechanical Principles (0.53), and perhaps Speed of Identification (0.44). Fleishman named this factor "Visualization." In some cases (Factor IV), the name of the factor is rather obvious from the nature of the tests that "load on" it. In other cases it is not (as with Factor II).

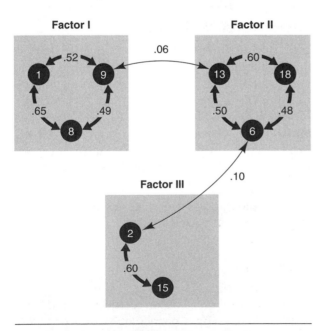

FIGURE 9.2 Three clusters (represented by boxes) of tests (shown as circles) that might result from a factor analysis. (Correlations between tests within a cluster are higher than correlations between tests in different clusters.)

	FACTORS									
Variable	**I**	**II**	**III**	**IV**	**V**	**VI**	**VII**	**VII**	**IX**	**h²**
1. Instrument comprehension	18	22	18	13	54	02	15	−01	20	48
2. Reaction time	60	−15	03	−03	08	007	16	−07	−09	43
3. Rate of movement	43	19	−02	−06	09	09	22	−01	14	31
4. Pattern comprehension	12	66	18	07	34	26	11	−07	08	69
5. Mechanical principles	03	53	22	52	09	07	06	12	05	63
6. General mechanics	05	19	12	65	14	02	11	−03	10	52
7. Speed of identification	27	44	14	17	21	27	01	00	00	61
8. Visual pursuit	14	23	38	05	25	23	10	16	17	40
9. Complex coord. trials 1-5	05	35	21	26	35	38	42	22	04	73
10. Complex coord. trials 12-16	23	16	23	21	19	47	46	41	22	86
11. Complex coord. trials 49-53	42	13	−03	22	19	38	47	52	−07	92
12. Complex coord. trials 60-64	43	12	01	20	19	34	40	58	06	89
13. Rotary pursuit	28	15	15	15	13	16	55	01	00	49
14. Plane control	16	07	−06	28	20	33	31	−11	20	41
15. Kinesthetic coordination	−01	−16	45	28	16	35	09	11	00	29
16. Unidimensional matching	14	16	34	14	08	19	45	14	06	45
17. Two-hand matching	16	21	14	15	−01	70	08	02	15	63
18. Discrimination reaction time	28	24	23	20	46	40	04	−16	00	63

TABLE 9.1. A Factor Matrix

Note. Decimal omitted. Factors are identified as follows: I = Speed of Arm Movement; II = Visualization; III = Perceptual Speed; IV = Mechanical Experience; V = Spatial Orientation; VI = Response Orientation; VII = Fine Control Sensitivity; VIII = Complex Coordination "Within Task" Factor; IX = Residual Factor; h² is called the communality, and is the sum of the squared factor loadings for that test (e.g., .18² + .22² + . . . + .20² = .48).

From Fleishman 1957.

Notice that a given test can load on two factors at the same time. An example is test 5 (Mechanical Principles), which loads on both Factor II (0.53) and Factor IV (0.52). One interpretation is that this test is made up of at least two abilities (Visualization, Mechanical Experience) and that it measures both of these abilities at the same time. This is in keeping with the idea that any given performance or skill (e.g., test 5) can be thought of as composed of many abilities.

Finally, the pattern of factor loadings is different for the various factors. That is, the tests that load highly on one factor are typically not the same tests that load highly on the other factors. Compare Factors I and II, for example. Here, the tests with the highest loadings on one have very low loadings on the other. This observation is really the same as that in figure 9.2, where each

of the factors appeared to represent a separate ability or group of abilities.

Motor Abilities Identified by Factor Analysis

The following list of abilities has been determined in a number of separate studies, using the methods outlined in the previous sections. The list is not exhaustive; it merely provides an idea of the kinds of abilities that have been inferred from these methods. These abilities all come from Fleishman's work (e.g., Fleishman, 1964, 1965, 1967; Parker & Fleishman, 1960) and bear the names given by him. After each we have provided an example of a "real-world" task in which this ability might be used, based largely on conjecture.

• **Control Precision.** This ability underlies the production of a movement for which the outcomes must be rapid and precise, but which is made with relatively large body segments. Example: swinging an ax.

- **Multilimb Coordination.** This ability underlies tasks for which a number of limb segments must be coordinated while moving simultaneously, such as the two hands, the two feet, or the hands and feet. Examples: juggling, playing a piano.

- **Response Orientation.** This ability underlies tasks for which rapid directional discriminations among alternative movement patterns must be made, and it is apparently related to the ability to select a correct movement in choice-RT situations. Examples: actions performed by a defensive lineman in American football or a hockey goalie.

- **Reaction Time.** This ability underlies tasks for which there is one stimulus and one response and which require the subject to react as quickly as possible after a stimulus in simple-RT situations. Example: sprint start.

- **Speed of Arm Movement.** This ability underlies tasks for which the limb must be moved from one place to another very quickly and the measure of performance is movement time (MT). Example: a jab in boxing.

- **Rate Control (Timing).** This ability underlies tasks for which the movement speed of the limbs must be adjusted to the movements of the environment so that the person's limbs are timed correctly. Example: tracking tasks, as in steering a race car.

- **Manual Dexterity.** This ability underlies tasks for which relatively large objects are manipulated, primarily with the hands and arms. Example: hammering a nail.

- **Finger Dexterity.** This ability underlies tasks for which small objects are manipulated, primarily with the fingers. Examples: repairing a wristwatch, sewing.

- **Postural Discrimination.** This ability underlies tasks for which subjects must respond to changes in postural cues, in the absence of vision, in making precise bodily adjustments. Example: walking in the dark.

- **Response Integration.** This ability underlies tasks for which the person must utilize and apply sensory cues from several sources into a single, integrated response. Example: throwing a pass in a football game.

- **Arm–Hand Steadiness.** This ability underlies tasks in which the person must be quiet and steady. Example: aiming in riflery or archery.

- **Wrist–Finger Speed.** This ability underlies tasks for which alternating movements (e.g., tapping) must be made as quickly as possible; it seems to represent the rapid coordination of the muscles required for up-and-down movements of the fingers and wrist. Example: piano trills.

- **Aiming.** This ability underlies tasks for which the subject must aim or point at a target, attempting to hit it with very quick movements. Example: dart throwing.

- **Physical Proficiency Abilities.** In addition to the abilities listed for the movement control area, other abilities have to do with physical or structural aspects of the body. Some of these as outlined by Fleishman (1964) are Extent (Static) Flexibility, Dynamic Flexibility, Static Strength, Dynamic Strength, Trunk Strength, Explosive Strength, Gross Body Coordination, Gross Body Equilibrium, and Stamina (Cardiovascular Endurance). These nine abilities can be thought of as underlying dimensions of physical fitness or physical proficiency, and they appear to be separate from the skills-oriented abilities listed.

Role of the Factors in Skills

How do these factors contribute to particular skills? It is interesting to consider that a number of factors seem to represent what we might call "quickness." For example, Response Orientation involves RT with more than one stimulus–response alternative (choice RT); Reaction Time refers to RT tasks involving only one stimulus–response alternative (simple RT); and Movement Time refers to making an arm movement quickly. Thus, "quickness" seems involved in each of these three kinds of tasks, yet they are represented by different underlying abilities. Also, note that Manual Dexterity and Finger Dexterity are separate abilities. Both pertain to the hands, but for different-sized objects. If so, then what does it mean to say that a person "has good hands"? To answer this question adequately, we would have to know about at least two different abilities. Clearly, the structure of human motor abilities is far more complicated than common sense would lead us to believe. Statements such as "John is good with his hands" must be combined with information about *how* the hands are used in order to be meaningful.

Edwin A. Fleishman

Certainly one of the most influential figures in the field of research on individual differences—particularly as it relates to motor behavior—has been Ed Fleishman (figure 9.3). In the years after World War II, when pilot performance and pilot selection procedures were being examined, Fleishman took a position at the Air Force Human Resources Research Center in San Antonio, Texas, from 1951 to 1956. There, he developed a program that linked correlational and experimental methods in the study of perceptual–motor abilities. During this period and afterward at Yale University and his later affiliations, Fleishman and his colleagues published numerous studies in which factor-analytic methods were used to examine the fundamental structure of human motor abilities. These studies identified and defined the abilities required by individuals to perform a variety of perceptual–motor tasks, ranging from those involving fine manipulations of objects to those involving gross and coordinated movements or complex timing operations (see Fleishman, 1954, 1972). Fleishman later broadened this focus to measures of physical fitness; he found that the abilities required for physical fitness are largely separate from those involving perceptual–motor skill. In this area he identified and defined the abilities involved in performing physically demanding tasks and specified the tests most diagnostic and reliable in measuring each ability (Fleishman, 1964).

With an understanding of the fundamental perceptual–motor abilities developed in his factor-analytic studies, Fleishman then sought to determine how these abilities could be used in the prediction of success in piloting and in many other occupations. Fleishman was also interested in how individual differences could be used in the study of learning (Fleishman & Rich, 1963) and retention (Fleishman & Parker, 1962) of complex perceptual–motor skills. He was one of the first to show that the particular combination of abilities involved in learning such skills changes at different stages of skill acquisition. In later years, Fleishman and Quaintance (1984) and Fleishman and Reilly (1992) developed methods for analyzing the ability requirements of jobs; these methods were based on his earlier taxonomic work and were extended to cognitive abilities. Fleishman showed that tests predicting job performance could be administered with the use of these methods.

Fleishman's work leaves a legacy for future efforts on solving problems of prediction. In 2004 he was awarded the American Psychological Foundation's Gold Medal Award for Life Achievement in the Application of Psychology (see American Psychological Association, 2004). A reading of this retrospective of his career provides a more complete picture of his immense contributions to psychology in general and to the field of motor behavior in particular.

FIGURE 9.3   Edwin A. Fleishman (b. 1927).
Courtesy of Edwin Fleishman.

Selected Bibliography

American Psychological Association. (2004). Gold Medal Award for Life Achievement in the Application of Psychology. *American Psychologist, 59,* 352-354.

Fleishman, E.A. (1954). Dimensional analysis of psychomotor abilities. *Journal of Experimental Psychology, 48,* 263-272.

Fleishman, E.A. (1972). Structure and measurement of psychomotor abilities. In R.N. Singer (Ed.), *The psychomotor domain: Movement behavior* (pp. 78-106). Philadelphia: Lea & Febiger.

Fleishman, E.A., & Quaintance, M.K. (1984). *Taxonomies of human performance: The description of human tasks.* Orlando, FL: Academic Press.

Fleishman, E.A., & Reilly, M.E. (1992). *Handbook of human abilities: Definitions, measurements, and task requirements.* Potomac, MD: Management Research Institute.

Note that the particular collection, or pattern, of these abilities appears to change markedly with only minor changes in the task or situation. For example, use of a choice-RT ability or a different simple-RT ability depends on the number of stimulus–response alternatives presented to the subject. The task remains generally the same with respect to the movements made, but the way in which the movement is signaled by the stimuli on the display is changed. Again, different abilities are used when the task is changed.

Finally, it has been tempting to align the human abilities defined by factor-analytic methods with the experimental research described in the first sections of this book. Fleishman and Bartlett (1969) discuss the hypothesis that the abilities are measures of separate ways in which humans process information. In some situations, this connection is easy to imagine, such as with simple- versus choice-RT abilities being differentiated on the basis of the need to resolve uncertainty. Similarly, abilities like Rate Control (or anticipation, timing) involve the processes related to analysis of incoming sensory information.

Criticisms of the Abilities Approach

The abilities approach has not been without its critics. One problem is methodological (see Kleine, 1982, 1985). There are many varieties of factor analysis and of other techniques (called "rotations") that are applied to factor-analytic outcomes to aid in interpretation. Choices about the way in which the same data are analyzed can change the nature of the factors that emerge. Fleishman's work in the armed forces has been criticized—unfairly, in our opinion—as limited in scope, dealing primarily with young servicemen. Rarely were women used as subjects; children were never included, nor were older people. Thus, the studies suffer some limitation in generalizability. Finally, the abilities that emerged from these studies have been based on skills for which the person is typically seated and using the hands (occasionally the feet as well), and for which the performance is noncompetitive. These kinds of performances are but one kind of action involved in the total spectrum of motor activity, and the abilities that emerged from these studies probably are somewhat limited as a result.

Ability Structures in Everyday Activities

The conclusions from the previous sections—that abilities are very specific—are often troublesome

to some because they do not appear to agree with a number of common observations. On playgrounds, for example, some children seem to be able to do well at nearly any motor task they try whereas others are nearly always ineffective, which makes abilities appear to be more general than they are. How can this apparent contradiction be rationalized?

A number of forces are at work to produce success in activities like sports. Some parents encourage their children to participate in many sports; for these children, this contributes to motor learning in a number of sport tasks and can provide the *appearance* of a strong general motor factor. Also, playground activities favor those children who are larger and more physically mature than average, leading mature children to practice many sports and relatively immature children perhaps to avoid sports. A kind of "rich get richer" phenomenon develops, whereby a little experience and encouragement can result in more experience, more encouragement, and so on. Such processes can be completely absent for other children.

Taxonomies

A *taxonomy* is a classification scheme used to assign things to various categories. We discussed a few of these classification methods in chapter 2, in connection with open versus closed skills and continuous versus discrete skills, for example. More elaborate systems for classification have been developed on the basis of the underlying structure of the abilities involved in motor tasks.

The basic notion is that one of the ways to classify tasks is in terms of the pattern of abilities that underlie them, rather than more superficial and obvious characteristics such as whether the performance is discrete or continuous. For example, performance on the pommel horse in gymnastics might be made up of Strength, Rate Control, and Multilimb Coordination, with each contributing a certain proportion to the whole. Again, the leader in the early development of this area was Fleishman (e.g., Fleishman & Stephenson, 1970). Two of these general taxonomic methods are described next (others are presented in Gawron, Drury, Czaja, & Wilkins, 1989).

Factor-Analytic Classifications

After a great deal of experience with the various motor tasks in previous factor analyses, the scientist sees that certain tests seem always to result in the emergence of certain factors or abilities. A good example is the various tests of rapid movement that, when included in factor analyses, typically produce a factor that is labeled Movement Speed. Such stable findings lead to the establishment of a particular MT test as the "best" measure of the ability of Movement Speed, with the "best" test being defined in terms of ease of administration, the sizes of the factor loadings, and so on. These tests are often elevated to the status of *reference tests*—the generally agreed-upon measures of a particular motor ability.

Now, if this reference test is included in another, subsequent factor analysis that involves tests for an entirely different activity (e.g., pilotry), we can understand the structure of this new task somewhat if we note the extent to which Movement Speed ability loads on the new task. If high loadings with the Movement Speed ability are obtained, then we can say that the new activity has an important Movement Speed component. By including other reference tests at the same time, each one representing a different predetermined ability, we can pinpoint the abilities represented in this new activity.

A good example is provided in the factor matrix shown in table 9.1. Tests 1 through 8 are tests of various kinds of skills, such as Instrument Comprehension, Reaction Time, and so on. These eight tests are the reference tests—items that had been studied extensively so that their underlying abilities were understood. Now notice that tests 9 through 12 are all based on the same apparatus, called the complex-coordination task (see figure 2.5*d*), in which the person manipulates an aircraft-type "joystick" and foot pedals to respond to a pattern of lights presented on a display.

What abilities underlie the complex-coordination task? For simplicity's sake, consider only the initial performance measures, trials 1 through 5 (test 9). The highest factor loadings for this task were for Factor VII (0.42) and Factor VI (0.38), with Factors II and V having slightly smaller loadings (0.35). We can therefore say that this task (at this stage of practice at any rate) is based on Fine Control Sensitivity (VII) and Response Orientation (VI), and to some extent Visualization (II) and Spatial Orientation (V). By comparison, none of the other factors seem to be involved very much. In this way, such a procedure "defines" this task in terms of its underlying ability structure, just as a recipe defines what a licorice milk shake is.

In theory, this procedure can be applied to any new task, such as the game of golf. We could use a large number (e.g., 50) of well-practiced and skilled golfers and administer reference tests to them, perhaps the eight tests we have mentioned. (We might wish to use somewhat different tests if there is reason to believe that some factor definitely is, or definitely is not, involved in golf.) Then, we administer a golf performance test and examine the reference tests and the golf test with factor analysis. The loadings that emerge should give an indication of the nature of the abilities involved in golf.

However, all of this is not as simple as we have perhaps made it sound. A major problem is having "good," well-understood reference tests in the first place. Fleishman's research has provided a start, but there are limitations to the generality of this work, as we have pointed out. And many abilities that might be involved in golf may not be detected, as they may not be represented by any of the reference tests. But with progressive additions to knowledge about the underlying abilities, the reference tests will become more numerous and more effective, making the task of discovering new tests easier in the future. This method has a great deal of potential for practical application for new jobs in industry, for which the nature of the abilities needs to be known.

Task Analysis

A considerably easier but less effective way to determine the nature of underlying abilities is through a series of procedures that has been termed *task analysis*. The essential idea is to analyze (i.e., break down) the task to consider what kinds of abilities might be involved in it. Look at the flowchart in figure 9.4, from Fleishman and Stephenson (1970; Fleishman, 1975). Consider a skill such as the throwing task performed by a shortstop in baseball. Begin at the top of the chart, asking whether or not speed is important to performance of this task. It is, so move to the right and ask whether accuracy is important also. Follow the arrow dictated by that decision. If baseball players or coaches are asked to use such procedures to evaluate throwing, researchers can arrive at a tentative understanding of the kinds of abilities required for this action. We would probably come to the decision that this task involves Control Precision, because speed, accuracy, and fine control are all needed for success.

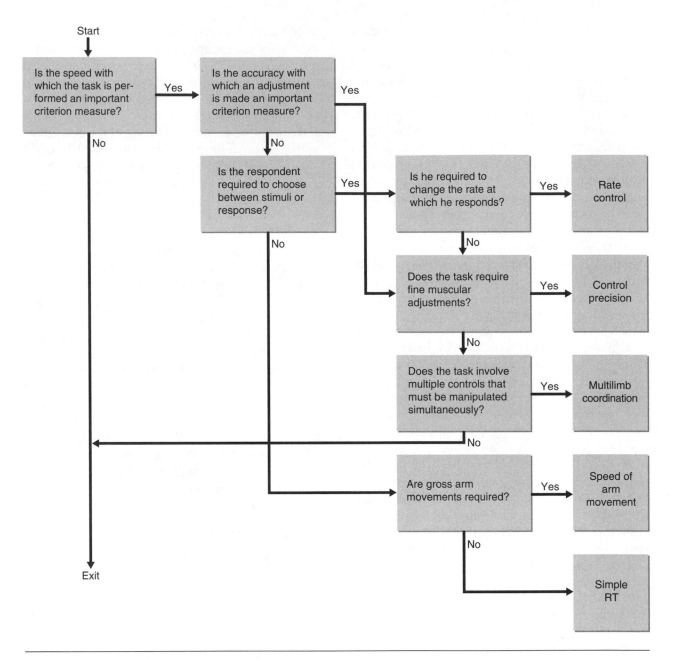

FIGURE 9.4 A binary flow diagram used to make decisions about abilities underlying particular tasks.

Adapted, by permission, from E.A. Fleishman and R.W. Stephenson, 1970, "Development of a taxonomy of human performance: A review of the third year's progress," *Technical Report No. 726-TPR3* (Washington, D.C.: American Institutes for Research).

These methods are only in the beginning stages of development and problems obviously exist, such as ambiguities that make it difficult to give satisfactory answers to the questions in the boxes.

Prediction

Companion to the research on abilities, the second major aspect of the work on individual differ-

ences is the problem of prediction. The fundamental problem is to be able to say (or predict) with some degree of accuracy what a person's score or level of skill will be on one task as a result of information about that person's measure on some other task or tasks.

These problems exist everywhere in the practical world. For example, insurance companies attempt to predict the probability that you will have a car accident on the basis of information such as age, gender, driving record, and where you live. Also, universities attempt to predict success in graduate school from tests that supposedly measure certain intellectual abilities (e.g., the Graduate Record Examination). More important to motor skills is the need to predict success in jobs or occupations.

Prediction in this sense implies the concept of *futurity*—forecasting some event or behavior before it happens. While this is the primary kind of application of individual-differences work, it is not the only way the idea of prediction is used. A second way involves the study of which tests best "predict" (or are correlated with) some other score that we already have in hand. Such techniques are intimately involved in the development of test batteries, and some of these procedures are described in the next section.

Test Battery Development: An Example

Suppose that you are a personnel director for a large company and that you want to predict success in some particular job in the company. For many jobs, this is easy. If you know the relevant *skills*, you can simply measure whether an applicant has these skills (e.g., plumbing skills). But a problem arises with a job for which the applicants have had no previous experience. Common examples involve accepting applicants into a flight training program in the Air Force or hiring a person to perform a particular assembly line job that exists only in your company. The problem is to determine whether or not the applicant has the necessary abilities to do this job after a training period, as no applicant would be expected to have the particular skill without prior experience.

Posing the Problem

Consider the occupation of dental technician, studied several years ago by Schmidt and Pew (1974). In this occupation, the primary task is to make fittings for the mouth, such as crowns, bridges, and artificial teeth, according to a dentist's prescription. The job involves use of the fingers and hands in the manipulation of tools and various materials such as gold, plastics, and wax. Employees usually perform their tasks seated at a workbench, and the job is relatively sedentary. The major problem giving rise to this study was that the firm requesting the analysis had a turn-over rate of 80% per year. The employees simply could not, or would not, continue in the job for very long, even though the pay was quite good. Management suspected that they were hiring people with the wrong abilities.

Task Analysis

The first step in developing a test battery was to perform a task analysis to generate an estimate of the skills involved on the job. The authors then asked what kinds of abilities might be required in these particular skills. Earlier studies provided a number of possibilities such as Manual Dexterity, Finger Dexterity, and Steadiness. These made up a preliminary group of reference tests that were probably involved. A second group of tests consisted of *face valid tests,* meaning that the performances involved in the tests closely mimicked some of the skills on the job, such as a test in which subjects matched two-dimensional pictures of teeth with three-dimensional models. A third group of tests concerned fundamental mechanisms in motor control, as discussed in the earlier chapters here. For example, to measure the consistency of muscular impulses, subjects were asked to make rapid ballistic movements of the fingers, with a goal MT of 100 ms; measures of timing consistency were emphasized. The Fitts tapping task was also used, as was aiming a stylus to a target.

The result of this process was 24 *predictor tests*—tests from which success on the job was to be predicted. These 24 predictor tests, about equally divided among the three categories described in the previous paragraph, were then administered to 44 of the current employees, all of whom had had at least one successful year on the job.

Criterion Variable

Probably the most critical aspect of the project was the development of a *criterion score.* This score was the best estimate of the employee's level of skill on the job. The supervisors were asked to rank the employees from "most skilled" to "least skilled," and to do this in a group session in which each employee's skill was discussed and a consensus about the final ordering was achieved. It was this rank that was to be predicted with the battery of tests, and this rank represented the measure that one would like to predict. In other occupations, the criterion score might have been one's yearly production level, quality of play in a sport as judged from game films, peer ratings of performance on the job, or any other measure providing a "best" estimate of success.

Validation

Next, the task was to determine which of the 24 predictor tests were the most valid (or useful) in predicting the criterion. First, the correlation between each of the predictor tests and the criterion was computed, and the authors rejected any test with a correlation less than 0.15. This preliminary screening left 14 tests that correlated 0.15 or greater with the criterion.

Next, the problem was to determine which tests, and in what combination, were most effective in predicting the criterion score. Decisions like this are based on a statistical procedure called *multiple regression* (see "Multiple Correlation").

Essentially, the method allows the determination of which predictor tests are the strongest predictors of the criterion score, minimizing duplication, and allows the generation of a regression equation that assigns a weight to each predictor.

In the present case, the final regression equation had the form

$$\text{RANK} = 0.599(\text{BA}) + 0.42(\text{TL}) + 0.56(\text{SS}) + 0.30(\text{RL}) \tag{9.1}$$

where the abbreviations (BA, TL, SS, and RL) are the predictor test names: Ballistic Aiming, Tapping (Left Hand), Spatial Scaling, and Rotated Letters, respectively. This regression equation had a multiple R of 0.50, meaning that the combination of tests shown correlated 0.50 with the criterion score (rank). This provided a preliminary battery of tests that could be used in the evaluation of new applicants. The potential employee

Multiple Correlation

Multiple-correlation methods are very similar to "regular" correlation measures, except that the multiple correlation (abbreviated R) is the correlation between some criterion score (a measure of what one is attempting to predict) and a weighted *combination* of what are called predictor scores (which are test scores from which one would like to predict the criterion). Imagine combining the predictor scores (for example, [1.0 × test 1] plus [2.5 × test 2] plus [8.0 × test 9] plus [5.5 × test 24] to form a single sum for each subject. If we correlated this weighted sum (now a single score) with the criterion score (another single score) using traditional correlation as described earlier, we would have a kind of multiple R. The only difference is that inherent in the multiple-correlation procedures is the automatic determination of the weights in the sum, so that the correlation between the *weighted* sum and the criterion score is maximized. That is, the multiple-correlation technique automatically adjusts the weights so as to achieve a maximum correlation between the predictors and the criterion, and thus it "decides" which ones of the predictors are most and least effective in predicting the criterion and in what combination. This procedure produces what is called a *regression equation*, which is the specification of the weights and the variables that best predict the criterion score.

Usually, the prediction is stronger with more tests. In the case of the example with the dental technicians, the prediction would be best if we were to use all 14 tests, but the time needed to measure 14 test performances on every new applicant would not be worth the effort. Thus, there is a trade-off between the number of tests and the size of the multiple R. Adding tests raises the R, but with each added test the multiple R is raised by a smaller and smaller amount, eventually to the point that adding another test does not yield enough more useful information to justify the effort. In the example cited here, the final battery involved four tests for which the multiple R was 0.50. The battery of four tests accounted for about $0.50^2 \times 100 = 25\%$ of the variance in the criterion score with the various predictors. Thus, about 75% of the abilities that were important for this job were *not* included in the battery of tests. This level of success (or lack of it) in prediction is unfortunately typical for many different situations—including the U.S. Air Force and prediction of pilot success, on which considerable effort, time, and money have been spent. This highlights the idea that effective prediction is difficult to achieve in the motor behavior area.

would perform the four tests; the weights would be applied as shown in the equation, and a predicted rank would be computed. Such a rank would be at least one basis for hiring or not hiring that person.

This general method can be applied to a variety of situations with only slight modification. The techniques are relatively time-consuming and expensive (because of testing time), however. The area of industrial personnel selection has used these techniques for years, and the armed services have employed them in pilot selection programs. A few professional football teams use batteries of tests that have been developed in ways like those described here, but this is more the exception than the rule.

Some Efforts at Prediction of Skill

With use of the basic methods just described, attempts have been made to develop batteries of tests that would predict success in various situations in the military, in industry, and in professional sport. Clearly the most systematic and large-scale effort in this regard has been the attempt to develop prediction batteries for U.S. Air Force and Navy pilots. A great deal of research has been directed toward the problem, mostly during the post-World War II years, the 1940s and 1950s. Fleishman was one of the most active researchers in this area, and some of his important findings are presented in the next section. For more information on these programs of research, see Fleishman (1956) or Adams (1953, 1956, 1987).

In this research, the criterion score is usually a measure of success in flight school. This in itself is a complex score, consisting of instructors' ratings, performances on knowledge tests, evaluations of "leadership" qualities, and subjective evaluations of personality. Typically, the research is done using a large group of potential pilot trainees, measuring a variety of motor and perceptual tests (the predictors) as well as the criterion score (success in flight school), and then using multiple-correlation methods to determine which predictors are the most useful for predicting success.

About 10 tests were identified in this program of work. Some of these seem to resemble the task of flying an airplane, whereas others are not so obviously linked. From the regression equations developed, the combination of these tests correlated approximately 0.70 with the criterion score of success in pilot school. This level of predictability is not particularly strong; it represents only somewhat better predictability than was seen in the example with dental technicians (50% in that case).

Individual-Difference Variables

In this final section we describe some research about certain kinds of individual-difference variables and the ways in which they relate to skilled performance. An individual-difference variable is usually some definable trait that can be measured in people, such as age, height, weight, gender, or ancestry. It has been of some interest to determine what relationships these variables have to the performance of certain kinds of skills. Such questions as "Do men outperform women on tests of pursuit tracking?" or "How much does movement speed decline as age increases beyond 40?" are tied to this general way of studying individual differences. Other individual-difference variables have to do with the ways in which people of different skill levels perform certain activities, such as sport skills.

Space does not permit a discussion of many of these individual-difference variables, so we concentrate on those that have been studied the most and that have the most interest and relevance for understanding human skilled performances. The discussion focuses on three important variables: age, neurological impairments, and expertise. Others have obvious importance but are not dealt with here, such as gender; race or country of national origin; sociological variables like number of siblings and birth order; and body configuration variables like height, eye color, weight, percentage of fat, and fitness. For more on these kinds of variables, see Noble (1978) or Singer (1975).

Effects of Age on Skilled Performance

The study of the effects of age has traditionally been divided according to two separate age categories. There are studies of what is called *motor development*, that is, of children as they mature and gain experience, usually from birth through the teenage years. A second category of studies involves *aging,* or the processes related to the effects of age on performance of individuals in the upper age categories, often considering adults 65 years of age and older. The kinds of changes in skills seen during these two age spans are markedly different, even though the variable of interest (age) is the same in both cases.

Motor Development

One major finding that emerges from the motor development research is that large and systematic gains occur in nearly every conceivable aspect of motor performance as age progresses from birth to about 18 years (Haywood & Getchell, 2009; Keogh & Sugden, 1985; Piek, 2006). These improvements can be divided into categories related to growth and strength (Malina, Bouchard, & Bar-Or, 2004), biomechanical changes (Zernicke & Schneider, 1993), posture (Woollacott & Sveistrup, 1994), capacity to anticipate and predict (von Hofsten, 1983), ability to process information from complex displays, speed of decision and movement, and accuracy in throwing (Halverson, Roberton, & Langendorfer, 1982), as well as many other specific areas of research (see also Gabbard, 2008; Payne & Isaacs, 2007). We could probably make the case that, in some way, most of the laboratory and real-life tasks studied involve the various abilities discussed in earlier sections of this chapter. And these abilities appear to develop, through maturation or experience or both, with increasing age up to about 18 years. So, it is not surprising at all that, on the average, older children typically outperform younger children.

One of the common hypotheses in the motor development literature today is the idea that as humans become older the capacity to process information increases (e.g., Thomas, 1980). Children appear to be relatively deficient in the rate and amount of information that they can process, which, as we discussed in earlier chapters, was an important limiting factor in motor control tests such as Fitts task. Children appear to have smaller capacities to hold information in short-term memory, shorter attention spans, and perhaps less effective mechanisms for processing information necessary for movement (e.g., feedback or environmental cues—see Thomas, 2000; Thomas, Thomas, & Gallagher, 1993). Therefore it is a logical theoretical prediction that motor performance improves as processing capacity increases with age.

Another view considers the development of motor skills within a dynamic systems approach (Newell, 1986; Thelen & Ulrich, 1991; see chapter 8). By this view, motor development (infant development in particular) involves the emergence of motor skills as a function of the complex interaction of the individual with the task and the environment in which the task is performed (Newell, 1986). The emergence of this view as a new paradigm in the study of motor development is probably most closely associated with the work of Esther Thelen.

Motor Performance in Older Adults

One of the fastest-growing areas in the behavioral and biological sciences is *gerontology,* or the study of aging. The primary concern here is with the upper age levels and the associated changes in the motor system that affect movement abilities in *healthy* older adults. Aging studies, like motor development studies, have been conducted on numerous variables related to motor behavior, such as postural control; coordination; rapid, aimed hand movements; tracking; timing; and learning. For a review of these variables and many others related to aging processes, readers can refer to Spirduso, Francis, and MacRae (2005). One of the most frequently studied questions is the effect of aging on RT. For example, Fozard, Vercruyssen, Reynolds, Hancock, and Quilter (1994) examined the changes in simple and choice RT in males and females who ranged from 20 to 90 years of age. As can be seen from the data in figure 9.6 (p. 318), there is a marginal slowing in simple RT with age, but a more dramatic slowing in choice RT. The decline in performance of tasks requiring speeded decisions, especially for tasks of increasing complexity, seems to be one of the most general findings in aging research (Salthouse, 1985; Spirduso, Francis, & MacRae, 2005).

Another consistent finding in the aging literature is that people move more slowly as they age. These effects are seen not only in tasks for which speed is measured directly, but also in tasks for which speed is evaluated indirectly. For example, in tasks requiring accuracy and speed, the overall score often suffers with increasing age because speed decreases. Or there may be a marked shift in the speed–accuracy trade-off, with speed decreasing and accuracy either increasing or being held constant. According to early thinking about these speed deficits with age, the slowing reflects the

Esther Thelen

FIGURE 9.5   Esther Thelen (1941-2004).
Photo courtesy of Indiana University.

The study of infant development, and particularly so the research on complex movement and behavior development, was influenced greatly by the remarkable work of Esther Thelen. With graduate training in both animal and human development, Thelen was unmoved by the dominant views of the day suggesting that the emergence of stereotypical movements in infants unfolded according to a predetermined, neural maturation process. For example, the newborn stepping reflex is characterized by "walking-like" rhythmic movements that are seen when the bottom of an infant's feet are stimulated, but these usually disappear from the infant's behavioral repertoire after 6 to 8 weeks of age. A dominant view was that the disappearance of the stepping reflex reflected the natural neural maturation of the infant's motor development. However, Thelen's research showed that the reflex "reappeared" when an infant was suspended in water. Conversely, the reflex "disappeared" when an infant who normally showed the reflex was fitted with small weights on their feet. The disappearance and reemergence of these reflexes, therefore, were not a matter simply of neural maturation. Rather, they reflected a much more complex interaction of the infant's sensory–motor system with the gravitational influences of the environment, suggesting that movements are largely determined as emergent behaviors.

Thelen's research and thinking extended beyond the boundaries of motor development to include perception and cognition. She viewed action as a process by which infants learn to solve problems. Her views therefore embodied cognition as part of a much more complex system of interactions of infants with their environment. She passed away in 2004, but her legacy lives on as a true paradigm shift in the study of infant development.

Selected Bibliography

Smith, L.B., & Thelen, E. (2003). Development as a dynamic system. *Trends in Cognitive Sciences, 7,* 343-348.

Thelen, E. (1995). Motor development. A new synthesis. *American Psychologist, 50,* 79-95.

Thelen, E., Schöner, G., Scheier, C., & Smith, L.B. (2001). The dynamics of embodiment: A field theory of infant perseverative reaching. *Behavioral and Brain Sciences, 24,* 1-34.

Esther Thelen Tributes

Galloway, G.C. (2005). In memoriam: Esther Thelen May 20, 1941–December 29, 2004. *Developmental Psychobiology, 47,* 103-107.

Smith, L.B. (2005). Lessons from Esther Thelen. *Journal of Motor Behavior, 37,* 83-84.

Spencer, J.P., Clearfield, M., Corbetta, D., Ulrich, B., Buchanan, P., & Schöner, G. (2006). Moving toward a grand theory of development: In memory of Esther Thelen. *Child Development, 77,* 1521-1538.

See also the papers in the special issue of *Infancy,* 2008, *13(3),* 197-283.

slowing in neurological activities in the CNS—not only those involved in nerve conduction times but also those involved in decision making and other aspects of information processing. Later studies suggested, however, that the slowing may also be related to the fact that older people appear to be more "cautious" than younger people (Welford,

1984). Being unwilling to make errors on a task makes a person—old or young—appear to be slow. Strategic factors are currently the subject of much continued research in aging and human performance (e.g., Morgan et al., 1994).

However, although the most obvious findings from aging research are the factors that *decline*

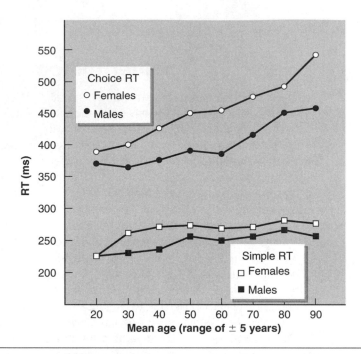

FIGURE 9.6   Effects of age and gender on simple and choice reaction time (RT).

Reprinted, by permission, from J.L. Fozard et al., 1994, "Age differences and changes in reaction time: The Baltimore longitudinal study of aging," *Journal of Gerontology: Psychological Sciences* 49: 182.

with age, these somewhat pessimistic findings do not represent the entire picture—there are many aspects of performance that are maintained well into advanced years. For example, Wishart and colleagues (2000) found that healthy adults over 80 years of age performed as accurately and consistently as 20-year-old subjects on an in-phase bimanual coordination task (see chapter 8), suggesting that the declines in motor performance may be attenuated in tasks that are highly automated. But cognition also serves a critical role. Older typists in an important study by Salthouse (1984) were slower to make alternate hand taps and in choice RTs, but equal to younger typists in typing speed. The older adults compensated for hypothesized declines in motor and sensory processes by accumulating more advance information about the information to be typed. Similar findings are emerging in older adults who have specific sport expertise too—maintenance in performance (or maintained performance relative to expected or typical declines) has been found for tasks that have important perceptual components, such as tennis (Caserta, Young, & Janelle, 2007). Thus, aging research also yields the very optimistic findings that perceptual and cognitive train-

ing can go a long way to offset the declines in the more physical accompaniments of aging (Starkes, Cullen, & MacMahon, 2004).

Individuals With Neurological Impairments

To this point in the book we have focused our discussion, with only a few exceptions, on the performance of persons who have an intact CNS. However, important information has also been discovered in numerous investigations examining movement in people who have had damage to the CNS. In chapter 6 we discussed Lashley's patient, who could accurately position his knee despite the absence of sensory feedback resulting from a gunshot wound (see also the neuropathy patient shown in figure 6.3). The primary purpose for studying individuals with particular neurological impairments is to gather information that might improve quality of life. However, a side benefit of this research is the comparison with information about performance by persons with a nonimpaired CNS. Such knowledge can lead not only to a better understanding of the effects of the specific impairment, but also to a theoretical advancement of specific roles of the CNS thought to be involved in the impairment.

We discuss some specific aspects of research in this area to illustrate the diversity of this work.

In most studies of individuals with very low cognitive functioning, the nature of the neurological impairment is unknown. Individuals with Down syndrome, however, have a known genetic disorder that is manifested in certain physical and cognitive impairments. Elliott, Weeks, and Elliott (1987) proposed a model in which hemispheric functioning in people with Down syndrome is partially reversed, compared to that in age-matched controls. According to the model, this reversal in functioning has implications regarding specific aspects of motor performance in these individuals, particularly with regard to speech perception and production (e.g., Heath & Elliott, 1999).

Persons with Parkinson's disease and Huntington's disease have provided important information about the role of the basal ganglia in movement (Prodoehl, Corcos, & Vaillancourt, 2009). Individuals with Parkinson's disease typically have slowness of movement, problems in movement initiation, and tremor. The basal ganglia pathology in Huntington's disease results in excessive movements. A research strategy that has been popular in recent years, for example, has applied what is known about bimanual coordination in young adults (chapter 8) and healthy older adults to contrast with information gathered about bimanual coordination performance in those with Parkinson's disease (Almeida, Wishart, & Lee, 2002; Byblow, Summers, Lewis, & Thomas, 2002; Lin, Sullivan, Wu, Kantak, & Winstein, 2007; Serrien, Steyvers, Debaere, Stelmach, & Swinnen, 2000) and Huntington's disease (Johnson et al., 2000; Serrien, Burgunder, & Wiesendanger, 2002). Studies of this type provide a greater depth of knowledge regarding the role of the CNS (and the basal ganglia in particular) in the control of movement than could be obtained if experiments were restricted solely to the study of nonimpaired individuals.

Another example of the use of knowledge about bimanual coordination in nonimpaired subjects is investigations of individuals who have undergone *callosotomies* (people with a surgically severed corpus callosum—the neural bundle that connects the two brain hemispheres). These studies have revealed that the tight coupling normally apparent in bimanual timed movements does not occur in individuals with a callosotomy

(e.g., Kennerly, Diedrichsen, Hazeltine, Semjen, & Ivry, 2002). Figure 9.7 illustrates a demonstration of the loss of interhemispheric connections in bimanual coupling. In this study (Franz, Eliassen, Ivry, & Gazzaniga, 1996), subjects drew three-sided rectangles that were oriented to be either spatially compatible (top half of figure 9.7) or incompatible (bottom half of figure 9.7). The effects are dramatic: The incompatible rectangles are nearly impossible for subjects with an intact corpus callosum to draw well (bottom left of figure 9.7), although the individual with a callosotomy was able to draw these symbols with little difficulty (bottom right of figure 9.7). These findings suggest an important role of the corpus callosum in tasks involving the control of both upper limbs (see chapter 8).

One of the most highly investigated patient groups comprises individuals who have suffered a stroke. In addition to the unilateral motor control deficits that often result from a stroke, these individuals demonstrate remarkable plasticity of the CNS in the recovery of lost function. For example, one of the most recent developments in the treatment of stroke has been termed *constraint-induced therapy*. This therapy is based on the principle that

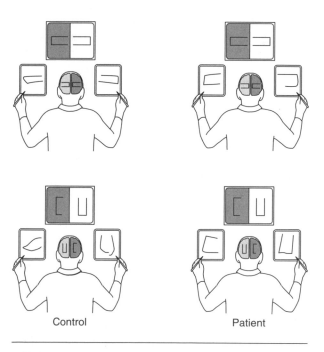

FIGURE 9.7   Spatial coordination in subject with an intact corpus callosum (left) and a callosotomy patient.

E.A. Franz, J.C. Eliassen, R.B. Ivry, and M.S. Gazzaniga, *Psychological Science*, "Dissociation of spatial and temporal coupling in the bimanual movements of callostomy patients," 7: 306-310, © 1996, Reprinted by permission of SAGE Publications.

self-generated, goal-directed movements involving the affected limb induce permanent changes in recovery due to a resultant reorganization of the CNS (see "Constraint-Induced Physical Therapy" on p. 350 for more details). Recent clinical trials have revealed quite impressive recovery of upper limb function in survivors of mild to moderate stroke, with retention of these changes up to two years poststroke (Wolf et al., 2006, 2008).

Comparative research investigations involving other patient groups have also been frequent in recent years (e.g., see the extended discussion of patient RS in "Neurological Disorders and Problems in Movement Control"). Such investigations have included the study of persons with Alzheimer's disease (e.g., Dick, Hsieh, Bricker, & Dick-Muehlke, 2003; Patterson & Wessel, 2002), with damage to the cerebellum (e.g., Spencer, Zelaznik, Diedrichsen, & Ivry, 2003), and with acquired brain injury (e.g., Holden, Dettwiler, Dyar, Niemann, & Bizzi, 2001). These investigations have provided valuable insights regarding the functioning of the motor control system in people with damage to the CNS, as well as a comparative analysis to advance our understanding of the CNS without damage.

Neurological Disorders and Problems in Movement Control

Recently we have become aware of a neurology patient (RS) who demonstrates some curious movement coordination disorders. These disorders seem especially interesting when considered in relation to some of the issues discussed in this chapter and chapter 8. RS, who is right-handed and in his late 60s, originally sought medical treatment because of clumsiness in his left hand and arm as well as balance problems. His right hand and arm seem to be nearly unaffected; conscious detection of tactile stimuli in the left hand seems not to be disrupted.

Testing (e.g., X-rays, MRIs, behavioral testing) revealed a rather diffuse pattern of neurological degeneration that apparently affects several brain structures, including the frontal cortex, basal ganglia, and cerebellum (see Ivry & Hazeltine, 1999; Mauk et al., 2000; Mauk & Buonomano, 2004). A conclusive diagnosis for RS is unclear, but a degenerative process called multiple systems atrophy has been suspected.

Following are some of the movement difficulties that RS experiences. Note the relationships of these deficiencies to some of the issues about motor control and coordination discussed throughout this book and particularly in the work of Franz and colleagues.

- RS has a marked decrement in left-hand fine motor control that is manifested in tasks such as typing, fastening buttons, picking up small objects with the fingers, using eating utensils, and tying shoelaces. Because consciously perceived tactile stimulation is essentially unaffected, these difficulties may then be due to some lack of nonconscious feedback control (full vision of the objects does not compensate for these difficulties). See the discussion of tactile feedback in chapter 5.

- Using a medical version of the Fitts tapping task (see Desrosiers et al., 1995), where the neurologist has the patient tap alternately between the examiner's finger and the patient's nose as quickly as possible, the number of taps RS could produce in 15 seconds with his left hand was only half the number that he produced with the nearly unaffected right hand.

- The tendency for the two hands to be coupled strongly to each other appears to be absent. (See the section on bimanual control in chapter 8.) In fact, even when RS tries to move his hands in the same pattern together, the left hand appears disconnected from the right and the patterns do not resemble each other. The coordination of the hands together as one, which is one of the most striking phenomena of "normal" motor behavior, seems almost totally absent in RS.

- Making a large (2 foot diameter, or 60 cm) horizontal circle with the right hand and arm displays the requisite coordination between the muscles controlling the elbow and shoulder. In attempting this task with the left hand and arm, RS seems to lack this intralimb coordination. This is also seen in an underhand ball toss with the left hand, where the timing of the ball's release is in gross error.

- We appear to control limbs with one hand in the "foreground" while the other hand automatically does some nearly trivial task in the "background." An example might be brushing teeth with the right hand and simultaneously dropping the toothpaste tube in a drawer with the left hand. When RS tries such a task combination, his left hand acts as if it is frozen over the open drawer and will not release the toothpaste tube until nearly full attention is directed to it.

These are just a few of the many ways in which motor control and coordination are disrupted by neurological damage. We find it interesting that some of the strongest and most obvious features of "normal" motor behavior and coordination (e.g., interjoint coordination in one arm, the almost trivially easy coupling of one hand to the other in rhythmic tasks) can be so easily lost.

Selected Bibliography

Desrosiers, J., Hébert, R., Bravo, G., & Dutil, E. (1995). Upper-extremity motor co-ordination of healthy elderly people. *Age and Ageing, 24,* 108-112.

Ivry, R.B., & Hazeltine, E. (1999). Subcortical locus of temporal coupling in the bimanual movements of a callosotomy patient. *Human Movement Science, 18,* 345-375.

Mauk, M.D., & Buonomano, D.V. (2004). The neural basis of temporal processing. *Annual Review of Neuroscience, 27,* 307-340.

Mauk, M.D., Medina, J.F., Nores, W.L., & Ohyama T. (2000). Cerebellar function: Coordination, learning or timing? *Current Biology, 10,* R522-R525.

Expert–Novice Differences

Issues regarding motor learning are the focus in the next part of the book. However, a growing research area that has become a topic of individual-differences research is the comparison of performances in people who possess varying levels of skill (Ericsson, 1996; Starkes & Allard, 1993; Starkes & Ericsson, 2003). The fundamental question concerns the ways in which experts perform *differently* than novices. This expert–novice research is characterized by various methodological approaches, each contributing unique information about the ways in which distinctions can be made among people of varying levels of skill in certain activities (Abernethy, Burgess-Limerick, & Parks, 1994; Chamberlin & Coelho, 1993). We briefly summarize some of these approaches.

Recall of Briefly Presented Information

Early work in cognitive psychology (Chase & Simon, 1973; DeGroot, 1946/1978) revealed that master chess players had excellent recall of games they had played previously. To examine this apparent superior "memory" under controlled experimental conditions, expert and novice chess players were briefly shown chessboards of games that had been partially completed; they were then asked to recall the information by reconstructing the pieces' locations on the game board after the pieces had been removed from view. As expected, the experts were much better than the novices at this recall task. However, when the "game" that was shown was in actuality a series of randomly arranged chess pieces, the experts were no better at reconstructing the board than were the novices. The arrangement of the pieces in an actual game had meaning and relevance to the expert, but not so for random patterns. The recall advantage was specific to the domain of the subject's expertise.

These important findings have been replicated in experts in other intellectual games (e.g., Scrabble; Tuffiash, Roring, & Ericsson, 2007) and in sports. For example, using a paradigm similar to the chess work, Abernethy, Neal, and Koning

(1994) compared expert and novice snooker players' recall of ball positions during an actual match. Although the experts were better at the task than the novices for recall of a partially completed game, no differences were found when the balls were scattered randomly on the table. Similar patterns of findings, in which the recall advantage for experts is specific to the nature of the expertise, have been reported for many other sports (see reviews in Chamberlin & Coelho, 1993; Starkes, Helsen, & Jack, 2001; Williams, Davids, & Williams, 1999).

Eye Movement Recordings

Eye movement recording devices allow the experimenter to analyze the parts of a visual display that a subject fixates using visual search during performance (see chapter 2). Researchers have used this technique to identify how experts and novices differ in terms of obtaining visual information from the environment, particularly when watching the actions of an opponent. A recent review of the literature suggests that, in general, experts tend to have fewer eye fixations on a target, but each has a longer duration than nonexperts (Mann, Williams, Ward, & Janelle, 2007). One particularly important time when these differences emerge is immediately prior to movement onset—what Vickers (2007) has called the quiet-eye effect. Experts in such sports as billiards, basketball, and golf are consistent in their tendency to have fewer eye fixations of longer duration than nonexperts. It is unclear, however, what purpose this quiet-eye period serves, although a probable role is given to facilitating movement preparation.

Occlusion Methods

Two methods of studying expertise involve adapting the visual displays that are seen by the subject. Although this research paradigm began many years ago with the use of film and videotape (e.g., Jones & Miles, 1978), more recent opportunities afforded by digital displays have provided researchers with precise methods of preventing the subject from viewing certain parts of a display. *Spatial occlusion* methods involve masking certain relevant and irrelevant parts of a display, such as the various parts of the arm and racket of a badminton opponent (Abernethy & Russell, 1987). *Temporal occlusion* methods are used to stop a display at critical points during an action (e.g., Salmela & Fiorito, 1979). A frequent experimental approach compares experts and nonexperts under these occlusion methods to assess a key temporal marker or an important spatial location in the display that differentiates the performance of the subjects. Presumably, the nature of the specific skills that define expertise for that sport underlies observed differences in performance (Williams & Ward, 2003).

A good example of this research was provided by Müller and colleagues (2006; 2010), who videotaped cricket bowlers from the perspective of the batter. Edited videos were shown to groups of expert, intermediate, and novice players, who made judgments about the location at which the ball would land under varying conditions. Temporal occlusion was manipulated by stopping the video at time markers during the bowler's delivery—either well before or shortly before ball delivery, at the point of release, or with no occlusion. Müller and colleagues found that only the experts could make use of the earliest time-occlusion information—intermediate players showed some moderate success (relative to the novices) when the video was occluded at the point of ball release, but novices only improved their accuracy well after the ball had been released. Spatial occlusion involved editing out parts of the display during the ball delivery up to the temporal marker of ball release, at which point the entire video was stopped. The features that were spatially occluded included relevant parts on some trials (e.g., hand and ball; bowling arm) and irrelevant parts on other trials (e.g., nonbowling arm; lower body) (see figure 9.8). The results revealed that a complex relationship existed for the pickup of advanced information; in impoverished viewing conditions, only the experts were able to predict with accuracy when relevant viewing data were available. The differences in performance between experts and nonexperts in occlusion experiments of this kind suggest that the acquisition of perceptual skills in sport is not a simple, quantitative change that occurs with practice. Rather, the acquisition of expertise requires the learning of specific perceptual cues to which information is acquired with increasingly earlier temporal landmarks.

Point-Light Displays

A different approach to the occlusion of information uses a paradigm in which whole-body images are replaced with visual markers (white dots against a black background). When these point-light displays are set in motion, they reveal information about movement kinematics to the viewer

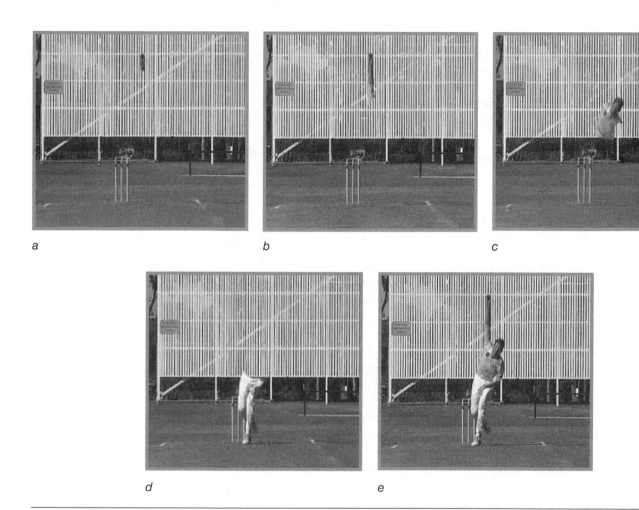

FIGURE 9.8 Five different types of spatial occlusion, which prevented subjects from seeing different body segments, were shown under five temporal occlusion conditions in a cricket batting task.

Reprinted from S. Müller et al., 2010, "Expertise and the spatio-temporal characteristics of anticipatory information pick-up from complex movement patterns," *Perception* 39: 745-760. By permission of authors.

who is sufficiently skilled to perceive that information accurately. The use of point-light information has therefore become another important paradigm in the identification of factors that differentiate the skills of expert and nonexpert athletes.

In a sense, most of us are "experts" in some types of perceptual identification from some types of point-light displays. People can often make the distinction between males and females, and between friends and strangers, simply from the information contained in these moving white dots. The identification of perceptual information in point-light displays of specific athletic actions, for example, would probably be observed only in the expert, by this thinking, and research using these tools is becoming more common (Shim, Carlton, Chow, & Chae, 2005; Williams, Ward, & Smeeton, 2004).

Domain Knowledge Reports

An alternative type of methodology for studying expert–novice differences is the analysis of self-report data. In this method the verbal reports of athletes engaged in certain sport-specific situations are subjected to a protocol analysis (e.g., French & Thomas, 1987). The objective of this analysis is to identify domain-specific differences in knowledge about certain tactics, procedures, rules, nuances, and so on that might distinguish the expert from the novice. Obviously, this qualitative type of information is not obtained through the more conventional methods that we have described. Studies of this type are becoming more frequent and provide a number of important details about factual knowledge and strategic differences between experts and novices (e.g., MacMahon & McPherson, 2009; McPherson, 1993, 1994; McPherson &

MacMahon, 2008; Starkes, Cullen, & MacMahon, 2004). One needs to be mindful, however, that even experts are subject to illusions and biases—what they "think" may be happening is often quite subjective and not always supported by objective data (e.g., Lee et al., 2008a).

Summary

The study of individual differences concerns the variations among individuals on various tasks or behaviors. This kind of research differs strongly from the experimental approach in which differences among individuals are ignored in order to concentrate on the average performances of larger groups of people affected by certain independent variables. Two major subdivisions of individual-differences research can be identified.

The major focus is on abilities, defined as stable, enduring characteristics or traits, probably genetically defined, that underlie certain movement skills or tasks. Since the 1930s, there have been many points of view about the structure of motor abilities. Some convergence has occurred on the idea that humans possess a relatively large number of separate motor abilities (perhaps 50 to 100), that these abilities are independent, and that any particular skill or task may have many of these abilities underlying it. Henry's specificity theory and Fleishman's work on factor-analytically determined abilities tend to point to this kind of conclusion. Both of these approaches indicate that the idea of a general motor ability defining proficiency on all motor tasks is surely not correct. However, some abilities might turn out to be more general than the other abilities mentioned here, though more research is needed in order to provide certainty about this.

A second major division of individual-differences research is related to *prediction*. Here, the relationships among scores on various tests (the *predictors*) are used to predict or estimate the scores on some other test (the *criterion*), such as the prediction of an applicant's probable success on the job from various measures of abilities. The development of predictive tests is time-consuming, and the effectiveness of such batteries in predicting some criterion behavior is disappointingly low even when a great deal of research funding and effort have been applied. The problem is that many abilities seem to exist, and these abilities are not well understood.

A large number of individual-difference variables have been studied. These variables provide an easy basis for classifying people, so that the performance on some task can be studied "as a function of" these variables. Three major research variables have attracted considerable research interest: (a) age effects, both from the point of view of growth and maturation and from the point of view of older age levels (gerontology); (b) the effects of neurological impairments; and (c) expert–novice differences.

Student Assignments

1. Prepare to answer the following questions during class discussion:
   a. Use the concept of specificity of individual differences to explain the performance characteristics of two video game experts whom you know.
   b. Add a novel example to each of the abilities listed in the textbook in the section "Motor Abilities Identified by Factor Analysis."
   c. Timing is one ability that may be generalizable. Discuss how this concept might be examined for musical performance in a large group of 10-year-old children.
2. Find a research article that contrasts the abilities of experts and novices in the performance of a motor skill.

Web Resources

A discussion of factor analysis:

   www.fact-index.com/f/fa/factor_analysis.html

Link to *Research Quarterly for Exercise and Sport*, a journal that published many of the early investigations of individual differences:

   www.aahperd.org/rc/publications/rqes/index.cfm

Notes

[1] The limiting factor is that the correlation between test X and test Y is theoretically less than the square root of the reliability of either test X and/or test Y; that is, $r_{xy} \leq \sqrt{r_{xx}}$ and/or $r_{xy} \leq \sqrt{r_{yy}}$. See Gullicksen (1950).

PART III

MOTOR LEARNING

At this point in the text we change the emphasis with respect to the treatment of motor skills. The concern so far has been with skilled performance—often at high levels of proficiency—and the numerous internal processes that make these performances possible. We now shift to a different, but related problem: the *learning* of skills as a result of practice or experience. The problem is different from the issue of skilled performance, because we will be focusing on the *changes* in skill, rather than the nature of skill at some particular level. As such, different methods and logic are needed to understand these performance changes; and in chapter 10, we document some of the more important methods used to understand the principles that have been discovered about motor learning. Chapters 11 and 12 describe how conditions of practice and augmented feedback influence learning. In chapter 13, we present the various ways in which the learning process has been conceptualized by researchers. This part closes in chapter 14 with a discussion of factors that influence retention (how learning is retained over periods of no practice) and transfer (how learned behavior can be applied in novel situations).

CHAPTER 10

MOTOR LEARNING CONCEPTS AND RESEARCH METHODS

Learning is a critical part of our existence. Think where humans would be if we could not profit by the experiences and practices in which we all engage. You would not be able to read the words on this page, we would not be able to type the words that appear here, and no one would be able to speak. In short, we would be simple creatures indeed if we were forced to behave in the world equipped only with the skills we inherited. The fact that we can acquire new knowledge and skills has led to a robust interest in the ways in which people learn, in the critical variables that determine how people will profit from experience or practice, and in the design of instructional programs.

We will not attempt to review the entire topic of learning. There are examples of learning in all organisms (even the simplest of single-celled organisms), and the learning that humans enjoy is the most complex of all. Thus, many forms of human learning are not discussed here, such as the learning of verbal materials, the learning of concepts, and the learning of interpersonal skills. We concentrate on the acquisition of motor skills as defined in chapter 2. Essentially, the concern will be with the effects of practice and experience on performance, in an attempt to understand the relevant variables that determine gains in proficiency.

Motor Learning Defined

Learning in general, and motor learning in particular, have been defined in a variety of ways. Four distinct characteristics are included in the definition: (1) Learning is a *process* of acquiring the capability for producing skilled actions. That is, learning is the set of underlying events, occurrences, or changes that happen when practice enables people to become more skilled at some task. (2) Learning occurs as a direct result of practice or experience. (3) Learning cannot be observed directly, as the processes leading to changes in behavior are internal and are usually not available for direct examination; rather, one must *infer* that learning processes occurred on the basis of the changes in behavior that can be observed. (4) Learning is assumed to produce *relatively permanent* changes in the *capability* for skilled behavior; for this reason, changes in behavior caused by easily reversible alterations in mood, motivation, or internal states (e.g., fatigue) are not thought of as due to learning.

A synthesis of these four characteristics produces the following definition: *Motor learning is a set of processes associated with practice or experience leading to relatively permanent changes in the capability for skilled movement.* We discuss these aspects in more detail next.

Motor Learning Is a Set of Processes

A *process* is a set of events or occurrences that, taken together, lead to some particular product, state, or change. For example, in reading we are interested in processes that transform visual information to provide meaning; in motor control we may focus on processes of retrieving a motor program from memory; and in physiology we can discuss processes that result in muscle hypertrophy. Similarly, practice and learning can be seen as a set of analogous processes that, taken together, lead to the acquisition of the capability for moving skillfully—with "skill" being defined as in chapter 1. These processes are *assumed;* in other words, we assume that some set of processes must have taken place in order for learning to have occurred with practice. However, what these processes are (exactly) is not specified, and in fact the nature of these processes is what learning theorists try to understand. Thus, an important focus is on what happens—in terms of the underlying processes—when people practice and acquire new skills.

Learning Produces an Acquired Capability for Skilled Movement (Habit)

The processes involved in learning—like all processes—generates or results in a product or internal state. In the case of motor learning, this state is an increased *capability* for moving skillfully in the particular situation. Notice that we have not defined learning as a change in *behavior* per se, as many have done (e.g., Morgan & King, 1971). In this sense, the goal of practice for the learner is to increase the "strength" or the "quality" of this internal state, so that the capability for skill will be maximized in future attempts. The researcher's goal is to understand the *nature* of the internal processes that have led to the increases in the state; thus, theorists propose hypothetical processes to account for learning in experimental settings. Also, the researcher wants to understand the nature of the state itself, perhaps in terms of the codes involved or the kinds of control it exerts on behavior; such knowledge will tend to provide an answer to the question of *what* was learned.

William James (1890) used the term "habit" for this internal capability for movement (with only minor reference to the usual use of the word), but it has been named in other ways by other theorists. Regardless of its label, the notion of some internal state that is the product of learning represents a critically important distinction. Defining learning as producing a *capability* for movement directs our focus to the internal state and the processes that have led to it, rather than simply to the behavioral changes. More importantly, the concept of a capability for movement implies that if the capability is "strong," then the skilled behavior may occur if the external conditions, motivation, and other surrounding factors are present; if the conditions are not favorable, then the skilled behavior might not occur—for example, if fatigue is present or motivation is low. That is, behavior may vary for a number of reasons, only some of which are a result of change in the internal capability for movement produced by practice. This concept provides a basis for the distinction between *learning versus performance,* which is a major theme of this chapter.

Numerous changes in humans can contribute to their capability for movement in skilled situations, but many of these have little to do with learning as defined here. For example, we know that increased maturation or growth can lead to improvements in skill, as older children generally outperform younger ones. Similarly, changes in strength or endurance from physiological training could contribute to certain kinds of skills, such as those used in weightlifting or soccer. However, we would not want to include such improvements in a definition of learning because practice or experience is not the basis for the changes in capability. We will be searching for situations in which changes in capability are primarily related to changes acquired through experience.

Motor Learning Is Not Directly Observable

It should be clear that motor learning is not directly observable. The processes that underlie changes in capability—and the nature of the capability itself—are highly complex phenomena in the central nervous system, such as changes in the ways sensory information is organized or changes in the patterning of muscular action. As such, they are rarely directly observable, and one must infer their existence from changes in motor behavior. This feature of motor learning makes it particularly difficult to study. Experiments must be designed carefully so that the observed changes in behavior allow the logical conclusion that there were associated changes in some internal state.

Motor Learning Is Relatively Permanent

Another important feature of motor learning is that it is relatively permanent. Something lasting occurs when one engages in practice and learns some activity—something that does not simply pass away in the next few minutes or hours. More dramatically, we could say that when you practice and learn, you will never be quite the same person as you were before. Learning has the effect of changing the learner (if only slightly) in a relatively permanent way.

With respect to skill learning, this distinction is important because it rules out the changes in skills that can come from a variety of temporary performance factors. For example, skills might improve if the person is in the "right" mood, if motivation is temporarily high, or if certain drugs are administered. Yet each of these changes in behavior will probably vanish when the temporary effect of the mood, for example, "wears off." Thus we should not attribute these changes in behavior to motor *learning*, because they are not sufficiently permanent.

An analogy may help to clarify this point. If you cool water sufficiently, you will find that it becomes solid (ice); you can reverse the effect completely to produce water again simply by warming the ice. This is not so with boiling an egg. Boiling an egg for 10 min produces changes that are not reversible when the egg is cooled. Some relatively permanent change has been made in the egg that was not the case with the water.

This analogy applies well to the concept of motor learning and performance. The nature of the water or of the egg can be observed directly, and they both behave in predictable ways when the independent variable (temperature) is applied. But beneath the surface is some unobservable change in the nature of the substance; in one case (the water), this change is completely reversible and not relatively permanent, while in the other (the egg), the change is not reversible. With human learning, many analogous variables can be applied in order to change the observed

behavior (skill), but these may or may not change the internal structure of the person in a relatively permanent way. If the effect of some independent variable can appear and disappear as the value of the variable is changed, then this change in behavior cannot be associated with anything relatively permanent, hence is not thought to be due to learning.

How permanent is "relatively permanent"? This is a vague concept, and scientists studying learning are rarely clear about it. But the intention of this discussion should be clear; learning should have some lasting effect.

Measuring Motor Learning

Given that motor learning is a set of processes that underlie the changes in a capability for movement, how can such a capability be measured in order to understand what variables affect it during practice? It will be helpful to consider a typical motor learning experiment to explain some of the major points in the measurement process.

Performance Curves

In a simple experiment on learning, a large group of individuals are asked to practice on some motor task, and the experimenter charts their performances as a function of "trials," resulting in a *performance curve*. For example, figure 10.1 is a graph from Fleishman and Rich (1963) showing performance on the two-hand coordination task. Subjects had to follow a moving target through movements of two crank handles, one controlling the forward–backward direction of a pointer and one controlling right–left movements (see figure 2.5d). The average time on target (in minutes) for a group of 20 subjects is plotted as a function of successive blocks of four 1 min trials. A clear trend can be seen for the scores to increase with practice, with the increases being somewhat more rapid at first and then leveling off later.

When the measure of performance is an error score, for example, the scores will decrease, as shown by the performance curve in figure 10.2. These data, from Quesada and Schmidt (1970), are from subjects' performances on a timing task. Here, the subject's task was to operate a switch when a moving pointer became aligned with a stationary one, and error was the time interval

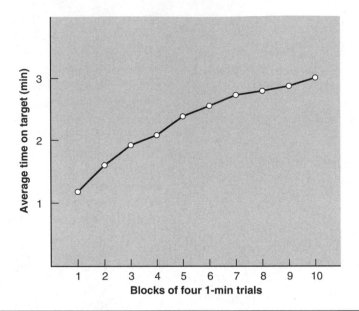

FIGURE 10.1   A performance curve showing increases in the score with practice.

Reprinted, by permission, from E.A. Fleishman and S. Rich, 1963, "Role of kinesthetic and spatial-visual abilities in perceptual motor learning," *Journal of Experimental Psychology* 66: 9. Copyright © 1963 by the American Psychological Association.

between the switch movement and the actual moment of coincidence. Average absolute error decreased rapidly at first, and more gradual decreases occurred later in practice.

Even though the two performance curves (figures 10.1 and 10.2) change in opposite ways with practice, they both represent gains in performance and almost certainly can be interpreted as caused by motor learning. Such effects are usually among the most powerful in the study of motor behavior. But what is usually of more interest than whether or not learning occurred is whether learning was

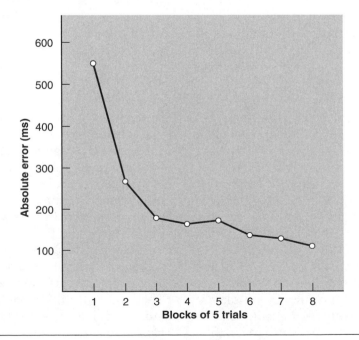

FIGURE 10.2   A performance curve showing decreases in the score with practice.

Adapted from D.C. Quesada and R.A. Schmidt, 1970, "A text of the Adams-Creamer decay hypothesis for the timing of motor responses," *Journal of Motor Behavior* 2: 273-283, adapted with permission of the publisher (Taylor & Francis Ltd, http://www.informaworld.com).

greater in one condition than in some other condition. Thus, the question of interest relates to the role of *variables that influence learning* of the motor task. In order to make meaningful inferences about whether or not condition *A* produced more learning than condition *B,* special procedures are needed to analyze these performance scores in motor learning experiments.

Motor Learning Experiments

Graphs such as those shown in figures 10.1 and 10.2 are often thought to represent the acquired capability for movement in the subjects during practice from trial to trial, and to some extent they probably do. For this reason, such curves are often loosely termed *learning* curves, as it is tempting to regard the changes in performance as reflecting the product of the internal capability for movement generated by learning. The notion that these curves "mirror" the internal state (the amount of habit) is oversimplified, however, and scientists are very cautious about interpreting the changes in curves like those in figures 10.1 and 10.2 as a reflection of the *amount* of motor learning. Some reasons for this caution are outlined next.

Performance Measures

The first reason performance curves perhaps should not be assumed to reflect learning is that skilled *performance*—not the *capability* for moving skillfully—is plotted as a function of trials. Since the capability (habit) cannot be measured directly, any change in habit that has occurred must be inferred from the changes in performance. Thus, it seems more logical to refer to the curves exemplified in figures 10.1 and 10.2 as *performance curves* rather than learning curves. As such, they reflect both the momentary changes in performance and the relatively permanent consequences of practice.

Between-Subject Variability

A second problem in making inferences about learning from performance curves is that they are insensitive to the differences among individuals that arise as a function of practice. Consider how a performance curve is produced. A large number of people (the larger the better, usually) is used. The first-trial scores for all of the subjects are averaged to obtain the data point for trial 1; trial 2 scores for all subjects are averaged to obtain the data point for trial 2, and so on. This averaging

procedure has a number of advantages, such as "smoothing" or "canceling out" many random (perhaps meaningless) variations in scores due to inattention, errors in measurement, and other factors not directly related to the internal habit changes. But at the same time, this averaging procedure tends to hide any differences that may have existed among people on a particular trial, or it may hide important trends in improvement with practice.

These effects can be particularly important in the study of learning. Consider two hypothetical subjects whose performances over a number of trials are shown in figure 10.3. Subject 2 seemed to improve in performance early in the sequence, with little change occurring later. Subject 1 has a difficult time improving in the task until later in practice, when finally performance improves markedly.

Now consider what happens if these two subjects' scores are averaged in ways that are typical for studies of larger groups. In figure 10.3, the center line is the average of the performances for the two subjects for each of the trials. The pattern of improvement with practice is considerably different now. It might be tempting to say that the average capability for responding accumulated gradually and consistently. This, of course, would be misleading, as neither of the subjects whose

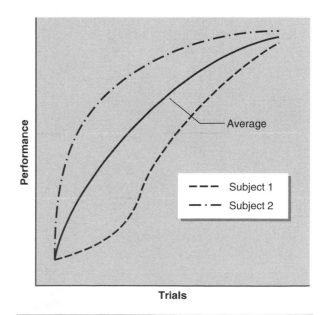

FIGURE 10.3 Hypothetical performance curves for two individuals, together with the curve representing the average of their performances.

data produced the average performance curve showed this trend. Thus, it could certainly be that learning does not occur gradually at all, as is usually evidenced by the individual performance curves. Rather, learning might sometimes occur as more of an abrupt "revolution" than a gradual "evolution" in the ways in which the subjects perform the task.

Within-Subject Variability

As mentioned previously, one of the important aspects of the averaging procedure is the reduction of errors in measurement and of factors that seem to obscure the "true" capabilities of the people on a particular trial. As seen in chapter 7, a typical finding is that people inherently vary from trial to trial, even if they are attempting to do the "same" thing each time. But is trial-to-trial variation for a particular person due to some meaningless random fluctuation in the motor system, or is it due to some meaningful change in the way the person attempted the task on a particular trial?

The problem can be better illustrated with an example. Consider the task of free-throw shooting in basketball when the subjects are relatively inexperienced. Certainly a great deal of variability exists in this task's performance from trial to trial, and much of this variability does not seem to represent fundamental changes in the ways that people attempt the task. If a large group of people is examined on this task, with performance scored as "correct" or "incorrect," each person will have a pattern of scores that shows a large number of apparently randomly ordered hits (baskets made) or misses, with somewhat more hits as practice continues. And different people will have the hits and misses scattered across the trials differently.

A performance curve can be plotted with these data, with the measure for a particular trial being the *probability of success* on that trial (figure 10.4). With this measure, the data point for trial 1 will be the total number of hits divided by the total number of attempts (i.e., the number of subjects)—that is, the proportion of subjects that shot successfully on trial 1; the method is similar for trial 2. When plotted, the average performance curve usually rises gradually, perhaps moving from 0.10 to 0.40 in 100 trials. From such a curve it is tempting to conclude that the *capability* for accurate shooting grew slowly as a result of practice. But note that not a single subject could

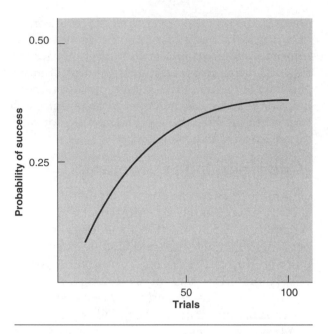

FIGURE 10.4 An average performance curve for which probability of success is the dependent measure. (On a particular trial, any given subject can receive only 0 or 1.)

have shown this pattern of performance! Indeed, there is no way that a given person could ever achieve a score of 0.20 on a particular trial, as a single subject can only achieve 1.0 (hit) or 0 (miss) on a single trial. Thus, the average performance curve in figure 10.4 obscures all the variations that occurred within people across trials and encourages us to draw conclusions about the learning process that may be incorrect.

Ceiling and Floor Effects

Ceiling and floor effects are a third kind of problem that can lead to erroneous conclusions about learning processes from group performance curves; these are present in many of the tasks used in motor learning experiments. In most tasks, absolute scores exist that no person will ever exceed. For example, there can be no fewer than zero errors on a trial, no less than 0 s for some movement-time task, and no more than 30 s for a time-on-target score in a 30 s performance trial. Thus, as people approach these *ceilings* (the limitation in score at the top of the scale) or *floors* (the limitation at the bottom of the scale), the changes in the performance levels of the people doing the task become increasingly *insensitive* to the changes in learning that may be occurring in the people as they practice. As a person approaches some ceiling or floor, it becomes increasingly "difficult" to improve performance; in gymnastics, for example, it is far "easier" to improve one's score from 6.0 to 6.5 than it is to improve from 9.0 to 9.5, when "perfect" is 10.0. Similarly, in golf it is much easier to reduce one's total by five strokes, say from 140 to 135, than it is to improve by five strokes from 75 to 70. In addition to these absolute scoring ceilings and floors, psychological or physiological floors and ceilings can be present. For example, the 4 min mile was at one time a barrier that we thought would remain unbroken. Now the barrier is considerably lower, but it could very well be that no human will ever break a 3 min mile. Will anyone ever long jump more than 30 ft? As performers approach these physiological limits, it becomes increasingly more difficult to improve.

Scoring Sensitivity and the Shape of Performance Curves

The primary problem is that the "rate" of progress (the slope of the performance curve) toward some ceiling (or floor) is usually quite arbitrary and dependent on the ways in which the task is measured. The rate does not seem directly linked to the rate of change in the capability for movement that underlies this change in behavior. A powerful example of this principle comes from a study by Bahrick, Fitts, and Briggs (1957, their "simple task"). The authors studied 25 male subjects on a continuous tracking task for ten 90 s practice trials. The pattern of the track that the subjects had to follow, and the movements of the lever that the subjects made when following it, were recorded for later analysis.

The authors then analyzed the single set of performances in three different ways. First, they assumed that the width of the target the subject had to follow was small, 5% of the total width of the screen. (There was, in fact, no target width as far as the subjects were concerned, as all they saw as a target during the performance trials was a thin line that moved on the screen.) By going over the tracking records and examining the number of seconds in a trial during which the subject was in this imaginary 5% target band, the authors obtained a separate measure of the "time on target" for every subject and trial. Then, the data from trial 1 were averaged for all the subjects to form the trial 1 data point in figure 10.5 for the curve marked "5%." The data for other trials for this target size were handled in a similar way.

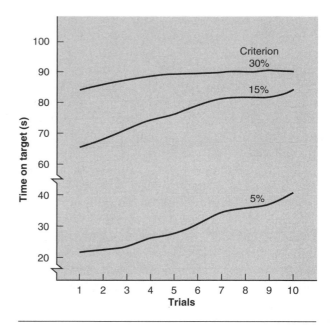

FIGURE 10.5   Time on target for a tracking task as a function of trials for three different scoring criteria. (The 5% criterion indicates that the target used for scoring was 5% of the screen width, and so on.)

Reprinted from H.P. Bahrick, P.M. Fitts, and G.E. Briggs, 1957, "Learning curves: facts or artifacts," *Psychological Bulletin* 54: 260.

The authors then performed this procedure a second time, scoring the subjects using a different tolerance for error (again, there was no target width as far as the subjects knew). Here, the target width was 15% of the width of the screen, and the subjects were evaluated in terms of the number of seconds during a trial the pointer was in this target zone. As the criterion of success was much more lenient (the "target" was wider, therefore hit more often), the time-on-target scores were naturally larger, forming a second performance curve marked "15%" in figure 10.5. Finally, the procedure was done again, this time with a very wide target that was 30% of the width of the screen. In figure 10.5 the performance curve for these data is labeled "30%."

The important point about the data in figure 10.5 is that all three curves are based on the *same* performances, but the differences between them are produced by the ways in which the experimenter has chosen to evaluate those performances. We might conclude (if we did not know that all the data came from the same performances on the same subjects) on the basis of the 5% curve that habit gains are a *positively accelerated* function of trials (because the shape of the curve is concave upward), and on the basis of the 30% curve that habit gains are a negatively accelerated function of trials (because the shape of the curve is concave downward). This is, of course, nonsense; only one pattern of habit gain emerged (whatever it was), but evidence about this gain was obtained in three different ways that gave three different answers about how the capability for performing progressed with practice.

The differences are apparently caused by the fact that making the criterion "easier" (moving from 5% to 30% target widths) moves the person through the range from floor to ceiling at different rates, depending on the *sensitivity* of the scores and the level of skill. Thus, despite the fact that the same learning occurred in all three curves from trial 1 to trial 10, very different amounts of *performance improvements* are displayed depending on which target zone one chooses to use. So, what is the pattern of habit change that occurred with practice? We have no idea, on the basis of these data, and we can conclude (erroneously) just about anything we choose merely by selecting the "right" target width to study (see also Wilberg, 1990).

Implications for Experiments on Learning

These considerations present strong limitations on what can be understood from experiments on learning, often making it impossible to provide clear interpretations about what happened to habit in the study. Consider this hypothetical example. We want to study whether children learn more than adults as a result of a given amount of practice at some new task. (We could as easily ask about males versus females, older versus younger adults, and so on.) We choose a task such as the pursuit rotor (figure 2.5a), which is foreign to both the children and the adults, and allow both groups to practice.

A finding that emerges consistently from the work on children's motor behavior is that adults nearly always perform better than children (although video game performance may be an exception). If we were to use a pursuit rotor with a very small target and a fast speed of rotation (a relatively "difficult" task), allowing the children and adults to practice for fifty 30 s trials, we might expect curves such as those that appear in figure 10.6a. Here, both hypothetical groups begin with nearly no time on target, but the adults improve more than the children because they are relatively

closer to hitting the target than are the children. With a little practice, their initial advantage in motor control begins to show up in terms of increased time on target, whereas the children show no such effects even though they may be moving slightly closer to the target. We may (erroneously) conclude that the adults learned more than the children because their performance gains were larger.

Now consider what happens if we do the "same" experiment, but with an "easy" version of the pursuit rotor task in which the target is large and the speed of rotation is slow (figure 10.6b). Now the adults begin very near ceiling, and the children are somewhere in the middle range. The adults have little capability to demonstrate continued improvement, whereas the children start in a sensitive area of the scoring range where a little practice produces maximum score gains. In this case, the gains in score are much larger for the children than for the adults. We might (again, erroneously) conclude that the children learned more than the adults.

This nonsense is caused by the marked differences in the sensitivity of the scoring system to changes in the subjects' behaviors and movement patterns—that is, in the sensitivity to changes in the level of habit of the subjects. The central region of the scoring system (around 15 s time on target) is very sensitive to changes in the subjects' habit, whereas the regions near the ceiling and floor tend to be relatively insensitive to such changes in habit. In fact, if we wanted to show that children and adults learned the same amount, we could easily choose a scoring criterion intermediate in "difficulty." So, given the choice of the sensitivity of the scoring system, we can produce just about any conclusion we desire about the relative amounts of learning in children and adults.

But games like this are not science, and it makes no sense to play them. Even so, scientists do not know how to resolve this particular problem, and thus we have no idea whether children learn more than adults or vice versa. The lesson is that such effects are always present in learning studies, and scientists have to be aware of the potential artifacts that they may produce in coming to their conclusions about learning (see also Estes, 1956; Sidman, 1952). Fortunately, experimental designs that minimize this kind of problem are available. Some of these designs are described in the next section.

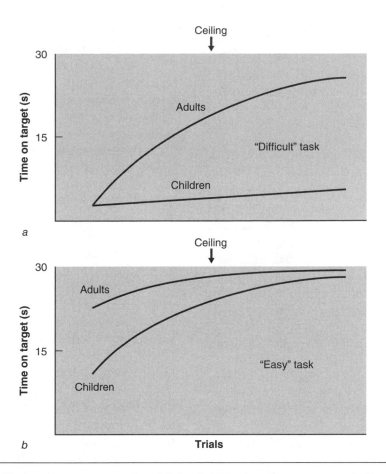

FIGURE 10.6 Hypothetical performance curves for adults' and children's performances on a "difficult" or an "easy" task. (Depending on the scoring criterion, one can [erroneously] conclude *[a]* that adults learn more than children or *[b]* that children learn more than adults.)

Designing Experiments on Learning

One of the major goals in the study of motor learning is to understand which independent variables are involved in maximizing learning, which variables impair learning, and which have no effect whatsoever. Clearly, such knowledge is important both for the development of useful theories of learning and for practical application in teaching and other learning situations.

Given the definition of learning and the limitations on the kinds of behavioral changes that scientists are willing to classify as learning changes, how do we go about deciding whether a certain variable influences learning or not? What follows is a discussion of a rather typical, but hypothetical, example of an experiment on motor learning. Imagine that one is interested in some "new" method for practice and wishes to contrast this

method with a more traditional "old" method, where the independent variable is the method used in practice. (Hundreds of other examples could have been chosen.) We begin by assigning participants from a large group of people at random to two groups. Then we administer one level of the independent variable (the "new" method) to one group and another level of the independent variable (the "old" method) to the other group, and record the performance levels achieved during considerable practice of a novel motor skill. It might seem logical that the answer to the question of which of the two methods produced more learning would be based on the performance levels achieved during practice, and especially at the end of practice. But, for the reasons discussed in the previous sections, we need a way to separate the relatively permanent effects of the independent variable from the transient effects on performance. To do this, researchers have typically used so-called transfer (or retention) designs.

Transfer or Retention Designs

Transfer or retention designs in their simplest form involve two related operations. First, the learners are provided a retention interval (or rest period away from practicing the task) of sufficient duration that the transient effects of the experimental variable (here, the practice method) will dissipate. It is difficult to say how long such an interval must be, but it is clear that we are interested in the lasting, relatively permanent effects of practice and not the momentary benefits afforded by the experimental variable. As a result, retention intervals of 24 h or more are commonly used before the subjects perform the transfer test. The second feature is that the learners are all tested under a *common* level of the independent variable—that is, under identical conditions. This is done so that any transient effects of the independent variable (especially ones that are different for the different experimental variables) will not return in the test to again hide the relatively permanent effects. Thus, in the retention test, we assume that the transient effects of the independent variable have dissipated, but that the relatively permanent effects of the variable have, by definition, remained, so that performance on the retention or transfer test will reveal differences in amount learned.

Transfer and retention designs are quite similar, and often the terms are used interchangeably by researchers to refer to the same test. In general, however, tests involving the same task as practiced in the acquisition phase are called retention tests, as they evaluate the extent to which a given skill has been retained over the retention interval. Transfer tests, on the other hand, typically involve new variations of the tasks practiced in acquisition (e.g., performing the task at a new speed, or with different lighting conditions), or they might involve essentially new tasks that have not been practiced before. The essential feature of both retention and transfer designs, however, is that the tasks and conditions are the same for the two groups.

Returning to the example of the "new" and "old" practice methods, the results might look something like those shown in shown in figure 10.7, where the curves in acquisition are plotted for each of four different hypothetical situations. In each of the four cases, the "new" method (the open circles in figure 10.7) exerts an effect that tends to increase the performance measure relative to the "old" method (the filled circles). We consider next some of the possible effects that could occur on retention or transfer tests, and the interpretations we could make.

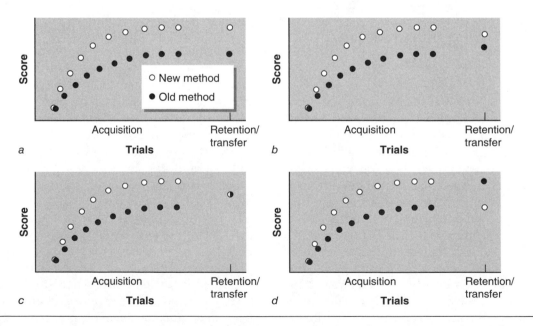

FIGURE 10.7 Hypothetical effects of an independent variable on performance (in acquisition) and learning (in retention or transfer): *(a)* Size of the performance effect in acquisition is maintained in retention or transfer; *(b)* size of the performance effect in acquisition is reduced somewhat in retention or transfer; *(c)* size of the performance effect in acquisition is eliminated in retention or transfer; and *(d)* the performance effect in acquisition is reversed in retention or transfer.

In the first case, shown in figure 10.7a, the levels of performance after the retention interval are essentially similar to those shown at the end of acquisition. Here we are forced to the conclusion that the "new" method is better than the "old" for learning. Further, all of the effect of the different methods in acquisition was apparently due to the variable's relatively permanent effects, and there was no transient effect to dissipate.

In the second case, in figure 10.7b, the "new method" group still outperforms the "old method" group on the retention test, but the differences are not as large as they were in acquisition. Still, though, we conclude that the "new" method produced more learning than the "old" because the performances still favor the "new" group in retention. We also see that not all of the difference present in acquisition was relatively permanent, as some of the advantage seen for the "new" group dissipated with rest, bringing the groups closer together than they were in acquisition. In the situation shown, we conclude that there is a learning advantage for the "new" method.

In the third case shown, in figure 10.7c, performance of the two groups in retention is essentially equivalent. Our decision rule leads to the conclusion that there is no learning benefit of the "new" method over the "old." During acquisition, the "old" method tends to produce somewhat depressed scores, whereas the "new" method tends to elevate performance. We see this by viewing the retention performances in relation to those in acquisition; the "new method" subjects have lost some of their gains in acquisition (which gains, therefore, must have been temporary), and the "old method" group shows gains (i.e., from acquisition to retention) presumably resulting from the dissipation of temporarily depressing effects in acquisition. Overall, though, because (and *only* because) the two groups performed similarly in the retention/transfer test, we argue that there was no learning benefit for the "new" versus "old" methods at all.

Finally, the case shown in figure 10.7d is an interesting one. Here, the groups on the retention test have *reversed* their orders relative to their performance in acquisition. Of course, we argue that the "old" method is better for learning than the "new," based on the better performance in retention. Yet, the "new"

method was better for performance in acquisition. Apparently, the "new" method involves many temporary benefits to performance, but these benefits do not survive until the retention test. The effect is stronger than that, however. With the "new" method—even though it is performing very well in acquisition—subjects are learning the task less effectively than with the "old" method, which we see only on the retention or transfer tests. It may seem that such reversals in performance level from acquisition to retention would never occur in real situations. However, there are several cases like this, highlighted in chapters 11 and 12, that force rather counterintuitive conclusions about the effects of practice.

Double-Transfer or -Retention Designs

There is a potential problem with using only one level of the independent variable for the transfer or retention test as was done in the previous examples. Consider figure 10.7d again, and further assume that all subjects switch to the "old" method in retention or transfer. This naturally favors the "old" practice method in acquisition, because those learning under the "old" conditions are tested under the same conditions while those learning under the "new" conditions must switch conditions in the transfer test. The same problem, but in reverse, would have occurred if we tested all subjects under the "new" conditions in retention/transfer.

One way to reduce this difficulty is to use so-called double-transfer designs, in which the two acquisition groups are each split into two subgroups for the retention test. For each of the acquisition groups, one of the subgroups has its retention test under "new" conditions and one under "old" conditions. This forms essentially four groups in the experiment—"new" and "old" in acquisition and "new" and "old" in retention. As we will see, these methods are frequently used to avoid problems in interpretation, and we give many examples of them in chapters 11 and 12.

Which Group Learned More?

Notice that in all of these cases, the fundamental question "Which group learned more?" was answered by an analysis of the performance levels in the retention or transfer test. We did not consider the level of performance in acquisition *at all* when considering the question of learning, because this performance confounds relatively permanent and transient effects of the independent variable. Nor did we use the difference between the performance at the end of acquisition and the performance in retention as a basis for the answer. Simply, the group that performs better on the retention or transfer test was concluded to have learned more.

Learning and Performance Variables

With the use of these experimental designs, it has been possible to classify experimental variables into essentially two categories. One of the categories is that of the *performance variable*. According to its definition, this kind of variable has effects on performance while it is present, but when the level is altered in transfer, the effect is altered as well. A performance variable is thus one that influences performance but not in a "relatively permanent" way. Using the analogy presented earlier, cooling water to make ice is only a "performance variable" and not a "learning variable" because the effect of the variable vanishes when it is taken away.

A *learning variable,* on the other hand, affects performance after the variable has been removed. That is, the variable influences performance in a "relatively permanent" way, affecting the learning of the task. Examples can be seen in the first hypothetical outcome in figure 10.7*a,* where the effect of the independent variable remains even when the level of the variable is changed. To extend our analogy, boiling an egg for 10 min is a "learning variable."

Finally, variables may be both learning *and* performance variables. Like the hypothetical examples in figure 10.7, many of the variables that will be examined influence performance when they are present, with some part of the effect dissipating when the variable is taken away. Yet some other part of the effect remains when the level of the variable is changed, suggesting that the variable also has affected learning in the task. Examples like this can be seen in the hypothetical situation in figure 10.7*b,* where not all of the effect of the independent variable has dissipated upon transfer. We will see other examples of effects like these in chapters 11 and 12.

Alternative Methods for Measuring Learning

Many situations exist in which the measurement of performance, and thus the measurement of learning, does not give a good estimate of the relative "amount" that someone has learned in practice. The problem is often that the performance scores have approached a ceiling or floor during the course of practice, so that all the subjects appear to be the same on the task because all the scores hover close to the ceiling or floor. In such situations, attempts to show that a given independent variable has effects on learning are thwarted because continued practice on the task can result in no changes, as the scores are already maximized or minimized.

These problems can arise in at least two different settings. One of these involves simple tasks, for which all subjects perform nearly maximally in only a few practice trials. Here, continued practice can result in no effects on the performance score. A second situation relates to a particular type of complex task—those that people have had a great deal of experience with in the past, such as driving a car. Because subjects are so well practiced, little improvement in skills will be evidenced as they continue to practice. The problem again is that subjects are so close to a performance ceiling that no additional improvements can be shown. Other examples are the performance of high-level sport skills and the performance of various highly skilled jobs in industry.

In chapter 2, we discussed secondary-task methods for the measurement of skills. The problem is similar to the present one, as the measures of the subject's behaviors on a particular task may not give a good indication of the level of skill this person possesses. The example we used was driving under the influence of fatigue. The accumulations of fatigue from long, uninterrupted stretches of driving were not observed in vehicle-control movements at all. However, decrements were observed as a function of the duration of the previous driving when subjects were asked to perform a simultaneous secondary task, suggesting that there was a decrement in "spare capacity" with increasing levels of fatigue (e.g., Brown, 1962, 1967).

Secondary Tasks and Alternative Learning Measures

The measurement of performance on a task often does not tell us much about the person's level of learning. Additional practice (e.g., driving a car) will probably result in some additional learning of the skill even at advanced levels of proficiency, but the experimenter may not be able to detect these effects because the subjects are so close to the performance ceiling or floor, as the case may be. By using secondary-task methods, one can often see these changes more clearly.

Assume that two groups of subjects practice a task and that they have reached a performance ceiling. Figure 10.8 shows some hypothetical curves that could result. Now, suppose that one of the groups (A) is told to discontinue practice, whereas the other group (B) continues to practice. Group B's performance is shown as a continuation of the earlier curve along the ceiling, as there can be no further improvements in the *score* after the ceiling has been reached. This procedure, in which a person practices further after having reached some criterion of success, is often called *overlearning*.

Did any learning of the task go on during the overlearning trials? Which of the two groups had learned more after all the practice had been completed? We might suspect that the contin-

ued practice at the ceiling did something to the subjects, but we have no way to make this conclusion from the performance curves shown in figure 10.8, as both groups have the same final score—essentially at the ceiling. We address these questions using this basic experimental design in the next three sections, so keep the situation indicated in figure 10.8 in mind. In each case, various methods with secondary tasks can be used to answer these questions.

Automaticity and Learning

One hypothesis that has received considerable empirical support is that skills become more *automatic* (see chapter 4) with practice, in the sense that systematically less interference with certain simultaneous secondary tasks will be shown. What would be the effect of imposing a simultaneous secondary task in the example shown in figure 10.8? We could (as Brown [1962] did) have the subjects do a mental task requiring the detection of a duplicated letter in a stream of auditorily presented letters. The measure of importance would be the extent to which the subjects could improve on this secondary task as they practice the main task. Some hypothetical results are presented in figure 10.9. We would probably see continued improvement in the accuracy of the secondary task, even during the overlearning trials for which the score for the main task was

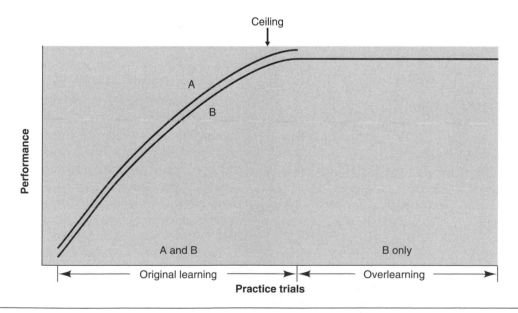

FIGURE 10.8 Hypothetical performance curves from original learning to a ceiling (groups A and B) and "overlearning" trials at the ceiling (group B only).

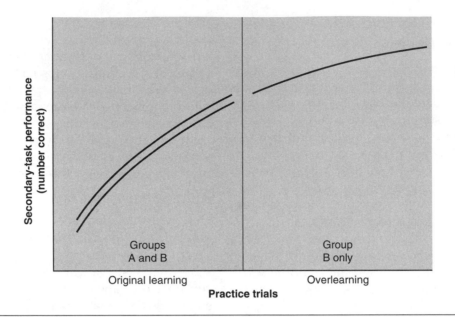

FIGURE 10.9 Hypothetical data from a secondary task measured during practice trials of the task shown in figure 10.8. (The secondary-task score continues to increase even though the main-task score is at a ceiling.)

essentially fixed at the ceiling. The improvement in the secondary task would suggest that learning was going on during the overlearning trials, with practice reducing the attentional load and allowing more accurate task performance. This technique has not been used often, but it is useful in situations like this.

Effort and Learning

Closely related to the notion of automaticity is the notion of *effort* (Kahneman, 1973). As people learn a motor skill, they appear to be able to do the task with less and less physical and mental effort, possibly because they learn to perform with more efficient movements or because they process information more efficiently. If so, then simultaneous physiological measures could be used to show that, during the overlearning trials in which the subjects are practicing the task at the ceiling, the effort in the task continues to be reduced with additional practice. Measures like oxygen consumption (assessed by techniques associated with physiology of exercise) or pupil dilation (also a measure of effort) are frequently associated with levels of effort. If we find less effortful performances during these overlearning trials, such data could be interpreted as showing that the continued practice trials produced some additional learning, and that it was manifested as a decrease in the effort expended.

Speed of Decision and Learning

Another method is effective in situations for which the main task involves decision making, such as in learning to make the correct movement when one of several different stimuli is presented. Early in the overlearning trials, subjects are just able, with much time and effort, to generate the correct response. But, later in overlearning, they can choose the correct answer more easily and far more quickly. What if, in addition to measuring whether or not the subject could make the correct response, we measured the *latency* with which the subject did so (Adams, 1976a)? We would probably see that the latency of the response (which is not yet at a floor) would decrease markedly even though the accuracy of the response did not change at all (since accuracy of performance was at the ceiling). This procedure will not work with all motor tasks, but it seems ideally suited to those situations in which there are time pressures to make accurate decisions, such as deciding where to throw a fielded baseball, or choosing a defensive maneuver in a dangerous driving situation. If such outcomes occurred, we would conclude that the decreased response latencies indicated a continuation of learning even though the subjects were at the ceiling, the learning being manifested as increases in *speed* with constant accuracy.

Memory and Learning

Inherent in the notion of learning is the concept of memory (chapter 14). In fact, most experimental psychologists define learning in terms of memory, saying that something has been learned when a person has a memory of it. In this sense, memory and habit are very similar constructs. Memory is evident when one has learned a skill or can perform it again at some time after the original-practice session.

With respect to the problem of overlearning, if the group with overlearning trials was practicing at the ceiling, the two groups should differ on a *retention* test given some weeks later, perhaps producing a pattern of results something like that shown in figure 10.10. Here, the group with overlearning trials should outperform the group without these trials on the first retention-test trial. Both groups would have lost, in this hypothetical example, some of what they had learned in the original session; but the group without the over-learning would be farther below the ceiling than the group with the overlearning trials, leading to the conclusion that a stronger memory (habit) for the task existed after the overlearning condition. Evidence for a stronger habit after a retention interval could indicate that learning continued during the overlearning trials, even though the ceiling prevented a change in performance scores in these trials.

In addition to data on the initial performance in the retention test, useful information can be found in the patterns of improvement during retention-test performance. Typically, group B would be expected to improve at a faster rate than group A, reattaining the ceiling somewhat more quickly as a result (and also because they had less loss in the first place). But another measure, first discussed long ago by Ebbinghaus (1913) and more recently by Nelson (1985) and Seidler (2007), is the *savings score* (see also chapter 14). Here, the amount of additional practice "saved" in reaching some criterion score (in this case, the ceiling) on the retention test is measured. From figure 10.10, if group A required, for example, 25 trials to reach the ceiling again, and group B reached the ceiling in about 10 additional trials, overlearning would have produced an average "savings" of 15 trials. Savings scores are also of considerable practical interest in industry and the military because they indicate the amount of additional (time-consuming and costly) practice that will be needed to return people to various criteria of "readiness" for a particular job.

Generalizability as a Learning Criterion

We normally think of learning as having the goal of improving our behavior on a *particular* movement (e.g., to serve more effectively in tennis),

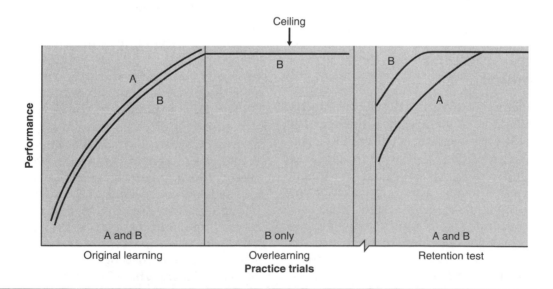

FIGURE 10.10 Retention as a measure of original learning. (Original learning and overlearning trials are shown at left, with hypothetical scores from a retention test shown at right; the finding that B outperforms A on the retention test indicates that B learned something during the "overlearning" trials even though no change in task performance could be seen.)

but broader benefits of practice should also be recognized. One of these is *generalizability*—the extent to which practice on one task contributes to the performance of other, related skills, perhaps in different contexts. As highlighted in chapter 6 in the section on generalized motor programs (GMPs), our capability to perform a task like throwing is not based on one particular throwing movement. Rather, we appear to be able to use a generalized throwing program for a variety of throwing tasks, but with the selection of appropriate parameters for the kind of object to be thrown as well as parameters to achieve the distance and trajectory of the throw. We could regard throwing practice as having the goal of contributing to one's *overall* throwing capability as well as to the skills actually practiced. In this sense, we can measure the effectiveness of a practice session not only by how well the particular skills practiced are acquired, but also by how well performance improves on similar skills (that are not practiced directly). This would involve measuring performance on other similar skills in a transfer test—analogous to the measurement of the retention characteristics of some task as in figure 10.10. The acquisition condition producing the most effective performance in this transfer test would be judged as having the highest generalizability. We can therefore think of the measurement of generalizability as another in a group of alternative measures of learning. The details of these evaluations are related to the measurement of *transfer*, which we consider in detail in chapter 14.

Summary of Alternative Learning Assessments

All these methods are consistent with the fundamental notion that learning is the set of internal, unobservable processes that occur with practice or experience, resulting in a changed underlying capability for moving. Therefore, it is not surprising that even when obvious changes do not occur in the main task, these learning processes can be demonstrated by a variety of other means, such as decreases in the interference created for other simultaneous activities, reduction in effort, increases in the speed with which a main task demanding accuracy is completed, changes in retention capabilities, or alterations in generalizability to other similar skills. These techniques highlight the idea that learning is internal and

complex, having many forms in many different situations. Above all, we stress here the deficiency in the oversimplified idea that learning is merely a change in behavior on the task in question. It is clearly a much more complex set of processes than that.

Issues About the "Amount" of Learning

On the basis of experiments on learning, researchers are often tempted to make statements phrased in terms of the *amount* of learning that has occurred as a result of practice. For example, we might wish to say that a group of subjects practicing with one condition learned 20% less than a group with another condition. Or you may wish to say that Luc learned twice as much as Jack on this task. Do such statements really have any meaning?

The problem is that habit is a construct that cannot be observed directly. Usually little basis exists for making quantitative statements about it, because it can only be estimated from performance scores. Recall the experiment by Bahrick and colleagues (1957) discussed earlier. By a simple change in the way the task was scored (change in the strictness of the criterion of success), the authors obtained almost any scores they wanted, and they could easily change the shapes of the performance curves. For example, looking back at the data from their experiment in figure 10.5, we computed that the subjects with the 5% scoring criterion improved 86% as a result of practice, that the same subjects improved 29% with the 15% criterion, and that they improved 8% with the 30% criterion. How can we assess the "amount" of habit gain that occurred here? Will we say that it was 8%, 29%, or 86%? That decision is purely arbitrary, and we would be equally wrong in making any of these claims.

The best one can do is to make statements about the *relative* amounts that two groups have learned, or about the relative amounts that two people have learned, essentially with statements like "group A learned more than group B." The issues are somewhat different for the case in which groups are compared to each other versus the case in which individuals are compared against each other, so we discuss these two situations in turn.

Group Differences

Figure 10.11*a* is a typical example of the transfer paradigm discussed earlier, where practice tends to increase the scores on the task. Here, the experimenter does not really have any idea about *how much* learning occurred, but can make statements about two things: the fact that both groups learned, and the fact that group A learned more than did group B. Because the two groups began practice on trial 1 with the same level of performance, and because, during the course of practice, they progressed to different levels of performance, the conclusion that group B learned less than group A in this case seems unavoidable. Remember that the test of the relative amount learned should always be on the transfer trials, as it is only there in the sequence that the temporary effects of the independent variable are equated for the two different levels of initial capability.

Now consider figure 10.11*b*, where the two groups *began* practice at different levels of per-formance and hence different levels of initial capability. This initial difference could be attributable to some systematic difference in the nature of the subjects (e.g., males vs. females or children vs. adults), or it could be attributable to simple random sampling effects, whereby the groups simply differ by chance. In either case, both groups learned, but we are in a difficult position with respect to saying which group learned more. You can see that both groups gained about the same amount in terms of the score on the task, but you have no way of knowing whether the amount of change in the capability (i.e., habit) was larger or smaller for group A or group B.

The problem is that the differences in the initial level of performance have confounded interpretation about which of the groups learned more. Thus, in designing these kinds of experiments it is essential, if this question is to be asked about the data, to be certain that the two groups of subjects are equated at the beginning of practice

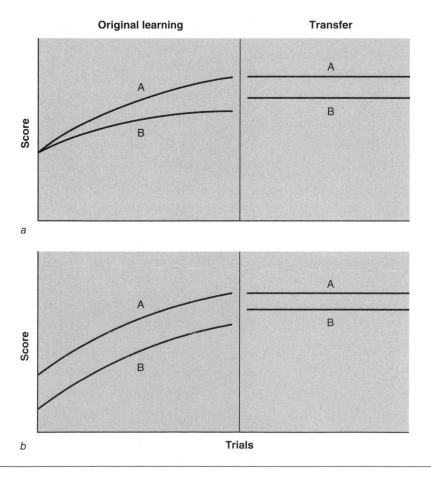

FIGURE 10.11 Outcomes from an experiment on learning in which the original level of proficiency for the two groups was *(a)* controlled or *(b)* not controlled.

so that differences in the performance on the transfer test can be attributed to changes in the amount learned.[1] This can be accomplished by administering a pretest on the learning task, ranking subjects from highest to lowest on this test, and then assigning the subjects with odd-numbered ranks to one group and those with even-numbered ranks to the other group. In this way the groups are almost exactly equal on the first trial, and the problem is eliminated. (Other matching techniques are available as well.)

There are some drawbacks to using a pretest. One is that the pretest provides some practice on the experimental task, which then reduces the size of the changes to be observed under the different levels of the independent variable. This procedure has the additional limitation that the first trials on a motor task are usually not strongly correlated with the last trials in the sequence—that is, with the final trials on which the relative amount of learning is assessed. Such correlations are frequently as low as 0.20. If so, then the variable that is matched (initial performance) is not going to influence the "equality" of the groups on the transfer trials to a very strong degree.

A second method is to use large groups that are randomly formed from some larger group. In this way the groups will be expected to differ due to chance effects; but if the groups are large (e.g., 25 people per group), then the chance differences in the group means on the motor task should be relatively small. This procedure has the advantage that it does not give subjects experience on the task before the independent variable is administered, but it has the disadvantage that chance differences can still occasionally occur. More on this issue can be found in Schmidt (1971a, 1972a).

Could you "correct for" the initial differences in performance (as seen, e.g., in figure 10.11b) by subtracting the initial difference from the differences that occurred in the transfer trials? While arithmetically this can be done, such procedures produce nearly meaningless interpretations of the relative amount learned. The problem is that the sensitivity of the scoring system to changes in the internal capability is different at various places on the performance scale. Thus, subtracting the initial differences in performance from the differences in performance at the end of practice will probably lead to an adjustment that is far too large. Because we have no idea how much too large this adjustment will be, and we have no way to find out, such adjustments probably should not be used.

Of course, these adjustments are exactly equivalent to computing "learning scores," or the differences between the initial and final performance for one group, and comparing these differences to the difference between the initial and final performance scores for the other group (Schmidt, 1971b). The use of "learning scores" or "gain scores" is not as prevalent as it was some years ago, largely for the reasons mentioned.

Individual Differences in Learning

The problem just raised is similar in many respects to that of comparing the amount learned by one person to the amount learned by another person. This is a common problem in the study of individual differences in learning, as sometimes it is of interest to determine whether or not some measure of an ability correlates with the amount that someone will *learn* (e.g., Bachman, 1961, and many others). Naturally, in order to compute the correlation, one must achieve a measure of the "amount learned" by each person. But we have just argued that such measures are not meaningful if they are based on the differences between the initial and final performance.

A second situation in which these kinds of measures are usually taken is in determining grades. Often, a measure of the student's initial level of proficiency is taken at the beginning of instruction, and another measure of proficiency is taken after the instruction has been completed; grades are then assigned on the basis of the difference between the initial and final performance levels, presumably in terms of "amount learned."

The fundamental problem with this technique is that the difference between initial and final performance is not an adequate measure of the "amount learned," for the reasons already discussed. Also, in philosophical and educational terms, in most aspects of life we are judged on the basis of what we can *do*, not on the basis of how much we have *improved*. If someone received an A in physics because she could pass the examinations at the end of the course, no one cares that she could have passed the examinations on the first day of class. Evaluating improvement scores in teaching or research settings is generally laced with difficulty, and should be avoided.

"Rate" of Learning

We have argued that using scores from acquisition data to calculate measures of "amount" of learning leads to many problems in interpretation. A problem similar to those already noted arises in the measure of "rate" of learning. The idea of a learning rate has been common in sport folklore ("so-and-so is a fast learner"). Attempts to measure the speed of acquisition are often based on the steepness or slope of the performance curve. For instance, look back at the plot of the two hypothetical subjects in figure 10.3. It might be tempting to say that subject 2 is a "faster" learner than subject 1 because the slope of the curve is much steeper in the early stages of practice. However, such conclusions fall prey to exactly the same problems as with trying to measure the *amount* of learning.

Understanding Learning and Performance Variables

The problem of identifying which of the many independent variables are critical for learning, and which are relevant only for performance, is important not only for development and testing of theories of motor learning, but also for application to a variety of practical situations. We treat these two issues briefly here but discuss them again throughout the remainder of the text.

Importance for Theory

Learning theories make predictions about how certain independent variables will affect learning. In such cases, experimental tests of the theory involve evaluations of, among other things, the extent to which one group of subjects learned more than some other. As we have argued, valid tests of such questions ultimately rest on which of the two groups performs most effectively on retention or transfer tests. Thus, such research designs become the key way in which theories of learning are tested in the laboratory. Many examples of this kind of theory testing are presented in the following chapters.

Importance for Application

A second practical outcome is that knowledge about which variables affect performance tempo-

rarily, and which affect learning, allows the production of more effective settings for instruction in various motor tasks in sport, industry, therapy, and so on. Naturally, if the goal of practice in such application areas is to maximize learning, variables that influence learning (as measured on retention or transfer tests) should be emphasized during practice, and variables that influence performance only temporarily can be ignored. The topic of this relation between research and practice, as it pertains specifically to issues of learning, will arise numerous times throughout the remainder of the book.

Summary

The study of motor learning is considerably different from the study of performance in that the focus is on the *changes* in performance that occur as a direct result of practice. Motor learning is defined as a set of internal processes associated with practice or experience leading to a relatively permanent change in the capability for skilled behavior, a state sometimes termed *habit*. Such a definition must be carefully worded to rule out changes in behavior that are due to maturation or growth, or to momentary fluctuations in performance attributable to temporary factors.

In the typical motor learning experiment, two or more groups of subjects practice a task under a different level of an independent variable. A common method of data analysis involves *performance curves*, or plots of average performance on each trial for a large number of subjects. These curves can hide a great deal of important information about learning, however, such as individual differences in learning or changes in strategies. They tend to characterize motor learning as a slow, constantly evolving process requiring continued practice, whereas other evidence suggests that learning is often sudden, insightful, or even "revolutionary." As a result, interpretations about the nature of learning from performance curves must be made carefully.

Learning experiments usually involve what is called a *transfer* (or *retention*) *design,* in which the groups of subjects practicing at different levels of the independent variable are transferred to a common level of that variable. These designs provide for the separation of the relatively permanent effects (due to learning) and the temporary effects of the independent variable. Those independent variables affecting performance "relatively permanently" are called *learning variables*, and those affecting performance only temporarily are called *performance variables*.

In many situations, the performance scores are near a ceiling or floor, at which no changes can occur because of task-imposed or biologically imposed limitations on performance. In such situations, a number of secondary-task methods can be used, such as measures of latency, measures of attention or effort, measures of retention, or measures of generalizability. Even with all the methods, it is seldom possible to speak meaningfully about the actual *amount* a person or a group has learned or the rate of learning.

Student Assignments

1. Prepare to answer the following questions during class discussion:

   a. Motor learning is defined in terms of four distinct characteristics. Use an example of learning a real motor skill to illustrate these four characteristics.

   b. In your own words, describe how you would explain to an athlete the distinction between performance and learning. Why might this distinction be important to the athlete?

   c. Using an example of research discussed in chapter 11 or 12, describe how an experimenter might devise a double-transfer design to assess learning.

2. Find a research article that illustrates one of the hypothetical learning and performance effects depicted in figure 10.7.

Web Resources

The *Measurement in Physical Education and Exercise Science* journal is devoted to measurement issues in kinesiology.

www.informaworld.com/smpp/title~content=
t775653683~db=all

The *Journal of the Learning Sciences* is devoted to the study of learning and education.

www.informaworld.com/smpp/title~content=
t775653672~db=all

Notes

[1] Some research examples presented in chapters 11 and 12 will *appear* to show group differences on the very first trial (e.g., Shea & Morgan. 1979). In these cases, however, it is important to recognize that the first data point on the graph does not correspond with the first trial but rather with the first *block* of trials, which may represent the average of 5-10 or more trials. Thus, the learning variable is revealing rapid effect on the performance of the groups, which we assume, were equated on trial 1.

CHAPTER 11

CONDITIONS OF PRACTICE

Time is a key constraint in many situations in which individuals are asked to learn (or relearn) motor skills. An insurance company may dictate that a maximum of nine rehabilitation sessions will be paid by insurance. A badminton practicum may involve three sessions per week for 14 weeks. A tool and die worker is given one training session to learn to use a new piece of equipment. A microsurgeon takes a two-day course involving a new technique before surgery on patients begins. In all of these situations that invoke specific temporal limitations on practice, the implicit understanding is that practice should be *organized* in a way that maximizes the amount of potential learning. To meet the demands of these time constraints, the learning facilitator must be aware of the variables, or the *conditions of practice*, that influence performance and learning, and adjust them so that learning will be maximized.

This chapter is about these variables and techniques, with the focus on the major ones that are important for motor learning. There are many such variables, and we have confined the discussion to those variables having the largest effects (i.e., those that make the biggest difference) and those that are usually under the direct control of the experimenter or teacher. With this emphasis, the material relates rather closely to the design of instructional settings such as would be seen in schools, in training for jobs in industry or the military, and in rehabilitation (e.g., see "Constraint-Induced Physical Therapy" on p. 350). Also, we stress those variables in which there is the greatest theoretical interest. This emphasis also provides a strong contribution to practical application, because well-established theories have many real-world implications (Kerlinger, 1973). Generally, the chapter is about attempts to understand the many variables that determine the effectiveness of the conditions of practice.

The Law of Practice

One practice variable dwarfs all the others in terms of importance and is so obvious that it need hardly be mentioned at all—the amount of practice. All other things being equal, more learning will occur if there are more practice trials. In fact, so pervasive is the effect on learning that this is simply called the *"law of practice."*

One of the most frequently observed characteristics about the change in performance that accompanies practice is that the improvements in (average) performance are generally large and rapid at first and become systematically smaller as practice continues. Thus, whether the measure of performance increases or decreases (see figures 10.1 and 10.2) with practice, performance curves are usually *negatively accelerated* functions of practice (i.e., the "rate" of improvement changes toward zero as practice continues). Although a few particular tasks might not show this kind of relationship, or certain performance phenomena might distort it considerably (e.g., fatigue), as a general rule the majority of the behaviors studied in motor learning seem to show practice curves with this overall form.

Time Scales for the Law of Practice

A negatively accelerated relation between performance and practice trials has many of the general features of a very common equation that is termed a *power function* (or log-linear function), in which the time, *T*, to complete an action (where performance is measured in terms of time) can be expressed as

$$T = a P^{-b} = a / P^b \qquad (11.1)$$

where *a* and *b* are constants, and *P* is some measure of the amount of practice (e.g., number of trials). Here, as practice increases and *P* becomes larger, the ratio a/P decreases, resulting in smaller time to complete the action, *T*; the larger the constant *b*, the more "rapid" are the decreases with practice. Analogous power functions can also be defined for tasks with scores that increase with practice, such as the pursuit rotor or Bachman ladder task (Bachman, 1966). For these the sign of *b* is simply reversed.

One important feature of power functions such as that in equation 11.1 is that the plot of the *logarithm* of performance *(T)* against the *logarithm* of the number of practice trials *(P)* will yield a *linear* function. For example, taking the logarithm of both sides of equation 11.1 yields

$$\text{Log } (T) = -b \,(\text{Log } P) + \text{Log } (a) \qquad (11.2)$$

Notice that, from the discussions of empirical equations earlier in the book, equation 11.2 is simply a special case of the standard equation for a linear function, $Y = a + b X$, where here *Y* is Log *(T)*, *a* is the constant Log *(a)*, and *X* is Log *(P)*. Therefore we can summarize equation 11.2 easily by saying that the relationship between Log *(T)* and Log *(P)* is linear, with an intercept of Log *(a)* and a slope of $-b$. Note again that many variables distort these performances (and hence these kinds of relationships) so that these power functions are not very useful for studying and measuring learning; but these functions are still good *general, rough* indicators of the relationship between practice and performance. They are, after all, just performance curves—not learning curves, as we stressed repeatedly in chapter 10.

Generality of the Law of Practice

Fitts (1964), and later Newell and Rosenbloom (1981), pointed out that practice on numerous tasks with widely differing movement measurements, goals, and measures of performance—motor tasks and verbal tasks alike—tended to follow this logarithmic power function. The first analysis of this kind was presented by Snoddy (1926). Subjects learned to draw figures while viewing only the mirror image of their drawing hand, with practice continuing over 100 days (one trial per day). The data, plotted in figure 11.1 using a power function, show a generally linear relationship, except perhaps for the first few data points. This is an example in which the score increases with practice. Another example comes from Crossman (1959) in a study of factory workers who made cigars using a small hand-operated jig. In figure 11.2 is a plot of the average time for cigar production against practice time (a decreasing function), also plotted as a power function. This plot is also generally linear, only flattening out near the region of high practice where the minimum cycle time of the machine itself became a factor in performance. Fitts (1964) and Newell and Rosenbloom (1981) provide more examples and a fuller discussion of power functions in learning.

An important interpretation of these logarithmic relationships is that the rate of improvement at any point in practice tends to be linearly related to the "amount left to improve" in the task. So, early in practice, when there is much learning left to accomplish, the speed of improvement is very rapid as compared to that at the end of practice when there is not so much "room for improvement" remaining. Furthermore, many of the experiments in support of the law of practice show that improvements continue to occur for years, even though these later gains may be very small. Consider, for example, the situation in Crossman's (1959, figure 11.2) data, where improvements can be seen even after seven years of practice, and after 10 million cigars were rolled! Data like these suggest that learning is never really completed, even in the simplest of tasks. Statements like, "John learned to drive last week" lose a great deal of their meaning when seen in this light.

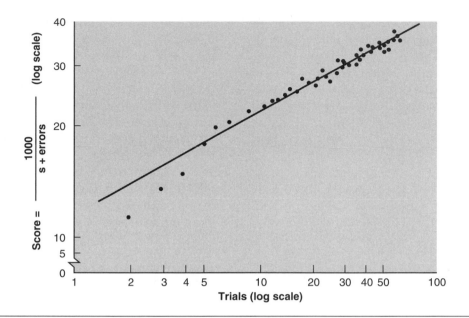

FIGURE 11.1   Scores in a mirror-tracing task as a function of extended practice.

Reprinted from G.S. Snoddy, 1926, "Learning and stability," *Journal of Applied Psychology* 10:1-36.

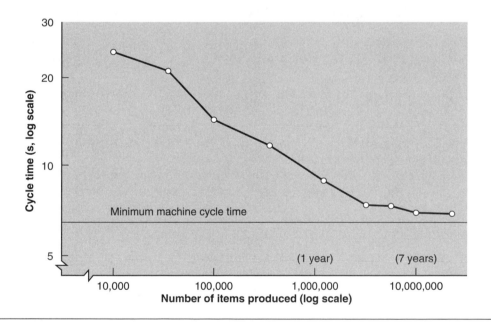

FIGURE 11.2   Completion time in making cigars as a function of extended practice.

Reprinted, by permission, from E.R.F.W. Crossman, 1959, "A theory of the acquisition of speed skill," *Ergonomic* 2: 153-166, reprinted by permission of the publisher (Taylor & Francis Ltd, http://www.informaworld.com).

Although the power function has been used to describe motor learning data sets for more than 80 years, it may not necessarily be the optimal function to describe the law of learning. A reanalysis of many of these earlier data sets by Heathcoat, Brown, and Mewhort (2000) revealed that the power function best described the averaged data of all participants of the experiment. As

we cautioned in chapter 10, however, group data can sometimes misrepresent the performance of the individuals for whom the data have been averaged (see figure 10.3 as an example). When the published data for each of the subjects were analyzed separately, Heathcoat and colleagues found strong evidence that an *exponential* function provided a better fit for the law of learning than a power function. Indeed, a replication of Snoddy's original experiment (1926) revealed much better fits for an exponential function than a power function (Stratton, Liu, Hong, Mayer-Kress, & Newell, 2007), leading these researchers to suggest that many different time scales may be used to describe learning, depending on the interactions of the individual with different aspects of the task and practice-related factors (Newell, Liu, & Mayer-Kress, 2001, 2009).

Regardless of which function best fits the data, it is important to remember that the law of practice is just a *description* of the relationship between practice trials and performance. As we discussed in chapter 10, this relationship may, but does not necessarily, provide a description of the progress of *learning*—that is, the underlying capability for performance that is the goal of practice and learning research. Later in this chapter we discuss various conditions that alter the shapes of these performance curves in practice, and we show how these performance alterations may not be closely related to the underlying changes in learning. The law of practice is interesting and robust, but we should be cautious in using it to generalize about the course of learning over practice.

Constraint-Induced Physical Therapy

In the fields of physical therapy and rehabilitation medicine, a relatively new approach has emerged in the treatment of individuals following a stroke. The patients who have volunteered for these studies are typically many months (sometimes over a year) poststroke, when the recovery of motor function in these individuals is typically considered to be finished. The new therapy consists of "constraining" the use of the less affected limb (the "better" limb), for example by asking the patient to wear a sling or a large oven mitt on the "good side" for many hours of the day. In this way the patient is "forced" to use the affected limb to carry out activities of daily living.

Experimental interventions of this type have been remarkably successful in facilitating further recovery of function in the affected limb (see reviews in Wolf, Blanton, Baer, Breshears, & Butler, 2002; Taub, Uswatte, & Pidikiti, 1999). Furthermore, the motor recovery from these interventions has been shown to be retained for at least two years (Wolf et al., 2006, 2008). There is some controversy, however, over the reasons why this type of therapy is effective.

One interpretation (e.g., Taub et al., 1999) suggests that, following a stroke, patients learn strategies that tend to "replace" the goal-directed movements that would normally have been done by the affected limb. Many of these strategies result in using the "better" limb more frequently, essentially resulting in a reduced *need* to use the affected limb in the future. According to Taub, each successful completion of an activity by means other than using the affected limb reinforces ("rewards") the *nonuse* of that limb. Thus, constraint-induced therapy is seen as a method to overcome "learned nonuse" by inducing the patient to use the affected limb.

An alternative view more closely resembles the principles of practice, suggesting that improvement in motor skill is a function of an increasing accumulation of practice trials, coupled with movement-produced feedback. By this rationale, the patient who compensates for the loss of function in the affected limb by discontinuing use of that limb has essentially ceased to accumulate practice trials, or is even reversing this trend (causing forgetting), which might make that limb's function even more degraded than normal. Constraint-induced therapy is seen as a method for improving the acquisition of motor skill by forcing the accumulation of more practice trials (similar in many respects to the definition of deliberate practice) (Wolf et al., 2002). Similarly, this notion is in keeping with the view that, among perhaps many other things, physical, occupational, and speech therapy consist of *practice*, whose principles are a part of the motor learning ideas we present here (Maas et al., 2008; McNeil, Robin, & Schmidt, 1997; Schmidt, 1991b; Winstein, 1991). Whatever the mechanism at work here, the implications of constraint-induced therapy for the efficacy of therapeutic intervention and theory development hold a great deal of promise.

Deliberate Practice

What does the term "practice" really mean? Ericsson, Krampe, and Tesch-Römer (1993) note that the term "practice" can take on various meanings, and they advocate the term *deliberate practice* to denote the kinds of activities that instructors, teachers, and therapists use on a daily basis. Specifically, Ericsson and colleagues define deliberate practice as "activities that have been specially designed to improve the current level of performance. . . . Deliberate practice requires effort and is not inherently enjoyable. Individuals are motivated to practice because practice improves performance" (p. 368). But research has not been conducted that compares the long-term effects of years of deliberate practice versus other forms of practice (e.g., play). So, it is unknown whether the laws of practice apply to deliberate practice only, or whether there are different functions for different forms of practice, and so on.

In the remainder of this chapter we will discuss methods of deliberate practice that can be modified, structured, improved, and otherwise changed so as to influence performance. Figure 11.3 provides a conceptual overview of these methods. Off-task practice considerations refer to those factors that are generally applied when the learner is *not* actively engaged in physical performance, such as the effects of modeling (or observation). On-task practice conditions generally refer to the methods by which the physical engagement in practice can be altered,

and how alterations affect performance and learning. Remember to always keep in mind the distinction between factors that influence temporary improvements in performance and those that have relatively permanent effects (i.e., on learning). This distinction is critical in a number of research areas discussed in this chapter and the next.

In the next sections we concentrate on the various ways in which learning can be enhanced when the learner is not physically engaged in practice of the actual task. Much of this discussion—but not all of it—concerns those factors that have been shown to operate before the practice session begins—involving the preparation of the learner for the upcoming practice sequence.

Motivation for Learning

Since practice is the most important factor in learning, as discussed in the previous section, an important point is that *motivation* is a primary determinant for engaging in practice at all and thus is important for learning. If the learner perceives the task as meaningless or undesirable, then learning of the task will probably be minimal. If the level of motivation is too low, people may not be sufficiently motivated to practice at all, and very little, if any, learning will be the result. Aside from this rather obvious conclusion, a number of reasonably complex determinants of learning exist as a function of motivational level.

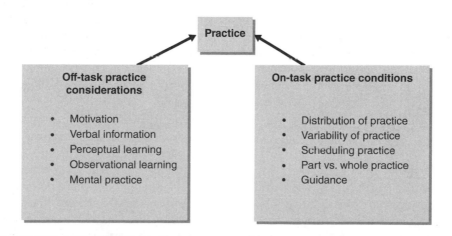

FIGURE 11.3   Practice can include on-task situations, as well as conditions in which the learner does not physically interact with the task.

Making the Task Seem Important

Before beginning the practice session, it is important that the learner see the task as one that is desirable to learn. Much of this kind of motivation appears already to be established in people because of culturally derived emphases on certain activities. But in many cases it is important to show why it would be useful to have a certain skill. A teacher once pointed out that the usual all-male games (e.g., tackle football) were fine for playing among young males, but that a time would come in life when less violent recreational skills might be preferred. Such a comment emphasized the importance of learning these other activities. Similarly, some might consider badminton a rather leisurely game that is played in the backyard on warm summer days—until, that is, they see a game involving highly skilled players. A person might be much more interested in learning these skills after seeing them performed by role models in world-class competition.

Goal Setting

Another frequently used motivational technique is goal setting, whereby performers try to attain goals that are set before they begin practicing. This technique has been studied extensively in research related to industrial and organizational psychology (for reviews see Locke & Latham, 1985, 2006; Tubbs, 1986), and more recently in sport (for reviews see Burton, Naylor, & Holliday, 2001; Locke, 1991; Weinberg, 1994) and rehabilitation (Gauggel & Fischer, 2001; Playford, Siegert, Levack, & Freeman, 2009), suggesting some important principles for performance and learning.

Probably the most intuitively appealing and most often used goal in all types of daily activities is the *do-your-best* goal. Encouragement such as "Try to get as many done as possible," "Do the best job you can," and "Give it 100% out there" is typical of these types of goals. However, research suggests that "do-your-best" goals are not as effective as other types of goals. Locke and Latham (1985) summarized the psychological research and suggested that specific, "difficult" goals produce stronger performance than either no goals or vague, ambiguous goals such as "do your best." Locke and Latham proposed four advantages of setting specific, "difficult" goals; these can be considered analogous to the advantages of setting an agenda for an important meeting. These

kinds of goals (1) focus one's activities, (2) help to regulate the effort directed toward these activities, (3) help maintain vigilance in attempting to reach the goals, and (4) serve as a referent against which achievement can be compared.

Goal-setting studies in sport and exercise research, however, have not consistently supported Locke and Latham's conclusion that specific, "difficult" goals are the most effective ones for performance. Problems specific to conducting research in sport and exercise in relation to goal setting may account for these inconsistent effects (see also Locke, 1991; Burton et al., 2001). Since sport and exercise tasks are often intrinsically motivating and competitive, subjects may have a vested interest in their outcome when they serve as participants in a research study. For example, participants who are told not to set a specific goal or are told to use a vague goal may, in fact, secretively set specific, perhaps "difficult" goals, thereby masking the potential impact of goal-setting variables. Thus, the smaller overall effects of goal setting in sport and exercise studies do not necessarily mean that goal setting is not an important factor in the performance of motor skills (cf. Burton et al., 2001; Weinberg, 1994). The fact that the tasks in these studies lend themselves to intrinsic goal setting may overshadow the experimenter's manipulations, making it difficult to detect the true effects of goal setting.

Kyllo and Landers' (1995) quantitative review (meta-analysis) of the literature suggests that one small but consistent finding does appear in the sport and exercise research. The authors found that *specific, absolute goals of moderate "difficulty"* were beneficial to the performance of sport and exercise tasks. In addition, there was evidence that setting short-term goals and setting a combination of short-term and long-term goals facilitated performance as compared to setting long-term goals only.

One limitation of the research literature is that performance and learning effects often have not been separated. Although most of the goal-setting literature is dominated by studies on performance, there have been some studies that do address goal-setting effects on learning. For example, Boyce (1992) examined three groups of subjects who set different goals while they were learning to shoot a rifle. One group was told to "do your best." Another group was encouraged to set their own specific goals. A third group was assigned specific goals that were made progressively higher on each practice day. The goal-setting procedures were established following a pretest and were applied on five days of practice sessions over a three-week period. A retention test assessed learning one week after the last practice session. The results, shown in figure 11.4, revealed that the group of subjects told to "do your best" performed slightly better than the other groups on the first practice day, but worse on the other days. These differences were maintained in a retention test, suggesting that the specific goal-setting procedures had beneficial effects on both performance *and* learning.

Verbal Information

Assuming that an individual is motivated to learn, many believe it important to give the person some information about the task to be learned before actually physically practicing the task. There are many ways to do this, of course, and some of these are discussed next.

Instructional Set

One of the most common ways of giving students an initial orientation to the new skill is through verbal instructions, usually presented by the teacher or instructor. An early study by Solley (1952) demonstrated the long-lasting effects of initial orientation. In this study, three groups of subjects practiced a two-step lunge to stab at a target. Over six days of practice, the various groups were encouraged to perform the action with an emphasis on either speed or accuracy or with an equal emphasis on speed and accuracy. The results were quite dramatic. The group instructed to emphasize accuracy was the most accurate over practice; the group instructed to emphasize speed was the fastest; and the group giving equal emphasis to speed and accuracy performed at intermediate levels on both measures. A strong feature of the study was that it included transfer tests over six additional days of practice, in which all groups were encouraged to give equal emphasis to speed and accuracy. The effects seen during practice were maintained in transfer, especially for performance speed—the instructional "set" had a lasting impact on both performance and learning.

Instructions can also provide useful and important information about the movement itself, such as the initial positions of the limbs in relation to an apparatus or an implement used, the stance, what to watch and listen for, and what to do. Perhaps more importantly, an overall "idea" or image of the movement can be conveyed that can serve as a representation for the first attempt.

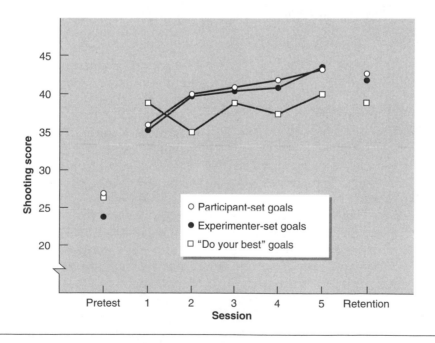

FIGURE 11.4   Effects of goal setting on learning a shooting task.

Adapted, by permission, from B.A. Boyce, 1992, "Effects of assigned versus participant-set goals on skill acquisition and retention of a selected shooting task," *Journal of Teaching in Physical Education* 11(2): 227.

Also, instructions can emphasize the ways in which one can recognize one's own errors—for example, "After the movement, check to see that your arm is straight." These kinds of instructions can serve to stimulate the development of error-detection capabilities (see chapter 13).

Focus of Attention

In chapter 4 we discussed the effects of instructed attentional focus on performance. Wulf and her colleagues have conducted a number of experiments using attentional focus instructions in learning experiments and have demonstrated powerful effects that are both immediate and long-lasting (for reviews see Wulf, 2007; Wulf & Prinz, 2001). Most of these studies used novice subjects who learned various sport-related skills or laboratory tasks. For example, in a study by Wulf, Weigelt, Poulter, and McNevin (2003), subjects learned to balance on a stabilometer (figure 2.5c) while holding a tube with both hands. In one experimental group (internal focus instructions), subjects were told to keep their *hands* held horizontal; subjects in the other group (external instructions) were told to hold the *tube* horizontal; and subjects in a control group were given no instructions. The results on the last trial of two days of practice (fourteen 90 s trials), four retention trials one day later, and three transfer trials (without the tube) on the stabilometer balance task are illustrated in figure 11.5. It is interesting to note that in both the external and internal groups, the instructions merely directed the subjects' attention to their hands, yet the effects were immediate and permanent: external focus of attention facilitated both performance and learning as compared to internal focus. These influences of attentional focus instructions on performance and learning have been replicated many times by Wulf and her colleagues, as well as by others (e.g., Hodges & Franks, 2000).

But as important as instructions are, they can sometimes bias performance in undesirable ways (Hodges & Franks, 2001) or are overused in learning situations. Words alone are relatively crude descriptions of the complex kinds of movements that a learner is attempting to achieve; just try to describe the actions in pole-vaulting, or in tying a bow-knot on your shoe, as examples. Only the most global, general aspects of the intended movement are going to be transmitted through

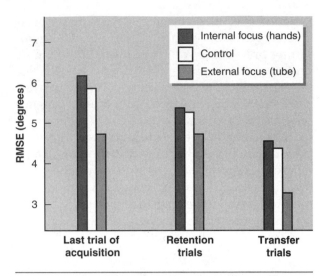

FIGURE 11.5 Effects of attentional focus instructions on stabilometer performance in acquisition, retention, and transfer. RMSE is root mean square *error* so lower scores are better.

verbal instructions. Also, memory limitations (chapter 3) suggest that a learner can remember only so many instructions, and few of these important points are assimilated on the first trials of practice. This problem seems even more critical when one is dealing with children, whose attentional skills and memory capacities are much weaker than those of adults.

One solution is to describe in words those aspects of the actions that are absolutely essential for the first trial or two, making sure that learners achieve them in early practice. A different approach, used by coaches for years, has been to use *analogies* to get the learner to think about how an action should be performed. For example, basketball instructors may tell the learner to finish the shot with a hand position "like reaching into a cookie jar." Compared to learning by explicit instructions, Liao and Masters (2001) found that learning table tennis with analogy instructions resulted in less verbalizable knowledge, but transfer performance that more strongly withstood the degrading effects of a secondary task. Similar findings have been found for learning basketball skills (Lam, Maxwell, & Masters, 2009).

Although more research in this area is warranted, the effects of attentional focus and analogy learning may have similar bases. In both areas, instructions having the more positive effects on learning (external focus and analogy learning) direct the learner's awareness away from how a movement should be regulated. And, as we see in the next section, awareness appears to be unnecessary at all for motor learning to occur.

Learning Without Awareness

One of the assumed benefits of verbal instructions is to make the learner aware of certain components of the task before practice begins. But, is this even necessary? Some research suggests that learning of some tasks can occur even though the subject is oblivious to the perceptual regularities of the task. In a classic study in this area, conducted by Wickens and Pew (see Pew, 1974b), subjects practiced a pursuit tracking task, having to move a lever in order to try to match a perceptual input signal on a computer monitor. A trial comprised three 20 s segments. During the first and last of these segments the perceptual signal was generated randomly by the computer, and the random sequence was different on each of the 24 trials completed during each session on 16 days of practice. However, the perceptual signal during the middle segment was always the same. Improvements on the repeated, middle segment were greater and occurred much faster than on the random segments. More importantly, however, interviews with the subjects after day 11 revealed that *none* had any idea that the middle portion of the trial was always repeating! It seems that the enhanced learning of the middle segment had occurred even though the subjects were unaware that any part of the task had been different from the others. These results have been replicated in experiments in which the first segment was repeated—again with *none* of the subjects being aware of any regularities in the perceptual stimuli (see Magill, 1998). Studies have also shown that these effects persist in transfer tests, again without the subjects' awareness (Wulf & Schmidt, 1997). The result of experiments in which learning occurs in the absence of explicit awareness or purpose by the learner has sparked considerable research interest and debate, lending support to the argument presented in the previous section of fundamental differences in the role of awareness in retention and transfer characteristics of motor skills (e.g., Gentile, 1998; Verdolini-Marston & Balota, 1994; see Hodges & Franks, 2002b; Masters, 2008, for reviews).

Knowledge of Mechanical Principles

How much should learners know about mechanical properties underlying a particular movement task? Will such knowledge, if provided before the learning of the task begins, be an aid to future performance and learning? Early work by Judd (1908) on dart throwing to targets submerged under water gave initial indications that such information was useful. Judd taught his learners the principles of refraction, whereby the light rays from the submerged target are bent so that the target is not really where it appears, and this provided initial advantages when the targets were moved to different depths of submersion. Similar results were obtained by Hendrickson and Schroeder (1941) in a task that required shooting an air gun at underwater targets.

Mechanical principles are also a part of instruction in sport skills, such as in swimming (propulsion) and billiards (ball spin, geometry). However, explicit knowledge of mechanical principles is not always necessary for performance of certain tasks. In an often cited example, Polanyi (1958) points to a champion cyclist who did not know the mechanical principles involved in the maintenance of balance on a bicycle, implying that such principles may not be critical for learning the task. The implication here is consistent with the point made in the preceding sections— that at least some learning can occur in the absence of explicit information (Krist, Fieberg, & Wilkening, 1993).

Perceptual Learning

One of the features of expertise in many open sporting events is the skill to use advance perceptual information (reviewed in chapter 9). Based on this evidence, another prepractice technique is to expose the learner to the environmental stimuli that will be experienced in the task. In this way, the temporal and spatial regularities can be presented, and the performance of the task with the actual stimuli may be more effective when the performer then begins to respond to the environmental stimuli physically (i.e., when the entire task is performed). As examples, a baseball batter can watch the flight of a curve ball a number of times before swinging at one; and a race car driver can walk through a road racing course before driving it.

Adams and Creamer (1962) used a technique like this in a laboratory situation. Subjects were to learn a tracking task that involved moving a lever to follow a stimulus dot in a regular sinewave pattern. Before practice on the task began, some subjects were asked to watch these stimuli and to respond by pressing a button every time the stimulus reversed direction, attempting to anticipate its movement. After considerable experience with this task, subjects were transferred to the task in which the same stimuli were used; but now, instead of pressing the button, they were required to make lever movements with the hand to follow the dot. Subjects who had experienced the perceptual pretraining were more accurate in tracking than were subjects who had not had this experience. Similar findings were produced by Trumbo, Ulrich, and Noble (1965) when subjects learned to name each stimulus position in a regular series. When subjects had learned to anticipate the order of stimulus positions through this naming activity, they were more effective in responding to those stimuli in a tracking task (see also Schmidt, 1968, for a review).

Perceptual training techniques represent a good off-task training option when physical practice is either not possible or not practical. Early research studies in which perceptual skills in sport were trained provided promising results (Abernethy, Wood, & Parks, 1999; Farrow & Abernethy, 2002; Williams & Grant, 1999). These studies indicate that there is potential for learning from perceptual inputs, especially if the learner attends to and responds to them in some way rather than merely watching them passively. Moreover, perceptual learning may be enhanced by methods that attract the observer's attention to the most relevant, advance perceptual information (Hagemann, Strauss, & Cañal-Bruland, 2006; Jackson & Farrow, 2005).

Observational Learning

Learning from a model (observational learning) is a specific kind of perceptual learning. One important way to use modeling is to demonstrate the skill so that learners can observe the elements of the action directly. Another variant is to use videotapes or photos of skilled performers. At a superficial level, these procedures seem to be the same, with the live or archived model providing information about the task to be learned and perhaps some essential details about technique. Shrewd entrepreneurs have seized upon the simplicity of this idea in marketing videotapes of expert athletes demonstrating their talents. But, while these specific techniques may seem to have intuitive appeal, there is reason to doubt the learning benefit they provide (Druckman & Bjork, 1991). Nevertheless, there is mounting evidence that observation is an effective method for learning motor skills (for reviews see Ferrari, 1996; McCullagh & Weiss, 2001; Maslovat, Hayes, Horn, & Hodges, 2010; Scully & Newell, 1985). In the following sections we discuss some of the important issues regarding observational learning.

People observe for different reasons. While one person may go to a concert solely to be entertained, another may be there to observe the musicians play, perhaps trying to pick up skills to practice later. An aspect of this latter situation—how and what information is learned from observation—is our interest in this section. Much of the early work credited Bandura with the theoretical framework for the development of this research (see Adams, 1987). However, some argue that Bandura's theory, which was developed to explain the acquisition of *social* behaviors, is not appropriate for understanding the learning of motor skills (e.g., Maslovat et al., 2010), and recent advances in research specifically involving motor skill observational learning have provided new insights. Research on perceptual learning (see previous section) provides evidence that acquisition of environmental regularities is an important aspect of skilled performance. And the discovery of the mirror neuron system in the brain has elicited much excitement and research regarding the possibility that specific neural mechanisms provide the foundation for learning through observation (Rizzolatti & Craighero, 2004; Rizzolatti & Fabbri-Destro, 2010). These developments in research and theory have resulted in a rapid increase in the amount of research conducted on observational learning in recent years.

What Is Learned?

One of the earliest studies on modeling effects showed quite clearly that movement *strategies* could be learned by observation. The task used by Martens, Burwitz, and Zuckerman (1976) involved trying to move a ball rolling on top of two rods by varying the distance between the rods. Two strategies for success were modeled. The "creeping" strategy was a conservative approach to the task whereby the distance between the rods was adjusted slowly in order to move the ball. This strategy typically produces consistent, but only moderately successful results. In contrast, the "ballistic" strategy involved a rapid and more violent adjustment of the rods. This strategy typically produces quite variable levels of achievement; yet when scores are high, they can be very high. When given the opportunity to perform the task, observers of these two different modeling strategies tended to imitate deliberately the actions they had observed. Similar beneficial effects for learning a three-ball juggling task by imitating the actions of the model were reported by Hayes, Ashford, and Bennett (2008).

Information that can be represented spatially can be modeled quite readily, especially if the spatial attributes are presented in a static, discrete manner. For example, the acquisition of sign language is a frequently used task for observational learning because the actions are discrete and also associated with a verbal label (e.g., Caroll & Bandura, 1990; Steffens, 2007; Weeks, Hall, & Anderson, 1996). Spatial sequences represent another type of task that appears to be readily learned through demonstration (e.g., Heyes & Foster, 2002; Kelly, Burton, Riedel, & Lynch, 2003). Modeling of dynamic skills is also effective. For example, a study of females with no prior dance training revealed more benefit after subjects watched videotaped ballet sequences than after they looked at a series of still photographs of the dance (Gray, Neisser, Shapiro, & Kouns, 1991). The investigators concluded that the modeled information contributed to learning the qualitative features of the ballet routine. These conclusions are supported by experiments that modeled skiing actions (Whiting, Bijlard, & den Brinker, 1987) and gymnastics rope skills (Magill & Schoenfelder-Zohdi, 1996). In one practical study in this area, medical students performed surgical techniques more accurately after watching a skilled surgeon perform the surgery, compared to students without the benefit of observation (Custers, Regehr, McCulloch, Peniston, & Reznick, 1999). This finding suggests that even very fine spatial information can be successfully learned through demonstration.

Watching another's motor behavior can have a more subtle influence on the observer, sometimes perhaps even without the observer's awareness.

Participants in a study by Mattar and Gribble (2005) watched a video of a model who learned to manipulate a robot arm in an environment where the movement path was deflected away from the target by an invisible force field provided by a robot (see figure 2.16). Observers who watched the model perform in the same force field environment as they would later perform the task were more effective than no-observation controls, even when attention was engaged in a secondary task.

Timing is another type of information that can be successfully learned through observation, and various methods for presenting temporal information have been used (Adams, 1986; Doody, Bird, & Ross, 1985; McCullagh & Little, 1989; Meegan, Aslin, & Jacobs, 2000; Zelaznik, Shapiro, & Newell, 1978; Zelaznik & Spring, 1976). For example, Zelaznik and colleagues provided one group of subjects with the recorded sounds of another subject making a correct timing movement prior to any practice. After the presentation of the modeled information, this group performed the timed movement more accurately than another group who had not listened to the sounds. The "listening group" could even improve slightly in the task without any knowledge of results. The interpretation of these findings is that the listening experience provided the subjects with a reference of correctness, and the reference allowed an evaluation of the auditory feedback produced by the movement and subsequent adjustments on the upcoming trials (see also Blandin & Proteau, 2000; Wrisberg & Schmidt, 1975). Timing information can also be successfully modeled when auditory and visual information is presented in a spatial timing task (e.g., Vogt, 1995).

Model Skill Level

One of the implicit assumptions regarding the use of videos that provide sport instruction is that highly skilled performers are more effective than unskilled models. This assumption may be true, depending on how the unskilled model demonstrates the task to be learned. The evidence suggests that the assumption is not true when people observe unskilled models *learn* a motor task. For instance, Pollock and Lee (1992) studied the effectiveness of demonstrations of a computer video game to groups of individuals who had had no prior practice on the task. Subjects either watched an expert perform the task or watched a novice who was learning the task for the first time (a *learning model*). After a series of modeling trials, the observers in both groups showed a substantial benefit of having watched their respective models (as compared to a no-model control group). However, there was no advantage to having viewed the expert model compared to the learning model. Similar findings were reported by McCullagh and Meyer (1997) using a weightlifting task.

A more surprising finding in this research is that, under some circumstances, the provision of a learning model can result in *stronger* observational learning than an expert model. This research area was initiated by Adams (1986), who used learning models to demonstrate the performance of a manual timing task. Adams found that observation alone was insufficient for learning this task. However, considerable learning was seen if the model's feedback from the experimenter (termed *knowledge of results*, KR) was also presented to the observer (Blandin, Lhuisset, & Proteau, 1999). In this dynamic observation environment, the observer can gain information (a) from the model about the movement performed (both visual and auditory), (b) from the augmented feedback presented to the model (as KR), and (c) from seeing the success of the model's attempt to use that feedback on the next performance of the task. In this way, the observer benefits not only

from "observing" the performance, but also from observing the processing operations of the model in the attempt to improve performance, which becomes increasingly important as the difficulty of the task is elevated (Laguna, 2008).

The research method used by Adams (1986) was extended by McCullagh and Caird (1990), who directly compared the effectiveness of learning models and expert models on Adams' task. Three observation groups were compared. One group had repeated exposures to a tape of a perfect execution of the timing goal. Two other groups watched a tape of a model who was learning the task; one group also received the model's KR and one did not. As illustrated in figure 11.6, the largest effects were found for those who observed the learning model and also received the model's KR (open squares). These subjects improved their performance consistently over the acquisition period, in the absence of any KR about their own performance, and both retained their performance levels and transferred to a novel timing goal better than either of the other observation groups.

These findings suggest an important application to modeling real-world tasks. Novice athletes are likely to gain relatively little insight from watching experts unless they are specifically cued regarding where to watch and what to look for (Janelle, Champenoy, Coombes, & Mousseau,

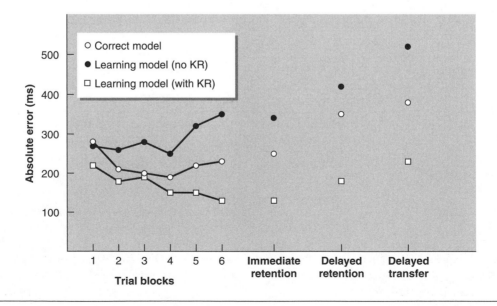

FIGURE 11.6 Effects of model skill level and availability of model's knowledge of results (KR) on learning.

Adapted, by permission, from P. McCullagh and J.K. Caird, 1990, "Correct and learning models and the use of model knowledge of results in the acquisition and retention of a motor skill," *Journal of Human Movement Studies* 18: 107-116.

2003). While viewing professional golf on television, for example, we likely get the greatest *learning* benefit when experts make mistakes. The mistakes occur so infrequently that the commentators usually replay the action and point out exactly what went wrong—what movement error resulted in the flubbed shot. In other words, the "model" demonstrated an incorrect action, which was accompanied by KR that identified the error. Thus, the issue of essential importance in this research may not be the skill level of the model at all, but rather about what type of information is being demonstrated—errors or perfect templates of an action. The research findings suggest that we learn more from observing mistakes than we do from correct performances.

Scheduling Observations

Although this part of the chapter is about "off-task" practice considerations, perhaps the most successful strategy in the use of models is to intersperse the demonstrated information with physical practice trials performed by the observer. Similar to the conclusion from the previous discussion, this scheduling of observation and physical practice has the advantage of engaging the learner more in the active problem-solving process of learning than would be the case if all demonstrations were presented prior to physical practice. This scheduling also has the advantage of providing the performer with some rest between physical trials, which, as we discuss in a later section, is also important for learning. The literature is quite consistent in showing that interspersing physical and modeled trials results in better learning (retention and transfer) than a single block of observations prior to physical practice of the task (Deakin & Proteau, 2000; Granados & Wulf, 2007; Shea, Wulf, & Whitacre, 1999; Shea, Wright, Wulf, & Whitacre, 2000; Weeks & Anderson, 2000). In this sense, interleaving information gained from off-task observation with on-task practice appears to optimize the benefits gained from observations.

Mental Practice

One of the most frequently used and advocated off-task methods to promote learning is *mental* practice, in which the performance of a task is mentally rehearsed, often using imagery techniques, in the absence of overt physical practice.

Experimental assessment of mental practice effects usually requires several different groups of subjects, at a minimum (Goginsky & Collins, 1996): All subjects are given a pretest on a task to be learned, followed by the experimental manipulation, then a posttest on the learning task. The mental practice manipulation often entails covert rehearsal of the task, sometimes involving strategies such as imagery. In this case, however, the learning that can be attributed only to mental practice effects cannot be inferred just from a retention test. Rather, one must demonstrate that performance on the posttest exceeded performance in a control group that did not perform intervening practice or that performed practice on an unrelated task. In addition, mental practice is usually compared to a third condition in which a group *physically* practices the task for the same amount of time as the mental practice group. Some experiments also include *combination* conditions with alternation between trials of mental and physical practice. Of course, many experiments use other variations of these mental practice manipulations (see reviews by Feltz & Landers, 1983; Feltz, Landers, & Becker, 1988; Lotze & Halsband, 2006).

Is Mental Practice as Effective as Physical Practice?

A nice demonstration of all these various practice conditions and their effects was provided in a complex study by Hird, Landers, Thomas, and Horan (1991). Twelve groups of subjects participated in the experiment. Six groups were asked to learn a pegboard task, inserting pegs of different colors and shapes as rapidly as possible into squares cut in a board. The other six groups performed the pursuit rotor task. For each task, subjects performed a pretest, seven sessions of training (on separate days), and a posttest. During the training sessions the 100% physical practice group performed eight trials on the task while the 100% mental practice group covertly practiced the task for the same amount of time. Three other groups involved combinations of practice, consisting of two, four, or six trials of physical practice combined with six, four, or two trials of mental practice (i.e., 75% physical practice [P], 25% mental practice [M]; 50P:50M; and 25P:75M groups). The control group performed an unrelated task (the stabilometer) for the same amount of time during these training sessions.

The difference in performance between the pretest and posttest for each group in Hird and colleagues' study is presented in figure 11.7.[1] The sets of findings for the two tasks are remarkably similar. The groups given mental practice (100%M) were more effective than the no-practice (control) groups, but not nearly as effective as the groups given the same amount of physical practice (100%P). In addition, the results for the combination groups showed that learning was enhanced with higher proportions of the training trials spent in physical, compared to mental, practice (e.g., compare the 75P:25M groups with the 25P:75M groups in figure 11.7).

The findings of Hird and colleagues (1991) have been replicated (Allami, Paulignan, Brovelli, & Boussaoud, 2008) and concur with the reviews of the mental practice literature conducted by Feltz and Landers (1983; Feltz et al., 1988; Lotze & Halsband, 2006). The results suggest that *whenever possible*, physical practice is preferable to mental practice for learning. However, when physically practicing a task is not possible, as when an individual is away from a clinical rehabilitation setting, then mental rehearsal is an effective method for augmenting learning (Dickstein & Deutsch, 2007; Mulder 2007).

Hypotheses About Mental Practice Effects

Why then, is mental practice effective for learning a motor skill? Certainly, one of the components of mental practice involves learning the *cognitive elements* in the task; that is, learning what to do (Heuer, 1985). Given the requirement of rehearsing mentally, the learner can think about what kinds of things could be tried, can predict the consequences of each action to some extent on the basis of previous experiences with similar skills, and can perhaps rule out inappropriate courses of action. This view suggests that not very much *motor* learning is happening in mental practice, the majority being the rapid learning associated with the cognitive elements of the task. Such a view fits well with data from Minas (1978, 1980), who used a serial throwing task in which subjects had to throw balls of different weights and textures into the proper bins. The main finding was that mental practice contributed to the learning of the sequence (the cognitive element) but did not contribute very much to learning the particular throwing actions (motor elements).

Another view, however, suggests that there is more to mental practice than the learning of

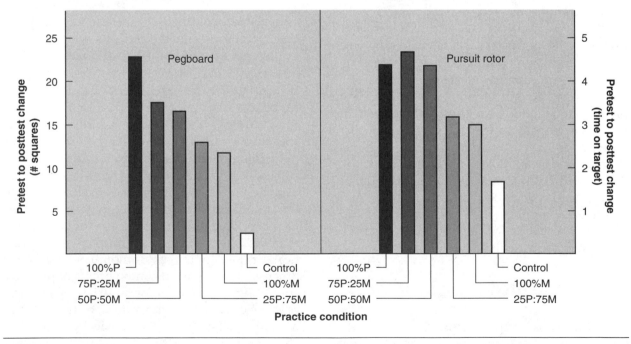

FIGURE 11.7 Effects of various combinations of physical and mental practice on pegboard and pursuit rotor tasks.

Adapted, by permission, from J.S. Hird et al., 1991, "Physical practice is superior to mental practice in enhancing cognitive and motor task performance," *Journal of Sport and Exercise Psychology* 13(3): 286-287.

the cognitive elements in a task. Some suggest that the motor programs for the movements are actually being run off during mental practice but that the learner simply turns down the "gain" of the program so that the muscular contractions are not visible. Research on so-called *implicit speech,* in which subjects are told to imagine speaking a given sentence, shows patterns of electromyographic activity from the vocal musculature that resemble the patterns evoked during actual speech. One possibility is that very small forces (not sufficient to cause movements) are produced and the performer receives Golgi tendon organ feedback about them (chapter 5), as the Golgi tendon organs are extremely sensitive to small loads. Another possibility is that the "movements" are sensed via feedforward and corollary discharge (i.e., "internal feedback"), generated when the motor programs are run off (chapter 5). Yet another possibility discussed earlier in this chapter is that *planning* a movement (which should be part of mental practice) is, in itself, beneficial to learning.

Most recent hypotheses about the effects of mental practice have focused on the specific role of *imagery.* Many researchers now agree that imagined actions share similarities with the actual movements being imaged. For example, performance times are similar for imaged and physically performed trials of the Fitts reciprocal tapping tasks with different indexes of difficulty (Cerritelli, Maruff, Wilson, & Currie, 2000; Decety & Jeannerod, 1996; Kohl & Fisicaro, 1995; Stevens, 2005). Similar effects are also observed in grasping tasks (Frak, Paulignan, & Jeannerod, 2001) and when a mass either is loaded or is imagined being loaded to a limb (Papaxanthis, Schieppati, Gentili, & Pozzo, 2002). Studies involving brain mapping techniques (chapter 2) also point to similar activation regions in the brain when movements are produced and imagined (Jeannerod, 2001; Jeannerod & Frak, 1999). Together with observations that apraxia patients sometimes fail to inhibit imagined movements (without awareness; Schwoebel, Boronat, & Branch Coslett, 2002), the findings suggest that imagery is a process by which actions are programmed as in normal movements but are *inhibited* from being executed. According to this view, at least some learning can be attributed solely to the motor programming process, in the absence of movement execution.

Distribution of Practice

Our discussion of on-task conditions of practice begins with one of the variables that instructors and therapists have under their control: the scheduling of periods of *work* (i.e., time spent in actual practice) and *rest* (i.e., time not practicing the task). This scheduling can be considered within the constraints of a short time frame, such as the amount of work and rest during a 45 min therapy session. Or the scheduling may be considered in terms of a longer time scale, as when one chooses the length and frequency of sessions per week. The question of importance concerns whether or not the frequency and length of rest periods have an effect on learning the skill being practiced in the work periods. What is the best way to distribute the time spent in work versus the time spent resting—or simply, what is the best *practice distribution*?

Defining "Massed" and "Distributed" Practice

Research on practice-distribution effects has frequently used the terms *massed practice* and *distributed practice.* In one sense, "massing" means to put things together—in this case, running work periods very close together with either no rest at all or very brief rest intervals between periods of work. By default, distributing practice means *spacing* these periods of work apart with longer intervals of rest. The labels are not truly satisfactory, however, because researchers often use these terms to describe the two extremes of practice distributions within a particular experiment, and because many experimenters use more than two distribution conditions (e.g., Ammons, 1950; Bourne & Archer, 1956). Thus, these terms must be considered relative to the context of other conditions within any particular experiment and relative to the context of other experiments.

The vast majority of the research on distribution-of-practice effects has been conducted using continuous tasks, for which the work period might be 20 or 30 s in duration. The task most commonly used for this research was the pursuit rotor tracking task (figure 2.5). However, tasks such as mirror tracing, the Bachman ladder (figure 2.8), and inverted-alphabet printing were also popular in the early research studies of this area. We first discuss the effects of practice distribution using continuous tasks. Only a few studies have been done using discrete tasks; however, the findings are quite different from those of studies using continuous tasks and are presented later.

Distribution-of-Practice Effects on Performance

Many experiments were done in the 1940s and 1950s on practice-distribution effects (for reviews, see Donovan & Radosevich, 1999; Lee & Genovese, 1988). Even though these experiments involved wide differences in methods (such as the length of work and rest periods, the number of trials), the results are remarkably similar. Put simply, the findings converge on a very straightforward statement about the effect on performance: *Given constant periods of work, short rest periods degrade performance relative to performance with longer rest periods.*

Findings from a study by Bourne and Archer (1956) are typical of the performance effects seen in experiments on practice distribution. The task was pursuit rotor tracking. Five different groups of subjects were compared; all groups had work periods of 30 s. In one group (the 0 s rest group), subjects practiced continuously for 21 trials, with no rest at all. For the other four groups, a period of rest was interspersed between each work period. One group had rest periods of 15 s, and the other three groups had rest periods of 30, 45, or 60 s.

Bourne and Archer found that longer rest periods resulted in more effective performances. Looking closely at the left side of figure 11.8, one can see that a systematic separation of the various distribution-of-practice groups had emerged by about trial 7 and that these differences became larger with further practice. Many other examples of effects like these have been documented, and reviews by McGeoch and Irion (1952), Bilodeau and Bilodeau (1961), Lee and Genovese (1988), and Donovan and Radosevich (1999) describe details of this literature.

Distribution-of-Practice Effects on Learning

For tasks such as the pursuit rotor, practice with little or no rest would likely cause muscular fatigue to develop; this fatigue could be expected to depress performance, and that seems to be evident by the results in figure 11.8. Thus, because

at least part of the decrement in performance displayed by these groups was due to temporary fatigue, not all of the performance depression could be attributed to differences in the relatively permanent development of skill. So, how much was due to learning?

To assess this issue, Bourne and Archer gave all of their subjects a 5 min rest period following the last acquisition trial. After this rest period, subjects performed a common transfer test in which all groups were shifted to a massed schedule—all trials were performed with 0 s rest between 30 s work periods. The rationale was that if muscular fatigue was responsible for *all* of the differences between groups during the acquisition trials, then the groups should be similar in performance after the dissipation of the fatigue. This was not the case, as can be seen in the right side of figure 11.8.

Several items in these transfer data are noteworthy. The most important is that substantial differences were maintained between the groups after the rest period, with initial transfer performance being increasingly more skilled for groups that had longer periods of rest between work periods during the acquisition trials. This finding suggests that the practice distribution had a relatively permanent effect, which is supported by many other studies in the literature (Lee & Genovese, 1988).

Another item worth noting in these data is that the differences between the groups on the first transfer trial (trial 22) are smaller than the differences between groups on the last acquisition trial (trial 21). Thus, some of the practice-distribution effect seen in the acquisition data was due to the temporary, detrimental influence of fatigue. Still, the differences due to changes brought about by learning remained large on the transfer trials. The last item to notice is that massing the transfer trials also had a depressing effect on performance. However, even after nine transfer trials with no rest (i.e., on trial 30), the groups that had initially practiced with some rest between trials still out-performed the group that had practiced with no rest.

We have used the Bourne and Archer (1956) study to illustrate the effects of practice distribution on performance and learning. It is a particularly good example of this effect because more than two distribution groups were used and because a transfer design was used to separate the temporary from the permanent effects of the practice variable. However, several conclusions drawn from this study require further discussion.

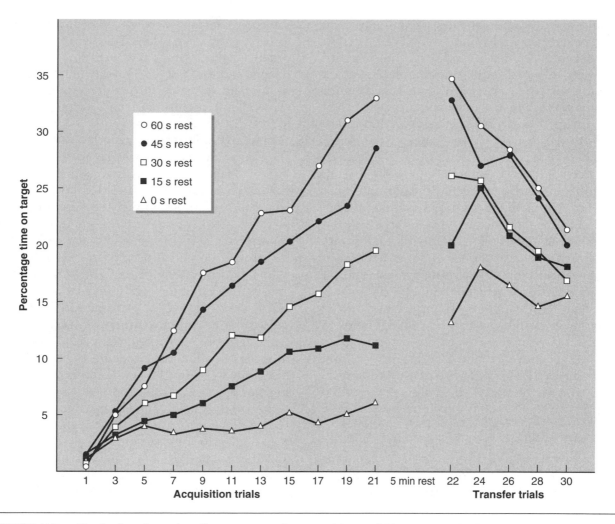

FIGURE 11.8 Distribution-of-practice effects on a pursuit rotor task in acquisition and transfer. Trials were 30 s in duration, and separate groups received either 0, 15, 30, 45, or 60 s of rest between practice trials. Transfer trials were performed with 0 s rest between trials.

Reprinted from L.E. Bourne and E.J. Archer, 1956, "Time continuously on target as a function of distribution of practice," *Journal of Experimental Psychology* 51: 27.

Length of the Retention Interval

One complicating factor about the Bourne and Archer experiment is that a 5 min rest period following continuous practice may not have been long enough to allow the temporary influence of muscular fatigue on performance to dissipate (Ammons, 1988; Lintern, 1988). Thus, the transfer trials may have been influenced by the same temporary effects that influenced acquisition performance (e.g., fatigue). Several studies have addressed this issue using longer rest intervals following practice (e.g., one day in Adams, 1952; 10 weeks in Reynolds & Bilodeau, 1952) and have shown that the learning effect remained even when these temporary effects had surely dissipated. These findings support the conclusion

about the learning difference from the Bourne and Archer study.

Do the Learning Effects "Wash Out"?

The Bourne and Archer data show that performance differences in transfer began to converge by trial 30 (after nine transfer trials). The convergence of effects in transfer has been argued by some to cast doubt on the "relative permanency" of the learning effect. An important study by Adams and Reynolds (1954) further calls this issue into question. In this study, distributed practice was defined as 30 s of work with 30 s rest. Massed practice involved the same trial duration but with only 5 s of rest. One group received 40 trials under distributed conditions. Four more groups received initial practice for 5, 10, 15, or 20 trials, respectively, under massed conditions; they then rested for 10 min, and finally transferred to the distributed-practice condition for the remainder of the 40 practice trials. Adams and Reynolds found that when the various massed-practice groups were shifted to distributed practice, they caught up (though not entirely) within a few trials to the level of performance of the group that had practiced entirely under distributed-practice conditions. A small flaw in the design, however, makes these effects difficult to interpret. The problem is that the groups that transferred to distributed-practice conditions received the benefit of a 10 min rest. The distributed group, which may have experienced some temporary fatigue effects, did not have such a rest. Thus, it is difficult to know whether or not the differences observed were temporary or permanent.

A clever design by Ammons (1950) helps to clarify this issue. Groups received rest periods that ranged from 0 s and 20 s to up to 12 min between each 20 s trial on the pursuit rotor task. One group even had *24 h* between each of the 36 practice trials. A 20 min rest period followed the 36th practice trial, after which subjects performed an additional 36 transfer trials with no rest between trials (many more transfer trials than had been used by Bourne & Archer [1956]). By the end of this transfer period, only small differences remained between the groups. However, Ammons (1950) asked subjects to return to the lab for *another* set of transfer trials one day later. The differences that had been seen on the first transfer test—and apparently washed out by the transfer trials—were "restored" after this additional rest period. These data are strong indicators that practice distribution has large effects on temporary performance levels *and* relatively permanent influences on learning.

Distributing Practice Over a Longer Time Scale

Perhaps of more direct significance to instructors and therapists are the effects of practice distribution when practice takes place on a much longer time scale. A few such studies have been performed, and the results are generally similar to those of the studies done in a single session. In a very early investigation of this type, right-handed subjects were asked to throw javelins with their left arm (Murphy, 1916). All subjects practiced on 34 separate days. Massed-practice

subjects performed on consecutive days (Monday to Friday) for seven weeks. The distributed group practiced three times per week for 12 weeks. Results at the end of the 34th day of practice and on a retention test performed three months later showed both performance and learning benefits for the distributed group.

Similar findings were reported by Baddeley and Longman (1978) for postal workers who were training to use a keyboard. In this study, separate groups of postal workers trained for 60 to 80 h using one of four schedules: Work periods were conducted either once or twice per day, and the duration of each work period was 1 or 2 h. The data for the practice period and for retention tests performed one, three, and nine months later showed that the condition that massed the practice the most (2 × 2) resulted in the lowest performance and learning (see figure 11.9). Although the other three groups did not differ in these retention tests, the effects of the "most distributed" group (1 × 1) are likely diminished because practice for this group was stopped after a total accumulation of 60 h, as compared to the 80 h of practice for the other three groups. These data appear to suggest that there is some generalizability of the results obtained in experiments of relatively short duration to studies involving practice and retention over much longer periods of time (see also Shea, Lai, Black, & Park, 2001).

Total Practice Time

From the previous sections, it would appear that it is not beneficial for learning to mass trials in a practice session. But there is another important variable that coexists with massing—the total *time* involved in practice. Recall that in the experiments presented so far, the number of practice trials was held constant; and because the amount of time between practice trials was different for the massed and distributed conditions, the overall practice time was allowed to vary. That is, a group receiving massed practice will have a shorter total practice period than will an equivalent group with distributed practice.

Consider the Baddeley and Longman (1978) study just described. Although the group that practiced for 2 h per session twice per day (2 × 2) showed the poorest acquisition and retention performance, their practice period was completed in one-half the time used by two groups (1 × 2 and 2 × 1) and one-quarter of the time used by

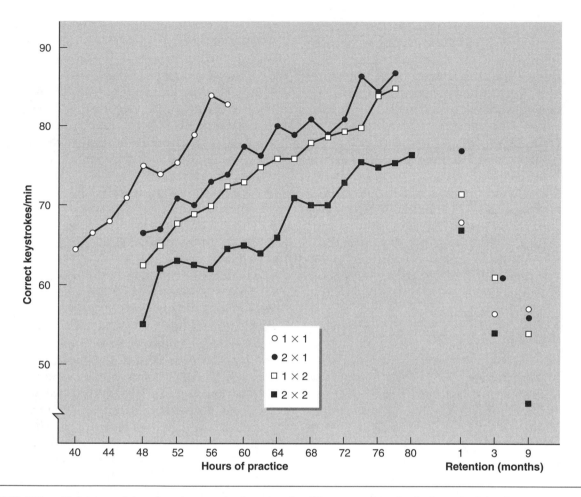

FIGURE 11.9 Training postal workers to use a keyboard under different practice-distribution schedules (1 × 1 refers to sessions conducted once per day of 1 h duration each; 2 × 2 refers to two sessions per day of 2 h duration each, etc.).

Data from Baddeley and Longman 1978.

the 1 × 1 group. Additional training for this 2 × 2 group would likely have resulted in improved performance and learning.

The issue of practice distribution and total practice time involves a *trade-off*. Distributed practice results in the most learning per time in training but requires the most total time to complete. Massed practice results in reduced benefits per time in training but requires the least total time. Thus, what is most *effective* for learning may not always be the most *efficient*, at least in terms of time required to optimize learning.

Safety Issues

Finally, it should be clear that massing has strong effects on performance of many tasks and that the risks of injury in dangerous tasks are likely to increase with massed practice. The laboratory tasks described here are not particularly

dangerous, but many tasks used in sport (e.g., giant swings on the horizontal bar) and industry (e.g., work with a hydraulic paper cutter) entail considerably more opportunity for serious injury if errors are made. And most certainly for people in rehabilitation, whose motor coordination has already been affected, the risk of injury is of vital concern to the therapist. Thus, caution should be used in designing training regimens in situations in which factors such as fatigue could put the learner at risk.

Discrete Tasks

The amount of evidence about discrete tasks is far less than for continuous tasks. Carron (1967, 1969) used a peg-turn task in which the subject moved 44 cm from a key to grasp a peg in a hole, turned the peg end-for-end to reinsert it into the hole, and then returned to the key again as quickly as possible. This movement was discrete and required a movement time (MT) of from 1,300 to 1,700 ms, depending on the level of skill of the performers. Carron had subjects learn this task under two conditions: distributed (the amount of rest between trials was 5 s) and massed (the amount of rest between trials was only 300 ms, with a 5 s rest every 10 trials). Carron found no effect of the massing conditions on performance of the task while the massing was present. When he tested the subjects 48 h later as a measure of learning, he found that the subjects in the massed condition actually performed slightly faster than the subjects in the distributed condition (1,430 vs. 1,510 ms), but it is probably more reasonable to say there were no real differences. For this discrete task, massing appeared to be neither a performance variable nor a learning variable, contrary to the rather strong effects of massing found for continuous tasks.

Lee and Genovese (1989) investigated this apparent continuous–discrete difference directly, in parallel experiments employing very similar timing tasks. For the continuous task, there was a tendency for subjects in the distributed conditions in acquisition to perform more effectively than those in the massed conditions. This effect carried over into the delayed (seven days) transfer test, so that practice under distributed conditions in acquisition resulted in more learning, regardless of whether the transfer-test conditions were distributed or massed. This was essentially the same as had been found with the other continuous tasks (see previous section). However, for the discrete task, there was a slight tendency for the massed condition to be more effective in acquisition. In a delayed transfer test performed under massed conditions, there was an advantage to the group that had massed practice in acquisition compared to distributed practice. This provides at least one example indicating that massed practice can be more effective for learning than distributed practice.

A different interpretation of the distribution-of-practice effect can be made when considered over a longer-term time scale. For example, in a golf putting study by Dail and Christina (2004), novice subjects performed 240 practice putts of 3.7 m distance. Subjects in the massed group performed all of their trials in one session, whereas the distributed group practiced 60 trials on each of four consecutive days. All subjects returned either 1, 7, or 28 days later for retention tests. The findings from the Dail and Christina study, presented in figure 11.10, revealed small but consistent advantages for distributed practice by about halfway through the practice trials. More importantly, these

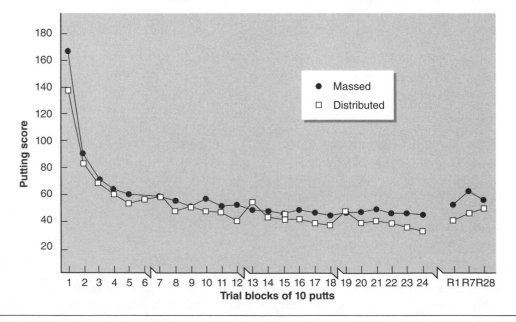

FIGURE 11.10 Effects of massed and distributed practice in a golf putting task.

performance advantages were maintained on each of the retention tests, conducted up to one month later (see also Shea, Lai, Black, & Park, 2000, experiment 2). Thus, it would appear that the effects of distributed practice on performance and learning in continuous and discrete tasks might have more similarities than previously thought.

Variability of Practice

Another factor that has been shown to affect learning is the amount of *variability* in a practice sequence. In one sense, this is obvious. Many tasks have inherent variability, such as fielding ground balls in baseball or steering a car down an unfamiliar road (so-called *open skills;* see chapter 2). An important part of learning such tasks is acquiring the capability to cope with novel situations; practicing under constant (unvarying) situations would probably not be appropriate. But in another sense, the effect of variable practice is not so obvious, especially when the task involves *closed skills,* for which the environmental conditions are always similar (e.g., archery, bowling). Here, because the criterion task to be learned is always performed under the same environmental conditions, it would seem that practice under these exact conditions would be most effective for learning. Yet the evidence suggests that varied practice may be important in closed tasks as well.

Much of the research on variability of practice has been conducted to test certain predictions of *schema theory* (Schmidt, 1975b; see chapter 13 for more on schema theory). One prediction was that transfer to novel tasks would be enhanced after practice in variable, as compared to constant, practice conditions. We discuss only a few of these studies; reviews of many more of these experiments are available (Lee, Magill, & Weeks, 1985; Shapiro & Schmidt, 1982; Van Rossum, 1990).

Variability-of-Practice Effects in Retention

One way to obtain an indication of the effect of practice variability is to assess retention performance after a period of time following the acquisition session (chapter 10). A few experimenters have done this by comparing the relative impacts of constant and varied practice on retention of the tasks that were practiced. There is a design complication with this type of study, however, as subjects in the different groups practice different tasks; thus what has been practiced and what is assessed in retention cannot be equated. But this does not pose a problem for results such as those we see in studies conducted by Shea and Kohl (1990, 1991).

Subjects in the Shea and Kohl experiments learned to generate a goal force by squeezing a handgrip that was connected to a force transducer. In one experiment (Shea & Kohl, 1991, experiment 1), subjects performed 100 trials to acquire a criterion force of 150 N. One group ("Criterion only" in figure 11.11) received only these acquisition trials. Another group ("Criterion + variable") received the same number of acquisition trials on the criterion task but, in addition, practiced goal forces that were ±25 or ±50 N relative to the criterion task (i.e., 100, 125, 175, and 200 N). Notice, however, that this variable-practice group not only had the same amount of specific practice as the criterion group, but also practiced at tasks that surrounded the criterion task—which confounds the role of the variable practice with the amount of additional practice. So, Shea and Kohl also included a third group of subjects ("Criterion + criterion") that practiced the criterion task, as well as performing additional practice trials on the criterion task, so that the total number of practice trials was equal to the total practiced by the variable group.

Performance on the criterion task for these groups in acquisition and in a retention test one day later is presented in figure 11.11. The criterion + variable practice group performed less accurately on the criterion task throughout most of the acquisition period in comparison to the other two groups. However, after a rest period of no practice, subjects in the criterion + variable practice group performed *more* accurately in a retention test on the criterion task than both the criterion-only group and the criterion + criterion group. These findings indicate that practice at tasks that were similar to (and that "surrounded") the criterion task actually *facilitated* its retention.

Variability-of-Practice Effects in Transfer

In one of the first studies investigating practice variability, McCracken and Stelmach (1977) had subjects move their right arm from a starting key

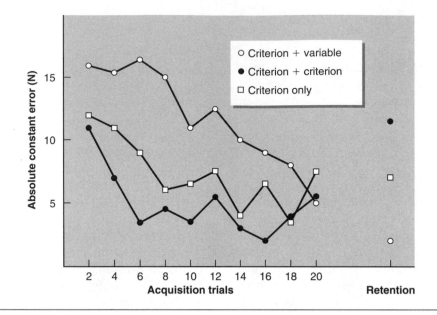

FIGURE 11.11 Effects of variable-practice conditions and a criterion-only practice condition during acquisition and retention (performance plotted only for the criterion task).

Reprinted with permission from *Research Quarterly for Exercise and Sport,* Vol. 62, pg.190, Copyright 1991, by the American Alliance for Health, Physical Education, Recreation and Dance, 1900 Association Drive, Reston, VA 20191.

to knock over a barrier, with a 200 ms goal MT from initiation to barrier contact. The distances to the barrier could be changed in different conditions (15, 35, 60, and 65 cm), with a constant 200 ms goal in the practice phase. Table 11.1 presents the details of the experimental design. A Constant group was actually made up of four subgroups, each of which had practice at only one of the barrier distances for 300 trials. The Variable group, on the other hand, had the same number of trials as the Constant group (i.e., 300), but these trials were varied in that all four barrier distances were practiced in a random order (75 trials of each).[2]

In a transfer-test phase, the two groups performed a *novel* (50 cm) distance, both immediately after training and after a two-day interval. With this design the authors evaluated the effect of variable versus constant practice on the performance of a variation that had never been performed previously. This transfer design addresses an effect of learning quite different from that studied in the retention design by Shea and Kohl (1991) discussed in the preceding section. In that research, Shea and Kohl assessed how well one *common* task, practiced by all the groups, was *retained* as a function of

TABLE 11.1. Experimental Design for an Experiment on Variability in Practice			
	ORIGINAL PRACTICE	TRANSFER-TEST PHASE	
Group	**300 Trials** **Day 1**	**Immediate** **Day 1**	**Delayed** **Day 2**
Constant			
Subgroup a	15 cm only	50 cm	50 cm
Subgroup b	35 cm only	50 cm	50 cm
Subgroup c	60 cm only	50 cm	50 cm
Subgroup d	65 cm only	50 cm	50 cm
Variable	15, 35, 60, 65 cm	50 cm	50 cm

Adapted from McCracken and Stelmach 1977.

the other tasks that had also been practiced. In the McCracken and Stelmach study, the primary research interest was the effect of varied versus constant practice on the capability to perform a *novel task.*

The results are shown in figure 11.12, where the absolute errors are plotted for the trials at the end of the acquisition phase, as well as for the trials on the two transfer-test phases. In the original-practice phase, the Constant group had less absolute error than the Variable group. This finding is similar to the results shown by Shea and Kohl (see figure 11.11). The critical contrasts, however, are in the transfer-test phases, when the task was novel for both groups. In immediate transfer, the order of the groups was reversed, with the Variable group now having less absolute error than the Constant group. This trend persisted into delayed transfer, 48 h later, but with the difference between groups being considerably smaller. Thus, it appeared that variability in practice (during the original-practice phase) allowed the subjects to learn the task more effectively, permitting them to perform a new version of it on the transfer phase with less error than the Constant group (see also Wrisberg & Ragsdale, 1979). Variable practice seemed to be important in generating a capacity to perform a novel version of this task. But this novel task (50 cm) was clearly within the original range of experience of the Variable group (i.e., from 15 to 65 cm), and one could argue that the Variable group had more practice than the Constant group at tasks closer to the transfer task. Would such effects also be seen if the novel transfer task was *outside* the range of previous experience?

Catalano and Kleiner (1984) used a timing task in which the subject was to press a button when a moving pattern of lights arrived at a coincidence point. Using a design much like that of McCracken and Stelmach (1977), they had a Variable group practice at speeds of 5, 7, 9, and 11 mph; a Constant group (with four subgroups) practiced at only one of these speeds. Then, on a subsequent transfer test, all subjects transferred to four *novel* light speeds that were outside the range of previous experience (i.e., 1, 3, 13, and 15 mph). The performance of the two groups on these transfer tests is shown in figure 11.13. The absolute errors were smaller for the Variable group than for the Constant group, and the differences were present even when the "distance" from the range of previous experience was quite large. Variable practice appeared to increase the "applicability" of the learning that occurred in acquisition, contributing to the performance of novel variations of the task that were well outside the range of the stimuli experienced in the acquisition phase. One cannot argue that the Variable group was more effective simply because the subjects had experienced the range of speeds involved in the transfer test, as neither group had experienced them. In other words, variable practice seemed to increase *generalizability,* an important criterion for motor learning as discussed in chapter 10 (see Roller, Cohen, Kimball, & Bloomberg, 2001, for a different demonstration of generalization following variable practice).

Other Factors Influencing Effects of Practice Variability

When adults are used as subjects, there is reasonably strong evidence that increased practice variability is beneficial for learning (as measured on novel transfer tests), and basically no evidence that variable practice is detrimental to learning (Shapiro & Schmidt, 1982). However, a number of studies show very small effects, and others show essentially no effects, casting some doubt on the "strength" or generality of these effects (Van Rossum, 1990). Overall, in practical settings it is reasonably safe to say that attempts to make the practice more variable for learners will result in

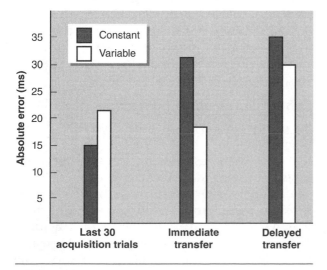

FIGURE 11.12 Performance in a ballistic-timing task as a function of variability in practice conditions.

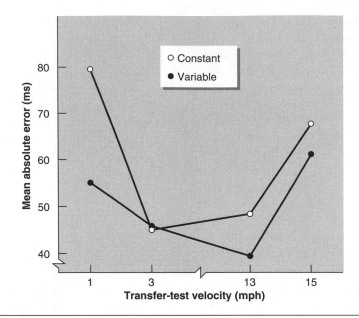

FIGURE 11.13 Mean absolute timing error during novel transfer-test velocities as a function of the variability in practice conditions in acquisition.

Reproduced and adapted from figure 2 with permission from authors and publisher from: Catalano, J.F., & Kleiner, B.M. Distant transfer in coincident timing as a function of variability of practice. *Perceptual and Motor Skills*, 1984, 58, 851-856. © Perceptual and Motor Skills 1984.

greater learning and generalizability. However, in the following paragraphs we discuss some of the issues that complicate this general statement.

Age of the Learner

The effects of practice variability seem to depend on the nature of the learners. Certainly the most obvious classification is that of children versus adults. In their review of the literature on practice variability, Shapiro and Schmidt (1982) noted that the advantage for variable versus constant practice for children was strong in nearly every study conducted. For example, using a strictly closed throwing skill with young children, Kerr and Booth (1977, 1978) found in two experiments that variable practice was more effective than constant practice when subjects were transferred to a novel version of the task. Even more surprising was the finding that for learning this novel variation of the task, practice at variations of the task approximating the novel task was more effective than was practicing the *novel task itself!* Practice variability appears to be a powerful variable in children's motor learning (see also Green, Whitehead, & Sugden, 1995; Wulf, 1991).

Nature of the Task

Similar to the practice-distribution effects, it appears that some of the differences in the effects of variability of practice may be accounted for by the nature of the task. For example, a study by Shea, Lai, Wright, Immink, and Black (2001) showed that the *relative timing* of a closed task was learned more effectively with practice conditions that promoted movement consistency (e.g., constant practice) compared to practice conditions that promoted variability. In contrast, learning the *absolute timing* of the task was better under variable- than consistent-practice conditions. These recent findings support the intriguing possibility that some aspects of the *same task* may be learned more effectively through constant-practice conditions and other aspects through variable-practice conditions (see Wulf & Shea, 2002, for more discussion).

Scheduling Variable Practice

We mentioned earlier that the effects of variable practice in adults have not always been consistent—some studies showing positive effects and others showing no effects. A review of those studies showing no effects by Lee and colleagues (1985) revealed an interesting pattern of findings. Many of these experiments had structured the variable-practice sessions such that most or all of the practice on any single variant of the task was conducted together, in what is called a *blocked practice sequence.* Although we will have much more to say about the effects of random and blocked practice in the next section, the conclusion drawn by Lee and colleagues (1985) was that for variable practice to be most effectively utilized (relative to constant practice), the order should be randomized, rather than blocked.

Interpreting Variability-of-Practice Effects

Most of the studies on variability have been done in the context of schema theory (chapter 13). The basic premise is that with practice, people develop rules (called *schemas*) about their own motor behavior. Think back to the ideas about the generalized motor program (chapter 6), indicating that a set of parameters must be applied to the program in order for it to be performed. Schema theory proposes that subjects learn a rule in the practice sequence. The rule is a relationship between all the past environmental outcomes that the person produced and the values of the parameters that were used to produce those outcomes. This rule is maintained in memory and can be used to select a new set of parameters for the next movement situation—even a novel variation—that involves the same motor program. Knowing the rule and what environmental outcome is to be produced, the person can select the parameters for the program that will produce it. The schema theory is related to variability in practice because the theory predicts that learning the rule will be more effective if the experience is varied rather than constant.

Another important finding from the literature on variability in practice is that the occurrence of learning during the acquisition phase was revealed by performance on a *novel* version of the task in transfer. This was true regardless of whether the novel version was inside (McCracken & Stelmach, 1977) or outside (Catalano & Kleiner, 1984) the range of variation experienced in the acquisition phase. As we will point out in chapter 13, such evidence suggests that what was learned was *not* some particular movement, but rather the (generalizable) capability to produce any of a variety of movements of this type. These results are explained well by schema theory, in that the variable practice produces a rule (or schema) for selecting parameters of the generalized motor program (e.g., for throwing), and this rule can be used for any novel movement using the same motor program.

Why should variable practice be more effective for children? One idea is that children are less experienced at motor skills than are older (adult) subjects, so the rules (schemas) that the children acquire in laboratory settings have already been achieved by the adults in their earlier experiences with motor tasks. Also, when the task used in the research is simple, it is possible that the adults already have at their disposal the rules (schemas) necessary to perform novel tasks whereas the children must learn some of the rules in the experimental setting. Here, then, variable practice is more effective for children than for the adults because the children have considerably "more to learn" than the adults.

Contextual Interference

The preceding section focused on practicing a number of task variations, compared to practice on only one task variation, as measured in retention and transfer tests (i.e., tests of learning). In this section we assume that variable practice is more useful for learning, and ask the question whether or not it makes a difference how the variable practice is *scheduled*.

Blocked Versus Random Practice

Research on the scheduling of practice for multiple tasks was popularized in the motor skills area with the study by Shea and Morgan (1979), although a few isolated studies of practice-scheduling effects had been published earlier (e.g., Pyle, 1919). The Shea and Morgan study was influenced considerably by the ideas of William Battig (see "William Battig and Contextual Interference"), and together, their work has made a substantial impact on research in motor learning and practical application to real-world skills. One of the main issues was the finding that variables that made the organization of practice more "difficult" during acquisition degraded performance during acquisition (not surprisingly), but also made performance in retention and transfer tests *more* effective. This latter effect was surprising and attracted considerable attention from researchers. Battig's notion was that *contextual interference*—which he defined as interference generated due to the context in which the skills were being practiced—produced decrements in performance during practice, but made the learning of these tasks more effective. This advantage for learning showed up in later tests of retention and transfer. Shea and Morgan (1979) operationalized Battig's notion of contextual interference in terms of the order of practice among several tasks during acquisition. Their notion was that, by randomizing the order in which several tasks were practiced, high levels of contextual interference would be generated, and the learning advantage of this interference would then be seen later in retention and transfer tests.

William Battig and Contextual Interference

Research on practice schedules owes a huge debt of gratitude to William F. Battig. Throughout a distinguished career, this cognitive psychologist maintained an interest in memory and learning, conducting studies using both verbal and motor tasks. Early in his research, Battig found that factors that make a task more "difficult" for the subject to perform actually enhanced remembering and transfer. For example, requiring (vs. not requiring) learners to pronounce nonsense "words" (e.g., XENF), whose letters corresponded to individual finger movements, made performance on *another* version of the finger task more effective (Battig, 1956).

Battig interpreted these and related findings in terms of the principle that "intertask facilitation is produced by intratask interference" (Battig, 1966, p. 227). *Intra*task interference referred to the performance decrement caused by attempting to keep multiple items in working memory at one time (e.g., the interference between the "word" pronunciations and the finger movements). By *inter*task transfer, Battig was referring to the beneficial transfer of learning to other motor tasks. These findings ran counter to intuition, as many researchers believed that transfer to other tasks would be strongest if the first task had been learned under the most optimal conditions for performance during practice.

But the field of psychology was not prepared to consider such radical ideas, perhaps because the concepts ran so counter to existing theories of memory and learning. Little attention was paid to Battig's ideas, even though he continued to publish more demonstrations of these counterintuitive findings (e.g., Battig, 1972; Hiew, 1977). A responsive chord was finally struck with the publication of Battig's expanded ideas on *contextual interference*. In this paper (Battig, 1979), he presented a wider framework that conceptualized the findings he had accumulated over the years. These ideas were expanded shortly thereafter to motor skill learning (Battig & Shea, 1980), where Battig's influence has made a very important mark.

Battig identified two important sources of interference that could arise during practice. One factor related to the *order* in which multiple items were studied or practiced. If the same task was practiced repeatedly, then only this one task needed to be held in working memory, and interference should be *low*. However, if practice involved frequent switching among multiple tasks, then interference should be *higher*. This source of interference has been the object of considerable study and is the focus of the present discussion on contextual interference. The other source of interference was the nature of the material to be practiced. If the items (or motor tasks) were quite similar, then the interference arising during practice would be *high* because of the increased confusion among them. Items or tasks that were quite different or distinct would cause lower interference. Battig showed that the presence of these factors both (a) degraded performance in acquisition and (b) facilitated performance in retention, transfer, or both.

Above all, the most important element of the contextual interference arising from a set of tasks or items to practice was *how the learner responded to the interference*. Battig suggested that subjects respond to situations of high or low interference with correspondingly high or low levels of elaborative and distinctive processing (which are effortful). These ideas have been expanded for motor behavior and motor learning by John Shea and his colleagues; today, they represent an important account of the contextual-interference effect.

In their study, Shea and Morgan (1979) used two kinds of practice sequences in acquisition, and learners practiced three different tasks. *Blocked practice* is a sequence in which all the trials on one task are done together, uninterrupted by practice on any of the other tasks. On the surface, a blocked practice sequence seems to make good "common sense," in that learners can concentrate on improving one task before moving on to the next task. For *random practice,* on the other hand, the same task is rarely repeated on consecutive trials. Notice that, in both practice sequences, the same number of trials is performed on each task, the only difference being the order in which the various task variations are presented. The task variations involved rapid arm movements to produce three different movement patterns, and were evaluated by measures of reaction time (RT) to initiate and the movement time (MT) to produce the pattern; total time (RT + MT) was also used. There were 54 trials in acquisition, 18 on each of the tasks. Retention and transfer tests were given after 10 min and 10 days, administered under both random and blocked conditions for different subgroups of subjects.

The Shea and Morgan results are shown in figure 11.14, here with total time as the dependent variable. The findings are very clear. Blocked practice resulted in an immediate performance advantage during acquisition compared to random practice (blocks 1-6, during acquisition, in figure 11.14). And, though the performance difference was reduced over blocks of trials, there remained an advantage favoring the blocked group at the end of practice.

The performances in the retention tests are presented on the right side of figure 11.14. Consider first the tests given under random conditions, seen as the solid lines in the figure; the first letter in the label gives the acquisition condition (R or B), and the second letter gives the retention condition (R or B). The group that received random practice in acquisition (R-R) far outperformed the group with blocked conditions in acquisition (B-R) in both the 10 min and 10-day random retention tests. That is, the performance advantage seen during acquisition was *reversed* when learning was assessed in these retention tests. Now examine the data for subjects in the blocked retention test (dotted lines). Here, the group with random conditions in acquisition (R-B) outperformed the group with blocked conditions in acquisition (B-B), but not by as large an amount as was seen for the R-R and B-R

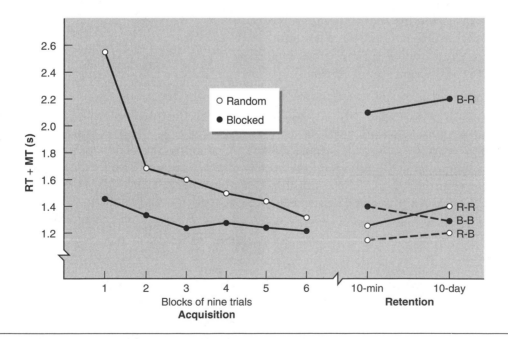

FIGURE 11.14 Blocked and random practice effects during practice and in various conditions of immediate and delayed retention.

groups. In summary, regardless of the scheduling in the retention trials, learning was always enhanced when practiced under random conditions. Random practice degraded performance in acquisition but facilitated learning. Similar findings were seen in transfer tests to novel patterns. These findings strongly supported Battig's ideas that contextual interference during practice would facilitate retention and transfer—that is, would facilitate learning.

These effects of blocked versus random practice on learning have been termed *contextual-interference effects* (or CI effects), based on Battig's original notions. However, notice that the CI manipulation is just one of many ways in which contextual interference could be generated or manipulated (or both) during practice (for reviews see Brady, 1998, 2004; Lee & Simon, 2004; Magill & Hall, 1990).

Generalizability of Contextual-Interference Effects

Issues about the *generalizability* of CI effects might be rephrased to ask the question, "How much faith should I put in the implications arising from the Shea and Morgan study?" Should random and blocked differences be expected to emerge under a variety of different conditions, using different tasks, for different subjects, and so on? Research suggests that, while there is overall rather wide generalizability, certain conditions tend to influence the size of the CI effect.

Task Influences

The original Shea and Morgan (1979) experiment used a laboratory task in which subjects were required to make rapid patterns of arm movements by knocking over small wooden barriers in response to a stimulus light. These findings have been replicated a number of times using similar task requirements (e.g., Del Rey, Liu, & Simpson, 1994; Lee & Magill, 1983b; Shea & Wright, 1991; Wright, 1991). Other laboratory studies have revealed similar results using tasks that emphasize the timing of actions (e.g., Lee & Magill, 1983b; Proteau, Blandin, Alain, & Dorion, 1994; Wulf & Lee, 1993), perceptual anticipation (e.g., Del Rey, 1989; Del Rey, Wughalter, & Whitehurst, 1982), force regulation (Enebo & Sherwood, 2005; Shea, Kohl, & Indermill, 1990; Shea, Shebilske, Kohl, & Gudadgnoli, 1991), force field adaptation (Osu, Hirai, Yoshioka, & Kawato,

2004; Overduin, Richardson, Lane, Bizzi, & Press, 2006), and error-detection capabilities (Sherwood, 1996), to list just a few.

Many studies of CI effects have used relatively simple laboratory tasks, leading some to suggest that the potential value of this research for practical situations would be greater if the findings were replicated in more complex tasks (e.g., Wulf & Shea, 2002). For example, Tsutsui, Lee, and Hodges (1998) showed that random practice facilitated the learning of new bimanual timing patterns—tasks that are difficult to acquire because of the inherent stability of competing in-phase and anti-phase patterns (see chapter 8). And Ollis, Button, and Fairweather (2005) found that random practice facilitated the learning of knot-tying skills, regardless of the complexity of the knots. In contrast, Albaret and Thon (1998) found that random practice facilitated learning only for a version of a drawing task that had the smallest number of component parts. No CI differences were found for the complex version of the task.

Despite some uncertainty about the role of task complexity, the typical CI effect has been replicated in a number of sport tasks (which are, arguably, more complex than laboratory tasks), such as badminton (Goode & Magill, 1986; Memmert, Hagemann, Althoetmar, Geppert, & Seiler, 2009; Wrisberg, 1991; Wrisberg & Liu, 1991), rifle shooting (Boyce & Del Rey, 1990), volleyball skills (Bortoli, Robazza, Durigon, & Carra, 1992), kayaking (Smith & Davies, 1995), snowboarding (Smith, 2002), and baseball batting (Hall, Domingues, & Cavazos, 1994). Moreover, it is important to note that CI effects have also been found in many other tasks as well, such as learning logic operations (Carlson & Yaure, 1990), automatic teller operations (Jamieson & Rogers, 2000), foreign language vocabulary (Schneider, Healy, & Bourne, 2002), artwork identification (Kornell & Bjork, 2008), and handwriting in children (Ste-Marie, Clark, Findlay, & Latimer, 2004).

In contrast to these replications of CI effects in "complex tasks" are a number of studies in which no differences were found, including investigations using tasks such as dart throwing (Meira & Tani, 2001; Moreno et al., 2003), volleyball skills (Jones & French, 2007), and gymnastics cartwheels (Smith, Gregory, & Davies, 2003). However, in most of these studies it was only rarely the case that blocked practice resulted in more learning than random practice (e.g., Shewokis &

Klopfer, 2000; see also Wulf & Shea, 2002, and a related discussion later in this section). In general, random practice has almost always been found to be as beneficial as, if not superior to, blocked practice for learning.

Subject Influences

In the preceding section we presented evidence that variability-of-practice differences were larger in children than in adults. The evidence relating to CI effects is not quite as clear, however, as some studies have shown these effects in children (e.g., Pollock & Lee, 1997; Ste-Marie et al., 2004; Wulf, 1991) whereas others have not (e.g., Brady, 2004; Del Rey, Whitehurst, & Wood, 1983; Jarus & Goverover, 1999; Pigott & Shapiro, 1984). There is some evidence that the magnitude of CI effects may also depend on experience. Del Rey and her colleagues have shown, for example, that transfer in an anticipation task after random practice is facilitated more for subjects with experience in open skills than for novices (Del Rey, 1989; Del Rey et al., 1982).

A particularly interesting finding was reported by Hall and colleagues (1994), whose subjects were college-level baseball players and thus already quite skilled at the task. All subjects performed two extra batting practice sessions

per week for six weeks. The batting sessions involved practice in which the pitcher threw 15 fastballs, 15 curves, and 15 change-ups. Groups of batters received these pitches in either a blocked or a random order over the entire six-week period. They also performed two transfer tests in which pitches were delivered in both random and blocked orders. The results are presented in figure 11.15, including the results for a control group that did not receive the extra batting practice. The control group performed more poorly on the transfer tests than did either practice group, suggesting that the extra batting practice was beneficial regardless of the order in which the pitches were thrown. However, the most interesting finding was the observed CI effect in practice and transfer. Notice in figure 11.15 that the performances of the blocked group on the blocked transfer test and of the random group on the random transfer test were nearly identical to their respective performances in the eighth practice session. It was when performance was assessed on the *common* transfer tests that the true value of the practice sequences in learning came through, as random practice facilitated transfer under both orderings of pitches. Thus, it would appear from this study that even highly skilled athletes benefited from random practice.

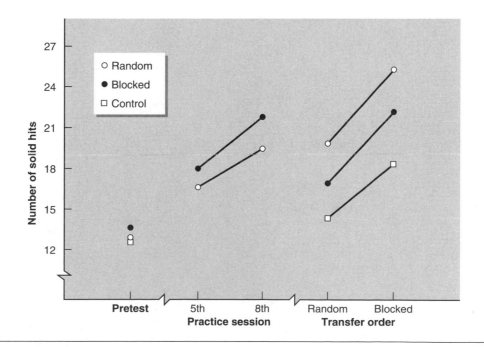

FIGURE 11.15 Blocked and random practice effects in baseball batting.

Reproduced and adapted from Figure 1 with permission of authors and publisher from: Hall, K.G., Domingues, D.A., & Cavazos, R. Contextual interference effects with skilled baseball players. *Perceptual and Motor Skills*, 1994, 78, 835-841. © Perceptual and Motor Skills 1994.

Other Practice Schedules

There are a wide variety of ways in which practice could be scheduled, given *X* tasks and *N* trials per task. Having *all* of the trials for one task performed in a drill-type sequence represents an extreme scheduling manipulation. Alternatively, *never* performing two consecutive trials on the same task might be considered the opposite extreme. A serial practice order might be considered "moderate," relative to these extremes, because it combines the predictability of blocked practice with the nonrepetitiveness of random practice (Lee & Magill, 1983b). In one study, however, as shown in figure 11.16, the performance of the serial group was nearly identical to that of the random group, leading to the suggestion that the lack of repetitiveness of random practice—and not its unpredictability—may be the key factor that both degrades acquisition performance and facilitates learning.

An important question is whether or not a practice schedule that represents some "middle ground" in terms of repetitiveness of practice might be beneficial to *both* performance and learning. Studies by Pigott and Shapiro (1984) and Al-Ameer and Toole (1993) support this possibility. In the Al-Ameer and Toole study, subjects practiced a task similar to that used by Shea and

Morgan (1979), under either random or blocked sequences. Results for both acquisition and retention replicated the Shea and Morgan findings. But Al-Ameer and Toole also added two groups that performed small, *randomized blocks of trials*, in which a subject would practice one task for two or three trials, then randomly switch to another task and practice that for two or three trials. This moderate CI condition, involving randomized blocks of either two or three trials, facilitated acquisition performance (relative to random practice), and was just as beneficial to learning as random practice. Landin and Hebert (1997) also found that serial alternation of blocks of trials was more effective than either blocked or random practice in the learning of basketball shooting skills.

These findings are important, as they suggest that it may be possible to reduce the acquisition performance decrement normally seen with random practice without sacrificing the long-term learning benefit as a consequence. The results are also important for applying the findings from these scheduling experiments to tasks involving daily activities. One obvious drawback with a completely random schedule is that constantly switching from one task to another may be impractical. For example, consider tasks that involve training a new worker on specific

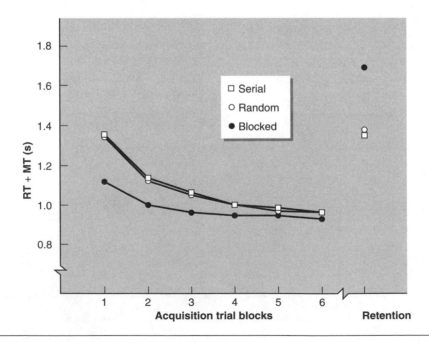

FIGURE 11.16 Comparison of blocked and random practice with a serial practice schedule.

Adapted, by permission, from T.D. Lee and R.A. Magill, 1983, "The locus of contextual interference in motor-skill acquisition," *Journal of Experimental Psychology: Learning, Memory, and Cognition*, 9: 739. Copyright © 1983 by the American Psychological Association.

job-related skills. If these tasks are performed in separate locations in a plant, it is logical to do at least *some* blocked practice before switching to a new task. The findings previously discussed regarding a randomized-blocks schedule suggest that this condition combines the positive effect in acquisition performance of a blocked practice with the beneficial learning effect of a random practice schedule.

Hypotheses on Contextual-Interference Effects

Before the first CI studies were published, learning researchers seemed to be quite satisfied with the general understanding that any practice variable that promoted effective performance in acquisition would also promote learning. The findings of Shea and Morgan (1979) caused many researchers to become much less comfortable with this general idea. How could a variable that slows improvement and retards the overall level of performance in practice be so potent in facilitating retention? This *performance–learning paradox* generated new thinking and debate, not only about why these scheduling effects occur, but also with regard to the motor learning process in general. Several hypotheses have been advanced to explain the advantages of random over blocked practice for learning. Though they may seem to present competing views, they probably have much in common to say about the learning process.

Elaborative Processing Hypothesis

One of these hypotheses, proposed by Shea and colleagues, holds that random practice forces the learner into more *elaborative* conceptual processing of the tasks to be learned (Shea & Morgan, 1979; Shea & Titzer, 1993; Shea & Zimny, 1983, 1988). During a random schedule, practice on one task is usually followed by practice on a completely different task. Thus, the preparation for action before movement and the evaluation of performance afterward may be quite different from the preparatory and evaluative processing that was completed on the previous trial. According to the elaborative processing view, random practice promotes more *comparative and contrastive* analyses of the actions required to complete these tasks. As a result, the representation of each task following random practice is more *memorable* than in blocked practice, in

which the opportunity for contrasting the different tasks is minimized because of the repetitive nature of the schedule. The advantages shown by random schedules in retention and transfer result from more *meaningful* representations of a given movement task and more elaborate distinctions between the various task versions (see also Kornell & Bjork, 2008).

Verbal reports from subjects involved in these experiments provide one line of evidence in support of the elaboration hypothesis. Post-experiment interviews indicated that subjects in the random condition understood the tasks in a qualitatively different way than did subjects who performed blocked practice (Shea & Zimny, 1983). Compared to those who had blocked practice, subjects in the random group reported a much larger number of elaborate mental representations for distinguishing the shapes of the various movement patterns (e.g., noting that one pattern was essentially a mirror image of another, or that a given pattern was the only one with a reversal in direction; Shea & Zimny, 1983). In contrast, subjects in the blocked group reported that they tended to run the movements off without much thought, more or less "automatically." Using a concurrent verbal report protocol, Zimny (reported in Shea & Zimny, 1988) found that subjects who were engaged in random practice made comments about specific tasks, as well as between-task comparisons, about twice as often as those engaged in blocked practice (see also Del Rey & Shewokis, 1993). These verbal report data support the enhanced contrastive value of random practice as predicted by the elaborative processing hypothesis.

A different type of support for the elaborative view was provided in a study in which physical practice trials were interspersed with three imagery practice trials (Gabriele, Hall, & Lee, 1989, experiment 1). For two groups, these imagery trials were performed on the task that had just been practiced physically (blocked imagery). In the other two groups, subjects imaged the three tasks, but these *had not* been performed on the preceding physical practice trial (random imagery). Regardless of whether the physical trials were practiced in a blocked or random order, random imagery facilitated retention more than blocked imagery, supporting the view that this contrastive processing during practice was beneficial for learning.

A more direct experimental manipulation of elaboration was examined in studies by Wright (1991; Wright, Li, & Whitacre, 1992). Using an arm movement task similar to that employed by Shea and Morgan (1979), four groups of subjects engaged in blocked practice. One group performed no additional processing, while subjects in the other groups performed selected cognitive activities between practice trials. After each practice trial, subjects in two of the groups were asked to describe verbally the order of movements of one of the tasks—either the task just completed or one of the other tasks. In the fourth group, subjects were asked to make specific comparisons between the task just performed and one of the other tasks. The prediction was that processing in this last condition would be most like the processing used by subjects in random practice. The prediction was supported, as subjects in the intertask processing condition were elevated in retention as compared to the other three groups. Interestingly, the additional processing in the other two groups with intervening cognitive descriptions did not improve retention at all, suggesting that the qualitative nature of the processing was more important than the quantity.

A more recent technique to study the elaboration hypothesis was introduced by Lin, Fisher, Winstein, Wu, and Gordon (2008; see also Lin, Winstein, Fisher, & Wu, 2010). They provided transcranial magnetic stimulation (TMS; see chapter 2) between blocked and random practice trials that was meant to prevent subjects from conducting elaborative processing. The typical CI effect was found for the control, blocked, and random practice groups. However, the random practice advantage was eliminated when TMS was applied between random practice trials. Lin and colleagues provided a strong rationale to support the argument that TMS prevented subjects in the random group from undertaking elaborative processing, thereby eliminating the CI effect.

Forgetting and Reconstruction Hypothesis

A different explanation for the CI effect was proposed by Lee and Magill (1983b, 1985). According to the *reconstruction* view, the action planning that occurs just prior to a practice trial is influenced by what has been done in the previous trial. In chapter 6, we presented the notion that in order to produce an action, the generalized motor program (GMP) must first be retrieved from long-term memory; it must be parameterized and otherwise readied for execution in the response-programming stage of information processing. Presumably only one action plan can be in working memory at a time.

In blocked practice, "action plan A" is constructed for task A and remains available in working memory for future trials on task A. However, since tasks are ordered intermittently in random practice, "action plan A" is no longer useful for the next task (say task B). Therefore, for the next trial, "action plan A" must be abandoned and "action plan B" must be prepared. When the random ordering determines that task A is to be performed again, the previously constructed "action plan A," which was abandoned from working memory, must be *reconstructed*. According to the hypothesis, the value of a practice trial depends on the reconstructive processing that was undertaken. Remembering the "solution" (the action plan) from a previous trial (as in blocked practice) promotes performance in acquisition, but does not promote the kind of processing that facilitates learning as measured in retention and transfer. In contrast, random practice causes a short-term "forgetting" of the action plan when a different task must be produced. This is detrimental to acquisition performance but beneficial to retention and transfer because it forces the subject to undertake reconstructive processing. Notice that this view of the CI effect is based on the same logic as a key explanation of the spacing effect in memory (see "When Forgetting Improves Remembering").

One prediction of the reconstruction view that has been empirically tested in a learning paradigm relates to the cause of short-term forgetting. The idea here is that on a given task, *any* activity between practice trials that causes short-term forgetting should promote learning. Note that this prediction is different from the elaborative processing view, which suggests that distinctiveness *increases* as the similarity of different tasks in working memory increases. Several studies have examined this prediction; the evidence, though not strong, has been generally positive in support of the reconstruction hypothesis (Lee & Magill, 1983a, 1987; Magill, 1988; Young, Cohen, & Husak, 1993).

A different approach to examining the reconstruction hypothesis was used in a study by Lee,

When Forgetting Improves Remembering

One of the puzzles about working memory is the curious statement that *"forgetting helps remembering"* (Cuddy & Jacoby, 1982). This statement sounds strange because forgetting (which we will discuss in chapter 14) is usually thought of as a *reduction* in the capability to remember; saying that "forgetting helps remembering" sounds like nonsense. However, the evidence from experiments on the *spacing effect* in verbal memory suggests that this statement is not as bizarre as it seems. In these experiments, subjects are typically given a long list of words that they are asked to study and recall some time later on a memory test. The list often comprises words presented only once, as well as words presented more than once. For the words presented more than once, they are sometimes repeated immediately (a zero "lag" condition) or at other times with a small or large number of words intervening between repetitions. The *spacing effect* refers to the finding that later recall of words that have been repeated with long lags is more effective than recall of words repeated with no lag or short lags.

Larry Jacoby (Cuddy & Jacoby, 1982; Jacoby, 1978; Jacoby & Dallas, 1981) proposed the idea that forgetting helps memory because the *processing* undertaken during study is determined by what is remembered about the material from the last processing of it. If the information is remembered well, then the material to be studied will not be fully processed on its second presentation. If the information has been forgotten, then the material will be more fully processed once again. The critical issue for Jacoby is that the value of a repetition lies in the degree to which it promotes full processing of the information on *each* presentation. Processing information is similar to solving a problem. The results of the processing constitute a solution, much like the solution obtained by multiplying two numbers together "in your head." If the same problem arises soon after the solution has been determined, then the mental arithmetic need not be undertaken again in order to solve the problem because the solution is readily available in working memory. However, if the solution has been forgotten, then full processing must be undertaken in order to solve the problem again. Memory, according to Jacoby, is a product of the processing activities. He summarized this idea when he wrote, "The means by which a solution is obtained influences subsequent retention performance: subsequent retention suffers when the solution is remembered" (Jacoby, 1978, p. 666).

Wishart, Cunningham, and Carnahan (1997). An important component of the prediction relates to the information in working memory when a trial is practiced. Instead of trying to induce short-term forgetting, Lee and colleagues attempted to introduce into working memory the information necessary for the upcoming trial's action plan by means of a model. If the action plan was provided by the model, then the problem-solving activity normally undertaken during random practice would be unnecessary, and the beneficial effects of random practice would be eliminated or at least reduced. The experimenters used a timing task, with subjects making patterns of key presses on a computer keyboard. The random and blocked practice groups performed in acquisition and retention as expected. A third, *random plus model* group also practiced in a random order; however, the computer generated a visual map of the task along with an auditory template of

the timing requirements, presented three times before each action.

The absolute constant error ($|CE|$) results are presented in figure 11.17. Two points of interest are noteworthy. First, even though practice was conducted in a random order, the performance of the group given modeled information was excellent. In fact, this random plus model group outperformed the blocked group on the very first block of practice trials. And, second, there was a strong negative influence of the model in immediate and delayed retention tests. The learning advantage normally seen following random practice was eliminated by the presence of the modeled information during practice. These findings were replicated and extended by Simon and Bjork (2002). In their study, the modeled information either matched the action plan requirements for the upcoming trial (as in Lee et al., 1997) or was inappropriate for the upcoming trial. The

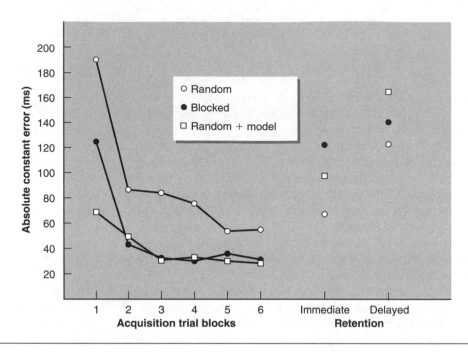

FIGURE 11.17 Elimination of the random practice decrement in practice and the random practice benefit in retention with a guiding model.

information provided by the inappropriate model was detrimental to acquisition performance but beneficial for retention, providing further evidence for the reconstruction hypothesis.

Another issue that is central to the reconstruction view deals with the nature of the planning activity. The hypothesis is that, for random practice, the action prepared for one task is inappropriate for a completely different task, and thus a new preparation is required. Experimenters have shown, for example, that more attentional capacity in general (Li & Wright, 2000) and motor programming time in particular (Immink & Wright, 1998, 2001) are required to prepare an action plan for an upcoming trial in random practice than in blocked practice. Measures of functional magnetic resonance imaging also show greater activity in the brain's planning regions in random practice (Cross, Schmitt, & Grafton, 2007). Research suggests also that random practice is more beneficial than blocked practice if task variations require learning different GMPs, or parameter learning when all tasks belong to the same GMP (Hall & Magill, 1995; Lee, Wulf, & Schmidt, 1992; Wulf & Lee, 1993). However, the evidence also suggests that blocked practice is more beneficial than random practice for relative timing learning

when only one GMP is practiced (Giuffrida, Shea, & Fairbrother, 2002; Lai & Shea, 1998; Lai, Shea, Wulf, & Wright, 2000; Shea, Lai, Wright, Immink, & Black, 2001). This latter result is inconsistent with the reconstruction view because it predicts that no differences between random and blocked practice should result. When only a rescaled action plan is required, the same relative timing can be maintained in memory on subsequent trials and little reconstructive process should be necessary (Magill & Hall, 1990; Lee et al., 1992).

Finally, Trachtman (2003) has used a paradigm that examines the benefit from the action planning per se. She used so-called "abort" trials, in which the action is planned and readied but at the last second is not executed. According to the reconstruction view, if the number of executed trials is held constant, additional abort trials should be beneficial to learning because of additional reconstructions provided. Trachtman's data fail to provide any evidence for the benefits of abort trials, however, and thus offer no support for the reconstruction view.

Evaluating the Hypotheses

On balance, there appears to be considerable support for both the elaborative processing account and the reconstruction view of the CI effect, although neither is able to explain all of the findings that now exist on the topic. One of the problems in comparing these hypotheses is that there are few situations in which different predictions can be contrasted. Thus, the hypotheses should not necessarily be seen as *competing* predictors of the CI effect, but perhaps rather as complementary theoretical views about the ways in which learners comply with the processing operations encouraged under different practice and task conditions.

Other Hypotheses

Of course, it is possible that both the elaboration and the reconstruction views are wrong. Wulf and Schmidt (1994a) argued that random practice is beneficial for learning because it makes response feedback (KR) *less useful* during practice—which, as we will discuss in chapter 12, is often an effective strategy for learning. Others have suggested that the detrimental effect in retention occurs because of greater *retroactive inhibition:* The early tasks practiced by the blocked group are more difficult to recall because of the interference caused by practicing the other tasks in the interim (Del Rey et al., 1994; Shea & Titzer, 1993). Another view downplays the role of cognitive factors and suggests instead that CI effects reflect a "difficulty" arising from an interaction among factors that include the learner, the task, and the environment (Davids, Button, & Bennett, 2008; Ollis et al., 2005). Lastly, some researchers have modeled these effects using a *connectionist* approach (Horak, 1992; Masson, 1990; Shea & Graf, 1994).

Practical Implications

Regardless of the theoretical explanation for these curious effects, it is clear that they are present in both laboratory and practical situations, that they lead to relatively large effects in learning, and that they should have important practical implications for the design of learning environments in sport, industry, and therapy. The "traditional" methods of continuous drill on a particular action (i.e., practicing one skill repeatedly until it is correct) are probably not the most effective way to learn. Rather, the evidence suggests that practicing a number of tasks in some nearly randomized order will be the most successful means of achieving the goal of stable retention and transfer. Of course, these findings highlight the learning–performance

distinction discussed earlier in this and the preceding chapter. Here we have a situation for which the conditions in acquisition that make performance most effective (blocked practice) are *not* the most effective for learning—an important general consideration for those designing workable practice sessions (Bjork, 1994; Schmidt & Bjork, 1992). Although the application for these ideas is strongly implicated (Dempster, 1988; Goettl, 1996), much work remains to be done on these issues with more complex tasks (Wulf & Shea, 2002) and various training settings before we can be confident about how to effectively apply these principles.

Two Caveats

If, indeed, beneficial effects of random practice are found to be useful for training settings, then another problem will need to be considered. In their research discussed earlier, Simon and Bjork (2001, 2002) asked their subjects during practice and just prior to retention to predict their level of success in performance on the delayed retention test. If subjects were aware that performance effects are misleading as predictors of retention, we would expect subjects in a blocked practice group to realize that their expected performance in retention would be poor. However, as illustrated in figure 11.18, Simon and Bjork (2001) found that this was not the case at all. Rather, blocked practice resulted in overestimated levels of retention—error in retention was more than *double* what had been predicted just prior to the retention trials (compare the open and filled circles in retention). This finding underscores a persistent problem, that performance effects are often mistaken for learning effects (Bjork, 1994). As a result of this problem, it is difficult to encourage students, instructors, and other training program organizers to use practice conditions that *appear* to be ineffective for learning during the training period. The implications are that some explanation *about* the learning process may be critical before the effects of CI and other practice-related phenomena can be successfully employed in training settings.

But, let's consider one more conundrum before ending this section. Presumably, if learners were poor judges of their own learning, then allowing them to regulate their own practice schedules would probably result in considerable blocked practice, and very little random practice. That seems to be true for some individuals. However,

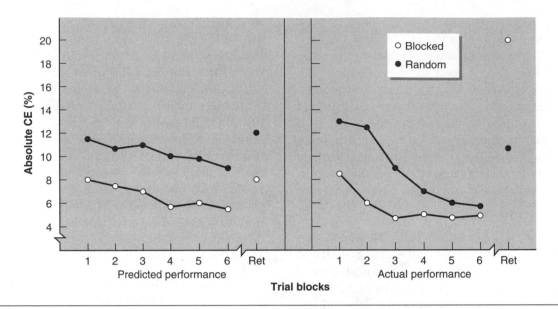

FIGURE 11.18 Effects of blocked and random practice for actual and predicted levels of performance and retention.

Adapted, by permission, from D.A. Simon and R.A. Bjork, 2001, "Metacognition in motor learning," *Journal of Experimental Psychology: Learning, Memory, and Cognition* 27: 910. Copyright © 2001 by the American Psychological Association.

some tend to choose a more random schedule and some a series of "mini-blocks" of trials; still others choose a progression from blocked to random practice (Keetch & Lee, 2007; Wu, 2007). However, regardless of the specific nature of the schedule that individuals choose, the very fact that they have self-regulated their own practice appears to provide a boost to learning when compared to yoked controls and experimenter-determined schedules. These findings offer a tantalizing suggestion that perhaps the optimal variability in learning multiple tasks occurs when it is self-determined by the learner (see also the section of self-regulated augmented feedback in chapter 12). Adaptive, or learner-contingent, schedules have also been explored recently as a means to tailor the schedule to the needs of the learner (Huang, Shadmehr, & Diedrichson, 2008; Choi, Qi, Gordon, & Schweighofer, 2008; Simon, Lee, & Cullen, 2008). We predict that the success of these types of practice schedules will be determined when the subject's long-term (learning) interests are tailored to the schedule, rather than to the interests of immediate performance gains.

Part Versus Whole Practice

A common technique for teaching motor skills is to break them down into smaller parts. Several reasons exist for breaking down tasks. One is to eliminate the burden of repeating the simpler parts of the entire task, and another applies when the task is very complex and cannot be grasped as a whole. Examples are numerous, such as practicing separately the arm and leg strokes in Red Cross swimming methods and practicing specific stunts in gymnastics that later become part of a larger routine. The ultimate test of whether or not these methods are effective is the amount of transfer from practice of the parts to the performance of the whole task. It seems obvious that if practice is given on the part, it would certainly transfer highly to the whole task, as the part would seem to be identical to one element of the whole. The problem with this idea is that practice on the part in isolation may change the motor programming of the part, so that for all practical purposes it is no longer the "same" as it is in the context of the total skill. The research suggests that whether or not part practice or whole practice is effective depends largely on the nature of the task (Wightman & Lintern, 1985).

Serial Tasks

Seymour (1954) conducted extensive research on industrial tasks that are serial in nature. One task consisted of a series of elements to be performed on a lathe. Some of the elements were difficult, requiring a great deal of practice to master; some were easy and could be accomplished on the first try. Seymour found that if the difficult parts were practiced separately, without any corresponding practice on the less difficult parts, there was considerable transfer of the part to the whole task. Similar findings were produced by Adams and Hufford (1962), who studied part practice of various discrete actions involved in aircraft flying, and Mané, Adams, and Donchin (1989), who studied multicomponent video games.

An interesting variation of the part-task technique was used by Dubrowski, Backstein, Abughaduma, Leidl, and Carnahan (2005) to train medical students in a surgical bone-plating task. This particular task involves multiple steps that are usually undertaken in a specific serial order. Practicing the parts of the task in the same order as required for surgery resulted in the most effective learning. However, Dubrowski and colleagues found that part practice was also effective, but only if repetitions of the parts were practiced in a random order—blocked practice severely degraded learning.

In some cases, transfer from part practice can be *greater than* 100%, meaning that the benefits afforded by some amount of practice on the parts in isolation can be greater than those obtained with an equal amount of time devoted to the whole task (see also Newell, Carlton, Fisher, & Rutter, 1989; Wightman & Sistrunk, 1987). One way of viewing these effects is that, in part-task practice, the learner does not have to spend time on the parts of the task that already have been mastered, and efficiency is improved because practice can be devoted to those parts of the task that need it most. The task can be reassembled in many ways, of course, but an efficient method is *backward chaining*, in which the last element in the sequence is systematically preceded by earlier and earlier parts until the whole chain is completed (Wightman & Lintern, 1985; Wightman & Sistrunk, 1987). Mere practice on a part isolated from the sequence does not appear to be as useful for transfer in serial tasks (Sheppard, 1984).

Continuous Tasks

For continuous tasks, in which the behavior continues more or less uninterrupted (as in walking or steering a car), the parts that can be isolated occur at the same time as other parts. This is, of course, in sharp contrast to the situation for serial tasks, in which discrete parts are sequentially organized. Also, in continuous tasks the parts must often be *coordinated* with each other; and breaking into this pattern of coordination to practice a part might not appear to be highly effective, as it is the coordination between the parts that must be learned. Swimming strokes have this characteristic, as the arm strokes, breathing, and kicking actions must be coordinated to form an effective whole.

Briggs and Brogden (1954) and Briggs and Waters (1958) used a lever-positioning task that required positioning in two dimensions (forward-backward, left-right) simultaneously and continuously, much like the positioning of the "joystick" that controls the motions of an airplane. They found that practice on the separate dimensions alone transferred to the whole task, but that this practice was less effective than practicing the whole task for the same period of time. It is possible that the most effective way to learn such tasks is to practice the whole, unless the task is highly complex or contains rather trivial elements.

Another situation that produces slightly different findings involves those tasks in which the parts *interact* while they are being performed simultaneously. As an example, one complex task involves the operations necessary to take a helicopter from the ground into flight. According to Zavala, Locke, Van Cott, and Fleishman (1965), the operator must handle four separate controls simultaneously. The first is a *cyclic pitch-control stick*, which is really a stick control for two dimensions in one (roll and pitch). When moved in a particular direction, it causes the helicopter to tilt in that direction. Thus, it can be used to control roll (side to side) and pitch (nose up or down) simultaneously. Second, a *collective pitch lever* is mounted to the left of the pilot, and up-and-down movements of this lever control the vertical component of the flight. Third, a *throttle* is located as a twist grip on the pitch control just mentioned; it controls the engine speed in the same way the accelerator in an automobile does. Fourth, *antitorque pedals* under the pilot's feet control the pitch of the small propeller at the tail of the helicopter, thus controlling its direction and compensating for the torque produced by the overhead rotors.

The problem for the person learning this task is that these components interact strongly. That is, when the throttle control is used to speed up the rotor or the pitch control is adjusted, there is a tendency for the helicopter to turn in the direction opposite the rotation of the rotor. This must be counteracted by an appropriately graded foot-pedal movement to maintain the proper heading. But also, the helicopter will increase its tendency to roll and attempt to dive; both of these motions must be counteracted by the adjustment of the cyclic-control stick. Thus, when the lift of the rotors is increased in the attempt to take off, *three* other adjustments must be made simultaneously to prevent it from turning upside down. The amount of control change in these three dimensions depends on the amount of lift that is imparted to the helicopter via the other pitch control. These control dimensions are said to *interact* because the setting of one of them depends on the setting applied to the others.

It would be tempting to take this highly complex task and break it down into separate parts. But this breakdown seems to sidestep the most important problem for the learner: how to *coordinate* these actions. Any one of the dimensions can easily be performed separately, but this practice would not seem to be very effective for learning the total task. In general, the limitations of part-to-whole transfer methods probably depend on the extent to which the parts of the task interact within the whole task. As for the helicopter, it would seem that an effective way to learn the task would be to practice in a ground-based simulator, where all dimensions would be learned together without the fear of an accident (see more on *simulators* in chapter 14).

Although experimental investigations of part–whole practice in learning to control a helicopter have not been conducted, the conclusions just mentioned are certainly supported by research on polyrhythm learning. Recall from chapter 8 that polyrhythms are complex bimanual timing sequences in which the rhythms tapped by the two hands have different metrical structures (the left hand tapping every 600 ms with the right hand tapping every 400 ms is an example of a 2:3 polyrhythm that has a simultaneous tap every 1,200 ms). Studies have shown that part-task training, in which the rhythms of each hand are practiced separately, results in virtually no transfer to the performance of the polyrhythm (Klapp, Martin, McMillan, & Brock, 1987; Klapp, Nelson, & Jagacinski, 1998; Summers & Kennedy, 1992; see Summers, 2002, for a review). An exception to

this finding was a study by Kurtz and Lee (2003), who found that independently practicing the motor parts of the rhythm while simultaneously listening to *both* auditory streams was effective in learning the rhythmic structure of the whole task. This finding suggests that part-task practice may be effective in learning a continuous task that has a perceptual component.

Discrete Tasks

Can we apply this evidence about part versus whole practice to discrete tasks whose MTs are very short (e.g., less than 1 s)? Probably not, as the evidence gives a different picture in these situations. For example, Lersten (1968) had subjects learn a hand movement task (the rho task) that required a rapid movement with two components. The subject grasped a handle and rotated it in the horizontal plane through 270° until it hit a stop, whereupon the subject was to release the handle and move forward to knock over a barrier. This was to be done as quickly as possible (MTs were about 600 ms). Thus, a circular component was followed by a linear component, both of which were practiced separately by part-practice groups. Another group of subjects practiced only the whole task. Lersten found that practice on the circular component alone transferred only about 7% to the performance of the circular phase in the context of the whole task. Other conditions produced no transfer to the whole task. Even more important, Lersten found that the practice on the linear component alone transferred *negatively* (about –8%) to the whole task. That is, practicing this linear component in isolation produced less transfer to the whole task than not practicing at all! Overall, the findings suggest that practicing these isolated components of the whole task produced essentially negligible transfer to the performance of the whole task.

Sequential Parts

How can these findings be explained? First, even though the task Lersten used was "serial" in nature, it must be seen as quite different from the serial tasks used by Seymour (1954) and others reviewed previously. One clear difference relates to the overall MT—Seymour's tasks had durations in the order of minutes, and Lersten's task lasted for only about 600 ms. It seems reasonable to assume that Lersten's task was governed by a single motor program that contained the instructions for both the circular and the linear components, as well as the instructions for the transition between the two (timing the release of the handle, for example). If so, then practicing the circular part in isolation would result in the subject's practicing a program different from that involved in the circular part within the context of the whole skill, because the isolated circular part did not entail a handle release. In contrast, the serial tasks that Seymour (1954) used might be thought of as a series of programs that have been strung together. Practicing one of them in isolation is the same as practicing that program in the context of the total skill, so part-to-whole transfer should be high from this perspective.

These ideas suggest that the major determinant of whether or not part-to-whole transfer will be effective is the extent to which the movement is governed by a single program. If the movement is very fast, it will almost certainly be governed by one motor program, and it should be practiced as a whole. Second, if the movement is slower but there is a "break" in the action that is easily adjusted, it is possible that the movement is governed by more than one program. An example is the break between the toss action and the hit action in a tennis serve; the toss seems programmed, but then there is a feedback-based break so that the hit program can be adjusted to the exact location and timing of the ball toss. In a springboard dive, the takeoff and tuck are probably programmed, but the timing of the "untuck" movements might be feedback based, determined by visual or vestibular information. These tasks could probably be split into their component parts for separate practice, and part-to-whole transfer would probably be higher.

Simultaneous Parts

A second situation occurs when the parts of the task are simultaneous, rather than serial as in Lersten's task. Many examples exist, such as playing the piano (left and right hands) or any other task for which one part of the body has to be coordinated with another. Transfer research on these questions is nearly nonexistent, though, and the decisions about part–whole transfer are mostly speculative.

First, it seems from the data presented in chapter 8 that rapid, discrete two-handed simultaneous movements must be controlled by a single program, with the program containing instructions for both hands (Heuer, Schmidt, & Ghodsian, 1995). Practicing the movements of one hand in isolation probably results in the development of a different program than practicing that "same" movement in the context of a total two-handed skill. For example, data from Konzem (1987) suggest that the motor program to make a V with the right hand is probably different from the program required to make a V with the right hand and γ with the left hand simultaneously. The principles underlying coordination of the separate limbs in an action are not well understood, and more work on this is needed; but it seems clear that breaking down a task into its components will not always result in large part-to-whole transfer.

Lead-Up Activities

A closely related question for the teaching of skills concerns the use of so-called lead-up activities. In these situations, certain simpler tasks are thought to be in some way fundamental to the learning of more complex tasks, so the simpler tasks are formally taught as a part of the procedure for learning the more complex task. These procedures are often used in gymnastics as the instructors talk of a progression of subtasks leading eventually to the complex goal action. The question can be thought of as one of transfer from the lead-up task to the goal movement. Such activities might have the disadvantage of being, by necessity, different from the goal action, and the motor transfer from them could be very small.

On the other hand, lead-up activities may have many positive aspects. Recall from our discussion earlier in the chapter that one effective "off-task" practice activity involves perceptual training, such as watching videos of opponents in open-skill sports. In this case, learning to use advance perceptual cues to anticipate a temporal or spatial event can facilitate the motor response process. Research shows that perceptual learning in the absence of overt motor responses can be an effective training technique.

Additionally, in many tasks (e.g., stunts in gymnastics) there is a strong element of fear. Lead-up activities, being simpler and less dangerous, may serve a useful role in reducing fear responses that can be detrimental to learning a more complex movement. This fear-reduction aspect is borne out in studies using "desensitization techniques," whereby people are taught to eliminate phobic responses (e.g., fear of snakes, or heights) by performing lead-up activities that bring them closer to the target fear (e.g., progressively more "realistic" snakes, eventually leading to an actual snake; see Bandura, 1969, or Bandura, Blanchard, & Ritter, 1969). Also, many lead-ups are designed with a particular action in mind. In gymnastics, again, the "kipping" action (a forceful, timed extension of the hip) is thought to be involved in a large number of skills. The idea is that learning to kip in one simple lead-up activity possibly will transfer to the "same" action in a more complex and dangerous activity.

Guidance

A technique frequently used in teaching and in rehabilitation involves *guidance*, whereby the learner is physically assisted through the task to be learned. Guidance refers to a variety of separate procedures, including physically pushing and pulling the learner through a movement sequence, preventing incorrect movements by means of physical limitations on the apparatus, or even verbally "talking someone through" a new situation. These guidance procedures tend to prevent the learner from making errors in the task.

What does the evidence on guidance suggest? Much of the early research on guidance by Holding (1970; Holding & Macrae, 1964; Macrae & Holding, 1965, 1966), Singer (1980; Singer & Pease, 1976; Singer & Gaines, 1975), and others (reviewed by Armstrong, 1970a), using various tasks and guidance procedures, showed considerable positive effects of guidance procedures on performance during acquisition. We should remember, however, that guidance almost certainly would usually have strong effects on *performance* during the trials in which it is administered. By its very nature, a guidance technique is a method that will prevent or severely limit the occurrence of errors. Of course, as we have discussed previously, performance gains during acquisition may not represent relatively permanent changes attributable to learning, and the important question is whether such performance gains will survive in a transfer test when the guidance is removed.

One of the definitive studies in this area was performed by Armstrong (1970b). He compared various forms of physical guidance in a task for which the learner was to make an elbow movement having a complex spatial–temporal pattern (see figure 6.21), with MTs of 3 or 4 s. Three of his groups are of specific interest here. One group practiced the task and received terminal, kinematic feedback (knowledge of performance, KP) after each trial. In addition, after the last in a block of 15 trials, subjects in this group were shown a plot of their last trial in combination with a template of the goal pattern. Another group was given concurrent, real-time visual feedback of the movement together with a perfect template of the goal movement. In a third group, the movement device moved by the subject was mechanically controlled such that deviations from the target path were physically restricted. Practice was conducted over three days, which also included a transfer test on the third day during which all subjects performed the task with no augmented information.

The results, presented in figure 11.19, were very dramatic. As can be seen, the guidance device restricted errors so that performance was nearly perfect throughout the entire practice period. The concurrent feedback was also quite effective in reducing performance error during practice, but clearly not as effective as the guidance device (although much more so than the terminal feedback). But Armstrong's results showed that the guidance effects provided only temporary boosts to performance. As can be seen on the right side of figure 11.19, the transfer trials were performed most accurately by the terminal-feedback group and very poorly by both the guidance- and concurrent-feedback groups. In fact, the latter two groups performed the transfer trials at almost the same level of performance as had the terminal KP group early in practice. Together with other results (e.g., Domingo & Ferris, 2009; Schmidt & Wulf, 1997; Singer & Pease, 1976), Armstrong's findings raise considerable doubt about the benefits of guidance techniques as learning aids.

There is research however, suggesting that *some* guidance can be beneficial when interspersed with active practice trials (Hagman, 1983; Sidaway et al., 2008; Winstein, Pohl, & Lewthwaite, 1994) or when used with complex tasks (Tsutsui & Imanaka, 2003; Wulf & Toole, 1999). Still other research has used guidance that is less physically restrictive than many traditional types of physical guidance. For example, a

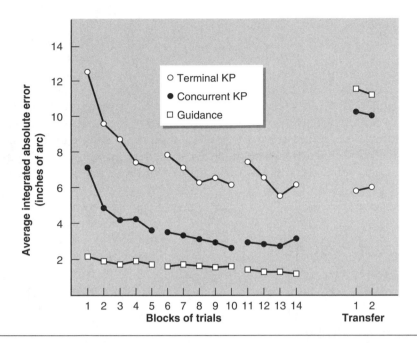

FIGURE 11.19 Comparison of physical guidance with terminal- and concurrent-feedback effects on acquisition and transfer.

Adapted from T.R. Armstrong, 1970, "Training for the production of memorized movement patterns," *Technical Report* 26: 15.

computer-operated steering mechanism allowed subjects in a study by Marchal Crespo and Reinkensmeyer (2008) to manipulate a wheelchair around a virtual environment under three training conditions: no guidance, fixed guidance, or a guidance-as-needed condition. This latter condition permitted subjects to perform the task without restriction until a tolerance for error in performance was reached, at which time the computer provided haptic guidance as it physically corrected the tracking device. This condition also eased the tolerance limits as proficiency on the task improved over trials.[3] Marchal Crespo and Reinkensmeyer found that providing some guidance without eliminating all errors provided positive transfer performance when all guidance was removed, as contrasted with the fixed-guidance and no-guidance conditions. These findings offer strong promise for the use of computers and robots in the training of functional motor skills (Reinkensmeyer & Patton, 2008) and in rehabilitative settings (Reinkensmeyer, Emken, & Cramer, 2004).

These various findings permit a number of tentative generalizations about guidance. First, guidance may be effective in early practice when the task is unfamiliar to the learners. Much of the apparent contribution of guidance procedures is involved in getting the movement "into the ballpark" so that later refinements can be made. Second, guidance may be most effective for tasks that are very slow in time (e.g., matching some perceived state such as a force or a position). Presumably guidance gives the learner an indication of the nature of the state that is to be matched, so that movements may be adjusted to match this state later. Direct and indirect lines of evidence, however, suggest that guidance will be less effective for tasks that are rapid and ballistic or for tasks that involve the learning of motor programs (e.g., Armstrong's spatial–temporal pattern).

A final aspect of guidance that is rarely studied is the prevention of injury and reduction of fear. As with Marchal Crespo and Reinkensmeyer's "guidance-as-needed" robot, providing guidance that is relatively "loose" until the individual produces an error can also be an effective way to help people learn a dangerous task. Gymnasts use manual assistance and spotting belts regularly to ensure that a mistake will not result in a serious fall. Similar "techniques" are used by parents when their children begin to ride a bicycle without the training wheels. An adult running down the street beside the child, either with a guiding hand or without, is an easily recognizable image of "guidance as needed." Such procedures provide a great deal of confidence for learners and are highly effective in reducing the fear and potential disruptions in skill learning. The key feature is that guidance is minimal, while fear of injury is nearly eliminated. Even so, there remains the problem of the guidance serving as a "crutch," so that when it is removed there will be a marked reduction in the skill level. Gymnasts say that it is difficult to perform a risky new skill "out of the spotting belt" for the first time, as the performer knows that now a mistake could cause a serious injury. Even so, it would seem that there is no substitute for practicing the skill on your own as soon as it is safe to do so.

Principles of Practice Specificity

Many of the issues addressed in this chapter reveal a common dilemma for those designing practice settings—deciding how to establish performance conditions in the acquisition phase that will best prepare the learner for the conditions under which the learning will be applied. The general hypothesis—that we should attempt to match those conditions in practice with those expected in the "test" performance—is an old one, based on empirical evidence and common sense. In motor behavior research it has been called the *specificity of learning hypothesis* (e.g., Barnett, Ross, Schmidt, & Todd, 1973), stemming from Henry's (1958/1968) work on individual differences (see chapter 9). The view holds that because skills are very specific (i.e., generally uncorrelated with each other), changing the conditions under which a task is performed will require a substantial shift in the underlying abilities. Therefore, because practicing a task under one set of conditions and then performing it as a criterion task under different conditions would require a shift in abilities, the conditions in practice and "test" can be equated whenever possible. However, note that similar ideas exist in the psychology of learning, originating with Thorndike's theory of identical elements (Thorndike, 1906; see also Healy, Wohldmann, Sutton, & Bourne, 2006).

Although this straightforward principle is very robust—that practice conditions should match the conditions expected later in retention or transfer—it is worthwhile to recall evidence presented earlier in the chapter that seems to violate this specificity effect. For example, distributed-practice conditions were superior for retention

than massed practice when the retention trials were conducted in a distributed fashion (which is consistent with specificity predictions), but also when the retention trials were *massed* (Bourne & Archer, 1956). Also, recall that random practice produced superior retention performance relative to blocked practice under conditions in which retention trials were either blocked or randomly ordered (e.g., Shea & Morgan, 1979). Both of these findings are opposite to a strict specificity prediction.

What is happening here? We suggest that these different practice effects are related to different types of specificity phenomena that emerge as a function of the interaction between conditions of practice and the conditions of retention (or transfer). We discuss different types of specificity next.

Sensory and Motor Specificity

Some motor learning researchers suggest that the internal representations for skills that are developed with practice are very specific to the conditions of practice. These effects are illustrated nicely in a series of studies by Proteau and his colleagues in which subjects aimed a stylus at a target (Proteau, 1992, 1995). Subjects in different conditions practiced this task with KR for varying numbers of trials (ranging from very few trials to several days of practice); they were then asked to perform transfer trials without KR. Various practice conditions were used that manipulated the amount of inherent visual feedback the subject was able to gather before, during, and after the movement. These conditions ranged from full vision of the subject's arm, the stylus, and the target, at one extreme, to conditions in which no visual feedback was provided. Various visual conditions have been included in other experiments (e.g., Blandin, Toussaint, & Shea, 2008; Elliott, Lyons, & Dyson, 1997; Proteau, 2005; Proteau & Isabelle, 2002; Soucy & Proteau, 2001; Tremblay & Proteau, 1998). In general, these studies show that, after practice, if the transfer test has required subjects to perform without visual feedback or vision of the target only, then the groups that perform the best are the ones that learned the task with the least amount of vision during practice. Typically, the weakest performance is by the group that had the most vision available during practice.

These findings may not seem too surprising, as we know that vision tends to dominate all other sensory modalities when it is available. Thus, when practicing with vision the subject may come to rely on its availability to support performance, and then will suffer when performing in the absence of vision. However, Proteau and his colleagues took their research one step further, showing that when vision was *added* in transfer, performance deteriorated considerably for the groups that had performed in the absence of vision during practice (Proteau, Marteniuk, & Lévesque, 1992). Findings such as these have led Proteau and colleagues to suggest that learning involves a sensorimotor representation that integrates the motor components with the sensory information available during practice. This representation results in specificity during transfer such that performance is optimized when the conditions during transfer require the same sensorimotor representation that was learned in practice.

Although the topic is not often discussed in relation to *motor learning,* there is evidence from exercise physiology studies that show a similar effect. For example, there are generally large specificity effects when training and performance comparisons involve the same types of exercise (e.g., isometric and concentric exercise), the same ranges of motion, and to a lesser degree, the same movement velocity (Morrissey, Harman, & Johnson, 1995; Sale & MacDougall, 1981). Physiological specificity effects have also been found by experimenters who manipulated levels of *arousal* in practice and retention (e.g., Movahedi, Sheikh, Bagherzadeh, Hemayattalab, & Ashayeri, 2007), suggesting that this practice for this type of specificity effect might represent a way to offset some of the test performance detriments due to "choking" (Oudejans & Pijpers, 2009).

Context Specificity

A logic similar to that in Proteau's research methods has been used to examine specificity of practice conditions in a more general way. This research has been done often in psychology and reveals a kind of "mixed bag" of specificity effects. For example, various environmental factors that compose a study *context* (room temperature, color, etc.) have an influence on remembering the information that has been learned. When a person attempts to recall the information later (e.g., in an exam), the same contextual information, if present, can serve as cues to help retrieve the information (Davies & Thomson, 1988; Smith & Vela, 2001).

The evidence for context specificity in motor learning is not abundant, although it does appear to be consistent with the general set of findings in cognitive psychology. For example, subjects in a study by Wright and Shea (1991) learned sequences of key-press patterns, with the computer monitor providing stimulus cues specific to each pattern (i.e., the information about which keys to press was presented in different colors, shapes, and positions on the screen and was accompanied by auditory cues specific for each pattern). Performance in retention was maximized when the cues were matched with the same patterns as had been practiced, leading to the conclusion that the stimulus information provided a *context* that was learned as part of the representation for the movement sequence (see also Wright & Shea, 1994).

A possible relation of this research to practical experience is the so-called *home advantage* in sport. A finding that appears in many team sports is that a higher proportion of wins (or points) is achieved when playing at home than when playing on the road. This finding has been well documented in the literature: It has been remarkably consistent for many years, across the various major team sports, and is found at both the college and professional levels (Carron, Loughhead, & Bray, 2005; Courneya & Carron, 1992). Several potential hypotheses for the home advantage seem to be ruled out, such as effects of travel, crowd size, and crowd aggressiveness. But it appears that one factor that cannot be ruled out is related to the idea of context specificity—that certain factors related to the court or field on which the game is played (and on which the home team practices) provide a home advantage. Perhaps the contextual information provided by the surroundings of the practice area constitutes a small advantage when games are played in the same venue. This hypothesis must be viewed quite cautiously, however, as the evidence that lends support to it is not strong (e.g., Pollard, 1986).

Transfer-Appropriate Processing

The specificity effects presented in the preceding sections seem to provide some guidelines for establishing determinants of the effectiveness of practice, when considered in light of the conditions under which retention or transfer will be conducted. However, trying to anticipate the conditions of retention or transfer, and then matching practice conditions to them, is often difficult if not impossible in the real world. A rather different kind of specificity in *learning* has to do with the *processing* that a learner undertakes during practice.

The concept of "transfer-appropriate processing" was first suggested by Morris, Bransford, and Franks (1977; Bransford, Franks, Morris, & Stein, 1979; see also Lee, 1988). The idea is that the effectiveness of practice activities can be evaluated only in relation to the goals and purposes of the transfer or retention test. That is, conditions in practice are said to be effective to the extent that they engage processing that is *appropriate* for performance on the retention or transfer test. We can evaluate "relative amount learned" only with respect to some particular transfer task or particular transfer conditions; acquisition conditions that might be effective for one transfer test might be ineffective for another because they stress different kinds of information-processing activities.

Evidence of transfer-appropriate processing was seen in a number of instances in this chapter. Distributed practice is more effective than massed practice for retention under both distributed and massed retention trials. Variable practice can be more effective for retention of a specific task than specific practice on that task alone. Random practice is usually more effective than blocked practice for both random and blocked retention orders. And we also saw that observational learning can be enhanced by watching a learning model (a model who is actually learning) as compared to an expert model (e.g., McCullagh & Caird, 1990; figure 11.6). The transfer-appropriate processing view explains this latter finding as follows: The observer sees how the learning model attempts to perform the task, receives information about the results of the model's performance, and sees how the model uses that information to make adjustments on the next attempt. In other words, the observer is drawn into the *same problem-solving process* that she will encounter when actually performing the task (Adams, 1986). In contrast, observing an expert engages the observer in a kind of processing that will be very different from the processing involved in the trial-and-error, problem-solving activities one performs when attempting to learn the motor skill.

The notion of transfer-appropriate processing addresses more than just the contextual or incidental similarities between practice and retention or transfer situations. Processing specificity suggests that it is the similarity of the underlying *processes* (not simply the *conditions*) between acquisition and transfer that will be the critical determinant of the effectiveness of practice. In these cases, the most effective practice conditions are those that require subjects to practice and learn the same underlying *processes* that will be ultimately used in the retention or transfer test. That is, practice will be most effective if it fosters the processes most appropriate to performance on the transfer test. Sometimes, of course, when the superficial environmental conditions described by the specificity of learning hypothesis are the same in practice and transfer, the underlying processes are the same as well. But often this is not the case.

In relation to all the practice variables noted previously, though the superficial conditions in acquisition versus transfer may differ, the gain provided by learning some new appropriate processing capability overshadows any switch in conditions, so that the overall result is improved performance on the transfer test. This hypothesis of processing specificity does not identify the nature of the appropriate processes learned in acquisition, however, and these still must be discovered by research.

Summary

This chapter deals with the major independent variables that affect the learning of motor skills and thus those variables that influence the design of instructional programs. Of most importance is the amount of practice itself, as illustrated by the law of practice. But one can do a considerable amount of learning apart from physically practicing a motor skill. Much of this learning involves the performer's trying to figure out what to do. Methods that engage the learner in information-processing activities and encourage problem solving will likely benefit learning, especially when used later in on-task practice. Procedures involving mental practice, perceptual training, and observational learning have all been shown to be effective "off-task" methods that facilitate learning.

The structure of practice also has very important influences on learning. Distributed practice facilitates performance and learning more than massed practice does, although these effects seem to be stronger for the learning of continuous tasks.

Practice sequences in which the task conditions are deliberately varied from trial to trial are slightly more effective than constant-practice conditions for adults and far more effective for children. Randomly ordered practice is detrimental to performance as compared to blocked practice, but facilitates retention and transfer. Decisions about whether to break down a task into its component parts for practice, or whether to practice the task as a whole, depend entirely on the nature of the task. If practicing the parts means changing the task itself, then whole practice will probably be more effective. And guidance can be a useful aid in some situations, but overuse of guidance techniques can also be detrimental to learning.

We have emphasized often that the value of practice sessions must be assessed in tests of retention and transfer. Complicating this evaluation of learning is the fact that performance in these tests is influenced by the relationship between the nature of practice conditions and the nature of the retention and transfer conditions. Specificity in learning suggests that the sensory, motor, contextual, and processing activities of the retention and transfer tests influence to a considerable extent the "value" that we attribute to certain practice conditions.

Student Assignments

1. Prepare to answer the following questions during class discussion:
   a. Describe one task that might be expected to benefit from distributed practice and another task that might be expected to benefit from massed practice.
   b. Describe an "alternative" practice schedule that combines the benefits to performance and learning that are typical of blocked and random practice.
   c. Describe the learning of two industrial tasks, one that would be expected to benefit more from part practice and another that would be expected to benefit more from whole practice.

2. Find a research article that examines the effects of mental practice in the performance or learning of a sport skill.

Web Resources

Distribution of practice in baseball:

http://baseballtips.com/practice.html

Some principles of practice for sailboat racing:

www.sailingscuttlebutt.com/news/04/ras/

Notes

[1] Although we are not in favor of change (pretest-posttest) scores to measure learning (see chapter 10), here these scores are similar to absolute retention scores because there were no differences between groups in the pretest. Thus, the change scores are essentially an absolute-retention score with a constant subtracted.

[2] Note that these variable-practice trials were conducted in a *random order*. This factor will become an important variable, as discussed in the next section.

[3] Note that this guidance-as-needed condition provides a type of bandwidth augmented feedback that is faded over trials, discussed in greater detail in chapter 12.

AUGMENTED FEEDBACK

Oned of the most important features of practice is the information learners receive about their attempts to produce an action. Some of this information is inherent in the movement production; we have examined this kind of sensory information in chapter 5; we can also consider information that is presented in an "augmented" form from the instructor, therapist, or coach. This chapter deals with this latter form of information.

Classifications and Definitions

Consider, as the broadest class, all the various kinds of sensory information that people can receive, including all those sources that have to do with the many diverse aspects of our lives. Of course, not all such information is related to our movements: the sound of wind in the trees as we walk through a forest is not relevant in this respect. Of the sources of information that are related to our movements, we can speak of those available (a) before the action, (b) during the action, and (c) after the action. Before the action, sensory information signals the position of your limbs, the sight of a ball flying toward you, the nature of the environmental setting, and so on. During the action, you receive sensory informa-

tion produced by the movement, such as the way it feels, sounds, and looks. After the action is completed, information is available regarding the result that the movement produced in the environment (e.g., the actions of a ball that has been struck) and, for a brief time, a memory for the how the movement felt, sounded, and looked. This latter class of information is usually termed *movement-produced feedback,* or simply *feedback.* The term "feedback" can be further subdivided into two broad classes: *inherent* feedback (sometimes called "intrinsic" feedback) and *augmented* (sometimes called "extrinsic") feedback.

Inherent Feedback

People can gain information about many aspects of their own movements through various sensory mechanisms. These forms of information are *inherent* to the individual during the action, and result from the movement's execution. For example, you know that an error was made in a basketball shot because you saw that the ball did not go into the basket. Also, the stinging sensations as you land on your back in a pool after a faulty dive inform you that something probably went wrong. Just about every movement we can make has associated with it certain sources of inherent feedback that provide a basis for evaluating those movements. Such feedback is usually rich and varied, containing substantial information regarding performance. Depending on the nature of the movement and the source of inherent feedback, sometimes the performer knows that something has gone wrong before the movement is even completed. The information provided as the movement is executed is sufficiently useful that the movement outcome can often be predicted even before it occurs. At other times the nature of the movement and the source of feedback are such that the evaluation of the movement must occur after it is completed.

In many situations, inherent feedback requires almost no evaluation at all; one sees that the bat missed the ball or one can feel the fall while walking on an icy sidewalk. Thus, some errors seem to be signaled immediately and clearly. But other aspects of inherent feedback are not so easily understood, and perhaps the performer must *learn* to recognize their occurrence and evaluate what the feedback means. Examples might be the gymnast learning to sense whether or not the knees are bent during a movement, or a patient with a recent hip replacement who is learning to put partial weight through the leg while walking with canes. It is thought that inherent feedback is compared to a learned reference of correctness, with this reference acting in conjunction with the feedback in an error-detection process. Without such a reference of correctness, many forms of inherent feedback probably cannot be used to detect errors.

Augmented Feedback

In contrast to inherent feedback, *augmented feedback* is information provided about the action that is supplemental to, or that augments, the inherent feedback. For example, you can receive infor-

mation from a buzzer when your car's engine exceeds a certain temperature—information that is not normally available during driving. Augmented information can be provided verbally, for example in the presentation of one's time after a 100 m race or the set of scores after a gymnastics or ice skating routine. Even though these various forms of information are not strictly verbal, they are in a form that is capable of being verbalized.

A number of useful dimensions for augmented feedback are summarized in table 12.1. First, one can distinguish between *concurrent* and *terminal* feedback. Concurrent feedback is delivered during the movement (e.g., the information about engine speed that the racing driver receives from the tachometer), while terminal feedback is postponed until after the movement has been completed (e.g., the gymnast's score). Another dimension of augmented feedback is the time at which it is delivered; it can be either *immediate* or *delayed* by some amount of time. The feedback can be verbal (or capable of being verbalized) or nonverbal (e.g., a buzzer indicating that the car's engine is too hot). Also, the performance can be sampled for a period of time, with the *accumulated* feedback indicating the average performance for the past few seconds; or the feedback can be *distinct*, representing each moment of the performance (e.g., feedback from a speedometer). (See Holding, 1965, Annett, 1969, and Singer, 1980, for additional dimensions.)

These various dimensions of augmented feedback should be considered independent of one another. For example, if the augmented feedback is terminal, it could be either verbal or nonverbal, and it might be delayed or immediate. These dimensions, then, should be thought of as separate descriptors of augmented feedback that

TABLE 12.1. Dimensions of Augmented Feedback	
Concurrent: Presented during the movement	**Terminal:** Presented after the movement
Immediate: Presented immediately after the relevant action	**Delayed:** Delayed in time after the relevant action
Verbal: Presented in a form that is spoken or capable of being spoken	**Nonverbal:** Presented in a form that is not capable of being spoken
Accumulated: Feedback that represents an accumulation of past performance	**Distinct:** Feedback that represents each performance separately
Knowledge of results (KR): Verbalized (or verbalizable) postmovement information about the outcome of the movement in the environment	**Knowledge of performance (KP):** Verbalized (or verbalizable) postmovement information about the nature of the movement pattern.

define most kinds of feedback commonly used.

Knowledge of Results

One of the important categories of augmented feedback is termed *knowledge of results (KR)*. Essentially, KR is verbal (or verbalizable), terminal (i.e., postmovement) feedback about the *outcome* of the movement in terms of the environmental goal. It forms one combination of the various possible dimensions of augmented feedback (verbal-terminal) shown in table 12.1. Examples are seen when the instructor says "You were 2 m off target that time" or a computer screen presents the symbolic information "long 12" (meaning that the movement was 12 units too long). Knowledge of results can be highly specific, or it can be very general. Knowledge of results can also contain a rewarding component, such as "very good."

It is important to be clear about the use of the term KR. First, note that KR is about movement *outcome* in terms of an environmental goal ("You missed the ball"). KR is *not* feedback about the movement itself ("Your elbow was bent"). Usually this distinction is easily made; in shooting a basketball, for example, the goal and the movement to produce it are clearly separable. But often these two aspects of feedback are difficult to distinguish—for example, in a situation in which the goal of a movement *is* the form of the movement itself, as in a gymnastics move. Occasionally, other terms are used for KR as defined here, such as *information feedback* (Bilodeau, 1966), *extrinsic feedback*, or *reinforcement* (which implies a reward). Despite these inconsistencies, the tendency is to use the term KR as we have defined it here: *verbal, terminal, augmented feedback about goal achievement.* (See the review by Salmoni, Schmidt, & Walter, 1984, for additional distinctions.)

Knowledge of Performance

As already mentioned, an additional kind of feedback information concerns the *movement pattern* that the learner has made (e.g., "Your elbow was bent"). Gentile (1972) called this type of feedback *knowledge of performance (KP)* to distinguish it from KR as defined previously (see table 12.1). Knowledge of performance is probably more related to the feedback that instructors give to their students, being directed toward the correction of improper movement patterns rather than just the outcome of the movement in the environment. Also, KP can refer to aspects of the movement about which the subject is only vaguely aware,

such as the behavior of a particular limb in a complex movement. And it can refer to processes in the body about which the subject is normally unaware, such as blood pressure or the activity of a particular motor unit—often referred to as *biofeedback* (Basmajian, 1989).

Research on Augmented Feedback

How do scientists conduct research to understand feedback and learning? What forms of feedback are useful in motor learning, and how are these forms of feedback most effectively presented to the learner? A major problem for such research is that, in most natural situations, it is difficult to *control* the information received by a performer, so the situation is not easy to study. For example, there are many sources of feedback in the task of shooting a basketball, and it is difficult to know which sources are being used at any one time and how they are being used. A typical strategy used by many researchers in motor behavior is to alter the environment or the task (or both) so that minimal feedback information is provided to the subject, and then provide augmented feedback information artificially (in the form of KR or KP) so that the effects can be studied directly. This technique usually involves experiments with tasks that are artificial and novel, but a basic understanding of the functioning of error information can result just the same.

Paradigms for Augmented-Feedback Research

Although many definitions exist (Kuhn, 1962), a *paradigm* often refers to a standardized way of gaining knowledge through research. The study of KR variables[1] in motor learning research was directly influenced by research in experimental psychology, and these traditions remain today (see "Origins of the KR Paradigm"). Seldom stated explicitly is the assumption that the (augmented) KR provided in these artificial learning situations is fundamentally like the (inherent) error information a person would normally receive in a more natural setting. Is it correct to say that the information "You moved 2 cm too far" in a blindfolded linear-positioning movement works fundamentally in the same way as the information received by observing visually a shot missing the basket in basketball? Certainly different processes are involved, but it is entirely possible that the use of the error information is the same in both situations, in that the information provides a basis for changing the movement on the next attempt in order to make it more accurate. If this assumption is correct, then this general method provides a way to come to an understanding of the way in which inherent feedback works to produce learning in natural environments.

The other side of the argument is that such research, using tasks that are so simple and artificial, may have little to tell us about the ways in which the rich and varied sources of inherent feedback work in more natural settings. For now, our assumption will be that the study of KR is one means to understanding the operation of inherent feedback in natural environments. However, you should remember that the principles might not be quite the same in these two situations.

The dominant paradigm for understanding the functions of feedback information in learning is a legacy from the historical influences of experimental psychology (discussed in "Origins of the KR Paradigm"). The KR paradigm frequently uses a movement task that is very simple; the most common task used in early research investigations was the linear-positioning task, for which the person must learn to move a slide or a lever to a given position, usually while blindfolded. In such tasks, the subject cannot evaluate performance outcome without some supplemental information because of the removal of the most potent source of inherent information (vision). If the instruction is to move 20 cm, the subject cannot know for certain whether a given attempt to move that distance was correct or not on the basis of inherent information. True,

Origins of the KR Paradigm

The classic learning theories of Pavlov, Watson, Thorndike, Guthrie, Tolman, Hull, and others during the first half of the 20th century established a framework for research that remains today. One of the dominant approaches was the instrumental conditioning paradigm, influenced largely by Thorndike. The main feature of this approach was the idea that if an animal's behavior was followed quite soon by reward, the behavior was elicited more frequently under these conditions in the future. In theory, an association ("bond") was formed between the situation and the behavior. The association was strengthened if the behavior was repeatedly "reinforced" (by the reward). Thus, the reward was considered instrumental to the occurrence of learning.

A key feature of the instrumental learning paradigm is the assessment of learning by means of experimental extinction—a phrase coined by Pavlov to refer to the *apparent* elimination of the learned response. Extinction is studied in the instrumental learning paradigm during a period of time when the previously rewarded behavior is no longer reinforced. Strength of the conditioned response is measured by the *resistance to extinction,* defined as the continued behavior in the absence of the reward.

The instrumental conditioning paradigm in the study of motor behavior began with Thorndike (1927). Over a period of nine practice sessions, Thorndike's subjects drew lines of 3, 4, 5, and 6 in. The first session was without KR. The next seven sessions saw performance improve steadily with KR. The last session, without KR, resulted in a marked deterioration in performance. In Thorndike's view, learning occurred through strengthening the connection between a stimulus (the movement goal) and a response to that stimulus (the movement), and KR was viewed as instrumental in strengthening that bond. The purpose of the no-KR trials was to study the "strength" of the bond via the resistance to extinction.

The rationale underlying Thorndike's line-drawing experiment was not to study the laws of motor learning, but rather to investigate the generality of his Law of Effect using a motor task. For our purposes, however, Thorndike's experiment is remembered for introducing the KR/no-KR paradigm to a later generation of researchers interested specifically in human motor learning. This influence may also be considered another one of Thorndike's legacies (cf. Adams, 1978).

the feedback from the limb is present to signal the movement details, but the individual likely does not have the reference of correctness against which to evaluate this source of inherent feedback. In some sense, the feedback has not been "calibrated" to the environment. With this kind of task, one can study the use of feedback or KR by "augmenting" information to the subject in a systematic way. The most elementary of these experiments might involve the contrast between providing KR and withholding KR altogether. A more refined experiment might manipulate the time of presentation of the KR, the way in which the KR is presented (e.g., on a computer monitor or verbally, by an experimenter), or the qualitative aspects of the KR (e.g., imprecise or precise). In this way, experiments that vary the nature of the feedback given to the learner can be done in the same ways as experiments about any other independent variable. Thus, the task used must allow control over the relative usefulness of the sources of inherent feedback.

Temporal Placement of KR

Many of the experiments on KR and motor learning are structured so that the temporal relation among the events in a trial is closely controlled. These events are shown in figure 12.1. The subject performs movement 1 (M_1); then, after a period of time called the *KR-delay interval,* the KR for that trial (KR_1) is delivered by the experimenter. The period of time from the presentation of KR until the next movement is termed the *post-KR delay,* during which it is presumed that the person is

processing the KR and planning the next movement. The sum of the KR-delay and post-KR-delay intervals is termed the *intertrial interval.* Usually the intertrial interval is on the order of 10 to 20 s, but of course these intervals can be practically any length to serve the purposes of a particular experimental situation.

Learning Versus Performance Effects

In the typical KR paradigm, the variables (such as amount of KR; absolute and relative frequency; precision; length of, and activity during, the KR-delay, post-KR-delay, and intertrial intervals) are typically manipulated over a series of *acquisition* trials, just as we have discussed in chapter 11. After these trials, all the conditions of the particular KR manipulation (preferably involving separate groups of subjects) are transferred to a common condition of KR for additional performance trials. By far the most common *transfer* test is a series of no-KR (or "KR withdrawal") trials. Although other paradigms have been used, the no-KR transfer test has a long history of use in experimental psychology, upon which much of motor behavior research in this area is based (see "Origins of the KR Paradigm").

Salmoni and colleagues (1984) provided a strong argument in support of the typical paradigm, in which a KR variable is manipulated during practice trials and the effects of that manipulation are evaluated in a common, no-KR transfer test. The authors argued that the two phases of the typical KR paradigm permitted a direct comparison of the effects of a KR variable on performance and

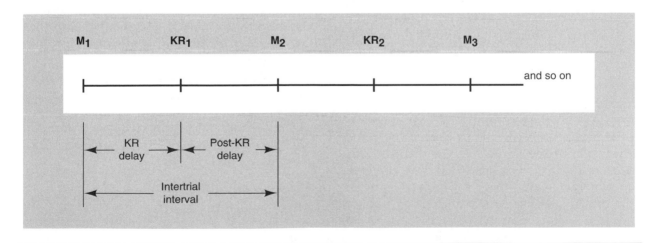

FIGURE 12.1   Temporal placement of events in the knowledge-of-results (KR) paradigm. M_1 refers to movement trial 1. KR_1 refers to the augmented feedback provided about results of movement trial 1.

learning (see chapter 10 for more explanation). Making a distinction similar to other distinctions between learning and performance (chapters 10 and 11), they argued that a KR variable that exerted an influence *only* while being manipulated was a performance variable. A KR variable that exerted an influence after the manipulation was withdrawn (and after the temporary influences had dissipated) was a learning variable.

Several arguments support the preference for the no-KR transfer test over other transfer tests in the assessment of KR effects on performance and learning. One argument is that learning can be addressed in a more steady state under no-KR than under KR trials, since continued improvements in performance are unlikely to occur in the absence of KR (Salmoni et al., 1984). A further contention is that a series of no-KR trials provides a more consistent estimate of performance capabilities and thus a more reliable account of learning effects, since performance is stabilized more in the absence than in the presence of KR (Rubin, 1978). Another argument is that the use of a no-KR test of learning is consistent with many practical applications: Augmented information supplied during training or rehabilitation is often unavailable when "real" performance is required (e.g., in a game situation or when a patient is away from the clinic).

Potential Applications of Augmented-Feedback Research

The vast majority of the research on augmented feedback and motor learning has involved information about movement outcome (KR). For a person who has had extensive practice at a sport or occupational activity, it would seem far more effective to provide information about the *patterns* of movement the person made—defined earlier here as KP. Why is there a focus on KR (movement outcome) when KP (movement pattern) is what will probably be most useful for application? Probably the most important reason is that in experiments on KR, the movement outcome can usually be measured easily and corrections on the next trial can be measured. But when the experimenter wants to give KP, there is more difficulty in measuring the pattern of movement and then noting how the pattern changed on the subsequent trial. Until late in the previous century, these procedures were tedious (using film analysis, strip-chart records, and so on),

and many motor behavior workers chose not to use them. However, with the use of computing technology and increased emphasis on biomechanical techniques, researchers have examined KP as a source of error information much more frequently. For now, we will assume that the mechanisms involved when the learner receives any type of augmented feedback are essentially the same. That is, we assume that what the learner does with these various kinds of information is identical, the major distinction being that these different kinds of information refer to different aspects of the movement. Thus, for example, the principles that have been discovered for KR would be applicable to situations when KP would be given. This could be incorrect, of course, but until evidence appears to the contrary, we think the assumption is reasonable.

Evaluating the Effects of Augmented Feedback

In this part of the chapter, some of the fundamental principles of augmented feedback for motor learning situations are presented. A number of conclusions can be drawn from the literature, probably because this area has received a great deal of study in motor skills research (for reviews see Adams, 1987; Magill, 2001; Salmoni et al., 1984; Swinnen, 1996; Wulf & Shea, 2004). Also, the effects found are very robust and large relative to those of other variables considered. First, we discuss a basic question: whether or not augmented feedback is a variable affecting performance, learning, or both. Then we discuss the research variables related to KP, and finally, we present the rather large and complex set of effects of KR variables on performance and learning.

Most of us probably suspect that KR has important effects on both performance and learning, so it is perhaps not crucial that we document these effects. But we have been fooled by our intuitions before, so we will review briefly some of the critical evidence on this issue.

Augmented Feedback Is a Learning Variable

Using the paradigm described in the previous section, Bilodeau, Bilodeau, and Schumsky (1959) employed a linear-positioning task with four groups of subjects. One group had KR after the first 19 of the 20 acquisition trials, and a second group received no KR at all in the 20 trials. Two other groups received KR for two and six trials, respectively, before having KR withdrawn for the remainder of the 20 practice trials. The main findings are shown in figure 12.2, where absolute error is plotted as a function of trials for these four groups. The group that had KR provided after trials 1 through 19 showed an initial sharp decrease in error, followed by a more gradual decrease. On the other hand, the group that had no KR at all showed essentially no change in performance over the 20 practice trials. For the remaining two groups, improvement occurred on trials that followed the administration of KR, but the improvement ceased when KR was withdrawn, with slight decrements in performance thereafter.

Did KR affect the learning in this task? As with any other variable that could affect learning or performance, these data can be interpreted in at least two ways. First, we could conclude that the 19-trial KR group learned more than the no-KR group, as evidenced by the fact that they performed more effectively during the practice phase. But another possibility is that KR had affected performance only temporarily, perhaps through some kind of motivational or "energizing" process. Thus, it could be that when these temporary effects of KR are allowed to dissipate with rest (as with fatigue effects), the temporary effects of KR will vanish and performance will regress to the original level (see chapter 10).

Bilodeau and colleagues provided a partial answer to this question when they transferred their no-KR group to the KR conditions for an additional five trials. In the right portion of figure 12.2, the absolute errors on these five trials are plotted together with those for the first five trials of group 19. The size of the errors, as well as the pattern of change with trials, was practically identical for these two sets of trials. That is, the no-KR group in this transfer condition performed nearly the same as group 19 at the beginning of their practice trials. Thus, we can say that the 20-trial no-KR practice sequence for this group did not produce any learning at all, and consequently that KR is a learning variable. And, KR is not just a variable that *affects* learning; rather, when KR is not present in such situations, learning does not occur at all. While Bilodeau and colleagues' study

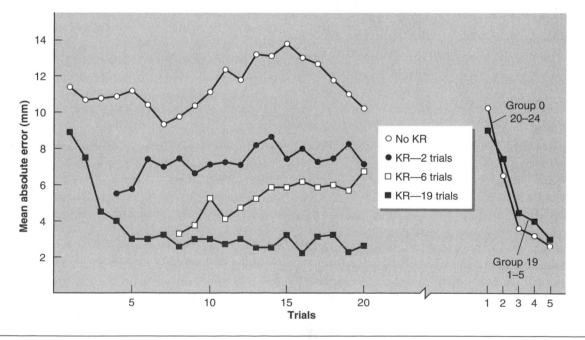

FIGURE 12.2 Absolute errors in a linear-positioning task as a function of knowledge of results (KR). (The group numbers indicate the number of presentations of KR received before KR withdrawal; group 0 switched to a KR condition shown at the right, where its performance is compared to group 19's first five trials replotted from left.)

Reprinted from E.A. Bilodeau, I.M. Bilodeau, and D.A. Schumsky, 1959, "Some effects of introducing and withdrawing knowledge of results early and late in practice," *Journal of Experimental Psychology* 58: 143.

uses a kind of transfer design, it does not use the typical transfer procedures we recommended earlier (chapter 10). Similar conclusions, however, have come from a number of other studies in which relative amount learned was evaluated on no-KR transfer tests (Bennett & Simmons, 1984; Newell, 1974; Trowbridge & Cason, 1932).

Knowledge of results does not always have such dramatic effects on learning motor skills, though, and the reasons often depend on the availability and usefulness of inherent feedback. For example, KR had only minimal effects on performance and learning for a tracking task in which KR was or was not provided after each trial (Archer, Kent, & Mote, 1956; Bilodeau, 1966). Similar effects have been found for learning an anticipation-timing task (Magill, Chamberlin, & Hall, 1991).

Does this mean that augmented information about errors is somehow not important for learning these tasks? Probably not. Rather, while practicing the task, subjects are able to detect their own errors through the inherent feedback (visual in these cases) provided during the normal course of the trial. This visual information probably serves the same function as the verbal KR did in the linear-positioning experiment described earlier. This observation is in accord with the idea that the presentation of information about errors to the learner is more effectively studied in situations in which learners are unable to evaluate accurately their inherent feedback to detect errors.

Augmented Feedback Is a Performance Variable

The evidence clearly points to (temporary) performance effects of KR in addition to the learning effects we have just described. For example, KR can be motivating, or "energizing," for the learners. Some early research shows that when KR is provided, subjects report that they are more interested in the task, they seem to put more effort into practice, and they persist longer after the KR is removed, in comparison to practicing without KR (Arps, 1920; Crawley, 1926; Elwell & Grindley, 1938). In relatively boring situations such as *vigilance* tasks, in which subjects are asked to spend hours monitoring a display for the appearance of a threatening object (e.g., in airport security monitoring), KR about the subject's performance has an "alerting" (or energizing) effect, and it can act to counteract sleep loss (Poulton, 1973). All these phenomena exert strong influences on performance, but weaker effects on learning (e.g., Szalma, Hancock, Warm, Dember, & Parsons, 2006).

Another temporary effect of KR is related to its informational properties, whereby KR informs the subject of the errors that have been made and then indicates what to do next. Thus, KR provides something like *guidance* for the learner. In chapter 11 we presented evidence that guidance is very effective for performance when it is present but that all or part of the beneficial effect can disappear when the guidance is removed (e.g., Armstrong, 1970a; see figure 11.19). In an analogous way, then, KR (acting as guidance) might provide strong informational support for performance when it is being administered, with the benefits disappearing as soon as the KR is removed or the task conditions are changed (Salmoni et al., 1984).

Untangling the Learning Versus Performance Effects

From the previous sections we have seen that variations in KR can have powerful effects on performance when KR is present, but there is good reason to question whether such effects are always "relatively permanent" to the extent that they can be thought of as learning effects. The scientific problem is to distinguish the variables that produce transient performance changes from those that produce relatively permanent changes. Transfer designs used as discussed in chapters 10 and 11 provide a good way to make this distinction in experiments on KR. However, except for a few studies (e.g., Annett, 1959; Griffith, 1931; McGuigan, 1959; Trowbridge & Cason, 1932), early feedback researchers did not take this learning–performance distinction seriously, apparently assuming that any variation of feedback that affected performance was automatically a learning variable. As we will see, there are many situations in which this assumption is simply incorrect.

Knowledge of Performance

We begin our analysis of augmented-feedback variables by looking at studies of information that is provided to learners about the patterns of actions they make. It was Gentile (1972) who termed these kinds of feedback "knowledge of performance." Many forms of KP are possible; they may range from rather casual comments about performance, made by a teacher or coach, to complex feedback generated by computer in a simulator and delivered to the learner online in computer-aided instruction. Some of these kinds of KP are discussed in the following sections.

Video Feedback

It would certainly seem reasonable to think of analog or digital video feedback as a powerful mode in which to present KP. From a motor skills viewpoint, a video will contain a record of the entire performance, and the individual can detect errors directly and attempt to correct them on the next trial. However, for all the logic leading to the use of video feedback, as well as its use in many sport situations, the research evidence suggests that this method of presenting KP, *by itself,* is rather ineffective. Rothstein and Arnold (1976) and Newell (1981) have reviewed this work, finding that numerous experiments fail to show positive effects of these techniques for motor learning. Some evidence even suggests that video feedback might actually hinder learning (Ross, Bird, Doody, & Zoeller, 1985). One suggestion is that video feedback might provide *too much* information, especially if the skill is complex and the viewer does not know which of the many details are important. In support of this notion, Rothstein and Arnold pointed out that studies using *cuing,* in which subjects were directed or taught to examine certain aspects of the display during a viewing, showed more positive effects of video feedback than did studies using undirected viewing.

The benefits of cued or directed viewing of video feedback were shown clearly in a study by Kernodle and Carlton (1992). Subjects practiced throwing a sponge ball with their nondominant arm. After each throw, they were provided with KR regarding the distance thrown (subjects closed their eyes on ball release, making the augmented feedback more important for learning) and were shown video feedback of the trial just completed. One group of subjects was provided only KR, while another group watched a video replay of their own performance, with no additional augmented information. Previous research, however, had shown that combining verbal KP with other forms of augmented feedback can be quite beneficial to learning (Wallace & Hagler, 1979). So, another group received a verbal cue to watch one particular aspect of the movement during the video feedback (e.g., "Focus on the hips during the throwing phase"). A final group, before watching the videotape, was given additional augmented feedback in the form of specific error-correction information (e.g., "Rotate the hips from left to right during the throwing phase"). Figure 12.3 illustrates the subjective ratings of throwing performance (or form) during no-feedback trials on five transfer tests over a four-week period.

The results were clear: The strongest learning effects were seen when the video feedback was

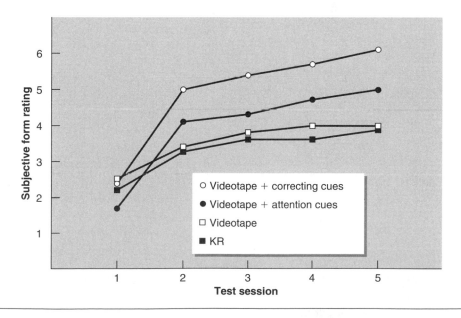

FIGURE 12.3 Throwing performance under various conditions of videotape replays.

Data from Kernodle and Carlton 1992.

accompanied by error-correcting cues, although considerable gains were achieved with the attention-focusing cues as well. The video feedback alone was no better than simply providing KR. Similar results were obtained when measures of distance thrown were analyzed.

It is important to remember that video can also be used to present the performance of a model (chapter 11). However, in both uses of videos as forms of augmented information, research has shown that they are most effective when supplemented with additional, attention-directing augmented information. Practically speaking, information provided in videos is most effective for learning when it is augmented by an instructor who can direct the learner's attention to important details and toward ignoring the irrelevant aspects. This is probably especially so if the learner is a novice, who has less knowledge than an experienced performer about what details in the video are important.

Kinematic Feedback

Recall that *kinematics* refers to measures of "pure motion" without regard to the forces that produced them (chapter 2). Feedback about kinematics involves various measures derived from movement such as position, time, velocity, and patterns of coordination. When coaches or teachers give information about movement patterning (e.g., "You bent your elbow that time"), they are really providing a (loosely measured) form of kinematic information, a form of KP. Expert music or dance instructors and sport coaches seem to be able to sense "what went wrong" and to provide verbal descriptors that can serve as suggestions for change in the movement. Of course, many different features of the movement can be described and used for feedback, and a major issue has been the discovery of what kinds of kinematic information would be most useful for learning and performance (e.g., Swinnen, 1996; Newell, 1991; Newell & Walter, 1981).

Early studies of kinematic information feedback were done by Lindahl (1945; see also Tiffin & Rogers, 1943), who analyzed patterns of foot-pedal actions in skilled industrial workers operating a cutting machine (see "Lindahl's Study Using Movement Kinematics" on p. 39). Lindahl determined the most effective pattern of foot motion from measurements of highly skilled workers and then used this pattern as a "gold standard" for providing feedback about foot action to new employees. Such kinematic feedback greatly facilitated training; in as few as 10 weeks of practice, new trainees could be brought to the level of employees who had nine months of experience. Knowledge of performance about the most effective patterns of actions—not easily observable without additional measurements of the fine details of foot movements, and not easily verbalizable—was apparently critical to the establishment of proper actions in the new performers.

A key feature of kinematic feedback is that it informs the subjects about some aspect of the movement pattern that is otherwise difficult to perceive. In some cases, a whole pattern of multijoint coordination is presented (e.g., by means of analog or digital video), showing important information about the movement of a particular joint in relation to another (e.g., Hatze, 1976). It is possible that the subject could gain this information on his own, but it is unlikely that a learner would focus on the particular aspects that the instructor considers to be critical. Other kinds of information cannot be sensed at all, however, such as relative timing differences in two joints or subtle changes in velocity; and kinematic feedback can allow the learner to become aware of these features. Also, feedback information about subtle aspects of the movement's goal has been shown to be useful; Phillips and Berkhout (1976) had subjects learn gearshifting and acceleration in a simulation of heavy truck driving, and showed that computer-aided feedback about smoothness of acceleration produced marked gains measured later on a no-feedback transfer test.

But how effective is kinematic KP when compared with other types of augmented feedback? Several studies have been conducted on this issue, and the findings reveal some interesting principles. Most of this research suggests quite clearly that the effectiveness of kinematic feedback depends on the nature of the task goal. For example, subjects were asked to draw geometric shapes on a tabletop in two experiments reported by Newell, Carlton, and Antoniou (1990). The task goal (a circle) was known in the first experiment, but in the second experiment the task goal was an unknown, irregular shape. The subjects were given one of three types of feedback: (1) KR about the error between their movement and the goal;

(2) a digital image of the pattern plus the KR; or (3) a digital image of the feedback of the produced movement superimposed on a template of the task goal, plus KR. Learning (as measured in a retention test without any augmented feedback) was not affected by the nature of the feedback when the task goal was well known to the subjects (the circle in experiment 1). However, when the task goal was unknown, there was a clear advantage for the group that received the KR plus the augmented feedback superimposed on the task goal. The benefit of augmented kinematic feedback may be optimized when its content specifies information that cannot otherwise be generated from sources such as inherent feedback or from other, less detailed sources of augmented feedback.

The role of task goal information and available sources of feedback may also be related to the findings reported by Swinnen, Walter, Lee, and Serrien (1993). Subjects in this study practiced a discrete, bimanual-coordination task in which the actions of the two limbs were not the same. The left limb was to produce a unidirectional elbow flexion movement. At the same time, a flexion–extension–flexion movement of the right elbow was to be performed. Without practice this coordination task is very difficult to perform, as there is a tendency to make the *same* actions with each arm (see chapter 8). Swinnen and colleagues (1993) found that the capability to perform each distinct limb goal improved little with practice in the absence of augmented feedback. Surprisingly, however, learning was facilitated equally well by KR (a simple outcome measure of coordination performance) and by the precise augmented kinematic feedback profiles of the two limbs. According to Swinnen and colleagues, the findings supported the idea that the limb coordination information provided by the KR was sufficient to enable subjects to explore new strategies to learn the task. Thus, it seemed that practice—and strategies brought about by information sources that affected practice—combined to determine the value of augmented feedback.

In this research, the effectiveness of kinematic feedback was assessed in tasks in which the feedback was identical to the goal of the movement. For example, augmented feedback about a dive or an ice skating jump could be related directly to the movement, as the quality of the movement *represents* the task goal. However, in other skills, the outcome of an action may be quite distinct from the motions that produced it. For example, many different movements can produce the same trajectory of a batted ball.

How does kinematic feedback about movements affect the acquisition of skills in which the movements are not isomorphic with the task goal? A computer-controlled analog of a baseball batting task was developed by Schmidt and Young (1991) to examine these issues. The task required subjects to "strike" a moving-light "object" by passing a movement lever through a coincidence point as the light went by. The goal was to maximize distance, as defined by a combination of the velocity and timing accuracy at the coincidence point. On the basis of research suggesting that a particular movement pattern produced the best outcome scores (Schmidt & Young, 1991), Young and Schmidt (1992) conducted a study to assess what kinematic feedback variables facilitated learning when presented in relation to the optimal movement pattern. Their findings revealed that each kinematic variable manipulated (mean or variability of the reversal point; mean or variability of the time of the reversal) tended to facilitate the acquisition of that kinematic variable in the production of the movement. However, only the kinematic feedback about the mean reversal point was more effective than outcome KR in maximizing performance outcome. The effects of KP appear to be enhanced, however, when an optimal movement pattern is not used as a reference criterion, again suggesting that the kinematic information may be most useful when it promotes active, problem-solving activities in the learner (Brisson & Alain, 1996a, 1996b).

Similar findings reveal that kinematic feedback facilitates specific motor learning outcomes in rehabilitation. For example, Cirstea, Ptito, and Levin (2006) examined three groups of patients with hemiparesis as they practiced an arm-pointing task without vision over 10 sessions and in a one-month retention test. Compared to a control group, the individuals who received KR about movement end point steadily learned and improved aiming precision, but not speed. However, the subjects who received KP about elbow and shoulder velocities mainly improved *these* performance outcomes. Thus, augmented information may contribute to learning specificity effects (see discussion in chapter 11).

These specificity effects may help to resolve the curiosity about the effectiveness of kinematic feedback relative to certain attentional focus manipulations. In previous sections of the book we discussed findings regarding the impact on performance (chapter 4) and learning (chapter 11) of instructions to focus one's attention. In most cases, research has shown that instructions to attend to an "external" source of information were beneficial for performance and learning, compared to instructions to focus on an "internal" source of information (Wulf, 2007). In the context of the present discussion, it might be correct to say that KP directs the learner to focus attention on an internal source (e.g., the motions of a limb), whereas KR directs the learner's attention to the impact of the movement on the environment (i.e., externally). From this perspective, even though KP might provide more information than KR, one might anticipate that KR holds an advantage over KP in terms of directing the learner's attention to a more appropriate focus.

As an example, subjects in a study by Shea and Wulf (1999) practiced the stabilometer and received concurrent feedback about the position of the platform relative to the horizontal. Some subjects were told that the feedback represented a line on the platform (external group) while others were told that this feedback represented their feet (internal feedback). The results over two days of practice and a no-feedback retention test (on day 3) are shown in figure 12.4. Compared to the internal group, the external group performed more accurately both early and later in practice. The differences were small at the start of the retention test, but the external group continued to improve their performance in the retention test compared to the internal group. These findings have been replicated in a tennis serve task (Wulf, McConnel, Gärtner, & Schwarz, 2002) and in stroke rehabilitation (Cirstea & Levin, 2007), although further work is necessary to dissociate the specific effects of attention-focusing instructions and augmented feedback. Nevertheless, these findings are important in that they provide the beginnings of a better understanding of both the potentially positive and negative influences of kinematic feedback on performance and learning.

Biofeedback

Going a step further, feedback can be given about features of the movement that are not perceived directly—a key feature of *biofeedback training*. If a particular biological process (e.g., blood pressure) is measured electronically and used as feedback, then subjects can learn to voluntarily control these (normally unconscious) processes (see Richter-Heinrich & Miller, 1982, for a review). Years ago, Basmajian (1963) gave subjects visual and auditory feedback of their own electromyograms (EMGs) and showed how such information

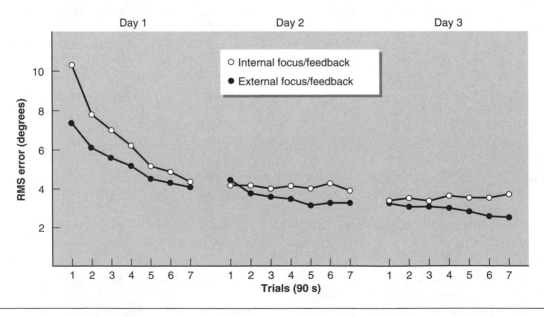

FIGURE 12.4 Effects of internal- versus external-focus feedback in acquisition (days 1 and 2) and in retention (day 3).

Reprinted from *Human Movement Science*, Vol. 18, C.H. Shea and G. Wulf, Enhancing motor learning through external-focus instruction and feedback, pages 553-571, Copyright 1999, with kind permission from Elsevier.

could allow the subject to learn to control a single motor unit, something that is not normally under voluntary control. This general idea has been tried (with only moderate success) in teaching subjects who are deaf to speak, with the subjects' sounds being transformed into visual information presented on a television screen (Nickerson, Kalikow, & Stevens, 1976). Mulder and Hulstijn (1985) showed that feedback information about the EMG from the muscles controlling the big toe contributed to learning toe movements, and that the gains remained even after the feedback was removed.

Brenner (1974) and Lang (1974) argued that there is a close relationship between these biofeedback procedures for training unconscious processes on the one hand and kinematic feedback for motor learning on the other. If such a relationship exists, however, then it is possible that biofeedback would be expected to have some adverse effect in motor learning as well (Yiu, Verdolini, & Chow, 2005). As we will see later, augmented feedback that is provided instantaneously with the completion of performance is beneficial for performance but can degrade learning. Clinical treatment of speech disorders, for example, is one research area in which continuous, instantaneous feedback may have an adverse effect on rehabilitation (for a review see Maas et al., 2008).

Kinetic Feedback

Whereas kinematic measures are variables describing pure motion, kinetic measures are descriptors of the *forces* that produce the kinematic variables. We have long recognized that muscular forces and the durations over which they act are fundamental outputs of the central structures thought to organize movements; the impulse-timing theory discussed in chapters 6 and 7 is one statement of that basic view. As a result, researchers have often thought that feedback in terms of kinetics would be a "natural" kind of information for the motor system to use for learning.

Some early work supports this view. English (1942) utilized force feedback from a trigger squeeze to facilitate riflery training. Howell (1956) had subjects learn a runner's sprint start and recorded forces applied against a strain gauge (a force sensor) that was attached to the foot plate in the starting blocks. The forces recorded during the time of the action provided a *force–time curve*, which was shown to subjects after each trial as a

form of kinetic feedback. Subjects could use this information to *optimize* the form of the force–time curve (i.e., to produce a maximum impulse). Newell and Walter (1981) and Newell, Sparrow, and Quinn (1985) have provided similar examples with other tasks. The effects of this extra information are relatively permanent too, as they persist in a short-term no-feedback retention test (Newell et al., 1985) as well as in tests that occur after a long delay interval (Broker, Gregor, & Schmidt, 1993; van Dijk, Mulder, & Hermens, 2007).

There is good reason to remain cautious about the benefits of using kinetic feedback for the attentional focus reasons mentioned in the previous sections. If the provision of kinetic feedback encourages the learner to adopt an internal focus of attention in performance, then the potential benefit of this rich form of augmented feedback might be overshadowed by the consequences of the ineffective attentional focus.

Knowledge of Results

We now turn our attention to the vast amount of research on KR—augmented information about the movement outcome. Experiments in this research area have frequently used very simple tasks, such as blindfolded limb-positioning tasks and timing tasks. The reason is that with these kinds of tasks, very little if any learning at all can occur in the absence of KR. In this way, the relative effectiveness of various manipulations of KR can be examined in terms of their impact on the learning process.

Precision of KR

The *precision* of KR refers to the degree of exactness of the information provided to the learner. For example, if the subject's goal was to make a 10 cm movement and the actual movement was 10.13 cm, KR could be provided in a variety of ways. At the most general or *qualitative* level, the subject could be told that the movement was either "right" or "wrong." However, differing degrees of precision could be substituted for these general feedback statements of "right" or "wrong."

In the case of "wrong," one could give more precise KR by saying "long" or "short," meaning that the person moved beyond or short of the target. One could give still more precise KR by saying "wrong by 1," meaning 1 mm off target.

Or, one could say "long 0.1," meaning that the movement was 0.1 mm too long, or "long 0.13," meaning that it was 0.13 mm too long. The KR could be even more precise than this, measuring movement accuracy to finer *quantitative* degrees (e.g., in nanometers).

In the case of "right," the experimenter would need to define, exactly, what movement outcome would satisfy the criterion that distinguished "right" from "wrong." In the early work of Trowbridge and Cason (1932), for example, lines were considered to be correct if drawn within 1/8 in. of the 3 in. goal. In such a case, the "correctness" of the movement is defined relative to a "bandwidth," defined as the degree of acceptable error tolerance around the goal. Various combinations of qualitative and quantitative forms of KR have been examined, and these manipulations have rather large effects on performance and learning.

Qualitative Versus Quantitative KR

The most basic question concerning the precision of KR is the kind of information that is presented. Information about the *direction* of the error is presented in some, but not all, forms of KR. Information can also be provided about the *magnitude* of the error, irrespective of direction. Some of these forms of KR have information about both factors (e.g., "long 13"). Generally, the evidence suggests that there is some benefit to providing information about magnitude of error, but this information is far more useful if the direction is also specified. Knowing that an error was made in a particular direction gives a strong indication of the ways in which the movement must be modified next time but information only about magnitude does not.

Another key issue is related to the precision of the KR, and the classic study in this area was conducted by Trowbridge and Cason (1932). Four groups practiced drawing 3 in. lines for 100 trials. One group never received KR. Another group received nonsense syllables after drawing each line (a control condition). A third group received qualitative KR in the form of "right" (if the line was within ±1/8 in. of the goal) or "wrong" from the experimenter. The last group was given precise, directional KR (longer or shorter) in terms of the exact deviation, in eighths of an inch, from the goal length. During both acquisition and a no-KR transfer test that followed immediately after practice, accuracy was greater for the precise and the right–wrong KR groups than for either the nonsense-KR or the no-KR group (figure 12.5). Furthermore, precise KR was more accurate than

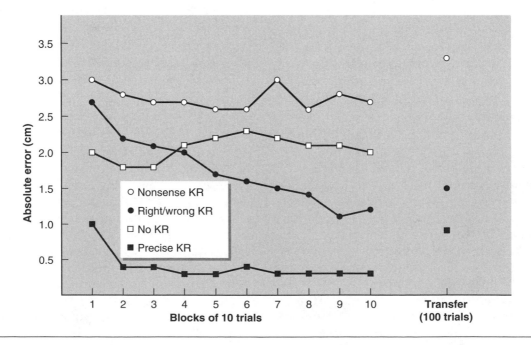

FIGURE 12.5 Qualitative and quantitative knowledge of results (KR) effects in acquisition and transfer. The No-KR group did not perform the transfer rest.

Data from Trowbridge and Cason 1932.

the right/wrong type of KR. These effects have been replicated often (Bennett & Simmons, 1984; Magill & Wood, 1986; Reeve, Dornier, & Weeks, 1990; Salmoni, Ross, Dill, & Zoeller, 1983), supporting the conclusion that precise, quantitative KR is generally more effective for learning than qualitative KR.

These techniques do not permit the separation of information about precision of KR from information about the direction of reported error. Studies conducted since the Trowbridge and Cason experiment have separated these effects and have generally shown that the more precise the KR, the more accurate the performance, up to a point, beyond which no further increases in accuracy are found as KR is made more precise (for reviews, see Newell, 1981; Salmoni et al., 1984). Subjects presumably know that they cannot be responsible for errors smaller than a certain size (e.g., 1 mm), as the movement control mechanisms themselves are more variable than this. Therefore, it is likely that subjects "round off" very precise KR to a more meaningful level of precision.

Bandwidth KR

An alternative to giving either qualitative or quantitative KR is provided by the *bandwidth KR* method (Sherwood, 1988). With this method

the nature of augmented feedback is determined by a bandwidth about the movement goal. In most studies using this method, qualitative KR in the form of "correct" or "right" is provided to the subject when the performance outcome lies *within* the boundaries of correctness as defined by the bandwidth (similar to the KR provided by Trowbridge & Cason [1932]). However, when performance *exceeds* the bandwidth, the experimenter provides the learner with specific KR that gives both the magnitude and the direction of error. This method is probably what many teachers and therapists do spontaneously—correcting relatively poor performance and rewarding relatively good performance.

Bandwidth KR has rather substantial effects on performance and learning. In fact, the research suggests that learning is facilitated as the bandwidth becomes *larger*. There is probably an optimal bandwidth size, although more research needs to be done to establish what this might be. Sherwood (1988) conducted one of the first studies in this area (see also Annett, 1959). Subjects were to learn to achieve a rapid elbow flexion movement time as close to 200 ms as possible. Subjects in a control (no bandwidth) group (0% BW in figure 12.6) were told their exact movement time after each trial. In two other

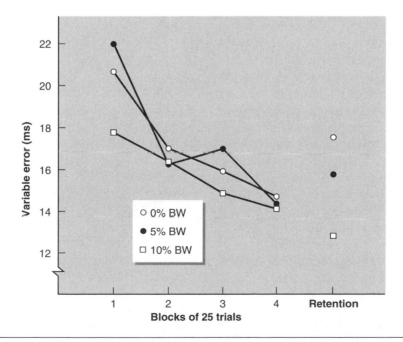

FIGURE 12.6   Bandwidth knowledge-of-results (KR) effects in acquisition and retention.

Reproduced and adapted from Table 1 and 2 with permission of author and publisher from: Sherwood, D.E. Effect of bandwidth knowledge of results on movement consistency. *Perceptual and Motor Skills*, 1988, 66, 535-542. © Perceptual and Motor Skills 1988.

conditions, subjects were given movement-time KR only if their outcomes exceeded a tolerance limit around the MT goal (±5% or ±10%). Performance inside the bandwidth received no *explicit* KR—which subjects had been instructed to interpret as meaning that their MT had been correct. Although these bandwidth conditions had no differential effects on acquisition performance, as can be seen in figure 12.6, the no-KR retention test performance was positively related to the size of the bandwidth.

Sherwood's experiment uncovered a number of important issues regarding KR and the learning process. For example, one consequence of the bandwidth KR procedure is that as the tolerance limits are increased (5% to 10%), the proportion of trials supplied with *error KR* diminishes. As will be seen later in this chapter, less frequent error KR in acquisition also improves learning. So, one question is whether or not the bandwidth effect is more than just a reduced KR frequency effect. To examine this question, Lee and Carnahan (1990a) used bandwidth groups of 5% and 10% together with *yoked* control groups; the control groups received KR on the same trials as their yoked counterparts in the bandwidth groups. However, the key difference was that a bandwidth subject interpreted no KR to be feedback that the previous trial performance had been "correct." For the yoked controls, the absence of KR revealed nothing about the previous trial. Lee and Carnahan found that the bandwidth groups performed more effectively in retention than did their respective control groups, suggesting that the provision of the "correct" KR gave an additional boost to learning beyond that normally associated with less frequent KR. Similar results were reported by Butler, Reeve, and Fischman (1996) and Wright, Smith-Munyon, and Sidaway (1997). Moreover, bandwidth KR facilitated learning more than a yoked relative-frequency control group in an observational learning paradigm, supporting a high cognitive function to the provision of "correct" feedback (Badets & Blandin, 2005).

Another potentially strong learning effect that could have been going on in the Sherwood (1988) study is that the distributions of error KR and correct KR change as skill improves—the proportion of trials followed by error KR is reduced and the proportion of "correct KR" trials is increased. This seems to be an important component of bandwidth KR effectiveness, as methods of reduc-

ing the size of the bandwidth over the course of practice, keeping the proportions of error and correct KR relatively constant, have been ineffective (Goodwin & Meeuwsen, 1995; Lai & Shea, 1999).

As suggested earlier, these effects make considerable sense and have been replicated in experiments in which a golf chipping task was learned (Smith, Taylor, & Withers, 1997). The essence is that, when assisting people in learning a new skill, you might provide help when they are doing something wrong, but not when they are correct (in other words, "If it ain't broke, don't fix it"). The key seems to be in deciding when is the best time to intervene and provide augmented feedback. If an optimal bandwidth exists for each person, its size would likely depend on a number of factors that may change with practice and task demands (Lee & Maraj, 1994).

Erroneous KR

Imagine a situation in which the provider of augmented feedback is *inaccurate* in giving the feedback. For example, in older bowling alleys, an illuminated indicator at the end of the lane provided KR in terms of how many pins were left standing after the first ball was bowled. Since there are times when one pin is hidden from the bowler's view by another pin, the augmented feedback from the pin indicator can reveal information that the bowler cannot directly see. But, if one or more of the indicator lights happened to malfunction, the bowler could get an incorrect impression of the number of pins that were still standing. That is the issue—what is the impact of KR when it is erroneous?

Buekers and Magill (1995) conducted studies on the effects of erroneous KR in an anticipation-timing task—a task for which inherent (visual) feedback is normally sufficient for learning to occur (Magill et al., 1991). Subjects in these studies were sometimes provided with incorrect augmented feedback, indicating that the accuracy of the previous anticipation had been 100 ms later than actually had been the case (e.g., someone who had been 65 ms *early* in anticipating the arrival of the stimulus would be told that she had been 35 ms *late*). The consequence of this *erroneous* feedback is a motor behavior whereby the subjects perform the task with a constant error (CE) of up to −100 ms. These effects are relatively long lasting, with large negative CEs occurring after one week in a no-KR retention test (Buekers, Magill,

& Hall, 1992; Vanvenckenray, Buekers, Mendes, & Helsen, 1999) and in transfer tests to novel stimulus speeds (McNevin, Magill, & Buekers, 1994). The findings have been replicated in other types of timing tasks (Ryan & Fritz, 2007; Ryan & Robey, 2002), as well as in a soccer ball kicking task in which visual feedback provided by a video was erroneous (Ford, Hodges, & Williams, 2007).

These erroneous-KR effects indicate that the accuracy of augmented feedback has very powerful effects on performance and learning, whereby subjects negate or discount the accuracy of their own error-detection capabilities in favor of trusting the validity of the (erroneous) augmented feedback. The impact of erroneous KR appears to be the strongest when it is presented on every practice trial during acquisition. Studies in which trials with erroneous KR are alternated with trials providing correct KR (Buekers, Magill, & Sneyers, 1994), and those in which trials with erroneous KR follow a practice period with correct KR (Buekers & Magill, 1995), show diminished performance effects and no learning effect of erroneous KR. Thus, *periodic* KR that is counterintuitive to inherent feedback may not be as disruptive to learning as the situation in which the learner is consistently faced with conflicting augmented information.

Schedules of KR

We saw in the previous section about bandwidth KR that determining when to give KR and what type of KR to give can have a large impact on performance and learning. These effects relate closely to a class of KR-*scheduling* variables over which the experimenter has specific control. As we will see, these variables also have profound learning and performance effects.

Relative- and Absolute-Frequency of KR

If error information is required for learning, we might reasonably expect that more KR will result in stronger learning. We can distinguish between two measures of the "amount" of KR that is provided: *absolute frequency* and *relative frequency* of KR. Absolute frequency of KR refers to the number of KR presentations received over the course of practice. If 80 practice trials are given, and the person receives KR after every other trial for a total of 40 presentations, then the absolute frequency of KR is 40. On the other hand, relative frequency of KR refers to the *percentage* of trials on

which KR is provided. It is the number of times KR is given divided by the total number of trials, multiplied by 100 for conversion to a percentage. In this example, the relative frequency of KR is $(40 / 80) \times 100 = 50\%$.

Which of these two KR-scheduling variables is the more critical for learning? Bilodeau and Bilodeau (1958) were the first to investigate this question, using a task in which subjects turned a knob to a target position in the absence of vision. For the four different groups, KR was provided after (a) every trial, (b) every third trial, (c) every fourth trial, or (d) every 10th trial, producing relative frequencies of KR of 100%, 33%, 25%, and 10%, respectively. The number of trials performed by these groups, however, was adjusted so that all groups were presented KR after 10 trials; therefore, the group with 100% relative frequency received 10 trials, the group with 33% relative frequency received 30 trials, and so on. Thus, the experiment involved groups that had different relative frequencies, but constant absolute frequencies (10) of KR.

The results for each of the four groups are presented in figure 12.7. Only the trials *immediately following* the presentation of KR are plotted. This is, of course, every trial for the group with 100% relative frequency of KR, only one-third of the trials for the group with 33% relative frequency, and so on. The amount of error on each trial, as well as the pattern of change of the errors as trials progressed, was nearly the same for the four groups. Even though the groups differed greatly in terms of the relative frequency of KR, when the absolute frequency was equated, no difference in performance was found between groups. For performance, the critical feature of KR in this experiment was the number of times that KR was given; the relative proportion of trials followed by KR appeared not to be an important variable. Another way to think of this is that the no-KR trials were meaningless, neither contributing to nor detracting from performance of the task. Motor learning researchers initially took the equal performances of the various groups in figure 12.7 to mean that absolute frequency is important for learning and that relative frequency is irrelevant.

But notice that the Bilodeau and Bilodeau study did not use a transfer design to separate the performance effects of relative frequency from the learning effects. Hence, we actually have no way of knowing whether varying relative frequency

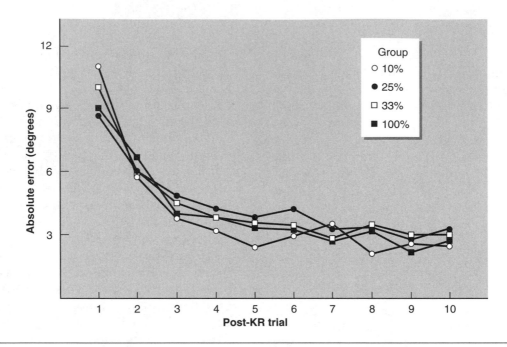

FIGURE 12.7 Absolute errors in positioning for trials immediately following knowledge of results (KR). (Group numbers indicate the percentage relative frequency of KR.)

Reprinted from E.A. Bilodeau and I.M. Bilodeau, 1958, "Variable frequency knowledge of results and the learning of simple skill," *Journal of Experimental Psychology* 55: 379.

affected learning. More recently, experimenters have included these transfer tests, and the effects on learning have been mixed. Some studies showed that reduced relative frequencies of KR produced learning effects that were *as large as* those in 100% KR conditions (e.g., Lee, White, & Carnahan, 1990, experiment 2; Sparrow & Summers, 1992, experiment 1; Winstein & Schmidt, 1990, experiment 1). Yet, using similar tasks and slightly modified methods, other experiments showed that reduced relative-frequency conditions produced *more* learning than 100% KR conditions (e.g., Lee et al., 1990; Sidaway et al., 2008; Sparrow & Summers, 1992; Sullivan, Kantak, & Burtner, 2008, adults; Vander Linden, Cauraugh, & Greene, 1993; Weeks & Kordus, 1998; Weeks, Zelaznik, & Beyak, 1993). Similar effects have also been found when the provision of KR is reduced in an observational learning paradigm (Badets & Blandin, 2004; Badets, Blandin, Wright, & Shea, 2006).

An example is provided in figure 12.8 (from Winstein & Schmidt, 1990, experiment 2). Notice that there are no differences between the 100% and 50% relative-frequency groups in acquisition, as Bilodeau and Bilodeau (1958) had found. However, in 5 min and 24 h no-KR retention tests, a clear learning effect was shown that favored the 50% group. Thus, it seems that instead of

being irrelevant for learning, reduced relative-frequency effects may be beneficial to learning!

This general result has surprised many because it says that the no-KR trials, instead of being meaningless for learning as they appeared to be in the Bilodeau and Bilodeau (1958) study, contributed to the learning in some way. This contradicted a long-held suspicion that practice without feedback was useless for learning. Further, this contribution was not manifested during practice when the KR was present, but was seen in a delayed retention test. Decreasing relative frequency certainly does not diminish learning and may actually facilitate it.

But there is one additional concern with these studies. When the relative proportion of trials that are followed by KR is reduced, a confounding variable arises. Compared to a 100% KR condition, if the total number of trials during practice is held constant, then reduced relative frequency of KR also results in reduced *absolute* frequency of KR. If the researcher decides to make the absolute frequency the same as in the 100% condition, then the total number of trials must be increased for the reduced relative-frequency group. In all the studies cited here, the total number of trials was kept constant. Thus, the effects of reduced relative frequency must be considered in light of

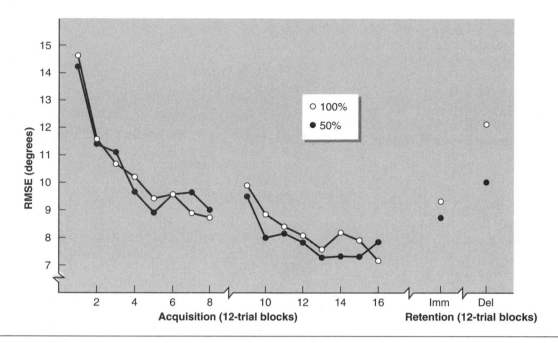

FIGURE 12.8 Effects of 100% versus 50% relative frequency of knowledge of results (KR) in acquisition and retention.

Reprinted, by permission, from C.J. Winstein and R.A. Schmidt, 1990, "Reduced frequency of knowledge of results enhances motor skill learning," *Journal of Experimental Psychology: Learning, Memory, and Cognition* 16; 910. Copyright © 1990 by the American Psychological Association.

the fact that fewer KR presentations were given. When we recall that learning increases with the number of KR presentations, perhaps it is not surprising that the effects of relative frequency are rather mixed. It may very well be that the positive effect of reducing the relative frequency has been offset by the negative effect of fewer KR presentations. This certainly contradicts the earlier conclusions that providing more feedback is all-critical for motor learning. And, note that delayed no-KR transfer tests were required in order to show these effects—further supporting the use of such transfer designs in motor learning research.

The effects of relative frequency appear to be clearer if the method used for reducing the presentations of KR is a "fading" procedure. Here, giving *fewer* KR presentations (trials constant) seems to greatly improve learning (Sullivan et al., 2008; Winstein & Schmidt, 1990; Wulf & Schmidt, 1989). The method usually involves providing KR relatively often during the initial stages of practice and then gradually withholding the presentation of KR more and more toward the end of practice. This method actually has an effect very similar to what naturally happens when using the bandwidth KR procedure, because skill improvements increase the likelihood that performance

will lie within the bandwidth so that the provision of error KR will be withheld.

However, one further complication arises when we consider the effects of reduced relative frequency as a function of the task that is learned. Experiments have shown that when subjects practice several versions of a generalized motor program, reduced relative frequency of KR facilitates the learning of invariances common to the movement pattern, but not the parameterization characteristics (Wulf, Lee, & Schmidt, 1994; Wulf & Schmidt, 1989; Wulf, Schmidt, & Deubel, 1993).

A possible explanation for the relative-frequency effect in motor learning was suggested by Salmoni and colleagues (1984; see also Schmidt, 1991a; Schmidt & Bjork, 1992; Schmidt & Shapiro, 1986; Winstein & Schmidt, 1990). When KR is given on every trial (relative frequency of 100%), this condition is very effective for performance when KR is present, because of a number of temporary factors already discussed (e.g., guidance, motivational, and energizing properties). However, the subject comes to rely too heavily on this information and fails to process information necessary for learning the task in a relatively permanent way; subjects use KR as a "crutch." Subjects in conditions of lower relative frequency, however, do not have such a strong performance enhancement from KR and so are "forced" to engage in other processes during the acquisition phase. These processes result in the subjects' learning something fundamentally *different*, such as the capability to detect one's own errors or to be consistent. Perhaps reducing the relative frequency also encourages one to make between-task comparisons, which might facilitate the abstraction of common movement attributes (Shea & Zimny, 1983; Wulf et al., 1994). This learning is not revealed during the acquisition phase because every-trial KR dominates performance, but it does contribute to performance on delayed no-KR transfer tests. According to this hypothesis, "too much" KR in acquisition is detrimental if the goal is to produce the movement without KR later, as it usually is. As we will see, this hypothesis can explain a number of seemingly contradictory findings in the KR literature and has been supported by some recent experiments to be discussed in sections that follow (e.g., Guadagnoli & Kohl, 2001).

A few practical implications are possible. First, KR is certainly important for learning, as the results generally say that increasing the amount of feedback, other things being equal, is beneficial to performance and learning. But KR can be given too often; in these cases learners come to rely too heavily on its motivating or guiding properties. This enhances performance during practice in which KR is present, but it is probably detrimental to learning as measured on a delayed test in which the learner must perform without KR. Also, relative frequency of KR should be large in initial practice, when guidance and motivation are critical; but then the instructor should systematically decrease relative frequency of KR as the performer becomes more proficient.

Trials Delay and Summary KR

The literature discussed so far has involved situations in which KR for a given trial is presented before the next trial (i.e., KR_n occurs before $trial_{n+1}$ in figure 12.1). However, what happens if the KR from a given trial occurs *after* the performance of the next few trials? Such a procedure, at first glance, would appear to be extremely disrupting for performance; it would be difficult for the learner to know which KR to associate with which movement, particularly when KR is increasingly separated from the trial to which it refers. We can probably think of practical situations in which this effect might occur—for example, when a learner performs a number of trials in a series, *after which* the instructor or therapist gives information about each trial or maybe about just one of the trials in the series. In such situations, the first trial in the sequence is separated from its KR by the intervening trials.

This method of giving KR was given the term *trials delay* by Bilodeau (1956, 1966, 1969). In contrast to what occurs in the usual KR paradigm, we see in figure 12.9 that one or more trials is interpolated between a given movement and its KR. In figure 12.9*a*, M_1 and KR_1 are separated by M_2—there is a one-trial delay between a given movement and its KR. In figure 12.9*b* there is a two-trial delay, with two trials separating a given

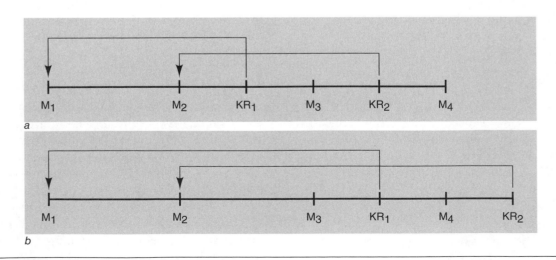

FIGURE 12.9 The trials-delay technique, showing a trials delay of (a) one and (b) two. (A given movement and its knowledge of results [KR] are separated by other trials of the same task.) M_1 refers to movement trial 1. KR_1 refers to the augmented feedback provided about results of movement trial 1.

movement and its KR. You can probably think of many different variations of this type of KR paradigm.

Bilodeau (1956) investigated the effects of trials delay using a lever-positioning task with blindfolded subjects. In two experiments, she varied the number of trials by which KR was delayed. In experiment 1, Bilodeau used zero-, one-, two-, and three-trials delay; in experiment 2, she used zero-, two-, and five-trials delay. Subjects were fully informed about this technique and were questioned to make certain that they understood how KR was being administered.

The data from the two experiments are shown in figure 12.10, where absolute error in positioning (for trials following KR) is plotted against trials for the various trials-delay conditions. For both experiments, performance accuracy systematically decreased as the trials delay was increased. This can be seen both in the "rate" of

approach to the final performance level and in the level of final performance. These findings differed somewhat from earlier ones by Lorge and Thorndike (1935), who had found that improvement in performance did not occur at all under the trials-delay method. But there can be little argument that trials delay is a variable that has drastic negative effects on performance. In the earlier literature (e.g., Bilodeau, 1966), the interpretation of these trials-delay effects was in terms of learning, but these experiments did not use transfer designs to separate the temporary and relatively permanent effects. However, Lavery (1962; Lavery & Suddon, 1962) and others (e.g., Anderson, Magill, & Sekiya, 1994, 2001; Anderson, Magill, Sekiya, & Ryan, 2005) have used transfer designs in the study of this variable (and modifications of it), and their surprising results have had important influences on our thinking about how KR operates.

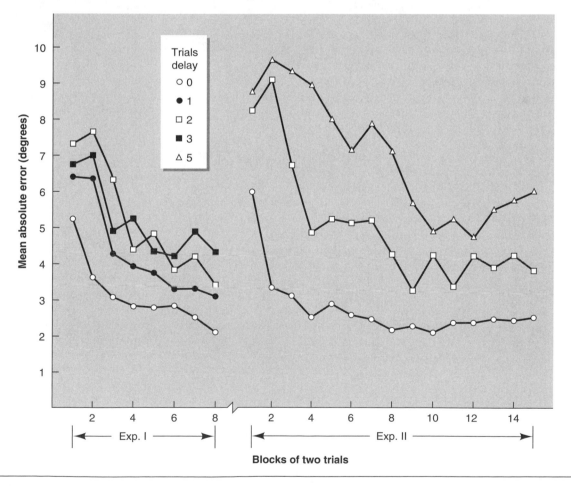

FIGURE 12.10 Absolute error in positioning as a function of the amount of trials delay in two experiments. (The group label indicates the number of trials separating a movement and its knowledge of results [KR].)

Lavery (1962) used several tasks in which a ball was propelled up a track to a target. Three methods were used to give KR. One was the usual condition in which KR is given after every trial, called "Immediate." A second method was "Summary," in which the performance on every trial in a 20-trial sequence was shown, but only after the 20th trial had been completed; no KR was given after each trial as in Immediate. This summary technique was more or less the same as the trials-delay technique, as the KR for trial 1 was separated from its trial by the other 19 movements in the block, trial 2 by the next 18, and so on. Finally, the third condition involved *both* the immediate postmovement KR and the summary, labeled "Both." After an initial no-KR practice day, five days of practice were given under these conditions.

Performance on all the tasks averaged together is shown in figure 12.11. In acquisition, the number of correct trials was far smaller for the Summary group than for the two groups with KR after each trial (i.e., Immediate and Both). The addition of the summary information to Immediate to create Both did not improve performance very much relative to providing the usual postmovement KR (Immediate), so it is clear that the major determinant of performance was the immediate KR. But we knew this before, as this pattern of results is similar to the pattern in the study by Bilodeau (1956) in that performance in acquisition (while KR was present) was hindered by the trials-delay technique.

Now consider the measure of relative amount learned in this experiment—the performance on the transfer trials on days 7, 8, 9, 10, 37, and 93 for which no KR was provided at any time. The group that was formerly least accurate (i.e., Summary) was now the most accurate, and the other two groups, which had been the most accurate

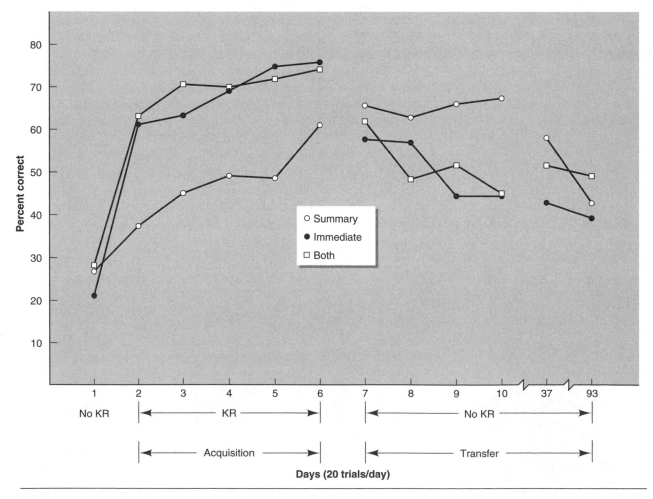

FIGURE 12.11 Percentage correct trials for various summary knowledge-of-results (KR) conditions. (Immediate had KR after every trial; Summary had KR about every trial presented after each block of 20 trials; and Both had both forms of KR.)

(i.e., Immediate and Both), were now the least accurate. Furthermore, the latter two groups appeared to have lost accuracy with each successive no-KR day, while the Summary group did not. The effects persisted to day 37 but were essentially gone by day 93.

Which group learned the most? Using the performance on the transfer/retention test as the measure of relative amount learned, as described earlier, we are forced to conclude that the Summary (trials delay) condition was more effective for learning than either the Immediate or the Both condition. Notice that this is yet another example showing that the most effective condition for performance in acquisition was the least effective for learning! The basic experiment was repeated by Lavery and Suddon (1962), but with the same trials-delay methods as used by Bilodeau (1956), and the results were nearly the same as the findings shown in figure 12.11.

At first glance, we might be drawn to the interpretation that the summary KR per se was in some way effective for learning, providing a benefit over and above the normally useful immediate-KR condition. But look again. If summary KR was "good" for learning, then we should expect the Both group (which also had summary KR) to have benefited in a similar way. To the contrary, though, we see that the Both group performed almost identically to the Immediate group, both in the acquisition phase and in the no-KR transfer phase. One view is that, when KR was added to the normally effective summary-KR procedure to form the Both group, it *lowered* the level of learning to that of the Immediate group. In our interpretation (see Salmoni et al., 1984; Schmidt, 1991a; Schmidt, Young, Swinnen, & Shapiro, 1989), it was not that summary KR was necessarily responsible for the beneficial effect seen in learning, but that immediate KR was *detrimental* to learning! This interpretation is in keeping with the guidance hypothesis that immediate KR provides "too much" information for learners, causing them to rely on it too heavily; thus the subject is not forced to learn the information-processing activities critical for performance when KR is removed in the transfer test. Summary KR provides much less guidance, and presumably forces the subject to learn the task in a somewhat different way, perhaps by prompting the learner to gather information through alternative feedback sources (Anderson et al., 2005).

Optimizing Summary Length

It would seem that summary KR could easily be overdone, with summaries of so many trials that the guidance properties of KR would be minimal. Such thinking leads to the idea that there could be an *optimal* number of trials to be summarized, and that this optimum might also vary with task complexity in some way. In an experiment by Schmidt and colleagues (1989), summary KR was provided as a graph of performance against trials and was given either after each trial (an immediate-KR procedure) or after 5, 10, or 15 trials. In a relatively simple movement-timing task, increased summary length systematically degraded performance in the acquisition phase when KR was present, as Lavery had found earlier. But surprisingly, in a delayed no-KR transfer test, the most accurate performance was achieved by the group that had (in acquisition) received the 15-trial summaries, with systematically increasing error as the acquisition summary length decreased. The effect appeared to be related to long-term retention, with systematically poorer retention as the summary length decreased. The longest summaries produce the most learning; no clear optimal summary length was evident. Similar findings were also reported by Gable, Shea, and Wright (1991), with subjects in a 16-trial condition performing most effectively and no evidence for an optimal summary size.

In another investigation using a more complex, anticipation-timing task with KP provided rather than KR, summaries given after either 1, 5, 10, or 15 trials (Schmidt, Lange, & Young, 1990) were used as in the study just described. Figure 12.12 shows the performance in acquisition and on 10 min and two-day delayed no-KP transfer tests. Again, increasing the summary length degraded the performance in the acquisition phase, with systematically lower scores as the summary length increased. But in the no-KP transfer tests, the most effective summary length for learning was five trials; shorter (one trial) and longer (10 and 15 trials) summaries showed less effective learning. A similar set of results was also reported by Yao, Fischman, and Wang (1994); acquisition performance was least effective for conditions with the longest summary lengths (using summaries of 1, 5, and 15 trials). In the no-KR retention test, however, the five-trial summary condition was superior to both the every-trial and 15-trial summary conditions (see figure 12.13 on p. 417).

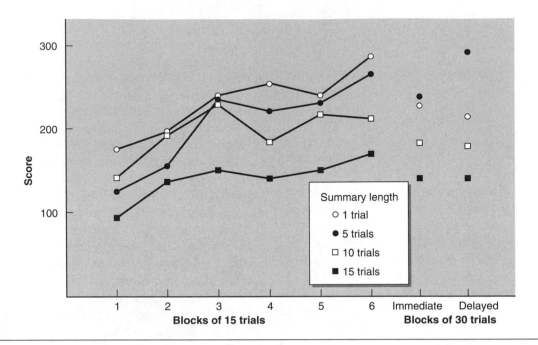

FIGURE 12.12 Performance score for various numbers of trials included in a summary-feedback presentation for acquisition (left) and immediate and delayed retention (right).

Reprinted from *Human Movement Science*, Vol. 9, R.A. Schmidt, C. Lange, and D.E. Young, "Optimizing summary knowledge of results for skill learning," pg. 334, Copyright 1990, with kind permission of Elsevier.

It seems clear from these studies that if optimal summary lengths do exist, these are likely to be task specific, perhaps in relation to the task's complexity. Such conclusions are supported in a clever experiment by Guadagnoli, Dornier, and Tandy (1996). In this study, Guadagnoli and colleagues had subjects learn simple and complex versions of a force production task. For the simple task, the largest (15 trials) summary condition produced the most learning; however, for the complex task, the smallest (one trial) summary group was optimal. These findings provide support for Schmidt and colleagues' (1990) suggestion that optimal summary-KR sizes are dependent on the amount of information provided in the summary, which is determined largely by the complexity of the task.

Statistical Summaries of KR

In many summary-KR experiments, performance on a series of trials is presented to the subject in the form of a graph that organizes the augmented feedback about *all* of the trials in summary fashion. When multiple KR presentations need to be given, the information is more readily understood when given graphically than when given numerically (Cauraugh, Chen, & Singer, 1993), perhaps

because the numeric information overloads the processing capabilities of the learner. However, there is an interesting variant of the summary procedure that has been called *average KR*. Here, instead of providing KR about a block of trials in the summary, the average of the block of trials is determined and this mean score is provided as KR. In this way, the average represents a *statistical summary* of the block of trials rather than a *graphical summary*. In the study by Yao and colleagues (1994) discussed in the previous section, two additional groups of subjects received summary KR that was provided as a statistical average of either 5 or 15 trials. The results for a temporal measure of performance are presented in figure 12.13 (the findings for a spatial measure were similar).

As described in the previous section, acquisition performance was related inversely to the summary size, and no-KR retention performance was most accurate for the five-trial summary group and least effective for the every-trial group. Of particular interest, however, was that the groups receiving average summaries performed similarly to the groups that received graphical summaries. This was consistent for both acquisition and retention and for both the five-trial and 15-trial summary

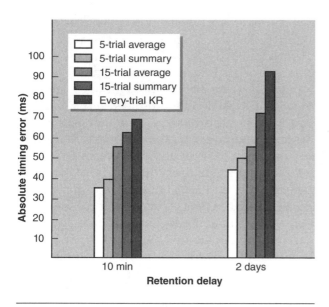

FIGURE 12.13 Absolute timing errors for various summary- and average-KR (knowledge of results) conditions.

conditions. These data suggest that the learning and performance effects of summary KR may be similar regardless of whether the summary is presented as a graph or as a statistical average (see also Weeks & Sherwood, 1994; Young & Schmidt, 1992). The similarity of effects of graphical and statistical forms of summary KR is also explained well by the guidance properties of KR, as the two methods work in similar ways to reduce the guiding properties of augmented feedback. But attempts to further tease apart the specific impact of KR summaries have had mixed success (Guay, Salmoni, & Lajoie, 1999; Guay, Salmoni, & McIlwain, 1992; Sidaway, Moore, & Schoenfelder-Zohdi, 1991; Wright, Snowden, & Willoughby, 1990).

Blocked Versus Random KR

Up to this point, most of the research we have reviewed has involved augmented feedback about one information source, such as KR for movement time or end-point accuracy. But consider the scheduling implications if there were many sources for which feedback could be provided. Suppose, for example, one were to provide KP about the gait of a stroke patient along with several forms of KP. Many potential sources of feedback could be used, but the amount of feedback would likely be overwhelming if all the feedback sources of information were provided at once. So, therapists intuitively withhold much of this feedback.

Now, suppose that only one source of feedback were used. On what basis is this one source to be chosen? Is it the one that has the most important impact on performance, the one that is most important for a safety concern, or the one that meets some other criterion? Moreover, if augmented feedback is provided relatively often, can it be about the same information source or different sources? These ideas have not been addressed frequently in research, although some interesting findings about scheduling have been reported using KR as augmented feedback (Lee & Carnahan, 1990b; Swanson & Lee, 1992).

Subjects performed a three-segment timing task in the Lee and Carnahan (1990b) study, with a specific timing goal for each segment. All subjects were given KR about one segment after each trial. The question was whether KR should be presented repeatedly on the *same* segment for a series of consecutive trials (blocked-KR schedule) or whether KR should be given about a *different* segment on each successive trial (random-KR schedule).[2] The results were rather surprising: The random-KR schedule was more effective for both performance *and* learning of the task. In acquisition, KR was beneficial when it was provided for a given segment, but performance deteriorated once KR was withdrawn from that segment (see also Swanson & Lee, 1992). Blocked KR focused learners only on the segment about which they were currently receiving KR, whereas random KR encouraged subjects to process information about all three segments on each trial.

These results suggest another way in which KR can have an overly directive or guiding function. In terms of the guidance hypothesis, blocked KR may have been directing the subject's attention to the one segment on which KR was being delivered, and treating that segment as just one part of the whole task. When KR was shifted elsewhere, it guided the subject to a different part of the task, again decomposing the task into parts. These conclusions should be considered with caution, however, until more research has been conducted using different tasks and feedback sources (e.g., Wulf, Hörger, & Shea, 1999).

Self-Regulated KR

To this point in the discussion of KR variables, we have directed our focus toward variables that are under the direct manipulation of the experimenter. We now turn our attention to a different experimental approach to deciding when to present KR (Huet, Camachon, Fernandez, Jacobs, & Montagne, 2009; Janelle, Barba, Frehlich, Tennant, & Cauraugh, 1997; Janelle, Kim, & Singer, 1995; Wulf & Toole, 1999). In this paradigm, subjects perform a movement task and are presented with the *option* of receiving augmented feedback or not. For example, subjects in a study by Janelle and colleagues (1997) practiced throwing a ball at a target with their nondominant limb. Transitional KP was provided in a manner similar to that in the Kernodle and Carlton (1992) study discussed earlier. A control group received no KP, and another group received a summary-KP statement after every fifth trial. The group of most importance here followed a self-regulated schedule, in which KP was provided only when subjects asked to receive the augmented feedback. The final group was another control group that was *yoked* to the self-regulated group—the KP delivery schedule for each subject in this yoked group was matched to a member of the self-regulated group. In this way, the yoked control subjects received the same number of KPs as the self-regulated subjects, and on the very same trials in the acquisition schedule sequence. The key difference was that the subject in the self-regulated group actively chose which trials would receive KR; the yoked controls did not.

The results of Janelle and colleagues' (1997) study are shown in figure 12.14. The augmented feedback was useful for learning, as all groups that received KP scored higher than the control group. Of more importance, though, the self-regulated KP schedule produced more effective performance in acquisition and retention than did the yoked controls and the summary-KP group.

Why might self-regulation have an effect that was stronger than a schedule identical in every aspect except for the fact that it was experimenter imposed? One of the leading hypotheses suggests that self-regulation allows subjects to tailor the delivery of augmented feedback to suit their immediate performance needs. Interviews of subjects who had practiced with a self-regulated schedule indicated that they tended to request KR after trials in which performance was believed to have been relatively effective, rather than after ineffective performances (Chiviacowsky & Wulf, 2002). In response to this finding, Chiviacowsky and Wulf (2005) performed a nice experimental test by comparing self-regulated conditions in which subjects made the determination to receive KR either before or after the trial. They found a benefit for learning when self-regulation occurred after the trial.

These findings, however, represent a puzzle in the literature. Self-regulation appears to facilitate

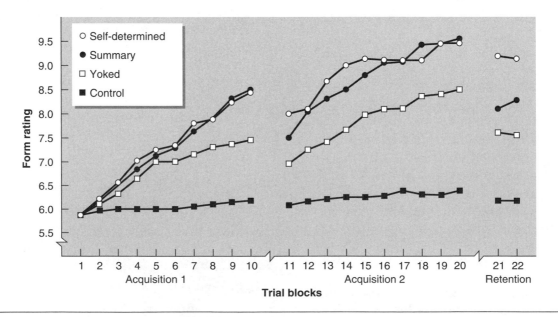

FIGURE 12.14 Effects of a learner-determined feedback schedule in acquisition and retention relative to a frequency-yoked control group, a no-feedback control group, and a summary-feedback group.

Reprinted with permission from *Research Quarterly for Exercise and Sport*, vol. 68, pgs. 269-279. Copyright 1997 by the American Alliance for Health, Physical Education, Recreation and Dance, 1900 Association Drive, Reston, VA 20191.

the learning process when practice conditions allow subjects to decide when to receive augmented feedback (this chapter) or when subjects are given control over the scheduling of trials for multiple tasks (chapter 11). But, recall also from chapter 11 that subjects often have very weak judgments about their own learning. For example, Simon and Bjork (2001) found that subjects in a blocked practice schedule severely overestimated their retention performance, and that random practice subjects underestimated their performance. Earlier, Baddeley and Longman (1978) found that subjects would have preferred to undergo a massed practice schedule, although it was the least effective schedule for learning. If the basis for self-regulation is to facilitate acquisition *performance*, then why is *learning* not detrimentally affected, as we have seen in situations such as the contextual-interference effect? How can these findings be reconciled?

One possibility suggests that the mere *decision* to receive augmented feedback or not engages the learner in the process of self-assessments during practice (see also Cleary, Zimmerman, & Keating, 2006). As we will discuss later on page 426 in "How Augmented Feedback Can Degrade Learning," factors that encourage the processing of inherent feedback are usually considered strong learning variables. Another suggestion, offered by Chiviacowsky and Wulf (2005), is that the strong tendency to request feedback after "good" trials could mean that the KR is serving a strong motivational role—confirming the learner's hunch that the trial's performance was indeed "good" (similar to the rationale underlying the bandwidth KR effect). Support for or rejection of these ideas awaits further research.

Temporal Locus of KR

The next two sections deal with the question of *when* KR is presented in the events prior to and following a practice trial. The question really concerns the three intervals defined in figure 12.1—the KR delay, the post-KR delay, and the intertrial interval—and the ways in which experimentally altering these intervals affects learning and performance. The problem is complicated by the fact that when one of the intervals is lengthened experimentally (e.g., KR delay) and another is held constant (e.g., post-KR delay), then the third interval (in this example, the intertrial interval) must also increase. The effects of the KR delay and the intertrial interval are then *confounded*, so that any resulting change in learning cannot logically be attributed exclusively to either one of them. This fact sometimes makes it difficult to be certain about the particular roles these intervals have in the learning process, as we see in the following sections.

KR-Delay Interval

The KR-delay interval is the amount of time KR is delayed after a movement. Many experimenters have examined feedback delays and motor learning, beginning with Lorge and Thorndike (1935). For a variety of reasons, scientists have always expected to find that increasing the KR delay degrades learning. One reason is that analogous effects in instrumental learning in animals are particularly strong (Lieberman, Vogel, & Nisbet, 2008). Delaying the reward (e.g., a pellet of food) slightly in time from the animal's bar-press movement has large effects on animal learning, and delaying the reward too much eliminates learning completely (Fantino & Logan, 1979; Tarpy & Sawabini, 1974). Scientists expected something like this for KR delay in human motor learning as well. A second reason is that because movement information is lost rapidly from memory (e.g., Adams & Dijkstra, 1966), learning should be less effective as the feedback delay from the associated movement is increased. This would seem to weaken the possibility for the learner to *associate* commands for the movement with its actual outcome—a concept critical to many early theoretical ideas about learning.

However, as reviewed by Salmoni and colleagues (1984), the experiments in human motor learning examining the delay of KR have almost uniformly failed to show that increasing the KR delay has any effect at all. For example, Lorge and Thorndike (1935) used delays of either 1, 2, 4, or 6 s and found no effect in an acquisition phase; but no transfer design was used here to evaluate effects on learning. Perhaps the delay was not sufficiently long. Other studies have used much longer delays ranging from a few seconds to a few minutes; one study even used a delay of one week! Whereas a few studies have shown small, somewhat inconsistent effects on performance, the majority of research has shown no effect (e.g., Schmidt & Shea, 1976). Recent work has used various transfer designs to assess the temporary versus relatively permanent effects of KR delay. There are numerous studies showing no effects, or at best very small effects, and we must doubt that delaying KR has a *detrimental* effect on motor learning.

In contrast, there is some evidence to suggest that detriments to learning can occur if the KR delay is *too short*. Swinnen, Schmidt, Nicholson, and Shapiro (1990) compared groups of subjects who received KR after each trial—either at a short delay after performance was completed (3.2 s) or *instantaneously* upon completion of the trial. As illustrated in figure 12.15, acquisition performance was not affected on the first day of practice by the KR conditions. Performance improvements increased steadily for the delayed-KR group on a second day of practice, but not for the instantaneous-KR group. Learning, as measured in no-KR retention tests after various time intervals, was also facilitated by having KR delayed for a short time. It seems that the instantaneous KR enhanced performance to a point, but retarded both continued improvement and retention after that.

The degrading effects of instantaneous KR are strikingly similar to the effects of concurrent KR, discussed in the previous chapter, in the study by Armstrong (1970b). Take another look at figure 11.19 (p. 387). In chapter 11 we discussed how guided practice degraded learning of a spatial–temporal pattern, relative to a terminal-feedback condition. Armstrong also included a condition in which augmented feedback was presented concurrently, as the subject performed the task. Although this concurrent feedback had a positive influence during practice, it severely degraded learning as seen in the transfer phase, suggesting that the concurrent feedback provided only a temporary boost to performance. These detrimental learning effects have been replicated often (Maslovat, Brunke, Chua, & Franks, 2009; Ranganathan & Newell, 2009; Schmidt & Wulf, 1997; Vander Linden et al., 1993); but they can be lessened by reducing the relative frequency of trials accompanied by concurrent feedback (Camachon, Jacobs, Huet, Buekers, & Montagne, 2007; Park, Shea, & Wright, 2000). This evidence supports the interpretation that frequent, concurrent feedback results in a learning effect that is

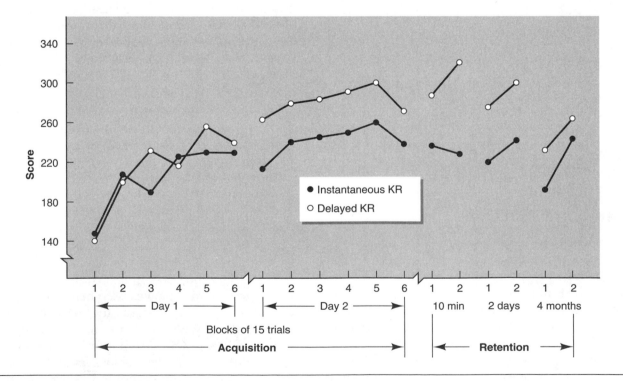

FIGURE 12.15 Performance scores of instantaneous- and delayed-KR (knowledge of results) conditions in acquisition and retention.

highly dependent on maintaining the provision of concurrent information to support performance.

Post-KR-Delay Interval

Next, consider the other portion of the intertrial interval—the post-KR-delay interval, or the time between the presentation of KR and the production of the next movement. In contrast to the hypothesis that the subject is trying to remember the aspects of the movement during the KR-delay interval, during the post-KR-delay interval it appears that other processes are occurring. In particular, KR has now been delivered, likely indicating that the movement was incorrect in some way. Now the learner must generate a movement that is *different* from the previous one, hopefully one that is more correct. So, in contrast to the hypothesis that during the KR-delay interval the learner is storing movement information, in the post-KR-delay interval the learner is thought to be an active and creative movement problem solver.

If the subject is actively processing KR to change the movement during post-KR delay, then shortening the post-KR-delay interval past a certain point should decrease learning in the task, as the person would not have sufficient time to develop an effective new movement. Some support for this view exists in the verbal learning literature using *concept-formation tasks* (e.g., Bourne & Bunderson, 1963; Bourne, Guy, Dodd, & Justesen, 1965; Croll, 1970; White & Schmidt, 1972). The literature on motor learning and performance, however, does not show close parallels to these findings for concept formation. In the acquisition phase, decreasing the post-KR-delay interval does have slight detrimental effects on performance accuracy in both adults (Weinberg, Guy, & Tupper, 1964) and children (Gallagher & Thomas, 1980), but no transfer designs were used in these studies to assess learning effects. When transfer designs are used, however, decreasing post-KR delay also degrades learning, but only when KR delay is held constant, not when the intertrial interval is held constant. Salmoni and colleagues (1984) argued, therefore, that it was the intertrial interval that seemed to be the important one for learning. But there is still some evidence that learning might be reduced when the post-KR delay is very short. Taken together, the evidence does not suggest that the length of this interval, per se, is very important for learning. But this is not to deny the role of processes that occur here,

as they could occur quite rapidly for these very simple motor tasks, and varying the length of the interval might not severely limit processing.

Intertrial Interval

The intertrial interval, or the sum of KR delay and post-KR delay (figure 12.1), has been the object of considerable *indirect* study—mainly because it covaries when either one of the intervals composing it varies, and not because of much interest in the intertrial interval per se. According to a review by Salmoni and colleagues (1984), there are many conflicting results on intertrial-interval effects for performance during the acquisition phase, obtained from a variety of experimental procedures; little generalization seems possible. McGuigan (1959) and Dees and Grindley (1951) have shown, however, that increasing the intertrial-interval length increases learning as measured on no-KR transfer tests, similar to distributed-practice effects discussed in chapter 11. Perhaps longer intertrial intervals result in increased forgetting of the *solution* to the motor problem generated on the previous trial and thus require an active generation of the motor program again on the next trial. These forced generations could be very important for the learning process, as has been inferred from the contextual-interference literature discussed in the previous chapter.

Interpolated Activities During KR Intervals

What is the effect of requiring the learner to perform various activities during otherwise "empty" KR intervals? This question is motivated by an information-processing viewpoint about KR according to which certain other activities could interfere with various processes that occur during these KR intervals and thus the effects should be seen in learning of the task. As we will see, however, various interpolated activities either have no influence, a positive effect, or a negative impact on learning, depending on the nature of the interpolated activity and the delay interval during which it is interpolated.

Interference During the KR-Delay Interval

The influence of various activities during the KR-delay interval may be referred to as "interfering" if they distract the learner from processing the inherent feedback from the performance just completed. For example, Shea and Upton (1976) had subjects perform linear-positioning movements, but *two* positions were to be practiced and learned on each trial rather than one. On a given trial, the subject would produce movement 1, then movement 2, then would engage in the performance of other movements (or would rest if in the other condition); then after 30 s the subject would receive KR about movement 1 and movement 2, then engage in the next trial, and so on. Filling the KR-delay interval increased absolute error on the acquisition trials, indicating that the extraneous movements had a negative effect on performance. And, in the no-KR transfer trials it seemed clear that the decrements in performance caused by the extraneous movements did, in fact, interfere with the learning of the tasks. Marteniuk (1986), Swinnen (1990), and Lieberman and colleagues (2008) provided similar results using more complex motor tasks.

What is happening here? One interpretation of these findings is that the subjects usually engaged in various information-processing activities during the KR-delay interval and that the requirement of the extraneous movements in some way interfered with this processing, degrading learning as it did. What kind of processing might this be? Marteniuk (1986) argued that the interference is from relatively high-level planning processes. But it is also possible that the subject must retain in short-term memory the sensory consequences of the movement until the KR is presented so that the two can be compared. The retention of information is important in order to develop an error-detection capability (capability to detect errors based on inherent feedback sources). If other movements are required, then there will be either a blocked capacity to hold the information in short-term memory or a reduced precision of the inherent feedback, resulting in less effective use of KR when it is presented.

Subjective Estimations During the KR-Delay Interval

Support for the interpretation just outlined is provided in situations in which subjects are *encouraged* to undertake error estimation during the KR-delay interval. Hogan and Yanowitz (1978) asked some subjects to estimate their own errors in a ballistic-timing task prior to receiving KR on each trial. In an acquisition

session with KR present, there were essentially no differences between these subjects and another group of subjects who did not estimate their errors. But in a transfer test without KR, the subjects who were estimating maintained performance nearly perfectly, whereas those subjects who did not estimate regressed systematically over trials. One interpretation is that the estimation conditions in acquisition forced the subjects to attend to their own movement-produced (inherent) feedback to a greater extent than the no-estimation conditions did, thus enabling them to acquire an error-detection capability. This capability was not particularly useful in acquisition because of the powerful guiding properties of KR. But in no-KR transfer, subjects who had gained this error-detection capability through estimation in acquisition were able to maintain performance, whereas the no-estimation subjects were relatively unaware of their own errors and drifted off target. Swinnen (1990; Swinnen et al., 1990) extended and refined the Hogan-Yanowitz paradigm in various ways, using different tasks and transfer tests, in an attempt to understand these phenomena more completely. Overall, there continues to be support for the notion that asking for error estimation in acquisition is effective for learning as measured on no-KR transfer tests.

But some additional experiments suggest that these effects might be more complex than originally conceptualized. Two recent studies have revealed this to be the case. In one study, Liu and Wrisberg (1997) investigated the effects of subjective estimations of movement form error in a throwing task by the nondominant limb (Kernodle & Carlton, 1992). Subjects in two groups saw the outcome of their throw either immediately or after a 13 s delay. In two other groups, the subjects provided subjective estimates of their throwing *form* either just after seeing the outcome of the throw or during the delay interval. As shown in figure 12.16, the performance of these two subjective estimation groups was more accurate in retention than that of the two groups who did not estimate their movement form. From the perspective suggested earlier, this result is rather surprising because in the immediate + estimation group, the subjective estimation occurred after the KR, not during the KR-delay interval, which is typical of most studies of this type. One view of the

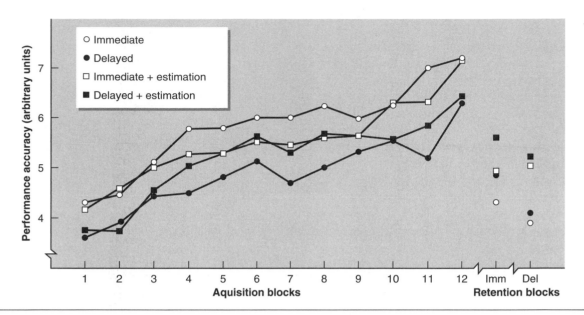

FIGURE 12.16 Combined effects of feedback delay and estimation in the acquisition and retention of a throwing task using the nondominant limb.

From J. Liu and C.A. Wrisberg. Adapted with permission from *Research Quarterly for Exercise and Sport,* vol. 68, pgs. 145-151. Copyright 1997 by the American Alliance for Health, Physical Education, Recreation and Dance, 1900 Association Drive, Reston, VA 20191.

results is that merely estimating something that will be confirmed or corrected by the augmented feedback is not enough—perhaps one needs to estimate something about the performance itself, which is then supplemented by other augmented information and used in the problem-solving process.

Another study (Guadagnoli & Kohl, 2001) offers a related idea regarding the combined effects of subjective estimation and reduced relative frequency of KR. Subjects performed 150 trials in a force-estimation task followed by a no-KR retention test one day later. Four groups were formed based on the factorial combination of relative frequency of KR (100% vs. 20%) and error estimation (every trial vs. no estimation). The 100% relative-frequency condition produced the most accurate retention, but only if accompanied by error estimation during practice (see figure 12.17). If KR was provided on every trial in the absence of any error estimation, then this condition produced the most error in retention. The performance of the other two groups showed that error estimation on every trial was only moderately effective when KR was presented on only 20% of the trials, but that reduced relative frequency was moderately effective even in the absence of error estimation (perhaps due to spontaneous estimation in this group).

These two experiments suggest that error estimation is an important factor in the use of augmented feedback in motor learning. The contribution of error estimation to learning appears to be diminished if it is not accompanied by augmented feedback (Guadagnoli & Kohl, 2001). Yet it also appears that estimating something about performance that encourages the learner to interpret the augmented feedback provides a boost to learning as well (Liu & Wrisberg, 1997).

The issues about error detection are important for theoretical reasons, but there is a strong practical application also. We can think of the self-detected error as a kind of substitute for KR, as it informs the subject about the size and direction of the error that was just made. It is unfortunate that nearly all the focus in learning environments is on performance and that there is almost no concern for the development of the learner's error-detection capacity (but see Schmidt & White, 1972). If procedures could be developed for increasing the strength of error detection, then learners could develop hypotheses about their performance that could then be checked against the objective information provided later in the form of augmented feedback from the teacher or coach. Effective teachers and coaches attempt to establish such error-detection

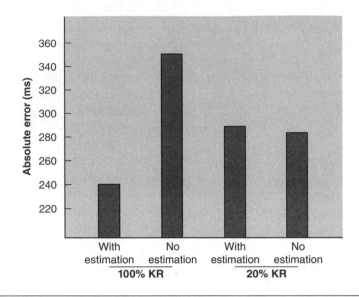

FIGURE 12.17 Combined effects of feedback frequency and estimation in the retention of a force production task.
Data from Guadagnoli and Kohl 2001.

capabilities that can be effectively used for self-evaluation when the teacher or coach is not present.

Interference During the Post-KR-Delay Interval

The focus of processing activities during the KR-delay interval is on movement-produced inherent feedback. During the post-KR delay, however, the processing activities are likely focused on using augmented feedback to alter movement behavior on the next attempt. A number of early experimenters who interpolated activities in the post-KR interval showed that performance was degraded (e.g., Boucher, 1974; Rogers, 1974; but see Magill, 1973), but these studies did not use transfer procedures to assess learning (see Schendel & Newell, 1976, for a discussion). Later experimenters who used transfer tests produced mixed results. Swinnen (1990) and Benedetti and McCullagh (1987) found that interference during the post-KR delay was detrimental as measured in a no-KR retention test; Lee and Magill (1983a, 1987) found no detrimental effects of interpolated activities measured in a transfer test; and Magill (1988) found that such activities were actually beneficial. The rather equivocal nature of these findings makes it difficult to infer practical applications. However, given the comparative strength of these effects, it would appear that instructors should be more concerned about extraneous activities in the KR-delay interval than in the post-KR-delay interval.

Theoretical Issues: How Does Augmented Feedback "Work"?

The previous sections have presented various separate facts in connection with the functioning of augmented feedback in motor learning situations. Some of these have obvious relevance for practical situations, whereas others have distinct implications for how we believe feedback operates in humans to facilitate learning. In this section, we consider some of these implications.

How Augmented Feedback Can Enhance Learning

The research presented in this chapter suggests three possible ways in which KR and KP operate to affect learning in a positive way, and theories of learning have generally adopted one or more of these positions. Both KR and KP are considered to have *informational, motivational,* and *associational* functions. These concepts are considered next.

Informational Functions

In previous sections we have drawn attention to a number of features that are common to KR in human motor learning situations and reward in animal learning situations. Both KR and reward are presented contingent on the nature of the movement, and both are given after the movement. What is the evidence that KR and reward are really different?

That KR and reward might be similar is not a new idea at all, and it is the foundation of the Law of Effect, from Thorndike (1927; see Adams, 1978, 1987). This law states that the organism tends to repeat rewarded movements and to extinguish (or avoid) movements followed either by no reward or by punishment. For motor learning, according to this concept, KR indicating small errors or no error was thought to be a type of "reward," and KR indicating large errors was thought of as "punishment." In this way, the movements followed by nonreward were eliminated, and those followed by reward (i.e., zero or small error) tended to be repeated, leading to decreasing errors with practice.

However, numerous lines of evidence suggest that humans do not use KR as proposed by this interpretation of the Law of Effect. First, when KR is not presented (on no-KR trials), subjects tend to *repeat* the given movements rather than to eliminate them. Only when KR is presented do subjects change their movement behaviors, and then quite clearly in the direction of the target. It would seem that subjects are not using the KR as a reward, but rather as *information* about what to do next. In addition, even a short delay of reward in animal learning severely retards acquisition, and delaying reward by 30 s or so can eliminate learning. Of course, we do not find these effects at all in humans, as the delay of KR seems to have no effect on motor learning. Thus, reward in laboratory rats and KR in humans seem to involve fundamentally different principles of operation (see "Elwell and Grindley on Knowledge of Results").

For these major reasons, the current belief about augmented feedback is that it produces learning more by the provision of *information* about what was wrong with the previous trials—and by *prescriptive* means to improve

performance (Newell, 1991)—than through the rewarding of correct movements and the "punishment" of incorrect ones. This interpretation would seem to contradict the findings from manipulations of bandwidth KR; in these experiments, information conveying to the subject that performance was correct gave an additional boost to learning in comparison to the learning in no-KR trials (Lee & Carnahan, 1990a). We suggest that the boost to learning came from the information content provided by this "no error" type of feedback. That subjects resist making changes to performance on the basis of what could be "noise" might be a way of avoiding the negative influences of too-frequent augmented feedback (see "Inducing Maladaptive Corrections").

One further suggestion is that KR has *optimal* informational value when the learner is *uncertain* about the reliability of his inherent sources of information. A dictionary provides a useful analogy here. The dictionary is like KR in that it is an externally available, objective, and reliable source of knowledge, providing augmented information such as the spelling or meaning of a word. The decision to consult a dictionary arises because we have questioned the reliability of our inherent knowledge; we do not consult the dictionary otherwise. Thus, the dictionary provides the means for assessing (and improving) the reliability of our spelling knowledge. One hypothesis arising from this analogy is that augmented feedback can be optimally useful when the subject asks for it—a concept that has received support from recent experiments (see the earlier section on self-regulated KR).

Motivational Functions

As mentioned earlier, receiving information like KR and KP can play a strong motivating, or "energizing," role. Augmented feedback may make the task seem more interesting, keep the learner alert, cause the learner to set higher performance goals, and generally make boring tasks more enjoyable. Some of the effects of motivation are probably performance phenomena, which can be expected to subside when the feedback is withdrawn after training. But there is an indirect learning effect that should not be ignored. When learners are highly motivated, they are inclined to practice more often, longer, and with more intensity and seriousness. Of course, deliberate

ELWELL AND GRINDLEY ON KNOWLEDGE OF RESULTS

They said it . . .

Elwell and Grindley (1938) provided the first major challenge to Thorndike's ideas regarding the role of KR in motor learning; this is developed more completely in three subsequent papers (Dees & Grindley, 1951; MacPherson, Dees, & Grindley, 1948, 1949). They suggested that KR provided more than just a rewarding function, and their arguments formed the basis for what was later called the *informational* role of KR. The authors stated:

"In the acquisition of a muscular skill, such as that described in the present paper, the learning cannot be regarded merely as the strengthening of the tendency to repeat movements which have been 'rewarded' (by a high score). If a subject missed the bull's-eye he tried, next time, to correct for his error by altering his response in the appropriate direction. . . . Knowledge of results, when the movement was not completely successful (i.e., when it did not result in a bull's-eye) introduces also a tendency towards a specific kind of variation of the response which has just been made. We may call this the 'directive effect' of knowledge of results." (p. 51)

practice per se is a critical variable for learning, and any factor that increases it will almost surely enhance learning (Ericsson, 1996; Ericsson, Krampe, & Tesch-Römer, 1993). Recent evidence suggests that there may be a more direct effect on learning as well (Chiviacowsky & Wulf, 2007; Lewthwaite & Wulf, 2010), which may require revised views of the motivational role of feedback in the future.

Associational Functions

A different view is that KR is associational—providing associations between stimuli and movements. One version of this concept is provided within schema theory (Schmidt, 1975b), according to which KR is thought to operate associationally as well as in the ways that Adams (1971) has suggested (both theories are discussed in more detail in chapter 13). In schema theory, with respect to rapid movements that are presumably controlled by motor programs, the person associates the KR received on a trial (a measure of what happened in the environment) with the parameters of the generalized motor program (GMP) that were issued to produce that outcome in the environment. With practice, the learner comes to develop a rule (or schema) about the relationship between what the limbs were "told to do" and "what they did when told to do it." On this basis, knowing what kinds of internal commands tend to produce certain kinds of movements, the learner has a way of selecting the parameters of the movement on future trials. Thus, in this view, KR serves more than a guid-ance function toward the target; it also provides a rule about the relationship between internal commands and the outcomes that were produced in the environment.

How Augmented Feedback Can Degrade Learning

Another view of how KR works is that it guides the learner to making the correct movement. Thus, when the learner makes a movement, KR informs the person about how the movement was inadequate, and the learner then changes the movement to one that (hopefully) will be more adequate. Augmented feedback thus carries inherent "instructions" about which aspects of the movement should be changed, as well as about the directions those changes should take. According to this position, KR does not provide any direct strengthening of the movement but creates it indirectly by guiding the person to the proper action. Once the proper actions are being produced, other processes take over to help the person learn the task.

This view is fundamental to Adams' (1971) learning theory, which says that KR presented after each trial of a slow positioning movement guides the person toward the correct location. Then, as the learner achieves positions close to the target, she also receives kinesthetic feedback associated with the proper position, and this feedback forms an internal representation of being at the target (a reference of correctness). This internal representation becomes stronger with each successive trial near the target and thus provides an increasingly effective means for detecting errors. Thus, according to Adams, KR has a guidance role in driving the subject closer and closer to the target so that a reference of correctness can be formed.

Considered in this way (as envisaged by Adams, 1971), the guiding influences of augmented feedback on learning should always be positive. As we have seen, however, in some experiments the KR effects showed that increased guidance *degraded* learning (leading to doubts about Adams' theory; see chapter 13). We consider reasons why feedback can degrade learning in the next sections (see also Salmoni et al., 1984; Schmidt, 1991a; Schmidt & Bjork, 1992).

Blocking Other Processing Activities

When augmented feedback is provided frequently, immediately, or otherwise in such a way that various processing activities are not undertaken, then there will likely be a decrement in learning. One of the negative influences of augmented feedback may be to *block* the processing of inherent sources of feedback, which then leads to the failure to learn error-detection capabilities for this task. Augmented feedback is often a very salient source of information, and one that will be attended to even when doing so may not be in the learner's best interest (Buekers et al., 1992). The presentation of instantaneous KP (Swinnen et al., 1990), which was discussed earlier, is an example of a case in which the saliency of the augmented feedback is maximized. We interpret results of this type as suggesting that the augmented feedback blocked the processing of alternative sources of information and reduced the learning effectiveness of the practice session as measured in retention.

Inducing Maladaptive Corrections

One of the fundamental views about the directive function of augmented feedback is that it tells the learner what went wrong and how to fix it. As we found in our discussion of precision of KR, more precise KR can be beneficial, but only up to a point. The idea is similar here. When each trial is followed by information about errors, there is a tendency for the subject to make a change for the next trial based on that error. The problem is that motor performance is variable, and a change meant to correct a very small error might actually make the error larger on the next trial. The idea is that KR induces movement variability, not all of which is adaptive in producing improved learning. Sometimes augmented feedback can have maladaptive corrective properties (R.A. Bjork, personal communication), in which case withholding feedback (and stabilizing performance) seems to be beneficial for learning. Presenting information that encourages a subject to correct an action that was essentially accurate may have a detrimental impact on learning (Schmidt, 1991a; Schmidt & Bjork, 1992).

Bandwidth KR effects illustrate how maladaptive corrections may be avoided. Under bandwidth KR conditions, there exists a zone of acceptable error within which movement is considered correct. Defining the actual width of the band of correctness, as well as what would be considered maladaptively corrective and what would be considered too imprecise, is a challenge for future research. However, we suspect that an *optimal KR bandwidth* may be closely related to the precision of an individual's motor control capabilities, although even within an individual this is likely to change (e.g., with learning and aging).

Summary

Feedback is that class of sensory information that is movement related, and it can be classified into two basic categories—*inherent* (intrinsic to the task) and *augmented* (supplementary to the task). Two major classes of augmented feedback include KP, which is information about the form of the movement, and KR, which is verbal postmovement information about performance outcome. Much research suggests that the provision of augmented information is the single most important variable for motor learning (except for practice itself, of course).

Information about the learner's movements (KP) can be given through video feedback, recordings of the force–time characteristics of the movement (kinetics), or representations of the movement trajectories (kinematics); and all these appear to have positive effects on performance and perhaps on learning. The impact of KP on learning appears to be strongest when it precisely specifies information that is critical for movement efficiency and that cannot be obtained from other sources of feedback.

Research on KR precision shows that performance improves with increases in precision up to a point, with no further increases in performance thereafter. Presenting combinations of qualitative and quantitative KR, based upon a goal-related bandwidth of correctness, has strong implications for both application and theory.

Early research indicated that the *relative frequency* of KR (the percentage of trials on which KR was given) was irrelevant for learning, whereas the absolute frequency (the number of KR presentations given) was the critical determinant. More recent data using transfer designs contradict this position, indicating that both are clearly important. Trials on which no KR is given appear to contribute to learning in the task, but not as much as the KR trials do. The trials-delay and summary-KR procedures, in which the KR for a given movement is separated from the movement by other trials, were shown to produce detrimental effects on motor performance but positive effects on learning.

The effect of delaying KR, that is, the effect of the interval from the movement until KR is presented, has been found to be negligible for learning most motor tasks, as long as KR is not presented too soon after performance. Filling this interval with activities not related to the task degrades learning. However, filling this interval with activities related to the task, such as subjective estimation processes, enhances learning. If the post-KR-delay interval—the interval from the KR until the next movement—is too short, subjects appear to have difficulty generating a new and different movement on the next trial. However, filling this interval has uncertain effects on learning.

Augmented feedback appears to have several possible mechanisms for enhancing learning. It acts as *information*. It acts to form *associations* between movement parameters and resulting action. And it acts in a *motivational* role. Augmented feedback also has a guidance property that can enhance performance but degrade learning.

Student Assignments

1. Prepare to answer the following questions during class discussion:

   a. Choose any skilled trade that would require motor learning (e.g., carpenter). Provide examples for each of the different kinds of inherent and augmented feedback that could be useful in learning this trade.

   b. Using one of the augmented-feedback examples from the answer in 1a, describe how the temporal locus of presenting this information to the learner would affect learning.

   c. Models, physical guidance devices, and augmented feedback are methods of providing external sources of information to the learner. Compare and contrast these methods in terms of their potential effect in a learning environment.

2. Find a research article (published in the past five years) that examines the influence of knowledge of performance on the performing or learning of a motor skill.

Web Resources

This Web site describes augmented feedback teaching devices to facilitate motor learning:

www.thespeedstik.com/

This Web site offers golf swing training aids:

www.dwquailgolf.com/training/your_pro_swing_trainer.html

Notes

[1] Although we have distinguished between various types of augmented feedback, of which KR is one, we will generally refer to many aspects of this work in relation to the term KR. However, exceptions will be made when a clear distinction is necessary.

[2] Note the differences between the use of these terms and the use of random and blocked practice in chapter 11. In that work, the same task is repeated in blocked practice, and switching between tasks occurs in random practice. In the Lee and Carnahan experiment, the same task is performed on each trial, but KR is given either about the same segment over a series of trials (blocked KR) or about a different segment on successive trials (random KR).

CHAPTER 13

THE LEARNING PROCESS

So far in the discussion of motor learning, our major concern has been the most important empirical findings about the acquisition of skills. It is time now to consider the underlying reasons for these findings and to ask about the nature of the motor learning processes that cause the motor system to behave in the ways identified in previous chapters. A part of this process is theoretical, in that we search for a fundamental understanding—stated as theories—of how the system "works" when it learns. But part of it is practical, in that a solid understanding of the system's function provides suggestions for practical application to situations that have not actually been studied; there is nothing as practical as a good theory (Kerlinger, 1973).

In this chapter, we consider the many ways in which various people have conceptualized the motor learning process. All these theoretical perspectives have as their basic goal an understanding of the changes in skill that occur with practice. However, we will see that a phenomenon as broad and common as this can be explained in various ways and at a number of levels of analysis (biomechanical, cognitive, and so on). At the same time, we will see that the concepts basic to these various theoretical ideas are already familiar from previous chapters, having to do with such notions as the building of new motor programs, changes in attentional requirements, the development of error-detection processes, and the like.

The chapter is divided into three major sections. The first section presents some fundamental ideas about the learning process. With this information in mind, together with information from the previous two chapters, we then present various theoretical views about motor learning. Two of these, which are considered major theoretical advances in the history of motor learning research, are presented in the second section of the chapter. The third section presents different perspectives on the learning process—perspectives that in one form or another can be considered major hypotheses about learning.

Characteristics of the Learning Process

Without a doubt, the most notable thing that happens when people practice is that they demonstrate increased proficiency in the task. Sometimes this is so obvious that it hardly needs to be mentioned, while in other cases the changes are more subtle and require special methods, observation, and rationale in order to be examined. In this section we describe a number of ways in which the learning process has been characterized, in terms of the various descriptions of the ways individuals change in their capability to perform a motor skill with practice.

Stages of Motor Learning

Many have noticed that learners appear to pass through relatively distinct stages (or phases) as they practice a skill. Bryan and Harter (1897, 1899) were among the first to study the acquisition of skill in considerable detail (see "Bryan and Harter's Hierarchy of Habits"). Learning was defined as a two-stage process by Snoddy (1926). Subjects in Snoddy's research learned to make hand movements but saw their hand only in a mirror—a task that requires abilities needed by a dentist, for example. According to Snoddy (1926), the *adaptation* stage involved acquisition of the neuromuscular pattern required to perform the task. Once the pattern was learned, the *facilitation* stage

involved improving the efficiency of the pattern. Other two-stage views were later suggested by Adams (1971) and Gentile (1972). A three-stage view of learning was suggested by Fitts (1964; Fitts & Posner, 1967) and later Anderson (1982, 1995). These three stages, referred to as the *cognitive, fixation,* and *autonomous stages,* are discussed in more detail in this section. As you read these explanations, however, remind yourself that these stages are not discrete and fixed stages, but have "fuzzy" borders (see Anson, Elliott, & Davids, 2005, for an excellent discussion of Fitts' stages of learning).

Stage 1: Cognitive

When the learner is new to a task, the primary problem to be solved concerns *what is to be done*—that is, what actions need to be taken in order to achieve the goal of the task? Naturally, considerable cognitive activity is required so that

Bryan and Harter's Hierarchy of Habits

A fascinating early set of studies regarding the perceptual and motor changes that occur with learning was conducted by William Lowe Bryan (a psychologist) and Noble Harter (a telegrapher and student of Bryan's). The result of their shared interests was two landmark papers regarding the acquisition of telegraphic skills (Bryan & Harter, 1897, 1899). In these papers, Bryan and Harter presented the results of experiments that compared novice and expert telegraphers, as well as data they obtained by charting the acquisition of telegraphy skill over many months of practice. These papers present many interesting findings (Lee & Swinnen, 1993), but we will focus on one in particular.

Skill, in Bryan and Harter's view, was a process of achieving a *hierarchy of habits.* At the most basic level, telegraphy involves the ability to discriminate (perceptually and motorically) between *units* of time. A dot is one "unit" of continuous auditory signal. A dash is three "units" of continuous time. One unit of no signal occurs between dots and dashes within a letter (e.g., the letter *G* is a dash-dash-dot). Three continuous units of no signal denotes that a new letter is beginning, and six units marks a new word. This "language" of telegraphy lent itself well to Bryan and Harter's view of learning as a hierarchy of habits. The discrimination of time was learned quickly.

The alphabet became the next challenge. This, too, is usually learned quickly, and performance in sending and receiving code improves rapidly. However, Bryan and Harter then noticed something peculiar about the practice curves of some of their subjects: Periods of time would go by during which little or no improvement occurred at all, which were followed later by rapid improvements. They called these periods *plateaus* in performance that occur prior to the formation of a new, advanced capability. They proposed that rather than hearing dots and dashes, with learning, the telegraphers "hear" letters. With further practice they then "hear" words, and, for the most skilled, even larger units of a sentence. Presumably, the plateaus in performance occur because the maximum performance capability of one habit places a limit on performance, which is then lifted when a higher-order habit is formed. Although some of Bryan and Harter's views have been challenged at times (e.g., Keller, 1958), many of the basic concepts of progression through stages and to higher orders of skill have been retained in a number of conceptualizations of skill acquisition that remain popular today.

the learner can determine appropriate strategies to try to get the movement in the "ballpark." Effective strategies are retained, and inappropriate ones are discarded. As a result, the performance gains during this stage are dramatic and generally larger than at any other stage in the learning process. Performance is usually very inconsistent, perhaps because the learner is trying many different ways of solving the problem. The use of instructions, models, augmented feedback, and various other training techniques (discussed in chapters 11 and 12) is most effective during this stage because they assist the learner in this problem-solving process. Probably most of the improvements in the cognitive stage can be thought of as verbal–cognitive in nature, the major gains being in terms of what to do rather than in the motor patterns themselves. Adams (1971) termed this stage the *verbal–motor stage*.

Stage 2: Fixation

The second stage of motor learning begins when the individual has determined the most effective way of doing the task and starts to make more subtle adjustments in *how the skill is performed*. Performance improvements are more gradual, and movements become more consistent in the fixation stage. This stage can persist for quite a long time, with the performer gradually producing small changes in the motor patterns that will allow more effective performance. Many writers (e.g., Adams, 1971; Fitts, 1964) think that the verbal aspects of the task have largely dropped out by this stage, with the performer concentrating on *how to do* the action rather than on which (of many) movement patterns should be produced. This stage and the next (autonomous) are equivalent to what Adams called the *motor stage*.

Stage 3: Autonomous

After many months, perhaps years, of practice, the learner enters the autonomous stage, so named because the skill has become largely *automatic* in the sense discussed in chapter 4. That is, the task can now be performed with less interference from other ongoing activities. It is easy to find examples of high-level performers engaging in secondary tasks without interference—for example, the concert pianist who can shadow digits or do mental arithmetic without interference while sight-reading and playing piano music (e.g., Allport, Antonis, & Reynolds,

1972; Shaffer, 1971, 1980). Automaticity is usually evidenced with respect to particular kinds of simultaneous tasks, primarily those that we could class as verbal-cognitive; some other motor task could in fact interfere with a performance in the autonomous stage, as discussed in chapter 4 in detail. Even so, the performer gives the impression that she is performing without having to "pay attention" to the actions. This stage has the benefit of allowing the person to process information from other aspects of the task, such as the strategy in a game of tennis or the form or style of movement in ice skating or dance.

A major problem for motor behavior research is that this stage, which is of immense importance for understanding high-level skills, is only rarely studied in experiments on motor learning. The reasons are probably obvious. In paradigms in which subjects practice on laboratory tasks, such practice should continue for months before even approaching the levels of skill shown by high-level musicians, athletes, and industrial workers. It is very difficult to convince subjects to devote this kind of effort in experiments. Alternatively, we could use other, more natural tasks that learners are practicing anyway; but it is difficult to manipulate and control the many variables that would need to be used for a scientific understanding of the learning processes.

Some efforts at understanding the principles of automaticity have been made in this direction by Schneider and colleagues (Schneider & Fisk, 1983; Schneider & Shiffrin, 1977) in reaction-time (RT) tasks, and by Logan (1985, 1988) using speeded-decision tasks. Unfortunately, research involving more complex motor tasks is rarely taken to this stage of learning (but see Jabusch, Alpers, Kopiez, Vauth, & Altenmüller, 2009, for a recent exception).

Individual Differences and Motor Learning

Some important hypotheses for motor learning are framed in the language and methods of individual-differences research (see chapter 9). Beginning with the concept that a given motor performance is based on some small set of underlying motor abilities, one hypothesis simply states that this set of abilities changes in its makeup as practice continues. The abilities themselves do not change; this would violate the assumption (discussed in chapter 9) that abilities are to a large extent genetically defined and unmodifiable by practice. But what *does* change, according to this view, is the particular collection of abilities that underlie the skill being learned.

Studies Using Individual-Difference Variables

Fleishman and Hempel (1955) and Fleishman and Rich (1963) contributed important investigations in this area. In the Fleishman-Rich study, subjects practiced the two-hand coordination task, in which two crank handles had to be manipulated to cause a pointer to follow a moving target on a target board (figure 2.5). Separate from the practice on this test, the subjects were given two additional tests. In one, they were asked to lift small weights and to judge the weight relative to a standard weight. This test was called *kinesthetic sensitivity* because it seemed related to how

sensitive the person was to applied tensions. A second test called *spatial orientation* was a paper-and-pencil test related to a subject's perception of orientation in space.

First, Fleishman and Rich divided their group of people into two, on the basis of their performance on the kinesthetic sensitivity test; then they plotted the groups' performances separately for the two-hand coordination test. As seen in figure 13.1*a*, the subjects classified as high and low on the kinesthetic sensitivity measure were not different on the two-hand coordination test in early trials; but later in practice, the subjects high in kinesthetic sensitivity began to outperform those low in kinesthetic sensitivity. The interpretation of these results is that kinesthetic sensitivity is an ability that increases in importance with practice, at least for this task. Next, consider the spatial orientation measure (figure 13.1*b*). The subjects classified as high on this test were

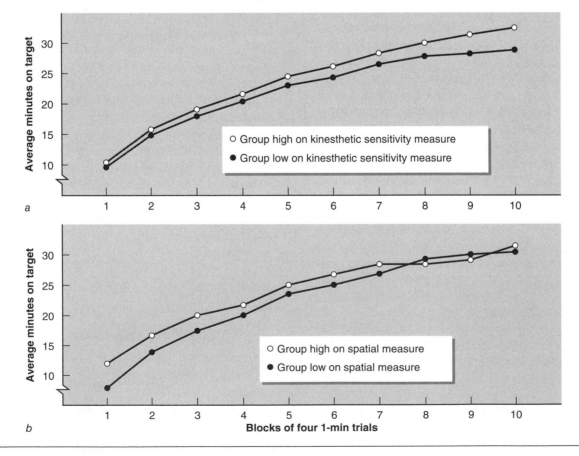

FIGURE 13.1   Performance on the two-hand coordination test as a function of practice trials. *(a)* Groups classed as high and low on a kinesthetic sensitivity test are plotted separately; *(b)* groups classed as high and low on a spatial orientation test are plotted separately.

stronger performers on the two-hand coordination test than subjects classed as low, but only for initial performance. This result is interpreted as evidence that spatial orientation is an ability that is important for early proficiency in this task but appears to have little to do with performance in later practice.

Another way to view these results is that, for the two-hand coordination test, there is some *collection* of abilities that underlies it on trial 1. This collection includes some abilities related to the spatial orientation measure, and it does not include abilities related to kinesthetic sensitivity. As practice continues, the collection of abilities (but not the abilities themselves) changes, so that at the end of practice the task is made up of a somewhat different set of abilities. This collection could include some of the same abilities as in early practice, but it now has abilities related to kinesthetic sensitivity and does not have any abilities related to spatial orientation. Practice results in a shift in the abilities underlying a task (see also Bartram, Banerji, Rothwell, & Smith, 1985).

Practice and the Predictability of Skilled Performance

If the collection of abilities underlying a particular performance becomes rearranged systematically with practice, then the *prediction* of success in the skill will be based on different ability measures in early versus late practice. Fleishman and Rich (1963, figure 13.1) showed that, early in learning (but *not* later in learning), performance on the two-hand coordination test could be predicted (to some extent) from the spatial relations test; that is, the subjects *high* on this measure outperformed those classified as *low*. However, late in practice (but *not* early in practice), the two-hand coordination test performance could be predicted from kinesthetic sensitivity. This notion of prediction implies that the *correlation* between the two-hand coordination test and, for example, the kinesthetic sensitivity test would be zero in initial practice and larger in later practice. More generally, the hypothesis that the collection of abilities underlying some skill will change with practice says that the correlations between measures of various abilities and the criterion task performance will change with practice.

Intertrial Correlation Analyses

Take any motor task and measure a large number of subjects on each of a series of trials. Then correlate the performances obtained on every trial with those on every other trial and arrange these correlation values in an *intertrial correlation matrix*. Such a matrix is shown in table 13.1, reproduced from Jones' (1962, 1966) work on the two-hand coordination test. The bottom half of the matrix is omitted for simplicity (it is the mirror image of the top half). There are a number of interesting features of tables like this, as has been pointed out by Jones (1966).

Remoteness Effects First, notice that across any row of the table, the correlations become systematically smaller; they drop from 0.79 to 0.70 in the first row, from 0.87 to 0.82 in the second row, and so on. The top row represents the correlations of

---

TABLE 13.1. An Intertrial Correlation Matrix

Trial	1	2	3	4	5	6	7	8
1	—	.79	.77	.74	.73	.71	.71	.70
2		—	.87	.87	.84	.82	.82	.82
3			—	.91	.89	.87	.85	.86
4				—	.91	.88	.86	.88
5					—	.89	.90	.90
6						—	.93	.93
7							—	.94
8								—

Note. The boxed-in section forms the diagonal of the matrix, and the shaded portion is the "superdiagonal."

Adapted from Jones 1966.

trial 1 with trial 2, trial 1 with trial 3, trial 1 with trial 4, and so on up to trial 1 with trial 8. Thus, the number of trials between the two trials being correlated increases as we move to the right along any row. As a general rule, as the number of intervening trials increases, the correlation decreases. This effect is often called the *remoteness effect,* because the correlations between the trials depend on how "remote" (how far apart) the trials are from each other.

What is the meaning of the remoteness effect? First, remember that the correlation between two tests (in this case, two trials of the "same" test) is related to the number of common abilities they share. As two tests become more separated in the practice sequence, and become less correlated, the argument is that these performances are becoming dependent on fewer and fewer of the same abilities. In this sense, the remoteness effect is just another way to say that the motor abilities change with practice, as did Fleishman's research, discussed in the previous section.

Adjacent-Trial Effects   Examine the data in table 13.1 again, this time concentrating on the correlations between adjacent trials—that is, between trials 1 and 2, between trials 2 and 3, and so on. These correlations can be found on what is called the *superdiagonal* (the shaded area), or the line of correlations that lies just above the diagonal of the matrix (unfilled squares in table 13.1). Notice that, as the adjacent trials are chosen later and later in the sequence, the correlations steadily increase. The correlation between trials 1 and 2 is 0.79, whereas the correlation between trials 7 and 8 is 0.94, the highest in the matrix. This is another well-known finding. The change in these adjacent-trial correlations along the superdiagonal suggests that performances become systematically more stable, in terms of their underlying ability structure, as practice continues.

Practice as a Process of Simplification   An even more restrictive descriptor of the intertrial correlation matrix is what is called the superdiagonal form, for which any four arbitrarily chosen correlations within the matrix must possess a particular mathematical relationship with each other. (A discussion of the nature of this relationship is beyond the scope of this text, but see Jones, 1966.) The important point is that this superdiagonal form is derived from the hypothesis that the number of abilities systematically decreases with

practice. In this sense, the task becomes "simpler" (in the sense of having fewer underlying abilities) with increased practice.

Individual Differences and Stages of Learning

A variation of Fitts' stages of learning view by Ackerman (1988, 1989, 1990, 1992; Ackerman & Cianciolo, 2000) suggests that, early in practice, performing the task should be based on abilities having to do with thinking, reasoning, mechanical knowledge, and so on. General intellectual abilities (information-processing skills) are the most important determiners of individual differences in performance during the cognitive stage of skill acquisition. Later in practice, these abilities should not be involved as much; and perhaps other abilities such as movement speed, RT, strength, and steadiness become the most important. Once the idea of the task has been acquired, the role of general intelligence as a determiner of individual differences drops off, replaced by more "motor" abilities during the fixation stage in performance.

Predicting Individual Differences During Different Stages   According to Ackerman's theory, the correlation between tests of intellectual, perceptual-speed, and psychomotor abilities will differ during different stages in learning. These predictions are illustrated in the three graphs in figure 13.2. Figure 13.2*a* suggests that the correlation between general intellectual ability and task performance will be highest during the cognitive stage (stage 1) and will drop off quickly thereafter. The correlation between perceptual-speed tests and task performance should be low during the cognitive and autonomous stages (stages 1 and 3) but much higher during the fixation stage (stage 2), as presented in figure 13.2*b*. Figure 13.2*c* depicts very little contribution of psychomotor abilities until the autonomous stage (stage 3), at which point increasingly higher correlations are predicted.

Evidence for Ackerman's Integrated Model   Ackerman asked subjects to perform a simple-RT task for six sessions, during which subjects pressed a key on a numeric keypad in response to the number shown on a screen (e.g., press the "1" key in response to the number "1"). As would be expected, subjects had little difficulty in figuring out what to do in this task and there-

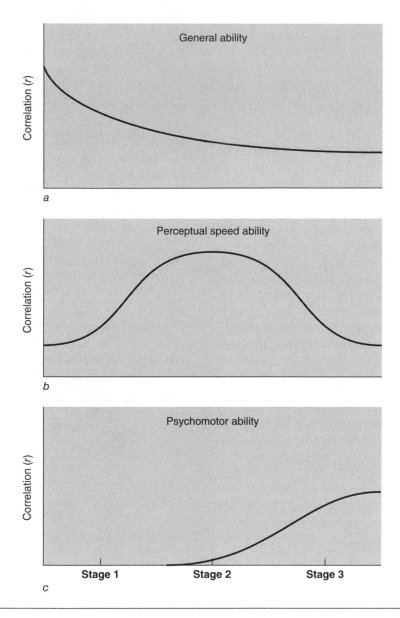

FIGURE 13.2 Predicted correlation of individual differences in general intellectual, speed, and psychomotor abilities at different stages of learning.

Reprinted, by permission, from P.L. Ackerman, 1990, "A correlational analysis of skill specific city. Learning, abilities, and individual differences," *Journal of Experimental Psychology: Learning, Memory and Cognition* 16: 887. Copyright © 1990 by the American Psychological Association.

fore would be expected to perform as if starting in stage 2 of practice rather than in stage 1. The correlations of task performance with general and perceptual-speed abilities are presented in figure 13.3. As can be seen, the correlations are higher for perceptual speed than for general ability in the training phase, as is predicted for stage 2. Moreover, the general trend taken by these correlations over the six sessions is similar to the predicted correlations illustrated in figure 13.2 for stage 2 of practice.

Then, in session 7, Ackerman transferred his subjects from the simple, compatible stimulus–response (S-R) mappings to less compatible mappings in which subjects pressed the key designated by a two-letter abbreviation system; the first letter indicated the numeric keypad *row* (e.g., L = lower row), and the second letter indicated the numeric keypad *column* (e.g., M = middle column). Thus, the stimulus "LM" (lower middle) indicates that the "2" key should be pressed; a "UR" denotes the "9" key. The rationale was that this incompatible mapping would require considerable cognitive activity initially in practice, forcing the learner back into stage 1. On the right side of figure 13.3, the correlations between RT performance and the abilities tests were much higher early in transfer for the general ability, but were similar to those for perceptual-speed ability later in practice. Again, the shape of these functions over practice in the transfer phase appears rather similar to the predictions seen in figure 13.2 for phase 1 of practice.

These findings provide support for Ackerman's theory. In addition, Ackerman (1988) found support for the psychomotor abilities predictions when he reanalyzed data sets from Fleishman (1956; Fleishman & Hempel, 1955, 1956). These data showed that the correlations between the rate of arm movement (a psychomotor ability) and three different performance tasks *increased* with practice, as predicted by the theory (see also Adams, 1957). More recent studies (Ackerman & Cianciolo, 2000), using a flight-simulator task, have provided additional support for the predictions shown in figure 13.2, *a* and *c*. However, the prediction that perceptual-speed abilities become most important during phase 2 of skill acquisition (figure 13.2*b*) was not supported.

Error-Detection Capabilities

It is well known that a major outcome of practice is the capability to produce more effective movement behaviors, but an additional outcome of practice is that learners become more capable of *evaluating* their own movement behaviors. That is, it seems that a learner develops a kind of *error-detection* capability with practice that, in many instances, can be used as feedback to inform the individual about his own errors.

For example, one of the distinguishing features of expert jugglers seems to be their ability to detect errors in the way that the hand releases the object. If the force is too large or too small (affecting the amplitude of the throw), or if the angle of release is slightly off line (affecting the location where it will be caught by the other hand), then spatial and timing adjustments will have to be made in order to maintain the juggling pattern. Beek and Lewbel (1995) argued that novices and experts differ in the type of information they use and how quickly they detect an error; novices tend to use visual feedback of the object in flight, while experts can detect an error by monitoring the sensory feedback as (or even before) the object leaves the hand. Thus, some of the skill differences between novices and experts can be accounted for by the "advance" information an expert processes indicating that

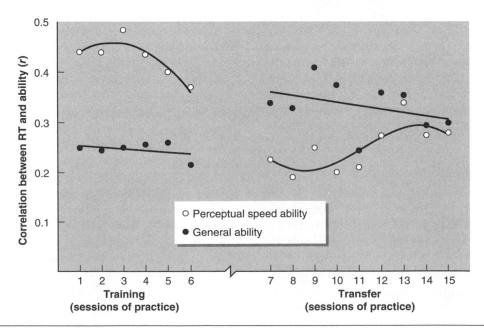

FIGURE 13.3 Test of theoretical predictions illustrated in figure 13.2.

Reprinted, by permission, from P.L. Ackerman, 1988, "Determinants of individual differences during skill acquisition: Cognitive abilities and information processing," *Journal of Experimental Psychology: General* 117: 299. Copyright © 1988 by the American Psychological Association.

an error has occurred (or will occur). Another interpretation is that experts possess the ability to monitor the *motor commands* sent to the body parts that execute the movements, by comparing using these commands to an internal model of the expected sensory consequences (Wolpert & Ghahramani, 2000).

Studying the acquisition of error-detection mechanisms in skills is complicated, however, because different types of skills produce different results. A major distinction is between rapid and slow movements, examined next.

Objective–Subjective Correlations in Rapid Movements

Schmidt and White (1972) used a ballistic-timing task in which the subjects moved a slide 23 cm, with a follow-through, so that the movement time (MT) was as close to 150 ms as possible. The subject made a movement, then guessed the MT outcome score in milliseconds, and then was given knowledge of results (KR, or the actual score) in milliseconds. The subject's guess was subtracted from the subject's actual score, and was termed *subjective error.* The actual score was subtracted from the goal score and termed *objective error.* If an increased capability to detect errors is acquired with practice, then the agreement between the subject's subjective and objective scores should increase.

The statistic used to estimate this agreement was based on correlations (see section in chapter 2 for review). For a block of 10 trials, each subject would have 10 objective scores and 10 subjective scores. These pairs of scores were correlated for each subject separately for each of 17 blocks of trials in the experiment. The idea was that, if the error-detection capability was weak, almost no agreement would exist between the objective and subjective errors, and the correlation should be near zero. But if error detection increased in accuracy with practice, then the objective and subjective scores should agree to a greater extent, and the magnitude of the correlation statistic (r) should increase over blocks of trials.[1]

The average within-subject correlations are presented in figure 13.4. On the first block, the average correlation was about 0.28, indicating a relatively weak association between objective and subjective errors. But as practice continued, the average correlation increased to the point that on day 2 the values approached 1.0. This evidence suggests that the learners became more and more sensitive to their own errors through the development of error-detection processes (see also Rubin, 1978).[2]

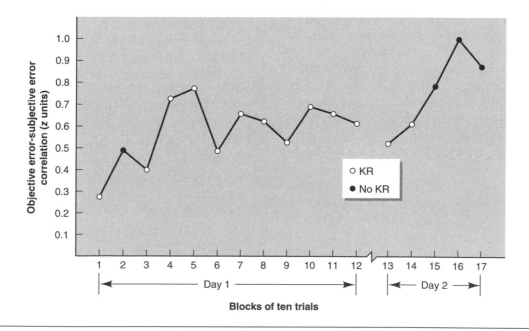

FIGURE 13.4   Average within-subject correlation between objective and subjective error as a function of practice trials. (Increased correlation is interpreted as gains in capability to detect errors; correlations are transformed to Z' units.)

Reprinted, by permission, from R.A. Schmidt and J.L. White, 1972, "Evidence for an error detection mechanism in motor skills: A test of Adams' closed-loop theory," *Journal of Motor Behavior* 4: 143-153, reprinted with permission of the publisher (Taylor & Francis Ltd, http://www.informaworld.com).

Objective–Subjective Correlations in Slow Movements

This is not so with slow movements. It appears that, for some slow movements at least, the error-detection processes may be responsible for actually *producing* the action. Because there is ample time to use feedback, it is thought that the subject in a positioning movement evaluates intrinsic feedback against the learned reference of correctness and moves to the position recognized as correct (Adams, 1971). If so, the error-detection capacity, being used to position the limb at the target, cannot then be used again after the movement as a basis for telling the experimenter about the error in positioning; if it were used, the errors would all be close to zero, as the action is based on that position that "feels like" it has minimum error. Then, if the subject is asked to report the error in positioning, she will have no idea whether or not the movement was on target.

Schmidt and Russell (1974) performed an experiment analogous to that of Schmidt and White but using a slow, linear-positioning task. In contrast to Schmidt and White (figure 13.4), Schmidt and Russell found consistently low within-subject correlations between objective and subjective errors, with most of the correlations being only about 0.20 even after 100 trials of practice. These findings suggest that the error-detection processes were used to position the limb in the slow task and that further estimates of error after completion of movement were based largely on guesswork by the subjects (see also Nicholson & Schmidt, 1991, who used timing tasks). These ideas figure heavily in the concepts of schema theory, presented in the next section of this chapter.

In the 1970s, two important papers were published on the motor learning process—*closed-loop theory* (Adams, 1971) and *schema theory* (Schmidt, 1975b). Because of the impact that these theories had on subsequent motor learning research, we describe them in some detail next.

Closed-Loop Theory

Adams (1971) developed his closed-loop theory of motor learning using a well-established set of empirical laws of motor learning, most of which were based on slow, linear-positioning movements. He believed that the principles of performance and learning that applied to these movements were the same as for any other kind of movement, and that using a well-established set of empirical laws from positioning movements would produce a solid basis for theorizing.

A Feedback Emphasis

Adams believed that all movements are made by comparing the ongoing feedback from the limbs to a *perceptual trace*—the reference of correctness, stored in memory, which is learned during practice. When the person makes a positioning movement, inherent feedback is produced that represents the particular locations of the limb in space. These stimuli "leave a trace" in the central nervous system (hence the name perceptual *trace*). With repeated practice, the person comes closer and closer to the target over trials; and on each trial another trace is laid down, so that eventually a kind of "collection" of traces develops. With practice (and KR), the learner's movements become increasingly closer to the target and with increasing consistency. Therefore, each trial provides feedback that tends to represent the *correct* movement with increasing frequency. In turn, the collection of perceptual traces comes to represent the feedback qualities of the correct movement. Then, on subsequent trials, the learner moves to that position in space for which the difference between the ongoing (inherent) feedback produced and the perceptual trace is minimized. Because the perceptual trace associated with the correct movement becomes stronger with each KR trial, the errors in performance decrease with practice.

Adams' theory assured a guidance role for KR (although his writings do not use this term). Learners, according to Adams, are not passive recipients of reward, but rather are actively engaged in verbalization and hypothesis formation about the task to be learned. To Adams, KR provides information to solve the motor problem. After a trial, KR is given that provides information about how the next movement should be made to more closely achieve the task goal. In early learning, the learner uses KR in relation to the perceptual trace to make the movement more precise, so that KR guides the movement to the target on successive trials. In such a view, KR does not produce learning directly. Rather, it creates the appropriate situation (i.e., being on target) so that the actual learning processes can operate. The movement's feedback produces an increment in "strength" for the perceptual trace.

We created the graphs in figure 13.5 to illustrate the learning process in Adams' theory. In the early stage of learning (figure 13.5*a*, top graph), the subject produces some correct movements but produces many incorrect movements, too. Thus, the movement feedback provides an increment to learning of the correct perceptual trace, but this trace is based on other, incorrect traces as well. In this stage of learning, performance is likely to be inaccurate and variable because of the spread of trace strengths among correct and incorrect perceptual traces. With the guidance of KR, the learner produces more and more correct movements, which has the effect of strengthening the correct perceptual trace and reducing the *relative* strength of incorrect perceptual traces, as illustrated in the middle and bottom graphs (figure 13.5, *b* and *c*). The reduction in relative strength of these incorrect perceptual traces improves the likelihood that the correct perceptual trace will guide the limb to the goal position with increasing frequency (i.e., less variability).[3]

One of the interesting implications of Adams' theory is that errors produced during the course of training are harmful to learning. This is the case because when an error is made, the resulting feedback is necessarily different from the feedback associated with a correct movement, and thus will increment the strength of an incorrect perceptual trace. The relative strength of the correct perceptual trace will be degraded a little bit as well. One prediction, then, is that guidance should be particularly useful as a training method, as it prevents errors.

Adams also sought to explain how learners develop error-detection capabilities. He argued that after the movement was completed, the individual could compare the feedback received against the perceptual trace, the difference representing the movement error that the person could report to the experimenter or use as self-evaluation in the form of subjective reinforcement. Presumably, this subjective reinforcement could be used to keep the movement on target without KR; and, according to the theory, keeping the movement on target can provide gains in learning because the feedback continues to

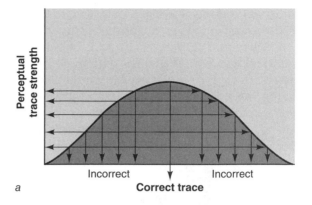

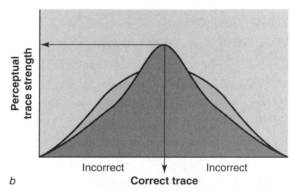

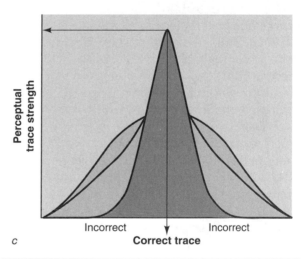

FIGURE 13.5 Adams' theory, represented as a growth in perceptual trace strength. As skill develops (from top to bottom panel), the correct perceptual trace accumulates proportionally more repetitions, and the shape of the distribution becomes more peaked at the mode.

add to the perceptual trace, again without KR in later learning.

Contrary to earlier closed-loop theorists, Adams realized that in order for the system to have the capacity to detect its own errors, two memory states must be present—one to produce the action and one to evaluate the outcome. What if the same state that produced the movement also evaluated it? If the movement were chosen incorrectly, the feedback from the movement and the reference of correctness would always match, producing a report of no error on every attempt. In Adams' theory, the movement is selected and initiated by another memory state that Adams called the *memory trace*—a "modest motor program" responsible for choosing the direction of the action, initiating it, and giving it a "shove" toward the target. The perceptual trace then takes over the control of the movement to stop it at the final target location.

Limitations and Contradictory Evidence

One characteristic of "good" theories is that there should be no contradictions among the logically derived predictions. Contradiction does appear to exist in Adams' theory, though, regarding subjective reinforcement for *slow* positioning movements. Adams viewed the perceptual trace as providing (a) the basis for placing the limb at the correct target location and (b) a basis for the performer to detect how far that movement was away from the target location after the movement has been completed. Schmidt (1975b) argued that, if the perceptual trace is used to position the limb, then no additional information can be available about the amount of actual error produced. As discussed previously, Schmidt and Russell (1974; Nicholson & Schmidt, 1991) provided evidence that no error-detection mechanism exists after the completion of slow positioning movements, even after 100 trials of practice, contrary to Adams' predictions. However, Schmidt and White (1972; Nicholson & Schmidt, 1991) found strong error-detection mechanisms after *rapid* movements, for which the perceptual trace presumably cannot be used to guide the limb during the movement. Adams did not make a distinction between these fast and slow movements, yet the evidence shows that they develop and use error-detection mechanisms very differently (e.g., Newell, 1976b).

Certainly one of the most damaging lines of evidence with respect to Adams' theory is the work on deafferentation in animals (Taub, 1976) and humans (Lashley, 1917), reviewed in chapter 6. Organisms deprived of all sensory feedback from the limbs can move reasonably skillfully, and they can even learn new actions (e.g., Taub & Berman, 1968). If the only mechanism for controlling skilled actions involved feedback in

relation to a perceptual trace, then these animals should not have been able to produce the actions they did. Adams (1976b) has countered this argument by saying that the animals may have shifted to some other source of feedback, such as vision, to substitute for the lost sensations from the responding limbs. This may be the case for some of these studies, but it does not apply to all of them (e.g., Polit & Bizzi, 1978, 1979; Taub & Berman, 1968). Also, Adams' theory does not account for the data from various species showing the existence of central (spinal) pattern generators—structures apparently capable of generating complex actions without feedback from the responding limbs (see chapter 6). The failure to recognize the role of open-loop processes in movement control is a serious drawback for Adams' theory.

A second line of evidence against Adams' theory was provided by the literature on variability of practice. Because the perceptual trace is the feedback representation of the correct action, making movements *different* from the correct action (in variable practice) should not increase perceptual trace strength. Thus, Adams' theory predicts that variability of practice should be less effective for learning the criterion target than is practice at the target itself. In chapter 11 we reviewed this literature and found no clear evidence that variable practice was less effective than practice at the transfer target; and often the evidence said that variability in practice was superior to practicing the transfer target itself (e.g., Shea & Kohl, 1991). Because Adams' theory explicitly claims that experience at the target location is critical for the development of the perceptual trace, this evidence is quite damaging to his position.

Lastly, the role of KR in Adams' theory was to guide the learner to making the correct movement. However, as we reviewed in chapter 12, there is clear evidence that, when KR serves a guidance role, it has a degrading influence on learning, not the enhanced effect as would be predicted by Adams' theory.

Summary

At the time Adams' theory was proposed, it represented a major step forward for motor learning, as it presented a plausible, empirically based theory for researchers to evaluate. We believe that such evaluations have shown the theory to have a number of limitations, as outlined here, and that it no longer accounts for much of the currently available evidence on motor learning. But the theory served its intended purpose. It generated substantial research and thinking, and it paved the way for newer theories that account for the older data together with newer data. Thus, it remains as a key legacy in the growth of motor learning research.

Schema Theory

Largely because of dissatisfaction with Adams' theory, Schmidt (1975b) formulated a theory that was considered a "rival" to Adams'. The primary concern with Adams' position was the lack of emphasis on open-loop control processes, and the schema theory has a strong open-loop component. Yet, at the same time, many aspects of Adams' theory are very appealing, such as the emphasis on subjective reinforcement, the concern for slow movements, and the need to have one memory state that is responsible for producing the movement and another state that is responsible for evaluating it. Thus, schema theory borrowed heavily from Adams and others by retaining the most effective parts and replacing, changing, or eliminating defective ones. Also, the new theory was based heavily on knowledge about motor control and used these concepts in conjunction with ideas about learning processes to attempt to explain the learning of both rapid and slower movements (see also Schmidt, 1980, 2003).

Recall and Recognition Memory

Schema theory holds that there are two states of memory, a *recall memory* responsible for the production of movement and a *recognition memory* responsible for movement evaluation. For rapid, ballistic movements, recall memory is involved with the motor programs and parameters, structured in advance to carry out the movement with minimal involvement from peripheral feedback. Recognition memory, on the other hand, is responsible for evaluating the inherent feedback after the movement is completed, thereby informing the subject about the amount and direction of errors. Such structures satisfy the goal of having the memory state that produces the action be different from the memory state that evaluates its correct-

ness, also one of the strengths of Adams' theory.

According to schema theory, recall memory is not thought to have an important role in slow positioning movements. The major problem for the learner is the comparison between movement-produced feedback and the reference of correctness. In these movements, the recall state merely pushes the limb along in small bursts, with the person stopping when the movement-produced feedback and the reference of correctness match. Here, in these slow movements, the agent that produces the action is the same as the agent that evaluates it; hence no postmovement subjective reinforcement can exist as is the case for rapid movements. We have already presented evidence that rapid movements do, and slow movements do not, provide postmovement subjective reinforcement (Nicholson & Schmidt, 1991; Schmidt, Christenson, & Rogers, 1975).

Schema Learning

The *schema* concept is an old one in psychology, having been introduced by Head (1926) and later popularized by Bartlett (1932). For these researchers, the schema was an abstract memory representation thought of as a rule, concept, or generalization. Schmidt (1975b) attempted to use the basic idea of the schema (or rule) to form a theory of how motor skills are learned.

At the heart of Schmidt's view of schema learning is the idea that movements are made by first selecting a generalized motor program (GMP), structured with invariant features (such as relative timing), then adding parameters as required in order to specify the particular way that the program is to be executed for any one particular instance (see chapter 6 for details). After a GMP is selected and a movement is made by adding the parameters, four types of information are available for brief storage in short-term memory: (1) information about the initial conditions (bodily positions, weight of thrown objects, and so on) that existed before the movement was made; (2) the parameters assigned to the GMP, (3) augmented feedback about the outcome of the movement; and (4) the sensory consequences of the movement—how the movement felt, looked, sounded, and so on. These four sources of information are stored only long enough that the performer can abstract two schemas. These abstract rules of how the sources of information are interrelated are called the recall and recognition schemas.

Recall Schema

The first of these relationships is termed the *recall schema* because it is concerned with movement production. Figure 13.6 represents the kind of process that occurs, according to the recall-schema idea. On the horizontal axis are the outcomes in the environment, such as the distance a ball traveled after being thrown. On the vertical axis are the parameters that an individual assigned to the GMP. The co-occurrence of the parameter and the movement outcome produces a data point on the graph. With repeated movements using different parameters and producing different outcomes, other data points are established. As the number of throws accumulates, a *relationship* between the size of the parameter and the nature of the movement outcome is established; this relationship is represented by the *regression line* drawn through the points.[4] With each successive movement using the program, a new data point is produced and the relationship is refined slightly. After each new movement, the various sources of information are lost from working memory, so all that remains of the movement is the updated rule, termed the recall schema in LTM.

But this is not the entire story. The relationship also includes information about the initial con-

ditions of the movement, shown in figure 13.7. Here, the relationship between the parameters used and the outcome produced will depend on the nature of the initial conditions, such as different objects to be thrown. These different initial conditions are represented as different regression lines in figure 13.7.

How does the individual use the recall schema? On a future trial using this GMP, the person sets as a goal the desired environmental outcome, labeled point A on figure 13.7. Also, the particular initial conditions are noted (e.g., the weight of the object to be thrown), which might fit into the category represented by line 2 in figure 13.7. Then, with use of the relationship established by past experience, the rule is employed to select the parameter (labeled point B) that will come closest to accomplishing that goal. The value of this parameter is then applied to the GMP to produce the action.

Recognition Schema

The recognition schema, for movement evaluation, is thought to be formed and used in a way similar to the recall schema. Here the schema is composed of the relationship between the initial conditions, the environmental outcomes, and the *sensory consequences*. This relationship is represented as the

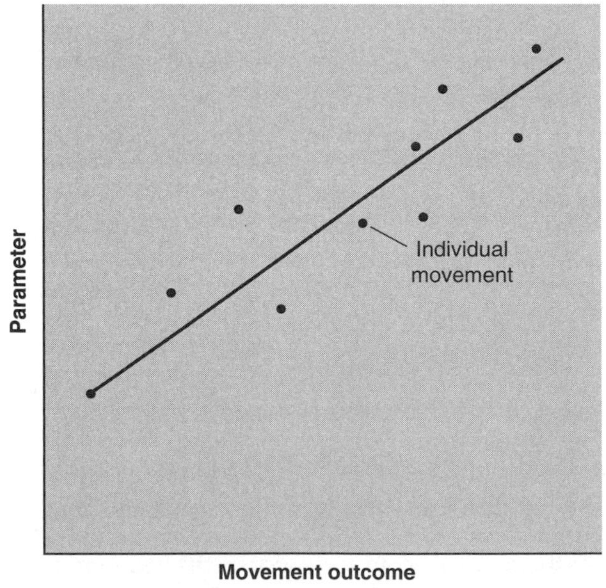

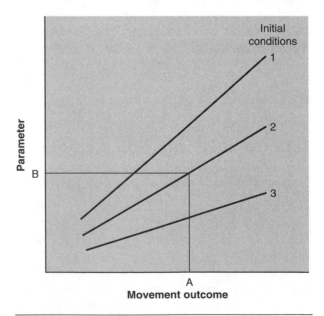

FIGURE 13.6   The hypothetical relationship between movement outcomes in the environment and the parameters used to produce them.

FIGURE 13.7   The hypothetical relationship between movement outcomes in the environment and the parameters that were used to produce them for various initial conditions: the recall schema.

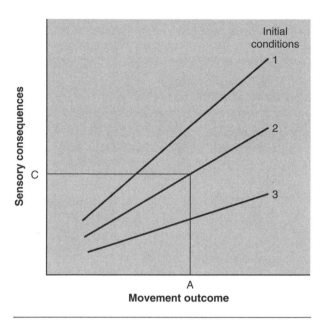

FIGURE 13.8 The hypothetical relationship between movement outcomes in the environment and the sensory consequences produced for various initial conditions: the recognition schema.

Human motor behavior: an introduction by R.A. Schmidt. Copyright 1982 by TAYLOR & FRANCIS GROUP LLC - BOOKS. Reproduced with permission of TAYLOR & FRANCIS GROUP LLC - BOOKS in the format Textbook via Copyright Clearance Center.

three lines shown in figure 13.8. Before the movement, the individual selects a movement outcome and determines the nature of the initial conditions. Then, with the recognition schema, the person can estimate the sensory consequences that will occur if that movement outcome is produced. These, called the *expected sensory consequences* (labeled point C), serve as the basis for movement evaluation. The expected sensory consequences are analogous to Adams' perceptual trace.

Some Predictions About Schema Learning

The theory says that we acquire skills, at least in part, by learning *rules* about the functioning of our bodies—forming relationships between how our muscles are activated, what they actually do, and how those actions feel. Thus, movements for which any of the four stored sources of information are missing will result in degraded learning of the rules. One of the most critical of the sources is movement outcome information (augmented feedback, such as KR); if the person does not receive augmented information about the movement outcome, then even if the other sources of information are present, no strengthening of the

schema can occur because the location on the horizontal axis will not be known. Similarly, if sensory consequences are missing (e.g., as in temporary deafferentation), then no recognition schema development can occur. In passive movements, no parameters are issued to the GMP (indeed, no GMP is selected to be run off), so no recall schema updating can occur.

Also, note that, according to schema theory, there are positive benefits from the production of movements whether they are correct or not. This is so because the schema is the rule based on the relationship among all stored elements, and this relationship is present just as much for incorrect movements as for correct ones. Adams' theory, you may remember, views errors as disruptive, as they degrade the relative strength of the correct perceptual trace (see figure 13.5).

Variability of Practice

The theory predicts that practicing a variety of movement outcomes with the same program (i.e., by using a variety of parameters) will provide a widely based set of experiences upon which a rule or schema can form. When the range of movement outcomes and parameters is small, all the data points such as those shown in figure 13.6 are clustered in one place, and less certainty exists about the placement of the line.[5] When a *new* movement is required, greater error will occur in estimating the proper parameters, expected sensory consequences, or both. Shapiro and Schmidt (1982) found considerable evidence that practice variability is a positive factor in motor learning, especially for children (see "Variability of Practice" in chapter 11).

Novel Movements

Schema theory also predicts that a particular movement outcome (specified by a particular value of the parameter) need not have been produced previously in order to be produced in the future. This is so because the basis for producing a new movement is a *rule* about parameter selection based on the performance of earlier similar movements. Research has shown that, after varied practice, novel movements can be produced about as accurately as they can be if the novel movement had been practiced repeatedly, and sometimes *more* accurately (see the section on variability of practice in chapter 11). This evidence suggests that motor learning may be primarily rule learning and not the learning of specific movements. Such ideas have been used for a long time in

Especial Skills

The *set shot* in basketball provides an interesting "test" of schema theory. The set shot is characterized as a deliberate shooting motion in which the player's feet never leave the ground. The set shot is not typically used in game action because it is relatively easy to block. However, it is the type of shot that is used for a free throw and is executed many, many times in practice, almost exclusively from the free throw line. An interesting question, then, is this: Do years of free throw practice establish a GMP, in which time and force parameters appropriate for the free throw distance must be generated when a free throw is to be performed (as predicted by schema theory)? Or does this practice result in a motor program that is specific for the free throw? Or do both processes occur? Keetch, Schmidt, Lee, and Young (2005) examined this question using skilled players from college basketball teams—subjects who probably had performed many thousands of free throws in practice and games. The players were asked to perform set shots at distances of 9 to 21 ft (the official free throw distance is 15 ft) from the basket, from locations on the floor 2 ft apart. Several key predictions were of interest, based on the combined predictions of schema theory and the principles of force variability (as presented in chapter 6; Schmidt, Zelaznik, Hawkins, Frank, & Quinn, 1979). First, a negatively sloped regression line that relates the success of the shot to the distance from the basket was expected. The GMP would need to be parameterized with increased levels of force as the distance increased, thereby increasing the force variability in the movement output and increasing error. Second, schema theory predicts that the accuracy between 9 and 21 ft would fall on or very close to this negatively sloped regression line, because of the principles reviewed earlier in this section about the recall schema.

The results of the study are illustrated in the left side of figure 13.9, with the mean data points fitted by a regression line. The findings support all but one of the predictions: The regression line nicely fits four of the five data points. However, the key finding, which does not support schema theory, occurred at the distance of 15 ft—the foul line. From this distance, the players' success was considerably higher than predicted based on the schema regression. A similar effect of distance has been found in skilled baseball pitchers—who were much more accurate (than predicted) at the regulation pitching distance compared to other distances, including distances *just one foot* closer or farther from home plate than the normal pitching distance (60.5 ft; Simons, Wilson, Wilson, & Theall, 2009). But, when these basketball skills were performed by novices (Breslin et al., 2010) or by experts using jump shots (where the feet do leave the floor), all of the data points fit nicely on the regression line, as predicted by schema theory (see the right panel in figure 13.9). There was no advantage for a jump shot taken from the foul line, presumably because jump shots are not practiced more frequently at the foul line than at any other location as set shots are.

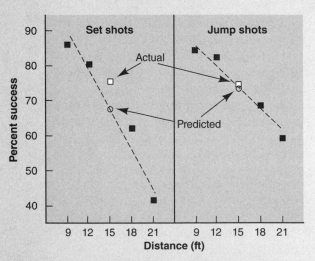

FIGURE 13.9 Schema theory accurately predicts the performance of a 15 ft jump shot (right panel) but severely underestimates the performance of a 15 ft set shot (left panel)—a free throw.

Reprinted, by permission, from K.M. Keetch, R.A. Schmidt, T.D. Lee, and D.E. Young, 2005. "Especial skills: Their emergence with massive amounts of practice," *Journal of Experimental Psychology: Human Perception and Performance* 31: 970-978. Copyright © 2005 by the American Psychological Association.

What do these results suggest? For the set shots, something specific and unique to the free throw distance had been learned through many years of practice at this distance. This specific capability facilitated performance only for the set shot and only at the 15 ft distance taken at an angle straight on to the basket, making it an "especial" skill—a rather special skill existing within a class of basketball set-shot skills. Note that this particular finding is not consistent with the schema view, as the theory gives no specific preference for any particular parameterization, regardless of the number of specific practice instances that have been executed. This study illustrates many questions of practical interest that have been discussed at a theoretical level in this and previous chapters, such as force-variability principles, variable practice, schema theory, and specificity of learning.

movement-education situations with children, where the pupils are presumably developing a set of rules or schemas about their motor behaviors and consequently being helped to be more proficient performers in novel situations in the future (Nicholson & Schmidt, 1991; Schmidt, 1976b, 1977).

Error Detection

Schema theory predicts that there should be no capability for error detection after a slow movement, whereas such capability should exist after a rapid movement. This is the case because the error-detection capability is actually used to produce the slow movement, leaving behind no capability with which to detect errors. Based on the information about closed-loop processes presented in chapter 5, if the movement was rapid (as was the case in the Schmidt & White, 1972, study), the subject would compare the feedback from the movement to the reference of correctness to define an error after the movement was completed. The error-detection process is not responsible for producing the action, and it evaluates the correctness of the action only *after* the movement has been completed. For reasons discussed before, there is insufficient time for the performer to take in the feedback, evaluate it, and make corrections before the movement is completed. According to the theory, the recall schema is thought to produce the movements, and the recognition schema is responsible for comparing the movement-produced feedback with the learned reference of correctness for evaluating the movement afterward. As mentioned during the discussion of Adams' theory, empirical evidence supports this prediction (Schmidt & Russell, 1974; Schmidt & White, 1972).

Limitations and Logical Problems

The emphasis of schema theory on the GMP concept represents both a major strength and major limitation of the theory. While we believe that the evidence strongly supports the GMP view (see chapter 6), the theory is mute in terms of how the program is formed in the first place, and this deficiency is readily acknowledged as a major problem with the theory (Schmidt, 2003). The following sections highlight other limitations.

Knowledge-of-Results Frequency

Strengthening of the schema depends on the subject's knowledge of the movement outcome, so higher levels of KR relative frequency would be expected to enhance schema learning as compared to lower levels. When relative KR frequency effects on overall learning were evaluated in chapter 12, the results appeared to contradict this schema theory prediction because reduced frequencies either had no effect on learning or in some cases enhanced it, rather than degrading it, especially so if the KR was "faded" over trials (Sullivan, Kantak, & Burtner, 2008; Winstein & Schmidt, 1990). These findings are further complicated by KR variables that appear to influence the learning of parameters and invariances in different ways, which is also contrary to schema theory (Shea & Wulf, 2005).

Contextual Interference and Cognitive Operations

One key prediction of schema theory is that variable practice would result in stronger rule learning than nonvariable (or constant) practice, and evidence supports that general prediction (but note the discussion in "Especial Skills"). However, schema theory makes no prediction about *how* the variable practice should be scheduled. Recall from the discussion of random versus blocked practice effects in chapter 11 that the amount of variable practice in these studies was equal. Because they share a common breadth of practice variability, schema theory fails to predict the learning differences that occur between random and blocked practice (Lee, Magill, &

Weeks, 1985). The explanations for contextual-interference effects stress the importance of cognitive operations during practice, which highlights a more general limitation of schema theory, as the theory provides no rationale for learning effects due to cognitive operations such as imagery, mental practice, and observational learning (Shea & Wulf, 2005; Sherwood & Lee, 2003).

Summary

Schema theory has provided an alternative to Adams' closed-loop theory of motor learning. Compared to Adams' theory, it has the advantage that it accounts for more kinds of movements; it seems to account for error-detection capabilities more effectively and seems to explain the production of novel movements in open-skills situations. Some logical problems need to be solved, and it is not clear that this can be done without discarding the entire theoretical structure (Petrynski, 2003; Schmidt, 2003; Shea & Wulf, 2005). There are some apparent failures of the evidence to agree with the theoretical predictions as well (e.g., Klein, Levy, & McCabe, 1984; Keetch et al., 2005). While the theory was a step forward, it should be clear that it does not provide a complete understanding of the data on motor learning. Even so, the theory provides a useful framework for thinking about skill learning because it is consistent with the literature on the GMP.

Differing Theoretical Perspectives of Motor Learning

The ideas presented next are probably best described as hypotheses about the learning of motor skills. They really do not satisfy the basic criteria for consideration as *theories* for a number of reasons. First, many of them are directed at only certain kinds of tasks, such as continuous tasks, positioning tasks, and tracking; and more generality is usually required for a theory. As well, some of these theoretical perspectives concern only a few experimental variables, and theories (such as closed-loop theory and schema theory) are usually thought to have more complete structures that are capable of explaining the effects of a variety of independent variables. Further, an important ingredient of a theory is

that it makes testable predictions that can be falsified by experimental testing. Nevertheless, the theoretical perspectives that we consider next represent important advances in furthering our understanding of the complex interaction of processes involved in motor learning.

Cognitive Perspectives

Although both closed-loop theory (Adams, 1971) and schema theory (Schmidt, 1975) emphasized the role of memory structures in skill, the learning process depended on movement repetition and feedback. The development of the perceptual trace in Adams' theory and the recall and recognition schema in Schmidt's theory were mechanistic processes. Research conducted since these theories were published, on learning variables such as the contextual-interference effect (chapter 11) and various augmented-feedback effects (chapter 12), suggests that the role of cognitive processes in learning might be more complex than originally conceptualized in Adams' and Schmidt's theories.

Both of the major hypotheses regarding the contextual-interference effect suggest that cognitive processes play a key role. In the elaboration hypothesis, explicit contrasts and comparisons of the tasks to be learned were thought to benefit learning. In the reconstruction view, it was the process of planning a different action to be performed that boosted learning. In both hypotheses, learning was more effective if the elaboration or reconstruction was made more *difficult* (i.e., in random practice), suggesting that the *effort* with which the cognitive processes were undertaken had a critical impact on learning (Lee, Swinnen, & Serrien, 1994; Sherwood & Lee, 2003; Vickers, Livingston, Umeris-Bohnert, & Holden, 1999).

This cognitive emphasis suggested that something more was occurring during learning than executing movements and receiving inherent feedback, which could not explain the differences between random and blocked practice. In both practice conditions the subjects received the same amount of practice on the same tasks. The effects on learning of augmented-feedback variables such as concurrent feedback (chapter 12) also fit a cognitive perspective well. Movements that are produced with the assistance of concurrent feedback experience the same efferent commands and intrinsic feedback as nonguided movements. However, as argued in the KR-guidance hypothesis (Salmoni, Schmidt, & Walter, 1984; Schmidt, 1991), such variables tend to *minimize* the learner's need for evaluation of subjective information and other cognitive operations that are ordinarily undertaken in the preparation for the next trial.

The effects of these practice variables on the learning process are complex, however—they appear to have a strong dependence on the nature of the task and the experience level of the subject (Wulf & Shea, 2002). Some of these complexities were conceptualized in a theoretical framework by Guadagnoli and Lee (2004), who suggested that cognitive processing during practice is affected by the degree to which the subject is *challenged* during the practice period. The nature of the task, the conditions of practice, and the experience level of the learner interact to determine the amount of challenge present during acquisition trials. For example, random practice is considered more challenging than blocked practice and therefore should benefit learning. But, driving on a busy highway would be more challenging than driving in a deserted parking lot—and certainly much more challenging for the novice learner than the semiskilled driver. The framework suggests that variables such as random practice and concurrent feedback are effective to the degree that they challenge the cognitive processes of the learner. The framework suggests, however, that there exists a *point* at which these cognitively challenging practice conditions may not be needed. Indeed, they may be detrimental to learning if used for tasks that are already inherently challenging. Similarly, learning may be sufficiently challenged in individuals whose performance capabilities are put to the test merely by the demands of the task. In such cases, nonchallenging practice conditions (e.g., blocked practice or concurrent KR) would be expected to facilitate, rather than be detrimental to learning.

Although the Guadagnoli and Lee framework has provided an explanation for some of the complex relationships for learner, task, and practice variables that exist in the literature, it has limitations. Certainly, the concept of *task difficulty*, though frequently discussed as an important factor in the motor learning literature, remains a construct with an elusive definition. As well, the framework stops short of identifying exactly what cognitive processes are being challenged and how these processes change over the course of learning. Nevertheless, it is clear from the many studies conducted in the past several decades that the effects on learning of practice and augmented-feedback variables are much more complex than at first believed. The challenge-point framework represents an attempt to characterize the complexity of these relationships within a cognitive perspective. Some empirical explorations of the framework support its explanatory power, especially with individuals who have a compromised motor system (Lin, Sullivan, Wu, Kantak, & Winstein, 2007; Onla-or & Winstein, 2008; Sullivan et al., 2008).

Hierarchical Control Perspectives

As people learn, at least with some tasks, a change occurs such that motor control is shifted to progressively "lower" levels in the nervous system. The idea that motor behavior is hierarchical means that some "higher" level in the system is responsible for decision making and some "lower" level is responsible for carrying out the decisions. With respect to the information-processing analysis, the decision-making processes of the system are considered to be at a "higher" level in the hierarchy than the motor programming level. The hierarchical control perspective suggests that with practice, control is *shifted* from the "higher" to the "lower" levels in the system.

A good example that demonstrates research in this perspective was a study by Pew (1966), who used a tracking task in which the subject controlled the movement of a dot on a monitor by pressing one or the other of two buttons. Pressing the right button caused the dot to accelerate to the right, and the acceleration could be halted and reversed by pressing the left button, which caused the dot to accelerate to the left. If no button was pressed, the dot accelerated off the screen in one direction or another. The subject's task was to keep the dot in the center (this is called a compensatory tracking task).

A record from one of the subjects, with the velocity and position of the dot shown for early and late practice, is presented in figure 13.10. In early practice (figure 13.10*a*), the subject was making about three button presses per second, and the dot was never positioned near the center of the screen for very long. In this mode of control the subject pressed the button, waited for the visual feedback from the screen, decided that the dot was accelerating off the screen, then planned a movement to reverse it, pressed the other button, and so on. Here, the subject is using the executive (e.g., the information-processing stages) level predominantly, so that the "highest" level in the system is consistently involved in the production of every movement.

Compare figure 13.10*a* to figure 13.10*b*, which is from the same subject but later in practice. Here the motor behavior is quite different. First, the rate of responding is much faster, about eight movements per second. Next, the dot is much closer to the target because the button was pressed to reverse the direction of the dot before the dot was very far away from the target. Although we cannot be absolutely certain, the mode of control appears to have changed. It appears that now a long string of movements is prestructured as a unit, perhaps governed by a motor program. Thus, a separate decision from the executive level is no longer required for the control of each button press. Pew viewed this finding as evidence for the hypothesis that with practice, the subject shifted the control from an executive-based level to the lower-level control of the motor program, freeing the decision mechanism for other activities and making the movement more effective. Now, instead of controlling every button press, the executive level was controlling *groups* of button presses. With some subjects, the durations of the right and left buttons were adjusted, perhaps as a kind of "parameter" of the programmed activities.

It is easy to see the advantages of shifting the control from the decision-making level to the motor program level. Foremost is the freeing of the attentional mechanisms for use on higher-order aspects of the task (e.g., strategy), for doing other simultaneous tasks, or for simply resting so that the organism does not become fatigued. This freeing of attention is one of the major events that occur when people learn, and it is discussed further in later sections of this chapter.

Progression–Regression Hypothesis

Of particular relevance to tracking tasks is a hypothesis presented by Fitts, Bahrick, Noble, and Briggs (1959) about how changes in motor behavior occur with practice. In many tracking tasks, both in the laboratory and in the outside world, the movements of the track to be followed are made up of a number of components that can be described according to the physical principles of motion. At the simplest level is the position of the track at any moment. The next most complex aspect of the track is its velocity at any moment. A third and yet more complex aspect of the track is its acceleration at any moment. In designing servo systems to regulate some mechanical system, engineers can devise a simple system that responds to (a) only the position of the track,

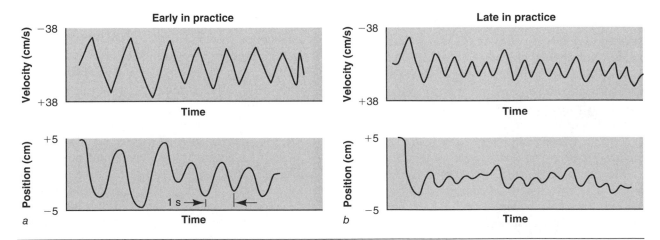

FIGURE 13.10 Performance records from a button-press tracking task in *(a)* early and *(b)* late practice. (Top records show instantaneous velocity, and bottom records show position with target represented as zero; responding is more rapid and more accurate in later practice.)

(b) the position and velocity, or (c) the position, velocity, and acceleration. With each increase in the number of components being tracked, progressive increases are required in the complexity (and expense) of the mechanical or electronic devices that are to track them.

The *progression–regression hypothesis* for humans presented by Fitts and colleagues (1959) holds that, when the learner practices a tracking task, a progression develops in the learner's behavior in the direction of acting more and more like a complex tracking system. Early in practice, the person responds only to the simplest elements of the display (position). With increased practice, the learner becomes able to use velocity information, and even later comes to use information about acceleration as well. The regression portion of the hypothesis refers to what happens to the learner under stressful conditions or when forgetting of the movement has occurred (perhaps as a result of a long layoff). According to the hypothesis, the person regresses to a simpler level of control (from acceleration to velocity, or from velocity to position), with systematically reduced tracking performance as a consequence. Thus, the hierarchical nature of learning involves progressing to levels of more complex information, although performance effects may show reversals in the shift between levels in the hierarchy (regressing to less complex information).

A number of experimenters have studied learning in tracking tasks with respect to the progression–regression hypothesis. Fuchs (1962) found that the role of position cues in tracking decreased with practice, while the role of acceleration cues increased; and these effects were reversed when a secondary task was added to induce stress (see also Garvey, 1960). More recently, researchers have improved on the methods used in the earlier work and have provided additional evidence for a shift in movement control consistent with the hypothesis (Hah & Jagacinski, 1994; Jagacinski & Hah, 1988; Marteniuk & Romanow, 1983).

At least for tracking tasks, learners appear to respond to systematically different aspects of the track with practice and to reverse these trends with stress. We should be careful not to go too far with these conclusions, because we have no independent way of knowing exactly which stimuli were being used here. But the evidence is certainly consistent with the progression–regression hypothesis, and it contributes to an understanding of the hierarchical nature of the underlying changes in motor control when skill is achieved with practice or reduced under stress or with forgetting.

Making Movements Automatic

For more than a century (e.g., James, 1890), the idea of automaticity has been that, as a by-product of learning, skilled performers become able to perform with minimal attention cost and minimal interference from other cognitive information-processing activities. In chapter 4, we qualified this basic idea considerably, saying that "automatic" responding appears to involve a lack of interference with respect to particular secondary tasks; the notion that a given task is interference free for *all* secondary tasks is not supported by the evidence (Neumann, 1987). However, it does seem likely that the interference from many simultaneous cognitive information-processing activities is decreased, or even eliminated, with practice, thus freeing the individual to engage in other higher-order aspects of the task—such as planning strategies in tennis or race car driving, or projecting an affective emotional style in acting, music, or dance.

Automaticity can be considered in essentially two ways. First, and most common, is the idea that specialized information-processing structures are learned with practice and that they handle portions of the processing requirements of the overall task, such as feature detection and movement selection (e.g., Logan, 1988; Neumann, 1987; Schneider & Fisk, 1983; Schneider & Shiffrin, 1977; Shiffrin & Schneider, 1977). Each process can occur when the appropriate stimulus conditions are presented and essentially triggered into action without awareness; indeed, sometimes the process cannot even be prevented (Schneider, 1985). By handling information processing in this way, the performer decreases the interference with other cognitive activities that compete for the same common resources. If, in a given task, all these processes can be so acquired, then the task can be thought of as "automatic," in the sense that the entire movement can occur without interference from particular groups of secondary tasks. In this view, the organism does not decrease the amount of environmental information processing that must be accomplished; rather, it processes this information differently—via specialized structures—and more quickly and with less interference from other simultaneous tasks.

However, another view is possible (see Schmidt, 1987). In at least some kinds of tasks (e.g., predictable and stereotyped), a major process of learning appears to be a shift from high-level conscious control to a lower-level programming control, as discussed in a previous section. With predictable tasks, the regularities of the environmental information can be learned and therefore can be anticipated during performance. If so, then the person does not have to process this information directly, but rather preprograms long sequences of action based on the prediction of the environmental information. Musicians "memorize" sheet music so that they are not dependent on it, and experienced drivers no longer have to watch their feet as they move from accelerator to brake in the car. Thus, being able to avoid processing environmental information frees those (conscious) information-processing activities for other tasks and makes the task appear "automatic," at least with respect to particular kinds of activities. In this view, the person does not necessarily process information any more effectively or faster, but rather learns to avoid having to process information by shifting to motor programming modes of control.

Of course, it could be that both of these viewpoints are correct but that each is relevant for a different class of movement tasks (e.g., those that have predictable and those that have unpredictable environmental information). Even within a particular skill, one can imagine specialized structures for detecting environmental information; then, sequences of preprogrammed output could be generated that reduce the reliance on such information for the next few hundred milliseconds. Both viewpoints provide ways of conceptualizing the acquisition of automaticity in high-level motor learning, and they present interesting issues for research in motor skills.

Creating Motor Programs

Of course, we know that many changes occur in our movements when they are subjected to practice, with actions tending to become more consistent, smoother, less effortful, and more routine or automatic with experience. These are all powerful changes, and in the next sections we consider some of the experimental evidence for them.

The Acquisition of Movement Pattern Consistency One important change in movement behavior with practice is that the movement outcomes tend to become more consistent, predictable, and certain with experience. Recall that variable error and other measures of variability (chapter 2) were devised to capture this aspect of motor behavior. In the study of these phenomena, the patterns of movement are measured by various kinematic procedures (e.g., video analysis, position–time records, computer simulation). Changes in the trial-to-trial consistency of these measures have been noted in an impressive variety of tasks, such as driving (Lewis, 1956), throwing (Stimpel, 1933), handwheel cranking (Glencross, 1973), table tennis (Tyldesley & Whiting, 1975), tracking (Darling & Cooke, 1987; Franks & Wilberg, 1984), keyboarding (Salthouse, 1986), bimanual coordination (Lee, Swinnen, & Verschueren, 1995), and many others. Such generalizations perhaps seem to be particularly appropriate with respect to the acquisition of closed skills, which have as a major goal the production of a consistent action in a stable (or predictable) environment—the kinds of skills for which stable motor programs are most highly suited. These changes in movement pattern consistency probably represent some of the most persistent phenomena in the motor learning area.

The Acquisition of Sequencing: The Gearshift Analogy Another hierarchical change in movement control with practice involves the ways in which movements are sequenced. MacKay (1976, personal communication) suggested that motor programs might be generated by stringing together smaller programmed units of behavior so that eventually this string of behavior is controllable as a single unit—such as in learning to shift gears in a car.[6] As you may remember, the act of shifting gears when you were first learning was a slow, jerky, step-by-step process; you lifted your foot from the accelerator, then depressed the clutch, and then moved the shift lever (probably in three distinct movements as well), until the entire act was completed (or until the car rolled to a stop going up a hill). Contrast this behavior to that of a race car driver, who appears to shift gears in a single, rapid action. Not only does the movement occur much more quickly, but also the elements of the action are performed with precise timing, and the actions of the hands and both feet are coordinated in relatively complex ways. In relation to the behavior of the early learner, the action seems to be controlled in a very different way, perhaps as a single programmed unit.

MacKay suggested that the various elements are learned in a progressive way to form the entire action. Figure 13.11 is a diagram of how this might work. Assume there are seven elements in the entire sequence and that these are at first controlled one at a time, each by a separate motor program. With some practice, the first two elements might come to be controlled as a single unit; the next three elements could compose another unit, and the last two could compose a third. Finally, with considerable experience, the entire sequence might be controlled as a single unit. This view is of a type of hierarchical control in that it specifies how the program is structured from the beginning, progressively growing in length by adding parts. Other possibilities exist as well (Marteniuk & Romanow, 1983).

We should be able to see evidence of the changes in these structures by using a fundamental principle of variability: The variability (inconsistency) of the elements *within* a unit should be considerably smaller than the variability between units. In figure 13.11 (middle practice), if we were to measure the interval from the end of element 2 to the beginning of element 3, the relative variability of this interval (expressed as the SD of the interval divided by the mean interval length) from

trial to trial would be greater than the variability from the end of element 3 to the beginning of element 4. This is the case because the first two elements (2 and 3) are in different units (controlled by different programs), while the latter two (3 and 4) are supposedly controlled by the same program. Turning this logic around, if we found intervals in the sequence in which temporal variability was very high, this could be taken as evidence that the behaviors occurring at the opposite ends of this interval of time are members of different motor programs. This is similar to the method used by Young and Schmidt (1990, 1991) and Schmidt, Heuer, Ghodsian, & Young (1998) to investigate the acquisition of new bimanual coordination programs (see also chapter 8).

Combinations of Reflexes Another way that motor programs are thought to be formed in practice is through the combination of fundamental reflexes (Easton, 1972, 1978). According to this viewpoint, higher levels in the motor system are capable of tuning or adjusting lower spinal levels so that the existing reflexes (e.g., the stretch reflex) can be controlled in ways that result in skilled actions. Thus, rather than hypothesizing that the motor system builds a set of commands that come to exist as a stored motor program, Easton held that the "commands" are really ways of controlling the preexisting reflexes. Such emphases

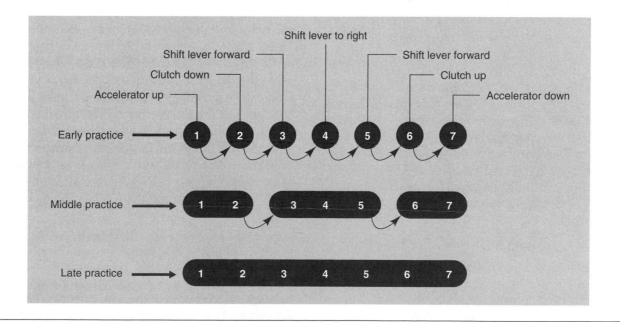

FIGURE 13.11 The gearshift analogy. (Initially, seven elements are each controlled by separate programs; later, they become grouped so that they are organized into a few units or even into a single unit.)

Adapted from MacKay, 1976, personal communication.

on reflexes are also seen in the views of Fukuda (1961) and Hellebrandt, Houtz, Partridge, and Walters (1956), as discussed in chapter 5; but here, while the reflexes are thought to be of assistance to the overall programmed action when increased force or speed is required, they are not the fundamental basis of it. But Easton's viewpoint also has a great deal in common with the ideas of Greene (1972), Turvey (1977), and others, all of whom argue that rapid movements consist of controlling structures that are constrained to act as a single unit, perhaps by tuning of spinal systems or by utilization of reflexes. These ideas share much in common with the theoretical perspectives of the Russian physicist Bernstein (see p. 8), whose ideas on learning are presented next.

The Bernstein Perspective

Suppose you were asked to throw a ball overhand with your nondominant arm. In all likelihood, your performance would look quite clumsy—the movements of the body would lack the fluid motion that characterizes a throwing motion with the dominant arm. The motions of the nondominant arm would probably be described as much more fixed and restricted in the range of motion. This example characterizes an important concept of learning initiated by the work of Bernstein (1967). The concept is that learning involves a process of *solving the degrees of freedom problem*—discovering ways in which the independent parts of the moving body can be organized in order to achieve a task goal. In Bernstein's perspective, learning occurred in three stages, although the stages that he proposed were different than the stages discussed earlier in the chapter (Adams, 1971; Fitts, 1964). According to Bernstein (1967), the stages of learning involve (a) freezing degrees of freedom, (b) releasing and reorganizing degrees of freedom, and (c) exploiting the mechanical and inertial properties of the body.

Stage 1: Freezing Degrees of Freedom

Bernstein suggested that early in practice the learner attempts to "freeze" as many of the degrees of freedom as possible, allowing as few as possible of the body parts to move independently. With practice, more and more of the degrees of freedom are "thawed out"—individual body parts appear to move either

with more independence or with a different dependency. In the earlier example of throwing with the nondominant arm, one possible strategy for the performer would be to *fix* or limit the degrees of freedom involved in the act. This is done in order to reduce the contribution of their independent variability, and hence reduce the complexity of the action. In this way, the performer can achieve a relatively crude level of success at the task by reducing the number of ways in which things can go wrong. In a nice demonstration of this stage of learning, Southard and Higgins (1987) showed that people who learned a racquetball shot initially restricted the motion of the elbow and wrist and performed the shot with a more whole-arm action. A similar set of findings was reported by Hodges, Hayes, Horn, and Williams (2005) over 10 days of practice in a soccer-chip task. Participants gradually achieved more initial successes at the task as the range of motion at the hip was reduced with practice.

Stage 2: Releasing and Reorganizing Degrees of Freedom

According to Bernstein's arguments, in stage 2 of learning, the *constraints* on the degrees of freedom are loosened, allowing both for greater independent motion and for a higher level of success. Bernstein's introspections about the learning process have received support in a study by Vereijken, van Emmerik, Whiting, and Newell (1992), for example. Subjects practiced a ski simulator task that required whole-body movements to move a platform from side to side over curved metal rails (see figure 2.9, p. 36). The sides of the platform were anchored to a frame by rubber springs; when the springs were subjected to force from the "skier," the platform would oscillate from one side of the frame to the other. Subjects practiced this task over seven days, attempting to produce large-amplitude displacements of the platform.

Changes in some of the kinematic measures of performance are presented in figure 13.12. In this figure we can see that in the pretest, the platform movements were made with quite *restricted* angular movements of the hip, knee, and ankle. At this early stage of learning, subjects seemed to "freeze" the range of motion of the lower limb and trunk, perhaps just to get *any* movement of the platform at all. By the end of the first day, the

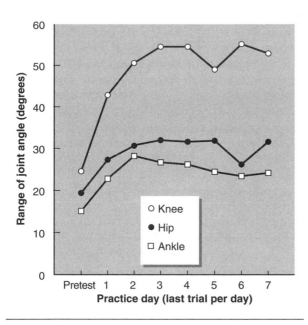

FIGURE 13.12 Changes in the frequency and amplitude of movements during practice of the ski simulator task.

range of motion of each of the joints had been extended considerably, resulting in much larger amplitudes of the platform but with reduced frequency. By the end of the seventh day, oscillation frequency had increased dramatically, along with further increases in amplitudes and joint ranges of motion. Thus, greater success in displacement and frequency of platform oscillations was achieved with greater range in the motion of the lower limbs and trunk—supporting Bernstein's suggestion that practice results in a release of the degrees of freedom (Vereijken, Whiting, & Beek, 1992; see also Arutyunyan, Gurfinkel, & Mirskii, 1968, 1969; Newell, van Emmerik, & Sprague, 1993).

Note, however, that the concept of releasing degrees of freedom has not received universal acceptance among researchers. For example, a study of violinists by Konczak, vander Velden, and Jaeger (2009) revealed that shoulder motions of the bowing arm were actually *reduced* as a function of practice, indicating that the degrees of freedom underwent freezing, not freeing, as a function of practice. We can hypothesize at least two other exceptions. First, in learning to windsurf, the performer gradually learns to freeze the degrees of freedom in the knees and hips, so that most of the controlling actions are in the shoulders and arms—actions used to manipulate the sail's orientation to the wind.

Second, in learning to do a handstand on the still rings, the learner comes to freeze the degrees of freedom in the knees, hips, and trunk, so that balance control is ultimately achieved primarily by movements of the wrists. Unfortunately, very few studies have addressed this stage of Bernstein's perspective on learning, revealing a gap in empirical evidence.

Overall, we think that these ideas (about freezing and freeing degrees of freedom) form a useful description of learning's effect on movement control in *some* tasks. However, the counter-examples described here indicate that this does not provide a universal account of all motor learning.

Another key concept suggested by Bernstein was that independent degrees of freedom are assembled into functional units that act together. When two or more independently moving degrees of freedom "combine" to perform as one functional movement, the independent parts are said to be coupled—they act as *coordinative structures* (or *functional synergies*) to coordinate the independent parts to work as if they were a single unit. This is perhaps exemplified by the gearshifting concepts presented earlier in this chapter (see figure 13.11).

Another good example of coupling independent degrees of freedom occurs when you try rubbing your stomach while patting your head. In this task you are asking the two limbs to perform two different actions. How does your motor system deal with each limb when performing this task? Most likely, if you have never practiced the task before, you will find it difficult because of the strong tendency to perform similar actions with each limb—either patting both the head and the stomach or rubbing both (chapter 8). However, research suggests that with practice, you can overcome the tendency to couple these parts as a coordinative structure.

A series of studies that demonstrated the effects of practice on bimanual coordination was conducted by Walter and Swinnen (1990, 1992, 1994; Swinnen, Walter, Lee, & Serrien, 1993; Swinnen, Walter, Pauwels, Meugens, & Beirinckx, 1990). Subjects were asked to initiate rapid, discrete actions of the left and right limbs simultaneously. The left arm moved a lever toward the body with a single, rapid elbow flexion movement. The right arm also moved a lever toward the body. However, midway through the movement the right arm was required to reverse the direction of its movement twice. Thus, the subject's task was to produce a unidirectional, flexion movement of the left arm and a flexion–extension–flexion movement of the right arm, the arms starting and moving simultaneously (figure 8.9, p. 275).

As with the task of rubbing your stomach while patting your head, Walter and Swinnen found that subjects tended to perform similar actions with the two limbs: There was a *less* pronounced reversal for the limb that the subject intended to reverse, and there was evidence of a reversal in the limb that the subject did *not* intend to reverse (Swinnen, Walter, & Shapiro, 1988). Thus, neither of the limb movements was performed as intended. Rather the functional unit was of two limbs performing similar, albeit hybrid, actions of the individual goals; this was seen via high (within-subject) correlations among the kinematics of the two limbs. Learning was viewed in terms of the success with which each limb performed its own goal with practice. Learning was enhanced if it was supplemented with augmented feedback (Swinnen et al., 1990, 1993), as we would expect from our understanding of feedback effects in chapter 12.

Learning was also enhanced under *adapted* conditions, whereby the actions were performed slowly at first and then were gradually increased in speed (Walter & Swinnen, 1992). Related findings have been provided in experiments involving the acquisition of handwriting skills (Newell & van Emmerik, 1989) and dart throwing (McDonald, van Emmerik, & Newell, 1989), as well as in bimanual aiming tasks involving asymmetric amplitudes (Sherwood, 1990; Sherwood & Canabal, 1988).

One interpretation of these findings is that, by overcoming the existing coupling of degrees of freedom, the limbs are somehow *uncoupled* in a way that allows them to move more or less independently. This interpretation has some controversy, however, as others have shown that learning a new bimanual pattern actually results in an *increased* dependence between the hands: that learning results in the development of new bimanual GMPs involving tight, complex linkages between the limbs (Schmidt et al., 1998). This controversy is complicated by the evidence that the duration of the movement task has a large role in the control and learning of coordinated actions (chapter 8). More research is needed to address these issues.

Stage 3: Exploiting the Mechanical–Inertial Properties of the Limbs

The final stage of Bernstein's perspective on learning is the alteration of movement control so that the motor system can take advantage of (or exploit) the built-in mechanical–inertial properties of the limbs. This notion is tied strongly to mass–spring control, discussed in chapter 7, in which certain spring-like properties of the limb system can be used to the performer's advantage to reduce the need for complex computations and information processing, to reduce energy costs, or to make the movement faster and more forceful.

Schneider, Zernicke, Schmidt, and Hart (1989) studied this question using film analysis of rapid three-joint arm movements together with a biomechanical analysis that allowed the estimation of torques in each of the participating joints. Near the middle of this maximum-speed movement, the subject was to reverse his hand movement at a target, at which the arm was briefly extended upward at about 45°. Early in practice, the subjects tended to use a shoulder flexion torque at the target (reversal point), as if they were holding their arm up against gravity. But later in practice, the shoulder flexion torque tended to drop out, to be replaced by an *extension* torque. Now the limb appeared to be "thrown" at the target, to be "caught" by the shoulder *extensors* in order to reverse its direction and bring it back down quickly. Certainly, the structure of the GMP had changed markedly across practice, employing systematically different muscle groups for essentially the same set of positions early and late in practice. There were many other changes in movement trajectories and in the forces produced as well (see also Spencer & Thelen, 1999).

A different type of analysis was performed by Gray, Watts, Debicki, and Hore (2006), who reported on the differences between the baseball throwing motions of the dominant (skilled) and nondominant (unskilled) arms. Their analyses revealed evidence of restricted ranges of motion for the movements of the unskilled arm, providing additional support for Bernstein's stage 1 (freezing degrees of freedom). However, one of the strengths of Gray and colleagues' (2006) study was the comparison of the unskilled arm mechanics and the mechanics of the skilled arm, thereby revealing the effects of practice and learning. Their analyses showed that, compared to the unskilled arm, the skilled arm tended to exploit interaction torques at various joints to achieve higher arm velocities.

The interpretation of these studies was that the motor system learned to use various passive inertial properties of the system, and that the benefit could be realized not only in terms of increased speed but also in terms of decreased energy costs. These studies clearly support Bernstein's hypothesis and reveal many interesting changes that occur in the movement control processes during the third stage of learning (see also Newell & Vaillancourt, 2001a).

The Haken-Kelso-Bunz Model (Again)

The HKB model of movement coordination was discussed in detail in chapter 8. As mentioned there, the performance of discrete tasks appears to be fundamentally different when compared to performance of continuous tasks. We have discussed several times in previous chapters that discrete skills are dependent on a motor program for their execution. In contrast, continuous motor skills are more dependent on interactions with the environmental stimuli for their regulation. Therefore, it should not be surprising that perspectives on the learning of continuous motor tasks differ in many respects from those constructs developed to explain the learning of discrete tasks.[7]

In chapter 8 we presented evidence that there are two preferred coordination patterns by which continuous oscillations of two limbs or fingers can be reliably produced—*in-phase* and *anti-phase* coordination (the observed coordination pattern is measured in terms of the relative phase lag between the individual cycles; 0° or 180° in these two instances; see chapter 2 for review). Much of the research conducted on coordination dynamics uses the Haken-Kelso-Bunz (1985) model as a basis (see chapter 8). Basically, the HKB model states that intrinsic stabilities of the motor system attract moving degrees of freedom to perform in accordance with one of the system's naturally stable states. For the oscillating-fingers research presented in chapter 8, the strong tendency was to coordinate the fingers in an in-phase or an anti-phase pattern. Of course, theoretically, there are an infinite number of bimanual coordination patterns that can be produced. However, if the system were not amenable to change, then we

would forever be locked into performing only these two patterns. But research suggests that new patterns can be learned, leading to a number of important issues about the learning process as a consequence (Swinnen & Wenderoth, 2004).

Recall from chapter 2 that studies of motor learning often devised experimental tasks that were as unique as possible to the learner. The reasons for this were straightforward—if subjects came into the laboratory with skills already learned (e.g., typing skills), then it would decrease the skill that could be gained during the earliest stages of learning. Traditional motor learning tasks such as the pursuit rotor (figure 2.5, p. 32) and the Bachman ladder (figure 2.8, p. 35) satisfied these criteria because it was highly unlikely that subjects had ever learned skills that were remotely similar to the skills required to perform these "novel" tasks. These advantages however, must be weighed against the major disadvantage that learning does not occur against the background of a "blank slate"—we can never know how learning this new task is influenced by the skills that the learner possessed prior to practice.

The self-organization approach, which was critical in the development of the HKB model, overcame some of the problems associated with "novel tasks" and provided many advantages for the study of motor learning. The approach both exploited the requirements for a learning task and provided a unique window into the influence of previously acquired skills on new learning (see also Kelso & Zanone, 2002; Schöner, Zanone, & Kelso, 1992; Zanone & Kelso, 1994, 1997). Because in-phase and anti-phase coordination are known and measurable *stable* patterns that exist prior to practice, the performance of new bimanual coordination patterns could be evaluated over the course of practice trials and compared to the performance of these existing skills.

In one experiment (Zanone & Kelso, 1992; see also Kelso & Zanone, 2002; Zanone & Kelso, 1997), subjects attempted to coordinate the relative phasing of the index fingers on both hands by rhythmically oscillating them in time to two blinking lights, which alternated in 90° relative phase. Before, during, and after each of five days of practice, Zanone and Kelso had subjects perform a type of transfer test in which the visual metronomes started by blinking simultaneously (in 0° relative phase) and then increased in phase offset by 15° after every 20 s until 180° relative phase had been reached. The main finding was that the 90° pattern was learned and became relatively stable with practice. An unexpected finding, though, was that some subjects showed a *reduced* stability for the anti-phase (180°) pattern as practice trials accumulated on the 90° pattern. This finding provided support for Zanone and Kelso's argument that learning does not involve simply adding a new skill to a subject's repertoire. Rather, learning occurs against the background of an individual's existing skills, resulting not only in the acquisition of new patterns but also in a change in the previously stabilized patterns. This latter finding is a controversial one, however, as it implies that new learning may result in the *unlearning* of previously acquired skills. Other studies suggest that the destabilization of the anti-phase pattern is only a performance bias, not a permanent destabilization in performance (Fontaine, Lee, & Swinnen, 1997; Lee et al., 1995; Smethurst & Carson, 2001), reminiscent of our previous discussions on the learning–performance distinction.

Another finding with use of this approach is also of interest. In the study by Lee and colleagues (1995), which used many of the same methods as Zanone and Kelso's (1992), when learning a 90° pattern, subjects showed strong influences of the existing stable patterns. As an example, the progress in learning for one subject is illustrated in figure 13.13. The panels in this figure represent a plot of the relative motion of the right limb together with the relative motion of the left limb. Recall that plots of this type were presented in chapter 2, for in-phase and anti-phase coordination (figure 2.13, p. 42).

For the 90° pattern investigated by Lee and colleagues, the "correct" plot was represented as an ellipse (overlaid in the top left panel of figure 13.13).[8] All subjects practiced the ellipse pattern during three days of practice. There are two observations in particular to note in this figure. First, for most subjects the initial performance trials were performed in anti-phase; much of the initial stages of learning involved "breaking away" from the attraction to perform this bimanual task as a previously acquired stable pattern. This process was revealed over the practice trials on day 1, with fewer and fewer anti-phase cycles being produced and coordination moving toward 90°. A second important finding concerned the initial trial on day 2, illustrated

in the lower-left. Here, the subjects showed a short-lived performance bias that reverted to anti-phase. This result is interesting because it showed an effect that was very much like that predicted by the progression–regression hypothesis (regression to a previously mastered level of learning). It also is consistent with a phenomenon to be discussed in chapter 14 termed *warm-up decrement,* in which retention loss has a dramatic impact on performance. But, note here that the decrement was very specific, as performance reverted to a previously stable pattern, not to an *unstable* state.

The application of the HKB model and new experimental paradigm to the study of motor learning by Zanone and Kelso (1992) has generated considerable interest. Investigators have studied the role of many different variables with the purpose of discovering how new coordination patterns develop as a function of practice. For example, an existing coordination pattern may help to either stabilize or destabilize a new pattern (Fontaine, Lee, & Swinnen, 1997; Hurley & Lee, 2006; Kostrubiec & Zanone, 2002; Wenderoth & Bock, 2001; Wenderoth, Bock, & Krohn, 2002) in ways that are different than the retention of that pattern (Tallet, Kostrubiec, & Zanone, 2008). The acquisition of a stabilized new pattern appears to be greatly accelerated if movements are unpaced (Kovacs, Buchanan, & Shea, 2009), perhaps due to the influences of discovery learning processes (Hodges & Franks, 2002a; Hodges & Lee, 1999). And other factors, similar to those seen with more traditional approaches to the study of practice (chapters 11 and 12) and transfer (chapter 14), have been recast within a self-organization framework (Faugloire, Bardy, & Stoffregen, 2009; Lay, Sparrow, & O'Dwyer, 2005; Ronsse, Miall, & Swinnen, 2009), broadening the conceptual approaches to viewing these more traditional ideas.

Summary

The empirical laws of motor learning presented in previous chapters are the focus of hypotheses or theories that are directed at explaining them, and this chapter presents some of the more important of these formulations. Learners appear to pass through various stages (or phases) when they practice a skill: a *cognitive stage* in which

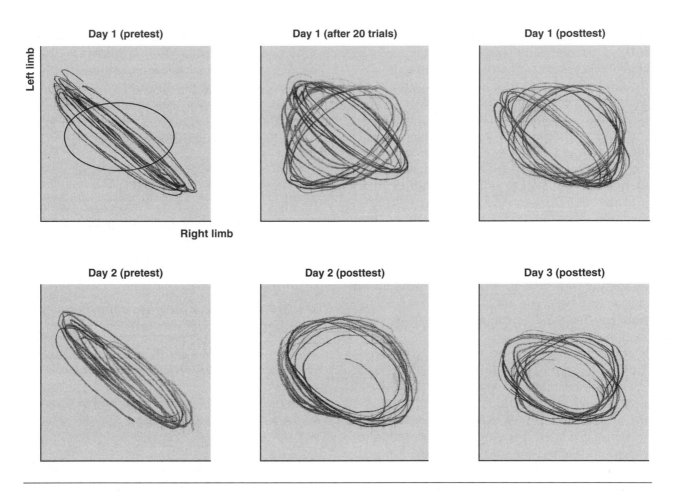

Left limb

Day 1 (pretest)　　**Day 1 (after 20 trials)**　　**Day 1 (posttest)**

Right limb

Day 2 (pretest)　　**Day 2 (posttest)**　　**Day 3 (posttest)**

FIGURE 13.13 Effects of practice on the development of a novel bimanual timing skill. The goal is to produce a relative timing represented by an oval-shaped Lissajous figure.

emphasis is on discovering what to do, a *fixation stage* in which the concern is with perfecting the movement patterns, and an *autonomous stage* in which the attentional requirements of the movement appear to be reduced or even eliminated. A major direction for understanding skill learning has been provided by the individual-differences tradition. A significant finding is that the set of abilities underlying a skill appears to change with practice, so that the collection of abilities underlying a skill is systematically different in practiced and unpracticed subjects. The change is in the direction of less involvement of cognitive abilities and greater involvement of motor abilities with practice. These characteristics of abilities and learning provide insight into why accurate prediction of high-level motor behavior is so difficult to achieve.

Two major theories of motor learning are *closed-loop theory* and *schema theory*. Closed-loop theory holds that the learner acquires a reference of correctness (called the *perceptual trace*) through practice and that the improvements in skill result from the increased capability of the performer to use the reference in closed-loop control. Schema theory is based on the idea that slow movements are feedback based, with rapid movements being program based; with learning, the subject develops rules (or schemas) that allow for the generation of novel movements. Both theories can claim a number of lines of experimental support, but neither is capable of explaining all the evidence on motor learning.

Several other theoretical perspectives have spawned a number of hypotheses about the learning process. The *cognitive perspective* suggests that processes involved in the planning and evaluation of movement affect learning, especially so when performance difficulties challenge these cognitive processes. The *hierarchical control perspective* holds that the control of the skill is systematically shifted from higher-level control processes to lower-level processes involving motor programming. Motor programs are assumed to be constructed through practice, but it is not known how such structuring occurs. In the progression–regression hypothesis, learning to track is viewed as a progression toward higher-order control, with regression to a previously achieved level of skill the result of stress or forgetting. The *Bernstein perspective* addresses his three stages of learning, in which, at least for some tasks, degrees of freedom are initially "frozen," then later released and reorganized with learning. In a later stage of learning, the mechanical–inertial properties of movement can be exploited for movement control that is more precise, faster, or more efficient (or some combination of these).

The self-organization view (HKB model) stresses the importance of interactions between a person's sensory–motor system and the world in which actions are performed. The examination of humans who are learning new coordination patterns of relative phasing has contributed an important method for studying the evolution of skills against the background of existing skills. The method emphasizes changes in stabilities and instabilities, both temporary and long-term.

Student Assignments

1. Prepare to answer the following questions during class discussion:
   a. Using any sport skill, describe the skill characteristics of an athlete who is in the Fitts phases of learning: the cognitive phase, the associative phase, and the autonomous phase.
   b. Using the same sport skill as in question 1a, describe the skill characteristics of an athlete who is in the Bernstein stages of learning: the freezing degrees of freedom stage, the releasing and reorganizing degrees of freedom stage, and the exploiting the mechanical–inertial properties stage.
   c. Compare and contrast closed-loop theory (Adams, 1971) and schema theory (Schmidt, 1975) in terms of

their memory requirements and predictions regarding transfer to novel variations of a learned skill.
2. Find a research article that was designed to specifically test a prediction of either closed-loop theory (Adams, 1971) or schema theory (Schmidt, 1975).

Web Resources

The following link provides a list of Web sites on learning theory (psychology):

> www.nova.edu/~burmeist/learning_theory. html

This British Web site provides many good links to information about skills learning:

> http://news.bbc.co.uk/sportacademy/hi/ sa/learning_centre/newsid_2151000/ 2151977.stm

Notes

[1] Note that the unit of measurement for the *y*-axis in figure 13.4 is Z, not *r*. This is a typical transformation performed on correlation values prior to statistical analysis because the *r* data are not normally distributed (the scores are truncated at the two extremes, $r = +1$ and -1), which violates an assumption for analyses of variance. The Z-transformation provides a normal distribution to the data.

[2] Other statistics have been used to estimate error-detection capabilities as well, such as the absolute error between objective and subjective scores (Newell, 1974) and *d'* in signal-detection analyses (Rubin, 1978).

[3] We have assumed normal distribution here, with the mode represented as the correct perceptual trace. With learning, the shape of the distribution of incremented perceptual traces moves from platykurtic (flat) to leptokurtic (peaked). Of course, other distributions are also possible. For example, in learning to play golf, many more people have trouble with slicing the ball than with hooking the ball. In this case, the shape of the distribution would be expected to change in both kurtosis and skewness, as a function of learning.

[4] Learning in Adams' theory was represented by changes in the normal distribution—a more pronounced mode and reduced variability. In schema theory, learning is represented by a regression-line analogy. A more *powerful* regression equation is developed with learning—one that has reduced residual variability and for which the

regression coefficient (R^2) approaches 1 (see discussion at end of chapter 2).

[5] In terms of the regression-line analogy, the predicted success of a novel variation of the regression line is reduced considerably when extended to parameters *beyond* those actually experienced in practice. Therefore, greater breadth in the variability of practice should extend the predictability of the schema to novel parameters.

[6] The term "gearshift analogy" is probably incorrect from a historical point of view. A similar idea was proposed by Jastrow before cars even had gearshifts: "At the outset each step of the performance is separately and distinctly the object of attention and effort; and as practice proceeds and expertness is gained . . . the separate portions thereof become fused into larger units, which in turn make a constantly diminishing demand upon consciousness" (Jastrow, 1906, p. 42).

[7] The HKB model described in this section represents one of several perspectives that consider how an individual's sensory–motor system interacts on various levels with the environment to influence the regulation of movement. An overview of various approaches is provided in Turvey and Fonseca (2009), Beer (2009), and Latash, Scholz, and Schöner (2007).

[8] In this study the left and right limbs were to produce different amplitudes at a 90° phase lag. In other studies, in which subjects learn 90° phase lags with equal amplitudes, the left limb–right limb figure to be produced is a circle.

CHAPTER 14

RETENTION AND TRANSFER

At one point in the process of revising this text, the two authors got together to discuss some ideas over a long bike ride on the beach in Venice, California. Although the second author had not ridden a bike in many years and, indeed, had never ridden this particular bike before, he managed to avoid causing any serious harm to the sunbathers and volleyball players gathered on the beach that warm spring day. Should we be surprised that the skill of bike riding is retained and transferred so easily? And what factors might influence how well we retain and transfer these and other types of motor skills? Such concerns about how well skills are retained over time and how well they transfer to different situations are of both theoretical and practical importance—theoretical because of the need to understand how the motor system is structured so that skills can be produced "on demand," and practical because usually much time and effort have gone into the learning of the skills, and we need to know how such investments can be protected from loss. This chapter is about the empirical relationships and principles concerned with *retention* and *transfer.*

Fundamental Distinctions and Definitions

You may have the impression that motor learning and motor memory are two different aspects of the same problem, one having to do with gains in skill, the other with maintenance of skill. This is so because psychologists and others tend to use the metaphor of memory as a *place* where information is stored, such as a computer hard drive or a library. Statements like "I have a good memory for names and dates," or "The subject placed the phone number in long-term memory," are representative of this use of the term. The implication is that some set of processes has led to the acquisition of the materials, and now some other set of processes is responsible for keeping them "in" memory.

Memory

A common meaning of the term *motor memory* is "the persistence of the acquired capability for performance." In this sense, habit and memory are conceptually similar. Remember, the usual test for learning of a task concerns how well the individual can perform the skill on a retention or transfer test. That is, a skill has been learned if and only if it can be retained "relatively permanently" (see chapter 10). If you can still perform a skill after not having practiced it for a year (or even for a day or just a few minutes), then you have a memory of the skill. In this sense, memory is the *capability* for performance, not a location where that capability is stored. Depending on one's theoretical orientation about motor learning, memory could be a motor program, a reference of correctness, a schema, or an intrinsic coordination pattern (Amazeen, 2002). From this viewpoint, as you can see, learning and memory are just "different sides of the same behavioral coin," as Adams (1976a, p. 223) put it (see also Adams, 1967).

Forgetting

Another term used in this context is *forgetting*. The term is used to indicate the opposite of learning, in that learning refers to the acquisition of the capability for movement whereas forgetting refers to the loss of such capability. It is likely that the processes and principles having to do with gains and losses in the capability for moving will be different, but the terms refer to the different directions of the change in this capability. "Forgetting" is a term that has to do with theoretical constructs, just as "learning" does. Memory is a construct, and forgetting is the loss of memory; so forgetting is a concept at a theoretical, rather than a behavioral, level of thinking.

As shown in table 14.1, the analogy to the study of learning is a close one. At the theoretical level, learning is a gain in the capability for skilled action, while forgetting is the loss of same. On the behavioral level, learning is evidenced by relatively permanent gains in performance, while forgetting is evidenced by relatively permanent losses in performance, or losses in retention. So, if you understand what measures of behavior suggest about learning, then you also understand the same about forgetting.

Retention and Transfer

Retention refers to the persistence or lack of persistence of the *performance*, and is considered at the behavioral level rather than at the theoretical level (table 14.1). It might or might not tell us whether memory has been lost. The test on which decisions about retention are based is called the *retention test*, performed at a period of time after practice trials have ended (the *retention interval*). If performance on the retention test is as proficient as it was immediately after the end of the practice session (or acquisition phase), then we might be inclined to say that no memory loss (no forgetting) has occurred. If performance on the retention test is poor, then we may decide that a memory loss has occurred. However, because the test for memory (the retention test) is a test of *performance*, it is subject to all the variations that cause performances to change in temporary ways—just as in the study of learning. Thus, it could be that performance is poor on the retention test for some temporary reason (fatigue, anxiety), and so one could falsely conclude that a memory loss has occurred. (At this point it might be helpful to review the learning–performance distinction presented in chapter 10.)

For all practical purposes, a retention test and a *transfer test* are very similar. In both cases, the interest is in the persistence of the acquired capability for performance (habit). The two types of tests differ only in that the transfer test has subjects (all or some) switching to different tasks or conditions, whereas the retention test usually involves retesting subjects on the same task or conditions.

TABLE 14.1. The Analogous States of Motor Learning and Motor Forgetting

	Theoretical level	Behavioral level
Motor learning	Acquiring the capability for moving, gains in memory	Relatively permanent gains in performance with practice
Motor forgetting	Losing the capability for moving, or forgetting, loss of memory	Relatively permanent losses in performance, or retention losses

Measuring Retention and Transfer

Tests of retention and transfer provide indicators about the persistence of an acquired habit during an absence from practice, or about the way in which previous practice influences performance on a new task. Unfortunately, straightforward conclusions from such tests are not always possible. Next, we present the most common and important of the various methods and measures of retention and transfer that have been devised by researchers, and we suggest which ones provide the most useful information.

Retention of Learning

In motor memory research, a number of different measures of retention have been used, and these different methods provide somewhat different interpretations about the underlying forgetting processes. The most common of these methods are *absolute retention* and various measures of *relative retention*.

Absolute Retention

By far the most simple (and scientifically justifiable) measure of retention is absolute retention, defined simply as the level of performance on the initial trial(s) of the retention test. Figure

14.1 shows the hypothetical scores of a group of subjects who practiced the pursuit rotor task (see figure 2.5, p. 32) for 30 trials and then, after a retention interval, performed a retention test involving 30 additional trials. The absolute-retention score is 20, because performance in trial 1 of retention is approximately 20 s of time on target (20 s TOT). Notice that the absolute-retention score is not based in any way on the level of performance attained in the practice trials.

Relative Retention

Various measures of relative retention are possible, such as those using a *difference score* and those using *percentage scores*. These measures express in various ways the absolute-retention score *relative to* scores obtained during the practice trials.

Difference Score Probably the most common relative-retention score is a difference score that supposedly represents the "amount" of loss in skill over the retention interval. It is computed by taking the difference between the performance levels at the end of the practice session and the beginning of the retention test. In the example given in figure 14.1, the difference score is 5 s, as the group performed with a TOT of 25 s before the retention interval and 20 s afterward. Such measures are aesthetically pleasing to many investigators because they seem (erroneously, however) to represent the forgetting processes more or less directly.

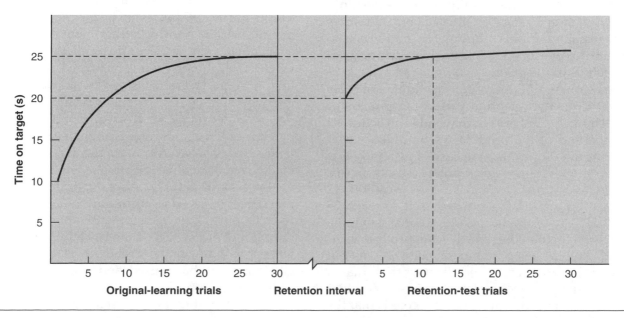

FIGURE 14.1 Hypothetical performance curves on the pursuit rotor for original-learning and retention-test trials.

Percentage Score A second kind of relative-retention score is a percentage score, which represents the "amount" lost in retention over the retention interval relative to the amount of improvement that occurred on the task in the practice session. That is, the percentage score is the difference score (as defined earlier) divided by the amount of change in performance during the practice session (another difference score), then multiplied by 100 for conversion into a percentage. In the example in figure 14.1, the percentage score is the difference score (5 s) divided by the amount of performance change during the practice trials (25 − 10 = 15 s) and multiplied by 100, or 5 / 15 × 100 = 33.3%. The meaning usually given to the percentage score in this case is that one-third of the amount of original improvement during practice was lost over the retention interval. Be careful, though, because such estimates are sensitive to temporary factors that alter performance during practice (e.g., fatigue, random practice) and thus alter the size of the denominator. However, these scores are sometimes useful when one wishes to compare (usually informally) the retention on two different skills, perhaps with different scoring systems.

Savings Score A third measure of retention, which was introduced long ago by Ebbinghaus (1913) and has regained popularity in recent years (e.g., Keisler & Willingham, 2007; Krakauer & Shadmehr, 2006; Seidler & Noll, 2008), involves the "savings" in relearning. That is, after a retention interval, one measures the number of trials required for the subjects to reach the level of proficiency achieved in original practice. In the example in figure 14.1, the savings score would represent the number of trials *"saved"* in the retention test in the process of reaching the 25 s of TOT that had been achieved at the end of the practice session. Notice that the number of trials to relearn is generally less than the total number of practice trials; in this case (as opposed to 30 trials in acquisition) 12 retention-test trials were required to reach 25 s TOT. Therefore, in the retention session, the subject regained the same level of proficiency as had been achieved in the practice session—but in this instance it required 18 fewer trials than it did in the practice session (savings = 30 − 12 = 18 trials). The idea of a savings score is that the more complete the retention, the faster should

be the "rate" of relearning, even if the first trial or so show poor performance (due, for example, to warm-up decrement, discussed later).

Contrasting the Various Retention Measures

While it may seem that these various methods merely provide subtle differences in the measurement of a single process (forgetting), this is not the case. According to an analysis of the problem some years ago (Schmidt, 1971a, 1972a), the relative-retention scores are flawed by a variety of factors. The basis of the problem is that all these scores come from *performance* measures, with changes in performance being used to infer something about the changes in the internal state (habit or memory) that underlies performance. Therefore, all the problems with performance curves that we mentioned with respect to the measurement of learning (ceiling and floor effects, for example, in chapter 10) also apply to the measurement of forgetting. In particular, difference scores are subject to a variety of influences that cloud interpretations about forgetting, casting doubt on their usefulness. Moreover, the percentage score is based on two difference scores, one divided by the other to gain the percentage, clouding the issue even further. The savings score suffers a similar problem since the assessment of "savings in relearning" itself employs a difference score in its computation.

The problem is not just a technical or academic one (Schmidt, 1971a). Some of the most fundamental variables in forgetting have empirical effects that seem to depend completely on the ways in which retention is measured. If forgetting in figure 14.1 is measured by the absolute-retention method, then numerous studies show that absolute retention increases as the amount of practice increases, just as we might suspect. But if forgetting is measured by the relative-retention methods, then relative retention (computed from the *same* set of data) *decreases* as the amount of practice increases (see Schmidt, 1972a). Thus, the relationship between forgetting of skills and the amount of practice would be completely different depending on how retention is measured. Obviously, this has caused, and will continue to cause, many confusing situations for students who are attempting to understand the principles of motor forgetting. The absolute-retention score minimizes these problems, and it is the most simple and straightforward one to use.

Transfer of Learning

Transfer is usually defined as the gain (or loss) in the capability for performance in one task as a result of practice or experience on some other task. Thus, we might ask whether practicing a task like badminton would produce benefits or losses (or neither) for another task such as tennis. If it turns out that the performance of tennis is more effective after badminton experience than it would have been with no previous badminton experience, then we would say that the skills acquired in badminton have "transferred to" the skills involved in tennis. It is as if something that is learned in the badminton situation can be carried over to (or applied to) the task of playing tennis (Schmidt & Young, 1987).

Transfer Experiments

Experiments on the transfer of learning can use a variety of experimental designs, but we will not consider them all here (see Ellis, 1965, for a complete description). In the simplest of all designs, assume that there are just two groups of subjects (groups I and II). In table 14.2, group I practices task A for some arbitrary number of practice trials, after which this group is transferred to practice on task B. Group II does *not* practice task A at all, but merely begins practicing task B.

You can think of tasks A and B as any two activities; they could be different tasks such as badminton and tennis, or they could be two slightly different variations of the *same* task, such as the pursuit rotor at different speeds. Thus, when the two groups begin practice of task B, the only systematic difference between them is whether or not they have had previous experience on task A.

TABLE 14.2. A Simple Design for an Experiment on Proactive Transfer of Learning

Group	Transfer task	Test
I	Task A	Task B
II	--	Task B
III	Task Z	Task B

Positive and Negative Transfer   Consider the possible results of such an experiment as shown in figure 14.2. Here, the task of interest is task B, so task A performance is not graphed. In figure 14.2, group I, which had task A prior to task B, performs task B more effectively than does group II, which did not have the experience with task A. In this case, we conclude that experience on task A has provided increased capability for task B, equal to 30 units on trial 1 of task B. When the practice on task A enhances subsequent performance on task B, we say that *positive transfer* occurred from task A to task B.

Now consider what happens with another hypothetical group (group III). As seen in table 14.2, group III practices task Z (rather than task A as group I did) prior to trials on task B. In figure 14.2 the performance for group III is less skilled in relation to that of group II by 20 units on trial 1 of task B. For the reasons just mentioned, we conclude that experience on task Z has interfered with group III's capability for performance on task B. In this case, we would say that *negative transfer* occurred from task Z to task B.

Proactive and Retroactive Transfer   In the examples given so far, the transfer seemed to

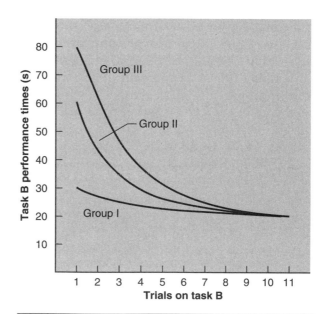

FIGURE 14.2   Performances on task B for a group with no prior experience (II) or with prior practice on task A (group I) or task Z (group III). If group I outperforms group II, then positive transfer has occurred. If group III performs more poorly than group II, negative transfer has occurred.

work "forward" in time from task A or Z to task B. This is termed *proactive* transfer. However, we can also consider *retroactive transfer,* that is, transfer that seems to work "backward" in time. Consider the more complex experimental design shown in table 14.3. Here, two different treatment groups (groups IV and V) both perform task B. Then, group IV performs task Q while group V performs nothing. Later, both groups return to task B for a retention test. If the retention performance on task B is more effective for group IV than for group V, we say that positive retroactive transfer occurred from task Q to task B; practicing task Q seemed to "enhance" the capability already shown on task B. Alternately, if the performance of task B on the retention test is less effective for group IV than for group V, we say that negative retroactive transfer (or interference) occurred; here, practicing task Q seemed to degrade the capability for the previously practiced task B.

The retroactive- and proactive-transfer designs are similar in that they both consider the performance on the *initial* trials of task B in the retention test (or the test phase in table 14.2) to be the critical data indicating transfer. Some measures of these different performances are described in the next sections.

Measurement of Transfer

The "amount" of transfer from one task to another can be assessed in a number of ways, all of which suffer from the basic problems raised many times earlier about the measurement of performance, learning, and forgetting; thus none of these methods will be very satisfactory in measuring transfer. Rather they are used to describe the relationships among curves such as those in figure 14.2 and are occasionally helpful in discussion of the results of different transfer experiments.

Percentage Transfer   One method of estimating the amount of transfer is to consider the gain in performance as a result of experience on task A as a percentage of the "total amount learned" by

group II in the experiment. The data from groups I and II are illustrated again in figure 14.3. On trial 1 the difference between the two groups is 30 units (labeled as points X and Y). At the end of practice, group II's performance level is 20 units (point C) and has therefore improved by 40 units (60 − 20). The amount of improvement in task B by group II can be represented as the total improvement shown in task B (or $X − C$). Thus, group I's experience with task A has provided 30 out of the possible 40 units of improvement, or 75% transfer. In terms of a more general formula,

$$\text{Percent transfer} = (X − Y) / (X − C) \times 100 \quad (14.1)$$

in which $X = 60$, $Y = 30$, and $C = 20$ score units. The formula can also be used for negative transfer as shown in figure 14.2. Here, the values X and C remain the same, but Y (the initial performance level on task B by group III) is larger than it was for group I (i.e., 80). Being careful to keep the signs of the numbers straight, and noting that the numerator of the equation is a negative number

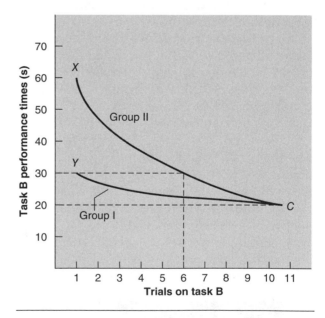

FIGURE 14.3   The calculation of percentage transfer.

TABLE 14.3. A Retroactive Transfer Design			
Group	**Initial practice**	**Transfer task**	**Retention test**
IV	Task B	Task Q	Task B
V	Task B	--	Task B

(i.e., $X − Y$, or $60 − 80$, or $−20$), we calculate transfer as $−20 / 40 3 100 = −50\%$.

Roughly speaking, we can interpret the percentage transfer as the percentage of gain (or loss) on task B as a result of prior practice on task A. Positive transfer of 100% would imply that the performance on the first trial of task B for group I is at the final level of performance (i.e., point C in figure 14.3) demonstrated by group II. Transfer of 0% would mean that the two groups are the same in initial performance on task B (i.e., both at level X).

The reason this measure is inadequate, of course, is that the amount of improvement on task B (i.e., $X − C$) will depend on the amount of practice provided, on the scoring system used for task B, on the nature of the subjects, and on countless other arbitrary factors that affect the shapes of performance curves. But using percentage transfer measures can serve a useful purpose in describing the relationships among the curves; just be careful not to take the finding of, say, 75% transfer too literally.

Savings Score   Another, far less frequently used method for describing the amount of transfer is a savings score, as already discussed. Here, the savings score represents the amount of practice time "saved" (i.e., reduced) on task B by having first practiced task A. In figure 14.3, group I (which had practiced task A previously) begins its performance of task B at a level of performance equivalent to that shown by group II after six trials. It is possible to say that group I "saved" six trials in the learning of task B by having first learned task A. But this is not the whole story; the "savings" on task B are almost certainly compensated for by a "loss," because task A had to be practiced, and the practice time on task A is usually going to be longer than the amount of time "saved" on task B. That is, for learning task B, usually nothing is as efficient as practicing task B (see chapter 11 for discussion on practice specificity).

Such "savings" begin to have importance when the financial cost of practice is considered. A common example is in learning to fly an airplane, such as the McDonnell Douglas MD-11. To practice in the actual MD-11 aircraft would be very costly, so computer-based simulators that closely resemble the airplane cockpit are frequently used for practice (see figure 14.15, and the related discussion, later in the chapter). Here, the time "spent" in the simulator (task A) is inexpensive relative to the time "saved" in learning to fly the MD-11 (task B), and it is safer as well. In such situations, the effectiveness of a simulator-based training program is often evaluated in terms of financial savings, such savings being the number of hours saved on task B (the MD-11) multiplied by the number of dollars per hour of practice on task B. In the case of the MD-11, dollar amounts of savings can be very large.

Retention and Motor Memory

One of the most frequently studied theoretical issues in psychology—an issue that people often disagree about—concerns memory. Is memory a result of some processing of an event, or does memory refer to the processing *itself*? Are there different types of memory, such as memories for movements, for sensations, for smells, and the like, or is there just one memory, whose *retention characteristics* are a product of the nature and type of processing that is conducted? Questions such as these are hotly debated topics. For example, a scan of the chapters in Byrne (2008) reveals an extremely wide diversity of topics, studied at many different levels of analysis. For the most part, these topics are beyond our present purposes. Rather, we present some of the evidence about the retention (this section) and retention loss (next section) of motor skills.

Retention of Skill for Continuous Tasks

That many motor skills are nearly never forgotten is almost a cliché. Examples such as swimming and riding a bicycle, in which performance after many years of no intervening practice is nearly as proficient as it was originally, are frequently cited. Ideas about such examples, though, are seldom based on acceptable experimental methods; fortunately, many laboratory examples of these situations have been studied, and these results seem to say the same thing.

Although many studies could be cited to illustrate the point, we consider a representative study with long retention intervals by Fleishman and Parker (1962). They used a three-dimensional compensatory tracking task (the Mashburn task, figure 2.5*b*, p. 32), with movements of the hands in forward–backward and left–right dimensions and movement of the feet in a left–right dimension. Subjects practiced in sessions for 17 days, and then separate groups performed retests after either 9, 14, or 24 months.

The scores for practice and retention tests are shown in figure 14.4, where scores for all three retention groups have been averaged together in the practice session. After the different retention intervals, the various groups were nearly equivalent, and none had shown any appreciable losses in proficiency even after two years of layoff. Some tendency was seen for the two-year group to have slightly less proficiency than the groups with shorter retention intervals, but the differences were very small and the losses were regained completely in three sessions. These small differences are not very meaningful when one compares the retention-test performance to the level of performance at the start of practice. Certainly, this continuous task was retained nearly perfectly for two years.

Other studies, using different continuous tasks, have shown very similar effects. Meyers (1967), using the Bachman ladder climb task, demonstrated nearly no loss in performance for retention intervals of up to 12 weeks. Ryan (1962),

using the pursuit rotor and stabilometer tasks, found nearly no retention losses after retention intervals of 21 days; later, he found only small losses in performance on the stabilometer task with retention intervals of up to one year (Ryan, 1965). There are many other examples, and the generalization continues to hold. Continuous motor tasks are extremely well retained over very long retention intervals, just as the cliché about the bicycle would have us believe.

Retention of Skill for Discrete Tasks

While there is ample evidence of nearly complete retention of continuous skills, the picture appears to be quite different for discrete skills. Consider an example by Neumann and Ammons (1957). The subject sat in front of a large display with eight pairs of switches arranged in an inside and an outside circle of eight switches each. The subject was to turn the inner switch "on" and then discover which switch in the outer circle was paired with it; a buzzer sounded when the correct match was made. Subjects learned the task to a criterion of two consecutive errorless trials, and then retention intervals of 1 min, 20 min, two days, seven weeks, and one year were imposed for different groups of subjects.

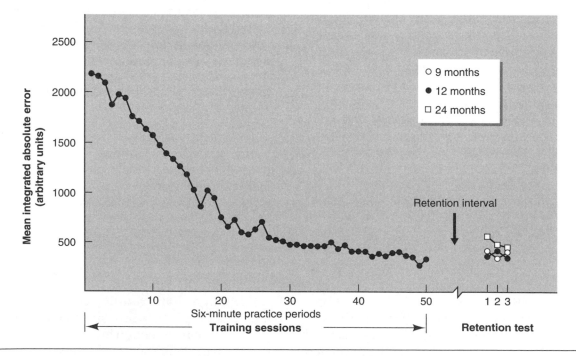

FIGURE 14.4   Mean performance on a three-dimensional tracking task in original learning and after three retention intervals.

Reprinted from E.A. Fleishman and J.F. Parker, 1962, "Factors in the retention and relearning of perceptual motor skill," *Journal of Experimental Psychology* 64: 218.

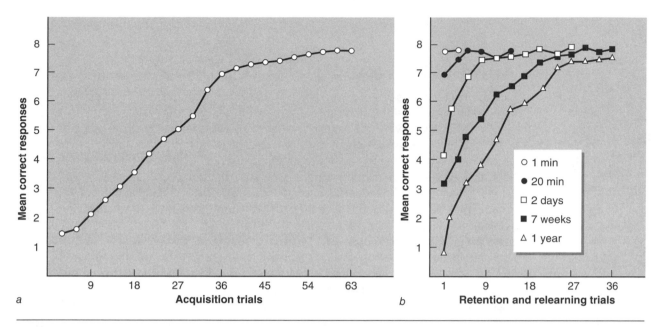

FIGURE 14.5 Mean performance of a discrete task in original learning and after various retention intervals.

Reprinted, by permission, from E. Neumann and R.B. Ammons, 1957, "Acquisition and long term retention of a simple serial perception motor skill," *Journal of Experimental Psychology* 53: 160.

The main findings are presented in figure 14.5. Some losses in performance appeared after only 20 min, and the losses became progressively greater as the length of the retention interval increased. In fact, after one year, the performance was actually less correct than the initial performance in practice had been, suggesting that the forgetting was essentially complete. However, notice that in all cases the improvements during the retention trials were more rapid than in the original-practice session (as indicated by comparing the slopes of the relearning and practice session curves), indicating that some memory for the skill was retained, which facilitated performance in these relearning trials.

Continuous Versus Discrete Tasks

Why is there such a large difference in the retention characteristics of continuous and discrete skills, with continuous tasks having nearly perfect retention and discrete tasks having such poor retention? A number of hypotheses have been proposed to explain these differences, and they are discussed next.

Verbal–Cognitive Components

One hypothesis is that verbal–cognitive components are somehow more quickly forgotten than motor components; because discrete tasks seem to

have a heavier emphasis on verbal–cognitive elements (learning which switch in the inner circle is paired with which switch in the outer circle in the Neumann & Ammons study, for example), there is more loss for the discrete tasks over time. Ideas similar to this have generated considerable interest among neuropsychologists who study differences in the retention characteristics of various tasks (e.g., see "Retention of Motor Skills in Amnesia").

However, while it is true that most of the discrete tasks that have been studied in retention situations seem highly verbal-cognitive (e.g., Schendel & Hagman, 1982), there is no reason that discrete tasks must be so. Certainly, one can think of many discrete tasks that have relatively little reliance on verbal–cognitive abilities (e.g., throwing, striking, pole-vaulting). What would be the retention characteristics of a discrete task that was highly "motor" in nature? Lersten (1969) used an arm movement task (the rho task) in which a circular and a linear movement component had to be performed as quickly as possible. He found approximately 80% loss (of the original amount of improvement) in the circular phase, and a 30% loss for the linear component, with retention intervals of one year. Similarly, Martin (1970) used a task in which the subjects moved the hand over two barriers and then returned to

Retention of Motor Skills in Amnesia

The examination of amnesia patients has provided some surprising information about the retention of motor skills compared to other types of information. Two patients are particularly noteworthy. One famous patient (H.M.) was studied by neuropsychologists for many years following an operation on the temporal lobes in his brain. The result of the surgery was a devastating memory deficit, leaving him unable to retain information in memory for more than very brief durations. H.M. was able to learn motor skills, however, such as mirror tracing and pursuit rotor tracking. Remarkably, H.M. showed impressive retention of these motor skills after periods of no practice, despite the fact that he could not remember ever having practiced these tasks or the experimenters who had conducted the experiments (Milner, Corkin, & Teuber, 1968)!

Memory in a patient with Alzheimer's disease (M.T.) was documented during the play of two rounds of golf with neuropsychologist Daniel Schacter. This patient had been diagnosed with a progressively deteriorating memory disorder, and at the time of the golf "experiments" showed extremely poor performance on standard tests of verbal memory. What makes M.T.'s case interesting is that his golf skill had remained relatively unimpaired. According to Schacter (1983), he remained "able to execute a complex set of acquired perceptual-motor procedures in a relatively fluent manner . . . generally hit the ball straight and frequently hit it for respectable distances . . . frequently sank putts up to 5 or 6 feet long, and twice holed putts from over 20 feet" (p. 239). Nevertheless, M.T.'s memory deficits caused frequent problems in playing golf. For example, if M.T. was the second person of the twosome to hit his tee shot and left the teeing area immediately, then he had a good probability of finding his ball. However, if he teed off first, he usually had no idea where the ball had gone and occasionally had forgotten that he had already played his tee shot!

The existence of motor retention for newly acquired learning in people with amnesia (H.M.) and for a previously acquired skill (M.T.) in the presence of severe retention deficits for other types of information is a type of memory *dissociation*. Similar dissociations for preserved retention of motor skill, combined with memory loss for information about the details of the practice session, have since been documented for healthy subjects (e.g., Hikosaka et al., 2002; Verdolini-Marston & Balota, 1994). These dissociations have been explained by some theorists as supporting the view that the retention of (or memory for) motor skills is fundamentally different from the retention of other types of information, such as verbal knowledge (e.g., Roediger, 1990; Schacter, 1987). Various dichotomies have been used to describe this distinction, such as implicit versus explicit memory and declarative versus procedural memory, representing a continuing source of experimental and theoretical curiosity in contemporary research.

a starting switch as quickly as possible, finding approximately 50% retention loss over a four-month retention interval. The large amount of loss in retention for discrete skills that can be considered "mostly motor" is similar to the loss experienced by Neumann and Ammons' subjects (figure 14.5), suggesting that there is more to these effects in retention than just the "motorness" of the tasks.

Amount of Practice

One of the major factors determining absolute retention is the amount of original practice, with retention increasing as the amount of original practice increases. In tracking, for example, there are many instances within a trial lasting 30 s in duration in which the pointer and track become separated, with each instance requiring a separate adjustment. Thus, a single "trial" may require many separate "discrete" actions. Contrast this situation to that for discrete tasks, for which a trial typically consists of a single adjustment or action. It stands to reason, therefore, that with the same number of learning trials, the continuous task receives far more practice than the discrete task. The extra amount of practice, according to this hypothesis, leads to increased retention, since it is well known that absolute retention is directly related to the amount of original practice.

What is a "Trial"?

Another notion, related to the one just presented, is that the definition of *trial* is quite arbitrary; a trial can refer to both a 200 ms reaction-time (RT) performance and a 2 min duration performance on a tracking task. This poses a problem for defining the amount of original practice for the task, and it is also a problem in connection with the retention test. Remember, the level of absolute retention is measured in terms of the performance on the first few "trials" of retention-test performance. If a "trial" is a 2 min performance, there could be a great deal of relearning *occurring within* a trial for the continuous task, with no relearning within a trial for a rapid discrete performance. So the initial movements within the first trial for the continuous task could show considerable retention loss, but the experimenter might not detect it because the error in the initial performance would be "averaged" with the later portions of the trial on which performance was more proficient. Because this could not occur for the discrete task, it is possible that the amount of forgetting is typically underestimated for the continuous task and not for the discrete task, making the two kinds of tasks appear to be different in their retention characteristics when they might otherwise not be. Fleishman and Parker (1962) found a great deal of improvement within a continuous-task trial, as might be suspected.

Retention of Generalized Motor Programs Versus Parameters

Another possible difference in the forgetting of continuous and discrete tasks is that researchers might be examining different characteristics of the task. Evidence of this was found in a study by Swinnen (1988), who had subjects learn an elbow flexion–extension–flexion task with a goal movement time (MT) of 650 ms. Following 60 trials of practice (with knowledge of results, KR), no-KR retention tests were given after intervals from 10 min to five months. Swinnen analyzed separately the retention of absolute timing (related to the movement parameter) and relative timing (related to the generalized motor program, GMP) and found that absolute timing decayed rapidly, supporting much of the research in this area for discrete tasks. In contrast, the GMP information

suffered no loss in relative timing accuracy. These findings suggest that at least some information from learning discrete tasks is retained quite well. Moreover, these findings make sense from a schema theory view (Schmidt, 1975b). One has no need to retain parameter information over long periods of time, because that information is used only briefly to update the schema. In contrast, schema theory suggests that the retention characteristics of GMPs are quite strong so that the invariant features of the action can be recalled and parameterized as needed. Certainly, much more work could be done to explore the ideas introduced in Swinnen's experiments.

Retention Loss

In this section we present four different research methods used to investigate retention loss in motor performance, followed by a discussion of related theoretical and experimental issues about the processes through which retention loss occurs. Each method highlights some important features about performance loss that are revealed under different task conditions.

Iconic Memory and Motor Performance

As we discussed in chapter 5, motor performance benefits considerably from the availability of visual information, especially for actions that require precise end-point accuracy, such as manual aiming (e.g., typing; moving a cursor). However, there is considerable evidence to suggest that *continuous* visual information is unnecessary in order to maintain accuracy. The reason is that our memory for the immediate visual environment can "fill in" the gaps if the continuous supply of vision is cut off. For example, suppose you took aim at the bull's-eye in dart throwing and the room lights suddenly went out just before you started moving the dart. How would performance be affected? Research using experiments that closely resemble this situation suggests that performance would depend on the length of time you were in the dark before throwing the dart.

Studies by Elliott and his colleagues suggest that motor performance deteriorates quickly because persistence of the visual information (the icon) fades rapidly from sensory memory

(Sperling, 1960). For example, in a study by Elliott and Madalena (1987), subjects moved a stylus to a target under various conditions of available room light. A control condition provided subjects with continuous visual feedback of the target and stylus. In another condition, the room lights were extinguished as the subjects initiated their movements; thus the entire movement (durations of 200-500 ms) was made in the absence of any direct visual information. The other three conditions also involved movements without visual information available; however, these movements were made after the room lights had been extinguished for 2, 5, or 10 s.

As figure 14.6 shows, subjects could perform the aiming movements well without visual information if the entire movement was *completed* within half a second after the room lights were turned off. Performance was markedly disrupted, however, after a wait in the dark of 2 s or more. Elliott and Madalena (1987) interpreted these findings to suggest that a very short-lived memory for visual information can support performance rather accurately (see chapter 3; reviews by Elliott, 1990, 1992; also Farrell & Thomson, 1998). However, the information is prone to forgetting due to a *decay* of the icon—a process whereby rapid information loss is attributable to the passage of time.

The findings of Elliott and Madalena (1987) and others (e.g., Binsted, Rolheiser, & Chua, 2006) indicate that motor performance can be supported for a brief time by a short-term sensory store, which loses information quite rapidly. These findings suggest a process similar to that proposed in the oldest theory of forgetting, the *trace-decay* theory. It is a passive theory of memory loss caused by disuse—information is forgotten because it is not practiced and therefore "decays" with time. The memory of an item, event, or skill is thought to be represented as a trace in the central nervous system, with the strength of this trace weakening over time. When the information or skill in memory is needed at some future time, performance accuracy is related to the current strength of the trace. This idea accounts well for the common effects of disuse and, of course, for the fact that time, per se, seems to be a strong factor in forgetting.

Considerable research on trace-decay effects in slow, linear-positioning tasks has been conducted using what is called the *short-term motor*

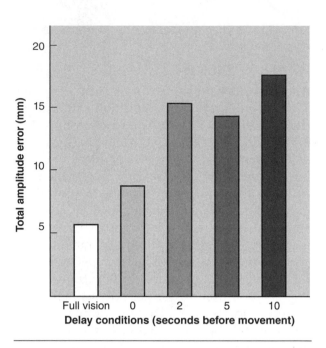

FIGURE 14.6 Total amplitude error in aiming under conditions of vision and without vision under various delay conditions.

Data from Elliott and Madalena 1987.

memory paradigm (chapter 3). This involves the presentation of a movement, followed by recall of that movement after very brief time intervals, often only a few seconds in duration. These studies used methods that paralleled methods in experiments in memory for verbal materials, early investigations having been conducted by Brown (1958) and Peterson and Peterson (1959). In one of the first motor studies, Adams and Dijkstra (1966) had subjects move to a stop that defined a target position, then return to a starting location for a retention interval, and finally, estimate the defined target position but with the stop removed. Subjects were blindfolded and not given KR about their movement accuracy. In addition, subjects were given various numbers of "reinforcements," whereby movement to the target position was presented 1, 6, or 15 times before the retention interval.

The major findings are presented in figure 14.7. The absolute errors on the recall trials are presented as a function of the number of "reinforcements" and the length of the retention interval. As the length of the retention interval increased, the error in recall also increased, with the increases being nearly maximized by the time the retention interval was 80 s in length and

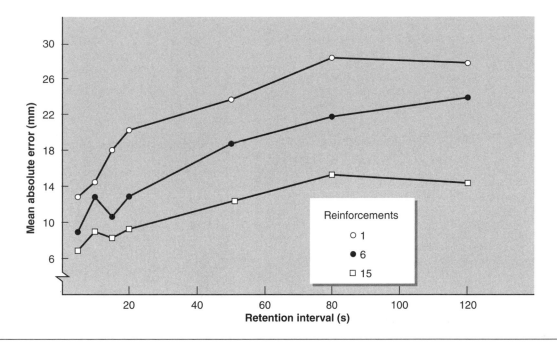

FIGURE 14.7 Mean absolute error in positioning as a function of the retention-interval length and the number of "reinforcements."

Reprinted, by permission, from J.A. Adams and S. Dijkstra, 1966, "Short-term memory and motor responses," *Journal of Experimental Psychology* 71: 317. Copyright © 1966 by the American Psychological Association.

with no important increases thereafter. Similar to memory for verbal items, memory for these linear-positioning movements appears to have a forgetting process that is nearly completed in about 1 min. Also, the rate of forgetting appears to be slowed by "reinforcements," or practice; the errors were systematically smaller with more repetitions of the target position.

One interpretation of these results is that the movement to the stop created a short-term memory representation of the feedback qualities of the correct position. Further, it appeared that, although this representation was weakened over the course of the empty retention interval, it was strengthened by repetition. These factors combined to determine the "strength" of the representation against which the feedback was compared at the retention test—weakened by time, but strengthened by repetitions. It is also possible that forgetting can occur by means other than trace decay. This idea is presented in the next example.

Brief Postmovement Memory

Now consider a very different and clever memory-related paradigm, developed by Rosenbaum and his colleagues (Rosenbaum, Weber, Hazelett,

& Hindorff, 1986; see also Rosenbaum, 2009). The subject's task is easy to simulate: The basic requirement is to speak aloud as many letters as possible in 10 s, alternating between a loud voice and a soft voice with each spoken letter. For example, in one condition the subject would shout the letter *A*, then softly speak the letter *b*, then shout *C*, softly speak *d*, then start over again by shouting *A*, and so on (*AbCdAbCd . . .*). Notice that a loud vocalization was always required for the letters *A* and *C*, and a soft vocalization was always required for *b* and *d*. And this is true for any *even*-numbered memory set. Now compare this to an *odd*-numbered memory set, such as *AbCaBcAbCaBc*. Notice now that the stress on a specific letter *switches* to the opposite stress on each repeated cycle. This feature is consistent for all *odd*-numbered memory sets.

The speed and error data from Rosenbaum and colleagues' (1986) experiment are presented in figure 14.8. As you would expect, more letters in the even-numbered memory sets (2, 4, 6, 8) were produced in 10 s than in the odd-numbered sets (3, 5, 7, 9) (figure 14.8*a*). Also, trials on which errors occurred were more frequent for the odd-numbered than the even-numbered sets (figure 14.8*b*).

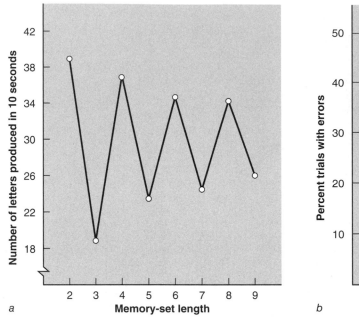
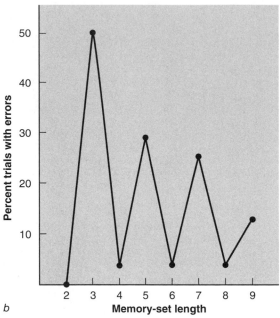

FIGURE 14.8   *(a)* Total number of letters spoken and *(b)* percentage of trials with errors as a function of memory set length.

Adapted from *Journal of Memory and Language*, Vol. 25, D.A. Rosenbaum, R.J. Weber, W.M. Hazelett, and V. Hindorff, "The parameter remapping effect in human performance: Evidence from tongue twisters and finger fumblers," pg. 713, Copyright 1986, with permission of Elsevier.

What do these findings suggest about motor memory? One view is that this task required subjects to vocalize letters (all having different learned GMPs) with different parameterizations—in this case the specific parameter of interest was whether the letter is spoken loudly or softly. Once the letter was produced, the parameter used for that instance was retained in memory. If the next vocalization of that same letter required the same parameter (i.e., as in an even-numbered memory set), the accurate representation that remained in memory *facilitated* performance. However, if the opposite parameter was required (i.e., as in an odd-numbered memory set), the memory of the previous parameter for that letter *interfered* with performance because the remembered parameter needed to be changed. Thus, a strong memory representation either facilitated or degraded performance, depending on the task demands.

But notice something else in the speed and error data in figure 14.8. As the length of the memory set increased, the size of the performance difference between the even- and odd-numbered sets was reduced. The memory-set effect, which previously had either facilitated or degraded performance, was *reduced* when more letters intervened between the repetitions of any one

letter. We expect that if the length of the memory sets had been extended even further (e.g., to 25 and 26 letters), the performance differences between the odd- and even-numbered letter strings might have been eliminated completely. This finding suggests a *weakening* of the influence of a previous performance on selecting a parameter for a subsequent performance, which is dependent on the memory-set size.

Two possible influences seem to be occurring in Rosenbaum and colleagues' (1986) study. As the length of the memory set increased, the *time* between any two vocalizations of the same letter increased, resulting in a decay of the representation for the previous parameter. The mere passage of time is not all that happened, though, because as the memory-set size increased, more intervening letters were spoken, which caused more *interference* with the memory for any specific previously spoken letter. Thus, another cause of forgetting may have had something to do with these events, rather than mere passage of time as trace-decay theory would have it.

Interference theory suggests that memory is actively degraded by other events. Such interference, according to the theory, can be of two basic kinds: *proactive interference* and *retroactive interference* (Underwood, 1957). The most common research method involves an experimental paradigm in which the interfering event occurs between the time of the storage of the to-be-remembered information and the time of the attempted recall—that is, during the retention interval. The term *retroactive* implies that the interference "works backward" on the memory; of course, it does not work backward at all, but it does nevertheless serve to disrupt the recall of something that occurred before the interference.[1] Interference can also occur in a less obvious way when something that happens before the criterion memory task causes interference with the recall of that criterion information. The term *proactive* implies that the information already "in memory" interferes with more recently acquired information.

Using the short-term motor memory paradigm described in chapter 3, experimenters have attempted to assess the mechanisms causing forgetting in relation to interference theory. With respect to *proactive interference*, neither Adams and Dijkstra (1966) nor Posner and Konick (1966) found evidence that later positions to be remembered in a sequence were less accurate than earlier ones, which would be expected if the proactive interference from the earlier movements were disrupting the memory of the later positions. Such findings had been shown in verbal behavior. One reason these proactive effects may not have occurred in the motor studies is that the intertrial intervals were very long (2 min in Adams & Dijkstra's study; figure 3.21 on p. 90), possibly providing an opportunity for forgetting of an earlier movement before a later movement could be presented.

Ascoli and Schmidt (1969) studied proactive effects by concentrating the prior movements into a short period of time. They presented either zero, two, or four positions just prior to the presentation of a criterion movement (the movement to be remembered). A retention interval of either 10 or 120 s followed the criterion movement, then recall of the criterion movement was attempted, and finally a recall of the preliminary movements (if any) was done. Figure 14.9 presents absolute errors in recall for the two retention intervals and for the various numbers of prior movements. Errors increased as the length of the retention interval increased. But of more interest was the finding that the four-prior-position condition showed more error than either the zero- or two-prior-position condition. A major effect was seen

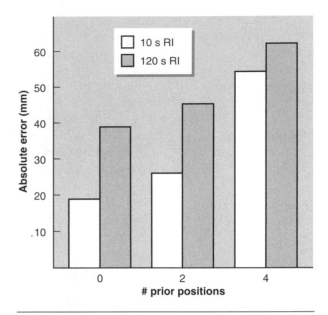

FIGURE 14.9   Mean absolute error in positioning as a function of the retention-interval length and the number of previous positions.

Adapted, by permission, from K.M. Ascoli and R.A. Schmidt, 1969, "Proactive interference in short-term motor retention," *Journal of Motor Behavior* 1: 29-35, adapted with permission of the publisher (Taylor & Francis Ltd, http://www.informaworld, com).

for constant error, with increased prior positions making the movements systematically too short. The data can be interpreted to mean that proactive interference is a factor in the retention of these positioning movements, supporting the interference theory (see also Stelmach, 1969).

With respect to *retroactive interference*, some earlier researchers failed to find effects of activities placed between the presentation and the recall of the test movements, casting serious doubt on the application of interference theory to memory for movements. But none of these studies reported constant errors, and the finding that proactive interference had its major effects on constant error raised the possibility that retroactive effects would be seen in the same way. In a reanalysis of earlier data, Pepper and Herman (1970) found that movements produced during the retention interval tended to have negative effects on movement accuracy when measured in terms of constant error. Subsequently, Patrick (1971) and Milone (1971) also provided evidence for retroactive interference.

Cue-Separation Techniques

What does the performer remember and recall in these positioning tasks? One possibility is that the person remembers the sensory qualities of the target position and attempts to match these sensations through a closed-loop process during the recall movement. That is, the person might be attempting to move to that position that is *recognized* as correct (see "Schema Theory," p. 441). Another possibility, however, is that the person remembers the distance moved, rather than the location of the target, and remembers a motor program that will move the limb a certain distance. These two possible cues (location vs. distance cues) were confounded in the earlier experiments on motor short-term memory. However, Keele and Ells (1972), Marteniuk (1973), and Laabs (1973) used a simple, but clever, method for unraveling these two potential cues (see figure 14.10 for an illustration).

For example, Laabs (1973) had subjects move to a stop for the presentation of the stimulus materials (as in the Adams & Dijkstra study). Then he formed two different conditions for recall. In both of these conditions, subjects began at a *different* starting position for the recall movement. In one condition, subjects were asked to recall the same *location* on the curvilinear track as before, so the distance of the recall movement was different from that of the presentation movement, rendering memory for distance unreliable. In the other condition, the subject was asked to move the same *distance* as in the presentation movement, so the location of the presentation movement was unreliable to the subject for recall.

Laabs' major findings were that accuracy was far greater in the condition in which the location cue was recalled than in the one in which the distance cue was recalled. Subsequent research has suggested that subjects have a difficult time remembering cues about movement distance and that positioning movements are probably based on some memory of location. However, retroactive-interference effects for location and distance information may occur in complex ways in some instances (Imanaka & Abernethy, 1991, 1992; Imanaka, Abernethy, & Quek, 1998; Walsh, Russell, Imanaka, & James, 1979).

The Preselection Effect

In the usual paradigm for motor short-term memory studies, the subject is asked to move to a stop that is defined by the experimenter; thus the subject does not have any advance knowledge about where the movement end point is located until she contacts the stop. Marteniuk (1973) and Stelmach, Kelso, and Wallace (1975) introduced a new method when they asked subjects to choose their own movement end points. In

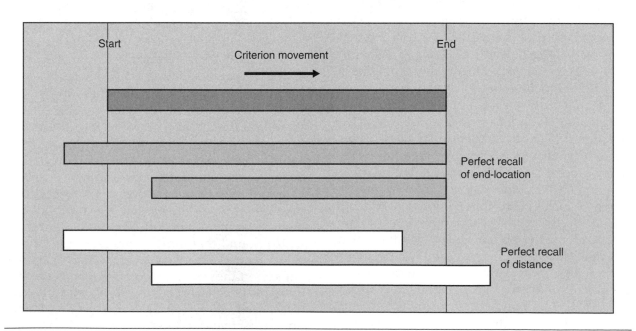

FIGURE 14.10 Illustration of the motor short-term memory paradigm used to separate the effects of end-location and distance cues.

Adapted, by permission, from K. Imanaka, B. Abernethy, and J.J. Quek, 1998, The locus of distance-location interference in movement reproduction: Do we know any more 25 years on? In *Motor behavior and human skill*, edited by J.P. Piek (Champaign, IL: Human Kinetics), 33.

effect, the instruction was to move to a position of the subject's choice (a stop was not provided); then the subject returned to the starting position and was asked to reproduce the position after a retention interval. This so-called *preselection* method led to much more accurate recall than the experimenter-defined method. Note that these findings have some similarity to recently studied effects in learning when subjects are allowed to regulate their own practice schedule (chapter 11) or augmented feedback presentations (chapter 12). The key commonality may be related to the active involvement of the learner in remembering and learning processes.

When the subject is faced with these reproduction situations, it is likely that the nature of the methods will influence the way in which the person stores the information. For example, if the person does not know where the target will be (in the standard paradigm), this could force the individual to process sensory cues about the target location, perhaps leading to a strategy wherein the recall of the movement is produced through closed-loop processes. In the preselection method, however, the performer can generate a movement plan in advance, perhaps programming it, and thus can ignore the sensory consequences of the movement—simply rerunning the program at the retention test. This may also suggest that memory for programs or parameterizations may be more stable than memory about the feedback for correct locations.

Spacing of Repetitions

Earlier we presented the findings of the Adams and Dijkstra (1966) study, in which many repetitions of the movement reduced the loss of information during the retention interval. These findings have been replicated often (reviewed in Lee & Weeks, 1987), suggesting that a memory representation is stronger or more resistant to forgetting with "practice." A curious finding, however, is that the repetition effect is enhanced if the repetitions themselves do not occur immediately but instead are spaced apart—especially so if some interference occurs between these repetitions (e.g., Lee & Weeks, 1987; Weeks, Reeve, Dornier, & Fober, 1991). One explanation for this *spacing effect* is that the forgetting that occurs between repetitions actually serves to *enhance* memory on the retention test (see p. 379, "When Forgetting Improves Remembering"). This find-

ing is similar to the contextual-interference effect discussed in chapter 11, suggesting that common underlying factors may be involved.

Warm-Up Decrement

To this point in the chapter, the focus has been on memory losses. But as mentioned earlier, not all decrements seen in a retention test are due to memory losses, as evidenced by such temporary factors as loss of motivation, day-to-day fluctuations in performance, effects of drugs, and illness. Many of these have been discussed with respect to the measurement of performance (chapter 2) and learning (chapter 10), and they are all involved in motor retention as well. But a special kind of decrement in motor performance has a small literature of its own, and it deserves special mention. This effect is called *warm-up decrement*.

The phenomenon can be easily introduced with an example. Adams (1952, 1961) studied a large group of subjects on the pursuit rotor task, providing thirty-six 30 s trials per day for five days; the results are shown in figure 14.11. The typical improvement with practice during a session of trials is seen, but also seen is a relatively large decrement in performance after each 24 h rest period. This decrement appears to be quite severe, and it is equivalent in size to the gains experienced in 5 to 10 trials. It is also rather short-lived, being eliminated in only a few practice trials. The phenomenon has been known for a long time and has been found in nearly every motor task that has been studied (see Adams, 1961, for a review). This decrement was thought to be related in some way to the need to "warm up" (probably not in the usual sense of warming up the muscles) for the task again after the rest, and the phenomenon came to be called *warm-up decrement*. It can be of potential importance when people are asked to perform after a rest period, as occurs with the worker operating a dangerous machine after a coffee break, the athlete going into the game from the bench, or a surgeon's first operation of the day (Kahol, Satava, Ferrara, & Smith, 2009).

Two major classes of explanation for warm-up decrement can be described. A *forgetting hypothesis* holds that the loss in skill is due to forgetting of the type mentioned in the previous sections. On the other hand, various versions of the *set hypothesis* argue that the loss in skill is due to a relatively temporary loss of bodily adjustments

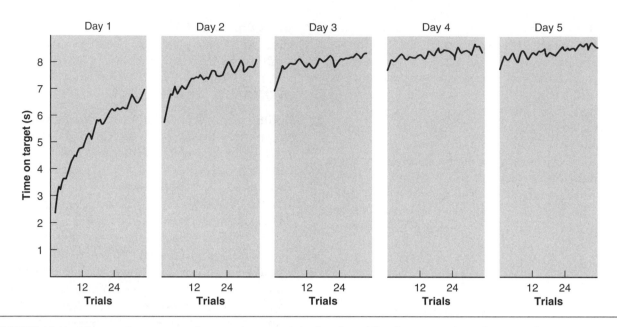

FIGURE 14.11 Mean performance on the pursuit rotor task for five days. (The decrements in performance from the end of one day until the beginning of the next are termed "warm-up decrement.")

Reprinted from J.A. Adams, 1961, "The second facet of forgetting: A review of warm-up decrement," *Psychological Bulletin* 58: 260.

or states. These views and the evidence for them are contrasted in the following sections.

Warm-Up Decrement as Forgetting

One major hypothesis, and probably the earliest and simplest explanation to be considered, is that warm-up decrement is simply another form of forgetting—that is, the loss of memory for the skill. In this view, the rest period allows certain forgetting processes to occur, with the initial phases of these processes being relatively rapid. These account for the rather large performance decrements seen with only a few minutes of rest. The improvements in performance with resumed practice are, in this view, due to relearning of the task whose memory was weakened over the rest period. This view does not seem to hold well for continuous skills, which as we have discussed, are retained well for long periods of time but also show substantial warm-up decrements. In general, there appears to be little support for a memory-loss explanation of warm-up decrement (Stratton, Liu, Hong, Mayer-Kress, & Newell, 2007).

Warm-Up Decrement as a Loss of Set

In another view, the loss of skill is related to the loss of *set*—one or more temporary internal states that underlie and support the skill in question. Set could consist of postural adjustments, orienta-

tion of attention to the feedback channel that is relevant for the task (e.g., vision vs. kinesthesis), adjustments in emotional state, and many more. According to this view, warm-up decrement is caused by the loss (or disruption) of these adjustments (set) over the rest period. The hypothesis says that *memory* of the skill is not lost over the rest period; or perhaps very small memory losses do occur, but they are far too small to account for the large decrements seen. With practice resumed on the task after the rest, performance is improved because the internal set (or adjustments) that supports the skill is reinstated.

Early Evidence on the Set Hypothesis The set hypothesis seemed reasonable for many years, as it is easy to imagine how such a process might disrupt skills with rest, especially in the face of the nearly perfect retention of skills like those in the pursuit rotor task. Yet no evidence existed for these set-loss phenomena until Irion's (1948) data with verbal skills suggested a way to study the problem. Irion's idea was that it should be possible to reinstate a lost set through certain activities that are related to the action in question but that cannot be thought of as contributing specifically to the memory for it. Irion used verbal learning as the main task, with two groups; both practiced the verbal task, then had a rest, then resumed practice again. One of the groups remained inactive during the rest period. The other group engaged in color naming during the end of the rest period—an activity presented on the same apparatus and having the same rhythms as the verbal-learning task but using none of the learned items from the main task. If the set hypothesis is correct, color naming should reinstate the lost set produced by the rest, and the initial performance on the verbal-learning task should be more accurate than for the group that simply rested. It was. Because color naming cannot be argued to increase memory strength for the verbal task, the implication is that color naming reinstated the lost set, in some way *preparing* the subjects for the upcoming verbal task.

Numerous studies were done to evaluate the set hypothesis with motor skills, but with few successes. In one such investigation, Ammons (1951) used the pursuit rotor; during the rest he had subjects watch another active subject or follow the target area with the finger, for example, in an attempt to eliminate warm-up decrement. No procedures were found that would eliminate it (see Adams, 1955). These data seemed to say that either (a) the set hypothesis was wrong for motor behavior or (b) the appropriate non-memory-set–reinstating activities had not been studied. In either case, the set hypothesis was not well supported. This evidence is reviewed more completely by Adams (1961, 1964) and by Nacson and Schmidt (1971).

Recent Evidence on the Set Hypothesis Nacson and Schmidt (1971) tested the set hypothesis and provided considerable support for it. Their idea was that during practice, various supportive mechanisms are adjusted constantly so that performance is maximized; then, during rest, these functions are adjusted to levels most compatible with resting, leading to an ineffective pattern of adjustment when the task is resumed. Practicing a task requiring the same adjustments (set) as the main task just before returning to it should reinstate those adjustments, leading to a reduction in warm-up decrement, just as Irion (1948) had found with color naming.

The task used by Nacson and Schmidt (1971) involved a right-hand force production; the subject had to learn to squeeze a handle with a 21 kg force, with KR given after each trial and 10 s rest between trials. After trial 20, a 10 min rest was given, and then practice resumed for another 10 trials. The independent variable was the nature of the activities presented in the 10 min rest period. One group (Rest) was allowed to rest for 10 min. Another group (Exp) had 5 min of rest, followed by 5 min of another force-estimation task; this task, though, involved the left arm rather than the right arm, elbow flexors rather than the gripping action, and a different level of force (9 kg). So it could not be argued that this task would contribute to the memory of the right-hand grip task. After 18 trials of this task with the same intertrial interval and KR, subjects were shifted immediately to the right-hand grip task for the retention test.

The absolute errors in the main (right-hand gripping) task are shown in figure 14.12 for the two groups before and after the rest period. The group that simply rested (Rest) for 10 min showed the typical warm-up decrement after the rest; but the group with the left-hand activities (Exp) showed very little warm-up decrement, suggesting that the activities in the rest period reinstated the lost set. Similar findings have been shown for a linear-positioning task (with a positioning task as the warm-up task) by Nacson and Schmidt (1971; Schmidt & Nacson, 1971), and by Schmidt and Wrisberg (1971) using a movement-speed task (with another movement-speed task as the warm-up task). These data also argue against the hypothesis that warm-up decrement is simply forgetting; a forgetting hypothesis cannot explain why a different warm-up task (which seems to have no memory elements in common with the main task) should produce improvements in main-task performance.

Other data (Schmidt & Nacson, 1971) showed that the reinstated set was rather transient in nature. If as few as 25 s of rest were inserted between the reinstatement of the set and the resumption of practice on the main task, the set was completely lost again. Also, activities can be designed that will *increase* warm-up decrement even more than resting does. For example, Schmidt and Nacson (1971) showed that a grip strength task (with maximum force) performed just before the resumption of practice on a linear-positioning task caused a very large increase in error on the first postrest trial, suggesting that the maximum-grip task required a set that was incompatible with the set for linear positioning. Other experiments indicate that *imagery* practice of the task just prior to the resumption of performance can reduce the warm-up decrement,

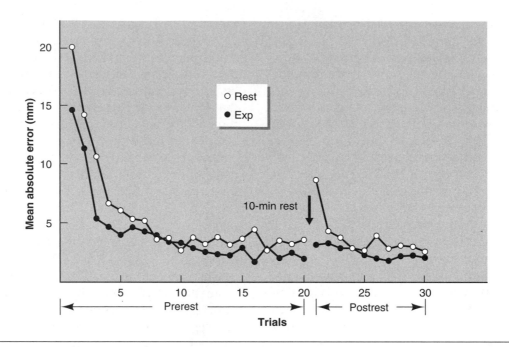

FIGURE 14.12 Absolute error in a force-estimation task for original learning and after a 10 min rest. Group Rest rested during the interval, and group Exp performed a left-hand force-estimation task; error is measured as a polygraph pen displacement.

Adapted, by permission, from J. Nacson and R.A. Schmidt, 1971, "The activity-set hypothesis for warm-up decrement," *Journal of Motor Behavior* 3: 1-15, adapted with permission of the publisher (Taylor & Francis Ltd, http://www.informaworld.com).

although the nature of the reduction seems to be task specific (Ainscoe & Hardy, 1987; Anshel & Wrisberg, 1988, 1993; Wrisberg & Anshel, 1993).

In sum, these findings suggest that warm-up decrement is caused by some loss of internal adjustments (or set) over the rest period. These adjustments are critical to effective performance in the task, but they are not a part of the memory for it. Just as a race car needs to attain the proper temperature before maximal performance can be achieved, so too, it appears, must the human be brought into the proper state of (temporary) adjustment for high-level skilled performance. It is not clear exactly what is being adjusted in these experiments, but probable candidates are the level of arousal, the rhythm and timing for the trial cycle, attention to the proper focus and sources of feedback, and so on.

These findings have considerable relevance for high-level performances, especially after performance is interrupted by rest or when major changes in tasks are required. For example, in golf, there are probably different sets for driving and putting, each of which must be reestablished before each shot. Watch professional golfers before they execute a swing; or watch professional basketball players before they take a free throw. Most players carry out a "preshot routine"—a sequence of actions and thoughts that are specific to each athlete, but done consistently by that athlete from shot to shot. It is tempting to suggest that the preshot routine is a method that reinstates the set and helps to overcome warm-up decrement (Boutcher & Crews, 1987), and some evidence exists to support the contention (Mack, 2001). However, much more research could be done to more fully investigate the idea.

Consolidation

An old concept in motor learning research, which dates back well over a century (see McGaugh, 2000, for a historical review), has received renewed interest in recent years. Much of the current work is being conducted at the cellular level of analysis with animals, and is beyond the scope of discussion here. However, a significant amount of research has also been conducted at the behavioral level, with intriguing results.

The basic idea is that practice produces a memory for motor skill that is unstable for a period of time but that stabilizes, or "consolidates," during a critical period afterward. A frequently used method to examine consolidation uses a variant of the retroactive-interference paradigm discussed earlier. In this paradigm, one group learns task A, then immediately practices a second task (B). Another group undergoes the same learning procedures, except that a time interval is inserted prior to learning task B, which presumably allows for the consolidation of task A. Retention of task A is measured later for both groups.

This paradigm was used, for example, by Walker, Brakefield, Hobson, and Stickgold (2003) to examine the retention characteristics of a finger-sequencing task. Subjects who learned a different sequence (task B) immediately after practicing an initial sequence (task A) performed much less skillfully 24 h later in the retention trials of task A than subjects who delayed practice of task B by 6 h after initial practice of task A. This suggested that the 6 h rest allowed some consolidation of task A, rendering it less vulnerable to interference from task B. Moreover, these consolidation effects appear to be larger if the consolidation interval includes a period of sleep (Stickgold & Walker, 2006).

These findings are not without some controversy, however, as failures to find consolidation effects appear to be related to task-specific differences and experimental design issues (e.g., Criscimagna-Hemminger & Shadmehr, 2008; Krakauer & Shadmehr, 2006). These consolidation effects are also difficult to reconcile with variability-of-practice effects discussed in chapter 11, in which retention and transfer following practice on a single task are *less effective* than with practice on multiple tasks (e.g., Shea & Kohl, 1991). Nevertheless, the renewed interest in these retention issues has escalated motor learning research in a number of experimental laboratories, representing a current "hot topic" in the literature.

Transfer of Learning

A number of decisions about the design of practice sessions are based heavily on an understanding of transfer of learning—the gain (or loss) in proficiency in one skill as a result of practice on some other skill. Often, the task actually practiced in a session is not the activity of primary interest, the real concern being for some other task believed to be related to this activity. One example is the use of drills, in basketball for example. The instructor usually does not really care whether the student can perform these drills, per se, well; rather, the instructor assumes that, by practicing them, the student will learn something that will transfer to some other task that is of primary interest (e.g., performance in a basketball game). For drills to be successful, one must be certain that what is learned in practice on the drill transfers to performance of the desired *criterion task*.

Another example is the common method whereby the task is broken down into its components for practice. The assumption is that practice on the parts will transfer to the whole task (see chapter 11). Still another example is the use of simulators of various kinds, such as a pitching machine to simulate a "real" pitcher in baseball, a dummy for training resuscitation skills, or a simulator to duplicate an aircraft cockpit. Does practice on these simulators result in improved performance on the criterion task—that is, do learning skills using the simulator *transfer*? The choices about whether or not to use these methods, and about how they should be structured, if used, depend heavily on an understanding of transfer of learning. We consider some of the principles of motor transfer next.

Basic Principles of Transfer

Many studies using different techniques and tasks have produced a vast array of different and sometimes contradictory findings on transfer (see Cormier & Hagman, 1987, for a review). Two major points emerge from the work on motor skills. First, the amount of transfer seems to be quite small and positive unless the tasks are practically identical. Second, the amount of transfer depends on the "similarity" between the two tasks (Schmidt & Young, 1987).

Motor Transfer Is Small

When the transfer from one task to a completely different task—sometimes called *intertask transfer*—is studied, we typically find that the transfer is small or negligible. Such evidence comes from studies concerned with attempts to train some behavior or trait in one situation by providing presumably related experiences in different situations. For example, investigations by Lindeburg (1949) and Blankenship (1952) showed that "quickening exercises" (various laboratory tasks that require rapid decision and action) provided no transfer to other tasks that required quickness. This is certainly not surprising in light of what is known about the specificity of motor abilities (see chapter 9), as the activities in the quickening exercises probably used different motor abilities than the task to which the exercises were supposed to have contributed (see "The Myth of General Vision Training" on p. 486). Evidence suggests that general traits such as quickness, balance, and coordination cannot be improved by the use of different activities supposedly involving that trait; and we would not expect that an *ability* would be improved by practice anyway.

What if the tasks are more similar? Here, the transfer among tasks tends to be higher than for the previous situation, but still the amount of transfer is typically small. For example, figure 14.13 presents results from Lordahl and Archer (1958). Different groups of subjects practiced the pursuit rotor task on one day at 40, 60, or 80 rpm for 30 trials. All groups then switched to the 60 rpm version of the task for evaluation of the transfer effects on the next day. The group that had 60 rpm in both the training trials and the transfer trials was used as the standard against which the transfer in the other two groups was assessed (i.e., it served the role of group II in figure 14.2). Using the calculation for the percentage transfer introduced earlier in this chapter, the transfer from the 40 and 80 rpm versions of the task to the 60 rpm version was 12% and 31%, respectively, on the very first trial.

And, as can be seen in figure 14.13, both groups required considerable practice on day 2 to achieve the same level of performance as attained by the 60–60 group at the end of day 1 practice. Namikas and Archer (1960), using the same procedures, found somewhat higher transfer, ranging from 42% to 64%. Remember that in these experiments the transfer is between the pursuit rotor and *itself*, with only the speed of rotation changed to define the different "tasks." It is somewhat surprising that the transfer is so small, but numerous other experiments show essentially the same thing.

These generally small transfer effects seem to fit with a number of other phenomena that we have discussed already. First, the transfer findings coincide with the ideas about individual differences. An important concept in chapter 9 was that motor abilities are both numerous and specific, and that even similar tasks appear to correlate very weakly with each other (with the possible exception of timing skills). If so, then in transfer experiments when the task is changed in even a small way (e.g., changing the turntable speed of the pursuit rotor), it is likely that different and unrelated abilities are called into play. Thus, there might be low transfer among even very similar tasks because the abilities involved are almost completely different.

These findings also fit well with the GMP notion. In chapter 6, a major idea was that two tasks with different relative timing characteristics were assumed to be governed by different GMPs.

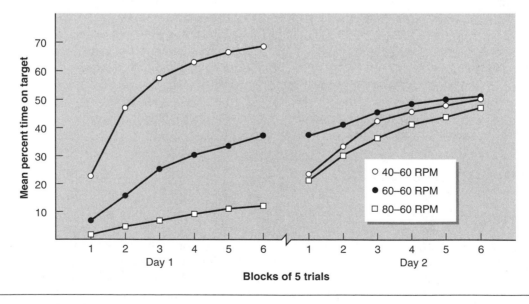

FIGURE 14.13 Mean time on target in pursuit tracking. Separate groups practiced on day 1 at speeds of 40, 60, or 80 rpm and transferred to 60 rpm on day 2.

Data from Lordahl and Archer 1958.

If a shift in conditions requires subjects to abandon one GMP in favor of another, then they will be performing two different GMPs in the two different variations of the "same" motor task. This is analogous to speeding up a treadmill so that jogging is substituted for walking, each activity having its own program (e.g., Shapiro, Zernicke, Gregor, & Diestel, 1981). It is difficult to say how wide the range of conditions produced by a given GMP might be, but we suspect that many GMPs exist and that they are shifted rather freely when the conditions change. Viewed in this way, it is not surprising that the tasks do not transfer to each other very strongly.

Transfer Depends on Similarity

A second and related concept is that transfer depends on the similarity of the two tasks being considered. The idea of similarity is certainly not new, as Thorndike (1906) and Woodworth (1901) proposed that transfer depends on the number of "identical elements" that exist in common between two tasks. If one task had elements that were totally different from the elements in another task, then no transfer would be expected. Transfer would be 100% if the two tasks had all their elements in common. The problem with this theory was that it never specified what an "element" was and how it could be operationalized, so the theory cannot be put to empirical test. In the previous paragraphs, the implication is that the "elements" could be (a) abilities in common between the two tasks, (b) GMPs that are used for the two tasks, or (c) both. And other possibilities exist.

The theories of transfer have been improved considerably since the publication of this next idea. A major contribution was Osgood's (1949) *transfer surface,* which provided a description of the amount of transfer of *verbal* learning as a joint function of the similarity of the stimulus elements and the response elements. Holding (1976) presented a related idea for motor skills. In all these cases, the notion of similarity is a dominant theme, as it always has been. But these recent theories are not completely satisfactory, as a large number of transfer phenomena do not appear to be explained by them. The problem seems to be related to our lack of understanding about what "similarity" is and what the "elements" are that are supposedly transferred across various tasks. Perhaps research with abilities and motor programs will contribute to this area, but to date this possibility has not been realized. The conclusion from a look at this literature is that motor transfer is still not well understood at all (Schmidt & Young, 1987).

Negative Transfer

We have mentioned that transfer is not always positive and that losses can occur in one skill as a result of experience on another. This is called *negative transfer.* Many people believe that negative transfer is relatively common and that the skill losses it produces can be quite large. Almost cliché is the story that tennis in the summer ruined the person's badminton game in the winter, presumably because the two tasks are quite similar yet somewhat incompatible (e.g., the wrist action in the two strokes is different). But the research on transfer nearly always shows low but positive transfer; negative transfer is seldom the outcome. However, negative transfer can be produced if the proper conditions are presented, such as those provided by Lewis, McAllister, and Adams (1951). Lewis and colleagues used the Mashburn task, in which a two-dimensional arm control and a foot control are operated simultaneously to match the positions of lights on a display. After subjects practiced for a varying number of trials (either 10, 30, or 50) with the usual configuration of the task, they were switched to a condition in which the control–display relationships were reversed. For example, in order to move the light on the display to the left, the lever had to be moved to the right rather than to the left as had been the case before. All three dimensions of the task (right-left, backward-forward, right foot–left foot) were reversed. This is analogous to driving a car in which the "normal" movements of the controls are suddenly backward (e.g., steering wheel turned clockwise to go left, brake pedal released to stop). After 10, 20, 30, or 50 trials on this reversed task, subjects were switched back to the original configuration of the task to examine whether skill on it had been lost or gained. This is a retroactive-transfer design (as shown in table 14.3).

The differences on the main task between the number of matches before and after reversed-task practice are plotted in figure 14.14 (see p. 485). A decrement score of zero means that the standard task was performed just as well after the reversed task as before, meaning that no negative (or positive) retroactive transfer occurred; larger decrement scores imply more negative transfer. Transfer was generally negative, and negative transfer increased as the number of reversed-task trials increased. This is what one might expect,

The Myth of General Vision Training

A quick search of the Internet will reveal a growing industry that markets various "training programs" designed to improve vision. Some of these programs make the further claim that improvements in vision will transfer to improvements in performance, most notably sport performance. These claims are rather impressive, if not surprising, given that the amount of motor transfer between two tasks is normally small and restricted to training tasks that are highly similar to the transfer task (e.g., Lordahl & Archer, 1958; Schmidt & Young, 1987). However, a close look at the "evidence" provided in support of these programs quickly reveals it to be weak, biased, and perhaps even fraudulent.

Sport vision training programs generally make the following claims: (1) Superior athletes have superior visual skills; (2) visual skills can be improved with training; and (3) visual skills that are trained in sport vision programs will result in superior sport performance (Abernethy & Wood, 2001; Starkes, Helsen, & Jack, 2001; Williams & Grant, 1999). The first claim, that superior athletes have superior *visual* skills, has little to no support. Instead, the evidence suggests that superior athletes often have a *perceptual advantage*—that is, experts process specific sport-related perceptual information faster and more precisely than less skilled athletes (Starkes et al., 2001; Williams & Ward, 2003). Experts are similar to less skilled athletes in speed and precision in processing perceptual information (and visual information in general) that is not specific to the nature of their expertise (Starkes & Ericsson, 2003).

The second claim, that general visual skills can be trained, is misleading. There does appear to be evidence that some improvement can be gained from general visual skills training, but this benefit is limited to individuals with visual defects. In their review of the literature, Abernethy and Wood (2001) conclude that there is no evidence that visual skills can be improved in *athletes* as appears to be the case for individuals with compromised vision.

The last claim, that general visual skills training programs can improve sport performance, appears highly suspect or fraudulent. The "strongest" support is provided by case testimonials, usually by athletes who have undergone the training program. However, testimonials are not experimental evidence, and any *perceived* benefit could be due to expected improvements (i.e., a Hawthorne effect). As we have suggested many times in this book, *transfer* is a highly selective and specific process. There is no evidence at all, for example, that intensive "training" to respond to a stimulus light in the midst of a complicated array will facilitate auto racing performance. Tracking a swinging ball with ocular and finger pursuit movements will not improve forearm shots in tennis. And, trying to identify an alphanumeric character presented in a tachistoscopic display will never help a batter to distinguish between a fastball and a curveball. The conclusion regarding this third claim—that general vision training can improve sport performance—appears to be an overwhelming "no!" based on theory and empirical evidence (Abernethy & Wood, 2001).

as the amount of interference from this reversed task should be larger if it is learned more completely. (There was also an effect of the number of original-practice trials of the task with standard controls, but it is far from clear what this means; see Schmidt, 1971a, for a more complete discussion of this effect.) This is an example of clear and unmistakable negative retroactive transfer; similar findings have been produced in other studies using similar procedures (see Lewis, 1953; Schmidt, 1971a; Schmidt & Young, 1987).

However, the negative transfer produced in these studies seemed mainly cognitive and may not have had much to do with *motor* negative transfer. The reversed conditions probably left the subjects confused about what to do (which way to move) and may not have disrupted the motor control processes in the task at all. This argument is not strong, though, as it is difficult to know what the relevant motor and cognitive processes are in such tasks. Yet it seems logical to assume that a major portion of the problem for the subjects on returning to the standard task was confusion about what the limbs controlling each of the three dimensions of the task were supposed to do.

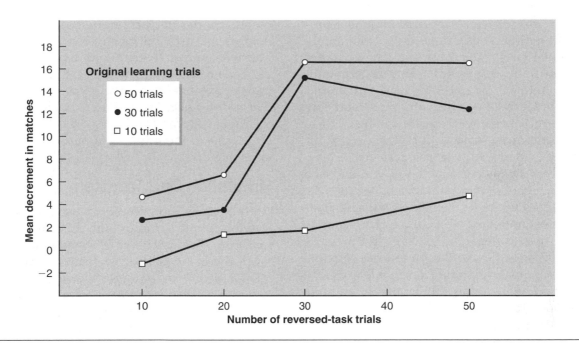

FIGURE 14.14 Retroactive negative transfer (interference) as a function of amount of practice on the reversed task and the amount of original practice on the standard task.

Reprinted from D. Lewis, D.E. McAllister, and J.A. Adams, 1951, "Facilitation of interference in performance on the modified mashburn apparatus: I. The effects of varying the amount of original learning," *Journal of Experimental Psychology* 41: 53.

Negative Transfer of Timing

Some studies suggest, however, that negative transfer of limb control can be quite large. For example, Shapiro (1977, 1978) had subjects learn complex patterns of movements with a particular relative timing. Later, subjects were instructed to speed up the movement, maintaining the same relative timing, which they had no trouble doing. But when they were told to *ignore* the temporal pattern they had learned earlier, subjects had a great deal of difficulty producing a new temporal structure. Instead, they sped up the original temporal structure, more or less as one would speed up a phonograph record. (These studies are discussed in more detail in chapter 6.) This can be seen as a kind of negative transfer, where the prior experience with the "old" temporal structure interfered with producing the "new" pattern at maximal speed. This might turn out to be an important finding for understanding transfer. Schmidt and Young (1987) suggest that tasks whose relative timing and sequencing are the same will tend to transfer to each other positively; two tasks whose sequencing is the same, but whose timing is different, will tend to transfer to each other negatively; most tasks with neither sequencing nor timing in common transfer to each other hardly at all.

Similar effects for learning new coordination-timing patterns were described in chapter 13. Strong negative-transfer effects are exerted by the existing, stable patterns (in-phase and anti-phase patterns) when one attempts to learn a new pattern, such as a 90° relative-phase coordination (Zanone & Kelso, 1992; Lee, Swinnen, & Verschueren, 1995). This suggests that some negative transfer can result from the experiences that subjects bring into the laboratory (i.e., before learning any specific task). Certainly much more can be discovered about negative transfer effects from this kind of research.

Another example involves second-language learners; here we consider the production of a particular language's speech sounds (but not its grammar or vocabulary) as a motor skill. Common experience tells us that the difficulty in producing a particular speech sound in English, for example, is critically related to the speaker's first language. The same acoustic goal is often produced differently by speakers whose native language is French versus German; these difficulties represent negative transfer from French (or German) to English. (One of us, R.A.S., was never able to perform the common "ui" sound in Dutch [e.g., "bruin"], despite much practice.) If negative transfer were *not* occurring, these pronunciation difficulties would not be common to a particular language group, and we would not expect to find, for example, French accents in English. Yet such accents are clearly differentiated from German accents, and are remarkably persistent across many years of speaking English. These phenomena seem to represent some of our strongest evidence for negative transfer.

Finally, it seems reasonable to think that two tasks, each containing a number of "elements," may have some similar elements leading to positive transfer and have other, dissimilar elements contributing to negative transfer. In Shapiro's (1977, 1978) studies, at the same time negative transfer of relative timing occurred, positive transfer of sequencing might also have been occurring. Other aspects of the task might not transfer at all—positively or negatively. This idea can be seen in many tasks in sports, for example handball and racquetball. There appear to be many common elements between these two games, such as the angles that the ball bounces off the walls of the court and the strategies of the game, all of which might lead to positive transfer (e.g., Smeeton, Ward, & Williams, 2004). Yet at the same time, other elements of the game would appear to lead to negative transfer, such as the exact positioning of the body just before

the shot, or the limb actions in the shot itself. The point is that whether or not two tasks transfer positively or negatively might depend on a kind of "balance sheet" on which the elements that transfer positively are "weighed" against those that transfer negatively. This is not an adequate theory of transfer, but it may help to conceptualize some of the things that happen when two tasks interact.

Simulation and Transfer

An important and commonly used method for training people in motor (and cognitive) tasks is *simulation*. The main feature of simulations is that they provide a practice task that is (supposedly) related to some *criterion task* (whose performance is the overall goal of the learning process) in some way. For example, pilots may practice procedural skills on ground-based devices that mimic the cockpit of the airplane, as seen in figure 14.15. The reasoning is that the practice of these skills in the simulator will transfer to the actual skills in the airplane (the criterion task). Many aspects of simulators were reviewed in Sweezy and Andrews (2001).

Physical Simulators

Many examples of simulators in learning situations could be mentioned. At one end of the scale are

FIGURE 14.15 The MD-11 flight simulator.

expensive and highly sophisticated devices that simulate large and complex systems (see figure 14.15). For example, the simulators for learning to fly are often elaborate, with very detailed and specific replications of the cockpit area, instrumentation, and so on. The pilot or learner is often given simulated displays showing airport runways; the instrumentation is complete and functioning; and the "feel" of the controls is as identical as possible to that in the real aircraft. In some simulators, even movements of the cockpit as a whole simulate the effect of control movements and the movements of the aircraft in a storm. In these situations, the information displayed on the gauges and dials is produced by a computer, and the learner's responses are monitored as well; these are then used to move the simulator, its displays, or both. Comparable devices are used to simulate the behavior of a weapons system, and simulators for controlling the behavior of nuclear power plants have been developed. As you might imagine, these devices are very expensive to produce, operate, and update.

Some of the early medical simulators were less expensive and could be used to train procedural skills, such as resuscitation. Low-fidelity mannequins such as Resusci-Annie were the precursor to higher-fidelity simulators that remain in use today for resuscitation and many other types of medical diagnosis and treatment training (Cooper & Taqueti, 2009; Perkins, 2007). The use of minimally invasive surgical procedures (e.g., laparoscopic surgery) seems to require simulators for training; these kinds of simulators are by now quite common and generally supported in the medical community (Sturm et al., 2008).

At the other end of the scale, simulation devices can be made that are relatively simple and inexpensive. Many of us learned to drive a car by practicing on driver simulators that had not-so-realistic configurations of an automobile's controls, so that we could learn the proper motions before we tried them in a real car. Some dental schools still use plaster-of-Paris models of the jaw—dentists-in-training practice dental skills with the "jaw" on a workbench or even in the position it would be in if it were the upper jaw of a patient. A simulator can require almost no apparatus; for example, you can practice golf putting on a living room rug with a glass lying on its side on the floor.

Physical simulators provide a number of advantages, such as decreased cost or time of training (or both), increased safety, and the increased convenience of having the simulator available for use at any time in any weather. And yet simulators have a number of serious drawbacks. First, the "worth" of any simulation device has to be measured in terms of the amount of transfer that it provides to the criterion task. If the simulator does not provide transfer to the criterion task, the device is essentially useless in terms of the purpose for which it was originally intended. Thus, the evaluation of simulation devices usually places heavy emphasis on transfer of learning from the device to the criterion task (Alessi, 1988; Lintern, Sheppard, Parker, Yates, & Nolan, 1989; Schendel, Heller, Finley, & Hawley, 1985; Sturm et al., 2008).

One point that consistently emerged from our earlier discussion is that motor transfer is generally quite small unless the training and criterion tasks are so similar as to be practically identical. From these basic research findings, as well as from the literature on the specificity of individual differences (chapter 9) and specificity of learning (chapter 11), it might be predicted that many simulators will not transfer well to the criterion tasks for which they were designed. Certainly a critical part of simulator evaluation is the conduct of a transfer experiment, perhaps with various versions of the simulator, to evaluate the amount of transfer that is actually produced. Transfer should increase from the simulator to the criterion task to the extent that the two are similar. Recognition of this fact has led the designers of simulation devices to make them very realistic—for example, the simulated airplane cockpit that moves as the actual aircraft would if it were in a storm. Much effort is devoted to making the controls feel as they do in the airplane, with proper resistances, feedback, and so on to maximize the similarity. This makes good sense. If differences between simulator and criterion task are too great, it is possible that separate motor control mechanisms might be learned in the two situations, producing no transfer to the criterion task.

Simulation devices are usually excellent for teaching *procedural skills*, the proper order of a sequence of activities, and the like. These aspects of the overall task are important, and considerable time can be "saved" by using simulators at early stages of practice, as sequence knowledge appears to be transferable between different effector systems (Fendrich, Healy, & Bourne, 1991;

Keele, Jennings, Jones, Caulton, & Cohen, 1995). There is less certainty that the motor elements of the task are so easily simulated, however.

Simulations are often applied rather blindly without regard for the kinds of transfer that will be produced. Many examples are seen in athletics, in which certain kinds of behaviors are simulated in various drill procedures. The use of blocking dummies in American football may be helpful in the early stages of learning a play when the athletes have questions about where to go and whom to block, but there would seem to be little utility in using them beyond this point. Players would seem to require practice in blocking other players who do not wish to be blocked; this is, of course, very difficult to simulate. It is difficult to evaluate the effectiveness of these various procedures because we have no research about the transfer of these drills to game situations. Our guess is that the faith placed in many of these procedures is probably overdone. Certainly it would make sense to examine any such drills or simulations very carefully.

Virtual Simulators

In contrast to the traditional type of physical simulators for use in training new skills are simulators that use computer-based technologies to train the perceptual–motor attributes of criterion tasks. *Virtual environments* often simulate the perceptual (visual, auditory, and haptic) demands of a task, together with a simulated effector system, and display these on a computer monitor. The actions of a subject can be mapped in terms of the actions of the simulated effector system, with the expected (computer generated) consequences displayed. One advantage of such devices is that they are much less costly to produce than many of the physical simulators already discussed. And, once developed, these computer programs should be modifiable so that newer versions need not be built again from scratch.

In recent years, one of the fields that has been developing virtual environments the fastest is the medical field. Arnold and Farrell (2002) critically reviewed the early evidence and concluded that virtual reality was, at the time, unverified as a positive training aid for surgical motor skills. The potential for positive motor skills transfer, however, has been elevated by the use of robotic devices that provide simulated haptic and proprioceptive feedback (see figure 2.16, p. 44). For example, robotic devices can provide the medical

student with visual, auditory, and haptic feedback as a cut is made through bone or other tissue, thereby providing numerous sources of augmented information during training. Although researchers still await conclusive evidence about how to optimize virtual reality training (Fialkow & Goff, 2009; van der Meijden & Schijven, 2009), we suspect that the attempt to make training as task specific as possible can only be a positive advance for motor transfer. That said, we know from the literature on augmented feedback (chapter 12) that complex and sophisticated feedback in simulators can be detrimental for learning if it is not used appropriately.

In contrast to expensive, high-fidelity training simulators, some researchers and practitioners are now using commercially available hardware and software to explore skill transfer. For example, the Nintendo Wii is a hugely popular gaming system that combines many different types of part- and whole-body movements together with interactive visual and haptic feedback experiences. Physical therapists, for example, have employed the Wii to motivate active participation in movement-related activities, and have reported positive effects for an individual with cerebral palsy (Deutsch, Borbely, Filler, Huhn, & Guarrera-Bowlby, 2008). And in a rather surprising finding of transfer generality, extensive video gaming experience appears to be causally related to enhancements in visual attention (Dye, Green, & Bavelier, 2009; Green & Bavelier, 2003, 2006). The capability for using inexpensive yet sophisticated gaming systems in these studies represents an exciting new development for future skills transfer research.

Summary

Learning, memory, retention, and transfer are very closely related concepts. Motor memory is the persistence of the acquired capability for responding, and losses in memory are called forgetting. Forgetting is usually measured by performance losses on a retention test, administered after a retention interval. Different measures of retention can be computed, although the absolute-retention measure is the most useful.

A variant of the learning experiment is the transfer experiment, in which the effect of practicing one task on the performance of some other (criterion) task is evaluated. Transfer is often measured as a percentage, indicating the proportion of performance improvement in one task that was achieved by practice on the other task. Studies of transfer are important for evaluating training, simulation, and other instructional issues.

Continuous skills are retained nearly perfectly over long retention intervals. Discrete skills, on the other hand, can show marked performance losses during the same retention intervals. The reasons for this difference in retention are not clear, but they are probably not based on the tendency for continuous tasks to be more "motor" than discrete tasks. Perhaps the difference has its basis in the idea that continuous tasks, with more practice time in a typical experiment, are more resistant to forgetting because they are learned more completely.

The loss of information related to motor performance can occur in various possible ways. Information might decay from memory due to a passive process, or might be lost due to retroactive or proactive interference. Warm-up decrement is a retention loss caused by the imposition of a short rest in a series of practice trials. Research supports the set hypothesis to explain it, which holds that warm-up decrement is a loss, during rest, of a pattern of temporary nonmemory adjustments critical to performance. Consolidation of motor memories, a field of study that has recently reemerged, suggests that the interfering effects of learning a competing task are time dependent.

Two basic principles of transfer are (a) that motor transfer is usually small but positive and (b) that motor transfer depends on the similarity between tasks. Considerable difficulty exists in understanding the underlying basis of similarity, however. Negative transfer can be produced under certain conditions, but it is probably mostly cognitive in nature. Devices such as simulators and virtual environments provide promise for positive transfer, although their value seems to be highly specific to the similarity between the training and transfer tasks.

Student Assignments

1. Prepare to answer the following questions during class discussion:

   a. Using practical examples of discrete and continuous skills, illustrate the differences in expected retention characteristics.

   b. Describe three workplace examples in which warm-up decrement might be expected to occur after a lunch break.

   c. Suggest a computer simulation game that could be used to train physicians who are learning a microsurgery technique. Describe three key features of the simulation that should be particularly effective for learning.

2. Find a research article that was designed to examine the short-term retention characteristics of movement information.

Web Resources

This Web site provides a history of virtual reality:

http://archive.ncsa.illinois.edu/Cyberia/VETopLevels/VR.History.html

More on virtual reality applications:

http://human-factors.arc.nasa.gov/web/hf101/reference.html

Notes

[1] Robert Bjork tells us that Stanford University's first president, David Starr Jordan, who was an ichthyologist (i.e., he studied fish), once said that every time he learned the name of a new student he forgot the name of a fish—a clear example of retroactive interference.

Logarithms to the Base 2

Number	.0	.1	.2	.3	.4	.5	.6	.7	.8	.9
0.		−3.32	−2.32	−1.74	−1.32	−1.00	−0.74	−0.51	−0.32	−0.15
1.	0.00	0.14	0.26	0.38	0.49	0.58	0.68	0.77	0.85	0.93
2.	1.00	1.07	1.14	1.20	1.26	1.32	1.38	1.43	1.49	1.54
3.	1.58	1.63	1.68	1.72	1.77	1.81	1.85	1.89	1.93	1.96
4.	2.00	2.04	2.07	2.10	2.14	2.17	2.20	2.23	2.26	2.29
5.	2.32	2.35	2.38	2.41	2.43	2.46	2.49	2.51	2.54	2.56
6.	2.58	2.61	2.63	2.66	2.68	2.70	2.72	2.74	2.77	2.79
7.	2.81	2.83	2.85	2.87	2.89	2.91	2.93	2.94	2.96	2.98
8.	3.00	3.02	3.04	3.05	3.07	3.09	3.10	3.12	3.14	3.15
9.	3.17	3.19	3.20	3.22	3.23	3.25	3.26	3.28	3.29	3.31
10.	3.32	3.34	3.35	3.36	3.38	3.39	3.41	3.42	3.43	3.45
11.	3.46	3.47	3.49	3.50	3.51	3.52	3.54	3.55	3.56	3.57
12.	3.58	3.60	3.61	3.62	3.63	3.64	3.66	3.67	3.68	3.69
13.	3.70	3.71	3.72	3.73	3.74	3.75	3.77	3.78	3.79	3.80
14.	3.81	3.82	3.83	3.84	3.85	3.86	3.87	3.88	3.89	3.90
15.	3.91	3.92	3.93	3.94	3.94	3.95	3.96	3.97	3.98	3.99
16.	4.00	4.01	4.02	4.03	4.04	4.04	4.05	4.06	4.07	4.08
17.	4.09	4.10	4.10	4.11	4.12	4.13	4.14	4.15	4.15	4.16
18.	4.17	4.18	4.19	4.19	4.20	4.21	4.22	4.22	4.23	4.24
19.	4.25	4.26	4.26	4.27	4.28	4.29	4.29	4.30	4.31	4.31
20.	4.32	4.33	4.34	4.34	4.35	4.36	4.36	4.37	4.38	4.39
21.	4.39	4.40	4.41	4.41	4.42	4.43	4.43	4.44	4.45	4.45
22.	4.46	4.47	4.47	4.48	4.49	4.49	4.50	4.50	4.51	4.52
23.	4.52	4.53	5.54	4.54	4.55	4.55	4.56	4.57	4.57	4.58
24.	4.58	4.59	4.60	4.60	4.61	4.61	4.62	4.63	4.63	4.64
25.	4.64	4.65	4.66	4.66	4.67	4.67	4.68	4.68	4.69	4.69
26.	4.70	4.71	4.71	4.72	4.72	4.73	4.73	4.74	4.74	4.75
27.	4.75	4.76	4.77	4.77	4.78	4.78	4.79	4.79	4.80	4.80
28.	4.81	4.81	4.82	4.82	4.83	4.83	4.84	4.84	4.85	4.85
29.	4.86	4.86	4.87	4.87	4.88	4.88	4.89	4.89	4.90	4.90
30.	4.91	4.91	4.92	4.92	4.93	4.93	4.94	4.94	4.94	4.95
31.	4.95	4.96	4.96	4.97	4.97	4.98	4.98	4.99	4.99	5.00
32.	5.00	5.00	5.01	5.01	5.02	5.02	5.03	5.03	5.04	5.04
33.	5.04	5.05	5.05	5.06	5.06	5.07	5.07	5.07	5.08	5.08
34.	5.09	5.09	5.10	5.10	5.10	5.11	5.11	5.12	5.12	5.13
35.	5.13	5.13	5.14	5.14	5.15	5.15	5.15	5.16	5.16	5.17
36.	5.17	5.17	5.18	5.18	5.19	5.19	5.19	5.20	5.20	5.21
37.	5.21	5.21	5.22	5.22	5.22	5.23	5.23	5.24	5.24	5.24
38.	5.25	5.25	5.26	5.26	5.26	5.27	5.27	5.27	5.28	5.28
39.	5.29	5.29	5.29	5.30	5.30	5.30	5.31	5.31	5.31	5.32
40.	5.32	5.33	5.33	5.33	5.34	5.34	5.34	5.35	5.35	5.35

Note. To find the Log_2 (23.5), for example, enter the row labeled 23, then move to the right under the column headed .5; the result is 4.55.

GLOSSARY

abilities—Stable characteristics or traits, genetically defined and unmodifiable by practice or experience, that underlie certain skilled performances.

absolute constant error (|CE|)—The absolute value of CE for each subject; a measure of amount of bias without respect to its direction.

absolute error (AE)—The average absolute deviation of a set of scores from a target value; a measure of overall error.

absolute frequency of knowledge of results—The absolute number of presentations of KR given in a sequence of trials.

absolute retention—A measure of retention based on the level of performance on the retention test.

accumulated feedback—Information presented after a series of movements that represents a summary of those performances.

action-centered interference—A view of attention that localizes interference effects at the response-selection stage.

Adams' theory—A closed-loop theory of motor learning proposed by Adams (1971), focusing heavily on the learning of slow positioning movements.

adjacent-trial effect—With intertrial correlation matrices, the tendency for the correlations between adjacent trials to increase with practice.

alpha motor neuron—Large efferent neuron responsible for innervation of the extrafusal fibers of the skeletal musculature.

anti-phase—A coordination pattern in which two movement components oscillate in 180° relative phase.

arousal—An internal state of alertness or excitement.

associative phase—The second of three phases of learning proposed by Fitts, in which learners establish motor patterns.

attention—A limited central resource that can be allocated to a few processes at a time.

augmented feedback—Feedback added to that typically received in the task (also called extrinsic feedback).

automatic processing—Information processing that is relatively fast, that is done in parallel with other processes, and that requires minimal effort and attention (compare with controlled processing).

autonomous phase—The third of three phases of learning proposed by Fitts, in which learners have greatly reduced the attention demands of the task.

average knowledge of results—A type of summary-KR method that presents the results of two or more trials as a statistical average.

average velocity—The speed of a movement, or the movement distance divided by the movement time.

bandwidth KR—Tolerance limits on errors that define when to provide qualitative or quantitative KR.

Bernstein perspective—A view of motor control and learning that originated with the work of Russian physiologist Nikolai Bernstein (1896-1966).

bit—The amount of information required to reduce the original amount of uncertainty by half; short for **bi**nary dig**it.**

blocked practice—A practice sequence in which all of the trials on one task are done together, uninterrupted by practice on any of the other tasks; low contextual interference.

capacity interference—Interference between tasks caused by limitations in attention.

ceiling effect—A limitation, imposed either by the scoring system or by physiological–psychological sources, that places a *maximum* on the score that a performer can achieve in a task.

central pattern generators—Mechanisms in the spinal cord, capable of providing oscillatory behavior, thought to be involved in the control of locomotion and other tasks.

change blindness—A failure to perceive changes in the environment as a consequence of directing attention to another object or event.

changing component abilities hypothesis—The hypothesis that the set of abilities underlying a skill shifts systematically as practice continues.

choice reaction time—RT for a task in which the response to be made is dependent on the stimulus presented.

chunking—The combining of individual elements in memory into larger units.

clock variance—The variance in timing due to central timekeeping processes; from the Wing-Kristofferson model.

closed-loop system—A control system employing feedback, a reference of correctness, a computation of error, and subsequent correction in order to maintain a desired state; sometimes called a servomechanism or servo.

closed skills—Skills that are performed in stable or predictable environmental settings.

cocktail party problem—The phenomenon, described by Cherry (1953), whereby humans can attend to a single conversation at a noisy gathering, neglecting other inputs.

cognitive phase—The first of three phases of learning proposed by Fitts, in which learners' performances are heavily based on cognitive or verbal processes.

cognitive psychology—A psychological tradition in which the behavior of the individual is described in terms of information processes.

component interaction—A characteristic of some tasks in which the adjustment on one part of the task requires an adjustment of some other part.

concurrent feedback—Feedback that is presented simultaneously with an action.

consciousness—The mechanism or process by which humans are aware of sensations, elements in memory, actions, or internal events.

constant error (CE)—With respect to sign, the average error of a set of scores from a target value; a measure of average bias.

contextual interference—The interference in performance and learning that arises from performing one task in the context of other tasks.

continuation—A task in which the subject's goal is to continue periodic finger taps after the removal of a pacing signal, usually following a series of synchronization taps.

continuous skills—Skills that appear to have no recognizable and inherent beginning or end.

controlled processing—Information processing that is relatively slow, that is done serially with other processes, and that requires effort and attention (compare with automatic processing).

coordination—Behavior of two or more degrees of freedom in relation to each other to produce skilled activity.

correct rejection—An outcome that results when the operator correctly decides that a signal was absent; from signal-detection theory.

correlation coefficient (r)—A statistical measure of the degree of linear association between two variables.

cost–benefit analysis—A method by which the benefits from anticipating correctly can be weighed against the "cost" of anticipating incorrectly.

criterion—A cutoff point set by an operator for deciding when a signal will be judged as present; related to beta in signal-detection theory.

criterion variable—In studies of prediction, the variable or score that is predicted from the predictor variables; the "best" obtainable measure of the construct that is to be predicted.

Crossman-Goodeve theory—A theory about Fitts' law that assumed a series of constant-duration movements, each interspersed with feedback-based corrections; an intermittent-control theory of rapid movement.

cuff technique—A method of temporary deafferentation in which blood flow to the limb is eliminated by a blood pressure cuff, rendering the afferent neurons anoxic so that they cannot deliver sensory information.

current or contemporary control—Woodworth's idea that the later portions of a movement were controlled by a feedback-based "homing in" process that allowed a target to be achieved.

deafferentation—Eliminating, usually by surgery (dorsal rhizotomy), the sensory input to the spinal cord while leaving efferent output intact.

degrees of freedom—The number of separate independent dimensions of movement in a system that must be controlled.

degrees of freedom problem—The difficulty in explaining the simultaneous control of multiple, independently moving body parts.

deliberate practice—Identified by Ericsson as practice that is not inherently enjoyable and is undertaken for the sole purpose of improving performance.

differential approach—That approach to the study of behavior that focuses on individual differences, abilities, and prediction.

difficulty—Depending on the particular paradigm, either the ratio of the amplitude to the target widths (Fitts, 1954) or the ratio of the movement amplitude to MT (Schmidt, Zelaznik, & Frank, 1978; Schmidt, Zelaznik, Hawkins, Frank, & Quinn, 1979).

directional preference—In bimanual coordination, the tendency to synchronize the timing of two limbs in the same direction in a plane of motion.

discrete skills—Skills that have an inherent and definite beginning and end.

discrimination reaction time—RT for a task in which a number of stimuli can be presented, but where a response is made only if a particular stimulus occurs.

distributed practice—A sequence of practice and rest periods in which the time in practice is often equal to or less than the time at rest.

dorsal rhizotomy—The cutting of the dorsal roots at various segmental levels of the spinal cord, resulting in deafferentation from the associated areas of the body.

dorsal root—The collection of nerve fibers from the periphery into a bundle near the posterior side of the spinal cord at each spinal level; the major peripheral sensory input to the cord.

dorsal visual stream—Processing involving the posterior parietal cortex; provides information for the visual control of movement; sometimes termed ambient vision.

d-prime (d')—A measure of sensitivity in decision making; from signal-detection theory.

dynamic-pattern theory—A view that describes coordination as a self-organizing process of pattern formation.

early responding—Processing all of the aspects of a movement in advance so that the movement can occur at or before the stimulus.

ecological viewpoint—A point of view emphasizing the study of movement in natural environments.

effective target width (W_e)—The size of the target area that the performer actually uses in a series of aiming movements, calculated as the standard deviation of the movement end points.

effector anticipation—Predicting the duration of internal processes and subsequent external movement so that some portion of the movement can be made coincident with some anticipated external event.

egocentric preference—In bimanual coordination, the tendency to synchronize the timing of two limbs toward and away from the center of the body.

elaborative processing hypothesis—A view of random–blocked practice effects that emphasizes the comparative and contrastive value of tasks in short-term memory.

electromyography (EMG)—Recording of the electrical activity from muscles.

empirical equation—An equation describing the outcome of an experiment in which a functional mathematical relationship is estimated from empirical observations.

ensemble—The combination of the various sources of sensory information that enable accurate perception of movement and position.

equilibrium point—For a given level of muscle activation, the hypothetical joint angle at which the torques from the two opposing muscle groups are equal and opposite.

equilibrium-point models (α and λ)—Limb-control models in which a movement end point is produced through the specification of an equilibrium point between the agonist and the antagonist muscle groups.

ergonomics—The study of human beings in work environments (also called human factors).

error in execution—An error in which the planned spatial–temporal goal of a movement is appropriate, but the movement deviates from the desired path because of factors occurring during execution.

error in selection—An error in which the chosen spatial–temporal goal is inappropriate given the nature of the environment.

expected sensory consequences—A construct in schema theory; the anticipated feedback sensations that should be received if the movement is correct.

extrafusal fibers—The muscle fibers of the major skeletal muscles, exclusive of the fibers in the muscle spindles.

factor analysis—A complex statistical procedure wherein a large number of separate tests are grouped into a smaller number of factors, each of which is thought to represent an underlying ability.

factor loading—In factor analysis, the statistical values indicating the extent to which the tests measure the various factors.

false alarm—An outcome that results when the operator incorrectly decides that a signal was present, when in truth the signal was absent; from signal-detection theory.

feedback—Sensory information that results from movement.

feedforward control—The sending of information ahead to ready a part of the system for incoming sensory feedback or for a future motor command.

Fitts' law—Mathematical description of the speed–accuracy trade-off in which the average MT is linearly related to $Log_2 (2A/W)$.

floor effect—A limitation, imposed either by the scoring system or by physiological–psychological limits, that places a *minimum* on the score that a performer can achieve in a task.

force variability—The within-subject variability in a series of forces produced either in static or in dynamic contractions.

foreperiod—The interval between a warning signal and the presentation of the stimulus to respond.

forgetting—The loss of memory, or the loss of the acquired capability for responding.

functional magnetic resonance imaging (fMRI)—A technique used to detect areas of the brain that have increased blood flow, indicating active information processing.

functional stretch reflex—A stretch reflex with a latency of from 50 to 80 ms, modified by instruction and mediated in higher brain centers; sometimes called the long-loop reflex.

gain—The relationship between the amount of input to a system and the output produced by it; usually expressed as a ratio.

gamma motor neurons—Small efferent neurons that innervate the intrafusal muscle fibers of the muscle spindle.

gearshift analogy—An idea about the learning of motor programs, analogous to learning to shift gears in an automobile.

generalized motor program—A motor program whose expression can be varied depending on the choice of certain parameters.

general motor ability—An early concept in which a single ability was thought to account for major portions of the individual differences in motor behavior.

goal setting—A motivational technique in which subjects are encouraged to set performance goals.

Golgi tendon organs—Small stretch receptors located at the musculotendinous junctions, providing precise information about muscle tension.

guidance—Techniques in which the behavior of the learner is limited or controlled by various means to prevent errors.

habit—The acquired capability for moving; an unobservable internal state that underlies skilled performance.

Haken-Kelso-Bunz (HKB) model—A self-organizational model of coordination as patterns of degrees of freedom that spontaneously organize, dissolve, and reorganize as a function of environmental interactions.

Hick's law—A mathematical statement that choice RT is linearly related to the Log_2 of the number of stimulus–response alternatives, or to the amount of information that must be processed in order to choose a response.

hierarchical control model—The idea that with practice, the control of the response shifts systematically from attention-demanding higher levels to less attention-demanding motor program levels.

hit—An outcome that results when the operator correctly decides that a signal was present; from signal-detection theory.

impulse—From physics, the aggregate of forces applied over time; the area under a force–time curve, or the integral of force over time.

impulse-timing model—A model of motor programming in which movement trajectory is controlled by impulses that determine the amplitude and timing of applied forces.

impulse-variability theory—A theory of rapid actions in which the variability in the muscular impulses leads directly to the variations or errors in movement control.

inattention blindness—A failure to perceive objects in the environment as a consequence of directing attention to other objects or events.

index of difficulty (ID)—In Fitts' law, the Log_2 $(2A/W)$, or the theoretical "difficulty" of a movement.

individual differences—Stable, enduring differences among individuals on some variable or task.

individual differences in learning—Stable, enduring differences among individuals in the amount of or rate of skill acquisition.

information—The content of a message that serves to reduce uncertainty.

information-processing viewpoint—The study of movement in which the human is viewed as a processor of information, focusing on storage, coding, retrieval, and transformation of information.

inherent feedback—That feedback normally received in the conduct of a particular task (also called intrinsic feedback).

inhibition of return (IOR)—A delay in responding to a previously cued (orienting) stimulus, when the SOA is 300 ms or longer.

initial adjustment—Woodworth's term for the initial open-loop portion of an aiming movement.

initial conditions—A construct in schema theory; the nature of the task and environment prior to the production of a movement.

in-phase—A coordination pattern in which two movement components oscillate in 0° relative phase.

intercept (*a*)—One of the constants for linear empirical equations; the value on the *Y*-axis when *X* is zero.

interference theory—A theory that forgetting is caused by interference from other learned materials.

interneurons—Neurons originating and terminating wholly within the spinal cord that connect various segments of it; some are thought to be involved in the spinal generators.

intertrial correlation matrix—A table or matrix of correlations among scores on all pairs of trials in a practice sequence.

intertrial interval—The interval of time between one movement and the next in the KR paradigm.

intrafusal fibers—The small muscle fibers lying at the polar ends of the muscle spindle.

invariant characteristic—The relationship between joint position and joint torque established by the central nervous system.

inverted-U principle—A description of the relationship between arousal and performance that resembles an inverted U when graphed.

ironic effect—A result in which the specific intention to avoid a motor behavior produces that very behavior.

joint receptors—Common term for a number of different receptors that are located in the joint capsules, presumably providing information about joint position.

kinematic feedback—Feedback about the movement characteristics or movement pattern produced.

kinetic feedback—Feedback about the force characteristics of a movement.

knowledge of performance (KP)—Augmented feedback based on some aspect of the movement's kinematics.

knowledge of results (KR)—Augmented feedback related to the nature of the result produced in relation to the environmental goal.

KR delay—The interval between the production of a movement and the presentation of KR.

law of practice—The finding that the log of the performance measure tends to change linearly with the log of the amount of practice.

lead-up tasks—Tasks or activities that are typically presented to prepare learners for a more important or more complex task or activity.

learning—A set of internal processes associated with practice or experience leading to relatively permanent changes in the capability for skill.

learning curve—A label sometimes applied to the performance curve, in the belief that the changes in performance mirror changes in learning.

learning score—A difference score, computed as the difference between the initial and final levels of performance on a task; sometimes used in estimating the amount of change in performance as a result of practice.

learning variable—An independent variable that affects learning.

length–tension diagram—A graph of the tension produced by a contracting muscle as a function of its length.

Log₂ *(N)* —The power to which the base, 2, must be raised to achieve *N*.

long-loop reflex—A stretch reflex with a latency of from 50 to 80 ms, modified by instructions and mediated in higher brain centers; sometimes called the functional stretch reflex.

long-term memory—A functionally limitless memory store for abstractly coded information, facts, concepts, and relationships; presumably storage for movement programs.

magnet effect—Identified by von Holst as the tendency of one effector's rhythmic oscillation to become interdependent with that of another oscillating limb.

maintenance tendency—Identified by von Holst as the tendency of one effector to maintain an independent rhythmic oscillation while another effector is oscillating.

massed practice—A sequence of practice and rest periods in which the rest time is much less than the practice time.

memory—The persistence of habit; the acquired capability for skill.

memory trace—A construct in Adams' closed-loop theory; a modest motor program for determining and initiating the movement.

mental practice—A practice method in which performance on the task is imagined or visualized without overt physical practice.

mesencephalic preparation—A surgical preparation in which the spinal cord is cut at the midbrain, essentially separating higher centers from the spinal cord; the Shik preparation.

miss—An outcome that results when the operator incorrectly decides that a signal was absent, when in truth the signal was present; from signal-detection theory.

modeling—A technique for demonstrating the task to be practiced.

modular—A view of individual differences that organizes brain activities in terms of functions (such as timekeeping) rather than tasks.

moment of inertia—A physical quantity defining an object's resistance to rotational forces; the mass of the object multiplied by the square of the distance of the center of the object's mass from the point of rotation.

monosynaptic stretch reflex—A segmental reflex produced by stretch of a muscle and its spindles connecting monosynaptically with the alpha motor neurons of the same muscle; it has a latency of about 30 to 50 ms in humans.

motivation—An internal state that tends to direct or energize the system toward a goal.

motor behavior—An area of study stressing primarily the principles of human skilled movement generated at a behavioral level of analysis.

motor control—An area of study dealing with the understanding of the neural, physical, and behavioral aspects of biological (e.g., human) movement.

motor development—A field of study concerning the changes in motor behavior occurring as a result of growth, maturation, and experience.

motor learning—A set of internal processes associated with practice or experience leading to relatively permanent changes in the capability for motor skill.

motor memory—The memory for movement or motor information.

motor neuron pools—Collections of alpha motor neuron cell bodies in the gray matter of the cord that serve motor units in the same, or anatomically related, muscles.

motor program—An abstract representation that, when initiated, results in the production of a coordinated movement sequence.

motor reaction time—The interval between the first change in EMG and the movement's initiation.

motor variance—The variance in timing due to motor-implementation processes; from the Wing-Kristofferson model.

movement—Changes in joint angles, the position of the entire body, or both.

movement outcome—A construct in schema theory; the result of the movement in the environment, usually signaled by intrinsic feedback or KR.

movement time (MT)—The interval between the initiation of a movement and its termination.

multiple correlation—A statistical procedure in which the weightings of predictor variables are adjusted so that their (weighted) sum correlates maximally with some criterion variable.

muscle spindle—Small spindle-shaped structures, located in parallel with the extrafusal fibers, that provide information about muscle length.

negative transfer—The loss in capability for one task as a result of practice or experience in some other task.

objectivity—The aspect of measurement related to the extent to which two observers assign the same score.

occlusion method—Technique used to assess perceptual skill by deleting selective spatial or temporal information in a display.

open-loop system—A control system with preprogrammed instructions to a set of effectors; it does not use feedback information and error-detection processes.

operant techniques—Methods for learning in which certain behaviors are reinforced or rewarded, leading to an increase in the probability that they will occur again.

optimized-submovement model—A view of the speed–accuracy trade-off that optimizes the duration of an initial impulse and, if necessary, one or more corrective impulses.

parallel processing—A type of information processing in which at least two processes occur simultaneously.

parameter—A value specified to the generalized motor program that defines the particular expression of the pattern of activity.

part practice—The learning technique in which the task is broken down into its parts for separate practice.

perceptual anticipation—Anticipation of the arrival of a signal through internal mechanisms or processes.

perceptual narrowing—The focusing of attention so that specific sources of information are more likely to be received but rare, or peripheral, events are more likely to be missed.

perceptual trace—A construct in Adams' closed-loop theory; a reference of correctness in memory that has been learned from feedback at the correct target position.

performance curve—A plot of the average performance of a group of subjects for each of a number of practice trials or blocks of trials.

performance variable—An independent variable that affects performance temporarily.

perturbation—An unexpected physical event that changes the movement or the movement goal.

phase transition—An abrupt shift from one coordination pattern to another.

phasing—The temporal structure of a sequence, usually measured by the ratios of element durations and the overall movement duration; relative timing.

point-light display—Technique used to assess perceptual identification based on limited information.

point-to-point computation—Models of limb control in which the coordinates of each point in a limb's trajectory are achieved sequentially by the motor system at the time of response execution.

polyrhythm—The rhythm produced when two effectors simultaneously produce their own, nonharmonic rhythms (e.g., three beats with one finger combined with two beats of another finger).

positive transfer—The gain in capability on one task as a result of practice or experience on some other task.

post-KR delay—The interval of time between the presentation of KR and the next movement.

precision of KR—The level of accuracy with which KR describes the movement outcome produced.

prediction—The process in which the score on a criterion variable is estimated from one or more predictor variables based on the association between them.

predictor variable—The variable(s) from which a criterion variable is predicted.

premotor reaction time—The interval from the stimulus presentation to the initial change in EMG.

preparation—Reorganization of attention and information processing so that a signal can be received and responded to quickly.

preprogramming—The process of preparing a motor program for initiation.

preselection effect—In short-term motor memory work, the phenomenon whereby the memory for subject-selected movements is stronger than for experimenter-selected movements.

proactive interference—In the interference theory, a source of forgetting caused by learning imposed before the original learning of some to-be-remembered task.

probe technique—A secondary-task method that uses RT to assess the attention demands of some primary task.

progression–regression hypothesis—The idea that learning produces a progression to more complex control strategies and that stress or forgetting produces a regression to more simple levels.

psychological refractoriness—The delay in the response to the second of two closely spaced stimuli.

random practice—A practice sequence in which the tasks being practiced are ordered (quasi-) randomly across trials; high contextual interference.

reach/grasp action—An action that coordinates the limb transport component with the opening and closing of the grasp component.

reaction time (RT)—The interval between the presentation of an unexpected stimulus and the initiation of a response.

recall schema—A construct in schema theory; the relationship among past parameters, past initial conditions, and the movement outcomes produced by these combinations.

receptor anticipation—Anticipation of the arrival of a stimulus based on sensory information indicating its time of arrival.

recognition schema—A construct in schema theory; the relationship among past initial conditions, past movement outcomes, and the sensory consequences produced by these combinations.

reconstruction hypothesis—A view of random–blocked practice effects that emphasizes the role of previously forgotten action plans or "solutions" to the motor problem.

reflex-reversal phenomenon—The phenomenon by which a given stimulus can produce two different reflexive responses depending on the function of the limb in a movement.

regression line—The line of best fit in plots of two variables, whose slope and intercept are usually determined by regression analysis.

relative force—An invariant feature of the motor program that defines the relationships among the forces produced in the various actions in a movement.

relative frequency of KR—The percentage of trials for which KR is provided; the absolute frequency divided by the number of trials.

relative phase—A measure of temporal coordination that expresses the position of one limb within its cycle relative to the other limb within its cycle.

relative retention—Measures of retention in which the performance on the retention test is evaluated in relation to the level of performance reached in original learning.

reliability—The aspect of measurement related to the repeatability of a score.

remoteness effect—In intertrial correlation matrices, the tendency for trials that are progressively more separated in the practice sequence to correlate systematically lower with each other.

response-chaining hypothesis—A movement control theory which holds that each element in a sequence is triggered by movement feedback from a previous element.

response-programming stage—A stage of information processing in which the previously chosen response is transformed into overt muscular action.

response-selection stage—A stage of information processing in which the response associated with the presented stimulus is selected.

response time—The interval from the presentation of a stimulus to the completion of a movement; the sum of reaction time and movement time.

retention interval—The interval between the end of original learning and the retention test.

retention test—A performance test administered after a retention interval for the purpose of assessing learning.

retroactive interference—In interference theory, a source of forgetting caused by practice imposed between the original learning and the retention test for a to-be-remembered task.

root mean square error (RMSE)—The square root of the average squared deviations of a set of values from a target value; typically used as a measure of tracking proficiency.

savings score—A statistic used in transfer experiments, representing the "savings" in practice time on one task resulting from experience on some other task.

scattergram—A graph on which subjects' scores on two tests are jointly represented as data points.

schema—The basis for schema theory; a rule, concept, or relationship formed on the basis of experience.

secondary-task method—A collection of experimental methods whereby learning on a main task can be estimated by the use of simultaneous secondary measures of performance.

selective attention—A mechanism for directing attention or capacity to a given stimulus input.

self-organization—From dynamic-pattern theory; a view that describes motor control as emerging from the interaction of the components of the movement system.

self-regulation—Technique used in motor learning studies in which the learners determine how to schedule practice or feedback.

sensitivity—That aspect of measurement dealing with the likelihood of detecting changes in a dependent measure in relation to varying experimental conditions.

sequencing—An invariant feature of motor programs in which the order of elements is fixed.

serial processing—A style of information processing in which processing activities are arranged sequentially in time.

serial tasks—Movements combining a series of discrete elements, with the order of elements being important.

set—A nonmemory pattern of adjustments that supports performance.

set hypothesis—A hypothesis holding that warm-up decrement is caused by loss of set.

short-term memory—A memory store with a capacity of about seven elements, capable of holding moderately abstract information for up to 30 s; analogous to consciousness; a "work space" for processing.

short-term sensory store—A functionally limitless memory store for holding literal information for only about 1 s.

signal detection theory (SDT)—A method of analyzing two-choice decisions, resulting in two types of correct decision (hits and correct rejections) and two types of errors (misses and false alarms).

similarity—A construct in most theories of transfer, indicating the extent to which certain aspects of two tasks are the same.

Simon effect—A type of stimulus–response compatibility effect in which irrelevant directional or location information interferes with the action.

simple reaction time—Reaction time from a task in which a single action is produced in response to a single presented stimulus.

simplification hypothesis—The idea that the factor structure of a skill becomes progressively simpler with practice.

simulator—A training device in which certain features of a task are duplicated, allowing for practice that resembles the transfer task.

single-channel hypothesis—A theory of attention suggesting that the system can process only a single stimulus leading to a response at any given time.

skills—Movements that are dependent on practice and experience for their execution, as opposed to being genetically defined.

slope (b)—One of the constants of a linear equation; the inclination of the line.

spacing effect—In memory experiments, the finding that repetitions of the criterion task that are increasingly separated in time are remembered more effectively.

spatial anticipation—The anticipation of which of several possible stimuli will occur; also called event anticipation.

spatial–temporal goal—A subgoal for the performer in which a pattern of limb movement defined in terms of both space and time is selected; the major product of running a motor program.

specificity of individual differences—Henry's theory of the structure of motor abilities, according to which motor tasks are thought to be composed of many independent abilities.

specificity of learning—The concept that the similarity of the environmental conditions in practice to those in transfer, has a strong positive influence on transfer performance.

speed–accuracy trade-off—The general principle describing a person's tendency to decrease the accuracy of a movement when its speed is increased.

startle reaction—A rapid (<100 ms) reaction to an unexpected, often very loud, stimulus; used to study the involuntary release of motor programs.

state anxiety—A temporary state of worry or concern about a particular situation or activity.

static contraction—Contraction in which the muscle is not changing length as it is producing force; sometimes called *isometric* contraction.

stiffness—A characteristic of muscles and springs defined as the change in tension divided by the change in length; the slope of the length–tension relationship.

stimulus-identification stage—A stage of information processing in which the stimulus is identified and features or patterns are abstracted; often divided into separate encoding and identification stages.

stimulus onset asynchrony (SOA)—The interval of time between the onsets of two stimuli, as in the double-stimulation paradigm.

stimulus–response compatibility—The degree to which the stimuli and associated responses in a set are "naturally" related to each other.

stimulus–response viewpoint—A tradition in psychology and motor behavior stressing the responses produced as a function of stimuli presented, without regard to the intervening mental events or processes.

storage problem—A problem with early notions of motor programming in which the number of necessary programs was so large that their storage in the central nervous system seemed impossible.

stress—A motivational state that tends to direct the individual away from some particular situation.

Stroop effect—A delay in responding due to competition from automatically processed information.

structural interference—Interference among tasks caused by the simultaneous use of the same receptors, effectors, or processing systems.

subjective reinforcement—A construct in Adams' closed-loop theory; the subject's self-generated error signal, based on comparing feedback against a reference of correctness.

summary KR—Augmented information about each of a set of performance trials presented after the set is completed.

synchronization—A task in which the subject's goal is to make periodic finger taps that coincide with those of a pacing signal.

task analysis—A process of determining the underlying abilities and structure of a task or occupation.

tau (τ)—Time-to-contact information based on the rate of expansion of the approaching object on the retina of the eye.

taxonomy—A system of classification.

temporal anticipation—The anticipation of when a given stimulus will arrive or when a movement is to be made.

temporal variability—The inconsistency of some event with respect to time.

terminal feedback—Feedback given after the movement's completion.

time to contact (T_c)—Information about the time remaining until a moving object arrives at the eye.

total variability (E)—The standard deviation of a set of scores about a target value; a measure of overall accuracy.

trace-decay theory—A theory holding that forgetting is caused by the spontaneous "decay" or weakening of memory over time.

trait anxiety—A general tendency to be anxious or stressed that is characteristic of a particular individual.

transcranial magnetic stimulation (TMS)—A technique used to excite or inhibit processing in a specific area of the brain.

transfer-appropriate processing—The concept that practice is most effective when arranged so that the processing capability learned is appropriate for that in some goal criterion task or conditions.

transfer design—An experimental design for measuring learning effects, in which all treatment groups are transferred to a common level of the independent variable.

trials-delay technique—A procedure in which the presentation of KR for a movement is delayed; during this interval the learner practices one or more other movements.

triggered reaction—A coordinated response to an environmental stimulus whose latency is shorter than RT yet longer than that of the long-loop reflex.

unit of action—A "piece" of behavior that can be utilized repeatedly in various actions, producing essentially the same movements (but scaled to the environment) each time.

validity—That aspect of measurement related to the extent to which a test measures what the experimenter wanted it to measure.

variability in practice—A prediction of schema theory; transfer is predicted to be facilitated when goals are systematically varied from trial to trial during practice.

variable error (VE)—The standard deviation of a set of scores about the subject's own average score; a measure of movement consistency.

variable error in timing (VE_t)—The within-subject standard deviation of the duration of some process or event.

ventral visual stream—Processing involving the inferotemporal cortex; responsible for providing cognitive information about objects in the environment; sometimes called focal vision.

verbal pretraining—The presentation of stimulus or display elements of the task in isolation so that they can be more easily responded to later in whole-task performance.

vestibular apparatus—The receptors in the inner ear that are sensitive to the orientation of the head with respect to gravity, to rotation of the head, and to balance.

visual illusion—A perceptual effect that causes an inaccurate visual representation of a display.

visual proprioception—Gibson's concept that vision can serve as a strong basis for perception of movements and positions of the body in space.

warm-up decrement—The decrement in performance occurring when practice is resumed after a brief rest period.

whole practice—The learning technique in which the task is practiced in its entirety (i.e., not broken into parts).

wineglass effect—A slip of a held object through the fingertips that triggers an increased grip force within approximately 30 ms.

Wing-Kristofferson model—An open-loop, hierarchical model of timing performance involving a central timekeeper level and a motor implementation level.

REFERENCES

Abbs, J.H., & Gracco, V.L. (1983). Sensorimotor actions in the control of multi-movement speech gestures. Trends in Neuroscience, 6, 391-395.

Abbs, J.H., Gracco, V.L., & Cole, K.J. (1984). Control of multi-movement coordination: Sensorimotor mechanisms in speech motor programming. Journal of Motor Behavior, 16, 195-232.

Abbs, J.H., & Winstein, C.J. (1990). Functional contributions of rapid and automatic sensory-based adjustments to motor output. In M. Jeannerod (Ed.), Attention and performance XIII (pp. 627-652). Hillsdale, NJ: Erlbaum.

Abernethy, B. (1988). Dual-task methodology and motor skills research: Some applications and methodological constraints. Journal of Human Movement Studies, 14, 101-132.

Abernethy, B. (2001). Attention. In R.N. Singer, H.A. Hausenblas, & C.M. Janelle (Eds.), Handbook of sport psychology (2nd ed.) (pp. 53-85). New York: Wiley.

Abernethy, B., & Burgess-Limerick, R. (1992). Visual information for the timing of skilled movements: A review. In J.J. Summers (Ed.), Approaches to the study of motor control and learning (pp. 343-384). Amsterdam: Elsevier.

Abernethy, B., Burgess-Limerick, R., & Parks, S. (1994). Contrasting approaches to the study of motor expertise. Quest, 46, 186-198.

Abernethy, B., Hanna, A., & Plooy, A. (2002). The attentional demands of preferred and non-preferred gait patterns. Gait & Posture, 15, 256-265.

Abernethy, B., Neal, R.J., & Koning, P. (1994). Visual-perceptual and cognitive differences between expert, intermediate, and novice snooker players. Applied Cognitive Psychology, 8, 185-211.

Abernethy, B., & Russell, D.G. (1987). Expert-novice differences in an applied selective attention task. Journal of Sport Psychology, 9, 326-345.

Abernethy, B., & Wood, J.M. (2001). Do generalized visual training programmes for sport really work? An experimental investigation. Journal of Sports Sciences, 19, 203-222.

Abernethy, B., Wood, J.M., & Parks, S. (1999). Can the anticipatory skills of experts be learned by novices? Research Quarterly for Exercise and Sport, 70, 313-318.

Abrams, R.A., Meyer, D.E., & Kornblum, S. (1989). Speed and accuracy of saccadic eye movements: Characteristics of impulse variability in the oculomotor system. Journal of Experimental Psychology: Human Perception and Performance, 15, 529-543.

Abrams, R.A., Meyer, D.E., & Kornblum, S. (1990). Eye-hand coordination: Oculomotor control in rapid aimed limb movements. Journal of Experimental Psychology: Human Perception and Performance, 16, 248-267.

Ackerman, P.L. (1988). Determinants of individual differences during skill acquisition: Cognitive abilities and information processing. Journal of Experimental Psychology: General, 117, 288-318.

Ackerman, P.L. (1989). Individual differences and skill acquisition. In P.L. Ackerman, R.J. Sternberg, & R. Glaser (Eds.), Learning and individual differences: Advances in theory and research (pp. 165-217). New York: Freeman.

Ackerman, P.L. (1990). A correlational analysis of skill specificity: Learning, abilities, and individual differences. Journal of Experimental Psychology: Learning, Memory, and Cognition, 16, 883-901.

Ackerman, P.L. (1992). Predicting individual differences in complex skill acquisition: Dynamics of ability determinants. Journal of Applied Psychology, 77, 598-614.

Ackerman, P.L., & Cianciolo, A.T. (2000). Cognitive, perceptual-speed, and psychomotor determinants of individual differences during skill acquisition. Journal of Experimental Psychology: Applied, 6, 259-290.

Adam, J.J., Mol, R., Pratt, J., & Fischer, M.H. (2006). Moving farther but faster: An exception to Fitts's law. Psychological Science, 17, 794-798.

Adamovich, S.V., & Feldman, A.G. (1984). Model of the central regulation of the parameters of motor trajectories. Biophysics, 29, 338-342.

Adams, J.A. (1952). Warm-up decrement in performance on the pursuit-rotor. American Journal of Psychology, 65, 404-414.

Adams, J.A. (1953). The prediction of performance at advanced stages of training on a complex psychomotor task (Research Bulletin 53-49). Lackland Air Force Base, TX: Human Resources Research Center.

Adams, J.A. (1955). A source of decrement in psychomotor performance. Journal of Experimental Psychology, 49, 390-394.

Adams, J.A. (1956). An evaluation of test items measuring motor abilities (Research Rep. AFPTRC-TN-56-55). Lackland Air Force Base, TX: Human Resources Research Center.

Adams, J.A. (1957). The relationship between certain measures of ability and the acquisition of a psychomotor criterion response. Journal of General Psychology, 56, 121-134.

Adams, J.A. (1961). The second facet of forgetting: A review of warm-up decrement. Psychological Bulletin, 58, 257-273.

Adams, J.A. (1964). Motor skills. Annual Review of Psychology, 15, 181-202.

Adams, J.A. (1967). Human memory. New York: McGraw-Hill.

Adams, J.A. (1968). Response feedback and learning. Psychological Bulletin, 70, 486-504.

Adams, J.A. (1971). A closed-loop theory of motor learning. Journal of Motor Behavior, 3, 111-150.

Adams, J.A. (1976a). Issues for a closed-loop theory of motor learning. In G.E. Stelmach (Ed.), Motor control: Issues and trends (pp. 87-107). New York: Academic Press.

Adams, J.A. (1976b). Learning and memory: An introduction. Homewood, IL: Dorsey.

Adams, J.A. (1977). Feedback theory of how joint receptors regulate the timing and positioning of a limb. Psychological Review, 84, 504-523.

Adams, J.A. (1978). Theoretical issues for knowledge of results. In G.E. Stelmach (Ed.), Information processing in motor control and learning (pp. 229-240). New York: Academic Press.

Adams, J.A. (1986). Use of the model's knowledge of results to increase the observer's performance. Journal of Human Movement Studies, 12, 89-98.

Adams, J.A. (1987). Historical review and appraisal of research on the learning, retention, and transfer of human motor skills. Psychological Bulletin, 101, 41-74.

Adams, J.A., & Bray, N.W. (1970). A closed-loop theory of paired-associate verbal learning. Psychological Review, 77, 385-405.

Adams, J.A., & Creamer, L.R. (1962). Anticipatory timing of continuous and discrete responses. Journal of Experimental Psychology, 63, 84-90.

Adams, J.A., & Dijkstra, S. (1966). Short-term memory for motor responses. Journal of Experimental Psychology, 71, 314-318.

Adams, J.A., & Hufford, L.E. (1962). Contributions of a part-task trainer to the learning and relearning of a time-shared flight maneuver. Human Factors, 4, 159-170.

Adams, J.A., & Reynolds, B. (1954). Effect of shift in distribution of practice conditions following interpolated rest. Journal of Experimental Psychology, 47, 32-36.

Adrian, E.D., & Buytendijk, F.J.J. (1931). Potential changes in the isolated brain stem of the goldfish. Journal of Physiology, 71, 121-135.

Aglioti, S., DeSouza, J.F.X., & Goodale, M.A. (1995). Size contrast illusions deceive the eye but not the hand. Current Biology, 5, 679-685.

Aiken, L.R. Jr. (1964). Reaction time and the expectancy hypothesis. Perceptual and Motor Skills, 19, 655-661.

Ainscoe, M., & Hardy, L. (1987). Cognitive warm-up in a cyclical gymnastics skill. International Journal of Sport Psychology, 18, 269-275.

Al-Ameer, H., & Toole, T. (1993). Combinations of blocked and random practice orders: Benefits to acquisition and retention. Journal of Human Movement Studies, 25, 177-191.

Albaret, J.-M., & Thon, B. (1998). Differential effects of task complexity on contextual interference in a drawing task. Acta Psychologica, 100, 9-24.

Alessi, S.M. (1988). Fidelity in the design of instructional simulators. Journal of Computer-Based Instruction, 15, 40-47.

Alexander, R.M. (2003). Principles of animal locomotion. Princeton, NJ: Princeton University Press.

Allami, N., Paulignan, Y., Brovelli, A., & Boussaoud, D. (2008). Visuo-motor learning with combination of divergent rates of motor imagery and physical practice. Experimental Brain Research, 184, 105-113.

Allport, A. (1987). Selection for action: Some behavioral and neurophysiological considerations of attention and action. In H. Heuer & A.F. Sanders (Eds.), Perspectives on perception and action (pp. 395-419). Hillsdale, NJ: Erlbaum.

Allport, A. (1993). Attention and control: Have we been asking the wrong questions? In D.E. Meyer & S. Kornblum (Eds.), Attention and performance XIV. Cambridge, MA: MIT Press.

Allport, D.A., Antonis, B., & Reynolds, P. (1972). On the division of attention: A disproof of the single channel hypothesis. Quarterly Journal of Experimental Psychology, 24, 225-235.

Alm, H., & Nilsson, L. (1995). The effects of a mobile telephoning task on driver behaviour in a car following situation. Accident Analysis and Prevention, 27, 707-715.

Almeida, Q.J., Wishart, L.R., & Lee, T.D. (2002). Bimanual coordination deficits with Parkinson's disease: The influence of movement speed and external cueing. Movement Disorders, 17, 30-37.

Amazeen, P.G. (2002). Is dynamics the content of a generalized motor program for rhythmic interlimb coordination? Journal of Motor Behavior, 34, 233-251.

Amazeen, P.G., Amazeen, E.L., & Turvey, M.T. (1998). Breaking the reflectional symmetry of interlimb coordination dynamics. Journal of Motor Behavior, 30, 199-216.

Amazeen, P.G., Schmidt, R.C., & Turvey, M.T. (1995). Frequency detuning of the phase entrainment dynamics of visually coupled rhythmic movements. Biological Cybernetics, 72, 511-518.

Ambrose, A. (1997). Cellular telephones and traffic accidents (correspondence). New England Journal of Medicine, 337, 127-129.

Ammons, R.B. (1950). Acquisition of motor skill: III. Effects of initially distributed practice on rotary pursuit performance. Journal of Experimental Psychology, 40, 777-787.

Ammons, R.B. (1951). Effects of pre-practice activities on rotary pursuit performance. Journal of Experimental Psychology, 41, 187-191.

Ammons, R.B. (1988). Distribution of practice in motor skill acquisition: A few questions and comments. Research Quarterly for Exercise and Sport, 59, 288-290.

Anderson, D.I., Magill, R.A., & Sekiya, H. (1994). A reconsideration of the trials-delay of knowledge of results paradigm in motor skill learning. Research Quarterly for Exercise and Sport, 65, 286-290.

Anderson, D.I., Magill, R.A., & Sekiya, H. (2001). Motor learning as a function of KR schedule and characteristics of task intrinsic feedback. Journal of Motor Behavior, 33, 59-66.

Anderson, D.I., Magill, R.A., Sekiya, H., & Ryan, G. (2005). Support for an explanation of the guidance effect in motor skill learning. Journal of Motor Behavior, 37, 231-238.

Anderson, J.R. (1982). Acquisition of cognitive skill. Psychological Review, 89, 369-406.

Anderson, J.R. (1990). Cognitive psychology and its implications (3rd ed.). New York: Freeman.

Anderson, J.R. (1995). Learning and memory: An integrated approach. New York: Wiley.

Andres, R.O., & Hartung, K.J. (1989). Prediction of head movement time using Fitts' Law. Human Factors, 31, 703-713.

Angel, R.W. (1977). Antagonist muscle activity during rapid arm movements: Central versus proprioceptive influences. Journal of Neurology, Neurosurgery, and Psychiatry, 40, 683-686.

Angel, R.W., & Higgins, J.R. (1969). Correction of false moves in pursuit tracking. Journal of Experimental Psychology, 82, 185-187.

Annett, J. (1959). Learning a pressure under conditions of immediate and delayed knowledge of results. Quarterly Journal of Experimental Psychology, 11, 3-15.

Annett, J. (1969). Feedback and human behavior. Middlesex, England: Penguin.

Anshel, M.H., & Wrisberg, C.A. (1988). The effect of arousal and focused attention on warm-up decrement. Journal of Sport Behavior, 11, 18-31.

Anshel, M.H., & Wrisberg, C.A. (1993). Reducing warm-up decrement in the performance of the tennis serve. Journal of Sport and Exercise Psychology, 15, 290-303.

Anson, G., Elliott, D., & Davids, K. (2005). Information processing and constraints-based views of skill acquisition: Divergent or complementary? Motor Control, 9, 217-241.

Anzola, G.P., Bertolini, G., Buchtel, H.A., & Rizzolatti, G. (1977). Spatial compatibility and anatomical factors in simple and choice reaction times. Neuropsychologica, 15, 295-302.

Arbib, M.A. (1981). Perceptual structures and distributed motor control. In V. Brooks (Ed.), Handbook of physiology: Section 1: The nervous system. Vol. 2. Motor control, part 2 (pp. 1449-1480). Baltimore: American Physiological Society.

Archer, E.J., Kent, G.W., & Mote, F.A. (1956). Effect of long-term practice and time-on-target information feedback on a complex tracking task. Journal of Experimental Psychology, 51, 103-112.

Armstrong, T.R. (1970a). Feedback and perceptual-motor skill learning: A review of information feedback and manual guidance training techniques (Tech. Rep. No. 25). Ann Arbor, MI: University of Michigan, Department of Psychology.

Armstrong, T.R. (1970b). Training for the production of memorized movement patterns (Tech. Rep. No. 26). Ann Arbor, MI: University of Michigan, Department of Psychology.

Arnold, P., & Farrell, M.J. (2002). Can virtual reality be used to measure and train surgical skills? Ergonomics, 45, 362-379.

Arps, G.F. (1920). Work with knowledge of results versus work without knowledge of results. Psychological Monographs, 28, 1-41.

Arutyunyan, G.A., Gurfinkel, V.S., & Mirskii, M.L. (1968). Investigation of aiming at a target. Biophysics, 13, 536-538.

Arutyunyan, G.A., Gurfinkel, V.S., & Mirskii, M.L. (1969). Organization of movements on execution by man of an exact postural task. Biophysics, 14, 1162-1167.

Asatryan, D.G., & Feldman, A.G. (1965). Biophysics of complex systems and mathematical models. Functional tuning of nervous system with control of movement or maintenance of a steady posture—I. Mechanographic analysis of the work of the joint on execution of a postural task. Biophysics, 10, 925-935.

Aschersleben, G. (2002). Temporal control of movements in sensorimotor synchronization. Brain and Cognition, 48, 66-79.

Aschersleben, G., & Müsseler, J. (1999). Dissociations in the timing of stationary and moving stimuli. Journal of Experimental Psychology: Human Perception and Performance, 25, 1709-1720.

Ascoli, K.M., & Schmidt, R.A. (1969). Proactive interference in short-term motor retention. Journal of Motor Behavior, 1, 29-35.

Ashmead, D.H., Davis, D.L., & Northington, A. (1995). Contribution of listeners' approaching motion to auditory distance perception. Journal of Experimental Psychology: Human Perception and Performance, 21, 239-256.

Assaiante, C., Marchand, A.R., & Amblard, B. (1989). Discrete visual samples may control locomotor equilibrium and foot positioning in man. Journal of Motor Behavior, 21, 72-91.

Atkeson, C.G., & Hollerbach, J.M. (1985). Kinematic features of unrestrained vertical arm movements. Journal of Neuroscience, 5, 2318-2330.

Atkinson, R.C., & Shiffrin, R.M. (1971). The control of short-term memory. Scientific American, 225, 82-90.

Attneave, F. (1959). Applications of information theory to psychology: A summary of basic concepts, methods, and results. New York: Holt, Rinehart & Winston.

Augustyn, J.S., & Rosenbaum, D.A. (2005). Metacognitive control of action: Preparation for aiming reflects knowledge of Fitts's law. Psychonomic Bulletin & Review, 12, 911-916.

Baars, B.J. (1986). The cognitive revolution in psychology. New York: Guilford.

Baars, B.J. (1997). In the theatre of consciousness: The workspace of the mind. New York: Oxford University Press.

Bachman, J.C. (1961). Specificity vs. generality in learning and performing two large muscle motor tasks. Research Quarterly, 32, 3-11.

Bachman, J.C. (1966). Influence of age and sex on the amount and rate of learning two motor tasks. Research Quarterly, 37, 176-186.

Bachrach, A.J. (1970). Diving behavior. In Scripps Institute of Oceanography, Human performance and scuba diving. Proceedings of the Symposium on Underwater Physiology, La Jolla, CA. Chicago: Athletic Institute.

Baddeley, A. (2003). Working memory: Looking back and looking forward. Nature Reviews: Neuroscience, 4, 829-839.

Baddeley, A.D., & Longman, D.J.A. (1978). The influence of length and frequency of training session on the rate of learning to type. Ergonomics, 21, 627-635.

Baddeley, A.D., & Weiskrantz, L. (Eds.). (1993). Attention: Selection, awareness, and control: A tribute to Donald Broadbent. Oxford: Clarendon Press.

Badets, A., & Blandin, Y. (2004). The role of knowledge of results frequency in learning through observation. Journal of Motor Behavior, 36, 62-70.

Badets, A., & Blandin, Y. (2005). Observational learning: Effects of bandwidth knowledge of results. Journal of Motor Behavior, 37, 211-216.

Badets, A., Blandin, Y., Wright, D.L., & Shea, C.H. (2006). Error detection processes during observational learning. Research Quarterly for Exercise and Sport, 77, 177-184.

Bahrick, H.P., Fitts, P.M., & Briggs, G.E. (1957). Learning curves—facts or artifacts? Psychological Bulletin, 54, 256-268.

Baird, K.M., Hoffmann, E.R., & Drury, C.G. (2002). The effects of probe length on Fitts' law. Applied Ergonomics, 33, 9-14.

Balakrishnan, R. (2004). "Beating" Fitts' law: Virtual enhancements for pointing facilitation. International Journal of Human-Computer Studies, 61, 857-874.

Balasubramaniam, R. (2006). Trajectory formation in timed repetitive movements. In M.L. Latash & F. Lestienne (Eds.), Progress in motor control IV (pp. 47-54). New York: Springer.

Balasubramaniam, R., & Turvey, M.T. (2005). The lambda-based equilibrium point (EP) hypothesis 1990-1999. In M.F. Levin (Ed.), Forty years of the equilibrium point hypothesis (pp. 375-378). Quebec: Tristar.

Balasubramaniam, R., Wing, A.M., & Daffertshofer, A. (2004). Keeping with the beat: Movement trajectories contribute to movement timing. Experimental Brain Research, 159, 129-134.

Baldissera, F., Cavallari, P., & Civaschi, P. (1982). Preferential coupling between voluntary movements of ipsilateral limbs. Neuroscience Letters, 34, 95-100.

Baldissera, F., Cavallari, P., Marini, G., & Tassone, G. (1991). Differential control of in-phase and anti-phase coupling of rhythmic movements of ipsilateral hand and foot. Experimental Brain Research, 83, 375-380.

Baldissera, F., Cavallari, P., & Tesio, L. (1994). Coordination of cyclic coupled movements of hand and foot in normal subjects and on the healthy side of hemiplegic patients. In S.P. Swinnen, H. Heuer, J. Massion, & P. Casaer (Eds.), Interlimb coordination: Neural, dynamical, and cognitive constraints (pp. 229-242). San Diego: Academic Press.

Baldo, M.V.C., Ranvaud, R.D., & Morya, E. (2002). Flag errors in soccer games: The flash-lag effect brought to real life. Perception, 31, 1205-1210.

Band, G.P.H., & van Boxtel, G.J.M. (1999). Inhibitory motor control in stop paradigms: Review and reinterpretation of neural mechanisms. Acta Psychologica, 101, 179-211.

Band, G.P.H., van der Molen, M.W., & Logan, G.D. (2003). Horse-race model simulations of the stop-signal procedure. Acta Psychologica, 112, 105-142.

Bandura, A. (1969). Principles of behavior modification. New York: Holt, Rinehart & Winston.

Bandura, A., Blanchard, E.B., & Ritter, B. (1969). Relative efficacy of desensitization and modeling approaches for inducing behavioral, affective, and attitudinal changes. Journal of Personality and Social Psychology, 13, 173-199.

Bard, C., Turrell, Y., Fleury, M., Teasdale, N., Lamarre, Y., & Martin, O. (1999). Deafferentation and pointing with visual double-step perturbations. Experimental Brain Research, 125, 410-416.

Barnett, M.L., Ross, D., Schmidt, R.A., & Todd, B. (1973). Motor skills learning and the specificity of training principle. Research Quarterly, 44, 440-447.

Barnsley, R.H., Thompson, A.H., & Legault, P. (1992). Family planning: Football style. The relative age effect in football. International Review for the Sociology of Sport, 27, 77-86.

Barrett, N.C., & Glencross, D.J. (1989). Response amendments during manual aiming movements to double-step targets. Acta Psychologica, 70, 205-217.

Bartlett, F.C. (1932). Remembering: A study in experimental and social psychology. Cambridge: Cambridge University Press.

Bartlett, F.C. (1958). Thinking: An experimental and social study. New York: Basic Books.

Bartlett, N., & Bartlett, S. (1959). Synchronization of a motor response with an anticipated sensory event. Psychological Review, 66, 203-218.

Bartlett, R., & Darling, W.G. (2002). Opposite effects on perception and action induced by the Ponzo illusion. Experimental Brain Research, 146, 433-440.

Bartram, D., Banerji, N., Rothwell, D., & Smith, P. (1985). Task parameters affecting individual differences in pursuit and compensatory tracking performance. Ergonomics, 28, 1633-1652.

Basmajian, J.V. (1963). Control and training of individual motor units. Science, 141, 440-441.

Basmajian, J.V. (1989). Biofeedback: Principles and practice for clinicians (3rd ed.). Baltimore: Williams & Wilkins.

Battig, W.F. (1956). Transfer from verbal pretraining to motor performance as a function of motor task complexity. Journal of Experimental Psychology, 51, 371-378.

Battig, W.F. (1966). Facilitation and interference. In E.A. Bilodeau (Ed.), Acquisition of skill. New York: Academic Press.

Battig, W.F. (1972). Intratask interference as a source of facilitation in transfer and retention. In R.F. Thompson & J.F. Voss (Eds.), Topics in learning and performance (pp. 131-159). New York: Academic Press.

Battig, W.F. (1979). The flexibility of human memory. In L.S. Cermak & F.I.M. Craik (Eds.), Levels of processing in human memory (pp. 23-44). Hillsdale, NJ: Erlbaum.

Battig, W.F., & Shea, J.B. (1980). Levels of processing of verbal materials: An overview. In P. Klavora & J. Flowers (Ed.), Motor learning and biomechanical factors in sport (pp. 24-33). Toronto: University of Toronto.

Baumeister, R.F. (1984). Choking under pressure: Self-consciousness and paradoxical effects of incentives on skillful performance. Journal of Personality and Social Psychology, 46, 610-620.

Bayley, N. (1935). The development of motor abilities during the first three years. Monographs of the Society for Research in Child Development, 1, 1-26.

Bean, C.H. (1912). The curve of forgetting. Archives of Psychology, 3, 1-45.

Bear, M.F., Connors, B.W., & Paradiso, M.A. (2001). Neuroscience: Exploring the brain (2nd ed.). Baltimore: Lippincott Williams & Wilkins.

Beatty, J., & Wagoner, B.L. (1978). Pupillometric signs of brain activation vary with level of cognitive processing. Science, 199, 1216-1218.

Beauchet, O., Annweiler, C., Dubost, V., Allali, G., Kressig, R.W., Bridenbaugh, S., Berrut, G., Assal, F., & Herrmann, F.R. (2009). Stops walking when talking: A predictor of falls in older adults? European Journal of Neurology, 16, 786-795.

Beek, P.J., & Lewbel, A. (1995, November). The science of juggling. Scientific American, 273, 92-97.

Beer, R.S. (2009). Beyond control: The dynamics of brain-body-environment interaction in motor systems. In D. Sternad (Ed.), Progress in motor control (pp. 7-24). Berlin: Springer.

Beevor, C.E., & Horsely, V. (1887). A minute analysis (experimental) of the various movements produced by stimulating in the monkey different regions of the cortical centre for the upper limb as defined by Professor Ferrier. Philosophical Transactions, 178, 153.

Beevor, C.E., & Horsely, V. (1890). A record of the results obtained by electrical excitation of the so-called motor cortex and internal capsule in the orangutang. Philosophical Transactions, 181, 129.

Beilock, S.L. (2008). Math performance in stressful situations. Current Directions in Psychological Science, 17, 339-343.

Beilock, S.L. (2010). Choke: What the secrets of the brain reveal about getting it right when you have to. New York: Free Press.

Beilock, S.L., Bertenthal, B.I., McCoy, A.M., & Carr, T.H. (2004). Haste does not always make waste: Expertise, direction of attention, and speed versus accuracy in performing sensorimotor skills. Psychonomic Bulletin & Review, 11, 373-379.

Beilock, S.L., & Carr, T.H. (2001). On the fragility of skilled performance: What governs choking under pressure? Journal of Experimental Psychology: General, 130, 701-725.

Beilock, S.L., Carr, T.H., MacMahon, C., & Starkes, J.L. (2002). When paying attention becomes counterproductive: Impact of divided versus skill-focused attention on novice and experienced performance of sensorimotor skills. Journal of Experimental Psychology: Applied, 8, 6-16.

Beilock, S.L., Kulp, C.A., Holt, L.E., & Carr, T.H. (2004). More on the fragility of performance: Choking under pressure in mathematical problem solving. Journal of Experimental Psychology: General, 133, 584-600.

Belen'kii, V.Y., Gurfinkel, V.S., & Pal'tsev, Y.I. (1967). Elements of control of voluntary movements. Biofizika, 12, 135-141.

Benedetti, C., & McCullagh, P. (1987). Post-knowledge of results delay: Effects of interpolated activity on learning and performance. Research Quarterly for Exercise and Sport, 58, 375-381.

Bennett, D.M., & Simmons, R.W. (1984). Effects of precision of knowledge of results on acquisition and retention of a simple motor skill. Perceptual and Motor Skills, 58, 785-786.

Berkinblit, M.B., & Feldman, A.G. (1988). Some problems of motor control. Journal of Motor Behavior, 20, 369-373.

Berkinblit, M.B., Feldman, A.G., & Fukson, O.I. (1986). Adaptability of innate motor patterns and motor control mechanisms. Behavioral and Brain Sciences, 9, 585-638.

Bernstein, N.A. (1947). On the structure of movements. Moscow: State Medical Publishing House.

Bernstein, N.A. (1967). The co-ordination and regulation of movements. Oxford: Pergamon Press.

Bernstein, N.A. (1996). On dexterity and its development. In M.L. Latash & M.T. Turvey (Eds.), Dexterity and its development (pp. 3-244). Mahwah, NJ: Erlbaum.

Bernstein, N.A., & Popova, T.S. (1930). Studies on the biodynamics of the piano strike: Paper 1. Studies of the rhythmic octave strike using the kymocyclographic method. Proceedings of the piano-methodological section of the State Institute of Music Science (Vol. 1) (pp. 5-47). Moscow: Muzgiz. (In Russian; English translation published 2003 in Motor Control, 7, 3-45)

Biguer, B., Jeannerod, M., & Prablanc, C. (1982). The coordination of eye, head, and arm movements during reaching at a single visual target. Experimental Brain Research, 46, 301-304.

Biguer, B., Prablanc, C., & Jeannerod, M. (1984). The contribution of coordinated eye and head movements in hand pointing accuracy. Experimental Brain Research, 55, 462-469.

Bilodeau, E.A. (Ed.). (1966). Acquisition of skill. New York: Academic Press.

Bilodeau, E.A., & Bilodeau, I.M. (1958). Variable frequency of knowledge of results and the learning of a simple skill. Journal of Experimental Psychology, 55, 379-383.

Bilodeau, E.A., & Bilodeau, I.M. (1961). Motor-skills learning. Annual Review of Psychology, 12, 243-280.

Bilodeau, E.A., Bilodeau, I.M., & Schumsky, D.A. (1959). Some effects of introducing and withdrawing knowledge of results early and late in practice. Journal of Experimental Psychology, 58, 142-144.

Bilodeau, I.M. (1956). Accuracy of a simple positioning response with variation in the number of trials by which knowledge of results is delayed. American Journal of Psychology, 69, 434-437.

Bilodeau, I.M. (1966). Information feedback. In E.A. Bilodeau (Ed.), Acquisition of skill (pp. 255-296). New York: Academic Press.

Bilodeau, I.M. (1969). Information feedback. In E.A. Bilodeau (Ed.), Principles of skill acquisition (pp. 255-285). New York: Academic Press.

Binsted, G., Rolheiser, T.M., & Chua, R. (2006). Decay in visuomotor representations during manual aiming. Journal of Motor Behavior, 38, 82-87.

Bizzi, E. (1974). The coordination of eye-head movements. Scientific American, 231(4), 100-106.

Bizzi, E., Accornero, N., Chapple, W., & Hogan, N. (1982). Arm trajectory formation in monkeys. Experimental Brain Research, 46, 139-143.

Bizzi, E., Hogan, N., Mussa-Ivaldi, F.A., & Giszter, S. (1992). Does the nervous system use equilibrium-point control to guide single and multiple joint movements? Behavioral and Brain Sciences, 15, 603-613.

Bizzi, E., Kalil, R.E., & Tagliasco, V. (1971). Eye-head coordination in monkeys: Evidence for centrally patterned organization. Science, 173, 452-454.

Bizzi, E., Polit, A., & Morasso, P. (1976). Mechanisms underlying achievement of final head position. Journal of Neurophysiology, 39, 435-444.

Bjork, R.A. (1994). Institutional impediments to effective training. In D. Druckman & R.A. Bjork (Eds.), Learning, remembering, believing (pp. 295-306). Washington, DC: National Academy Press.

Blakemore, S.-J., Frith, C.D., & Wolpert, D.M. (1999). Spatio-temporal prediction modulates the perception of self-produced stimuli. Journal of Cognitive Neuroscience, 11, 551-559.

Blakemore, S.-J., Wolpert, D.M., & Frith, C.D. (1998). Central cancellation of self-produced tickle sensation. Nature Neuroscience, 1, 635-640.

Blakemore, S.-J., Wolpert, D.M., & Frith, C.D. (2000). Why can't you tickle yourself? Neuroreport, 11, R11-R16.

Blandin, Y., Lhuisset, L., & Proteau, L. (1999). Cognitive processes underlying observational learning of motor skills. Quarterly Journal of Experimental Psychology, 52A, 957-979.

Blandin, Y., & Proteau, L. (2000). On the cognitive basis of observational learning: Development of mechanisms for the detection and correction of errors. Quarterly Journal of Experimental Psychology, 53A, 846-867.

Blandin, Y., Toussaint, L., & Shea, C.H. (2008). Specificity of practice: Interaction between concurrent sensory information and terminal feedback. Journal of Experimental Psychology: Learning, Memory, and Cognition, 34, 994-1000.

Blankenship, W.C. (1952). Transfer effects in neuromuscular responses involving choice. Unpublished master's thesis, University of California, Berkeley.

Blix, M. (1892-1895). Die Länge und Spannung des Muskels. Skandinavische Archiv Physiologie, 3, 295-318; 4, 399-409; 5, 150-206.

Blouin, J., Gauthier, G.M., Vercher, J.L., & Cole, J. (1996). The relative contribution of retinal and extraretinal signals in determining the accuracy of reaching movements in normal subjects and a deafferented patient. Experimental Brain Research, 109, 148-153.

Bogacz, S. (2005). Understanding how speed affects performance of polyrhythms: Transferring control as speed increases. Journal of Motor Behavior, 37, 21-34.

Bogaerts, H, & Swinnen, S.P. (2001). Spatial interactions during bimanual coordination patterns: The effect of directional compatibility. Motor Control, 5, 183-199.

Bonnet, C., Carello, C., & Turvey, M.T. (2009). Diabetes and postural stability: Review and hypotheses. Journal of Motor Behavior, 41, 172-190.

Book, W.F. (1908). The psychology of skill. University of Montana Studies in Psychology (Vol. 1). (Reprinted, New York: Gregg, 1925)

Bootsma, R.J., Marteniuk, R.G., MacKenzie, C.L., & Zaal, F.T.J.M. (1994). The speed-accuracy trade-off in manual prehension: Effects of movement amplitude, object size and object width on kinematic characteristics. Experimental Brain Research, 98, 535-541.

Bootsma, R.J., & van Wieringen, P.C.W. (1990). Timing an attacking forehand drive in table tennis. Journal of Experimental Psychology: Human Perception and Performance, 16, 21-29.

Boring, E.G. (1950). A history of experimental psychology. New York: Appleton-Century-Crofts.

Bortoli, L., Robazza, C., Durigon, V., & Carra, C. (1992). Effects of contextual interference on learning technical sports skills. Perceptual and Motor Skills, 75, 555-562.

Boucher, J.L. (1974). Higher processes in motor learning. Journal of Motor Behavior, 6, 131-137.

Boucher, L., Palmeri, T.J., Logan, G.D., & Schall, J.D. (2007). Inhibitory control in mind and brain: An interactive race model of countermanding saccades. Psychological Review, 114, 376-397.

Bourne, L.E. Jr., & Archer, E.J. (1956). Time continuously on target as a function of distribution of practice. Journal of Experimental Psychology, 51, 25-33.

Bourne, L.E. Jr., & Bunderson, C.V. (1963). Effects of delay of informative feedback and length of postfeedback interval on concept identification. Journal of Experimental Psychology, 65, 1-5.

Bourne, L.E. Jr., Guy, D.E., Dodd, D.H., & Justesen, D.R. (1965). Concept identification: The effects of varying length and informational components of the intertrial interval. Journal of Experimental Psychology, 69, 624-629.

Boutcher, S.H., & Crews, D.J. (1987). The effect of a preshot attentional routine on a well-learned skill. International Journal of Sport Psychology, 18, 30-39.

Bowditch, H.P., & Southard, W.F. (1882). A comparison of sight and touch. Journal of Physiology, 3, 232-244.

Boyce, B.A. (1992). Effects of assigned versus participant-set goals on skill acquisition and retention of a selected shooting task. Journal of Teaching in Physical Education, 11, 220-234.

Boyce, B.A., & Del Rey, P. (1990). Designing applied research in a naturalistic setting using a contextual interference paradigm. Journal of Human Movement Studies, 18, 189-200.

Boyd, I.A., & Roberts, T.D.M. (1953). Proprioceptive discharges from stretch-receptors in the knee-joint of the cat. Journal of Physiology, 122, 38-59.

Brady, F. (1998). A theoretical and empirical review of the contextual interference effect and the learning of motor skills. Quest, 50, 266-293.

Brady, F. (2004). Contextual interference: A meta-analytic study. Perceptual and Motor Skills, 99, 116-126.

Bransford, J.D., Franks, J.J., Morris, C.D., & Stein, B.S. (1979). Some general constraints on learning and memory research. In L.S. Cermak & F.I.M. Craik (Eds.), Levels of processing in human memory (pp. 331-354). Hillsdale, NJ: Erlbaum.

Brebner, J., Shepard, M., & Cairney, P. (1972). Spatial relationships and S-R compatibility. Acta Psychologica, 36, 1-15.

Brenner, J. (1974). A general model of voluntary control applied to the phenomenon of learned cardiovascular change. In P.A. Obrist, A.H. Black, J. Brenner, & L.V. DiCara (Eds.), Cardiovascular psychophysiology: Current issues in response mechanisms, biofeedback, and methodology (pp. 365-391). Chicago: Aldine.

Breslin, G., Hodges, N.J., Kennedy, R., Hanlon, M., & Williams, A.M. (2010). An especial skill: Support for a learned parameters hypothesis. Acta Psychologica, 134, 55-60.

Bridgeman, B. (1996). Extraretinal signals in visual orientation. In W. Prinz & B. Bridgeman (Eds.), Handbook of perception and action. Vol. 1: Perception (pp. 191-223). San Diego: Academic Press.

Bridgeman, B., Gemmer, A., Forsman, T., & Huemer, V. (2000). Processing spatial information in the sensorimotor branch of the visual system. Vision Research, 40, 3539-3552.

Bridgeman, B., Kirch, M., & Sperling, A. (1981). Segregation of cognitive and motor aspects of visual information using induced motion. Perception & Psychophysics, 29, 336-342.

Briem, V., & Hedman, L.R. (1995). Behavioural effects of mobile telephone use during simulated driving. Ergonomics, 38, 2536-2562.

Briggs, G.E., & Brogden, W.J. (1954). The effect of component practice on performance of a lever-positioning skill. Journal of Experimental Psychology, 48, 375-380.

Briggs, G.E., & Waters, L.K. (1958). Training and transfer as a function of component interaction. Journal of Experimental Psychology, 56, 492-500.

Brisson, T.A., & Alain, C. (1996a). Should common optimal movement patterns be identified as the criterion to be achieved? Journal of Motor Behavior, 28, 211-223.

Brisson, T.A., & Alain, C. (1996b). Optimal movement pattern characteristics are not required as a reference for knowledge of performance. Research Quarterly for Exercise and Sport, 67, 458-464.

Broadbent, D.E. (1958). Perception and communication. London: Pergamon Press.

Brodie, E.E., & Ross, H.E. (1985). Jiggling a lifted weight does aid discrimination. American Journal of Psychology, 98, 469-471.

Broker, J.P., Gregor, R.J., & Schmidt, R.A. (1993). Extrinsic feedback and the learning of kinetic patterns in cycling. Journal of Applied Biomechanics, 9, 111-123.

Brookhuis, K.A., de Vries, G., & de Waard, D. (1991). The effects of mobile telephoning on driving performance. Accident Analysis and Prevention, 23, 309-316.

Brooks, V.B. (1975). Roles of cerebellum and basal ganglia and control of movements. Le Journal Canadien Des Sciences Neurologiques, 2, 265-277.

Brooks, V.B. (1979). Motor programs revisited. In R.E. Talbott & D.R. Humphrey (Eds.), Posture and movement (pp. 13-49). New York: Raven Press.

Brooks, V.B. (1986). The neural basis of motor control. New York: Oxford University Press.

Brown, I.D. (1962). Measuring the "spare mental capacity" of car drivers by a subsidiary auditory task. Ergonomics, 5, 247-250.

Brown, I.D. (1967). Measurement of control skills, vigilance, and performance on a subsidiary task during 12 hours of car driving. Ergonomics, 10, 665-673.

Brown, I.D., Tickner, A.H., & Simmons, D.C.V. (1969). Interference between concurrent tasks of driver and telephoning. Journal of Applied Psychology, 53, 419-424.

Brown, J. (1958). Some tests of the decay theory of immediate memory. Quarterly Journal of Experimental Psychology, 10, 12-21.

Brown, T.G. (1911). The intrinsic factors in the act of progression in the mammal. Proceedings of the Royal Society of London. Series B, Containing Papers of a Biological Character, 84, 308-319.

Bruce, D. (1994). Lashley and the problem of serial order. American Psychologist, 49, 93-103.

Bruno, N. (2001). When does action resist visual illusions? Trends in Cognitive Sciences, 5, 379-382.

Bruno, N., Bernardis, P., & Gentilucci, M. (2008). Visually guided pointing, the Müller-Lyer illusion, and the functional interpretation of the dorsal-ventral split: Conclusions from 33 independent studies. Neuroscience & Biobehavioral Reviews, 32, 423-437.

Bruno, N., & Franz, V.H. (2009). When is grasping affected by the Müller-Lyer illusion? A quantitative review. Neuropsychologia, 47, 1421-1433.

Bryan, W.L., & Harter, N. (1897). Studies in the physiology and psychology of the telegraphic language. Psychological Review, 4, 27-53.

Bryan, W.L., & Harter, N. (1899). Studies on the telegraphic language: The acquisition of a hierarchy of habits. Psychological Review, 6, 345-375.

Buchanan, J.J., & Kelso, J.A.S. (1993). Posturally induced transitions in rhythmic multijoint limb movements. Experimental Brain Research, 94, 131-142.

Buekers, M.J., & Magill, R.A. (1995). The role of task experience and prior knowledge for detecting invalid augmented feedback while learning a motor skill. Quarterly Journal of Experimental Psychology, 48A, 84-97.

Buekers, M.J., Magill, R.A., & Hall, K.G. (1992). The effect of erroneous knowledge of results on skill acquisition when augmented information is redundant. Quarterly Journal of Experimental Psychology, 44A, 105-117.

Buekers, M.J., Magill, R.A., & Sneyers, K.M. (1994). Resolving a conflict between sensory feedback and knowledge of results, while learning a motor skill. Journal of Motor Behavior, 26, 27-35.

Burgess, P.R., & Clark, F.J. (1969). Characteristics of knee joint receptors in the cat. Journal of Physiology, 203, 317-335.

Burgess-Limerick, R., Neal, R.J., & Abernethy, B. (1992). Against relative timing invariance in movement kinematics. Quarterly Journal of Experimental Psychology, 44A, 705-722.

Burton, D., Naylor, S., & Holliday, B. (2001). Goal setting in sport: Investigating the goal effectiveness paradox. In R.N. Singer, H.A. Hausenblas, & C.M. Janelle (Eds.), Handbook of sport psychology (2nd ed.) (pp. 497-528). New York: Wiley.

Butler, M.S., Reeve, T.G., & Fischman, M.G. (1996). Effects of the instructional set in the bandwidth feedback paradigm on motor skill acquisition. Research Quarterly for Exercise and Sport, 67, 335-359.

Byblow, W.D., Lewis, G.N., Stinear, J.W., Austin, N.J., & Lynch, M. (2000). The subdominant hand increases the efficacy of voluntary alterations in bimanual coordination. Experimental Brain Research, 131, 366-374.

Byblow, W.D., Summers, J.J., Lewis, G.N., & Thomas, J. (2002). Bimanual coordination in Parkinson's disease: Deficits in movement frequency, amplitude, and pattern switching. Movement Disorders, 17, 20-29.

Byrne, J. (Ed.). (2008). Learning and memory: A comprehensive reference (4 vols.). Oxford: Elsevier.

Caird, J.K., Willness, C.R., Steel, P., & Scialfa, C. (2008). A meta-analysis of the effects of cell phones on driver performance. Accident Analysis and Prevention, 40, 1282-1293.

Camachon, C., Jacobs, D.M., Huet, M., Buekers, M., & Montagne, G. (2007). The role of concurrent feedback in learning to walk through sliding doors. Ecological Psychology, 19, 367-382.

Canic, M.J., & Franks, I.M. (1989). Response preparation and latency in patterns of tapping movements. Human Movement Science, 8, 123-139.

Card, S.K., English, W.K., & Burr, B.J. (1978). Evaluation of mouse, rate-controlled isometric joystick, step keys, and text keys for text selection on a CRT. Ergonomics, 21, 601-613.

Cardinal, B.J., & Thomas, J.R. (2005). The 75th anniversary of Research Quarterly for Exercise and Sport: An analysis of status and contributions. Research Quarterly for Exercise and Sport, 76 (Suppl. 2), S122-S134.

Carey, D.P. (2001). Do action systems resist visual illusions? Trends in Cognitive Sciences, 5, 109-113.

Carlsen, A.N., Chua, R., Inglis, J.T., Sanderson, D.J., & Franks, I.M. (2004). Prepared movements are elicited early by startle. Journal of Motor Behavior, 36, 253-264.

Carlsen, A.N., Dakin, C.J., Chua, R., & Franks, I.M. (2007). Startle produces early response latencies that are distinct from stimulus intensity effects. Experimental Brain Research, 176, 199-205.

Carlson, R.A., & Yaure, R.G. (1990). Practice schedules and the use of component skills in problem solving. Journal of Experimental Psychology: Learning, Memory, and Cognition, 16, 484-496.

Carlton, L.G. (1979). Control processes in the production of discrete aiming responses. Journal of Human Movement Studies, 5, 115-124.

Carlton, L.G. (1981a). Processing visual feedback information for movement control. Journal of Experimental Psychology: Human Perception and Performance, 7, 1019-1030.

Carlton, L.G. (1981b). Visual information: The control of aiming movements. Quarterly Journal of Experimental Psychology, 33A, 87-93.

Carlton, L.G. (1992). Visual processing time and the control of movement. In L. Proteau & D. Elliott (Eds.), Vision and motor control (pp. 3-31). Amsterdam: Elsevier.

Carlton, L.G. (1994). The effects of temporal-precision and time-minimization constraints on the spatial and temporal accuracy of aimed hand movements. Journal of Motor Behavior, 26, 43-50.

Carlton, L.G., Carlton, M.J., & Kim, K.H. (1997). Visuo-motor delays with changing environmental conditions. Unpublished manuscript.

Carlton, L.G., Chow, J.W., Ekkekakis, P., Shim, J., Ichiyama, R., & Carlton, M.J. (1999). A Web-based digitized video image system for the study of motor coordination. Behavior Research Methods, Instruments & Computers, 31, 57-62.

Carlton, L.G., & Newell, K.M. (1988). Force variability and movement accuracy in space-time. Journal of Experimental Psychology: Human Perception and Performance, 14, 24-36.

Carnahan, H. (1992). Eye, head and hand coordination during manual aiming. In L. Proteau & D. Elliott (Eds.), Vision and motor control (pp. 179-196). Amsterdam: Elsevier.

Carnahan, H., & Marteniuk, R.G. (1991). The temporal organization of hand, eye, and head movements during reaching and pointing. Journal of Motor Behavior, 23, 109-119.

Carroll, W.R., & Bandura, A. (1990). Representational guidance of action production in observational learning: A causal analysis. Journal of Motor Behavior, 22, 85-97.

Carron, A.V. (1967). Performance and learning in a discrete motor task under massed versus distributed conditions. Unpublished doctoral dissertation, University of California, Berkeley.

Carron, A.V. (1969). Performance and learning in a discrete motor task under massed vs. distributed practice. Research Quarterly, 40, 481-489.

Carron, A.V., Loughhead, T.M., & Bray, S.R. (2005). The home advantage in sport competitions: Courneya and Carron's (1992) conceptual framework a decade later. Journal of Sports Sciences, 23, 395-407.

Carson, R.G., Byblow, W.D., Abernethy, B., & Summers, J.J. (1996). The contribution of inherent and incidental constraints to intentional switching between patterns of bimanual coordination. Human Movement Science, 15, 565-589.

Carson, R.G., Goodman, D., Kelso, J.A.S., & Elliott, D. (1995). Phase transitions and critical fluctuations in rhythmic coordination of ipsilateral hand and foot. Journal of Motor Behavior, 27, 211-224.

Carson, R.G., Riek, S., Smethurst, C.J., Párraga, J.F., & Byblow, W.D. (2000). Neuromuscular-skeletal constraints upon the dynamics of unimanual and bimanual coordination. Experimental Brain Research, 131, 196-214.

Carter, M.C., & Shapiro, D.C. (1984). Control of sequential movements: Evidence for generalized motor programs. Journal of Neurophysiology, 52, 787-796.

Carter, M.C., & Smith, J.L. (1986). Simultaneous control of two rhythmical behaviors. I. Locomotion and paw-shake response in normal cat. Journal of Neurophysiology, 56, 171-183.

Caserta, R.J., Young, J., & Janelle, C.M. (2007). Old dogs, new tricks: Training the perceptual skills of senior tennis players. Journal of Sport and Exercise Psychology, 29, 479-497.

Castellote, J.M., Kumru, H., Queralt, A., & Valls-Solé, J. (2007). A startle speeds up the execution of externally guided saccades. Experimental Brain Research, 177, 129-136.

Casteneda, B., & Gray, R. (2007). Effects of focus of attention on baseball batting performance in players of differing skill levels. Journal of Sport and Exercise Psychology, 29, 60-77.

Castiello, U. (1996). Grasping a fruit: Selection for action. Journal of Experimental Psychology: Human Perception and Performance, 22, 582-603.

Castiello, U. (2005). The neuroscience of grasping. Nature Reviews: Neuroscience, 6, 726-736.

Castiello, U., Bennett, K.M.B., & Stelmach, G.E. (1993). Reach to grasp: The natural response to perturbation of object size. Experimental Brain Research, 94, 163-178.

Castiello, U., & Umiltà, C. (1988). Temporal dimensions of mental effort in different sports. International Journal of Sport Psychology, 19, 199-210.

Catalano, J.F., & Kleiner, B.M. (1984). Distant transfer in coincident timing as a function of practice variability. Perceptual and Motor Skills, 58, 851-856.

Cattell, J.M. (1886). The time it takes to see and name objects. Mind, 11, 63-65.

Cattell, J.M. (1893). Aufmerksamkeit und reaction. Philosophische Studien, 8, 403-406. English translation in R.S. Woodworth (1947), Psychological research (Vol. 1) (pp. 252-255). Lancaster, PA: Science Press.

Cauraugh, J.H., Chen, D., & Singer, R.N. (1993). Graphic versus numeric knowledge of results: Which mode? Research Quarterly for Exercise and Sport, 64, 213-216.

Cavallo, V., & Laurent, M. (1988). Visual information and skill level in time-to-collision estimation. Perception, 17, 623-632.

Cerritelli, B., Maruff, P., Wilson, P., & Currie, J. (2000). The effect of an external load on the force and timing components of mentally represented actions. Behavioural Brain Research, 108, 91-96.

Chabris, C.F., & Simons, D.J. (2010). The invisible gorilla: And other ways our intuitions deceive us. New York: Crown.

Chalmers, D.J. (1995, December). The puzzle of conscious experience. Scientific American, 273(6), 80-86.

Chamberlin, C.J., & Coelho, A.J. (1993). The perceptual side of action: Decision-making in sport. In J.L. Starkes & F. Allard (Eds.), Cognitive issues in motor expertise (pp. 135-157). Amsterdam: Elsevier.

Chambers, J.W. Jr., & Schumsky, D.A. (1978). The compression block technique: Use and misuse in the study of motor skills. Journal of Motor Behavior, 10, 301-311.

Chan, T., & Chan, K. (1995). Effect of frequency ratio and environmental information on spatial coupling: A study of attention. Ecological Psychology, 7, 125-144.

Chapanis, A. (1951). Theory and methods for analyzing errors in man-machine systems. Annals of the New York Academy of Sciences, 51, 1179-1203.

Chapanis, A. (1965). Man-machine engineering. Belmont, CA: Wadsworth.

Chapanis, A. (1999). The Chapanis chronicles: 50 years of human factors research, education, and design. Santa Barbara, CA: Agean.

Chapman, S. (1968). Catching a baseball. American Journal of Physics, 36, 868-870.

Chase, W.G., & Simon, H.A. (1973). Perception in chess. Cognitive Psychology, 4, 55-81.

Cheng, D.T., Luis, M., & Tremblay, L. (2008). Randomizing visual feedback in manual aiming: Reminiscence of the previous trial condition and prior knowledge of feedback availability. Experimental Brain Research, 189, 403-410.

Cherry, E.C. (1953). Some experiments on the recognition of speech, with one and two ears. Journal of the Acoustical Society of America, 25, 975-979.

Chisholm, S.L., Caird, J.K., & Lockhart, J. (2008). The effects of practice with MP3 players on driving performance. Accident Analysis and Prevention, 40, 704-713.

Chiviacowsky, S., & Wulf, G. (2002). Self-controlled feedback: Does it enhance learning because performers get feedback when they need it? Research Quarterly for Exercise and Sport, 73, 408-415.

Chiviacowsky, S., & Wulf, G. (2005). Self-controlled feedback is effective if it is based on the learner's performance. Research Quarterly for Exercise and Sport, 76, 42-48.

Chiviacowsky, S., & Wulf, G. (2007). Feedback after good trials enhances learning. Research Quarterly for Exercise and Sport, 78, 40-47.

Cho, Y.S., & Proctor, R.W. (2003). Stimulus and response representations underlying orthogonal stimulus-response compatibility effects. Psychonomic Bulletin & Review, 10, 45-73.

Choi, Y., Qi, F., Gordon, J., & Schweighofer, N. (2008). Performance-based adaptive schedules enhance motor learning. Journal of Motor Behavior, 40, 273-280.

Christina, R.W. (1992). The 1991 C.H. McCloy research lecture: Unraveling the mystery of the response complexity effect in skilled movements. Research Quarterly for Exercise and Sport, 63, 218-230.

Chua, R., & Elliott, D. (1993). Visual regulation of manual aiming. Human Movement Science, 12, 365-401.

Cirstea, M.C., & Levin, M.F. (2007). Improvement of arm movement patterns and endpoint control depends on type of feedback during practice in stroke survivors. Neurorehabilitation and Neural Repair, 21, 398-411.

Cirstea, M.C., Ptito, A., & Levin, M.F. (2006). Feedback and cognition in arm motor skill reacquisition after stroke. Stroke, 37, 1237-1242.

Claxton, G. (1975). Why can't we tickle ourselves? Perceptual and Motor Skills, 41, 335-338.

Cleary, T.J., Zimmerman, B.J., & Keating, T. (2006). Training physical education students to self-regulate during basketball free throw practice. Research Quarterly for Exercise and Sport, 77, 251-262.

Cohen, J.D., Dunbar, K., & McClelland, J.L. (1990). On the control of automatic processes: A parallel distributed processing account of the Stroop effect. Psychological Review, 97, 332-361.

Cohen, J., & Schooler, J.W. (Eds.). (1996). Scientific approaches to consciousness. Mahwah, NJ: Erlbaum.

Cohen, L. (1971). Synchronous bimanual movements performed by homologous and non-homologous muscles. Perceptual and Motor Skills, 32, 639-644.

Cohen, P.J. (1997). Cellular telephones and traffic accidents (correspondence). New England Journal of Medicine, 337, 127-129.

Cole, K.J., & Abbs, J.H. (1988). Grip force adjustments evoked by load force perturbations of a grasped object. Journal of Neurophysiology, 60, 1513-1522.

Collet, C., Guillot, A., & Petit, C. (2010). Phoning while driving I: A review of epidemiological, psychological, behavioural and physiological studies. Ergonomics, 53, 589-601.

Collet, C., Guillot, A., & Petit, C. (2010). Phoning while driving II: A review of driving conditions influence. Ergonomics, 53, 602-616.

Collier, G.L., & Ogden, R.T. (2004). Adding drift to the decomposition of simple isochronous tapping: An extension of the Wing-Kristofferson model. Journal of Experimental Psychology: Human Perception and Performance, 30, 853-872.

Consiglio, W., Driscoll, P., Witte, M., & Berg, W.P. (2003). Effect of cellular telephone conversations and other potential interference on reaction time in a braking response. Accident Analysis and Prevention, 35, 495-500.

Cooke, J.D. (1980). The organization of simple, skilled movements. In G.E. Stelmach & J. Requin (Eds.), Tutorials in motor behavior (pp. 199-212). Amsterdam: Elsevier.

Cooke, N.J. (2008). Preface to the special 50th anniversary issue of Human Factors. Human Factors, 50, 347-350.

Cooper, J.M., & Strayer, D.L. (2008). Effects of simulator practice and real-world experience on cell-phone–related driver distraction. Human Factors, 50, 893-902.

Cooper, J.B., & Taqueti, V.R. (2009). A brief history of the development of mannequin simulators for clinical education and training. Postgraduate Medical Journal, 84, 563-570.

Corcos, D.M. (1984). Two-handed movement control. Research Quarterly for Exercise and Sport, 55, 117-122.

Corcos, D.M., Jaric, S., & Gottlieb, G.L. (1996). Electromyographic analysis of performance enhancement. In H.N. Zelaznik (Ed.), Advances in motor learning and control (pp. 123-153). Champaign, IL: Human Kinetics.

Cordo, P.J., & Nashner, L.M. (1982). Properties of postural adjustments associated with rapid arm movements. Journal of Neurophysiology, 47, 287-302.

Cormier, S.M., & Hagman, J.D. (Eds.). (1987). Transfer of learning: Contemporary research applications. New York: Academic Press.

Courneya, K.S., & Carron, A.V. (1992). The home advantage in sport competitions: A literature review. Journal of Sport and Exercise Psychology, 14, 13-27.

Court, M.L.J., Bennett, S.J., Williams, A.M., & Davids, K. (2005). Effects of attentional strategies and anxiety constraints on perceptual-motor organisation of rhythmical arm movements. Neuroscience Letters, 384, 17-22.

Crago, P.E., Houk, J.C., & Hasan, Z. (1976). Regulatory actions of human stretch reflex. Journal of Neurophysiology, 39, 925-935.

Craik, F.I.M., & Jacoby, L.L. (1996). Aging and memory: Implications for skilled performance. In W.A. Rogers, A.D. Fisk, & N. Walker (Eds.), Aging and skilled performance: Advances in theory and applications (pp. 113-137). Mahwah, NJ: Erlbaum.

Craik, K.J.W. (1948). The theory of the human operator in control systems: II. Man as an element in a control system. British Journal of Psychology, 38, 142-148.

Cratty, B.J. (1964). Movement behavior and motor learning. Philadelphia: Lea & Febiger.

Crawley, S.L. (1926). An experimental investigation of recovery from work. Archives of Psychology, 13, 85.

Creamer, L.R. (1963). Event uncertainty, psychological refractory period, and human data processing. Journal of Experimental Psychology, 66, 187-194.

Creem, S.H., & Proffitt, D.R. (2001). Defining the cortical visual systems: "What", "where", and "how." Acta Psychologica, 107, 43-68.

Crick, F., & Koch, C. (2003). A framework for consciousness. Nature Neuroscience, 6, 119-126.

Criscimagna-Hemminger, S.E., & Shadmehr, R. (2008). Consolidation patterns of human motor memory. Journal of Neuroscience, 28, 9610-9618.

Croll, W.L. (1970). Children's discrimination learning as a function of intertrial interval duration. Psychonomic Science, 18, 321-322.

Cronbach, L.J. (1957). The two disciplines of scientific psychology. American Psychologist, 12, 671-684.

Cross, E.S., Schmitt, P.J., & Grafton, S.T. (2007). Neural substrates of contextual interference during motor learning support a model of active preparation. Journal of Cognitive Neuroscience, 19, 1854-1871.

Crossman, E.R.F.W. (1959). A theory of the acquisition of speed skill. Ergonomics, 2, 153-166.

Crossman, E.R.F.W., & Goodeve, P.J. (1963/1983). Feedback control of hand-movements and Fitts' law. Paper presented at the meeting of the Experimental Psychology Society, Oxford, July, 1963. Published in Quarterly Journal of Experimental Psychology, 1983, 35A, 251-278.

Cruse, H., Dean, J., Heuer, H., & Schmidt, R.A. (1990). Utilization of sensory information for motor control. In O. Neumann & W. Prinz (Eds.), Relationships between perception and action: Current approaches (pp. 43-79). Berlin: Springer-Verlag.

Cuddy, L.J., & Jacoby, L.L. (1982). When forgetting helps memory. An analysis of repetition effects. Journal of Verbal Learning and Verbal Behavior, 21, 451-467.

Custers, E.J.F.M., Regehr, G., McCulloch, W., Peniston, C., & Reznick, R. (1999). The effects of modeling on learning a simple surgical procedure: See one, do one or see many do one? Advances in Health Sciences Education, 4, 123-143.

Dail, T.K., & Christina, R.W. (2004). Distribution of practice and metacognition in learning and retention of a discrete motor task. Research Quarterly for Exercise and Sport, 75, 148-155.

Daniels, G.L., & Newell, K.M. (2003). Attentional focus influences the walk-run transition in human locomotion. Biological Psychology, 63, 163-178.

Darling, W.G., & Cooke, J.D. (1987). Changes in the variability of movement trajectories with practice. Journal of Motor Behavior, 19, 291-309.

Davids, K., Button, C., & Bennett, S. (2008). Dynamics of skill acquisition: A constraints-led approach. Champaign, IL: Human Kinetics.

Davies, G.M., & Thomson, D.M. (1988). Memory in context: Context in memory. New York: Wiley.

Davis, R. (1959). The role of "attention" in the psychological refractory period. Quarterly Journal of Experimental Psychology, 11, 211-220.

Deakin, J.M., & Proteau, L. (2000). The role of scheduling in learning through observation. Journal of Motor Behavior, 32, 268-276.

Decety, J., & Jeannerod, M. (1996). Mentally simulated movements in virtual reality: Does Fitts's law hold in motor imagery? Behavioural Brain Research, 72, 127-134.

Dees, V., & Grindley, G.C. (1951). The effect of knowledge of results on learning and performance: IV. The direction of the error in very simple skills. Quarterly Journal of Experimental Psychology, 3, 36-42.

deGroot, A.D. (1946/1978). Thought and choice in chess. The Hague: Mouton. (Original work published in 1946)

DeJaeger, D., & Proteau, L. (2003). The relative efficacy of different forms of knowledge of results for the learning of a new relative timing pattern. Quarterly Journal of Experimental Psychology, 56A, 621-640.

De Jong, R., Coles, M.G.H., Logan, G.D., & Gratton, G. (1990). In search of the point of no return: The control of response processes. Journal of Experimental Psychology: Human Perception and Performance, 16, 164-182.

Del Rey, P. (1989). Training and contextual interference effects on memory and transfer. Research Quarterly for Exercise and Sport, 60, 342-347.

Del Rey, P., Liu, X., & Simpson, K.J. (1994). Does retroactive inhibition influence contextual interference effects? Research Quarterly for Exercise and Sport, 65, 120-126.

Del Rey, P., & Shewokis, P. (1993). Appropriate summary KR for learning timing tasks under conditions of high and low contextual interference. Acta Psychologica, 83, 1-12.

Del Rey, P., Whitehurst, M., & Wood, J.M. (1983). Effects of experience and contextual interference on learning and transfer by boys and girls. Perceptual and Motor Skills, 56, 581-582.

Del Rey, P., Wughalter, E.H., & Whitehurst, M. (1982). The effects of contextual interference on females with varied experience in open sport skills. Research Quarterly for Exercise and Sport, 53, 108-115.

Dempster, F.N. (1988). The spacing effect: A case in the failure to apply the results of psychological research. American Psychologist, 43, 627-634.

Denier van der Gon, J.J., & Thuring, J.P. (1965). The guiding of human writing movements. Kybernetik, 2, 145-148.

Department of Transportation. (2000). Denial of Motor Vehicle Defect Petition, DP99-004. Federal Register, 65, No. 83, 25026-25037.

Desmurget, M., & Grafton, S. (2000). Forward modeling allows feedback control for fast reaching movements. Trends in Cognitive Sciences, 4, 423-431.

Desmurget, M., Prablanc, C., Arzi, M., Rossetti, Y., Paulignan, Y., & Urquizar, C. (1996). Integrated control of hand transport and orientation during prehension movements. Experimental Brain Research, 110, 265-278.

Desrosiers, J., Hébert, R., Bravo, G., & Dutil, E. (1995). Upper-extremity motor co-ordination of healthy elderly people. Age and Ageing, 24, 108-112.

Deutsch, D. (1983). The generation of two isochronous sequences in parallel. Perception & Psychophysics, 34, 331-337.

Deutsch, J.E., Borbely, M., Filler, J., Huhn, K., & Guarrera-Bowlby, P. (2008). Use of a low-cost, commercially available gaming console (Wii) for rehabilitation of an adolescent with cerebral palsy. Physical Therapy, 88, 1196-1207.

Deutsch, J.A., & Deutsch, D. (1963). Attention: Some theoretical considerations. Psychological Review, 70, 80-90.

Dewhurst, D.J. (1967). Neuromuscular control system. IEEE Transactions on Biomedical Engineering, 14, 167-171.

Dick, M.B., Hsieh, S., Bricker, J., & Dick-Muehlke, C. (2003). Facilitating acquisition and transfer of a continuous motor task in healthy older adults and patients with Alzheimer's disease. Neuropsychology, 17, 202-212.

Dickstein, R., & Deutsch, J.E. (2007). Motor imagery in physical therapist practice. Physical Therapy, 87, 942-953.

Diedrich, F.J., & Warren, W.H. Jr. (1995). Why change gaits? Dynamics of the walk-run transition. Journal of Experimental Psychology: Human Perception and Performance, 21, 183-202.

Diedrich, F.J., & Warren, W.H. Jr. (1998a). The dynamics of gait transitions: Effects of grade and load. Journal of Motor Behavior, 30, 60-78.

Diedrich, F.J., & Warren, W.H. Jr. (1998b). Dynamics of human gait transitions. In D.A. Rosenbaum & C.E. Collyer (Eds.), Timing of behavior: Neural, psychological, and computational perspectives (pp. 323-343). Cambridge, MA: MIT Press.

Dietz, V., & Duysens, J. (2000). Significance of load receptor input during locomotion: A review. Gait & Posture, 11, 102-110.

Domingo, A., & Ferris, D.P. (2009). Effects of physical guidance on short-term learning of walking on a narrow beam. Gait & Posture, 30, 464-468.

Donders, F.C. (1969). On the speed of mental processes. In W.G. Koster (Ed. & Trans.), Attention and performance II. Amsterdam: North-Holland. (Original work published in 1868)

Donovan, J.J., & Radosevich, D.J. (1999). A meta-analytic review of the distribution of practice effect: Now you see it, now you don't. Journal of Applied Psychology, 84, 795-805.

Doody, S.G., Bird, A.M., & Ross, D. (1985). The effect of auditory and visual models on acquisition of a timing task. Human Movement Science, 4, 271-281.

Drazin, D.H. (1961). Effects of foreperiod, foreperiod variability, and probability of stimulus occurrence on simple reaction time. Journal of Experimental Psychology, 62, 43-50.

Drewing, K., & Aschersleben, G. (2003). Reduced timing variability during bimanual coupling: A role for sensory information. Quarterly Journal of Experimental Psychology, 56A, 329-350.

Drews, F.A., Pasupathi, M., & Strayer, D.L. (2008). Passenger and cell phone conversations in simulated driving. Journal of Experimental Psychology: Applied, 14, 392-400.

Driver, J., Davis, G., Russell, C., Turatto, M., & Freeman, E. (2001). Segmentation, attention and phenomenal visual objects. Cognition, 80, 61-95.

Druckman, D., & Bjork, R.A. (1991). In the mind's eye: Enhancing human performance. Washington, DC: National Academy Press.

Druckman, D., & Bjork, R.A. (1994). Learning, remembering, believing: Enhancing human performance. Washington, DC: National Academy Press.

Drury, C.G., & Hoffmann, E.R. (1992). A model for movement time on data-entry keyboards. Ergonomics, 35, 129-147.

Drury, C.G., & Woolley, S.M. (1995). Visually-controlled leg movements embedded in a walking task. Ergonomics, 38, 714-722.

Dubrowski, A. Backstein, D., Abughaduma, R., Leidl, D., & Carnahan, H. (2005). The influence of practice schedules in the learning of a complex bone-plating surgical task. American Journal of Surgery, 190, 359-363.

Dudink, A. (1994). Birth date and sporting success. Nature, 368, 592.

Duffy, E. (1962). Activation and behavior. New York: Wiley.

Dunbar, K.N., & MacLeod, C.M. (1984). A horse race of a different color: Stroop interference patterns with transformed words. Journal of Experimental Psychology: Human Perception and Performance, 10, 622-639.

Duncan-Johnson, C.C., & Donchin, E. (1982). The P300 component of the event-related brain potential as an index of information processing. Biological Psychology, 14, 1-52.

Dunlap, K. (1910). Reactions to rhythmic stimuli, with attempt to synchronize. Psychological Review, 17, 399-416.

Duysens, J., & Van de Crommert, H.W.A.A. (1998). Neural control of locomotion; part 1: The central pattern generator from cats to humans. Gait & Posture, 7, 131-141.

Dye, M.W.G., Green, C.S., & Bavelier, D. (2009). Increasing speed of processing with action video games. Current Directions in Psychological Science, 18, 321-326.

Easterbrook, J.A. (1959). The effect of emotion on cue utilization and the organization of behavior. Psychological Review, 66, 183-201.

Easton, T.A. (1972). On the normal use of reflexes. American Scientist, 60, 591-599.

Easton, T.A. (1978). Coordinative structures—the basis for a motor program. In D.M. Landers & R.W. Christina (Eds.), Psychology of motor behavior and sport (pp. 63-81). Champaign, IL: Human Kinetics.

Ebbinghaus, H.D. (1913). Memory: A contribution to experimental psychology (H.A. Ruger & C.E. Bussenius, Trans.). New York: Teachers Colleges. (Original work published in 1885)

Eccles, D.W., & Tenenbaum, G. (2004). Why an expert team is more than a team of experts: A social-cognitive conceptualization of team coordination and communication in sport. Journal of Sport and Exercise Psychology, 26, 542-560.

Eimer, M., Nattkemper, D., Schröger, E., & Prinz, W. (1996). Involuntary attention. In O. Neumann & A.F. Sanders (Eds.), Handbook of perception and action. Vol. 3: Attention (pp. 155-184). San Diego: Academic Press.

Elliott, D. (1990). Intermittent visual pickup and goal directed movement: A review. Human Movement Science, 9, 531-548.

Elliott, D. (1992). Intermittent versus continuous control of manual aiming movements. In L. Proteau & D. Elliott (Eds.), Vision and motor control (pp. 33-48). Amsterdam: Elsevier.

Elliott, D., & Allard, F. (1985). The utilization of visual feedback information during rapid pointing movements. Quarterly Journal of Experimental Psychology, 37A, 407-425.

Elliott, D., Binsted, G.,& Heath, M. (1999). The control of goal-directed limb movements: Correcting errors in the trajectory. Human Movement Science, 18, 121-136.

Elliott, D., Chua, R., & Pollock, B.J. (1994). The influence of intermittent vision on manual aiming. Acta Psychologica, 85, 1-13.

Elliott, D., Hansen, S., Grierson, L.E.M., Lyons, J., Bennett, S.J., & Hayes, S.J. (2010). Goal-directed aiming: Two components but multiple processes. Psychological Bulletin, 136, 1023-1044.

Elliott, D., Helsen, W.F., & Chua, R. (2001). A century later: Woodworth's (1899) two-component model of goal-directed aiming. Psychological Bulletin, 127, 342-357.

Elliott, D., Lyons, J., & Dyson, K. (1997). Rescaling an acquired discrete aiming movement: Specific or general motor learning? Human Movement Science, 16, 81-96.

Elliott, D., & Madalena, J. (1987). The influence of premovement visual information on manual aiming. Quarterly Journal of Experimental Psychology, 39A, 541-559.

Elliott, D., & Roy, E.A. (Eds.). (1996). Manual asymmetries in motor performance. Boca Raton, FL: CRC Press.

Elliott, D., Weeks, D.J., & Elliott, C.L. (1987). Cerebral specialization in individuals with Down's syndrome. American Journal on Mental Retardation, 92, 263-271.

Elliott, D., Zuberec, S., & Milgram, P. (1994). The effects of periodic visual occlusion on ball catching. Journal of Motor Behavior, 26, 113-122.

Ellis, H.C. (1965). The transfer of learning. New York: Macmillan.

Ellis, R.R., Flanagan, J.R., & Lederman, S.J. (1999). The influence of visual illusions on grasp position. Experimental Brain Research, 125, 109-114.

Ells, J.G. (1973). Analysis of temporal and attentional aspects of movement control. Journal of Experimental Psychology, 99, 10-21.

Elwell, J.L., & Grindley, G.C. (1938). The effect of knowledge of results on learning and performance. British Journal of Psychology, 29, 39-54.

Enebo, B., & Sherwood, D.E. (2005). Experience and practice organization in learning a simulated high-velocity low-amplitude task. Journal of Manipulative and Physiological Therapeutics, 28, 33-43.

English, H.B. (1942). How psychology can facilitate military training—a concrete example. Journal of Applied Psychology, 26, 3-7.

Ericsson, K.A. (Ed.). (1996). The road to excellence: The acquisition of expert performance in the arts and sciences, sports, and games. Mahwah, NJ: Erlbaum.

Ericsson, K.A., Chase, W.G., & Faloon, S. (1980). Acquisition of a memory skill. Science, 208, 1181-1182.

Ericsson, K.A., Krampe, R.Th., & Tesch-Römer, C. (1993). The role of deliberate practice in the acquisition of expert performance. Psychological Review, 100, 363-406.

Espenschade, A. (1940). Motor performance in adolescence including the study of relationships with measures of physical growth and maturity. Monographs of the Society for Research in Child Development, 5, 1-126.

Estes, W.K. (1956). The problem of inference from curves based on group data. Psychological Bulletin, 53, 134-140.

Evarts, E.V. (1972). Contrasts between activity of precentral and postcentral neurons of cerebral cortex during movement in the monkey. Brain Research, 40, 25-31.

Evarts, E.V. (1973). Motor cortex reflexes associated with learned movement. Science, 179, 501-503.

Fagg, A.H., & Arbib, M.A. (1998). Modeling parietal-premotor interactions in primate control of grasping. Neural Networks, 11, 1277-1303.

Fantino, E., & Logan, C.A. (1979). The experimental analysis of behavior: A biological perspective. San Francisco: Freeman.

Farnsworth, P.R., & Poynter, W.F. (1931). A case of unusual ability in simultaneous tapping in two different times. American Journal of Psychology, 43, 633.

Farrell, J.E. (1975). The classification of physical education skills. Quest, 24, 63-68.

Farrell, M.J., & Thomson, J.A. (1998). Automatic spatial updating during locomotion without vision. Quarterly Journal of Experimental Psychology, 51A, 637-654.

Farrow, D., & Abernethy, B. (2002). Can anticipatory skills be learned through implicit video-based perceptual training? Journal of Sports Sciences, 20, 471-485.

Farrow, D., Baker, J., & MacMahon, C. (2008). Developing sport expertise: Researchers and coaches put theory into practice. New York: Routledge.

Faugloire, E., Bardy, B.G., & Stoffregen, T.A. (2009). (De)stabilization of required and spontaneous postural dynamics with learning. Journal of Experimental Psychology: Human Perception and Performance, 35, 170-187.

Fecteau, J.H., & Munoz, D.P. (2003). Exploring the consequences of the previous trial. Nature Reviews: Neuroscience, 4, 435-443.

Feigenberg, I.M., & Latash, L.P. (1996). N.A. Bernstein: The reformer of neuroscience. In M.L. Latash & M.T. Turvey (Eds.), Dexterity and its development (pp. 247-275). Champaign, IL: Human Kinetics.

Feldman, A.G. (1966a). Functional tuning of the nervous system with control of movement or maintenance of a steady posture—II. Controllable parameters of the muscles. Biophysics, 11, 565-578.

Feldman, A.G. (1966b). Functional tuning of the nervous system during control of movement or maintenance of a steady posture—III. Mechanographic analysis of the execution by man of the simplest motor tasks. Biophysics, 11, 667-675.

Feldman, A.G. (1986). Once more on the equilibrium-point hypothesis (λ model) for motor control. Journal of Motor Behavior, 18, 17-54.

Feldman, A.G. (2009). Origin and advances of the equilibrium-point hypothesis. In D. Sternad (Ed.), Progress in motor control (pp. 637-643). Berlin: Springer.

Feldman, A.G., & Latash, M.L. (2005). Testing hypotheses and the advancement of science: Recent attempts to falsify the equilibrium point hypothesis. Experimental Brain Research, 161, 91-103.

Feldman, A.G., & Levin, M.F. (1995). The origin and use of positional frames of reference in motor control. Behavioral and Brain Sciences, 18, 723-806.

Feldman, A.G., & Levin, M.F. (2009). The equilibrium-point hypothesis – past, present and future. In D. Sternad (Ed.), Progress in motor control (pp. 699-726). Berlin: Springer.

Feldman, A.G., Ostry, D.J., Levin, M.F., Gribble, P.L., & Mitnitski, A.B. (1998). Recent tests of the equilibrium-point hypothesis (λ model). Motor Control, 2, 189-205.

Feltz, D.L., & Landers, D.M. (1983). The effects of mental practice on motor skill learning and performance: A meta-analysis. Journal of Sport Psychology, 5, 25-57.

Feltz, D.L., Landers, D.M., & Becker, B.J. (1988). A revised meta-analysis of the mental practice literature on motor skill learning. In D. Druckman & J.A. Swets (Eds.), Enhancing human performance: Issues, theories, and techniques. Background papers (part III, chapter 5, pp. 1-65). Washington, DC: National Academy Press.

Fendrich, D.W., Healy, A.F., & Bourne, L.E. Jr. (1991). Long-term repetition effects for motoric and perceptual procedures. Journal of Experimental Psychology: Learning, Memory, and Cognition, 17, 137-151.

Ferrari, M. (1996). Observing the observer: Self-regulation in the observational learning of motor skills. Developmental Review, 16, 203-240.

Ferrier, D. (1888). Discussions on cerebral localization. Transactions of the Congress of American Physicians and Surgeons, 1, 337-340.

Fialkow, M.F., & Goff, B.A. (2009). Training the next generation of minimally invasive surgeons. Journal of Minimally Invasive Gynecology, 16, 136-141.

Fischer, M.H. (2001). How sensitive is hand transport to illusory context effects? Experimental Brain Research, 136, 224-230.

Fischer, M.H., Pratt, J., & Neggers, S.F.W. (2003). Inhibition of return and manual pointing movements. Perception & Psychophysics, 65, 379-387.

Fischman, M.G. (1984). Programming time as a function of number of movement parts and changes in movement direction. Journal of Motor Behavior, 16, 405-423.

Fischman, M.G., Christina, R.W., & Anson, J.G. (2008). Memory drum theory's C movement: Revelations from Franklin Henry. Research Quarterly for Exercise and Sport, 79, 312-318.

Fischman, M.G., Stodden, D.F., & Lehman, D.M. (2003). The end-state comfort effect in bimanual grip selection. Research Quarterly for Exercise and Sport, 74, 17-24.

Fitch, H.L., Tuller, B., & Turvey, M.T. (1982). The Bernstein perspective: III. Tuning of coordinative structures with special reference to perception. In J.A.S. Kelso (Ed.), Human motor behavior: An introduction (pp. 271-281). Hillsdale, NJ: Erlbaum.

Fitts, P.M. (1954). The information capacity of the human motor system in controlling the amplitude of movement. Journal of Experimental Psychology, 47, 381-391.

Fitts, P.M. (1964). Perceptual-motor skills learning. In A.W. Melton (Ed.), Categories of human learning (pp. 243-285). New York: Academic Press.

Fitts, P.M., Bahrick, H.P., Noble, M.E., & Briggs, G.E. (1959). Skilled performance (Contract No. AF 41 [657]-70). Columbus, OH: Ohio State University, Wright Air Development Center.

Fitts, P.M., & Deininger, R.L. (1954). S-R compatibility: Correspondence among paired elements within stimulus and response codes. Journal of Experimental Psychology, 48, 483-492.

Fitts, P.M., & Jones, R.E. (1947). Analysis of factors contributing to 460 "pilot error" experiences in operating aircraft controls (Memorandum Rep. TSEA4-694-12, Aero Medical Laboratory). Drayton, OH: Wright Patterson Air Force Base.

Fitts, P.M., & Peterson, J.R. (1964). Information capacity of discrete motor responses. Journal of Experimental Psychology, 67, 103-112.

Fitts, P.M., & Posner, M.I. (1967). Human performance. Belmont, CA: Brooks/Cole.

Fitts, P.M., & Seeger, C.M. (1953). S-R compatibility: Spatial characteristics of stimulus and response codes. Journal of Experimental Psychology, 46, 199-210.

Flach, J.M., Guisinger, M.A., & Robison, A.B. (1996). Fitts's law: Nonlinear dynamics and positive entropy. Ecological Psychology, 8, 281-325.

Flegal, K.E., & Anderson, M.C. (2008). Overthinking skilled motor performance: Or why those who teach can't do. Psychonomic Bulletin & Review, 15, 927-932.

Fleishman, E.A. (1956). Psychomotor selection tests: Research and application in the United States Air Force. Personnel Psychology, 9, 449-467.

Fleishman, E.A. (1957). A comparative study of aptitude patterns in unskilled and skilled psychomotor performances. Journal of Applied Psychology, 41, 263-272.

Fleishman, E.A. (1964). The structure and measurement of physical fitness. Englewood Cliffs, NJ: Prentice Hall.

Fleishman, E.A. (1965). The description and prediction of perceptual-motor skill learning. In R. Glaser (Ed.), Training research and education (pp. 137-175). New York: Wiley.

Fleishman, E.A. (1967). Individual differences and motor learning. In R.M. Gagne (Ed.), Learning and individual differences (pp. 165-191). Columbus, OH: Merrill.

Fleishman, E.A. (1975). Toward a taxonomy of human performance. American Psychologist, 30, 1127-1149.

Fleishman, E.A. (2004). Gold medal award for life achievement in the application of psychology. American Psychologist, 59, 352-354.

Fleishman, E.A., & Bartlett, C.J. (1969). Human abilities. Annual Review of Psychology, 20, 349-380.

Fleishman, E.A., & Hempel, W.E. Jr. (1955). The relation between abilities and improvement with practice in a visual discrimination reaction task. Journal of Experimental Psychology, 49, 301-312.

Fleishman, E.A., & Hempel, W.E. Jr. (1956). Factorial analysis of complex psychomotor performance and related skills. Journal of Applied Psychology, 40, 96-104.

Fleishman, E.A., & Parker, J.F. (1962). Factors in the retention and relearning of perceptual motor skill. Journal of Experimental Psychology, 64, 215-226.

Fleishman, E.A., & Rich, S. (1963). Role of kinesthetic and spatial-visual abilities in perceptual-motor learning. Journal of Experimental Psychology, 66, 6-11.

Fleishman, E.A., & Stephenson, R.W. (1970). Development of a taxonomy of human performance: A review of the third year's progress (Tech. Rep. No. 726-TPR3). Silver Springs, MD: American Institutes for Research.

Folk, C.L., & Gibson, B.S. (Eds.). (2001). Attraction, distraction and action: Multiple perspectives on attentional capture. Amsterdam: Elsevier.

Fontaine, R.J., Lee, T.D., & Swinnen, S.P. (1997). Learning a new bimanual coordination pattern: Reciprocal influences of intrinsic and to-be-learned patterns. Canadian Journal of Experimental Psychology, 51, 1-9.

Ford, P., Hodges, N.J., & Williams, A.M. (2005). Online attentional-focus manipulations in a soccer-dribbling task: Implications for the proceduralization of motor skills. Journal of Motor Behavior, 37, 386-394.

Ford, P., Hodges, N.J., & Williams, A.M. (2007). Examining action effects in the execution of a skilled soccer kick by using erroneous feedback. Journal of Motor Behavior, 39, 481-490.

Forssberg, H., Grillner, S., & Rossignol, S. (1975). Phase dependent reflex reversal during walking in chronic spinal cats. Brain Research, 85, 103-107.

Fowler, B., Duck, T., Mosher, M., & Mathieson, B. (1991). The coordination of bimanual aiming movements: Evidence for progressive desynchronization. Quarterly Journal of Experimental Psychology, 43A, 205-221.

Fowler, B., Meehan, S., & Singhal, A. (2008). Perceptual-motor performance and associated kinematics in space. Human Factors, 50, 879-892.

Fowler, C.A., Richardson, M.J., Marsh, K.L., & Shockley, K.D. (2008). Language use, coordination, and the emergence of cooperative action. In A. Fuchs & V.K.

Jirsa (Eds.), Coordination: Neural, behavioral and social dynamics (pp. 261-279). Berlin: Springer.

Fozard, J.L., Vercruyssen, M., Reynolds, S.L., Hancock, P.A., & Quilter, R.E. (1994). Age differences and changes in reaction time: The Baltimore longitudinal study of aging. Journal of Gerontology: Psychological Sciences, 49, P179-P189.

Fraise, P. (1969). Why is naming longer than reading? Acta Psychologica, 30, 96-103.

Frak, V., Paulignan, Y., & Jeannerod, M. (2001). Orientation of the opposition axis in mentally simulated grasping. Experimental Brain Research, 136, 120-127.

Frank, J.S., Williams, I.D., & Hayes, K.C. (1977). The ischemic nerve block and skilled movement. Journal of Motor Behavior, 9, 217-224.

Franks, I.M., & Harvey, T. (1997). Cues for goalkeepers: High-tech methods used to measure penalty shot response. Soccer Journal, 42(3), 30-33, 38.

Franks, I.M., Nagelkerke, P., Ketelaars, M., & van Donkelaar, P. (1998). Response preparation and control of movement sequences. Canadian Journal of Experimental Psychology, 52, 93-102.

Franks, I.M., & Stanley, M.L. (1991). Learning the invariants of a perceptual motor skill. Canadian Journal of Psychology, 45, 303-320.

Franks, I.M., & Wilberg, R.B. (1984). Consistent reproduction of movement sequences during acquisition of a pursuit tracking task. Perceptual and Motor Skills, 58, 699-709.

Franz, E.A. (1997). Spatial coupling in the coordination of complex actions. Quarterly Journal of Experimental Psychology, 50A, 684-704.

Franz, E.A., Eliassen, J.C., Ivry, R.B., & Gazzaniga, M.S. (1996). Dissociation of spatial and temporal coupling in the bimanual movements of callosotomy patients. Psychological Science, 7, 306-310.

Franz, E.A., Zelaznik, H.N., & McCabe, G. (1991). Spatial topological constraints in a bimanual task. Acta Psychologica, 77, 137-151.

Franz, E.A., Zelaznik, H.N., & Smith, A. (1992). Evidence of common timing processes in the control of manual, orofacial, and speech movements. Journal of Motor Behavior, 24, 281-287.

Franz, E.A., Zelaznik, H.N., Swinnen, S.P., & Walter, C.B. (2001). Spatial conceptual influences on the coordination of bimanual actions: When a dual task becomes a single task. Journal of Motor Behavior, 33, 103-112.

Franz, V.H., Bülthoff, H.H., & Fahle, M. (2003). Grasp effects of the Ebbinghaus illusion: Obstacle avoidance is not the explanation. Experimental Brain Research, 149, 470-477.

French, K.E., & Thomas, J.R. (1987). The relation of knowledge development to children's basketball performance. Journal of Sport Psychology, 9, 15-32.

Fritsch, G., & Hitzig, E. (1870). Über die elektrische Erregbarkeit des Grosshirns. Archiv Anatomie Physiologie, 37, 300-332.

Fuchs, A.H. (1962). The progression-regression hypothesis in perceptual-motor skill learning. Journal of Experimental Psychology, 63, 177-182.

Fuchs, A.H. (1998). Psychology and "The Babe." Journal of the History of Behavioral Sciences, 34, 153-165.

Fuchs, A., & Jirsa, V.K. (2000). The HKB model revisited: How varying the degree of symmetry controls dynamics. Human Movement Science, 19, 425-449.

Fukson, O.I., Berkinblit, M.B., & Feldman, A.G. (1980). The spinal frog takes into account the scheme of its body during the wiping reflex. Science, 209, 1261-1263.

Fukuda, T. (1961). Studies on human dynamic postures from the viewpoint of postural reflexes. Acta Oto-Laryngologica, 161, 1-52.

Fullerton, G.S., & Cattell, J. (1892). On the perception of small differences. University of Pennsylvania Philosophical Series, No. 2.

Gabbard, C.P. (2008). Lifelong motor development (5th ed.). San Francisco: Benjamin/Cummings.

Gable, C.D., Shea, C.H., & Wright, D.L. (1991). Summary knowledge of results. Research Quarterly for Exercise and Sport, 62, 285-292.

Gabriele, T.E., Hall, C.R., & Lee, T.D. (1989). Cognition in motor learning: Imagery effects on contextual interference. Human Movement Science, 8, 227-245.

Gagnon, C., Mathieu, J., & Desrosiers, J. (2004). Standardized finger-nose test validity for coordination assessment in an ataxic disorder. Canadian Journal of Neurological Sciences, 31, 484-489.

Gallagher, J.D., & Thomas, J.R. (1980). Effects of varying post-KR intervals upon children's motor performance. Journal of Motor Behavior, 12, 41-46.

Gallistel, C.R. (1980). The organization of action: A new synthesis. Hillsdale, NJ: Erlbaum.

Gandevia, S.C., & Burke, D. (1992). Does the nervous system depend on kinesthetic information to control natural limb movements? Behavioral and Brain Sciences, 15, 614-632.

Gandevia, S.C., Proske, U., & Stuart, D.G. (Eds.). (2002). Sensorimotor control of movement and posture. New York: Kluwer Academic/Plenum Press.

Ganel, T., Tanzer, M., & Goodale, M.A. (2008). A double dissociation between action and perception in the context of visual illusions: Opposite effects of real and illusory size. Psychological Science, 19, 221-225.

Gao, L., & Zelaznik, H.N. (1991). The modification of an already programmed response: A new interpretation of Henry and Harrison (1961). Journal of Motor Behavior, 23, 221-223.

Garvey, W.D. (1960). A comparison of the effects of training and secondary tasks on tracking behavior. Journal of Applied Psychology, 44, 370-375.

Gauggel, S., & Fischer, S. (2001). The effect of goal setting on motor performance and motor learning in brain-damaged patients. Neuropsychological Rehabilitation, 11, 33-44.

Gawron, V.J., Drury, C.G., Czaja, S.J., & Wilkins, D.M. (1989). A taxonomy of independent variables affecting human performance. International Journal of Man-Machine Studies, 31, 643-672.

Gelfan, S., & Carter, S. (1967). Muscle sense in man. Experimental Neurology, 18, 469-473.

Gelfand, I.M., Gurfinkel, V.S., Tomin, S.V., & Tsetlin, M.L. (1971). Models of the structural-functional organization of certain biological systems. Cambridge, MA: MIT Press.

Gentile, A.M. (1972). A working model of skill acquisition with application to teaching. Quest, 17, 3-23.

Gentile, A.M. (1998). Implicit and explicit processes during acquisition of functional skills. Scandinavian Journal of Occupational Therapy, 5, 7-16.

Gentile, A.M. (2000). Skill acquisition: Action, movement, and neuromotor processes. In J.H. Carr & R.H. Shepherd (Eds.), Movement science: Foundation for physical therapy in rehabilitation (2nd ed.) (pp. 111-180). Gaithersburg, MD: Aspen.

Gentilucci, M., Chieffi, S., Scarpa, M., & Castiello, U. (1992). Temporal coupling between transport and grasp components during prehension movements: Effects of visual perturbation. Behavioural Brain Research, 47, 71-82.

Gentner, D.R. (1987). Timing of skilled motor performance: Tests of the proportional duration model. Psychological Review, 94, 255-276.

Ghez, C., & Krakauer, J. (2000). The organization of movement. In E.R. Kandel, J.H. Schwartz, & T.M. Jessell (Eds.), Principles of neural science (pp. 653-673). New York: McGraw-Hill.

Ghez, C., & Thach, W.T. (2000). The cerebellum. In E.R. Kandel, J.H. Schwartz, & T.M. Jessell (Eds.), Principles of neural science (pp. 832-852). New York: McGraw-Hill.

Gibson, J.J. (1958). Visually controlled locomotion and visual orientation in animals. British Journal of Psychology, 49, 182-194.

Gibson, J.J. (1966). The senses considered as perceptual systems. Boston: Houghton Mifflin.

Gibson, J.J. (1979). The ecological approach to visual perception. Boston: Houghton Mifflin.

Gielen, C.C.A.M., Schmidt, R.A., & van den Heuvel, P.J.M. (1983). On the nature of intersensory facilitation of reaction time. Perception & Psychophysics, 34, 161-168.

Gielen, C.C.A.M., van den Oosten, K., & ter Gunne, F.P. (1985). Relation between EMG activation and kinematic properties of aimed arm movements. Journal of Motor Behavior, 17, 421-442.

Gilbreth, F.B. (1909). Bricklaying system. New York: Myron C. Clark.

Giuffrida, C.G., Shea, J.B., & Fairbrother, J.T. (2002). Differential transfer benefits of increased practice for constant, blocked, and serial practice schedules. Journal of Motor Behavior, 34, 353-365.

Gladwell, M. (2002). The tipping point: How little things can make a big difference. New York: Little, Brown.

Gladwell, M. (2008). Outliers: The story of success. New York: Little, Brown.

Glencross, D.J. (1973). Temporal organization in a repetitive speed skill. Ergonomics, 16, 765-776.

Glencross, D., & Barrett, N. (1992). The processing of visual feedback in rapid movements: Revisited. In J.J. Summers (Ed.), Approaches to the study of motor control and learning (pp. 289-311). Amsterdam: Elsevier.

Glover, S. (2002). Visual illusions affect planning but not control. Trends in Cognitive Sciences, 6, 288-292.

Glover, S. (2004). Separate visual representations in the planning and control of action. Behavioral and Brain Sciences, 27, 3-78.

Glover, S.R., & Dixon, P. (2001). Dynamic illusion effects in a reaching task: Evidence for separate visual representations in the planning and control of reaching. Journal of Experimental Psychology: Human Perception and Performance, 27, 560-572.

Goettl, B.P. (1996). The spacing effect in aircraft recognition. Human Factors, 38, 34-49.

Goggin, N.L., & Meeuwsen, H.J. (1992). Age-related differences in the control of spatial aiming movements. Research Quarterly for Exercise and Sport, 63, 366-372.

Goginski, A.M., & Collins, D. (1996). Research design and mental practice. Journal of Sports Sciences, 14, 381-392.

Goodale, M.A., & Humphrey, G.K. (2001). Separate visual pathways for action and perception. In E.B. Goldstein (Ed.), Blackwell handbook of perception (pp. 312-343). Malden, MA: Blackwell.

Goodale, M.A., & Milner, A.D. (1992). Separate visual pathways for perception and action. Trends in Neurosciences, 15, 20-25.

Goodale, M.A., Milner, A.D., Jakobson, L.S., & Carey, D.P. (1991). A neurological dissociation between perceiving objects and grasping them. Nature, 349, 154-156.

Goodale, M.A., & Servos, P. (1996). Visual control of prehension. In H.N. Zelaznik (Ed.), Advances in motor control and learning (pp. 87-121). Champaign, IL: Human Kinetics.

Goode, S., & Magill, R.A. (1986). Contextual interference effects in learning three badminton serves. Research Quarterly for Exercise and Sport, 57, 308-314.

Goodman, D., & Kelso, J.A.S. (1980). Are movements prepared in parts? Not under compatible (naturalized) conditions. Journal of Experimental Psychology: General, 109, 475-495.

Goodman, D., Kobayashi, R.B., & Kelso, J.A.S. (1983). Maintenance of symmetry as a constraint in motor control. Canadian Journal of Applied Sport Science, 8, 238.

Goodwin, G.M., McCloskey, D.I., & Matthews, P.B.C. (1972). The contribution of muscle afferents to kinaesthesia shown by vibration induced illusions of movement and by the effects of paralyzing joint afferents. Brain, 95, 705-748.

Goodwin, J.E., & Meeuwsen, H.J. (1995). Using bandwidth knowledge of results to alter relative frequencies during motor skill acquisition. Research Quarterly for Exercise and Sport, 66, 99-104.

Gordon, A.M., & Soechting, J.F. (1995). Use of tactile afferent information in sequential finger movements. Experimental Brain Research, 107, 281-292.

Gordon, J., & Ghez, C. (1991). Muscle receptors and spinal reflexes: The stretch reflex. In E.R. Kandel, J.H. Schwartz, & T.M. Jessell (Eds.), Principles of neural science (3rd ed.) (pp. 564-580). Amsterdam: Elsevier.

Gordon, J., Ghilardi, M.F., & Ghez, C. (1995). Impairments of reaching movements in patients without proprioception. I. Spatial errors. Journal of Neurophysiology, 73, 347-360.

Gottlieb, G.L. (1998). Rejecting the equilibrium-point hypothesis. Motor Control, 2, 10-12.

Gottlieb, G.L. (2000). A test of torque-control and equilibrium-point models of motor control. Human Movement Science, 19, 925-931.

Gottlieb, G.L., Corcos, D.M., & Agarwal, G.C. (1989). Strategies for the control of voluntary movements with one mechanical degree of freedom. Behavioral and Brain Sciences, 12, 189-250.

Gottsdanker, R. (1970). Uncertainty, timekeeping, and simple reaction time. Journal of Motor Behavior, 2, 245-260.

Gottsdanker, R. (1973). Psychological refractoriness and the organization of step-tracking responses. Perception & Psychophysics, 14, 60-70.

Gottsdanker, R., & Stelmach, G.E. (1971). The persistence of psychological refractoriness. Journal of Motor Behavior, 3, 301-312.

Gould, D., & Krane, V. (1992). The arousal-athletic performance relationship: Current status and future directions. In T.S. Horn (Ed.), Advances in sport psychology (pp. 119-141). Champaign, IL: Human Kinetics.

Goulding, M. (2009). Circuits controlling vertebrate locomotion: Moving in a new direction. Nature Reviews: Neuroscience, 10, 507-518.

Granados, C., & Wulf, G. (2007). Enhancing motor learning through dyad practice: Contributions of observation and dialogue. Research Quarterly for Exercise and Sport, 78, 197-203.

Granit, R. (1970). The basis of motor control. New York: Academic Press.

Gray, J.T., Neisser, U., Shapiro, B.A., & Kouns, S. (1991). Observational learning of ballet sequences: The role of kinematic information. Ecological Psychology, 3, 121-134.

Gray, R. (2002). "Markov at the Bat": A model of cognitive processing in baseball batters. Psychological Science, 13, 543-548.

Gray, R. (2004). Attending to the execution of a complex sensorimotor skill: Expertise differences, choking, and slumps. Journal of Experimental Psychology: Applied, 10, 42-54.

Gray, R. (2009a). A model of motor inhibition for a complex skill: Baseball batting. Journal of Experimental Psychology: Applied, 15, 91-105.

Gray, R. (2009b). How do batters use visual, auditory, and tactile information about the success of a baseball swing? Research Quarterly for Exercise and Sport, 80, 491-501.

Gray, S., Watts, S., Debicki, D., & Hore, J. (2006). Comparison of kinematics in skilled and unskilled arms of the same recreational baseball players. Journal of Sports Sciences, 24, 1183-1194.

Green, C.S., & Bavelier, D. (2003). Action video game modifies visual selective attention. Nature, 423, 534-537.

Green, C.S., & Bavelier, D. (2006). Effect of action video games on the spatial distribution of visuospatial attention. Journal of Experimental Psychology: Human Perception and Performance, 32, 1465-1478.

Green, D.M., & Swets, J.A. (1966). Signal detection theory and psychophysics. New York: Wiley.

Green, D.P., Whitehead, J., & Sugden, D.A. (1995). Practice variability and transfer of a racket skill. Perceptual and Motor Skills, 81, 1275-1281.

Green, M. (2000). "How long does it take to stop?" Methodological analysis of driver perception-brake times. Transportation Human Factors, 2, 195-216.

Greene, L.S., & Williams, H.G. (1993). Age related differences in timing control of repetitive movements: Application of the Wing-Kristofferson model. Research Quarterly for Exercise and Sport, 64, 32-38.

Greene, P.H. (1972). Problems of organization of motor systems. In R. Rosen & F.M. Snell (Eds.), Progress in theoretical biology (Vol. 2). New York: Academic Press.

Greenwald, A.G., & Schulman, H.G. (1973). On doing two things at once: Elimination of the psychological refractory period effect. Journal of Experimental Psychology, 101, 70-76.

Griffith, C.R. (1931). An experiment on learning to drive a golf ball. Athletic Journal, 11, 11-13.

Grillner, S. (1972). The role of muscle stiffness in meeting the changing postural and locomotor requirements for force development by the ankle extensors. Acta Physiologica Scandinavica, 86, 92-108.

Grillner, S. (1975). Locomotion in vertebrates: Central mechanisms and reflex interaction. Physiological Reviews, 55, 247-304.

Grillner, S. (2007). Biological pattern generation: The cellular and computational logic of networks in motion. Neuron, 52, 751-766.

Grillner, S., & Wallén, P. (1985). Central pattern generators for locomotion, with special reference to vertebrates. Annual Review of Neuroscience, 8, 233-261.

Grillner, S., & Wallén, P. (2002). Cellular bases of a vertebrate locomotion system—steering, intersegmental and segmental co-ordination and sensory control. Brain Research Reviews, 40, 92-106.

Grosjean, M., Shiffrar, M., & Knoblich, G. (2007). Fitts's law holds for action perception. Psychological Science, 18, 95-99.

Guadagnoli, M.A., Dornier, L.A., & Tandy, R.D. (1996). Optimal length for summary knowledge of results: The influence of task-related experience and complexity. Research Quarterly for Exercise and Sport, 67, 239-248.

Guadagnoli, M.A., & Kohl, R.M. (2001). Knowledge of results for motor learning: Relationship between error estimation and knowledge of results frequency. Journal of Motor Behavior, 33, 217-224.

Guadagnoli, M.A., & Lee, T.D. (2004). Challenge point: A framework for conceptualizing the effects of various practice conditions in motor learning. Journal of Motor Behavior, 36, 212-224.

Guay, M., Salmoni, A., & Lajoie, Y. (1999). The effects of different knowledge of results spacing and summarizing techniques on the acquisition of a ballistic movement. Research Quarterly for Exercise and Sport, 70, 24-32.

Guay, M., Salmoni, A., & McIlwain, J. (1992). Summary knowledge of results for skill acquisition: Beyond Lavery and Schmidt. Human Movement Science, 11, 653-673.

Guiard, Y. (1993). On Fitts's and Hooke's laws: Simple harmonic movement in upper-limb cyclical aiming. Acta Psychologica, 82, 139-159.

Guiard, Y. (1997). Fitts' law in the discrete vs. cyclical paradigm. Human Movement Science, 16, 97-131.

Gullicksen, H. (1950). Theory of mental tests. New York: Wiley.

Guthrie, E.R. (1952). The psychology of learning. New York: Harper & Row.

Haffenden, A.M., & Goodale, M.A. (1998). The effect of pictorial illusion on prehension and perception. Journal of Cognitive Neuroscience, 10, 122-136.

Haffenden, A.M., Schiff, K.C., & Goodale, M.A. (2001). The dissociation between perception and action in the Ebbinghaus illusion: Nonillusory effects of pictorial cues on grasp. Current Biology, 11, 177-181.

Hagemann, N., Strauss, B., & Cañal-Bruland, R. (2006). Training perceptual skill by orienting visual attention. Journal of Sport and Exercise Psychology, 28, 143-158.

Haggard, P. (2008). Human volition: Towards a neuroscience of will. Nature Reviews: Neuroscience, 9, 934-946.

Haggard, P., Clark, S., & Kalogeras, J. (2002). Voluntary action and conscious awareness. Nature Neuroscience, 5, 382-385.

Haggard, P., & Wing, A. (1995). Coordinated responses following mechanical perturbation of the arm during prehension. Experimental Brain Research, 102, 483-494.

Hagman, J.D. (1983). Presentation- and test-trial effects on acquisition and retention of distance and location. Journal of Experimental Psychology: Learning, Memory, and Cognition, 9, 334-345.

Hah, S., & Jagacinski, R.J. (1994). The relative dominance of schemata in a manual tracking task: Input patterns, system dynamics, and movement patterns. Journal of Motor Behavior, 26, 204-214.

Haigney, D., & Westerman, J. (2001). Mobile (cellular) phone use and driving: A critical review of research methodology. Ergonomics, 44, 132-143.

Haken, H., Kelso, J.A.S., & Bunz, H. (1985). A theoretical model of phase transitions in human hand movements. Biological Cybernetics, 51, 347-356.

Hall, K.G., Domingues, D.A., & Cavazos, R. (1994). Contextual interference effects with skilled baseball players. Perceptual and Motor Skills, 78, 835-841.

Hall, K.G., & Magill, R.A. (1995). Variability of practice and contextual interference in motor skill learning. Journal of Motor Behavior, 27, 299-309.

Hallett, M. (2007). Transcranial magnetic stimulation: A primer. Neuron, 55, 187-199.

Halverson, L.E., Roberton, M.A., & Langendorfer, S. (1982). Development of the overarm throw: Movement and ball velocity changes by seventh grade. Research Quarterly for Exercise and Sport, 53, 198-205.

Hammerton, M. (1989). Tracking. In D.H. Holding (Ed.), Human skills (2nd ed.) (pp. 171-195). Chichester: Wiley.

Hancock, G.R., Butler, M.S., & Fischman, M.G. (1995). On the problem of two-dimensional error scores: Measures and analyses of accuracy, bias, and consistency. Journal of Motor Behavior, 27, 241-250.

Hancock, P.A., Lesch, M., & Simmons, L. (2003). The distraction of phone use during a critical driving maneuver. Accident Analysis and Prevention, 35, 501-514.

Hasan, Z., & Enoka, R.M. (1985). Isometric torque-angle relationship and movement-related activity of human elbow flexors: Implications for the equilibrium-point hypothesis. Experimental Brain Research, 59, 441-450.

Hasher, L., & Zacks, R.T. (1988). Working memory, comprehension, and aging: A review and a new view. In G.H. Bower (Ed.), The psychology of learning and motivation (Vol. 22) (pp. 193-225). New York: Academic Press.

Hatze, H. (1976). Biomechanical aspects of a successful motion optimization. In P.V. Komi (Ed.), Biomechanics V-B (pp. 5-12). Baltimore: University Park Press.

Hay, J.F., & Jacoby, L.L. (1996). Separating habit and recollection: Memory slips, process dissociations, and probability matching. Journal of Experimental Psychology: Learning, Memory, and Cognition, 22, 1323-1335.

Hay, L. (1981). The effect of amplitude and accuracy requirements on movement time in children. Journal of Motor Behavior, 13, 177-186.

Hayes, S.J., Ashford, D., & Bennett, S.J. (2008). Goal-directed imitation: The means to an end. Acta Psychologica, 127, 407-415.

Haynes, J.D., & Rees, G. (2006). Decoding mental states from brain activity in humans. Nature Reviews: Neuroscience, 7, 523-534.

Haywood, K.M., & Getchell, N. (2009). Life span motor development (5th ed.). Champaign, IL: Human Kinetics.

Head, H. (1926). Aphasia and kindred disorders of speech. Cambridge: Cambridge University Press.

Healy, A.F., Wohldmann, E.L., Sutton, E.M., & Bourne, L.E. Jr. (2006). Specificity effects in training and transfer of speeded responses. Journal of Experimental Psychology: Learning, Memory, and Cognition, 32, 534-546.

Heath, M., & Elliott, D. (1999). Cerebral specialization for speech production in persons with Down syndrome. Brain and Language, 69, 193-211.

Heathcote, A., Brown, S., & Mewhort, D.J.K. (2000). The power law repealed: The case for an exponential law of practice. Psychonomic Bulletin & Review, 7, 185-207.

Hellebrandt, F.A., Houtz, S.J., Partridge, M.J., & Walters, C.E. (1956). Tonic reflexes in exercises of stress in man. American Journal of Physical Medicine, 35, 144-159.

Hellyer, S. (1963). Stimulus-response coding and amount of information as determinants of reaction time. Journal of Experimental Psychology, 65, 521-522.

Helmuth, L.L., & Ivry, R.B. (1996). When two hands are better than one: Reduced timing variability during bimanual movement. Journal of Experimental Psychology: Human Perception and Performance, 22, 278-293.

Helsen, W., Starkes, J.L., & Buekers, M.J. (1997). Effects of target eccentricity on temporal costs of point of gaze and the hand in aiming. Motor Control, 1, 161-177.

Helsen, W.F., Starkes, J.L., & van Winckel, J. (2000). Effects of a change in selection year on success of male soccer players. American Journal of Human Biology, 12, 729-735.

Hendrickson, G., & Schroeder, W.H. (1941). Transfer of training in learning to hit a submerged target. Journal of Educational Psychology, 32, 205-213.

Henry, F.M. (1953). Dynamic kinesthetic perception and adjustment. Research Quarterly, 24, 176-187.

Henry, F.M. (1959). Reliability, measurement error, and intraindividual difference. Research Quarterly, 30, 21-24.

Henry, F.M. (1961). Reaction time–movement time correlations. Perceptual and Motor Skills, 12, 63-66.

Henry, F.M. (1968). Specificity vs. generality in learning motor skill. In R.C. Brown & G.S. Kenyon (Eds.), Classical studies on physical activity (pp. 331-340). Englewood Cliffs, NJ: Prentice Hall. (Original work published in 1958)

Henry, F.M. (1975). Absolute error vs "E" in target accuracy. Journal of Motor Behavior, 7, 227-228.

Henry, F.M. (1980). Use of simple reaction time in motor programming studies: A reply to Klapp, Wyatt, and Lingo. Journal of Motor Behavior, 12, 163-168.

Henry, F.M., & Harrison, J.S. (1961). Refractoriness of a fast movement. Perceptual and Motor Skills, 13, 351-354.

Henry, F.M., & Rogers, D.E. (1960). Increased response latency for complicated movements and a "memory drum" theory of neuromotor reaction. Research Quarterly, 31, 448-458.

Hepp-Reymond, M.-C., Chakarov, V., Schulte-Mönting, J., Huethe, F., & Kristeva, R. (2009). Role of proprioception and vision in handwriting. Brain Research Bulletin, 79, 365-370.

Herrick, C.J. (1924). Origin and evolution of the cerebellum. Archives of Neurology and Psychiatry, 11, 621-652.

Herslund, M.B., & Jørgensen, N.O. (2003). Looked-but-failed-to-see-errors in traffic. Accident Analysis and Prevention, 35, 885-891.

Heuer, H. (1985). Wie wirkt mentale Übung [How does mental practice operate]? Psychologische Rundschau, 36, 191-200.

Heuer, H. (1988). Testing the invariance of relative timing: Comment on Gentner (1987). Psychological Review, 95, 552-557.

Heuer, H. (1991). Invariant relative timing in motor-program theory. In J. Fagard & P.H. Wolff (Eds.), The development of timing control and temporal organization in coordinated action (pp. 37-68). Amsterdam: Elsevier.

Heuer, H. (1996). Coordination. In H. Heuer & S.W. Keele (Eds.), Handbook of perception and action. Vol. 2: Motor skills (pp. 121-180). San Diego: Academic Press.

Heuer, H., & Schmidt, R.A. (1988). Transfer of learning among motor patterns with different relative timing. Journal of Experimental Psychology: Human Perception and Performance, 14, 241-252.

Heuer, H., Schmidt, R.A., & Ghodsian, D. (1995). Generalized motor programs for rapid bimanual tasks: A two-level multiplicative-rate model. Biological Cybernetics, 73, 343-356.

Heyes, C.M., & Foster, C.L. (2002). Motor learning by observation: Evidence from a serial reaction time task. Quarterly Journal of Experimental Psychology, 55A, 593-607.

Hick, W.E. (1952). On the rate of gain of information. Quarterly Journal of Experimental Psychology, 4, 11-26.

Hiew, C.C. (1977). Sequence effects in rule learning and conceptual generalization. American Journal of Psychology, 90, 207-218.

Higuchi, T., Takada, H., Matsuura, Y., & Imanaka, K. (2004). Visual estimation of spatial requirements for locomotion in novice wheelchair users. Journal of Experimental Psychology: Applied, 10, 55-66.

Hikosaka, O., Rand, M.K., Nakamura, K., Miyachi, S., Kitaguchi, K., Sakai, K., Lu, X., & Shimo, Y. (2002). Long-term retention of motor skill in macaque monkeys and humans. Experimental Brain Research, 147, 494-504.

Hill, L.B. (1934). A quarter century of delayed recall. Pedagogical Seminary and Journal of Genetic Psychology, 44, 231-238.

Hill, L.B. (1957). A second quarter century of delayed recall or relearning at 80. Journal of Educational Psychology, 48, 65-68.

Hill, L.B., Rejall, A.E., & Thorndike, E.L. (1913). Practice in the case of typewriting. Pedagogical Seminary, 20, 516-529.

Hills, B.L. (1980). Vision, visibility and perception in driving. Perception, 9, 183-216.

Hird, J.S., Landers, D.M., Thomas, J.R., & Horan, J.J. (1991). Physical practice is superior to mental practice in enhancing cognitive and motor task performance. Journal of Sport and Exercise Psychology, 13, 281-293.

Hodges, N.J., & Franks, I.M. (2000). Attention focusing instructions and coordination bias: Implications for learning a novel bimanual task. Human Movement Science, 19, 843-867.

Hodges, N.J., & Franks, I.M. (2001). Learning a coordination skill: Interactive effects of instruction and feedback. Research Quarterly for Exercise and Sport, 72, 132-142.

Hodges, N.J., & Franks, I.M. (2002a). Learning as a function of coordination bias: Building upon pre-practice behaviours. Human Movement Science, 21, 231-258.

Hodges, N.J., & Franks, I.M. (2002b). Modelling coaching practice: The role of instruction and demonstration. Journal of Sports Sciences, 20, 793-811.

Hodges, N.J., Hayes, S., Horn, R.R., & Williams, A.M. (2005). Changes in coordination, control and outcome as a result of extended practice on a novel motor skill. Ergonomics, 48, 1672-1685.

Hodges, N.J., & Lee, T.D. (1999). The role of augmented information prior to learning a bimanual visual-motor coordination task: Do instructions of the movement pattern facilitate learning relative to discovery learning? British Journal of Psychology, 90, 389-403.

Hoffmann, E.R., & Sheikh, I.H. (1991). Finger width corrections in Fitts' Law: Implications for speed-accuracy research. Journal of Motor Behavior, 23, 259-262.

Hoffmann, E.R., Tsang, K.K., & Mu, A. (1995). Data-entry keyboard geometry and keying movement times. Ergonomics, 38, 940-950.

Hogan, J.C., & Yanowitz, B.A. (1978). The role of verbal estimates of movement error in ballistic skill acquisition. Journal of Motor Behavior, 10, 133-138.

Holden, M.K., Dettwiler, A., Dyar, T., Niemann, G., & Bizzi, E. (2001). Retraining movement in patients with acquired brain injury using a virtual environment. Studies in Health Technology and Informatics, 81, 192-198.

Holding, D.H. (1965). Principles of training. Oxford: Pergamon.

Holding, D.H. (1970). Learning without errors. In L.E. Smith (Ed.), Psychology of motor learning (pp. 59-74). Chicago: Athletic Institute.

Holding, D.H. (1976). An approximate transfer surface. Journal of Motor Behavior, 8, 1-9.

Holding, D.H., & Macrae, A.W. (1964). Guidance, restriction, and knowledge of results. Ergonomics, 7, 289-295.

Hollands, M.A., Marple-Horvat, D.E., Henkes, S., & Rowan, A.K. (1995). Human eye movements during visually guided stepping. Journal of Motor Behavior, 27, 155-163.

Hollerbach, J.M. (1978). A study of human motor control through analysis and synthesis of handwriting. Unpublished doctoral dissertation, Massachusetts Institute of Technology, Cambridge.

Hollerbach, J.M. (1981). An oscillation theory of handwriting. Biological Cybernetics, 39, 139-156.

Hollerbach, J.M., & Flash, T. (1982). Dynamic interactions between limb segments during planar arm movement. Biological Cybernetics, 44, 67-77.

Hollingworth, H.L. (1909). The inaccuracy of movement. Archives of Psychology, 13, 1-87.

Holmes, G. (1939). The cerebellum of man. Brain, 62, 1-30.

Hommel, B., & Prinz, W. (Eds.). (1997). Theoretical issues in stimulus-response compatibility. Amsterdam: Elsevier.

Horak, M. (1992). The utility of connectionism for motor learning: A reinterpretation of contextual interference in movement schemas. Journal of Motor Behavior, 24, 58-66.

Horrey, W.J., & Wickens, C.D. (2006). The impact of cell phone conversations on driving using meta-analytic techniques. Human Factors, 48, 196-205.

Houk, J.C. (1979). Regulation of stiffness by skeletomotor reflexes. Annual Review of Physiology, 41, 99-114.

Houk, J.C., & Henneman, E. (1967). Responses of Golgi tendon organs to active contractions of the soleus muscle of the cat. Journal of Neurophysiology, 30, 466-481.

Houk, J.C., & Rymer, W.Z. (1981). Neural control of muscle length and tension. In V.B. Brooks (Ed.), Handbook of physiology: Section 1: The nervous system. Vol. 2. Motor control (pp. 257-323). Bethesda, MD: American Physiological Society.

Howard, L.A., & Tipper, S.P. (1997). Hand deviations away from visual cues: Indirect evidence for inhibition. Experimental Brain Research, 113, 144-152.

Howell, M.L. (1953). Influence of emotional tension on speed of reaction and movement. Research Quarterly, 24, 22-32.

Howell, M.L. (1956). Use of force-time graphs for performance analysis in facilitating motor learning. Research Quarterly, 27, 12-22.

Hoyt, D.F., & Taylor, C.R. (1981). Gait and the energetics of locomotion in horses. Science, 292, 239-240.

Huang, V.S., Shadmehr, R., & Diedrichsen, J. (2008). Active learning: Learning a motor skill without a coach. Journal of Neurophysiology, 100, 879-887.

Hubbard, A.W., & Seng, C.N. (1954). Visual movements of batters. Research Quarterly, 25, 42-57.

Huet, M., Camachon, C., Fernandez, L., Jacobs, D.M., & Montagne, G. (2009). Self-controlled concurrent feedback and the education of attention towards perceptual invariants. Human Movement Science, 28, 450-467.

Hughes, C.M.L., & Franz, E.A. (2008). Goal-related planning constraints in bimanual grasping and placing of objects. Experimental Brain Research, 188, 541-550.

Hull, C.L. (1943). Principles of behavior. New York: Appleton-Century-Crofts.

Hurley, S.R., & Lee, T.D. (2006). The influence of augmented feedback and prior learning on the acquisition of a new bimanual coordination pattern. Human Movement Science, 25, 339-348.

Huxley, H.E. (1969). Structural organization and the contraction mechanism in striated muscle. In S. Devons (Ed.), Biology and the physical sciences (pp. 114-138). New York: Columbia University Press.

Hyman, I.E. Jr., Boss, S.M., Wise, B.M., McKenzie, K.E., & Caggiano, J.M. (2010). Did you see the unicycling clown? Inattentional blindness while walking and talking on a cell phone. Applied Cognitive Psychology, 24, 597-607.

Hyman, R. (1953). Stimulus information as a determinant of reaction time. Journal of Experimental Psychology, 45, 188-196.

Imanaka, K., & Abernethy, B. (1991). The mediating effect of learning on the interference between location and distance recall from motor short-term memory. Acta Psychologica, 77, 153-165.

Imanaka, K., & Abernethy, B. (1992). Interference between location and distance information in motor short-term memory: The respective roles of direct kinesthetic signals and abstract codes. Journal of Motor Behavior, 24, 274-280.

Imanaka, K., Abernethy, B., & Quek, J.-J. (1998). The locus of distance-location interference in movement reproduction: Do we know any more 25 years on? In J.P. Piek (Ed.), Motor behavior and human skill (pp. 29-55). Champaign, IL: Human Kinetics.

Immink, M.A., & Wright, D.L. (1998). Contextual interference: A response planning account. Quarterly Journal of Experimental Psychology, 51A, 735-754.

Immink, M.A., & Wright, D.L. (2001). Motor programming during practice conditions high and low in contextual interference. Journal of Experimental Psychology: Human Perception and Performance, 27, 423-437.

Irion, A.L. (1948). The relation of "set" to retention. Psychological Review, 55, 336-341.

Irion, A.L. (1966). A brief history of research on the acquisition of skill. In E.A. Bilodeau (Ed.), Acquisition of skill (pp. 1-46). New York: Academic Press.

Irwin, M., Fitzgerald, C., & Berg, W.P. (2000). Effect of the intensity of wireless telephone conversations on reaction time in a braking response. Perceptual and Motor Skills, 90, 1130-1134.

Ishigami, Y., & Klein, R.M. (2009). Is a hands-free phone safer than a handheld phone? Journal of Safety Research, 40, 157-164.

Ivry, R., & Corcos, D.M. (1993). Slicing the variability pie: Component analysis of coordination and motor dysfunction. In K.M. Newell & D.M. Corcos (Eds.), Variability and motor control (pp. 415-447). Champaign, IL: Human Kinetics.

Ivry, R.B., & Keele, S.W. (1989). Timing functions of the cerebellum. Journal of Cognitive Neuroscience, 1, 136-152.

Ivry, R.B., Keele, S.W., & Diener, H.C. (1988). Dissociation of the lateral and medial cerebellum in movement timing and movement execution. Experimental Brain Research, 73, 167-180.

Ivry, R.B., Richardson, T.C., & Helmuth, L.L. (2002). Improved temporal stability in multi-effector movements. Journal of Experimental Psychology: Human Perception and Performance, 28, 72-92.

Jabusch, H.-C., Alpers, H., Kopiez, R., Vauth, H., & Altenmüller, E. (2009). The influence of practice on the development of motor skills in pianists: A longitudinal study in a selected motor task. Human Movement Science, 28, 74-84.

Jackson, G.M., German, K., & Peacock, K. (2002). Functional coupling between the limbs during bimanual reach-to-grasp movements. Human Movement Science, 21, 317-333.

Jackson, G.M., Jackson, S.R., & Kritikos, A. (1999). Attention for action: Coordinating bimanual reach-to-grasp movements. British Journal of Psychology, 90, 247-270.

Jackson, R.C., & Farrow, D. (2005). Implicit perceptual training: How, when, and why? Human Movement Science, 24, 308-325.

Jacoby, L.L. (1978). On interpreting the effects of repetition: Solving a problem versus remembering a solution. Journal of Verbal Learning and Verbal Behavior, 17, 649-667.

Jacoby, L.L., & Dallas, M. (1981). On the relationship between autobiographical memory and perceptual learning. Journal of Experimental Psychology: General, 110, 306-340.

Jacoby, L.L., Ste-Marie, D., & Toth, J.P. (1993). Redefining automaticity: Unconscious influences, awareness, and control. In A. Baddeley & L. Weiskrantz (Eds.), Attention: Selection, awareness, and control: A tribute to Donald Broadbent (pp. 261-282). Oxford: Clarendon Press.

Jagacinski, R.J., & Flach, J.M. (2003). Control theory for humans: Quantitative approaches to modeling performance. Mahwah, NJ: Erlbaum.

Jagacinski, R.J., & Hah, S. (1988). Progression-regression effects in tracking repeated patterns. Journal of Experimental Psychology: Human Perception and Performance, 14, 77-88.

Jagacinski, R.J., & Monk, D.L. (1985). Fitts' law in two dimensions with hand and head movements. Journal of Motor Behavior, 17, 77-95.

Jakobson, L.S., & Goodale, M.A. (1991). Factors affecting higher-order movement planning: A kinematic analysis of human prehension. Experimental Brain Research, 86, 199-208.

James, W. (1890). The principles of psychology (Vol. 1). New York: Holt.

Jami, L. (1992). Golgi tendon organs in mammalian skeletal muscle: Functional properties and central actions. Physiological Reviews, 72, 623-666.

Jamieson, B.A., & Rogers, W.A. (2000). Age-related effects of blocked and random practice schedules on learning a new technology. Journal of Gerontology: Psychological Sciences, 55B, P343-P353.

Janelle, C.M. (1999). Ironic mental processes in sport: Implications for sport psychologists. Sport Psychologist, 13, 210-220.

Janelle, C.M., Barba, D.A., Frehlich, S.G., Tennant, L.K., & Cauraugh, J.H. (1997). Maximizing performance feedback effectiveness through videotape replay and a self-controlled learning environment. Research Quarterly for Exercise and Sport, 68, 269-279.

Janelle, C.M., Champenoy, J.D., Coombes, S.A., & Mousseau, M.B. (2003). Mechanisms of attentional cueing during observational learning to facilitate skill acquisition. Journal of Sports Sciences, 21, 825-838.

Janelle, C.M., Kim, J., & Singer, R.N. (1995). Subject-controlled performance feedback and learning of a closed motor skill. Perceptual and Motor Skills, 81, 627-634.

Janelle, C.M., Singer, R.N., & Williams, A.M. (1999). External distraction and attentional narrowing: Visual search evidence. Journal of Sport and Exercise Psychology, 21, 70-91.

Janis, I., Defares, P., & Grossman, P. (1983). Hypervigilant reactions to threat. In H. Selye (Ed.), Selye's guide to stress research (pp. 1-43). New York: Van Nostrand Reinhold.

Janssen, L., Beuting, M., Meulenbroek, R., & Steenbergen, B. (2009). Combined effects of planning and execution constraints on bimanual task performance. Experimental Brain Research, 192, 61-73.

Jaric, S., & Latash, M.L. (2000). The equilibrium-point hypothesis is still doing fine. Human Movement Science, 19, 933-938.

Jarus, T., & Goverover, Y. (1999). Effects of contextual interference and age on acquisition, retention, and transfer of motor skill. Perceptual and Motor Skills, 88, 437-447.

Jasiewicz, J., & Simmons, R.W. (1996). Response timing accuracy as a function of movement velocity and distance. Journal of Motor Behavior, 28, 224-232.

Jastrow, J. (1906). The subconscious. Boston: Houghton-Mifflin.

Jeannerod, M. (1981). Intersegmental coordination during reaching at natural visual objects. In J. Long & A. Baddeley (Eds.), Attention and performance IX (pp. 153-169). Hillsdale, NJ: Erlbaum.

Jeannerod, M. (1984). The timing of natural prehension movements. Journal of Motor Behavior, 16, 235-254.

Jeannerod, M. (1996). Reaching and grasping: Parallel specification of visuomotor channels. In H. Heuer & S.W. Keele (Eds.), Handbook of perception and action. Vol. 2: Motor skills (pp. 405-460). San Diego: Academic Press.

Jeannerod, M. (1997). The cognitive neuroscience of action. Oxford: Blackwell.

Jeannerod, M. (2001). Neural simulation of action: A unifying mechanism for motor cognition. NeuroImage, 14, 103-109.

Jeannerod, M., & Frak, V. (1999). Mental imaging of motor activity in humans. Current Opinion in Neurobiology, 9, 735-739.

Jeannerod, M., & Jacob, P. (2005). Visual cognition: A new look at the two-visual systems model. Neuropsychologia, 43, 301-312.

Jeannerod, M., & Marteniuk, R.G. (1992). Functional characteristics of prehension: From data to artificial neural networks. In L. Proteau & D. Elliott (Eds.), Vision and motor control (pp. 197-232). Amsterdam: Elsevier.

Jeeves, M.A. (1961). Changes in performance at a serial reaction task under conditions of advance and delay of information. Ergonomics, 4, 329-338.

Jeka, J.J., & Kelso, J.A.S. (1989). The dynamic pattern approach to coordinated behavior: A tutorial review. In S.A. Wallace (Ed.), Perspectives on the coordination of movement (pp. 3-45). Amsterdam: Elsevier.

Jenison, R.L. (1997). On acoustic information for motion. Ecological Psychology, 9, 131-151.

Jervis, C., Bennett, K., Thomas, J., Lim, S., & Castiello, U. (1999). Semantic category interference effects upon the reach-to-grasp movement. Neuropsychologia, 37, 857-868.

Johansson, R.S., & Flanagan, J.R. (2009). Coding and use of tactile signals from the fingertips in object manipulation tasks. Nature Reviews: Neuroscience, 10, 345-359.

Johansson, R.S., & Westling, G. (1984). Roles of glabrous skin receptors and sensorimotor memory in automatic control of precision grip when lifting rougher or more slippery objects. Experimental Brain Research, 56, 550-564.

Johansson, R.S., & Westling, G. (1988). Programmed and triggered actions to rapid load changes during precision grip. Experimental Brain Research, 71, 72-86.

Johansson, R.S., & Westling, G. (1990). Tactile afferent signals in the control of precision grip. In M. Jeannerod (Ed.), Attention and performance XIII (pp. 677-713). Hillsdale, NJ: Erlbaum.

Johansson, R.S., & Westling, G. (1991). Afferent signals during manipulative tasks in man. In O. Franzen & J. Westman (Eds.), Somatosensory mechanisms (pp. 25-48). London: Macmillan.

Johnson, K.A., Bennett, J.E., Georgiou, N., Bradshaw, J.L., Chiu, E., Cunnington, R., & Iansek, R. (2000). Bimanual co-ordination in Huntington's disease. Experimental Brain Research, 134, 483-489.

Jones, C.M., & Miles, T.R. (1978). Use of advance cues in predicting the flight of a lawn tennis ball. Journal of Human Movement Studies, 4, 231-235.

Jones, L.L., & French, K.E. (2007). Effects of contextual interference on acquisition and retention of three volleyball skills. Perceptual and Motor Skills, 105, 883-890.

Jones, M.B. (1962). Practice as a process of simplification. Psychological Review, 69, 274-294.

Jones, M.B. (1966). Individual differences. In E.A. Bilodeau (Ed.), Acquisition of skill (pp. 109-146). New York: Academic Press.

Jones, S.K. (1993). A modular approach to individual differences in skill and coordination. In J.L. Starkes & F. Allard (Eds.), Cognitive issues in motor expertise (pp. 273-293). Amsterdam: Elsevier.

Jonides, J., Naveh-Benjamin, M., & Palmer, J. (1985). Assessing automaticity. Acta Psychologica, 60, 157-171.

Jordan, M.I. (1995). The organization of action sequences: Evidence from a relearning task. Journal of Motor Behavior, 27, 179-192.

Judd, C.H. (1908). The relation of special training to general intelligence. Educational Review, 36, 28-42.

Kahneman, D. (1973). Attention and effort. Englewood Cliffs, NJ: Prentice Hall.

Kahol, K., Satava, R.M., Ferrara, J., & Smith, M.L. (2009). Effect of short-term pretrial practice on surgical proficiency in simulated environments: A randomized trial of the "preoperative warm-up" effect. Journal of the American College of Surgeons, 208, 255-268.

Kandel, E.R., Schwartz, J.H., & Jessell, J.M. (Eds.). (2000). Principles of neural science. New York, McGraw-Hill.

Kao, J.C., Ringenbach, S.D., & Martin, P.E. (2003). Gait transitions are not dependent on changes in intralimb coordination variability. Journal of Motor Behavior, 35, 211-214.

Karlin, L., & Kestenbaum, R. (1968). Effects of number of alternatives on the psychological refractory period. Quarterly Journal of Experimental Psychology, 20, 167-178.

Karwowski, W. (Ed.). (2001). International encyclopedia of ergonomics and human factors. London: Taylor & Francis.

Keele, S.W. (1968). Movement control in skilled motor performance. Psychological Bulletin, 70, 387-403.

Keele, S.W. (1973). Attention and human performance. Pacific Palisades, CA: Goodyear.

Keele, S.W. (1981). Behavioral analysis of movement. In V. Brooks (Ed.), Handbook of physiology: Section 1: The nervous system. Vol. 2. Motor control, part 2 (pp. 1391-1414). Baltimore: American Physiological Society.

Keele, S.W. (1986). Motor control. In K.R. Boff, L. Kaufman, & J.P. Thomas (Eds.), Handbook of perception and performance (pp. 30.1-30.60). New York: Wiley.

Keele, S.W. (1998). Programming or planning conceptions of motor control speak to different phenomena than dynamical systems conceptions. In J.P. Piek (Ed.), Motor behavior and human skill (pp. 403-405). Champaign, IL: Human Kinetics.

Keele, S.W., Cohen, A., & Ivry, R. (1990). Motor programs: Concepts and issues. In M. Jeannerod (Ed.), Attention and performance XIII (pp. 77-110). Hillsdale, NJ: Erlbaum.

Keele, S.W., & Ells, J.G. (1972). Memory characteristics of kinesthetic information. Journal of Motor Behavior, 4, 127-134.

Keele, S.W., & Hawkins, H.L. (1982). Explorations of individual differences relevant to high level skill. Journal of Motor Behavior, 14, 3-23.

Keele, S.W., & Ivry, R.B. (1987). Modular analysis of timing in motor skill. In G.H. Bower (Ed.), The psychology of learning and motivation (Vol. 21) (pp. 183-228). New York: Academic Press.

Keele, S.W., Ivry, R., & Pokorny, R.A. (1987). Force control and its relation to timing. Journal of Motor Behavior, 19, 96-114.

Keele, S.W., Jennings, P., Jones, S., Caulton, D., & Cohen, A. (1995). On the modularity of sequence representation. Journal of Motor Behavior, 27, 17-30.

Keele, S.W., Pokorny, R.A., Corcos, D.M., & Ivry, R. (1985). Do perception and motor production share common timing mechanisms: A correlational analysis. Acta Psychologica, 60, 173-191.

Keele, S.W., & Posner, M.I. (1968). Processing of visual feedback in rapid movements. Journal of Experimental Psychology, 77, 155-158.

Keetch, K.M., & Lee, T.D. (2007). The effect of self-regulated and experimenter-imposed practice schedules on motor learning for tasks of varying difficulty. Research Quarterly for Exercise and Sport, 78, 476-486.

Keetch, K.M., Lee, T.D., & Schmidt, R.A. (2008). Especial skills: Specificity embedded within generality. Journal of Sport and Exercise Psychology, 30, 723-736.

Keetch, K.M., Schmidt, R.A., Lee, T.D., & Young, D.E. (2005). Especial skills: Their emergence with massive amounts of practice. Journal of Experimental Psychology: Human Perception and Performance, 31, 970-978.

Keisler, A., & Willingham, D.T. (2007). Non-declarative sequence learning does not show savings in relearning. Human Movement Science, 26, 247-256.

Keller, F.S. (1958). The phantom plateau. Journal of the Experimental Analysis of Behavior, 1, 1-13.

Kellogg, R.T. (2003). Cognitive psychology (2nd ed.). Thousand Oaks, CA: Sage.

Kelly, J.P. (1991). The sense of balance. In E.R. Kandel, J.H. Schwartz, & T.M. Jessell (Eds.), Principles of neural science (3rd ed.) (pp. 500-511). Amsterdam: Elsevier.

Kelly, S.W., Burton, A.M., Riedel, B., & Lynch, E. (2003). Sequence learning by action and observation: Evidence for separate mechanisms. British Journal of Psychology, 94, 355-372.

Kelso, B.A. (1984). The effects of extended practice on aiming movements in terms of Fitts' Law. Unpublished master's thesis, York University.

Kelso, J.A.S. (1977). Motor control mechanisms underlying human movement reproduction. Journal of Experimental Psychology: Human Perception and Performance, 3, 529-543.

Kelso, J.A.S. (1982). Concepts and issues in human motor behavior: Coming to grips with the jargon. In J.A.S. Kelso (Ed.), Human motor behavior: An introduction (pp. 21-58). Hillsdale, NJ: Erlbaum.

Kelso, J.A.S. (1984). Phase transitions and critical behavior in human bimanual coordination. American Journal of Physiology: Regulatory, Integrative and Comparative Physiology, 15, R1000-R1004.

Kelso, J.A.S. (1992). Theoretical concepts and strategies for understanding perceptual-motor skill: From information capacity in closed systems to self-organization in open, nonequilibrium systems. Journal of Experimental Psychology: General, 121, 260-261.

Kelso, J.A.S. (1995). Dynamic patterns: The self-organization of brain and behavior. Cambridge, MA: MIT Press.

Kelso, J.A.S. (2008). Haken-Kelso-Bunz model. Scholarpedia, 3(10), 1612.

Kelso, J.A.S., Buchanan, J.J., & Wallace, S.A. (1991). Order parameters for the neural organization of single, multijoint limb movement patterns. Experimental Brain Research, 85, 432-444.

Kelso, J.A.S., & Engstrøm, D.A. (2005). The complementary nature. Cambridge, MA: MIT Press.

Kelso, J.A.S., Holt, K.G., & Flatt, A.E. (1980). The role of proprioception in the perception and control of human movement: Toward a theoretical reassessment. Perception & Psychophysics, 28, 45-52.

Kelso, J.A.S., & Jeka, J.J. (1992). Symmetry breaking dynamics of human multilimb coordination. Journal of Experimental Psychology: Human Perception and Performance, 18, 645-668.

Kelso, J.A.S., Putnam, C.A., & Goodman, D. (1983). On the space-time structure of human interlimb coordination. Quarterly Journal of Experimental Psychology, 35A, 347-375.

Kelso, J.A.S., Scholz, J.P., & Schöner, G. (1986). Nonequilibrium phase transitions in coordinated biological motion: Critical fluctuations. Physics Letters A, 118, 279-284.

Kelso, J.A.S., Scholz, J.P., & Schöner, G. (1988). Dynamics governs switching among patterns of coordination in biological movement. Physics Letters A, 134, 8-12.

Kelso, J.A.S., Southard, D.L., & Goodman, D. (1979). On the coordination of two-handed movements. Journal of Experimental Psychology: Human Perception and Performance, 5, 229-238.

Kelso, J.A.S., & Stelmach, G.E. (1976). Central and peripheral mechanisms in motor control. In G.E. Stelmach (Ed.), Motor control: Issues and trends (pp. 1-40). New York: Academic Press.

Kelso, J.A.S., Stelmach, G.E., & Wannamaker, W.M. (1976). The continuing saga of the nerve compression block technique. Journal of Motor Behavior, 8, 155-160.

Kelso, J.A.S., Tuller, B., Vatikiotis-Bateson, E., & Fowler, C.A. (1984). Functionally specific articulatory cooperation following jaw perturbations during speech: Evidence for coordinative structures. Journal of Experimental Psychology: Human Perception and Performance, 10, 812-832.

Kelso, J.A.S., & Zanone, P.-G. (2002). Coordination dynamics of learning and transfer across different effector systems. Journal of Experimental Psychology: Human Perception and Performance, 28, 776-797.

Kennerley, S.W., Diedrichsen, J., Hazeltine, E., Semjen, A., & Ivry, R.B. (2002). Callosotomy patients exhibit temporal uncoupling during continuous bimanual movements. Nature Neuroscience, 5, 376-381.

Keogh, J., & Sugden, D. (1985). Movement skill development. New York: Macmillan.

Kerlinger, F.N. (1973). Foundations of behavioral research (2nd ed.). New York: Holt, Rinehart & Winston.

Kernodle, M.W., & Carlton, L.G. (1992). Information feedback and the learning of multiple-degree-of-freedom activities. Journal of Motor Behavior, 24, 187-196.

Kerr, B. (1973). Processing demands during mental operations. Memory & Cognition, 1, 401-412.

Kerr, B. (1975). Processing demands during movement. Journal of Motor Behavior, 7, 15-27.

Kerr, B., Condon, S.M., & McDonald, L.A. (1985). Cognitive spatial processing and the regulation of posture. Journal of Experimental Psychology: Human Perception and Performance, 11, 617-622.

Kerr, R. (1973). Movement time in an underwater environment. Journal of Motor Behavior, 5, 175-178.

Kerr, R. (1978). Diving, adaptation, and Fitts Law. Journal of Motor Behavior, 10, 255-260.

Kerr, R., & Booth, B. (1977). Skill acquisition in elementary school children and schema theory. In D.M. Landers & R.W. Christina (Eds.), Psychology of motor behavior and sport—1976 (Vol. 2). Champaign, IL: Human Kinetics.

Kerr, R., & Booth, B. (1978). Specific and varied practice of motor skill. Perceptual and Motor Skills, 46, 395-401.

Khan, M.A., Franks, I.M., Elliott, D., Lawrence, G.P., Chua, R., Bernier, P.M., Hansen, S., & Weeks, D.J. (2006). Inferring online and offline processing of visual feedback in target-directed movements from kinematic data. Neuroscience & Biobehavioral Reviews, 30, 1106-1121.

Klapp, S.T. (1977a). Reaction time analysis of programmed control. Exercise and Sport Sciences Reviews, 5, 231-253.

Klapp, S.T. (1977b). Response programming, as assessed by reaction time, does not establish commands for particular muscles. Journal of Motor Behavior, 9, 301-312.

Klapp, S.T. (1979). Doing two things at once: The role of temporal compatibility. Memory & Cognition, 7, 375-381.

Klapp, S.T. (1981). Temporal compatibility in dual motor tasks II: Simultaneous articulation and hand movements. Memory & Cognition, 9, 398-401.

Klapp, S.T. (1995). Motor response programming during simple and choice reaction time: The role of practice. Journal of Experimental Psychology: Human Perception and Performance, 21, 1015-1027.

Klapp, S.T. (1996). Reaction time analysis of central motor control. In H.N. Zelaznik (Ed.), Advances in motor learning and control (pp. 13-35). Champaign, IL: Human Kinetics.

Klapp, S.T., & Erwin, C.I. (1976). Relation between programming time and duration of the response being programmed. Journal of Experimental Psychology: Human Perception and Performance, 2, 591-598.

Klapp, S.T., Hill, M.D., Tyler, J.G., Martin, Z.E., Jagacinski, R.J., & Jones, M.R. (1985). On marching to two different drummers: Perceptual aspects of the difficulties. Journal of Experimental Psychology: Human Perception and Performance, 11, 814-827.

Klapp, S.T., Martin, Z.E., McMillan, G.G., & Brock, D.T. (1987). Whole-task and part-task training in dual motor tasks. In L.S. Mark, J.S. Warm, & R.L. Huston (Eds.), Ergonomics and human factors (pp. 125-130). New York: Springer-Verlag.

Klapp, S.T., Nelson, J.M., & Jagacinski, R.J. (1998). Can people tap concurrent bimanual rhythms independently? Journal of Motor Behavior, 30, 301-322.

Klavora, P. (1977). An attempt to derive inverted-U curves based on the relationship between anxiety and athletic performance. In D.M. Landers & R.W. Christina (Eds.), Psychology of motor behavior and sport—1976 (pp. 369-377). Champaign, IL: Human Kinetics.

Klein, R.M. (2000). Inhibition of return. Trends in Cognitive Sciences, 4, 138-147.

Klein, R.M. (2004). Orienting and inhibition of return. In M.S. Gazzaniga (Ed.), The cognitive neurosciences (3rd ed.) (pp. 545-560). Cambridge, MA: MIT Press.

Klein, R., Levy, S., & McCabe, J. (1984). The parameter preferences of acquired motor programs for rapid, discrete movements: I. Transfer of training. Memory & Cognition, 12, 374-379.

Kleine, D. (1982). Psychomotorik und Intelligenz. Theoretische und empirische Untersuchungen unter Berücksichtigung von Übungseffekten im Psychomotorikberich [Psychomotor skills and intelligence. Theoretical and empirical studies with consideration of training effects in psychomotor information]. Unpublished doctoral dissertation, Free University of Berlin.

Kleine, D. (1985). Psychomotor performance and intellectual abilities. An analysis of the changes in the relationship during practice. Paper presented at the VIth International Congress for Sport Psychology, Copenhagen.

Klemmer, E.T. (1956). Time uncertainty in simple reaction time. Journal of Experimental Psychology, 51, 179-184.

Knapp, B. (1963). Skill in sport: The attainment of proficiency. London: Routledge & Kegan Paul.

Kohl, R.M., & Fisicaro, S.A. (1995). Imaging goal-directed movement. Research Quarterly for Exercise and Sport, 66, 17-31.

Konczak, J., vander Velden, H., & Jaeger, L. (2009). Learning to play the violin: Motor control by freezing, not freeing degrees of freedom. Journal of Motor Behavior, 41, 243-252.

Konzem, P.B. (1987). Extended practice and patterns of bimanual interference. Unpublished doctoral dissertation, University of Southern California.

Kornblum, S., Hasbroucq, T., & Osman, A. (1990). Dimensional overlap: Cognitive basis for stimulus-response compatibility—a model and taxonomy. Psychological Review, 97, 253-270.

Kornell, N., & Bjork, R.A. (2008). Learning concepts and categories: Is spacing the "enemy of induction"? Psychological Science, 19, 585-592.

Kostrubiec, V., & Zanone, P.-G. (2002). Memory dynamics: Distance between the new task and existing behavioural patterns affects learning and interference in bimanual coordination in humans. Neuroscience Letters, 331, 193-197.

Kots, Y.M. (1977). The organization of voluntary movement: Neurophysiological mechanisms. New York: Plenum Press.

Koustanaï, A., Boloix, E., Van Elslande, P., & Bastien, C. (2008). Statistical analysis of "looked-but-failed-to-see" accidents: Highlighting the involvement of two distinct mechanisms. Accident Analysis and Prevention, 40, 461-469.

Kovacs, A.J., Buchanan, J.J., & Shea, C.H. (2009). Bimanual 1:1 with 90° continuous relative phase: Difficult or easy! Experimental Brain Research, 193, 129-136.

Kovacs, A.J., Buchanan, J.J., & Shea, C.H. (2010). Impossible is nothing: 5:3 and 4:3 multi-frequency bimanual coordination. Experimental Brain Research, 201, 249-259.

Krakauer, J., & Ghez, C. (2000). Voluntary movement. In E.R. Kandel, J.H. Schwartz, & T.M. Jessell (Eds.), Principles of neural science (pp. 756-799). New York: McGraw-Hill.

Krakauer, J.W., & Shadmehr, R. (2006). Consolidation of motor memory. Trends in Neurosciences, 29, 58-64.

Krist, H., Fieberg, E.L., & Wilkening, F. (1993). Intuitive physics in action and judgment: The development of knowledge about projectile motion. Journal of Experimental Psychology: Learning, Memory, and Cognition, 19, 952-966.

Kucera, H., & Francis, W.N. (1967). Computational analysis of present-day American English. Providence, RI: Brown University Press.

Kugler, P.N., Kelso, J.A.S., & Turvey, M.T. (1980). On the concept of coordinative structures as dissipative structures: I. Theoretical lines of convergence. In G.E. Stelmach & J. Requin (Eds.), Tutorials in motor behavior (pp. 3-47). Amsterdam: Elsevier.

Kugler, P.N., & Turvey, M.T. (1987). Information, natural law, and the self-assembly of rhythmic movement. Hillsdale, NJ: Erlbaum.

Kuhn, T.S. (1962). The structure of scientific revolutions. Chicago: University of Chicago Press.

Kunde, W., & Weigelt, M. (2005). Goal congruency in bimanual object manipulation. Journal of Experimental Psychology: Human Perception and Performance, 31, 145-156.

Kurtz, S., & Lee, T.D. (2003). Part and whole perceptual-motor practice of a polyrhythm. Neuroscience Letters, 338, 205-208.

Kvålseth, T.O. (1980). An alternative to Fitts' law. Bulletin of the Psychonomic Society, 16, 371-373.

Kveraga, K., Boucher, L., & Hughes, H.C. (2002). Saccades operate in violation of Hick's law. Experimental Brain Research, 146, 307-314.

Kyllo, L.B., & Landers, D.M. (1995). Goal setting in sport and exercise: A research synthesis to resolve the controversy. Journal of Sport and Exercise Psychology, 17, 117-137.

Laabs, G.J. (1973). Retention characteristics of different reproduction cues in motor short-term memory. Journal of Experimental Psychology, 100, 168-177.

Laban, R. (1956). Principles of dance and movement notation. London: MacDonald and Evans.

LaBerge, D. (1973). Identification of two components of the time to switch attention: A test of a serial and a parallel model of attention. In S. Kornblum (Ed.), Attention and performance IV (pp. 71-85). New York: Academic Press.

Lackner, J.R., & DiZio, P.A. (2000). Aspects of body self-calibration. Trends in Cognitive Sciences, 4, 279-288.

Laguna, P.L. (2008). Task complexity and sources of task-related information during the observational learning process. Journal of Sports Sciences, 26, 1097-1113.

Lai, Q., & Shea, C.H. (1998). Generalized motor program (GMP) learning: Effects of reduced frequency of knowledge of results and practice variability. Journal of Motor Behavior, 30, 51-59.

Lai, Q., & Shea, C.H. (1999). Bandwidth knowledge of results enhances generalized motor program learning. Research Quarterly for Exercise and Sport, 70, 79-83.

Lai, Q., Shea, C.H., Wulf, G., & Wright, D.L. (2000). Optimizing generalized motor program and parameter learning. Research Quarterly for Exercise and Sport, 71, 10-24.

Lam, W.K., Maxwell, J.P., & Masters, R.S.W. (2009). Analogy versus explicit learning of a modified basketball shooting task. Performance and kinematic outcomes. Journal of Sports Sciences, 27, 179-191.

Lamble, D., Kauranen, T., Laasko, M., & Summala, H. (1999). Cognitive load and detection thresholds in car following situations: Safety implications for using mobile (cellular) telephones while driving. Accident Analysis and Prevention, 31, 617-623.

Landin, D., & Hebert, E.P. (1997). A comparison of three practice schedules along the contextual interference continuum. Research Quarterly for Exercise and Sport, 68, 357-361.

Lang, P.J. (1974). Learned control of human heart rate in a computer directed environment. In P.A. Obrist, A.H. Black, J. Brenner, & L.V. DiCara (Eds.), Cardiovascular psychophysiology: Current issues in response mechanisms, biofeedback, and methodology (pp. 392-405). Chicago: Aldine.

Langer, E.J. (1989). Mindfulness. New York: Addison-Wesley.

Langfeld, H.S. (1915). Facilitation and inhibition of motor impulses: A study in simultaneous and alternating finger movements. Psychological Review, 22, 453-478.

Langolf, G.D., Chaffin, D.B., & Foulke, J.A. (1976). An investigation of Fitts' law using a wide range of movement amplitudes. Journal of Motor Behavior, 8, 113-128.

Lashley, K.S. (1917). The accuracy of movement in the absence of excitation from the moving organ. American Journal of Physiology, 43, 169-194.

Lashley, K.S. (1942). The problem of cerebral organization in vision. In J. Cattell (Ed.), Biological symposia. Vol. VII. Visual mechanisms (pp. 301-322). Lancaster, PA: Jaques Cattell Press.

Lashley, K.S. (1951). The problem of serial order in behavior. In L.A. Jeffress (Ed.), Cerebral mechanisms in behavior: The Hixon symposium (pp. 112-136). New York: Wiley.

Laszlo, J.I. (1967). Training of fast tapping with reduction of kinaesthetic, tactile, visual and auditory sensations. Quarterly Journal of Experimental Psychology, 19, 344-349.

Laszlo, J.I., & Bairstow, P.J. (1979). The compression-block technique: A reply to Chambers and Schumsky (1978). Journal of Motor Behavior, 11, 283-284.

Latash, M.L. (1993). Control of human movement. Champaign, IL: Human Kinetics.

Latash, M.L. (1999). Mirror writing: Learning, transfer, and implications for internal inverse models. Journal of Motor Behavior, 31, 107-111.

Latash, M.L. (2008a). Evolution of motor control: From reflexes and motor programs to the equilibrium-point hypothesis. Journal of Human Kinetics, 19, 3-24.

Latash, M.L. (2008b). Neurophysiological basis of movement (2nd ed.). Champaign, IL: Human Kinetics.

Latash, M.L., & Gutman, S.R. (1993). Variability of fast single-joint movements and the equilibrium-point hypothesis. In K.M. Newell & D.M. Corcos (Eds.), Variability and motor control (pp. 157-182). Champaign, IL: Human Kinetics.

Latash, M.L., Scholz, J.P., & Schöner, G. (2007). Toward a new theory of motor synergies. Motor Control, 11, 276-308.

Latash, M.L., & Zatsiorsky, V.M. (Eds.). (2001). Classics in movement science. Champaign, IL: Human Kinetics.

Lavery, J.J. (1962). Retention of simple motor skills as a function of type of knowledge of results. Canadian Journal of Psychology, 16, 300-311.

Lavery, J.J., & Suddon, F.H. (1962). Retention of simple motor skills as a function of the number of trials by which KR is delayed. Perceptual and Motor Skills, 15, 231-237.

Lay, B.S., Sparrow, W.A., & O'Dwyer, N.J. (2005). The metabolic and cognitive energy costs of stabilising a high-energy interlimb coordination task. Human Movement Science, 24, 833-848.

Leavitt, J.L. (1979). Cognitive demands of skating and stick-handling in ice hockey. Canadian Journal of Applied Sports Science, 4, 46-55.

Lederman, S.J., & Klatzky, R.L. (1997). Haptic aspects of motor control. In M. Jeannerod (Ed.), Handbook of neuropsychology (Vol. 11) (pp. 131-148). Amsterdam: Elsevier.

Lederman, S.J., & Klatzky, R.L. (2009). Haptic perception: A tutorial. Attention, Perception, & Psychophysics, 71, 1439-1459.

Lee, D.N. (1976). A theory of visual control of braking based on information about time-to-collision. Perception, 5, 437-459.

Lee, D.N. (1980). Visuo-motor coordination in space-time. In G.E. Stelmach & J. Requin (Eds.), Tutorials in motor behavior (pp. 281-295). Amsterdam: North-Holland.

Lee, D.N. (1990). Getting around with light or sound. In R. Warren & A.H. Wertheim (Eds.), Perception and control of self-motion (pp. 487-505). Hillsdale, NJ: Erlbaum.

Lee, D.N. (1998). Guiding movement by coupling taus. Ecological Psychology, 10, 221-250.

Lee, D.N. (2009). General tau theory: Evolution to date. Perception, 38, 837-850.

Lee, D.N., & Aronson, E. (1974). Visual proprioceptive control of standing in human infants. Perception & Psychophysics, 15, 529-532.

Lee, D.N., Georgopolous, A.P., Clark, M.J.O., Craig, C.M., & Port, N.L. (2001). Guiding contact by coupling the taus of gaps. Experimental Brain Research, 139, 151-159.

Lee, D.N., Lishman, J.R., & Thomson, J.A. (1982). Regulation of gait in long jumping. Journal of Experimental Psychology: Human Perception and Performance, 8, 448-459.

Lee, D.N., & Young, D.S. (1985). Visual timing of interceptive action. In D. Ingle, M. Jeannerod, & D.N. Lee (Eds.), Brain mechanisms and spatial vision (pp. 1-30). Dordrecht: Martinus Nijhoff.

Lee, D.N., Young, D.S., Reddish, P.E., Lough, S., & Clayton, T.M.H. (1983). Visual timing in hitting an accelerating ball. Quarterly Journal of Experimental Psychology, 35A, 333-346.

Lee, J.D. (2008). Fifty years of driving safety research. Human Factors, 50, 521-528.

Lee, J.D., Caven, B., Haake, S., & Brown, T.L. (2001). Speech-based interaction with in-vehicle computers: The effect of speech-based e-mail on drivers' attention to the roadway. Human Factors, 43, 631-640.

Lee, R.G., Murphy, J.T., & Tatton, W.G. (1983). Long latency myotatic reflexes in man: Mechanisms, functional significance, and changes in patients with Parkinson's disease or hemiplegia. In J. Desmedt (Ed.), Advances in neurology (pp. 489-508). Basel: Karger.

Lee, T.D. (1988). Transfer-appropriate processing: A framework for conceptualizing practice effects in motor learning. In O.G. Meijer & K. Roth (Eds.), Complex movement behaviour: "The" motor-action controversy (pp. 201-215). Amsterdam: Elsevier.

Lee, T.D. (1998). On the dynamics of motor learning research. Research Quarterly for Exercise and Sport, 69, 334-337.

Lee, T.D. (2004). Intention in bimanual coordination performance and learning. In V.K. Jirsa & J.A.S. Kelso (Eds.), Coordination dynamics: Issues and trends (pp. 41-56). Berlin: Springer.

Lee, T.D., Almeida, Q.J., & Chua, R. (2002). Spatial constraints in bimanual coordination: Influences of effector orientation. Experimental Brain Research, 146, 205-212.

Lee, T.D., Blandin, Y., & Proteau, L. (1996). Effects of task instructions and oscillation frequency on bimanual coordination. Psychological Research, 59, 100-106.

Lee, T.D., & Carnahan, H. (1990a). Bandwidth knowledge of results and motor learning: More than just a relative frequency effect. Quarterly Journal of Experimental Psychology, 42A, 777-789.

Lee, T.D., & Carnahan, H. (1990b). When to provide knowledge of results during motor learning: Scheduling effects. Human Performance, 3, 87-105.

Lee, T.D., & Genovese, E.D. (1988). Distribution of practice in motor skill acquisition: Learning and performance effects reconsidered. Research Quarterly for Exercise and Sport, 59, 277-287.

Lee, T.D., & Genovese, E.D. (1989). Distribution of practice in motor skill acquisition: Different effects for discrete and continuous tasks. Research Quarterly for Exercise and Sport, 60, 59-65.

Lee, T.D., Ishikura, T., Kegel, S., Gonzalez, D., & Passmore, S. (2008a). Head-putter coordination patterns in expert and less-skilled golfers. Journal of Motor Behavior, 40, 267-272.

Lee, T.D., Ishikura, T., Kegel, S., Gonzalez, D., & Passmore, S. (2008b). Do expert golfers really keep their heads still while putting? Annual Review of Golf Coaching, 2, 135-143.

Lee, T.D., & Magill, R.A. (1983a). Activity during the post-KR interval: Effects upon performance or learning? Research Quarterly for Exercise and Sport, 54, 340-345.

Lee, T.D., & Magill, R.A. (1983b). The locus of contextual interference in motor-skill acquisition. Journal of Experimental Psychology: Learning, Memory, and Cognition, 9, 730-746.

Lee, T.D., & Magill, R.A. (1985). Can forgetting facilitate skill acquisition? In D. Goodman, R.B. Wilberg, & I.M. Franks (Eds.), Differing perspectives in motor learning, memory, and control (pp. 3-22). Amsterdam: Elsevier.

Lee, T.D., & Magill, R.A. (1987). Effects of duration and activity during the post-KR interval on motor learning. Psychological Research, 49, 237-242.

Lee, T.D., Magill, R.A., & Weeks, D.J. (1985). Influence of practice schedule on testing schema theory predictions in adults. Journal of Motor Behavior, 17, 283-299.

Lee, T.D., & Maraj, B.K.V. (1994). Effects of bandwidth goals and bandwidth knowledge of results on motor learning. Research Quarterly for Exercise and Sport, 65, 244-249.

Lee, T.D., & Simon, D.A. (2004). Contextual interference.

In A.M. Williams & N.J. Hodges (Eds.), Skill acquisition in sport: Research, theory and practice (pp. 29-44). London: Routledge.

Lee, T.D., & Swinnen, S.P. (1993). Three legacies of Bryan and Harter: Automaticity, variability and change in skilled performance. In J.L. Starkes & F. Allard (Eds.), Cognitive issues in motor expertise (pp. 295-315). Amsterdam: Elsevier.

Lee, T.D., Swinnen, S.P., & Serrien, D.J. (1994). Cognitive effort and motor learning. Quest, 46, 328-344.

Lee, T.D., Swinnen, S.P., & Verschueren, S. (1995). Relative phase alterations during bimanual skill acquisition. Journal of Motor Behavior, 27, 263-274.

Lee, T.D., & Weeks, D.J. (1987). The beneficial influence of forgetting on short-term retention of movement information. Human Movement Science, 6, 233-245.

Lee, T.D., White, M.A., & Carnahan, H. (1990). On the role of knowledge of results in motor learning: Exploring the guidance hypothesis. Journal of Motor Behavior, 22, 191-208.

Lee, T.D., Wishart, L.R., Cunningham, S., & Carnahan, H. (1997). Modeled timing information during random practice eliminates the contextual interference effect. Research Quarterly for Exercise and Sport, 68, 100-105.

Lee, T.D., Wulf, G., & Schmidt, R.A. (1992). Contextual interference in motor learning: Dissociated effects due to the nature of task variations. Quarterly Journal of Experimental Psychology, 44A, 627-644.

Lee, W.A. (1980). Anticipatory control of postural and task muscles during rapid arm flexion. Journal of Motor Behavior, 12, 185-196.

Lenoir, M., Musch, E., Thiery, E., & Savelsbergh, G.J.P. (2002). Rate of change of angular bearing as the relevant property in a horizontal interception task during locomotion. Journal of Motor Behavior, 34, 385-401.

Leob, G.E., & Ghez, C. (2000). The motor unit and muscle action. In E.R. Kandel, J.H. Schwartz, & T.M. Jessell (Eds.), Principles of neural science (pp. 674-694). New York, McGraw-Hill.

Leonard, J.A. (1953). Advance information in sensori-motor skills. Quarterly Journal of Experimental Psychology, 5, 141-149.

Leonard, J.A. (1954). An experiment with occasional false information. Quarterly Journal of Experimental Psychology, 6, 79-85.

Leonard, J.A. (1959). Tactual choice reactions: I. Quarterly Journal of Experimental Psychology, 11, 76-83.

Lersten, K.C. (1968). Transfer of movement components in a motor learning task. Research Quarterly, 39, 575-581.

Lersten, K.C. (1969). Retention of skill on the Rho apparatus after one year. Research Quarterly, 40, 418-419.

Leuba, J.H., & Chamberlain, E. (1909). The influence of the duration and of the rate of arm movements upon the judgment of their length. American Journal of Psychology, 20, 374-385.

Lewis, D. (1947). Positive and negative transfer in motor learning. American Psychologist, 2, 423.

Lewis, D. (1953). Motor skills learning. In A.B. Nadel (Ed.), Symposium on psychology of learning basic to military training problems (HR-HTD 201/1, pp. 45-84). Washington, DC: Department of Defense.

Lewis, D., McAllister, D.E., & Adams, J.A. (1951). Facilitation and interference in performance on the modified Mashburn apparatus: I. The effects of varying the amount of original learning. Journal of Experimental Psychology, 41, 247-260.

Lewis, R.E.F. (1956). Consistency and car driving skill. British Journal of Industrial Medicine, 13, 131-141.

Lewthwaite, R., & Wulf, G. (2010). Social-comparative feedback affects motor skill learning. Quarterly Journal of Experimental Psychology, 63, 738-749.

Li, Y., & Wright, D.L. (2000). An assessment of the attention demands during random- and blocked-practice schedules. Quarterly Journal of Experimental Psychology, 53A, 591-606.

Liao, C.M., & Masters, R.S.W. (2001). Analogy learning: A means to implicit motor learning. Journal of Sports Sciences, 19, 307-319.

Libet, B. (1985). Unconscious cerebral initiative and the role of conscious will in voluntary action. Behavioral and Brain Sciences, 8, 529-566.

Lieberman, D.A., Vogel, A.C.M., & Nisbet, J. (2008). Why do the effects of delaying reinforcement in animals and delaying feedback in humans differ? A working memory analysis. Quarterly Journal of Experimental Psychology, 61, 194-202.

Lin, C.-H., Fisher, B.E., Winstein, C.J., Wu, A.D., & Gordon, J. (2008). Contextual interference effect: Elaborative processing or forgetting–reconstruction? A post hoc analysis of transcranial magnetic stimulation–induced effects on motor learning. Journal of Motor Behavior, 40, 578-586.

Lin, C.-H., Sullivan, K.J., Wu, A.D., Kantak, K., & Winstein, C.J. (2007). Effect of task practice order on motor skill learning in adults with Parkinson disease: A pilot study. Physical Therapy, 87, 1120-1131.

Lin, C.-H., Winstein, C.J., Fisher, B.E., & Wu, A.D. (2010). Neural correlates of the contextual interference effect in motor learning: A transcranial magnetic stimulation investigation. Journal of Motor Behavior, 42, 223-232.

Lindahl, L.G. (1945). Movement analysis as an industrial training method. Journal of Applied Psychology, 29, 420-436.

Lindeburg, F.A. (1949). A study of the degree of transfer between quickening exercises and other coordinated movements. Research Quarterly, 20, 180-195.

Lindemann, O., Abolafia, J.M., Girardi, G., & Bekkering, H. (2007). Getting a grip on numbers: Numerical magnitude priming in object grasping. Journal of Experimental Psychology: Human Perception and Performance, 33, 1400-1409.

Lintern, G. (1988). Distributed practice: Are there useful insights for application or theory? Research Quarterly for Exercise and Sport, 59, 298-302.

Lintern, G., Sheppard, D.J., Parker, D.L., Yates, K.E., & Nolan, M.D. (1989). Simulator design and instructional features for air-to-ground attack: A transfer study. Human Factors, 31, 87-99.

Liu, J., & Wrisberg, C.A. (1997). The effects of knowledge of results delay and the subjective estimation of movement form on the acquisition and retention of a motor skill. Research Quarterly for Exercise and Sport, 68, 145-151.

Locke, E.A. (1991). Problems with goal-setting research in sports—and their solution. Journal of Sport and Exercise Psychology, 13, 311-316.

Locke, E.A., & Latham, G.P. (1985). The application of goal setting to sports. Sport Psychology Today, 7, 205-222.

Locke, E.A., & Latham, G.P. (2006). New directions in goal-setting theory. Current Directions in Psychological Science, 15, 265-268.

Lococo, K., & Tucker, M.E. (in press). Pedal application errors. Washington, DC: NHTSA, U.S. Department of Transportation.

Logan, G.D. (1982). On the ability to inhibit complex movements: A stop-signal study of typewriting. Journal of Experimental Psychology: Human Perception and Performance, 8, 778-792.

Logan, G.D. (1985). Skill and automaticity: Relations, implications, and future directions. Canadian Journal of Psychology, 39, 367-386.

Logan, G.D. (1988). Toward an instance theory of automatization. Psychological Review, 95, 492-527.

Logan, G.D. (1994). On the ability to inhibit thought and action: A user's guide to the stop signal paradigm. In D. Dagenbach & T.H. Carr (Eds.), Inhibitory processes in attention, memory, and language (pp. 189-239). San Diego: Academic Press.

Logan, G.D., & Cowan, W.B. (1984). On the ability to inhibit thought and action: A theory of an act of control. Psychological Review, 91, 295-327.

Lordahl, D.S., & Archer, E.J. (1958). Transfer effects on a rotary pursuit task as a function of first-task difficulty. Journal of Experimental Psychology, 56, 421-426.

Lorge, I., & Thorndike, E.L. (1935). The influence of delay in the after-effect of a connection. Journal of Experimental Psychology, 18, 186-194.

Lotter, W.S. (1960). Interrelationships among reaction times and speeds of movement in different limbs. Research Quarterly, 31, 147-155.

Lotze, M., & Halsband, U. (2006). Motor imagery. Journal of Physiology – Paris, 99, 386-395.

Maas, E., Robin, D.A., Austermann Hula, S.N., Freedman, S.E., Wulf, G., Ballard, K.J., & Schmidt, R.A. (2008). Principles of motor learning in treatment of motor speech disorders. American Journal of Speech-Language Pathology, 17, 277-298.

Mack, M.G. (2001). Effects of time and movements of the preshot routine on free throw shooting. Perceptual and Motor Skills, 93, 567-573.

MacKay-Lyons, M. (2002). Central pattern generation of locomotion: A review of the evidence. Physical Therapy, 82, 69-83.

MacKenzie, I.S. (1989). A note on the information-theoretic basis of Fitts' law. Journal of Motor Behavior, 21, 323-330.

MacKenzie, I.S., & Buxton, W. (1994). The prediction of pointing and dragging times in graphical user interfaces. Interacting with Computers, 6, 213-227.

MacLeod, C.M. (1991). Half a century of research on the Stroop effect: An integrative review. Psychological Bulletin, 109, 163-203.

MacLeod, C.M., & Dunbar, K. (1988). Training and Stroop-like interference: Evidence for a continuum of automaticity. Journal of Experimental Psychology: Learning, Memory, and Cognition, 14, 126-135.

MacLeod, C.M., & MacDonald, P.A. (2000). Interdimensional interference in the Stroop effect: Uncovering the cognitive and neural anatomy of attention. Trends in Cognitive Sciences, 4, 383-391.

MacMahon, C., & McPherson, S.L. (2009). Knowledge base as a mechanism for perceptual-cognitive tasks: Skill is in the details! International Journal of Sport Psychology, 40, 565-579.

MacMahon, C., & Starkes, J.L. (2008). Contextual influences on baseball ball-strike decisions in umpires, players, and controls. Journal of Sports Sciences, 26, 751-760.

MacNeilage, P.F. (1970). Motor control of serial ordering of speech. Psychological Review, 77, 182-196.

MacPherson, S.J., Dees, V., & Grindley, G.C. (1948). The effect of knowledge of results on learning and performance: II. Some characteristics of very simple skills. Quarterly Journal of Experimental Psychology, 1, 68-78.

MacPherson, S.J., Dees, V., & Grindley, G.C. (1949). The effect of knowledge of results on learning and performance: III. The influence of time intervals between trials. Quarterly Journal of Experimental Psychology, 1, 167-174.

Macrae, A.W., & Holding, D.H. (1965). Method and task in motor guidance. Ergonomics, 8, 315-320.

Macrae, A.W., & Holding, D.H. (1966). Transfer of training after guidance or practice. Quarterly Journal of Experimental Psychology, 18, 327-333.

Magill, R.A. (1973). The post-KR interval: Time and activity effects and the relationship of motor short-term memory theory. Journal of Motor Behavior, 5, 49-56.

Magill, R.A. (1988). Activity during the post-knowledge of results interval can benefit motor skill learning. In O.G. Meijer & K. Roth (Eds.), Complex movement behaviour: "The" motor-action controversy (pp. 231-246). Amsterdam: Elsevier.

Magill, R.A. (1998). Knowledge is more than we can talk about: Implicit learning in motor skill acquisition. Research Quarterly for Exercise and Sport, 69, 104-110.

Magill, R.A. (2001). Augmented feedback in motor skill acquisition. In R.N. Singer, H.A. Hausenblas, & C.M. Janelle (Eds.), Handbook of sport psychology (2nd ed.) (pp. 86-114). New York: Wiley.

Magill, R.A., Chamberlin, C.J., & Hall, K.G. (1991). Verbal knowledge of results as redundant information for learning an anticipation timing skill. Human Movement Science, 10, 485-507.

Magill, R.A., & Hall, K.G. (1990). A review of the contextual interference effect in motor skill acquisition. Human Movement Science, 9, 241-289.

Magill, R.A., Schmidt, R.A., Young, D.E., & Shapiro, D.C. (1987). Unpublished data, University of California, Los Angeles.

Magill, R.A., & Schoenfelder-Zohdi, B. (1996). A visual model and knowledge of performance as sources of information for learning a rhythmic gymnastics skill. International Journal of Sport Psychology, 27, 7-22.

Magill, R.A., & Wood, C.A. (1986). Knowledge of results precision as a learning variable in motor skill acquisition. Research Quarterly for Exercise and Sport, 57, 170-173.

Malina, R., Bouchard, C., & Bar-Or, O. (2004). Growth, maturation, and physical activity (2nd ed.). Champaign, IL: Human Kinetics.

Mané, A.M., Adams, J.A., & Donchin, E. (1989). Adaptive and part-whole training in the acquisition of a complex perceptual-motor skill. Acta Psychologica, 71, 179-196.

Mann, D.T.Y., Williams, A.M., Ward, P., & Janelle, C.M. (2007). Perceptual-cognitive expertise in sport: A meta-analysis. Journal of Sport and Exercise Psychology, 29, 457-478.

Maraj, B.K.V., Elliott, D., Lee, T.D., & Pollock, B.J. (1993). Variance and invariance in expert and novice triple jumpers. Research Quarterly for Exercise and Sport, 64, 404-412.

Marchal Crespo, L., & Reinkensmeyer, D.J. (2008). Haptic guidance can enhance motor learning of a steering task. Journal of Motor Behavior, 40, 545-556.

Marder, E., Bucher, D., Schulz, D.J., & Taylor, A.L. (2005). Invertebrate central pattern generation moves along. Current Biology, 15, R685-R699.

Marsden, C.D., Merton, P.A., & Morton, H.B. (1972). Servo action in human voluntary movement. Nature, 238, 140-143.

Marteniuk, R.G. (1973). Retention characteristics of motor short-term memory cues. Journal of Motor Behavior, 5, 249-259.

Marteniuk, R.G. (1974). Individual differences in motor performance and learning. Exercise and Sport Sciences Reviews, 2, 103-130.

Marteniuk, R.G. (1976). Information processing in motor skills. New York: Holt, Rinehart & Winston.

Marteniuk, R.G. (1986). Information processes in movement learning: Capacity and structural interference effects. Journal of Motor Behavior, 18, 55-75.

Marteniuk, R.G., Leavitt, J.L., MacKenzie, C.L., & Athenes, S. (1990). Functional relationships between grasp and transport components in a prehension task. Human Movement Science, 9, 149-176.

Marteniuk, R.G., MacKenzie, C.L., & Baba, D.M. (1984). Bimanual movement control: Information processing and interaction effects. Quarterly Journal of Experimental Psychology, 36A, 335-365.

Marteniuk, R.G., MacKenzie, C.L., Jeannerod, M., Athenes, S., & Dugas, C. (1987). Constraints on human arm movement trajectories. Canadian Journal of Psychology, 41, 365-378.

Marteniuk, R.G., & Romanow, S.K.E. (1983). Human movement organization and learning as revealed by variability of movement, use of kinematic information, and Fourier analysis. In R.A. Magill (Ed.), Memory and control of action (pp. 167-197). Amsterdam: Elsevier.

Martens, R., Burwitz, L., & Zuckerman, J. (1976). Modeling effects on motor performance. Research Quarterly, 47, 277-291.

Martens, R., & Landers, D.M. (1970). Motor performance under stress: A test of the inverted-U hypothesis. Journal of Personality and Social Psychology, 16, 29-37.

Martin, H.A. (1970). Long-term retention of a discrete motor task. Unpublished master's thesis, University of Maryland, College Park.

Martin, J.H., & Jessell, T.M. (1991). Modality coding in the somatic sensory system. In E.R. Kandel, J.H. Schwartz, & T.M. Jessell (Eds.), Principles of neural science (3rd ed.) (pp. 341-352). Amsterdam: Elsevier.

Maslovat, D., Brunke, K.M., Chua, R., & Franks, I.M. (2009). Feedback effects on learning a novel bimanual coordination pattern: Support for the guidance hypothesis. Journal of Motor Behavior, 41, 45-54.

Maslovat, D., Hayes, S.J., Horn, R., & Hodges, N.J. (2010). Motor learning through observation. In D. Elliott & M.A. Khan (Eds.), Vision and goal-directed action: Neurobehavioural perspectives (pp. 315-339). Champaign, IL: Human Kinetics.

Massaro, D.W. (1989). Experimental psychology: An information processing approach. San Diego: Harcourt Brace Jovanovich.

Masson, M.E.J. (1990). Cognitive theories of skill acquisition. Human Movement Science, 9, 221-239.

Masters, R.S.W. (1992). Knowledge, knerves and know-how: The role of explicit versus implicit knowledge in the breakdown of a complex motor skill under pressure. British Journal of Psychology, 83, 343-358.

Masters, R.S.W. (2008). Applying implicit (motor) learning. In D. Farrow, J. Baker, & C. MacMahon (Eds.), Developing elite sports performers: Lessons from theory to practice (pp. 89-103). Routledge: London.

Masters, R.S.W., & Maxwell, J. (2008). The theory of reinvestment. International Review of Sport and Exercise Psychology, 1, 160-183.

Mates, J., & Aschersleben, G. (2000). Sensorimotor synchronization: The impact of temporally displaced auditory feedback. Acta Psychologica, 104, 29-44.

Mattar, A.A.G., & Gribble, P.L. (2005). Motor learning by observing. Neuron, 46, 153-160.

McCarthy, G., & Donchin, E. (1981). A metric for thought: A comparison of P300 latency and reaction time. Science, 211, 77-80.

McCartt, A.T., Hellinga, L.A., & Bratiman, K.A. (2006). Cell phones and driving: Review of research. Traffic Injury Prevention, 7, 89-106.

McCloy, C.H. (1934). The measurement of general motor capacity and general motor ability. Research Quarterly, 5 (Suppl. 5), 45-61.

McCloy, C.H. (1937). An analytical study of the stunt type test as a measure of motor educability. Research Quarterly, 8, 46-55.

McCracken, H.D., & Stelmach, G.E. (1977). A test of the schema theory of discrete motor learning. Journal of Motor Behavior, 9, 193-201.

McCullagh, P., & Caird, J.K. (1990). Correct and learning models and the use of model knowledge of results in the acquisition and retention of a motor skill. Journal of Human Movement Studies, 18, 107-116.

McCullagh, P., & Little, W.S. (1989). A comparison of modalities in modeling. Human Performance, 2, 107-116.

McCullagh, P., & Meyer, K.N. (1997). Learning versus correct models: Influence of model type on the learning of a free-weight squat lift. Research Quarterly for Exercise and Sport, 68, 56-61.

McCullagh, P., & Weiss, M.R. (2001). Modeling: Considerations for motor skill performance and psychological responses. In R.N. Singer, H.A. Hausenblas, & C.M. Janelle (Eds.), Handbook of sport psychology (2nd ed.) (pp. 205-238). New York: Wiley.

McDonald, P.V., van Emmerik, R.E.A., & Newell, K.M. (1989). The effects of practice on limb kinematics in a throwing task. Journal of Motor Behavior, 21, 245-264.

McEvoy, S.P., Stevenson, M.R., & Woodward, M. (2007). The contribution of passengers versus mobile phone use to motor vehicle crashes resulting in hospital attendance by the driver. Accident Analysis and Prevention, 39, 1170-1176.

McGarry, T., Chua, R., & Franks, I.M. (2003). Stopping and restarting an unfolding action at various times. Quarterly Journal of Experimental Psychology, 56A, 601-620.

McGarry, T., & Franks, I.M. (1997). A horse race between independent processes: Evidence for a phantom point of no return in the preparation of a speeded motor response. Journal of Experimental Psychology: Human Perception and Performance, 23, 1533-1542.

McGarry, T., & Franks, I.M. (2000). Inhibitory motor control in stop paradigms: Comment on Band and van Boxtel (1999). Acta Psychologica, 105, 83-88.

McGarry, T., & Franks, I.M. (2003). On the nature of stopping an earlier intended voluntary action. Motor Control, 7, 155-198.

McGarry, T., Inglis, T., & Franks, I.M. (2000). Against a final ballistic process in the control of voluntary action: Evidence using the Hoffman reflex. Motor Control, 4, 469-485.

McGaugh, J.L. (2000). Memory: A century of consolidation. Science, 287, 248-251.

McGeoch, J.A., & Irion, A.L. (1952). The psychology of human learning. New York: Longmans.

McGraw, M.B. (1935). Growth: A study of Johnny and Jimmy. New York: Appleton-Century.

McGraw, M.B. (1939). Later development of children specially trained during infancy: Johnny and Jimmy at school age. Child Development, 10, 1-19.

McGuigan, F.J. (1959). The effect of precision, delay, and schedule of knowledge of results on performance. Journal of Experimental Psychology, 58, 79-84.

McKnight, A.J., & McKnight, A.S. (1993). The effect of cellular phone use upon driver attention. Accident Analysis and Prevention, 25, 259-265.

McLeod, P. (1977). A dual task response modality effect: Support for multiprocessor models of attention. Quarterly Journal of Experimental Psychology, 29, 651-667.

McLeod, P. (1980). What can probe RT tell us about the attentional demands of movement? In G.E. Stelmach & J. Requin (Eds.), Tutorials in motor behavior (pp. 579-589). Amsterdam: Elsevier.

McLeod, P. (1987). Visual reaction time and high-speed ball games. Perception, 16, 49-59.

McLeod, P., & Dienes, Z. (1993). Running to catch the ball. Nature, 362, 23.

McLeod, P., & Dienes, Z. (1996). Do fielders know where to go to catch the ball or only how to get there? Journal of Experimental Psychology: Human Perception and Performance, 22, 531-543.

McLeod, P., Reed, N., & Dienes, Z. (2001). Toward a unified fielder theory: What we do not yet know about how people run to catch a ball. Journal of Experimental Psychology: Human Perception and Performance, 27, 1347-1355.

McLeod, P., Reed, N., & Dienes, Z. (2003). How fielders arrive in time to catch the ball. Nature, 426, 244-245.

McLeod, P., Reed, N., & Dienes, Z. (2006). The generalised optic acceleration cancellation theory of catching. Journal of Experimental Psychology: Human Perception and Performance, 32, 139-148.

McNeil, M.R., Robin, D., & Schmidt, R.A. (1997). Apraxia of speech: Definition, differentiation, and treatment. In M.R. McNeil (Ed.), Clinical management of sensorimotor speech disorders (pp. 311-344). New York: Thieme Medical.

McNevin, N., Magill, R.A., & Buekers, M.J. (1994). The effects of erroneous knowledge of results on transfer of anticipation timing. Research Quarterly for Exercise and Sport, 65, 324-329.

McPherson, S.L. (1993). Knowledge representation and decision-making in sport. In J.L. Starkes & F. Allard (Eds.), Cognitive issues in motor expertise (pp. 159-188). Amsterdam: Elsevier.

McPherson, S.L. (1994). The development of sport expertise: Mapping the tactical domain. Quest, 46, 223-240.

McPherson, S.L., & MacMahon, C. (2008). How baseball players prepare to bat: Tactical knowledge as a mediator of expert performance in baseball. Journal of Sport and Exercise Psychology, 30, 755-778.

Mechsner, F. (2004). A perceptual-cognitive approach to bimanual coordination. In V.K. Jirsa & J.A.S. Kelso (Eds.), Coordination dynamics: Issues and trends (pp. 177-195). Berlin: Springer.

Mechsner, F., Kerzel, D., Knoblich, G., & Prinz, W. (2001). Perceptual basis of bimanual coordination. Nature, 414, 69-73.

Mechsner, F., & Knoblich, G. (2004). Do muscles matter for coordinated action? Journal of Experimental Psychology: Human Perception and Performance, 30, 490-503.

Meegan, D.V., Aslin, R.N., & Jacobs, R.A. (2000). Motor timing learned without motor training. Nature Neuroscience, 3, 860-862.

Meegan, D.V., Glazebrook, C.M., Dhillon, V.P., Tremblay, L., Welsh, T.N., & Elliott, D. (2004). The Müller-Lyer illusion affects the planning and control of manual aiming movements. Experimental Brain Research, 155, 37-47.

Meegan, D.V., & Tipper, S.P. (1998). Reaching into cluttered visual environments: Spatial and temporal influences of distracting objects. Quarterly Journal of Experimental Psychology, 51, 225-249.

Meijer, O.G. (2001). Making things happen: An introduction to the history of movement science. In M.L. Latash & V.M. Zatsiorsky (Eds.), Classics in movement science (pp. 1-57). Champaign, IL: Human Kinetics.

Meira, C.M. Jr., & Tani, G. (2001). The contextual interference effect in acquisition of dart-throwing skill tested on a transfer test with extended trials. Perceptual and Motor Skills, 92, 910-918.

Melton, A.W. (Ed.). (1947). Apparatus tests. Washington, DC: U.S. Government Printing Office.

Memmert, D., Hagemann, N., Althoetmar, R., Geppert, S., & Seiler, D. (2009). Conditions of practice in perceptual skill learning. Research Quarterly for Exercise and Sport, 80, 32-43.

Memmert, D., & Furley, P. (2007). "I spy with my little eye!": Breadth of attention, inattentional blindness, and tactical decision making in team sports. Journal of Sport and Exercise Psychology, 29, 365-381.

Merkel, J. (1885). Die zeitlichen Verhaltnisse det Willensthaütigkeit. Philosophische Studien, 2, 73-127. (Cited in Woodworth, R.S., 1938, Experimental psychology. New York: Holt)

Merton, P.A. (1953). Speculations on the servo control of movement. In G.E.W. Wolstenholme (Ed.), The spinal cord. London: Churchill.

Merton, P.A. (1972). How we control the contraction of our muscles. Scientific American, 226, 30-37.

Meyer, D.E., Abrams, R.A., Kornblum, S., Wright, C.E., & Smith, J.E.K. (1988). Optimality in human motor performance: Ideal control of rapid aimed movements. Psychological Review, 95, 340-370.

Meyer, D.E., Smith, J.E.K., Kornblum, S., Abrams, R.A., & Wright, C.E. (1990). Speed-accuracy tradeoffs in aimed movements: Toward a theory of rapid voluntary action. In M. Jeannerod (Ed.), Attention and performance XIII (pp. 173-226). Hillsdale, NJ: Erlbaum.

Meyer, D.E., Smith, J.E.K., & Wright, C.E. (1982). Models for the speed and accuracy of aimed movements. Psychological Review, 89, 449-482.

Meyers, J.L. (1967). Retention of balance coordination learning as influenced by extended lay-offs. Research Quarterly, 38, 72-78.

Michaels, C.F., & Oudejans, R.R.D. (1992). The optics and actions of catching fly balls: Zeroing out optic acceleration. Ecological Psychology, 4, 199-222.

Michon, J.A. (1966). Tapping regularity as a measure of perceptual motor load. Ergonomics, 9, 401-412.

Michon, J.A. (1967). Timing in temporal tracking. Soesterberg, The Netherlands: Institute for Perception, RNO-TNO.

Miller, G.A. (1956). The magical number seven, plus or minus two: Some limits on our capacity for processing information. Psychological Review, 63, 81-97.

Miller, G.A. (2003). The cognitive revolution: A historical perspective. Trends in Cognitive Sciences, 7, 141-144.

Miller, G.A., Galanter, E., & Pribram, K.H. (1960). Plans and the structure of behavior. New York: Holt, Rinehart & Winston.

Milner, A.D., & Goodale, M.A. (1993). Visual pathways to perception and action. In T.P. Hicks, S. Molotchnikoff, & T. Ono (Eds.), Progress in brain research (Vol. 95). Amsterdam: Elsevier.

Milner, A.D., & Goodale, M.A. (1995). The visual brain in action. Oxford: Oxford University Press.

Milner, A.D., & Goodale, M.A. (2008). Two visual systems re-viewed. Neuropsychologia, 46, 774-785.

Milner, B., Corkin, S., & Teuber, H.L. (1968). Further analysis of the hippocampal amnesic syndrome: 14 year follow up study of H.M. Neuropsychologica, 6, 215-234.

Milone, F. (1971). Interference in motor short-term memory. Unpublished master's thesis, Pennsylvania State University, University Park.

Minas, S.C. (1978). Mental practice of a complex perceptual-motor skill. Journal of Human Movement Studies, 4, 102-107.

Minas, S.C. (1980). Acquisition of a motor skill following guided mental and physical practice. Journal of Human Movement Studies, 6, 127-141.

Mohler, B.J., Thompson, W.B., Creem-Regehr, S.H., Pick, H.L., & Warren, W.H. (2007). Visual flow influences gait transition speed and preferred walking speed. Experimental Brain Research, 181, 221-228.

Monno, A., Temprado, J.J., Zanone, P.-G., & Laurent, M. (2002). The interplay of attention and bimanual coordination dynamics. Acta Psychologica, 110, 187-211.

Montagne, G., & Laurent, M. (1994). The effects of environment changes on one-handed catching. Journal of Motor Behavior, 26, 237-246.

Mon-Williams, M., Tresilian, J.R., Coppard, V.L., & Carson, R.G. (2001). The effect of obstacle position on reach-to-grasp movements. Experimental Brain Research, 137, 497-501.

Moors, A., & De Houwer, J. (2006). Automaticity: A theoretical and conceptual analysis. Psychological Bulletin, 132, 297-326.

Moray, N. (1970). Attention: Selective processes in vision and hearing. New York: Academic Press.

Moreno, F.J., Ávila, F., Damas, J., Garciá, J.A., Luis, V., Reina, R., & Ruíz, A. (2003). Contextual interference in learning precision skills. Perceptual and Motor Skills, 97, 121-128.

Morgan, C.T., & King, R.A. (1971). Introduction to psychology (4th ed.). New York: McGraw-Hill.

Morgan, M., Phillips, J.G., Bradshaw, J.L., Mattingley, J.B., Iansek, R., & Bradshaw, J.A. (1994). Age-related motor slowness: Simply strategic? Journal of Gerontology: Medical Sciences, 49, M133-M139.

Morris, C.D., Bransford, J.D., & Franks, J.J. (1977). Levels of processing versus transfer appropriate processing. Journal of Verbal Learning and Verbal Behavior, 16, 519-533.

Morris, M.E., Summers, J.J., Matyas, T.A., & Iansek, R. (1994). Current status of the motor program. Physical Therapy, 74, 738-748.

Morrissey, M.C., Harman, E.A., & Johnson, M.J. (1995). Resistance training modes: Specificity and effectiveness. Medicine and Science in Sports and Exercise, 27, 648-660.

Most, S.B., Scholl, B.J., Clifford, E.R., & Simons, D.J. (2005). What you see is what you set: Sustained inattentional blindness and the capture of awareness. Psychological Review, 112, 217-242.

Movahedi, A., Sheikh, M., Bagherzadeh, F., Hemayattalab, R., & Ashayeri, H. (2007). A practice-specificity-based model of arousal for achieving peak performance. Journal of Motor Behavior, 39, 457-462.

Mowbray, G.H. (1960). Choice reaction times for skilled responses. Quarterly Journal of Experimental Psychology, 12, 193-202.

Mowbray, G.H., & Rhoades, M.V. (1959). On the reduction of choice reaction times with practice. Quarterly Journal of Experimental Psychology, 11, 16-23.

Mowrer, O.H. (1940). Preparatory set (expectancy): Some methods of measurement. Psychological Monographs, 52, No. 233.

Mulder, T. (2007). Motor imagery and action observation: Cognitive tools for rehabilitation. Journal of Neural Transmission, 114, 1265-1278.

Mulder, T., & Hulstijn, W. (1985). Delayed sensory feedback in the learning of a novel motor task. Psychological Research, 47, 203-209.

Müller, S., Abernethy, B., Eid, M., McBean, R., & Rose, M. (2010). Expertise and the spatio-temporal characteristics of anticipatory information pick-up from complex movement patterns. Perception, 30, 745-760.

Müller, S., Abernethy, B., & Farrow, D. (2006). How do world-class cricket batsmen anticipate a bowler's intention? Quarterly Journal of Experimental Psychology, 59, 2162-2186.

Munoz, D.P., & Everling, S. (2004). Look away: The anti-saccade task and the voluntary control of eye movement. Nature Reviews: Neuroscience, 5, 218-228.

Murata, A. (1999). Extending effective target width in Fitts' law to a two-dimensional pointing task. International Journal of Human-Computer Interaction, 8, 457-469.

Murata, A., & Iwase, H. (2001). Extending Fitts' law to a three-dimensional pointing task. Human Movement Science, 20, 791-805.

Murphy, H.H. (1916). Distribution of practice periods in learning. Journal of Educational Psychology, 7, 150-162.

Musch, J., & Grondin, S. (2001). Unequal competition as an impediment to personal development. A review of the relative age effect in sport. Developmental Review, 21, 147-167.

Muybridge, E. (1887). Animal locomotion: An electro-photographic investigation of consecutive phases of animal movements. Philadelphia: Lippincott.

Muybridge, E. (1979). Muybridge's complete human and animal locomotion: All 781 plates from the 1887 Animal Locomotion. New York: Dover.

Nacson, J., & Schmidt, R.A. (1971). The activity-set hypothesis for warm-up decrement. Journal of Motor Behavior, 3, 1-15.

Namikas, G., & Archer, E.J. (1960). Motor skill transfer as a function of intertask interval and pretransfer task difficulty. Journal of Experimental Psychology, 59, 109-112.

Napier, J.R. (1956). The prehensile movements of the human hand. Journal of Bone and Joint Surgery, 38B, 902-913.

Nashner, L., & Berthoz, A. (1978). Visual contribution to rapid motor responses during postural control. Brain Research, 150, 403-407.

Nashner, L.M., & Woollacott, M. (1979). The organization of rapid postural adjustments of standing humans: An experimental-conceptual model. In R.E. Talbott & D.R. Humphrey (Eds.), Posture and movement (pp. 243-257). New York: Raven Press.

Navon, D., & Gopher, D. (1979). On the economy of the human processing system. Psychological Review, 86, 214-255.

Néda, Z., Ravasz, E., Brechet, Y., Vicsek, T., & Barabási, A.-L. (2000). The sound of many hands clapping. Nature, 403, 849-850.

Neisser, U. (1967). Cognitive psychology. New York: Appleton-Century-Crofts.

Neisser, U., & Becklen, R. (1975). Selective looking: Attending to visually specified events. Cognitive Psychology, 7, 480-494.

Nelson, T.O. (1985). Ebbinghaus's contribution to the measurement of retention: Savings during relearning. Journal of Experimental Psychology: Learning, Memory, and Cognition, 11, 472-479.

Neumann, E., & Ammons, R.B. (1957). Acquisition and long-term retention of a simple serial perceptual-motor skill. Journal of Experimental Psychology, 53, 159-161.

Neumann, O. (1987). Beyond capacity: A functional view of attention. In H. Heuer & A.F. Sanders (Eds.), Perspectives on perception and action (pp. 361-394). Hillsdale, NJ: Erlbaum.

Neumann, O. (1996). Theories of attention. In O. Neumann & A.F. Sanders (Eds.), Handbook of perception and action. Vol. 3: Attention (pp. 389-446). San Diego: Academic Press.

Neumann, O., & Sanders, A.F. (Eds.). (1996). Handbook of perception and action. Vol. 3: Attention. San Diego: Academic Press.

Newell, A., & Rosenbloom, P.S. (1981). Mechanisms of skill acquisition and the law of practice. In J.R. Anderson (Ed.), Cognitive skills and their acquisition (pp. 1-55). Hillsdale, NJ: Erlbaum.

Newell, K.M. (1974). Knowledge of results and motor learning. Journal of Motor Behavior, 6, 235-244.

Newell, K.M. (1976a). More on absolute error, etc. Journal of Motor Behavior, 8, 139-142.

Newell, K.M. (1976b). Motor learning without knowledge of results through the development of a response recognition mechanism. Journal of Motor Behavior, 8, 209-217.

Newell, K.M. (1980). The speed-accuracy paradox in movement control: Error of time and space. In G.E. Stelmach (Ed.), Tutorials in motor behavior. Amsterdam: Elsevier.

Newell, K.M. (1981). Skill learning. In D.H. Holding (Ed.), Human skills. New York: Wiley.

Newell, K.M. (1986). Constraints on the development of coordination. In M.G. Wade & H.T.A. Whiting (Eds.), Motor development in children: Aspects of coordination and control (pp. 341-360). Boston: Nijhoff.

Newell, K.M. (1991). Motor skill acquisition. Annual Review of Psychology, 42, 213-237.

Newell, K.M., & Carlton, L.G. (1985). On the relationship between peak force and peak force variability in isometric tasks. Journal of Motor Behavior, 17, 230-241.

Newell, K.M., & Carlton, L.G. (1988). Force variability in isometric responses. Journal of Experimental Psychology: Human Perception and Performance, 14, 37-44.

Newell, K.M., Carlton, M.J., & Antoniou, A. (1990). The interaction of criterion and feedback information in learning a drawing task. Journal of Motor Behavior, 22, 536-552.

Newell, K.M., Carlton, L.G., Carlton, M.J., & Halbert, J.A. (1980). Velocity as a factor in movement timing accuracy. Journal of Motor Behavior, 12, 47-56.

Newell, K.M., Carlton, M.J., Fisher, A.T., & Rutter, B.G. (1989). Whole-part training strategies for learning the response dynamics of microprocessor driven simulators. Acta Psychologica, 71, 197-216.

Newell, K.M., Carlton, L.G., & Hancock, P.A. (1984). Kinetic analysis of response variability. Psychological Bulletin, 96, 133-151.

Newell, K.M., Carlton, L.G., & Kim, S. (1994). Time and space-time movement accuracy. Human Performance, 7, 1-21.

Newell, K.M., Carlton, L.G., Kim, S., & Chung, C. (1993). Space-time accuracy of rapid movements. Journal of Motor Behavior, 25, 8-20.

Newell, K.M., Hoshizaki, L.E.F., Carlton, M.J., & Halbert, J.A. (1979). Movement time and velocity as determinants of movement timing accuracy. Journal of Motor Behavior, 11, 49-58.

Newell, K.M., Liu, Y.-T., & Mayer-Kress, G. (2001). Time scales in motor learning and development. Psychological Review, 108, 57-82.

Newell, K.M., Liu, Y.-T., & Mayer-Kress, G. (2008). Landscapes beyond the HKB model. In A. Fuchs & V.K. Jirsa (Eds.), Coordination: Neural, behavioral and social dynamics (pp. 27-44). Berlin: Springer.

Newell, K.M., Liu, Y.-T., & Mayer-Kress, G. (2009). Time scales, difficulty/skill duality, and the dynamics of motor learning. In D. Sternad (Ed.), Progress in motor control (pp. 457-476). Berlin: Springer.

Newell, K.M., & McDonald, P.V. (1992). Practice: A search for task solutions. In American Academy of Physical Education, Enhancing human performance in sport: New concepts and developments (The Academy Papers, No. 25, pp. 51-59). Champaign, IL: Human Kinetics.

Newell, K.M., Sparrow, W.A., & Quinn, J.T. Jr. (1985). Kinetic information feedback for learning isometric tasks. Journal of Human Movement Studies, 11, 113-123.

Newell, K.M., & Vaillancourt, D.E. (2001a). Dimensional change in motor learning. Human Movement Science, 20, 695-715.

Newell, K.M., & Vaillancourt, D.E. (2001b). Woodworth (1899): Movement variability and theories of motor control. In M.L. Latash & V.M. Zatsiorsky (Eds.), Classics in movement science (pp. 409-435). Champaign, IL: Human Kinetics.

Newell, K.M., & van Emmerik, R.E.A. (1989). The acquisition of coordination: Preliminary analysis of learning to write. Human Movement Science, 8, 17-32.

Newell, K.M., van Emmerik, R.E.A., & Sprague, R.L. (1993). Stereotypy and variability. In K.M. Newell & D.M. Corcos (Eds.), Variability and motor control (pp. 475-496). Champaign, IL: Human Kinetics.

Newell, K.M., & Walter, C.B. (1981). Kinematic and kinetic parameters as information feedback in motor skill acquisition. Journal of Human Movement Studies, 7, 235-254.

Nicklaus, J., & Bowden, K. (1974). Golf my way. New York: Simon & Schuster.

Nichols, T.R., & Houk, J.C. (1976). Improvement of linearity and regulation of stiffness that results from actions of stretch reflex. Journal of Neurophysiology, 39, 119-142.

Nicholson, D.E., & Schmidt, R.A. (1991). Timing-task duration determines post-response error-detection capabilities. Paper presented at NASPSPA annual meeting, Monterey, CA.

Nickerson, R.S. (1973). Intersensory facilitation of reaction time: Energy summation or preparation enhancement? Psychological Review, 80, 489-509.

Nickerson, R.S., Kalikow, D.N., & Stevens, K.N. (1976). Computer-aided speech training for the deaf. Journal of Speech and Hearing Disorders, 41, 120-132.

Nideffer, R.M. (1976). The inner athlete: Mind plus muscle for winning. New York: Crowell.

Noble, C.E. (1968). The learning of psychomotor skills. Annual Review of Psychology, 19, 203-250.

Norman, D.A. (1969). Memory while shadowing. Quarterly Journal of Experimental Psychology, 21, 85-93.

Norman, D.A. (1976). Memory and attention (2nd ed.). New York: Wiley.

Norman, D.A. (1981). The categorization of action slips. Psychological Review, 88, 1-15.

Norman, D.A., & Bobrow, D.G. (1975). On data-limited and resource-limited processes. Cognitive Psychology, 7, 44-64.

Norman, J. (2002). Two visual systems and two theories of perception: An attempt to reconcile the constructivist and ecological approaches. Behavioral and Brain Sciences, 25, 73-144.

Obhi, S.S., Matkovich, S., & Gilbert, S.J. (2009). Modification of planned actions. Experimental Brain Research, 192, 287-292.

Ogden, G.D., Levine, J.M., & Eisner, E.J. (1979). Measurement of workload by secondary tasks. Human Factors, 21, 529-548.

Ojha, H.A., Kern, R.W., Lin, C.-H., & Winstein, C.J. (2009). Age affects the attentional demands of stair ambulation: Evidence from a dual-task approach. Physical Therapy, 89, 1080-1088.

Ollis, S., Button, C., & Fairweather, M. (2005). The influence of professional expertise and task complexity upon the potency of the contextual interference effect. Acta Psychologica, 118, 229-244.

Onla-or, S., & Winstein, C.J. (2008). Determining the optimal challenge point for motor skill learning in adults with moderately severe Parkinson's disease. Neurorehabilation and Neural Repair, 22, 385-395.

Osgood, C.E. (1949). The similarity paradox in human learning: A resolution. Psychological Review, 56, 132-143.

Osman, A., Kornblum, S., & Meyer, D.E. (1990). Does motor programming necessitate response execution? Journal of Experimental Psychology: Human Perception and Performance, 16, 183-198.

Osu, R., Hirai, S., Yoshioka, T., & Kawato, M. (2004). Random presentation enables subjects to adapt to two opposing forces on the hand. Nature Neuroscience, 7, 111-112.

Otto-de Haart, E.G., Carey, D.P., & Milne, A.B. (1999). More thoughts on perceiving and grasping the Müller-Lyer illusion. Neuropsychologia, 37, 1437-1444.

Oudejans, R.R.D., Michaels, C.F., Bakker, F.C., & Davids, K. (1999). Shedding some light on catching in the dark: Perceptual mechanisms for catching fly balls. Journal of Experimental Psychology: Human Perception and Performance, 25, 531-542.

Oudejans, R.R.D., & Pijpers, J.R. (2009). Training with anxiety has a positive effect on expert perceptual–motor performance under pressure. Quarterly Journal of Experimental Psychology, 62, 1631-1647.

Oudejans, R.R.D., Verheijen, R., Bakker, F.C., Gerrits, J.C., Steinbrückner, M., & Beek, P.J. (2000). Errors in judging "offside" in football. Nature, 404, 33.

Oude Nijhuis, L.B., Janssen, L., Bloem, B.R., vanDijk, J.G., Gielen, S.C., Borm, G.F., & Overeem, S. (2007). Choice reaction times for human head rotations are shortened by startling acoustic stimuli, irrespective of stimulus direction. Journal of Physiology, 584, 97-109.

Overduin, S.A., Richardson, A.G., Lane, C.E., Bizzi, E., & Press, D.Z. (2006). Intermittent practice facilitates stable motor memories. Journal of Neuroscience, 26, 11888-11892.

Paillard, J., & Bruchon, M. (1968). Active and passive movements in the calibration of position sense. In S.J. Freedman (Ed.), The neuropsychology of spatially oriented behavior. New York: Dorsey.

Papaxanthis, C., Schieppati, M., Gentili, R., & Pozzo, T. (2002). Imagined and actual arm movements have similar durations when performed under different conditions of direction and mass. Experimental Brain Research, 143, 447-452.

Park, J.-H., & Shea, C.H. (2002). Effector independence. Journal of Motor Behavior, 34, 253-270.

Park, J.-H., & Shea, C.H. (2003). Effect of practice on effector independence. Journal of Motor Behavior, 35, 33-40.

Park, J.-H., & Shea, C.H. (2005). Sequence learning: Response structure and effector transfer. Quarterly Journal of Experimental Psychology, 58A, 387-419.

Park, J.-H., Shea, C.H., &Wright, D.L. (2000). Reduced frequency concurrent and terminal feedback: A test of the guidance hypothesis. Journal of Motor Behavior, 32, 287-296.

Parker, J.F. Jr., & Fleishman, E.A. (1960). Ability factors and component performance measures as predictors of complex tracking behavior. Psychological Monographs, 74 (Whole No. 503).

Partridge, L.D. (1979). Muscle properties: A problem for the motor physiologist. In R.E. Talbott & D.R. Humphrey (Eds.), Posture and movement (pp. 189-229). New York: Raven Press.

Partridge, L.D. (1983). Neural control drives a muscle spring: A persisting yet limited motor theory. Experimental Brain Research Supplementum, 7, 280-290.

Partridge, L.D., & Benton, L.A. (1981). Muscle, the motor. In V.B. Brooks (Ed.), Handbook of physiology: Vol. 2. Motor control (pp. 43-106). Bethesda, MD: American Physiological Society.

Pashler, H. (1993, January-February). Doing two things at the same time. American Scientist, 81(1), 48-49.

Pashler, H. (1994). Dual-task interference in simple tasks: Data and theory. Psychological Bulletin, 116, 220-244.

Pashler, H. (1999). The psychology of attention. Cambridge, MA: MIT Press.

Patla, A.E. (1989). In search of laws for the visual control of locomotion: Some observations. Journal of Experimental Psychology: Human Perception and Performance, 15, 624-628.

Patla, A.E. (1997). Understanding the roles of vision in the control of human locomotion. Gait & Posture, 5, 54-69.

Patla, A.E. (1998). How is human gait controlled by vision? Ecological Psychology, 10, 287-302.

Patla, A.E., Frank, J.S., Allard, F., & Thomas, E. (1985). Speed-accuracy characteristics of saccadic eye movements. Journal of Motor Behavior, 17, 411-419.

Patla, A.E., Rietdyk, S., Martin, C., & Prentice, S. (1996). Locomotor patterns of the leading and the trailing limbs as solid and fragile obstacles are stepped over: Some insights into the role of vision during locomotion. Journal of Motor Behavior, 28, 35-47.

Patla, A.E., Robinson, C., Samways, M., & Armstrong, C.J. (1989). Visual control of step length during overground locomotion: Task-specific modulation of the locomotor synergy. Journal of Experimental Psychology: Human Perception and Performance, 15, 603-617.

Patrick, J. (1971). The effect of interpolated motor activities in short-term motor memory. Journal of Motor Behavior, 3, 39-48.

Patterson, J.T., & Wessel, J. (2002). Strategies for retraining functional movement in persons with Alzheimer disease: A review. Physiotherapy Canada, 54, 274-280.

Paulignan, Y., & Jeannerod, M. (1996). Prehension movements: The visuomotor channels hypothesis revisited. In A.M. Wing, P. Haggard, & J.R. Flanagan (Eds.), Hand and brain: The neurophysiology of psychology of hand movements (pp. 265-282). San Diego: Academic Press.

Paulignan, Y., Jeannerod, M., MacKenzie, C., & Marteniuk, R. (1991). Selective perturbation of visual input during prehension movements. 2. The effects of changing object size. Experimental Brain Research, 87, 407-420.

Paulignan, Y., MacKenzie, C., Marteniuk, R., & Jeannerod, M. (1991). Selective perturbation of visual input during prehension movements. 1. The effects of changing object position. Experimental Brain Research, 83, 502-512.

Payne, V.G., & Isaacs, L.D. (2007). Human motor development: A lifespan approach (7th ed.). Columbus, OH: McGraw-Hill.

Pearson, K. (1976). The control of walking. Scientific American, 235, 72-86.

Pearson, K., & Gordon, J. (2000a). Locomotion. In E.R. Kandel, J.H. Schwartz, & T.M. Jessell (Eds.), Principles of neural science (pp. 739-755). New York: McGraw-Hill.

Pearson, K., & Gordon, J. (2000b). Spinal reflexes. In E.R. Kandel, J.H. Schwartz, & T.M. Jessell (Eds.), Principles of neural science (pp. 713-736). New York: McGraw-Hill.

Pellecchia, G., Shockley, K., & Turvey, M.T. (2005). Concurrent cognitive task modulates coordination dynamics. Cognitive Science, 29, 531-557.

Pélisson, D., Prablanc, C., Goodale, M.A., & Jeannerod, M. (1986). Visual control of reaching movements without vision of the limb II. Evidence of fast unconscious processes correcting the trajectory of the hand to the final position of double-step stimulus. Experimental Brain Research, 62, 303-311.

Peper, C.E., Ridderikhoff, A., Daffertshofer, A., & Beek, P.J. (2004). Explanatory limitations of the HKB model: Incentives for a two-tiered model of rhythmic interlimb coordination. Human Movement Science, 23, 673-697.

Pepper, R.L., & Herman, L.M. (1970). Decay and interference effects in the short-term retention of a discrete motor act. Journal of Experimental Psychology, 83 (Monograph Suppl. 2).

Perel, M. (1976). Analyzing the role of driver/vehicle incompatibilities in accident causation using police reports (Tech. Rep. No. DOT H5-806-509). Washington, DC: U.S. Department of Transportation.

Perenin, M.-T., & Vighetto, A. (1988). Optic ataxia: A specific disruption in visuomotor mechanisms I. Different aspects of the deficit in reaching for objects. Brain, 111, 643-674.

Perkins, G.D. (2007). Simulation in resuscitation training. Resuscitation, 73, 202-211.

Perkins-Ceccato, N., Passmore, S.R., & Lee, T.D. (2003). Effects of focus of attention depend on golfers' skill. Journal of Sports Sciences, 21, 593-600.

Peters, M. (1977). Simultaneous performance of two motor activities: The factor of timing. Neuropsychologica, 15, 461-464.

Peters, M. (1985). Performance of a rubato-like task: When two things cannot be done at the same time. Music Perception, 2, 471-482.

Peterson, L.R., & Peterson, M.J. (1959). Short-term retention of individual verbal items. Journal of Experimental Psychology, 58, 193-198.

Petrynski, W. (2003). Róne rodzaje odpowiedzi czucioworuchowych w schemacie Schmidta [Various kinds of sensory-motor performances in the Schmidt's scheme]. Antropomotoryka, 13, 97-110.

Pew, R.W. (1966). Acquisition of hierarchical control over the temporal organization of a skill. Journal of Experimental Psychology, 71, 764-771.

Pew, R.W. (1970). Toward a process-oriented theory of human skilled performance. Journal of Motor Behavior, 2, 8-24.

Pew, R.W. (1974a). Human perceptual-motor performance. In B.H. Kantowitz (Ed.), Human information processing: Tutorials in performance and cognition (pp. 1-39). Hillsdale, NJ: Erlbaum.

Pew, R.W. (1974b). Levels of analysis in motor control. Brain Research, 71, 393-400.

Phillips, J.R., & Berkhout, J. (1976). Uses of computer-assisted instruction in developing psychomotor skills related to heavy machinery operation (Contract Rep. DAHC-19-75G0009). Alexandria, VA: U.S. Army Research Institute.

Piek, J. (2006). Infant motor development. Champaign, IL: Human Kinetics.

Pigott, R.E., & Shapiro, D.C. (1984). Motor schema: The structure of the variability session. Research Quarterly for Exercise and Sport, 55, 41-45.

Plamondon, R., & Alimi, A.M. (1997). Speed/accuracy tradeoffs in target-directed movements. Behavioral and Brain Sciences, 20, 279-349.

Playford, E.D., Siegert, R., Levack, W., & Freeman, J. (2009). Areas of consensus and controversy about goal setting in rehabilitation: A conference report. Clinical Rehabilitation, 23, 334-344.

Pohl, P.S., Winstein, C.J., & Fisher, B.E. (1996). The locus of age-related movement slowing: Sensory processing in continuous goal-directed aiming. Journal of Gerontology: Psychological Sciences, 51B, P94-P102.

Polanyi, M. (1958). Personal knowledge: Towards a post-critical philosophy. London: Routledge and Kegan Paul.

Polit, A., & Bizzi, E. (1978). Processes controlling arm movements in monkeys. Science, 201, 1235-1237.

Polit, A., & Bizzi, E. (1979). Characteristics of motor programs underlying arm movements in monkeys. Journal of Neurophysiology, 42, 183-194.

Pollard, R. (1986). Home advantage in soccer: A retrospective analysis. Journal of Sports Sciences, 4, 237-248.

Pollock, B.J., & Lee, T.D. (1992). Effects of the model's skill level on observational motor learning. Research Quarterly for Exercise and Sport, 63, 25-29.

Pollock, B.J., & Lee, T.D. (1997). Dissociated contextual interference effects in children and adults. Perceptual and Motor Skills, 84, 851-858.

Pons, T.P., Garraghty, P.E., Ommaya, A.K., Kaas, J.H., Taub, E., & Mishkin, M. (1991). Massive cortical reorganization after sensory deafferentation in adult macaques. Science, 252, 1857-1860.

Populin, L., Rose, D.J., & Heath, K. (1990). The role of attention in one-handed catching. Journal of Motor Behavior, 22, 149-158.

Posner, M.I. (1969). Reduced attention and the performance of "automated" movements. Journal of Motor Behavior, 1, 245-258.

Posner, M.I. (1978). Chronometric explorations of mind. Hillsdale, NJ: Erlbaum.

Posner, M.I., & Cohen, Y. (1984). Components of visual orienting. In H. Bouma & D.G. Bouwhuis (Eds.), Attention and performance X: Control of language processes (pp. 531-556). Hillsdale, NJ: Erlbaum.

Posner, M.I., & Keele, S.W. (1969). Attentional demands of movement. Proceedings of the 16th Congress of Applied Psychology. Amsterdam: Swets and Zeitlinger.

Posner, M.I., & Konick, A.F. (1966). On the role of interference in short-term retention. Journal of Experimental Psychology, 72, 221-231.

Posner, M.I., Nissen, M.J., & Ogden, W.C. (1978). Attended and unattended processing modes: The role of set for spatial location. In H.L. Pick & I.J. Saltzman (Eds.), Modes of perceiving and processing information (pp. 137-157). Hillsdale, NJ: Erlbaum.

Posner, M.I., & Petersen, S.E. (1990). The attention system of the human brain. Annual Review of Neuroscience, 13, 25-42.

Posner, M.I., & Snyder, C.R. (1975). Attention and cognitive control. In R.L. Solso (Ed.), Information processing and cognition. Hillsdale, NJ: Erlbaum.

Poulton, E.C. (1950). Perceptual anticipation and reaction time. Quarterly Journal of Experimental Psychology, 2, 99-112.

Poulton, E.C. (1957). On prediction in skilled movements. Psychological Bulletin, 54, 467-478.

Poulton, E.C. (1973). The effect of fatigue upon inspection work. Applied Ergonomics, 4, 73-83.

Poulton, E.C. (1974). Tracking skill and manual control. New York: Academic Press.

Pratt, J., & Abrams, R.A. (1994). Action-centered inhibition: Effects of distractors on movement planning and execution. Human Movement Science, 13, 245-254.

Pratt, J., & Abrams, R.A. (1996). Practice and component submovements: The roles of programming and

feedback in rapid aimed limb movements. Journal of Motor Behavior, 28, 149-156.

Pratt, J., Adam, J.J., & Fischer, M.H. (2007). Visual layout modulates Fitts's law: The importance of first and last positions. Psychonomic Bulletin & Review, 14, 350-355.

Proctor, R.W., & Dutta, A. (1995). Skill acquisition and human performance. Thousand Oaks, CA: Sage.

Proctor, R.W., & Reeve, T.G. (Eds.). (1990). Stimulus-response compatibility: An integrated perspective. Amsterdam: Elsevier.

Proctor, R.W., & Van Zandt, T. (1994). Human factors in simple and complex systems. Boston: Allyn & Bacon.

Prodoehl, J., Corcos, D.M., & Vaillancourt, D.E. (2009). Basal ganglia mechanisms underlying precision grip force control. Neuroscience & Biobehavioral Reviews, 33, 900-908.

Proteau, L. (1992). On the specificity of learning and the role of visual information for movement control. In L. Proteau & D. Elliott (Eds.), Vision and motor control (pp. 67-103). Amsterdam: Elsevier.

Proteau, L. (1995). Sensory integration in the learning of an aiming task. Canadian Journal of Experimental Psychology, 49, 113-120.

Proteau, L. (2005). Visual afferent information dominates other sources of afferent information during mixed practice of a video-aiming task. Experimental Brain Research, 161, 441-456.

Proteau, L., Blandin, Y., Alain, C., & Dorion, A. (1994). The effects of the amount and variability of practice on the learning of a multi-segmented motor task. Acta Psychologica, 85, 61-74.

Proteau, L., & Isabelle, G. (2002). On the role of visual afferent information for the control of aiming movements toward targets of different sizes. Journal of Motor Behavior, 34, 367-384.

Proteau, L., Marteniuk, R.G., & Lévesque, L. (1992). A sensorimotor basis for motor learning: Evidence indicating specificity of practice. Quarterly Journal of Experimental Psychology, 44A, 557-575.

Provins, K.A. (1958). The effect of peripheral nerve block on the appreciation and execution of finger movements. Journal of Physiology, 143, 55-67.

Purdy, W.C. (1958). The hypothesis of psychophysical correspondence in space perception. PhD thesis, Cornell University, Ithaca, NY.

Pyle, W.H. (1919). Transfer and interference in card-distributing. Journal of Educational Psychology, 10, 107-110.

Quesada, D.C., & Schmidt, R.A. (1970). A test of the Adams-Creamer decay hypothesis for the timing of motor responses. Journal of Motor Behavior, 2, 273-283.

Quinn, J.T. Jr., Schmidt, R.A., Zelaznik, H.N., Hawkins, B., & McFarquhar, R. (1980). Target-size influences on reaction time with movement time controlled. Journal of Motor Behavior, 12, 239-261.

Quinn, J.T. Jr., & Sherwood, D.E. (1983). Time requirements of changes in program and parameter variables in rapid ongoing movements. Journal of Motor Behavior, 15, 163-178.

Rack, P.M.H., & Westbury, D.R. (1969). The effects of length and stimulus rate on tension in the isometric cat soleus muscle. Journal of Physiology, 204, 443-460.

Radlo, S.J., Janelle, C.M., Barba, D.A., & Frehlich, S.G. (2001). Perceptual decision-making for baseball pitch recognition: Using P300 latency and amplitude to index attentional processing. Research Quarterly for Exercise and Sport, 72, 22-31.

Raibert, M.H. (1977). Motor control and learning by the state-space model (Tech. Rep. No. AI-TR-439). Cambridge: Massachusetts Institute of Technology, Artificial Intelligence Laboratory.

Ranganathan, R., & Newell, K.M. (2009). Influence of augmented feedback on coordination strategies. Journal of Motor Behavior, 41, 317-330.

Raynor, A.J., Yi, C.J., Abernethy, B., & Jong, Q.J. (2002). Are transitions in human gait determined by mechanical, kinetic or energetic factors? Human Movement Science, 21, 785-805.

Reason, J. (1990). Human error. Cambridge: Cambridge University Press.

Reason, J., & Mycielska, K. (1982). Absent-minded? The psychology of mental lapses and everyday errors. Englewood Cliffs, NJ: Prentice Hall.

Redelmeier, D.A., & Tibshirani, R.J. (1997). Association between cellular-telephone calls and motor vehicle collisions. New England Journal of Medicine, 336, 453-458.

Reed, E.S. (1988). Applying the theory of action systems to the study of motor skills. In O.G. Meijer & K. Roth (Eds.), Complex movement behaviour: "The" motor-action controversy (pp. 45-86). Amsterdam: Elsevier.

Reed, N., McLeod, P., & Dienes, Z. (2010). Implicit knowledge and motor skill: What people who know how to catch don't know. Consciousness and Cognition, 19, 63-76.

Reeve, T.G., Dornier, L.A., & Weeks, D.J. (1990). Precision of knowledge of results: Consideration of the accuracy requirements imposed by the task. Research Quarterly for Exercise and Sport, 61, 284-290.

Reinhart, W. (1994). The effect of countermeasures to reduce the incidence of unintended acceleration accidents (Paper No. 94 S5 O 07). Washington, DC: NHTSA, U.S. Department of Transportation.

Reinkensmeyer, D.J., Emken, J., & Cramer, S. (2004). Robotics, motor learning, and neurologic recovery. Annual Review of Biomedical Engineering, 6, 497-525.

Reinkensmeyer, D.J., & Patton, J.L. (2009). Can robots help the learning of skilled actions? Exercise and Sport Sciences Reviews, 37, 43-51.

Rensink, R.A. (2002). Change detection. Annual Review of Psychology, 53, 245-277.

Repp, B.H. (2001). Phase correction, phase resetting, and phase shifts after subliminal timing perturbations in sensorimotor synchronization. Journal of Experimental Psychology: Human Perception and Performance, 27, 600-621.

Repp, B.H. (2005). Sensorimotor synchronization: A review of the tapping literature. Psychonomic Bulletin & Review, 12, 969-992.

Reynolds, B., & Bilodeau, I.M. (1952). Acquisition and retention of three psychomotor tests as a function of distribution of practice during acquisition. Journal of Experimental Psychology, 44, 19-26.

Richardson, M.J., Marsh, K.L., Isenhower, R.W., Goodman, J.R.L., & Schmidt, R.C. (2007). Rocking together: Dynamics of intentional and unintentional interpersonal coordination. Human Movement Science, 26, 867-891.

Richardson-Klavehn, A., & Bjork, R.A. (1988). Measures of memory. Annual Review of Psychology, 39, 475-543.

Richter-Heinrich, E., & Miller, N. (Eds.). (1982). Biofeedback—basic problems and clinical applications. Amsterdam: Elsevier.

Riek, S., Tresilian, J.R., Mon-Williams, M., Coppard, V.L., & Carson, R.G. (2003). Bimanual aiming and overt attention: One law for two hands. Experimental Brain Research, 153, 59-75.

Rizzolatti, G., & Craighero, L. (2004). The mirror-neuron system. Annual Review of Neuroscience, 27, 169-192.

Rizzolatti, G., & Fabbri-Destro, M. (2010). Mirror neurons: From discovery to autism. Experimental Brain Research, 200, 223-237.

Roberts, J.R., Jones, R., Mansfield, N.J., & Rothberg, S.J. (2005). Evaluation of impact sounds on the "feel" of a golf shot. Journal of Sound and Vibration, 287, 651-666.

Robertson, S.D., Zelaznik, H.N., Lantero, D.A., Bojczyk, K.G., Spencer, R.M., Doffin, J.G., & Schneidt, T. (1999). Correlations for timing consistency among tapping and drawing tasks: Evidence against a single timing process for motor control. Journal of Experimental Psychology: Human Perception and Performance, 25, 1316-1330.

Robinson, G.H., & Kavinsky, R.C. (1976). On Fitts' law with two-handed movement. IEEE Transactions on Systems, Man, and Cybernetics, 6, 504-505.

Rock, P.B., & Harris, M.G. (2006). Tau-dot as a potential control variable for visually guided braking. Journal of Experimental Psychology: Human Perception and Performance, 32, 251-267.

Roediger, H.L. (1990). Implicit memory: Retention without remembering. American Psychologist, 45, 1043-1056.

Roediger, H.L. (Ed.). (2008a). Cognitive psychology of memory (Vol. 2 of Learning and memory: A comprehensive reference). Oxford: Elsevier.

Roediger, H.L. (2008b). Relativity of remembering: Why the laws of memory vanished. Annual Review of Psychology, 59, 225-254.

Roediger, H.L., & McDermott, K.B. (1993). Implicit memory in normal human subjects. In H. Spinnler & F. Boller (Eds.), Handbook of neuropsychology (Vol. 8) (pp. 63-131). Amsterdam: Elsevier.

Rogers, C.A. Jr. (1974). Feedback precision and postfeedback interval duration. Journal of Experimental Psychology, 102, 604-608.

Rogers, D.K., Bendrups, A.P., & Lewis, M.M. (1985). Disturbed proprioception following a period of muscle vibration in humans. Neuroscience Letters, 57, 147-152.

Roller, C.A., Cohen, H.S., Kimball, K.T., & Bloomberg, J.J. (2001). Variable practice with lenses improves visuo-motor plasticity. Cognitive Brain Research, 12, 341-352.

Romaiguère, P., Hasbroucq, T., Possamaï, C., & Seal, J. (1993). Intensity to force translation: A new effect of stimulus-response compatibility revealed by analysis of response time and electromyographic activity of a prime mover. Cognitive Brain Research, 1, 197-201.

Ronsse, R., Miall, R.C., & Swinnen, S.P. (2009). Multisensory integration in dynamical behaviors: Maximum likelihood estimation across bimanual skill learning. Journal of Neuroscience, 29, 8419-8428.

Rose, D.J., & Christina, R.W. (1990). Attention demands of precision pistol-shooting as a function of skill level. Research Quarterly for Exercise and Sport, 61, 111-113.

Rosenbaum, D.A. (1980). Human movement initiation: Specification of arm, direction, and extent. Journal of Experimental Psychology: General, 109, 444-474.

Rosenbaum, D.A. (1983). The movement precuing technique: Assumptions, applications, and extensions. In R.A. Magill (Ed.), Memory and control of action (pp. 231-274). Amsterdam: Elsevier.

Rosenbaum, D.A. (2009). Human motor control (2nd ed.). San Diego: Academic Press.

Rosenbaum, D.A. (2005). The Cinderella of psychology: The neglect of motor control in the science of mental life and behavior. American Psychologist, 60, 308-317.

Rosenbaum, D.A., Cohen, R.G., Jax, S.A., Weiss, D.J., & van der Wel, R. (2007). The problem of serial order in behavior: Lashley's legacy. Human Movement Science, 26, 525-554.

Rosenbaum, D.A., Loukopoulos, L.D., Meulenbroek, R.G.J., Vaughan, J., & Engelbrecht, S.E. (1995). Planning reaches by evaluating stored postures. Psychological Review, 102, 28-67.

Rosenbaum, D.A., Marchak, F., Barnes, H.J., Vaughan, J., Slotta, J.D., & Jorgensen, M.J. (1990). Constraints for action selection: Overhand versus underhand grips. In M. Jeannerod (Ed.), Attention and performance XIII (pp. 321-342). Hillsdale, NJ: Erlbaum.

Rosenbaum, D.A., Meulenbroek, R.G.J., Vaughan, J., & Jansen, C. (2001). Posture-based motion planning: Applications to grasping. Psychological Review, 108, 709-734.

Rosenbaum, D.A., & Patashnik, O. (1980). Time to time in the human motor system. In R.S. Nickerson (Ed.), Attention and performance VIII (pp. 93-106). Hillsdale, NJ: Erlbaum.

Rosenbaum, D.A., van Heugten, C.M., & Caldwell, G.E. (1996). From cognition to biomechanics and back: The end-state comfort effect and the middle-is-faster effect. Acta Psychologica, 94, 59-85.

Rosenbaum, D.A., Vaughan, J., Barnes, H.J., & Jorgensen, M.J. (1992). Time course of movement planning: Selection of handgrips for object manipulation. Journal of Experimental Psychology: Learning, Memory, and Cognition, 18, 1058-1073.

Rosenbaum, D.A., Weber, R.J., Hazelett, W.M., & Hindorff, V. (1986). The parameter remapping effect in human performance: Evidence from tongue twisters and finger fumblers. Journal of Memory and Language, 25, 710-725.

Ross, D., Bird, A.M., Doody, S.G., & Zoeller, M. (1985). Effects of modeling and videotape feedback with knowledge of results on motor performance. Human Movement Science, 4, 149-157.

Rossignol, S., Dubuc, R., & Gossard, J.P. (2006). Dynamic sensorimotor interactions in locomotion. Physiological Review, 86, 89-154.

Roth, K. (1988). Investigations on the basis of the generalized motor programme hypothesis. In O.G. Meijer & K. Roth (Eds.), Complex motor behavior: "The" motor-action controversy (pp. 261-288). Amsterdam: Elsevier.

Rothstein, A.L. (1973). Effect of temporal expectancy of the position of a selected foreperiod within a range. Research Quarterly, 44, 132-139.

Rothstein, A.L., & Arnold, R.K. (1976). Bridging the gap: Application of research on videotape feedback and bowling. Motor Skills: Theory Into Practice, 1, 35-62.

Rothwell, J.C., Traub, M.M., Day, B.L., Obeso, J.A., Thomas, P.K., & Marsden, C.D. (1982). Manual motor performance in a deafferented man. Brain, 105, 515-542.

Rubin, W.M. (1978). Application of signal detection theory to error detection in ballistic motor skills. Journal of Experimental Psychology: Human Perception and Performance, 4, 311-320.

Ryan, E.D. (1962). Retention of stabilometer and pursuit rotor skills. Research Quarterly, 33, 593-598.

Ryan, E.D. (1965). Retention of stabilometer performance over extended periods of time. Research Quarterly, 36, 46-51.

Ryan, L.J., & Fritz, M.S. (2007). Erroneous knowledge of results affects decision and memory processes on timing tasks. Journal of Experimental Psychology: Human Perception and Performance, 33, 1468-1482.

Ryan, L.J., & Robey, T.B. (2002). Learning and performance effects of accurate and erroneous knowledge of results on time perception. Acta Psychologica, 111, 83-100.

Sack, A.T., & Linden, D.E.J. (2003). Combining transcranial magnetic stimulation and functional imaging in cognitive brain research: Possibilities and limitations. Brain Research Reviews, 43, 41-56.

Sainburg, R.L. (2005). Handedness: Differential specializations for control of trajectory and position. Exercise and Sport Sciences Reviews, 33, 206-213.

Sale, D., & MacDougall, D. (1981). Specificity in strength training: A review for the coach and athlete. Canadian Journal of Applied Sport Sciences, 6, 87-92.

Salesse, R., Oullier, O., & Temprado, J.J. (2005). Plane of motion mediates the coalition of constraints in rhythmic bimanual coordination. Journal of Motor Behavior, 37, 454-464.

Salmela, J.H., & Fiorito, P. (1979). Visual cues in ice hockey goaltending. Canadian Journal of Applied Sport Science, 4, 56-59.

Salmoni, A.W., Ross, D., Dill, S., & Zoeller, M. (1983). Knowledge of results and perceptual-motor learning. Human Movement Science, 2, 77-89.

Salmoni, A.W., Schmidt, R.A., & Walter, C.B. (1984). Knowledge of results and motor learning: A review and critical reappraisal. Psychological Bulletin, 95, 355-386.

Salmoni, A.W., Sullivan, S.J., & Starkes, J.L. (1976). The attention demands of movements: A critique of the probe technique. Journal of Motor Behavior, 8, 161-169.

Salthouse, T.A. (1984). Effects of age and skill in typing. Journal of Experimental Psychology: General, 113, 345-371.

Salthouse, T.A. (1985). A theory of cognitive aging. Amsterdam: Elsevier.

Salthouse, T.A. (1986). Effects of practice on a typing-like keying task. Acta Psychologica, 62, 189-198.

Sanders, A.F. (1980). Stage analysis of reaction processes. In G.E. Stelmach & J. Requin (Eds.), Tutorials in motor behavior (pp. 331-354). Amsterdam: Elsevier.

Sanders, M.S., & McCormick, E.J. (1993). Human factors in engineering and design (7th ed.). New York: McGraw-Hill.

Sanes, J.N. (1990). Motor representations in deafferented humans: A mechanism for disordered movement performance. In M. Jeannerod (Ed.), Attention and performance XIII (pp. 714-735). Hillsdale, NJ: Erlbaum.

Sanes, J.N., Mauritz, K.-H., Dalakas, M.C., & Evarts, E.V. (1985). Motor control in humans with large-fiber sensory neuropathy. Human Neurobiology, 4, 101-114.

Savelsbergh, G., & Davids, K. (2002). "Keeping the eye on the ball": The legacy of John Whiting (1929-2001) in sport science. Journal of Sports Sciences, 20, 79-82.

Savelsbergh, G.J.P., van der Kamp, J., Williams, A.M., & Ward, P. (2005). Anticipation and visual search behaviour in expert soccer goalkeepers. Ergonomics, 48, 1686-1697.

Savelsbergh, G.J.P., & Whiting, H.T.A. (1996). Catching: A motor learning and developmental perspective. In H. Heuer & S.W. Keele (Eds.), Handbook of perception and action. Vol. 2: Motor skills (pp. 461-501). San Diego: Academic Press.

Savelsbergh, G.J.P., Whiting, H.T.A., & Bootsma, R.J. (1991). Grasping tau. Journal of Experimental Psychology: Human Perception and Performance, 17, 315-322.

Savelsbergh, G.J.P., Whiting, H.T.A., & Pijpers, J.R. (1992). The control of catching. In J.J. Summers (Ed.), Approaches to the study of motor control and learning (pp. 313-342). Amsterdam: Elsevier.

Savelsbergh, G.J.P., Whiting, H.T.A., Pijpers, J.R., & van Santvoord, A.A.M. (1993). The visual guidance of catching. Experimental Brain Research, 93, 148-156.

Schaal, S., Sternad, D., Osu, R., & Kawato, M. (2004). Rhythmic arm movement is not discrete. Nature Neuroscience, 1, 1137-1144.

Schacter, D.L. (1983). Amnesia observed: Remembering and forgetting in a natural environment. Journal of Abnormal Psychology, 92, 236-242.

Schacter, D.L. (1987). Implicit memory: History and current status. Journal of Experimental Psychology: Learning, Memory, and Cognition, 13, 501-518.

Schellekens, J.M.H., Kalverboer, A.F., & Scholten, C.A. (1984). The micro-structure of tapping movements in children. Journal of Motor Behavior, 16, 20-39.

Schendel, J.D., & Hagman, J.D. (1982). On sustaining procedural skills over a prolonged retention interval. Journal of Applied Psychology, 67, 605-610.

Schendel, J.D., Heller, F.H., Finley, D.L., & Hawley, J.K. (1985). Use of the Weaponeer Marksmanship Trainer in predicting M16A1 rifle qualification performance. Human Factors, 27, 313-325.

Schendel, J.D., & Newell, K.M. (1976). On processing the information from knowledge of results. Journal of Motor Behavior, 8, 251-255.

Schlager, N. (Ed.). (1994). When technology fails: Significant technological disasters, accidents and failures of the twentieth century. Detroit: Gale Research.

Schmidt, R.A. (1967). Motor factors in coincident timing. Unpublished doctoral dissertation, University of Illinois, Urbana.

Schmidt, R.A. (1968). Anticipation and timing in human motor performance. Psychological Bulletin, 70, 631-646.

Schmidt, R.A. (1969a). Intra-limb specificity of motor response consistency. Journal of Motor Behavior, 1, 89-99.

Schmidt, R.A. (1969b). Movement time as a determiner of timing accuracy. Journal of Experimental Psychology, 79, 43-47.

Schmidt, R.A. (1969c). Consistency of response components as a function of selected motor variables. Research Quarterly, 40, 561-566.

Schmidt, R.A. (1971a). Proprioception and the timing of motor responses. Psychological Bulletin, 76, 383-393.

Schmidt, R.A. (1971b). Retroactive interference and amount of original learning in verbal and motor tasks. Research Quarterly, 42, 314-326.

Schmidt, R.A. (1972a). The case against learning and forgetting scores. Journal of Motor Behavior, 4, 79-88.

Schmidt, R.A. (1972b). The index of preprogramming (IP): A statistical method for evaluating the role of feedback in simple movements. Psychonomic Science, 27, 83-85.

Schmidt, R.A. (1975a). Motor skills. New York: Harper & Row.

Schmidt, R.A. (1975b). A schema theory of discrete motor skill learning. Psychological Review, 82, 225-260.

Schmidt, R.A. (1976a). Control processes in motor skills. Exercise and Sport Sciences Reviews, 4, 229-261.

Schmidt, R.A. (1976b). Movement education and the schema theory. In E. Crawford (Ed.), Report of the 1976 conference June 3-8. Cedar Falls, IA: National Association for Physical Education of College Women.

Schmidt, R.A. (1977). Schema theory: Implications for movement education. Motor Skills: Theory Into Practice, 2, 36-38.

Schmidt, R.A. (1980). Past and future issues in motor programming. Research Quarterly for Exercise and Sport, 51, 122-140.

Schmidt, R.A. (1983). On the underlying structure of well-learned motor responses: A discussion of Namikas and Schneider and Fisk. In R.A. Magill (Ed.), Memory and control of action (pp. 145-165). Amsterdam: Elsevier.

Schmidt, R.A. (1985). The search for invariance in skilled movement behavior. Research Quarterly for Exercise and Sport, 56, 188-200.

Schmidt, R.A. (1987). The acquisition of skill: Some modifications to the perception-action relationship through practice. In H. Heuer & A.F. Sanders (Eds.), Perspectives on perception and action (pp. 77-103). Hillsdale, NJ: Erlbaum.

Schmidt, R.A. (1988). Motor and action perspectives on motor behaviour. In O.G Meijer & K. Roth (Eds.), Complex movement behaviour: "The" motor-action controversy (pp. 3-44). Amsterdam: Elsevier.

Schmidt, R.A. (1989a). Toward a better understanding of the acquisition of skill: Theoretical and practical contributions of the task approach. In J.S. Skinner, C.B. Corbin, D.M. Landers, P.E. Martin, & C.L. Wells (Eds.), Future directions in exercise and sport science research (pp. 395-410). Champaign, IL: Human Kinetics.

Schmidt, R.A. (1989b). Unintended acceleration: A review of human factors contributions. Human Factors, 31, 345-364.

Schmidt, R.A. (1990). Distinguished scholar award to Jack Ashton Adams. NASPSPA Newsletter, 15, 4-5.

Schmidt, R.A. (1991a). Frequent augmented feedback can degrade learning: Evidence and interpretations. In J. Requin & G.E. Stelmach (Eds.), Tutorials in motor neuroscience (pp. 59-75). Dordrecht: Kluwer.

Schmidt, R.A. (1991b). Motor learning principles for physical therapy. In M.J. Lister (Ed.), Contemporary management of motor control problems: Proceedings of the II step conference (pp. 49-63). Alexandria: Foundation for Physical Therapy.

Schmidt, R.A. (1993). Unintended acceleration: Human performance considerations. In B. Peacock & W. Karwowski (Eds.), Automotive ergonomics (pp. 431-451). London: Taylor & Francis.

Schmidt, R.A. (1994). Movement time, movement distance, and movement accuracy: A reply to Newell, Carlton, and Kim. Human Performance, 7, 23-28.

Schmidt, R.A. (2003). Motor schema theory after 27 years: Reflections and implications for a new theory. Research Quarterly for Exercise and Sport, 74, 366-375.

Schmidt, R.A., & Bjork, R.A. (1992). New conceptualizations of practice: Common principles in three paradigms suggest new concepts for training. Psychological Science, 3, 207-217.

Schmidt, R.A., Christenson, R., & Rogers, P. (1975). Some evidence for the independence of recall and recognition in motor behavior. In D.M. Landers, D.V. Harris, & R.W. Christina (Eds.), Psychology of motor behavior and sport II. State College, PA: Penn State HPER Series.

Schmidt, R.A., Gielen, C.C.A.M., & van den Heuvel, P.J.M. (1984). The locus of intersensory facilitation of reaction time. Acta Psychologica, 57, 145-164.

Schmidt, R.A., & Gordon, G.B. (1977). Errors in motor responding, "rapid" corrections, and false anticipations. Journal of Motor Behavior, 9, 101-111.

Schmidt, R.A., Heuer, H., Ghodsian, D., & Young, D.E. (1998). Generalized motor programs and units of action in bimanual coordination. In M. Latash (Ed.), Progress in motor control, Vol. 1: Bernstein's traditions in movement studies (pp. 329-360). Champaign, IL: Human Kinetics.

Schmidt, R.A., Lange, C., & Young, D.E. (1990). Optimizing summary knowledge of results for skill learning. Human Movement Science, 9, 325-348.

Schmidt, R.A., & McGown, C. (1980). Terminal accuracy of unexpectedly loaded rapid movements: Evidence for a mass-spring mechanism in programming. Journal of Motor Behavior, 12, 149-161.

Schmidt, R.A., McGown, C., Quinn, J.T., & Hawkins, B. (1986). Unexpected inertial loading in rapid reversal movements: Violations of equifinality. Human Movement Science, 5, 263-273.

Schmidt, R.A., & Nacson, J. (1971). Further tests of the activity-set hypothesis for warm-up decrement. Journal of Experimental Psychology, 90, 56-64.

Schmidt, R.A., & Pew, R.W. (1974). Predicting motor-manipulative performances in the manufacture of dental appliances (Tech. Rep. to Heritage Laboratories). Romulus, MI: University of Michigan.

Schmidt, R.A., & Russell, D.G. (1972). Movement velocity and movement time as determiners of degree of preprogramming in simple movements. Journal of Experimental Psychology, 96, 315-320.

Schmidt, R.A., & Russell, D.G. (1974). Error detection in positioning responses. Unpublished manuscript, University of Michigan, Ann Arbor.

Schmidt, R.A., & Shapiro, D.C. (1986). Optimizing feedback utilization in motor skill training (Tech. Rep. Contract No. MDA903-85-K-0225). Alexandria, CA: U.S. Army Research Institute.

Schmidt, R.A., & Shea, J.B. (1976). A note on delay of knowledge of results in positioning responses. Journal of Motor Behavior, 8, 129-131.

Schmidt, R.A., & Sherwood, D.E. (1982). An inverted-U relation between spatial error and force requirements in rapid limb movements: Further evidence for the impulse-variability model. Journal of Experimental Psychology: Human Perception and Performance, 8, 158-170.

Schmidt, R.A., Sherwood, D.E., Zelaznik, H.N., & Leikind, B.J. (1985). Speed-accuracy trade-offs in motor behavior: Theories of impulse variability. In H. Heuer, U. Kleinbeck, & K.-H. Schmidt (Eds.), Motor behavior: Programming, control, and acquisition (pp. 79-123). Berlin: Springer-Verlag.

Schmidt, R.A., & White, J.L. (1972). Evidence for an error detection mechanism in motor skills: A test of Adams' closed-loop theory. Journal of Motor Behavior, 4, 143-153.

Schmidt, R.A., Wood, C.T., Young, D.E., & Kelkar, R. (1996). Evaluation of the BIC J26 child guard lighter (Tech. Rep.). Los Angeles: Failure Analysis Associates, Inc.

Schmidt, R.A., & Wrisberg, C.A. (1971). The activity-set hypothesis for warm-up decrement in a movement-speed task. Journal of Motor Behavior, 3, 318-325.

Schmidt, R.A., & Wulf, G. (1997). Continuous concurrent feedback degrades skill learning: Implications for training and simulation. Human Factors, 39, 509-525.

Schmidt, R.A., & Young, D.E. (1987). Transfer of movement control in motor learning. In S.M. Cormier & J.D. Hagman (Eds.), Transfer of learning (pp. 47-79). Orlando, FL: Academic Press.

Schmidt, R.A., & Young, D.E. (1991). Methodology for motor learning: A paradigm for kinematic feedback. Journal of Motor Behavior, 23, 13-24.

Schmidt, R.A., Young, D.E., Swinnen, S., & Shapiro, D.C. (1989). Summary knowledge of results for skill acquisition: Support for the guidance hypothesis. Journal of Experimental Psychology: Learning, Memory, and Cognition, 15, 352-359.

Schmidt, R.A., Zelaznik, H.N., & Frank, J.S. (1978). Sources of inaccuracy in rapid movement. In G.E. Stelmach (Ed.), Information processing in motor control and learning (pp. 183-203). New York: Academic Press.

Schmidt, R.A., Zelaznik, H.N., Hawkins, B., Frank, J.S., & Quinn, J.T. Jr. (1979). Motor-output variability: A theory for the accuracy of rapid motor acts. Psychological Review, 86, 415-451.

Berlin: Springer.

Schmidt, R.C., Carello, C., & Turvey, M.T. (1990). Phase transitions and critical fluctuations in the visual coordination of rhythmic movements between people. Journal of Experimental Psychology: Human Perception and Performance, 16, 227-247.

Schmidt, R.C., Christianson, N., Carello, C., & Baron, R. (1994). Effects of social and physical variables on between-person visual coordination. Ecological Psychology, 6, 159-183.

Schmidt, R.C., & O'Brien, B. (1997). Evaluating the dynamics of unintended interpersonal coordination. Ecological Psychology, 9, 189-206.

Schmidt, R.C., & Richardson, M.J. (2008). Dynamics of interpersonal coordination. In A. Fuchs & V.K. Jirsa (Eds.), Coordination: Neural, behavioral and social dynamics (pp. 281-308).

Schmidt, R.C., Shaw, B.K., & Turvey, M.T. (1993). Coupling dynamics in interlimb coordination. Journal of Experimental Psychology: Human Perception and Performance, 19, 397-415.

Schneider, D.M., & Schmidt, R.A. (1995). Units of action in motor control: Role of response complexity and target speed. Human Performance, 8, 27-49.

Schneider, G.E. (1969). Two visual systems. Science, 163, 895-902.

Schneider, K., Zernicke, R.F., Schmidt, R.A., & Hart, T.J. (1989). Changes in limb dynamics during the practice of rapid arm movements. Journal of Biomechanics, 22, 805-817.

Schneider, V.I., Healy, A.F., & Bourne, L.E. Jr. (2002). What is learned under difficult conditions is hard to forget: Contextual interference effects in foreign vocabulary acquisition, retention, and transfer. Journal of Memory and Language, 46, 419-440.

Schneider, W. (1985). Training high-performance skills: Fallacies and guidelines. Human Factors, 27, 285-300.

Schneider, W., Dumais, S.T., & Shiffrin, R.M. (1984). Automatic processing and attention. In R. Parasuraman & R. Davies (Eds.), Varieties of attention (pp. 1-27). New York: Academic Press.

Schneider, W., & Fisk, A.D. (1983). Attention theory and mechanisms for skilled performance. In R.A. Magill (Ed.), Memory and control of action (pp. 119-143). Amsterdam: Elsevier.

Schneider, W., & Shiffrin, R.M. (1977). Controlled and automatic human information processing: I. Detection, search, and attention. Psychological Review, 84, 1-66.

Scholz, J.P., & Kelso, J.A.S. (1990). Intentional switching between patterns of bimanual coordination depends on the intrinsic dynamics of the patterns. Journal of Motor Behavior, 22, 98-124.

Scholz, J.P., Kelso, J.A.S., & Schöner, G. (1987). Nonequilibrium phase transitions in coordinated biological motion: Critical slowing down and switching time. Physics Letters A, 123, 390-394.

Schöner, G., Zanone, P.G., & Kelso, J.A.S. (1992). Learning as change of coordination dynamics: Theory and experiment. Journal of Motor Behavior, 24, 29-48.

Schutz, R. (1977). Absolute, constant, and variable error: Problems and solutions. In D. Mood (Ed.), The measurement of change in physical education (pp. 82-100). Boulder, CO: University of Colorado Press.

Schutz, R.W., & Roy, E.A. (1973). Absolute error: The devil in disguise. Journal of Motor Behavior, 5, 141-153.

Schweickert, R. (1993). Information, time, and the structure of mental events: A twenty-five-year review. In D.E. Meyer & S. Kornblum (Eds.), Attention and performance XIV (pp. 324-341). Cambridge, MA: Bradford.

Schwoebel, J., Boronat, C.B., & Branch Coslett, H. (2002). The man who executed "imagined" movements: Evidence for dissociable components of the body schema. Brain and Cognition, 50, 1-16.

Scripture, E.W. (1894). Tests of mental ability as exhibited in fencing. Studies From the Yale Psychological Laboratory, 2, 122-124.

Scully, D.M., & Newell, K.M. (1985). Observational learning and the acquisition of motor skills: Toward a visual perception perspective. Journal of Human Movement Studies, 11, 169-186.

Sears, T.A., & Newsom-Davis, J. (1968). The control of respiratory muscles during voluntary breathing. Annals of the New York Academy of Sciences, 155, 183-190.

Seibel, R. (1963). Discrimination reaction time for a 1023-alternative task. Journal of Experimental Psychology, 66, 215-226.

Seidler, R.D. (2007). Aging affects motor learning but not savings at transfer of learning. Learning & Memory, 14, 17-21.

Seidler, R.D., & Noll, D.C. (2008). Neuroanatomical correlates of motor acquisition and motor transfer. Journal of Neurophysiology, 99, 1836-1845.

Semjen, A., & Ivry, R.B. (2001). The coupled oscillator model of between-hand coordination in alternate-hand tapping: A reappraisal. Journal of Experimental Psychology: Human Perception and Performance, 27, 251-265.

Senders, J.W. (1998). Analysis of an intersection. Ergonomics in Design, 6, 4-6.

Seow, S.C. (2005). Information theoretic models of HCI: A comparison of the Hick-Hyman Law and Fitts' Law. Human-Computer Interaction, 20, 315-352.

Sergent, V., Hellige, J.B., & Cherry, B. (1993). Effects of responding hand and concurrent verbal processing on time-keeping and motor-implementation processes. Brain and Cognition, 23, 243-262.

Serrien, D.J., Bogaerts, H., Suy, E., & Swinnen, S.P. (1999). The identification of coordination constraints across planes of motion. Experimental Brain Research, 128, 250-255.

Serrien, D.J., Burgunder, J.-M., & Wiesendanger, M. (2002). Control of manipulative forces during unimanual and bimanual tasks in patients with Huntington's disease. Experimental Brain Research, 143, 328-334.

Serrien, D.J., Steyvers, M., Debaere, F., Stelmach, G.E., & Swinnen, S.P. (2000). Bimanual coordination and limb-specific parameterization in patients with Parkinson's disease. Neuropsychologia, 38, 1714-1722.

Serrien, D.J., & Swinnen, S.P. (1997a). Coordination constraints induced by effector combination under isofrequency and multifrequency conditions. Journal of Experimental Psychology: Human Perception and Performance, 23, 1493-1510.

Serrien, D.J., & Swinnen, S.P. (1997b). Isofrequency and multifrequency coordination patterns as a function of the planes of motion. Quarterly Journal of Experimental Psychology, 50A, 386-404.

Serrien, D.J., & Swinnen, S.P. (1999). Intentional switching between behavioral patterns of homologous and nonhomologous effector combinations. Journal of Experimental Psychology: Human Perception and Performance, 25, 1253-1267.

Servos, P., Carnahan, H., & Fedwick, J. (2000). The visuomotor system resists the horizontal-vertical illusion. Journal of Motor Behavior, 32, 400-404.

Seymour, W.D. (1954). Experiments on the acquisition of industrial skills. Occupational Psychology, 28, 77-89.

Shadmehr, R., & Krakauer, J.W. (2008). A computational neuroanatomy for motor control. Experimental Brain Research, 185, 359-381.

Shaffer, L.H. (1971). Attention in transcription skill. Quarterly Journal of Experimental Psychology, 23, 107-112.

Shaffer, L.H. (1980). Analyzing piano performance: A study of concert pianists. In G.E. Stelmach & J. Requin (Eds.), Tutorials in motor behavior (pp. 443-455). Amsterdam: Elsevier.

Shaffer, L.H. (1984). Timing in solo and duet piano performances. Quarterly Journal of Experimental Psychology, 36A, 577-595.

Shannon, C.E., & Weaver, W. (1949). The mathematical theory of communication. Urbana, IL: University of Illinois Press.

Shapiro, D.C. (1977). A preliminary attempt to determine the duration of a motor program. In D.M. Landers & R.W. Christina (Eds.), Psychology of motor behavior and sport—1976 (pp. 17-24). Champaign, IL: Human Kinetics.

Shapiro, D.C. (1978). The learning of generalized motor programs. Unpublished doctoral dissertation, University of Southern California, Los Angeles.

Shapiro, D.C., & Schmidt, R.A. (1982). The schema theory: Recent evidence and developmental implications. In J.A.S. Kelso & J.E. Clark (Eds.), The development of movement control and co-ordination (pp. 113-150). New York: Wiley.

Shapiro, D.C., & Walter, C.B. (1982). Control of rapid bimanual aiming movements: The effect of a mechanical block. Society for Neuroscience Abstracts, 8(2), 733.

Shapiro, D.C., Zernicke, R.F., Gregor, R.J., & Diestel, J.D. (1981). Evidence for generalized motor programs using gait pattern analysis. Journal of Motor Behavior, 13, 33-47.

Shapiro, K. (2001). The limits of attention: Temporal constraints on human information processing. New York: Oxford University Press.

Shea, C.H., Guadagnoli, M.A., & Dean, M. (1995). Response biases: Tonic neck response and aftercontraction phenomenon. Journal of Motor Behavior, 27, 41-51.

Shea, C.H., & Kohl, R.M. (1990). Specificity and variability of practice. Research Quarterly for Exercise and Sport, 61, 169-177.

Shea, C.H., & Kohl, R.M. (1991). Composition of practice: Influence on the retention of motor skills. Research Quarterly for Exercise and Sport, 62, 187-195.

Shea, C.H., Kohl, R., & Indermill, C. (1990). Contextual interference: Contributions of practice. Acta Psychologica, 73, 145-157.

Shea, C.H., Lai, Q., Black, C., & Park, J.-H. (2000). Spacing practice sessions across days benefits the learning of motor skills. Human Movement Science, 19, 737-760.

Shea, C.H., Lai, Q., Wright, D.L., Immink, M., & Black, C. (2001). Consistent and variable practice conditions: Effects on relative timing and absolute timing. Journal of Motor Behavior, 33, 139-152.

Shea, C.H., Shebilske, W.L., Kohl, R.M., & Guadagnoli, M.A. (1991). After-contraction phenomenon: Influ-ences on performance and learning. Journal of Motor Behavior, 23, 51-62.

Shea, C.H., Wright, D.L., Wulf, G., & Whitacre, C. (2000). Physical and observational practice afford unique learning opportunities. Journal of Motor Behavior, 32, 27-36.

Shea, C.H., & Wulf, G. (1999). Enhancing motor learning through external-focus instruction and feedback. Human Movement Science, 18, 553-571.

Shea, C.H., & Wulf, G. (2005). Schema theory: A critical appraisal and reevaluation. Journal of Motor Behavior, 37, 85-101.

Shea, C.H., Wulf, G., & Whitacre, C. (1999). Enhancing training efficiency and effectiveness through the use of dyad training. Journal of Motor Behavior, 31, 119-125.

Shea, J.B., & Graf, R.C. (1994). A model for contextual interference effects in motor learning. In C.R. Reynolds (Ed.), Cognitive assessment: A multidisciplinary perspective (pp. 73-87). New York: Plenum Press.

Shea, J.B., & Morgan, R.L. (1979). Contextual interference effects on the acquisition, retention, and transfer of a motor skill. Journal of Experimental Psychology: Human Learning and Memory, 5, 179-187.

Shea, J.B., & Titzer, R.C. (1993). The influence of reminder trials on contextual interference effects. Journal of Motor Behavior, 25, 264-274.

Shea, J.B., & Upton, G. (1976). The effects on skill acquisition of an interpolated motor short-term memory task during the KR-delay interval. Journal of Motor Behavior, 8, 277-281.

Shea, J.B., & Wright, D.L. (1991). When forgetting benefits motor retention. Research Quarterly for Exercise and Sport, 62, 293-301.

Shea, J.B., & Zimny, S.T. (1983). Context effects in memory and learning movement information. In R.A. Magill (Ed.), Memory and control of action (pp. 345-366). Amsterdam: Elsevier.

Shea, J.B., & Zimny, S.T. (1988). Knowledge incorporation in motor representation. In O.G. Meijer & K. Roth (Eds.), Complex movement behaviour: "The" motor-action controversy (pp. 289-314). Amsterdam: Elsevier.

Sheppard, D.J. (1984). Visual and part-task manipulations for teaching simulated carrier landings (Rep. No. 81-C-0105-9). Orlando, FL: Naval Training Equipment Center.

Sherrington, C.S. (1906). The integrative action of the nervous system. New Haven, CT: Yale University Press.

Sherwood, D.E. (1988). Effect of bandwidth knowledge of results on movement consistency. Perceptual and Motor Skills, 66, 535-542.

Sherwood, D.E. (1990). Practice and assimilation effects in a multilimb aiming task. Journal of Motor Behavior, 22, 267-291.

Sherwood, D.E. (1991). Distance and location assimilation effects in rapid bimanual movement. Research Quarterly for Exercise and Sport, 62, 302-308.

Sherwood, D.E. (1994). Interlimb amplitude differences, spatial assimilations, and the temporal structure of rapid bimanual movements. Human Movement Science, 13, 841-860.

Sherwood, D.E. (1996). The benefits of random variable practice for spatial accuracy and error detection in a rapid aiming task. Research Quarterly for Exercise and Sport, 67, 35-43.

Sherwood, D.E., & Canabal, M.Y. (1988). The effect of practice on the control of sequential and simultaneous actions. Human Performance, 1, 237-260.

Sherwood, D.E., & Lee, T.D. (2003). Schema theory: Critical review and implications for the role of cognition in a new theory of motor learning. Research Quarterly for Exercise and Sport, 74, 376-382.

Sherwood, D.E., & Schmidt, R.A. (1980). The relationship between force and force variability in minimal and near-maximal static and dynamic contractions. Journal of Motor Behavior, 12, 75-89.

Sherwood, D.E., Schmidt, R.A., & Walter, C.B. (1988). The force/force-variability relationship under controlled temporal conditions. Journal of Motor Behavior, 20, 106-116.

Shewokis, P.A., & Klopfer, D. (2000). Some blocked practice schedules yield better learning than random practice schedules with anticipation timing tasks. Journal of Human Movement Studies, 38, 57-73.

Shiffrin, R.M., & Schneider, W. (1977). Controlled and automatic human information processing: II. Perceptual learning, automatic attending, and a general theory. Psychological Review, 84, 127-190.

Shik, M.L., & Orlovskii, G.N. (1976). Neurophysiology of a locomotor automatism. Physiological Reviews, 56, 465-501.

Shik, M.L., Orlovskii, G.N., & Severin, F.V. (1968). Locomotion of the mesencephalic cat elicited by stimulation of the pyramids. Biofizika, 13, 143-152.

Shim, J., Carlton, L.G., Chow, J.W., Chae, W-S. (2005). The use of anticipatory visual cues by highly skilled tennis players. Journal of Motor Behavior, 37, 164-175.

Shinar, D., Tractinsky, N., & Compton, R. (2005). Effects of practice, age, and task demands, on interference from a phone task while driving. Accident Analysis and Prevention, 37, 315-326.

Shirley, M.M. (1931). The first two years (Vol. 1). Minneapolis: University of Minnesota Press.

Shockley, K., Baker, A.A., Richardson, M.J., & Fowler, C.A. (2007). Articulatory constraints on interpersonal postural coordination. Journal of Experimental Psychology: Human Perception and Performance, 33, 201-208.

Shockley, K., Santana, M.V., & Fowler, C.A. (2003). Mutual interpersonal postural constraints are involved in cooperative conversation. Journal of Experimental Psychology: Human Perception and Performance, 29, 326-332.

Shockley, K., & Turvey, M.T. (2006). Dual-task influences on retrieval from semantic memory and coordination dynamics. Psychonomic Bulletin & Review, 13, 985-990.

Short, M.W., & Cauraugh, J.H. (1999). Precision hypothesis and the end-state comfort effect. Acta Psychologica, 100, 243-252.

Shumway-Cook, A., & Woollacott, M.H. (2007). Motor control: Translating research into clinical practice (3rd ed.). Baltimore: Lippincott Williams & Wilkins.

Sidaway, B., Ahn, S., Boldeau, P., Griffin, S., Noyes, B., & Pelletier, K. (2008). A comparison of manual guidance and knowledge of results in the learning of a weight-bearing skill. Journal of Neurologic Physical Therapy, 32, 32-38.

Sidaway, B., Moore, B., & Schoenfelder-Zohdi, B. (1991). Summary and frequency of KR presentation effects on retention of a motor skill. Research Quarterly for Exercise and Sport, 62, 27-32.

Sidaway, B., Sekiya, H., & Fairweather, M. (1995). Movement variability as a function of accuracy demand in programmed serial aiming responses. Journal of Motor Behavior, 27, 67-76.

Sidman, M. (1952). A note on functional relations obtained from group data. Psychological Bulletin, 49, 263-269.

Siegmund, G.P., Inglis, J.T., & Sanderson, D.J. (2001). Startle response of human neck muscles sculpted by readiness to perform ballistic head movements. Journal of Physiology, 535, 289-300.

Simon, D.A., & Bjork, R.A. (2001). Metacognition in motor learning. Journal of Experimental Psychology: Learning, Memory, and Cognition, 27, 907-912.

Simon, D.A., & Bjork, R.A. (2002). Models of performance in learning multisegment movement tasks: Consequences for acquisition, retention, and judgments of learning. Journal of Experimental Psychology: Applied, 8, 222-232.

Simon, D.A., Lee, T.D., & Cullen, J.D. (2008). Win-shift, lose-stay: Contingent switching and contextual interference in motor learning. Perceptual and Motor Skills, 107, 407-418.

Simon, J.R. (1969a). Reactions toward the source of stimulation. Journal of Experimental Psychology, 81, 174-176.

Simon, J.R. (1969b). Stereotypic reaction information processing. In L.E. Smith (Ed.), Psychology of motor learning (pp. 27-50). Chicago: Athletic Institute.

Simon, J.R. (1990). The effects of an irrelevant directional cue on human information processing. In R.W.

Proctor & T.G. Reeve (Eds.), Stimulus-response compatibility: An integrated perspective (pp. 31-86). Amsterdam: Elsevier.

Simon, J.R., & Rudell, A.P. (1967). Auditory S-R compatibility: The effect of an irrelevant cue on information processing. Journal of Applied Psychology, 51, 300-304.

Simons, D.J. (2000). Attentional capture and inattentional blindness. Trends in Cognitive Sciences, 4, 147-155.

Simons, D.J., & Chabris, C.F. (1999). Gorillas in our midst: Sustained inattentional blindness for dynamic events. Perception, 28, 1059-1074.

Simons, D.J., & Levin, D.T. (1998). Failure to detect changes to people in a real-world interaction. Psychonomic Bulletin & Review, 5, 644-649.

Simons, D.J., & Rensink, R.A. (2005). Change blindness: Past, present, and future. Trends in Cognitive Sciences, 9, 16-20.

Simons, J.P., Wilson, J.M., Wilson, G.J., & Theall, S. (2009). Challenges to cognitive bases for an especial motor skill at the regulation baseball pitching distance. Research Quarterly for Exercise and Sport, 80, 469-479.

Singer, R.N. (1975). Motor learning and human performance (2nd ed.). New York: Macmillan.

Singer, R.N. (1980). Motor learning and human performance (3rd ed.). New York: Macmillan.

Singer, R.N. (2000). Performance and human factors: Considerations about cognition and attention for self-paced and externally-paced events. Ergonomics, 43, 1661-1680.

Singer, R.N., & Gaines, L. (1975). Effects of prompted and trial-and-error learning on transfer performance of a serial motor task. American Educational Research Journal, 12, 395-403.

Singer, R.N., & Pease, D. (1976). A comparison of discovery learning and guided instructional strategies on motor skill learning, retention, and transfer. Research Quarterly, 47, 788-796.

Sittig, A.C. (1986). Kinesthesis and motor control. Unpublished doctoral dissertation, University of Utrecht, Holland.

Sittig, A.C., Denier van der Gon, J.J., & Gielen, C.C.A.M. (1985a). Separate control of arm position and velocity demonstrated by vibration of muscle tendon in man. Experimental Brain Research, 60, 445-453.

Sittig, A.C., Denier van der Gon, J.J., & Gielen, C.C.A.M. (1985b). Different control mechanisms for slow and fast human arm movements. Neuroscience Letters, 22, S128.

Skoglund, S. (1956). Anatomical and physiological studies of the knee joint innervation in the cat. Acta Physiologica Scandinavica, 36 (Suppl. 124).

Slater-Hammel, A.T. (1960). Reliability, accuracy and refractoriness of a transit reaction. Research Quarterly, 31, 217-228.

Small, A.M. (1990). Foreword. In R.W. Proctor & T.G. Reeve (Eds.), Stimulus-response compatibility: An integrated perspective (pp. v-vi). Amsterdam: Elsevier.

Smeeton, N.J., Ward, P., & Williams, A.M. (2004). Do pattern recognition skills transfer across sports? A preliminary analysis. Journal of Sports Sciences, 22, 205-213.

Smeets, J.B.J., & Brenner, E. (1999). A new view on grasping. Motor Control, 3, 237-271.

Smeets, J.B.J., & Brenner, E. (2001). Action beyond our grasp. Trends in Cognitive Sciences, 5, 287.

Smeets, J.B.J., Brenner, E., & Biegstraaten, M. (2002). Independent control of the digits predicts an apparent hierarchy of visuomotor channels in grasping. Behavioural Brain Research, 136, 427-432.

Smeets, J.B.J., Brenner, E., de Grave, D.D.J., & Cuijpers, R.H. (2002). Illusions in action: Consequences of inconsistent processing of spatial attributes. Experimental Brain Research, 147, 135-144.

Smeets, J.B.J., Brenner, E., & Martin, J. (2009). Grasping Occam's razor. In D. Sternad (Ed.), Progress in motor control (pp. 499-522). Berlin: Springer.

Smeets, J.B.J., Brenner, E., Trébuchet, S., & Mestre, D.R. (1996). Is judging time-to-contact based on "tau"? Perception, 25, 583-590.

Smethurst, C.J., & Carson, R.G. (2001). The acquisition of movement skills: Practice enhances the dynamic stability of bimanual coordination. Human Movement Science, 20, 499-529.

Smethurst, C.J., & Carson, R.G. (2003). The effect of volition on the stability of bimanual coordination. Journal of Motor Behavior, 35, 309-319.

Smith, J.L. (1969). Fusimotor neuron block and voluntary arm movement in man. Unpublished doctoral dissertation, University of Wisconsin, Madison.

Smith, J.L. (1977). Mechanisms of neuromuscular control. Los Angeles: UCLA Printing and Production.

Smith, J.L. (1978). Sensorimotor integration during motor programming. In G.E. Stelmach (Ed.), Information processing in motor control and learning (pp. 173-182). New York: Academic Press.

Smith, J.L., Bradley, N.S., Carter, M.C., Giuliani, C.A., Hoy, M.G., Koshland, G.F., & Zernicke, R.F. (1986). Rhythmical movements of the hindlimbs in spinal cat: Considerations for a controlling network. In M.E. Goldberger, A. Gorio, & M. Murray (Eds.), Development and plasticity of the mammalian spinal cord (pp. 362-374). Padova: Liviana Press.

Smith, J.L., Roberts, E.M., & Atkins, E. (1972). Fusimotor neuron block and voluntary arm movement in man. American Journal of Physical Medicine, 5, 225-239.

Smith, M.C. (1969). The effect of varying information on the psychological refractory period. In W.G. Koster (Ed.), Attention and performance II (pp. 220-231). Amsterdam: North-Holland.

Smith, P.J.K. (2002). Applying contextual interference to snowboarding skills. Perceptual and Motor Skills, 95, 999-1005.

Smith, P.J.K., & Davies, M. (1995). Applying contextual interference to the Pawlata roll. Journal of Sports Sciences, 13, 455-462.

Smith, P.J.K., Gregory, S.K., & Davies, M. (2003). Alternating versus blocked practice in learning a cartwheel. Perceptual and Motor Skills, 96, 1255-1264.

Smith, P.J.K., Taylor, S.J., & Withers, K. (1997). Applying bandwidth feedback scheduling to a golf shot. Research Quarterly for Exercise and Sport, 68, 215-221.

Smith, S.M., & Vela, E. (2001). Environmental context-dependent memory: A review and meta-analysis. Psychonomic Bulletin & Review, 8, 203-220.

Smith, W.M., & Bowen, K.F. (1980). The effects of delayed and displaced visual feedback on motor control. Journal of Motor Behavior, 12, 91-101.

Smits-Engelsman, B.C.M., Van Galen, G.P., & Duysens, J. (2002). The breakdown of Fitts' law in rapid, reciprocal aiming movements. Experimental Brain Research, 145, 222-230.

Snoddy, G.S. (1926). Learning and stability: A psychophysical analysis of a case of motor learning with clinical applications. Journal of Applied Psychology, 10, 1-36.

Snoddy, G.S. (1935). Evidence for two opposed processes in mental growth. Lancaster, PA: Science Press.

Solley, W.H. (1952). The effects of verbal instruction of speed and accuracy upon the learning of a motor skill. Research Quarterly, 23, 231-240.

Sonstroem, R.J., & Bernardo, P. (1982). Intraindividual pregame state anxiety and basketball performance: A reexamination of the inverted-U curve. Journal of Sport Psychology, 4, 235-245.

Soucy, M.-C., & Proteau, L. (2001). Development of multiple movement representations with practice: Specificity versus flexibility. Journal of Motor Behavior, 33, 243-254.

Southard, D., & Higgins, T. (1987). Changing movement patterns: Effects of demonstration and practice. Research Quarterly for Exercise and Sport, 60, 348-356.

Sparrow, W.A., & Summers, J.J. (1992). Performance on trials without knowledge of results (KR) in reduced relative frequency presentations of KR. Journal of Motor Behavior, 24, 197-209.

Spencer, J.P., & Thelen, E. (1999). A multimuscle state analysis of adult motor learning. Experimental Brain Research, 128, 505-516.

Spencer, R.M., Zelaznik, H.N., Diedrichsen, J., & Ivry, R.B. (2003). Disrupted timing of discontinuous but not continuous movements by cerebellar lesions. Science, 300, 1437-1439.

Sperling, G. (1960). The information available in brief visual presentations. Psychological Monographs, 74 (11, Whole No. 498).

Sperry, R.W. (1950). Neural basis of the spontaneous optokinetic response produced by visual inversion. Journal of Comparative and Physiological Psychology, 43, 482-489.

Spijkers, W., & Heuer, H. (1995). Structural constraints on the performance of symmetrical bimanual movements with different amplitudes. Quarterly Journal of Experimental Psychology, 48A, 716-740.

Spijkers, W.A.C., & Lochner, P. (1994). Partial visual feedback and spatial end-point accuracy of visual aiming movements. Journal of Motor Behavior, 26, 283-295.

Spirduso, W.W., Francis, K.L., & MacRae, P.S. (2005). Physical dimensions of aging (2nd ed.). Champaign, IL: Human Kinetics.

Stahl, J.S. (2001). Eye-head coordination and the variation of eye-movement accuracy with orbital eccentricity. Experimental Brain Research, 136, 200-210.

Starkes, J.L. (1987). Attention demands of spatially locating position of a ball in flight. Perceptual and Motor Skills, 64, 127-135.

Starkes, J.L., & Allard, F. (Eds.). (1993). Cognitive issues in motor expertise. Amsterdam: Elsevier.

Starkes, J.L., Cullen, J.D., & MacMahon, C. (2004). A life-span model of the acquisition and retention of expert perceptual-motor performance. In A.M. Williams & N.J. Hodges (Eds.), Skill acquisition in sport: Research, theory, and practice (pp. 259-281). New York: Routledge.

Starkes, J.L., & Ericsson, K.A. (2003). Expert performance in sport: Advances in research on sport expertise. Champaign, IL: Human Kinetics.

Starkes, J.L., Helsen, W., & Elliott, D. (2002). A ménage à trois: The eye, the hand and on-line processing. Journal of Sports Sciences, 20, 217-224.

Starkes, J.L., Helsen, W., & Jack, R. (2001). Expert performance in sport and dance. In R.N. Singer, H.A. Hausenblas, & C.M. Janelle (Eds.), Handbook of sport psychology (2nd ed.) (pp. 174-201). New York: Wiley.

Steffens, M.C. (2007). Memory for goal-directed sequences of actions: Is doing better than seeing? Psychonomic Bulletin & Review, 14, 1194-1198.

Stelmach, G.E. (1969). Prior positioning responses as a factor in short-term retention of a simple motor task. Journal of Experimental Psychology, 81, 523-526.

Stelmach, G.E., Kelso, J.A.S., & Wallace, S.A. (1975). Preselection in short-term motor memory. Journal of Experimental Psychology: Human Learning and Memory, 1, 745-755.

Stelmach, G.E., & Requin, J. (Eds.). (1980). Tutorials in motor behavior. Amsterdam: North-Holland.

Stelmach, G.E., & Requin, J. (Eds.). (1992). Tutorials in motor behavior II. Amsterdam: Elsevier.

Ste-Marie, D.M., Clark, S.E., Findlay, L.C., & Latimer, A.E. (2004). High levels of contextual interference enhance handwriting skill acquisition. Journal of Motor Behavior, 36, 115-126.

Sternad, D. (2001). Kurt Wachholder: Pioneering electrophysiological studies of voluntary movements. In M.L. Latash & V.M. Zatsiorsky (Eds.), Classics in movement science (pp. 375-407). Champaign, IL: Human Kinetics.

Sternad, D. (2002). Wachholder and Altenburger 1927: Foundational experiments for current hypotheses on equilibrium-point control in voluntary movements. Motor Control, 6, 299-318.

Sternad, D., & Corcos, D. (2001). Effect of task and instruction on patterns of muscle activation: Wachholder and beyond. Motor Control, 5, 307-336.

Sternberg, S. (1969). The discovery of processing stages: Extensions of Donders' method. In W.G. Koster (Ed.), Attention and performance II (pp. 276-315). Amsterdam: North-Holland.

Sternberg, S., Monsell, S., Knoll, R.L., & Wright, C.E. (1978). The latency and duration of rapid movement sequences: Comparisons of speech and typewriting. In G.E. Stelmach (Ed.), Information processing in motor control and learning (pp. 117-152). New York: Academic Press.

Stevens, J.A. (2005). Interference effects demonstrate distinct roles for visual and motor imagery during the mental representation of human action. Cognition, 95, 329-350.

Stevens, L.T. (1886). On the time-sense. Mind, 11, 393-404.

Stewart, D., Cudworth, C.J., & Lishman, J.R. (1993). Misperception of time-to-collision by drivers in pedestrian accidents. Perception, 22, 1227-1244.

Stickgold, R., & Walker, M.P. (2006). Memory consolidation and reconsolidation: What is the role of sleep? Trends in Neurosciences, 28, 408-415.

Stimpel, E. (1933). Der Wurk [The throw]. Neue Psychologische Studien, 9, 105-138.

Stratton, S.M., Liu, Y.T., Hong, S.L., Mayer-Kress, G., & Newell, K.M. (2007). Snoddy (1926) revisited: Time scales of motor learning. Journal of Motor Behavior, 39, 503-515.

Strayer, D.L., Drews, F.A., & Crouch, D.J. (2006). A comparison of the cell phone driver and the drunk driver. Human Factors, 48, 381-391.

Strayer, D.L., Drews, F.A., & Johnston, W.A. (2003). Cell phone-induced failures of visual attention during simulated driving. Journal of Experimental Psychology: Applied, 9, 23-32.

Strayer, D.L., & Johnston, W.A. (2001). Driven to distraction: Dual-task studies of simulated driving and conversing on a cellular telephone. Psychological Science, 12, 462-466.

Stroop, J.R. (1935). Studies of interference in serial verbal reactions. Journal of Experimental Psychology, 18, 643-662.

Stuart, D.G., Mosher, C.G., Gerlack, R.L., & Reinking, R.M. (1972). Mechanical arrangement and transducing properties of Golgi tendon organs. Experimental Brain Research, 14, 274-292.

Stuart, D.G., Pierce, P.A., Callister, R.J., Brichta, A.M., & McDonagh, J.C. (2001). Sir Charles S. Sherrington: Humanist, mentor, and movement neuroscientist. In M.L. Latash & V.M. Zatsiorsky (Eds.), Classics in movement science (pp. 317-374). Champaign, IL: Human Kinetics.

Studenka, B.E., & Zelaznik, H.N. (2008). The influence of dominant versus non-dominant hand on event and emergent motor timing. Human Movement Science, 27, 29-52.

Sturm, L.P., Windsor, J.A., Cosman, P.H., Cregan, P., Hewett, P.J., & Maddern, G.J. (2008). A systematic review of skills transfer after surgical simulation training. Annals of Surgery, 248, 166-179.

Sullivan, K.J., Kantak, S.S., & Burtner, P.A. (2008). Motor learning in children: Feedback effects on skill acquisition. Physical Therapy, 88, 720-732.

Summers, J.J. (1975). The role of timing in motor program representation. Journal of Motor Behavior, 7, 229-241.

Summers, J.J. (Ed.). (1992). Approaches to the study of motor control and learning. Amsterdam: Elsevier.

Summers, J.J. (2002). Practice and training in bimanual coordination tasks: Strategies and constraints. Brain and Cognition, 48, 166-178.

Summers, J.J. (2004). A historical perspective on skill acquisition. In A.M. Williams & N.J. Hodges (Eds.), Skill Acquisition in sport: Research, theory and practice (pp. 1-26). London: Routledge.

Summers, J.J., & Anson, J.G. (2009). Current status of the motor program: Revisited. Human Movement Science, 28, 566-577.

Summers, J.J., & Kennedy, T. (1992). Strategies in the production of a 5:3 polyrhythm. Human Movement Science, 11, 101-112.

Summers, J.J., & Pressing, J. (1994). Coordinating the two hands in polyrhythmic tapping. In S.P. Swinnen, H. Heuer, J. Massion, & P. Casaer (Eds.), Interlimb coordination: Neural, dynamical, and cognitive constraints (pp. 571-593). San Diego: Academic Press.

Summers, J.J., Rosenbaum, D.A., Burns, B.D., & Ford, S.K. (1993). Production of polyrhythms. Journal of Experimental Psychology: Human Perception and Performance, 19, 416-428.

Summers, J.J., Todd, J.A., & Kim, Y.H. (1993). The influence of perceptual and motor factors on bimanual coordination in a polyrhythmic tapping task. Psychological Research, 55, 107-115.

Swanson, L.R., & Lee, T.D. (1992). Effects of aging and schedules of knowledge of results on motor learning.

Journal of Gerontology: Psychological Sciences, 47, P406-P411.

Sweezy, R.W., & Andrews, D.H. (Eds.). (2001). Readings in simulation and training: A 30-year perspective. Santa Monica, CA: Human Factors and Ergonomics Society.

Swets, J.A. (1964). Signal detection and recognition by human observers. New York: Wiley.

Swets, J.A., Dawes, R.M., & Monahan, J. (2000). Psychological science can improve diagnostic decisions. Psychological Science in the Public Interest, 1, 1-26.

Swift, E.J., & Schuyler, W. (1907). The learning process. Psychological Bulletin, 4, 307-310.

Swinnen, S.P. (1988). Learning and long-term retention of absolute and relative time. Unpublished manuscript, Catholic University of Leuven, Belgium.

Swinnen, S.P. (1990). Interpolated activities during the knowledge-of-results delay and post-knowledge-of-results interval: Effects on performance and learning. Journal of Experimental Psychology: Learning, Memory, and Cognition, 16, 692-705.

Swinnen, S.P. (1992). Coordination of upper-limb movement: A neuro-dynamics account. In G.E. Stelmach & J. Requin (Eds.), Tutorials in motor behavior II (pp. 695-711). Amsterdam: Elsevier.

Swinnen, S.P. (1996). Information feedback for motor skill learning: A review. In H.N. Zelaznik (Ed.), Advances in motor learning and control (pp. 37-66). Champaign, IL: Human Kinetics.

Swinnen, S.P. (2002). Intermanual coordination: From behavioural principles to neural-network interactions. Nature Reviews: Neuroscience, 3, 350-361.

Swinnen, S.P., Dounskaia, N., Verschueren, S., Serrien, D.J., & Daelman, A. (1995). Relative phase destabilization during interlimb coordination: The disruptive role of kinesthetic afferences induced by passive movement. Experimental Brain Research, 105, 439-454.

Swinnen, S.P., Heuer, H., Massion, J., & Casaer, P. (Eds.). (1994). Interlimb coordination: Neural, dynamical, and cognitive constraints. San Diego: Academic Press.

Swinnen, S.P., Jardin, K., & Meulenbroek, R. (1996). Between-limb asynchronies during bimanual coordination: Effects of manual dominance and attentional cueing. Neuropsychologia, 34, 1203-1213.

Swinnen, S.P., Jardin, K., Meulenbroek, R., Dounskaia, N., & Hofkens-van den Brandt, M. (1997). Egocentric and allocentric constraints in the expression of patterns of interlimb coordination. Journal of Cognitive Neuroscience, 9, 348-377.

Swinnen, S.P., Jardin, K., Verschueren, S., Meulenbroek, R., Franz, L., Dounskaia, N., & Walter, C.B. (1998). Exploring interlimb constraints during bimanual graphic performance: Effects of muscle grouping and direction. Behavioural Brain Research, 79-87.

Swinnen, S.P., Schmidt, R.A., Nicholson, D.E., & Shapiro, D.C. (1990). Information feedback for skill acquisition: Instantaneous knowledge of results degrades learning. Journal of Experimental Psychology: Learning, Memory, and Cognition, 16, 706-716.

Swinnen, S.P., Walter, C.B., Lee, T.D., & Serrien, D.J. (1993). Acquiring bimanual skills: Contrasting forms of information feedback for interlimb decoupling. Journal of Experimental Psychology: Learning, Memory, and Cognition, 19, 1328-1344.

Swinnen, S.P., Walter, C.B., Pauwels, J.M., Meugens, P.F., & Beirinckx, M.B. (1990). The dissociation of interlimb constraints. Human Performance, 3, 187-215.

Swinnen, S.P., Walter, C.B., & Shapiro, D.C. (1988). The coordination of limb movements with different kinematic patterns. Brain and Cognition, 8, 326-347.

Swinnen, S.P., & Wenderoth, N. (2004). Two hands, one brain: Cognitive neuroscience of bimanual skill. Trends in Cognitive Sciences, 8, 18-25.

Szalma, S.L., Hancock, P.A., Warm, J.S., Dember, W.N., & Parsons, K.S. (2006). Training for vigilance: Using predictive power to evaluate feedback effectiveness. Human Factors, 48, 682-692.

Tallet, J., Kostrubiec, V., & Zanone, P.-G. (2008). The role of stability in the dynamics of learning, memorizing, and forgetting new coordination patterns. Journal of Motor Behavior, 40, 103-116.

Tarpy, R.M., & Sawabini, F.L. (1974). Reinforcement delay: A selective review of the last decade. Psychological Bulletin, 81, 984-997.

Taub, E. (1976). Movement in nonhuman primates deprived of somatosensory feedback. Exercise and Sport Sciences Reviews, 4, 335-374.

Taub, E., & Berman, A.J. (1968). Movement and learning in the absence of sensory feedback. In S.J. Freedman (Ed.), The neuropsychology of spatially oriented behavior. Homewood, IL: Dorsey Press.

Taub, E., Uswatte, G., & Pidikiti, R. (1999). Constraint-induced movement therapy: A new family of techniques with broad application to physical rehabilitation. A clinical review. Journal of Rehabilitation Research Development, 36, 237-251.

Taylor, T.L., & Klein, R.M. (1998). On the causes and effects of inhibition of return. Psychonomic Bulletin & Review, 5, 625-643.

Teasdale, N., Forget, R., Bard, C., Paillard, J., Fleury, M., & Lamarre, Y. (1993). The role of proprioceptive information for the production of isometric forces and for handwriting tasks. Acta Psychologica, 82, 179-191.

Telford, C.W. (1931). The refractory phase of voluntary and associative responses. Journal of Experimental Psychology, 14, 1-36.

Temprado, J.J. (2004). A dynamical approach to the interplay of attention and bimanual coordination. In V.K. Jirsa & J.A.S. Kelso (Eds.), Coordination dynamics: Issues and trends (pp. 21-39). Berlin: Springer.

Temprado, J.J., & Laurent, M. (2004). Attentional load associated with performing and stabilizing a between-persons coordination of rhythmic limb movements. Acta Psychologica, 115, 1-16.

Terzuolo, C.A., & Viviani, P. (1979). The central representation of learning motor programs. In R.E. Talbott & D.R. Humphrey (Eds.), Posture and movement (pp. 113-121). New York: Raven Press.

Terzuolo, C.A., & Viviani, P. (1980). Determinants and characteristics of motor patterns used for typing. Neuroscience, 5, 1085-1103.

Thelen, E., & Ulrich, B.D. (1991). Hidden skills: A dynamic systems analysis of treadmill stepping during the first year. Monographs of the Society for Research in Child Development, Serial No. 223, 56(1).

Thomas, J.R. (1980). Acquisition of motor skills: Information processing differences between children and adults. Research Quarterly for Exercise and Sport, 51, 158-173.

Thomas, J.R. (1997). Motor behavior. In J.D. Massengale & R.A. Swanson (Eds.), The history of exercise and sport science (pp. 203-292). Champaign, IL: Human Kinetics.

Thomas, J.R. (2000). Children's control, learning, and performance of motor skills. Research Quarterly for Exercise and Sport, 71, 1-9.

Thomas, J.R., Nelson, J.K., & Silverman, S.J. (2005). Research methods in physical activity (5th ed.). Champaign, IL: Human Kinetics.

Thomas, J.R., Thomas, K.T., & Gallagher, J.D. (1993). Developmental considerations in skill acquisition. In R.N. Singer, M. Murphey, & L.K. Tennant (Eds.), Handbook of research on sport psychology (pp. 73-105). New York: Macmillan.

Thorndike, E.L. (1906). The principles of teaching, based on psychology. New York: Seiler.

Thorndike, E.L. (1914). Educational psychology. New York: Columbia University.

Thorndike, E.L. (1927). The law of effect. American Journal of Psychology, 39, 212-222.

Thorndike, E.L., & Woodworth, R.S. (1901). The influence of improvement in one mental function upon the efficiency of other functions. Psychological Review, 8, 247-261.

Tiffin, J., & Rogers, H.B. (1943). The selection and training of inspectors. Personnel, 22, 3-20.

Tipper, S.P., Lortie, C., & Baylis, G.C. (1992). Selective reaching: Evidence for action-centered attention. Journal of Experimental Psychology: Human Perception and Performance, 18, 891-905.

Todd, J.T. (1981). Visual information about moving objects. Journal of Experimental Psychology: Human Perception and Performance, 7, 795-810.

Törnros, J.E.B., & Bolling, A.K. (2005). Mobile phone use – effects of handheld and hands-free phones on driving performance. Accident Analysis and Prevention, 37, 902-909.

Torre, K., & Balasubramaniam, R. (2009). Two different processes for sensorimotor synchronization in continuous and discontinuous rhythmic movements. Experimental Brain Research, 199, 157-166.

Trachtman, D. (2003). Contextual interference and the role of response retrieval during learning. Unpublished doctoral dissertation, University of California, Los Angeles.

Tränkle, U., & Deutschmann, D. (1991). Factors influencing speed and precision of cursor positioning using a mouse. Ergonomics, 34, 161-174.

Trbovich, P., & Harbluk, J.L. (2003). Cell phone communication and driver visual behaviour: The impact of cognitive distraction. Conference on Computer-Human Interactions, April 8, 2003, Fort Lauderdale, FL.

Treisman, A.M. (1969). Strategies and models of selective attention. Psychological Review, 76, 282-299.

Tremblay, L., & Proteau, L. (1998). Specificity of practice: The case of powerlifting. Research Quarterly for Exercise and Sport, 69, 284-289.

Tresilian, J.R. (1995). Perceptual and cognitive processes in time-to-contact estimation: Analysis of prediction-motion and relative judgment tasks. Perception & Psychophysics, 57, 231-245.

Tresilian, J.R. (1997). Correcting some misperceptions of time-to-collision: A critical note. Perception, 26, 229-236.

Tresilian, J.R. (1999). Visually timed action: Time-out for "tau"? Trends in Cognitive Sciences, 3, 301-310.

Trevarthen, C.B. (1968). Two mechanisms of vision in primates. Psychologische Forschung, 31, 299-337.

Trowbridge, M.H., & Cason, H. (1932). An experimental study of Thorndike's theory of learning. Journal of General Psychology, 7, 245-260.

Trumbo, D., Ulrich, L., & Noble, M.E. (1965). Verbal coding and display coding in the acquisition and retention of tracking skill. Journal of Applied Psychology, 49, 368-375.

Tsutsui, S., & Imanaka, K. (2003). Effect of manual guidance on acquiring a new bimanual coordination pattern. Research Quarterly for Exercise and Sport, 74, 104-109.

Tsutsui, S., Lee, T.D., & Hodges, N.J. (1998). Contextual interference in learning new patterns of bimanual coordination. Journal of Motor Behavior, 30, 151-157.

Tubbs, M.E. (1986). Goal setting: A meta-analytic examination of empirical evidence. Journal of Applied Psychology, 71, 474-483.

Tuffiash, M., Roring, R.W., & Ericsson, K.A. (2007). Expert performance in SCRABBLE: Implications for the study of the structure and acquisition of complex skills. Journal of Experimental Psychology: Applied, 13, 124-134.

Tuller, B., & Kelso, J.A.S. (1989). Environmentally-specified patterns of movement coordination in normal and split-brain subjects. Experimental Brain Research, 75, 306-316.

Turvey, M.T. (1977). Preliminaries to a theory of action with reference to vision. In R. Shaw & J. Bransford (Eds.), Perceiving, acting, and knowing (pp. 211-265). Hillsdale, NJ: Erlbaum.

Turvey, M.T. (1990). Coordination. American Psychologist, 45, 938-953.

Turvey, M.T., & Carello, C. (1996). Dynamics of Bernstein's level of synergies. In M.L. Latash & M.T. Turvey (Eds.), Dexterity and its development (pp. 339-376). Mahwah, NJ: Erlbaum.

Turvey, M.T., & Fonseca, S. (2009). Nature of motor control: Perspectives and issues. In D. Sternad (Ed.), Progress in motor control (pp. 93-123). Berlin: Springer.

Turvey, M.T., Rosenblum, L.D., Schmidt, R.C., & Kugler, P.N. (1986). Fluctuations and phase symmetry in coordinated rhythmic movements. Journal of Experimental Psychology: Human Perception and Performance, 12, 564-583.

Turvey, M.T., Schmidt, R.C., & Rosenblum, L.D. (1989). "Clock" and "motor" components in absolute coordination of rhythmic movements. Neuroscience, 33, 1-10.

Tyldesley, D.A., & Whiting, H.T.A. (1975). Operational timing. Journal of Human Movement Studies, 1, 172-177.

Ulrich, B.D., & Reeve, T.G. (2005). Studies in motor behavior: 75 years of research in motor development, learning, and control. Research Quarterly for Exercise and Sport, 76 (Suppl. 2), S62-S70.

Ulrich, R., & Wing, A.M. (1991). A recruitment theory of force-time relations in the production of brief force pulses: The parallel force unit model. Psychological Review, 98, 268-294.

Umiltà, C., & Nicoletti, R. (1990). Spatial stimulus-response compatibility. In R.W. Proctor & T.G. Reeve (Eds.), Stimulus-response compatibility (pp. 89-116). Amsterdam: Elsevier.

Umiltà, C., Priftis, K., & Zorzi, M. (2009). The spatial representation of numbers: Evidence from neglect and pseudoneglect. Experimental Brain Research, 192, 561-569.

Underwood, B.J. (1957). Interference and forgetting. Psychological Review, 64, 49-60.

Underwood, B.J. (1975). Individual differences as a crucible in theory construction. American Psychologist, 30, 128-134.

Underwood, G., & Everatt, J. (1996). Automatic and controlled information processing: The role of attention in the processing of novelty. In O. Neumann & A.F. Sanders (Eds.), Handbook of perception and action. Vol. 3: Attention (pp. 185-227). San Diego: Academic Press.

Ungerleider, L.G., & Mishkin, M. (1982). Two cortical visual systems. In D.J. Ingle, M.A. Goodale, & R.J.W. Mansfield (Eds.), Analysis of visual behavior (pp. 549-586). Cambridge, MA: MIT Press.

Vallbo, A.B. (1974). Human muscle spindle discharge during isometric voluntary contractions: Amplitude relations between spindle frequency and torque. Acta Physiologica Scandinavica, 90, 319-336.

Valls-Solé, J., Kumru, H., & Kofler, M. (2008). Interaction between startle and voluntary reactions in humans. Experimental Brain Research, 187, 497-507.

Valls-Solé, J., Rothwell, J.C., Goulart, F., Cossu, G., & Muñoz, E. (1999). Patterned ballistic movements triggered by a startle in healthy humans. Journal of Physiology, 516, 931-938.

van Boxtel, G.J.M., & Band, G.P.H. (2000). Inhibitory motor control in stop paradigms: Reply to McGarry and Franks (2000). Acta Psychologica, 105, 79-82.

Van Caekenberghe, I., Segers, V., De Smet, K., Aerts, P., & De Clercq, D. (2010). Influence of treadmill acceleration on actual walk-to-run transition. Gait & Posture, 31, 52-56.

Van de Crommert, H.W.A.A., Mulder, T., & Duysens, J. (1998). Neural control of locomotion: Sensory control of the central pattern generator and its relation to treadmill training. Gait & Posture, 7, 251-263.

Vander Linden, D.W., Cauraugh, J.H., & Greene, T.A. (1993). The effect of frequency of kinetic feedback on learning an isometric force production task in nondisabled subjects. Physical Therapy, 73, 79-87.

van der Meijden, O.A.J., & Schijven, M.P. (2009). The value of haptic feedback in conventional and robot-assisted minimal invasive surgery and virtual reality training: A current review. Surgical Endoscopy, 23, 1180-1190.

van Dijk, H., Mulder, T., & Hermens, H.J. (2007). Effects of age and content of augmented feedback on learning an isometric force-production task. Experimental Aging Research, 33, 341-353.

van Donkelaar, P. (1999). Pointing movements are affected by size-contrast illusions. Experimental Brain Research, 125, 517-520.

Van Rossum, J.H.A. (1990). Schmidt's schema theory: The empirical base of the variability of practice hypothesis. A critical analysis. Human Movement Science, 9, 387-435.

Vanvenckenray, J., Buekers, M.J., Mendes, R.S., & Helsen, W.F. (1999). Relearning movements: Modifications of an incorrectly timed reversal movement. Perceptual and Motor Skills, 89, 195-203.

Vaughan, C.L., & O'Malley, M.J. (2005). Froude and the contribution of naval architecture to our understanding of bipedal locomotion. Gait & Posture, 21, 350-362.

Verbruggen, F., & Logan, G.D. (2008). Response inhibition in the stop-signal paradigm. Trends in Cognitive Sciences, 12, 418-424.

Vercher, J.L., Magenes, G., Prablanc, C., & Gauthier, G.M. (1994). Eye-head-hand coordination in pointing at visual targets: Spatial and temporal analysis. Experimental Brain Research, 99, 507-523.

Verdolini-Marston, K., & Balota, D.A. (1994). Role of elaborative and perceptual integrative processes in perceptual-motor performance. Journal of Experimental Psychology: Learning, Memory, and Cognition, 20, 739-749.

Vereijken, B., van Emmerik, R.E.A., Whiting, H.T.A., & Newell, K.M. (1992). Free(z)ing degrees of freedom in skill acquisition. Journal of Motor Behavior, 24, 133-142.

Vereijken, B., Whiting, H.T.A., & Beek, W.J. (1992). A dynamical systems approach to skill acquisition. Quarterly Journal of Experimental Psychology, 45A, 323-344.

Verwey, W.B., & Dronkert, Y. (1996). Practicing a structured continuous key-pressing task: Motor chunking or rhythm consolidation? Journal of Motor Behavior, 28, 71-79.

Vicente, K.J., & Wang, J.H. (1998). An ecological theory of expertise effects in memory recall. Psychological Review, 105, 33-57.

Vickers, J. (2007). Perception cognition, and decision training. Champaign, IL: Human Kinetics.

Vickers, J.N., Livingston, L.F., Umeris-Bohnert, S., & Holden, D. (1999). Decision training: The effects of complex instruction, variable practice and reduced delayed feedback on the acquisition and transfer of a motor skill. Journal of Sports Sciences, 17, 357-367.

Vince, M.A., & Welford, A.T. (1967). Time taken to change the speed of a response. Nature, 213, 532-533.

Vincent, W.J. (2005). Statistics in kinesiology (3rd ed.). Champaign, IL: Human Kinetics.

Vogt, S. (1995). On relations between perceiving, imaging, and performing in the learning of cyclical movement sequences. British Journal of Psychology, 86, 191-216.

von Hofsten, C. (1983). Catching skills in infancy. Journal of Experimental Psychology: Human Perception and Performance, 9, 75-85.

von Holst, E. (1954). Relations between the central nervous system and the peripheral organs. British Journal of Animal Behavior, 2, 89-94.

von Holst, E. (1973). On the nature of order in the central nervous system. In R. Martin (Trans.), The selected papers of Erich von Holst. The behavioural physiology of animals and man (Vol. 1) (pp. 3-32). London: Methuen. (Original work published in 1937)

von Holst, E., & Mittelstaedt, H. (1950). Das reafferenzprinzip [The reafference principle]. Naturwissenschaften, 37, 464-476.

Vorberg, D., & Wing, A. (1996). Modeling variability and dependence in timing. In H. Heuer & S.W. Keele (Eds.), Handbook of perception and action. Vol. 2: Motor skills (pp. 181-262). San Diego: Academic Press.

Wadman, W.J., Denier van der Gon, J.J., Geuze, R.H., & Mol, C.R. (1979). Control of fast goal-directed arm movements. Journal of Human Movement Studies, 5, 3-17.

Walker, M.P., Brakefield, T., Hobson, J.A., & Stickgold, R. (2003). Dissociable stages of human memory consolidation and reconsolidation. Nature, 425, 616-620.

Walker, N., Philbin, D.A., & Fisk, A.D. (1997). Age-related differences in movement control: Adjusting submovement structure to optimize performance. Journal of Gerontology: Psychological Sciences, 52B, P40-P52.

Wallace, R.J. (1971). S-R compatibility and the idea of a response code. Journal of Experimental Psychology, 88, 354-360.

Wallace, S.A. (1996). Dynamic pattern perspective of rhythmic movement: An introduction. In H.N. Zelaznik (Ed.), Advances in motor learning and control (pp. 155-194). Champaign, IL: Human Kinetics.

Wallace, S.A., & Hagler, R.W. (1979). Knowledge of performance and the learning of a closed motor skill. Research Quarterly, 50, 265-271.

Wallace, S.A., & Weeks, D.L. (1988). Temporal constraints in the control of prehensile movements. Journal of Motor Behavior, 20, 81-105.

Wallace, S.A., Weeks, D.L., & Kelso, J.A.S. (1990). Temporal constraints in reaching and grasping behavior. Human Movement Science, 9, 69-93.

Walsh, W.D., Russell, D.G., Imanaka, K., & James, B. (1979). Memory for constrained and preselected movement location and distance: Effects of starting position and length. Journal of Motor Behavior, 11, 201-214.

Walter, C.B., & Swinnen, S.P. (1990). Asymmetric interlimb interference during the performance of a dynamic bimanual task. Brain and Cognition, 14, 185-200.

Walter, C.B., & Swinnen, S.P. (1992). Adaptive tuning of interlimb attraction to facilitate bimanual decoupling. Journal of Motor Behavior, 24, 95-104.

Walter, C.B., & Swinnen, S.P. (1994). The formation and dissolution of "bad habits" during the acquisition of coordination skills. In S.P. Swinnen, H. Heuer, J.

Massion, & P. Casaer (Eds.), Interlimb coordination: Neural, dynamical, and cognitive constraints (pp. 491-513). San Diego: Academic Press.

Walter, C.B., Swinnen, S.P., & Franz, E.A. (1993). Stability of symmetric and asymmetric discrete bimanual actions. In K.M. Newell & D.M. Corcos (Eds.), Variability and motor control (pp. 359-380). Champaign, IL: Human Kinetics.

Wann, J.P. (1996). Anticipating arrival: Is the tau margin a specious theory? Journal of Experimental Psychology: Human Perception and Performance, 22, 1031-1048.

Wann, J.P., & Land, M. (2000). Steering with or without the flow: Is the retrieval of heading necessary? Trends in Cognitive Sciences, 4, 319-324.

Wann, J.P., & Nimmo-Smith, I. (1990). Evidence against the relative invariance of timing in handwriting. Quarterly Journal of Experimental Psychology, 42A, 105-119.

Warren, W.H. Jr. (1998). Visually controlled locomotion: 40 years later. Ecological Psychology, 10, 177-219.

Warren, W.H. Jr., & Whang, S. (1987). Visual guidance of walking through apertures: Body-scaled information for affordances. Journal of Experimental Psychology: Human Perception and Performance, 13, 371-383.

Warren, W.H. Jr., & Yaffe, D.M. (1989). Dynamics of step length adjustment during running: A comment on Patla, Robinson, Samways, and Armstrong (1989). Journal of Experimental Psychology: Human Perception and Performance, 15, 618-623.

Warren, W.H. Jr., Young, D.S., & Lee, D.N. (1986). Visual control of step length during running over irregular terrain. Journal of Experimental Psychology: Human Perception and Performance, 12, 259-266.

Waterson, P., & Sell, R. (2006). Recurrent themes and developments in the history of the Ergonomics Society. Ergonomics, 49, 743-799.

Weber, E. (1846). Muskelbewegung [Muscle movement]. In R. Wagner (Ed.), Handworterbuch der Physiologie (Vol. 3, Pt. 2, pp. 1-122). Braunschweig: Bieweg.

Weeks, D.L., & Anderson, L.P. (2000). The interaction of observational learning with overt practice: Effects on motor skill learning. Acta Psychologica, 104, 259-271.

Weeks, D.J., Chua, R., & Elliott, D. (2000). Perceptual-motor behavior in Down syndrome. Champaign, IL: Human Kinetics.

Weeks, D.L., Hall, A.K., & Anderson, L.P. (1996). A comparison of imitation strategies in observational learning of action patterns. Journal of Motor Behavior, 28, 348-358.

Weeks, D.L., & Kordus, R.N. (1998). Relative frequency of knowledge of performance and motor skill learning. Research Quarterly for Exercise and Sport, 69, 224-230.

Weeks, D.J., & Proctor, R.W. (1990). Salient-features coding in the translation between orthogonal stimu-lus and response dimensions. Journal of Experimental Psychology: General, 119, 355-366.

Weeks, D.J., Reeve, T.G., Dornier, L.A., & Fober, G.W. (1991). Inter-criterion interval activity and the retention of movement information: A test of the forgetting hypothesis for contextual interference effects. Journal of Human Movement Studies, 20, 101-110.

Weeks, D.L., & Sherwood, D.E. (1994). A comparison of knowledge of results scheduling methods for promoting motor skill acquisition and retention. Research Quarterly for Exercise and Sport, 65, 136-142.

Weeks, D.J., Zelaznik, H., & Beyak, B. (1993). An empirical note on reduced frequency of knowledge of results. Journal of Human Movement Studies, 25, 193-201.

Wegner, D.M. (1994). Ironic processes of mental control. Psychological Review, 101, 34-52.

Wegner, D.M. (2009). How to think, say, or do precisely the worst thing for any occasion. Science, 325, 48-50.

Wegner, D.M., Ansfield, M.E., & Pilloff, D. (1998). The putt and the pendulum: Ironic effects of the mental control of action. Psychological Science, 9, 196-199.

Weigelt, M., Kunde, W., & Prinz, W. (2006). End-state comfort in bimanual object manipulation. Experimental Psychology, 53, 143-148.

Weinberg, D.R., Guy, D.E., & Tupper, R.W. (1964). Variation of postfeedback interval in simple motor learning. Journal of Experimental Psychology, 67, 98-99.

Weinberg, R.S. (1994). Goal setting and performance in sport and exercise settings: A synthesis and critique. Medicine and Science in Sports and Exercise, 26, 469-477.

Weinberg, R.S., & Gould, D. (2011). Foundations of sport and exercise psychology (5th ed). Champaign, IL: Human Kinetics.

Weinberg, R.S., & Ragan, J. (1978). Motor performance under three levels of trait anxiety and stress. Journal of Motor Behavior, 10, 169-176.

Weir, P.L., Weeks, D.J., Welsh, T.N., Elliott, D., Chua, R., Roy, E.A., & Lyons, J. (2003). Influence of terminal action requirements on action-centered distractor effects. Experimental Brain Research, 149, 207-213.

Weiskrantz, L., Elliott, J., & Darlington, C. (1971). Preliminary observations on tickling oneself. Nature, 230, 598-599.

Weiss, A.D. (1965). The locus of reaction time change with set, motivation, and age. Journal of Gerontology, 20, 60-64.

Welch, J.C. (1898). On the measurement of mental activity through muscular activity and the determination of a constant of attention. American Journal of Physiology, 1, 283-306.

Welford, A.T. (1952). The "psychological refractory period" and the timing of high-speed performance—a review and a theory. British Journal of Psychology, 43, 2-19.

Welford, A.T. (1968). Fundamentals of skill. London: Methuen.

Welford, A.T. (1984). Psychomotor performance. Annual Review of Gerontology and Geriatrics, 4, 237-273.

Welford, A.T., Norris, A.H., & Shock, N.W. (1969). Speed and accuracy of movement and their changes with age. Acta Psychologica, 30, 3-15.

Welsh, T., Almeida, Q., & Lee, T.D. (2005). The effects of spatial orientation between the upper limbs and postural stability on bimanual coordination. Experimental Brain Research, 161, 265-275.

Welsh, T.N., & Pratt, J. (2008). Actions modulate attentional capture. Quarterly Journal of Experimental Psychology, 61, 968-976.

Weltman, G., & Egstrom, G.H. (1966). Perceptual narrowing in novice divers. Human Factors, 8, 499-505.

Wenderoth, N., & Bock, O. (2001). Learning of a new bimanual coordination pattern is governed by three distinct processes. Motor Control, 5, 23-35.

Wenderoth, N., Bock, O., & Krohn, R. (2002). Learning a new bimanual coordination pattern is influenced by existing attractors. Motor Control, 6, 166-182.

Westling, G., & Johansson, R.S. (1984). Factors influencing the force control during precision grip. Experimental Brain Research, 53, 277-284.

Westwood, D.A., Dubrowski, A., Carnahan, H., & Roy, E.A. (2000). The effect of illusory size on force production when grasping objects. Experimental Brain Research, 135, 535-543.

Wetzel, M.C., & Stuart, D.G. (1976). Ensemble characteristics of cat locomotion and its neural control. Progress in Neurobiology, 7, 1-98.

White, R.M. Jr., & Schmidt, S.W. (1972). Preresponse intervals versus postinformative feedback intervals in concept identification. Journal of Experimental Psychology, 94, 350-352.

Whiting, H.T.A. (1969). Acquiring ball skill: A psychological interpretation. London: Bell.

Whiting, H.T.A. (Ed.). (1984). Human motor actions: Bernstein reassessed. Amsterdam: Elsevier.

Whiting, H.T.A., Bijlard, M.J., & den Brinker, B.P.L.M. (1987). The effect of the availability of a dynamic model on the acquisition of a complex cyclical action. Quarterly Journal of Experimental Psychology, 39A, 43-59.

Whiting, H.T.A., Gill, E.B., & Stephenson, J.M. (1970). Critical time intervals for taking in flight information in a ball-catching task. Ergonomics, 13, 265-272.

Wickens, C.D. (1976). The effects of divided attention on information processing in manual tracking. Journal of Experimental Psychology: Human Perception and Performance, 2, 1-13.

Wickens, C.D. (1980). The structure of attentional resources. In R.S. Nickerson (Ed.), Attention and performance VIII (pp. 239-257). Hillsdale, NJ: Erlbaum.

Wickens, C.D., & Hollands, J.G. (2000). Engineering psychology and human performance (3rd ed.). Upper Saddle River, NJ: Prentice Hall.

Wickens, C.D., & McCarley, J.S. (2008). Applied attention theory. Boca Raton, FL: CRC Press.

Wiener, N. (1948). Cybernetics. New York: Wiley.

Wightman, D.C., & Lintern, G. (1985). Part-task training for tracking and manual control. Human Factors, 27, 267-283.

Wightman, D.C., & Sistrunk, F. (1987). Part-task training strategies in simulated carrier landing final-approach training. Human Factors, 29, 245-254.

Wilberg, R.B. (1990). The retention and free recall of multiple movements. Human Movement Science, 9, 437-479.

Wilde, H., & Shea, C.H. (2006). Proportional and nonproportional transfer of movement sequences. Quarterly Journal of Experimental Psychology, 59, 1626-1647.

Williams, A.M. (2000). Perceptual skill in soccer: Implications for talent identification and development. Journal of Sports Sciences, 18, 737-750.

Williams, A.M., Davids, K., & Williams, J.G. (1999). Visual perception and action in sport. London: E & FN Spon.

Williams, A.M., & Grant, A. (1999). Training perceptual skill in sport. International Journal of Sport Psychology, 30, 194-220.

Williams, A.M., & Ward, P. (2003). Perceptual expertise: Development in sport. In J.L. Starkes & K.A. Ericsson (Eds.), Expert performance in sport: Advances in research on sport expertise (219-247). Champaign, IL: Human Kinetics.

Williams, A.M., Ward, P., & Smeeton, N.J. (2004). Perceptual and cognitive expertise in sport: Implications for skill acquisition and performance enhancement. In A.M. Williams & N.J. Hodges (Eds.), Skill acquisition in sport: Research, theory and practice (pp. 328-347). London: Routledge.

Williams, H.G., Woollacott, M.H., & Ivry, R. (1992). Timing and motor control in clumsy children. Journal of Motor Behavior, 24, 165-172.

Wilson, A.D., & Bingham, G.P. (2008). Identifying the information for the visual perception of relative phase. Perception & Psychophysics, 70, 465-476.

Wilson, A.D., Bingham, G.P., & Craig, J.C. (2003). Proprioceptive perception of phase variability. Journal of Experimental Psychology: Human Perception and Performance, 29, 1179-1190.

Wilson, D.M. (1961). The central nervous control of flight in a locust. Journal of Experimental Biology, 38, 471-490.

Wimmers, R.H., Beek, P.J., & van Wieringen, P.C.W. (1992). Phase transitions in rhythmic tracking movements: A case of unilateral coupling. Human Movement Science, 11, 217-226.

Wing, A.M. (1980). The long and short of timing in response sequences. In G.E. Stelmach & J. Requin (Eds.), Tutorials in motor behaviour (pp. 469-486). Amsterdam: Elsevier.

Wing, A.M. (2002). Voluntary timing and brain function: An information processing approach. Brain and Cognition, 48, 7-30.

Wing, A.M., & Fraser, C. (1983). The contribution of the thumb to reaching movements. Quarterly Journal of Experimental Psychology, 35A, 297-309.

Wing, A.M., & Kristofferson, A.B. (1973a). The timing of interresponse intervals. Perception & Psychophysics, 13, 455-460.

Wing, A.M., & Kristofferson, A.B. (1973b). Response delays and the timing of discrete motor responses. Perception & Psychophysics, 14, 5-12.

Wing, A.M., Turton, A., & Fraser, C. (1986). Grasp size and accuracy of approach in reaching. Journal of Motor Behavior, 18, 245-260.

Winstein, C.J. (1991). Designing practice for motor learning: Clinical implications. In M.J. Lister (Ed.), Contemporary management of motor control problems: Proceedings of the II step conference (pp. 65-76). Alexandria: Foundation for Physical Therapy.

Winstein, C.J., & Garfinkel, A. (1989). Qualitative dynamics of disordered human locomotion: A preliminary investigation. Journal of Motor Behavior, 21, 373-391.

Winstein, C.J., Pohl, P.S., & Lewthwaite, R. (1994). Effects of physical guidance and knowledge of results on motor learning: Support for the guidance hypothesis. Research Quarterly for Exercise and Sport, 65, 316-323.

Winstein, C.J., & Schmidt, R.A. (1990). Reduced frequency of knowledge of results enhances motor skill learning. Journal of Experimental Psychology: Learning, Memory and Cognition, 16, 677-691.

Wishart, L.R., Lee, T.D., Murdoch, J.E., & Hodges, N.J. (2000). Effects of aging on automatic and effortful processes in bimanual coordination. Journal of Gerontology: Psychological Sciences, 55B, P85-P94.

Wolf, S.L., Blanton, S., Baer, H., Breshears, J., & Butler, A.J. (2002). Repetitive task practice: A critical review of constraint-induced movement therapy in stroke. Neurologist, 8, 325-338.

Wolf, S.L., Winstein, C.J., Miller, J.P., Taub, E., Uswatte, G., Morris, D., Guiliani, C., Light., K.E., & Nichols-Larsen, D. (2006). Effect of constraint-induced movement therapy on upper extremity function 3 to 9 months after stroke: The EXCITE randomized clinical trial. Journal of the American Medical Association, 296, 2095-2104.

Wolf, S.L., Winstein, C.J., Miller, J.P., Thompson, P.A., Taub, E., Uswatte, G., Morris, D., Blanton, S., Nichols-Larsen, D., & Clark, P.C. (2008). Retention of upper limb function in stroke survivors who have received constraint-induced movement therapy: The EXCITE randomised trial. Lancet Neurology, 7, 33-40.

Wolpert, D.M., & Ghahramani, Z. (2000). Computational principles of movement neuroscience. Nature Neuroscience, 3, 1212-1217.

Wolpert, D.M., Ghahramani, Z., & Flanagan, J.R. (2001). Perspectives and problems in motor learning. Trends in Cognitive Sciences, 5, 487-494.

Wolpert, D.M., Miall, R.C., & Kawato, M. (1998). Internal models in the cerebellum. Trends in Cognitive Sciences, 2, 338-347.

Woodman, T., & Hardy, L. (2001). Stress and anxiety. In R.N. Singer, H.A. Hausenblas, & C.M. Janelle (Eds.), Handbook of sport psychology (2nd ed.) (pp. 290-318). New York: Wiley.

Woodrow, H. (1932). The effect of rate of sequence upon the accuracy of synchronization. Journal of Experimental Psychology, 15, 357-379.

Woods, T. (2001). How I play golf. New York: Warner Books.

Woodworth, R.S. (1899). The accuracy of voluntary movement. Psychological Review Monographs, 3 (Whole No. 13).

Woodworth, R.S. (1903). Le mouvement. Paris: Doin.

Woodworth, R.S. (1938). Experimental psychology. New York: Holt.

Woodworth, R.S., & Schlosberg, H. (1954). Experimental psychology (rev. ed.). New York: Holt, Rinehart & Winston.

Woollacott, M.H., & Jensen, J.L. (1996). Posture and locomotion. In H. Heuer & S.W. Keele (Eds.), Handbook of perception and action. Vol. 2: Motor skills (pp. 333-403). San Diego: Academic Press.

Woollacott, M.H., & Shumway-Cook, A. (2002). Attention and the control of posture and gait: A review of an emerging area of research. Gait & Posture, 16, 1-14.

Woollacott, M.H., & Sveistrup, H. (1994). The development of sensorimotor integration underlying posture control in infants during the transition to independent stance. In S.P. Swinnen, H. Heuer, J. Massion, & P. Casaer (Eds.), Interlimb coordination: Neural, dynamical, and cognitive constraints (pp. 371-389). San Diego: Academic Press.

Worringham, C.J. (1992). Some historical roots of phenomena and methods in motor behavior research. In G.E. Stelmach & J. Requin (Eds.), Tutorials in motor behavior II (pp. 807-825). Amsterdam: Elsevier.

Wraga, M., Creem, S.H., & Proffitt, D.R. (2000). Perception-action dissociations of a walkable Müller-Lyer configuration. Psychological Science, 11, 239-243.

Wright, C.E. (1990). Generalized motor programs: Reexamining claims of effector independence in writing. In M. Jeannerod (Ed.), Attention and performance XIII (pp. 294-320). Hillsdale, NJ: Erlbaum.

Wright, C.E., & Meyer, D.E. (1983). Conditions for a linear speed-accuracy trade-off in aimed movements. Quarterly Journal of Experimental Psychology, 35A, 279-296.

Wright, D.L. (1991). The role of intertask and intratask processing in acquisition and retention of motor skills. Journal of Motor Behavior, 23, 139-145.

Wright, D.L., Black, C., Park, J.-H., & Shea, C.H. (2001). Planning and executing simple movements: Contributions of relative-time and overall-duration specification. Journal of Motor Behavior, 33, 273-285.

Wright, D.L., Li, Y., & Whitacre, C. (1992). The contribution of elaborative processing to the contextual interference effect. Research Quarterly for Exercise and Sport, 63, 30-37.

Wright, D.L., & Shea, C.H. (1991). Contextual dependencies in motor skills. Memory & Cognition, 19, 361-370.

Wright, D.L., & Shea, C.H. (1994). Cognition and motor skill acquisition: Contextual dependencies. In C.R. Reynolds (Eds.), Cognitive assessment: A multidisciplinary perspective (pp. 89-106). New York: Plenum Press.

Wright, D.L., & Shea, C.H. (2001). Manipulating generalized motor program difficulty during blocked and random practice does not affect parameter learning. Research Quarterly for Exercise and Sport, 72, 32-38.

Wright, D.L., Smith-Munyon, V.L., & Sidaway, B. (1997). How close is too close for precise knowledge of results? Research Quarterly for Exercise and Sport, 68, 172-176.

Wright, D.L., Snowden, S., & Willoughby, D. (1990). Summary KR: How much information is used from the summary? Journal of Human Movement Studies, 19, 119-128.

Wrisberg, C.A. (1991). A field test of the effect of contextual variety during skill acquisition. Journal of Teaching in Physical Education, 11, 21-30.

Wrisberg, C.A., & Anshel, M.H. (1993). A field test of the activity-set hypothesis for warm-up decrement in an open skill. Research Quarterly for Exercise and Sport, 64, 39-45.

Wrisberg, C.A., & Liu, Z. (1991). The effect of contextual variety on the practice, retention, and transfer of an applied motor skill. Research Quarterly for Exercise and Sport, 62, 406-412.

Wrisberg, C.A., & Ragsdale, M.R. (1979). Further tests of Schmidt's schema theory: Development of a schema rule for a coincident timing task. Journal of Motor Behavior, 11, 159-166.

Wrisberg, C.A., & Schmidt, R.A. (1975). A note on motor learning without post-response knowledge of results. Journal of Motor Behavior, 7, 221-225.

Wu, W.F.W. (2007). Self-control of learning multiple motor skills. Unpublished doctoral thesis, Louisiana State University.

Wulf, G. (1991). The effect of type of practice on motor learning in children. Applied Cognitive Psychology, 5, 123-134.

Wulf, G. (2007). Attention and motor skill learning. Champaign, IL: Human Kinetics.

Wulf, G., Hörger, M., & Shea, C.H. (1999). Benefits of blocked over serial feedback on complex motor skill learning. Journal of Motor Behavior, 31, 95-103.

Wulf, G., & Lee, T.D. (1993). Contextual interference in movements of the same class: Differential effects on program and parameter learning. Journal of Motor Behavior, 25, 254-263.

Wulf, G., Lee, T.D., & Schmidt, R.A. (1994). Reducing knowledge of results about relative versus absolute timing: Differential effects on learning. Journal of Motor Behavior, 26, 362-369.

Wulf, G., McConnel, N., Gärtner, M., & Schwarz, A. (2002). Feedback and attentional focus: Enhancing the learning of sport skills through external-focus feedback. Journal of Motor Behavior, 34, 171-182.

Wulf, G., McNevin, N.H., & Shea, C.H. (2001). The automaticity of complex motor skill learning as a function of attentional focus. Quarterly Journal of Experimental Psychology, 54A, 1143-1154.

Wulf, G., & Prinz, W. (2001). Directing attention to movement effects enhances learning: A review. Psychonomic Bulletin & Review, 8, 648-660.

Wulf, G., & Schmidt, R.A. (1989). The learning of generalized motor programs: Reducing the relative frequency of knowledge of results enhances memory. Journal of Experimental Psychology: Learning, Memory and Cognition, 15, 748-757.

Wulf, G., & Schmidt, R.A. (1994a). Contextual-interference effects in motor learning: Evaluating a KR-usefulness hypothesis. In J.R. Nitsch & R. Seiler (Eds.), Movement and sport: Psychological foundations and effects. Vol. 2. Motor control and motor learning (pp. 304-309). Sankt Augustin, Germany: Academia Verlag.

Wulf, G., & Schmidt, R.A. (1994b). Feedback-induced variability and the learning of generalized motor programs. Journal of Motor Behavior, 26, 348-361.

Wulf, G., & Schmidt, R.A. (1996). Average KR degrades parameter learning. Journal of Motor Behavior, 28, 371-381.

Wulf, G., & Schmidt, R.A. (1997). Variability of practice and implicit motor learning. Journal of Experimental Psychology: Learning, Memory, and Cognition, 23, 987-1006.

Wulf, G., Schmidt, R.A., & Deubel, H. (1993). Reduced feedback frequency enhances generalized motor program learning but not parameterization learning. Journal of Experimental Psychology: Learning, Memory, and Cognition, 19, 1134-1150.

Wulf, G., & Shea, C.H. (2002). Principles derived from the study of simple skills do not generalize to complex skill learning. Psychonomic Bulletin & Review, 9, 185-211.

Wulf, G., & Shea, C.H. (2004). Understanding the role of augmented feedback: The good, the bad and the ugly. In A.M. Williams & N.J. Hodges (Eds.), Skill Acquisition in sport: Research, theory and practice (pp. 121-144). London: Routledge.

Wulf, G., & Toole, T. (1999). Physical assistance devices in complex motor skill learning: Benefits of a self-controlled practice schedule. Research Quarterly for Exercise and Sport, 70, 265-272.

Wulf, G., Weigelt, M., Poulter, D.R., & McNevin, N.H. (2003). Attentional focus on supra-postural tasks affects balance learning. Quarterly Journal of Experimental Psychology, 56A, 1191-1211.

Yamanishi, J., Kawato, M., & Suzuki, R. (1980). Two coupled oscillators as a model for the coordinated finger tapping by both hands. Biological Cybernetics, 37, 219-225.

Yantis, S. (1993). Stimulus-driven attention capture. Current Directions in Psychological Science, 2, 156-161.

Yao, W., Fischman, M.G., & Wang, Y.T. (1994). Motor skill acquisition and retention as a function of average feedback, summary feedback, and performance variability. Journal of Motor Behavior, 26, 273-282.

Yardley, L., Gardner, M., Leadbetter, A., & Lavie, N. (1999). Effect of articulatory and mental tasks on postural control. Neuroreport, 10, 215-219.

Yerkes, R.M., & Dodson, J.D. (1908). The relation of strength of stimulus to rapidity of habit-formation. Journal of Comparative Neurology and Psychology, 18, 459-482.

Yiu, E. M-L., Verdolini, K., & Chow, L.P.Y. (2005). Electromyographic study of motor learning for a voice production task. Journal of Speech, Language, and Hearing Research, 48, 1254-1268.

Young, D.E., Cohen, M.J., & Husak, W.S. (1993). Contextual interference and motor skill acquisition: On the processes that influence retention. Human Movement Science, 12, 577-600.

Young, D.E., & Schmidt, R.A. (1990). Units of motor behavior: Modifications with practice and feedback. In M. Jeannerod (Ed.), Attention and performance XIII (pp. 763-795). Hillsdale, NJ: Erlbaum.

Young, D.E., & Schmidt, R.A. (1991). Motor programs as units of movement control. In N.I. Badler, B.A. Barsky, & D. Zeltzer (Eds.), Making them move: Mechanics, control, and animation of articulated figures (pp. 129-155). San Mateo, CA: Morgan Kaufmann.

Young, D.E., & Schmidt, R.A. (1992). Augmented kinematic feedback for motor learning. Journal of Motor Behavior, 24, 261-273.

Young, M.S., & Stanton, N.A. (2007). Back to the future: Brake reaction times for manual and automated vehicles. Ergonomics, 50, 46-58.

Zaal, F.T.J.M., Bingham, G.P., & Schmidt, R.C. (2000). Visual perception of mean relative phase and phase variability. Journal of Experimental Psychology: Human Perception and Performance, 26, 1209-1220.

Zaichkowsky, L.D., & Baltzell, A. (2001). Arousal and performance. In R.N. Singer, H.A. Hausenblas, & C.M. Janelle (Eds.), Handbook of sport psychology (2nd ed.) (pp. 319-339). New York: Wiley.

Zanone, P.-G., & Kelso, J.A.S. (1992). Evolution of behavioral attractors with learning: Nonequilibrium phase transitions. Journal of Experimental Psychology: Human Perception and Performance, 18, 403-421.

Zanone, P.-G., & Kelso, J.A.S. (1994). The coordination dynamics of learning: Theoretical structure and experimental agenda. In S.P. Swinnen, H. Heuer, J. Massion, & P. Casaer (Eds.), Interlimb coordination: Neural, dynamical, and cognitive constraints (pp. 461-490). San Diego: Academic Press.

Zanone, P.-G., & Kelso, J.A.S. (1997). The coordination dynamics of learning and transfer: Collective and component levels. Journal of Experimental Psychology: Human Perception and Performance, 23, 1454-1480.

Zavala, A., Locke, E.A., Van Cott, H.P., & Fleishman, E.A. (1965). The analysis of helicopter pilot performance (Tech. Rep. AIR-E-29-6/65-TR). Washington, DC: American Institutes for Research.

Zehr, E.P. (2005). Neural control of rhythmic human movement: The common core hypothesis. Exercise and Sport Sciences Reviews, 33, 54-60.

Zehr, E.P., & Stein, R.B. (1999). What functions do reflexes serve during human locomotion? Progress in Neurobiology, 58, 185-205.

Zelaznik, H.N., & Hahn, R. (1985). Reaction time methods in the study of motor programming: The precuing of hand, digit, and duration. Journal of Motor Behavior, 17, 190-218.

Zelaznik, H.N., Hawkins, B., & Kisselburgh, L. (1983). Rapid visual feedback processing in single-aiming movements. Journal of Motor Behavior, 15, 217-236.

Zelaznik, H.N., Mone, S., McCabe, G.P., & Thaman, C. (1988). Role of temporal and spatial precision in determining the nature of the speed-accuracy trade-off in aimed-hand movements. Journal of Experimental Psychology: Human Perception and Performance, 14, 221-230.

Zelaznik, H.N., Schmidt, R.A., & Gielen, C.C.A.M. (1986). Kinematic properties of rapid aimed hand movements. Journal of Motor Behavior, 18, 353-372.

Zelaznik, H.N., Shapiro, D.C., & McColsky, D. (1981). Effects of a secondary task on the accuracy of single aiming movements. Journal of Experimental Psychology: Human Perception and Performance, 7, 1007-1018.

Zelaznik, H.N., Shapiro, D.C., & Newell, K.M. (1978). On the structure of motor recognition memory. Journal of Motor Behavior, 10, 313-323.

Zelaznik, H.N., Spencer, R.M., & Doffin, J.G. (2000). Temporal precision in tapping and circle drawing movements at preferred rates is not correlated: Further evidence against timing as a general-purpose ability. Journal of Motor Behavior, 32, 193-199.

Zelaznik, H.N., Spencer, R.M.C., Ivry, R.B., Baria, A., Bloom, M., Dolansky, L., Justice, S., Patterson, K., & Whetter, E. (2005). Timing variability in circle drawing and tapping: Probing the relationship between event and emergent timing. Journal of Motor Behavior, 37, 395-403.

Zelaznik, H.N., & Spring, J. (1976). Feedback in response recognition and production. Journal of Motor Behavior, 8, 309-312.

Zernicke, R.F., & Roberts, E.M. (1978). Lower extremity forces and torques during systematic variation of non-weight bearing motion. Medicine and Science in Sports, 10, 21-26.

Zernicke, R.F., & Schneider, K. (1993). Biomechanics and developmental neuromotor control. Child Development, 64, 982-1004.

SUBJECT INDEX

Note: Page numbers followed by an italicized *f* or *t* refer to the figure or table on that page, respectively.

ABOUT THE AUTHORS

Richard A. Schmidt, PhD, is professor emeritus in the department of psychology at UCLA. He currently runs his own consulting firm, Human Performance Research, working in the area of human factors and human performance. Known as one of the leaders in research on motor behavior, Dr. Schmidt has more than 35 years' experience in this area and has published widely.

The originator of schema theory, Dr. Schmidt founded the *Journal of Motor Behavior* in 1969 and was editor for 11 years. He authored the first edition of *Motor Control and Learning* in 1982, followed up with a second edition of the popular text in 1988, and collaborated with Tim Lee for the third edition in 1999 and fourth edition in 2005.

Photo courtesy of Anne Hillinger.

The authors and their wives: Dick Schmidt, Laurie Wishart, Gwen Gordon, and Tim Lee.

Dr. Schmidt received an honorary doctorate from Catholic University of Leuven, Belgium, in recognition of his work. Schmidt is a member of the North American Society for the Psychology of Sport and Physical Activity (of which he was president in 1982), the Human Factors and Ergonomics Society, and the Psychonomic Society. Dr. Schmidt has received the C.H. McCloy Research Lectureship from the American Alliance for Health, Physical Education, Recreation and Dance.

His leisure-time activities include sailboat racing, amateur Porsche racing, and skiing.

Timothy D. Lee, PhD, is a professor in the department of kinesiology at McMaster University in Hamilton, Ontario, Canada. He has published extensively in motor behavior and psychology journals since 1979. More recently, he has contributed as an editor to *Journal of Motor Behavior* and *Research Quarterly for Exercise and Sport* and as an editorial board member for *Psychological Review*. Since 1984 his research has been supported by grants from the Natural Sciences and Engineering Research Council of Canada.

Dr. Lee is a member and past president of the Canadian Society for Psychomotor Learning and Sport Psychology (SCAPPS) and a member of the North American Society for the Psychology of Sport and Physical Activity (NASPSPA), the Psychonomic Society, and the Human Factors and Ergonomics Society. In 1980 Dr. Lee received the inaugural Young Scientist Award from SCAPPS; in 1991-92 he received a Senior Research Fellowship by the Dienst Onderzoekscoordinatie, Catholic University in Leuven, Belgium; and in 2005 he presented a prestigious Senior Scientist Lecture at NASPSPA.

In his leisure time, Dr. Lee enjoys playing hockey and golf. He has maintained a lifelong fascination with blues music and would one day love to put years of motor learning study into practice by learning to play blues guitar.